Psychology

CONTEXTS & APPLICATIONS

THIRD EDITION

Jane S. Halonen

JAMES MADISON UNIVERSITY

John W. Santrock

UNIVERSITY OF TEXAS AT DALLAS

McGraw-Hill College

Boston   Burr Ridge, IL   Dubuque, IA   Madison, WI   New York   San Francisco   St. Louis
Bankon   Bogata   Caracas   Lisbon   London   Madrid   Mexico City   Milan
New Delhi   Seoul   Singapore   Sydney   Taipei   Tornonto

McGraw-Hill College

A Division of The **McGraw·Hill** *Companies*

PSYCHOLOGY: CONTEXTS & APPLICATIONS, THIRD EDITION

Copyright © 1999 by The McGraw-Hill Companies, Inc. All rights reserved. Previous edition © 1996 Times Mirror Higher Education Group, Inc. All rights reserved. Printed in the United States of America. Except as permitted under the United States Copyright Act of 1976, no part of this publication may be reproduced or distributed in any form or by any means, or stored in a data base or retrieval system, without the prior written permission of the publisher.

 This book is printed on recycled, acid-free paper containing 10% postconsumer waste.

1 2 3 4 5 6 7 8 9 0 QPD/QPD 9 3 2 1 0 9 8

ISBN 0-697-37648-6

Editorial director: *Jane E. Vaicunas*
Senior sponsoring editor: *Joseph Terry*
Developmental editor: *John Haley*
Marketing manager: *James Rozsa*
Project manager: *Susan J. Brusch*
Production supervisor: *Sandra Hahn*
Design manager: *Stuart D. Paterson*
Photo research coordinator: *John C. Leland*
Art editor: *Joyce Watters*
Supplement coordinator: *David A. Welsh*
Compositor: *GTS Graphics, Inc.*
Typeface: *10/12 Minion*
Printer: *Quebecor Printing Book Group/Dubuque, IA*

Cover/interior design: *Becky Lemna*
Cover image: *G.K. & Vikki Hart/The Image Bank, Inc.*

The credits section for this book begins on page 647 and is considered an extension of the copyright page.

Library of Congress Cataloging-in-Publication Data

Halonen, Jane S.
     Psychology: contexts & applications / Jane S. Halonen, John W. Santrock.—3rd ed.
          p.   cm.
     Prev. ed. has subtitle: contexts of behavior.
     Includes bibliographical references and index.
     ISBN 0-697-37648-96
     1. Psychology.   I. Santrock, John W.   II. Title.
BF121.H195   1999
150—dc21   98-15014
                                        CIP

INTERNATIONAL EDITION
Copyright © 1999. Exclusive rights by The McGraw-Hill Companies, Inc. for manufacture and export. This book cannot be re-exported from the country to which it is consigned by McGraw-Hill. The International Edition is not available in North America. When ordering this title, use ISBN 0-07-115988-6.

www.mhhe.com

Brief Contents

Contents

List of Boxes

Sociocultural Worlds

Applications in Psychology

Self-Assessment

Improving Personal and Cognitive Skills

Resources for Psychology and Improving Humankind

Preface

We wrote *Psychology: Contexts and Applications,* third edition, with two goals in mind: (1) Present the field of psychology as a science in as solid and interesting a way as possible. (2) Make this book one that students will love by including real-world information and challenges that motivate students to learn.

The third edition represents a continuation of presenting psychology as a science and emphasizing the contextual dimensions of psychology. However, as evidenced in the change in title from *Psychology: Contexts of Behavior* to *Psychology: Contexts and Applications,* we have extensively revised the book to include information about applications. A second major change is that the book is considerably shorter than the second edition. We shortened the book based on your input about the optimal length of an introductory psychology book and your belief that most books have become too long and too expensive for students. Let's examine the themes of the third edition.

CONTEXTS

A contexts theme has been an important and well-received aspect of the first edition of this book. It is continued in the book's third edition in the following ways:

- A separate chapter on sociocultural diversity, including material on culture, ethnicity, gender, and religion
- A Sociocultural Worlds box in each chapter
- Addition of recent research, applications, and skills material on diversity

APPLICATIONS

The applications material in the third edition has been expanded. It now includes:

- A new chapter, Chapter 16, on "Applied Psychology." This chapter gives students a broad picture of applications by focusing on industrial/organizational psychology, environmental psychology, sport psychology, forensic psychology, and educational psychology
- An Applications box in each chapter

- Unique chapter endpieces called "Resources for Psychology and Improving Humankind," which includes not only recommended books, but also phone numbers, agencies, brochures, and Web sites that can benefit students when they want more information about a topic.

A unique feature of the third edition is an emphasis on applying psychology to improve students' personal and cognitive skills. This emphasis includes:

- An important new chapter-ending feature called "Thinking It Over." This stimulates students to develop their skills in critical thinking (think more deeply and logically, and obtain evidence to support arguments), creative thinking (come up with unique solutions and brainstorm with other students), active learning (carry out projects and design research studies), and reflective thinking (contemplate and analyze personal issues and problems). Each chapter includes an exercise in each of these four domains.

   Most introductory psychology texts include one or more critical thinking exercises in each chapter. However, the systematic inclusion of thinking activities in four different domains gives students opportunities to stretch their thinking in more diverse ways.
- One or more Self-Assessments in each chapter. This highly popular feature encourages students to evaluate themselves on some aspect of psychology related to the chapter's contents. For example, in Chapter 8, "Human Development," students complete a self-assessment on their identity development; in Chapter 11, "Abnormal Psychology," they complete Self-Assessments on anxiety and depression. The Self-Assessments are not fluffy, pop psychology types of self-evaluations. For example, in Chapter 1, "The Scope and Methods of Psychology," the Self-Assessment focuses on getting students to evaluate critically such pop-psychology beliefs. And in Chapter 2, "Biological Foundations and the Brain," the Self-Assessment includes items that help students to examine false beliefs and stereotypes about the brain that are commonly portrayed in the media. Such Self-Assessments help students to understand better the importance of psychology's scientific base.
- One or more "Improving Personal and Cognitive Skills" inserts in each chapter. They are designed to help students become more successful and function more effectively in their world. For example, in Chapter 4, "States of Consciousness," students will read "What Can People Do If They Have A Substance Abuse Problem?" and in Chapter 9, "Motivation and Emotion," they will study "Strategies for Setting Goals," and "Managing Your Anger."
- A "Learning to Learn" Prechapter, which focuses on improving students' thinking and study skills, including memory and time management skills.

PSYCHOLOGY AS A SCIENCE

Although this book has two main themes (contexts and applications), the science base of psychology was not sacrificed. Foremost in our efforts to introduce psychology to students is to portray its scientific nature. In each chapter, we thoroughly examined the research that was presented in the second edition and made every effort to revise it and update it based on an extensive number of reviews and our evaluation of current research.

Ch. 1: The Scope and Methods of Psychology
- Evolutionary psychology
- Placebo effect, experimenter bias, and double-blind studies

Ch. 2: Biological Foundations and the Brain
- Contemporary material on the relative contributions of heredity and environment
- Buss' views on evolutionary psychology
- Brain damage, plasticity, and repair
- The brains of the Mankato Nuns

Ch. 3: Sensation and Perception
- Psychophysics
- Signal detection
- Perceptual expectations
- Stereograms

Ch. 4: States of Consciousness
- Hazards of college drinking

Ch. 5: Learning
- Bandura's ideas on self-efficacy

Ch. 6: Memory
- Comparison of Baddeley's contemporary working memory model with Atkinson and Shiffrin's traditional model
- Update on repressed memory
- Memory and study strategies

Ch. 7: Thinking, Language, and Intelligence
- Thinking critically about behavior and critical thinking pitfalls
- Csikszentmihalyi's ideas on creativity
- How creative works emerge
- How to talk with babies
- Working with linguistically and culturally diverse children
- Winner's ideas on gifted children

Ch. 8: Human Development
- AIDS in infants
- Being a competent parent
- Vulnerability of early maturing girls
- Identity's components
- Improving the lives of adolescents
- Gay and lesbian parents

Ch. 9: Motivation and Emotion
- Goal-setting and planning in achievement
- Strategies for setting goals
- Managing anger
- Emotional intelligence

Ch. 10: Personality
- More extensive discussion of trait theories and research, including the big five model
- Evaluating trait perspectives
- Strategies for raising self-esteem
- Evaluating the Rorschach test

Ch. 11: Abnormal Psychology
- Self-assessment of anxiety
- Managing suicide threats

Ch. 12: Therapies
- Self-talk
- Conquering depression
- *Consumer Reports* survey on mental health treatment

Ch. 13: Health, Stress, and Coping
- Sexually transmitted diseases
- College version of Life Events measure
- Assertive behavior

Ch. 14: Social Psychology
- Self-monitoring assessment
- Cults
- Overcoming loneliness

Ch. 15: Human Commonality and Diversity
- Improving the lives of African American and Latino youth
- Sex hormone research
- Male role strain
- Improving women's and men's lives
- Psychology and religion

Ch. 16: Applied Psychology
- Industrial/organizational psychology
- Human factors (engineering) psychology
- Interviewing strategies
- Communication strategies
- Environmental psychology
- Forensic psychology
- Sport psychology
- Educational psychology
- Improving the English and computer literacy of Latino children

THE NEW CHAPTERS

The second edition had nineteen chapters. The third edition has sixteen. We combined the introductory and methods chapter from the second edition into a single chapter now called "The Scope and Methods of Psychology." We worked very hard at streamlining and fine-tuning the writing so that content was not lost. This proved to be a very effective strategy and even allowed us to add some important new information such as the evolutionary perspective, placebo effects, experimenter bias, and double-blind studies. To increase student understanding, examples of depression research were woven throughout the discussion of the scientific method and research strategies.

The second edition had two chapters on human development. The new edition has a single chapter. We think you will find that Chapter 8, "Human Development," is a solid presentation of the field. Co-author John Santrock has authored leading books in the fields of life-span development, child development, and adolescence. Chapter 8 presents thorough coverage of the field in all periods of development. Among the important new contemporary topics discussed are being a competent parent, the risks of early maturation for girls, the components of identity, strategies for developing a positive identity, and how to die young as late in life as possible. Some instructors are concerned that introductory psychology books do not have adequate coverage of adult development and aging. You will find that Chapter 8 has thorough coverage of these important dimensions of human development, presenting a good balance of children's development and adults' development.

The second edition had a chapter on gender and a chapter on human sexuality. The gender material has been moved into Chapter 15, "Human Commonality and Diversity," and the sexuality discussion is now in chapter 9, "Motivation and Emotion," and Chapter 13, "Health, Stress, and Coping." We believe you will find that the coverage of gender and sexuality in this new edition is solid. Gender continues to be woven throughout the book as an important theme.

Chapter 16, "Applied Psychology," is a new chapter that significantly expands the applications material in the book. As mentioned earlier, students will read about a wide range of applied psychology topics including industrial/organizational psychology, environmental psychology, sport psychology, forensic psychology, and educational psychology. Among the high-interest topics in this chapter are students' motivation to enter the field of psychology as a career, how to "knock 'em dead" on a job interview, how to communicate effectively, whether students' career interests match the fastest-growing jobs, changing environmentally damaging behavior, characteristics of defendants and juries in trials like those of O. J. Simpson and Timothy McVeigh, and how to improve performance in sports.

WRITING AND PEDAGOGY

We spent considerable time making this a book that has a student-friendly writing style and a pedagogical system that helps students to learn the material. Every section, paragraph, sentence, figure, table, and legend went under the microscope of a very talented and experienced developmental editor, John Haley, who has worked on many successful introductory psychology texts. With his input and that of an extensive review team, the writing was amplified, trimmed, and clarified.

The pedagogical system includes an extensive number of chapter-beginning, within-chapter, and chapter-ending features. These include chapter outlines and previews at the beginning of chapters, clear definitions of key terms and in-chapter reviews within each chapter, and visual concept maps and thinking exercises at the end of each chapter. To examine the complete learning system, turn to the section later in the Preface called For the Student.

THE ANCILLARY PACKAGE

The supplements listed here may accompany *Psychology: Contexts and Applications,* third edition. Please contact your local McGraw-Hill representative for details concerning policies, prices, and availability, as some restrictions may apply.

Study Guide, prepared by Steven A. Schneider, Pima Community College (0-697-37667-2). Each chapter of the study guides contains an extended outline and learning objectives coordinated with the test bank and instructor's manual; fill-in-the-blank key term checks with answers and definitions provided at the end of each chapter; a guided review through the chapter; concept check exercises to recall main ideas from each chapter; thought exercises to encourage reflection about the "Sociocultural Worlds" and "Applications" features in each chapter; and expanded multiple choice practice tests, each keyed to a specific learning objective.

Instructor's Manual, prepared by Todd Zakrajsek, Southern Oregon University (07-0-303486-X). The Instructor's Manual includes chapter outlines and learning objectives as well as three complete lectures in each chapter. Each lecture will take about 1 to 1.5 hours to deliver, depending on the instructor. Each lecture contains a minimum of one active learning exercise, a classroom demonstration, or a detailed discussion topic summary that may be used as an alternative to a portion of the lecture. Suggestions are provided for portions of the lecture to eliminate to make room for the alternative activity. This allows an instructor to do all the lectures if he or she wishes (right out of the Instructor's Manual) or a combination of lectures, classroom demonstrations, and active learning exercises all integrated with each other and the text.

Test Bank, prepared by Cynthia Gray of Alverno College (0-697-37669-9). The Test Bank features 2,000 multiple-choice items keyed to learning objectives from the Instructor's Manual and student Study Guide. In keeping with the new theme of the text, a large number of application-oriented items are included in addition to factual and conceptual questions. Many of the items also reflect the text's focus on human diversity.

Computerized Test Banks, available in Windows (0-07-303488-6) and Macintosh (0-07303487-8) formats. Items from the text bank are easily available to instructors. MicroTest III, a powerful but easy-to-use test-generating program by Chariot Software Group, facilitates both selection of questions from the test bank and printing tests and answer keys. Instructors can customize questions, headings, and instructions and add or import their own questions.

Overhead Transparencies (0-07-303489-4). A set of full-color overhead transparency acetates with images from the textbook.

PowerPoint Slides (0-07-303491-6). Full-color, dynamic slides that enhance lectures and classroom presentation of material from the textbook.

The multimedia package also includes the **PRISM CD-ROM** for students (0-07-303464-9), the **Presentation Manager CD-ROM** for instructors (0-07-303490-8), and the **McGraw-Hill Learning Architecture** for instructors and students (0-07-450944-6). A number of other supplements, including *The Critical Thinker, Annual Editions, Taking Sides,* and **The Active Learner CD-ROM,** also may be available. Please consult your McGraw-Hill sales representative for the details about these supplements.

ACKNOWLEDGMENTS

We owe a special debt to the outstanding reviewers of this new edition:

Sally Browder, Lyon College

L. William Cheney, Community College of Rhode Island

Gloria Fisher, Mississippi College

E. Keith Gerritz, Wilmington College of Ohio

Patricia Guth, Westmoreland Community College

Vivian Hamilton, Portland Community College–Sylvania campus

Kevin Keating, Broward Community College North

Christopher Kilmartin, Mary Washington College

Gary King, Rose State College

Patricia Levy, University of Southern Colorado

Joel Morgovsky, Brookdale Community College

Maria Parrilla Vasquez, Weber State University

Bobby J. Poe, Belleville Area College

Paul Rowland, Southern Oregon State University

Ed Sabin, St. Louis University

Patricia A. Santoro, Frostburg State University

Leon Scott, Westmar University

Paul Smith, Alverno College

Chris Spatz, Hendrix College

Joanne Stephenson, Union University

Freddie Thomason, Wallace State College

Judy Zimmerman, Portland Community College

We also are indebted to the reviewers of the first two editions of the text:

Jeannette Altarriba, SUNY–Albany

Bruce Bain, University of Alberta, Edmonton

Lou Banderet, Northeastern University

Robert Bell, Texarkana Community College

Deborah Best, Wake Forest University

Richard Brislin, East-West Center, University of Hawaii

Eugene Butler, Quinisigamond Community College

Thomas Cadwallader, Indiana State University

Luetilla M. Carter, Oakwood College

Toby Klinger Connet, Johnson City Community College

Katherine Covell, University College of Cape Breton

Robert Cox, Shelby State Community College

Jagannath P. Das, University of Alberta

Florence Denmark, Pace University

Nancy Denney, University of Wisconsin, Madison

Larry Dohrn, San Antonio Community College

Peter Flynn, North Essex Community College

Pauline Ginsberg, Utica College of Syracuse University

Randall Gold, Cuesta College

Sandra Graham, UCLA

Peter Gram, Pensacola Junior College

Algea Harrison, Oakland University

James Hart, Edison State Community College

Morton Heller, Winston Salem State University

Janet E. Helms, University of Maryland

Nils Hovik, Lehigh Community College

Jeanette Ickovics, Yale University

Mary Kite, Ball State University

Claudia Kittock, Cambridge Community College

Rick Kribs, Motlow State Community College

Stan Kuczaj, Southern Methodist University

V. K. Kumar, West Chester University

Ed Lawson, State University of New York, Fredonia

David Matsumoto, San Francisco State University

Lyla Maynard, Des Moines Area Community College

Jodi Mindell, St. Joseph's University

John Moritsugu, Pacific Lutheran University

Dirk W. Mosig, University of Nebraska

Steve Myers, Washburn University

Mary Ellen O'Connor, University of Tulsa

Michele Paludi, CUNY Hunter College

Paul Pederson, Syracuse University

Linda Petioff, Central Community College

David Pittenger, Marietta College

Retta Poe, Western Kentucky University

Marilyn J. Reedy, Alverno College

Harriet W. Richard, Northern Kentucky University

Marshall Segall, Syracuse University

Tod Sloan, University of Tulsa

Martha Spiker, University of Charleston

Joseph Trimble, Western Washington University

Boika S. Twe, Sinclair Community College

Shirley A. Vaugh, Henry Ford Community College

Cynthia Whissell, Laurentian University

For example, a brief overview of new content includes:

We especially want to thank a number of outstanding psychologists who contributed information that served as a foundation for several chapters in the book. They include:

Alice O'Toole, *University of Texas at Dallas:* Chapter 3, Sensation and Perception

James Bartlett, *University of Texas at Dallas,* Chapter 6, Memory, and Chapter 7, Thinking, Language, and Intelligence

Raymond Paloutzian, *Westmont College:* Chapter 15: Sociocultural Diversity (Section on Religion)

David Neufelt, *Hutchinson Community College:* Chapter 16: Applied Psychology (sections on industrial/organizational psychology and human factors/engineering psychology)

Robert Gifford, *University of Victoria:* Chapter 16: Applied Psychology (Section on Environmental Psychology)

Don Hockenbury, *Tulsa Junior College:* Statistical Appendix (Analyzing the Data)

We had superb support from some talented librarians—Jackie Rice and Mary Georgia Matlock, among others. Thanks also to our new publisher, McGraw-Hill, for believing in this book and providing the support necessary to make this third edition truly exciting for students taking their first psychology course. A final note of thanks go to our spouses—Brian Halonen and Mary Jo Santrock—for their enthusiastic support of our work, for their patient tolerance of our work habits, and for their companionship and unfailing humor.

About the Authors

Jane S. Halonen earned her Ph.D. in Clinical Psychology from the University of Wisconsin–Milwaukee. She is head of the psychology department at James Madison University. She has served as a consultant to numerous psychology departments and has edited *Teaching Critical Thinking in Psychology*. She is past President of the Council of Teachers of Undergraduate Psychology and a fellow and program chair for Division Two of the American Psychological Association. Jane also was a private practice clinician in Milwaukee where she worked with families and children around issues of loss and change.

John W. Santrock received his Ph.D. from the University of Minnesota. He is a member of the psychology department at the University of Texas at Dallas. He has also held teaching positions at the University of Charleston and the University of Georgia. His research on father custody is widely cited and used in expert witness testimony to promote flexibility and alternative considerations in custody disputes. He is also the author of several textbooks in developmental psychology published by McGraw-Hill.

Learning to Learn in Psychology

Learning should be a joy and full of excitement. It is

life's greatest adventure.

—TAYLOR CALDWELL
American Writer, 20th Century

STUDYING PSYCHOLOGY

The study of psychology involves three things: acquiring a specialized knowledge base about behavior, learning new ways of thinking about behavior, and developing attitudes and motivations consistent with the science of psychology.

The Knowledge Base

Psychology is rich in language that communicates findings about patterns of behavior. Concepts and terms deftly communicate complex behavior patterns. You will find that in this text we have printed key concepts in bold type to make them stand out and help you organize your reading.

As a science, psychology systematically explores behavior, generating principles to explain behavior. What regularities and irregularities exist in behavior, and how do we account for them? Psychologists search for the factors (or variables) that most plausibly account for behavior. They create hypotheses that propose explanations, and they design research in various formats to test their hypotheses, generating evidence to confirm them. Sometimes psychologists propose complex explanations of behavior, called theories, based on the research evidence. Where one theory does not adequately explain behavior, psychologists offer competing explanations.

In addition to specialized content areas of psychology, certain perspectives in psychology have dominated the development of psychological research since the foundation of the discipline. Important perspectives in psychology include the behavioral, psychoanalytic, humanistic, evolutionary, neurobiological, cognitive, and sociocultural perspectives. Chapter 1, "The Scope and Methods of Psychology," describes each of these approaches in more detail. What is important is that you recognize that these perspectives foster multiple explanations of behavior, a hallmark of psychological thinking.

Psychologists organize the knowledge in their discipline in specialized fields of psychology. This book is no exception. We will explore the major subfields of psychology in separate chapters, citing relevant research studies and human stories as we discuss psychological concepts and principles.

Psychological researchers specialize in selected fields and contribute to the knowledge in that field through creative research designs. In addition to books and popular articles, psychologists publish in professional journals for their specialized interest areas. The "literature" of psychology is organized and accessible through an indexing system published as *Psychological Abstracts,* which can assist you in tracking down information relevant to specific questions you have about behavior. The index in *Psychological Abstracts* is organized according to psychological concepts. An electronic database of psychological research called *Psychlit* also may be available in your library. Ask your librarian to show you how to use *Psychlit* or *Psychological Abstracts* if you have a research paper to complete in this course.

Thinking Skills

You will find that this text takes seriously the obligation to improve your thinking skills. Throughout the text you will find opportunities to practice new thinking skills as you apply what you learn in psychology. At the end of each chapter, in a feature called "Thinking It Over," we encourage you to build a portfolio of experiences in which you practice various forms of thinking that will make you a better learner and psychological thinker.

Critical Thinking.   Experts differ on how to define critical thinking: however, definitions usually include grasping the deeper meaning of problems, exploring different approaches and perspectives, asking relevant questions, and making accurate inferences. Psychologists think critically when they explain, predict, or modify behavior. For example, clinical psychologists analyze complex human experiences and identify strategies that provide help for clients. As you build a strong knowledge base of psychological concepts, principles, and perspectives and apply these ideas to your own life, your critical thinking will improve.

Creative Thinking. Research psychologists regularly demonstrate creativity when they come up with new ways to explain and predict behaviors. When you connect ideas to arrive at a new way of looking at behavior, you are engaged in creative thinking. These activities might involve artistic forms, such as drawing, creating stories, or making up scenarios. You might demonstrate creative thinking by brainstorming with others or generating unique ideas on your own.

Experiential Learning. Experiential learning involves "learning by doing." Exploring how psychological principles can be used to solve problems will help you experience the range of solutions that psychologists use. Applied psychologists adopt psychological principles in a variety of contexts to foster behavior change. The active learning exercises will encourage you to participate in field trips, talk with psychology professionals, apply research findings, and explore other practical applications of psychology.

Reflective Thinking. Many students discover that learning about psychology offers them new insights about their own behavior. The reflective thinking activities promote insight through journal-writing assignments at the end of the chapter and self-assessment activities in the chapter. In many cases you will be able to compare your responses on self-assessment activities with the results of others who have completed the assessment. Your insights from journal writing and self-assessments can help you identify some new goals for your personal development.

Attitudes

Psychologists also show characteristic attitudes about behavior that you may discover could be contagious as the result of your study. For example, psychologists are curious about what makes people tick. They like to think about what motivates people to act or refrain from acting. As a result of your studies in your first course in psychology, you may discover that you will be more routinely observant and have more questions about the behavior of others. (Your friends might also feel pestered by the questions that you generate!)

Psychologists believe that it is easy to fall into the trap of thinking that there is only one answer to a problem or one side to an issue. For example, when you witness your niece laughing in a manner that reminds you of your sister, you may be inclined to think of the laugh as "inherited." Your interpretation favors "nature," the contribution made from genes. However, it is quite likely that your sister has raised your niece, exposing your niece to her distinctive laugh all her life. The effect of the environment on behavior is referred to as the "nurture" side of the argument. How do we know which is the more powerful influence? We won't. Both influences are involved, and we would be hard pressed to determine which has greater impact. The *nature-nurture controversy* is complex, and we will revisit it throughout the text. However, it effectively illustrates the tendency we might have to produce simplistic explanations that don't completely account for complex problems.

According to psychologists, most behaviors are complex occurrences and simple explanations rarely account for them fully. For example, a friend might tell you, "My marriage didn't work because he couldn't let go of his mother." The husband's inability to relinquish his strong attachment to his mother may have been one cause of the divorce, but there were probably others as well—perhaps economic problems, religious differences, sexual difficulties, personality conflicts, and so on. One of psychology's great lessons is that behavior is multiply determined.

Most psychologists maintain a skeptical or disbelieving stance about simplistic behavioral claims. Psychologists seek to sort fact from fantasy by critically questioning the nature of mind and behavior. They generally prefer to rely on objective or research-based evidence to support behavioral claims rather than subjective accounts or personal testimony. They often seek multiple points of view in order to comprehend complex behavior. They actively pursue alternate explanations as a way of expanding the factors that might be implicated.

We might not discover some answers to behavioral questions until some time in the distant future. Psychologists refer to this acceptance of unresolved questions as *tolerance of ambiguity.* Psychologists not only expect and tolerate ambiguity, but enjoy the challenge of it.

Psychologists also try hard to avoid being judgmental. Because we can't be completely confident of identifying all of the causes of behavior, psychologists believe that there is value in slowing down and being extremely careful when forming conclusions, especially when determining blame. We routinely won't have all the information we need to be certain in our conclusions. Therefore, the judgments we pose are tentative rather than definite. Psychologists often begin their answers to queries about behavior with the phrase *"It depends on"* as a reflection of these qualities. This response can be frustrating until you recognize that this tentative approach is a hallmark of psychological ways of thinking.

Despite the nonjudgmental attitude, psychologists are unwilling to accept information at face value. They challenge the positions of others, whether to seek clarification, to suggest improvements, to identify inadequacies in stated positions, or propose alternatives. Psychology is a changing discipline; as we begin a new century, psychologists will continue to contribute new ideas, concepts, and theories about mind and behavior.

IMPROVING YOUR STUDY SKILLS

This might be your very first exposure to the scientific study of behavior called psychology. You might feel some anxiety about performing well in the course. On the other hand, you may have had the opportunity to study psychology before in another context so you have greater confidence about your abilities. With the adventure that lies ahead, you will want to make the best use of your study time to master the concepts and skills psychology has to offer. Let's explore a case study that will help you begin to exercise psychological ways of thinking while we address the practical problem of developing effective study skills.

> A student named Tom came to his professor's office about 2 weeks before the final exam in an introductory psychology course. He had a *D* average in the course and wanted to know what was causing him to get such a low grade. It turned out that he wasn't doing well in any of his classes. What questions would you ask to discover the causes of his poor performance?

Several *hypotheses* (scientific hunches) may come to mind. Each question below highlights a possible *variable* (factor) that might influence Tom's behavior.

- Is Tom doing his reading? (preparation)
- Is he getting enough sleep? (fatigue)
- Does he like the professor? (emotion)

The following sections explore several possibilities for helping both Tom and you improve your study skills. But first, take a moment to complete the Self-Assessment. This will preview the areas we will explore and help you gain some insight into your own study skill strengths and weaknesses.

How Should I Manage My Time?

If you suspected that Tom managed his time poorly, you would be right. Eventually the conversation between Tom and his professor turned to his study techniques and what he could do to get better grades on his final exams.

The professor asked Tom to put together a study schedule for the four final exams he was getting ready to take in 2 weeks. He planned to study a total of 4 hours for his psychology exam; he scheduled only 1 of those hours for the night before the exam and allotted no study time to the morning before the exam (the exam was in the late afternoon.).

The professor assured Tom that although the psychology exam probably was not the most difficult one he would ever take in college, learning the material would require more than 4 hours of study time if he wanted to improve his grade for the course. Tom wasn't just bad at managing time—he was terrible! True, he had a part-time job in addition to the credit hours he was taking, but as he mapped out how he used his time during the day, Tom quickly became aware that he was wasting big chunks of it.

Self-Assessment

Taking Stock of Your Learning Strategies

We take seriously the importance of your ability to develop your self-reflection skills in this course. In every chapter of the book, you will find self-assessments like this one to help you develop insights into your own behavior.

At the end of each chapter, you also will find other opportunities to practice thinking skills related to the content of the chapter.

In this first exercise, review the elements of effective learning and, for each of them, indicate whether you think it is an area of strength you already demonstrate in your approach to new courses or it may be an area in which you could use some improvement. After you complete this exercise on learning strategies, read on about how to strengthen your abilities as a student in psychology to prepare you for this course.

Strength	Could be improved	
___	___	I manage my time effectively to complete course assignments.
___	___	I use study environments that reduce distractions.
___	___	I can concentrate on my studies without losing too much time to daydreaming.
___	___	I read my text carefully to capture critical concepts and ideas

Strength	Could be improved	
___	___	I listen carefully and make meaningful notes during lecture and classroom activities.
___	___	I organize and reorganize ideas to help me grasp main points and key concepts rather than memorize everything I read or hear.
___	___	I rehearse materials until they are "overlearned" to enhance my effectiveness on objective tests.
___	___	I devote a sufficient amount of time using properly spaced study sessions in order to avoid last-minute cramming for tests.
___	___	I involve myself personally by looking for how the ideas presented in class connect with and apply to my personal life.
___	___	I ask questions about the ideas that are confusing or seem inaccurate or incomplete to me.
___	___	I actively evaluate how successful my approach is to the course, based on feedback from my instructor, and make corrections to improve my effectiveness.

One week is 168 hours. Students vary in how they invest those hours. A typical full-time college student sleeps 50 hours, attends class between 12 and 20 hours, and eats 11 hours in every week. Students divide the remaining hours between study, work and family obligations, and leisure pursuits.

Tom attends class for 19 hours. In his situation, we must also allot 15 hours a week for his part-time job and 6 hours a week for transportation to and from school, work, and home. Tom finds that his main activities account for 101 hours of the week. Even though he works, he still has 67 hours in which to strike a balance between study and his other commitments.

The degree of success that you experience depends on how much time you allocate to study as well as how efficiently you use that time. One general rule that you might find helpful is to spend 1 hour outside of class for every hour in class. Although this strategy doesn't guarantee success, it definitely serves as an improvement over Tom's approach to study. If you have fewer competing obligations, you might find that a 2:1 ratio of study hours to classroom hours will be even more powerful in enhancing your success as a student.

You might find it helpful to fill out a weekly schedule of your activities to see where your time goes. Figure P.1 provides an example of one student's daily time schedule, along with comments about how and where time could be used more effectively, based on the ideas presented in this chapter. Examine this schedule and then construct your own model in figure P.2. Where are there opportunities to reshape how you use your time more effectively? Effective study often involves shorter, well-spaced study sessions than one intensive period of study. Where can you schedule shorter periods of study into your busy life?

Look carefully at your schedule to determine where there might be "holes" that you can fill with review activities. (This approach is sometimes referred to as the "Swiss cheese" method of time management.) But don't overlook scheduling, and sticking to, longer blocks of time that you devote exclusively to studying.

Time		Time used	Activity-Description
Start	End		
7:45	8:15	:30	Dress
8:15	8:40	:25	Breakfast
8:40	9:00	:20	Nothing
9:00	10:00	1:00	Psychology-Lecture
10:00	10:40	:40	Coffee-Talking
10:40	11:00	:20	Nothing
11:00	12:00	1:00	Economics-Lecture
12:00	12:45	:45	Lunch
12:45	2:00	1:15	Reading-Magazine
2:00	4:00	2:00	Biology-Lab
4:00	5:30	1:30	Recreation-Volleyball
5:30	6:00	:30	Nothing
6:00	7:00	1:00	Dinner
7:00	8:00	1:00	Nap
8:00	8:50	:50	Study-Statistics
8:50	9:20	:30	Break
9:20	10:00	:40	Study-Statistics
10:00	10:50	:50	Rap session
10:50	11:30	:40	Study-Accounting
11:30	11:45	:15	Ready for bed
11:45	7:45	8:00	Sleep

Paste on mirror 3 × 5 cards. Laws of economics; psychological terms; statistical formulas—study while brushing teeth, etc.

Look over textbook assignment and previous lecture notes to establish continuity for today's psychology lecture.

Break too long and too soon after breakfast. Should work on psychology notes just taken; also should look over economics assignment.

Should re-work the lecture notes on economics while still fresh in mind. Also, look over biology assignment to recall the objective of the upcoming lab.

Use this time for reading a magazine or newspaper.

Not a good idea. Better finish work, then get a good night's sleep.

Break—too long.

Good as a reward if basic work is done.

Insufficient time allotted, but better than no time.

While brushing teeth, study the 3 × 5 cards. Replace cards that have been mastered with new ones.

*F*IGURE P.1

Record of One Day's Activities and Suggestions for Better Time Management

Some students object to the use of a study schedule. They are afraid that a schedule will make them too rigid; however, more successful students usually follow organized schedules in order to manage their time efficiently. One compelling advantage in scheduling your time is the enhanced sense of control you will feel over your life; if you waste less time, you will have much more free time for personal activities and will spend fewer hours feeling guilty or unproductive.

How can you learn to live with a schedule? Try taking 5 minutes every morning to chart your plan for the day. Before you go to bed at night, review your day to see how well you met your schedule. Try to make this review a regular part of your routine. Your review will help you pinpoint problems that need to be solved or changes that must be made in your schedule to ensure your success. With a few weeks of practice, you should notice that this review becomes a more natural part of your daily routine.

What happens if you blow it? Like any new healthy habit, effective time management takes some time to learn. Don't let a minor deviation from the plan derail your good intentions to improve your study skills. Don't be too harsh in your evaluation. Recommit yourself to better time management tomorrow. As each week goes by, you may notice less strain in managing your time effectively.

What's the Most Effective Study Environment?

There are many distractions that keep you from studying or remembering what you have studied. Select your place of study carefully, paying close attention to the features of the environment that will allow you to do your best work.

Some students find that they work best if they consistently study in the same place. Ideally, this area should be well lighted without glare and should be a comfortable temperature. A quiet environment is more conducive to effective concentration than a noisy environment. Noise is one of the main distractions to effective study. Turn off the stereo, radio, or television while you are studying to minimize distraction. However, your

| Time | | Time | |
Start	End	used	Activity-Description

𝓕IGURE P.2

Constructing Your Own Time Management Schedule

Make up a time management schedule for one day in your life. If you need more lines, transfer the schedule to another sheet of paper and add them. After creating the schedule, reflect on what you learned about how efficient you are in organizing your time.

options about where you study may be limited. If your situation involves interruption and noise, soft music and earphones will mask many of these distractions. When you read chapter 13, "Health, Stress, and Coping," you may find other ideas that will help you in selecting a stress-reduced environment that will promote your best efficiency and productivity.

The library may be just the right place to maximize your ability to concentrate. Go there to study, especially if there are people where you live who are likely to distract you. If you live on campus, you may want to explore other quiet areas that you can adopt for your study purposes. For example, some residence halls maintain quiet rooms that will promote a nondistracting environment. However, don't rule out other, less obvious possibilities. Some students report success in studying while riding on public transportation and find this practice a reliable one to increase their study time, especially if long rides are required.

Some individuals need a private, personal study area to maximize their efficiency. This area often includes your own desk—a specific place for pens, paper, and books. If you plan to organize your studies around your desk, you may find it helpful to use your desk *only* for studying. If you nap or daydream extensively at your desk, it can act as a cue for more napping and daydreaming. Use your desk as a cue for studying. When you choose to nap or spend some time daydreaming, go somewhere else.

How Can I Maximize My Reading Effectiveness?

Many students approach the challenge of reading the text as just so many pages to plow through. There is a difference between *reading to read* (to complete the required number of pages) and *reading to learn*. Reading to learn from a text is enhanced if you approach the text as a conversation the author is having with you about the concepts and principles in psychology. As in any effective conversation, you must pay attention, figure out how the parts of the conversation fit together, and make some judgments as you go about acquiring other information you need in order to understand the author's intent.

The following strategies can help you maximize your ability to understand and retain what you read.

Preview and Plan.   Look at the number of pages you need to digest and plan how to read the assignment. If the task is very long, determine where there are appropriate breaks you can take. Plan how to reward yourself for sticking to the task. Make sure you have access to a dictionary if the vocabulary looks challenging. The purpose of previewing is to help you plan your reading strategy.

Skim.   Look at the structure of the assignment and extract the main ideas in what you will cover. Look at the headings. Read the paragraphs that introduce a new section. Examine review or summary features. Glance at the terms in the chapter to determine their familiarity. When you skim, you begin to develop a foundation for the main ideas the chapter has to offer.

Read to Comprehend.   There is no way around the hard work involved in learning the material in a textbook. However, there are some things you can do to make your reading to understand the assignment more efficient and effective.

Pay attention to the sections of the assignment as meaningful units. Take one section at a time. Read each unit until you are satisfied that you know the ideas.

Don't skip over what you don't understand. Think about confusing parts in the context of what you are reading. What clues can you pick up from the surrounding material that can help you understand? Draw pictures or make notes in the margins of your text. Find a classmate to discuss the ideas that are challenging.

Work on your reading speed. Practice taking in more words as your eye sweeps the line of print. Don't mouth the words as you read, this practice only slows you down. It will make you abandon your reading sooner. Good readers tend to be faster readers.

What happens if you are reading along and suddenly realize you haven't been paying attention? Don't worry. This happens even to the best readers. Retrace your steps to the last material that is meaningful to you and start again. If you get lost again, it is a sign that you might need to take a short break. Coming back refreshed will help you stay on task.

Read to Retain.   Most students need to read assignments more than once if they are going to learn what the assignment has to offer. When you read to retain the ideas, practice reading analytically. Think about personal examples that can illustrate the concepts. Question how the parts of the assignment go together. Identify whether you agree with the ideas expressed in the chapter. Set aside a portion of your notes where you record your observations about the reading. By actively constructing your own meaning in the reading, you will provide many more ways to help you recall the critical ideas at test time.

Review.   After you have used the techniques suggested so far, you need to *review* the material you have read at least several times before you take a test. Just because you have read a chapter, do not think that you will be able to recall all of its information. By reciting the information, thinking critically about the key ideas, and continuing to review the material, you will improve your test performance. At the end of each chapter in this book, we will encourage you to go back and once again read the in-chapter reviews to obtain an overall summary of the chapter.

How Can I Better Listen and Concentrate in Class?

Unfortunately much of the knowledge offered in your courses might pass through your mind like grains of sand washed through a sieve. You need to do more than just memorize or passively absorb new information in class. You must attend, listen carefully, and take notes that will serve you well outside of class.

Being There.   What about attendance? Instructors vary in the importance they place on your regular attendance; however, the vast majority are likely to treat each and every class hour as an important learning experience they have carefully planned to assist your learning. You would not skip a chapter in this book if you knew that you were responsible for the chapter on a later test, so it is not a good idea to skip a class just to reach the allowed number of cuts or to cram for an exam. Some students believe that, because they go to class and listen passively, they can get by in test situations without devoting further study time. However, by preparing for the lecture, using learning strategies actively during the lecture, and doing simple follow-up work on what you have heard, you should be able to improve your performance in the course.

Listening Carefully. What goes on in the classroom is just as important as what is in this textbook. Listening to lecture or attending out other kinds of class activities can also be regarded as a conversation in which you are an active participant, if you are going to reap maximum benefits for your learning.

In preparing for a lecture, motivate yourself by telling yourself that it is important for you to stay alert and listen carefully. Make sure that you get sufficient rest and have eaten recently enough that your body won't distract you from listening. A regular exercise program can also heighten your alertness.

One approach to improve your involvement with the lecture is to listen with the intention of making connections between what you already know and what you are listening to in the lecture. As you listen to lecture or class discussion, actively process the ideas being presented. To assist you in developing this ability, the following questions may help:

- Did I understand this portion?
- What's the main point?
- Does this remind me of anything in my own personal experience?
- Does this content relate to other ideas I've learned in this or other courses?
- Do the points seem accurate and valid, or is something missing?
- Do I like or agree with the ideas proposed?

Initially, this approach may feel cumbersome; however, this deeper level of processing will help you build a more enduring content base for future testing and future life applications. This approach will also prepare you effectively to participate in any class discussions.

Despite good intentions, occasionally you might find yourself daydreaming instead of concentrating. Daydreaming is a natural occurrence that takes you away from the task at hand. As you will read in chapter 4, "States of Consciousness," some amount of daydreaming may be inevitable in any period set aside for work. However, daydreaming can sometimes get out of hand. Even though daydreaming can be pleasant and restful, the consequences of extensive daydreaming can be poor test or course grades.

How can you reduce the amount of time you spend daydreaming? Analyze the trends in your daydreaming. Are you trying to solve some problem? Or are you spending time thinking about something over which you have virtually no control? Promise yourself that you will pursue specific problems more intently after your study period is over.

When daydreaming problems are serious, some students have found a mild punishment technique to be helpful. Wear a rubber band around your wrist. When you recognize that you are off-task, snap the rubber band and refocus your attention on the task at hand. Then congratulate yourself at the end of a successful study period for your improved self-discipline.

If the problems that prompt you to daydream seem overwhelming, and you simply cannot avoid thinking about them, you may want to contact the student counseling service at your college or university. Most college and university counseling centers not only have counselors who help students with personal problems, but they often have study skills counselors who help students personalize more successful approaches to their studies.

Taking Effective Notes. Note taking can serve as an effective method to focus your attention. Some students approach taking notes as a stenographer might. They try to record every word without evaluating its significance or importance. They assume that the material will make more sense to them later if they have as much as possible of the material verbatim. This approach does work for a few students; however, most feel frustrated later when they review the massive quantity of information they have recorded, because it might not make sense and will feel overwhelming.

Instead, experiment with note-taking forms to see which serves you best. Some students find that recording notes in a simple narrative paragraph serves very well to capture key ideas and stimulate further questions. Others may find that mapping or outlining helps to organize the content and clarify how each point relates to others in the lecture. Striving to capture general ideas rather than minute details tends to be more effective.

There is no one right way to take notes. You need to develop a system that feels comfortable for you. For example, you can leave a wide margin to make your own notes or ask questions that you wish to follow up on later. You can skip lines to show the end of one idea and the beginning of another. Use abbreviations to save time so you can listen more. Table P.1 offers some examples of abbreviations that will be helpful in a psychology class. The list is not exhaustive. Keep in mind that you can customize your notes by developing your own abbreviations for terms you find yourself using regularly. Draw pictures if they help you personalize what you hear. Regardless of the specific features that you incorporate into your own note-taking style, write legibly so that, when you review, you will know what you have written.

𝒯ABLE P.1
**Some Abbreviations
You Can Use in
Psychology Classes**

ψ = psychology ("psi")
env = environmental
Fr = Freud
ⓑ = behavior
s'o = schizophrenia
dev = development
→ = leads to
∴ = therefore
sig = significant
cog = cognitive
sc = sociocultural
prsp = perspective

In addition, some students rewrite and reorganize their notes as a method of rehearsing main ideas. You may want to consolidate your notes during your first free time after class by underlining the key ideas. Reviewing these highlights before the next class period will improve your ability to recall the information. You will also prepare yourself effectively for what will be said in the upcoming class or questions that the instructor may pose.

How Should I Prepare for Tests?

In most cases, your grade in this course will depend on how well you do on the exams spaced periodically throughout the semester. Well-constructed tests can serve as very accurate representations of the quality of your learning, although even well-constructed examinations won't be able to reflect everything that you have learned.

Students have mixed feelings about tests. Tests can be time-consuming, nerve-racking, and "tricky"; however, doing well on a test for which you have prepared well provides a special thrill. To enhance your course performance, we will address several areas.

Identifying the Test Format. Find out what kind of testing you will be confronting. Will the challenge be an objective test comprised of multiple-choice questions? How many questions? What kind of format? Usually such tests emphasize term recognition and information recall. Therefore, preparation for such tests relies most heavily on memorization.

On the other hand, some instructors will evaluate your knowledge using *productive* measures, such as essay tests. In this kind of challenge, the teacher might emphasize *higher-order* thinking skills. Teachers might ask you to construct or defend an argument, to make comparisons between two approaches, to find flaws in an experiment, or to identify underlying values in a theoretical position. These tasks are appropriate critical thinking challenges for those just learning the discipline.

Preparing the Content. Regardless of the examination format, your grade in this course will depend on how well you perform in testing situations. Complete all of your textbook reading several days before an examination. All of your classroom notes should be in order so you can review them easily. Complete and hand in all term papers or projects so that you are free to concentrate on organizing and consolidating the information in the manner that fits the testing format.

If you have been following an effective routine for managing your time, taking notes, keeping up, and building in opportunities to recite and review what you have learned, you should be well positioned to consolidate what you have learned for the examination. Develop a summary system, which follows closely what you did for each chapter or lecture. Several days before the exam, review several chapters and a number of lectures. Try putting them together in an overall system the last day or so before the exam.

Some students find it helpful to develop their own multiple-choice questions for practice. This experience may help you think about the content as your professor might.

Should you cram for an exam? If you have not studied much until several days before the exam, you will probably have to do some intensive studying prior to the test. However, cramming can never replace methodical, consistent study throughout the course. Studying in shorter sessions that are distributed over time will produce superior results compared to cramming.

Practicing the Test Skills. Memorizing new ideas is a foundation skill in this and other courses you will be taking. How can you remember course terms and principles more effectively?

First, make up your mind to remember. If you really want to improve your memory, you can; but you must motivate yourself to improve. Second, keep refreshing your memory of the content you are trying to learn. Almost everything tends to fade unless you periodically think about it. Periodic rehearsal of what you have heard in class or read in this book will help you store the information and retrieve it not just for testing situations but for other practical purposes as well. Third, organize, outline, or otherwise structure what you want to remember. Pick out the main points in the material you are studying and arrange them in a meaningful pattern, outline, or image. Recite and repeat them until you can recall them on command. Select, organize, and repeat—these are time-tested steps for helping you remember.

You can adopt a number of strategies for improving your memory in learning psychology. One powerful approach is to relate what you have read to your own life. By drawing more connections to unfamiliar material, you make the ideas more accessible and more interesting. Chapter 6, "Memory," will address several other approaches to improving memory. If this approach intrigues you, skip ahead to that chapter and read how these techniques can help you organize and recall psychological concepts.

If you will be confronting testing situations that require more than memorization, you need other preparation strategies. If your teacher asks you to write essay questions, ask the instructor for sample questions. Ask what kinds of thinking will be required. Try to anticipate what kinds of questions could be crafted by the instructor to fit the material. If you practice thinking about these potential questions, you aren't likely to be surprised by the particular combinations of ideas that your instructor may develop. Write out some questions for practice to increase your rehearsal time and build your confidence.

Preparing Yourself. To ensure success on an exam, you need to be physically and psychologically ready in addition to having facts, ideas, and principles in mind. First, you need rest; second, you need confidence. If you create mountains of work for yourself, especially by not studying until the last minute, you will rob yourself of sleep, food, and exercise, leaving both your mind and your body in poor shape to perform well on an exam. If you find that anxiety significantly interferes with your performance, you may want to seek assistance from the student counseling center to develop strategies to minimize this interference. On the other hand, if you have managed more systematic approaches to your studies, you will be less likely to panic and will be more likely to develop a confident attitude about the test.

Learning from the Test. Some students believe that when the test is over, the learning is over. However, reviewing the test results and listening to instructor feedback will help you develop your study skills in several ways. First, determine which strategies were truly helpful in organizing the better features of your test performance. Second, revise incorrect ideas for future testing challenges or other practical uses. Finally, consider other approaches you might take to increase the quality of your future performance. These alternatives may include seeking additional tutoring, asking for a conference with the instructor to seek further feedback, or developing a study group with your peers in the class.

SUMMING UP

Through planning, study, and review, you will be able to learn psychology efficiently and effectively. Practice your thinking skills as you read your text and study, as you participate in class, and as you go about your everyday activities. By increasing your knowledge about behavior, you will not only build an impressive knowledge base but improve the skills that will help you observe, describe, explain, and predict behavior.

Overview

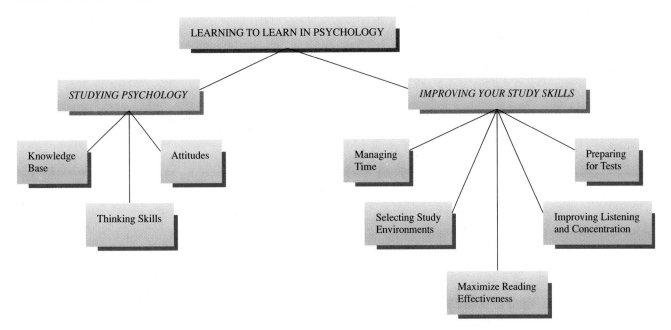

In this prechapter, "Learning to Learn in Psychology," you initially read about studying psychology, with an emphasis on three things: acquiring a specialized knowledge base about psychology, learning to think about behavior, and developing attitudes and motivations consistent with the science of psychology. Then you read about ways to improve your study skills, which included managing time, selecting study environments, maximizing reading effectiveness, improving listening and concentration, and preparing for tests.

1

The Scope and Methods of Psychology

OUTLINE

BOXES

Science is not an inhuman or superhuman activity. It's something that humans invented and it speaks to one of our great needs—to understand the world around us.

—MAXINE SINGER
American Geneticist, 20th Century

PREVIEW

What leads one person, so full of promise, to commit brutal acts of violence and another to turn poverty and trauma into a rich, literary harvest? How can we attempt to explain why one person can pick up the pieces of a life shattered by tragedy, such as a loved one's death, whereas another comes unhinged by life's minor hassles? Why is it some people are whirlwinds—involved in their work and with family and friends, with time left over for community organizations—whereas others hang out on the sidelines, mere spectators in life? Explaining such curiosities is an important goal of psychology. In this first chapter, we will introduce you to the field of psychology, explore its scientific base, and challenge you to think critically about behavior.

The Stories of Ted Kaczynski and Alice Walker

Ted Kaczynski grew up in a middle-class family in Illinois. He sprinted through high school—a young genius who was so bright that he did not even bother with his junior year—and enrolled at Harvard when he was only 16. In high school Ted had made only passing efforts at social contact, and in college he continued to be a loner. One of his roommates at Harvard said that Ted had a special way of avoiding people by quickly shuffling by them and slamming the door behind him.

After graduating from Harvard, Kaczynski went to graduate school in mathematics at the University of Michigan and obtained his Ph.D. Then he became an assistant professor at the University of California at Berkeley. His colleagues there remember him as aloof and unsociable. He had no friends, he made no allies, and he did no networking.

Theodore Kaczynski, the Unabomber, traced his difficulties to growing up as a genius in a kid's body and not fitting in when he was a child.

Alice Walker won the Pulitzer Prize for her book *The Color Purple*. Like the characters in her book (especially the women), Walker overcame pain and anger to triumph and celebrate the human spirit.

After several years at Berkeley, Kaczynski resigned his teaching post and moved to a rural area of Montana where he lived a spartan existence in a crude shack for 25 years. In 1996, the shy hermit was arrested and charged with being the notorious Unabomber, America's most wanted killer. Authorities said that over the course of 17 years Kaczynski had built and sent 16 mail bombs that killed 3 people and left 23 others wounded and maimed. Neighbors and acquaintances were shocked. They could not conceive that the quiet former college professor was the Unabomber. Ted Kaczynski traced his own difficulties to growing up as a genius in a kid's body and sticking out like a sore thumb in his world.

A decade before the first Unabomber mail bomb was sent, Alice Walker was battling racism in Mississippi. She had won her first writing fellowship, but rather than use the money to follow her dream of moving to Senegal, Africa, she put herself into the heart and heat of the civil rights movement. Walker grew up knowing the brutal effects of poverty and racism. Born in 1944, she was the eighth child of Georgia sharecroppers who earned $300 a year. When Walker was 8, her brother accidentally shot her in the left eye with a BB gun. By the time her parents got her to the hospital a week later (they had no car), she was blind in that eye and it had developed a disfiguring layer of scar tissue. Despite the counts against her, Walker went on to become an essayist, a poet, an award-winning novelist, a short-story writer, and a social activist who, like her characters (especially the women), has overcome pain and anger. Alice Walker was awarded the Pulitzer Prize for her novel *The Color Purple*. ❖

INTRODUCING PSYCHOLOGY

If you have every wondered what makes people tick, you have asked yourself psychology's central question. In this book, you will explore not only the dimensions of what makes us human, but what makes us grow and change—or what makes us stumble and fail. You will learn about the methods psychologists use to explain human nature as well as the progress psychology has made in understanding behavior. A special feature of this book is how sociocultural factors, such as culture, ethnic background, gender, and economic circumstances, influence what people think and how they behave.

Psychology is uniquely qualified to help us make sense of a complex and challenging world. One day's edition of the *New York Times* is packed with more information than a person who lived in the Middle Ages acquired during a lifetime. The media bombard us daily with studies, surveys, and "expert" opinions. Access to the Internet produces even more input for us to consider and absorb. Psychology can help us critically examine, understand, and evaluate this flood of information.

One crucial benefit of getting a background in psychology is the practical assistance it can provide in our daily lives. For example, consider these findings:

- Both divorced and unhappily married people are more vulnerable to disease than are happily married people (Kiecolt-Glaser & others, 1993). This finding suggests that stressful relationships put individuals at risk for psychological and physical problems.
- Parents who are nurturant and firm are more likely to have children who cope well with stress than are parents who neglect or overcontrol their children (Baumrind, 1991).
- Moderate aerobic exercise not only improves most people's physical health, but it also reduces their anxiety and improves their self-concept (Moses & others, 1989).

As you can see, knowledge of research in psychology can help people live more satisfying and fulfilling lives.

Psychology can also improve the quality of our professional lives. The U.S. workforce is becoming increasingly diverse. By the year 2000, more than 80 percent of people entering the job market will be women and members of ethnic minority groups (Schultz & Schultz, 1998). This shift in the workforce requires greater awareness of similarities and differences among different kinds of people. Our prosperity as a country might depend on how effectively we manage the strains of new patterns in the workplace.

Psychology can help us untangle complex questions about how the world is changing. As our need to import and export goods increases, we are becoming more interdependent with other parts of the globe. We must understand other cultures for our mutual benefit. For example, psychology can help us learn about how North Americans and Latin Americans differ in their expectations for promoting stronger trade relations. We can learn from the Japanese what factors help them maintain low homicide rates despite their crowded metropolitan conditions. We can look to other industrialized countries in the world for ideas about reducing our high rate of teenage pregnancy. Theories of behavior need to reflect the experience of *all* people, both within and across national boundaries (Church & Lonner, 1998).

Although we will explore many questions about behavior, psychologists do not have all the answers. Psychology is still a very young science, and as you will see, many issues are very complex. Although it might not give us a solution for every problem, psychology can contribute enormously to our knowledge about why people are the way they are, why they think and act the way they do, and how they can cope more effectively with their lives. Psychologists are enthusiastic about the potential of the science to improve our lives as we begin the twenty-first century. This is an exciting time of discovery in the field of psychology.

Defining Psychology

Which kind of couple is more likely to have a long-lasting marriage—couples who live together before they marry, or couples who wait until after the wedding ceremony to begin living together? Common sense might tell you "practice makes perfect." If so, you might think that living together before marriage is the best bet. However, one research study suggests that couples who do *not* live together before marriage have a higher success rate than those who "practiced" married life (Teachman & Polonko, 1990). As you can see, psychology doesn't accept commonsense assumptions about human nature, however reasonable these assumptions sound. Psychologists rigorously test assumptions and gather evidence to explain behavior.

Psychology *is the scientific study of behavior and mental processes in context.* Psychology emphasizes observing, describing, explaining, and predicting behavior. Let's further examine the important elements in our definition of psychology: behavior, mental processes, science, and context.

Behavior *is everything that we do that can be directly observed.* This includes two people *kissing*, a baby *crying*, a student *studying*. Psychologists strive to describe behavior in simple and precise terms. They use verbs *(kissing, crying, studying)* to communicate observable actions.

Mental processes are trickier to define. These covert behaviors include *thoughts, feelings, and motives that each of us experiences privately but that cannot be observed directly.* Although we cannot directly observe and describe thoughts and feelings, they are no less real because of that. For example, mental processes include the *thoughts* you have when you anticipate kissing someone, the heart-fluttering *feelings* you have when your lips touch, and the *memories* the kiss may stir of someone who was a better kisser.

Because we can't observe these processes directly in others, we often *infer* the mental processes that support observable behavior. Psychologists are also careful to distinguish

psychology
The scientific study of behavior and mental processes in context.

behavior
Everything that organisms can do that can be directly observed.

mental processes
Thoughts, feelings, and motives that each person experiences privately but that cannot be observed directly.

behavior ("They are *kissing*") from inferences about behavior ("They must really like each other"). Inferences help us to interpret the meaning of a behavior, but different people can draw different inferences from the same behavior. And inferences can be dead wrong. For example, you might feel compelled to kiss Aunt Minnie at a family reunion even though you really don't like her. Someone watching you kiss your aunt might infer that you do like her, but that judgment would be wrong—that person's interpretation of your behavior does not accurately reflect your real feelings. As you can see, describing behavior is a relatively straightforward process but drawing inferences about unobservable mental processes is not. Your ability to interpret and predict behavior depends on making *sound* (that is, truthful and logical) inferences.

The **science of psychology** *uses systematic methods to observe, describe, explain, and predict behavior.* Psychology's methods involve hard work. Psychologists carefully plan and conduct research to generate meaningful data about behavior. Psychologists *observe* behavior in natural and laboratory environments. They *describe* these regular patterns of behavior using psychological terminology or concepts. After psychologists gather data, they want to *explain* what they have found. As is true of all sciences, psychologists strive to discover why something happens. This enables them to *predict* behavior.

Let's explore how this might work in an applied setting. Suppose you are working in a grocery store and you notice some patterns in consumer behavior that intrigue you. For example, you observe that people tend to linger near large sale signs, they shop faster when they have children along, and they often pick up small items near the cashier line. You make careful notes in which you describe this consumer behavior and begin to get some ideas about how you can increase sales of some items. You systematically vary sales conditions and note the impact each strategy has on what shoppers purchase. Eventually you can predict which sales strategies will work and which will be a waste of time. Careful observation and description set the stage for explaining and predicting behavior.

The fourth key aspect of our definition of psychology is **context,** *the historical, economic, social, and cultural factors that influence mental processes and behavior.* People do not act, or react, in a vacuum. Everything we think, say, or do is influenced by where we come from, the people we interact with, what has happened to us in the past, and what we think might happen to us in the future (Gopaul-McNicol & Brice-Baker, 1998).

> *Some things are very important and some are very unimportant. To know the differences is what we are given life to find out.*
> —ANNA F. TREVISAN, *American Biographer, 20th Century*

Exploring Psychology's History

Ever since our ancestors first gathered around fires to share their experiences, humans have tried to explain why things are the way they are. Most events were attributed to the pleasure or displeasure of the gods. When two people fell in love, they were pierced by Cupid's arrows. When a volcano erupted, the gods were angry. As we became more sophisticated, myth and superstition gave way to philosophy and rational speculations about the underlying principles of experience.

Forerunners of Psychology. Psychology has been mainly an enterprise of Western cultures. However, history that involves psychological issues has many global ties. For example, the first recorded evidence of behavior being measured for an applied purpose is from China in 2000 B.C. The Emperor Ta Yu developed methods for testing the competence of government officials before making promotion decisions.

Early Greek philosophers contributed many ideas that are basic to psychology. Socrates (469–399 B.C.) urged us to know ourselves. Aristotle (384–322 B.C.) encouraged us to use logic to make inferences about the mind as well as to observe behavior

science of psychology
The science that uses systematic methods to observe, describe, explain, and predict human behavior.

context
The historical, economic, social, and cultural factors that influence mental processes and behavior.

The Beginning of Psychology as a Science

Wilhelm Wundt established the first research laboratory in psychology at Germany's University of Leipzig in 1879. To help you place Wundt's achievement in history, consider that Alexander Graham Bell invented the telephone in 1876.

method of introspection

The process in which specially trained people systematically observe and analyze their own mental experience.

structuralism

An approach to psychology that emphasizes classifying sensations in order to discover the mind's structures.

functionalism

An approach to psychology that emphasizes the functions of the mind and behavior in adapting to the environment.

systematically. Direct observation remains an important dimension of psychology today.

Philosophical traditions in the Western world began to challenge Greek assumptions about the nature of knowledge. In the sixteenth and seventeenth centuries, philosophers debated many issues relevant to psychology. For example, they questioned whether knowledge is inborn or a product of our environment. This was a prelude to psychology's enduring interest in the *nature-nurture controversy.* That is, is a person's behavior due more to nature (biology, heredity) or to nurture (experience, environment)? Although such philosophical speculation fueled a great deal of intellectual passion, it did not produce many concrete answers.

Science emerged from philosophy in the sixteenth century. British scientist Francis Bacon argued that understanding nature requires more than direct observation alone. He advocated questioning and testing assumptions whenever possible. However, it was not until the late nineteenth century that the traditions of philosophy and science converged to produce the systematic examination of behavior that came to be known as psychology.

Psychology's Emergence in Europe.   Most historians credit Wilhelm Wundt with establishing the first scientific laboratory dedicated to studying behavior (see figure 1.1). Wundt opened his laboratory in Leipzig in 1879. His approach involved the **method of introspection,** *in which specially trained people systematically observe and analyze their own mental experience.* Wundt's goal was to demonstrate how sensations, feelings, and "volitions" (tendencies to respond) combined to produce immediate experience (Bolles, 1993). Wundt and his students used introspection to study reaction times, perceptual problems, and the chemical senses of taste and smell. Some of Wundt's many students brought psychology to America where it flourished.

Psychology Comes to North America.   Englishman Edward Bradford Titchener established a laboratory at Cornell University in 1892 to continue Wundt's traditions. However, he drifted from Wundt's beliefs. Titchener came to believe that perceptions should be analyzed into elemental sensations. This approach, which became known as **structuralism,** *emphasizes classifying sensations in order to discover the mind's structure.*

Another important figure in early American psychology was William James, who authored the first psychology textbook, published in 1890. James also used the method of introspection but rejected the quest to discover the mind's structures. Instead, James studied the mind's functions. James argued that our minds are characterized more accurately as a continuous flow of information about experience than as discrete structures. He was more interested in the *how* of behavior than the *what* of the mind. James's approach, which became known as **functionalism,** *emphasizes the functions of the mind and behavior in adapting to the environment.*

Early in the twentieth century, two distinct breeds of psychologists started to become apparent. They have been referred to as the "hardheaded" and the "softhearted" (Kimble, 1984). The hardheaded are experimental psychologists, like Wilhelm Wundt and William James, who generate knowledge through research. The softhearted are psychologists who use the principles of psychology to help others in clinical and applied settings. In some universities, experimental and clinical psychologists maintain a kind of rivalry. However, clinical psychologists receive experimental training as part of the "scientist-practitioner" model endorsed by the American Psychological Association. Thus, the distinction between experimentalists and clinicians sometimes is artificial.

As research flourished in psychology, hardheaded psychologists began to be uncomfortable with the limitations of introspection. John Watson (1913) argued that psychologists should observe behavior directly rather than infer mental processes. He also encouraged the science to look beyond internal, mental factors. Watson believed that psychologists should study overt behavior and environmental influences.

Softhearted psychologists became taken with the clinical methods of Sigmund Freud early in the century. Freud encouraged individuals to talk about their problems to help them expose and correct early trauma. Although his theory is controversial, Freud left a powerful legacy that spawned hundreds of approaches used by clinicians today. Next, as we explore psychology's contemporary perspectives, you will read further about both clinical and experimental approaches in exploring behavior.

eview

Introducing Psychology, Defining and Exploring the History of Psychology

Psychology can serve many functions, among them providing a better understanding of how people behave and think. Psychology is the scientific study of behavior and mental processes in contexts. Behavior is everything we do that can be directly observed. Mental processes are the thoughts, feelings, and motives that we experience privately but that cannot be directly observed. As a science, psychology uses systematic methods to observe, describe, explain, and predict behavior. Contexts are the settings in which mental processes and behavior occur, settings that involve historical, economic, social, and cultural factors. Recently there has been a renewed interest in contexts in psychology. The contexts of mental processes and behavior are discussed extensively in this text.

Thinking about psychological concepts began with the early Greek philosophers, such as Socrates and Aristotle. Psychology began as a science when Wilhelm Wundt developed the first scientific laboratory of psychology in 1879 in Leipzig, Germany. Wundt's student, E. B. Titchener, established an experimental laboratory in America and began the approach called structuralism. William James, one of the first American psychologists, developed an approach that became known as functionalism. Many of the early psychologists, such as Wundt and James, used introspection, the technique whereby specially trained individuals carefully observe and analyze their own mental experience.

Psychologists such as John Watson began to challenge introspection and argue that psychologists should observe behavior more directly. Two distinct branches of psychology became apparent early in the twentieth century—"hardheaded" research and "softhearted" clinical psychology.

Contemporary Perspectives

As this century nears its close, psychology is rich in perspectives. Seven important perspectives in contemporary psychology are the behavioral, psychoanalytic, humanistic, neurobiological, cognitive, evolutionary, and sociocultural. Each perspective represents a distinctive way of looking at behavior. Each tends to emphasize certain elements in explaining behavior, and each also might omit or diminish other factors that contribute to behavior. We will briefly describe each of these approaches and also return to them in later chapters.

Abstract principles of psychology can be difficult to remember. Throughout this book, we will illustrate psychology's perspectives by providing applications of the ideas. Here we will explore how each of these frameworks helps us shed light on the lives of Ted Kaczynski and Alice Walker.

> There are few things more exciting to me than a psychological reason.
> —WILLIAM JAMES, *American Psychologist, 19th/20th Century*

behavioral perspective

A perspective that emphasizes the scientific study of observable behavioral responses and their environmental determinants.

The Behavioral Perspective. The **behavioral perspective** *emphasizes the scientific study of observable behavioral responses and their environmental determinants.* Under the intellectual leadership of John B. Watson and B. F. Skinner, behaviorism dominated psychological research during the first half of the twentieth century.

Behaviorists emphasize that what we *do* is the ultimate test of who we are. They also stress that rewards and punishments determine our behavior. For example, we behave in a well-mannered fashion for our parents because of the controls they place on us. We work hard at our jobs because of the money we receive for our effort. We don't do these things, say behaviorists, because of an inborn motivation to be competent people—we do them because of the environmental conditions we have experienced and continue to experience (Skinner, 1938).

What Can the Behavioral Perspective Tell Us About Ted Kaczynski and Alice Walker? Behaviorists would tell us not to look inside Kaczynski and Walker to try to find out what makes them tick. According to behaviorists, inner motives and feelings cannot be directly observed, so they won't really help us understand behavior. Behaviorists don't deny that our thoughts and feelings exist. However, they emphasize that feedback from the environment is more important in determining behavior. Behaviorists trying to explain Kaczynski's and Walker's behavior would examine their learning history. Perhaps Kaczynski was rewarded for his intellectual mastery but punished for his social efforts. Walker was positively reinforced for the hard work she put into her writing. This encouraged her to work even harder to produce truly distinctive work.

psychoanalytic perspective

A perspective that emphasizes unconscious thought, conflict between biological instincts and society's demands, and early family experiences.

The Psychoanalytic Perspective. The **psychoanalytic perspective** *emphasizes unconscious thought, the conflict between biological instincts and society's demands, as well as early family experiences.* This approach stresses that unlearned biological instincts, especially sexual and aggressive impulses, influence the way people think, feel, and act. These instincts, buried deep within the unconscious mind, are often at odds with society's demands. Although Freud saw much of psychological development as instinctual, he argued that early relationships with parents are the chief forces that shape an individual's personality. Freud's ideas were controversial when he introduced them in Vienna around the turn of the century. However, his ideas flourished, and many clinicians still find value in his insights about human behavior.

What Can the Psychoanalytic Perspective Tell Us About Ted Kaczynski and Alice Walker? The psychoanalytic perspective suggests that Kaczynski and Walker are likely to be unaware of why they behave the way they do. That is, there might be unconscious reasons, derived from early family experience, for why Kaczynski sent mail bombs and Walker writes such sensitive novels. It also says that they experience considerable conflict between their biological needs and the demands of reality—for instance, that Kaczynski succumbed to his aggressive impulses and Walker successfully exploited her experiences with aggression in her writing.

humanistic perspective

A perspective that emphasizes a person's capacity for personal growth, freedom to choose a destiny, and positive qualities.

The Humanistic Perspective. The **humanistic perspective** *emphasizes a person's capacity for personal growth, freedom to choose a destiny, and positive qualities.* Humanistic psychologists stress that people have the ability to control their lives and not be manipulated by the environment (Maslow, 1971; Rogers, 1961). They believe that, rather than being driven by unconscious sexual and aggressive impulses, people have the ability to live by higher human values, such as altruism and free will. They also think we have tremendous potential for conscious self-understanding and that we can help others achieve self-understanding by being warm, nurturant, and supportive toward them. Many aspects of this optimistic approach to defining human nature survive in clinical practice today.

What Can the Humanistic Approach Tell Us About Ted Kaczynski and Alice Walker? Humanists would exalt in Alice Walker's personal triumph over challenging conditions. They would also speculate that Kaczynski likely did not receive adequate nurturance and support as a child or as an adult. According to the humanistic approach, Walker chose the right human values to guide her life, whereas Kaczynski selected the wrong ones and failed to live up to his true human potential.

neurobiological perspective

A perspective that emphasizes that the brain and nervous system play central roles in understanding behavior, thought, and emotion.

The Neurobiological Perspective. The **neurobiological perspective** *emphasizes that the brain and nervous system play central roles in understanding behavior, thought, and emotion.* Neurobiologists believe that thoughts have a physical basis in the brain (Squire, 1992). Electrical impulses zoom throughout the brain's cells, releasing chemical substances as we think, feel, and act. Our remarkable capacities as human beings would not be possible without the brain and nervous system, which constitute the most complex, intricate, and elegant system imaginable. This perspective has continued to grow in importance in psychology, supported by progress in technologies that unlock the body's secrets.

What Can the Neurobiological Perspective Tell Us About Ted Kaczynski and Alice Walker? Possibly something went wrong with Kaczynski's brain that contributed to his crimes. (A court-appointed psychiatrist diagnosed Kaczynski as paranoid schizophrenic, a condition that is widely considered to be a neurobiological disorder.) Possibly his shyness was inherited. His social isolation may have induced other physiological effects. Neurobiologists are intrigued by the neural circuitry that underlies virtually all behaviors, including Walker's brilliant writing efforts. They also would be interested in how Walker adapted to having vision in only one eye.

The Cognitive Perspective. In the 1950s, cognitive psychology emerged as a significant framework for understanding behavior. Cognitive psychologists challenged behaviorism's narrow perspective. The word *cognition* comes from the Latin for "to know." The **cognitive perspective** *emphasizes the mental processes involved in knowing: how we direct our attention, how we perceive, how we remember, and how we think and solve problems.* A cognitive psychologist views the mind as an active and aware problem-solving system (Ellis & Hunt, 1999; Simon, 1990).

cognitive perspective

A perspective that emphasizes the mental processes involved in knowing: how we direct our attention, how we perceive, how we remember, and how we think and solve problems.

What Can the Cognitive Perspective Tell Us About Ted Kaczynski and Alice Walker? Cognitive psychologists would be intrigued by Kaczynski's brilliant mind that enabled him to obtain a Ph.D. in mathematics and by Walker's literary gifts. They also would be interested in the decisions Kaczynski and Walker made and the problems they solved or failed to solve throughout their lives. Why did Kaczynski decide to become a hermit? How did he cognitively stitch together his Unabomber plot? Why did Walker choose to become a writer and social activist? How much was she motivated by her dreams of going to Africa?

The Evolutionary Perspective. Although Charles Darwin introduced the theory of evolution in 1859, his ideas about evolution only recently emerged as a popular framework for explaining behavior. The **evolutionary perspective** *emphasizes the importance of adaptation, reproduction, and the "survival of the fittest."* Evolutionary processes favor organisms that are best adapted to survive and reproduce in a particular environment. The evolutionary perspective focuses on conditions that allow individuals to thrive or to fail.

evolutionary perspective

A perspective that emphasizes the importance of adaptation, reproduction, and "survival of the fittest."

What Can the Evolutionary Perspective Tell Us About Ted Kaczynski and Alice Walker? Kaczynski's few attempts at romance met with dismal failure and kept him from passing on his genetic legacy through reproduction and parenting. His misbegotten actions are evidence of how poorly adapted he is to contemporary life. In contrast, Walker's thriving career as a writer attests to her ability to cope with the challenges of modern life.

The Sociocultural Perspective. The sociocultural approach is one of psychology's newest frameworks for examining behavior. The **sociocultural perspective** *emphasizes that culture, ethnicity, and gender, among other sociocultural contexts, are essential to understanding behavior.* From this perspective, behavior cannot be fully understood unless the context in which that behavior occurs is considered (Bronfenbrenner & Morris, 1998).

sociocultural perspective

A perspective that emphasizes that culture, ethnicity, and gender, among other sociocultural contexts, are essential to understanding behavior.

Students in wheelchairs or with other limitations face challenges in the physical environment, and in social contexts, that influence their adaptation.

culture

The behavior patterns, beliefs, and other products of a particular group of people; these include the values, work patterns, music, dress, diet, and rituals that are passed on from generation to generation.

ethnicity

A characteristic based on cultural heritage, nationality, race, religion, and language.

ethnic identity

Identification based on membership in an ethnic group.

gender

The sociocultural dimension of being female or male.

Culture *refers to a people's behavior patterns, beliefs, and other products— including the values, work patterns, music, dress, diet, and rituals that are passed on from generation to generation.* The culture of a group influences the identity, learning, and social behavior of its members (Brislin, 1993; Shweder & others, 1998; 1994; Triandis, 1994). For example, some cultures encourage eating insects and grubs, some cultures find the taste of root beer appalling. Some cultures discourage overt digestive noises in the company of others, others support a hardy burp after a meal as an expression of gratitude to the host. Dietary practices are just one of many dimensions of behavior that are strongly influenced by culture.

Ethnicity *is based on cultural heritage, nationality, race, religion, and language.* Ethnicity is central to the development of **ethnic identity,** *identification based on membership in an ethnic group.* For example, ethnicity is a prominent factor in the daily lives of most Native Americans. In contrast, a child who was adopted at birth might not have a clear idea about her ethnicity, but she might be raised with the Irish Catholic identity of her adopted parents. To explore ethnicity further, turn to Applications in Psychology, where you will read about the increasing ethnic diversity in American society.

Gender *is the sociocultural dimension of being female or male.* Few aspects of our existence are more central to our identity and social relationships than gender (Denmark & Paludi, 1998). Our gender-related attitudes and behavior seem to be changing, but it is not clear how much change has occurred or how much is desirable.

Other sociocultural contexts also influence behavior. For example, college students who are confined to wheelchairs or who are blind or deaf face obstacles to obtaining an education. In contrast to the obvious barriers faced by these students, the challenges that homosexuals face might be more subtle. It is stressful to have to worry about where and when you can safely express affection to others to avoid suspicion and recrimination. Sexual orientation, physical status and size, religious beliefs, and even political affiliations all can influence behavior in a given sociocultural context.

What Can the Sociocultural Perspective Tell Us About Ted Kaczynski and Alice Walker? A sociocultural psychologist would be interested in Kaczynski's being a loner in a culture where violence is commonplace—and in how Walker's African American and female heritage shaped her experiences. Walker's life especially calls attention to the struggle many ethnic minorities and females face.

Which Perspective Is Correct? You are likely, frequently, to wonder what perspective is correct throughout your studies in psychology. Although this introduction to psychology's seven main perspectives has been brief, you can see how each perspective might offer a piece of the puzzle in understanding behavior. All of these approaches to psychology have something to contribute to our understanding. They all have the potential to be truthful ways of looking at behavior, just as blueprints, floor plans, and photographs can all be useful ways of looking at a house. Some perspectives are better for some purposes. A floor plan, for instance, is more useful than a photograph for deciding how much lumber to buy, just as the neurobiological perspective is probably more useful than the humanistic perspective for understanding the brain's role in mental retardation. However, no single perspective is likely to be sufficient for explaining behavior.

Applications in Psychology

The Changing Tapestry of American Culture

In 1989 one-fifth of all children and adolescents in the United States under the age of 17 were members of ethnic minority groups—African American, Latino, Native American (American Indian), and Asian American. By the year 2000, one-third of all school-age children will fall into this category. This changing demographic tapestry promises national diversity, but it also carries the challenge of extending the American dream to people of all ethnic and minority groups. Historically ethnic minorities have found themselves at the bottom of the economic and social order. They have been disproportionately among the poor and the inadequately educated. Today, for instance, half of all African American children and one-third of all Latino children live in poverty, and the school dropout rate for minority youths is as high as 60 percent in some urban areas. Our social institutions can play an enormous part in helping correct these discrepancies. By becoming more sensitive to ethnic issues and by improving services to people of ethnic minority and low-income backgrounds, schools, colleges, social services, health and mental health agencies, and the courts can help bring minorities into the mainstream of American life (Jones, 1994).

An especially important fact for social planners to keep in mind is the tremendous diversity within each ethnic group. We're accustomed to thinking of American society as a melting pot of cultures—Anglo-Americans, African Americans, Latinos, Native Americans, Asian Americans, Italian Americans, Polish Americans, and so on. However, just as there are no cultural characteristics common *across* all American ethnic groups, there is no cultural characteristic common to all African Americans or all Latinos, for instance.

African Americans make up the largest ethnic minority group in the United States. African Americans are distributed throughout the social class structure, although a disproportionate number are poor.

Latinos also are a diverse group of individuals. Not all Latinos are Catholic. Many are, but some are not. Not all Latinos have a Mexican heritage. Many do, but others have cultural ties with South American countries, with Puerto Rico or other Caribbean countries, or with Spain.

Native Americans, with 511 distinct tribal units, also are an extremely diverse and complicated ethnic group (Trimble & Fleming, 1989). So are Asian Americans, with more than 30 distinct groups under this designation (Wong, 1982). Within each of these 511 Native American tribes and 30 Asian American groups, there is considerable diversity and individual variation (Ho, 1992).

America has embraced many cultures, and, in the process, the cultures have often mixed their beliefs and identities. Some elements of the cultures of origin are retained, some are lost, and some are mixed with the American culture. As the number of ethnic minority groups continues to increase rapidly in the next decade, one of psychology's most important agendas is to understand better the role that culture and ethnicity play in the ways we think and act (McLoyd, 1998).

The tapestry of American culture has changed dramatically in recent years. Nowhere is the change more noticeable than the increasing ethnic diversity of America's citizens. Ethnic minority groups—African American, Latino, Native American, and Asian American, for example—will make up approximately one-third of all individuals under the age of 17 in the United States by the year 2000. Two of psychology's challenges are to become more sensitive to race and ethnic origin and to provide improved services to ethnic minority individuals.

$\mathcal{I}$mproving Personal and Cognitive Skills

Sharpening the Saw

Sometimes you can spot people who have studied psychology just by the questions they ask about behavior. Just as carpenters keep their tools well honed, psychological thinkers use questions as tools to help them make good judgments about behavior.

- *"What exactly do you mean by . . . ?"*
  Once you have considered behavior carefully, you recognize that it is important to *describe* it precisely. Starting with precise descriptions can help you interpret behavior accurately or make on-target predictions.
- *"I wonder why that happens . . . ?"*
  Thinking like a psychologist involves trying to *explain*

behavior. Showing curiosity about what motivates people to do what they do is a hallmark of people interested in psychology.
- *"What is your evidence to back up your claim?"*
  When an explanation about the causes of behavior is at issue, personal testimony is not sufficient. When you think like a psychologist, you need to see the data that back up claims before you believe them.
- *"Is there another way to explain the behavior?"*
  When you don't have data to support an explanation, you may be able to generate other ideas. Coming up with alternative explanations for the cause of a behavior is a skill that psychologists value highly.

Despite the differences in the perspectives psychologists use to explain behavior, some characteristics are common to all psychological thinking. See Improving Personal and Cognitive Skills ("Sharpening the Saw") to help you identify some of the kinds of thinking promoted by the study of psychology.

At this point we have discussed a number of important perspectives in psychology and a number of individuals who were pioneers in various areas of the field. For a glimpse at some of psychology's pioneers, see figure 1.2. Most of these people and their views will be described later at appropriate places in this book. In our discussion so far, you have read about how varied psychology's perspectives are. As you will discover next, psychology's many fields also are varied.

Psychology's Specializations and Careers

You might have the preconceived notion that psychologists mainly analyze people lying on a couch or watch rats run through mazes. Some psychologists do analyze people's problems, and other observe how animals learn. But the field of psychology is much more diverse than these two examples suggest.

Areas of Specialization.   Students who go on to graduate school in psychology specialize in specific areas of psychology. These areas include the following:

- *Clinical and counseling psychology.* This is the most widely practiced specialization. It involves diagnosing and treating people with psychological problems. Clinical psychologists are different from psychiatrists. A clinical psychologist typically has a doctorate in psychology, which requires 4 or 5 years of graduate work, including an internship in a mental health facility. By contrast, **psychiatry** *is a branch of medicine practiced by physicians with an M.D. degree who specialize in abnormal psychology and therapy.* One important difference between clinical psychologists and psychiatrists is that psychiatrists can prescribe drugs, clinical psychologists cannot.
- *Experimental psychology.* This area involves pure research that emphasizes the use of precise, careful experiments. Experimental psychologists often explore the areas of learning, memory, sensation, and perception.
- *Neuroscience and physiological psychology.* Scientists in these areas investigate the role of the brain and nervous system in determining behavior. These psychologists are more likely than other psychologists to use animals in their research.

psychiatry
A branch of medicine practiced by physicians with an M.D. degree who specialize in abnormal psychology and therapy.

Wilhelm Wundt
(1832–1920)

William James
(1842–1910)

Alfred Binet
(1857–1911)

Ivan Pavlov
(1849–1936)

Ruth Howard
(1900–)

B. F. Skinner
(1904–1990)

Erik Erikson
(1902–1994)

Abraham Maslow
(1908–1970)

Carl Rogers
(1902–1987)

Albert Bandura
(1925–)

Sandra Bem
(1944–)

Eleanor Maccoby
(1917–)

1879: Wilhelm Wundt develops the first psychology laboratory at the University of Leipzig.

1890: William James publishes *Principles of Psychology*, which promotes functionalism.

1891: Mary Calkins establishes a laboratory for psychology at Wellesley.

1892: E. B. Titchener popularizes structuralism in the United States. G. Stanley Hall founds the American Psychological Association at Clark University.

1894: Margaret Washburn becomes the first woman to receive a Ph.D. in psychology.

1900: Sigmund Freud publishes *The Interpretation of Dreams*, reflecting his psychoanalytic view.

1905: Alfred Binet (with Theodore Simon) develops the first intelligence test to assess French schoolchildren.

1906: The Russian Ivan Pavlov publishes the results of his learning experiments with dogs.

1913: John Watson publishes his volume on behaviorism, promoting the importance of environmental influences.

1934: Ruth Howard becomes the first African American woman to receive a Ph.D. in psychology.

1938: B. F. Skinner publishes *The Behavior of Organisms*, expanding the view of behaviorism.

1939: Mamie Phipps Clark and Kenneth Clark conduct research on African American children's self-conceptions and identity. Later, in 1971, Kenneth Clark becomes the first African American president of the American Psychological Association.

1945: Karen Horney criticizes Freud's psychoanalytic theory as male-biased and presents her sociocultural approach.

1950: Erik Erikson publishes *Childhood and Society*, a psychoanalytic revision of Freud's views.

1954: Abraham Maslow presents the humanistic view, emphasizing the positive potential of the individual.

1954: Gordon Allport writes his now classic book, *The Nature of Prejudice*.

1958: Herbert Simon presents his information-processing view.

1961: Carl Rogers publishes *On Becoming a Person*, highlighting the humanistic approach.

1961: Albert Bandura presents ideas about social learning theory, emphasizing the importance of imitation.

1964: Roger Sperry publishes his split-brain research, showing the importance of the brain in behavior.

1969: John Berry, a Canadian psychologist, presents his ideas on the importance of cross-cultural research in psychology.

1974: Sandra Bem and Janet Spence develop tests to assess androgyny and promote the competence of females; Eleanor Maccoby (with Carol Jacklin) calls attention to the importance of sex and gender in understanding behavior and analyzing gender similarities and differences.

1977: Judith Rodin (with Ellen Langer) conducts research showing the powerful influence of perceived control over one's environment on behavior.

Mary Calkins
(1863–1930)

G. Stanley Hall
(1844–1924)

Margaret
Washburn
(1871–1939)

John B. Watson
(1878–1958)

Mamie Clark
(1917–1983)

Karen Horney
(1885–1952)

Gordon Allport
(1897–1967)

Sigmund Freud
(1856–1939)

Roger Sperry
(1913–1994)

John Berry
(1939–)

Judith Rodin
(1944–)

Herbert Simon
(1916–)

Figure 1.2

Important Pioneers and Theorists in Psychology's History

- *Developmental psychology.* Developmental psychologists study how people develop from conception to death. They explore the biological, cognitive, and socioemotional dimensions of our development as infants, children, adolescents, and adults.
- *Social psychology.* Social psychologists focus on people's interactions, relationships, attitudes, and group behavior.

- *Cross-cultural psychology.* Cross-cultural psychologists examine the role of culture in understanding behavior. They study whether behavior is culture-universal or culture-specific.
- *Psychology of women.* Psychologists in this area conduct research or therapy with women. They also advocate eliminating discrimination against women. To read about women and ethnic minorities in psychology, see Sociocultural Worlds.
- *Industrial and organizational psychology.* This area focuses on the workplace, including its workers and organizations who employ them. Industrial/organizational psychologists give hiring tests, study the best ways to train employees, investigate how to improve work conditions, and analyze how management and employees can get along better.
- *Forensic psychology.* Forensic psychologists work in the legal arena assisting in jury selection, evaluating disability claims, and providing expert testimony during court trials.
- *School and educational psychology.* This area is concerned with children's learning and adjustment in school. Psychologists who work in this area might administer psychological tests, conduct research, and/or teach in colleges and universities.

Sociocultural Worlds

Women and Ethnic Minorities in Psychology

Until recently psychology, like so many professions, kept women out (Kimmel, 1992). During its first 75 years, few women broke through to psychology's inner sanctum. In fact, the first American woman to complete requirements for a doctorate in psychology, Christine Ladd-Franklin, was denied the degree in 1892 simply because she was a woman. Mary Calkins's history is another example of the barriers women faced. In 1891 she introduced psychology into Wellesley College's curriculum and established its first psychology laboratory. In 1892 she returned to Harvard for additional training. By 1894 Mary Calkins had developed a technique for investigating memory and had completed the requirements for a doctoral degree. Her Harvard psychology professors enthusiastically recommended that she be awarded the degree, but the administration refused because Calkins was a woman (Furumoto, 1989).

The first woman actually to be awarded a doctorate in psychology was Margaret Washburn in 1894. By 1906 about 1 in every 10 psychologists was a woman. In the mid-1980s in the United States, the number of men and women receiving a doctorate in psychology was approximately equal (Furumoto & Scarborough, 1986). In 1992, more women than men earned doctorates in psychology: 1,914 women earned doctorates, compared to 1,338 men.

Similarly, discrimination has barred many individuals from ethnic minority groups from entering the field of psychology. The first African American to become a professor of psychology was Gilbert Jones, who obtained his doctorate at the University of Jena in Germany in 1909. Ethnic minority women, especially, faced overwhelming odds. It wasn't until 1934 that an African American woman, Ruth Howard at the University of Minnesota, finally received a doctorate in psychology. Over a period of about 50 years, the 10 universities with the most prestigious programs in psychology granted several thousand doctoral degrees, yet by 1969 these universities had awarded only 8 doctoral degrees to African American students (Albee, 1988). Few Latinos have been awarded doctoral degrees—recent surveys indicate that less than 2 percent of all psychologists are Latino (Cervantes, 1987). George Sanchez is one of the few. His pioneering research demonstrated that intelligence tests can be culturally biased against ethnic minority children. There are also very few Native American psychologists (McShane, 1987).

Over the past 25 years, the women's movement and the civil rights movement helped put the rights and needs of women and ethnic minorities on politicians' agendas and led to social change (Bronstein & Quina, 1988). Similarly psychologists, especially those belonging to these groups, began to reexamine psychology's basic premises and to question its relevance to their own experiences and concerns. This reexamination sparked new inquiry into populations that previously had been omitted from psychological research and the mainstream theories of psychology. Such journals as *Psychology of Women Quarterly, Sex Roles,* the *Hispanic Journal of Behavioral Science,* and the *Journal of Black Psychology* address the growing interest in gender and ethnic minority issues.

In recognizing the dearth of ethnic minority psychologists, the American Psychological Association has formed the Committee on Ethnic Minority Affairs to ensure that the concerns of its ethnic group members are heard. The Association of Black Psychologists directly involves its members in issues that are important to the African American community (Jones, 1987). The Asian American Psychological Association identifies resources, develops ideas for education and training, and fosters scientific research on issues of importance to the Asian American community (Suinn, 1987).

Careers in Psychology. You might already be wondering whether to major in psychology. Studying psychology as an undergraduate can give you a sound preparation for what lies ahead in your life. It will help you learn how to understand, predict, and have more control over the events in your own life. You also will gain a solid academic background that can enable you to enter various careers or go on to graduate programs, not just in psychology but also in other areas like business and law.

Some students report having decided against majoring in psychology because they heard that they wouldn't be able to get a job with a degree in psychology. A bachelor's degree in psychology does not automatically lead to fame and fortune, but it is a very marketable degree for a wide range of jobs. These include parent-educator, drug-abuse counselor, mental health aide, teacher for children with mental retardation, and staff member at a crisis hotline center. An undergraduate degree in psychology provides excellent training for many jobs in business, especially in the areas of sales, personnel, and training.

Although a master's degree or doctorate is not absolutely necessary for finding employment in psychology, you can greatly expand your opportunities (and your income) by obtaining a graduate degree. Also, because there are so few ethnic minority psychologists, job opportunities are increasing for qualified ethnic minority applicants.

All psychologists, whether they teach at a college or university, or whether they work in a clinical capacity helping people with their problems, have gone through training that stresses the scientific nature of psychology. Next we will explore psychology's scientific base.

eview

Contemporary Perspectives: Specializations and Careers in Psychology

Psychology's seven main contemporary perspectives are the behavioral, psychoanalytic, humanistic, neurobiological, cognitive, evolutionary, and sociocultural. The behavioral perspective emphasizes the scientific study of observable behavioral responses and their environmental determinants. The psychoanalytic perspective focuses on the unconscious mind, conflicts between biological instincts and society's demands, and early family experiences. The humanistic perspective emphasizes a person's capacity for growth, freedom to choose one's own identity, and positive qualities. The neurobiological perspective stresses that the brain and nervous system play central roles in determining behavior. The cognitive perspective focuses on cognitive (thought) processes such as attention, memory, thinking, and problem solving. The evolutionary perspective emphasizes the importance of adaptation and reproduction in explaining behavior. And the sociocultural perspective argues that culture, ethnicity, gender, and other contextual factors are key dimensions in understanding behavior.

Psychology has many areas of specialization. These include clinical and counseling psychology, experimental psychology, neuroscience and physiological psychology, developmental psychology, social psychology, cross-cultural psychology, psychology of women, industrial/organizational psychology, and school/educational psychology. Majoring in psychology as an undergraduate can provide you with a sound background for a number of careers. A graduate degree in psychology further expands your job opportunities.

CONDUCTING PSYCHOLOGICAL RESEARCH

Some people have difficulty thinking of psychology as being a science in the same way that physics, chemistry, and biology are sciences. Can a discipline that studies why people are attracted to each other, how they reason about moral values, and how ethnicity affects identity be equated with disciples that examine gravity, the molecular structure of a compound, or the flow of blood in the circulation system? Science is not defined by *what* it investigates but by *how* it investigates. Whether you explore photosynthesis, butterflies, Saturn's moons, or the reasons why people bite their fingernails, it is the way you investigate that makes the approach scientific or not.

In this section of the chapter we will examine the characteristics of the scientific method, specific research strategies used in psychology, and the ethical concerns involved in psychological research.

The Scientific Method

scientific method

A strategy designed to obtain accurate information. It includes these steps: Identify and analyze a problem, develop tentative explanations, collect data, draw conclusions, and confirm or revise theory.

The **scientific method** *is a strategy designed to obtain accurate information. It includes the following steps: identify and analyze a problem, develop tentative explanations, collect data, draw conclusions, and confirm or revise theory.* To help you understand how the scientific method works, we will apply it to a common psychological disorder: depression.

Identify and Analyze a Problem. The scientific method's first step consists of identifying and analyzing a problem. What problem do you want to solve? You need to go beyond a general description of the problem. This involves isolating, focusing on, and defining what you want to study. Peter Lewinsohn and his colleagues (1992) chose to study the problem of how to reduce depression.

Develop Tentative Explanations. After you have identified and analyzed a problem, the next step is to discover the most important factors, or variables, that are involved. To do this, psychologists often construct a **theory,** *which is a coherent set of ideas that helps to explain data and make predictions.* A theory has **hypotheses,** *which are assumptions that can be tested to determine their accuracy.* Lewinsohn and his colleagues hypothesized that taking a course on coping with depression will decrease the participants' depression. One of the course's components consists of teaching depressed individuals to control their negative thoughts.

theory

A coherent set of ideas that helps to explain data and make predictions.

hypotheses

Assumptions that can be tested to determine their accuracy.

> *There is nothing quite as practical as a good theory.*
> KURT LEWIN, *American Social Psychologist, 20th Century*

data

Information that is obtained from systematic observation.

Collect Data. After you have developed an hypothesis, the next step in the scientific method is to collect **data,** *information that is obtained from systematic observation.* Lewinsohn and his colleagues observed how effectively people who completed the depression course monitored their moods and engaged in productive work.

Draw Conclusions. After data have been collected, the next step in the scientific method is to analyze the data and draw some conclusions. At this point researchers ask, "What do the data mean?" (Note here that we are using the word *data* as a plural that takes plural verb forms.) Researchers usually use some type of statistical analysis to determine the results of the study. This helps them determine whether their observations are significant or merely due to chance. A brief overview of statistical procedures appears in the appendix at the end of this book. Lewinsohn and his colleagues statistically analyzed the data they obtained. Based on the analysis, they concluded that the course on coping with depression reduced the subject's depression.

Confirm or Revise Theory. The final step in the scientific method involves revising theory. Psychologists have developed a number of theories about why people become depressed and how they can cope with depression. The results obtained by Lewinsohn and his colleagues confirm the importance of cognitive factors in depression. Other aspects of depression are discussed in chapter 11 ("Abnormal Psychology") and chapter 12 ("Therapies"). A summary of the steps in the scientific method applied to Lewinsohn's study of depression is presented in figure 1.3.

Identify and Analyze a Problem	Develop Tentative Explanations	Collect Data	Draw Conclusions	Confirm and Revise Theories
Depression is a common problem. Lewinsohn and his colleagues chose the problem of how to reduce depression.	This often consists of proposing a new theory or using an existing theory to develop an hypothesis (or hypotheses). Lewinsohn and his colleagues hypothesized that people who take a coping with depression course will become less depressed, especially if they learn to control their negative thoughts.	Lewinsohn and his colleagues observed how effectively individuals who completed the course on coping with depression monitored their moods and engaged in productive work.	The researchers analyzed the data statistically to determine that the positive effects of the course were real and not just due to chance.	The research confirmed the theory that cognitive factors play an important role in depression.

𝒻IGURE 1.3

The Main Steps in the Scientific Method Applied to a Study of Depression

Research Strategies in Psychology

Psychologists must make several decisions in designing effective research strategies. Who will they study? Where will the research take place? What measures will be used? What depth of explanation is desired?

Selecting Participants.   Some research focuses on just one person; most studies involve more than one individual. In most cases, the researcher first defines the **population,** *the complete group of organisms (animal or human) that will be represented by the research participants.* For example, a researcher interested in depression might define the target population as middle-class White men in the Midwest, single mothers in an urban community, or first-year students attending a specific college.

The next step involves selecting a **sample,** *a representative group drawn from the population.* Psychologists regularly use a **random sample,** *a sample that is obtained by a method that gives every member of the population an equal chance of being selected for study.* For example, a depression researcher might send a questionnaire to 5 percent of the first-year students at a given college who were selected randomly to participate in the study. Results from a random sample can be generalized to describe the characteristics of the target population as a whole.

In some cases a researcher's interest in a particular characteristic shapes how a sample is selected (Meltzoff, 1998). For example, if a researcher wanted to explore how ethnicity influences depression, the selected sample might include equal numbers of Hispanics, African Americans, Caucasians, and so on, even if these equal proportions don't reflect these groups' proportions in the population from which the participants were drawn. The nature of the research question determines how participants should be selected.

Many subjects in psychological research have come from introductory psychology classes like the one you are taking now. You might have an opportunity to be a research participant through this class. We encourage you to participate in this research if it is available, because it gives you an opportunity to discover firsthand how psychologists conduct research. However, one criticism of research with college freshmen and sophomores is that its results might not be representative of the general population, which consists of people of other ages, education levels, and cultures.

Choosing a Research Setting.   Another important research decision is determining the context in which the study will be conducted. Will behavior be studied in a laboratory or in a more natural setting? A **laboratory** *is a controlled setting where many of the complex factors of the "real world" have been removed.* A laboratory allows the researcher to control the potential causes of behavior in a study. However, laboratory research has some drawbacks. The participants know that they are being studied and might therefore act in

population

The complete group of organisms from which the sample is selected.

sample

The group of organisms (human or animal) being studied.

random sample

A sample obtained by a method that gives every member of the population an equal chance of being selected for study.

laboratory

A controlled setting where many of the complex factors of the "real world" have been removed.

unnatural ways. For example, some might be more helpful, others less helpful, than they normally are. Some people might not be willing to go to a university laboratory to be studied. Finally, some problems, such as the factors that contribute to falling in or out of love, are too challenging to study in a laboratory.

Although naturalistic settings do not allow as much control, they can give rise to more realistic behavior. Psychologists study people in such naturalistic settings as homes, schools, day-care centers, parks, residence halls, shopping malls, soccer games, and other places people live in or frequent.

Selecting Measures. Another important research decision is choosing one or more measures to use in collecting data. Systematic measures include direct observation, interviews, and psychological tests.

Direct Observation. The fictional detective Sherlock Holmes chided his assistant Watson, "You see but you do not observe." We look at things all of the time, but casually watching a friend walk across the campus is not scientific observation. Unless you are a trained observer and practice your skills regularly, you do not know what to look for, you might not remember what you saw, and you might not communicate your observations effectively. For direct observation to be effective, we have to know what we are looking for, whom we are observing, when and where we will observe, how the observations will be made, and in what form they will be recorded.

Consider depression. What constitutes depressed behavior? How will we know it when we see it? Does it involve a blank emotional stare? a saddened look? How long do blank stares and saddened looks have to last? Do we want to study the subjects' behavior at home, in a laboratory, or both? A common way to record observations is to write them down, using shorthand or symbols. However, psychologists increasingly use tape recorders, video cameras, and one-way mirrors to make their observations more efficient.

interview

A measure researchers use that involves asking questions to find out about a person's experiences and attitudes.

social desirability

The tendency of participants to tell the interviewer what they think is socially acceptable or desirable rather than what they truly feel or think.

questionnaires (or surveys)

Measures similar to interviews except that the respondents read the questions and mark their answers on paper rather than verbally responding to the interviewer.

standardized tests

Tests that require people to answer a series of written or oral questions. The tests have two distinct characteristics. First, an individual's score is totaled to produce a single overall score. Second, the individual's score is compared to the scores of large numbers of other similar people to determine how the individual responded relative to others.

Interviews and Questionnaires. Sometimes the best and quickest way to get information from people is to ask them for it. An **interview** *is a measure researchers use that involves asking questions to find out about a person's experiences and attitudes.* Most interviews occur face-to-face, although they can take place over the telephone. Interviews vary in their structure. Some interview questions are open-ended, such as "Are you depressed a lot?" Other interview questions are more structured and ask for more specific detail. For example, "How many days have you been depressed in the last two months? Select from the following: 0, 1–2, 3–5, 6–10, 10–30, 30–60." One shortcoming of an interview is the factor of **social desirability,** *the tendency of participants to tell the interviewer what they think is socially acceptable or desirable rather than what they truly feel or think.* For example, June might not want to disclose the real torment her husband's abuse has caused when she is interviewed as part of a study on family factors involved in depression.

Questionnaires (or surveys) *are similar to structured interviews except that the respondents read the questions and mark their answers on paper or some other medium rather than verbally responding to the interviewer.* A major advantage of questionnaires is that they can be given to large numbers of people easily. Good surveys have concrete, specific, and unambiguous questions. Social desirability is a problem for questionnaires just as it is for interviews.

Standardized Tests. **Standardized tests** *require people to answer a series of written or oral questions. The tests have two distinctive features. First, an individual's score usually is totaled to produce a single overall score. Second, the individual's score is compared to the scores of large numbers of other similar people to determine how the individual responded relative to others.* Scores on standardized tests are often reported in percentiles. For example, a student who scores in the 92nd percentile of the SAT has scored higher than 92 percent of individuals who have taken the test. The most widely used standardized tests include the Stanford-Binet intelligence test and the Minnesota Multiphasic Personality Inventory

(MMPI). A standardized measure widely used to assess depression is the Beck Depression Inventory.

The main advantage of standardized tests is that they provide information about individual differences among people. One disadvantage is that information obtained from standardized tests does not always predict behavior in nontest situations. For example, a person might perform poorly on a standardized intelligence test in an office setting but show a much higher level of intelligence in a more relaxed setting, such as at home. Further, immigrants and ethnic minority individuals sometimes perform poorly on intelligence tests because of difficulties with the language in which the test is administered. More about intelligence tests appears in chapter 7 ("Thinking, Language, and Intelligence") and more about personality tests is discussed in chapter 10 ("Personality").

Research Strategies and Depth of Explanation. Another research decision involves choosing a method that gives the desired depth of explanation. Researchers can choose from three strategies: descriptive, correlational, and experimental.

The Descriptive Method. Science begins with description. Everyone observes and describes people, but psychologists strive to do this systematically and objectively. **Descriptive methods** *involve systematic and objective description of behavior.* What are some examples of descriptive methods? They can involve any of the measures we have just described. Thus, a psychologist might directly observe depressed people, interview them, or give them a psychological test. Suppose that the psychologist notes that the people observed, interviewed, or given tests not only are depressed but also are more likely to be women than men and seem to exaggerate their weaknesses and underestimate their strengths. Such observations might encourage the psychologist to pursue research that offers deeper insights into depression.

A special type of descriptive research is the **case study,** *an in-depth look at one individual. It is used mainly by clinical psychologists when the unique aspects of a person's life cannot be duplicated, for either practical or ethical reasons.* Some fascinating case studies involve individuals who have had traumatic experiences. A 26-year-old schoolteacher met a woman with whom he fell intensely in love. But several months after their love affair began, he became depressed, drank heavily, and talked about committing suicide. The suicidal ideas turned into images of murder and suicide. His actions became bizarre. On one occasion he punctured the tires on his loved one's car. On another, he stood on the side of the road where she passed frequently in her car, extending his hand in his pocket so she would think he was holding a gun. His feelings for the woman vacillated between love and hate. Only 8 months after meeting her, he shot her while he was a passenger in the car she was driving, then ran to a telephone booth and called his priest. The woman died (Revitch & Schlesinger, 1978). This case reveals how depression and bizarre thinking sometimes precede violent acts, even murder.

Although case histories provide dramatic, in-depth portrayals of people's lives, caution needs to be exercised when generalizing from this information. The subject of a case study is unique, with a genetic makeup and experiences like no other person's.

The Correlational Method. The **correlational method,** *in which the goal is to describe the strength of the relation between two or more events or characteristics,* provides a deeper level of explanation than the descriptive method. The correlational method is useful because the more strongly two events are correlated (related, or associated), the more effectively we can predict one from the other. Continuing with our theme of applying research methods to the study of depression, suppose that researchers give the Beck Depression Inventory to a group of adults to assess their level of depression. They also give the adults a questionnaire that includes questions about their exercise habits. They discover a relationship between depression and lack of exercise: the more the adults exercised, the less depression they reported.

descriptive method

Systematic and objective description of behavior.

case study

An in-depth look at one individual. This method is used mainly by clinical psychologists when the unique aspects of a person's life cannot be duplicated for either practical or ethical reasons.

correlational method

A method in which the goal is to describe the strength of the relation between two or more events or characteristics.

In this study, can we conclude that exercising *causes* people to have less depression? No. Why doesn't this significant correlation between the two mean that one causes the other? The correlation could mean that the exercise causes these people to feel less depression, but it also could mean that being depressed causes people to exercise less. And a third possibility exists: Although lack of exercise and depression are significantly correlated, it might be that neither causes the other. Possibly a third factor, such as a genetic tendency, job stress, conflict in close relationships, or loss of income, underlies their association. Figure 1.4 shows these possible explanations of correlational data.

To ensure that your understanding of correlation is clear, let's consider another example. In a study, researchers find that people who have a lot of money have higher self-esteem than those who make less money. We mistakenly could interpret this to mean that making a lot of money causes us to have high self-esteem. What are the other two interpretations we need to consider? (1) Possibly high self-esteem causes people to make a lot of money, and (2) possibly a third factor, such as education or social upbringing, causes both making a lot of money and self-esteem. Throughout this text you will read about studies that were based on the correlational method. Always keep in mind how easy it is to mistakenly infer causality when two events or characteristics are merely correlated.

The Experimental Method.   The experimental method produces the deepest level of explanation (see figure 1.5). The **experimental method** *allows psychologists to determine*

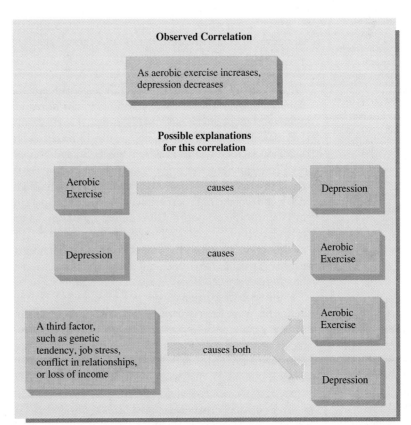

$\mathcal{F}$IGURE 1.4

Possible Explanations of Correlational Data

From an observed correlation between two events, it cannot be concluded that the first event causes the second event. Other causal possibilities are that the second event causes the first event or that a third, unknown event causes the correlation between the first two events.

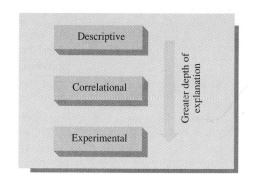

$\mathcal{F}$IGURE 1.5

Research Methods and Depth of Explanation

The descriptive research method provides the least depth of explanation, the experimental method the most. *Why does the experimental research method produce the greatest depth of explanation?*

experiment

A carefully regulated procedure in which one or more factors believed to influence the behavior being studied is manipulated and all other factors are held constant.

random assignment

Assignment of subjects to experimental and control groups by chance. This practice reduces the likelihood that the experiment's results will be due to any preexisting differences between the groups.

experimental group

The group whose experience is being manipulated in an experiment.

control group

The comparison group in an experiment; it is treated in every way like the experimental group except for the manipulated factor.

baseline

A basis for comparison that depicts behavior in the absence of the manipulated factor.

independent variable

The manipulated, influential, experimental factor. The label *independent* is used because this variable can be changed independently of other factors.

dependent variable

The factor that is measured in an experiment. It can change as the independent variable is manipulated. The label *dependent* is used because this variable depends on what happens to the subjects in the experiment.

behavior's causes. Psychologists accomplish this task by performing an **experiment,** *a carefully regulated procedure in which one or more factors believed to influence the behavior being studied are manipulated and all other factors are held constant.* If the behavior under study changes when a factor is manipulated, we say that the manipulated factor *causes* the behavior to change. Psychologists use the experimental method to determine cause and effect, something that the correlational method cannot do. *Cause* is the factor being manipulated. *Effect* is the behavior that changes because of the manipulation. Remember that researchers measure, but do not manipulate, behavior in the correlational method. However, in the experimental method, researchers actively manipulate factors to determine their effects on behavior.

To illustrate the experimental method, let's continue with a study in the area of depression. Suppose that the researchers hypothesize that regular aerobic exercise will reduce depression. They select as their participants 50 adult women volunteers who are 30 to 40 years of age and have been diagnosed with depression. The researchers randomly assign the participants to two groups. **Random assignment** *occurs when psychologists assign participants to experimental and control groups by chance. This practice reduces the likelihood that the experimenter's results will be due to any preexisting differences between the groups.* For example, random assignment greatly decreases the probability that the two groups will differ on factors such as health, intelligence, and socioeconomic status.

The depressed women who are assigned to the aerobic exercise program are called the **experimental group,** *which is the group whose experience is manipulated.* In this study, the depressed women in the experimental group participate in aerobic exercise four times a week in 1-hour sessions under the direction of a professional aerobics instructor. The exercise program lasts for 4 months. The depressed women who do not participate in the aerobic exercise program are called the **control group,** *a comparison group that is treated in every way like the experimental group except for the manipulated factor.* The control group serves as a **baseline,** *a basis for comparison that depicts behavior in the absence of the manipulated factor.* The **independent variable** *is the manipulated, influential, experimental factor. The label* independent *is used because this variable can be changed independently of other factors.* In the study of depression and aerobic exercise, access to exercise (aerobic exercise vs. no exercise) is the independent variable. Researchers have a vast array of options open to them in choosing an independent variable. The researchers could have chosen to manipulate the depressed women's thinking. They also could have given them a drug. The **dependent variable** *is the factor that is measured in an experiment. It can change as the independent variable is manipulated. The label* dependent *is used because this variable depends on what happens to the participants in the experiment.* In the study of depression and aerobic exercise, the dependent variable is the participants' level of depression. (Note that the dependent variable is the same for all participants in the study.) In this study, at the end of the 4 months, we find that the experimental group's depression is lower, on the average, than the control group's. We conclude that the aerobic exercise program caused the lower depression. Figure 1.6 illustrates the experimental method applied to this study of depression and aerobic exercise.

Despite the experimental method's power to determine cause, caution must be exercised when using it. Expectancies and biases can, often unknowingly, infiltrate an experiment and produce results that are misleading.

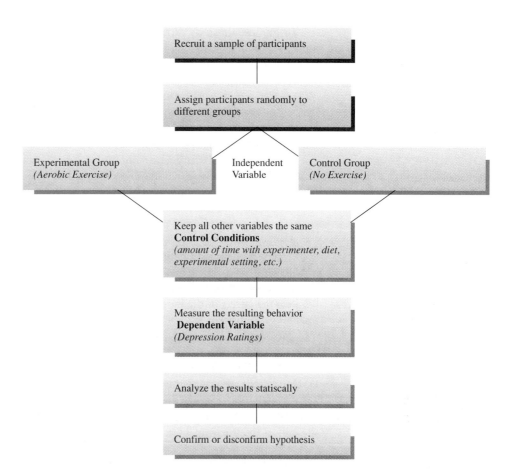

Recruit a sample of participants

Assign participants randomly to different groups

Experimental Group
(Aerobic Exercise)

Independent Variable

Control Group
(No Exercise)

Keep all other variables the same
Control Conditions
(amount of time with experimenter, diet, experimental setting, etc.)

Measure the resulting behavior
Dependent Variable
(Depression Ratings)

Analyze the results statiscally

Confirm or disconfirm hypothesis

$\mathcal{F}$IGURE 1.6

The Experimental Method

This example of the experimental method focuses on the effects of aerobic exercise on depression.

placebo effect

Subjects' expectations, rather than the experimental treatment, produce the desired outcomes.

experimenter bias

The researcher's expectations influence the outcome of the research.

Let's look at another study of depression to see how expectancies and biases might be involved. In this study, the researchers hypothesize that a new drug will lower depression. They randomly assign the participants to the experimental group (the group of participants who receive the drug) and the control group (the participants who do not receive the drug). After 2 months, the experimental group shows less depression than the control group. It sounds like we could conclude that the drug caused lower depression. However, the effects might be due to the participants' expectations that they will recover because they have taken the drug, and not due to the drug itself. Possibly because they expect to be less depressed, they become less depressed. The **placebo effect** *occurs when participants' expectations, rather than the experimental treatment, produce the desired outcome.*

How might this placebo effect be reduced? In the study of depression and a drug, the researchers can give the control group a *placebo,* such as a sugar pill. The control group participants are not told that what they are receiving is a placebo. Thus, in this study, the experimental and control groups both think that they are getting a drug. In any study, researchers try to minimize the participants' expectancies or cancel them out across the groups by making them as identical as possible.

Participants are not the only ones who can have expectancies that influence the outcome of a study; the experimenters can also. **Experimenter bias** *occurs when the researcher's expectations influence the outcome of the research.* If in the study of depression and aerobic exercise, the experimenters had expectations that the aerobic exercise program was going to reduce depression, possibly they treated the experimental and control groups in subtly different ways in addition to having them exercise or not exercise. Perhaps they were highly enthusiastic toward the experimental group and were not enthusiastic with the control group, and perhaps this enthusiasm, rather than exercise, contributed to lower depression in the experimental group. Possibly the experimenter got to know several of the people in the exercise group, but not in the control group, on a personal basis and this helped to lower their depression.

In one classic study, Robert Rosenthal (1966) turned college students into experimenters, randomly assigning them rats from the same litter. Half of the students were told that their rats were "maze bright," the other half were told that their rats were "maze dull." The students then conducted experiments to test their rats' ability to learn how to navigate mazes. The results were striking. The "maze-bright" rats ran the mazes better than the "maze-dull" rats. The only explanation for the results is that the college students' expectations affected either the performance of the rats or the way they perceived the rats' performance. In a number of subsequent studies, Rosenthal (1994) demonstrated that an experimenter's expectations influence not only rodent behavior but also human behavior. Rosenthal's stream of research findings demonstrates the importance of **replication**, *repeating research strategies to confirm original findings.* Robust results should be replicable.

A possible solution to the problem of expectancy effects is to conduct a **double-blind study**, *in which neither the subjects nor the researchers are aware of which subjects are in the experimental group and which are in the control group until the results are calculated.* If the study of depression and a drug is conducted in a double-blind manner, the experimenter and the participants would be kept in the dark about which group is receiving the drug and which is receiving the placebo. A double-blind study allows researchers to separate the effects of the independent variable from both the participants' and the experimenter's enthusiasm for it.

Ethics in Research

Psychologists have adopted a formal code of ethics to encourage humane and appropriate research practices (Vadum & Rankin, 1998). Despite this code, challenges persist regarding the ethical treatment of participants in psychological research. We will explore the ethical treatment of both human and animal subjects.

Ethical Treatment of Human Participants.   As you read about some of the classic research in psychology later in this book, you might be surprised and dismayed by some of the things psychologists have done to investigate behavior. For example, social psychologists have sometimes placed participants in situations where the participants thought they might have been harming others (Milgram, 1965; Zimbardo & others, 1972). Such experiments might have been psychologically risky for the participants.

Psychologists are increasingly recognizing that they need to take considerable caution to ensure the well-being of participants in a psychological study. Today colleges and universities have review boards that evaluate research proposals to determine whether the research will protect the participants from harm and will serve their best interests (Hoagwood, Jensen, & Fisher, 1996; Rosnow, 1995). The research proposal must be approved by the board before the research begins. Some of the research studies that you will read about in this book likely would not be approved by research review boards if they were proposed in the same form today.

The code of ethics of the American Psychological Association clarifies how to protect research participants from mental and physical harm (Canter & others, 1994). Researchers are required to keep the participants' needs foremost in mind when designing and conducting a study. These guidelines include **informed consent:** *participants must be told what their participation involves as well as whether there is any risk.* Participants must agree to participate, and they retain the right to withdraw from the study at any time.

Deception, *intentionally misleading a participant about the purpose of a research study,* is another issue that psychologists have debated extensively (Koocher & Keith-Spiegel, 1996). Revealing the purpose of a study beforehand can substantially alter participant behavior and make the researcher's data useless. For example, suppose a psychologist tells you she is investigating study strategies in college, when she really wants to collect data on cheating. By deceiving you, she might get a more accurate impression of the decisions you make about academic honesty. In all studies for which deceptive strategies are approved, psychologists must ensure that the deception will not harm the participant. The psychologist also must **debrief** *the participants by telling them the complete nature of the study as soon as possible after it is over* (Whitley, 1996).

replication

Repeating research strategies to confirm original findings.

double-blind study

A study in which neither the subjects nor the experimenters know which subjects are in the experimental group and which are in the control group until the results are calculated.

informed consent

Participants in a research study are informed of what their participation involves as well as whether any risk is present, and have the right to withdraw from the study at any time.

deception

Intentionally misleading a participant about the purpose of a research study.

debriefing

Informing research participants about the complete nature of the study as soon as possible after the research is over.

Ethical Treatment in Animal Research. For generations, some psychologists have used animals as the focus of their behavioral research. About 5 percent of all APA members use animals in their research. Rats and mice are by far the most widely used, accounting for 90 percent of all animals used in psychological research. In addition to exploring animal behavior in its own right, many such studies have provided a better understanding of human behavior.

Neal Miller (1985), a leading figure in biofeedback studies related to health, listed the following areas in which animal research has directly benefited humans:

- Rehabilitating neuromuscular disorders
- Alleviating the effects of stress and pain
- Testing drugs for the treatment of anxiety and mental illness
- Understanding drug addiction and relapse
- Facilitating weight gain in premature infants
- Reducing memory deficits caused by old age or illness

Many critics of animal research—animal welfare and rights activists—question whether the gains in knowledge are warranted (Dawkins, 1990). It is true that researchers sometimes use procedures that would be unethical with humans, but animal abuse is not as common as animal activist groups charge. Animal researchers are subject to a stringent set of standards that address such matters as the housing, feeding, and psychological well-being of animals (Herzog, 1995). Researchers must weigh the potential benefits of their research against the possible harms to the animal. They also must avoid inflicting unnecessary pain.

eview

Conducting Psychological Research

Psychology is a science because it uses the scientific method to discover accurate information about behavior. The scientific method consists of the following steps: (1) identify and analyze a problem, (2) develop a tentative explanation (which often involves theories and hypotheses), (3) collect data, (4) draw conclusions, and (5) conform or revise theory.

Psychologists must make several decisions when designing effective research strategies. One decision is to determine who the participants in the study will be—how large the sample will be, whether it will be a random sample, and whether results based on the sample will generalize to the larger population. Another decision involves choosing a research setting. One basic decision is whether to conduct the study in a laboratory (a controlled setting where many of the complex factors of the "real world" are removed) or in a more naturalistic setting. Yet another decision includes selecting measures to use in collecting information. One choice is to use direct observation in a systematic way. Another choice is to use an interview or questionnaire. Another option is to conduct a case study. And some studies include a standardized test. Each of these measures has strengths and weaknesses.

Another research decision involves choosing a method that gives the desired depth of explanation. The descriptive method provides systematic and objective descriptions of behavior. The correlational method, in which the goal is to describe the strength of relation between two or more events or characteristics, yields a deeper level of explanation than the descriptive method; however, we cannot conclude from a correlational study that one event caused the other. The deepest level of explanation is provided by the experimental method, which allows psychologists to determine behavior's causes. They accomplish this by performing an experiment, a carefully regulated procedure in which one or more factors believed to influence the behavior being studied are manipulated and all other factors are held constant. An experiment involves random assignment of participants to experimental and control groups. Experiments involve at least one independent variable (the manipulated, influential variable) and one dependent variable (the measured variable). Despite the experimental method's power to determine cause, experimenters must be cautious about factors that can make the data useless; these factors include participants' and experimenters' expectancies and biases. The placebo effect occurs when participants' expectations, rather than the independent variable, produce the desired outcome. Experimenter bias occurs when the researcher's own expectations influence the outcome of the research. A possible solution to the problem of expectancy effects is the double-blind study.

Ethical treatment of subjects is another important research issue. Psychologists have adopted a formal code of ethics to encourage humane and appropriate treatment of subjects. The code's guidelines include the use of informed consent, guidelines governing the use of deception, and debriefing of subjects. Strict ethical guidelines govern the safety and treatment of animal subjects.

THINKING CRITICALLY ABOUT BEHAVIOR

People don't change. Love is blind. Birds of a feather flock together. Communicating with spirits is possible. Such statements about human nature spark the psychologist's curiosity and **skepticism,** *the tendency to doubt the validity of claims in the absence of evidence.* Psychologists seek to sort fact from fancy by critically questioning the nature of mind and behavior. In this section we will explore how understanding psychology's principles and methods can help you become more effective at evaluating the truthfulness of the flood of claims you hear about behavior.

Making Sense of Behavior Claims

Headlines and advertising promotions often proclaim wondrous insights about human behavior that interest the public. For example, headlines on the tabloids you find in grocery store checkout aisles often tout a new miracle cure or weight-loss procedure. How can you use your knowledge of scientific methods to sort through the amazing claims and distinguish what is true from what is false?

Imagine this situation: Dr. Ralph Conman makes a guest appearance on a popular television talk show in which he describes the "amazing" results of a research study he has just completed. He has been investigating what makes children grow up to become productive, creative adults. He discloses to his host that children who have imaginary friends and frequently play with dolls and plush animals end up being more creative adults. Dr. Conman advocates that parents encourage their young children to create imaginary companions and play with dolls and plush animals to stimulate their creativity.

Should you rush out to the toy store and buy new imagination "helpers" to put the special children in your life on the path to becoming creative adults? Try to poke some holes in Dr. Conman's arguments before you read the recommendations below.

- *Find out how important terms are defined and measured.* What exactly did Dr. Conman mean by "creative adulthood"? How did he determine whether one child was more "imaginative" than another? In this study, as in all studies, you need to evaluate whether the researcher's definitions and measurements are sound.
- *Understand the nature of the sample before you generalize.* Sometimes the media make too much of research results that involve a small number of participants who constitute a narrowly defined sample (Kazdin, 1998). These conditions warrant caution because the results might not generalize to the larger population. Dr. Conman might have studied only three or four children. He might also have studied only children from a privileged socioeconomic group, or only boys or only girls. Unless you know that the research participants are comparable to those whose behavior you wish to predict or to influence, reserve your judgment.
- *Do not predict individual behavior from group results.* Most psychological research focuses on the behavior of groups of people. As a consumer of psychological information, you want to know what the information means for you individually. However, you might not be able to apply the results of a group finding to an individual case. Dr. Conman might be reporting "average" results that mask a wide range of individual performances.
- *Resist interpreting the results of a single study as definitive.* The popular press eagerly publishes reports of research that appear to be groundbreaking with far-reaching implications. Although such findings do occur, it is rare for a single study to provide earth-shattering and conclusive answers (Stanovich, 1992). Substantial answers to research questions usually emerge after many scientists have conducted studies and drawn similar conclusions. Children's creativity has been an area of vigorous research in psychology for many years. You would need to find out whether Dr. Conman's conclusions fit with the evidence already amassed on this topic before you become enthusiastic about his results. Avoid accepting the results of a single study as the definitive authority until they are confirmed by a body of research.
- *Differentiate correlational research from experimental research.* Drawing inappropriate causal conclusions is easy to do, so you need to find out how the research was designed and conducted. What kind of research method did Dr. Conman use to pro-

skepticism

The tendency to doubt the validity of claims in the absence of evidence.

duce his results? Most studies on children's creativity are *correlational*. That is, Dr. Conman probably studied existing patterns and drew conclusions about correlational data. He probably did not manipulate the possession of imaginary companions and dolls as an independent variable, as would have been done had the study involved the experimental method.

Let's assume that Dr. Conman derived his conclusions from a well-designed correlational study. Because the study was correlational, its results are open to multiple interpretations. As proposed by Dr. Conman, children with imaginary companions and toys could grow up to be creative adults. Or perhaps creative adults have clearer memories than their less creative counterparts about the nature of the play they engaged in as children. Or imaginative play in childhood and creative adulthood might both be influenced by a third factor—such as a loving home and competent schooling. We cannot know for certain which interpretation is accurate, because this was a correlational study.

- *Evaluate the credibility of the source.* The findings of research studies are not automatically accepted by the research community. Psychologists submit their work to professional journals, where their methods and results are reviewed by experts in that area. The reviewers decide whether or not the study is worthy of being published. Media reports do not have the same constraints. However, we can generally put more trust in reports about research in respected media, like the *New York Times* or *Newsweek,* than in reports in tabloids, such as the *National Inquirer* or *World Weekly News.*

  Also, just because Dr. Conman has the title *Dr.* does not automatically mean that his research is credible. Individuals who create careers in psychology by conducting research can use the title *Dr.* if they have earned a doctorate of philosophy (Ph.D.) degree. But even researchers with Ph.D.'s can produce suspect findings if they have biasing motives. For example, suppose Dr. Conman's research was funded by a grant from a major discount toy wholesaler. His results might have been inflated by experimenter bias.

- *Be skeptical of simplistic claims.* Most human behavior is complex. It is quite unlikely that the development of human creativity could be boiled down to whether or not a child had imaginary companions and access to plush toys. One should especially be suspicious when claims are dramatic. Creative adults, such as gifted novelists, emerge from childhood experiences far more complex than a lapful of "Beanie Babies."

Psychology versus Pseudoscience

You probably know your astrological sign. You might even know the "characteristics" of your sign. But have you ever wondered how much faith you should place in this approach to explaining behavior and predicting your future? From a scientific standpoint, none.

Astrology *uses the position of the stars and planets at the time of birth to describe, explain, and predict a person's behavior.* Researchers have repeatedly demonstrated that astrology has no scientific merit. When astrologers' predictions are successful, it is because

astrology

A pseudopsychology that uses the position of the stars and planets at the time of a person's birth to describe, explain, and predict the person's behavior.

Why does the science of psychology urge you to be skeptical of astrology?

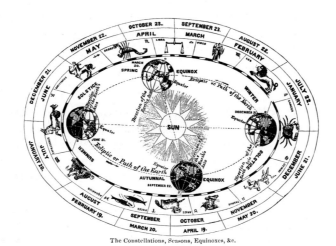

The Constellations, Seasons, Equinoxes, &c.

they are usually so vague that they are virtually guaranteed to happen. For example, "Money is likely to be a source of concern for you this month" is a fairly safe prediction. Do you know many people for whom this would be an inaccurate prediction? Astrologers' more specific predictions ("An unidentified flying object will land on the field during the halftime activities of Monday Night Football on October 2, 2000") virtually never hold up.

Astrology is a **pseudopsychology,** *a nonscientific system that resembles psychology but lacks scientific support.* Pseudopsychologies like astrology tend to produce descriptions, explanations, and predictions that either cannot be directly tested or, when tested, turn out to be false.

Graphology, *the use of handwriting analysis to describe, explain, and predict behavior,* is also a pseudopsychology. Surprisingly, there has been a dramatic increase in the use of graphology as a selection measure for employee screening (Hines, 1988). As indicated in figure 1.7, graphology's claims are not supported by scientific evidence.

Although psychologists pride themselves on being open-minded on most matters, they generally reject the claims of pseudosciences as not being scientifically grounded. The popularity of telephone psychic services is especially distressing to people trained in the scientific study of behavior. Spending hard-earned money on unfounded advice demonstrates a lack of critical thinking. You might feel good initially as you listen to a long list of your "positive qualities" (the longer the list, the more money the "psychic" will make). However, you are unlikely to find effective solutions by turning to pseudosciences. To determine how much you believe in pseudopsychological phenomena, complete the Self-Assessment. To fine-tune your thinking skills, study the box titled Improving Personal and Cognitive Skills (""Consumer Protection").

> *Thank God for fools; without them, where would the rest of us be?*
> —MARK TWAIN, *American Writer and Humorist, 19th/20th Century*

pseudopsychology

A nonscientific system that resembles psychology but lacks scientific support.

graphology

A pseudopsychology that uses handwriting analysis to describe, explain, and predict behavior.

𝓕IGURE 1.7

Graphology

At least 3,000 firms in the United States use graphology when hiring individuals. In other countries, such as Israel and Japan, the use of graphological analysis is even more widespread. Shown here are examples of the type of analysis graphologists use. If the research investigation of graphological claims is so negative, why is graphology so widely used and accepted? Graphological analysis has a mysterious, powerful ring to it. People are easily impressed by so-called experts and assume they know what they are talking about. Positive, unscientific reports of graphologists' abilities frequently appear in magazines and business commentaries. People are fascinated by graphology and want to believe that their handwriting, because it is highly individual, reveals something about themselves. Also, graphologists' predictions, like those of palmists and astrologers, are usually very general and difficult to disprove.

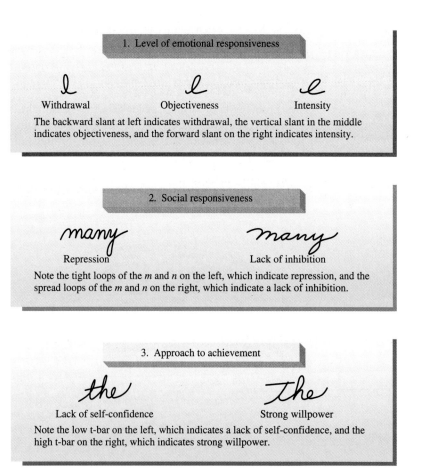

1. Level of emotional responsiveness

Withdrawal   Objectiveness   Intensity

The backward slant at left indicates withdrawal, the vertical slant in the middle indicates objectiveness, and the forward slant on the right indicates intensity.

2. Social responsiveness

Repression   Lack of inhibition

Note the tight loops of the *m* and *n* on the left, which indicate repression, and the spread loops of the *m* and *n* on the right, which indicate a lack of inhibition.

3. Approach to achievement

Lack of self-confidence   Strong willpower

Note the low t-bar on the left, which indicates a lack of self-confidence, and the high t-bar on the right, which indicates strong willpower.

Self-Assessment

Beliefs: Déjà Vu to Rock Crystals

For each of the following items, indicate whether it is something you believe in, something you are not sure about, or something you do not believe in.

	Believe	Not Sure	Do Not Believe
Déjà vu, or the feeling that you have been somewhere or done something before	_____	_____	_____
ESP, or extrasensory perception	_____	_____	_____
Telepathy, or communication between minds without using the traditional five senses	_____	_____	_____
Houses can be haunted	_____	_____	_____
Extraterrestrial beings have visited Earth at some time in the past	_____	_____	_____
Clairvoyance, or the power of the mind to know the past and predict the future	_____	_____	_____
Astrology, or that the position of the stars and planets can affect people's lives	_____	_____	_____
Ghosts, or that spirits of dead people can come back in certain places and situations	_____	_____	_____
That people can hear from or communicate mentally with someone who has died	_____	_____	_____
Telekinesis, or the ability of the mind to move or bend objects using just mental energy	_____	_____	_____
Witches	_____	_____	_____
Channeling, or allowing a "spirit being" to temporarily assume control of a human body during a trance	_____	_____	_____
That pyramids have a special healing power	_____	_____	_____
That rock crystals have a special healing power	_____	_____	_____

SCORING

If after reading our critique of pseudopsychologies, you still responded that you believe in any of these psychic phenomena, spend some time talking with other students in the class about this topic. Their comments might give you some insights that you had not previously thought about. You also might read some articles in the journal *Skeptical Inquirer*, which publishes criticisms of the pseudopsychologies.

Improving Personal and Cognitive Skills

Consumer Protection

How do you know whether you can believe what you hear? When confronted with a research claim about behavior, practice asking questions that will help you be an effective critical thinker and consumer of psychological information:

1. *Who did the research?*
    Was the research completed by a reputable researcher?
    Was it published in a respectable, peer-reviewed journal?
2. *What kind of evidence supports the claim?*
    Is personal testimony its only form of support?
    How does this research fit with the body of knowledge on the behavior?
3. *What was the nature of the research sample?*
    How big was the sample?
    What were the characteristics of the people in the sample?
4. *How was the research designed?*
    Did the researchers use descriptive, correlational, or experimental methods?
    How well-defined were the concepts in the study?
5. *Do the conclusions seem valid?*
    Do the conclusions follow logically from the design?
    Are there other explanations that might account for the results?

 eview

Thinking Critically About Behavior

Making sense of the variety of claims about behavior that appear in the popular press can be challenging. Thinking critically about behavior will help you be less susceptible to accepting false cause-and-effect claims. Some strategies you can adopt to clarify research findings include these: (1) Find out how important terms are defined and measured. (2) Understand the nature of the sample before you generalize. (3) Do not predict individual behavior from group results. (4) Resist interpreting the results of a single study as definitive. (5) Differentiate correlational from experimental research. (6) Evaluate the credibility of the source. (7) Be skeptical about simplistic claims.

Pseudopsychologies are nonscientific systems that resemble psychology. Pseudopsychologies, such as astrology and graphology, lack scientific support. Their descriptions, explanations, and predictions either cannot be directly verified or, when tested, are found to be false. There is a clear danger in following the advice of the pseudopsychologies: you can become diverted from coping with your life in a rational and realistic way.

Overview

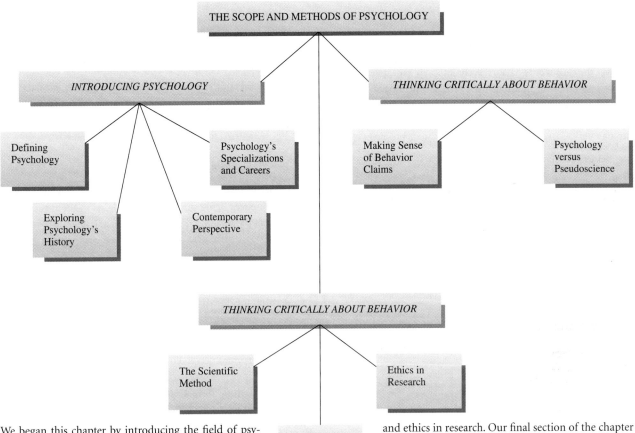

THE SCOPE AND METHODS OF PSYCHOLOGY

INTRODUCING PSYCHOLOGY

THINKING CRITICALLY ABOUT BEHAVIOR

Defining Psychology

Psychology's Specializations and Careers

Making Sense of Behavior Claims

Psychology versus Pseudoscience

Exploring Psychology's History

Contemporary Perspective

THINKING CRITICALLY ABOUT BEHAVIOR

The Scientific Method

Ethics in Research

Research Strategies in Psychology

We began this chapter by introducing the field of psychology. This included defining psychology, exploring psychology's history, describing contemporary perspectives, and presenting psychology's specializations and careers. Next, we studied the science base of psychology and how to conduct research in psychology. This involved understanding the scientific method, research strategies in psychology, and ethics in research. Our final section of the chapter emphasized thinking critically about behavior. Special attention was given to making sense of behavior claims and comparing psychology with pseudopsychology.

Remember that you can obtain a more extensive summary of the chapter by again studying the in-chapter reviews on pages 8, 16, 25, and 30.

Key Terms

Thinking It Over

Exercises . . .

. . . In Critical Thinking

Curiosity about behavior leads to asking questions that can help us uncover the causes of behavior. Psychological perspectives encourage certain kinds of questions (and ignore others). For example, Tim has trouble keeping up with his assignments. See if you can generate a question to represent each of the contemporary psychology perspectives below to help explain Tim's problem:

The Behavioral Perspective:

The Psychoanalytic Perspective:

The Humanistic Perspective:

The Neurobiological Perspective:

The Cognitive Perspective:

The Evolutionary Perspective:

The Sociocultural Perspective:

. . . In Creative Thinking

One way psychologists show creativity is by designing research studies. Suppose you wanted to explore what factors influence whether people will initiate a new relationship. Select one of the three methods described in this chapter for generating data (descriptive, correlational, or experimental) and describe how you might go about designing research to address this question. What are the advantages of the research strategy you chose?

. . . In Active Learning

Now that you are studying psychology, you probably will notice more references being made to psychologists in the media. Keep track of all the references you hear for 1 week. Identify what kind of psychologists you hear about as well as the activity they are engaged in. Jokes and cartoons count, too. If your impressions about psychologists were based only on what you heard during this week, what conclusions might you draw? How are these impressions different from the description in this textbook?

. . . In Reflective Learning

Astrology provides personality profiles that are usually pretty flattering. In a journal entry, write down your "sign" and identify the characteristics that the sign usually predicts for the "personality." For each characteristic cited, rate on a scale of 1 to 10 how accurately these characteristics describe your own personality. Does this description really do justice to who you think you are? Are there any characteristics you have that weren't included in the profile?

Resources for Psychology and Improving Humankind

American Psychological Association

750 First Street, NE
Washington, DC 20002-4242
202-336-5500

The American Psychological Association is the largest organization of psychologists in the United States. It publishes a number of journals on psychological topics and has books and brochures available. Undergraduate student members are welcome.

American Psychological Society

1010 Vermont Avenue, NW
Suite 1100
Washington, DC 20005
202-783-2077

The American Psychological Society promotes and advances research and applications in psychology. Student affiliate memberships are available.

Canadian Psychological Association/Société canadienne de psychologie

151 Slater Street, Suite 205
Ottawa ON K1P 5H3 CANADA
613-237-2144
e-mail: cpa@psychologyassoc.ca

The CPA is a national voluntary organization with over 4,000 members, representing the interests of psychologists and advocating the development of national standards and ethical principles. National conferences, scientific journals, and mainstream publications are used to disseminate information. Collaborative relationships are maintained with other provincial and national associations and with government departments in order to advance the objectives of the association.

Even the Rat Was White: A Historical View of Psychology (1976, 1994)

by Robert V. Guthrie
New York: Harper & Row

This critique of psychology rests on the premise that in its first century, psychology has systematically excluded important sociocultural factors, particularly race and ethnicity. Guthrie offers suggestions for the promotion of a more inclusive science of human behavior.

The Great Psychologists (1986)

by Robert Watson
Philadelphia: Lippincott

This fascinating book explores the early psychologists' views of mental processes and behavior.

How to Think Straight About Psychology (1993)

by Keith Stanovich
New York: HarperCollins

This excellent book explores how psychologists think about behavior. Special attention is given to creating and defending arguments based on scientific evidence.

Is Psychology the Major for You? (1987)

by P. J. Woods and C. S. Wilkinson
Washington, DC: American Psychological Association

This book is must reading for anyone interested in a career in psychology. The authors give insights into what it is like to work in a number of different areas of psychology, from clinical to experimental to industrial/organizational.

Library Use: A Handbook for Psychology (2nd ed.) (1992)

by Jeffrey Reed and Pam Baxter
Washington, DC: American Psychological Association

From this book you will learn about selecting, defining, and locating topics for library search in psychology. The topics chosen appeal to the interests of many psychology students, and you don't need to have highly technical knowledge to use the book.

Publication Manual of the American Psychological Association (1994, 4th ed.)

Washington, DC: American Psychological Association

This is the style manual used by researchers and students in psychology and other behavioral and social sciences. The manual provides publication information that includes the topics of organization, writing, submitting manuscripts, reducing bias in language, referencing, and general policies and ethics in scientific publication.

Untold Lives: The First Generation of American Women Psychologists (1987)

by Elizabeth Scarborough and Laurel Furumoto
New York: Columbia University Press

This well-crafted volume uses a research method called historiography to capture the struggles of America's pioneering women psychologists. The authors constructed the stories of the earliest women in psychology from correspondence, archives, and interviews and concluded that their collective experience documented harsh discriminatory practices that placed obstacles in the paths of talented women. The authors also review what aspects have changed for women in psychology since that time.

The Science Game (1993)

by Sandra Pyke and Neil Agnew
Englewood Cliffs, NJ: Prentice Hall

This popular book covers a number of important ideas about conducting research in psychology in an entertaining and informative way.

Internet Resources

Be sure to enter the Internet address exactly as it is written. Adding spaces or making any other changes will cause the address not to work. Also keep in mind that Websites often change addresses and they go off-line sometimes. We have visited these sites and hope they will be there when you try them. Try not to get too frustrated if you find a site no longer exists. In such instances, try to your Internet search feature.

http://galaxy.einet.net/galaxy/Social-Sciences/Psychology.html
A comprehensive site about the content and services of psychology, including active research departments.

http://www.hanover.edu:80/psych/hanpsyc.html
Participate in experiments and explore job possibilities among other activities posted on the web site.

http://psy.ucsd.edu/otherpsy.html
List of psychology departments around the world.

http://www.hanover.edu/psych/APS/aps.html
Web site for the American Psychology Society, which is dedicated to advancing the scientific aspects of psychology.

http://www.apa.org/
Web site for the American Psychological Association, a professional group that advocates for clinical practice and science.

http://www.psych-web.com/
A comprehensive site operated by Georgia Southern University, including career tips, research strategies, and special features.

http://www.cwu.edu/-warren/today.html
Explore what happened on today's date in history related to psychology via the American Psychological Association.

http://www.cwu.edu/-warren/today.html
Cyberlink explores electronic journals and databases researchers use in psychology.

http://www.tulsa.oklahoma.net/~jnichols/famous.html
Browse through famous historical figures in psychology.

http://www.tulsa.oklahoma.net/~jnichols/ethics.html
Investigate how psychologists adhere to ethical standards in research, teaching, and practice at the MegaPsych web site.

http://www.utc.edu/-psichi/Psichi.htm
Check out the national honorary society for excellence in undergraduate psychology study.

http://www.apa.org/pubinfo/pubinfo.html
APA offers some tips on how to apply psychology to concerns in daily life.

2

Biological Foundations and the Brain

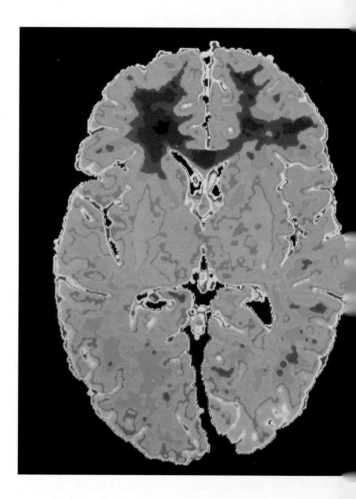

*The chess-board is the world. The pieces are the
phenomena of the universe. The rules of the game
are what we call the laws of nature.*

—THOMAS HUXLEY
English Biologist, 19th Century

PREVIEW

Shortly you will read about the bizarre similarities between Jim and Jim, identical twins who were separated at the age of 4 weeks and not reunited again until they were almost 40 years old. Their similarities raise questions about the role nature plays in human behavior and the biological foundations of our existence. How are characteristics transmitted from one generation to the next, for instance? How did the human species come to be? What exquisite systems give us our extraordinary ability to adapt to our world? These questions focus on biological perspectives and the nervous system, the main topics of this chapter.

The Story of the Jim and Jim Twins: Genetic Determinism or Mere Coincidence?

Jim Springer and Jim Lewis are identical twins. They were separated at the age of 4 weeks and didn't see one another again until they were 39 years old. Even so, they share uncanny similarities that read more like fiction that fact. For example, they have both worked as a part-time deputy sheriff, have vacationed in Florida, have driven Chevrolets, have had dogs named Toy, and have married and divorced women named Betty. In addition, one twin named his son James Allan, and the other named his son James Alan. Both like math but not spelling, and both enjoy carpentry and mechanical drawing. They have chewed their fingernails down to the nubs and have almost identical drinking and smoking habits. Both have had hemorrhoids, put on 10 pounds at about the same time, and first suffered headaches at the age of 18. They also have similar sleep patterns.

Jim and Jim have some differences as well. One wears his hair over his forehead, whereas the other wears it slicked back with sideburns. One expresses himself better

Jim Lewis *(left)* and Jim Springer *(right)*.

verbally; the other is more proficient in writing. For the most part, however, they are more alike than different.

The Jim and Jim twins are part of the Minnesota Study of Twins Reared Apart, directed by Thomas Bouchard and his colleagues. The researchers brought identical (genetically identical because they come from the same egg) and fraternal (genetically dissimilar because they come from two eggs) twins from all over the world to Minneapolis to investigate the psychological aspects of the twins' lives. For example, the twins were interviewed and asked more than 15,000 questions about their family and childhood environment, personal interests, vocational orientation, values, and aesthetic judgments. Detailed medical histories were obtained, including information about their smoking, diet, and exercise habits. The researchers also took chest X rays and gave heart stress tests and EEGs (brain wave tests). The twins were also given a number of personality, ability, and intelligence tests (Bouchard & others, 1981; McGue & Bouchard, 1989). Many argue that the many uncommon similarities discovered in the twin study are evidence of a genetic basis for habits, tastes, and behavior.

Critics of the Minnesota twin study dispute this conclusion. They point out that some of the separated twins had been together several months prior to their adoption, that some twins had been reunited prior to their testing (in some cases a number of years earlier), that adoption agencies often place twins in similar homes, and that even strangers who spend several hours together and start comparing their lives are likely to come up with coincidental similarities (Adler, 1991). Still, even in the face of such criticism, the Minnesota study demonstrates the interest scientists have shown in the genetic basis of behavior. ❖

PERSPECTIVES ON NATURE AND NURTURE

Biologists who study even the simplest animals agree that it is virtually impossible to separate the effects of an animal's genes from the effects of its environment (Mader, 1997). **Environment** *refers to all of the surrounding conditions and influences that affect the development of living things.* Environment includes the food that we eat, the air we breathe, and the many different physical and social contexts we experience—the cities and towns we live in; our relationships with parents, peers, and teachers; our continuing interactions at work, at home, and at play; and so on.

In the last chapter we introduced the concept of the nature-nurture controversy. The term **nurture** *is often used to describe an organism's environmental experiences.* The term **nature** *is often used to describe an organism's biological inheritance.* The interaction of nature *and* nurture, genes *and* environment, influences every aspect of mind and behavior to a degree. Neither factor operates alone (Nagashi, 1998). The debate about whether behavior is primarily influenced by nature or nurture has been a part of psychology since its beginning. Most psychologists do not take extreme positions on the nature-nurture controversy, but nonetheless debate is spirited.

environment

All of the surrounding conditions and influences that affect the development of living things.

nurture

A term often used to describe an organism's environmental experiences.

nature

A term often used to describe an organism's biological inheritance.

Sociocultural Worlds

Race and Ethnicity

Race, which originated as a biological concept, is a system for classifying plants and animals into subcategories according to specific physical and structural characteristics. *Race* is one of the most misused and misunderstood words in the English language (Atkinson, Morten, & Sue, 1999; Root, 1992). Loosely, it has come to mean everything from a person's religion to skin color.

Scholars have difficulty even determining how many races the human species comprises. Skin color, head shape, facial features, stature, and the color and texture of body hair are the physical characteristics most widely used to determine race. Racial classifications presumably were created to define and clarify the differences among groups of people; however, they have not been very useful. Many people argue that racial groupings are socially constructed on the basis of physical differences and are not biologically defensible (Van den Berghe, 1978).

One approach to classification specifies three main races: Mongoloid, or Asian; Caucasoid, or European; and Negroid, or African. However, some groups, such as Native Americans, Australians, and Polynesians, do not fit into any of the three main categories. Also, obvious differences *within* groups are not adequately explained. Arabs, Hindus, and Europeans, for instance, are physically different, yet they are all called Caucasian. Although there are some physical characteristics that distinguish "racial" groups, there are, in fact, more similarities than differences among such groups.

Too often we are socialized to accept as facts many myths and stereotypes about people whose skin color, facial features, and hair texture differ from ours. What people believe about race has profound social consequences. Until recently, for instance, African Americans were denied access to schools, hospitals, churches, and other social institutions attended by Whites.

Although scientists are supposed to be a fair-minded lot, some also have used racial distinctions to further their own biases. Some even claim that one racial group has a biological inheritance that gives it an adaptive advantage over other racial groups. Nineteenth-century biologist Louis Agassiz, for example, asserted that God had created Blacks and Whites as separate species. Also, in Nazi Germany, where science and death made their grisliest alliance, Jews and other "undesirables" were attributed with whatever characteristics were necessary to reinforce the conclusion that "survival of the fittest" demanded their elimination.

Social psychologist James Jones (1990, 1997) points out that thinking in racial terms has become embedded in cultures as an important factor in human interactions. For example, people often consider what race they will associate with when they decide on such things as where to live, who will make a suitable spouse, where to go to school, and what kind of job they want. Similarly, people often use race to judge whether or not another person is intelligent, competent, responsible, or socially acceptable. Children tend to adopt their parents' attitudes about race as they grow up, often perpetuating stereotypes and prejudice.

Physical and psychological characteristics vary not only across ethnic groups but also within them.

> *With a good heredity, nature deals you a fine hand at cards; and with a good environment, you learn to play the hand well.*
> —WALTER C. ALVAREZ, *Physician and Author, 20th Century*

Both genes and environment are necessary for a person to even exist. Without genes, there is no person; without environment, there is no person. Heredity and environment operate together—or cooperate—to produce a person's intelligence, temperament, height, weight, ability to pitch a baseball, read, and so on (Gottlieb, Wahlsten, & Lickliter, 1998). If an attractive, popular, intelligent girl is elected president of her senior class in high school, is her success due to heredity or to environment? Of course, the answer is both. Because how the environment influences a person depends on the person's genetically endowed characteristics, we say that the two factors *interact* (Mader, 1999).

The relative contributions of heredity and environment are not additive, as in such-and-such a percentage of nature, such-and-such a percentage of experience. That's the old view. Nor is it accurate to say that full genetic expression happens once, around conception or birth, after which we take our genetic legacy into the world to see how far it gets us. Genes produce proteins throughout the life span, in many different environments. Or they don't produce these proteins, depending on how harsh or nourishing those environments are. The interaction is so extensive that William Greenough (1997; Greenough & others, 1997) says that to ask which is more important, nature or nurture, is like asking which is more important to a rectangle, its length or its width.

Imagine for a moment that there were a cluster of genes somehow associated with youth violence (this is hypothetical because we don't know of any such combination). The child who carried this genetic mixture might inhabit a world of loving parents, regular nutritious meals, lots of books, and a series of gifted teachers. Or the child's world might consist of parental neglect, a neighborhood where gunshots and crime are everyday occurrences, and inadequate schooling. In which of these environments would the child's genes most likely manufacture the biological underpinnings of criminality? Also note that growing up with all of the "advantages" does not necessarily guarantee success. Children from wealthy families might have access to books, excellent schools, travel, and tutoring, but they might take such opportunities for granted and fail to develop the motivation to learn and achieve. In the same way, growing up "poor" or "disadvantaged" does not mean that one is "doomed."

More information about the roles of biology and experience in behavior is presented in Sociocultural Worlds, where we examine the biological and experiential aspects of race and ethnicity. Let's further explore the nature side of the equation by studying the biological topics of heredity and evolution.

The Genetic Perspective

All humans begin life as a single cell, a fertilized human egg, weighing about one-twenty-millionth of an ounce. This single cell develops into a human being made of trillions of cells. The nucleus of each human cell contains 46 **chromosomes,** *which are threadlike structures that come in 23 pairs, one member of each pair coming from each parent.*

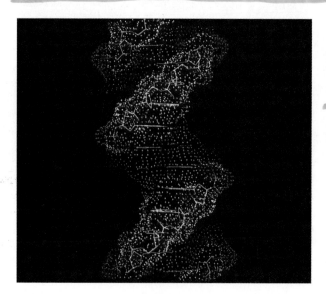

Chromosomes contain the remarkable genetic substance **deoxyribonucleic acid, or DNA,** *a complex molecule that contains genetic information* (see figure 2.1). **Genes,** *the units of heredity information, are short segments of DNA. Genes act as a blueprint for cells to reproduce themselves through cell division (called mitosis) and manufacture the proteins that maintain life.* Chromosomes, DNA, and genes can be mysterious. To help you turn mystery into understanding, see figure 2.2.

chromosomes

Threadlike structures, located in the nucleus of each human cell, that come in 23 pairs, one member of each pair coming from each parent.

deoxyribonucleic acid (DNA)

A complex molecule that contains genetic information.

genes

Short segments of DNA that are the units of hereditary information. Genes act as blueprints for cells to reproduce themselves through cell division called mitosis and manufacture the proteins that maintain life.

𝓕IGURE 2.1

The Remarkable Substance Known as DNA

Notice that a DNA molecule is shaped like a spiral staircase. Genes are short segments of the DNA molecule. The horizontal bars that look like the rungs of a ladder play a key role in locating the identity of a gene.

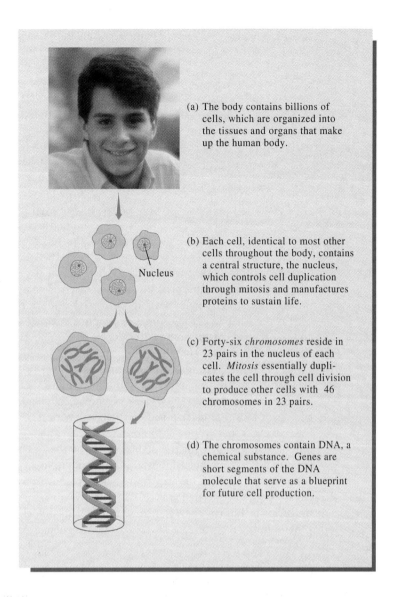

(a) The body contains billions of cells, which are organized into the tissues and organs that make up the human body.

Nucleus

(b) Each cell, identical to most other cells throughout the body, contains a central structure, the nucleus, which controls cell duplication through mitosis and manufactures proteins to sustain life.

(c) Forty-six *chromosomes* reside in 23 pairs in the nucleus of each cell. *Mitosis* essentially duplicates the cell through cell division to produce other cells with 46 chromosomes in 23 pairs.

(d) The chromosomes contain DNA, a chemical substance. Genes are short segments of the DNA molecule that serve as a blueprint for future cell production.

*F*IGURE 2.2

Concepts in Genetic Transmission

The frightening part about heredity and enviornment is that we parents provide both.

—NOTEBOOK OF A PRINTER

Although we have a long way to go before we unravel all the mysteries about the way genes work, some aspects of heritability are well understood (Rose, 1995). Every person has characteristics that reflect the genetic contributions from both parents, such as the physical characteristics of hair color and height. Behavioral characteristics, such as how shy or outgoing you are, also are believed to have a genetic component, although their transmission is more complex than height or hair color.

When genes combine to determine our characteristics, some genes are dominant over others. According to the **dominant-recessive genes principle,** *if one gene of a pair is dominant and one is recessive, the dominant gene exerts its effect, overriding the potential influence of the recessive gene. A recessive gene exerts its influence only if both genes of a pair are recessive.* If you inherit a recessive gene from only one parent, you may never know you carry the gene. In the world of dominant-recessive genes, brown eyes, far-sightedness, and dimples rule over blue eyes, near-sightedness, and freckles. If you inherit a recessive gene for a trait from both of your parents, you will show the trait. That's why two brown-eyed

dominant-recessive genes principle

The principle that if one gene of a pair is dominant and the other is recessive, the dominant gene exerts its effect, overriding the potential influence of the recessive gene. A recessive gene exerts its influence only if both genes of the pair are recessive.

parents can have a blue-eyed child. In each parent, the genes that govern eye color include a dominant gene for brown eyes and a recessive gene for blue eyes. Since dominant genes override recessive genes, the parents have brown eyes; however, both can pass on their recessive genes for blue eyes. With no dominant gene to override them, the recessive genes make the child's eyes blue.

Long before people wondered how brown-eyed parents could possibly bear a blue-eyed child, they wondered what determined a child's sex. Aristotle believed that, as the father's sexual excitement increased, so did the odds of producing a son. He was wrong, of course, but it was not until the 1920s that researchers confirmed the existence of human sex chromosomes, the genetic material that determines sex. As already mentioned, humans normally have 46 chromosomes arranged in pairs. The 23rd pair may have two X-shaped chromosomes to produce a female, or it may have both an X-shaped and a Y-shaped chromosome to produce a male. The 23rd pair of chromosomes also carries some sex-linked characteristics, such as color blindness or hairy ear rims, both of which are more common in men. This mechanism is illustrated in figure 2.3.

Most genetic transmission is more complex than these rather simple examples (McGue & Carmichael, 1995). Few psychological characteristics are the result of a single gene pair. Most are determined by the combination of different genes. Each of us has at least 50,000 genes in our chromosomes. When the 50,000 genes from one parent combine at conception with the 50,000 genes of the other parent, the number of possible combinations—in the trillions—is staggering. No wonder scientists are struck by the complexity of genetic transmission. Scientists have proposed the Human Genome Project (HGP), an international, 15-year project to map the human genome (the genetic blueprint of human characteristics) in order to unlock its mysteries. New discoveries of genetic linkages to disease have become a regular event due to the efforts of the HGP

FIGURE 2.3
Genetic Principles of
Reproduction

(a) Cell reproduction, called *meiosis,* produces special sex cells, called *gametes* (the male's sperm and the female's egg), that have only 23 unpaired chromosomes.

(b) Conception matches chromosomes from each partner into 23 pairs, one member of the chromosome pair from the mother's egg and one member from the father's sperm.

(c) Of the 23 pairs, one pair will determine the sex of the fertilized egg. In this illustration, the combination of an X from the mother and a Y from the father will result in a male child.

(Lee, 1991). These include discovering the genetic origins of certain forms of cancer. Identifying genetic makeup can help determine whether individuals are at risk for certain kinds of cancer.

The Evolutionary Perspective

The human genome represents a remarkable biological achievement. We share genetic patterns with many other species on Earth, despite the distinctive differences that make us "human"—such as advanced language and intelligence. Humans actually are relative newcomers to Earth (Sagan, 1980). If we compare evolutionary history to a calendar year, the beginning of the universe, sometimes referred to as "the Big Bang," took place on January 1, Earth did not form until mid September, life on Earth did not appear until late September, and humans did not show up until 10:30 P.M. on December 31!

> Who are we? We find that we live on an insignificant planet of a humdrum star lost in a galaxy tucked away in some forgotten corner of a universe in which there are far more galaxies than people.
>
> —CARL SAGAN, *American Astronomer, 20th century*

Despite our relatively brief existence on this planet, we have established ourselves as the most successful and dominant species. As our earliest ancestors left the forests to form hunting societies on the grassy savannas, their thinking and behavior changed. How did these changes in thinking and behavior come about?

natural selection

The evolutionary process that favors the individuals within a species that are best adapted to survive and reproduce in their particular environment.

Natural Selection. Over time, entire species can change through **natural selection,** *the evolutionary process that favors genes that code for design features that are most likely to lead to reproduction and survival.* Also known as "the survival of the fittest," natural selection lies at the heart of Charles Darwin's theory of evolution. Darwin, a nineteenth-century naturalist, sailed to South America to study a multitude of plant and animal species in their natural surroundings. He observed that most organisms reproduce at rates that should result in overpopulation, yet somehow populations remain nearly constant.

Darwin reasoned that each new generation must engage in an intense, constant struggle for food, water, and other resources. In the course of this struggle, many of the young would die. Those who survive would be those who had better adapted to their environment. The survivors would reproduce and, in turn, pass on some of their characteristics to the next generation. Over the course of many generations, the organisms with the characteristics needed for survival (speed and sharp claws in predators or thick fur in Arctic animals, for instance) would make up an increasingly larger percentage of the population. Over many, many generations, this process could modify the entire population. If environmental conditions were to change, however, other characteristics might be needed and would move the process in a different direction. Darwin published his observations and thoughts in *On the Origin of Species* (1859).

Generally, evolution proceeds at a very slow pace. The lines that led to the emergence of human beings and the great apes diverged about 14 million years ago. Modern humans, *Homo sapiens,* came into existence only about 50,000 years ago, and civilization as we know it began about 10,000 years ago. No sweeping evolutionary changes in humans have occurred since then—for example, our brains haven't become substantially bigger and we haven't learned to fly.

evolutionary psychology

A contemporary perspective that emphasizes the roles of evolution and psychological mechanisms in adaptive behavior.

Evolutionary Psychology. **Evolutionary psychology** *is a contemporary perspective that emphasizes the roles of both evolution and psychological mechanisms in adaptive behavior.* Evolutionary psychologists believe that the human mind evolved as a collection of independent mechanisms, or modules, that serve adaptive functions. Experts in the field of evolutionary psychology argue that research increasingly supports the evolution of these mechanisms because of the large number of adaptive problems humans had to solve in their past evolutionary environments (Buss, 1995; Pinker, 1997). What are some examples of these domain-specific, modular psychological mechanisms? They include:

- skills for understanding the concept of number
- mental maps for large territories
- the emotion of fear
- the ability to monitor one's own well-being
- a person's self-concept
- mating and feelings of sexual attraction and love

Evolutionary psychologists believe that their approach provides an umbrella for unifying the diverse fields of psychology. Not all psychologists agree. Some argue that it is unlikely that one approach can unify the diverse, complex field of psychology (Graziano, 1995). Others stress that evolutionary approaches do not account for cultural diversity (Paludi, 1995). At best, evolutionary psychology offers what are called *post hoc* (after-the-fact) explanations of diversity.

 eview

Perspectives on Nature and Nurture

The debate about whether behavior is primarily influenced by nature (heredity, biology) or nurture (environment, experience) has been a part of psychology since its beginning. Most psychologists don't take extreme positions on this controversy, but debate is spirited.

From the genetic perspective, the nucleus of each human cell contains 46 chromosomes, which are composed of DNA. Genes are short segments of DNA that act as blueprints for cells to reproduce and manufacture proteins that maintain life. Most genetic transmission involves combinations of genes.

From the evolutionary perspective, organisms who show better adaptation are more likely to survive; the survivors reproduce and pass on some of their characteristics to the next generation. Over the course of many generations, the organisms with the characteristics most needed for survival make up an increasingly large percentage of the population. Evolutionary psychology is a contemporary perspective that emphasizes the importance of both evolution and psychological mechanisms in adaptive behavior. Evolutionary psychologists believe the human mind evolved as a collection of independent mechanisms, or modules, that serve adaptive functions. Critics of evolutionary psychology argue that it does not adequately address sociocultural factors in behavior.

THE NERVOUS SYSTEM

neurons

Nerve cells, the basic units of the nervous system.

central nervous system (CNS)

The brain and spinal cord.

peripheral nervous system

A network of nerves that connects the brain and spinal cord to other parts of the body. Takes information to and from the brain and spinal cord and carries out the commands of the CNS to execute various muscular and glandular activities.

somatic nervous system

A division of the peripheral nervous system consisting of sensory nerves that convey information from the skin and muscles to the central nervous system about such matters as pain and temperature, and motor nerves, which tell muscles when to act.

Of all the aspects of the human body that evolved, none is more important than the nervous system. The purpose of the nervous system is to pass messages back and forth among cells. Highly organized, the nervous system is continuously processing information about everything we do—whether we are taking out the garbage, spotting a loved one across a crowded room, or preparing a speech. First we will take a *macro* view of the nervous system and examine how it is organized to execute such complex behaviors. Then we will explore a *micro* view of the nervous system by looking at the function of nerve cells, or **neurons,** *the basic units of the nervous system.*

Elegant Organization

The nervous system is divided into two parts: the central nervous system and the peripheral nervous system. Figure 2.4 displays the hierarchical organization of the nervous system's major divisions. The **central nervous system (CNS)** *is made up of the brain and spinal cord.* More than 99 percent of all neurons in the body are located in the CNS. The **peripheral nervous system** *is a network of nerves that connects the brain and spinal cord to other parts of the body. The peripheral nervous system takes information to and from the brain and spinal cord and carries out the commands of the CNS to execute various muscular and glandular activities.*

The two major divisions of the peripheral nervous system are the *somatic nervous system* and *autonomic nervous system.* The **somatic nervous system** *consists of sensory*

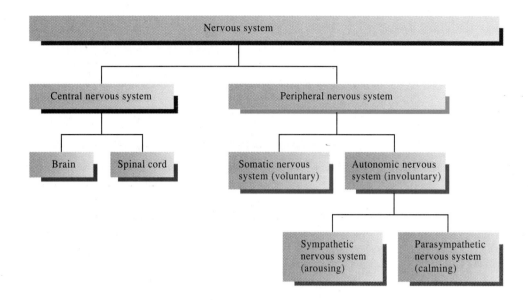

$\mathcal{F}$IGURE 2.4

Major Divisions of the Human
Nervous System

nerves, *which convey information from the skin and muscles to the CNS about such matters as pain and temperature, and motor nerves, which inform muscles when to act.* The **autonomic nervous system** *takes messages to and from the body's internal organs, monitoring such processes as breathing, heart rate, and digestion.* It also is divided into two parts, the **sympathetic nervous system,** *the division of the autonomic nervous system that arouses the body,* and the **parasympathetic nervous system,** *the division of the autonomic nervous system that calms the body* (see figure 2.5).

To get a better feel for how the human nervous system works, imagine that you are preparing to give a speech. As you go over your notes one last time, your peripheral nervous system carries information about the notes to your central nervous system. Your central nervous system processes the marks on the paper, interpreting the words as you memorize key points and plan ways to keep the audience interested. After studying the notes several minutes longer, you scribble a joke midway through them. Your peripheral nervous system is at work again, conveying the information that enables you to make the marks on the paper from your brain to the muscles in your arm and hand. The information transmitted from your eyes to your brain and from your brain to your hand is being handled by the somatic nervous system. Since this is your first speech in a while, you've got the jitters. As you think about getting up in front of the audience, your stomach feels queasy and your heart begins to thump. This is the sympathetic division of the autonomic nervous system functioning as you become aroused. You regain your confidence after reminding yourself that you know the speech. As you relax, 5 minutes into the speech, the parasympathetic division of the autonomic nervous system is working.

Neural Transmission

So far, we have discussed the nervous system's major divisions. However, there is much more to the intriguing story of how the nervous system processes information.

Neuron Pathways. Information flows to the brain, within the brain, and out of the brain along specialized nerve cells known as *afferent nerves, interneurons,* and *efferent nerves.* **Afferent nerves,** *or sensory nerves, carry information to the brain.* Afferent comes from the Latin word meaning "bring to." **Efferent nerves,** *or motor nerves, carry the brain's output.* The word *efferent* is derived from the Latin word meaning "bring forth." To see how afferent and efferent nerves work, let's consider a well-known reflex, the knee jerk. When your knee jerks in response to a tap just below your kneecap, afferent cells transmit information directly to efferent cells; the information processing is quick and simple.

The information involving the knee jerk reflex is processed at the spinal cord. This simple transaction does not require the brain's participation. More complex information

autonomic nervous system

The division of the peripheral nervous system that takes messages to and from the body's internal organs, monitoring such processes as breathing, heart rate, and digestion.

sympathetic nervous system

The division of the autonomic nervous system that arouses the body.

parasympathetic nervous system

The division of the autonomic nervous system that calms the body.

afferent nerves

Sensory nerves that carry information to the brain.

efferent nerves

Motor nerves that carry the brain's output.

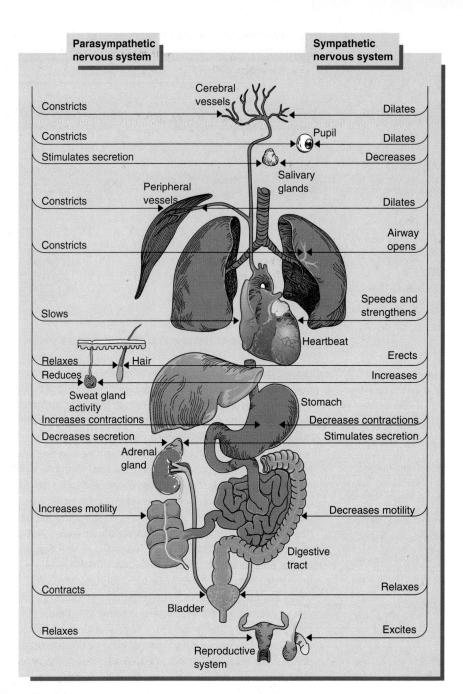

FIGURE 2.5

Autonomic Nervous System

Parasympathetic and sympathetic divisions. The sympathetic system is at work when we are aroused; the parasympathetic system is at work when we are calm. Both systems influence most organs. For example, the sympathetic system speeds and strengthens heartbeat; the parasympathetic system slows heartbeat.

interneurons

Central nervous system neurons that mediate sensory input and motor output. Interneurons make up most of the brain.

processing is accomplished by passing the information through systems of **interneurons**, *central nervous system neurons that mediate sensory input and motor output. Interneurons make up most of the brain.* For example, as you read the notes for your speech, the afferent input from your eye is transmitted to your brain, then is passed through many interneuron systems, which translate (process) the patterns of black and white into neural codes for letters, words, associations, and meanings. Some of the information is stored in the interneuron systems for future associations, and, if you read aloud, some is output as efferent messages to your lips and tongue.

Structure of the Neuron.   *Neurons* are nerve cells that handle information processing in the nervous system. There are about 100 billion neurons in the human brain. The average neuron is as complex as a small computer and has as many as 15,000 physical connections with other cells. At times the brain may be "lit up" with as many as a quadrillion connections.

cell body

The part of the neuron that contains the nucleus, which directs the manufacture of the substances the neuron uses for its growth and maintenance.

dendrite

The receiving part of the neuron, serving the important function of collecting information and orienting it toward the cell body.

axon

The part of the neuron that carries information away from the cell body to other cells.

myelin sheath

A layer of fat cells that encases most axons; it insulates the axon and helps nerve impulses travel faster.

ions

Electrically charged particles that include sodium (NA$^+$), chloride (Cl$^-$), and potassium (K$^+$). The neuron creates electrical signals by moving these charged ions back and forth through its membrane; the waves of electricity that are created sweep along the membrane.

resting potential

The stable, negative charge of an inactive neuron.

The three basic parts of the neuron are the cell body, the dendrites, and the axon (see figure 2.6). The neuron's **cell body** *contains the nucleus, which directs the manufacture of the substances the neuron uses for its growth and maintenance.* Most neurons are created very early in life and will not be replaced if they are destroyed, although their shape, size, and connections might change throughout the life span.

The **dendrite** *is the receiving part of the neuron, serving the important function of collecting information and orienting it toward the cell body.* Most nerve cells have a number of dendrites radiating from the cell body of the neuron, but there is only one axon. The **axon** *is the part of the neuron that carries information away from the cell body to other cells.* The axon typically is much thinner and longer than a dendrite and looks like an ultra-thin cylindrical tube. The axon of a single neuron may extend all the way from the top of the brain to the base of the spinal cord, a distance of over 3 feet. The axon terminates in small synaptic knobs called *terminal buttons,* the storage sites of neurotransmitters, which will be discussed in a later section.

A **myelin sheath,** *a layer of fat cells, encases most axons, insulating the nerve cell and helping nerve impulses travel faster.* The myelin coverings on the axons are not fully developed at birth. As babies grow and develop, their muscle coordination improves, indicating fuller myelination. The myelin sheaths develop as the brain and nerve cells grow larger, making it necessary for information to travel over long distances in the nervous system. This is similar to the appearance of freeways as cities grow. The newly developed roadways keep the fast-moving long-distance traffic from tangling up with slower-moving local traffic. The important role of the myelin sheath can easily be seen in diseases such as multiple sclerosis, in which deterioration of myelin diminishes nerve impulse transmission and leads to loss of muscle function.

The Nerve Impulse. Neurons send information down the axon as brief impulses, or waves, of electricity. Perhaps in a movie you have seen a telegraph operator sending a series of single clicks down a telegraph wire to the next station. That is what neurons do. To transmit information to other neurons, they send a series of single electrical clicks down their axons. By changing the rate and timing of the clicks, neurons can vary the nature of the message they send. As you reach to turn this page, hundreds of such clicks stream down the axons in your arm to tell your muscles when to flex and how vigorously.

To understand how a neuron, which is a living cell, creates and sends electrical signals, we need to examine this cell and the fluids in which it floats. A neuron is a balloon-like bag filled with one kind of fluid and surrounded by a slightly different kind of fluid. A piece of this balloonlike bag forms a long, hollow tube, which is the axon. The axon tube is very thin; a few dozen in a bundle would be about the thickness of a human hair.

To see how the neuron creates electrical signals, we must look at two things: the particles that float in the fluids and the actual wall of the cell, the membrane. The important particles in the fluids are **ions,** *electrically charged particles that include sodium (NA$^+$), chloride (Cl$^-$), and potassium (K$^+$). The neuron creates electrical signals by moving these charged ions back and forth through its membrane; the waves of electricity that are created sweep along the membrane.*

How does the neuron move these ions? The membrane, the wall of the neuron, is covered with hundreds of thousands of gates that open and close to let the ions pass in or out to the cell. Normally, when resting, or not sending information, the membrane gates for sodium are closed and those for potassium and chloride are partly open. Therefore, the membrane is in what is called a *semipermeable state,* and the ions separate; sodium is kept outside, lots of potassium ends up inside, and most of the chloride goes outside. Because the ions are separated, a charge is present along the membrane of the cell (figure 2.7 shows the movement of the sodium and potassium ions). **Resting potential** *is the stable, negative charge of an inactive neuron.* That potential is about one-fourteenth of a volt, so fourteen neurons could make a one-volt battery; an electric eel's 8,400 cells could generate 600 volts.

When a neuron gets enough stimulation to cause it to send a message, the sodium gates at the base of the axon open briefly, then shut again. While those gates are open, sodium rushes into the axon, carrying a positive electrical charge. That charge causes the next group of gates on the axon to flip open briefly. So it goes, all the way down the axon,

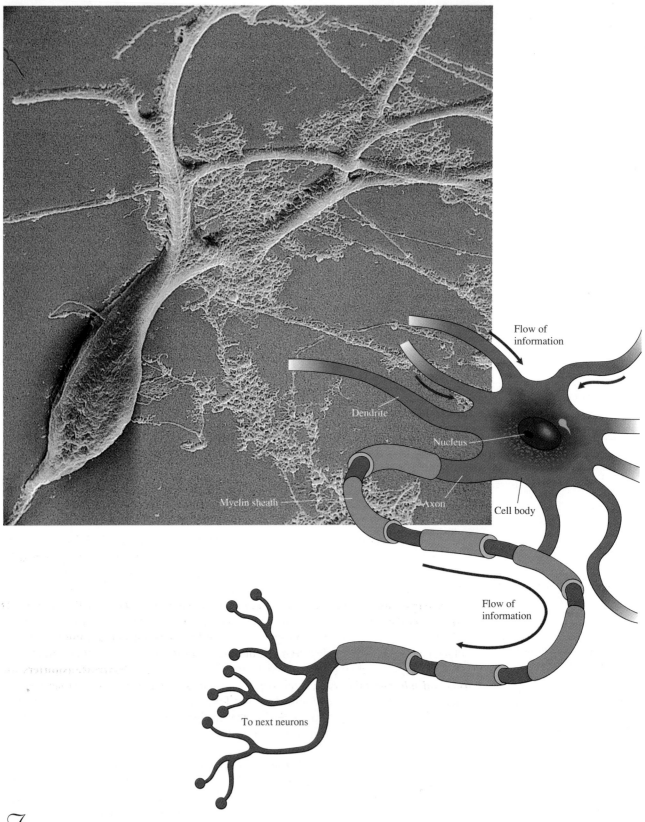

*F*IGURE 2.6

The Neuron

An actual neuron is shown in the large background photograph. Notice the branching dendrites at the top of the photo and the cell body in the lower left corner. The axon is just beginning to emerge from the cell body in the lower left corner of the photo. The graphic representation illustrates the flow of information across the neuron. The cell body receives information at the dendrites. Information leaves the cell body and travels to other neurons through the axon. A myelin sheath covers most axons and speeds information transmission. As it ends, the axon branches out, culminating in terminal buttons that store neurotransmitters.

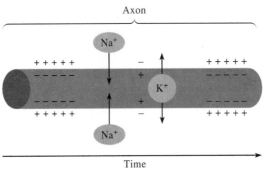

Axon

Na⁺

K⁺

Na⁺

Time

$\mathscr{F}$IGURE 2.7

Movement of Sodium and Potassium Ions Down the Axon and the Action Potential

Electrical/chemical changes in the neuron produce an action potential. The sodium and potassium ions are shown moving down the axon. As the nerve impulse moves down the axon, electrical stimulation of the membrane makes it more permeable to sodium ions (Na^+). Sodium rushes into the axon, carrying an electrical charge, and that charge causes the next group of gates on the axon to flip open briefly. So it goes, all the way down the axon. After the sodium gates close, potassium ions (K^+) flow out of the cell.

action potential

The brief wave of electrical charge that sweeps down the axon.

all-or-none principle

The principle that once the electrical impulse reaches a certain level of intensity, it fires and moves all the way down the axon, remaining at the same strength throughout its travel.

synapses

Tiny gaps between neurons. Most synapses are between the axon of one neuron and the dendrites or cell body of another neuron.

neurotransmitters

Chemical substances that carry information across the synaptic gap to the next neuron.

like a long row of cabinet doors opening and closing in sequence. After the sodium gates close, potassium ions flow out of the cell and bring the membrane charge back to the resting condition. **Action potential** *is the brief wave of electrical charge that sweeps down the axon.*

The wave of electrical charge that sweeps down the axon abides by the **all-or-none principle,** *which means that once the electrical impulse reaches a certain level of intensity, it fires and moves all the way down the axon, remaining at the same strength throughout its travel.* The electrical impulse traveling down an axon is much like a fuse on a firecracker. It doesn't matter whether a match or blowtorch is used to light the fuse; as long as a certain minimal intensity is reached, the spark travels quickly and at the same level of strength down the fuse until it reaches the firecracker. In the same manner, once stimulation exceeds minimum requirements, the neuron fires regardless of the intensity of the stimulation.

Synapses and Neurotransmitters.   What happens once the neural impulse reaches the end of the axon? Neurons do not touch each other directly; nevertheless, they manage to communicate. The story of the connection between one neuron and another is one of the most intriguing and highly researched areas of contemporary neuroscience.

Synapses *are tiny gaps between neurons. Most synapses are between the axon of one neuron and the dendrites or cell body of another neuron.* How does information get across this gap to the next neuron? The end of an axon branches out into a number of fibers, which end in structures called terminal buttons. Neurotransmitters are found in the tiny synaptic vesicles (chambers) located in the terminal buttons. **Neurotransmitters** *are chemical substances that carry information across the synaptic gap to the next neuron.* The molecules of these chemical substances wait for a nerve impulse to come down through the axon. Once the nerve impulse reaches the terminal buttons, the electrical signal causes these miniature, springlike molecules to contract, pulling the vesicles out to the edge of the terminal buttons. At the edge, the vesicles burst open, and the neurotransmitter molecules spew forth into the gap between the two neurons. In the synaptic gap, the neurotransmitter molecules bump about in random motion, and some land on receptor sites in the next neuron, where they open a gate and electrical signals begin to sweep through the next neuron. In effect, a message in the brain is "ferried" across the synapse by a neurotransmitter, which pours out of the end of the cell just as the message approaches the synapse. Synapses and neurotransmitters can be just as mysterious as genes and DNA. Turn to figure 2.8 for an illustration of this.

More than 50 neurotransmitters, each with a unique chemical makeup, have been discovered, and the list probably will grow to 100 or more in the near future. Interestingly, most creatures that have been studied, from snails to whales, use the same type of

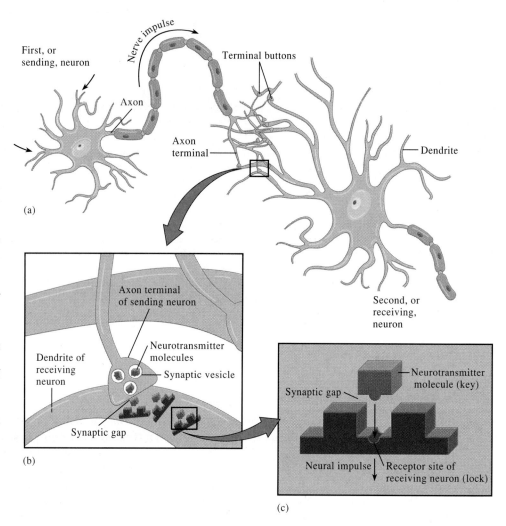

𝓕IGURE 2.8

How Synapses and Neurotransmitters Work

(a) When an axon reaches its destination, it branches out into a number of fibers that end in terminal buttons. There is a tiny gap between these terminal buttons at the tip of the axon terminal and the next neuron. *(b)* When it reaches the terminal buttons, the neural impulse releases tiny chemical molecules that are stored in synaptic vesicles in the knobs. These chemical substances are called neurotransmitters. They bump around in the synaptic gap between the sending and receiving neurons. Some of them land on receptor sites in the receiving neuron, where the neural impulse continues its travel.

(c) Neurotransmitter molecules fit like small keys in equally small locks, once they reach the receptor site in the receiving neuron. The key in the lock opens the "door," and the neural impulse begins its travel through the second neuron.

dopamine

A brain neurotransmitter that is related to movement, attention, learning, and mental health.

serotonin

A brain neurotransmitter that is involved in the regulation of sleep, mood, arousal, and pain.

endorphins

Natural opiates that are brain neurotransmitters; they are involved in pleasure and the control of pain.

neurotransmitter molecules as our own brains use. Neurotransmitters are either excitatory or inhibitory; they facilitate or disrupt the transfer of information from one neuron to another (Kolb, Whishaw, & Cice, 1998). Many animal venoms, such as that of the black widow spider, are neurotransmitter-like substances that disturb neurotransmission by interfering with muscle function.

Among the neurotransmitters that have important functions are dopamine, serotonin, and endorphins. **Dopamine** *is a brain neurotransmitter that is related to movement, attention, learning, and mental health.* Too little dopamine results in muscle tremors and unsteady walking, symptoms that are characteristic of Parkinson's disease. An excess of dopamine is associated with the severe mental disorder called schizophrenia, in which an individual loses contact with reality. **Serotonin** *is a brain neurotransmitter that is involved in the regulation of sleep, mood, arousal, and pain.* **Endorphins,** *natural opiates, are brain neurotransmitters that are involved in pleasure and the control of pain.* As early as the fourth century B.C., the Greeks used the wild poppy to induce euphoria. However, it was not until 2,000 years later that the formula behind opium's addictive action was discovered. In the early 1970s, scientists found that opium molecules plug into a sophisticated system of natural opiates in the brain's pathways (Pert & Snyder, 1973).

Review

The Nervous System

The elegantly organized nervous system is divided into two parts: the central nervous system (brain and spinal cord) and peripheral nervous system (connects brain and spinal cord to other parts of the body). The two major divisions of the peripheral nervous system are the somatic nervous system (sensory and motor nerves) and the autonomic nervous system (which connects with the body's internal organs). The autonomic nervous system is divided into parts: the sympathetic nervous system (which arouses body) and the parasympathetic nervous system (which calms body).

Information flows to the brain (via afferent nerves), away from the brain (via efferent nerves), and within the brain (via interneurons that make up most of the brain). Neurons are nerve cells. The neuron's three basic parts are the cell body, dendrite (receiving part), and axon (sending part). An insulating myelin sheath encases most axons; the sheath helps information (nerve impulses) travel faster.

Neurons send information down the axon as brief impulses, or waves, of electricity. Understanding how this works requires knowledge of ions (electrically charged particles), resting potential (that

stable negative charge of an inactive neuron), action potential (a brief wave of electrical charge that sweeps down the axon), and the all-or-none principle.

Synapses are tiny gaps between neurons. Neurotransmitters are chemical substances that carry information across the synaptic gap to the next neuron. More than fifty neurotransmitters have been discovered, including dopamine, serotonin, and endorphins.

THE CENTRAL NERVOUS SYSTEM

Most of the information we have covered about the brain has been about one or two cells. Earlier you learned that about 99 percent of all neurons in the nervous system are located in the brain and the spinal cord; however, neurons do not simply float in the brain. Connected in precise ways, they constitute the various structures of the brain.

As a human embryo develops inside the womb, the central nervous system begins as a long, hollow tube on the embryo's back. At 3 weeks or so after conception, the brain forms into a large mass of neurons and loses its tubular appearance. The elongated tube changes shape and develops into three major divisions: the hindbrain, which is the portion of the brain adjacent to the spinal cord; the midbrain, which is above the hindbrain; and the forebrain, which is at the highest region of the brain (see figure 2.9).

*F*IGURE 2.9

Embryological Development of the Nervous System

In the photograph on the right, you can see the primitive, tubular appearance of the nervous system at 6 weeks in the human embryo. The drawing shows the major brain regions and spinal cord as they appear early in the development of a human embryo.

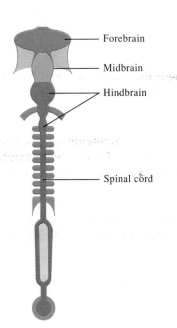

— Forebrain

— Midbrain

— Hindbrain

— Spinal cord

The nervous system's command center, the brain, controls all your thoughts and movements. It weighs about 3 pounds and is slightly larger than a grapefruit. With a crinkled outer layer, it looks like an oversized, shelled walnut. Inside, the brain resembles undercooked custard or a ripe avocado. In this section, we will examine the structure and function of the parts of the brain and spinal cord.

The Hindbrain

The **hindbrain,** *located at the rear of the skull, is the lowest portion of the brain. The three main parts of the hindbrain are the medulla, cerebellum, and pons* (figure 2.10 shows the location of these brain structures as well as some of the forebrain's main structures). The **medulla** *begins where the spinal cord enters the skull. It helps control breathing and regulates a portion of the reflexes that allow us to maintain an upright posture.* The **cerebellum** *extends from the rear of the hindbrain and is located just above the medulla. It consists of two rounded structures thought to play important roles in motor control.* Leg and arm movements are coordinated at the cerebellum, for example. When we play golf, practice the piano, or perfect our moves on the dance floor, the cerebellum is hard at work. If a higher portion of the brain commands us to write the number 7, it is the cerebellum that integrates the muscular activities required to do so. If the cerebellum becomes damaged, our movements become uncoordinated and jerky. The **pons** *is a bridge in the hindbrain that contains several clusters of fibers involved in sleep and arousal.*

The Midbrain

The **midbrain,** *located between the hindbrain and forebrain, is an area where many nerve fiber systems ascend and descend to connect the higher and lower portions of the brain. In particular, the midbrain relays information between the brain and the eyes and ears.* The ability to attend to an object visually, for example, is linked to one bundle of neurons in the midbrain. (Parkinson's disease, a deterioration of movement that produces rigidity and tremors in the elderly, damages a section near the bottom of the midbrain.) We will examine the role of the reticular formation and the basal ganglia in organizing and coordinating behavior.

The **reticular formation** *is a diffuse collection of neurons involved in stereotyped behavior, such as walking, sleeping, or orienting to sudden noise.* The nerve fibers originate in the medulla of the hindbrain and terminate at the thalamus, which sits atop the brain stem.

The **basal ganglia** *are small groups of neurons in the midbrain that send their axons to a remarkable variety of brain regions, perhaps explaining their involvement in high-level integrative functions.* Individuals with damage to the basal ganglia suffer from unwanted movement (such as jerking of limbs).

It is not the hindbrain or midbrain that separates humans from animals, however. In humans, it is the forebrain that becomes enlarged and specialized.

The Forebrain

You try to understand what all of these terms mean and what all of these parts of the brain do. You talk with friends and plan a party for this weekend. You remember that it has been 6 months since you went to the dentist. You are confident that you will do well on the next exam in this course. All of these experiences, and millions more, would not be possible without the **forebrain.** *Among its most important structures are the thalamus, the hypothalamus and endocrine system, the limbic system, and the cerebrum,* each of which we will discuss in turn.

The Thalamus. The **thalamus** *is about the size of a peach pit and sits at the top of the brain stem in the central core of the brain. It serves as a very important relay station, functioning much like a telephone switchboard between the diverse areas of the cortex and the reticular formation.* One area of the thalamus orients information from the sense receptors (hearing, seeing, and so on) and might be involved particularly in the perception of

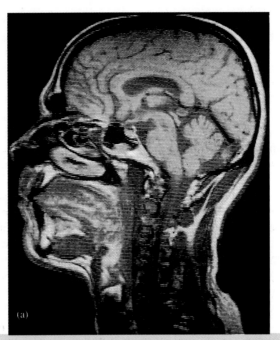

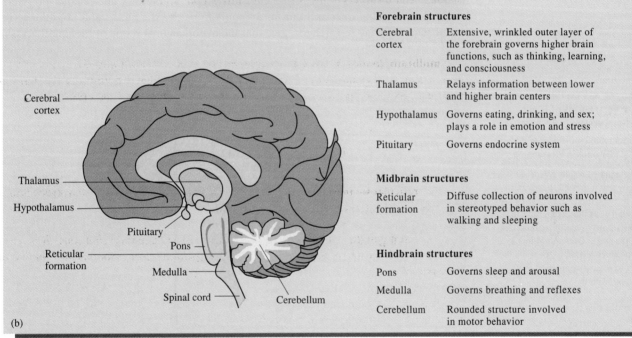

Forebrain structures

Cerebral cortex	Extensive, wrinkled outer layer of the forebrain governs higher brain functions, such as thinking, learning, and consciousness
Thalamus	Relays information between lower and higher brain centers
Hypothalamus	Governs eating, drinking, and sex; plays a role in emotion and stress
Pituitary	Governs endocrine system

Midbrain structures

Reticular formation	Diffuse collection of neurons involved in stereotyped behavior such as walking and sleeping

Hindbrain structures

Pons	Governs sleep and arousal
Medulla	Governs breathing and reflexes
Cerebellum	Rounded structure involved in motor behavior

(b)

*𝓕*IGURE 2.10

Structure and Regions in the Human Brain

(a) This image of a cross-section of the brain includes some of the brain's most important structures, which we will discuss shortly. As we discuss these structures, you might find it helpful to refer to this figure to obtain a visual image of what the structures look like. *(b)* This drawing reproduces the main structures in the forebrain and the hindbrain and corresponds to the image of the brain shown in *(a)*.

hypothalamus

An area just below the thalamus that monitors three enjoyable activities—eating, drinking, and sex; it also helps to direct the endocrine system through the pituitary gland; and it is involved in emotion, stress, and reward.

pain. Other regions coordinate sleep and wakefulness as well as motor movements (see figure 2.10 for the location of the thalamus).

The Hypothalamus. The **hypothalamus,** *much smaller than the thalamus and about the size of a kidney bean, is located just below the thalamus. The hypothalamus monitors three enjoyable activities—eating, drinking, and sex; it helps direct the endocrine system through the pituitary gland; and it is involved in emotion, stress, and reward.*

Perhaps the best way to describe the hypothalamus is in terms of its being a regulator and motivator. It is sensitive to changes in the blood and neural input, and it responds to these by influencing the secretion of hormones and neural outputs. For example, if the temperature of blood circulating near the hypothalamus is increased by just 1 or 2 degrees, certain cells in the hypothalamus increase their rate of firing. As a result, a chain of events is set into motion. Circulation in the skin and sweat glands increases immediately to release perspiration from the body. The cooled blood circulating to the hypothalamus slows down the activity of some of the neurons there, stopping the process when the temperature is right—37.1 degrees Centigrade. These temperature-sensitive neurons function like a finely tuned thermostat to restore the body to a balanced state.

The hypothalamus is also involved in emotional states and plays an important role in handling stress. The hypothalamus acts on the pituitary gland, located just below it, to integrate sensory signals such as hunger, aggression, and pleasure. When certain areas of the hypothalamus are electrically stimulated, feelings of pleasure result.

In a classic experiment, James Olds and Peter Milner (1954) implanted an electrode in the hypothalamus of a rat's brain. When the rat ran to a corner of an enclosed area, its hypothalamus received a mild electric shock. The researchers thought the rat would steer clear of the corner to avoid the shock. Much to their surprise, the rat kept returning. Olds and Milner believed they had discovered a pleasure center in the hypothalamus.

In similar experiments, Olds (1958) later found that rats would press bars until they dropped from exhaustion just to feel pleasure. Figure 2.11 shows one rat that pressed a bar more than 2,000 times an hour for 24 hours to receive the pleasurable stimulus to its hypothalamus. Today researchers agree that the hypothalamus is one of the links between

ℱIGURE 2.11

Results of the Experiment by Olds (1958) on the Role of the Hypothalamus in Pleasure

The graphed results of one rat show that it pressed the bar more than 2,000 times an hour for a period of 24 hours to receive the stimulus to its hypothalamus. One of the rats in Olds and Milner's experiments is shown pressing the bar to receive stimulation to its hypothalamus.

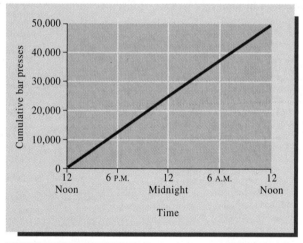

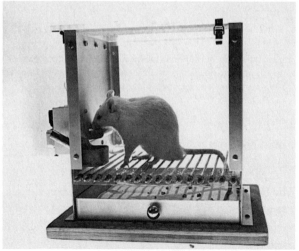

the brain and pleasure, but they know that other areas of the brain also are important (Kornetsky, 1986).

An area adjacent to the hypothalamus has been linked with the intense pleasure and craving triggered by cocaine use. This finding has important implications for treating drug addiction. Researchers hope eventually to develop drugs that mimic or block an addictive drug's effects on the brain. There also is increasing evidence that the pleasure or reward a drug induces outweighs the fear of pain or suffering that withdrawal produces (Wise & Rompre, 1989). The Olds and Milner experiments illustrate this: when the rats pressed the bar, the pleasure they received overrode the pain from the electric shock. Similarly, when cocaine users talk about the drug, they highlight its ability to heighten pleasure in a variety of activities, including eating and sex. They tend to overlook the discomfort that comes as the drug's effects wear off.

The hypothalamus also governs the release of hormones by the endocrine system. The **endocrine system** *consists of the hypothalamus and other endocrine glands that release their chemical products directly into the bloodstream.* **Hormones** *are chemical messengers manufactured by the endocrine glands.* The bloodstream conveys hormones to all parts of the body, and the membrane of every cell has receptors for one or more hormones.

The endocrine glands consist of the hypothalamus and the pituitary gland at the base of the brain, the thyroid and parathyroid glands at the front of the neck, the adrenal glands just above the kidneys, the pancreas in the abdomen, the ovaries in the female's pelvis, and the testes in the male's scrotum (see figure 2.12). Each gland manufactures and secretes hormones that are specialized in their effect on the central nervous system.

The **pituitary gland** *is an important endocrine gland that sits at the base of the skull and is about the size of a pea; the pituitary gland controls growth and regulates other glands.* The anterior (front) part of the pituitary is known as the master gland because most of its hormones direct the activity of target glands elsewhere in the body. For example, follicle-stimulating hormone (FSH) produced by the pituitary monitors the level of sex

endocrine system

The hypothalamus and other endocrine glands that release their chemical products into the bloodstream.

hormones

Chemical messengers manufactured by the endocrine glands.

pituitary gland

An important endocrine gland that sits at the base of the skull and is about the size of a pea; this gland controls growth and regulates other glands.

$\mathcal{F}$IGURE 2.12

The Major Endocrine Glands

The pituitary gland releases hormones that regulate the hormone secretions of the other glands. The pituitary gland is itself regulated by the hypothalamus.

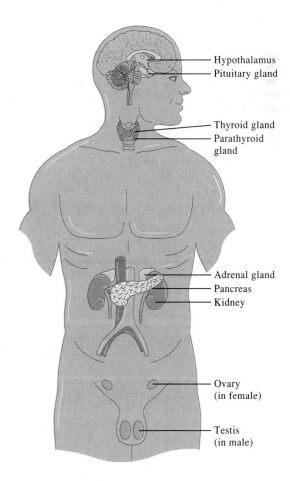

- Hypothalamus
- Pituitary gland
- Thyroid gland
- Parathyroid gland
- Adrenal gland
- Pancreas
- Kidney
- Ovary (in female)
- Testis (in male)

limbic system

A loosely connected network of structures under the cerebral cortex that plays an important role in memory and emotion.

amygdala

A limbic system structure that is involved in emotion and the discrimination of objects that are important in the organism's survival. These include appropriate food, mates, and social rivals.

hippocampus

A limbic system structure that has a special role in the storage of memories.

cerebral cortex (cerebrum)

The most recently evolved part of the brain; covering the rest of the brain like a cap, it is the largest part of the brain and makes up about 80 percent of its volume.

occipital lobe

The portion of the cerebral cortex at the back of the head that is involved in vision.

temporal lobe

The portion of the cerebral cortex that is just above the ears and is involved in hearing.

frontal lobe

The portion of the cerebral cortex that is behind the forehead and is involved in the control of voluntary muscles and in intelligence.

parietal lobe

The portion of the cerebral cortex at the top of the head and toward the rear; it is involved in processing bodily sensations.

hormones in the ovaries of females and the testes of males. Although most pituitary hormones influence specific organs, growth hormone (GH) acts on all tissues to produce growth during childhood and adolescence. Dwarfs have too little of this hormone, giants too much.

Limbic System. The **limbic system,** *a loosely connected network of structures under the cerebral cortex, plays important roles in both memory and emotion.* Its two principal structures are the amygdala and hippocampus (see figure 2.13)

The **amygdala** *(the name is Latin for "almond shape") is a limbic system structure that is involved in emotion and in the discrimination of objects that are important in the organism's survival. These include appropriate food, mates, and social rivals.* Neurons in the amygdala often fire selectively at the sight of such stimuli. Lesions in the amygdala can cause animals to attempt to eat, fight, or mate with inappropriate objects like chairs.

The **hippocampus** *is a limbic system structure that has a special role in the storage of memories.* Individuals suffering extensive hippocampal damage simply cannot retain any new conscious memories after the damage. It is fairly certain, though, that memories are not stored "in" the limbic system. Instead, the limbic system seems to control what parts of all the information passing through the cortex should be retained as durable, lasting neural traces in the cortex.

The Cerebral Cortex (Cerebrum). The **cerebral cortex (cerebrum)** *is a region of the forebrain that is the most recently evolved part of the brain. It is the largest part of the brain in volume (about 80 percent) and covers the lower portions of the brain like a large cap.* Let's look at the cerebral cortex in more detail.

The wrinkled surface of the *cerebral cortex* is divided into halves, called *hemispheres.* Each hemisphere is divided into four lobes—occipital, temporal, frontal, and parietal—each conveniently named for the main skull bone that covers it (see figure 2.14). These landmarks help us map the surface of the brain, but the lobes are not strictly functional regions. Nonetheless, they are often used in somewhat loose ways to describe the brain's functions. For example, the **occipital lobe,** *the portion of the cerebral cortex at the back of the head, is involved in vision;* the **temporal lobe,** *the portion of the cerebral cortex just above the ears, is involved in hearing;* the **frontal lobe,** *the portion of the cerebral cortex behind the forehead, is involved in the control of voluntary muscles and in intelligence;* and the **parietal lobe,** *the portion of the cerebral cortex at the top of the head and toward the rear, is involved in processing body sensations.*

In the same way that each cerebral cortex lobe is associated with different processes, regions within each lobe have different jobs. Scientists have determined this primarily through topographic mapping. Wilder Penfield (1947), a neurosurgeon at the Montreal Neurological Institute, pioneered mapping the brain. He worked with a number of patients who had very serious forms of epilepsy, a neurological disease that produces a storm of electrical activity across the cortex. Although Penfield sometimes surgically

*𝓕*IGURE 2.13

Limbic System

The limbic system includes the amygdala, which is involved in emotion and the discrimination of objects that are important to the organism's survival; the hippocampus, which is involved in memory and learning; part of the hypothalamus, which is involved in controlling motivational states; and part of the thalamus, which relays information from the senses to the higher levels of the cerebrum.

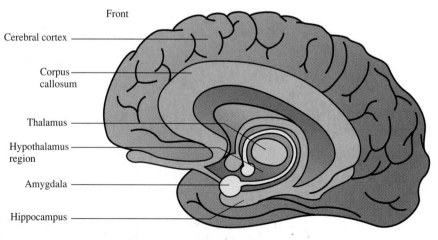

Front

Cerebral cortex

Corpus callosum

Thalamus

Hypothalamus region

Amygdala

Hippocampus

Right hemisphere

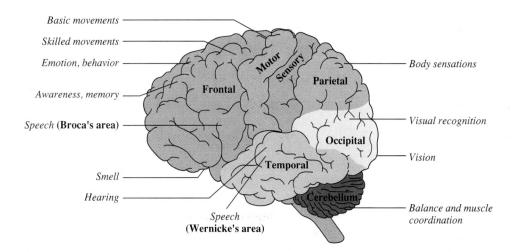

Basic movements
Skilled movements
Emotion, behavior
Awareness, memory
Speech (Broca's area)
Smell
Hearing
Speech (Wernicke's area)

Motor
Sensory
Frontal
Parietal
Occipital
Temporal
Cerebellum

Body sensations
Visual recognition
Vision
Balance and muscle coordination

*𝓕*IGURE 2.14

The Brain's Four Lobes

Shown here are the locations of the four lobes of the cerebral cortex (occipital, temporal, frontal, and parietal) and the cerebellum.

removed portions of the epileptic patients' brains to reduce their symptoms, he was concerned that such surgery might impair some of the patients' ability to function normally. Penfield's solution was to map the cerebral cortex during surgery. Penfield gave the patients a local anesthetic so they would remain awake during the operation. As he stimulated certain sensory and motor areas of the brain, different parts of the patient's body moved. For both sensory and motor areas, there is a point-to-point relation between a body part and a location on the cerebral cortex (see figure 2.15). The face and hands have proportionally more space on the cerebral cortex than other body parts because they are capable of finer perceptions and movements.

> My own brain is to me the most unaccountable of machinery—always buzzing, humming, soaring, roaring, diving, and then buried in the mud.
> —VIRGINIA WOOLF, *English Novelist, 20th Century*

So far our description of the cerebral cortex has focused on sensory and motor areas, but more than 75 percent of the cerebral cortex is made up of areas called the association cortex (see figure 2.16). The **association cortex** *(or association areas) is involved in our highest intellectual functions, such as problem solving and thinking.* The neurons in the association cortex communicate with each other and with neurons in the motor cortex. By observing brain-damaged people and using topographic mapping techniques, scientists have found that the association cortex is involved in linguistic and perceptual processes. Interestingly, damage to a specific part of the association cortex does not necessarily lead to a specific loss of function. With the exception of language areas, which *are* localized, loss of function seems to depend more on the extent of damage to the association areas than to the specific location of the damage. The largest portion of the association cortex is located in the frontal lobe, beneath the forehead. An individual whose frontal lobes have been damaged does not lose sensory or motor control but may become "a different person," leading researchers to believe that the frontal lobes are linked with personality (see figure 2.17, p. 58). This area may be most directly related to thinking and problem solving. Early experiments suggested that the frontal lobe is the center of intelligence, but more recent research indicates that damage to the frontal lobes may not result in a loss of intelligence. The ability to make plans, think creatively, and make decisions are other mental processes associated with the frontal lobe.

Split-Brain Research and the Cerebral Hemispheres

The brain is split into two halves, and these two halves have been involved in some fascinating research as well as speculation about what role they play in brain functioning.

Split-Brain Research. For many years, scientists speculated that the **corpus callosum,** *a large bundle of axons that connects the brain's two hemispheres,* had something to do with

association cortex

Areas of the brain that are involved in our highest intellectual functions, such as problem solving and thinking; also called association areas.

corpus callosum

A large bundle of axons that connects the brain's two hemispheres.

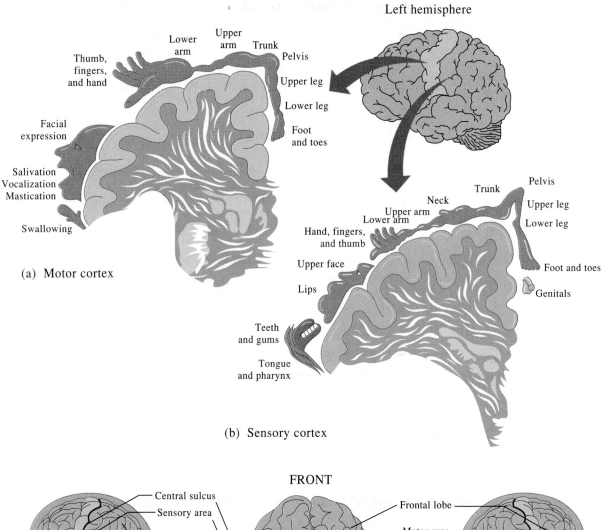

Left hemisphere

Lower arm Upper arm Trunk
Thumb, fingers, and hand Pelvis
Upper leg
Lower leg
Facial expression Foot and toes
Salivation
Vocalization
Mastication
Swallowing

(a) Motor cortex

Neck Trunk Pelvis
Upper arm Upper leg
Lower arm Lower leg
Hand, fingers, and thumb
Upper face Foot and toes
Lips Genitals
Teeth and gums
Tongue and pharynx

(b) Sensory cortex

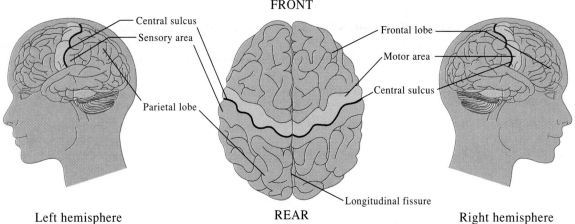

FRONT

Central sulcus
Sensory area
Parietal lobe

Frontal lobe
Motor area
Central sulcus

Longitudinal fissure

Left hemisphere REAR Right hemisphere

$\mathcal{F}$IGURE 2.15

Locations of the Motor and Sensory Areas on the Cerebral Cortex

This figure shows (a) the motor areas involved with the control of voluntary muscles and (b) the sensory areas involved with cutaneous and certain other senses. The body is disproportionately represented on the parietal and frontal lobes, with the hands and face receiving the most representation. Organization is inverse—functions represented at the top of the parietal lobe occur in the lower regions of the body, for example.

relaying information between the two sides. Roger Sperry and his colleagues confirmed this in experiments in which they cut the corpus callosum in cats. They also severed certain nerve endings leading from the eyes to the brain. After the operations, Sperry and Myers trained the cats to solve a series of visual problems with one eye blindfolded. After each cat learned the task, with only one eye uncovered, its other eye was covered and the animal was tested again. The split-brain cat behaved as if it had never learned the task. It seems that the memory was stored only in the left hemisphere, which could no longer directly communicate with the right hemisphere.

Further evidence of the corpus callosum's function has come from experiments with patients who have severe, even life-threatening, forms of epilepsy. Epilepsy's electrical storms flash uncontrollably across the corpus callosum. One of the most famous cases is that of "W. J." Neurosurgeons severed the corpus callosum of this epileptic patient in a final attempt to reduce his unbearable seizures. Sperry (1968) examined W. J. and found that the corpus callosum functions the same in humans as in animals—cutting the corpus callosum seems to leave patients with two separate minds that learn and operate independently. The right hemisphere receives information from the left side of the body, and the left hemisphere receives information from the right side of the body. When you hold an object in your left hand, for example, the right hemisphere of your brain detects the object. When you hold an object in your right hand, the left hemisphere of your brain detects the object (see figure 2.18). In a normal corpus callosum, both hemispheres receive this information.

The most extensive and consistent research findings on the brain's hemispheres involve language. In most right-handed individuals in whom the corpus callosum is intact, the left hemisphere controls the ability to use language, whereas the right hemisphere is unable to translate sensations into words. The split-brain patients in Sperry's (1974) experiments, such as W. J., could verbally describe sensations that were received by the left hemisphere—that is, a stimulus in the right visual field, but they could not verbally describe sensations that were received by the right hemisphere—a stimulus in the left visual field. Because the corpus callosum was severed, the information could not be communicated from one hemisphere to the other. More recent investigations of split-brain patients document that language is rarely processed in the right hemisphere (Gazzaniga, 1986).

Hemispheric Specialization. There has been lots of speculation over the past few years about the brain's hemispheric specialization, the notion being that the hemispheres function in different ways and that some psychological processes are restricted to one

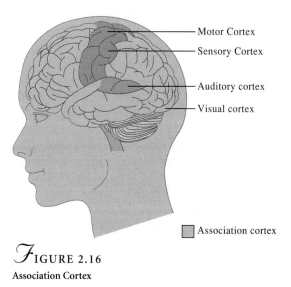

$\mathcal{F}$IGURE 2.16

Association Cortex

The very large areas of the cerebral cortex, called the association cortex or association areas, do not respond when electrically stimulated, unlike the motor and sensory areas. Neurons in the association cortex communicate with neurons in other areas of the association cortex and with sensory and motor areas. Neuroscientists believe that the association areas are involved in thinking and problem solving.

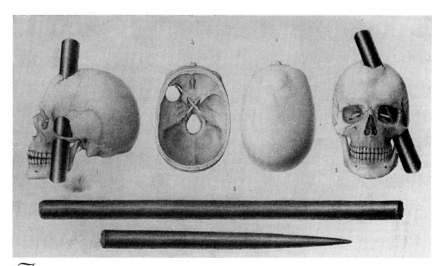

$\mathcal{F}$IGURE 2.17

The Injury to Phineas T. Gage

Phineas T. Gage, a 25-year-old foreman who worked for the Rutland and Burlington Railroad in Vermont, met with an interesting experience on September 13, 1848. Phineas and several co-workers were using blasting powder to construct a roadbed. The crew drilled holes in the rock and gravel, poured in the blasting powder, and then tamped down the powder with a steel rod. The powder blew up while Phineas was still tamping it down, driving the iron up through the left side of his face and out through the top of his head. Phineas was thrown to the ground, but, amazingly, he was still conscious and able to talk. His co-workers placed him on an ox cart and drove him almost a mile to his hotel. Phineas got out of the cart himself and walked up the flight of stairs to his room. A physician was called, and he discovered he could put the entire length of his index finger through the cylindrical hole in Phineas's skull.

Though the wound in Phineas's skull healed in a matter of weeks, he became a different person. He had been a mild-mannered, hard-working, emotionally calm individual prior to the accident. He was well liked by all who knew him. Afterward, he became obstinate, moody, irresponsible, selfish, and incapable of participating in any planned activities. Phineas's misfortune illustrates the brain's importance in determining the nature of personality.

hemisphere. In fact, Americans commonly use the terms *left-brained* and *right-brained* to describe which hemisphere is dominant. According to the media and popular books, the left hemisphere is rational, logical, and Western, whereas the brain's right hemisphere is creative, intuitive, and Eastern.

Everyone seems to accept this—everyone, that is, except the scientists who have researched left and right hemisphere functions. To them, the concept of the brain as split into tidy halves—one the source of creativity, the other the source of logical thinking—is too simplistic (Dolnick, 1988). Jerre Levy, a neuroscientist at the University of Chicago, points out that no complex function—making music, creating art, reading, and so on—can be assigned to one hemisphere. Complex thinking in normal people involves communication between both sides of the brain (Efron, in press).

How did the left-brain/right-brain myth get started? It actually had its origin in Sperry's classic studies of split-brain patients. Remember that Sperry examined people whose corpus callosum had been severed and found that after surgery the two sides of the brain learned and operated independently. As his findings made their way into the media, the complexity of Sperry's research was lost and his findings became oversimplified. Media reports indicated that, when a writer works on a novel, the left hemisphere is busy while the right is silent. In creating an oil painting, the right brain is working while the left is quiet. People appeared either right-brained (artistic) or left-brained (logical). An example of the either/or oversimplification of the brain's left and right hemispheres is shown in the drawing of how the brain divides its work (see figure 2.19).

Roger Sperry discovered that the left hemisphere is superior in the kind of logic used to prove geometric theorems, but, in the logic of everyday life, our problems involve integrating information and drawing conclusions. In these instances, the right brain's func-

Jerre Levy has conducted extensive research on the nature of hemispheric function in the brain.

Fixation point

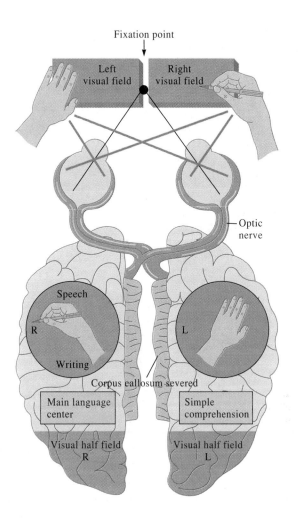

FIGURE 2.18

Visual Information in the Split Brain

Although both eyes take in the full visual field, the organization of the eye and brain are specialized. For example, images in the right visual field (such as the hand holding the pen) fall on the left side of both retinas and then are channeled to the left hemisphere by way of the optic nerves. Images seen in the right visual field reach only the left hemisphere and images seen in the left visual field reach only the right hemisphere in the initial stages of processing. Visual information in both hemispheres is then shared via the corpus callosum. Following split-brain surgery in which the corpus callosum is severed, each hemisphere has access only to the information originally processed from the corresponding visual field for which it is responsible.

Brandi Binder is evidence of the brain's hemispheric flexibility and resilience. Despite having the right side of her cortex removed because of a severe case of epilepsy, Brandi engages in many activities often portrayed as only "right-brain" activities. She loves music, math, and art, and is shown here working on one of her paintings.

tions are crucial. In virtually all activities, there is an interplay between the brain's hemispheres (Hellige, 1990). For example, in reading, the left hemisphere comprehends syntax and grammar, which the right does not. However, the right brain is better at understanding a story's intonation and emotion. The same is true for music and art. Pop psychology assigns both to the right brain. In some musical skills, such as recognizing chords, the right hemisphere is better. In others, such as distinguishing which of two sounds is heard first, the left hemisphere takes over. Enjoying or creating music requires the use of both hemispheres.

Further evidence of the brain's hemispheric flexibility and resilience involves teenager Brandi Binder (Nash, 1997). When she was 6, she developed such a severe case of epilepsy that surgeons at UCLA had to remove the right side of her cortex. Binder lost virtually all of the control she had established over muscles on the left side of her body, the side controlled by the right side of her brain. Yet today, after years of therapy ranging from leg lifts to math to music training, Binder is an A student. She loves music, math, and art, which usually are associated with the right side of the brain. Her recuperation is not 100 percent—for example, she never has regained the use of her right arm—but her recovery is remarkable and shows that if there is a way to compensate, the brain will find it.

There is so much more to understanding brain function and organization than to characterize people as right- or left-brained. After all, we are trying to understand the most complex piece of matter in the known universe.

His Brain and Her Brain.   Do the left and right hemispheres develop differently in girls and boys? According to one theory, the male brain is more "lateralized," that is, its hemispheres are specialized in their abilities, while females use both hemispheres more symmetrically, because in the female brain the corpus callosum supposedly is larger and

HOW THE BRAIN DIVIDES ITS WORK

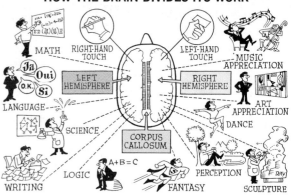

Is left-brain, right-brain specialization all-or-none, as this drawing implies? No.

© Roy Doty, *Newsweek.*

*ℱ*IGURE 2.19

Stereotyped Myths About Left-Brain, Right-Brain

Popular visions of right-brain, left-brain specialization suggest that artist Andy Warhol's and singer Aretha Franklin's right brains are responsible for their artistic and music talents, and that astronaut Guion Stewart Bluford's and physicist Albert Einstein's left brains are responsible for their gifts. Is this popular vision overdramatized? Yes, extensively.

aphasia

An inability to recognize or express language.

houses more fibers (Geschwind & Behan, 1982). In this theory, effects of testosterone (a hormone dominant in males) on the prenatal brain produce superior right-hemisphere talents, such as artistic, musical, or math skills. Right-hemisphere dominance is also said to explain the male's excellence in some tests of visuospatial ability, such as the ability to visualize three-dimensional objects. Males also have been said to have greater left-brain specialization as well. Females' skills, especially those involving language, are said to be more evenly divided between the left and right hemispheres. One interesting source of support for this view comes from differences in damage after stroke; males are three times more likely than females to develop **aphasia,** *inability to recognize or express language,* after left-hemisphere damage.

Gender expert Carol Tavris (1992) believes that talk of a gender dichotomy regarding brain function has been taken too far. She says that females and males, on the average, might differ in the physiology of their brains, but most brain researchers today believe the two hemispheres complement each other to the extent that one side can sometimes take over the functions of a side that has been damaged. And specific skills often involve components from both sides: One side has the ability to tell a joke, the other side the ability to laugh at one. Math abilities involve both visuospatial skills and reasoning skills. The right hemisphere is involved in creating art, the left hemisphere in appreciating and analyzing art.

Tavris also documented that most of the brain studies examining sex differences have been based on animals, with unknown generalizability to humans. And she commented

Improving Personal and Cognitive Skills

Some Tips for Conquering the Brain

There is no getting around the fact that this chapter includes a lot of terms you will need to know to do well on a test of the chapter's material. Here are some strategies you can use to help you remember the key concepts in this chapter:

- *Focus on the brain's organization.*
  The brain's systems are organized in a hierarchy. Concentrate on this hierarchy as you learn the brain's functions. Remembering the organization should help you remember the functions. At the *micro* level, the brain is made up of neurons. At that level, the brain consists of large systems, such as the somatic and autonomic nervous systems. The cortex of the brain is also organized symmetrically into two halves—left and right hemispheres.
- *Look for three-dimensional models.*
  It may be easier to understand the intricacy of brain function if you can "see" what the various parts of the nervous system look like. If you can't find good models available in science stores, build your own. A clay model of the brain or

a model of the neuron made of candy may help you distinguish the various features of the nervous system.

- *Personalize the concepts.*
  Think up some personalized examples that can help jog your memory. For example, imagine putting salt (sodium chloride) on a banana (rich in potassium) to help you remember the ions involved in neural transmission. Imagine that your thalamus is a telephone switchboard to help you remember its information-relaying function. Exaggerate the pronunciation of the terms in ways that provide clues to function. For example, exaggerating the pronunciation of *occipital* as ŏk-*sēé*pĭ-tl can help you remember that the function of the occipital lobes is managing vision. Think of other ways you can personalize concepts that are hard to learn.
- *Plan to devote some study time to mastery.*
  You are going to need some concentrated study time to learn the challenging concepts in this chapter. Read the chapter carefully, highlighting all the terms that you will need to master. Pay attention to the lecture and class activities and go over your notes after each lecture. Study your notes several times before the day you will be tested. Distributed practice over time will help you master the concepts efficiently.

that perhaps the most damaging blow to attempts at basing gender differences on brain differences is that the supposed sex differences that they are trying to account for—in verbal, spatial, and math abilities—are rapidly fading. Researchers and the public often err in focusing on very small differences rather than on the extensive overlap between females and males.

In summary, there are some anatomical differences in the brains of females and males. However, there are far more similarities than differences between female and male brains, and there is little evidence that the brain differences that do exist cause substantial behavioral differences in females and males. Such behavioral differences, which are often small, may be due to environmental influences and social experiences. Similarity rather than dissimilarity was the rule rather than the exception in a recent study of metabolic activity in the brains of females and males (Gur & others, 1995). The exceptions involved emotional expression (more active in females) and physical expression (more active in males).

Localization and Integration of Function

phrenology

Gall's pseudoscientific idea that the bumps on the skull are associated with personality and intelligence.

Early in the nineteenth century, the realization that certain parts of the brain are responsible for certain types of behavior began to emerge. **Phrenology** *was an approach developed by a German physician named Franz Joseph Gall, who argued that the bumps on the skull were associated with personality and intelligence.* Gall mapped out a large number of psychological functions: benevolence, destructiveness, mirthfulness, and individuality, for example (see figure 2.20).

Gall's basic idea was right; different brain regions do have different functions. Where Gall went wrong (besides thinking that skull bumps accurately reflect brain shape) was in the types of psychological functions he assigned to different brain regions. Despite the inaccuracy of Gall's predictions, phrenology was used extensively during criminal proceedings. This practice highlights the ways in which science can reinforce prevailing belief systems in a sociocultural context. Gall's phrenology maps were ultimately rejected by scientists of his time, but the notion that functions are localized has prevailed.

The degree to which functions are localized in the brain remains an important issue. Today psychologists believe that although a particular structure of the brain might be involved with one psychological function more than another, for the most part psychological function is based not on a specific structure, but rather on the interaction of *various* areas of the brain.

How do all of the various brain regions cooperate to produce the wondrous complexity of thought and behavior that characterize humans? Part of the answer to this question, such as how the brain solves a murder mystery or writes a poetic essay, is beyond the grasp of neuroscience. Still, we can get a sense of integrative brain function by considering something like the act of escaping from a burning building. Gall and his phrenologists might have argued that such behavior was controlled by an "escaping from danger" center in the brain. Let's compare that view with a more contemporary one.

Imagine you are sitting at your desk writing letters when fire breaks out behind you. The sound of crackling flames is relayed from your ear, through the thalamus, to your auditory cortex, and on to the auditory association cortex. At each stage, the stimulus energy has been processed to extract information, and at some stage, probably at the association cortex level, the sounds are finally matched with something like a neural memory representing previous sounds of fires you have heard. The association "fire" sets new machinery in motion. Your attention (guided in part by the reticular formation) swings to the auditory signal being held in your association cortex, and simultaneously (again guided by reticular systems) your head turns toward the noise. Now your visual association cortex reports in: "Objects matching flames are present." In other association regions, the visual and auditory reports are synthesized ("We have things that look and sound like fire"), and neural associations representing potential actions ("flee") are activated. However, firing the neurons that code the plan to flee will not get you out of the chair. The basal ganglia must become engaged, and from there the commands will arise to set the brain stem, motor cortex, and cerebellum to the task of actually transporting you out of the room.

Which part of your brain did you use to escape? Virtually all systems had a role; each was quite specific, and together they generated the behavior. By the way, you would probably remember an event such as a fire in your room. That is because your limbic circuitry would have activated when the significant association "fire" was first

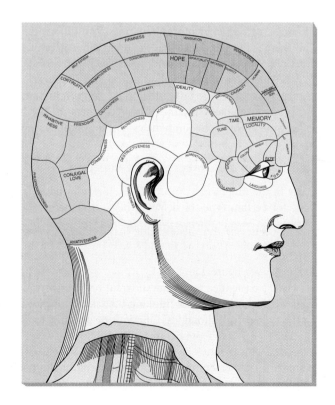

*F*IGURE 2.20

Phrenology Map Based on Gall's System

Gall was the father of the pseudo-science of phrenology. He believed that the brain was made up of about 30 "organs," each responsible for a single trait. Phrenology swept the United States and Europe, spawning phrenological societies, books, pamphlets, and sideshows. The craze attracted Edgar Allan Poe, Karl Marx, and Queen Victoria, who got a phrenologist to examine the royal children's cranial knobs. One fanatic proclaimed, "Phrenologist after phrenologist may die, but phrenology will never perish"; perish it did, however, when evidence failed to support it.

Self-Assessment

A Fanciful Tour of the Brain

See how well you can do with the following behaviors—real and imaginary—to reinforce your learning about brain function.

1. Snap your fingers next to the part of the cerebral cortex that processes sound. *This is called the _____ lobe.*
2. Stand on one foot while pointing to the cerebellum. *What purpose does the cerebellum serve?*
3. Furrow your brow to show the part of the brain where you do your most sophisticated thinking. *This is called the _____ lobe.*
4. Is your mouth dry? Are you thirsty? *Your _____ might be demanding some water.*
5. Scratch the spot on your head that processes itches. *This is the _____ lobe.*

6. Using your left hand, point to the area on the cortex that helps you point with your left hand. *Voluntary behavior is controlled by the _____ lobe.*
7. Close your eyes. *You have just shut off input to the _____ lobe.*
8. Suppose you had trouble opening your eyes. You are getting sleepy. *Your _____ may require a nap.*
9. Imagine that you wake up to find yourself a foot taller. *You would suspect a serious malfunction in your _____.*
10. You are angry because none of your clothes fit. *Your foul mood is governed by _____.*

Check the answer key. How well did you do? Review the concepts that were fuzzy before you move on to the next chapter.

Answer Key

1. temporal; 2. balance; 3. frontal; 4. hypothalamus; 5. parietal (sensory cortex); 6. frontal (motor cortex) on the right side of the head; 7. occipital; 8. pons; 9. pituitary; 10. amygdala or limbic system

triggered. The next time the sounds of crackling flames reach your auditory association cortex, the associations triggered will include those of this most recent escape. In sum, there is considerable integration of function in the brain.

At this point we have discussed many different aspects of biology and the brain. To evaluate your understanding of brain function, complete the Self-Assessment.

Review

The Central Nervous System

The nervous system can be divided into three levels: hindbrain (lowest portion of brain, consisting of the medulla, cerebellum, and pons), midbrain (between hindbrain and forebrain, where many fiber systems ascend and descend; includes the reticular formation, which is involved in walking, sleeping, or turning to a sudden noise); and the forebrain (the brain's highest level; includes the thalamus, hypothalamus and endocrine system, the limbic system, and the cerebrum).

The thalamus sits at the top of the brain stem and is an important relay station for information. The hypothalamus is located just below the thalamus and monitors eating, drinking, and sex. It also helps to direct the endocrine system, via the pituitary gland, and it is involved in emotion, stress, and reward. The limbic system, a loosely connected network of

structures under the cerebral cortex, plays important roles in memory and emotion. Its two main structures are the amygdala and the hippocampus.

The cerebral cortex (cerebrum) is the largest part of the brain in volume (about 80 percent) and covers the lower portions of the brain like a cap. The cerebral cortex is divided into two halves called hemispheres. Each hemisphere is divided into four lobes: occipital (involved in vision), temporal (involved in hearing), frontal (involved in the control of voluntary muscles and in intelligence), and parietal (involved in processing bodily sensations). Penfield mapped out the locations of motor and sensory areas on the cerebral cortex. The association cortex is involved in the highest intellectual functions.

The corpus callosum is a large bundle of fibers that connects the brain's two

hemispheres. Split-brain research, pioneered by Sperry, consists of severing the corpus callosum. This led to the conclusion that language is primarily a left-hemisphere function. In normal people, the two hemispheres work together to process information. A number of myths have developed about left-brain/right-brain functions. Although there are some anatomical differences in the brains of females and males, there are more similarities than differences.

Gall's phrenology tried to associate bumps on the skull with personality and intelligence. Gall's strategy was wrong, but different brain regions do have different functions. Even so, most psychological functions are not governed by a single structure in the brain. Rather, brain functioning works through an integration of information in a number of brain structures.

BRAIN DAMAGE, PLASTICITY, AND REPAIR

A healthy and properly functioning brain makes possible the amazing variety and complexity of human behavior. But what if the brain is damaged badly through injury or illness? Does it have the capacity to repair itself? Are there external ways we can restore some or all of the brain's functioning after it has been damaged?

The Brain's Plasticity and Capacity for Repair

Brain damage can produce horrific effects, including paralysis, sensory loss, memory loss, and personality deterioration. When such damage occurs, can the brain recover some or all of its functions? Recovery from brain damage varies considerably (Garraghty, 1996).

Plasticity *is the brain's capacity to modify and reorganize itself following damage.* In one study, researchers surgically removed part of monkeys' somatosensory cortex. Later the somatosensory cortical map shifted to intact adjacent parts of the parietal lobes, restoring the body's ability to experience sensations (Fox, 1984).

The human brain shows the most plasticity in young children before cortical regions' functions become entirely fixed (Kolb, 1989). For example, if the speech areas in an infant's left hemisphere are damaged, the right hemisphere assumes much of this language function. However, after age 5, damage to the left hemisphere can permanently disrupt language.

A key factor in recovery is whether some, or all, of the neurons in an affected area are just damaged or completely destroyed (Ashe & Aramakis, 1998). If the neurons are not completely destroyed, brain function often becomes restored over time. Unlike some fish and amphibians, our central nervous system cannot regenerate neurons. Once a human neuron is lost, it is gone forever.

Even though new neurons can't be regenerated in humans, other repair mechanisms exist (Azar, 1996), including these:

- *Collateral sprouting:* The axons of some healthy neurons adjacent to damaged cells grow new branches.
- *Substitution of function:* The damaged region's function is taken over by another area, or areas, of the brain. This is what happened in the example of the right hemisphere taking over the speech function of the damaged left hemisphere in infants.

To read further about the brain's plasticity, see the fascinating story of the Mankato nuns in Applications in Psychology.

Brain Tissue Implants

The brain's capacity to repair itself may restore some lost functions following damage, but not in all cases. In recent years, considerable excitement has been generated about **brain implants,** *which involve implanting healthy tissue into damaged brains.* The potential success of brain grafts is much better when brain tissue from the fetal stage (an early stage in prenatal development) is used. The neurons of the fetus are still growing and have a much higher probability of making connections with other neurons than do the neurons of adults. In a number of studies, researchers have damaged part of a rat's (or some other animal's) brain, waited until the animal recovered as much as possible by itself, and assessed its behavioral deficits. Then they took the corresponding area from a fetal rat's brain and transplanted it into the damaged brain of the adult rat. In these studies, the rats that received the brain transplants demonstrated considerable behavioral recovery (Dunnett, 1989).

Might such brain grafts be successful with humans suffering from brain damage? One problem is finding donors. Aborted fetuses are a possibility, but the use of fetal tissue raises ethical issues. Another possibility has been attempted with individuals who have Parkinson's disease, a neurological disorder that affects about a million people in the United States. Parkinson's disease impairs coordinated movement to the point that just

Actress Patricia Neal suffered a stroke when she was 39 years old. The stroke paralyzed one of her legs and left her unable to read, write, or speak. However, an intensive rehabilitation program and the human brain's plasticity allowed her to recover her functioning and resume her acting career 4 years later.

plasticity
The brain's capacity to modify and reorganize itself following damage.

brain implant
The implantation of healthy tissue into a damaged brain.

walking across a room can be a major ordeal. Brain grafters have tried to substitute adrenal gland tissue for brain tissue. Why adrenal gland tissue? Parkinson's disease damages neurons in an area of the brain that secretes the neurotransmitter dopamine. Adrenal gland cells produce dopamine. Early reports of adrenal gland transplants in Parkinson's patients were promising, but the long-term effects have been less so (Lewis, 1988).

The potential for brain grafts also exists for individuals with Alzheimer's disease, which is characterized by a progressive decline in intellectual functioning. Brain destruction in Alzheimer's disease involves the degeneration of neurons that function in memory.

*A*pplications in Psychology

The Brains of the Mankato Nuns

Nearly 700 nuns in a convent in Mankato, Minnesota, are the largest group of brain donors in the world. By examining the nuns' donated brains, as well as others, neuroscientists are beginning to understand that the brain has a remarkable capacity to change and grow, even in old age. The Sisters of Mankato lead an intellectually challenging life, and brain researchers recently have found that stimulating the brain with mental exercises can cause neurons to increase their dendritic branching (Snowden, 1995) (see figure 2.A).

The capacity of the brain to change offers new possibilities for preventing and treating brain diseases, helping to explain why some individuals can do the following:

- Delay the onset of Alzheimer's disease symptoms for years. The more educated people are, the less likely they are to develop Alzheimer's—probably because intellectual activity develops surplus brain tissue that compensates for tissue damaged by the disease.
- Recover better from strokes. Researchers have found that even when areas of the brain are permanently damaged by stroke, new message routes can be created to get around the blockage or to resume the function of that area.
- Feel sensation in missing limbs. Scientists no longer believe that complaints about pain in amputated body parts are psychosomatic. These sensations, which eventually fade, likely are the brain's way of keeping once-busy neurons active, providing evidence that areas of the brain no longer useful can be taken over by nearby regions of the cortex.

*F*IGURE 2.A

The Brains of the Mankato Nuns

Sister Marcella Zachman *(inset, left)* finally stopped teaching at age 97. Now, at 99, she helps ailing nuns exercise their brains by quizzing them on vocabulary or playing a card game called Skip-Bo, at which she deliberately loses. Sister Mary Esther Boor *(inset, right),* also 99 years of age, is a former teacher who keeps alert by doing puzzles and volunteering to work the front desk. *Large photo:* A technician holds the brain of a deceased Mankato nun. The nuns donate their brains for research that explores the effects of stimulation on brain growth. This research is supported by the National Institutes of Aging.

Such degenerative changes can be reversed in rats (Gage and Bjorklund, 1986). However, as yet no success has been reported with brain implants with Alzheimer's patients. Nonetheless, such implants might someday be possible in humans.

TECHNIQUES FOR STUDYING THE BRAIN

Earlier we discussed research by Wilder Penfield and James Olds in which electrodes were inserted into living persons' brains in order to study brain functions. Neuroscientists no longer have to perform surgery on living patients or cadavers to study the brain. Sophisticated techniques allow researchers to "look inside" the brain while it is at work (Haier, 1998). Let's examine some of these fascinating techniques.

High-powered microscopes are widely used in neuroscience research. Neurons are stained with the salts of various heavy metals such as silver and lead. These stains coat only a small portion of any group of neurons. The stains allow neuroscientists to view and study every part of a neuron in microscopic detail.

Also widely used, the **electroencephalograph (EEG)** *records the electrical activity of the brain. Electrodes placed on the scalp detect brain-wave activity, which is recorded on a chart known as an electroencephalogram.* This device has been used to assess brain damage, epilepsy, and other problems.

Not every recording of brain activity is made with electrodes. In single-unit recording, a portrayal of a single neuron's electrical activity, a thin wire or needle is inserted in or near an individual neuron (Seidemann & others, 1996). The wire or needle transmits the neuron's electrical activity to an amplifier, which allows researchers to gather information about the activity.

For years X rays have been used to determine damage inside or outside our bodies, both in the brain and in other locations. But a single X ray of the brain is hard to interpret because it shows the three-dimensional nature of the brain's interior in a two-dimensional image. **Computer-assisted axial tomography (CAT scan)** *is three-dimensional imaging obtained from X rays of the head that are assembled into a composite image by computer.* The CAT scan provides valuable information about the location of damage due to a stroke, language disorder, or loss of memory.

Positron-emmission tomography (PET scan) *measures the amount of glucose in various areas of the brain, then sends this information to a computer.* Because glucose levels vary

electroencephalograph (EEG)

An instrument that records the electrical activity of the brain; electrodes placed on an individual's scalp record brain-wave activity, which is reproduced on a chart known as an electroencephalogram.

computer-assisted axial tomography (CAT scan)

A three-dimensional imaging technique in which pictures obtained by passing X rays through the head are assembled by a computer into a composite image.

positron-emission tomography (PET scan)

An imaging technology that measures the amount of specially treated glucose in various areas of the brain, then sends this information to a computer.

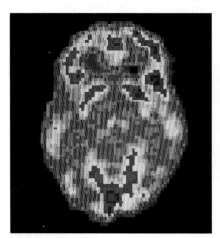 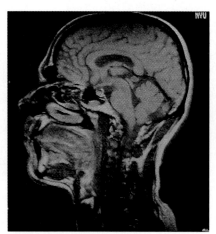 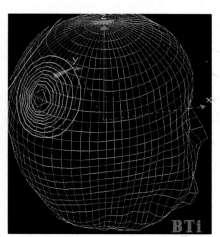

FIGURE 2.21

Contemporary Scanning Devices for Examining the Brain

Each scanning device has its strengths and weaknesses. For example, PET accurately tracks brain function but can't resolve structures less than 0.5 inches apart. MRI can't detect brain functions but can distinguish structures just 0.05 inches apart.

magnetic resonance imaging (MRI)

An imaging technique that involves creating a magnetic field around a person's body and using radio waves to construct images of the person's tissues (such as brain tissues) and biochemical activity.

superconducting quantum interference device (SQUID)

A brain-scanning device that senses tiny changes in magnetic fields.

with the levels of activity throughout the brain, tracing the amounts of glucose generates a picture of activity level throughout the brain (Fiez & others, 1996).

Another technique is **magnetic resonance imaging (MRI),** *which involves creating a magnetic field around a person's body and using radio waves to construct images of the person's brain tissues and biochemical activities.* MRI provides very clear pictures of the brain's interior, does not require injecting the brain with a substance, and does not pose a problem of radiation overexposure.

Also, the **superconducting quantum interference device (SQUID)** *is a brain-scanning device that senses tiny changes in magnetic fields.* When neurons fire, they create an electrical current; electrical fields include magnetic fields, so magnetic changes indicate neural activity. Figure 2.21 displays images from three of the brain-scanning instruments we have discussed—MRI, PET, and SQUID.

eview

Brain Damage, Plasticity, and Repair; Techniques for Studying the Brain

Recovery from brain damage varies considerably. Plasticity is the brain's capacity to modify and reorganize itself after damage. If neurons in the central nervous system are destroyed, they cannot be regenerated. Plasticity is greater in young children than in adults. Collateral sprouting and substitution of function are two mechanisms of repair in the brain. Brain grafts involve transplanting healthy tissue into damaged brains. The most successful brain grafts involve the use of fetal brain tissue, but this procedure raises ethical issues. Brain implants hold potential for treating individuals with Parkinson's disease and Alzheimer's disease, but so far brain implants have been much more successful in rats than in humans.

Among the most widely used techniques to study the brain are high-powered microscopes, the electroencephalograph, single-unit recordings, the CAT scan, the PET scan, magnetic resonance imaging (MRI), and SQUID.

Overview

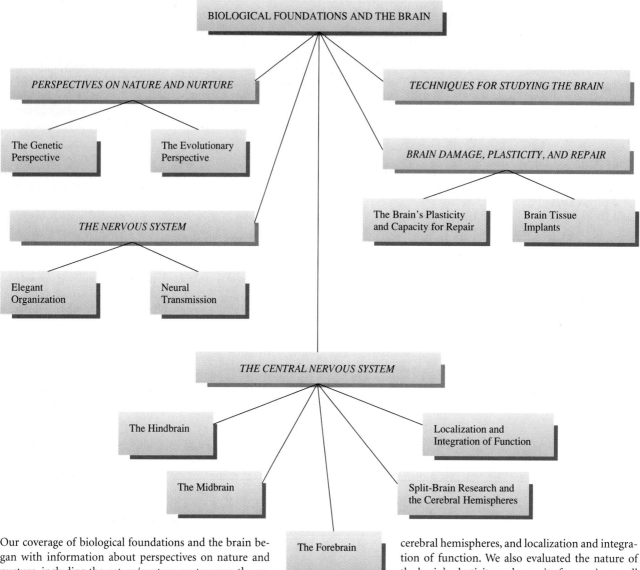

BIOLOGICAL FOUNDATIONS AND THE BRAIN

PERSPECTIVES ON NATURE AND NURTURE

The Genetic Perspective

The Evolutionary Perspective

THE NERVOUS SYSTEM

Elegant Organization

Neural Transmission

TECHNIQUES FOR STUDYING THE BRAIN

BRAIN DAMAGE, PLASTICITY, AND REPAIR

The Brain's Plasticity and Capacity for Repair

Brain Tissue Implants

THE CENTRAL NERVOUS SYSTEM

The Hindbrain

The Midbrain

The Forebrain

Localization and Integration of Function

Split-Brain Research and the Cerebral Hemispheres

Our coverage of biological foundations and the brain began with information about perspectives on nature and nurture, including the nature/nurture controversy, the genetic perspective, and the evolutionary perspective. Then we turned our attention to the nervous system, examining its elegant organization and the nature of neural transmission. We studied the following aspects of the central nervous system: the hindbrain, the midbrain, the forebrain, split-brain research, the cerebral hemispheres, and localization and integration of function. We also evaluated the nature of the brain's plasticity and capacity for repair, as well as brain tissue implants. And we learned about number of intriguing techniques for studying the brain.

Remember that you can obtain a more detailed summary of the chapter by again studying the in-chapter reviews on pages 42, 49, 63, and 67.

Key Terms

environment 36
nurture 36
nature 36
chromosomes 38
deoxyribonucleic acid (DNA) 38
genes 38
dominant-recessive genes principle 39
natural selection 41
evolutionary psychology 41
neurons 42
central nervous system (CNS) 42
peripheral nervous system 42
somatic nervous system 42
autonomic nervous system 43
sympathetic nervous system 43

parasympathetic nervous system 43
afferent nerves 43
efferent nerves 43
interneurons 43
cell body 45
dendrite 45
axon 45
myelin sheath 45
ions 45
resting potential 45
action potential 47
all-or-none principle 47
synapses 47
neurotransmitters 47
dopamine 48
serotonin 48
endorphins 48
hindbrain 50
medulla 50
cerebellum 50

pons 50
midbrain 50
reticular formation 50
basal ganglia 50
forebrain 50
thalamus 50
hypothalamus 51
endocrine system 53
hormones 53
pituitary gland 53
limbic system 54
amygdala 54
hippocampus 54
cerebral cortex (cerebrum) 54
occipital lobe 54
temporal lobe 54
frontal lobe 54
parietal lobe 54
association cortex 55
corpus callosum 55

aphasia 60
phrenology 61
plasticity 64
brain implant 64
electroencephalograph (EEG) 66
computer-assisted axial tomography (CAT scan) 66
positron-emission tomography (PET scan) 66
magnetic resonance imaging (MRI) 67
superconducting quantum interference device (SQUID) 67

Thinking It Over

Exercises . . .

. . . In Critical Thinking

Bouchard's research on identical twins reared apart offers some compelling evidence in support of the genetic determination of personality. Propose some alternative explanations that might account for Bouchard's findings that could weaken the position that personality characteristics are genetically determined.

. . . In Creative Thinking

Draw upon any musical or poetic skills you might have lurking somewhere on your cortex and construct a poem, a rap song, a country and Western number, or a tune in another style that could help you remember how different parts of your brain work. If you choose a familiar song as the foundation for your creation, you might find it easier to learn the connection between the terminology and their respective definitions.

. . . In Active Learning

Because the material about the brain is difficult to visualize, it helps to see the real thing. If your campus is close to a science museum, take a field trip and see what exhibits they have that will help you understand the brain and its functions. If no science museum is nearby, perhaps your instructor can arrange a trip to a biology lab where they are performing dissections. See how many brain parts you can identify and how many of their functions you can remember.

. . . In Reflective Learning

Consider the various techniques we have described to examine the functions of the brain. If you had the opportunity to participate in research in which your own brain functions could be charted, would you willingly subject yourself to the procedures? Which of these techniques would you find challenging to undergo?

Resources for Psychology and Improving Humankind

Brain, Mind, and Behavior (2nd ed.) (1985)

by F. E. Bloom, A. Lazerson, & L. Hofstader
New York: W. H. Freeman

This book is part of a multimedia teaching package involving the Public Broadcasting System's series "The Brain." The beauty of the brain is captured in both well-written essays and photographs.

Genetics Society of Canada/Société de génétique du Canada

151 Slater Street #907
Ottawa, ON K1P 5H4 CANADA
613-232-9459

The Genetics Society is a professional membership organization for geneticists; they publish their own research journal.

Human Growth Foundation

7777 Leesburg Pike
Falls Church, VA 22043
703-883-1773

This organization seeks to promote better understanding of human growth problems caused by pituitary gland irregularities. Information about hormone-related problems is available, as are recommendations for educational programs.

Huntington's Disease Society of America

104 W. 22nd Street, 6th Floor
New York, NY 10011-2420
800-345-4372

This organization is for individuals and volunteers concerned with Huntington's disease, an inherited and terminal neurological condition that causes progressive brain and nerve deterioration. Audiovisual materials, referral services, and general information are available.

The Mismeasure of Man (1981)

by Stephen J. Gould
New York: Norton

Gould is one of the best contemporary scientist-writers. In this book, he gives fascinating insights into the nature of biological and cultural evolution.

National Genetics Foundation

555 West 57th Street
New York, NY 10019
212-586-5800

This foundation provides information about birth defects, the genetic basis of disorders, and their treatment.

Parkinson Foundation of Canada

710-390 Bay Street
Toronto, ON M5H 2V2 CANADA
416-366-0099
1-800-565-3000

The foundation is dedicated to heightening public awareness, raising funds for research, developing and distributing literature and materials to individuals and organizations across Canada, and providing services to support persons with Parkinson's, their families, and caregivers. Their newsletter, *Network,* is published five times a year.

Parkinson's Educational Program

3900 Birch Street, No. 105
Newport Beach, CA 92660

This program serves as a clearinghouse for information about Parkinson's disease, a neurological disorder. It assists in establishing support groups throughout world. Educational materials are available.

The Twins Foundation

P.O. Box 9487
Providence, RI 02940
401-274-6910

For information about twins and multiple births, contact this organization.

Internet Resources

http://www.brown.edu/Departments/Psychiatry/NPlinks.shtml
Brown University operates a comprehensive site about neurological resources.

http://www.hbp.scripps.edu/Home.html
National Science Foundation's update on the Human Brain Project.

http://agora.leeds.ac.uk/comir/resources/links.html
Medical imaging resources available on the net.

http://www.med.harvard.edu/AANLIB/home.html
Harvard exhibits the power of neuroimaging.

http://www.nlm.nih.gov/
National Library of Medicine includes links to relevant databases.

http://wwwl.biostr.washington.edu/Brain Project.html
University of Washington provides brain maps.

http://www.tbilaw.com/
Provides background on the nature of brain injury.

http://www.ornl.gov/TechResources/HumanGenome/home.html
Review of the Human Genome Project.

http://gdbwww.gdb.org/gdb/ideo/docs/ideogram.html
Provides a map of the human genome.

http://www.talkorigins.org/faqs/faq-intro-to-biology.html
Answers to most frequently asked questions about evolution.

http://acupuncture.com/Acup/Comparison.htm
Compares the principles of western and eastern medicine.

3

Sensation and Perception

OUTLINE

BOXES

The setting sun, and music at close,

As the last taste of sweets,

is sweetest last,

Write in remembrance more

than things long past.

—William Shakespeare

English Playwright and Poet, 16th Century

P R E V I E W

*E*ach of us has a number of sensory and perceptual systems for detecting, processing, and interpreting our environment. Sensing and perceiving involve a complex and sophisticated visual system, an auditory system that is an elaborate engineering marvel compacted into a space the size of an Oreo cookie, and other processes that inform us about soft caresses and excruciating pain, sweet and sour tastes, floral and peppermint odors, and whether our world is upside down or right side up. Before we tackle each of the senses in greater detail, we need to know more about the nature of sensation and perception, that is, how we detect and perceive the world.

❖

The Story of Virgil: To See and Not See

*I*magine the enormous thrill of suddenly regaining your sight after nearly a lifetime of blindness. Colors and shapes, faces of loved ones, images that go with familiar sounds, smells, and feels—you could experience it all. Most of us imagine the restoration of sight would be like a miracle. However, Virgil's experience makes us reconsider.

A patient of renowned neurologist Oliver Sacks (1993), Virgil was born just after the start of World War II. He lost his sight at the age of 3 when he was simultaneously infected with meningitis (inflammation of the brain), polio, and cat-scratch fever. Eventually he recovered his motor function and could have recovered his vision. However, cataracts had formed, leaving him functionally blind by the age of 6. Despite this setback, he went to a school for the blind and learned to read Braille. As an adult he supported himself as a massage therapist at the YMCA, had significant social relationships, and had a passion for baseball, including a comprehensive knowledge of the game's statistics. Most people described him as passive but content with his life and limitations.

In 1991, Virgil became engaged to Amy, a woman he had known for about 20 years. Amy saw Virgil's life as rather dull. She began to encourage him to explore having cataract surgery. Although the possibility of sight was remote because his retinas might have deteriorated, she pushed for the surgery in the hopes that, after 45 years of blindness, he would be able to see for the wedding. Virgil was passive in this situation as well; he agreed to go along with the procedure without being particularly eager for the change.

Amy's diary describes the moment when the bandages were removed as more strange than dramatic. According to Virgil, all was a blur of meaningless lights and colors. Out of the confusion, a voice asked, "Well?" Only at that moment did the shapes and shadows converge into the image of his surgeon's face. Although his visual system was transmitting images, he had no experience with imagery to make sense of what he saw. Although he had sustained some damage to his visual system, he was able to see movement, shapes, and colors. His physicians predicted his vision would be stable.

You might be expecting a happy ending in which Virgil and Amy lived happily ever after. However, Virgil experienced many difficulties in adjusting to his new sensory world. He had trouble recognizing letters and preferred Braille. He seemed unable to integrate details into a meaningful whole. For example, he failed to recognize his own dog when seen from different angles. It took him a long time to understand how trunks and leaves go together to form the visual image of a tree. Faces were especially challenging. It seemed that Virgil couldn't sustain looking at faces to interpret facial expressions. He no longer found his job satisfying. The bodies he knew well by touch now were somewhat repugnant because he could see the skin imperfections that he hadn't noticed when he was blind.

To make matters worse, his health deteriorated. His childhood bout of polio had left him with some lung problems that compromised his breathing. He also gained a substantial amount of weight. Eventually he was stricken with pneumonia and became gravely ill, requiring intensive care and a constant tether to oxygen. During this period Virgil alternated between functional blindness and periods in which he claimed he couldn't see but behaved as though he could. For example, he could reach for objects or avoid them even though he said he couldn't see them.

When he emerged from the hospital, he was sufficiently weakened that he had to leave his job and move out of his home at the YMCA. His rehabilitation specialists reported that he had lost all of the vision the operations had restored. Subsequent tests indicated that he was totally blind; he had lost even the few functions he had had prior to the surgery. Dr. Sacks believed that the loss could be the result of three factors. Perhaps the sensitive retinas at the back of the eyes simply burned out. Perhaps his obesity had led to gradual oxygen starvation of visual tissues. But perhaps psychological factors were also responsible. Virgil was not at home in the sighted world. His brief access to vision also interfered with his competence in the area of touch. His serious illness allowed him to return to the world of touch—but as an unemployed, dependent, chronically ill, and decidedly depressed man.

As has been reported in many case histories of the newly sighted, the euphoria of seeing is soon replaced with a sense of chaos and frustration that makes adaptation challenging. Sacks believed that "one must die as a blind person to be born again as a sighted person." ❖

DETECTING AND PERCEIVING THE WORLD

How do you know that grass is green and that smell is sweet, that a sound is a sigh, that the lights around the shore are dim? You know these things because of your abilities to sense and perceive stimuli in the environment. All outside information comes into us through our senses. Without vision, hearing, touch, taste, smell, and other senses, your brain would be isolated from the world; you would live in a dark silence—a tasteless, colorless, sensationless void. Without perceptual abilities to organize incoming stimulation, the world would be chaotic. Let's examine the concepts of sensation and perception in greater detail.

Defining Sensation and Perception

sensation

The process of detecting and encoding stimulus energy in the world.

Sensation *is the process of detecting and encoding stimulus energy in the world.* Stimuli emit physical energy—light, sound, and heat, for example. The sense organs detect this energy and then transform, or transduce, it into a code that can be transmitted to the brain. The first step in "sensing" the world is the work of receptor cells, which respond to certain forms of energy. For example, the retina of the eye is sensitive to light, and special cells in the ear are sensitive to the vibrations that make up sound. The physical energy is transduced into electrical impulses; the information carried by these electrical impulses travels through nerve fibers that connect the sense organs with the central nervous system. Information about the external world then travels to the appropriate area of the cerebral cortex.

> *Thought is astonishing, but sensation is equally wonderful.*
> —VOLTAIRE, *French Philosopher, 18th Century*

perception

The brain's process of organizing and interpreting sensory information to give it meaning.

Perception *is the process of organizing and interpreting sensory information.* The retinas in our eyes record a fast-moving silver object in the sky, but they do not "see" a passenger jet; our eardrum vibrates in a particular way, but it does not "hear" a Beethoven symphony. Organizing and interpreting what is sensed, that is, "seeing" and "hearing" meaningful patterns in sensory information, is perception.

> *People only see what they are prepared to see.*
> —RALPH WALDO EMERSON, *American Poet, Essayist, 19th Century*

In our everyday lives, the two processes of sensation and perception are virtually inseparable. When the brain receives information, for example, it automatically interprets and responds to the information. Because of this, most contemporary psychologists refer to sensation and perception as a unified information-processing system (Goldstein, 1996).

Psychophysics and Sensory Thresholds

How different do the percentages of fat have to be for you to taste a difference between "low-fat" and "regular" versions of your favorite ice cream? How close does an approaching bumblebee have to get before you can hear its buzzing? Can you tell by the smell when cookies are ready to come out of the oven? Can you be persuaded to take action based on seeing or hearing things that don't penetrate your conscious awareness? These are questions explored in the specialized branch of psychology called **psychophysics,** *the formal study of psychological reactions to physical stimulation.*

psychophysics

The formal study of psychological reactions to physical stimuli.

Psychophysics. The term *psychophysics* has an interesting origin (Bolles, 1992). Long before the first experimental laboratory was founded in Germany in 1879, a German physics professor named Gustav Fechner became fascinated with visual phenomena. Unfortunately, his curiosity about unusual visual effects lured him to stare too long at the sun. As a consequence, he became virtually blind. His recovery took several years, further hampered by his erratic psychological functioning. He became reclusive and began spending all of his time in bed, often making notes and writing poetry. On October 22, 1850, Fechner had an insight so compelling that he rose from his bed and made a note crucial to the history of psychology. He envisioned a technique for measuring reactions to sensory stimuli that he believed would help him create a bridge between the physical world and psychological experience. Fechner abandoned his sickbed and devoted the following decade to careful experiments exploring that link. One of his most important contributions is the concept of the difference threshold.

Difference Threshold. An artist might detect the difference between two very similar shades of color. A tailor might determine a difference in the texture of two fabrics by feeling them. How different must the colors and textures be for those people to determine the difference? The **difference threshold,** *or just noticeable difference (jnd), is the smallest difference in stimulation required to discriminate one stimulus from another 50 percent of the time.*

One important aspect of difference thresholds is that the threshold increases with the magnitude of the stimulus. For example, you might notice when someone living with you turns up the volume on the stereo by even a small amount when the music is playing softly. But if the volume is turned up an equal amount when the music is playing very loudly, you might not notice. This relationship was first observed by German physiologist E. H. Weber, and it became known as **Weber's law,** *which states that two stimuli must differ by a constant proportion (rather than a constant amount) for their difference to be detected.* Weber's law generally holds true. For example, when we add 1 candle to 60 candles, we can notice a difference in the overall brightness of the candles; when we add 1 candle to 120 candles, we do not notice a difference. We discover, though, that adding 2 candles to 120 does produce a difference in brightness. Adding 2 candles to 120 candles is the same proportion as adding 1 candle to 60 candles. Fechner designated this proportion as *s*. The exact proportion varies with the type of stimulus involved. For example, a change in a tone's pitch of 3 percent can be detected, but a 20 percent change in taste and a 25 percent change in smell might be required before a person can detect a difference in taste or smell.

Comparing the perceived differences between two stimuli was not the only thing psychophysicists explored in the early days of psychology. They also investigated how intense a stimulus must be for it to be perceived. This concept is called the absolute threshold.

Absolute Threshold. Take your watch off and place it on the table next to you. Listen carefully and see if you can hear it ticking. As you move closer, the ticking gets louder. As you move away, the ticking fades. If you hold your position, the ticking will appear to fade in and out of your awareness. This simple demonstration illustrates the principle of the **absolute threshold,** *the minimum amount of sensory energy we can detect 50 percent of the time.* When a stimulus has less energy than this absolute threshold (also called *limen*), we cannot reliably detect its presence; when the stimulus is greater than the absolute threshold, we can detect it more reliably.

Under ideal circumstances, our senses have very low absolute thresholds. Demonstrate this by taking a sharp pencil and carefully lifting a single hair from your forearm. For most of us, this small pressure on the skin is easy to detect. Table 3.1 describes the minimum stimulus intensity necessary for the senses.

𝒯able 3.1

Approximate Absolute Thresholds for Five Senses

Vision	A candle flame at 30 miles on a dark, clear night
Hearing	A ticking watch at 20 feet under quiet conditions
Taste	A teaspoon of sugar in 2 gallons of water
Smell	One drop of perfume diffused throughout three rooms
Touch	The wing of a fly falling on your cheek from a distance of 1 centimeter

Source: Adapted from Galanter, 1962.

People have different thresholds. Some people have better hearing than others, and some people have better vision than others. Figure 3.1 shows one person's absolute threshold for detecting a clock's ticking sound. Using the same clock, another person might have an absolute threshold at 26 feet, the absolute threshold for another might be at 22 feet, and for another at 17 feet.

---

difference threshold

Also called the just noticeable difference (jnd); the smallest difference in stimulation required to discriminate one stimulus from another 50 percent of the time.

Weber's law

The principle that two stimuli must differ by a constant proportion (rather than a constant amount) for their difference to be detected.

absolute threshold

The minimum amount of sensory energy that we can detect 50 percent of the time.

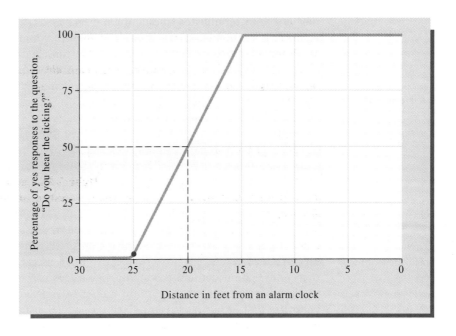

$\mathscr{F}$IGURE 3.1

Determining the Absolute Threshold

Absolute threshold is the stimulus value a person detects 50 percent of the time. Here the individual's absolute threshold for detecting the ticking of a clock is 20 feet. People have different absolute thresholds. Another individual tested with the ticking clock might have an absolute threshold of 22 feet, for example.

When psychophysics began, psychologists believed that the phenomenon of the absolute threshold was relatively straightforward. More recent studies in psycho-physics have concluded that interpreting sensory stimulation is a far more complicated process.

Signal Detection Theory.   **Signal detection theory** *states that sensitivity to sensory stimuli depends on the strength of the sensory stimulus, the respondent's sensory abilities, and a variety of psychological and contextual factors.* These factors include the respondent's past experiences, expectancies, and motivation. In essence, signal detection theorists argue that no absolute threshold exists. For example, when you are absorbed in studying, you might

signal detection theory

The theory that no absolute threshold exists—but that, rather, sensitivity to sensory stimuli depends on the strength of the sensory stimulus, the respondent's sensory abilities, and a variety of psychological and contextual factors.

How might signal detection theory be important in interpreting X-rays?

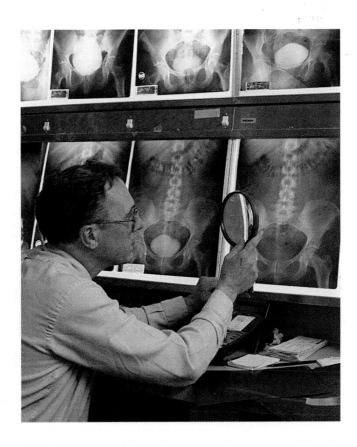

not hear your roommate's question about history class. However, chances are that you will hear your roommate announce that the pizza you ordered has arrived.

Signal detection can have more important consequences than whether you hear your roommate announce the arrival of your pizza. Air traffic controllers' signal detection mistakes can cost hundreds of lives. Reading and misreading X rays also illustrate signal detection in a medical context.

Signal detection researchers have found that people vary in how conservative or liberal they are in reporting that a signal is present. Conservative responders say a stimulus is present only when they are very sure it is there. By contrast, liberal responders say a stimulus is present even with a faint indication that it is there. Context affects whether people are conservative or liberal in their responses. A peacetime radar operator is more likely to be a conservative responder than a wartime radar operator is.

Subliminal Perception. Can we be influenced by sensations that are too faint for us to detect them at a conscious level? **Subliminal perception** *is the perception of stimuli below the threshold of awareness.* In 1957, a report in *Life* magazine astonished the public. It said that more than 45,000 unknowing movie viewers had been manipulated by subliminal messages. According to the report, the messages *Eat Popcorn* and *Drink Coca-Cola* repeatedly were flashed on the screen during the movies at rates too fast to be detected consciously. The sale of both products was reported to have increased dramatically.

The success of this manipulation intrigued advertisers, who hoped to apply this concept to increase consumer buying, and frightened consumers, who feared what they could be made to do without being aware that they were being manipulated. However, it appears that the original study was a fabrication by marketers (Rogers, 1992–1993). Despite the false claims, many people were persuaded that subliminal perception was a real threat. Researchers have not been able to replicate studies that claim to have found subliminal effects (Pratkanis & Greenwald, 1988).

A more recent example of interest in subliminal perception focuses on subliminal messages in rock music. Some rock groups allegedly have inserted satanic messages played backward into their records and tapes. When the record is played backward, supposedly the message cannot be heard consciously but influences behavior in a subliminal way. Yet another recent use of subliminal perception involves the widespread sale of subliminal self-help tapes that are designed to get people to quit smoking, lose weight, reduce stress,

subliminal perception

Perception of stimuli below the threshold of awareness.

Mötley Crüe's *Shout at the Devil* album has been a target of groups who believe that backward messages are embedded in the songs. The protestors say that this album embeds the phrase *Backward mask where are you, oh. Lost in error, Satan.* However, researchers have been unable to find any evidence that any such satanic messages are encoded in the music—or that, if they are, they can influence behavior.

and so on. There is no evidence that either backward satanic messages in rock music or subliminal self-help tapes influence behavior in any way (Moore, 1995).

Is the idea of subliminal perception entirely without merit? No. Sensory information too faint to be recognized consciously can be detected by sensory receptors and transmitted to the brain beneath the level of conscious awareness (Fowler & others, 1981). However, being aroused by a subliminal perception is not the same as being persuaded to take action (Greenwald, 1996).

Sensory Reactions

How we process sensory information has a direct influence on behavior. We will examine three kinds of behaviors—sensory adaptation, sensation seeking, and sensory deprivation—that involve reactions to sensation.

Sensory Adaptation. Naked except for capes that hang to their knees, two Ona Indians wade in freezing water as they use a bow and arrow to kill fish for their dinner. Darwin encountered the Ona Indians when he rounded Cape Horn on the southern tip of South America. At night they slept naked on the wet, virtually frozen ground. The ability of these Indians to endure the freezing temperatures, wearing little or no clothing, reflects the principle of **sensory adaptation,** *diminished sensitivity to prolonged stimulation.* You have experienced sensory adaptation countless times in your life—adapting to the temperature of a shower, to the water in a swimming pool, to the heat of jalapenos, to loud sounds of rock music, or to the rank smell of a locker room. Sensory adaptation is vividly demonstrated when you enter a darkened theater. Initially you can't see a thing. Gradually your eyes become adapted to the dark. When you return to the light, your eyes might feel uncomfortable until they become adapted to the light. Over time we become less responsive and less sensitive to these sensory experiences; this is due to sensory adaptation.

Sensory adaptation, also called *habituation,* is a mixed blessing. When we are exposed to unpleasant stimuli, such as rotting garbage or sneakers gone bad, habituation rescues us from being preoccupied with unpleasant stimulation. However, the charming smell of roses fades and the superb taste of a gourmet meal also loses its impact all too quickly, due to habituation. On a larger scale, we can gradually get used to conditions that might not be particularly healthy. For example, our senses readily adapt to increasing levels of pollution, and individuals in urban areas might have habituated to the sound of car alarms to such a degree that they no longer pay attention to them. In our original example with the Ona Indians, there is some risk that reduced sensitivity to cold might occasionally result in tissue damage from unhealthy, prolonged exposure.

Let's return to the dilemma of the advertiser. Rather than attempting to influence through subliminal perception, most advertisers try to capture our attention by creating stimuli with louder sound levels, provocative visual images, or creative messages that break through our habituated patterns of processing commercial messages.

Sensation Seeking. When you go out to eat, do you go to the same restaurant and order your favorite dish? Or do you make a point of going someplace new and try the most unusual offerings on the menu? If you go to an amusement park, do you prefer the giant roller-coaster to a peaceful people-watching walk around the park? Researchers believe that people can develop consistent preferences regarding the amount of sensory input they pursue. **Sensation seeking** *is behavior motivated by the need for varied, novel, and complex sensations and experiences* (Zuckerman, 1979). To test your sensation-seeking tendencies, turn to the Self-Assessment.

People with high sensation-seeking needs can seek thrills in either constructive or destructive ways (Farley, 1989). For example, writing a novel or managing an A average are constructive thrills. Breaking laws and taking sexual risks are destructive thrills that can entail huge personal penalties.

Sensory Deprivation. Imagine that you are in your fourth month of your assignment as a member of a science team in the Arctic Circle. It is unspeakably cold. Almost

sensory adaptation
Diminished sensitivity to prolonged exposure to a stimulus.

sensation seeking
Behavior motivated by the need for varied, novel, and complex sensations and experiences.

Self-Assessment

Sensation Seeking

Instructions

For each of the following items, decide which of the two choices best describes your likes and feelings. If neither choice applies, choose the one that *most* describes you. Answer all items.

1. a. I like the tumult of sounds in a busy city.
    b. I prefer the peace and quiet of the country.
2. a. I dislike the sensations one gets when flying.
    b. I enjoy many of the rides in amusement parks.
3. a. I would like a job that would require a lot of traveling.
    b. I would prefer a job in one location.
4. a. I often wish I could be a mountain climber.
    b. I can't understand people who risk their necks climbing mountains.
5. a. I get bored seeing the same old faces.
    b. I like the comfortable familiarity of everyday friends.
6. a. I like to explore a strange city or section of town by myself, even if it means getting lost.
    b. I prefer a guide when I am in a place I don't know well.
7. a. I find people who disagree with my beliefs more stimulating than people who agree with me.
    b. I don't like to argue with people whose beliefs are sharply divergent from mine, since such arguments are never resolved.
8. a. I prefer more subdued colors in decoration.
    b. I like to decorate with bright colors.
9. a. When I have nothing to do or look at for any length of time, I get very restless.
    b. I often enjoy just relaxing and doing nothing.
10. a. Most people spend entirely too much money on life insurance.
    b. Life insurance is something that no one can afford to be without.
11. a. I don't like to drink coffee because it overstimulates me and keeps me awake.
    b. I like to drink coffee because of the lift it gives me.
12. a. The worst social sin is to be rude.
    b. The worst social sin is to be a bore.
13. a. The most important goal of life is to live it to the fullest and experience as much of it as you can.
    b. The most important goal of life is to find peace and happiness.
14. a. If I were a salesperson, I would prefer working on commission if I had a chance to make more money than I could on a salary.
    b. If I were a salesperson, I would prefer a straight salary rather than the risk of making little or nothing on a commission basis.
15. a. I like sharp or spicy foods.
    b. I prefer foods with a minimum of seasoning.

Scoring

Count one point for sensation seeking for each of the following: 1a, 2b, 3a, 4a, 5a, 6a, 7a, 8b, 9a, 10a, 11b, 12b, 13a, 14a, 15a.

Interpretation

If you answered 11 or more items this way, you probably have a strong motivation for sensation seeking. If you answered 5 items or less this way, you probably have a weak motive for sensation seeking. If you responded this way 6 to 10 times, you probably are in the average range of sensation seekers. The older one gets, the more sensation seeking scores go down. These items represent an abbreviated version of Zuckerman's Sensation Seeking Scale.

---

sensory deprivation

The absence of normal external stimulation for extended periods of time.

everything you see is white. Conversation is at a minimum. Would you thrive in this environment? Your tolerance for the assignment would depend on your ability to cope with **sensory deprivation,** *the absence of normal external stimulation for extended periods of time.*

Research in sensory deprivation has produced dramatically different conclusions. Heron (1957) discovered that long periods of sensory deprivation induced hallucination, disorientation, and emotional distress. He placed volunteers in small soundproof rooms and blocked their sensory input by having them wear goggles and gloves. They could leave their confined space only for eating and toileting. Most volunteers could not manage the isolation for more than 2 days. However, an analysis of the demand characteristics of the research has made the findings questionable. Curiosity about the effects of sensory deprivation was heightened in the 1950s by the brainwashing treatments used on prisoners during the Korean War. In Heron's study the volunteers' sensitivity and fear about the risks involved in the procedure may have heightened their sense of danger.

More recently, sensory deprivation has been used as a therapeutic alternative. For example, a 24-hour restriction of sensory input called restricted environmental stimulation therapy (REST) has been proposed as therapy for individuals who have become overloaded with stimulation (Suedfield & Coren, 1989). You may have experienced periods in which you felt overwhelmed by stimulation. Coming home from work or school after a day that was too intense can make you crave peace and quiet. The appeal of staying in bed all day or taking a restful vacation underscores the importance of having controlled sensory deprivation experiences now and then.

eview

Detecting and Perceiving the World

Sensation is the process of detecting and encoding stimulus energy in the world. Perception is the process of organizing and interpreting sensory information. Most contemporary psychologists refer to sensation and perception as a unified information-processing system. A basic problem for any sensory system is to detect varying degrees of energy in the environment. Each of us has an absolute threshold, or minimum amount of energy

we can detect in any sensory mode. Psychophysics is the formal study of the psychological experience of the physical world.

The difference threshold, or just noticeable difference (jnd), is the smallest difference in stimulation required to discriminate one stimulus from another 50 percent of the time.

Signal detection theory suggests that psychological factors influence whether or

not we detect signals properly. Subliminal perception is the perception of stimuli below the threshold of awareness; this is a controversial topic.

Sensory adaptation is weakened sensitivity due to prolonged stimulation. People differ in the amount of stimulation they seek. Sensory deprivation appears to have therapeutic uses.

SENSATION

The brain continuously receives sensory information during our waking hours. Vision, hearing, smell, touch, and taste are obvious sensory channels through which we process input. We also manage upright posture and orientation in space as part of our kinesthetic senses. We will examine each of these sensory abilities in turn.

O for a life of Sensations rather than Thoughts!

—JOHN KEATS

The Visual System

We see a world of shapes and sizes, some stationary, others moving, some in black and white, others in color. *How* do we see this way? What is the machinery that enables us to experience this marvelous landscape?

light
A form of electromagnetic energy that can be described in terms of wavelengths.

wavelength
The distance from the peak of one wave to the peak of the next.

The Visual Stimulus and the Eye.   To understand our sense of vision, we need to know some basic facts about light, the energy that makes vision possible. **Light** *is a form of electromagnetic energy that can be described in terms of wavelengths.* Waves of light are much like the waves formed when a pebble is tossed into a lake. The **wavelength** *is the distance from the peak of one wave to the peak of the next.* Visible light's wavelengths range from about 400 to 700 nanometers (a nanometer is one-billionth of a meter and is abbreviated *nm*). The difference between visible light and other forms of electromagnetic energy is its wavelength. Outside the range of visible light are longer radio and infrared radiation waves, and shorter ultraviolet and X rays (see figure 3.2). These other wavelengths continually bombard us, but we do not see them. Why do we see only the narrow band of the electromagnetic spectrum between 400 and 700 nanometers? The most likely answer is that our visual system evolved in the sun's light. Thus, our visual system is able to perceive the spectrum of energy emitted by the sun. By the time sunlight reaches the earth's surface, it is strongest in the 400 to 700 nanometer range.

This narrow band of the electromagnetic spectrum strikes our eyes, which have a number of structures to handle the incoming light. By looking closely at your eyes in a

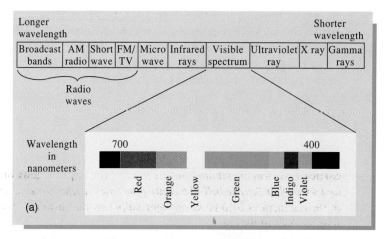

Longer wavelength									Shorter wavelength
Broadcast bands	AM radio	Short wave	FM/TV	Micro wave	Infrared rays	Visible spectrum	Ultraviolet ray	X ray	Gamma rays

Radio waves

Wavelength in nanometers   700   400

Red   Orange   Yellow   Green   Blue   Indigo   Violet

(a)

(b)

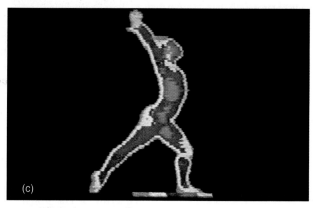

(c)

𝓕IGURE 3.2

The Electromagnetic Spectrum and Visible Light

(a) Visible light is only a narrow band in the electromagnetic spectrum. Visible light's wavelengths range from about 400 to 700 nanometers; X rays are much shorter and radio waves are much longer. *(b)* Most ultraviolet rays are absorbed by the ozone in the earth's upper atmosphere. The small fraction that reaches the earth is the ingredient in sunlight that tans the skin (and can cause skin cancer). *(c)* The electromagnetic radiation just beyond red in the spectrum (infrared) is felt as heat by receptors in the skin.

sclera

The white outer part of the eye, which helps to maintain the shape of the eye and to protect it from injury.

iris

The colored part of the eye, which can range from light blue to dark brown.

pupil

The opening, which appears black, in the center of the iris.

mirror, you notice three parts—the sclera, iris, and pupil (figure 3.3 shows the main structure of the eye).

The **sclera** *is the white outer part of the eye that helps to maintain the shape of the eye and to protect it from injury.* The **iris** *is the colored part of the eye, which can range from light blue to dark brown.* The **pupil,** *which appears black, is the opening in the center of the iris.* The iris contains muscles that function to control the size of the pupil, and hence, the amount of light that gets into the eye. This allows the eye to function optimally under different conditions of illumination, which can range in the course of a normal day from the darkest of basements to the brightest of summer sunshine. To get a good "picture" of

𝓕IGURE 3.3

Main Structures of the Eye

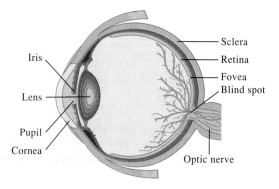

Iris

Lens

Pupil

Cornea

Sclera

Retina

Fovea

Blind spot

Optic nerve

the world, the amount of light that enters the eye needs to be adjustable. In this sense, the pupil acts like the aperture of a camera, opening to let in more light when it is needed and closing to let in less light when there is too much.

You can demonstrate changes in the size of your own pupil by looking at your eyes in the mirror and turning the room lights up and down. (You obviously need to try this in a room with sufficient light to see your eyes even when the lights are turned all the way down.) As you turn down the room lights, the pupil will begin to enlarge to let in more light; as you turn the room lights back up, the pupil opening will shrink to let in less light.

If the eye is to act like a camera, in addition to having the right amount of light, the image has to be in focus at the back of the eye. Two structures serve this purpose. The **cornea** *is a clear membrane just in front of the eye.* The **lens of the eye** *is a transparent and somewhat flexible ball-like entity filled with a gelatinous material. The function of both of these structures is to bend the light falling on the surface of the eye just enough to focus it at the back of the eye.* The curved surface of the cornea does most of this bending, while the lens "fine-tunes" the focus as needed. When you are looking at faraway objects, the lens has a relatively flat shape. This is because the light reaching the eye from far-away objects is parallel and the bending power of the cornea is sufficient to keep things in focus. The light reaching the eye from objects that are close, however, is more scattered and so more bending of the light is required to achieve focus. This focusing is done by a process called **accommodation,** *in which the lens changes its curvature.* Without this fine-tuning ability, it would be difficult to focus on objects that are close to us, like needle-work or reading. With age, the lens of the eye begins to lose its flexibility, and hence its ability to change from its normal flattened shape to the rounder shape needed to bring close objects into focus. This is why many people with normal vision throughout their young adult life require reading glasses when they get older.

The parts of the eye that we have discussed so far work together to get the best possible picture of the world. All of this effort, however, would be for naught without a method for keeping or "recording" the images we take of the world. In a camera, film serves just such a purpose. Film is made of a material that responds to light. Likewise, the **retina** *is the light-sensitive surface in the back of the eye. It consists of light receptors called rods and cones, and different kinds of neurons that you will read about shortly.* The analogy between the film of a camera and the retina, however, vastly underestimates the complexity and elegance of the retina's design. Even after decades of intense study, the full marvel of this structure is far from understood.

Because the retina is so important to vision, we need to study its makeup more closely. There are two kinds of receptors in the retina: rods and cones. They serve to turn the electromagnetic energy of light into a form of energy that can be processed by the nervous system. This process is referred to as transduction. **Rods** *are receptors in the retina that are exquisitely sensitive to light but are not very useful for color vision.* Thus, they function well under low illumination; as you might expect, they are hard at work at night. **Cones** *are the receptors that we use for color perception.* There are three types of cones, each maximally sensitive to a different range of wavelengths or hues. As we will see shortly, our color perception operates by being able to compare the responses of these three cone systems to a stimulus. Like the rods, cones are light sensitive. However, they require a larger amount of light than the rods to respond, and so they operate best in daylight or under high illumination.

The rods and cones in the retina are receptors that transduce light into neural impulses by means of a photochemical reaction. The breakdown of the chemicals produces a neural impulse that is first transmitted to the bipolar cells and then moves down to the ganglion cells (see figure 3.4). The nerve impulse then passes along the axons of the ganglion cells, which make up the optic nerve.

Rods and cones are involved in different aspects of vision and differ both in how they respond to light and in their distribution on the surface of the retina. The most important part of the retina is the **fovea,** *which is a minute area in the center of the retina where vision is at its best. The fovea is able to resolve much finer detail than any other part of the retina and contains only cones.* The fovea is vitally important to many visual tasks (try reading out of the corner of your eye!). By contrast, rods are found almost everywhere on the

---

cornea

A clear membrane just in front of the eye; its function is to bend the light falling on the surface of the eye just enough to focus it at the back of the eye.

lens of the eye

The transparent and somewhat flexible ball-like entity filled with a gelatinous material; its function is to bend the light falling on the surface of the eye just enough to focus it at the back of the eye.

accommodation

The action of the lens of the eye to increase or decrease its curvature.

retina

The light-sensitive surface in the back of the eye that houses light receptors called rods and cones.

rods

Receptors in the retina that are exquisitely sensitive to light but are not very useful for color vision.

cones

Receptors for color perception.

fovea

A minute area in the center of the retina where vision is at its best.

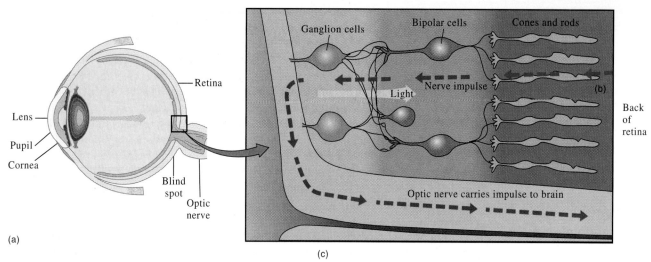

(a)

(c)

$\mathcal{F}$IGURE 3.4

Three Stages of Transmission of Light Information Through the Eye

(a) In the first stage, light passes (from left to right in this representation) through the cornea, pupil, and lens and then falls on the retina, a light-sensitive surface in the back of the eye. *(b)* Once light triggers a photochemical reaction in the rods and cones at the back of the retina, the direction of light processing reverses to create the second stage. The photochemical reaction of the rods and cones activates the bipolar cells, which in turn activate the ganglion cells at the front of the retina. *(c)* In the final stage, the ganglion cells intersect to become the optic nerve, which carries information to the parts of the brain that process visual information.

retina except in the fovea. As their name suggests, rods are long and cylindrical. Since they require little light to respond, they work best under conditions of low illumination. Because of this light sensitivity and the rods' location on the retina, we are able to detect fainter spots of light on the peripheral retina than at the fovea. It has been known for centuries that if you want to see a very faint star, you should gaze slightly to the right or left of the star.

Cones are shorter and fatter than rods and are concentrated in the fovea, but they can also be found on the peripheral retina. Because we know that rods are used in poorly lit conditions and that the fovea has no rods, we can conclude that vision is poor for objects registered on the fovea at night. A summary of some of the main characteristics of rods and cones is presented in table 3.2.

$\mathcal{T}$a b l e   3 . 2

Characteristics of Rods and Cones

Characteristics	Rods	Cones
Type of vision	Black and white	Color
Light conditions	Dimly lighted	Well lighted
Shape	Thin and long	Short and fat
Distribution	Not on fovea	On fovea

Finally, there is one place on the retina that contains neither rods nor cones. Not surprisingly, this area is called the **blind spot;** *it is the place on the retina where the optic nerve leaves the eye on its way to the brain.* We cannot see anything that reaches only this part of the retina. To experience your blind spot, see figure 3.5.

From Eye to Brain and Neural-Visual Processing.   The optic nerve leads out of the eye toward the brain carrying information about light. Stimuli in the left visual field are

blind spot

The area of the retina where the optic nerve leaves the eye on its way to the brain.

𝓕IGURE 3.5
The Eye's Blind Spot

There is a normal blind spot in your eye, a small area where the optic nerve leads to the brain. To find your blind spot, hold this book at arm's length, cover your left eye, and stare at the red pepper with your right eye. Move the book slowly toward you until the yellow pepper disappears. To find the blind spot in your left eye, cover your right eye, concentrate on the yellow pepper, and adjust the distance of the book until the red pepper disappears.

registered in the right half of the retina in both eyes, and stimuli in the right visual field are registered in the left half of the retina in both eyes. At the point called the optic chiasm the optic nerve fibers divide, and approximately half of the nerve fibers cross over the midline of the brain. The visual information originating in the right halves of the two retinae is then transmitted to the left side of the occipital lobe in the back of the brain. And the visual information originating in the left halves of the retinae is transmitted to the right side of the occipital lobe. What all of these crossings mean is that what we see in the left side of our visual field ends up in the right side of our brain, and what we see in the right visual field ends up in the left side of our brain (see figure 3.6).

The visual cortex in the occipital lobe combines information from both eyes and is responsible for higher levels of visual processing. David Huble and Torsten Wiesel (1965) won a Nobel Prize for their discovery that some neurons detect different features of the visual field. By recording the activity of a *single* neuron in a cat while it looked at patterns that varied in size, shape, color, and movement, the researchers found that the visual cortex has neurons that are individually sensitive to different types of lines and angles. For example, one neuron might show a sudden burst of activity when stimulated by lines of a particular angle; another neuron might fire only when moving stimuli appear; yet another neuron might be stimulated when the object in the visual field has a combination of angles, sizes, and shapes.

Color Vision.   We spend a lot of time thinking about color—the color of the car we want to buy, the color we are going to paint the walls of our room, the color of the clothes we wear. We can change our hair color or even the color of our eyes to make us look more attractive.

What Is Color?   The human eye registers light wavelengths between 400 and 700 nm, which we see as different colors of light. This is what was shown in figure 3.2. However, light waves themselves have no color. The sensations of color reside in the visual system of the observer. So, when we talk about red light, we refer to the wavelengths of light that evoke the sensation of red. Objects appear a certain color to us because they reflect specific wavelengths of light to our eyes. These wavelengths are split apart into a spectrum of colors when the light passes through a prism, as in the formation of a rainbow. We can remember the colors of the light spectrum by thinking of an imaginary man named ROY G. BIV, for the colors red, orange, yellow, green, blue, indigo, and violet.

If you go into a paint store and ask for some red paint, the salesperson will probably ask you what kind of red paint you want—dark or light, pinkish or more crimson, pastel or deep, and so on. These variations in the shade of red are due to differences in their hue, saturation, and brightness.

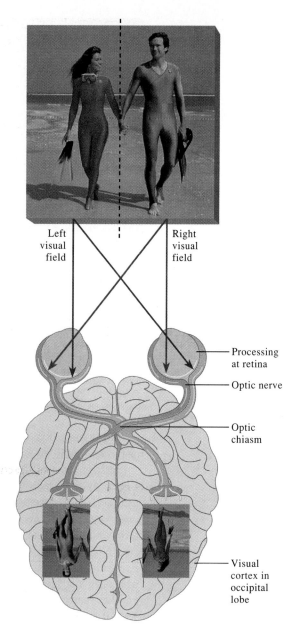

$\mathcal{F}$IGURE 3.6

Visual Pathways to and Through the Brain

Light from each side of the visual field falls on the opposite side of each eye's retina. Visual information then travels along the optic nerve to the optic chiasm, where most of the visual information crosses over to the other side of the brain. From there visual information goes to the occipital lobe at the rear of the brain. What all of the crossings mean is that what we see in the left side of our visual field (in this figure, the woman) ends up in the right side of our brain, and what we see in the right visual field (the man) ends up on the left side of our brain.

Left visual field

Right visual field

Processing at retina

Optic nerve

Optic chiasm

Visual cortex in occipital lobe

hue

A characteristic of color based on its wavelength content.

saturation

A characteristic of color based on its purity.

brightness

A characteristic of color based on its intensity.

additive mixture

The mixing of light beams from different parts of the color spectrum.

A color's **hue** *is based on its wavelength.* As shown in figure 3.2, the longest wavelengths seen by the human eye (about 700 nm) appear as red; the shortest (about 400 nm) appear as violet. A color's **saturation** *is based on its purity.* The purity of a color is determined by the amount of white light added to a single wavelength of color. The color tree shown in figure 3.7 can help us understand saturation. Colors that are very pure have no white light. They are located outside of the color tree. As we move toward the color tree's interior, notice how the saturation of color changes. The closer we get to the tree's center, the more white light has been added to the single wavelength of a particular color. That is, the deep colors at the edge fade into the more pastel colors toward the center. When saturation is added to hue, we see a much larger range of colors—pink and crimson as well as basic red, for example. However, another dimension also is involved in color—brightness. A color's **brightness** *is based on its intensity.* White has the most brightness, black the least.

When we mix colors, we get different results, depending on whether we mix light or pigments (any substance, such as paint, that produces color) (see figure 3.8). An **additive mixture** *of color refers to mixing beams of light from different parts of the color spectrum.*

Through additive mixing, we can produce virtually the entire color circle by using any three widely spaced colors. Television is an example of additive mixing—only three colors are involved—red, blue, and green. If you look at a color television screen through a magnifying glass, you will notice that a yellow patch of light is actually a combination of tiny red and green dots. Look at the other patches of color on a television screen with a magnifying glass to observe their composition.

subtractive mixture

The mixing of pigments rather than of beams of light.

In contrast, a **subtractive mixture** *of color refers to mixing pigments rather than beams of light.* An artist's painting is an example of subtractive mixing. When blue and yellow are mixed on the television screen, a gray or white hue appears, but, when an artist mixes a dab of blue paint with a dab of yellow paint, the color green is produced. In a subtractive color mixture, each pigment absorbs (subtracts) some of the light falling on it and reflects the rest of the light. When two pigments are mixed, only the light that is not absorbed or subtracted from either one emerges (Wasserman, 1978).

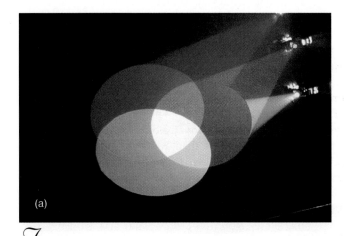

ℱIGURE 3.8

Comparing the Mixing of Light with the Mixing of Pigments

(a) Additive color mixtures occur when lights are mixed. For example, red and green lights when combined yield yellow. The three colors together give white. *(b)* Subtractive color mixtures occur when pigments are mixed or light is shown through colored filters placed over one another. Most of the time, a mixture of blue-green and yellow produces green, and a mixture of complementary colors produces black.

Theories of Color Vision. For centuries scientists have puzzled over how the human eye sees the infinite variety of color in the world. Though we can distinguish among 319 colors, no one believes that we have 319 kinds of cones in our retinas (Bartley, 1969). Instead, even the earliest theorists assumed that our retinas respond to a few primary colors and then relay the information to the brain, where it is synthesized into the many different hues we perceive. However, early theorists disagreed about which colors the retina was selecting. Two main theories were proposed, and each turned out to be right.

The first color vision theory we discuss is based on what you just learned about the three kinds of cone receptors in the retina. The **trichromatic theory** *states that color perception is based on the existence of three types of receptors, each of which is maximally sensitive to different, but overlapping, ranges of wavelengths.* The trichromatic theory of color vision was proposed by Thomas Young in 1802 and extended by Hermann von Helmholtz in 1852. The theory is based on the results of experiments on human color-matching abilities. These experiments

---

trichromatic theory

The theory that color perception is based on the existence of three types of receptors, each of which is maximally sensitive to different, but overlapping, ranges of wavelengths.

Species differ in their ability to see colors. Dogs do not have color vision. Birds, however, can detect bright colors and are attracted to brightly colored flowers.

show that a person with normal vision can match any color in the spectrum by combining three other wavelengths. In this type of experiment, individuals are given a light of a single wavelength and are asked to combine three other single-wavelength lights to match the first light. They can do this by changing the relative intensities of three lights until the color of the combination light is indistinguishable from the color of the first light. Young and Helmholtz reasoned that if the combination of any three wavelengths in different intensities is indistinguishable from any single pure wavelength, the visual system must be basing its perception of color on the relative responses of three receptor systems. To understand how this works, imagine that we have one kind of receptor mechanism for each wavelength in the spectrum of visible light and that each receptor responds to only one wavelength. The color represented by a wavelength of 550 nm would be registered in our visual system whenever the receptor type that was sensitive to 550 nm responded. With this system there is no way to match any color perceptually with any other set of colors, since only one type of receptor response could signal that color. By contrast, with three kinds of receptors that respond best to different overlapping ranges of wavelengths, by adjusting the relative intensities of any combination of three wavelengths we can exactly match the response that is produced for any single wavelength.

These color matching experiments were carried out long before anything was known about the physiological properties of receptors in the retina. The existence of three types of color receptors, or cones, corresponding to green, red, and blue, with different color-sensitive properties was confirmed in the 1960s, more than 100 years after the proposal of the trichromatic theory of color perception (Wald & Brown, 1965)!

Convincing support for the trichromatic theory is found in the study of defective color vision, often referred to as **"color blindness."** The term *color blind* is of somewhat misleading because it suggests that a color-blind person cannot see color at all. Complete color blindness is rare; most people who are color blind, the vast majority of whom are men, can see some colors but not others. The nature of color blindness depends on which of the three kinds of cones (green, red, or blue) is inoperative. For example, in the most common form of color blindness, the green cone system malfunctions in some way. Green is indistinguishable from certain combinations of blue and red. Color-matching experi-

---

color blindness

Defective color vision.

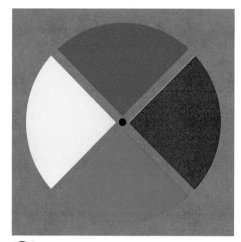

$\mathcal{F}$IGURE 3.9

Negative Afterimage—Complementary Colors

If you gaze steadily at the dot in the colored panel on the left for a few moments, then shift your gaze to the gray box on the right, you will see the original hues change into their complementary colors. The blue appears as yellow, the red as green, the green as red, and the yellow as blue. This pairing of colors has to do with the fact that color receptors in the eye are apparently sensitive as pairs; when one color is turned off (when you stop staring at the panel), the other color in the receptor is briefly "turned on." The afterimage effect is especially noticeable when you spend time painting walls or objects in bright colors.

dichromats

People with only two kinds of cones; they do not have normal color vision.

trichromats

People with normal color vision; they have three kinds of cone receptors.

afterimages

Sensations that remain after a stimulus is removed.

opponent-process theory

The theory that cells in the visual system respond to red-green and blue-yellow colors; a given cell might be excited by red and inhibited by green, while another cell might be excited by yellow and inhibited by blue.

ments performed by people with this form of color blindness show that they need only two other colors to match a pure color and hence have dichromatic color perception. **Dichromats** *are people with only two kinds of cones.* **Trichromats** *are people with normal color vision, and who have three kinds of functional cone receptors.*

The German physiologist Ewald Hering was not completely satisfied with the trichromatic theory of color vision. Hering observed that some colors cannot exist together whereas others can. For example, it is easy to imagine a greenish-blue or a reddish-yellow, but nearly impossible to imagine a reddish-green or a bluish-yellow. Hering also observed that trichromatic theory could not adequately explain **afterimages,** *sensations that remain after a stimulus is removed.* See figure 3.9 to experience an afterimage. Color afterimages are common and they involve complementary colors. Such information led Hering to propose that the visual system treats colors as complementary pairs: red-green and blue-yellow. One example of afterimages that many people are familiar with occurs after prolonged exposure to a computer terminal screen with green lettering, such as those used in many businesses. After working with a computer like this all day, it is not unusual for white objects and walls to appear reddish. Conversely, if you look at red long enough, eventually a green afterimage will appear; if you look at yellow long enough, eventually a blue afterimage will appear.

Hering's view is called **opponent-process theory,** *which states that cells in the visual system respond to red-green and blue-yellow colors; a given cell might be excited by red and inhibited by green, while another cell might be excited by yellow and inhibited by blue.* Researchers have found that opponent-process theory does explain afterimages (Hurvich & Jameson, 1969; Jameson & Hurvich, 1989). If you stare at red, for instance, your red-green system seems to "tire," and when you look away, it rebounds and gives you a green afterimage. Also, if you mix equal amounts of opponent colors, such as blue and yellow, you see gray.

Our tour of the visual system has been an extensive one—you have read about the light spectrum, the structures of the eye, neural visual processing, and the marvels of color vision. Next, you will study the second most researched sensory system, our hearing.

 eview

The Visual System

Light is a form of electromagnetic energy that can be described in terms of wavelengths. The receptors in the human eye are sensitive to wavelengths from 400 to 700 nm. Key external parts of the eye are the sclera, iris, pupil, and cornea. The lens focuses light rays on the retina, the light-sensitive mechanism in the eye. Chemicals in the retina break down light into neural impulses. The optic nerve transmits neural impulses to the brain. Because of the crossover of neural fibers, what we see in the left visual field is registered in the right side of the brain and vice versa. Visual information reaches the occipital lobe of the brain, where it is stored and further integrated. Hubel and Wiesel discovered that neurons in the visual cortex can detect features of our visual world, such as line, angle, and size.

Objects appear colored because they reflect certain wavelengths of light between 400 and 700 nm. Important properties of color are hue, saturation, and brightness. Mixing colors of light involves an additive mixture; mixing pigments involves a subtractive mixture. Scientists have found support for two theories of color vision. The Young-Helmholtz theory states that the retina's cones are sensitive to one of three colors—red, green, or blue. The Young-Helmholtz theory explains color blindness but not afterimages. The opponent-process theory does explain afterimages. It states that information is coded into pairs of opposite colors—blue-yellow or red-green.

The Auditory System

Just as light provides us with information about the environment, so does sound. Think about what life would be like without music, the rushing sound of ocean waves, or the gentle voice of someone you love. Sounds in the world tell us about the approach of a person behind us, an approaching car, the force of the wind outside, the mischief of a 2-year-old, and, perhaps most importantly, about the kinds of information that we transmit through language and song.

The Nature of Sound.   At a rock concert you may have felt the throbbing pulse of loud sounds or sensed that the air around you was vibrating. Bass instruments are especially effective at creating mechanical pulsations, even causing the floor or seat to vibrate on occasion. When a bass is played loudly we can sense air molecules being pushed forward in waves from the speaker. **Sounds,** *or sound waves, are vibrations in the air that are processed by our auditory (or hearing) system.*

Remember that we described light waves as being much like the waves fanned when a pebble is tossed into a lake, with concentric circles moving outward from where the pebble entered the water. Sound waves are similar. They vary in wavelength, which determines the **frequency** *of the sound waves or the number of cycles (or full wavelengths) that pass through a point in a given time* (see figure 3.10). **Pitch** *is the perceptual interpretation of the frequency of sound.* High-frequency sounds are perceived as having a high pitch, low-frequency sounds are perceived as having a low pitch. A soprano voice sounds high-pitched, a bass voice sounds low-pitched. As with the wavelengths of light, human sensitivity is limited to a range of sound frequencies. It is common knowledge that dogs, for example, can hear higher frequencies than humans can.

Sound waves vary not only in frequency, but also in amplitude. The sound wave's **amplitude** *is measured in decibels (dB), the amount of pressure produced by a sound wave relative to a standard;* the typical standard is the weakest sound the human ear can detect. Thus, zero decibels would be the softest noise detectable by humans. Noise rated at 80 decibels or higher, if heard for prolonged periods of time, can cause permanent hearing loss. A quiet library is about 40 decibels, a car horn about 90 decibels, a rock band at close range 120 decibels, and a rocket launching 180 decibels. **Loudness** *is the perception of a sound wave's amplitude.* In general, the higher the amplitude of the sound wave, the louder the sound is perceived to be. In the world of amplitude, this means that air is moving rapidly for loud sounds and slowly for soft sounds.

So far we have been describing a single sound wave with just one frequency. This is similar to the single-wavelength, or pure colored, light we just discussed in the context

sounds

Vibrations of air that are processed by the auditory (hearing) system; also called sound waves.

frequency

With respect to sound waves, the number of cycles (full wavelengths) that pass through a point in a given time.

pitch

The perceptual interpretation of sound's frequency.

amplitude

Measured in decibels (dB), the amount of pressure produced by a sound wave relative to a standard.

loudness

The perception of a sound wave's amplitude.

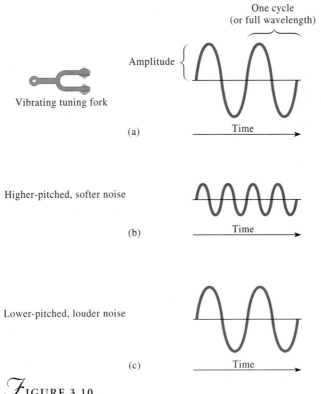

One cycle
(or full wavelength)

Amplitude

Vibrating tuning fork

(a)

Time

Higher-pitched, softer noise

(b)

Time

Lower-pitched, louder noise

(c)

Time

$\mathcal{F}$IGURE 3.10

Frequency and Amplitude of Sound Waves

(a) A tuning fork is an instrument with two prongs that produces a tone when struck. You may have seen one in a music classroom or science laboratory. The vibrations of the tuning fork cause air molecules to vibrate like a musical instrument, producing a sound wave pattern like the one shown. Wavelength determines the frequency of the sound wave, which is the number cycles, or full wavelengths, that can pass through a point in a given time. In the tuning fork example, two cycles (full wavelengths) have occurred in the time frame shown. *(b)* In the sound wave shown here, four cycles have occurred in this time frame, so this sound wave has a higher frequency than the sound wave with the tuning fork; hence, it has a higher pitch. Its small amplitude is indicative of softer sounds. The amplitude of the sound wave is the change in pressure created by the sound wave and is reflected in the sound wave's height. *(c)* This sound wave has a larger amplitude than the sound wave shown with the tuning fork; thus, it sounds louder. The reduced frequency of the wave indicates a lower pitch.

of color matching. Most sounds, however, including those of speech and music, are complex sounds. **Complex sounds** *are those in which numerous frequencies of sound blend together.* **Timbre** *is the tone color or perceptual quality of a sound.* Timbre differences are what make the difference between a trumpet and a trombone playing the same note, and are also responsible for the quality differences we hear between human voices.

Structures and Functions of the Ear. What happens to sound waves once they reach your ear? How do various structures of the ear transform sound waves of expanded and compressed air so they can be understood by the brain as sound? The function of the ear is analogous to the function of the eye. The ear serves the purpose of transmitting a high-fidelity version of sounds in the world to the brain for analysis and interpretation. Just as an image needs to be in focus and sufficiently bright for the brain to interpret it, a sound needs to be transmitted in a way that preserves information about its location (think how confusing life would be if you could hear sounds without being able to determine where they are coming from!); its frequency, which helps us distinguish the voice of a child from that of an adult; and its timbre, which allows us to identify the voice of a friend on the telephone.

The ear is divided into the *outer ear, middle ear,* and *inner ear* (the major structures of the ear are shown in figure 3.11). The **outer ear** *consists of the pinna and the external auditory canal.* The pinna is the outer visible part of the ear (elephants have very large

complex sounds

Sounds in which numerous frequencies of sound blend together.

timbre

The tone color or perceptual quality of a sound.

outer ear

The pinna and the external auditory canal.

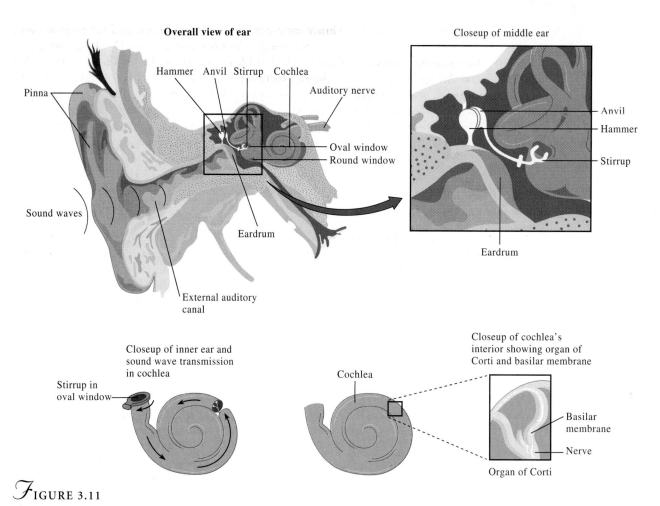

Overall view of ear

Pinna

Hammer Anvil Stirrup Cochlea

Auditory nerve

Oval window
Round window

Sound waves

Eardrum

External auditory
canal

Closeup of middle ear

Anvil
Hammer

Stirrup

Eardrum

Closeup of inner ear and
sound wave transmission
in cochlea

Stirrup in
oval window

Cochlea

Closeup of cochlea's
interior showing organ of
Corti and basilar membrane

Basilar
membrane

Nerve

Organ of Corti

ℱIGURE 3.11

Major Structures of the Human Ear and the Transmission of Sound Waves

Sound waves are funneled through the external auditory canal to the eardrum in the middle ear. Three bony structures in the middle ear—hammer, anvil, and stirrup—concentrate sound waves so they can be further processed in the inner ear. The stirrup relays the eardrum's vibrations through the oval window to the cochlea, a snail-like, fluid-filled structure, where sound waves are further processed before the auditory information moves on to the auditory nerve to be transmitted to the brain. The organ of Corti runs the entire length of the cochlea and contains the basilar membrane at its base. The movement of sound waves in the cochlear fluid causes the basilar membrane to vibrate and its hair cells to bend. The vibrating hair cells stimulate nearby nerve cells, which join to form the auditory nerve.

middle ear

An area of the ear with these four main parts: eardrum, hammer, anvil, and stirrup.

ones). Its shape helps us to localize sounds by making the sound different in front of us than behind us. The pinnae of many animals such as dogs are movable and serve a more important role in sound localization than do the pinnae of humans. Dogs will prick up their ears toward the direction of a faint and interesting sound.

After passing the pinna, sound waves are then funneled through the external auditory canal to the middle ear. The **middle ear** *has four main parts: eardrum, hammer, anvil, and stirrup.* The *eardrum* is the first structure that sound touches in the middle ear. The eardrum is a membrane that vibrates in response to a sound. The vibrations are then transmitted by the three smallest bones in the human body—the hammer, anvil, and stirrup—to the inner ear. The middle ear bones translate the sound waves in air into sound waves in fluid (lymph) so they can be processed further in the inner ear. Most us know that sound travels far more easily in air than in fluids. When we are swimming underwater, loud shouts from the side of the pool are barely detectable to us. Sound waves entering the ear travel in air until they reach the inner ear, at which point they begin to be transmitted through body fluids. At this border between air and fluid, sounds meet the same kind of resistance that shouts directed at an underwater swimmer meet when they hit the surface of the water. The hammer, anvil, and stirrup form a connected chain of bones that act like a lever to amplify the sound waves before they reach the liquid-filled inner ear.

92   *Chapter 3   Sensation and Perception*

inner ear

The oval window, cochlea, and
organ of Corti.

cochlea

A long, tubular, fluid-filled structure in the inner ear that is coiled
up like a snail.

basilar membrane

A membrane that is housed inside
the cochlea and runs its entire
length.

organ of Corti

A part of the ear that runs the
length of the cochlea and sits on
the basilar membrane. It contains
the ear's sensory receptors, which
change the energy of sound waves
into nerve impulses that can be
processed by the brain.

place theory

The theory of hearing that states
that each frequency produces vibrations at a particular spot on the
basilar membrane.

frequency theory

The theory of hearing that states
that the perception of a sound's
frequency is due to how often the
auditory nerve fires.

volley theory

The theory of hearing that states
that high frequencies can be signaled by teams of neurons that fire
at different offset times to create an
overall firing rate that could signal
a very high frequency.

auditory nerve

The nerve that carries neural impulses to the brain's auditory areas.

The main parts of the **inner ear** *are the oval window, cochlea, and the organ of Corti.* The stirrup is connected to the *oval window,* which is a membrane like the eardrum and transmits the waves to the cochlea. The **cochlea** *is a long tubular fluid-filled structure that is coiled up like a snail.* The **basilar membrane** *is housed inside the cochlea and runs its entire length.* The **organ of Corti,** *also running the length of the cochlea, sits on the basilar membrane and contains the ear's sensory receptors, which change the energy of the sound waves into nerve impulses that can be processed by the brain.* Hairlike sensory receptors in the organ of Corti are stimulated by vibrations of the basilar membrane. Sound waves traveling in the fluid of the inner ear cause these hairlike receptors to move. The movement generates nerve impulses, which vary with the frequency and extent of the membrane's vibrations. These nerve impulses are interpreted as sound by the brain.

One of the auditory system's mysteries is how the inner ear registers the frequency of sound. Two theories have been proposed to explain this mystery: place theory and frequency theory. **Place theory** *is a theory of hearing that states that each frequency produces vibrations at a particular spot on the basilar membrane.* Georg von Békésy won a Nobel Prize in 1961 for his research on the basilar membrane. Von Békésy (1960) studied the effects of vibration applied at the oval window on the basilar membrane of human cadavers. Through a microscope, he saw that this stimulation produced a traveling wave on the basilar membrane. A traveling wave is like the ripples that appear in a pond when you throw in a stone. However, since the cochlea is a long tube, the ripples can travel only in one direction, from the end of the cochlea, where the oval window is located, to the far tip of the cochlea. High-frequency vibrations create traveling waves that maximally displace (or move) the area of the basilar membrane next to the oval window; low-frequency vibrations maximally displace areas of the membrane closer to the tip of the cochlea.

Place theory adequately explains high-frequency sounds but fares poorly with low-frequency sounds. A high-frequency sound stimulates a very precise area on the basilar membrane. By contrast, a low-frequency sound causes a large part of the basilar membrane to be displaced, so it is hard to localize the "maximal displacement" of the basilar membrane. Because humans can hear low-frequency sounds better than can be predicted by looking at the precision of the basilar membrane's response to these sounds, some other factors must be involved. **Frequency theory** *states that the perception of a sound's frequency is due to how often the auditory nerve fires.* Higher-frequency sounds cause the auditory nerve to fire more often than lower frequency sounds do. One problem with frequency theory is that a single neuron has a maximum firing rate of about 1,000 times per second. Because of this limitation, frequency theory cannot be applied to tones with frequencies that would require a neuron to fire more than 1,000 times per second.

To deal with this limitation, a modification of place theory called **volley theory** *states that high frequencies can be signaled by teams of neurons that fire at different offset times to create an overall firing rate that could signal a very high frequency.* The term *volley* was used because the neurons fire in a sequence of rhythmic volleys at higher frequencies. The alteration in neural firing makes possible perception of frequencies above 1,000 times per second. Thus, frequency theory can better explain the perception of low-frequency sounds, and place theory can better explain the perception of high-frequency sounds. There is some evidence that the auditory system uses both place and frequency theory (Goldstein, 1994). And so, it is possible that both are correct but that sounds of high and low frequencies might be signaled with different coding schemes.

Neural-Auditory Processing. As we saw in the visual system, once energy from the environment is picked up by our receptors, it must be transmitted to the brain for processing and interpretation. An image on the retina does not a Picasso make—likewise, a pattern of receptor responses in the cochlea does not a symphony make! In the retina, we saw that the responses of the rod and cone receptors feed into ganglion cells in the retina and leave the eye via the optic nerve. In the auditory system, the **auditory nerve** *carries neural impulses to the brain's auditory areas.* Auditory information moves up the auditory pathway in a more complex manner than does visual information in the visual pathway. Many synapses occur in the ascending auditory pathway, with some fibers crossing over the midline and others proceeding directly to the hemisphere on the same side as the ear of reception. The auditory nerve extends from the cochlea to the brain stem, with some fibers crossing over the midline. The cortical destination of most of these fibers is the temporal lobes of the brain (beneath the temples of the head).

> It is extraordinary how music sends one back into memories of the past—and it is the same with smells.
>
> —GEORGE SAND, *French Writer, 19th Century*

Now that we have described the visual and auditory systems in some detail, we turn to the other sensory systems—the skin senses, the chemical senses (smell and taste), the kinesthetic senses, and the vestibular sense.

The Haptic System

You are at an amusement park. Your mouth and fingers feel sticky from the cotton candy you just ate. The sun is hot, warming your skin and scalp. A cool breeze softens the effect of the sun. Eager to get in line for the loop-to-loop ride, you grab your partner's hand. It is cold and clammy. As you strap yourself into your seat, you feel the pressure of the special harness as you wonder for just a moment whether this was such a good idea. In just moments, you'll be upside down, feeling the force of gravity and counterforce. At ride's end, you will feel exhilarated or nauseated. All of these sensations involve the touch, kinesthetic, and vestibular senses of the haptic system. According to J. J. Gibson (1966), the haptic system provides information about the body in relation to its environment.

Touch. Many of us think of our skin as a canvas rather than a sensory organ. We color it with cosmetics, dyes, and tattoos. We modify it with face lifts, hair transplants, and fake fingernails. The skin is an efficient container for our internal organs. It is "waterproof, dustproof, and miraculously—until we grow old—always the right size" (Montague, 1971, p. 5). Although we usually don't realize it, the skin is actually our largest sensory system. It drapes over the body with receptors for pressure, temperature, and pain.

With a rubber band, lightly touch the following parts of your body: the bottom of your foot, your leg, your nose, and your forefinger. You should be able to sense that these different parts of your body do not have the same sensitivity to touch. The body's most sensitive areas are in the head region (nose and upper lip, for example), and the least sensitive areas are in the foot region (sole of the foot, for example) (Weinstein, 1968). Women are more sensitive to touch over most of their bodies than men are.

Temperature. Do you feel too hot or too cold right now, or do you feel about right? Our bodies have a regulatory system that keeps the body's temperature at about 98.6 degrees Fahrenheit, and the skin plays an important role in this regulatory system. Some years ago, it was found that we have separate locations on our skin that sense warmth and cold (Dallenbach, 1927). The forehead is especially sensitive to heat, the arm is less sensitive, and the calf is the least sensitive.

Pain. For all living things, avoiding harm is critical for a strategy of survival, and pain is part of that strategy. Pain is information that warns us, protects us, and instructs us about what is harmful in the world. The importance of pain for humans is clearly illustrated by 7-year-old Sarah, who was born with an insensitivity to pain. She constantly hurts herself but does not realize it. A wound on her knee is protected from further harm by a cast on her leg. Her arm is bandaged to heal a bruise on her elbow. Sarah has something wrong with the nerve pathways that normally transmit signals to the brain that it interprets as pain.

Aside from a few people like Sarah, we all experience pain. Even so, we can never be sure whether another person is experiencing pain. You might infer from her expression or behavior that your friend is in pain, but you cannot directly experience her pain.

pain threshold

The stimulation level at which pain is first perceived.

Many stimuli can cause pain. Pain can be caused by intense stimulation of any one of our senses—too much light, very loud sounds, extreme temperatures, for example. However, like other perceptions, our perception of pain reflects our subjective judgments. Among other factors, our expectations, moods, and body's makeup influence how we perceive pain. If we expect something to hurt us, we are more likely to perceive pain, and if our body has a weak spot, we are more likely to experience pain there. **Pain threshold** *is the stimulation level at which pain is first perceived.* Because our perception of pain reflects subjective judgments, pain thresholds vary considerably from one person to another, from one point in time to another, and from one cultural group to another. Information about cultural and ethnic variations in reaction to pain appears in Sociocultural Worlds.

How is pain transmitted to the brain? Consider the situation when you miss a nail with a hammer and smash your thumb—it almost hurts just to think about it. The pain message begins with the release of chemicals usually found in or near the nerve endings in the skin (among these are chemicals known as substance P and bradykinin). These chemicals sensitize the nerve endings and help transmit the pain message from your thumb to your brain. The pain signal is converted into a series of electrochemical impulses that travel through the peripheral nervous system to the central nervous system and up the spinal cord. From there the pain signal becomes a cascade of chemical messages as it relays through the brain to the thalamus. Then, the pain message is routed to the cerebral cortex, where the pain's intensity and specific location are identified. It is also in the cerebral cortex that the pain is symbolically interpreted. In the case of martyrs and patriots, the pain may even be welcome (Restak, 1988). In our case of hitting the thumb with a hammer, it is undoubtedly not welcome. One other important fact about afferent information processing is that sound is processed faster than touch is. The crunch of the thumb beneath the hammer will be heard before the pain is felt.

gate-control theory

The theory that the spinal column contains a neural gate that can be opened (allowing the perception of pain) or closed (blocking the perception of pain).

Although pain messages are interpreted in the brain, understanding how we experience pain involves a closer look at the spinal cord. Ronald Melzack and Patrick Wall (1965, 1983) pointed out that the nervous system can process only a limited amount of sensory information of any kind—pain, touch, or anything else—at a given moment. They discovered that, when too much information moves through the nervous system, certain neural cells in the spinal column stop the signal. **Gate-control theory** *is Melzack and Wall's theory that the spinal column contains a neural "gate" that can be opened (allowing the perception of pain) or closed (blocking the perception of pain).* In the case of the throbbing thumb you hammered, you quickly grab a bunch of ice cubes and press them against your thumb. The pain lessens. According to gate-control theory (see figure 3.12), the ice sent signals to the spinal cord and slammed the gate in the face of competing pain signals. The brain also, in turn, can send information down the spinal cord and influence whether a gate is open or closed. In this way, emotions, attitudes, hypnosis, and neurotransmitters can influence how much pain we sense. The gate in gate-control theory is not a physical gate that opens and shuts; rather, the gate is the inhibition of neural impulses.

acupuncture

A technique in which thin needles are inserted at specific points in the body to produce effects such as local anesthesia.

When the spinal cord receives a strong peripheral signal, such as the prick of an acupuncture needle, it, too, can turn on the interneuron and close the gate. **Acupuncture** *is a technique in which thin needles are inserted at specific points in the body to relieve specific symptoms* (see figure 3.13). Interestingly, the point of stimulation may be some distance from the symptom being treated. For example, when acupuncture is used as an anesthetic in abdominal surgery, four acupuncture needles are placed in the pinna of each ear. Although acupuncture is still considered somewhat unorthodox in the United States, the technique is used widely in China in dentistry and occasionally in abdominal surgery. How does acupuncture reduce the sensation of pain? The gate-control mechanisms may be partly responsible, and neurotransmitters, such as endorphins, might also play a role. To read further about ways to reduce pain, see Improving Personal and Cognitive Skills ("Overcoming Acute Pain").

> *Physical pain however great ends in itself and falls away like dry husks from the mind whilst moral discords and nervous horrors sear the soul.*
> —ALICE JAMES, *American Writer, 19th Century*

Sociocultural Worlds

Cultural and Ethnic Differences in Reactions to Pain

In a remote village, a cart slowly wends its way along a dusty road. A man swings from a pole in the cart; ropes from two large steel hooks embedded in the man's back attach him to the pole. The man is not being punished or tortured; he is blessing the children and crops in a centuries-old ritual practiced in certain parts of India. His role is an honor. The man does not seem to be suffering; instead, he appears to be in a state of exaltation. What's more, his wounds heal rapidly after the hooks are removed, even with little medical treatment (see figure 3.A).

How does the man unflinchingly withstand such pain? Experiences such as these have been described as hypnotic, inducing an altered state of consciousness (which is discussed extensively in chapter 4). Aside from culturally variant religious roles, studies of several ethnic and cultural groups have shown differences in how people in more usual states of mind react to pain. In one investigation, Jewish patients tended to postpone taking an analgesic until after the determination of their diagnosis and future prognosis, whereas Italian patients were more likely to request immediate pain relief (Weisenberg, 1982).

Another example of cultural differences regarding pain is how Haitian Americans react to both familiar and unfamiliar symptoms. Any symptom that resembles an illness a relative died from, for instance, is a red flag for Haitian Americans to seek medical attention immediately. Conversely, they are likely to dismiss any sign of illness if there is no family history of that particular symptom. For example, Joseph, a Haitian American teacher from Port-au-Prince who migrated to New York, had no family history of diabetes; his diabetic condition remained undiagnosed until he fell into a coma and was hospitalized (Laguerre, 1981).

Stoicism, or resistance to emotion, may also have cultural roots. Both Navajo and Chinese American patients have been described as "stoic." Navajos and Chinese Americans may be reluctant to breach the barriers between their culture and Western medical practices. This reluctance might keep them from seeking medical assistance and might increase their psychological tolerance of pain. Their impassive demeanor might be learned: As they observe how others react, they adopt the culturally appropriate response to pain.

Social class might be another factor that influences a person's ideas about illness and wellness. People from poor neighborhoods might not have access to adequate health care through an HMO or good health insurance. As a result, they might adapt to a higher threshold to define unbearable pain. For example, a person who must take a day off from work without pay, find a physician or clinic, and pay immediately for medical services might wait until a symptom becomes severe before seeking treatment.

Although cross-cultural research on the perception of pain may yield some intriguing findings, several caveats are warranted. First, even when differences among groups are found, as in the comparison between Jewish and Italian patients, there are differences within groups as well. Not all of the Italian patients in the study moaned, groaned, and wanted immediate medication—many did, but some did not. Second, many studies on cultural and ethnic variations in reactions to pain are based on findings from a small number of people who are not always carefully selected to be truly comparable on all dimensions except the one difference the researcher is studying. Third, researchers in this area have not attended to the effects of mixing cultures. For instance, are Italians who live in the Little Italy section of an urban area more likely to show a desire for early medication than Italians who live in more integrated areas?

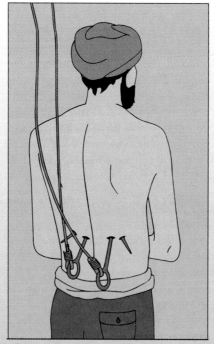
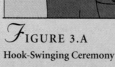

ℱIGURE 3.A

Hook-Swinging Ceremony

(Left) Two steel hooks are inserted into the back of an Asian Indian participating in a hook-swinging ceremony. *(Right)* The man hangs onto ropes as a cart takes him from village to village. After he blesses each child and farm field in the village, he swings freely, suspended by the hooks in his back.

FIGURE 3.12

Gate-Control Theory of Pain

(a) When you hit your thumb with a hammer, pain signals travel along afferent neurons to the *(b)* inter-neurons (special neurons that mediate sensory input and motor output) in the spinal cord and then on to *(c)* the sensory cortex of the parietal lobe of the cerebral cortex. Gate-control theory suggests that pain can be mediated by applying a peripheral stimulus (such as acupuncture) that sends competing information coming into the spinal cord. This turns on the interneuron and closes the gate in the pain pathway. The gate can also be closed by other kinds of signals coming down the spinal cord from the brain. For example, hypnosis and the excitement of athletic competition can also close the gate.

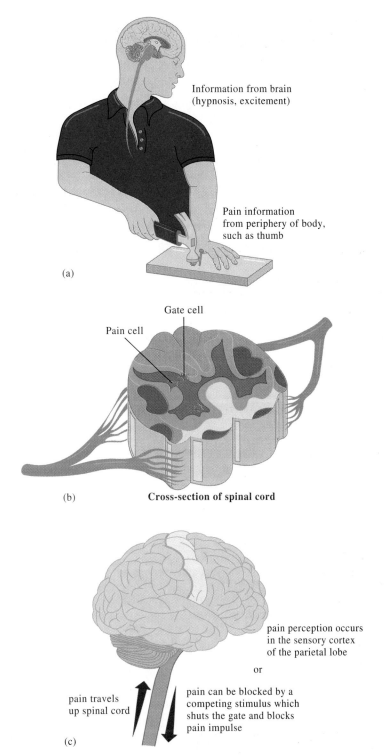

Information from brain (hypnosis, excitement)

Pain information from periphery of body, such as thumb

(a)

Gate cell

Pain cell

(b)   **Cross-section of spinal cord**

pain perception occurs in the sensory cortex of the parietal lobe

or

pain travels up spinal cord

pain can be blocked by a competing stimulus which shuts the gate and blocks pain impulse

(c)

kinesthetic senses

Senses that provide information about movement, posture, and orientation.

vestibular sense

The sense that provides information about balance and movement.

semicircular canals

Canals in the inner ear that contain the sensory receptors that detect body motion, such as tilting of the head or body.

The Kinesthetic and Vestibular Senses. Your body has two kinds of senses that provide information to your brain about your movement and orientation in space: **kinesthetic senses** *provide information about movement, posture, and orientation,* and the **vestibular sense** *provides information about balance and movement.* The vestibular sense tells you whether your body is tilted, moving, slowing down, or speeding up. It works in concert with the kinesthetic senses to coordinate your proprioceptive feedback, which is the information about the position of your limbs and body parts in relation to other body parts. The **semicircular canals,** *located in the inner ear, contain sensory receptors that detect body motion, such as tilting of the head or body* (see figure 3.14). These canals consist of three circular tubes that lie

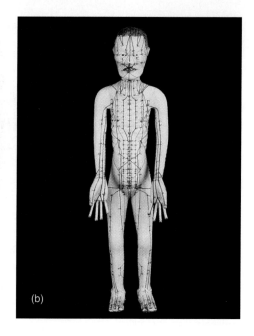

$\mathcal{F}$IGURE 3.13

Acupuncture

(a) A woman is being treated for pain by an acupuncturist. *(b)* Acupuncture points are carefully noted on this nineteenth-century Japanese papier-mâché figure. In their adaptation of the Chinese methodology, the Japanese identified 660 points.

(a)

(b)

in three planes of the body—left-right, up-down, and front-back. The tubes provide feedback to the brain when the body or head tilts in one of these three directions.

Because the semicircular canals and the vestibular sense inform us about our equilibrium, this sense is sometimes called the *equilibratory sense.* The most accepted view of why we are able to maintain our equilibrium and orientation is that the brain is constantly receiving information about the body's motion and position from three sources: the inner ear, the eyes, and other sensors in various parts of the body. Information from these sources is fed into the brain, which compares it with stored information about motion and position. There are occasions when we might wish our equilibratory sense were not so sensitive. When motion sickness occurs, these various sources send contradictory messages. For example, passengers on a ship's deck can see the rail of the ship ris-

$\mathcal{I}$mproving Personal and Cognitive Skills

Overcoming Acute Pain

Pain is one of our most valuable sensory features. Without the ability to feel pain, we would be in constant danger, because pain signals that something is physically wrong. In contrast to other kinds of sensory stimulation, pain does not habituate. *Acute pain,* which involves intense and time-limited pain reactions to physical damage, demands attention—a bandage, a trip to the emergency room, a visit with the dentist—to address the source of pain. However, when you have taken the available medical steps to fix the problem, the pain may linger. Beyond aspirin and acupuncture, what are some behavioral methods for managing acute pain?

- *Distraction.* When you must receive an injection, do you focus on the needle as it is about to plunge into your flesh? Or do you avert your eyes and concentrate on something else? The latter strategy is likely to be more helpful in reducing pain, because attention can magnify the sensation.

- *Focused breathing.* The next time you stub your toe, try breathing in short, fast breaths (similar to the breathing practiced in Lamaze childbirth classes). Focused breathing may successfully close the pain gate and diminish your agony.

- *Relaxation.* Creating a relaxed response despite pain combines the previous techniques with a sense of control over your body that can reduce pain. You can learn relaxation procedures from a relaxation audiotape that will train you on how to progressively relax muscle groups in your body until you can use the skill on your own.

- *Counterstimulation.* If you pinch your cheek in the aftermath of a bad cut, you will mute your pain. By offering counterstimulation, you can close the pain gate in the spinal cord. Applying ice to a sprained or swollen area not only reduces pain but can keep the swelling down.

- *Hypnosis.* Hypnosis does appear to offer relief from acute pain, though it is less clear how effective it is for chronic pain.

ing and falling as they watch the waves. The roll of the deck makes them feel like they are riding a roller coaster. The brain is not accustomed to all of this contradictory information. Over time, though, the brain recognizes that stored information is no longer relevant to the current discordant input. Two to three days usually is long enough to adjust to sensory conflict, but it can take longer.

The Chemical System

In the spring of 1985, a group of chemists practically turned American society upside down simply by shifting a few carbon, hydrogen, and oxygen atoms, or so it seemed when the Coca-Cola Company changed the formula for Coke. The uproar forced the company to bring back the original flavor that summer—even after spending millions of dollars

*F*IGURE 3.14

The Semicircular Canals and Vestibular Sense

(a) This is a photograph of the semicircular canals located in the ear. The semicircular canals play an important role in the vestibular sense. The three canals are roughly perpendicular to each other in three planes of space. Any angle of head rotation is registered by hair cells in one or more semicircular canals in both ears. *(b)* The semicircular canals provide feedback to this gymnast's brain as her body and head tilt in different directions.

advertising the virtues of the new Coke. The chemists at the Coca-Cola Company were dealing with the savor system, comprised of taste (gustation) and smell (olfaction). Both taste and smell differ from other senses—seeing, hearing, and the skin senses, for example—because they react to *chemicals,* whereas other senses react to *energy.* Together, smell and taste determine the flavors we experience when we ingest food and drink.

Taste. It won't be the prettiest sight you've ever seen, but try this anyway. Take a drink of milk and allow it to coat your tongue. Then go to a mirror, stick out your tongue, and look carefully at its surface. You should be able to see rounded bumps above the surface of your tongue (Matlin, 1983). Those bumps, called **papillae**, *contain your taste buds, the receptors for the taste sense.* Although the quantities of taste buds vary, taste buds are distributed on your tongue, around your mouth, and even in your throat.

Taste buds respond to four main qualities: sweet, bitter, salty, and sour. All areas of the tongue can detect each of these four tastes. Although many researchers have attempted to map zones of sensitivity on the tongue, clinical cases suggest that such concentrated areas do not exist. For example, individuals who have lost their tongues to cancer surgery still report taste sensitivity, which would not be possible if the tongue were more specialized in its transduction of the characteristics of food (Bartoshuk, 1994).

The efficiency of taste buds seems to vary according to genetic inheritance. For example, some individuals cannot tolerate sodas because of a heightened sensitivity to a bitter aftertaste. Others might happily guzzle the soda with no experience of an aftertaste. Research on these sensitivities has identified three categories of response to bitter tastes: nontasters, tasters, and supertasters, who show heightened responsiveness to bitter stimuli.

Babies are born with an innate preference for sweet tastes and a dislike of bitter substances. In addition, women appear to have greater sensitivity to sweet and bitter substances when they are pregnant or menstruating, suggesting that estrogen may be implicated in this gender-linked sensitivity. This causal relation is supported by initial observations that elderly women seem to have fewer papillae, reducing their effectiveness in sensing food characteristics (Bartoshuk, 1994). Older individuals' loss of interest in food could be the natural consequence of deteriorating taste bud responsiveness. This developmental outcome might explain why older individuals season their foods more heavily—as compensation for their diminished ability to taste.

Smell. Smell is an important but mysterious sense. We take the time to see a sunset or a play, to hear a symphony or a rock concert, and to feel the tension leave our muscles during a massage. However, many of us do not take the time to indulge our sense of smell (Matlin, 1988). Smell can kindle pleasure or trigger discomfort—when we inhale the aroma of a fresh flower or when we encounter a skunk, for example. The nose actually serves two purposes. We sample the air from the outside world when we smell the scent of a fresh flower or the distinctly unpleasant aroma of the skunk. But we also sample the air from the inside of the mouth to enhance the taste of wine or the goodness of chocolate.

We detect the scent of a fresh flower or a skunk when airborne molecules of an odor reach tiny receptor cells in the roof of the nasal cavity. The **olfactory epithelium,** *located at the top of the nasal cavity, is the sheet of receptor cells for smell.* These receptor sites are covered with millions of minute, hairlike antennae that project through mucus in the nasal cavity and make contact with air on its way to the throat and lungs. Ordinarily only a small part of the air you inhale passes the smell receptors. That is why we sometimes have to sniff deeply to get the full odor of an interesting or alarming smell—the bouquet of a fine wine or the odor of escaping gas, for example. Doing so changes the normal flow of air so that more air, with its odorous molecules, contacts the receptors.

You just read about how taste can be classified into four main categories: sweet, sour, salty, and bitter. Are there agreed-upon main categories of odors too? Some researchers argue that there are seven primary odors—floral, peppermint, ethereal (as in the gas ether), musky, camphoraceous (such as the odor of mothballs), pungent, and putrid (Amoore, 1970). However, the consensus is that olfactory researchers have yet to demon-

papillae
Bumps on the surface of the tongue that contain taste buds, which are the receptors for taste.

olfactory epithelium
Tissue located at the top of the nasal cavity that contains a sheet of receptor cells for smell.

strate that different categories of smell have distinct chemical makeups and receptor sites on the olfactory epithelium.

Unlike the sense of taste, in which infants show immediate preferences at birth and even in utero, babies do not show innate preferences for smell. Preferences for smell must be learned from consequences or by modeling (Bartoshuk, 1994).

> *Smell is the potent wizard that transports us across thousands of miles and all the years we have lived.*
>
> —HELEN KELLER, *American Essayist, 20th Century*

How good are you at recognizing smells? Without practice, most people do a rather poor job of identifying odors; however, the human olfactory sense can be improved. Perfumers, as perfume testers are called, can distinguish between 100 and 200 fragrances. If you have or have had a dog, though, you probably know that canines have a keener sense of smell than humans do. One reason is that a dog's smell receptors are located along the main airflow route and its smell-receptor sites are 100 times larger than a human's.

We have examined all the sensory systems that bring stimulation from the environment to the brain for further processing. Next, we will explore the nature of perception, by which we give meaning to the sensations we experience.

The Auditory System, the Haptic System, and the Chemical System

Sound waves vary in frequency, amplitude, and complexity; the perceptions are pitch, loudness, and timbre, respectively. The ear comprises the outer ear, the middle ear, and the inner ear. The basilar membrane, located inside the cochlea in the inner ear, is where vibrations are changed into nerve impulses. There are three main theories of hearing. Place theory emphasizes a particular place on the basilar membrane; frequency theory stresses the frequency of auditory nerve firing; and volley theory is a modification and expansion of frequency theory to handle high-frequency sounds. Frequency theory is better for explaining lower-frequency sounds, volley and place theories for higher-frequency sounds.

The haptic system involves touch, the kinesthetic senses, and the vestibular sense. Skin contains three important senses: pressure, temperature (warmth, cold), and pain. Pain has the important adaptive function of informing us when something is wrong with our body. No theory of pain is completely accepted. Gate-control theory has been given considerable weight. The kinesthetic senses provide information about movement, posture, and orientation. The vestibular sense provides information about balance and movement. The chemical senses—taste and smell—differ from other senses in that they react to chemicals rather than energy.

PERCEPTION

Earlier in this chapter, you learned that perception is the brain's process of organizing and interpreting sensory information to give it meaning. When perception goes to work, sensory receptors have received energy from stimuli in the external world and sensory organs have processed and transformed the information so it can be transmitted to the brain. Perception is a creation of the brain; it is based on input from sensory organs, such as the eye, ear, and nose. However, perception goes beyond this input. The brain uses previous information as a basis for making educated guesses, or interpretations, about the state of the outside world. Usually the interpretations are accurate and useful. For example, on the basis of a continuous increase in size, we can conclude that a train is coming toward us. Sometimes, though, the interpretations or inferences are wrong; the result is an illusion—we see something that is not there. To evaluate your perceptual expectations, see Improving Personal and Cognitive Skills ("Breaking Academic Perceptual Sets"). Our exploration of perceptual worlds evaluates the following questions: How do we perceive shape, depth, motion, and constancy? What are perceptual illusions and why do we see these illusions? Is perception innate or learned? What is extrasensory perception? Is it real?

*I*mproving Personal and Cognitive Skills

Breaking Academic Perceptual Sets

According to psychologist Ellen Langer (1997), students are inclined to develop "mindlessness" when their well-learned lessons—or *perceptual sets*—restrict rather than help their learning. Langer describes mindlessness as "hardening of the categories" or inflexible mindsets that people use to govern their own behavior. Mindful learning involves the willingness to create new categories, accept new information, and examine ideas from more than one perspective. Langer recommends the following actions to overcome the stifling effects of perceptual sets about learning:

- *Practice doesn't always make perfect.* Beware of the downside of overlearning a task. For example, overlearning a piano solo can result in a mechanical, lifeless performance. An overrehearsed speech also is likely to be lifeless and unmoving.
- *Pay attention using "soft vigilance."* Focusing intensely on one thing at a time creates a static, too-stable atmosphere. Varying the target of your attention can encourage a more creative response.

- *Rethink work versus play.* By categorizing one set of activities as "work" and another as "play," you encourage negativity in relation to the activities you categorize as work. Nearly any activity—even studying—can be more pleasurable if you adopt a positive attitude.
- *Recognize the advantages of forgetting.* Rather than punish yourself for your bad memory or absentmindedness, reconsider the value of forgetting. Because you forget, you can reexperience forgotten pleasures all over again. Forgetting also allows you not to be tormented by painful experiences.
- *Travel when you can.* Immersing yourself in another culture can make you question many of the commonplace practices and values in your own culture—such as driving patterns, eating practices, and friendship choice. Your college program may offer travel opportunities that will challenge the perceptual sets you have developed about how people ought to live and behave.

Principles of Perception

Whether we are organizing the diverse sounds of the instruments of an orchestra to appreciate a movement in a symphony or interpreting the complex visual action of a soccer game, perception determines how we will experience the environment. Perceptual processes, regardless of the sensory mode in which they operate, have four characteristics; they are *automatic, selective, contextual,* and *creative.* We do not have to be purposeful in organizing our sensory input. It happens *automatically.* Quickly read aloud the phrase in the triangle in figure 3.15 for an illustration of this characteristic. Perceptual preferences tend to influence what we experience, leading to perceptual *selectivity.* Leaving out a portion of the message within the triangle demonstrates how selective we can be. Perception is *contextual* and *creative.* Our expectations that we will be scared in a haunted house enhance our fearful reactions to the sights and sounds within, as our imagination dreams up frightful possibilities. In total, these characteristics contribute to the development of a

*F*IGURE 3.15

A Demonstration of the Automatic and Selective Qualities of Perception

Are you certain you read the contents accurately? How many words are in the triangle?

perceptual set

Expectations that influence how perceptual elements will be interpreted.

contour

A location at which a sudden change of brightness occurs.

figure-ground relationship

The principle by which we organize the perceptual field into stimuli that stand out (figure) and those that are left over (ground).

perceptual set, *expectations that influence how perceptual elements will be interpreted.* Perceptual sets act as filters as we process information about the environment. The Self-Assessment shows you an example of how expectations influence perception.

> *Blessed is he who expects nothing, for he shall never be disappointed.*
> —JONATHAN SWIFT, *English Satirist, 17th/18th Century*

Shape Perception.   Think about the world you see and its shapes—buildings against the sky, boats on the horizon, letters on this page. We see these shapes because they are marked off from the rest of what we see by **contour,** *a location at which a sudden change of brightness occurs.* Think about the letters on this page again. As you look at the page, you see letters, which are shapes, in a field or background, the white page. The **figure-ground relationship** *is the principle by which we organize the perceptual field into stimuli that stand out (figure) and those that are left over (ground).* Some figure-ground relationships, though, are highly ambiguous, and it is difficult to tell what is figure and what is

$\mathcal{S}$elf-Assessment

Perceptual Expectations

Sometimes our perceptions are strongly influenced by what we expect to see. This influence is sometimes referred to as *top-down processing*. To see the power of how top-down processing shapes perception, place your hand over the bottom set of cards. Now as quickly as you can, count how many aces of spades you see on the twelve cards in the top set.

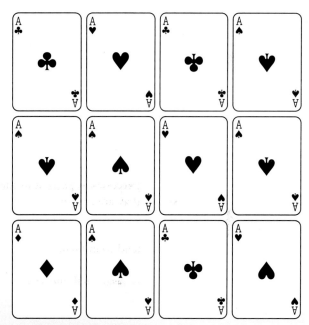

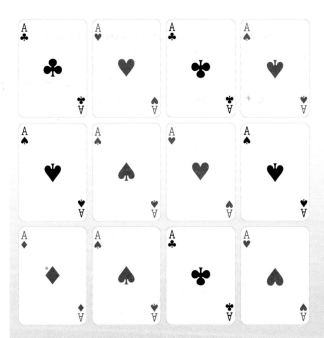

Now place your hand over the set of cards above. Quickly count the number of aces of spades in the twelve cards in the next column.

Scoring and Interpretation

Most people report that they see 2 or 3 aces of spades in the set of twelve cards in the left column. However, if you look closely, there are 5. Two of the aces of spades are black, and three are red. When people look at the set of twelve cards in this column they are more likely to count 5 aces of spades. Why the difference in what we perceive? The answer involves our perceptual expectations. We expect aces of spades to be black because they are black in a regular deck of cards. We don't expect them to be colored red, so it is easy to skip right over the red ones. Interestingly, young children are more accurate at this perceptual task than adults. Why? Because they have not built up the perceptual expectation that aces of spades are black.

SOURCE: Adapted from Grasha & Kirschenbaum (1986). *Adjustment and Competence.* St. Paul, MN: West Pub, p. 144.

$\mathcal{F}$IGURE 3.16

Reversible Figure-Ground Pattern

Either a goblet or a pair of silhou-etted faces in profile can be seen.

ground. A well-known ambiguous figure-ground relationship is shown in figure 3.16. As you look at the figure, your perception is likely to shift between seeing two faces or a single goblet. Another example of figure-ground ambiguity is found in the work of artist M. C. Escher, which keeps us from favoring one figure over another, seemingly because spatial location and depth cues are not provided (see figure 3.17).

One group of psychologists has been especially intrigued by how we perceive shapes in our world—the Gestalt psychologists. **Gestalt psychology** *is an approach that states that people naturally organize their perceptions according to certain patterns; Gestalt is a German word that means "configuration" or "form." One of Gestalt psychology's main principles is that the whole is not equal to the sum of its parts.* For example, when you watch a movie, the motion you see in the film cannot be found in the film itself; if you examine the film, you see only separate frames—but you see many of them per second. When you watch the film, you perceive a whole that is very different from the individual pictures that are its parts. Figure 3.18 also illustrates this fundamental principle of Gestalt psychology.

Gestalt psychology

An approach that states that people naturally organize their perceptions according to certain patterns. *Gestalt* is a German word that means "configuration" or "form." One of Gestalt psychology's main principles is that the whole is not equal to the sum of its parts.

$\mathcal{F}$IGURE 3.17

Sophisticated Use of Figure-Ground Relationship in Escher's Woodcut *Relativity* (1938)

The figure-ground relationship just described is another Gestalt principle. Three other Gestalt principles are closure, proximity, and similarity. The principle of *closure* states that, when individuals see a disconnected or incomplete figure, they fill in the spaces and see it as a complete figure (see figure 3.19a). The principle of *proximity* states that, when individuals see objects close to each other, they tend to group them together (see figure 3.19b). The principle of *similarity* states that, the more similar objects are, the more likely we are to group them together (see figure 3.19c). By turning to figure 3.20, you can observe some of the basic principles of Gestalt psychology in a famous artist's work.

Depth Perception. The images we see of the world appear on our retinas in two-dimensional form, yet we see a three-dimensional world. **Depth perception** *is the ability to perceive objects three-dimensionally.* Look at the setting you are in. You don't see it as flat. You see some objects farther away, some closer. Some objects overlap. The scene you are looking at and the objects in it have depth. How do we see depth? We use both binocular and monocular cues. **Binocular cues** *are depth cues that are based on both eyes working together.* **Monocular cues** *are depth cues based on each eye working independently.*

People with vision in only one eye do not have binocular cues for depth perception available to them, but they still see a world of depth. They can still see depth because of monocular cues that can be perceived by one eye only. Following are four monocular cues:

1. *Linear perspective.* The farther an object is from the viewer, the less space it takes up in the visual field. As an object recedes in the distance, parallel lines in the object converge.
2. *Texture gradient.* Texture becomes denser the farther away it is from the viewer.

depth perception
The ability to perceive objects three-dimensionally.

binocular cues
Depth cues that are based on both eyes working together.

monocular cues
Depth cues based on each eye working independently.

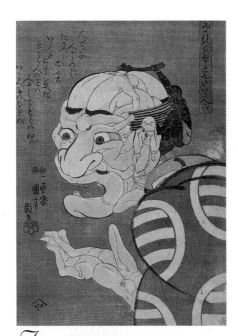

FIGURE 3.18

Example of the Gestalt Principle That the Whole Does Not Equal the Sum of the Parts

In *A Kindly Man of Fearful Aspect* by Kuniyoshi Ichiyusai, the configuration of the whole is clearly qualitatively different than the sum of its parts.

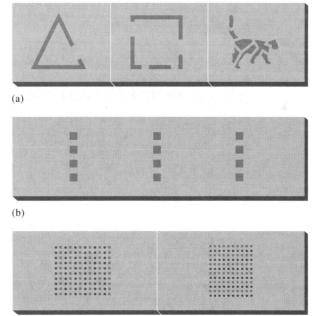

(a)

(b)

(c)

FIGURE 3.19

Gestalt Principles of Closure, Proximity, and Similarity

(a) Closure: when we see disconnected or incomplete figures, we fill in the spaces and see them as complete figures. *(b)* Proximity: when we see objects that are near each other, they tend to be seen as a unit. You are likely to perceive the grouping as 3 columns of 4 squares, not 1 set of 12 squares. *(c)* Similarity: when we see objects that are similar to each other, they tend to be seen as a unit. In this display, you are likely to see vertical columns of circles and squares in the left box but horizontal rows of circles and squares in the right box.

Gestalt Principles of Closure, Proximity, and Similarity in Picasso's *The Nude Woman,* 1910

Look at the painting and think about some of the Gestalt principles of perception that are incorporated. The nude is an incomplete figure. You have to fill in the spaces to make it a complete figure (principle of closure). Both the principles of proximity and similarity cause you to see the two objects toward the bottom of the painting as feet.

retinal or binocular disparity

Perception in which the individual sees a single scene even though the images on the eyes are slightly different.

convergence

A binocular cue for depth perception in which the eyes turn inward as an object gets closer. When eyes converge or diverge, information is sent to the brain, which interprets the information about the inward (object is closer) or outward (object is further away) eye movement.

apparent movement

The illusion of movement that occurs when we perceive a stationary object as moving.

stroboscopic motion

The illusion of movement created when the image of an object is flashed on and off in rapid succession at slightly different places on the retina.

movement aftereffects

An illusion of movement that occurs when we watch continuous movement in one direction and then look at a stationary surface, which then appears to move in the opposite direction.

3. *Relative size.* Objects farther away create a smaller retinal image than those nearby.
4. *Interposition.* An object that partially conceals or overlaps another object is perceived as closer.

Located several inches apart above your nose, your two eyes see the world from slightly different locations. **Retinal or binocular disparity** *is the perception in which an individual sees a single scene, even though the images on the eyes are slightly different.* The brain blends the two sets of overlapping information it receives from the retinas into a single image that gives the proper impression of depth and distance. Retinal disparity is one binocular cue that helps us see depth. **Convergence** *is a binocular cue for depth perception in which the eyes turn more inward as an object gets closer. When the eyes converge or diverge, information is sent to the brain, which interprets the information about the inward (object is closer) or outward (object is farther away) eye movement.* To experience convergence, hold your finger at arm's length and then slowly move it to a point between your eyes. As you move your finger closer, you have to turn your eyes inward to follow it.

Stereoscopic information presented in a single two-dimensional image illustrates the principle of depth perception that involves disparity. These types of displays have become very popular in recent years. They can now be found in art books, in greeting cards, and on posters (see figure 3.21).

Depth perception is especially intriguing to artists. Their challenge is to depict the three-dimensional world on a two-dimensional canvas. As shown in figure 3.22, artists often use monocular cues to give the feeling of depth to their paintings. Indeed, monocular cues have become so widely used by artists that they have also been called *pictorial cues.*

Motion Perception. During the course of everyday life, we perceive objects that move—other people, animals, cars, and planes. How do we perceive motion? Why are we able to perceive motion? First, we have neurons that are specialized to detect motion. Second, feedback from our body tells us whether we are moving or someone or something in our environment is moving. For example, you move your eye muscles as you track the motion of a ball coming toward you. This keeps the image of the ball on the same place on the retina even though the ball is moving. Third, the environment we see is rich in cues that give us information about movement. For example, when we run we can tell that the background is moving.

Psychologists are interested in both real movement and **apparent movement,** *an illusion of movement that occurs when an object is stationary but we perceive it to be moving.* Two forms of apparent motion are stroboscopic motion and movement aftereffects. **Stroboscopic motion** *is the illusion of movement created when the image of an object is flashed on and off rapidly in succession at slightly different places on the retina*—motion pictures are a form of stroboscopic motion. Films present a series of stationary images flashed on a screen at a high speed. When the images of different objects in the film are in slightly different positions in successive frames, we perceive the objects moving. If we took the film and cut it into frames and rearranged the frames, we would not perceive the smooth apparent movement of the objects in the film. Instead, we would see the objects that appear and disappear in the stationary images. **Movement aftereffects** *happen when we watch continuous movement in one direction and then look at a stationary surface, which appears to move in the opposite direction.* Figure 3.23 provides an opportunity to experience movement aftereffects.

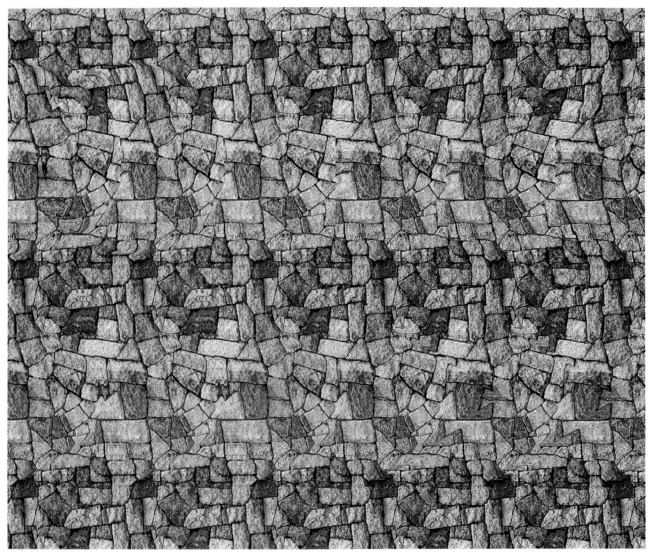

$\mathcal{F}$IGURE 3.21

A Stereogram

Seen in the right way, this figure contains 3 three-dimensional objects: a sphere in the top left, a pyramid in the top right, and a curved pointed conical figure in the center at the bottom. They may take a moment or two to see, but when you see them, they will be astoundingly clear and three-dimensional. There are two ways to see the three-dimensional objects in this figure. Technique 1: Cross your eyes by holding your finger up between your face and the figure. Look at the tip of your finger, and then slowly move your finger back and forth, toward and away from the figure, being careful to maintain focus on your finger. When the correct distance is reached, the three-dimensional objects will pop out at you. Technique 2: Put your face very close to the figure, so that it is difficult to focus or converge your eyes. Wait a moment, and begin to pull your face very slowly back from the figure. The picture should appear blurred for a bit, but when a good distance is reached should snap into three-dimensionality. Regardless of the technique you try, be patient! You may have to try one or both of these techniques a few times.

size constancy

Recognition that an object remains the same size even though the retinal image of the object changes.

shape constancy

Recognition that an object remains the same shape even though its orientation to us changes.

Perceptual Constancy. Retinal images are constantly changing as we experience our world. Even though the stimuli that fall on the retinas of our eyes change as we move closer to or farther away from objects, or as we look at objects from different orientations and in light or dark settings, we perceive objects as unchanging. We experience three types of perceptual constancies: size constancy, shape constancy, and brightness constancy. **Size constancy** *is the recognition that an object remains the same size even though the retinal image of the object changes* (see figure 3.24). **Shape constancy** *is the recognition that an object remains the same shape even though its orientation to us changes.* Look around the room in which you are reading this book. You probably see objects of various shapes—chairs and tables, for example. If you walk around the room, you will see these objects from different sides and angles. Even though the retinal image of the object

*F*IGURE 3.22

Raphael's *Fire in the Borgo*

The Renaissance masters used depth cues to give their paintings a three-dimensional appearance. Notice the detailed attention to perspective, such as how the roofs above the columns extend backward. Notice also the smaller size of the people in the distance and the overlapping of people and buildings.

brightness constancy

Recognition that an object retains the same degree of brightness even when different amounts of light fall on it.

changes as you walk, you still perceive the objects as being the same shape. **Brightness constancy** *is the recognition that an object retains the same degree of brightness even when different amounts of light fall on it.* For example, regardless of whether you are reading this book indoors or outdoors, the white pages and the black print do not look any different to you in terms of their whiteness or blackness.

How are we able to resolve the discrepancy between a retinal image of an object and its actual size, shape, and brightness? Experience is important. For example, no matter how far away you are from your car, you know how large it is. Not only is familiarity important in size constancy, but so are binocular and monocular distance cues. Even if we have never previously seen an object, these cues provide us with information about an object's size. Many visual illusions are influenced by our perception of size constancy.

*F*IGURE 3.23

Movement Aftereffects

This is an example of a geometric pattern that produces afterimages in which motion can be perceived. If the center of the pattern is fixated for approximately 10 seconds and then the afterimage is projected on a plain white surface, rotary motion is usually perceived.

$\mathcal{F}$IGURE 3.24

Size Constancy

Why do these hot air balloons look as if they are different sizes, yet when asked, people would say they are all about the same size?

visual illusion

An illusion that occurs when two objects produce exactly the same retinal image but are perceived as different images.

Perceptual Illusions

A **visual illusion** *occurs when two objects produce exactly the same retinal image but are perceived as different images.* Illusions are incorrect, but they are not abnormal. They can provide insight into how our perceptual processes work. More than 200 types of illusions have been discovered; we will study five.

One of the most famous is the Müller-Lyer illusion, shown in figure 3.25. The two lines are exactly the same length, although *b* looks longer than *a*. Another illusion is the horizontal-vertical illusion (see figure 3.26), in which the vertical line looks longer than the horizontal line, even though the two are equal. The Ponzo illusion is another line illusion in which the top line looks much longer than the bottom line (see figure 3.27).

Why do these line illusions trick us? One reason is that we mistakenly use certain cues for maintaining size constancy. For example, in the Ponzo illusion, we see the upper line as being farther away (remember that objects higher in a picture are perceived as being farther away). The Müller-Lyer illusion, though, is not as easily explained. We may

$\mathcal{F}$IGURE 3.25

Müller-Lyer Illusion

The two lines are exactly the same length, although *(b)* looks longer than *(a)*.

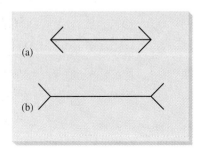

𝓕IGURE 3.26

The Horizontal-Vertical Illusion

The vertical line looks longer than the horizontal line, but they are the same length.

make our judgments about the lines by comparing incorrect parts of the figures. For example, when people were shown the Müller-Lyer illusion with the wings painted a different color than the horizontal lines, the illusion was greatly reduced (Coren & Girus, 1972). Shortly we also will discuss how cultural experiences influence an individual's perception of the Müller-Lyer illusion.

Another well-known illusion is the moon illusion (see figure 3.28). The moon is 2,000 miles in diameter and 289,000 miles away. Since both the moon's size and its distance from us are beyond our own experience, we have difficulty judging how far away it really is. When the moon is high in the sky, directly above us, little information is present to help us judge its distance—no texture gradients or stereoscopic cues exist, for example. However, when the moon is on the horizon, we can judge its distance in relation to familiar objects—trees and buildings, for example—which make it appear farther away. The result is that we estimate the size of the moon as much larger when it is on the horizon than when it is overhead (Hershenson, 1989).

The devil's tuning fork is another fascinating illusion. Look at figure 3.29 for about 30 seconds, then close the book. Now try to draw the tuning fork. You undoubtedly found this a difficult, if not impossible, task. Why? Since the figure's depth cues are ambiguous, you had problems interpreting it correctly.

Is Perception Innate or Learned?

One long-standing question in psychology is whether perception is innate (inborn, unlearned) or learned. Researchers have tried to unravel this nature-nurture question on depth perception in a number of ways: through experiments with infants, studies of individuals (like Virgil, whom you read about at the beginning of the chapter) who recover from blindness, and cross-cultural studies about how people perceive their world.

The Visual Cliff. An experiment by Eleanor Gibson and Richard Walk (1960) indicates that, by at least 6 months of age, infants have an understanding of depth. Gibson and Walk constructed a miniature cliff with a shallow side and a drop-off that was covered by firm glass (see figure 3.30). This structure is known as a *visual cliff*. Infants old enough to crawl (6 months and older) were placed on the shallow side. The infants stayed in place and did not venture out onto the glass-covered drop-off, indicating that they perceived depth. However, infants at 6 months are old enough to have encountered many situations where they could have *learned* to perceive depth, so the visual cliff experiment failed to provide convincing evidence that depth perception is innate. Whether or not infants younger than 6 months perceive depth is controversial.

Other studies have shown that, during the first month of life, human infants turn away to avoid objects that move directly toward them but do not turn away when objects move toward them at angles at which they would not collide with them (Ball & Tronick, 1971). Also, animals with little visual experience—including day-old goats and just-hatched chicks—respond just as 6-month-old infants do; they remain on the visual cliff's shallow side and do not venture out onto the glass-covered drop-off. These studies suggest that some of the ability to perceive depth is innate.

𝓕IGURE 3.27

Ponzo Illusion

The top line looks much longer than the bottom line, but they are equal in length.

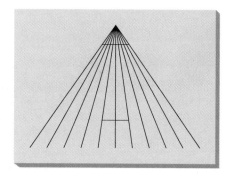

$\mathcal{F}$IGURE 3.28

The Moon Illusion

The moon illusion is that when the moon is on the horizon *(a)*, it looks much larger than when it is high in the sky, directly above us *(b). Why does the moon look so much larger on the horizon?*

carpentered-world hypothesis
The hypothesis that people who live in cultures in which straight lines, right angles, and rectangles predominate (in the West, rooms and buildings are usually rectangular, and many environmental features, such as city streets, have right-angle corners) should be more susceptible to illusions, such as the Müller-Lyer illusion, involving straight lines, right angles, and rectangles than are people who live in noncarpentered cultures.

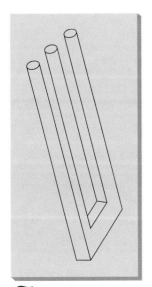

$\mathcal{F}$IGURE 3.29

Devil's Tuning Fork

Recovery from Blindness. In further attempts to determine whether or not depth perception is innate, psychologists have also studied people who were born blind, or became blind shortly after birth, and whose sight later was restored by medical procedures. If the ability to interpret sensory information is innate, such people should be able to see their world clearly after they recover from the operation. Consider S. B., blind since birth, who had a successful corneal transplant at the age of 52 (Gregory, 1978). Soon after his bandages were removed, S. B. was able to recognize common objects, identify the letters of the alphabet, and tell time from a clock. However, S. B. had some perceptual deficiencies. Although his eyes functioned effectively, S. B. had difficulty perceiving objects he had not previously touched (see figure 3.31).

The findings for formerly blind persons also do not answer the question of whether perception is innate or learned. Some people recognize objects soon after their bandages are removed; others require weeks of training before they recognize such simple shapes as a triangle. Neural connections, such as those between the eyes and the brain, can deteriorate from disuse, so a person whose sight has been restored after a lifetime of blindness may have an impaired ability to perceive visual information. Further, previously blind adults, unlike infants, have already experienced the world through their nonvisual senses, such as touch and hearing, and those perceptual systems may continue to contribute to their perception after they regain their vision.

Culture and Perception. Whereas our biological inheritance equips us with some elegant perceptual capabilities, our experiences also contribute to how we perceive the world. Some cross-cultural psychologists have proposed that the demands of various cultures lead to a greater emphasis on certain senses (Wober, 1966). For example, hunters who have to stalk small game animals might develop their kinesthetic senses more than office workers in highly industrialized nations do.

Cross-cultural psychologists have been especially interested in how people from different cultures perceive visual illusions (Segall & others, 1990). The **carpentered-world hypothesis** *states that people who live in cultures in which straight lines, right angles, and rectangles predominate (in which rooms and buildings are usually rectangular, and many objects, such as city streets, have square corners) should be more susceptible to illusions involving straight lines, right angles, and rectangles (such as the Müller-Lyer illusion) than people who live in noncarpentered cultures are.* People who live in a carpentered world have learned to interpret nonrectangular figures as rectangular, to perceive figures in perspective, and

The Zulu live in isolated regions of southeastern Africa in a world of open spaces and curves. Their huts are round with round doors, and they even plow their fields in curved, rather than straight, furrows. As the carpentered-world hypothesis would predict, the Zulu are not very susceptible to the Müller-Lyer illusion.

to interpret them as two-dimensional representations of three-dimensional objects. This tendency enhances the Müller-Lyer illusion (see figure 3.25). For example, the Zulu in isolated regions of southeastern Africa live in a world of open spaces and curves. Their huts are round with round doors, and they even plow their fields in curved, rather than straight, furrows. According to the carpentered-world hypothesis, the Zulu would not be very susceptible to the Müller-Lyer illusion. Cross-cultural psychologists have found this to be the case (Segall, Campbell, & Herskovits, 1963).

Another example in which culture shapes perception is found in Pygmies who live in the dense rain forests of the African Congo. Because of the thick vegetation, the Pygmies rarely see objects at long distances. Anthropologist Colin Turnbull (1961) observed that, when the Pygmies traveled to the African plains and saw buffalo on the horizon, they thought the animals were tiny insects and not huge buffalo. The Pygmies' lack of experience with distant objects probably accounts for their inability to perceive size constancy.

𝓕IGURE 3.30
Visual Cliff

The visual cliff was developed by Eleanor Gibson and Richard Walk (1960). The infant shown here hesitates as he moves onto the glass-covered drop-off, the deep side of the visual cliff. In the study, even when coaxed by their mothers, the infants were still reluctant to venture out onto the deep drop-off, indicating they could perceive depth.

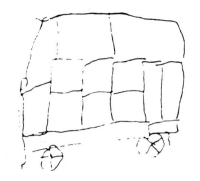

FIGURE 3.31

S. B.'s Drawings of a Bus After His Recovery from Blindness

S. B. drew the bus at the top 48 days after a corneal transplant restored his vision, and he drew the bus at the bottom a year after the operation. Both drawings reflect more detail for the parts of the bus S. B. used or touched while he was blind than the parts he did not use or touch. In the bottom drawing, notice the absence of the front of the bus, which S. B. never touched.

Both nature and nurture are responsible for the way we perceive the world. One view of how the two influences interact to shape perception is that all people, regardless of culture, have the same perceptual processes and the same potential for perceptual development, but cultural factors determine what is learned and at what age (Kagitcibasi & Berry, 1989). So far we have discussed perception in terms of shape, depth, constancy, illusion, and whether or not perception is innate or learned. However, we will also briefly discuss another, curious realm of perceptual phenomena—extrasensory perception.

Extrasensory Perception

Our eyes, ears, mouth, nose, and skin provide us with sensory information about the external world. Our perceptions are based on our interpretation of this sensory information. Some people, though, claim they can perceive the world through something other than normal sensory pathways. Literally, **extrasensory perception (ESP)** *is perception that occurs without the use of known sensory processes.* The majority of psychologists do not believe in ESP; however, a small number of psychologists do investigate it (Persinger & Krippner, in press).

Extrasensory experiences fall into four main categories. The first is **telepathy,** *which involves the transfer of thought from one person to another.* For example, this skill is supposedly possessed by people who can "read" another person's mind. If two people are playing cards and one person can tell what cards the other person picks up, telepathy is taking place (see figure 3.32). **Precognition** *involves "knowing" events before they happen.* For example, a fortune teller might claim to see into the future and tell you what will happen to you in the coming year. **Clairvoyance** *involves the ability to perceive remote events that are not in sight.* For example, a person at a movie theater "sees" a burglar breaking into his house at that moment. **Psychokinesis,** *closely associated with ESP, is the mind-over-matter phenomenon of being able to move objects without touching them,*

extrasensory perception
Perception that occurs without the use of known sensory processes.

telepathy
The transfer of thought from one person to another.

precognition
Knowing events before they occur.

clairvoyance
The ability to perceive remote events that are not in sight.

psychokinesis
Closely associated with ESP; the mind-over-matter phenomenon of being able to move objects without touching them, such as mentally getting a chair to rise off the floor or shattering a glass merely by staring at it.

FIGURE 3.32

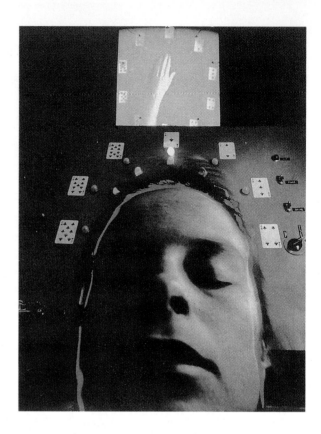

An Experimental situation Involving an Attempt to Demonstrate Telepathy

At the top *(blue insert);* a person in one room tries to "send" a message through thought to a person (the subject) in another room. The sender selects a card and then attempts to relay the information mentally to the subject. The subject then selects a card, and it is compared to the one previously chosen by the sender to see if the cards match. If the mind-to-mind communication occurs beyond chance, then it would be argued that telepathy has taken place.

such as mentally getting a chair to rise off the floor or shattering a glass merely by concentrating on doing so.

One of the most famous claims of ESP involved Uri Geller, a psychic who supposedly performed mind-boggling feats. Observers saw Geller correctly predict the number on a die rolled in a closed box eight out of eight times, reproduce drawings that were hidden in sealed envelopes, bend forks without touching them, and start broken watches. Although he had worked as a magician, Geller claimed his supernatural powers were created by energy sent from another universe. Careful investigation of Geller's feats revealed they were nothing more than a magician's tricks. For example, in the case of the die, Geller was allowed to shake the box and open it himself, giving him an opportunity to manipulate the die (Randi, 1980).

> *A psychic is an actor playing the role of a psychic.*
> —DARYL BEM, *American Psychologist, 20th Century*

Through their astonishing stage performances, many psychics are very convincing. They seemingly are able to levitate tables, communicate with spirits, and read an audience member's mind. Many psychics, such as Uri Geller, are also magicians, who have the ability to perform sleight-of-hand maneuvers and dramatic manipulations that go unnoticed by most human eyes. One magician's personal goal, though, is to expose the hoaxes of such psychics. James Randi (1980) has investigated a number of psychics' claims and publicized their failures, as discussed in Applications in Psychology.

Not only have magicians, such as Randi, investigated some psychics' claims, but scientists have also examined ESP in experimental contexts. Some ESP enthusiasts believe that the phenomenon is more likely to occur when a subject is totally relaxed and deprived of sensory input. In this kind of ESP experiment, the subject lies down, and half a Ping-Pong ball is affixed over each eye with cotton and tape. An experimenter watches through a one-way mirror from an adjacent room, listening to and recording the subject's statements. At an agreed-upon time, someone from another location concentrates on trying to receive a message from the subject's mind.

Applications in Psychology

Debunking Psychics' Claims

A woman reports that she has power over the goldfish in a huge 50-gallon tank. She claims that she can will them to swim to either end of the tank. As soon as she wills it, the fish take off.

Under the careful scrutiny of James Randi, this woman's account turned out to be just another fish story. The woman had written Randi, a professional magician, who has a standing offer of $10,000 to anyone whose psychic claims withstand his analysis. In the case of the woman and her goldfish, Randi received a letter from her priest validating her extraordinary power. Randi talked with the priest, who told him that the woman would put her hands in front of her body and then run to one end of the tank. The fish soon followed. Because the fish could see out of the tank just as we can see into it, Randi suggested that she put opaque brown wrapping paper over one end of the tank and then try her powers. The woman did and called Randi about the result, informing him that she had discovered something new about her power: that her mind could not penetrate the brown paper. The woman believed that she had magical powers and completely misunderstood why Randi had asked her to place the brown paper over the fish tank.

No one has claimed Randi's $10,000 prize, but he has been called to investigate several hundred reports of supernatural and occult powers. Faith healers have been among those he has evaluated. Randi has witnessed individuals yelling and dancing up and down, saying they are healed of such maladies as cancer and diabetes. When asked how they know they are healed, they usually say it is because they no longer have the disease or because the faith healer told them so. On checking back with the "healed" a week later, Randi has found diabetics taking insulin and a cancer patient resuming radiation therapy. In some cases, their health has dramatically worsened, as in the case of a diabetic who had to be taken to the hospital because he had stopped his insulin treatment. When asked if they still believed in the faith healer's treatment, it is not unusual to hear these individuals say that they just did not believe strongly enough.

Randi makes the distinction between the tricks of magicians, such as himself, and the work of psychics and faith healers. He says that magic is done for entertainment, the other for swindling.

Magician James Randi (right) has investigated a number of psychics' claims. No one has yet won Randi's standing offer of $10,000 to anyone whose psychic claims withstand his analysis.

Carl Sargent (1987) has used this procedure in a number of telepathy experiments and reported a great deal of success. In one experiment, Sargent had a "sender" mentally transmit an image of one of four pictures selected from 1 of 27 randomly selected sets of four pictures. Immediately afterward, the experimenter and the subject examined a duplicate set of four pictures and together judged and ranked their degree of correspondence with the subject's recorded impression. Experimental psychologist Susan Blackmore (1987) was skeptical about Sargent's success in ESP experiments, so she visited his laboratory at Cambridge University in England and observed a number of his telepathy sessions. With the subject shown four pictures, the success rate expected by chance was 25 percent (one of four pictures). In the experimental sessions Blackmore observed, the subjects' hit rate was 50 percent, far exceeding chance.

Sargent supposedly invokes a number of elaborate procedures to protect randomization, experimenter bias, unbiased selection by the subject, and so on. Blackmore was still skeptical, finding some disturbing flaws in the way Sargent's experiments were conducted. In some sessions, he randomized the pictures himself, putting himself where he could manipulate the order of the pictures. In other sessions, he came in while the subject was judging the pictures and "pushed" the subject toward the picture that had been "transmitted by the sender."

No one has been able to replicate the high hit rates in Sargent's experiments. Proponents of ESP, such as Sargent, claim they have demonstrated the existence of ESP, but critics, like Blackmore, demand to see or experience the same phenomena themselves. Replication is one of the hallmarks of scientific investigation, yet replication has been a major thorn in the side of ESP researchers. ESP phenomena have not been reproducible when rigorous experimental standards have been applied (Hines, 1988).

In the next chapter, we will explore many other aspects of our awareness, both of the external world and the internal world. Sleep, dreams, altered states of consciousness, and the influence of drugs on mental processes and behavior are discussed in chapter 4.

eview

Perception

Shape is perceived because it is marked off by contour. An important aspect is figure-ground relationship. Gestalt psychologists have developed a number of principles of perceptual organization, a fundamental one being that the whole is not equal to the sum of its parts. Depth perception is our ability to perceive objects as three-dimensional. To see a world of depth, we use binocular cues, such as retinal disparity and convergence, and monocular cues (also called pictorial cues), such as linear perspective, texture gradient, relative size, and interposition. Perceptual constancy includes size, shape, and brightness. Experience with objects and with distance cues helps us see objects as unchanging.

Illusions occur when two objects produce exactly the same retinal image but are perceived as different images. Among the more than 200 visual illusions are the Müller-Lyer illusion and the moon illusion. Perceptual constancies and cultural experiences are among the factors responsible for illusions.

Is perception innate or learned? Experiments using the visual cliff with young infants and animals indicate that some of the ability to perceive depth is innate. Investigations of formerly blind adults are inconclusive with regard to whether perception is innate or learned. Our experiences contribute to how we perceive the world. People in different cultures do not always perceive the world in the same way. The carpentered-world hypothesis and varying abilities to respond to depth cues in two-dimensional drawings across cultures reveal how experiences influence perception.

Extrasensory perception is perception that does not occur through normal sensory channels. Four main forms are telepathy, precognition, clairvoyance, and psychokinesis. The claims of ESP enthusiasts have not held up to scientific scrutiny.

Overview

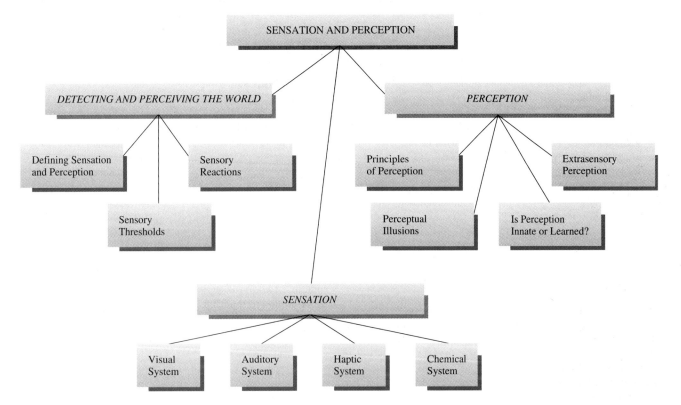

We began this chapter by studying how we sense and interpret the environment, defining sensation and perception, and also reading about sensory thresholds and sensory adaptation. Our coverage of sensation focused on the following sensory systems: visual, auditory, haptic (touch, as well as the kinesthetic and vestibular senses), and chemical (taste and smell). To learn about the nature of per-

ception, we discussed some principles of perception, illusions, whether perception is innate or learned, and extrasensory perception. Remember that you can obtain an overall summary of the chapter by again reading the in-chapter reviews on pages 81, 90, 101, and 116.

Key Terms

Thinking It Over

Exercises . . .

. . . In Critical Thinking

You explored the contemporary sensory research involved in signal detection. See if you can generate five practical examples of signal detection in your daily life. For example, children often learn that when their parents call them using their first, middle, and last names, this is a signal that they are in trouble. Or you might look for certain signals from a loved one and feel dismayed when the signals aren't there. What signal detection examples can you come up with?

. . . In Creative Thinking

This chapter provided several examples of how perceptual sets influence us to distort incoming information. Come up with your own perceptual stimulus that demonstrates the power of top-down processing. For example, can you think of other phrases, similar to *Once upon a time,* that could be used to test this phenomenon?

. . . In Active Learning

Take a tour of an art exhibit on campus or at a nearby gallery. See how many perceptual principles you can identify in the works on display. For example, how does the artist use cues of texture or brightness to create a compelling image? What strategies does the artist use to portray depth? Are there other principles you can identify that are useful tools for successful artists?

. . . In Reflective Learning

Think about your reliance on your sensory abilities. What would life be like for you if you suddenly lost your ability to use one of your senses? Losing which sensory system would create the greatest hardship for you? All of the senses are vital to living life as fully as possible, but do you treasure some senses more than others?

Resources for Psychology and Improving Humankind

Human Behavior in Global Perspective (1990)

by Marshall Segall, Pierre Dasen, John Berry,
and Ype Poortinga
New York: Pergamon

Segall's research has made important contributions to an understanding of cultural influences on perception. An entire chapter of this book is devoted to how culture affects our perception of visual illusions.

National Alliance of Blind Students

1115 15th Street NW, Suite 720
Washington, DC 20005
800-424-8666

This is an organization for postsecondary blind students that seeks to improve their educational opportunities and protect their rights.

National Association of the Deaf

814 Thayer Avenue
Silver Spring, MD 20910
301-587-1788

This association serves adult deaf persons, parents of deaf children, professionals, students, and others interested in deafness. The group publishes *Deaf American* and provides information about various books on American Sign Language.

National Federation of the Blind

1320 Johnston Street
Baltimore, MD 21230
410-659-9314

This organization seeks to establish the complete equality and integration of the blind into society. It publishes *Braille Monitor,* a monthly magazine, and a number of educational brochures. Job opportunities for the blind are listed.

Pseudoscience and the Paranormal (1988)

by Terence Hines
Buffalo, NY: Prometheus

This comprehensive book documents the lack of scientific evidence in many different areas such as graphology (use of handwriting to determine personality), UFO abductions, telepathy, astrology, and firewalking.

Seeing: Illusion, Brain, and Mind (1980)

by J. P. Frisby
New York: Oxford University Press

This fascinating book presents many different illusions and describes attempts to explain them.

The Story of My Life (1970)

by Helen Keller
New York: Airmont

This fascinating account of Helen Keller's life as a blind person provides insights into blind people's perception of the world and how they use other senses.

The Book of Natural Pain Relief (1995)

by L. Chartan
New York: Harper

This book discusses contemporary nonpharmaceutical interventions for both chronic and short-term pain. It includes an extensive discussion of psychological factors that can cause and enhance pain.

When Hearing Gets Hard (1993)

by E. Suss
New York: Bantam

This book explores psychological aspects of hearing loss and provides some physiological background on the causes of hearing loss.

Internet Resources

http://magic.hofstra.edu:7003/immortal/index.html/
Offers a profile of Beethoven including how his deafness affected his life.

http://www.gallaudet.edu/-nicd/
Gallaudet University provides a resource page for the Deaf.

http://www.nih.gov/nidcd/
The National Institute on Deafness updates research on sensory problems.

http://ificinfo.health.org/insight/exper.htm
Investigate how you can determine if you are a supertaster by visiting this site.

http://www.nih.gov/nidcd/smltaste.htm
Explore the nature of smell and taste disorders.

http://lwaber.swmed.edu/popgen/colorblind.htm
Dr. Oliver Sacks discusses the genetic background of colorblindness.

http://www.lava.net/-dewilson/web/color.html
A discussion about the mechanics of colorblindness.

http://www.mhnet.org/guide/blind.htm
Comprehensive resources for the Blind.

http://www.blind.net/bg200000.html
A review of the major causes of blindness.

http://robotics.eecs.berkeley.edu/-nicolson/tactile.html
Sample research related to touch from robotics lab at Berkeley.

http://www.textras.bc.ca/webball/ondeck/perception.html
Apply perception principles to becoming a better hitter in baseball.

http://www.fink.com/papers/impossible.html
Explore a variety of perceptual illusions called impossible figures.

http://www.rit.edu/-jjk6447/espintro.html
Evaluate your extrasensory powers at this site.

4

States of Consciousness

The ultimate gift of conscious life is a sense of the

mystery that encompasses it.

—LEWIS MUMFORD
American Writer and Philosopher, 20th Century

*T*his chapter is about the many different states of consciousness we can experience. We will explore what consciousness is, what happens when we are asleep, why we dream, how hypnosis works, and the effects of drugs on behavior. Regarding sleep, most of us take this nightly sojurn for granted. However, as you will read next, the experiences of Colin Kemp reveal some of the dramatic things that can take place while we are asleep.

The Story of Colin Kemp: A Fatal Night Terror

*I*t was August 1985, and Colin Kemp, a 33-year-old salesman in Caterham, England, went to sleep as usual. About 2 hours later, two Japanese soldiers appeared in his bedroom. They started to chase him. One soldier had a knife; the other a gun. Kemp ran away from them as fast as he could, but he wasn't fast enough. Kemp wrestled with the knife-wielding soldier. The other soldier aimed his gun at Kemp's head. Kemp tripped him, gripped his neck, and began choking him, but he slipped away. He turned, aimed the gun at Kemp, and fired. Kemp awoke in a state of panic, sweat pouring down his head. In a frenzy of terror, he turned to his wife, who was lying next to him in bed. She was dead. Kemp had strangled her, not a Japanese soldier.

At his trial 9 months later, Kemp said he was asleep when he killed his wife. He pleaded not guilty to the murder charge because he had intended to kill a Japanese soldier, not his wife. Psychiatrists testified on Kemp's behalf, instructing the jury that Kemp was having a night terror at the time he killed his wife. A **night terror** *is characterized by sudden arousal from sleep and intense fear, usually accompanied by a number of physiological reactions, such as rapid heart rate and breathing, loud screams, heavy perspiration, and physical movement.* In most instances, individuals have little or no memory of what happens during a night terror.

night terror

A state characterized by sudden arousal from sleep and intense fear, usually accompanied by a number of physiological reactions.

Kemp experienced night terrors on two occasions prior to the fatal event. Both times intruders chased him during his sleep. In one of the night terrors, he punched at his wife. She awakened and asked what was happening. The second time, he kicked her in the back. Strangling someone to death is a much more elaborate and sustained activity than kicking an individual in the back. Is it possible that an action like Kemp's—strangling someone to death—could actually take place during sleep? The jury apparently thought so, because they acquitted Kemp. They saw his act as an *automatic* one. That is, although Kemp was capable of the action, the jury concluded that he was not *conscious* of what he was doing (Restak, 1988). ❖

THE NATURE OF CONSCIOUSNESS

For much of the twentieth century, psychologists shunned the slippery, subjective trappings of consciousness that intrigued their predecessors in the late nineteenth century. Instead, they focused on overt behaviors of individuals and the rewards and punishments that determined those behaviors (Skinner, 1938; Watson, 1913). However, recently psychologists have granted respectability to the study of consciousness in cognitive science. For the first time in many decades psychologists from many different fields are interested in consciousness, including its relation to unconsciousness (Bowers, 1992).

Consciousness

consciousness

Awareness of external and internal stimuli or events.

Psychologists do not always agree on what the nature of conscious thought is or how it works in concert with or apart from unconscious thought. Although there is still disagreement about the nature of consciousness, we will define **consciousness** *as awareness of both external and internal stimuli or events.* External events include what you attend to as you go through your day—the comment your best friend makes about your new hairstyle, the car in front of you that swerves to miss a dog, the music you are listening to on your CD player, and so on. Internal events include your awareness of your sensations—your headache has returned, you are breathing too fast, your stomach is rumbling—as well as your thoughts and feelings—you're having trouble in biology this semester, you are anxious about the exam next week, you are happy that your friends are going with you to the game tonight.

The contents of our awareness may change from one moment to the next, since information can move rapidly in and out of consciousness. Many years ago, William James (1890/1950) described the mind as a **stream of consciousness**—*a continuous flow of changing sensations, images, thoughts, and feelings.* Your mind races from one topic to the next, from thinking about the person who is approaching you, to how well you feel, to what you are going to do tomorrow, to where you are going for lunch.

stream of consciousness

A continuous flow of changing sensations, images, thoughts, and feelings.

William James was interested in charting the shifting nature of our stream of consciousness. In contrast, Sigmund Freud (1900/1953) believed that unconscious thoughts exert more powerful influences on our behavior. **Unconscious thought** *is Freud's concept of a reservoir of unacceptable wishes, feelings, and thoughts that are beyond conscious awareness.* Unconscious thought in the Freudian sense has nothing to do with being unconscious after being knocked out by a blow on the head in a boxing match, being anesthetized, or falling into a coma.

unconscious thought

Freud's concept of a reservoir of unacceptable wishes, feelings, and thoughts that are beyond conscious awareness.

According to Freud, unconscious thoughts are too laden with sexual and aggressive meaning for consciousness to admit them. For example, a young man who is nervous around women breaks into a cold sweat as a woman approaches him. He is unconscious that his fear of women springs from the cold, punitive way his mother treated him when he was a child. Freud believed that one of psychotherapy's main goals is to bring unconscious thoughts into conscious awareness so their disruptive influence can be modified.

Freud accurately recognized the complexity of consciousness. It is not simply a matter of being aware or unaware. Consciousness comes in different forms and levels. Sometimes consciousness is highly focused and alert; at other times it is more passive (Baars, 1989). Even sleep, once thought to be completely passive and unconscious, has active and at least minimally conscious properties.

controlled processes

The most alert states of consciousness, in which individuals actively focus their efforts toward a goal.

Controlled processes *represent the most alert state of consciousness in which individuals actively focus their effort toward a goal.* Controlled processes require focused attention and interfere with other ongoing activities. Consider Anne, who is learning how to use her new personal computer. She is completely absorbed in reading the tutorial manual that accompanies the computer—she doesn't hear her roommate humming to herself or the song on the radio. This state of focused awareness is what is meant by controlled processes.

automatic processes

A form of consciousness that requires minimal attention and does not interfere with other ongoing activities.

In contrast, **automatic processes** *are a form of consciousness that requires minimal attention and does not interfere with other ongoing activities.* Once Anne learns how to use the software, maneuvers on the computer keyboard become almost automatic; that is, she doesn't have to concentrate so hard on how to perform each of the steps required to get the computer to do what she wants. Two weeks ago she had to stop and concentrate on which keys to press to move a paragraph from one page to another. Now her fingers fly across the computer keyboard when she needs to move a block of material. This kind of consciousness involves automatic processes. Automatic processes require less conscious effort than controlled processes do. Our automatic behaviors when we are awake should be thought of as lower in awareness than controlled processes, rather than not conscious at all. Since Anne pushed the right keys at the right time on her computer keyboard, she apparently was aware at a certain level of what she was doing.

daydreaming

A form of consciousness that involves a low level of conscious effort.

Daydreaming *is another form of consciousness that involves a low level of conscious effort.* It is a little like dreaming when we are awake. Daydreams usually start spontaneously when what we are doing requires less than our full attention. Mind wandering is probably the most obvious type of daydreaming. We regularly take brief side trips into our own private realms of imagery and memory even as we read, listen, or work. When we daydream, we drift off into a world of fantasy. We imagine ourselves on dates, at parties, on television, at faraway places, at another time in our lives. Sometimes our daydreams are about ordinary, everyday events, such as paying the rent, getting a new hairstyle, or dealing with someone at work. This semiautomatic thought flow can be useful. As you daydream while you brush your teeth, iron your clothes, or walk to the store, you might be making plans or solving a problem. Daydreams can remind us of important things ahead. Daydreaming keeps our minds active while helping us to cope, to create, and to fantasize.

Altered States of Consciousness

The states of consciousness we have described so far are normal, everyday occurrences in our lives. In contrast, an **altered state of consciousness** *occurs when a person is in a mental state that noticeably differs from normal awareness. Drugs, meditation, traumas, fatigue, hypnosis, and sensory deprivation produce altered states of consciousness.* Whether a state of consciousness is described as normal or altered depends on how the word *normal* is defined. Someone who has drunk a caffeinated soda to increase alertness, for instance, is considered to be in a normal state of consciousness. However, someone who takes a drug that induces hallucinations, such as LSD, is considered to be in an altered state of consciousness. For a discussion of the role that altered states of consciousness played in the origin of some of the world's great religions, see Sociocultural Worlds.

altered state of consciousness

A mental state that is noticeably different from normal awareness. Drugs, meditation, traumas, fatigue, hypnosis, and sensory deprivation produce altered states of consciousness.

Western cultures tend to regard altered states of consciousness with some suspicion. Our strong bias toward rational and logical processes encourages us to view many kinds of exotic states as pathological. However, exotic altered states of consciousness involving trance states or possession appear to be a natural occurrence in about 90 percent of all societies (Bourguignon & Evascu, 1977). The bias against such phenomena has discouraged psychology from vigorously examining them, except when they could be simulated in the lab. Disconnecting an altered state from its cultural context might substantially alter its impact and significance (Ward, 1994).

Ritual possession appears to be widely practiced all over the globe. In our own culture, charismatic Christian churches believe that the Holy Spirit takes possession of the believer. Similarly, voodoo proponents in the Caribbean, Sasale dancers in Niger, and devil dancers in Sri Lanka all demonstrate the characteristics of ritual possession, including

Sociocultural Worlds

Altered States of Consciousness and the World's Religions

- Yemenite Jews in a Jerusalem synagogue—wrapped in their prayer shawls, barefoot, sitting cross-legged, and swaying back and forth—recite the Torah.
- Dar Jo and Lai Sarr, Zen monks, explore the Buddha-nature at the center of their beings through zazen meditation, meditative walking, and chanting sutras.
- Coptic Christians in Cairo, Egypt, emit an eerie and spine-tingling cry of spiritual fervor.
- Muslims in Pakistan fast from dawn to dusk during the month of Ramadan, consistent with the fourth pillar of Islam.

Today billions of people around the world guide their lives by the tenets of Judaism, Christianity, Islam, and Buddhism (Hood, 1995). Most religions involve the practice of altered states of consciousness as expected parts of religious ritual, whether the altered state is derived through meditation, prayer, fasting, or substance use.

Many of the world's great religions began with a moment of revelation, an ecstatic moment infused with such mystery, power, and beauty that it forever altered the founding prophet's consciousness (Paloutzian, 1996). God called Abraham, bidding him to leave his homeland in Mesopotamia to seek a promised land known as Canaan. There he founded a religious faith, Judaism, whose followers were to enjoy a special relationship with the creator of heaven and earth. In the Christian religion, death could not vanquish Jesus in A.D. 29; following his death, Jesus appeared in a revelation to Paul, who then became a believer in Christ's resurrection and traveled widely to preach Christianity. In the Islamic religion, Muhammad saw a vision and heard a voice in the year A.D. 610 that would alter his life; the angel Gabriel came to Muhammad and said, "Muhammad, thou art a messenger of God."

Mystical revelation did not play a role in the creation of Buddhism. In the late fifth century B.C., Siddhartha Gautama (Buddha) developed enlightenment without assistance from any teachers or divine revelation. The Buddhist path to enlightenment involves meditating—turning inward to discover that within oneself is the origin of the world, the end of the world, and the way to all goals.

Regardless of whether you believe in the teachings of one or more of the world's religions, you can recognize the importance of altered states of consciousness as a critical component in the foundation or practice of the religions of the world. *Can you identify how altered states of consciousness might play a role in your own religious tradition?*

Among those who practice altered states of consciousness in the world's religions are *(a)* Zen monks who explore the Buddha-nature at the center of their beings and *(b)* Moslems in Pakistan who fast from dawn to dusk during the month of Ramadan as the fourth pillar of Islam.

uncontrollable body movements, unusual eye movements, and personality transformation consistent with the expectations of the religion. Most ritual transformation is induced by "sensory bombardment—repetitive clapping, singing, and chanting" (Ward, 1994, p. 62).

Rejecting ritual possession as a legitimate area of study overlooks the adaptive features of this form of altered consciousness (Ward, 1989). Participating in such rituals offers psychological and biological benefits. Participants report feelings of rejuvenation and contentment upon the ritual's completion. The sudden emotional release involved in the ritual compares favorably to the release clients pursue in psychotherapy. By completing the ritual a participant may gain prestige as well as be liberated from the normal expectations that typically govern behavior. Sharing the experience of ritualized possession encourages social cohesion in the group.

As you can see, our states of consciousness are many, varied, and complex. A summary of some of the main forms of consciousness is presented in figure 4.1. Now we will turn our attention to the fascinating world of sleep and dreams.

SLEEP AND DREAMS

Each night something lures us from work, from play, and from our loved ones into a solitary state. Sleep claims about one-third of the time in our lives, more than any other pursuit. This alluring realm of mental escapades we enter each night has intrigued philosophers and scientists for centuries. Those who first investigated sleep were primarily interested in its role as a springboard for dreams. We no longer regard sleep as the complete absence of consciousness. Now we know that sleep involves much more.

Cycles of Sleep and Wakefulness

We are unaware of most of our body's rhythms—for example, the rise and fall of hormones in the bloodstream, accelerated and decelerated cycles of brain activity, highs and lows in body temperature (Monk, 1989). Both wakefulness and sleep exhibit reliable cycles of activity. We will explore both types of cycles in turn.

circadian rhythm

A daily behavioral or physiological cycle, such as the 24-hour sleep/wake cycle.

Circadian Rhythms   Some rhythms are *circadian* (the word comes from the Latin words *circa* meaning "about" and *dies* meaning "day"). A **circadian rhythm** *is a daily behavioral or physiological cycle; an example is the 24-hour sleep/wake cycle.*

The natural circadian rhythm of most animals, including humans, is 25 to 26 hours, but our internal clocks easily adapt to the 24-hour rhythms (light, sounds, warmth) of the turning earth. When we are isolated from environmental cues, our sleep/wake cycles continue to be rather constant but slightly longer than 24 hours. For example, in 1972 French scientist Michel Siffre isolated himself in Midnight Cave near Del Rio, Texas, for 6 months. What were Siffre's days and nights like when he was completely isolated from clocks, calendars, the moon, the sun, and all the normal markers of time? Siffre's (1975) days closely resembled a 24-hour cycle, but they were slightly longer and more varied toward the end of his 6-month stay in the cave.

Our own circadian rhythms can become desynchronized when we take a cross-country or transoceanic flight. If you fly from Los Angeles to new York and then go to bed at 11 P.M. Eastern Standard time, you may have trouble falling asleep because your body is still on West Coast time. Even if you sleep for 8 hours that night, you may find it hard to wake up at 7 A.M. (which would be 4 A.M. in Los Angeles).

amplitude

The height of a wave.

frequency

The number of wave cycles per second.

Sleep Cycles.   Not only are our daily patterns of alertness cyclical. We also cycle through predictable stages of sleep.

The invention of the electroencephalograph (described in chapter 2) led to some major breakthroughs in understanding the nature of sleep, including the important fact that the brain is active, rather than inactive, during sleep. The brain's electrical activity shows specific patterns throughout the period of sleep. The EEG patterns vary in **amplitude,** *the height of the wave,* and **frequency,** *the number of cycles per second.* See figure 4.2 for a depiction of

High level awareness	Controlled processes	High level of awareness, focused attention required		This student is using controlled processes that require focused concentration.
Lower-level awareness	Automatic processes	Awareness, but minimal attention required	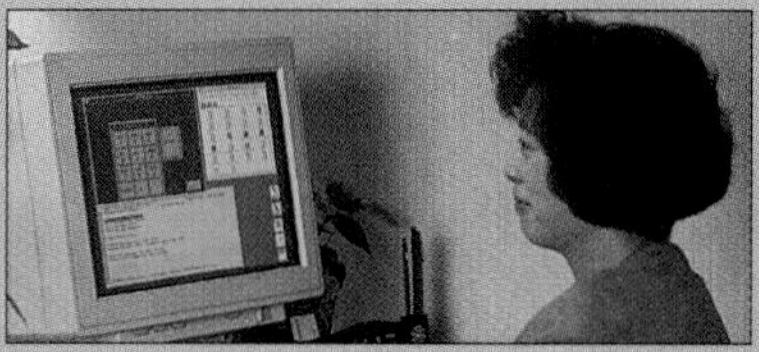	This woman is an experienced computer operator. Her maneuvers with the keyboard are automatic, requiring minimal awareness.
	Daydreaming	Low level of awareness and conscious effort, somewhere between active consciousness and dreaming while asleep		Our daydreams often start spontaneously when what we are doing requires less than our full attention.
	Altered states of consciousness	A mental state noticeably different from normal awareness; produced by drugs, trauma, fatigue, hypnosis, meditation, and sensory deprivation		Shown here is a woman being hypnotized.
	Sleep and dreams	No longer thought of as the absence of consciousness, but they are at very low levels of consciousness	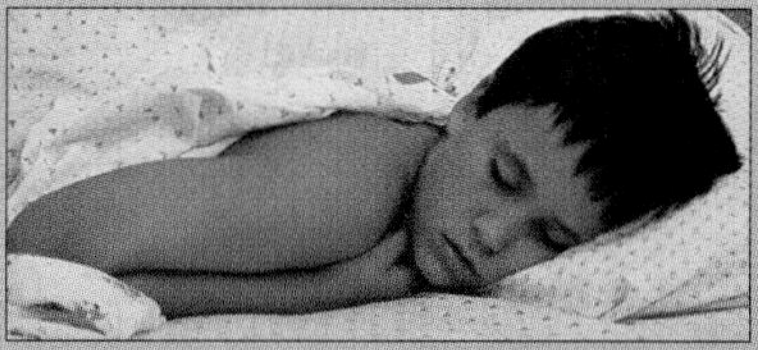	All of us dream while we sleep, but some of us dream more than others.
No awareness	Unconscious mind (Freudian)	Reservoir of unacceptable wishes, feelings, and memories, often with sexual and aggressive overtones, that are too anxiety provoking to be admitted to consciousness		The woman shown lying on the couch is undergoing psycho-analytic therapy to reveal her unconscious thoughts.
	Unconscious (non-Freudian)	Being knocked unconscious by a blow or when we are anesthetized; deep prolonged unconciousness characterizes individuals who go into a coma as the result of injury, disease, or poison		Unconsciousness can result from an injury, such as a blow to the head.

$\mathcal{F}$IGURE 4.1

Forms of Consciousness and Levels of Awareness and Unawareness

these characteristics. Brain waves show gradual changes from one stage to the next; sleep researchers designated five phases of sleep to correspond to the dominant patterns observed in each of these phases. Figure 4.3 describes the EEGs typical of these phases.

Imagine that you are a volunteer in research to study sleep patterns in college students. You have EEG monitors attached in various locations on your head to measure the electrical activity of your brain as you drift off to sleep. As you read your final homework

FIGURE 4.2

A Comparison Between Two EEG Patterns

Two examples of electrical activity in the brain (measured by EEG) that demonstrate the characteristics of amplitude (height of curve) and frequency (cycles per second).

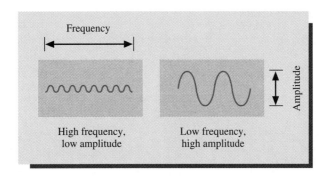

Frequency

High frequency, low amplitude

Low frequency, high amplitude

Amplitude

beta waves

The EEG pattern for high-frequency electrical activity in the brain, characteristic of periods of concentration.

alpha waves

The EEG pattern of individuals who are in a relaxed or drowsy state.

delta waves

The EEG pattern characteristic of deepening sleep and progressive muscle relaxation.

theta waves

Low-frequency and low-amplitude EEG patterns that characterize stage 1 sleep.

sleep spindles

Brief bursts of higher-frequency brain waves during sleep

assignment, your EEG measurements will probably reflect **beta waves,** *high-frequency electrical activity in the brain characteristic of periods of concentration.* When you shut off the lights, yawn, and stretch, your EEG patterns are likely to change slowly to **alpha waves,** *the EEG pattern of individuals who are in a relaxed or drowsy state.* Both of these patterns occur in awake individuals.

As you fall asleep, you begin the first of several cycles of sleep stages that will occur over the course of sleeping. Slower brain waves called **delta waves,** *characteristic of deepening sleep and progressive muscle relaxation,* begin to emerge and intensify throughout the four stages of sleep. These waves exhibit larger amplitude and greater irregularity as sleep deepens.

During light sleep in stage 1, which lasts up to 10 minutes, slower brain waves begin to emerge; **theta waves,** *low-frequency and low-amplitude EEG patterns,* characterize stage 1 sleep. In this stage people can awaken us fairly easily.

In stage 2 sleep, which lasts up to 20 minutes, the EEG pattern reflects the presence of **sleep spindles,** *brief bursts of higher-frequency waves.* During this stage EEG patterns may show responsiveness to external stimulation or internal sensation. Otherwise, electrical activity continues to slow down in stage 2.

In stage 3, which lasts up to 40 minutes, delta-wave activity becomes prominent. Delta-wave patterns dominate the deep sleep that occurs in stage 4. A sleeper who awakens during this stage often appears confused. Sleepwalking, sleeptalking, and bedwetting are most likely to occur in this deep state of sleep.

During the first 70 minutes of sleep, the sleeper spends most of the time in stages 3 and 4 in delta-wave activity. After stage 4, the patterns of electrical activity change again. The sleeper drifts up through the sleep stages toward wakefulness. Instead of reentering stage 1, however, the sleeper enters a form of sleep called "rapid eye movement" (REM)

"MY PROBLEM HAS ALWAYS BEEN AN OVERABUNDANCE OF ALPHA WAVES"

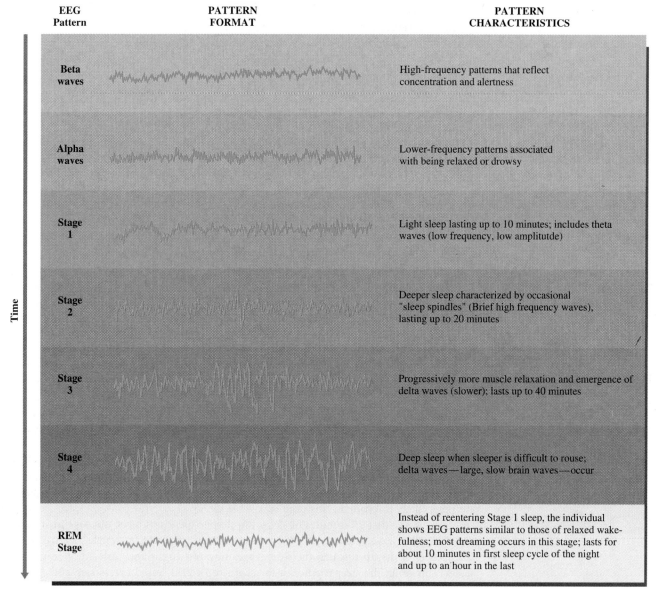

EEG Pattern	PATTERN FORMAT	PATTERN CHARACTERISTICS
Beta waves		High-frequency patterns that reflect concentration and alertness
Alpha waves		Lower-frequency patterns associated with being relaxed or drowsy
Stage 1		Light sleep lasting up to 10 minutes; includes theta waves (low frequency, low amplitutde)
Stage 2		Deeper sleep characterized by occasional "sleep spindles" (Brief high frequency waves), lasting up to 20 minutes
Stage 3		Progressively more muscle relaxation and emergence of delta waves (slower); lasts up to 40 minutes
Stage 4		Deep sleep when sleeper is difficult to rouse; delta waves—large, slow brain waves—occur
REM Stage		Instead of reentering Stage 1 sleep, the individual shows EEG patterns similar to those of relaxed wakefulness; most dreaming occurs in this stage; lasts for about 10 minutes in first sleep cycle of the night and up to an hour in the last

(left axis: Time)

FIGURE 4.3

Characteristics and Format of EEG Recordings During Stages of Wakefulness and Sleep

REM sleep

A periodic stage of sleep during which dreaming occurs.

sleep. **REM sleep** *is a periodic stage of sleep during which dreaming occurs.* During REM sleep, the EEG pattern shows fast, high-intensity waves similar to those of the alpha waves of relaxed wakefulness. During REM sleep, the eyeballs move up and down and from left to right (Benbadis & others, 1995) (see figure 4.4)

> *Sleep that knits up the ravelled sleave of care . . .*
> *Balm of hurt minds, nature's second course,*
> *Chief nourisher in life's feast.*
> —WILLIAM SHAKESPEARE, *English Playwright, 16th/17th Century*

Sleepers awakened during REM sleep are more likely to report having dreamed than are sleepers awakened at any other stage. Even people who claim that they rarely dream frequently report dreaming when they are awakened during REM sleep (McCarley, 1989). The longer the period of REM, the more likely a person will report dreaming. Dreams do occur during slow-wave or non-REM sleep, but the frequency of dreams in the other stages is relatively low (Webb, 1978).

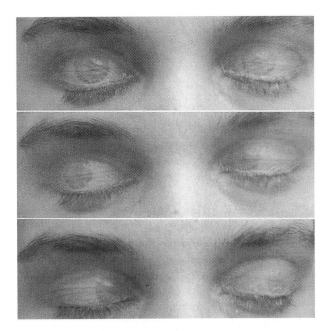

ℱIGURE 4.4

REM Sleep

During REM sleep, our eyes move rapidly as if we were observing the images we see moving in our dreams.

The REM period is distinctive in other ways as well. While dreaming in REM, the body is severely limited in its capacity to execute voluntary behavior. Psychologists presume that this paralysis acts as a safeguard by allowing fairly vivid dreaming without the challenges associated with acting out the action in the dream. In contrast, dreams that occur during stage 4 deep sleep do not have the motor paralysis protection. Many sleep researchers believe such dreams prompt sleepwalking and talking because these motor safeguards are not in place.

So far we have described a normal cycle of sleep, consisting of our stages plus REM sleep. As we move into later sleep cycles during the period, there are several important points to remember about the nature of these cycles (see figure 4.5). One cycle lasts about 90 minutes, and cycles recur several times during the night. The amount of deep sleep (stage 4) is much greater in the first half of a night's sleep than in the second half. Later cycles of sleep might not even include stages 3 or 4. The majority of REM sleep takes

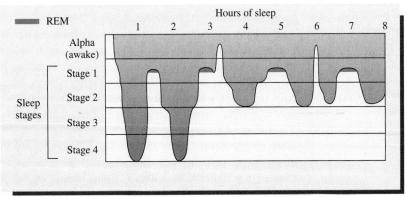

ℱIGURE 4.5

Normal Sleep Patterns of Young Adults

This graph illustrates six sleep cycles as they might occur over an 8-hour period of sleep in the young adult. The graph reflects that the sleeper descends from a relaxed, wakeful state into sleep, moving into stage 1 (light sleep) through stage 4 (deep sleep) during the first hour. The first cycle is complete when the sleeper reenters stage 1, during which the first of several REM sleep experiences occurs. Notice that slow-wave sleep, especially in stage 4, is less frequent during the latter part of the sleep period. Notice that REM sleep also increases during this period. In this example, the sleeper wakes up briefly after 3 hours and again just before the end of the sixth hour.

place during the latter part of a night's sleep when the REM period becomes progressively longer. The night's first REM period might last for only 10 minutes; the final REM period can last as long as an hour. Finally, REM patterns change over the course of the lifetime. As infants, we spend significantly more time in REM. As we grow older, we spend proportionately more time in lighter sleep stages rather than in deep sleep.

Why We Sleep and Sleep Deprivation

Sometimes sleep is irresistible and forces us to abandon the pleasures of conscious life. At other times we stave off sleep's powerful pull. In this section, we will explore theories about why we sleep and what happens when we don't get enough sleep.

Why We Sleep. For many years, researchers thought sleep occurred in the absence of enough sensory stimulation to keep the brain awake. They believed that without stimulation the brain just slowed down, producing sleep. However, researchers realized that sleep comes and goes without any obvious change in the amount of environmental stimulation. Theorists suggested we might have an internal "activating system" in the reticular formation that keeps the brain activated, or awake, all day. According to this theory, fatigue of the so-called activating system, or accumulation of "sleep toxin" that chemically depresses the activating system, might induce sleep (Monnier & Hosli, 1965).

The contemporary view of sleep is radically different. As you have learned, the brain does not stop during sleep but instead carries out complex processes that produce both REM and non-REM sleep behaviors. In fact, at the cellular level, many neurons fire faster during sleep than in a waking state (Jones, 1989).

The puzzle is not completely solved, but some of the major pieces of the brain's machinery involved in sleep have been identified. Non-REM sleep, for example, requires the participation of neurons in both the forebrain and medulla. REM sleep is a period of especially intense brain activity, also requiring the cooperation of a number of brain systems (Hobson, 1992).

There are two theories about why we sleep—repair theory and ecological theory. **Repair theory** *states that sleep restores, replenishes, and rebuilds our brains and bodies, which somehow are worn out or used up by the day's waking activities.* This idea fits with the feeling of being "worn out" before we sleep and "restored" when we wake. Aristotle proposed a repair theory of sleep centuries ago, and most experts today believe in a version of repair.

Ecological theory *is a relatively recent view of why we sleep. This evolution-based approach argues that the main purpose of sleep is to prevent animals from wasting their energy and harming themselves during the parts of the day or night to which they have not adapted.* For example, it was not adaptive for our ancestors to fumble around in the dark, risking accidents or attack by large predators, such as lions and tigers, so, like chimpanzees that slept safely in treetops, our ancestors presumably hid and slept through the night.

Both repair theory and ecological theory have some merit. Perhaps sleep was originally most important for keeping us out of trouble but has since evolved to allow for certain repair processes.

Sleep Deprivation. How long can people go without sleep and still function? The effects of profound sleep loss are difficult to study, because preventing a person from sleeping causes stress. After 2 or 3 days without sleep, people tend to become irritable, lose concentration, and show other signs of stress (Webb, 1978). In one recent study, individuals' performance of physical work tasks declined substantially after 48 hours of sleep deprivation (Rodgers & others, 1995).

How much sleep do we need each night? Some sleep researchers, such as William Dement (1993) and Mary Carskadon (1993), believe that Americans do not get enough sleep. Two dramatic examples illustrate the impact of sleep deprivation:

*   The 1989 *Exxon Valdez* oil spill in Alaska, in which the third mate, who was piloting the ship, fell asleep

repair theory

The theory that sleep restores, replenishes, and rebuilds our brains and bodies, which are somehow worn out by the day's waking activities.

ecological theory

A relatively recent view of sleep that is based on the theory of evolution. It argues that the main purpose of sleep is to prevent animals from wasting their energy and harming themselves during the parts of the day or night to which they have not adapted.

- The 1979 Three Mile Island nuclear plant accident, in which fatigued workers at 4 A.M. did not respond to a mechanical failure warning

Carskadon (1993) says that the human brain has an inherent daily rhythm of sleepiness that for most people consists of two time periods: a main one between 2 A.M. and 6 A.M. and another during midafternoon. Many cultures acknowledge the afternoon period with culturally endorsed napping or siesta during which businesses close and social activities diminish.

Sleep experts say that sleep deficits have gradually developed in this century in response to the flexibility in lifestyle that followed the introduction of electric lights. In 1910, adolescents 13 through 17 years old averaged 9½ hours of sleep a night; today they average 7½ to 8 hours a night. We do not know all of the consequences of chronic sleep loss, but 25 percent of adolescents report that they fall asleep in school at least once a week, and more than 10 percent say they are late for school at least once a week because they overslept. Surveys indicate that less than half of American adults get 8 hours of sleep each day and that one-fourth get less than 7 hours.

The exact amount of sleep a person needs does vary from individual to individual, but Carskadon (1993) argues that almost all adults need to get at least 7 hours of sleep a night to avoid accumulating a sleep debt. She believes that most adults need 8 hours. So, although some highly motivated individuals can function reasonably well even after no sleep for several days, the vast majority of us should get at least 7 to 8 hours of sleep on a regular basis to function competently.

So far we have discussed normal aspects of sleep. Next we'll see that sleep is not always predictable. There are many ways sleep can go awry.

Sleep Disorders

Most people go to bed, fall asleep, and have a restful night. However, some people have fitful nights and want to sleep much of the day. Others sleepwalk, sleeptalk, have nightmares or night terrors, or have breathing problems while they sleep.

insomnia

A common sleep problem; the inability to sleep.

Insomnia. **Insomnia** *is a common sleep problem; put simply, it is the inability to sleep.* Insomnia may involve a problem in falling asleep, waking up during the night, or waking up too early. As many as one in five Americans has insomnia (Zorick, 1989). It is more common among women, older adults, thin people, depressed or stressed people, and people who are poor.

We spend large sums of money, especially on drugs, trying to sleep better. Many sleep experts now believe that physicians have been too quick to prescribe sedatives for insomniacs (Nicholson, Bradley, & Pasco, 1989). Sedatives reduce the amount of time a person spends in stage 4 and REM sleep and may disrupt the restfulness of sleep. There is a danger of overdose, and over time sedatives lose their effectiveness, requiring ever greater dosages to achieve the same effect (Syvalahti, 1985). Sedatives and nonprescription sleeping pills should be used with caution and only for short-term sleep problems. See Improving Personal and Cognitive Skills ("Getting the Sleep You Need") for additional help for insomnia.

somnambulism

Sleepwalking; it occurs during the deepest stages of sleep.

Sleepwalking and Sleeptalking. **Somnambulism** *is the formal term for sleepwalking; somnambulism occurs during the deepest stages of sleep.* For many years, experts believed that somnambulists were acting out their dreams. However, somnambulism occurs during stages 3 and 4 of sleep, the time when a person usually does not dream. Although some adults sleepwalk, sleepwalking is most common in children. Most children outgrow the problem without having to seek professional help. Except for the danger of accidents while wandering about in the dark, there is nothing abnormal about sleepwalking. Contrary to popular belief, it is not only safe but wise to awaken sleepwalkers, because they might harm themselves as they roam through the night.

Another quirky night behavior is sleeptalking. Most sleeptalkers are young adults, but sleeptalkers come in all ages. If you were to interrogate a sleeptalker, could you find out

$\mathcal{I}$mproving Personal and Cognitive Skills

Getting the Sleep You Need

If you are having trouble falling asleep and sleeping soundly, instead of taking sleeping pills try the following:

- *Drink a glass of milk before bedtime.*
  Milk and milk products help some people sleep better.
- *Avoid caffeine, nicotine, and alcohol before bedtime.*
  Caffeine and nicotine can raise your energy level too much before you try to drift off. Alcohol might initially help you fall asleep, but it also will likely awaken you after several hours of sleep.
- *Adopt a regular schedule before going to bed.*
  Standardizing your routine in the evening signals your brain and body that it is time for "lights out."
- *Do something relaxing at bedtime.*
  Listen to soft music. Share a cup of herbal tea with a part-ner or roommate. Avoid emotionally charged discussions—they will get you aroused and cause you to have trouble falling asleep.
- *Exercise regularly.*
  Get into a regular exercise routine, but don't exercise in the last several hours before you go to bed. Exercising just before you go to bed will make you feel too alert to fall asleep.
- *Make sure your sleeping area is good for sleeping.*
  Sleep on a comfortable bed in an area with minimal light, minimal sound, and a comfortable temperature.
- *Be a good time manager.*
  This will let you get 7 to 8 hours of sleep every night. If you don't manage your time effectively, you might find yourself staying up too late to try to get things done that you could have accomplished earlier in the day.

what he did last Thursday night? Probably not. Although he might make fairly coherent statements, the sleeptalker is soundly asleep. Most likely, the sleeptalker will mumble a response to your question, but don't count on its truthfulness.

nightmare

A frightening dream that awakens the sleeper from REM sleep.

Nightmares and Night Terrors. A **nightmare** *is a frightening dream that awakens the sleeper from REM sleep.* A nightmare's content invariably involves some danger—the dreamer is chased, robbed, raped, murdered, or thrown off a cliff. Nightmares are common. Most of us have had them, especially when we were children. Even most adults experience a nightmare occasionally. Nightmares are usually so vivid that we can remember them if someone awakens us, although they account for only a small portion of our dream world.

Recall from the opening of the chapter that night terrors are characterized by sudden arousal from sleep and intense fear, usually accompanied by a number of physiological reactions, such as rapid heart rate and breathing, loud screams, heavy perspiration, and physical movement. Night terrors are less common than nightmares, and the person usually has little or no recall of an accompanying dream. Also unlike nightmares, night terrors occur in slow-wave, non-REM sleep.

narcolepsy

The overpowering urge to fall asleep.

Narcolepsy. **Narcolepsy** *is the overpowering urge to fall asleep.* The urge is so strong that the person may fall asleep while talking or standing up. Narcoleptics immediately enter REM sleep rather than moving through the first four sleep stages. Researchers suspect it is an inherited disorder, since narcolepsy runs in families.

sleep apnea

A sleep disorder in which individuals stop breathing because their windpipe fails to open or brain processes involved in respiration fail to work properly.

Sleep Apnea. **Sleep apnea** *is a sleep disorder in which individuals stop breathing while they are asleep because their windpipe fails to open or brain processes involved in respiration fail to work properly.* They wake up periodically during the night so they can breathe better, although they are not usually aware of their awakened state. During the day, these people may feel sleepy because they were deprived of sleep at night. This disorder is most common among infants and people over the age of 65.

In our tour of sleep, we have seen that dreams usually occur during REM sleep. Let's now explore the fascinating world of dreams in greater detail.

Review

Consciousness and Sleep

Consciousness is awareness of both external and internal stimuli and events. Consciousness is a rich, complex landscape of the mind, consisting of processes at varying levels of awareness. Among the many forms of consciousness are controlled processes, automatic processes, daydreaming, altered states of consciousness, sleep and dreams, unconscious thought (Freudian), and unconsciousness (non-Freudian, such as in an anesthetized state).

Important dimensions of sleep include the kinds of sleep, circadian rhythms, why we sleep, the neural basis of sleep, and sleep disorders. Various kinds of sleep can be measured by an electroencephalograph (EEG), which measures the brain's electrical activity. Alpha waves occur when we are in a relaxed state. When we sleep, we move from light sleep in stage 1 to deep sleep in stage 4 (delta waves). Then we go directly into REM sleep, where dreams occur. Each night we go through a number of these sleep cycles.

A circadian rhythm refers to cycles that are about 24 hours long. The human sleep/wake cycle is an important circadian rhythm. This cycle can become desynchronized. In some experiments, people have isolated themselves in caves for months; these people continue to have an approximate 24-hour cycle, although at times the cycle is slightly longer. People differ in how much sleep they need each night.

We sleep mainly for two reasons—for restoration and repair (repair theory) and to keep us from wasting energy and harming ourselves during the times of the day or night to which we are not adapted (ecological theory). Although some highly motivated individuals can go several days without sleep and function reasonably well, most people need at least 7 to 8 hours of sleep a day on a regular basis to function competently. A contemporary concern is that people have increasingly gotten less sleep as the twentieth century has progressed. Early views of sleep emphasized the role of environmental stimulation and subsequently an internal activating system in the reticular formation. The contemporary view is radically different: the brain is actively engaged in producing sleep behaviors and different neurotransmitters are involved. Among the most prominent sleep disorders are insomnia, sleepwalking and sleeptalking, nightmares and night terrors, narcolepsy, and sleep apnea.

Dreams

Ever since the dawn of language, dreams have been imbued with historical, personal, and religious significance (Dement, 1976). As early as 5000 B.C., Babylonians recorded and interpreted their dreams on clay tablets. Egyptians built temples in honor of Serapis, the god of dreams. People occasionally slept there, hoping Serapis would make their dreams more enjoyable. Dreams are described at length in more than seventy passages in the Bible, and in many less-developed cultures dreams are an extension of reality. For example, there is an account of an African chief who dreamed that he had visited England. On awakening, he ordered a wardrobe of European clothes. As he walked through the village in his new wardrobe, he was congratulated for having made the trip. Similarly Cherokee Indians who dreamed of being bitten by a snake were treated for the snakebite.

> Sleep has its own world
> And a wide realm of wild reality,
> And dreams in their development have breath,
> And tears, and tortures, and the touch of joy.
>
> —Lord Byron, *English Poet, 19th Century*

Today we still try to figure out what dreams mean. Much of the interest stems from psychoanalysts who have probed the unconscious mind to understand the symbolic content of dreams. Although there is concrete information regarding sleep stages, there is very little scientific data to explain why we dream or what dreams mean.

Why We Dream.   Many of us dismiss the nightly excursion into the world of dreams as a second-rate mental activity, unworthy of our rational selves. By focusing only on the less mysterious waking world, we deny ourselves the opportunity of chance encounters with distant friends, remote places, dead relatives, gods, and demons. But what, if anything, do our dreams really mean? Four approaches have been developed to explain dreams.

Dreams as Wish Fulfillment. In Freud's (1900/1953) theory, we dream for *wish fulfillment.* After analyzing clients' dreams in therapy, Freud concluded that dreams are unconscious attempts to fulfill needs, especially those involving sex and aggression, that cannot be expressed, or that go ungratified, during waking hours. For example, people who are sexually inhibited while awake would likely have dreams with erotic content; those who have strong aggressive tendencies and hold in anger while awake would likely have dreams filled with violence and hostility. Freud also stressed that dreams often contain memories of infancy and childhood experiences, and especially of events associated with parents. He said our dreams frequently contain information from the day or two preceding the dream. In his view, many of our dreams consist of combinations of these distant, early experiences with our parents and more recent daily events. He emphasized that the task of dream interpretation is complicated because we successfully disguise our wish fulfillment in dreams.

> *Our unconscious is like a vast subterranean factory with intricate machinery that is never idle, where work goes on day and night from the time we are born until the moment of our death.*
>
> —MILTON SAPIRSTEIN, *American Psychiatrist and Writer, 20th Century*

Through the centuries, artists have been adept at capturing the enchanting or nightmarish characteristics of our dreams. *(Left)* Dutch painter Hieronymus Bosch (1450–1516) captured the both enchanting and frightening world of dreams in *The Garden of Delights. (Above)* In *The Nightmare,* Henry Fuseli (1741–1825) portrayed the frightening world of nightmarish dreams by showing a demon sitting on a woman having a nightmare.

Freud believed that, in disguising our wish fulfillment, our dreams create a great deal of symbolism. Do you dream about elongated objects—sticks, tree trunks, umbrellas, neckties, and snakes? If so, Freud would have said, you are dreaming about male genitals. Do you dream about small boxes, ovens, cavities, ships, and rooms? Freud would have claimed your dreams were about female genitals. Freud thought that, once a therapist understood a client's symbolism, the nature of a dream could then be interpreted.

Dreams as Problem Solving. Whether or not dreams are an arena in which we can play out our ungratified needs, they are a mental realm where we can solve problems and think creatively. Scottish author Robert Louis Stevenson (1850–1894), for example, claimed he got the idea for *Dr. Jekyll and Mr. Hyde* in a dream. Elias Howe, attempting to invent a machine that sewed, reportedly dreamed he was captured by savages carrying spears with holes in their tips. On waking, Howe realized he should place the hole for the thread at the end of the needle, not the middle. Dreams might spark such gifts of inspiration because they weave together, in unique and creative ways, current experiences with the past.

Rosalind Cartwright (1978, 1989) studied the role of dreaming in problem solving. Participants in her study were awakened just after they had completed a period of REM sleep and then were questioned about their dreams. The first dream of the night, it turns out, often reflects a realistic view of a problem. The second dream usually deals with a similar experience in the recent past. Frequently the third dream goes back to an earlier point in the dreamer's life. The next several dreams often take place in the future. It is at this point, Cartwright says, that problem solving begins. However, many sleepers never get this far in a night's dreaming, and others just keep repeating the problem.

Dreams as Entertainment. Our dreams sometimes easily complete in vividness with feature films. However, the action in dreams can shift without rationale to include remnants of the day. Creating dreams might give us an opportunity to narrate our experience, no matter how nonsensical the "script" turns out to be.

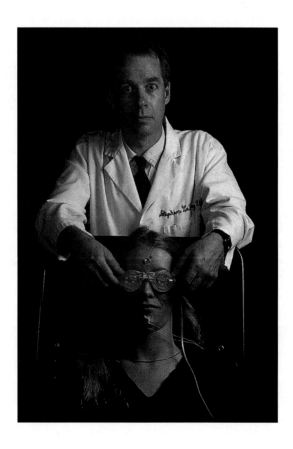

One of Stephen LaBerge's strategies for studying lucid dreaming is to ask volunteers to wear a sleep mask with sensors that turn on a red flashing light when REM sleep appears. The drowsy individual detects the flashing red light, then usually goes back to sleep after the light is turned off. The red light alerts dreamers that they were dreaming.

lucid dreams

A class of dreams in which a person "wakes up" mentally but remains in the sensory landscape of the dream world.

Can we banish evil, fly high and fast, or create a happy ending for our dreams at will? According to Stanford researcher Stephen LaBerge (1992), in the landscape of "lucid dreams," you can actually learn to take control of your dreams. **Lucid dreams** *are a class of dreams in which a person "wakes up" mentally but remains in the sensory landscape of the dream world.* During a lucid dream, the sleeper is consciously aware that the dream is taking place and can gain some control over dream content.

LaBerge describes a number of techniques to increase lucid dreaming. If you awaken from a dream in the middle of the night, immediately return to the dream in your imagination. Then envision yourself recognizing the dream. Tell yourself that the next time you dream you want to recognize that you are dreaming. If your intention is strong and clear enough, when you return to sleep you might discover that you are in a lucid dream.

activation-synthesis view

The view that dreams have no inherent meaning but, rather, reflect the brain's efforts to make sense out of or find meaning in the neural activity that takes place during REM sleep. In this view, the brain has considerable random activity during REM sleep, and dreams are an attempt to synthesize the chaos.

Dreams as Meaningless Brain States. According to the **activation-synthesis view,** *dreams are powered by the spontaneous firing of neurons. In this view, dreams have no inherent meaning; rather, they reflect the brain's efforts to make sense out of or find meaning in the neural activity that takes place during sleep.* In this view, the brain's activity involves a great deal of random activity. Dreams are an attempt to make sense out of this chaos (McCarley, 1989). Some of our senses, like vision and sound, are very active in REM sleep, the period during which people mainly dream. Other senses—pain, taste, and smell—hardly function at all. Our limbs don't move when the brain tells them to when we are dreaming. The sudden, uncoordinated eye movements of REM might make the dream world move in odd ways (for instance, you might dream you are floating on a magic carpet over an undulating landscape). In sum, in the activation-synthesis view, dreams are merely a glitzy side show, not the main act (Hooper & Teresi, 1993).

The Nature of Dreams. The world of dreams raises some intriguing questions. Do we dream in color? Why can't we remember all of our dreams? Do animals dream?

Some people say they dream only in black and white, but virtually everyone's dreams contain color. However, we often forget the color by the time we awaken and recall the dream. Some people claim that certain colors have fixed meanings in their dreams—white for purity, red for passion, green for vitality, black for evil or death, for example. However, no evidence has been found to support this belief. Red may stand for passion in one dream, danger in another, and anger in yet another dream.

Everyone dreams, but some of us remember our dreams better than others do. It's not surprising that we don't remember all of our dreams, since dreaming occurs at such a low level of consciousness. Psychoanalytic theory suggests we forget most of our dreams because they are threatening, but there is no evidence to support this belief. We remember our dreams best when we are awakened during or just after a dream. Similarly the dreams we have just before we awaken are the ones we are most likely to remember. People whose sleep cycles have long periods between their last REM stage and awakening are more likely to report that they don't dream at all or rarely remember their dreams.

It is impossible to say for certain whether or not animals dream; we know they have periods of REM sleep, so it is possible that they do. However, dogs' twitching and howling during sleep, for instance, should not be taken as evidence that they are dreaming. Since dogs can't report their dream content, we can't assume that the markers for human dreaming also apply to dog dreaming.

 eview

Dreams

Understanding dreams requires knowledge of how dreams are interpreted, the role of culture in dreams, whether we dream in color, whether animals dream, why we can't remember all of our dreams, and whether we can influence what we dream about. Freud's psychoanalytic view states that dreams are wish fulfillment of unmet needs in our waking state. Freud believed that dreams often involve a combination of daily residue and early childhood experiences. He stressed that dreams have rich symbolic content. A second view of dreams states that dreams are thinking activities and attempts to solve problems. A third view, the activation-synthesis view, states that dreams are the brain's way of trying to make sense out of neural activity during REM sleep.

HYPNOSIS

A young cancer patient is about to undergo a painful bone marrow transplant procedure. A doctor directs the boy's attention, asking him to breathe with him and listen carefully. The boy becomes absorbed in a pleasant fantasy—he is riding a motorcycle over a huge pizza, dodging anchovies and maneuvering around chunks of mozzarella. Minutes later the procedure is over. The boy is relaxed and feels good about his self-control (Long, 1986). The doctor successfully used hypnosis as a technique to help the young cancer patient control pain.

Hypnosis *is a psychological state of altered attention and awareness in which the individual is unusually receptive to suggestions.* Hypnosis has been used since the beginning of recorded history. It has been associated with religious ceremonies, magic, the supernatural, and many erroneous theories.

In the eighteenth century, Austrian physician Anton Mesmer cured his patients by passing magnets over their bodies. Mesmer said the problems were cured by "animal magnetism," an intangible force that passes from therapist to patient. In reality, the cures were due to a form of hypnotic suggestion. Mesmer's claims were investigated by a committee appointed by the French Academy of Science. The committee agreed that Mesmer's treatment was effective. However, they disputed his theoretical claims about animal magnetism and prohibited him from practicing in Paris. Mesmer's theory of animal magnetism was called mesmerism, and even today we use the term *mesmerized* to mean hypnotized or enthralled. Today hypnosis is recognized as a legitimate process in psychology and medicine, although much is yet to be learned about how it works.

Features of the Hypnotic State

There are four steps used to induce hypnosis. First, the hypnotist minimizes distraction and makes the subject comfortable. Second, the hypnotist tells the subject to concentrate on something specific, such as an imagined scene or the ticking of a watch. Third, the hypnotist describes what to expect in the hypnotic state (for example, relaxation or a pleasant floating sensation). Fourth, the hypnotist suggests certain events or feelings he or she knows will occur or observes occurring (for instance, "Your eyes are getting tired"). When the suggested effects occur, the subject interprets them as being caused by the hypnotist's suggestions and accepts them as an indication that something is happening. This increases the subject's expectations that the hypnotism will make things happen in the future and makes the subject even more suggestible.

An important characteristic of the hypnotic state is the subject's suggestibility. When individuals are hypnotized, they readily accept and respond to ideas offered by the hypnotist. **Posthypnotic suggestion** *is a suggestion, made by the hypnotist while the subject is in a hypnotic state, that the subject carries out after emerging from the hypnotic state.* **Posthypnotic amnesia,** *induced by the hypnotist's suggestion, is the subject's inability to remember what took place during hypnosis.*

hypnosis
A psychological state of altered attention and awareness in which the individual is unusually receptive to suggestions.

posthypnotic suggestion
A suggestion, made by the hypnotist while the subject is in a hypnotic state, that the subject carries out after emerging from the hypnotic state.

posthypnotic amnesia
The subject's inability to remember what took place during hypnosis, induced by the hypnotist's suggestions.

Individual Differences in Hypnosis

Do you think you could be hypnotized? What about your friends—are they more likely or less likely to be influenced by hypnosis than you are? For as long as hypnosis has been studied, about 200 years, some people have appeared to be more easily hypnotized than others. In fact, about 10 to 20 percent of the population are very susceptible to hypnosis, 10 percent or less cannot be hypnotized at all, and the remainder fall somewhere in between (Hilgard, 1965). There is no simple way to tell whether you can be hypnotized, but if you have the capacity to immerse yourself in imaginative activities—listening to a favorite piece of music or reading a novel, for example—you are a likely candidate. People who are susceptible to hypnosis become completely absorbed in what they are doing, removing the boundaries between themselves and what they are experiencing in their environment.

Theories of Hypnosis

Ever since Anton Mesmer proposed his theory of animal magnetism, psychologists have been trying to figure out why hypnosis works. Contemporary theorists are divided on their answers to the following question. Is hypnosis a special cognitive state, or is it simply a form of learned social behavior?

Ernest Hilgard (1977) argued that hypnosis is a special cognitive state. He proposed that hypnosis creates a **hidden observer,** *a part of the person that is aware of what is happening during hypnosis yet remains passive.* He discovered this dual involvement during a classroom demonstration in which he hypnotized a blind student. Hilgard hypnotically induced deafness in the blind student and showed that the student was completely unresponsive to what was going on around him. Then another student asked the person whether he was really as unresponsive as he seemed. Being a flexible teacher, Hilgard asked the blind and "deaf" person if there was a part of him that could hear. He was told to raise his finger if there was such a part of him. Surprisingly, the finger rose. Hilgard then told the individual that he would not be able to hear what this part of himself said. The second part of the person's awareness was able to report everything that happened during the hypnosis. Hilgard's inquiries revealed that approximately half of a group of highly hypnotizable subjects had a hidden observer but were unaware of it until they went through a similar procedure.

Special process theory *is Hilgard's theory that hypnotic behavior involves a special cognitive state that is different from normal cognitive states during nonhypnotic behavior, and that hypnotic responses are involuntary and involve a hidden observer.* The brain appears to create partitions or filters that prevent conscious remembrance of events.

Psychologist Ernest Hilgard developed the hidden observer theory of hypnosis, which stresses that part of a hypnotized individual's mind is aware of what is happening; that part remains a passive, or hidden, observer until called on to comment.

hidden observer

A part of the person that is aware of what is happening during hypnosis yet remains passive.

special process theory

Hilgard's theory that hypnotic behavior involves a special cognitive state that is different from normal cognitive states during nonhypnotic behavior, and that hypnotic responses are involuntary and involve a hidden observer.

nonstate view

The view that hypnotic behavior is similar to other forms of social behavior and can be explained without appealing to special processes. Hypnotic behavior is purposeful, goal-directed action that is best understood by the way subjects interpret their situation and how they try to present themselves.

A conflicting perspective, the **nonstate view,** *says that hypnotic behavior is similar to other forms of social behavior and can be explained without resorting to special processes. According to this perspective, hypnotic behavior is purposeful, goal-directed action that is best understood by the way subjects interpret their situation and how they try to present themselves.* The nonstate view recognizes that "good" hypnotic subjects often act as if they have lost control over their behavior, but these aspects of behavior are interpreted as voluntary rather than automatic (Spanos, 1988). These hypnotic volunteers might appear to surrender their voluntary control to conform to the situational demands. However, in the nonstate view, they are not partitioned into an actor and an observer like Hilgard suggested.

Applications of Hypnosis

Hypnosis is widely used in psychotherapy, medicine and dentistry, criminal investigation, and sports. Hypnosis has been used in psychotherapy to treat alcoholism, somnambulism, and suicidal tendencies. The least effective, yet most widely used, applications of hypnosis are to help people stop overeating and quit smoking. Hypnotists direct their clients to stop these behaviors. However, dramatic results rarely are achieved unless the client is already highly motivated to change. Hypnosis is most effective as an adjunct to various forms of psychotherapy, which we will discuss in chapter 12.

eview

Hypnosis

Hypnosis is a psychological state of altered attention in which the subject is unusually receptive to suggestion. The history of hypnosis began with Austrian physician Anton Mesmer and his belief in animal magnetism; a present view is the hidden-observer view. Regardless of how hypnosis is induced, it includes these features: the subject is made comfortable and distracting stimuli are reduced; the individual is told to concentrate on something that takes him or her away from the immediate environment; and suggestions are made about what the subject is expected to experience in the hypnotic state. About 10 to 20 percent of the population are highly susceptible to hypnosis, about 10 percent cannot be hypnotized at all, and the remainder fall in between.

These are two broad, competing theories about hypnosis. In the special process view, hypnotic behavior is qualitatively different from normal behavior. It is involuntary and dissociation between cognitive systems and amnesiac barriers is believed to be involved. Hilgard's hidden observer theory is an important perspective. The alternative, nonstate view argues that hypnotic behavior is similar to other forms of social behavior and can be explained without special processes. From this perspective, goal-directed action is purposeful and understood by the way subjects interpret their role and how they try to present themselves. Hypnosis has been widely applied, with mixed results, to a variety of circumstances, including psychotherapy, medicine and dentistry, criminal investigation, and sports.

PSYCHOACTIVE DRUGS AND ADDICTION

During one phase of his medical career, Sigmund Freud experimented with therapeutic uses of cocaine. He was searching for possible medical applications, such as a painkiller for eye surgery. He soon found that the drug induced ecstasy. He even wrote to his fiancée and told her how just a small dose of cocaine produced lofty, wonderful sensations. As it became apparent that some people become psychologically addicted to cocaine, and after several died from overdoses, Freud quit using the drug. Just what are psychoactive drugs?

Like Freud, many people turn to psychoactive drugs to alter their conscious experiences. In this portion of the chapter, we will explore the nature of psychoactive drugs and the dangers of addiction.

psychoactive drugs

Substances that act on the nervous system to alter our states of consciousness, modify our perceptions, and change our moods.

Psychoactive Drugs

Psychoactive drugs *act on the nervous system to alter our state of consciousness, modify our perceptions, and change our moods.* Ever since our ancient ancestors first sat entranced in front of a communal fire, humans have searched for substances that would produce pleasurable sensations and alter their states of consciousness. Among the substances that alter consciousness are alcohol, hemp and cactus plants, mushrooms, poppies, and tobacco, an herb that has been smoked and sniffed for more than 400 centuries.

Human beings are attracted to psychoactive substances because they help them adapt to or escape from an ever-changing environment. Smoking, drinking, and taking drugs reduce tension and frustration, relieve boredom and fatigue, and in some cases help us to escape from the harsh realities of the world. Psychoactive drugs provide us with pleasure by giving us tranquillity, joy, relaxation, kaleidoscopic perceptions, surges of exhilaration, and prolonged heightened sensation. They sometimes have practical uses, like the use of amphetamines to stay awake all night to study for an exam. We might also take drugs because we are curious about their effects, in some cases because of sensational accounts in the media. We may wonder if drugs can provide us with unique, profound experiences. We also take drugs for social reasons, hoping they will make us feel more at ease and happier in our interactions and relationships with others.

In our culture, however, the use of psychoactive drugs for such personal gratification and temporary adaptation carries a high price tag: drug dependence, personal and social disorganization, and a predisposition to serious and sometimes fatal diseases. What might initially have been intended as enjoyment and adaptation can eventually turn into sorrow and maladaptation. For example, drinking might initially help people relax and forget about their worries. But then they might begin to drink more and more, until the drinking becomes an addiction that destroys relationships and careers and leads to physical and psychological damage, including permanent liver damage and major depression.

Addiction

tolerance

The state in which a greater amount of a drug is needed to produce the same effect.

addiction

Physical dependence on a drug.

withdrawal

An addict's undesirable intense pain and craving for an addictive drug when the drug is withdrawn.

psychological dependence

The need to take a drug to cope with problems and stress.

People who are first starting to use a psychoactive drug usually need only a small dose to produce its intended effect. However, as a person continues to take a psychoactive drug, the body develops a **tolerance,** *which means that a greater amount of the drug is needed to produce the same effect.* The first time someone takes 5 milligrams of Valium, for example, the drug will make them feel very relaxed. But after taking the pill every day for 6 months, the person might need to take 10 milligrams to achieve the same calming effect.

Addiction *is physical dependence on a drug.* **Withdrawal** *is the undesirable intense pain and craving that an addicted person feels when the addicting drug is withdrawn.* **Psychological dependence** *is the need to take a drug to cope with problems and stress.* In both physical addiction and psychological dependence, the psychoactive drug plays a powerful role in the user's life. Some drugs have a greater potential for addiction or psychological dependence than others, as we will see in our discussion of different types of psychoactive drugs.

Alcohol

We do not always think of alcohol as a drug, but it is an extremely powerful one. Alcohol acts upon the body primarily as a depressant and slows down the brain's activities. This might seem surprising, since people who normally tend to be inhibited might begin to talk, dance, or socialize after a few drinks, but people "loosen up" after one or two drinks because the areas in the brain involved in controlling inhibition and judgment *slow down.* As people drink more, their inhibitions become even further reduced and their judgments become increasingly impaired. Activities requiring intellectual functioning and skill, such as driving, become impaired as more alcohol is consumed. Eventually the drinker becomes drowsy and falls asleep. With extreme intoxication, a person may even lapse into a coma and die. Each of these effects varies with how the person's body metabolizes alcohol, body weight, the amount of alcohol consumed, and whether previous drinking has led to tolerance.

Alcohol Use and Abuse. Alcohol is the most widely used drug in our society. A 1992 Gallup poll revealed that 64 percent of American adults drank beer, wine, or liquor at least occasionally—down from 71 percent in the late 1970s. More than 13 million people in the United States call themselves alcoholics. Alcoholism is the third leading killer in the United States. Each year approximately 25,000 people are killed, and 1.5 million injured, by drunk drivers. More than 60 percent of homicides involve the use of alcohol by either the offender or the victim, while 65 percent of aggressive sexual acts against women involve the use of alcohol by the offender. Alcohol costs the United States more than $40 billion each year in health costs, lost productivity, accidents, and crimes.

> *Alcohol is a good preservative for everything but brains.*
> —MARY PETTIBONE POOLE, *American Writer, 20th Century*

Of special concern is the high rate of alcohol abuse by adolescents and college students in the United States. In the 1990s, drug use by young adolescents has increased considerably, and alcohol is the substance they abuse the most.

Almost half of U.S. college students say that they binge drink (that is, have had 5 or more drinks in a row at least once in the last 2 weeks) (Johnston, O'Malley, & Bachman, 1996a). Can binge drinking have negative effects on students' lives? In a recent national survey on 140 campuses, binge-drinking students were eleven times more likely to fall behind in school and twice as likely to have unprotected sex than college students who did not drink. A more extensive list of binge-drinking college students' problems is shown in figure 4.6. The Self-Assessment can help you judge whether you are a substance abuser.

Nature/Nurture and Alcoholism. If you struggle to manage your alcohol use, chances are good that you are not the only person in your family who has this problem. Family studies consistently find a high frequency of alcoholism in the first-degree relatives of alcoholics (Cotton, 1979). In one review of research on family alcoholism, when the father was an alcoholic, both sons and daughters had increased rates of alcoholism; when the mother was an alcoholic, increased rates of alcoholism occurred only for daughters (Pollock & others, 1987). Twin studies of alcoholism have revealed a modest influence of

$\mathcal{S}$elf-Assessment

Do You Abuse Drugs?

For each of the following items, mark the response that you believe is most true of yourself.

		Yes	No
1.	I have gotten into problems because of using drugs.	___	___
2.	Using alcohol or other drugs has made my college life unhappy at times.	___	___
3.	Drinking alcohol or taking other drugs has been a factor in my losing a job.	___	___
4.	Drinking alcohol or taking other drugs has interfered with my preparation for exams.	___	___
5.	Drinking alcohol or taking drugs is jeopardizing my academic performance.	___	___
6.	My ambition is not as strong since I started drinking a lot or taking drugs.	___	___
7.	Drinking or taking other drugs has caused me to have difficulty sleeping.	___	___
8.	I have felt remorse after drinking or using other drugs.	___	___
9.	I crave a drink or other drugs at a definite time of the day.	___	___
10.	I want a drink or another drug the next morning.	___	___
11.	I have had a complete or partial loss of memory as a result of drinking or using other drugs.	___	___
12.	Drinking or using other drugs is affecting my reputation.	___	___
13.	I have been in a hospital or institution because of drinking or taking other drugs.	___	___

Scoring

College students who responded "yes" to any of these items from the Rutgers Collegiate Abuse Screening Test were more likely to be substance abusers than those who answered "no." If you responded "yes" even to just 1 of the 13 items on this drug-abuse screening test, you may have problems with substance abuse—consider going to your college health or counseling center for further screening.

SOURCE: After Bennett & others (1993), p. 526.

The Troubles that "Frequent Binge Drinkers" Create for ...

Themselves[1] (% of those surveyed who admitted having had the problem)		and Others[2] (% of those surveyed who had been affected)	
Missed a class	61	Had study or sleep interrupted	68
Forgot where they were or what they did	54	Had to care for drunken student	54
Engaged in unplanned sex	41	Been insulted or humiliated	34
Got hurt	23	Experienced unwanted sexual advances	26
Had unprotected sex	22	Had serious argument	20
Damaged property	22	Had property damaged	15
Go into trouble with campus or local police	11	Been pushed or assaulted	13
Had five or more alcohol-related problems in school year	47	Had at least one of above problems	87

$\mathcal{F}$IGURE 4.6

The Hazardous Consequences of
Binge Drinking in College

[1]"Frequent binge drinkers" were defined as those who had had at least four or five drinks at one time on at least three occasions in the previous two weeks.
[2]These figures are from colleges where at least 50% of students are binge drinkers.
Source: Survey of 140 U.S. colleges by the Harvard School of Public Health.

heredity (Sher, 1991), while adoption studies document the contribution of biological relatives' alcoholism to alcoholism in male adoptees (Sher, 1993). Research along these lines has persuaded many psychologists that heredity plays an important role in certain forms of alcoholism (Goodwin, 1988). However, the precise genetic mechanism has not yet been identified.

Although the family, twin, and adoption studies reveal a genetic influence on alcoholism, they also indicate that environmental factors play an important role. For example, family studies indicate that many alcoholics do not have close relatives who are alcoholics (Sher, 1993). Adoption studies suggest that heredity and environment interact for at least one form of alcoholism (environmentally dependent susceptibility), and some alcoholics do not have alcoholic biological parents. The large cultural variations in alcohol use also underscore that the environment plays an important role in alcoholism. Like other behaviors and problems, alcoholism is multiply determined, has multiple pathways, and can be effectively treated in multiple ways (Sobell & Sobell, 1992, in press). Applications in Psychology describes contrasting views on treating alcoholism.

$\mathcal{A}$pplications in Psychology

Contrasting Views on Treating Alcoholism

Alcoholism exacts a horrible toll on the drinker and the drinker's family, but the damage doesn't stop there. Drunk driving, workplace losses, and overburdened health care systems are only some of the larger-scale loss issues related to alcohol abuse. The search for effective methods of intervention has never been more intense. Among the treatments for alcoholism are twelve-step programs, cognitive therapy, and life-skills training programs. *Twelve-step programs,* such as Alcoholics Anonymous (AA), emphasize the importance of confession, group support, and spiritual commitment to God to help individuals cope with alcoholism. The twelve steps represent the heart of AA's principles, providing a precise guide for members to use in their recovery. AA's list of the twelve steps is presented in table 4.A.

Alcoholics Anonymous groups are open and free to anyone, alcoholics as well as nonalcoholics. The AA organization reports that 29 percent of AA members stay sober for more than 5 years. The age range of members is from teenagers to the elderly. The principles of AA have been revised and adopted by a number of other self-help groups, such as Narcotics Anonymous, Gamblers Anonymous, and Al-Anon. AA meetings often include extensive personal testimonies by AA members.

In a recent book (Ellis & Velton, 1992), cognitive therapist Albert Ellis, with his colleague Emmett Velton, tailored rational emotive therapy to the treatment of alcoholics. They believe that the way to treat alcoholism is by replacing maladaptive thought patterns with adaptive ones. In contrast to AA's emphasis on spiritual commitment and powerlessness, they argue that self-control and personal responsibility rather than control by a higher power will help alcoholics increase their sobriety.

Rational Recovery (RR), a nonreligious self-help group for recovering alcoholics and their relatives, traces its roots directly to Ellis. RR teaches that problem drinking results from people's beliefs that they are powerless and incompetent. Using Ellis's approach, a moderator (usually an RR member who has recovered from alcoholism) helps guide group discussion and get members to think more rationally and act more responsibly. While AA stresses that alcoholics can never become recovered but are always in some phase of recovery, RR tells

members that recovery is not only possible but that their methods help members kick their drinking problem in a year or so. Two other self-help groups (unrelated to Ellis's approach) that have sprung up in recent years as alternatives to AA are the Secular Organization for Sobriety (SOS) and Women for Sobriety (WFS). Turned off by AA's religious emphasis, the new groups rely more on willpower and self-control than on a higher power.

Both of these approaches—Alcoholics Anonymous and Rational Recovery—have helped many individuals overcome their drinking and addiction problems. If you have a drinking problem and have not sought help, call one of these groups. Information about them is listed at the end of the chapter.

$\mathcal{T}$ a b l e 4 . A

AA's Twelve-Step Recovery Program

Following are the twelve steps as they were originally presented in the *Big Book, Alcoholics Anonymous.*

1. We admitted we were powerless over alcohol, that our lives had become unmanageable.
2. Came to believe that a Power greater than ourselves could restore us to sanity.
3. Made a decision to turn our will and our lives over to the care of God *as we understood Him.*
4. Made a searching and fearless moral inventory of ourselves.
5. Admitted to God, to ourselves, and to another human being the exact nature of our wrongs.
6. Were entirely ready to have God remove all these defects of character.
7. Humbly asked Him to remove our shortcomings.
8. Made a list of all persons we had harmed, and became willing to make amends to them all.
9. Made direct amends to such people wherever possible, except when to do so would injure them or others.
10. Continued to take personal inventory and when we were wrong promptly admitted it.
11. Sought through prayer and meditation to improve our conscious contact with God *as we understood Him,* praying only for knowledge of His will for us and the power to carry that out.
12. Having had a spiritual awakening as the result of these steps, we tried to carry this message to alcoholics, and to practice these principles in all our affairs.

Other Psychoactive Drugs

Now that we have discussed alcohol, let's explore the nature of a number of other psychoactive drugs.

Barbiturates and Tranquilizers. **Barbiturates,** *such as Nembutal and Seconal, are depressant drugs that induce sleep or reduce anxiety.* In heavy dosages, they can lead to impaired memory and decision making. When combined with alcohol (for instance, sleeping pills taken after a night of binge drinking), the result can be lethal. Barbiturates by themselves also can produce death in heavy dosages, which makes them the drug most often chosen in suicide attempts. Abrupt withdrawal from barbiturates can produce seizures.

Tranquilizers, *such as Valium and Xanax, are depressant drugs that reduce anxiety and induce relaxation.* They are among the most widely used drugs in the United States and can produce withdrawal symptoms when a person stops taking them.

Opiates. **Opiates,** *which consist of opium and its derivatives, depress the central nervous system's activity.* The most common opiate drugs—morphine and heroin—affect synapses in the brain that use endorphins as their neurotransmitter. When these drugs leave the brain, the affected synapses become understimulated. For several hours after taking an opiate, a person feels euphoric and relieved of pain and has an increased appetite for food and sex. Morphine is used medically as a painkiller. But the opiates are among the most physically addictive drugs, leading to craving and painful withdrawal when the drug becomes unavailable.

Recently, another hazardous consequence of opiate addiction has surfaced: AIDS. Most heroin addicts inject the drug intravenously. When they share their needles, blood from the needles can be passed on. When this blood comes from someone with AIDS, the virus can spread from the infected user to the uninfected user.

Stimulants. **Stimulants** *are psychoactive drugs that increase the central nervous system's activity.* The most widely used stimulants are caffeine, nicotine (in cigarettes), amphetamines, and cocaine. Coffee, tea, and caffeinated soft drinks are mild stimulants. Amphetamines and cocaine are much stronger stimulants.

Amphetamines are widely prescribed, often in the form of diet pills. They are also called "pep pills" and "uppers." Amphetamines increase the release of the neurotransmitter dopamine, which increases the user's activity level and pleasurable feelings.

Cocaine comes from the coca plant, native to Bolivia and Peru. For centuries Bolivians and Peruvians have chewed on the plant to increase their stamina. Today cocaine is either snorted or injected in the form of crystals or powder. The effect is a rush of euphoria, which eventually wears off, followed by depression, lethargy, insomnia, and irritability. Cocaine can even trigger a heart attack, stroke, or brain seizure.

When animals and humans chew coca leaves, small amounts of cocaine gradually enter the bloodstream, without any apparent adverse effects. However, when extracted cocaine is sniffed, smoked, or injected, it enters the bloodstream very rapidly, producing a rush of euphoric feelings that lasts for about 15 to 30 minutes. Because the rush depletes the supply of the neurotransmitters dopamine and norepinephrine in the brain, an agitated, depressed mood usually follows as the drug's euphoric effects decline.

Crack *is an intensified form of cocaine, consisting of chips of pure cocaine that are usually smoked.* Crack is believed to be one of the most addictive substances known, being much more addictive than heroin, barbiturates, and alcohol. Emergency-room admissions related to crack have soared from less than 600 cases in 1985 to more than 15,000 cases a year in the 1990s.

Treatments for cocaine addiction have not been very successful. Cocaine's addictive properties are so strong that 6 months after treatment, more than 50 percent of cocaine abusers return to the drug. Experts on drug abuse believe the best approach to reduce cocaine addiction is through prevention programs.

---

barbiturates

Depressant drugs, such as Nembutal and Seconal, that induce sleep or reduce anxiety.

tranquilizers

Depressant drugs, such as Valium and Xanax, that reduce anxiety and induce relaxation.

opiates

Opium and its derivatives, which depress the central nervous system's activity.

stimulants

Psychoactive drugs that increase the central nervous system's activity.

crack

An intensified form of cocaine that consists of chips of pure cocaine that are usually smoked.

𝓕IGURE 4.7

LSD-Induced Hallucination

Under the influence of hallucinogenic drugs, such as LSD, several users have reported seeing images that have a tunnel effect like the one shown here.

Marijuana. Marijuana is the dried leaves and flowers of the hemp plant *Cannibas sativa*, which originated in central Asia but is now grown in most parts of the world. The plant's dried resin is known as hashish. The active ingredient in marijuana is THC, which stands for the chemical delta-9-tetrahydrocannabinol. This ingredient does not resemble the chemicals of other psychoactive drugs and does not affect a specific neurotransmitter. Rather, marijuana disrupts the membranes of neurons and affects the functioning of a variety of neurotransmitters and hormones.

The physical effects of marijuana include increases in pulse rate and blood pressure, reddening of the eyes, coughing, and dryness of the mouth. Psychological effects include a mixture of excitatory, depressive, and mildly hallucinatory characteristics, making it difficult to classify the drug. Marijuana can trigger spontaneous unrelated ideas, distorted perceptions of time and place, increased sensitivity to sounds and colors, and erratic verbal behavior. Marijuana can also impair attention and memory. When used daily in large amounts, marijuana can also alter sperm count and change hormonal cycles; it might be involved in some birth defects. Marijuana use declined during the 1980s, but an upsurge in its use has occurred in the 1990s (Johnston, O'Malley, & Bachman, 1996).

hallucinogens

Psychoactive drugs that modify a person's perceptual experiences and produce hallucinatory visual images. Hallucinogens are also called psychedelic ("mind altering") drugs.

Hallucinogens. *Hallucinogens are psychoactive drugs that modify a person's perceptual experiences and produce visual images that are not real. Hallucinogens are also called psychedelic drugs, which means "mind altering."* LSD, PCP, and mescaline are examples of hallucinogens.

LSD (lysergic acid diethylamide) is a hallucinogen that even in low doses produces striking perceptual changes. Objects change their shape and glow. Colors become kaleidoscopic, fabulous images unfold as users close their eyes. Designs swirl, colors shimmer, bizarre scenes appear. Sometimes the images are pleasurable; sometimes they are grotesque. Figure 4.7 shows one kind of perceptual experience that a number of LSD users have reported. LSD can influence the user's perception of time as well. Time often seems to slow down dramatically, so that brief glances at objects are experienced as deep, penetrating, and lengthy examinations, and minutes often seem to be hours or days.

LSD's effects on the body can include dizziness, nausea, and tremors. LSD acts primarily on the neurotransmitter serotonin in the brain, though it can affect dopamine as well. Emotional and cognitive effects can include rapid mood swings and impaired attention and memory. LSD was popular in the late 1960s and early 1970s, but its popularity dropped after its unpredictable effects became well publicized. However, a recent increase in LSD use by high school and college students has been reported (Johnston, O'Malley, & Bachman, 1996). LSD may be a prime example of generational forgetting. Today's youth don't hear what an earlier generation heard—that LSD can cause bad trips and undesirable flashbacks.

When people have a problem with substance abuse, what can they do? The discussion in the Applications box on contrasting views of treating alcoholism can help. See also the recommendations in Improving Personal and Cognitive Skills ("How to Help People with Substance-Abuse Problems").

Improving Personal and Cognitive Skills

How to Help with Substance-Abuse Problems

Whether you or someone you care about is struggling with substance abuse, several strategies may help:

- *Look at the evidence.*
Chances are good that other people have expressed their concerns to the person with substance-abuse problems. Unfortunately, most substance abusers deny that they have a problem. Before rejecting the idea outright, evaluate the evidence.
- *Accept that the problem exists.*
Once you accept the possibility of a serious problem, it is easier to muster the energy needed to change or to help others change.
- *Seek qualified help.*
Most towns and campuses provide access to qualified substance-abuse counselors. A treatment program might

be covered by health insurance or might be available at no cost. Alcoholics Anonymous and other not-for-profit agencies might provide help.
- *Redesign social life.*
Substance abusers might not make significant progress in managing the problem until they rid themselves of people who sabotage their attempts to become drug-free.
- *Use the resources section at the end of this chapter.*
You will find phone numbers and information about organizations that can help people deal effectively with substance abuse.

Be willing to have it so; acceptance of what has happened is the first step to overcome the consequences of any misfortune.
—WILLIAM JAMES, *American Psychologist, 19th/20th Century*

Review

Psychoactive Drugs and Addictions

Psychoactive drugs act on the central nervous system to alter states of consciousness, modify perceptions, and alter mood. Psychoactive substances have been used since the beginning of recorded history for pleasure, utility, curiosity, and social reasons. Tolerance for a psychoactive drug develops when a greater amount of the drug is needed to produce the same effect. Physical withdrawal is the intense pain and craving that arise when an addicted person stops taking the addictive drug. Psychological dependence is the need to take a drug to cope with problems and stress.

Alcohol is an extremely powerful drug that acts on the body primarily as a depressant. Drinking makes people less inhibited and impairs their judgment, motor skills, and intellectual functioning. With extreme intoxication, the drinker

may lapse into a coma and even die. Effects of alcohol vary according to a number of factors. Alcohol is the most widely used drug in America and the third leading killer. A special concern is the high rate of alcohol consumption by high school and college students. People in many countries drink more than people in the United States do.

Barbiturates are depressant drugs that induce sleep or reduce anxiety. Tranquilizers are depressant drugs that reduce anxiety and induce relaxation. Opiates (opium and its derivatives) depress the central nervous system's activity. Stimulants are psychoactive drugs that increase central nervous system activity. The most widely used stimulants are caffeine, nicotine, amphetamines, and cocaine. Cocaine provides a euphoric rush that is followed by depres-

sion, lethargy, insomnia, and irritability. Cocaine can trigger a heart attack, stroke, or brain seizure. Crack is an intensified form of cocaine and is believed to be one of the most addictive drugs. Treatments for cocaine addiction have not been very successful. Marijuana's psychological effects include a mixture of excitatory, depressive, and mildly hallucinatory characteristics, making the drug difficult to classify. Marijuana affects a number of neurotransmitters and hormones, and can impair attention and memory. Hallucinogens are psychoactive drugs that modify a person's perceptual experiences and produce visual images that are not real. Hallucinogens are also called psychedelic ("mind altering") drugs. LSD, PCP, and mescaline are examples of hallucinogens. There has been a recent increase in use of LSD.

Overview

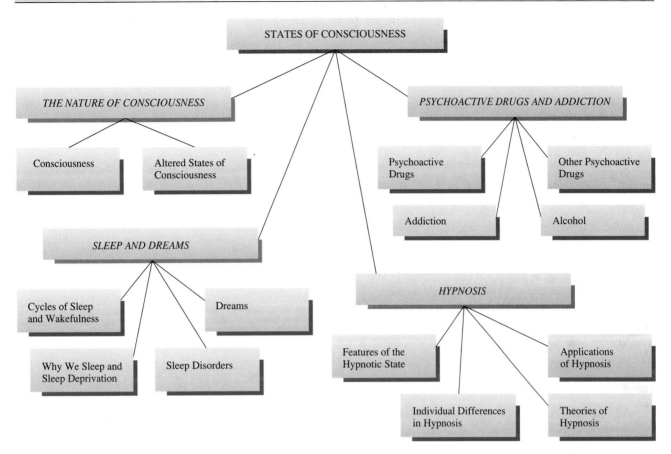

We began this chapter by exploring the nature of consciousness, and then studied about sleep and dreams—sleep and wake cycles, sleep theories, sleep deprivation, sleep disorders, and dreams. Next, we examined hypnosis, evaluating its features, individual differences, theories, and applications. In the final section of the chapter we read about psychoactive drugs and addiction. Don't forget that you can obtain an overall summary of the chapter by again reading the in-chapter reviews on pages 133, 137, 139, and 146.

Key Terms

Thinking It Over

Exercises in . . .

. . . In Critical Thinking

Many people believe that the lure of alcohol is so strong that alcoholics cannot afford to take even one drink once they have decided that they are alcoholics. Others believe that even alcoholics can learn to drink in moderation. Which side do you favor in this debate? Once you have identified your position, see if you can construct a compelling argument for the opposite side.

. . . In Creative Thinking

Monitor your dreams for one week. Take down the details of your dream life that you remember upon awakening each morning. Look for the possibility that the elements you are using in your dream have deeper meanings. Try to generate several hypotheses about the most prominent elements of your dreams. Do these elements symbolize other things? Or do your dreams feel more like a hodgepodge of ideas randomly assembled in your unconscious?

. . . In Active Learning

See if your instructor can arrange for a hypnotist to visit class. If possible, volunteer to be a subject for the hypnotist. Then decide which theory seems more accurate to you in explaining hypnotic behavior. Did you feel the presence of a hidden observer? Did you merely conform to the social demands of the situation? Or did you fail to succumb to the hypnotist's requests?

. . . In Reflective Learning

Social critics long have suggested that American culture regularly reinforces substance use and abuse. Advertising, movies, and even song lyrics might encourage the use of drugs and alcohol. For one week, monitor the entertainment channels you normally listen to. Record any references you hear to drug use. In a journal entry, reflect on the significance of the number of references you hear.

Resources for Psychology and Improving Humankind

Addiction Research Foundation/Foundation de la recherche sur la toxomanie

33 Russell St.
Toronto ON M5S 2S1 CANADA
416-595-6111
800-387-2916 (in Canada)

The Foundation's information line offers a tape on drug and alcohol abuse. The staff will discuss substance abuse issues. They maintain a reference library, an audiovisual desk, and a pharmacy, and they provide educational materials. They also provide information on treatment programs. Information is available in English, French, Cantonese, Greek, Hindi, Italian, Mandarin, Polish, Portuguese, Punjabi, Spanish, and Urdu.

Alcoholics Anonymous World Services

475 Riverside Drive
New York, NY
212-870-3400

Alcoholics Anonymous (AA) provides support groups for individuals with drinking problems or other addictive behaviors. Most communities have local chapters of AA.

Alliance for a Drug-Free Canada/Alliance pour un Canada sans drogues

P.O. Box 355 Station A
Toronto, ON M5W 1C5 CANADA
416-730-4217
800-563-5000 (in Canada)

American Narcolepsy Association

425 California Street
San Francisco, CA 94104
800-222-6085

This organization is devoted to improving the quality of life of individuals who suffer from narcolepsy or sleep apnea. The association maintains a library and publishes the quarterly newsletter *Eye Opener.*

Association for the Study of Dreams

P.O. Box 1600
Vienna, VA 22183
703-242-8889

This association provides an international, interdisciplinary forum for furthering knowledge about dreams. Medical professionals, psychologists, educators, and students are welcomed as members. The group publishes a quarterly newsletter.

Hypnosis: Questions and Answers (1986)

by B. Zilbergeld, M. Edlestein, and D. Araoz
New York: Norton

A number of experts answer questions about a wide range of topics pertaining to hypnosis.

Lucid Dreaming (1988)

by Stephen LaBerge
Los Angeles: Tarcher

If you want to try to increase your lucid dreaming, this book will tell you how. Easy-to-follow instructions are included, along with an examination of the nature of dreaming.

National Clearinghouse for Alcohol Information

P.O. Box 2345
1776 East Jefferson Street
Rockville, MD 20852

This clearinghouse provides information about a wide variety of issues related to drinking problems.

Rational Recovery Systems

P.O. Box 800
Lotus, CA 95651
916-621-4374

This organization uses the techniques of Albert Ellis's rational emotive therapy to teach individuals how to eliminate their addictive behavior. An increasing number of cities have Rational Recovery programs.

Sleep/Wake Disorders Canada/Affections du sommeil/eveil Canada

3089 Bathurst St. Suite 304
Toronto, ON M6A 2A4 CANADA
416-787-5374
800-387-9253

Sleep/Wake Disorders Canada is a national, self-help registered charity dedicated to helping the thousands of Canadians suffering from sleep/wake disorders. They have chapters across the country, and members work to improve the quality of life, alertness, and productivity of persons with sleep/wake disorders. SWDC offers information brochures, articles, booklets, and videos and publishes a quarterly newsletter, *Good/Night Good/Day.*

Internet Resources

http://www.nida.nih.gov/
National Institute on Drug Abuse provides comprehensive links for managing drug problems.

http://www.health.org/
Prevention On-line offers statistics and resources about substance abuse.

http://www.samhsa.gov/
Substance Abuse and Mental Health Service Administration home page.

file:///Int%202/Podunk/conciousness%20netsites
SleepNet offers advice on everything you wanted to know about sleep disorders but were too tired to ask.

http://www.pacificcoast.com/healthy/healthy.html
Healthy Sleep site offers tips on healthy sleep habits.

http://www.lucidity.com/
The Lucidity Institute explores the nature of dreams

http://www.lucidity.com/Tucson2.abs.html
Stephen LaBerge discusses dreaming and consciousness.

http://www.social.com/health/nhic/data/hr0300/hr0302.html
American Society of Clinical Hypnosis home page.

http://www.geocities.com/CapeCanaveral/9862/
A newsletter devoted to hypnosis and hypnotherapy.

http://nietzsche.physics.ubc.ca/~olav/MiscDocs/general Info.html
Learn about the use of sensory deprivation tanks.

5

Learning

OUTLINE

BOXES

Experience is the only teacher.

—RALPH WALDO EMERSON

American Poet and Essayist, 19th Century

PREVIEW

*P*sychologists explain our many experiences in terms of a few basic learning processes. We respond to things that happen to us, we act and then experience the consequences of our behavior, and we observe what others say and do. These aspects of experience form the three main types of learning we will study in this chapter: classical conditioning (responding), operant conditioning (acting), and observational learning (observing). As we study the nature of learning, you will discover that early approaches investigated the way experience and behavior are connected without referring to cognitive, or mental, processes. In recent years, cognitive processes have assumed a more important role in learning. We will discuss cognitive approaches to learning later in the chapter, but first we will further explore what learning is.

The Story of International Big Bird: Diplomat in Feathers

*H*e is over 8 feet tall, has big orange feet, and is covered with yellow feathers. He has spent years practicing basic skills, such as counting and rehearsing the letters in the alphabet, and asking questions of the other inhabitants of "Sesame Street." He definitely prefers the company of little people to adults. And he is a surprisingly effective teacher.

Television is a powerful vehicle for *observational learning* (learning by watching what other people do and say). Observational learning has changed drastically in the twentieth century because of television, which has touched the life of virtually every person in the United States. Television has been called a lot of names, not all of them

(Left) Big Bird, a surprisingly effective teacher; *(right)* Don Pimpon of Spain's "Barrio Sesamo" is a shaggy old codger who has traveled extensively and entertains with stories of his adventures. "Barrio Sesamo" helps young children in Spain learn social and cognitive skills.

good—*the one-eyed monster* or *the boob tube,* for example. Television has also been accused of interfering with children's academic growth, luring them away from schoolwork and books and making them passive learners. It has also been criticized for promoting violence. However, many psychologists believe that the influence is not entirely negative.

Big Bird's success demonstrated that television can contribute to children's learning. Television can introduce children to worlds that are different from the ones in which they live. "Sesame Street" was designed to improve children's cognitive and social skills (Green, 1995). Almost half of America's 2- to 5-year olds watch it regularly (Liebert & Sprafkin, 1988). "Sesame Street" uses fast-paced action, sound effects, music, and humorous characters to grab the attention of its young audience. With their eyes glued to the screen, young children learn basic academic skills. Studies have shown that regular "Sesame Street" viewers from low-income families, when they enter first grade, are rated by their teachers as better prepared for school than their counterparts who don't watch "Sesame Street" regularly (Bogatz & Ball, 1972; Wright, 1995).

Joan Ganz Cooney had no idea when her company, the Children's Television Workshop, created a home for Big Bird and his companions that they would become an influential force in learning for children, not just in the United States but in locations as distant as Kuwait, Israel, Latin America, and the Philippines. Since "Sesame Street" first aired in the United States in 1969, the show has been televised in eighty-four countries and has been adapted in thirteen foreign-language versions of the show. "Plaza Seesamo," shown in seventeen South and Central American countries as well as Puerto Rico, emphasizes diversity in cultures and lifestyles. Israel's "Rechove Sumsum" encourages children to learn how people from different ethnic and religious backgrounds can live in harmony. In the Netherlands, "Sesamstraat" teaches children about the concept of school from a 7-foot-tall blue bird named Pino. Whatever his color, Big Bird may be our best ambassador.

DEFINING LEARNING

When you think of learning, you might imagine yourself seated at a desk, pouring over books, trying hard to absorb facts so that you can do well on an examination. Studying does help you learn about and remember new ideas, but the concept of learning in this chapter emphasizes acquiring new behaviors and skills. Let's look at some examples to clarify this distinction.

In learning how to use a computer, you might make some mistakes along the way, but at a certain point you will get the knack of the behaviors that make the computer work efficiently. You will *change* from someone who cannot operate a computer into one who can. Usually, once you have learned to use a computer, your skills remain stable. (This is like learning to drive a car—once you have learned how, you do not have to repeat the process again.) Learning involves a *relatively permanent* influence on behavior. Through experience you also learned that you need to study in order to do well on a test or that you need to allow extra time when traveling during rush hour traffic. This contrasts with a full repertoire of behaviors that you didn't have to learn from experience. For example, no one taught you to blink or to swallow. Birds sing species-specific songs without training. These are examples of **fixed action patterns,** *behaviors that are driven by genetic inheritance and are species-specific.* Putting these pieces together, we arrive at a definition: **Learning** *is a relatively permanent change in behavior that occurs through experience.*

> *To learn is a natural pleasure.*
>
> —ARISTOTLE, *Greek Philosopher, 4th Century B.C.*

We need to draw one other distinction between behaviors that are learned versus behaviors that are unlearned. The capacities for some behaviors are inborn, or innate. For example, we do not have to be taught to swallow, to flinch at loud noises, or to blink when an object comes too close to our eyes. These behaviors are reflexes and do not have to be learned. However, most complex human behaviors cannot be considered innate. Learning is an important, complex process that promotes our adaptation to the challenges of our environment (Howard, 1995).

Psychologists argue about what is the best way to describe learning. Some believe that learning is a single but complex process. Others believe that we can distinguish different types of learning. We will begin by exploring the form of learning that psychologists call classical conditioning.

CLASSICAL CONDITIONING

It is a nice spring day. A father takes his baby out for a walk. The baby reaches over to touch a pink flower and is stung by a bumblebee sitting on the petals. The next day, the baby's mother brings home some pink flowers. She removes a flower from the arrangement and takes it over for her baby to smell. The baby cries loudly as soon as she sees the pink flower. The baby's panic at the sight of the pink flower illustrates the learning process of **classical conditioning,** *in which a neutral stimulus becomes associated with a meaningful stimulus and acquires the capacity to elicit a similar response.*

How Classical Conditioning Works

In the early 1900s, Russian physiologist Ivan Pavlov investigated the way the body digests food. As part of his experiments, he routinely placed meat powder in a dog's mouth, causing the dog to salivate. Pavlov began to notice that the meat powder was not the only stimulus that caused the dog to salivate. The dog also salivated in response to a number of stimuli associated with the food, such as the sight of the food dish, the sight of the individual who brought the food into the room, and the sound of the door closing when the food arrived. Pavlov recognized that the dog's association of these sights and sounds with the food was an important type of learning (which came to be called classical conditioning).

Pavlov wanted to know *why* the dog salivated to various sights and sounds before eating the meat powder. Pavlov observed that the dog's behavior included both learned and unlearned components. The unlearned part of classical conditioning is based on the fact that some stimuli automatically produce certain responses apart from any prior learning; in other words, the responses are inborn, or innate. **Reflexes** *are automatic stimulus-response connections that are "hard-wired" into the brain and body.* They include salivation in response to food, nausea in response to bad food, shivering in response to low temperature, coughing in response to the throat's being clogged, pupil constriction in response to light, and withdrawal in response to a blow, burns, or pain, among others. An **unconditioned stimulus (US)** *is a stimulus that produces a response without prior learning;* food was the US in Pavlov's experiments. An **unconditioned response (UR)** *is an unlearned response that is automatically associated with the US.* In Pavlov's experiments, the saliva that flowed from the dog's mouth was the UR in response to the food, which was the US. In the case of the baby and her pink

fixed action patterns
Behaviors that are driven by genetic inheritance and are species-specific.

learning
A relatively permanent change in behavior that occurs through experience.

classical conditioning
A form of learning in which a neutral stimulus becomes associated with a meaningful stimulus and acquires the capacity to elicit a similar response.

reflexes
Automatic stimulus-response connections that are "hardwired" into the brain.

unconditioned stimulus (US)
A stimulus that produces a response without prior learning.

unconditioned response (UR)
An unlearned response that is automatically associated with the unconditioned stimulus.

If a bee stings this young girl while she is holding a pink flower, how would classical conditioning explain her panic at the sight of pink flowers in the future?

flower, the baby did not have to learn to cry when the bee stung her. Pain reactions are reflexive, or unlearned; a child's crying occurs automatically in response to the pain of a bee sting. In this example, the bee's sting is the US and the crying is the UR.

conditioned stimulus (CS)

A previously neutral stimulus that elicits the conditioned response after being paired with the unconditioned stimulus.

conditioned response (CR)

The learned response to the conditioned stimulus that occurs after CS-US association.

In classical conditioning, the **conditioned stimulus (CS)** *is a previously neutral stimulus that elicits the conditioned response after being associated with the unconditioned stimulus.* The **conditioned response (CR)** *is the learned response to the conditioned stimulus that occurs after CS-US association* (Pavlov, 1927). While he was conducting studies on digestive processes in dogs, Pavlov observed that striking a tone from a tuning fork before giving meat powder to a dog stimulated the dog's saliva flow. Prior to its association with the food, the tone had no particular effect on the dog; that is, originally the tone was a neutral stimulus. However, once the dog began to associate the tone with the arrival of the food, the dog salivated when it heard the tone. The tone became a conditioned (learned) stimulus (CS), and the salivation a conditioned response (CR). Before conditioning (or learning), the tone and food were not related. After the association, the conditioned stimulus (the tone) elicited a conditioned response (salivation). For the unhappy baby, the flower was the CS and the crying was the CR after the baby associated the flower with the sting (UC). Figure 5.1 shows Pavlov's laboratory setting for studying classical conditioning and Pavlov demonstrating the procedure. A summary of how classical conditioning works is shown in figure 5.2.

Classical Conditioning Phenomena

Pavlov became intrigued with the associations dogs would make through conditioning. He began systematic study of classical conditioning phenomena and established many principles that are still accepted today. We will examine several of these phenomena, including generalization, discrimination, extinction, and spontaneous recovery.

(a)

(b)

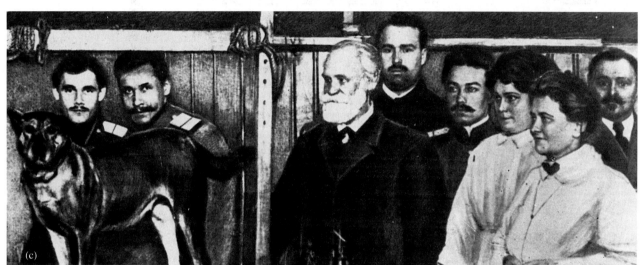

(c)

𝓕IGURE 5.1

Pavlov's Experimentation

(a) Surgical preparation for studying the salivary reflex: when the dog salivated, the saliva collected in a glass funnel attached to the dog's cheek. This way the strength of the salivary response could be measured precisely. *(b)* Shown here is Pavlov's experimental apparatus used to examine classical conditioning. *(c)* Pavlov (the white bearded gentleman in the center) is shown demonstrating the nature of classical conditioning to students at the Military Medical Academy in the Soviet Union.

generalization

In classical conditioning, the tendency of a new stimulus that is similar to the original conditioned stimulus to elicit a response that is similar to the conditioned response.

discrimination

In classical conditioning, the process of learning to respond to certain stimuli and not to others.

Generalization.   After many conditioning trials, Pavlov found that the dog salivated not only in response to the tone from the tuning fork, but to other sounds, such as a whistle. Pavlov did not pair these sounds with the unconditioned stimulus of the food. He discovered that the more similar the noise was to the original sound of the tone, the stronger the dog's salivary flow. In the example of conditioned fear of pink flowers, the baby not only cried at the sight of pink flowers, but she also learned to cry at the sight of red and orange flowers. **Generalization** *in classical conditioning is the tendency of a new stimulus that is similar to the original conditioned stimulus to elicit a response that is similar to the conditioned response.*

Discrimination.   Generalizing from one stimulus to another is not always beneficial. For example, a cat that generalizes from a minnow to a piranha has a major problem: In the one situation, the cat might retrieve dinner; in the other, the cat might become dinner. Therefore, in many situations it can be important to discriminate between stimuli. **Discrimination** *in classical conditioning is the process of learning to respond to certain stimuli and not to respond to others.* To produce discrimination among different stimuli, Pavlov gave food to the dog only after ringing the bell and not after any other sounds. In

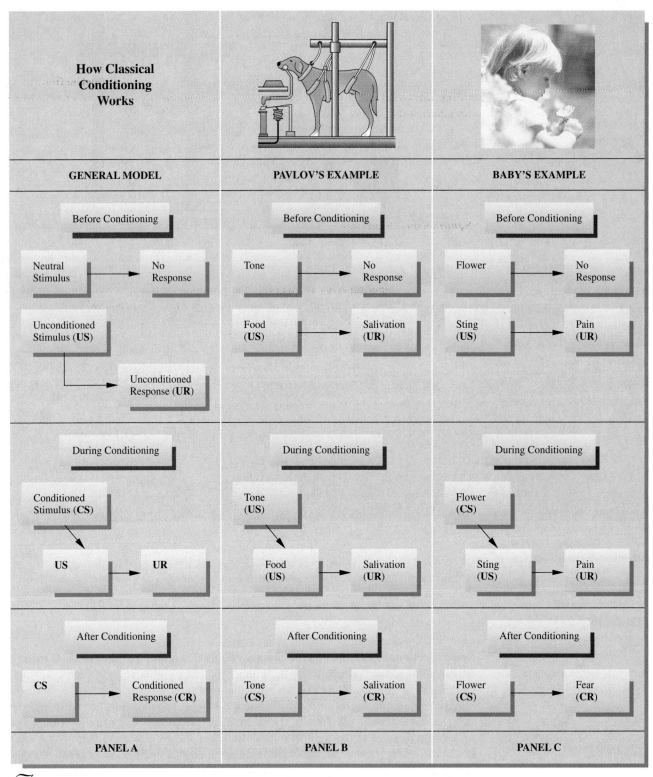

How Classical Conditioning Works

GENERAL MODEL	PAVLOV'S EXAMPLE	BABY'S EXAMPLE
Before Conditioning	**Before Conditioning**	**Before Conditioning**
Neutral Stimulus → No Response	Tone → No Response	Flower → No Response
Unconditioned Stimulus (US) → Unconditioned Response (UR)	Food (US) → Salivation (UR)	Sting (US) → Pain (UR)
During Conditioning	**During Conditioning**	**During Conditioning**
Conditioned Stimulus (CS) ↘ US → UR	Tone (US) ↘ Food (US) → Salivation (UR)	Flower (CS) ↘ Sting (US) → Pain (UR)
After Conditioning	**After Conditioning**	**After Conditioning**
CS → Conditioned Response (CR)	Tone (CS) → Salivation (CR)	Flower (CS) → Fear (CR)
PANEL A	PANEL B	PANEL C

FIGURE 5.2

Classical Conditioning Procedure

Panel A illustrates the general model of classical conditioning. Before any conditioning takes place, a neutral stimulus produces no response from the organism. However, the organism also shows an automatic or reflexive response, the unconditioned response (UR), to an unconditioned stimulus (US). When the neutral stimulus precedes the US, it begins to take on new meaning and becomes the conditioned stimulus (CS). If sufficient pairings of the CS and US occur, eventually the CS will elicit a response by itself. The conditioned response (CR) usually will be very similar to the UR that originally was elicited by the US. Panel B illustrates how this procedure worked to produce salivation in dogs (CR) to a tone struck from a tuning fork (CS). Panel C demonstrates how the pain (UR) from a bee sting (US) can lead to fear (CR) of flowers (CS).

this way the dog learned to distinguish between the bell and other sounds. Similarly, the baby did not cry at the sight of blue flowers, thus discriminating between blue and pink flowers.

Extinction.   When Pavlov rang the bell repeatedly in a single session and did not give the dog any food, eventually the dog stopped salivating. This result is **extinction,** *which in classical conditioning is the weakening of the conditioned response in the absence of the unconditioned stimulus.* Without continued association with the unconditioned stimulus (US), the conditioned stimulus (CS) loses its power to elicit the conditioned response (CR). Over time the baby encountered many pink flowers and was not stung by a bee. Consequently, her fear of pink flowers subsided and eventually disappeared. The pink flower (CS) lost its capacity to generate fear (CR) when the flower was no longer associated with bee stings (US) and the pain and fear they cause (UR).

Spontaneous Recovery.   Extinction is not always the end of the conditioned response. The day after Pavlov extinguished the conditioned salivation at the sound of a bell, he took the dog to the laboratory and rang the bell, still not giving the dog any meat powder. The dog salivated, indicating that an extinguished response can spontaneously appear again. **Spontaneous recovery** *is the process in classical conditioning by which a conditioned response can appear again without further conditioning.* In the case of the baby, even though she saw many pink flowers after her first painful encounter and was not "stung" by them, she showed some signs of fear of pink flowers from time to time. Over time, her conditioned fear (CR) of pink flowers (CS) diminished; she showed less tendency to recover her fear of pink flowers spontaneously, particularly because she didn't experience further painful stings (US). Figure 5.3 shows the sequence of extinction and spontaneous recovery. Spontaneous recovery can occur several times; however, as long as the conditioned stimulus is presented without the unconditioned stimulus, spontaneous recovery becomes weaker over time and eventually ceases to occur.

extinction

In classical conditioning, the weakening of the conditioned response in the absence of the unconditioned stimulus.

spontaneous recovery

The process in classical conditioning by which a conditioned response can appear again after a time delay without further conditioning.

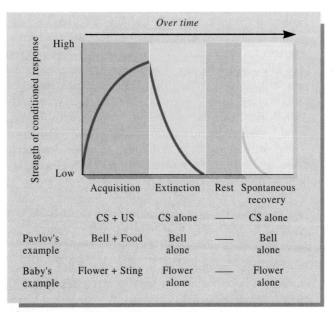

𝓕IGURE 5.3

The Strength of a Classically Conditioned Response During Acquisition, Extinction, and Spontaneous Recovery

During acquisition, the experimenter pairs the conditioned stimulus and the unconditioned stimulus. As seen in the graph, when this occurs over time, the strength of the conditioned response increases. During extinction, the experimenter presents the conditioned stimulus alone. This results in a decrease of the conditioned response. After a rest period, spontaneous recovery appears, although the strength of the conditioned response is not nearly as great at this point as it was after a number of CS-US pairings. When the experimenter presents the CS alone again after spontaneous recovery, the response extinguishes rapidly.

Applications in Human Classical Conditioning

Since Pavlov's accidental discovery, individuals have been conditioned to an impressive array of stimuli in the laboratory and in life. Because of classical conditioning, we jerk our hands away before they are burned by fire. We move out of the way of a rapidly approaching truck before it hits us. We escape if someone yells, "Fire!" Our capacity for making associations has a great deal of survival value.

Classical conditioning also explains some pleasant emotions. The sight of a rainbow, a sunny day, or a favorite song might produce special pleasure due to classical conditioning. If you have had a romantic experience, the location where that experience took place can become a conditioned stimulus. This is the result of the pairing of a neutral place (CS) with a pleasurable event (US). In the same vein, a pleasant interaction with someone who is quite different from other people you have known (for instance, who comes from another country or who is physically different) can also through classical conditioning, lead you to have positive expectations about others who are similar to that person.

Psychologists have also shown that classical conditioning can enhance the quality of life. For example, by imagining a tranquil scene—such as an abandoned beach with waves lapping onto the sand—a harried executive might relax as if she were actually lying on that beach. This result is due to her ability to make associations. Psychotherapists often recommend mental imagery about positive scenes to promote relaxation. Or using classical conditioning, a therapist might condition a client to react with revulsion at the sight of a cigarette.

phobias

Irrational fears.

However, sometimes classical conditioning can make life miserable, as when **phobias,** or *irrational fears,* develop. Classical conditioning provides an explanation of how we acquire irrational fears of pink flowers and other harmless objects. Behaviorist John Watson conducted an investigation to demonstrate classical conditioning's role in phobias. He showed a little boy named Albert a white laboratory rat to see if Albert was afraid of it. He was not. As Albert played with the rat, Watson banged a 4-foot steel bar with a hammer behind Albert's head to make a loud noise. As you might imagine, the noise caused little Albert to startle and cry. After only seven pairings of the loud noise with the white rat, Albert began to fear the rat even when the noise was not sounded. Albert's fear was generalized to a rabbit, a dog, and sealskin coat (see figure 5.4). Today we could not ethically conduct such an experiment because research review boards would have determined that the experiment lacked appropriate protection for little Albert. Especially noteworthy is the fact that Watson and his associate (Watson & Rayner, 1920) did not later remove Albert's fear of rats, so presumably this phobia could have remained with him after the experiment. Many of our fears—fear of the dentist after painful dental work, fear of driving after being in an automobile accident, and fear of dogs after being bitten, for example—can be learned through classical conditioning.

> *There is perhaps nothing so bad and so dangerous in life as fear.*
> —Jawaharlal Nehru, *Indian Political Leader, 20th Century*

counterconditioning

A classical conditioning procedure for weakening a conditioned response of fear by associating the fear-provoking stimulus with a new response that is incompatible with the fear.

If we can produce fears by classical conditioning, we should be able to eliminate them using conditioning procedures. **Counterconditioning** *is a classical conditioning procedure for weakening a conditioned response of fear by associating the fear-producing stimulus with a new response that is incompatible with the fear.* Though Watson did not eliminate little Albert's fear of white rats, an associate of Watson's, Mary Cover Jones (1924), did eliminate the fears of a 3-year-old boy named Peter. Peter had many of the same fears as Albert; however, Peter's fears were not produced by Jones. Among the things Peter feared were white rats, fur coats, frogs, fish, and mechanical toys. To eliminate these fears, a rabbit was brought into Peter's view but kept far enough away that it would not upset him. At the same time the rabbit was brought into view, Peter was fed crackers and milk. On each successive day, the rabbit was moved closer to Peter as he ate crackers and milk. Eventually Peter reached the point where he could eat the food with one hand and pet the rab-

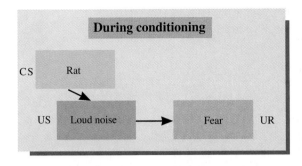

During conditioning

CS   Rat

US   Loud noise   →   Fear   UR

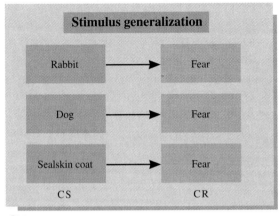

Stimulus generalization

Rabbit   →   Fear

Dog   →   Fear

Sealskin coat   →   Fear

CS   CR

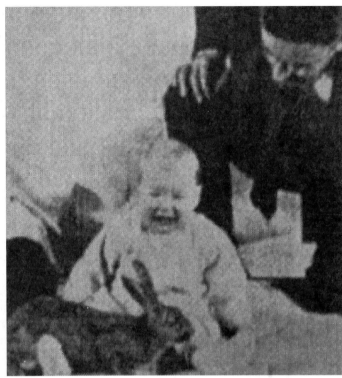

$\mathcal{F}$IGURE 5.4

Little Albert's Generalized Fear

In 1920, Watson and Rayner conditioned 9-month-old little Albert to fear a white rat by pairing the rat with a loud noise. When little Albert was subsequently placed with other stimuli similar to the white rat, such as the rabbit shown here with little Albert, he was afraid of them, too. This illustrates the principle of stimulus generalization in classical conditioning.

bit with the other. The feeling of pleasure produced by the crackers and milk was incompatible with his feeling of fear of the rabbit, and the fear was extinguished through counterconditioning.

Some of the behaviors we associate with certain health problems or mental disorders can involve classical conditioning. Classical conditioning can play a role in stress-related physical complaints, such as asthma, headaches, ulcers, and high blood pressure. We usually say that such health problems are caused by stress, but they are more properly said to be aggravated by stress. Often certain stimuli, such as a boss's critical attitude or a spouse's threat of divorce, become conditioned stimuli for physiological responses. Over time the frequent presence of the physiological responses may produce a health problem or disorder. A boss's persistent criticism might cause an employee to develop muscle tension, headaches, or high blood pressure. Anything associated with the boss, such as work itself, can then trigger stress responses in the employee (see figure 5.5).

Classical conditioning also explains how prejudices develop. For example, a child might get into an argument with a child from a different ethnic background. The child might generalize the bad experience to others from that ethnic background. In this way, the original negative feelings experienced with another person spreads to create negative feelings toward all people of that ethnic group.

Evaluation of Classical Conditioning

Several of Pavlov's principles have been challenged by more recent research in classical or Pavlovian conditioning (Rescorla, 1988). Pavlov proposed that repeated pairing of the CS and US would *eventually* produce a conditioned response. He believed that the interval between the CS and the US is one of the most important aspects of classical conditioning.

Classical Conditioning   **159**

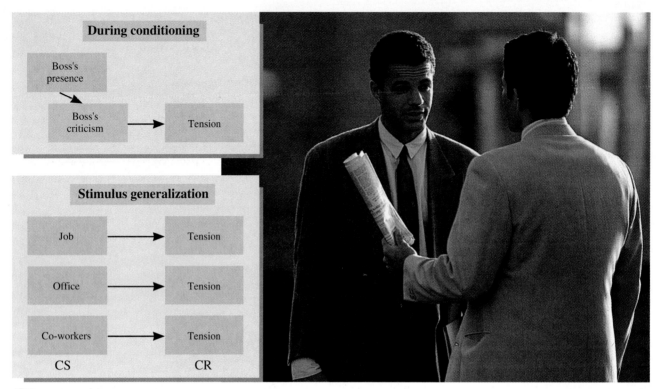

During conditioning

Boss's presence → Boss's criticism → Tension

Stimulus generalization

Job → Tension

Office → Tension

Co-workers → Tension

CS — CR

$\mathcal{F}$IGURE 5.5

How a Boss's Criticism Can Produce High Blood Pressure Through Classical Conditioning

stimulus substitution

Pavlov's theory of how classical conditioning works: The nervous system is structured in such a way that the CS and US bond together and eventually the CS substitutes for the US.

information theory

The contemporary explanation of how classical conditioning works: The key to understanding classical conditioning is the information the organism obtains from the situation.

latent learning

Changes in behavior that occur without direct experience.

The interval between the CS and the US defines the strength of association, or *contiguity,* of the stimuli. In many instances, optimal spacing between the CS presentation and the onset of the US is very short, a matter of seconds or even a fraction of a second (Kimble, 1961).

One of the most important differences between the contemporary view of classical conditioning and Pavlov's view involves the issue of how classical conditioning works. **Stimulus substitution** *was Pavlov's theory of how classical conditioning works; it states that the nervous system is structured in such a way that the CS and US bond together and eventually the CS substitutes for the US.* However, if the CS substitutes for the US, the two stimuli should produce similar responses. This does not always happen. Using a shock as a US often elicits flinching and jumping, whereas a light (CS) paired with a shock may cause the organism to be immobile, for example.

Information theory *is the contemporary explanation of how classical conditioning works. The key to understanding classical conditioning is in the information the organism obtains from the situation* (Rescorla & Wagner, 1972). Some years ago, E.C. Tolman (1932) speculated that the information value of a conditioned stimulus is important in telling the organism what will follow. He conducted research in which two groups of rats learned to run a maze. One group of rats was reinforced, the other was not. By the end of the training period, the rewarded rats committed few errors in running the maze. However, when rewards were offered to the previously unreinforced groups of rats, they also ran the maze efficiently. He referred to this behavior as **latent learning,** *changes in behavior that can take place without direct experience.* Tolman believed that the rats had learned the maze prior to being rewarded but rapidly changed their performance to receive the reward when the condition or conditioned stimulus changed. When rewards followed maze completion, the rats were able to distinguish the new learning contingency. In Tolman's view, the new contingency changed the rat's expectations about the task.

The contemporary view of classical conditioning sees the organism as an information seeker using logical and perceptual relations among events, along with preconceptions, to form a representation of the world (Rescorla, 1988). The contemporary view still

You will note that their ability to comprehend, assess and process information increases dramatically when Professor Podhertz throws in the cat.
© Leo Cullum, 1995.

recognizes contiguity between the CS and the US as important in classical conditioning, but it emphasizes that what is important about the CS-US connection is the information the stimuli give the organism.

Pavlov emphasized learning processes in terms of classical conditioning. Although classical conditioning helps us learn about our environment, we learn about our world in other ways, too. Classical conditioning emphasizes the organism's responding to the environment, a view that originally failed to capture the active nature of the organism and its influence on the environment. Next we will study a major explanation of learning that places more emphasis on the organism's *activity* in the environment—operant conditioning.

eview

The Nature of Learning and Classical Conditioning

Learning is a relatively permanent change in behavior due to experiences. How we respond to the environment (classical conditioning), how we act in the environment (operant conditioning), and how we observe the environment (observational learning) are the ways in which we learn new behavior. Early approaches emphasized connections between environment and behavior; many contemporary approaches stress that cognitive factors mediate environment-behavior connections.

Pavlov discovered that an organism learns the association between an unconditioned stimulus (US) and a conditioned stimulus (CS). The US automatically produces the UR (unconditioned response). After conditioning (CS-US pairing), the CS elicits the CR (conditioned response) by itself. Generalization, discrimination, and extinction also are involved. Classical conditioning has survival value for humans, as when we develop fear of hazardous conditions. Irrational fears often

are explained by classical conditioning. Counterconditioning has been used to eliminate fears. Pavlov explained classical conditioning in terms of stimulus substitution, but the modern explanation is based on information theory. Classical conditioning is important in explaining the way learning occurs in animals. It is not the only way we learn and misses the active nature of organisms in the environment.

OPERANT CONDITIONING

operant conditioning (instrumental conditioning)

A form of learning in which the consequences of behavior produce changes in the probability of the behavior's occurrence.

Classical conditioning excels at explaining how neutral stimuli become associated with unlearned, involuntary responses, but it might not be as effective in explaining voluntary behaviors, such as studying hard for a test, playing slot machines in Las Vegas, or teaching a pigeon to play Ping-Pong. Operant conditioning is usually better than classical conditioning at explaining *voluntary* behavior. The concept of operant conditioning was developed by the American psychologist B. F. Skinner (1938). **Operant conditioning** (or *instrumental conditioning*) *is a form of learning in which the consequences of behavior produce changes in the probability of the behavior's occurrence.* Skinner chose the term *operant* to describe the behavior of the organism—the behavior operates on the environment, and the environment in turn operates on the behavior. The consequences are *contingent,* or dependent, on the organism's behavior. For example, a simple operant might be pressing a lever that leads to the delivery of food; the delivery of food is contingent on pressing the lever.

We have mentioned one difference between classical and operant conditioning—classical conditioning is better at explaining learning that results from involuntary responding, whereas operant conditioning is better at explaining learning that results from voluntary responding. The emphasis in each form of learning is different as well. In classical conditioning, the emphasis is on the relation between the stimulus and the response. In operant conditioning, the emphasis is on the relation between the behavior (response) and its consequence. For example, suppose that we wanted to teach a dog to roll over. In operant conditioning, we would focus on the relation of the dog's trick behavior to the consequence (or rewarding stimulus), such as a pat on the head or a dog treat; the stimuli that govern behavior in operant conditioning *follow* the behavior. In classical conditioning, we are more likely to attend to the stimuli that *precede* the behavior. We might focus on developing discrimination between the cue for rolling over and the cue for sitting up if we were trying to apply classical conditioning procedures to dog training.

Thorndike's Law of Effect

Although B. F. Skinner has emerged as the primary figure in operant conditioning, E. L. Thorndike's experiments established the power of consequences in determining voluntary behavior. At about the same time Ivan Pavlov was conducting classical conditioning experiments with salivating dogs, American psychologist E. L. Thorndike was studying cats in puzzle boxes. Thorndike put a hungry cat inside a box and a piece of fish outside. To escape from the box, the cat had to learn how to open the latch inside the box. At first the cat made a number of ineffective responses. It clawed or bit at the bars and thrust its paw through the openings. Eventually the cat accidentally stepped on the treadle that released the door bolt. When the cat returned to the box, it went through the same random activity until it stepped on the treadle once more. On subsequent trials, the cat made fewer and fewer random movements, until it immediately clawed the treadle to open the door. The **law of effect,** *developed by Thorndike, states that behaviors followed by positive outcomes are strengthened, whereas behaviors followed by negative outcomes are weakened.*

The key question for Thorndike was how the correct stimulus-response bond strengthens and eventually dominates incorrect stimulus-response bonds. According to Thorndike, the correct S-R association strengthens and the incorrect association weakens because of the *consequences* of the organism's actions. Thorndike's view is called *S-R theory* because the organism's behavior is due to a connection between a stimulus and a response. As we see next, Skinners' operant conditioning approach expanded Thorndike's basic ideas.

law of effect

Developed by Robert Thorndike, this law states that behaviors followed by positive outcomes are strengthened, whereas behaviors followed by negative outcomes are weakened.

In 1948, Skinner wrote *Walden Two,* a novel in which he presented his ideas about building a scientifically managed society. Skinner envisioned a utopian society that could be engineered through behavioral control. Skinner viewed existing societies as poorly managed because people believe in myths such as free will. He pointed out that humans are no more free than pigeons are; denying that our behavior is controlled by environmental forces is to ignore science and reality, he argued. Skinner believed that in the long run we would be much happier when we recognized such truths, especially his concept that we could live a prosperous life under the control of positive reinforcement.

$\mathcal{F}$IGURE 5.6

Operant Conditioning in a Behavioral Laboratory

Shown here is a rat being conditioned in a Skinner box. Notice the elaborate machinery used to deliver food pellets as reinforcers and to keep track of the rat's behavior.

Skinner's Operant Conditioning

One of Skinner's basic beliefs was that the mechanisms of learning are the same for all species. This belief led him to an extensive study of animals in the hope that the basic mechanisms of learning could be understood with organisms more simple than humans. Skinner and other behaviorists have made every effort to study organisms under precisely controlled conditions so that the connection between the operant (a specific behavior) and the specific consequences could be examined in minute detail.

One of the ways in which Skinner achieved such control was the development in the 1930s of the Skinner box (see figure 5.6). A device in the box would deliver food pellets into a tray at random. After a rat became accustomed to the box, Skinner installed a lever and observed the rat's behavior. As the hungry rat explored the box, it occasionally pressed the lever and a food pellet would be dispensed. Soon after, the rat learned that the consequences of pressing the lever was positive—it would be fed. Further control was achieved by soundproofing the box to ensure that the consequence was the only influence on the organism. In many experiments the responses were mechanically recorded by a cumulative recorder and the food (the stimulus) was dispensed automatically. Such precautions were designed to avoid human error.

Skinner became a staunch advocate for the use of positive consequences to manage behavior. He created colorful demonstrations of this principle to support his viewpoint. For example, he taught pigeons to play table tennis and navigate torpedoes. Over the course of his animal studies, Skinner developed the basic principles of operant conditioning, which we will examine next.

reinforcement (reward)

A consequence that increases the probability that a behavior will occur.

positive reinforcement

Reinforcement in which the frequency of a response increases because the response is followed by a stimulus.

Reinforcement. **Reinforcement** *(reward) is a consequence that increases the probability that a behavior will occur. Reinforcement* means "to strengthen." In **positive reinforcement** *the frequency of a response increases because it is followed by a stimulus,* as in our example of the smile increasing talking. Similarly, complimenting someone you are attracted to might make that person more receptive to your advances and increase the probability that you will get to know the person better (see figure 5.7). The same principle of positive reinforcement is at work when an animal trainer teaches a dog to "shake hands" by giving it a piece of food when it lifts its paw.

"Once it became clear to me that, by responding correctly to certain stimuli, I could get all the bananas I wanted, getting this job was a pushover."
Jack Ziegler © 1998 from the Cartoon Bank. All rights Reserved.

negative reinforcement

Reinforcement in which the frequency of a response increases because the response either removes a stimulus or involves avoiding the stimulus.

punishment

A consequence that decreases the probability that a behavior will occur.

Conversely, in **negative reinforcement** *the frequency of a response increases because the response either removes a stimulus or involves avoiding the stimulus.* For example, your father nags at you to clean out the garage. He keeps nagging. Finally you get tired of the nagging and clean out the garage. Your response (cleaning out the garage) removed the unpleasant stimulus (nagging). Torture works the same way. An interrogator might say, "Tell me what I want to know and I will stop dripping water on your forehead." Taking aspirin is the same process: taking aspirin is reinforced when this behavior is followed by a reduction of pain (see figure 5.8).

Another way to remember the distinction between positive and negative reinforcement is that in *positive* reinforcement something is added, or obtained; in *negative* reinforcement something is *subtracted, avoided,* or *escaped.* For example, if you receive a sweater as a graduation present something has been added to increase your achievement behavior. But consider the situation when your parents criticize you for not studying hard enough. As you study harder, they stop criticizing you—something has been subtracted, in this case their criticism.

Punishment. **Punishment** *is a consequence that decreases the probability that a behavior will occur.* Richard Solomon (1964) stressed that punishment can be effective under certain conditions. He emphasized that to be effective, punishment needs to be immediate, consistent, and severe enough to alter the targeted behavior. He added that punishment is often misused because these principles are not followed.

𝓕IGURE 5.7

Positive Reinforcement

In positive reinforcement, the frequency of a response increases because it is followed by a stimulus. For example, in this stimulus situation, a male's flattering comments to a female have positive consequences, increasing the male's chances of getting to know the female better. His flattery is strengthened when he approaches other women in the future.

Positive reinforcement		
Behavior	Consequence +	Future behavior ↑
Flattering comments	Date responds with increased interest	Flattering increases

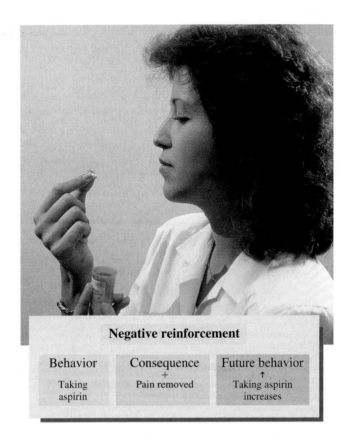

$\mathcal{F}$IGURE 5.8

Negative Reinforcement

In negative reinforcement, the frequency of behavior increases because the consequence of the behavior removes unpleasant stimuli or avoids the stimulus altogether. For example, aspirin removes or lessens pain, increasing the likelihood that one will take aspirin in the future at the first sign of a headache.

What are some of the circumstances when punishment might effectively be used? Punishment can be considered when positive reinforcement has not been found to work. Also, when the behavior that is being punished is viewed as more destructive than the punishment itself, then punishment might be justified. For example, some children engage in a behavior that is dangerous to their well-being, such as head banging. Punishment might reduce the destructive behavior. Nonetheless, as punishment is reduced, it is always wise to reinforce an alternative behavior so that undesirable behavior does not replace the punished response (Santrock, 1998).

Less severe forms of punishment create a negative consequence by removing opportunities for reward. *Time out* involves physically removing a child from a rewarding circumstance, such as play, for a specified period of time, say 5 to 10 minutes. Time-out procedures need to be adjusted according to the child's attention span and the severity of the behavior (see figure 5.9). *Response cost* is another punishment method. For example, an English professor might require students to complete one additional essay for each day they delay in turning in an assignment. When the response is inadequate (lateness), the penalty is the cost attached due to the additional writing.

Skinner believed that punishment is not especially effective in reducing the frequency of behavior and recommended positive reinforcement techniques as preferable. Punished individuals might learn to suppress the undesirable behavior rather than replace it with something more positive. When punishment is used, desirable as well as undesirable behaviors might be eliminated. For example, a child might stop interacting with other children altogether if he is slapped for biting another child. Punishment also can increase aggression. For example, a person who administers punishment is serving as an aggressive model, possibly inadvertently modeling how to behave in an aggressive, punitive way. Punishment can also lead to escape or avoidance. Punishment used with children is of special concern, because a significant proportion of child abuse evolves from excessive punishment used as an attempt to control children.

Negative reinforcement and punishment are easily confused because they both involve aversive or unpleasant stimuli, such as an electric shock or a slap in the face. To keep them straight, remember that negative reinforcement increases the probability a

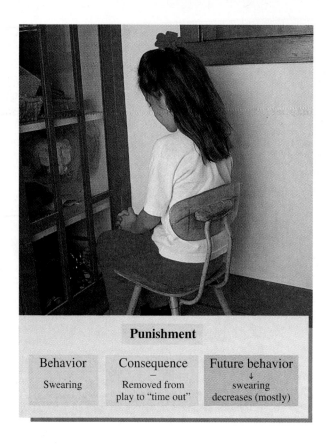

FIGURE 5.9

Punishment

In punishment, the frequency of a behavior usually decreases because the consequence of the behavior is undesirable. For example, a parent might teach a child not to swear by placing the child in time-out (consequence) when the child swears at a playmate (behavior). Punishment may not always work to reduce behavior so behavior modification specialists recommend using positive reinforcement to build preferred behaviors rather than using punishment alone to reduce inappropriate behaviors.

Punishment

Behavior	Consequence −	Future behavior ↓
Swearing	Removed from play to "time out"	swearing decreases (mostly)

response will occur, whereas punishment decreases the probability a response will occur. When an alcoholic consumes liquor to alleviate uncomfortable withdrawal symptoms, the probability of future alcohol use is increased. Avoiding withdrawal symptoms negatively reinforces drinking. However, if an inebriated alcoholic is seriously injured in a car wreck in which his drinking was a factor and he subsequently stops drinking, then punishment is involved because a behavior—drinking—was decreased.

Table 5.1 provides an overview of the distinctions among positive reinforcement, negative reinforcement, and punishment.

Table 5.1

Principles of Operant Conditioning

Process	Consequence	Effect on Behavior
Positive reinforcement	Pleasant +	Increases ↑
Negative reinforcement	Pleasant (by removing an aversive stimulus) +	Increases ↑
Punishment	Aversive −	Decreases (mostly) ↓

Time Interval. As with classical conditioning, in most situations learning is more efficient in operant conditioning when the interval between behavior and consequence is more likely on the order of seconds rather than minutes or hours. An especially important distinction to remember is that learning is more efficient under *immediate* rather than delayed consequences. To read further about the importance of time interval in learning, see Applications in Psychology.

shaping

The process of rewarding approximations of desired behavior.

Shaping and Chaining.   When a behavior is complex, the learning process in operant conditioning may be shortened if an *approximation* of the desired behavior is rewarded. **Shaping** *is the process of rewarding approximations of desired behavior.* In one situation,

$\mathscr{A}$pplications in Psychology

How Immediate and Delayed Consequences Influence Your Self-Control

- "That double-dutch chocolate dessert is just too good to pass up."
- "I know I should start exercising more but I guess I'm just too lazy to get started."
- "I've got an important paper due tomorrow morning. Why am I here at this party? Why don't I go home and write the paper?"

If you are like most people, self-control problems like these crop up in your life, unfortunately all too frequently. We often describe ourselves as not having enough willpower to handle these situations. Actually, many of these situations reflect a conflict between immediate and delayed consequences of behavior involving various combinations of reinforcers and punishers (Martin & Pear, 1988).

Immediate Small Reinforcers Versus Delayed Strong Punishers

One reason obesity is a major health problem is that eating is a behavior with immediate positive consequences—food tastes very good and quickly provides a pleasurable feeling. Although the potential delayed consequences of overeating (obesity and other possible health risks) are negative, immediate consequences are difficult to override. When the delayed consequences of behavior are punishing and the immediate consequences are reinforcing, the immediate consequences usually win, even when the immediate consequences are small reinforcers and the delayed consequences are major punishers. Smoking and drinking follow a similar pattern. The immediate consequences of smoking (the powerful combination of positive reinforcement—tension relief, energy boost—and negative reinforcement—removal of craving, "nicotine fit") are reinforcing for most smokers. The punishing aspects of smoking are primarily long-term including shortness of breath, a sore throat, coughing, emphysema, heart disease, lung cancer, and other cancers. The immediate pleasurable consequences of drinking override the delayed consequences of a hangover or even alcoholism.

Immediate Small Reinforcers Versus Delayed Stronger Reinforcers

Self-control problems also are brought about by the choice we face when we can obtain a small immediate reinforcer or wait

for a delayed but much-higher-valued reinforcer. For example, you can spend your money now on clothes, trinkets, parties, and the like or save your money and buy a house or car later. In another circumstance, you can play around now and enjoy yourself, which produces immediate small reinforcers, or you can study hard over a long period of time, which can produce delayed stronger reinforcers, such as good grades, scholarships to graduate school, and better jobs.

Immediate Punishers Versus Delayed Reinforcers

Why are some of us so reluctant to take up a new sport? To try a new dance step? To go to a social gathering? To do something different? One reason is that learning new skills often involves minor punishing consequences, such as initially looking stupid, not knowing what to do, having to put up with sarcastic comments from onlookers, and so on. In these circumstances, reinforcing consequences are often delayed. For example, it takes us a long time to become a good golfer or a good dancer and enjoy ourselves in these activities.

Immediate Weak Punishers Versus Strong Delayed Punishers

Why do so many of us postpone such activities as going to the dentist, scheduling minor surgery, or paying campus parking fines? In this kind of self-control problem, if we act immediately we experience a weak punisher—it hurts to get our teeth drilled, it is painful to have minor surgery, and it is not very pleasurable to pay a campus parking fine. However, the delayed consequences can be more punishing—our teeth can fall out, we might need major surgery, and our car might get towed away or we might get thrown in jail. All too often, though, immediate consequences win out in these self-control situations.

In these examples of different combinations of immediate and delayed consequences of our behavior, we have seen that immediate consequences often interfere with our ability to control our behavior. Later in the chapter, we offer some suggestions for ways to improve self-control through behavioral strategies.

parents used shaping to toilet train their 2-year-old son. The parents knew all too well that the grunting sound the child made signaled he was about to fill his diaper. In the first week they gave him candy if they heard the sound within 20 feet of the bathroom. The second week he was given candy only if he grunted within 10 feet of the bathroom, the third week only if he was in the bathroom, and the fourth week, he had to use the toilet to get the candy (Fischer & Gochros, 1975). It worked!

Chaining *is an operant conditioning technique used to teach a complex sequence, or chain, of behaviors. The procedure begins by shaping the final response in the sequence. Then you work backward until a chain of behaviors is learned.* For example, after the final response is learned, the next-to-last response is reinforced, and so on. Both shaping and chaining are used extensively by animal trainers to teach complex and unusual sequences of behavior. A dolphin that does three back flips, throws a ball through a hoop, places a hat on its head, and finally applauds itself learned the sequence of tricks in reverse order if its trainer used chaining. Figure 5.10 shows a sequence of behaviors a rat learned through the process of chaining. Shaping and chaining are also regularly used by coaches to help athletes acquire new skills.

Primary and Secondary Reinforcement. Positive reinforcement can be classified as either primary or secondary reinforcement. The difference between the two focuses on a distinction between inborn, unlearned, and learned aspects of behavior. **Primary reinforcement** *involves the use of reinforcers that are innately satisfying, that is, they do not take any learning on the organism's part to make them pleasurable.* Food, water, and sexual satisfaction are primary reinforcers.

Secondary reinforcement *acquires its positive value through experience; secondary reinforcers are learned or conditioned reinforcers.* Hundreds of secondary reinforcers characterize our lives. For example, secondary reinforcers include such social situations as get-

---

chaining

An operant conditioning technique used to teach a complex sequence, or chain, of behaviors. The procedure begins by shaping the final response in the sequence, then working backward until a chain of behaviors is learned.

primary reinforcement

The use of reinforcers that are innately satisfying (that is, they do not require any learning on the organism's part to make them pleasurable).

secondary reinforcement

Reinforcement that acquires its positive value through experience; secondary reinforcers are learned, or conditioned, reinforcers.

$\mathcal{F}$IGURE 5.10

An Example of Chaining

Starting at A, the rat climbs the ramp to B, crosses the drawbridge to C, climbs the ladder to D, crosses the tightrope to E, climbs the ladder to F, crawls through the tunnel to G, enters the elevator at H, descends to I, presses the lever at J, and then receives food. In chaining, the experimenter would reinforce lever pressing at J first, then movement from I to J, then descending from H to I to J, and so on.

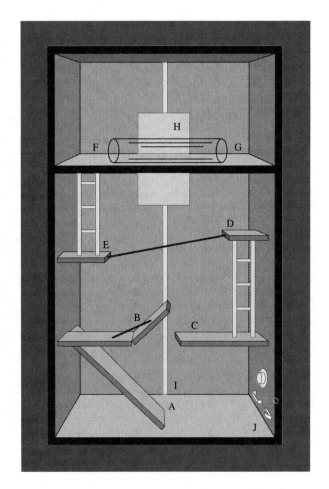

ting a pat on the back, praise, and eye contact. One popular story in psychology focuses on the use of eye contact as a secondary reinforcer to shape the behavior of a famous university professor, an expert on operant conditioning. Some students decided to train the professor to lecture from one corner of the classroom. They used eye contact as a reinforcer and began reinforcing successive approximations to the desired response. Each time the professor moved toward the appropriate corner, the students would look at him. If he moved in another direction, they looked away. By gradually rewarding successive approximations to the desired response, the students were able to get the professor to deliver his lecture from just one corner of the classroom. The well-known operant conditioning expert denies that this shaping ever took place. Whether it did or not, the story provides an excellent example of how secondary reinforcers can be used to shape behavior in real life circumstances (Chance, 1979).

Another example also helps us understand the importance of secondary reinforcement in our everyday lives. When a student is given $25 for an A on her report card, the $25 is a secondary reinforcer. It is not innate, and it increases the likelihood the student will work to get another A in the future. Money is often referred to as a *token reinforcer*. When an object can be exchanged for some other reinforcer, the object may have reinforcing value itself, so it is called a token reinforcer. Gift certificates and poker chips are other token reinforcers.

partial reinforcement

Intermittent reinforcement; responses are not reinforced every time they occur.

schedules of reinforcement

Timetables that determine when a response will be reinforced.

Schedules of Reinforcement.   In most of life's experiences, we are not reinforced every time we make a response. A golfer does not win every tournament she enters; a chess whiz does not win every match he plays; a student is not patted on the back each time she solves a problem. **Partial reinforcement** *(or intermittent reinforcement) simply means that responses are not reinforced each time they occur.* **Schedules of reinforcement** *are "timetables" that determine when a response will be reinforced.* The four main schedules of reinforcement are fixed-ratio, variable-ratio, fixed-interval, and variable-interval.

Slot machines are on a variable-ratio schedule of reinforcement. *What does this mean?*

fixed-ratio schedule

Reinforcement of a behavior after a set number of responses.

variable-ratio schedule

A timetable in which responses are rewarded an average number of times, but on an unpredictable basis.

fixed-interval schedule

Reinforcement of the first appropriate response after a fixed amount of time has elapsed.

variable-interval schedule

Reinforcement of a response after a variable amount of time has elapsed.

A **fixed-ratio schedule** *reinforces a behavior after a set number of responses.* For example, if you are playing the slot machines in Atlantic City and they are on a fixed-ratio schedule, you might get $5 back every 20 times you put money in the machine. It wouldn't take long to figure out that if you watched someone else play the machine 18 or 19 times, not get any money back, and then walk away, you should step up, insert your coin, and get back $5.

Consequently, slot machines are on a **variable-ratio schedule,** *a timetable in which responses are rewarded an average number of times, but on an unpredictable basis.* For example, a slot machine might pay off an average of every twentieth time, but unlike the fixed-ratio schedule, the gambler does not know when this payoff will be. The slot machine might pay off twice in a row and then not again until after 58 coins have been inserted. This averages out to a reward for every 20 responses, but when the reward is given is unpredictable.

The remaining two reinforcement schedules are determined by *time elapsed* since the last behavior was rewarded. A **fixed-interval schedule** *reinforces the first appropriate response after a fixed amount of time has elapsed.* For example, you might get a reward the first time you put money in a slot machine after every 10-minute period has elapsed. A **variable-interval schedule** *is a timetable in which a response is reinforced after a variable amount of time has elapsed.* On this schedule, the slot machines might reward you after 10 minutes, then after 2 minutes, then after 18 minutes, and so forth.

Which of these schedules is the most effective? The closer a schedule is to continuous reinforcement, the faster the individual learns. However, once behavior is learned, the intermittent schedules can be effective in maintaining behavior. The rate of behavior varies from one schedule to the next (Skinner, 1961). The fixed-ratio schedule produces a high rate of behavior with a pause occurring between the reinforcer and the behavior. This type of schedule is used widely in our lives. For example, if an individual is paid $100 for every ten lawns he mows, then he is on a fixed-ratio schedule. The variable-ratio schedule also elicits a high rate of behavior when the pause after the reinforcement is eliminated. This schedule usually elicits the highest response rate of all four schedules.

The interval schedules produce behavior at a lower rate than the ratio schedules do. The fixed-interval schedule stimulates a low rate of behavior at the start of an interval and a somewhat faster rate toward the end. This happens because the organism apparently recognizes that the behavior early in the interval will not be rewarded by that later behavior will be rewarded. A scallop-shaped curve characterizes the behavior pattern of an organism on a fixed-interval schedule. The variable-interval schedule produces a slow, consistent rate of behavior. Figure 5.11 provides a summary of how reinforcement schedules affect performance rates.

*𝓕*IGURE 5.11

Performance Curves Produced by Four Schedules of Reinforcement

The steeper the slope of the curve, the faster the response. Each pause indicated by a hash mark indicates the point at which reinforcement was given. Notice that the fixed-interval schedule reveals a scalloped effect rather than a straight line because the organism stops responding for a while after each reinforcement but quickly responds as the next reinforcement approaches. *Adapted from "Teaching Machines" by B. F. Skinner. Copyright © 1961 by Scientific American, Inc. All rights reserved.*

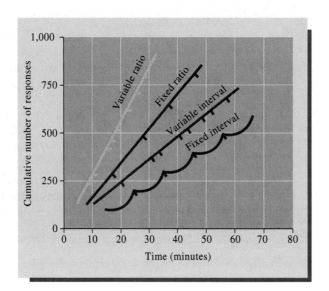

Extinction, Generalization, and Discrimination

One final principle of operant conditioning that Skinner articulated will sound familiar. In our discussion of classical conditioning we discovered that extinction is the weakening of the CS's tendency over time to elicit the CR when the CS is presented without the US. **Extinction** *in operant conditioning is a decrease in the tendency to perform a behavior that results in neither a positive nor a negative consequence.* For example, suppose you want to ask a question in your history class, but your history professor fails to notice your raised hand and continues with what she thinks is a fascinating lecture. Eventually your arm fatigues and you abandon your question. Your question-asking behavior weakens and disappears in this context. In the absence of a reinforcing or punishing consequence, an operant response will become extinguished (see figure 5.12).

In classical conditioning, generalization is the tendency of a stimulus similar to the conditioned stimulus to produce a response similar to the conditioned response. **Generalization** *in operant conditioning means giving the same response to similar stimuli.* For example, in one study pigeons were reinforced for pecking at a disc of a particular color (Guttman & Kalish, 1956). Stimulus generalization was tested by presenting the pigeons with discs of varying colors. The pigeons were most likely to peck at the disc closest in color to the original. An example of stimulus generalization in everyday life that is familiar to many parents involves an infant learning to say "doggie" to a hairy, four-legged creature with floppy ears and a friendly bark (Martin & Pear, 1996). Later, the infant sees a different kind of dog and says "doggie." This is an example of stimulus generalization because a previously reinforced response ("doggie") appeared in the presence of a new stimulus (a new kind of dog). Later, the infant sees a horse and says "doggie." This is another example of stimulus generalization, even though the infant's labeling is incorrect,

extinction

In operant conditioning, a decrease in the tendency to perform a behavior that no longer receives either positive or negative reinforcement.

generalization

In operant conditioning, giving the same response to similar stimuli.

$\mathcal{F}$IGURE 5.12

Extinction

In extinction, the frequency of a behavior declines because it has no effect or produces no consequence. For example, a student who volunteers to answer a question (behavior) but who is never called on (consequence) is likely to stop volunteering in the future.

Extinction		
Behavior	Consequence 0	Future behavior ↓
Asking questions	Teacher fails to call on student	Asking questions decreases

which indicates that not all instances of stimulus generalization are favorable and illustrates why discriminations need to be taught.

In classical conditioning, discrimination is the process of learning to respond to certain stimuli and not to others. **Discrimination** *in operant conditioning is the tendency to respond only to those stimuli that are correlated with reinforcement.* For example, you might look at two street signs, both made of metal, both the same color, and both with words on them. However, one sign says "Enter at your own risk," and the other reads "Please walk this way." The words serve as discriminative stimuli because the sign that says "Please walk this way" indicates that you will be rewarded for doing so, whereas the sign that says "Enter at your own risk," suggests that the consequences may not be positive. **Discriminative stimuli** *signal that a response will be reinforced.* Discrimination is one of the techniques used to teach animals to perform tricks. When Kent Burgess (1968) wanted to teach an Orca whale tricks, he used a whistle as the discriminative stimulus. Whenever the whistle sounded, the killer whale got fed. Burgess would blow the whistle immediately after a correct response and the Orca would approach the feeding platform where she would be fed. Using this tactic, Burgess taught the Orca to spout water, leap in the air, and so on (see figure 5.13).

Applications of Operant Conditioning

A preschool child repeatedly throws his glasses and breaks them. A high school student and her parents have intense arguments. A college student is deeply depressed. An elderly woman is incontinent. Operant conditioning procedures have helped such people adapt more successfully to their environment and cope more effectively with their problems.

Behavior modification *is the application of operant conditioning principles to changing human behavior; its main goal is to replace unacceptable responses with acceptable, adaptive ones.* Psychologists establish consequences for behavior to ensure that acceptable actions are reinforced and unacceptable ones are not. Advocates of behavior modification believe that many emotional and behavioral problems are caused by inadequate (or inappropriate) response consequences. A child who throws down his glasses and breaks them might be receiving too much attention from his teacher and peers for his behavior; they unwittingly reinforce an unacceptable behavior. In this instance, the parents and teachers would be instructed to divert their attention from the destructive behavior and transfer it to a more constructive behavior, such as working quietly or playing cooperatively with peers (Harris, Wolf, & Baer, 1964).

Consider another circumstance in which behavior modification can help people solve problems. Barbara and her parents were on a collision course. Things got so bad that her parents decided to see a clinical psychologist. The psychologist, who had a behavioral orientation for addressing clinical problems, talked with each family member, trying to get them to pinpoint the problem. The psychologist convinced the family to sign a behavioral contract that spelled out what everyone needed to do to reduce the conflict. Barbara agreed to (1) be home before 11 P.M. on weeknights, (2) look for a part-time job so she could begin to pay for some of her activities, and (3) refrain from calling her parents insulting names. Her parents agreed to (1) talk to Barbara in a low tone of voice rather

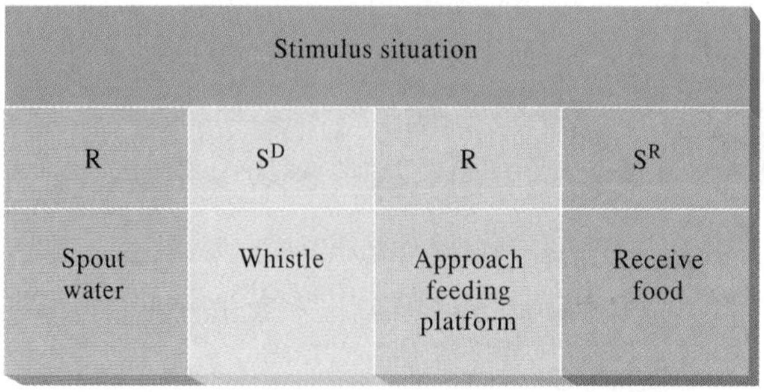

Sidebar definitions

discrimination

In operant conditioning, the tendency to respond only to those stimuli that are correlated with reinforcement.

discriminative stimuli

Stimuli that signal that a response will be reinforced.

behavior modification

The application of operant conditioning principles to change human behavior.

Figure

$\mathcal{F}$IGURE 5.13

Teaching Behavior to an Orca Whale

When spouting water was followed by a whistle, the whistle reinforced spouting and provided the signal for approaching the feeding platform to receive the reinforcing stimulus(S^R) of food.

Stimulus situation			
R	S^D	R	S^R
Spout water	Whistle	Approach feeding platform	Receive food

than yell if they were angry; (2) refrain from criticizing teenagers, especially Barbara's friends; and (3) give Barbara a small sum of money each week for gas, makeup, and socializing, but only until she found a job.

Also consider Sam, a 19-year-old college student, who has been deeply depressed lately. His girlfriend broke off their relationship of 2 years, and his grades have been dropping. He decides to go to a psychologist who has a behavioral orientation. The psychologist enrolls him in the Coping with Depression course developed by Peter Lewinsohn (1987). Sam learns to monitor his daily moods and increase his ratio of positive to negative life events. The psychologist trains Sam to develop more efficient coping skills and gets Sam to agree to a behavioral contract, just as the psychologist did with Barbara and her parents.

Mary is an elderly woman who lives in a nursing home. In recent months, she has become incontinent and is increasingly dependent on the staff for help with her daily activities. The behavioral treatment designed for Mary's problem involves teaching her to monitor her behavior and schedule going to the toilet. She is also required to do pelvic exercises. The program for decreasing Mary's dependence requires that the nursing home staff attend more to her independent behavior when it occurs and remove attention from dependent behavior whenever possible. Such strategies with the elderly have been effective in reducing problems with incontinence and dependence.

Psychologists use behavior modification to teach couples to communicate more effectively, to encourage fathers to engage in more competent caregiving with their infants, to train autistic children's interpersonal skills, to help individuals lose weight, and to reduce individuals' fear of social situations.

Evaluation of Operant Conditioning

Operant conditioning has been used in a variety of contexts to change human and animal behavior. Many clinical applications have produced dramatic changes in behavior that might not have been easily accomplished using other methods. Operant psychologists have been praised for their reliance on observable and measurable behavior, which enables them to provide clear documentation for the changes they report.

Yet operant conditioning is not without its critics, particularly in relation to many of the positions taken by B. F. Skinner. Skinner believed that behavior is determined solely by its consequences. His critics argue that his adherence to operant explanations is *reductionistic*. This means that operant conditioning reduces human experience to connections between behavior and consequences, disparaging matters of spirit and will. Among Skinner's more controversial stands was his insistence that humans have no free will (Skinner, 1971), that what appears to be freely chosen can, in fact, be predicted from the distinctive reinforcement history the organism has experienced.

Many psychologists believe that operant conditioning is effective only in explaining simple behaviors. Complex behaviors are likely to require other kinds of cognitive mediation in order to be sustained (Chance, 1988). However, Skinner proposed that operant theory had no room for cognitive processes and believed that the contemporary shifts toward cognitive psychology would ruin psychology (Skinner, 1990).

Operant techniques and those who use them have been criticized for manipulating behavior. Nowhere in psychology is the issue of control more pronounced. Skinner received national attention when he placed his daughter Deborah in a crib-sized "Skinner box" that responded to her infant needs. The "air-crib," as Skinner called it, functioned like a playpen and was completely enclosed, soundproofed, and temperature controlled. It not only allowed Skinner greater control over his daughter's behavior, but also allowed Deborah to exercise some control over the amount of stimulation she received. Despite Skinner's reports that his daughter was not adversely affected by the crib, many individuals protested its use. Critics suggest that the degree of control offered in operant conditioning techniques may challenge our sense of professional ethics as well as the protection of individual rights.

Operant Conditioning

Operant conditioning (instrumental conditioning) is a form of learning in which the consequences of a behavior produce changes in the probability of the behavior's occurrence. Operant conditioning focuses on what happens after a response is made, whereas classical conditioning emphasizes what occurs before a response is made. The key connection in classical conditioning is between two stimuli; in operant conditioning, it is between an organism's response and its consequences. Operant conditioning is often better at explaining voluntary behavior. Classical conditioning is often better at explaining involuntary behavior. Although Skinner has emerged as the primary figure in operant conditioning, E. L. Thorndike's experiments established the power of consequences in determining voluntary behavior. His view is referred to as S-R theory and involves the law of effect.

In operant conditioning, reinforcement (reward) is a consequence that increases the probability a behavior will occur. Operant conditioning can involve positive reinforcement and negative reinforcement. Also, punishment is a consequence that decreases the probability a behavior will recur. Punishment involves the use of noxious stimuli or aversive consequences to reduce responding.

Immediate consequences are more effective than delayed consequences. Shaping is the process of rewarding approximations of a desired behavior. Chaining involves establishing a complex sequence of responses. The final response in the sequence is learned first, then the next to the last, and so on. Primary reinforcement refers to innate reinforcers (such as food, water, and sex); secondary reinforcement refers to reinforcers that acquire positive value through experience (such as money and smiles). In schedules of reinforcement, a response will be reinforced on a fixed-ratio, variable-ratio, fixed-interval, or variable-interval schedule. These schedules have various degrees of effectiveness. Extinction in operant conditioning is a decrease in the tendency to perform a behavior that receives neither a positive nor a negative consequence. Generalization means giving the same response to similar stimuli. Discrimination is the process of responding in the presence of one stimulus that is reinforced by not responding in the presence of another stimulus that is not reinforced.

Behavior modification is the use of learning principles to change maladaptive or abnormal behavior. It focuses on changing behavior by following the behavior with reinforcement. Behavior modification is widely used to reduce maladaptive behavior.

Operant conditioning has been praised for its broad effectiveness in changing behavior and promoting rigorous methods of documenting behavior change. Critics describe operant conditioning as reductionistic. They also say it leaves out one of the most important areas of psychology: cognition. Operant conditioning has also been described as a manipulative strategy.

OBSERVATIONAL LEARNING

Does it make sense to teach a 15-year-old boy how to drive by either classical conditioning or operant conditioning procedures? Driving a car is a voluntary behavior, so classical conditioning doesn't really apply. In terms of operant conditioning, we would ask him to drive down the road and then reward his positive behaviors. Not many of us would want to be on the road, though, when some of his disastrous mistakes occur.

> We are in truth, more than half what we are by imitation.
> —LORD CHESTERFIELD, *English Politician, 18th Century*

Bandura's Model of Observational Learning

Albert Bandura (1986, 1994) believes that if we learned only in such a trial-and-error fashion, it would be exceedingly tedious and at times hazardous. Instead, many of our complex behaviors are the result of exposure to competent models who display appropriate behavior in solving problems and coping with their world.

observational learning

Learning that occurs when a person observes and imitates someone else's behavior; also called imitation or modeling.

Observational learning, *also called imitation or modeling, is learning that occurs when a person observes and imitates someone's behavior.* The capacity to learn behavior patterns by observation eliminates tedious trial-and-error learning. In many instances observational learning takes less time than operant conditioning.

The following experiment by Bandura (1965) illustrates how observational learning can occur by watching a model who is neither reinforced nor punished. The only requirement for learning is that the individual be connected in time and space with the model. The experiment also illustrates an important distinction between learning and performance.

An equal number of boys and girls of nursery-school age watched one of three films in which someone beat up an adult-sized plastic toy called a Bobo doll (see figure 5.14). In the first film, the aggressor was rewarded with candy, soft drinks, and praise for aggressive behavior; in the second film, the aggressor was criticized and spanked for the aggressive behavior; and in the third film, there were no consequences to the aggressor for the behavior. Subsequently, each child was left alone in a room filled with toys, including a Bobo doll. The child's behavior was observed through a one-way mirror. Children who watched the film where the aggressive behavior was reinforced or went unpunished imitated the behavior more than the children who saw that aggressive behavior was punished. As might be expected, boys were more aggressive than girls. The important point about these results is that observational learning occurred just as extensively when modeled aggressive behavior was not reinforced as when it was reinforced.

A second important point focuses on the distinction between *learning* and *performance*. Just because an organism does not perform a response does not mean it was not learned. When children were rewarded (in the form of stickers or fruit juice) for imitating the model, differences in the imitative behavior among the children in the three conditions were eliminated. In this experiment, all of the children learned about the model's behavior, but the performance of the behavior did not occur for some children until reinforcement was presented. Bandura believes that when an individual observes behavior but makes no observable response, the individual still may have acquired the modeled response in cognitive form.

Since his early experiments, Bandura (1986) has focused on some of the specific processes that influence an observer's behavior following exposure to a model. One of these is *attention.* Before a person can reproduce a model's actions, she must attend to what the model is doing or saying. You might not hear what a friend says if the stereo is blaring or you might miss the teacher's analysis of a problem if you are admiring someone sitting in the next row. Attention to the model is influenced by a host of characteristics. For example, warm, powerful, atypical people command more attention that do cold, weak, typical people.

Retention is considered next. To reproduce a model's actions, you must code the information and keep it in memory so that it can be retrieved. A simple verbal description or a vivid image of what the model did assists retention. Memory is such an important cognitive process that the next chapter is devoted exclusively to it.

Another process involved in observational learning is motor reproduction. People might attend to a model and code in memory what they have seen, but because of limitations in motor development they might not be able to reproduce the model's action. Thirteen-year-olds might see Michael Jordan do a reverse two-handed dunk but be unable to reproduce the pro's actions.

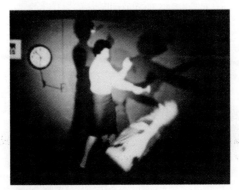 

ℱIGURE 5.14

Bandura's Study of Imitation and Children's Aggression

(a) An adult model behaves aggressively toward the Bobo doll by hitting it with a hammer. *(b)* A young girl imitates the model's aggressive behavior.

A final process in Bandura's conception of observational learning involves *reinforcement,* or incentive conditions. On many occasions we might attend to what a model says or does, retain the information in memory, and posess the motor capabilities to perform the action, but we might fail to repeat the behavior because of inadequate reinforcement. This was demonstrated in Bandura's (1965) study when those children who had seen a model punished for aggression reproduced the model's aggression only when they were offered an incentive to do so. A summary of Bandura's model of observational learning is shown in figure 5.15.

> *Children need models more than they need critics.*
> —JOSEPH JOUBERT, *French Essayist, 19th Century*

Role Models and Mentors

One practical aspect of observational learning is the significance of role models and mentors in modeling appropriate behavior. A **mentor** *is a role model who acts as an advisor, coach, and confidant.* A mentor can help someone become successful and master many of life's problems. Mentors can provide advice on career pursuits, suggest ways to cope with stressful circumstances, and listen to what's on a person's mind. For college students, a mentor might be a more advanced student, a graduate student, an instructor, or someone in the community the person respects and trusts.

Finding a good mentor or role model can be a particular problem for people from ethnic minority groups. See Sociocultural Worlds to explore the importance of this aspect of observational learning in the professional development of ethnic minority students.

mentor

A role model who acts as an advisor, coach, and confidant.

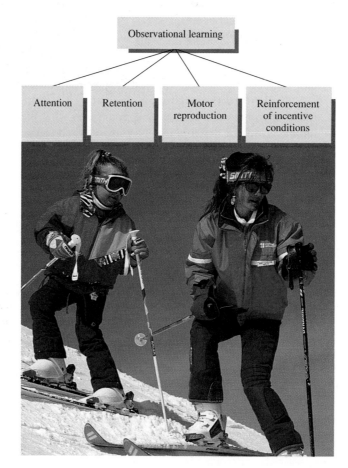

*F*IGURE 5.15

Bandura's Model of Observational Learning

Bandura argues that observational learning consists of four main processes: attention, retention, motor reproduction, and reinforcement or incentive conditions. Consider a circumstance involving learning to ski. You need to attend to the instructor's words and demonstrations. You need to remember what the instructor did and her tips for avoiding disasters. You also need the motor abilities to reproduce what the instructor has shown you, and praise from the instructor after you have completed a few moves on the slopes should improve your motivation to continue skiing.

Sociocultural Worlds

Ethnicity and Role Models

Many children from ethnic minority groups might be hard-pressed to observe competent role models with whom they can identify and from whom they can learn. A number of educators believe that the exposure of children and adolescents to competent role models is one way to reduce the high school dropout problem. Role models stimulate alternative ways of thinking about the future.

Television is one source of exposure to role models. However, historically television has underrepresented and misrepresented ethnic minorities (Pouissant, 1972). One study looked at portrayals of ethnic minorities in programs broadcast during children's heavy viewing hours (weekdays from 4 to 6 P.M. and from 7 to 11 P.M.) (Williams & Condry, 1989). The percentage of White characters in the programs far exceeded the percentage of Whites in the United States population. African Americans, Asian Americans, and Latinos were especially underrepresented. For example, only 0.6 percent of the characters were Latino, although the Latino population was 6.4 percent of the total U.S. population in 1989. Television usually presents less positive and less dignified portrayals of African American, Asian American, Latino, and Native American characters than of White characters (Condry, 1989). In their depictions on television, ethnic minorities tended to hold lower-status jobs and were more likely than Whites to be cast as criminals or victims.

Live role models, or *mentors*, can be even more influential examples for ethnic minorities. A mentor is an older, more experienced person who helps a younger person in a one-to-one relationship that goes beyond the formal obligations of a teaching or supervisory role. Mentors who are competent and caring provide young people with concrete images of who they can become and lend guidance and support to help enable them to fulfill their aspirations.

The Minority Achievement Committee (MAC) in Shaker Heights, Ohio, grew out of concern for the underachievement of young African American men. MAC began in 1991 when students began to identify what they needed to become successful. The program introduces struggling students to accomplished role models and promotes activities that help students transform their study habits and achievement. Managed entirely by students, MAC helps young African American males to build pride and academic competence. Students who have been mentored through this program have consistently improved their grade point averages. The highest achievers are honored with an awards ceremony and often return to the program to serve as role models for future generations of struggling students.

Mentoring programs, such as the Minority Achievement Committee (MAC) in Shaker Heights, Ohio, promote academic achievement and pride by providing older, successful students as effective role models.

If you have knowledge, let others light their candles at it.
—MARGARET FULLER, *American Social Critic, 19th Century*

Evaluation of Observational Learning

Anyone who has struggled to acquire a new skill by watching a master—whether the goal is to become a better golfer, a better driver, or a better writer—recognizes that observing does not always translate into learning. Simple behaviors may be more easily explained and copied by observation than complex behaviors are. Teachers recognize the importance of breaking down complex performances into smaller units in order to achieve mastery of the whole through modeling.

The effectiveness of observational learning depends on many factors. For example, a sailor described how he learned to tie a bowline when he was assigned to an aircraft carrier. The instructor had informed his new crew that he would demonstrate the knot once and that anyone unable to imitate the process would be thrown overboard. The focused attention and negative incentive resulted in rapid learning. Other influences involve the

Self-Assessment

Pavlov, Skinner, Bandura, and Me

So far in this chapter you have read about three kinds of learning: classical conditioning, operant conditioning, and observational learning. In this self-assessment, you will explore how these principles have shaped your own behavior.

Classical Conditioning

An example of how classical conditioning has influenced my behavior is _____
_____

Hint: You can use a phobia (learned irrational fear) or a case of conditioned taste aversion (food poisoning) if you cannot think of another example.

What is the US? _____

What is the UR? _____

What is the CS? _____

What is the CR? _____

Operant Conditioning

Three instances in which positive reinforcement strengthened my behavior:

behavior: _____   reinforcer: _____

behavior: _____   reinforcer: _____

behavior: _____   reinforcer: _____

An example of how negative reinforcement was useful to me is _____
_____
_____

My most memorable experience in which punishment decreased my behavior is _____
_____
_____

Was the punishment sufficient to change the behavior long-term? _____
_____
_____

An example of a situation in which my behavior was extinguished is _____
_____
_____

An example of how immediate and delayed consequences have influenced the success of my self-control is
_____
_____
_____

Observational Learning

In the last month, I engaged in the following instances of observational learning:

1. _____
2. _____
3. _____

Select the task that was most difficult to learn and rate (high-medium-low) the quality of your

Attention: _____

Retention: _____

Motor reproduction: _____

Reinforcement: _____

competence and attractiveness of the model (Berger, 1971) and the arousal level of the learner (Warden & Jackson, 1935).

When imitation fails, it might not be clear what the problem is. Is it insufficient exposure to the model? Is it that the model is insufficiently engaging? Is it that the rewards of performance are unclear? Ironically, we might know far less about the influences that promote or hinder observational learning than we know about classical and operant procedures (Chance, 1988).

Observational learning plays a substantial role in human behavior, although many other species function very well without developing this process. For example, dogs and cats show some capacity for observational learning, but not to the same extent as humans and other primates. Species lower on the evolutionary ladder have no capacity for observational learning (Chance, 1988). Bandura explained this difference as being due to lower species' inability to represent the observed behavior symbolically and to rehearse the new behavior covertly before performing it.

Bandura views observational learning as an information-processing activity. As a person observes, information about the world is transformed into cognitive representations that serve as guides for action. As we will see in the next section, interest in the cognitive factors of learning has increased dramatically in recent years. Before you go on to that section, though, this is a good time to review your understanding of classical conditioning, operant conditioning, and observational learning. The Self-Assessment will help you do this.

COGNITIVE FACTORS IN LEARNING

When we learn, we often cognitively represent or transform our experiences. In our excursion through learning we have had little to say about these cognitive processes, except in our description of observational learning. In the operant conditioning view of Skinner and the classical conditioning view of Pavlov, no room is given to the possibility that cognitive factors such as memory, thinking, planning, or expectations might be important in the learning process. Skinnerians point out that they do not deny the existence of thinking processes, but since they cannot be observed they may interfere with the discovery of important environmental conditions that govern behavior.

Many contemporary psychologists, including behavioral revisionists who recognize that cognition should not have been ignored in classical and operant conditioning, believe that learning involves much more than stimulus-response connections. The **S-O-R model** *is a model of learning that gives some importance to cognitive factors.* S stands for stimulus. O for organism, and R for response. The O sometimes is referred to as the "black box," because the mental activities of the organism cannot be seen and, therefore, must be inferred.

S-O-R model

A model of learning that gives some importance to cognitive factors. S stands for stimulus. O for organism, and R for response.

Bandura's Cognitive Model

Bandura (1994) described another model of learning that involves behavior, person, and environment. As shown in figure 5.16, behavior, person and cognitive factors, and environmental influences operate interactively. Behavior influences cognition and vice versa; the person's cognitive activities influence the environment; environmental experiences change the person's thought; and so on.

Let's consider how Bandura's model might work in the case of a college student's achievement behavior. As the student studies diligently and gets good grades, her behavior produces in her positive thoughts about her abilities. As part of her effort to make good grades, she plans and develops a number of strategies to make her studying more efficient. In these ways her behavior has influenced her thought, and her thought has influenced her behavior. At the beginning of the semester, her college made a special effort to involve students in a study skills program. She decided to join. Her success,

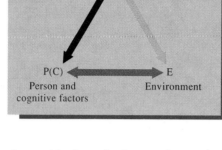

*F*IGURE 5.16

Bandura's Model of Reciprocal Influences of Behavior (B), Personal and Cognitive Factors (P[C]), and Environment (E)

The arrows reflect how relations between these factors are reciprocal rather than unidirectional. Examples of personal factors include intelligence, skills, and self-control.

along with that of other students who attended the program, has led the college to expand the program next semester. In these ways, environment influenced behavior, and behavior changed the environment. And the expectations of the college administrators that the study skills program would work made it possible in the first place. The program's success has spurred expectations that this type of program could work in other colleges. In these ways cognition changed environment, and the environment changed cognition.

self-efficacy

The expectation that one can master a situation and produce positive outcomes.

Bandura (1986, 1997) believes that an important person factor in learning is **self-efficacy,** the expectation that one can master a situation and produce positive outcomes. Self-efficacy is involved in people's success in solving problems and engaging in health-promoting behaviors like exercising and losing weight. Overweight individuals have more success with their diets if they believe they have the self-control to restrict their eating, for example. Self-efficacy, by itself, won't eliminate all of the problems you face. But the self-confidence it brings to challenging situations can motivate you to engage in positive actions. See Improving Personal and Cognitive Skills ("Developing Self-Efficacy").

Expectations and Cognitive Maps

E. C. Tolman says that when classical and operant conditioning occur the organism acquires certain expectations. In classical conditioning the young boy fears the rabbit because he expects it will hurt him. In operant conditioning a woman works hard all week because she expects to be paid on Friday.

In 1946, Tolman and his colleagues conducted a classic experiment to demonstrate the power of expectations in learning. Initially, rats ran on an elevated maze (see figure 5.17*a*). The rats started at *A*, ran across the circular table at *B*, through an alley at *CD*, then along the path to the food box at *G*. *H* represents a light that illuminated the path from *F* to *G*.

This maze was replaced by one with several false runways (see figure 5.17*b*). The rats ran down what had been the correct path before but found that it was blocked. Which of the remaining paths would the rats choose? We might anticipate that they would choose paths 9 and 10 because those were nearest the path that led to success. Instead, the rats explored several paths, running along one for a short distance, returning to the table, then trying out another one, and so on. Eventually, the rats ran along one path all the way to the end. This path was number 6, not 9 or 10. Path 6 ran to a point about 4 inches short of where the food box had been located previously. According to Tolman, the rats not only had learned how to run the original maze, they also had learned to expect food upon reaching a specific place.

In his paper "Cognitive Maps in Rats and Men," Tolman (1948) articulated his belief that organisms select information from the environment and construct a cognitive map of their experiences. A **cognitive map** *is an organism's mental representation of the structure of physical space.* In Tolman's maze experiment just described, the rats had developed a mental awareness of physical space and the elements in it. The rats used this cognitive map to find where the food was located.

cognitive map

An organism's mental representation of the structure of physical space.

𝒥mproving Personal and Cognitive Skills

Developing Self-Efficacy

What are some steps you can follow to develop self-efficacy? They include these (Watson & Tharp, 1996):

1. *Choose something you expect to be able to accomplish.*
   Later, as your sense of self-efficacy improves, you can tackle tougher projects. For example, a person who wants to stay sober concentrates on not drinking "one day at a time" instead of thinking "I'll never have a drink again."

2. *Distinguish between your past performance and your current project.*
   You may have learned to believe from past failures that you can't do certain things. Remind yourself that past failures are just that—in the past. You can now have a new sense of confidence and accomplishment. The only value in looking at past failures is to help you develop a better strategy for now and the future. For example, a person who repeatedly failed to lose 80 pounds on a diet should avoid thinking, "I'll always fail. This weight will never go away." Instead, the overweight person might look at past behavior and learn that failures came after a few days of starvation dieting. This can prompt the person to develop a new strategy of a more sensible diet combined with exercise.

3. *Keep good records.*
   Keeping records gives you concrete evidence of your successes. Consider Alan. Frustrated with being a poor student, he is trying to maintain a good study schedule. After sticking with the schedule for 4 days, he fails to follow it on the fifth day. He calls himself a failure. Then, he looks at his record keeping and sees that he has an 80 percent success rate because he stayed with his study plan on 4 of 5 days.

4. *Make a list of the situations in which you expect to have the most difficulty and the least difficulty.*
   Whenever possible, begin with the easier situations. Cope with the more difficult circumstances after you have experienced some successes in improving your self-efficacy. For example, Anita's list of things she wants to accomplish includes developing better study habits, reducing her anger, exercising more, spending less time partying, and getting more sleep. She looks at the list and decides that she is most likely to have success with exercising more and spending less time partying, so she moves those to the top of the list.

Tolman's idea of cognitive maps is alive and well today. When we move around in our environment, we develop a cognitive map of where things are located, on both small and large scales. We have a cognitive map of where rooms are located in our house or apartment, and we have a cognitive map of where we are located in the United States for example. A popular tradition is to draw a cognitive map reflecting our perception of the city or state in which we live, relative to the rest of the United States. Texans, for example, usually draw the state of Texas as being about three-fourths the size of the entire United States. In Manhattan, "The City" is often drawn about nine-tenths the size of the United States. Of course, such cognitive maps deliberately distort the physical world, reflecting the perceivers' egocentric interest in their city or state.

Tolman was not the only psychologist who was dissatisfied with the S-R view of learning. Gestalt psychologist Wolfgang Kohler thought that the cognitive process of insight learning was also an important form of learning.

Insight Learning

Wolfgang Kohler, a German psychologist, spent 4 months in the Canary Islands during World War I observing the behavior of apes. While there he conducted two fascinating experiments. One is called the "stick problem," the other the "box problem." Though these two experiments are basically the same, the solutions to the problems are different. In both situations, the ape discovers that it cannot reach an alluring piece of fruit, either because the fruit is too high or it is outside of the ape's cage and beyond its reach. To solve the stick problem, the ape has to insert a small stick inside a larger stick to reach the fruit. To master the box problem, the ape must stack several boxes to reach the fruit (see figure 5.18).

According to Kohler (1925), solving these problems does not involve trial and error or mere connections between stimuli and responses. Rather, when the ape realizes that his customary actions are not going to get the fruit, he often sits for a period of time and appears to ponder how to solve the problem. Then he quickly gets up, as if he had a

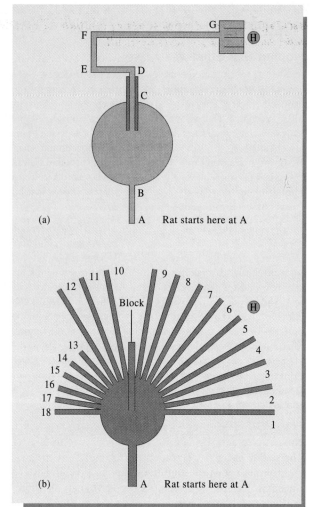

(a)

F ⎯⎯⎯⎯⎯⎯⎯⎯⎯ G

E ⎯ D

C

B

A   Rat starts here at A

12 11 10 9 8 7 6 5 4 3 2 1

13 14 15 16 17 18

Block

(H)

(b)   A   Rat starts here at A

𝓕IGURE 5.17

Tolman's Experiment on Expectations in Learning

In Tolman's classic experiment on the role of expectations in learning, initially rats ran on this elevated maze from A through G, with H representing a light that illuminated the path from F to G. After the rats ran the maze in *(a)*, they were placed in the maze shown in *(b)*. What path did the rats follow in *(b)*? Why?

𝓕IGURE 5.18

Kohler's Box Problem Involving Insight Learning

Sultan, one of Kohler's brightest chimps, is faced with the problem of reaching a cluster of bananas overhead. Suddenly he solves the problem by stacking boxes on top of one another to reach the bananas. Kohler called this type of problem solving "insight learning."

insight learning

A form of problem solving in which an organism develops a sudden understanding of a problem's solution.

sudden flash of insight, piles the boxes on top of one another, and gets the fruit. **Insight learning** *is a form of problem solving in which the organism develops a sudden insight or understanding of a problem's solution.*

Of course, humans also show insight. Think about those frustrating moments when your computer misbehaves. If you don't have access to a more experienced computer user, your situation is very much like Kohler's chimps trying to get the banana. After some pondering, you might develop an insight that will solve the problem. As a consequence, you will learn an operation or behavior that might help you avoid this problem in the future. You will read about more examples of insight in chapter 7's treatment of creativity.

BIOLOGICAL AND CULTURAL FACTORS IN LEARNING

Albert Einstein had many special talents. He combined enormous creativity with great analytic ability to develop some of this century's most important insights about the nature of matter and the universe. Genes obviously provided Einstein extraordinary intellectual skills to think and reason on a very high plane, but cultural factors also undoubtedly contributed to Einstein's genius. Einstein received an excellent, rigorous European education, and later in the United States he experienced the freedom and support believed to be important in creative exploration. Would Einstein have been able to fully develop his intellectual skills and make such brilliant insights if he had grown up in the more primitive cultures of his time or even in a Third World country today? Unlikely. Quite clearly both biological *and* cultural factors contribute to learning.

Biological Factors

We can't breathe under water, fish can't play table tennis, and cows can't solve math problems. The structure of an organism's body permits certain kinds of learning and inhibits others. For example, chimpanzees cannot learn to speak English because they lack the necessary vocal equipment. Some of us cannot solve difficult calculus problems, others of us can, and the differences do not all seem to be the result of experiences.

Some animals also learn readily in one situation but have difficulty learning in slightly different circumstances. The difficulty might not result from some aspect of the learning situation but from the predisposition of the organism (Seligman, 1970). **Preparedness** *is the species-specific biological predisposition to learn in certain ways but not in others.* For example, cats can escape from a cage by pulling a string to open the door or by pushing the door, but if they have to lick, their escape ability is greatly reduced.

preparedness

The species-specific biological predisposition to learn in certain ways but not in others.

instinctive drift

The tendency of animals to revert to instinctive behavior that interferes with learning.

Another example of biological influences on learning is **instinctive drift,** *the tendency of animals to revert to instinctive behavior that interferes with learning.* Consider the situation of Keller and Marion Breland (1961), students of B. F. Skinner, who used operant conditioning to train animals to perform at fairs, conventions, and in television advertisements. They used Skinner's techniques of shaping, chaining, and discrimination to teach pigs to cart large wooden nickels to a piggy bank and deposit them. They also trained raccoons to pick up a coin and place it in a metal tray. Although the pigs and raccoons, as well as other animals such as chickens, performed well at most of the tasks (raccoons became adept basketball players, for example—see figure 5.19), some of the animals began acting strangely. Instead of picking up the large wooden nickel and carrying it to the piggy bank, the pigs would drop the nickel on the ground, shove it with their snouts, toss it in the air, and then repeat these actions. The raccoons began to hold onto their coin rather than dropping it into the metal container.

When two coins were introduced, the raccoons rubbed them together in a miserly fashion. Somehow these behaviors overwhelmed the strength of the reinforcement that was given at the end of the day. Why were the pigs and the raccoons misbehaving? The pigs were rooting, an instinct which is used to uncover edible roots. The raccoons engaged in an instinctive food-washing response. Their instinctive drift interfered with learning.

This raccoon's skill in using its hands made it an excellent basketball player, but the raccoon had a much more difficult time taking money to the bank. *What factors explain why one behavior would be relatively easy to learn while the other would be more challenging?*

taste aversion

The conditioned avoidance of ingesting substances that cause nausea or other unpleasant reactions.

Dog owners sometimes must deal with the unpleasant consequences of instinctive drift. Although some breeds, such as rottweilers, pit bulls, and Dobermans, were selectively bred to be aggressive, many of these dogs have been adopted as family pets. However, in circumstances, such as competition for food or protection of young, these animals can revert to highly aggressive behavior.

A psychologist went to dinner with his wife and ordered filet mignon with Bérnaise sauce, his favorite dish. Afterward they went to the opera. Several hours later, he became very ill with stomach pains and nausea. Several weeks later, he tried to eat Bérnaise sauce but couldn't bear it. The psychologist's experience involves another biological constraint on learning called **taste aversion,** *the conditioned avoidance of ingesting substances that cause nausea or other unpleasant reactions.* (Alvarez & Lopez, 1996)

If an organism ingests a substance that poisons but does not kill it, the organism often develops considerable distaste for that substance. Rats that experience low levels of radiation after eating show a strong aversion to the food they were eating when the radiation made them ill. This aversion has been shown to last for as long as 32 days. Such long-term effects cannot be accounted for by classical conditioning, which would argue that a single pairing of the conditioned and unconditioned stimuli would not last that long. Radiation and chemical treatment of cancer often produces nausea in patients, and the resulting pattern of aversions often resembles those shown by laboratory animals.

Knowledge about taste aversion has been applied to balancing the ecological worlds of animals. For example, the livestock of farmers and ranchers may be threatened by wolves or coyotes. Instead of killing the pests or predators, the farmers feed them poisoned meat of their prey (cattle, sheep). The wolves and coyotes, poisoned but not killed, develop a taste aversion for cattle or sheep and, hence, are less of a threat to the farmers and ranchers. In this way, ranchers, farmers, cattle, sheep, wolves, and coyotes can live in a semblance of ecological balance.

Cultural Factors

In traditional views of learning, concepts such as culture have been given little or no attention. The behavioral orientation that dominated American psychology for much of the twentieth century does focus on the cultural contexts of learning, but the organisms in those contexts have often been animals. When humans have been the subjects, there has been little or no interest in the cultural context.

How does culture influence learning? Most psychologists agree that the principles of classical conditioning, operant conditioning, and observational learning are universal and are powerful learning processes in every culture. However, culture can influence the *degree* to which these learning processes are used, and it often determines the *content* of learning. For example, punishment is a universal learning process, but as we see next, its use and type show considerable sociocultural variation.

When behaviorism was dominant in the United States between 1910 and 1930, child-rearing experts regarded the infant as capable of being shaped into almost any kind of child. Desirable social behavior could be achieved if the child's antisocial behaviors were always punished and never indulged, and if positive behaviors were carefully conditioned and rewarded in a highly controlled and structured child-rearing regimen. The famous behaviorist John Watson (1928) authored a publication, *Infant Care,* that was the official government booklet for parents. This booklet advocated never letting children suck their thumb, and, if necessary, restraining the child by tying her hands to the crib at night and painting her fingers with foul-tasting liquids. Parents were advised to let infants "cry themselves out" rather than reinforce this unacceptable behavior by picking them up to rock and soothe them.

However, from the 1930s to 1960s, a more permissive attitude prevailed and parents were advised to be concerned with the feelings and capacities of the child. Since the 1960s there has been a continued emphasis on the role of parental love in children's socialization, but experts now advise parents to play a less permissive and more active role in shaping children's behavior. Experts stress that parents should set limits and make authoritative decisions in areas where the child is not capable of reasonable judgment. However, they should listen and adapt to the child's point of view, should explain their restrictions and discipline, but they should not discipline the child in a hostile, punitive manner.

Most child-rearing experts in the United States today do not advocate the physical punishment of children, but the United States does not have a law that prohibits parents from spanking their children. In 1979 Sweden passed a law forbidding parents from using physical punishment, including spanking and slapping, when disciplining their children (Ziegert, 1983). Physical punishment of children is treated as a punishable offense, just like any other attack on a person. The law is especially designed to curb child abuse. Sweden is the only industrial country in the world to pass such a law.

The United States probably could not pass this type of law. Many Americans would view such a law as totalitarian, and the law would likely stimulate protest from civil libertarians and others. An important factor in Sweden's "antispanking" law is its attitude toward rule of law. The United States enforces laws through punishment, but Sweden takes a softer approach, encouraging respect for law through education designed to change attitudes and behavior. When people, often teachers or doctors, suspect that a parent has spanked a child, they often will report the incident because they know that the state will try to provide the parent with emotional and educational support rather than assess a fine or send the parent to jail. Accompanying the antispanking law was a parenting guide—*Can One Manage to Raise Children Without Spanking or Slapping?*—that was widely available at day-care centers, preschool programs, physicians' offices, and other similar locations. The publication includes advice about why physical punishment is not a good strategy for disciplining children, along with specific information about better ways to handle children's problems.

> *Experience is the comb that Nature gives us when we are bald.*
> —BELGIAN PROVERB

The content of learning is also influenced by culture. We cannot learn about something we do not experience. A 4-year-old who has grown up among the Bushmen of the Kalahari Desert is unlikely to learn about taking baths or pouring water from one glass into another. Similarly a child growing up in Chicago is unlikely to be skilled at tracking animals or finding water-bearing roots in the desert. Learning usually requires practice, and certain behaviors are practiced much more often in some cultures than in others. In Bali many children are skilled dancers by the age of 6, whereas Norwegian children are much more likely to be good skiers and skaters by that age. Children growing up in a Mexican village famous for its pottery may work with clay day after day, whereas children in a nearby village famous for its woven rugs and sweaters rarely become experts at making clay pots (Price-Williams, Gordon, & Ramirez, 1969).

In this chapter, we have seen that learning is a pervasive aspect of life and has a great deal of adaptive significance for organisms. We have studied many forms of learning and have seen how cognitive, biological, and cultural factors influence learning. In the next chapter, we will become absorbed more deeply in the world of cognition as we explore the nature of memory.

Review

Observational Learning; Cognitive, Biological and Cultural Factors in Learning

Observational learning occurs when an individual observes someone else's behavior. Observational learning is also called imitation or modeling. In Bandura's model, four processes are important: Attention, retention, motor reproduction, and reinforcement. Being around positive role models and mentors makes observational learning work in your favor. Observational learning plays a substantial role in human behavior but is less influential in the behavior of lower species.

Many psychologists recognize the importance of studying how cognitive factors mediate environment-behavior connections. The S-O-R model reflects this, as does Bandura's contemporary model, which emphasizes reciprocal connections between behavior, person (cognition), and environment. Tolman reinterpreted classical and operant conditioning in terms of expectations. We construct cognitive maps of our experiences that guide our behavior; psychologists still study the nature of cognitive maps. Kohler, like Tolman, was dissatisfied with the S-R view of learning. He believed that organisms reflect and suddenly gain insight into how a problem should be solved.

Biological facts restrict what an organism can learn from experience. These constraints include physical characteristics, preparedness, instinctive drift, and taste aversion. Although most psychologists would agree that the principles of classical conditioning, operant conditioning, and observational learning are universal, cultural customs can influence the degree to which these learning processes are used, and culture often determines the content of learning.

Overview

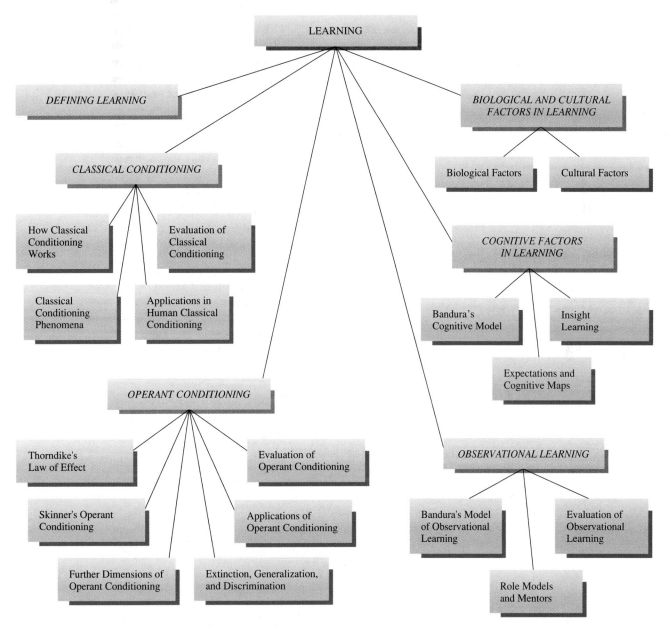

We began this chapter by defining learning and then turned our attention to three main forms of learning—classical conditioning, operant conditioning, and observational learning. Our coverage of classical conditioning focused on how it works, related classical conditioning phenomena, applications in human classical conditioning, classical conditioning in humans, and an evaluation of classical conditioning. Our discussion of operant conditioning emphasized Thorndike's law of effect, Skinner's operant conditioning, some further dimensions of operant conditioning, extinction, generalization, and discrimination, applications, and evalua-

tion of operant conditioning. We learned about observational learning, including Bandura's model, role models and mentors, and an evaluation of observational learning. We also explored cognitive factors in learning (Bandura's cognitive model, expectations and cognitive maps, and insight learning). We also discussed biological and cultural factors in learning.

Don't forget that you can obtain an overall summary of the chapter by again studying the in-chapter reviews on pages 161, 174, and 186.

Key Terms

fixed action patterns   153
learning   153
classical conditioning   153
reflexes   153
unconditioned stimulus (US)   153
unconditioned response (UR)   153
conditioned stimulus (CS)   154
conditioned response (CR)   154
generalization (classical conditioning)   155
discrimination (classical conditioning)   155

extinction (classical conditioning)   157
spontaneous recovery   157
phobias   158
counterconditioning   158
stimulus substitution   160
information theory   160
latent learning   160
operant conditioning   161
law of effect   162
reinforcement   163
positive reinforcement   163
negative reinforcement   164
punishment   164
shaping   167
chaining   168

primary reinforcement   168
secondary reinforcement   168
partial reinforcement   169
schedules of reinforcement   169
fixed-ratio schedule   170
variable-ratio schedule   170
fixed-interval schedule   170
variable-interval schedule   170
extinction (operant conditioning)   171
generalization (operant conditioning)   171
discrimination (operant conditioning)   172

discriminative stimuli   172
behavior modification   172
observational learning   174
mentor   176
S-O-R model   179
self-efficacy   180
cognitive map   180
insight learning   183
preparedness   183
instinctive drift   183
taste aversion   184

Thinking It Over

Exercises . . .

. . . In Critical Thinking

Watching television is a common observational learning activity. As you read in this chapter, Bandura conducted research to show how observational learning influences children's aggression. Your task now is to design a study to demonstrate whether children's television-viewing patterns influence their school achievement. In this study, how much control will you be able to have over the children's environment? Will you conduct a correlational or an experimental study? How will you define different patterns of television viewing? How will you measure academic achievement?

. . . In Creative Thinking

Suppose your next-door neighbor comes to you after she hears you have been taking a psychology class. Her little girl, Blair, has started throwing tantrums right and left. The mother can't even take the little girl shopping with her anymore. What creative suggestions can you offer the mother, based on what you learned in this chapter, to help her daughter improve her self-control?

. . . In Active Learning

You might not have thought much about the importance of finding a mentor to help you succeed while you are in college. To help get you started in finding a mentor, answer the following questions:

Who knows how to get things done on campus?

Who has great work and study habits?

Whose personal style do you admire the most?

Whose ideas do you find to be most stimulating?

Whose career interests are most like your own?

Once you have identified some possible mentors, take some time to talk over your conclusions with the people on your list. Where the chemistry feels good, you may have found a mentor.

. . . In Reflective Learning

Most child-rearing practices reflect the *zeitgeist,* or spirit of the times. Reflect on your life growing up with your parents. Did they use punishment to try to control your behavior? Were their practices consistent with the views of child-rearing that were current in those times, or did they depart from accepted practices? If you have children of your own, will you use parenting techniques similar to those your parents used or will you do something very different? Why?

Resources for Psychology and Improving Humankind

Behavior Modification: What It Is and How to Do It (1996, 5th ed.)

by G. Martin and R. Pear
Engelwood Cliffs, NJ: Prentice Hall

This excellent, easy-to-read book provides guidelines for using behavior modification to change behavior.

Conditioning and Learning (1996)

by Michael Domjan
Pacific Grove, CA: Brooks/Cole

A leading researcher in learning and conditioning, Domjan discusses contemporary perspectives with special emphasis on classical and instrumental conditioning. Chapter topics include stimulus control of behavior, avoidance learning, and punishment.

Don't Shoot the Dog (1991)

by K. Pryor
New York: Simon & Schuster

This is a practical guide for applying the principles of reinforcement to everyday life. Topics include training animals, managing employees, coping with intrusive roommates, and improving self-control.

Mentors (1992)

by T. Evans
Princeton, NJ: Peterson's Guides

This book describes how mentors can make a difference in children's lives, especially as a tutor in a one-to-one relationship.

National Center for the Study of Corporal Punishment

Temple University
253 Ritter Annex
Philadelphia, PA 19122
215-787-6091

This center provides information about the psychological and educational aspects of school discipline. It also provides legal advocacy to protest the use of corporal punishment and psychological abuse in schools. Consultation service for parents and teachers is available.

Self-Control (1995)

by Alexandra Logue
Upper Saddle River, NJ: Prentice Hall

This leading researcher evaluates specific areas of concern regarding self-control—eating, drug abuse, education, money, lying, depression, suicide, and aggression. Logue also lists places to contact for further information about some of the clinical problems covered in the text.

Social Foundations of Thought (1986)

by Albert Bandura
Englewood Cliffs, NJ: Prentice Hall

This book presents Bandura's cognitive social learning theory, which emphasizes reciprocal connections between behavior, environment, and person (cognition). Extensive coverage of observational learning is included.

Through Mentors

202-393-0512

This organization recruits mentors from corporations, government agencies, universities, and professional firms. The goal is to provide every youth in the District of Columbia with a mentor through high school. To learn how to become involved in a mentoring program or to start such a program, call the number above. Also, the National One-to-One Partnership Kit guides businesses in establishing mentoring programs (call 202-338-3844).

Walden Two (1948)

by B. F. Skinner
New York: Macmillan

Skinner once entertained the possibility of a career as a writer. In this provocative book, he outlines his ideas on how a more complete understanding of the principles of operant conditioning can produce a happier life. Critics argue that his approach is too manipulative.

Internet Resources

http://www.biozentrum.uni-wuerzburg.de/genetics/behavior/learning/behaviorism.html
Contrasts the history of operant and classical conditioning

http://www.sonic.net/~fredd/links.html
Phobia Links provides comprehensive resources on origin and treatment of phobia

http://www.kleinman.com/nyt/0907hyper.html
A humorous NY Times article on the impact of coping with phobias.

http://mmg2.im.med.umich.edu/~kleung/training.html
Train your dog using operant techniques.

http://www.cs.cmu.edu/~dst/Skinnerbots/index.html
The Skinnerbots apply operant conditioning to building robots.

http://www.mentalhealth.com/mag1/p5h-beh1.html
A discussion of learning applications to mental health.

http://www.parallaxweb.com/parenting/ttt.html
Tips on toilet training for "practically perfect parents."

http://www.mentors.net/
The Mentoring Resources Network home page.

http://www.psych101.com/behv/bandura.html
Read about Albert Bandura and related links in cognitive behaviorism

6

Memory

I come into the fields and spacious palaces of my

memory, where are treasures of countless images of

things of every manner.

—ST. AUGUSTINE
Christian Clergyman, 5th Century

*T*here are few moments when we are not steeped in memory. Memory can quietly stir, or spin off, with each step we take, each thought we think, each word we utter. Memory weaves the past into the present. It anchors the self in continuity. In this chapter, we will explore many different facets of memory: the nature of memory, the processes of memory, the biological and cultural contexts of memory, and strategies for improving memory.

The Story of S.:
A Man with Too Much Memory

*U*nlike the other reporters, when S. listened to his editor making detailed assignments, he never took notes. Feeling exasperated by what he saw as S.'s inattention, his editor challenged his professionalism. The editor was startled when S. reported not just the details of his own assignment but the details of others' assignments as well. S. was surprised himself. He thought everyone's memory operated in the same manner and until that point had never thought of himself as different or special.

Psychologist Alexander Luria (1968) chronicles the life of S., whose unique visual imagination allowed him to remember an extraordinary amount of detail. Luria had become acquainted with S. in the 1920s in Russia. He began some simple experiments to test S.'s memory by asking him to recall series of words or numbers, a standard method of testing memory skills. Luria concluded that S. had no apparent limits to his ability to recall. In such tests, most people can remember at most 5 to 9 numbers. Not only could S. remember as many as 70 numbers, he could recall them accurately in reverse order. S. also could report the sequence flawlessly with no warning or practice—even as long as fifteen years after his original exposure to the sequence. In addition, S. could describe what Luria had been wearing and where he had been sitting when S. learned the original list. Similar feats of recall included accurately reproducing passages from languages he didn't know after hearing the passage read only once.

How could S. manage such tasks? As long as each number or word was spoken slowly, S. could represent it as a visual image that was meaningful to him. These images were durable—S. easily remembered the image he created for each sequence long after he first learned the sequence. To erase an image, he enacted specific, mysterious rituals.

Although you might think S.'s ability would be very handy, S. often found it a serious liability. He moved from job to job, often feeling overwhelmed by the amount of detail he automatically involved in his work tasks. His propensity to create visual imagery interfered with normal information processing. He had trouble comprehending whole passages of text because he became bogged down in the details. To a casual observer, S. appeared to be disorganized and rather dimwitted—a person who talked too much and derailed social conversations by reporting the images that came unbidden to his mind. Ironically, he had a very poor memory for faces, finding them too flexible and changeable to recall. Worse, he experienced himself as being two people. He described himself as "I" when he felt in control of his memory and "he" when his imagery ran away with him. Luria concluded that S. had difficulty knowing which aspect of his life was more real: "the world of imagination in which he lived, or the world of reality in which he was merely a temporary guest" (p. 159). ❖

THE NATURE OF MEMORY

memory

The retention of information over time. Psychologists study how information is initially placed, or encoded, into memory; how it is retained, or stored, after being encoded; and how it is found, or retrieved, for a certain purpose later.

Memory *is the retention of information over time. Psychologists study how information is initially placed, or* encoded, *into memory; how it is retained, or* stored, *after being encoded; and how it is found, or* retrieved, *for a specific purpose later.* To explore the nature of memory, we will study memory's time frames and contents.

Time Frames of Memory

We remember some information for less than a second, some for half a minute, and other information for minutes, hours, years, even a lifetime. Because memory often functions differently across these varied time intervals, we can distinguish among different types of memory partly on the basis of their differing time frames. The three types of memory that vary according to their time frames are *sensory memory,* time frames of a fraction of a second to several seconds; *working memory* (also often called short-term memory), time frames of up to 30 seconds; and *long-term memory,* time frames of up to a lifetime (see figure 6.1).

sensory memory

Memory that holds information from the world in its original sensory form for only an instant, not much longer than the brief time for which one is exposed to the visual, auditory, and other sensations.

Sensory Memory. **Sensory memory** *holds information from the world in its original sensory form for only an instant, not much longer than the brief time for which one is exposed to the visual, auditory, and other sensations.* Sensory memory is very rich and detailed, but the information in it is very quickly lost unless certain processes are engaged in that transfer it into working or long-term memory.

*F*IGURE 6.1

The Time Frames of Memory

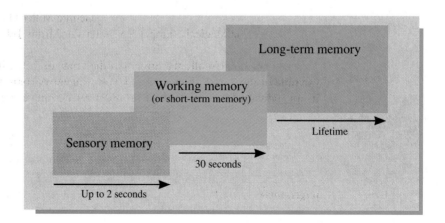

Life is all memory except for the one present moment that goes by so quick you can hardly catch it going.

—Tennessee Williams, *American Playwright, 20th Century*

Think about all the sights and sounds you encounter as you walk to class on a typical morning. Literally thousands of stimuli come into your fields of vision and hearing—cracks in the sidewalk, chirping birds, a noisy motorcycle, the blue sky, faces of hundreds of people. We do not process all of these stimuli, but we do process a number of them. In general, you process many more stimuli at the sensory level than you consciously notice. The sensory registers retain this information from your senses, including a large portion of what you think you ignore. But the sensory registers do not retain the information for very long.

Psychologists believe that sensory memory exists for all of the senses, but sensory memories for two senses—visual and auditory—have the strongest research base. Sensory memory for other senses, such as smell and touch have received little attention. **Echoic memory** *(from the word* echo*) is the name given to the auditory sensory registers in which information is retained for up to several seconds.* **Iconic memory** *(from the word* icon, *which means "image") is the name given to the visual sensory registers, in which information is retained only for about* 1/4 *second.*

The first scientific research on sensory memory focused on iconic memory. In his classic study in 1960, George Sperling presented his subjects with patterns of stimuli like those in figure 6.2. As you look at the letters, you have no trouble recognizing them. But Sperling flashed the letters on a screen for only very brief intervals, and about 1/20th of a second. After a pattern was flashed on the screen, the subjects could report only four or five letters. With such short exposure, reporting all nine letters was impossible.

But some of the participants in Sperling's study reported feeling that, for an instant, they could *see* all nine letters within a briefly flashed pattern. But they ran into trouble when they tried to *name* all the letters they had initially *seen*. One hypothesis to explain this experience is that all nine letters were initially processed by iconic sensory memory. This is why all nine letters were *seen*. However, forgetting was so rapid that the subjects could name only a handful of letters before they were lost from sensory memory.

Sperling decided to test this hypothesis. He reasoned that if all nine letters were actually processed in sensory memory, they should all be available for a brief time. To test this possibility, Sperling sounded a low, medium, or high tone just after a pattern of letters was shown. The subjects were told that the tone was the signal to report only the letters from the bottom, middle, or top row, respectively. Under these conditions, the subjects performed much better, suggesting a brief memory for most or all of the letters.

Working Memory. **Working memory,** *also sometimes called short-term memory, is a limited-capacity memory system in which information is retained for as long as 30 seconds, unless the information is rehearsed, in which case it can be retained longer.* Compared to sensory memory, working memory is limited in capacity, but is relatively longer in duration. Its limited capacity was examined by George Miller (1956) in a classic paper with a catchy title, "The Magical Number Seven, Plus or Minus Two." Miller pointed out that on many tasks individuals are limited in how much information they can keep track of without external aids. Usually the limit is in the range of 7 ± 2 items. The most widely cited example of the 7 ± 2 phenomenon involves **memory span,** which is the number of digits an individual can report back in order after a single presentation. Most college students can handle lists of 8 or 9 digits without making any errors. Longer lists, however, pose problems because they exceed your working memory capacity. If you rely on simple working memory to retain longer lists of items, you probably will make errors.

Of course, there are many examples where working memory seems to hold for much more than 5 or 6 units. For instance, consider a simple list of words: *hot, city, book, time, forget, tomorrow,* and *smile*. Try to hold these words in memory for a moment, then write them down. If you recalled all seven words, you succeeded in holding 34 letters in your

echoic memory

The auditory sensory registers in which information is retained for up to several seconds.

iconic memory

The visual sensory registers, in which information is retained for about 1/4 second.

working memory

Also sometimes called short-term memory, this is a limited-capacity memory system in which information is retained for as long as 30 seconds, unless the information is rehearsed, in which case it can be retained longer.

memory span

The number of digits an individual can report back in order following a single presentation of them.

$\mathcal{F}$IGURE 6.2

Sperling's Sensory Registers Experiment

This array of stimuli is similar to those flashed for about 1/20th of a second to subjects in Sperling's experiment. Trained subjects could reliably report any row, suggesting that iconic memory could hold as many as nine "bits" of information despite the subject's inability to name all nine.

working memory. Does this make you a genius with outrageous working memory skills? Or does it disprove the idea of limited capacity? The answer is neither. In demonstrating working memory for 34 letters, you "chunked" the letters into seven meaningful words. **Chunking** *is the grouping or "packing" of information into higher-order units that can be remembered as single units. Chunking expands working memory by making large amounts of information more manageable.* In demonstrating working memory for 34 letters, you "chunked" the letters into seven meaningful words. Since your working memory can handle seven chunks, you were successful in remembering 34 letters. Although working memory has limited capacity, chunking lets you make the most of it.

Another useful aid to working memory is **maintenance rehearsal,** *the conscious repetition of information that increases the length of time it stays in working memory* (Craik & Lockhart, 1972). To understand what we mean by maintenance rehearsal, imagine you are looking up a telephone number. If you can directly reach for the telephone, you will probably have no trouble dialing the number, because the entire combined action of looking up the number and dialing it can take place in the 30-second time frame of your working memory. But what if the telephone is not right by the phone book? Perhaps the phone book is in the kitchen and you want to talk privately on the extension in the den. You will probably *rehearse* the number as you walk from the kitchen to the den. Most of us experience a kind of "inner voice" that repeats the number again and again until we finally dial it. If someone or something interrupts our maintenance rehearsal, we may lose the information from short-term memory.

Working memory without maintenance rehearsal lasts half a minute or less, but if rehearsal is not interrupted, information can be retained indefinitely. Our rehearsal is often verbal, giving the impression of an inner voice, but it can also be visual or spatial, giving the impression of an inner eye. One way to use your visualization skills is to maintain the appearance of an object or scene for a period of time after you have viewed it. **Eidetic memory,** *also called photographic memory, involves especially vivid visual images. The small number of individuals who have eidetic memory can recall significantly more details of visual information than most people can.* S., who was described in the chapter-opening story, is one of those few people who have an eidetic memory. Individuals with eidetic memory say they literally "see" the page of a textbook as they attempt to remember information during a test. However, eidetic memory is so rare that it has been difficult to study. Some psychologists even doubt that it exists (Gray & Gummerman, 1975).

Rehearsal is an important aspect of working memory, but there is much more we need to know about this type of memory. Working memory is a kind of mental "workbench" that lets us manipulate and assemble information when we make decisions, solve problems, and comprehend written and spoken language. For example, in one study young

chunking

The grouping or "packing," of information into higher-order units that can be remembered as single units. Chunking expands working memory by making large amounts of information more manageable.

maintenance rehearsal

The conscious repetition of information that increases the length of time the information stays in working memory.

eidetic memory

Also called photographic memory; a form of memory involving especially vivid details. The small number of individuals who have eidetic memory can recall significantly more details of visual information than most of us can.

*𝓕*IGURE 6.3

A Model of Working Memory

In the model, the two slave systems—visuospatial scratchpad and phonological loop—help the executive do its job. The visuospatial scratchpad involves our spatial imagery skills; the phonological loop involves our spatial imagery skills, the phonological loop involves our language skills (Baddeley, 1986, 1990).

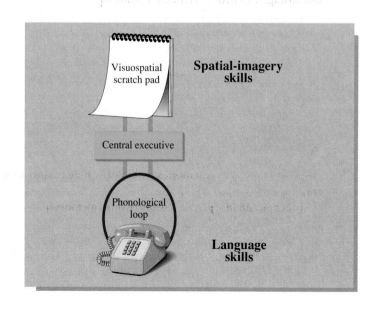

Working memory deficits are involved in Alzheimer's disease. The central executive of the working memory model may be the culprit, because Alzheimers' patients have considerable difficulty coordinating different mental activities—one of the central executive's functions.

children who were accurate readers had trouble comprehending what they had read (Yuill, Oakhill, & Parkin, 1989). Why couldn't this group of children comprehend what they read? Examination of their cognitive skills revealed that their poor working memory—their 30-second processing tool—was responsible for their poor comprehension.

One model of working memory is shown in figure 6.3 (Baddeley, 1990, 1993). In this model, working memory consists of a general "executive" and two "slave" systems that help the executive do its job. One of the slave systems is the phonological loop, which is specialized to process language information. This is where maintenance rehearsal occurs. The other slave system is the visuospatial scratchpad, which underlines some of our spatial imagery skills, such as visualizing an object or a scene. We will soon see that such visualization has powerful effects when we learn new information.

long-term memory

A type of memory that holds huge amounts of information for a long period of time, relatively permanently.

Long-Term Memory. **Long-term memory** *is a type of memory that holds huge amounts of information for a long period of time, relatively permanently.* In one study, people remembered the names and faces of their high school classmates with considerable accuracy for at least 25 years (Bahrick, Bahrick, & Wittlinger, 1975). The storehouse of long-term memory is indeed staggering. John von Neumann, a distinguished computer scientist, put the size at 2.8×10^{20} (280 quintillion) bits, which in practical terms means that our storage capacity is virtually unlimited. Von Neumann assumed we never forget anything; but even considering that we do forget things, we can hold several billion times more information than a large computer can. Even more impressive is the efficiency with which we retrieve information. It usually takes only a moment to search through this vast storehouse to find the information we want. Who discovered America? What was the name of your first date? When were you born? Who developed the first psychology laboratory? You can, of course, answer these questions instantly.

Contents of Memory

Just as different types of memory can be distinguished by how long they last—time frames of memory—memories within each time frame can be distinguished by their *content*. As we discussed earlier, the contents of sensory memory consist of memory for audition (echoic memory) and vision (iconic memory). Similarly, we learned that the contents of working memory vary according to at least two kinds of content—the articulatory loop, which holds information about speech, and the visuospatial scratchpad, which holds mental images. Therefore, it should be no surprise that the contents of long-term memory can also be differentiated. Indeed, many psychologists today accept the three-level hierarchy of long-term memory contents shown in figure 6.4 (Squire, 1987).

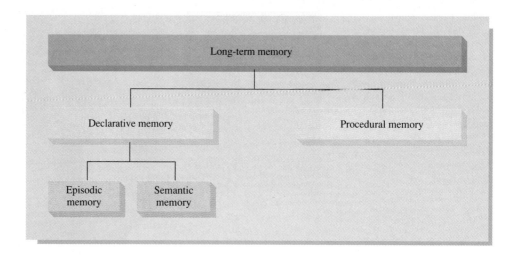

*F*IGURE 6.4
The Hierarchical Organization of
Long-Term Memory's Contents

In this hierarchical organization of long-term memory's contents, long-term memory is divided into the subtypes of declarative and procedural memory. Declarative memory is subdivided into episodic memory and semantic memory.

declarative memory

The conscious recollection of information, such as specific facts or events, and, at least in humans, information that can be verbally communicated.

procedural memory

Knowledge in the form of skills and cognitive operations about how to do something.

episodic memory

The retention of information about the where and when of life's happenings.

semantic memory

A person's general knowledge about the world.

Declarative and Procedural Memory.   **Declarative memory** *is the conscious recollection of information, such as specific facts or events that can be verbally communicated. Declarative memory has been called "knowing that," and, more recently, it has been called "explicit memory."* Examples of declarative (or explicit) memory include recounting the events of a movie you have seen and describing a basic principle of psychology to someone. However, you do not need to be talking to be using declarative memory. Simply sitting and consciously reflecting about Einstein's theory of relativity, or the date you had last weekend, involves declarative memory.

  Procedural memory *refers to knowledge in the form of skills and cognitive operations about how to do something. Procedural memory cannot be consciously recollected, at least not in the form of specific events or facts. This makes procedural memory difficult, if not impossible, to communicate verbally. Procedural memory has been called "knowing how" and, more recently, "implicit memory."* Examples of procedural (implicit) memory include the skills of playing tennis, riding a bicycle, and typing. They also include purely perceptual skills such as finding a product on a grocery store shelf. The first time you purchase a certain kind of product, it often takes a while to find it on the shelf, even if you know what aisle to walk down. But, with practice, the product "pops out" perceptually as you scan along an aisle. This sort of perceptual learning is a type of procedural memory.

Episodic and Semantic Memory.   Endel Tulving (1972) distinguishes between two subtypes of declarative memory: episodic and semantic. **Episodic memory** *is the retention of information about the where and when of life's happenings*—what it was like when your younger brother or sister was born, what happened to you on your first date, what you were doing when you heard about the bombing of the Oklahoma City federal building, what you had for breakfast this morning. Episodic memory is like an autobiographical filing system, organized in a manner that reflects each person's uniqueness.

> *How we remember, what we remember, and why we remember form the most personal map of our individuality.*
>
> —CHRISTINA BALDWIN, *American Author, 20th Century*

  Semantic memory *is a person's general knowledge about the world. It includes a person's fields of expertise* (such as knowledge of chess, for a skilled chess player); *general academic knowledge of the sort learned in school* (such as knowledge of geometry); *and "everyday" knowledge about meanings of words, famous individuals, important places, and common things* (such as who Nelson Mandela and Mahatma Gandhi are). *Semantic mem-*

Which kind of memory system—declarative or procedural—is at fault here?

THE FAR SIDE cartoon by Gary Larson is reprinted by permission of Chronicle Features, San Francisco, CA

ory knowledge is independent of the individual's personal identity with the past. For example, you can access a fact—such as "Lima is the capital of Peru"—and not have the foggiest notion of when and where you learned it.

Several examples help to clarify the distinction between episodic and semantic memory. In a certain type of amnesiac state, a person might forget entirely who she is—her name, family, career, and all other personal information about herself—yet be able to talk and demonstrate general knowledge about the world. Her episodic memory is impaired, but her semantic memory is functioning. An especially dramatic case of this type, a young man named K. C., was reported by Endel Tulving (1989). After suffering a motorcycle accident, K. C. lost virtually all use of his episodic memory. The loss was so profound that he was unable to consciously recollect a single thing that had ever happened to him. At the same time, K. C.'s semantic memory was sufficiently preserved that he could learn about his past as a set of facts, just as he would learn about another person's life. He could report, for example, that the saddest day of his life was when his brother died of drowning about 10 years before. This sounds as if K. C. had episodic memory, but further questioning revealed that he had no conscious memory of the drowning event. He simply knew about the drowning because he was able to recall—apparently through use of his semantic memory—what he had been told about his brother by other members of his family.

Traditional and Contemporary Models of Memory

Although there are several types of memory, (sensory, working, and long-term), they often work together when we perform tasks. Two models have been proposed to explain interactions among sensory, working, and long-term memory.

The Traditional Model—Atkinson and Shiffrin. The traditional model of memory was developed by Richard Atkinson and Richard Shiffrin (1968). In this **traditional information-processing model,** *memory involves a sequence of three stages—sensory registers, short-term (working) memory, and long-term memory* (see figure 6.5). Much information makes it no farther than the sensory registers, which means that it is retained only for a few seconds at most. However, some information—that to which we pay attention—is

traditional information-processing model

Atkinson and Shiffrin's model according to which memory involves a sequence of three stages—sensory registers, short-term (working) memory, and long-term memory.

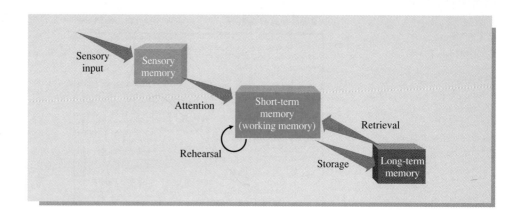

𝓕IGURE 6.5
The Traditional Information-
Processing Model of Memory

transferred to working memory. Information in working memory can be retained for about 30 seconds (or somewhat longer with the aid of rehearsal). Atkinson and Shiffrin claimed that the longer information is maintained in working memory through the use of rehearsal, the greater the chance it has of getting into long-term memory. Notice in figure 6.5 that retrieval is used to search long-term memory and bring information back into working memory.

contemporary model of working memory

Baddeley's model that emphasizes that long-term memory often precedes working memory and that working memory uses long-term memory in flexible ways.

The Contemporary Model—Baddeley.   The **contemporary working-memory model** *is Alan Baddeley's (1993) view that long-term memory often precedes working memory and that working memory uses long-term memory in flexible ways* (see figure 6.6). To get a better feel for the contemporary model of working memory, consider what you are doing right now—reading a book. Information flows into your sensory register, activating

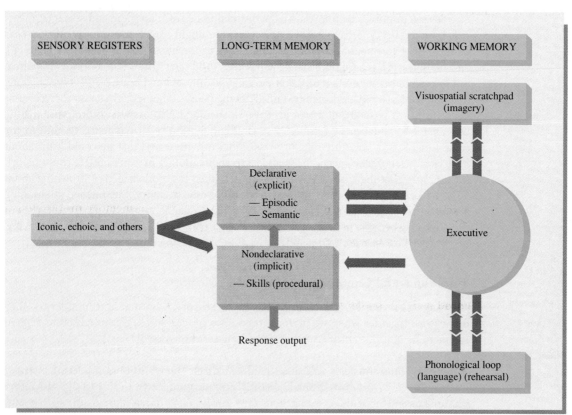

𝓕IGURE 6.6
The Contemporary Model of Working Memory

knowledge about visual features, words, and word meanings in declarative memory. Some of this activated knowledge reaches working memory. There the phonological loop and visuospatial scratchpad can be brought into play to improve comprehension. For example, in tackling a tough section of this text, you might find yourself going very slowly through a sentence, using rehearsal to "hold on" to the first words while you "take in" words that follow. The comprehension you achieve results in new learning, which is represented by the arrow from working memory back to the declarative portion of long-term memory in figure 6.6.

eview

The Nature of Memory, Time Frames of Memory, Contents of Memory, and Models of Memory

Memory is the retention of information over time. Psychologists study how information is encoded into memory, how it is stored, and how it is retrieved for some purpose later. Two important features of memory are its time frame and its contents. Time frames of memory include sensory memory, working memory, and long-term memory. Sensory memory holds information from the world in its original sensory form only for an instant, not much longer than the brief time for which it is exposed to the visual, auditory, and other senses. Visual sensory memory (iconic memory) retains information for about ¼ of a second, auditory sensory memory (echoic memory) for several seconds. Working memory, also called short-term memory, is a limited-capacity memory system in which information is retained for as long as 30 seconds, unless the information is rehearsed, in which case it can be retained longer. Compared to sensory memory, working memory is

limited in capacity but has a relatively long duration. According to George Miller, the limitation of working memory is 7 ± 2 units of information. Chunking can expand working memory, and maintenance rehearsal keeps information in working memory longer. In one model of working memory, an executive plus two slave systems—the phonological loop (which holds speech information) and the visuospatial scratchpad (which holds mental images)—are involved. Long-term memory is a relatively permanent type of memory that holds huge amounts of information for a long period of time.

Many psychologists today accept the model of a three-level hierarchical organization of memory in which long-term memory is subdivided into episodic and semantic memory. Declarative memory is the conscious recollection of information, such as specific facts or events, and, at least in humans, information that can be verbally communicated. Declarative memory

has been called "knowing that" and more recently, "explicit memory." Procedural memory cannot be consciously recollected, at least not in the form of specific events or facts, and this makes procedural memory difficult, if not impossible, to communicate verbally. Procedural memory has been called "knowing how" and, more recently, "implicit memory." Episodic memory is the retention of information about the where and when of life's happenings. Semantic memory is a person's general knowledge about the world.

Two models of memory are Atkinson and Shiffrin's traditional information-processing model and Baddeley's contemporary model of working memory. In the traditional model, memory involves a sequence of three stages—sensory registers, working memory, and long-term memory. In the contemporary model, long-term memory often precedes working memory, and working memory uses long-term memory in flexible ways.

THE PROCESSES OF MEMORY

memory processes

The encoding of new information into memory, the representation of information, and the retrieval of what was previously stored.

Psychologists who study memory are especially interested in **memory processes:** *the encoding of new information into memory, the representation of information, and the retrieval of what was previously stored.*

Encoding

encoding

The transformation of information in, and/or transfer of information into, a memory system.

Encoding *is the transformation and/or transfer of information into a memory system.* Information can be encoded into sensory memory and short-term or working memory. Here our main focus is on encoding information into long-term memory. In everyday language, encoding has much in common with learning. When you listen to a lecture, watch a movie, listen to music, or talk to a friend you are encoding information into your long-term memory. It is unlikely, though, that you are encoding all the information you receive. Psychologists are interested not only in how much encoding takes place, but also in the processes involved and their operating principles. Among the processes involved in encoding are attention, automatic and effortful processing, depth of processing and elaboration of information, organization, and imagery.

Attention. *Pay attention* is a phrase we hear all of the time. Just what is attention? When you take an exam, you attend to it. This implies that you have the ability to focus your mental effort on certain stimuli (the test questions) while excluding other stimuli. Thus, an important aspect of attention is selectivity. **Selective attention** *is the focusing of attention on a narrow band of information.* Sometimes we have difficulty ignoring information that is irrelevant to our interests or goals. For example, if a television set or stereo is blaring while you are studying, you might have trouble concentrating.

Not only is attention selective, it also is shiftable. If a professor asks you to pay attention to a certain question and you do so, your behavior indicates that you can shift the focus of your mental effort from one stimulus to another. If the telephone rings while you are studying, you shift your attention from studying to the telephone. However, an external stimulus is not necessary to elicit an attention shift. At this moment you can shift your attention from one topic to another virtually at will. You might think about the last time you ate at a Chinese restaurant, then think about yesterday's soccer game, then think about your date tonight.

As we have seen, attention is concentrated and focused mental effort, a focus that is both selective and shifting. Effort plays an important role in the two ways of encoding information—automatic and effortful processing.

Automatic and Effortful Processing. Research on attention sparked interest in the role of effort in encoding information. Encoding processes differ in how much effort they require. For example, imagine you are driving down the street and chatting with a friend. You're fine as long as the driving is easy and the concentration involves an everyday topic, such as gossip about a mutual acquaintance. But what if the streets are icy, or if the conversation turns serious and you find yourself in an intense argument? Something probably has to give—the driving or talking. If two or more activities are somewhat difficult, it is almost impossible to perform them simultaneously without overloading your focus of attention. In explaining the potential for overload, many cognitive psychologists believe that what is being focused in attention is a kind of mental energy for doing mental work. They believe the amount of this energy is limited, and because it is limited, overload can occur. This mental energy is defined as *capacity, cognitive resources,* or simply *effort.* Psychologists make a distinction between effortful processing and automatic processing. **Effortful processing** *requires capacity or resources to encode information in memory.* **Automatic processing** *does not require capacity, resources, or effort to encode information in memory.* Automatic processing occurs regardless of how people focus their attention (Hasher & Zacks, 1979).

Information about spatial aspects of the environment or frequency of events can be encoded automatically. For example, many students who are taking a test remember reading a certain piece of information on a specific page of the text. Such memory for location of written information is based not on conscious memorization strategies, but rather on automatic memory processes. However, many activities that are important for memory—organization, rehearsal, visualization, and elaboration, for example—do require mental effort. In a number of studies, this allocation of capacity, or effort, was related to having a good memory (Ellis, Thomas, & Rodriguez, 1984).

Now we consider some of the most important effortful processes—depth of processing and elaboration, organization, and imagery.

Depth of Processing and Elaboration. Earlier in the chapter, we saw that maintenance rehearsal acts as an aid to working memory. However, it is much less effective in improving long-term memory. Following this discovery, psychologists Fergus Craik and Robert Lockhart (1972) developed a new model of memory. **Levels of processing theory** *is Craik and Lockhart's theory that memory is on a continuum from shallow to deep. In this theory, deeper processing produces better memory.*

The sensory or physical features of stimuli are memorized at the *shallow* level. At an *intermediate* level of processing, more details are added. At the *deepest* level the most detail is added. For example, assume that you are hearing the story of Snow White and the Seven Dwarfs for the first time (see figure 6.7). If you encoded the story at a shallow level, you might recall it as a story about a housekeeper and a group of little men. At an inter-

---

selective attention

The focusing of attention on a narrow band of information.

effortful processing

Processing that requires capacity or resources to encode information in memory.

automatic processing

A process of encoding information in memory that does not require capacity, resources, or effort.

levels of processing theory

Craik and Lockhart's theory that memory processing occurs on a continuum from shallow to deep; in this theory, deeper processing produces better memory.

Tell me the story of Snow White and the Seven Dwarfs . . .	
SHALLOW PROCESSING	It's a story about a housekeeper and seven small men.
INTERMEDIATE PROCESSING	It's a tale about a bewitched princess caring for seven short coal miners.
DEEP PROCESSING	It's a fairy tale about an enchanted princess outcast from her home (by a Wicked Witch) who takes care of Dopey, Doc, Sneezy, Sleepy, Happy, Bashful, and Grumpy.

Depth of processing →

$\mathcal{F}$IGURE 6.7

Depth of Processing

According to the levels of processing theory of memory, deep processing of stimuli produces better memory of them.

elaboration

The extensiveness of information processing at any given depth in memory.

mediate level, you might be able to produce more details about the story—a wicked witch, a poison apple, a prince who saves the day. At the deepest level of processing you could distinguish Sneezy from Sleepy and describe your favorite aspects of the story. A number of studies have shown that people's memories improve when they make semantic associations with stimuli rather that merely attend to the shallow aspects of a stimulus. In other words, you're more likely to remember something when you process information at a deep, rather than a shallow, level.

However, cognitive psychologists soon recognized that there is more to a good memory than "depth." Within deep, semantic processing, psychologists discovered, the more extensive the processing, the better the memory (Craik & Tulving, 1975). **Elaboration** *is the extensiveness of information processing at any given depth in memory.* For instance, rather than memorizing the definition of *memory,* a better strategy is to come up with examples of how information enters your mind, how it is stored, and how you can retrieve it. Thinking of examples of a concept is a good way to understand it. Self-reference is another effective way to elaborate information. For example, if the word *win* is on a list of words

The more that you elaborate about an event, the better your memory of the event will be. For example, if you were at an open-air rock concert and you encoded information about how large the crowd was, who accompanied you, which songs you heard, how powerful the performances were, what the weather was like, and other vivid sights, sounds, and smells, you probably will remember the concert more clearly.

to remember, you might think of the last time you won a bicycle race. Or if the word *cook* appears, you might imagine the last time you cooked dinner. In general, deep elaboration—elaborate processing of meaningful information—is an excellent way to remember.

One reason that elaboration produces good memory is that is adds to the *distinctiveness* of the "memory codes" (Ellis, 1987). To remember a piece of information, such as a name, an experience, or a fact about geography, you need to search for the code that contains this information among the mass of codes contained in long-term memory. The search process is easier if the memory code is somehow unique. The situation is not unlike searching for a friend at a crowded airport. If your friend is 6 feet tall and has flaming red hair, it will be easier to find him or her in the crowd. Similarly, highly distinctive memory codes can be more easily differentiated. Also, as encoding becomes more elaborate, more information is stored. And as more information is stored, the more likely it is that this highly distinctive code will be easy to differentiate from other memory codes. For example, if you witness a bank robbery and observe that the getaway car is a red 1987 or 1988 Pontiac with tinted windows and spinners on the wheels, your memory of the car is more distinctive than that of a person who notices only that the getaway car is red.

Organization. Recall the 12 months of the year as quickly as you can. How long did it take you? What was the order of your recall? The answers to these questions probably are "4 to 6 seconds" and "natural order" (January, February, March, etc.). Now try to remember the months in alphabetical order. Did you make any errors? How long did it take you? There is a clear distinction between recalling the months naturally and recalling them alphabetically. This demonstration makes it easy to see that your memory for the months of the year is organized. Indeed, one of memory's most distinctive features is its organization.

An important feature of memory's organization is that sometimes it is hierarchical. A *hierarchy* is a system in which items are organized from general classes to more specific classes. An example of a hierarchy for the general category of minerals is shown in figure 6.8. In an experiment using conceptual hierarchies of words, such as those in figure 6.8, Gordon Bower and his colleagues (1969) showed the importance of organization in memory. Subjects who were presented the words in hierarchies remembered the words much better than did subjects who were given the words in random groupings. Other

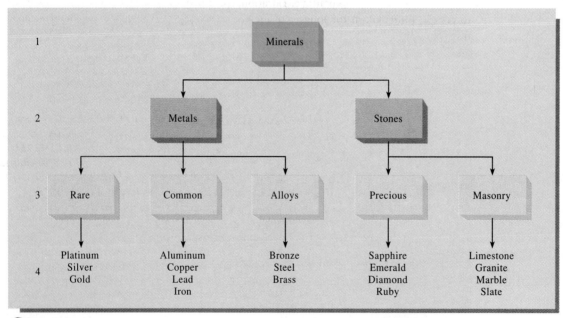

$\mathcal{F}$IGURE 6.8

Example of a Hierarchical Organization

FRANK & ERNEST reprinted by permission of UFS, Inc.

investigations have revealed that if people are simply encouraged to organize material, their memory of the material improves. This occurs even if no warning is given that memory will be tested (Mandler, 1980). This simple finding has implications for how you can better design your study activities (even for this course).

Imagery.   How many windows are in your apartment or house? If you live in a dorm room with only one or two windows, this question may be too easy. If so, how many windows were in the last home you lived in? Few of us have ever memorized this information, but many of us believe we can come up with a good answer, especially if we use imagery to "reconstruct" each room. We take a mental walk through the house, counting windows as we go.

For many years psychologists ignored the role of imagery in memory because it was believed to be too mentalistic by behaviorists. But studies by Allan Paivio (1971, 1986) documented how imagery can improve memory. Paivio argued that there are two ways a memory can be stored: as a verbal code or as an image code. For example, a picture can be remembered by a label (a verbal code) or a mental image. Paivio thinks that the image code, which is highly detailed and distinctive, produces better memory. Although imagery is widely accepted as an important aspect of memory, there is controversy over whether we have separate codes for words and images (Pylyshyn, 1973). More about imagery appears later in the chapter when we discuss strategies for improving memory. For now, just keep in mind that if you need to remember a list of things, forming mental images will help you out.

We have seen that semantic elaboration, organization, and imagery are effective ways to encode information for long-term memory storage but that maintenance rehearsal is not. Now we turn our attention to the ways we can represent information in memory storage.

eview

Encoding

Encoding is the transformation and/or transfer of information into a memory system. Information can be encoded into sensory memory and working memory, but the main focus is on encoding information into long-term memory. Among the important aspects of encoding are attention, automatic and effortful processing, depth of processing and elaboration, imagery, and organization.

Attention is the ability to focus on certain stimuli. Attention is both selective (the ability to focus and concentrate on a narrow band of information) and shifting. Automatic processes do not require capacity or resources; conversely, effortful processes require capacity or resources. Effortful processing includes depth of processing and elaboration, imagery, and organization. Craik and Lockhart developed the levels of processing view of memory, which stresses that memory is on a continuum from shallow to deep. In this view, deeper processing produces better memory. Elaboration refers to the extensiveness of processing at any depth and it leads to improved memory, making encoding more distinctive. Imagery involves sensations without an external stimulus present. One of the most pervasive aspects of memory is organization, which involves grouping or combining items. Information is often organized hierarchically. Paivio argued that we have two separate verbal and imaginal codes, but this is controversial. Imagery often improves memory.

Representation

Although we have talked about the time frames and content of memory, as well as the processes of encoding and retrieval, we have not tackled the question of how knowledge is represented in memory. Two approaches that have addressed this issue are network theories and schema theories.

Network Theories.   One of the first network theories claimed that our memories consist of a complex network of nodes that stand for labels or concepts (see figure 6.9). The network was assumed to be hierarchically arranged with more-concrete concepts (canary, for example) nestled under more-abstract concepts (bird). More recently, cognitive psychologists realized that such hierarchical networks were too neat to fit the way human cognition actually works (Shanks, 1991). For example, people take longer to answer the true-or-false statement "An ostrich is a bird" than they do to answer the statement "A canary is a bird." Memory researchers now envision the network as more irregular and distorted: a *typical* bird, such as a canary, is closer to the node or center of the category *bird* than is the atypical ostrich. Figure 6.10 shows an example of the revised model, which allows for the typicality of information while retaining the original notion of node and network.

We add new material to this network by placing it in the middle of the appropriate region. The new material is gradually tied in—by meaningful connections—to the appropriate nodes in the surrounding network. That is why if you cram for a test, you will not remember the information over the long term. The new material is not woven into the long-term web. In contrast, discussing the material or incorporating it into a research paper interweaves it and connects it to other knowledge you have. These multiple connections increase the probability that you will be able to retrieve the information many months or even years later.

Schema Theories.   Long-term memory has been compared to a library. Your memory stores information just as a library stores books. We retrieve information in a fashion

FIGURE 6.9

The Hierarchical Organization of Memory with Nodes (Branching Points) at Three Levels in the Hierarchy

Notice how the information becomes more detailed and specific as you move through the levels of the hierarchy in this model. Some psychologists have challenged this representation as too "clean" to portray the true complexity of our representation processes.

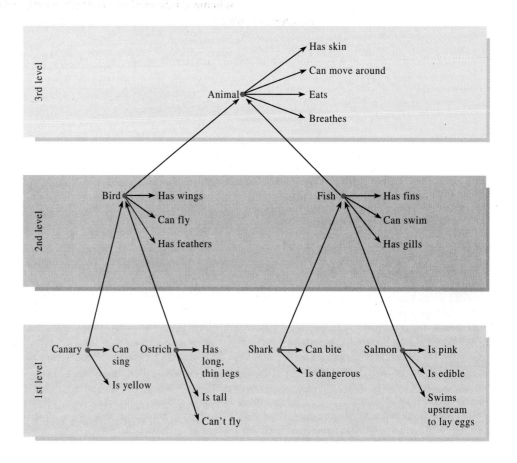

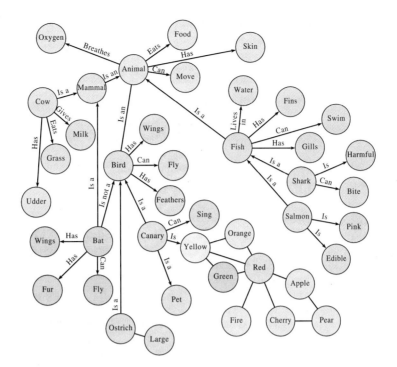

schema

Information—concepts, events,
and knowledge—that already exists
in a person's mind.

similar to the process we use to locate and check out a book. But the process of retrieving information from long-term memory is not as precise as the library analogy suggests. When we search through our long-term memory storehouse we don't always find the *exact* "book" we want, or we might find the book we want but discover that only several pages are intact. We have to *reconstruct* the rest.

When we reconstruct information, we often fit it into information that already exists in our mind. A **schema** *is information—concepts, events, and knowledge—that already exists in a person's mind.* Schemas from prior encounters with the environment influence the way we encode, make inferences about, and retrieve information. Unlike network theories, which assume that retrieval involves specific facts, schema theory claims that long-term memory searches are not very exact. We seldom find precisely what we want, or at least not all of what we want; hence, we have to reconstruct the rest. Our schemas support this reconstruction process, helping us fill in the gaps between our fragmented memories.

The schema theory of memory began with Sir Frederick Bartlett's (1932) studies of how people remember stories. Bartlett was concerned about how people's backgrounds determine what they encode and remember about stories. Bartlett chose stories that sounded strange and were difficult to understand. He reasoned that a person's background, which is encoded in schemas, would reveal itself in the person's reconstruction (modification and distortion) of the story's content. For example, one of Bartlett's stories was called "War of the Ghosts," an English translation of an American Indian folktale. The story contained events that were completely foreign to the experiences of the middle-class British research participants.

Summarized, the story goes like this: An Indian joins a war party that turns out to consist entirely of ghosts. They go off to fight some other Indians, and the main character gets hit but feels no pain. He returns to his people, describes his adventure, and goes to sleep. But in the morning he dies as something black comes out of his mouth.

What interested Bartlett was how differently the participants might reconstruct this and other stories from the original versions. The British participants used both their general schemas for daily experiences and their schemas for adventurous ghost stories in particular to reconstruct "War of the Ghosts." Familiar details from the story that "fit into" the participant's schemas were successfully recalled. But details that departed from the person's schemas were often extensively distorted. For example, the "something black" that came out of the Indian's mouth became blood in one reconstruction and condensed air in another.

There has been a flurry of interest in reconstructive memory, especially in the way people recall stories, give eyewitness testimony, remember their past, and recall conversations (Fivush, 1995). To learn more about the nature of reconstructive memory in eyewitness testimony see Sociocultural Worlds.

In memory each of us is an artist; each of us creates.
—PATRICIA HAMPL, *American Author, 20th Century*

Sociocultural Worlds

Eyewitness Testimony

In the legal arena, one person's memory of events given at testimony can be crucial in determining a defendant's future. For example, think about how our nation was gripped by the human drama that unfolded in the murder trial involving O. J. Simpson. Both defense and prosecution vigorously attempted to establish the credibility or faultiness of witnesses' memories. Much of the interest in eyewitness testimony focuses on distortion, bias, and inaccuracy in memory (Loftus, 1993a; Thompson & others, 1998).

Memory fades over time. That's why the amount of time that has passed between an incident and a person's recollection of it is a critical factor in eyewitness testimony. In one study, people were able to identify pictures with 100 percent accuracy after a 2-hour time lapse. However, 4 months later they achieved an accuracy of only 57 percent; chance alone accounts for 50 percent accuracy (Shepard, 1967).

Unlike a videotape, memory can be altered by new information. In one study, students were shown a film of an automobile accident (Loftus, 1975). Some of the students were asked how fast the white sports car was going when it passed a barn. Other students were asked the same question without any mention of a barn. In fact, there was no barn in the film. However, 17 percent of the students who heard the question that included the barn mentioned it in their answer; only 3 percent of those whose question did not include the barn mentioned that they saw it. New information, then, can add or even replace existing information in memory (Yarmey, 1998).

Studies have shown that people of one ethnic group are less likely to recognize individual differences among people of another ethnic group. Latino eyewitnesses, for example, may have trouble distinguishing among several Asian suspects. This makes identifying individuals from a police lineup or photographs an unreliable tool. In one investigation, clerks in small stores were asked to identify photographs of customers who had shopped there 2 hours earlier (Brigham & others, 1982). Only 33 percent of the customers were correctly identified. In another experiment, a mugging was shown on a television news program. Immediately after, a lineup of six suspects was broadcast and viewers were asked to phone in and identify which of the six individuals they thought committed the robbery. Of the 2,000 callers, more than 1,800 identified the wrong person. In addition, even though the robber was White, one-third of the viewers identified an African American or Latino suspect as the criminal.

Kato Kaelin's behavior on the stand during the O. J. Simpson trial suggested that his memory might be unreliable.

Identification of individuals from police lineups or photographs is not always reliable. People from one ethnic group often have difficulty recognizing differences among people of another ethnic group.

"Why? You cross the road because it's in the script—that's why!"

script

A schema for an event.

We have schemas not only for stories but also for scenes or spatial layouts (a beach or a bathroom) and common events (going to a restaurant, playing football, writing a term paper). A **script** *is a schema for an event* (Schank & Abelson, 1977). Consider a restaurant script. This script has information about physical features, people, and typical occurrences in restaurants. This kind of information is helpful when people need to figure out what is happening around them. For example, if you are enjoying your after-dinner coffee in a restaurant and a man in a tuxedo comes over and puts a piece of paper on the table, your script tells you that the man probably is a waiter who has just given you the check. Figure 6.11 shows some eating scripts in different cultures.

In one study, individuals in the United States and Mexico remembered according to script-based knowledge, consistent with common and familiar United States and Mexican cultural scripts (Harris, Schoen, & Hensley, 1992). For example, individuals in the United States remembered information about a dating script better when no chaperone was present on the date, while individuals in Mexico remembered the information better when a chaperone was present.

FIGURE 6.11

Eating Scripts

Shown here are representative scripts from a Japanese tea ceremony, an extravagant Western dinner, and an Ethiopian meal. *With which script do you feel most comfortable? least comfortable?*

The reason we use schemas and scripts to encode information in memory is so that the information can be more easily retrieved. Of course, even when we use such memory strategies, we might still forget some of the information. In the next section, we will explore the nature of retrieval and forgetting in memory.

Retrieval and Forgetting

Have you ever forgotten where you parked your car, your mother's birthday, or to meet a friend to study? Have you ever sat in a class taking an exam, unable to remember the answer to a question but remembering where the elusive concept was on the page? Psychologists have developed a number of theories about why we forget information and how we retrieve it (Schneider & Bjorklund, 1998).

Retrieval from Long-Term Memory. To retrieve something from our mental "data bank," we search our store of memory to find the relevant information. Just as with encoding, this search can be virtually automatic or it can require effort. For example, if someone asks you what your mother's first name is, the answer immediately springs to your lips; that is, retrieval is automatic. But if someone asks you the name of your first-grade teacher, it may take some time to dredge up the answer; that is, retrieval requires more effort. As appropriate information is found, it is pulled together to guide and direct a person's verbal and motor responses. Let's explore several concepts related to retrieval.

One glitch in retrieving information that we're all familiar with is the **tip-of-the-tongue phenomenon, or TOT state.** *It is a type of "effortful retrieval" that occurs when people are confident they know something but just can't quite seem to pull it out of memory.* In one study on the TOT state, participants were shown photographs of famous people and asked to say their names (Yarmey, 1973). The researcher found that people used two strategies to try to retrieve the name of a person they thought they knew. One strategy was to pinpoint the person's profession. For example, one participant correctly identified the famous person as an artist but the artist's name, Picasso, remained elusive. Another retrieval strategy was to repeat initial letters or syllables—such as *Monetti, Mona, Magett, Spaghetti,* and *Bogette*—in the attempt to identify singer Liza Minelli. The tip-of-the-tongue phenomenon suggests that without good retrieval cues, information encoded in memory can be difficult to find.

Understanding how retrieval works also requires knowledge of the **serial position effect:** *the effect of an item's position in a list on our recall of it. Recall is better for items at the beginning and at the end of a list.* If someone gave you the directions "Left on Mockingbird, right on Central, right on Stemmons, left on Balboa, and right on Parkside," you probably would remember "Left on Mockingbird" and "right on Parkside" more easily than the turns and streets in the middle. **Primacy effect** *refers to better recall for items at the beginning of a list.* **Recency effect** *refers to better recall for items at the end of the list.* Together with relatively low recall of items from the middle of the list, this pattern makes up the serial position effect. See figure 6.12 for a typical serial position effect that shows a weaker primacy effect and a stronger recency effect.

How can primacy and recency effects be explained? The first few items in the list are easily remembered because they are rehearsed more often that later items are (Atkinson & Shiffrin, 1968). Working memory is relatively empty when they enter, so there is little competition for rehearsal time. And since they get more rehearsal, they stay in working memory longer and more likely to be successfully encoded into long-term memory. In contrast, many items from the middle of the list drop out of working memory before being encoded into long-term memory. The last several items are remembered for different reasons. First, at the time these items are recalled, they may still be in working memory. Second, even if these items are not in working memory, their relative recency, compared to other list items, makes them easier to recall. For example, if you are a sports fan, try remembering at the end of the football season what football games you saw that year, or, at the end of the baseball season, what baseball games you saw. You probably will remember more recent games better than the earlier games. This represents a recency effect that extends far beyond the time span of working memory.

tip-of-the-tongue phenomenon, or TOT state

A type of effortful retrieval that occurs when people are confident they know something but just can't quite seem to pull it out of memory.

serial position effect

The effect of an item's position in a list on our recall of it; in particular, recall is superior for items at the beginning and at the end of a list.

primacy effect

Superior recall for items at the beginning of a list.

recency effect

Superior recall for items at the end of a list.

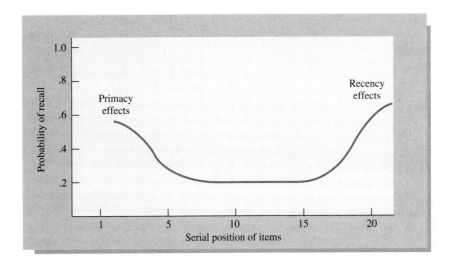

*F*IGURE 6.12

Serial Position Effect

When a person is asked to memorize a list of words, the words memorized last usually are recalled best, those at the beginning next best, and those in the middle least efficiently.

recall

A memory measure in which the individual must retrieve previously learned information, as on an essay test.

recognition

A memory measure in which the individual only has to identify (recognize) learned items, as on a multiple-choice test.

Two other factors involved in retrieval are (a) the nature of the cues that can prompt your memory, and (b) the retrieval task that you set for yourself. If effective cues for what you are trying to remember do not seem to be available, you need to create them. For example, if you have a "block" about remembering a new friend's name, you might go through the alphabet, generating names that begin with each letter. If you manage to stumble across the right name, you'll probably recognize it.

While cues help, your success in retrieving information also depends on the task you set for yourself. For instance, if you're simply trying to decide if something seems familiar, retrieval is probably a snap. Let's say you see a short, dark-haired woman walking toward you. You quickly decide she's someone who is in your English class. But remembering her name or a precise detail, such as when you met her, can be harder (Brown, Deffenbacher, & Sturgill, 1977). Such findings have implications for police investigations. A witness might be certain she has previously seen a face, yet she might have a hard time deciding if it was at the scene of the crime or in a mug shot.

The two factors just discussed—the presence or absence of good cues, and the retrieval task required—are involved in an important memory distinction: recall versus recognition memory. **Recall** *is a memory measure in which the individual must retrieve previously learned information, as on an essay test.* **Recognition** *is a memory measure in which the individual only has to identify ("recognize") learned items, as on a multiple-choice test.* Most college students prefer multiple-choice tests because they're easier than essay tests or fill-in-the-blank test. Recall tests, such as fill-in-the-blank tests, have poor retrieval cues. You are told to try to recall a certain class of information ("Discuss the factors that caused World War II"). In multiple-choice "recognition" tests, you merely judge whether a stimulus is familiar or not (does it match something you experienced in the past?).

You have probably heard people say they are terrible at remembering names but they "never forget a face." If you have made that claim yourself, actually try to *recall* a face. It's not so easy. Police officers know that witnesses can be terrible at describing a suspect, so they often bring in an artist to reconstruct the suspect's face. Recalling faces is difficult. If you think you are better at remembering faces rather than names, it is probably because you are better at recognition than recall.

Researchers have found that when people are faced with a recall task—a merciless professor gives a lengthy essay exam, for example—their memory improves when retrieval cues correspond to the situation when the information was encoded (Eich, 1990). For example, you'll probably recall information more easily when you take a test in the same room you heard the lecture and took notes in—that is, where the information was originally encoded. The strongest evidence for this conclusion is based on a study in which scuba divers learned information both on land and under water (Godden & Baddeley, 1975). They were then asked to recall the information. The scuba divers' recall was much better when the encoding and retrieval locations were constant (both on land or under water) (see figure 6.13). Although changing from land to under water or vice versa

$\mathcal{F}$IGURE 6.13

Relative Efficiency in Godden and Baddeley's Experiment on Encoding and Retrieval Cues

Divers recalled information better when encoding and retrieval locations were constant (both on land, both under water).

		Retrieval conditions	
		On land	In water
Encoding conditions	On land	+	−
	In water	−	+

cue-dependent forgetting

Forgetting information because of failure to use effective retrieval cues.

interference theory

The theory that we forget not because memories are actually lost from storage, but because other information gets in the way of retrieval of what we want to remember.

proactive interference

Interference that occurs when material that was learned earlier disrupts the recall of material learned later.

retroactive interference

Interference that occurs when material learned later disrupts the recall of material learned earlier.

adversely affects one's memory, less dramatic changes in environmental context, such as moving to a new room to take an exam, show weaker effects.

Cue-dependent forgetting *is a form of forgetting information because of failure to use effective retrieval cues.* Cue-dependent forgetting can explain why we sometimes fail to retrieve a needed fact on an exam even when we "know" that piece of information. These failures to retrieve what is stored in memory occur because we do not use the right cues. For example, you might forget the point of Sperling's experiment, described earlier, if "Sperling's experiment" is your only cue. But if you also use the cue "sensory memory" or "iconic memory," you might suddenly recollect what Sperling did and what he discovered.

Interference and Decay. The principle of cue-dependent forgetting is consistent with **interference theory**, *which states that we forget not because memories are actually lost from storage, but because other information gets in the way of retrieving what we want to remember.* There are two kinds of interference: proactive and retroactive.

Proactive interference *occurs when material that was learned earlier disrupts the recall of material learned later.* In this usage, *pro-* means "forward in time." For example, suppose you had a good friend 10 years ago named *Mary,* and last night you met someone at a party named *Marie.* You might find yourself calling your new friend *Mary* because the old information *(Mary)* interferes with retrieval of new information *(Marie).* **Retroactive interference** *occurs when material learned later disrupts retrieval of*

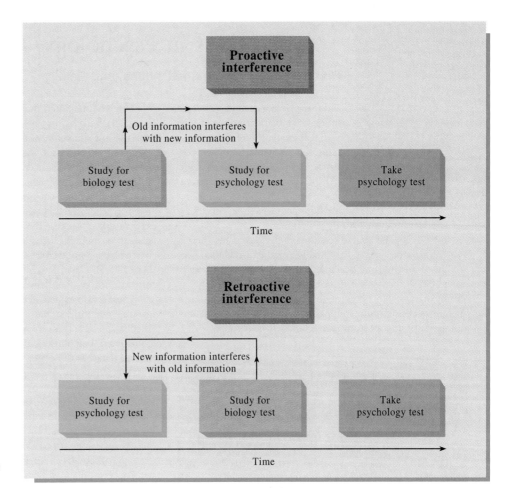

𝓕IGURE 6.14

Proactive and Retroactive Interference

Pro- means "forward," so in proactive interference old information has a forward influence by getting in the way of new material learned. *Retro-* means "backward," so in retroactive interference new information has a backward influence by getting in the way of material learned earlier. *How would this information help you organize your study period more effectively over the next few weeks?*

information learned earlier. Remember that *retro-* means "backward in time." Suppose you have become friends with *Marie* (and finally have gotten her name straight). If you find yourself sending a letter to your old friend *Mary,* you might address it to *Marie* because the new information *(Marie)* interferes with the old information *(Mary)* (see figure 6-14).

Proactive and retroactive interference *both* can be explained by cue-dependent forgetting. The reason that *Mary* interferes with *Marie,* and *Marie* interferes with *Mary* might be that the cue you are using to remember does not distinguish between the two memories. For example, if the cue you are using is "my good friend," it might evoke both names. This could result in retrieving the wrong name, or in a kind of blocking in which each name interferes with the other and neither comes to mind. Memory researchers have shown that retrieval cues (like "friend" in our example) can become overloaded, and when that happens we are likely for forget.

Although interference is involved in forgetting, it is not the whole story. **Decay theory** *states that when something new is learned a neurochemical "memory trace" is formed. However, over time this trace tends to disintegrate.* Decay theory suggests that the passage of time always increases forgetting.

Amnesia.   Consider the case of H. M. At the age of 27, H. M. underwent surgery to stop his epileptic seizures and emerged with his intelligence and most of his mental abilities

decay theory

The theory that when something new is learned, a neurochemical "memory trace" is formed, but over time this trace tends to disintegrate.

Applications in Psychology

Repressed Memories, Child Abuse, and Reality

There has been a dramatic increase in reported memories of childhood sexual abuse that were allegedly repressed for many years (Ceci & Bruck, 1998). With recent changes in legislation, people with recently discovered memories are suing alleged perpetrators for events that occurred 20, 30, even 40 or more years earlier.

In 1991, popular actress Roseanne's story was on the cover of *People* Magazine. She reported that her mother had abused her from the time Roseanne was an infant until she was 6 or 7 years of age, but she had only become aware of the abuse recently during therapy. Other highly publicized cases of repressed memories of child abuse coming into awareness during therapy dot the pages of popular magazines and self-help books.

Roseanne said that her mother abused her from the time she was an infant until she was 6 or 7 years old. *Why have many psychologists questioned some of the reports of activation of repressed memories?*

There is little doubt that childhood abuse is tragically common. Elizabeth Loftus (1993 b) and others (Kutchinsky, 1992) don't dispute that child abuse is a serious social problem. What Loftus takes issue with is the process therapists sometimes use to help their clients recall abuse. Loftus argues that therapists sometimes help clients "reconstruct" abuse "memories" that aren't real. Clients might develop false child-abuse memories because they perceive their therapist's expectations as plausible or because they have complete trust in their therapist. Some therapy clients who originally claimed to remember having been abused have later recanted their accusations and blamed their construction of "repressed memories" on the directiveness of their therapist.

There is also evidence that some repressed memories are genuine memories of past events. For instance, some therapy clients who have recovered repressed memories of abuse have confronted their abusers, and some of the accused have confirmed that they did commit the abuse.

How frequently are memories of abuse really repressed? At present, there aren't any completely satisfactory research methods that can help us discover the answer. Although Loftus has demonstrated the ease with which false memories can be implanted in unsuspecting individuals, her critics suggest that her research does not take into account the extent of the trauma endured by children during episodes of abuse, and intensity of trauma might correlate with likelihood of repression.

According to Loftus (1993b) psychotherapists, counselors, social service agencies, and law enforcement personnel need to be careful about probing for horrors on the other side of some amnesiac barrier. They should be cautious in their interpretation of uncorroborated repressed memories that return. Clarification, compassion, and gentle confrontation along with a demonstration of empathy are techniques that can be used to help individuals in their painful struggle to come to grips with their personal truths.

There is a final tragic risk of suggestive probing and uncritical acceptance of all allegations made by clients. These activities increase the probability that society in general will disbelieve the actual cases of child abuse that deserve extensive attention and evaluation. In general, any careless or uncritical acceptance of unreplicated findings in psychology, especially when they have a colorful element that attracts media attention, harms public attitudes toward the contributions of psychological research.

amnesia

The loss of memory.

anterograde amnesia

A memory disorder in which the
individual cannot form memories
of new information or events.

retrograde amnesia

A memory disorder that involves
memory loss for a segment of the
past but not for new events.

intact, but the part of his brain that was responsible for laying down new memories (the hippocampus) was damaged beyond repair. This damage resulted in **amnesia,** *the loss of memory.*

Although some types of amnesia clear up over time, H. M.'s amnesia endured. In the years following surgery, H. M.'s memory showed no improvement. The amnesia suffered by H. M. was anterograde in nature. **Anterograde amnesia** *is a memory disorder that affects the retention of new information or events. What was learned before the onset of the condition is not affected.* For example, H. M. could identify his friends, recall their names, and even tell stories about them—but only if he had known them before surgery. People who met H. M. after surgery remained virtual strangers, even if they spent thousands of hours with him. The vast majority of H. M.'s postsurgical experiences were never encoded in long-term memory. Oddly enough, H. M.'s short-term memory remained unchanged, and as indicated earlier, his overall intelligence, which was above average, remained intact.

Amnesia also occurs in a second form, known as **retrograde amnesia,** *which involves memory loss for a segment of the past but not for new events.* It is much more common than anterograde amnesia, and frequently occurs when the brain is assaulted by an electrical shock or a physical blow—such as a head injury to a football player. The key difference from anterograde amnesia is that the forgotten information is old (prior to the event that caused the amnesia), and the person's ability to acquire new memories is not affected.

Memory is more delible than ink.

—ANITA LOOS, *American Journalist, 20th Century*

Repression and Memory.   Repression is one of psychology's most controversial concepts. Long the province of clinical psychology, repression of threatening, anxiety-laden unconscious thoughts has caught the eye of memory researchers in cognitive psychology. Repression takes place when something shocking happens and the mind pushes the occurrence into some inaccessible part of the unconscious mind. At some later point in time, the memory might emerge in consciousness. Repression is one of the foundations on which the field of psychoanalysis rests. To read further about the nature of repressed memories, turn to Applications in Psychology.

 *R̄eview*

Repression, Retrieval, and Forgetting

Two theories of how knowledge is represented in memory are network and schema. Early network theories stressed that memories consist of a complex network of nodes that are hierarchically arranged. More recent network theories stress the role of meaningful nodes in the surrounding network. The concept of schema refers to information we have about various concepts, events, and knowledge. Schema theory claims that long-term memory is not very exact and that we reconstruct our past. Schemas for events are called scripts.

Retrieval involves getting information out of long-term memory. The search can be automatic or effortful. An interesting aspect is the tip-of-the-tongue phenomenon (TOT state), which occurs when we just can't quite pull something out of

memory. The implication of TOT is that, without good retrieval cues, stored information is difficult to find. The serial position effect influences retrieval—retrieval is superior for items at the beginning of a list (primacy effect) and at the end of a list (recency effect). One key factor that makes retrieval effortful is the absence of effective cues. A second factor is the nature of the retrieval task, which, along with the presence or absence of retrieval cues, distinguishes recall from recognition memory. Failure to use effective retrieval cues is one reason we forget, a phenomenon known as cue-dependent forgetting.

The principle of cue-dependent forgetting is consistent with interference theory. It states that we forget, not because memories are actually lost from storage, but because other information gets in the way

of what we want to remember. Proactive interference occurs when material that was learned earlier disrupts the recall of material learned later. Retroactive interference occurs when material learned later disrupts the retrieval of information learned earlier. Decay theory argues that, when something new is learned, a memory trace is formed. However, as time passes this trace begins to disintegrate.

Amnesia involves extreme memory deficits. There are two forms of amnesia. Anterograde amnesia is a memory disorder that affects the retention of new information and events. Retrograde amnesia is a memory disorder that involves memory loss for a segment of the past but not for new events. Memory researchers have recently become interested in repression, long a province of clinical psychology.

THE BIOLOGICAL AND CULTURAL CONTEXTS OF MEMORY

The forces of nature and nurture, of biology and experience, make us who we are and shape us as individuals. Memory is no exception. In this section, we explore the neurobiological basis of memory and memory's cultural dimensions.

The Neurobiological Origins of Memory

Karl Lashley (1950) spent a lifetime looking for a location in the brain where memories are stored. He trained rats to discover the correct pathway in a maze and then cut out a portion of the animals' brains and retested their memory of the maze pathway. After experimenting with thousands of rats, Lashley found that the loss of various cortical areas did not affect rats' ability to remember the maze's path. Lashley concluded that memories are not stored in a specific location in the brain.

Neural Circuits. Many neuroscientists today believe that memory is located in discrete sets or circuits of neurons. Brain researcher Larry Squire (1990), for example, says that most memories are probably clustered in groups of about 1,000 neurons. He points out that memory is distributed throughout the brain, in the sense that no specific memory center exists. Many parts of the brain and nervous system participate in the memory of a particular event. Yet memory is localized, in the sense that a limited number of brain systems and pathways are involved, and each probably contributes in different ways (Lynch, 1990).

Single neurons, of course, are at work in memory. Researchers who measure the electrical activity of single cells have found that some respond to faces, others to eye or hair color, for example. But for you to recognize your Uncle Albert, individual neurons that provide information about hair color, size, and other characteristics must act together.

Ironically, some of the answers to the complex questions about the neural mechanics of memory come from studies on a very simple experimental animal—the inelegant sea slug. Eric Kandel and James Schwartz (1982) chose this large snail-without-a-shell because of the simple architecture of its nervous system, which consists of only about 10,000 neurons.

The sea slug can hardly be called a quick learner or an animal with a good memory, but it is equipped with a reliable reflex. When anything touches the gill on its back, it quickly withdraws it. First the researchers repeatedly prodded the sea slug's gill. After

The inelegant sea slug with its elegant memory. *How and why do neurobiologists study the sea slug to learn about memory?*

awhile, it ignored the prodding and stopped withdrawing its gill. Next the researchers applied an electric shock to its tail when they touched the gill. After many rounds of the shock-accompanied prodding, the sea slug violently withdrew its gill at the slightest touch. The researchers found that the sea slug remembered this message for hours or even weeks.

More important than the discovery that sea slugs had memories was the finding that memory seems to be written in chemicals. Shocking the sea slug's gill releases the neurotransmitter serotonin at the synapses, and this chemical release basically provides a reminder that the gill was shocked. This "memory" informs the nerve cell to send out chemical commands to retract the gill the next time it is touched. If nature builds complexity out of simplicity, then the mechanism used by the sea slug might work in the human brain as well. Chemicals, then, might be the ink with which memories are written.

Broad-Scale Architecture.   While some neuroscientists are unveiling the cellular basis of memory, others are examining the broad-scale architecture of memory in the brain (Johnson, 1998). In a series of studies, Mortimer Mishkin and his colleagues (Mishkin & Appenzellar, 1987) examined the role of brain structures in the memories of monkeys. They assume that the same brain structures that are responsible for memory in monkeys are also responsible for memory in humans, an assumption that generates spirited debate.

In a typical experiment, Mishkin and his colleagues compare the memory of monkeys who have an intact brain with the memory of monkeys who have undergone surgery that has impaired some part of their brain. Impairment at any point in the "memory circuit" can produce deficits in memory. Damage to the amygdala and the hippocampus, two brain regions deep inside the brain at the tip of the brain stem, cause the most serious deficits in memory. However, damage to the thalamus and the mammillary body causes deficits as well, as does damage to the basal forebrain and the prefrontal cortex. Figure 6.15 shows the location of all six of these brain structures that are involved in the memory of monkeys.

Is there any evidence that these brain structures are responsible for memory in humans? Researchers have found that brain damage to humans with strokes, Alzheimer's disease, Korsakoff's syndrome, and operations intended to cure epilepsy involve the same brain structures in human memory. Recall the case of H. M., who was virtually unable to recall events that had occurred since his operation for epilepsy. H. M.'s hippocampus had been destroyed.

The "memory circuit" outlined by Mishkin and his colleagues appears to be involved in declarative memory only, not being responsible for procedural memory. The procedural memory of human amnesiacs such as H. M. also is preserved, which means that procedural memory likely has a memory circuit somewhere else in the brain. As yet, neuroscientists have not discovered this circuit. Ultimately, researchers may be able to link each type and subtype of memory we have discussed (episodic, semantic, priming, sensory memory, and working memory) to discrete brain circuits.

$\mathcal{F}$IGURE 6.15

Memory Circuit Involved in Declarative Memory

Mortimer Mishkin and his colleagues have demonstrated that the amygdala, hippocampus, thalamus, mammillary body, basal forebrain, and prefrontal cortex are involved in declarative memory. Neuroscientists call the combination of brain structures involved in memory a "memory circuit."

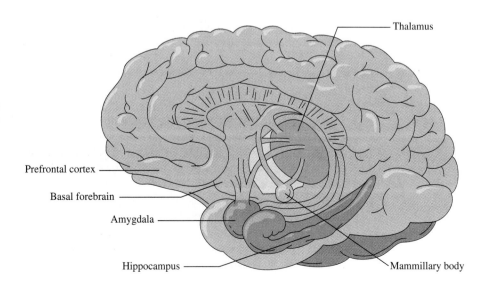

Thalamus

Prefrontal cortex

Basal forebrain

Amygdala

Hippocampus

Mammillary body

As neuroscientists discover the identity of memory circuits in the brain, might we reach a point at which the psychological study of memory becomes unimportant? That's unlikely. First, we are far from working out all of the complexities of the neurochemical underpinnings in human memory. And second, even if we were successful in unraveling the neurochemical mystery of memory, each person's private kingdom of memories will remain intact.

Cultural Influences on Memory

A culture sensitizes its members to certain objects and events in the environment, which in turn can influence the nature of memory (Mistry & Rogoff, 1994). Remember our discussion of schema theory? Sir Frederick Bartlett believed that a person's background, which is encoded in schemas, is revealed in the way the person reconstructs a story. This effect of background on memory is called the **culture specificity hypothesis.** *This hypothesis states that cultural experiences determine what is socially relevant in a person's life and, therefore, what the person is most likely to remember.* For example, imagine that you live on an island in the Pacific Ocean and make your livelihood by fishing. Your memory about how weather affects fishing is likely to be highly developed. On the other hand, as a Pacific Islander you would be hard-pressed to encode and recall the details of one hour of MTV. The culture specificity hypothesis also applies to subgroups within a culture. For example, many basketball fans can recount an impressive array of National Basketball Association (NBA) statistics. A devout gardener might know the informal and Latin names of all plants seen on a garden tour. Our specific interests in our culture and subculture shape how rich our memory stores are on any given topic.

IMPROVING MEMORY

With researchers discovering more about the biological and neurochemical bases of memory, it is possible that some day we will be able to take a memory pill that will help us recall information better. With no memory pill on the near horizon, though, what can we do to improve memory? As you will see, we can do a lot. We will start this section by examining how to improve memory for practical matters in everyday life. Then we will apply such strategies to improving your performance on tests.

Improving Practical Memory

Every day you must remember a mind-boggling collection of ideas, chores, and facts. For example, you might have to remember to put the dog out, take your vitamins, and fill your car with gas. You might have to memorize the steps for using the latest version of your word-processing program. You also meet a variety of individuals whose names you should probably commit to memory. Each day presents opportunities for adding new and helpful information to your memory as well as potentially embarrassing opportunities for your memory to fail.

General Memory Strategies. What are some things you can do to operate your memory efficiently? The following are some proven strategies.

- *Pay close attention.* When you attempt to learn something new, give it your undivided attention. Distraction sets up competing stimuli and makes your learning inefficient.
- *Rehearse and practice.* Overlearn ideas you want to store in long-term memory. For example, if you learn a new operation on the computer, repeat the procedure the next few days until it becomes a part of your routine. Remember, though, that by itself rehearsal increases short-term memory better than long-term memory.
- *Make a list, and check it twice.* Many people use memory aids, such as a well-constructed "to do" list, to keep them on task. This makes good sense, especially if your tasks exceed Miller's magic number of 7. Develop a ritual: Make a list and check it off at regular times during the day. This can help keep you on task.

Improving Personal and Cognitive Skills

Are You Sure About That?

Think back to the last time you had a disagreement with someone based partly on whose memory was more accurate. Your serious disagreement probably reflected different "realities" constructed out of the same experience. How does the nature of memory explain why two people can have different memories of the same experience?

1. *Differences in attention at the level of sensory memory and working memory.*
   Just because two people share the same physical space doesn't mean that they "take in" the same sensory information. They might extract different elements of the experience for further processing.

2. *Differences in the quality of working memory.*
   Individuals differ in the efficiency and effectiveness of their working memory. Some people seem to process information quickly; others labor harder to convert working-memory contents into long-term memory.

3. *Differences in strength of semantic long-term memory.*
   People differ in the kinds of ready access they have to different ideas in long-term memory. Some people develop expertise areas that others find boring or foolish. Expertise (well-developed semantic memory) can help solve problems or it can encourage the expert to reject others' viewpoints as less competent.

4. *Differences in schemas as a basis for attention and reconstruction.*
   Schemas are filters that affect how we evaluate information. We enter situations with different schemas that shape our expectations about how things will work. We might believe that our memories are accurate because our constructions fit best with our general expectations about how things *should have been.*

5. *Differences in the quality (and quantity) of episodic recall.*
   Some people have a knack for describing minute details. Others extract only larger impressions. These differences in style of recall show up with maddening frequency and feed into chronic differences of opinion.

So who is wrong and who is right? Regardless of how convinced we are that we have a handle on the truth and our partners are wrong (deluded, stupid, misguided, mentally unbalanced), we must conclude that there can always be other interpretations. Memory is vulnerable to error in many ways. This fact should temper our convictions about the accuracy of our own recall and help us have a more open-minded stance toward resolving differences of opinions.

It isn't so astonishing the number of things that I can remember, as the number of things I remember that aren't so.
—MARK TWAIN, *American Writer and Humorist, 19th Century*

- *Organize yourself to jog your memory.* For example, when you have errands to run, put reminders of the chores next to your wallet or purse. Under your car keys put books to be returned to the library or clothes to be taken to the dry cleaners.
- *Give yourself additional memory cues.* If you have the common problem of worrying that you left an electrical appliance plugged in, say out loud as you unplug the iron, "It's 9:05 and I'm unplugging the iron." The additional verbal cue can save you from having to return home to check. When you have only one thing to remember to do, wear your watch upside down. Every time you look at your watch, you will be cued about the one thing you wanted to remember to do.
- *When your memory fails, analyze what went wrong.* By spending some additional time analyzing, you might create some additional memory prompts that keep you from repeating the error.

Remembering Names. Most people have trouble remembering the names of new acquaintances. Several strategies can help you develop stronger social recall.

One simple approach when you are introduced to someone is to repeat the person's name immediately. You might say, "Tom Naylor? Hello, Tom." About 10 to 15 seconds later, look at the individual and repeat the name silently again. Do it again after 1 minute and then again after 3 minutes. The name will have a good chance of being retained in your long-term memory. This spacing strategy is effective because most forgetting occurs within a short time after you first learn a fact (Loftus, 1980).

A second approach is to scrutinize the name to see if you can break it into smaller units to help you make additional associations to it. For example, meeting Ms. Frankenheimer might make you think of hot dogs. Finally, adopt S.'s strategies and use visual imagery to help you remember. Imagine Ms. Frankenheimer wearing a hot dog hat! Your vivid imagination will help make her face and her name distinctive in your long-term memory.

Resolving Memory Differences. You have probably had some unpleasant arguments about "the way things were." See Improving Personal and Cognitive Skills ("Are You Sure About That?") to explore how differences in memory skills can contribute to interpersonal struggles.

Next we will explore how understanding memory processes can improve your academic preparation and test-taking skills.

Improving Academic Memory

By the time you finish college, your memory will be transformed by the concepts and skills you will have learned. Your memory will get a workout when you demonstrate your knowledge in test situations. Evaluate your current practices by completing the Self-Assessment. Now let's elaborate specific strategies to improve your study skills.

$\mathcal{S}$elf-Assessment

Memory and Study Strategies

Are you maximizing your memory and study strategies so that you can do well on tests? To find out, respond to the following items. Rate yourself from 1 (Not like me at all) to 5 (A lot like me).

	1	2	3	4	5
1. I memorize for understanding; I don't use rote memorization.					
2. I use effective organization strategies when I memorize. I review my notes after a lecture and put them in an organized form.					
3. I use imagery and word mnemonics.					
4. I distribute my learning over time so I don't have to cram.					
5. I use the recency effect in memory to my advantage.					
6. I overlearn, going over the material time and time again so I'm confident about retrieving it.					
7. I study 2 or 3 hours out of class each week for every hour I am in class.					
8. I am motivated and enthused about my classes and the material I have to remember.					
9. I am good at concentrating and eliminating distractions.					
10. I practice good physical health habits, such as exercising regularly and maintaining regular sleep patterns to avoid fatigue.					
11. I practice good mental health habits and don't get stressed out about tests.					

Scoring and Interpretation

Total your scores for the eleven items. If you scored 51–55, you are using good memory and study strategies to maximize your test performance. If you scored 46–50, you are using good memory and study strategies for the most part. However, you likely have several areas you can work on. For each item you marked 3 or less, put together a plan for improvement related to that item. If you scored 40–44, you are doing some things well, but have a lot of room for improvement in others. What can you do to improve your memory and study strategies? If you scored below 40, your failure to use effective memory and study strategies is likely having a negative impact on your test performance. Map out an organized plan to improve your memory and study strategies. Then follow the plan. If you have trouble putting the plan into action, contact the study skills service at your college for help.

Organize the Material.   We remember information better when we organize it hierarchically. For example, at the beginning of each chapter of this book we outline the main section headings. Then at the end of the chapter we provide a cognitive map—a hierarchical figure that shows the main topics you have studied.

When you take notes from a lecture, put your organizational skills to work. As soon as possible after the lecture, read your notes and organize them. Rewrite them in an outline form or create a cognitive map similar to those at the end of the chapters in this textbook. Do the same thing when you've finished reading a chapter or a section of a chapter.

Elaborate the Meaning.   You have already discovered that it is easier to memorize concepts in courses in which you have an intrinsic interest. In courses you don't like as well, for which memorizing feels like a chore, try to find a way to make the material more meaningful to you. Information that is memorized by rote rarely stays with us as long as meaningful information does. Search for personal connections to the material. When you elaborate the meaning of a concept to promote deep processing, you are memorizing for understanding.

mnemonics

Techniques for making memory more efficient.

method of loci

A mnemonic strategy in which information is associated with a well-known sequence of activities or locations.

pegword method

A mnemonic strategy that involves using a set of mental pegwords associated with numbers.

Use Mnemonics.   **Mnemonics** *are techniques that make memory more efficient.* They include strategies for remembering material using both imagery and words. Mnemonics are especially helpful when you need to remember lists.

One imagery strategy is called the **method of loci,** *in which information is associated with a well-known sequence of activities or locations.* Suppose you want to remember the components of long-term memory. Using the method of loci, you associate each concept with a concrete location. For example, you might envision your bedroom as the home of declarative memory and the bathroom as the home of procedural memory. While you are in the "bedroom," you open your diary to capture episodic memory. You thumb through your dictionary to capture semantic memory. By fixing on this sequence of images, you can recall the component parts of long-term memory.

Another imagery technique for memorizing is called the **pegword method,** *which involves using a set of mental pegs with numbers attached to them.* The standard pegword method rhyme is simple: "One is a bun, two is a shoe, three is a tree," and so on up to as many as twenty numbers. Once you repeat these rhymes to serve as a foundation, you can use them as mental pegs to memorize many things. Suppose you want to keep the order of the component parts of memory straight. Using the pegword strategy, you might envision the word *sensory* resting on a bun ("One bun is sensory"), next to a *work* boot ("Two shoe is working"), next to a long tree ("Three tree is long-term"). By maintaining these three images, you can keep the order straight. When you need to retrieve the order, you select the appropriate cue word, such as *bun* or *shoe.*

You can create other images or cartoons that can give you additional memory cues for the material you are trying to learn. Sometimes silly or even sexy images are the easiest to recall.

Some mnemonics involve wordplay rather than visual images. A simple mnemonic strategy for memorizing lists consists of creating a memorable word string using the first letter of each word in the list. You saw one example of this approach in the chapter on sensation and perception. *ROY G. BIV* represents the colors of the visible portion of the light-wave spectrum: red, orange, yellow, green, blue, indigo, and violet. Another example using this strategy encodes most important components of memory: The mnemonic *ARESIDORI* (Ellis, 1987) stands for *a*ttention, *r*ehearsal, *e*laboration, *s*emantic processing, *i*magery, *d*istinctiveness, *o*rganization, *r*etrieval, and *i*nterest.

Sometimes you can craft a memorable sentence to help you master the material. For example, if your task is to identify factors in retrieval and forgetting, this silly sentence might help: Right on *cue* Clara *primari*ly eats *serial* but *recent*ly she bit the *tip-of-her-tongue,* which *interfere*d with her plan to get her tooth *decay* fixed.

Consolidate Your Learning.   Regularly review what you need to learn. Go over your notes after a lecture. Examine them again at night. Study them again each week before the test. This systematic review distributes your learning over a longer period. It will

---

Improving Memory　　　　**219**

prepare you to benefit from a concentrated final tune-up just before the exam instead of being faced with having to learn everything at the last minute.

You've heard that it is not a good idea to cram for a test. The reason is that when you leave your learning to the last minute, you guarantee that your learning will be shallow and short- rather than long-term. Pulling all-nighters also can fatigue you, making your recall even less efficient.

Minimize Distraction.   Give your full attention to the material you want to remember. Schedule blocks of time dedicated to studying in a setting where you won't be interrupted. If you are in a noisy place and that's the best place you can study, take some steps to reduce the noise. For example, put on earphones and play soft instrumental music (without lyrics) in the background, just loud enough to block out distractions.

Remember, the *recency effect* states that you will best remember the information you learned most recently. If you have several tests in one week or even one day to study for, schedule your final study session in a subject as the last thing you do prior to that test.

Organize Yourself.   Successful students plan how to use their time effectively. A good strategy is to record your test schedule on an academic calendar. Then calculate backward to see how much time you are going to need for test preparation. Map out when you will do your regular cumulative review sessions and your final review session.

When planning your study sessions, pay attention to when you are likely to be at your best. Some of us are more alert in the morning, others in the afternoon, and yet others in the evening. Schedule your study sessions for the times when you feel the most alert and energetic. However, if you are "night person" and you must study or take a test in the morning, be sure to get a decent night's sleep and have a healthy breakfast to help you perform.

Review

Biological and Cultural Contexts of Memory; Improving Memory

The nature and nurture of memory involve the neurobiological basis of memory (nature) and the cultural dimensions of memory (nurture). In the study of memory's neurobiological basis, an important issue is the extent to which memory is localized or distributed. Single neurons are involved in memory, but some neuroscientists believe that most memories are stored in circuits of about a thousand neurons. There is no one specific memory center in the brain. Many parts of the brain participate in the memory of an event.

A culture sensitizes its members to certain objects and events in the environment. These cultural experiences can influence the content of a person's memory. The cultural specificity hypothesis describes the influence of a person's background on memory. This hypothesis also applies to subgroups within a culture.

Improving memory involves using the right strategies. We described a number of strategies for improving memory in practical matters as well as preparing for tests. Practical memory tips include paying attention, overlearning ideas, using "to do" lists, organizing yourself, using special cues, and analyzing what went wrong when memory fails. We also explored tips for remembering names and resolving arguments related to differing accounts of events.

Improving academic memory involves organizing the material, elaborating the meaning, using mnemonics, conducting review sessions, minimizing distraction, and organizing yourself.

Overview

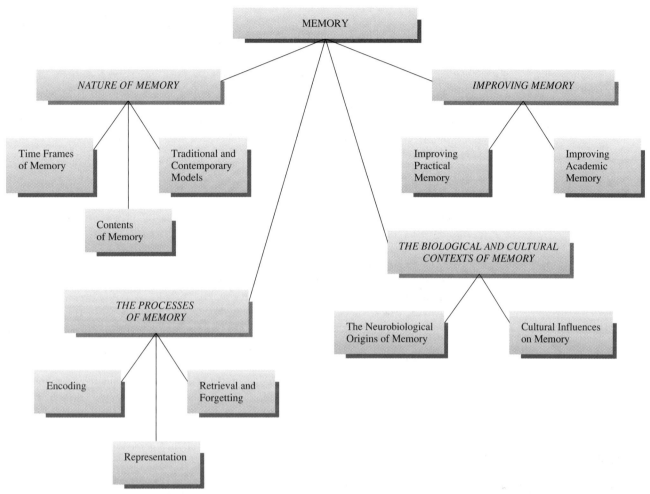

We began our exploration of memory by studying the nature of memory, which involved memory's time frames, memory's content, and traditional and contemporary models of memory. Our coverage of memory processes focused on encoding, representation, and retrieval and forgetting. We also examined memory's biological and cul-

tural contents, which include neurobiological origins and cultural influences. We also studied how to improve memory in practical and academic contexts.

Don't forget that you can obtain a more detailed summary of the chapter by again studying the in-chapter reviews on pages 199, 203, 213, and 220.

Key Terms

Thinking It Over

Exercises . . .

. . . In Critical Thinking

One major difference between American and Japanese education is the degree to which the two systems rely on the use of rote memorization. Japanese education relies extensively on rote memorization throughout different grade levels. American education has moved away from rote memorization as a primary cognitive strategy, placing more emphasis on reasoning and problem solving. What might be some advantages and disadvantages of both strategies? After you have completed your comparison, decide which strategy you prefer and explain why.

. . . In Creative Thinking

Get some practice in using visual mnemonic imagery by creating a picture that will help others quickly learn your name. Remember, the mnemonic needs to be vivid but uncomplicated. The mnemonic should contain memory cues that make it easy for a stranger to remember your name. Show your mnemonic to a friend and ask whether you have succeeded in creating an effective memory aid.

. . . In Active Learning

One popular party activity is called "The Rumor Chain." Get several volunteers to leave the room. The first volunteer is called back in, and a classmate reads either a complex news story or an unfamiliar fairy tale to the first volunteer. Then a second volunteer is called back into the room, and the first volunteer retells the story to the second volunteer. Repeat this sequence until all volunteers have had an opportunity to first listen to the story and then tell the story. The last volunteer tells the story to the rest of the class. Compare the "drift" in details from the original version to the version that emerges at the end of the chain. Speculate about the roles accurate listening and memory schemas play in communicating information.

. . . In Reflective Learning

Write down your very first memory from when you were a very young child. How clear are the details? Are there memory supports, such as family photos or stories, that bolster your recall? How accurate do you think this memory is? How might all of the years since this event occurred lead you to a reconstruction of the event that is different from what actually happened?

Resources for Psychology and Improving Humankind

Basic and Applied Memory Research, Vols. 1 and 2 (1996)

edited by Douglas Hermann, Cathy McEvoy, Chris Hertzog, Paula Hertel, and Marcia Johnson
Hillsdale, NJ: Erlbaum

A wide array of topics in basic and applied memory research are evaluated, including the practical application of memory research, memory and clinical problems, memory and study strategies, eyewitness memory, memory for faces, memory aids, amnesia, drugs and memory, and aging.

Human Memory (1990)

by A. Baddeley
Boston: Allyn & Bacon

The chapter you have just read highlighted Baddeley's contemporary working memory model. In his book, Baddeley extensively reviews research on memory to support the development of his memory model.

Memory and Cognition

edited by Gregory Loftus, U. of Washington

This research journal publishes articles on many aspects of memory and cognition. Topics of articles in recent issues of the journal include priming, distinctiveness, organization, autobiographical memory, schema theory, face processing, working memory, and retrieval processes.

The 36-Hour Day (1981)

by Nancy Mace and Peter Rabins
Baltimore: Johns Hopkins University Press

Alzheimer's is a widespread disorder in aging individuals. Its symptoms include memory loss. This book is a family guide to caring for persons with Alzheimer's.

Psychological Factors in Eyewitness Identification (1995)

edited by Siegried Sporer, Roy Malpass, and Guenter Koehnken
Hillsdale, NJ: Erlbaum

Researchers from different fields address a variety of issues involving eye witness identification. Among the topics discussed are voice recognition by humans and computers, children's memories, cross-racial identification, facial image reconstruction techniques, and person descriptions.

Remembering Our Past (1995)

edited by David Rubin
New York: Cambridge

Currently, there is increased interest in autobiographical memory. In this book, a number of contributors describe many dimensions of autobiographical memory.

Total Recall (1984)

by Joan Minninger
New York: Pocket Books

This book is full of helpful techniques for improving your memory. The author has given seminars on improving memory to a number of corporations, including IBM and General Electric. Tips on how to improve your memory draw on such important dimensions of memory as retrieval cues, depth of processing, linkages between short-term and long-term memory, episodic memory, and semantic memory. You also learn how to remember what you read, how to remember names and faces, how to remember dates and numbers, how to remember what you hear, and effective study strategies.

Your Memory: How It Works and How to Improve It (1988)

by K. L. Higbee
Englewood Cliffs, NJ: Prentice Hall

This practical book outlines strategies for using the principles of memory to remember all sorts of things in your personal life.

Internet Resources

http://dynamic.uoregon.edu/~jjf/trauma.html
Resources for trauma-related forgetting.

http://www.selfgrowth.com/memory.html
Self-Improvement On-line for better memory strategies.

http://www.well.com/user/smalin/miller.html
A reprint of George Miller's classic article on "7+/−2."

http://www.psych-web.com/mtsite/memory.html
Mindtools offers memory techniques and mnemonics.

http://advicom.net/~fitz/csicop/si/9503/memory.html
Elizabeth Loftus explores the phemenon of recovered memories.

http://braindance.com/frambdi6.htm
Memory strategies based on mind-mapping.

http://www.dartmouth.edu/dms/ptsd/RQ Spring 1996.html
A provocative article about what happens to memory under stress.

http://marlin.utmb.edu/~nkeele/
An exploration of the amygdala's role in memory.

7

Thinking, Language, and Intelligence

The mind is an enchanting thing.

—MARIANNE MOORE
American Poet, 20th Century

PREVIEW

*I*n this chapter, we will explore many aspects of cognition, including the cognitive revolution in psychology and the nature of thinking. We also will examine the fascinating landscape of intelligence and language. The story of Jay Leno, which follows, embodies some of the ideas about cognition that we will discuss in this chapter.

The Story of Jay Leno: Intelligence with a Difference

*J*ay Leno became the talk of the entertainment world when he was named the new permanent host of "The Tonight Show." He had served as a substitute host for the show for many years on Tuesday nights when Johnny Carson, legendary host for 30 years, was off. Leno polished his comedy skills on the road, sometimes playing as many as three hundred gigs per year. Admirers like his clean humor, political expertise, and affable nature. However, most people do not realize that Jay Leno rose to prominence despite a learning difference that influences his ability to use language.

Born James Douglas Muir Leno in Andover, Massachusetts, Leno had a blissful childhood (Stengel, 1992). His father, Angelo, was a successful insurance salesman whom Leno describes as "the funniest guy at the office." His mother, Catherine, worked in the home. He credits his parents with nurturing his sense of humor. He also describes his own humor as rising from his "female" side. He takes special pleasure in making women laugh, attested to by his strict avoidance of wife jokes.

School, however, was not much to his liking. He was the classroom cutup and prided himself on being able to make his teachers laugh. His fifth-grade teacher speculated that if Jay "used the effort toward his studies that he uses to be humorous, he would be an A student." In retrospect, Jay's humor might have served to cover up some insecurities he had about his academic skills.

He began experimenting with stand-up comedy when he was enrolled at Emerson College in Boston. He graduated and became a salesman for a Rolls-Royce

Jay Leno has succeeded in the field of entertainment despite his learning difference.

dealership but left the job to try his hand at comedy full-time after seeing a terrible comedian on "The Tonight Show." He knew he could do better. After a few appearances, Leno launched a career that ultimately led him into the spotlight as the permanent host of "The Tonight Show."

On rare occasions, Leno demonstrates the impact of his learning difference, dyslexia. People with dyslexia sometimes have difficulty with the order of letters in words. Refreshingly, Leno is open about his dyslexia. He tosses off verbal misfires with statements such as, "The things a dyslexic can do to language . . ." His ownership of the difficulties associated with dyslexia has inspired children and their families who struggle with the impact of learning differences on school performance. Like many other successful adults, Jay Leno demonstrates that a learning difference does not automatically produce failure or social stigma.. ❖

THE COGNITIVE REVOLUTION IN PSYCHOLOGY

Behaviorism was a dominant force in psychology until the late 1950s and 1960s, when many psychologists began to realize that they could not understand or explain human behavior without making reference to mental processes (Gardner, 1985). The term *cognitive psychology* became a label for approaches that sought to explain observable behavior by investigating mental processes and structures that cannot be directly observed.

Although behaviorists like John B. Watson had argued that psychology could not be a legitimate "scientific" discipline unless it restricted itself to the study and description of directly observable events, proponents of the cognitive revolution argued that scientific explanations usually explain the observable using terms or concepts that denote things that cannot be directly observed (Weimer, 1974). For example, Isaac Newton explained the behavior of falling objects using the concept of gravitational force, a force that could not be directly observed.

A number of factors stimulated the growth of cognitive psychology, but probably the most important was the development of computers. The first modern computer, developed by John von Neumann in the late 1940s, showed that inanimate machines could perform logical operations. This indicated that some mental operations might be modeled by computers, possibly telling us something about the way cognition works. Cognitive psychologists often use the computer as an analogy to help explain the relation between cognition and the brain. The physical brain is described as the computer's hardware and cognition as its software (see figure 7.1).

Although the development of computers played an important role in the cognitive revolution, inanimate computers and human brains function quite differently in some respects (Restak, 1988). For example, each brain cell, or neuron, is alive and can be altered in its functioning by many types of events in its biological environment. Current attempts to simulate neural networks greatly simplify the behavior of neurons. The brain derives information about the world through a rich system of visual, auditory, olfactory, gustatory, tactile, and vestibular sensory receptors that operate on analog signals. Most computers receive information from a human who has already digitally coded the information and represented it in a way that removes much of the ambiguity in the natural world. Attempts to use computers to process visual information or spoken language have achieved only limited success in highly constrained situations where much of the natural ambiguity is removed. The human brain also has an incredible ability to learn new rules, relationships, concepts, and patterns that it can generalize to novel situations. In comparison, current approaches to artificial intelligence are quite limited in their ability to learn and generalize.

Computers can do some things better than humans, and humans can do some things better than computers. Computers can perform complex numerical calculations much faster and more accurately than humans could ever hope to. Computers can also apply and follow some rules more consistently and with fewer errors than humans can and represent complex mathematical patterns better than humans can. Although a computer can simulate certain types of learning that may improve its ability to recognize patterns or use rules of thumb to make decisions, it does not have the means to develop new learning goals. Furthermore, the human mind is aware of itself; the computer is not. Indeed,

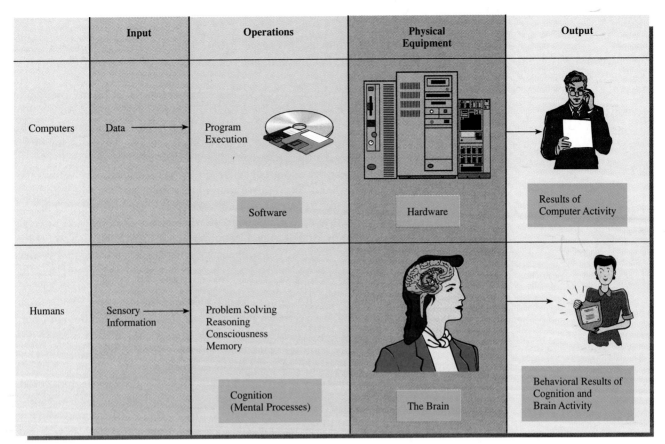

	Input	Operations	Physical Equipment	Output
Computers	Data →	Program Execution		
		Software	Hardware	Results of Computer Activity
Humans	Sensory Information →	Problem Solving Reasoning Consciousness Memory		
		Cognition (Mental Processes)	The Brain	Behavioral Results of Cognition and Brain Activity

$\mathcal{F}$IGURE 7.1

Computers and Human Cognition

The physical brain is analogous to a computer's hardware. Cognition (mental processes) is analogous to a computer's software.

artificial intelligence (AI)

The science of creating machines capable of performing activities that require intelligence when they are done by people.

expert systems

Computer-based systems for assessing knowledge and making decisions in advanced skill areas.

no computer is likely to approach the richness of human consciousness. In short, the brain's extraordinary capabilities will probably not be mimicked in a comprehensive manner by computers anytime in the near future.

The computer's role in cognitive psychology continues to increase, giving rise in recent years to a field called **artificial intelligence (AI),** *the science of creating machines capable of performing activities that require intelligence when they are done by people.* AI is especially helpful in tasks requiring speed, persistence, and a vast memory (Wagman, 1995). For example, today we have chess-playing programs that can beat even the best players our species has to offer.

These so-called **expert systems,** *computer-based systems for assessing knowledge and making decisions in advanced skill areas,* not only have been applied to playing chess, but have been designed to assist in the diagnosis of medical illnesses, diagnosing equipment failures, developing integrated circuits, evaluating loan applicants, advising students about what courses to take, and a broad range of other problems. These programs are especially beneficial when human experts are in short supply or are not available in the locations where they are needed. Expert systems also might help to preserve the expertise of talented individuals when they retire or die.

Expert systems attempt to mimic the way human experts think. But how do humans do their thinking?

THINKING

Information in memory is manipulated and transformed through thinking. We can think about the concrete, such as boats and beaches, and the abstract, such as freedom and independence. We can think about the past (life in the 1940s, 1960s, 1908s) and the future (life in the year 2000). We can think about reality (how to do better on the next test in this course) and fantasy (what it would be like to meet Catherine the Great or land a spacecraft on Jupiter).

Concept Formation

concepts

Categories used to group objects, events, and characteristics on the basis of common properties.

Regardless of the kind of thinking we engage in, our thinking is ruled by **concepts,** *which are categories used to group objects, events, and characteristics on the basis of common properties.*

We have a special ability to create categories to help us make sense of information in our world. We know that apples and oranges are fruits, but also that they have different tastes and colors. We know that Porsche 911s and Ford Escorts are automobiles, but also that they differ in cost, speed, and prestige. When individual things have so many differences, how are we able to group them together as, say, fruit or cars? The answer lies in our ability to ignore their differences and group them on the basis of common features. For example, Porsche 911s and Ford Escorts have four wheels and a steering wheel and provide transportation. These features are part of our *concept* of what an automobile is.

Why are concepts important? Without concepts, each object and event in our world would seem unique to us. Any kind of generalization would be impossible. Concepts allow us to relate experiences and objects. Weimaraners, cocker spaniels, and Labrador retrievers are all called sporting dogs by the American Kennel Club. The concept of sporting dogs gives us a way to compare dogs.

Concepts grease the wheels of memory, making it more efficient so we don't have to keep "reinventing the wheel" each time we come across a piece of information. For example, we don't have to relearn what the Dow Jones Industrial Average is each time we pick up a newspaper. We already know what the concept means. Concepts also provide clues about how to react to an object or experience. For example, if we see a bowl of pretzels, our concept of food lets us know it is okay to eat them. Concepts allow us to associate classes of objects or events.

Because concepts are so critical to our ability to make sense of our world, researchers have spent considerable time studying how concepts are formed. Figure 7.2 shows a typical research strategy that is used to test the type of concept formation called *hypothesis testing.*

We also can see the role of concept formation in more concrete, everyday examples. Suppose you are an avid tennis player but think you are losing too many matches because your serve is weak. Despite hours of practice, your serve just isn't getting any better. Your problem might be that you have only a vague concept of what a "killer serve" is really like. To get a feel for the concept and to see how the best players serve, you head for the tennis courts. Based on your observations, you develop a hypothesis about the mechanics of an excellent serve. For example, after hours of watching the "weekend pros" ace their opponents, you decide that the ball must be tossed high, so that the server has to stretch to reach it, and that the server needs to swing the racket like a baseball pitcher

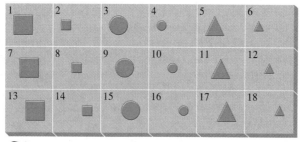

*F*IGURE 7.2

Example of a Concept Formation Task

This array of cards is presented to a subject. The researcher has selected a concept (such as "triangles only" or "any symbols that are not round"). The subject is asked to pick cards one at a time to try to determine, by trial and error, what the selected concept is. Each of the subject's selections represents a hypothesis about the concept's identity. The task is completed once the subject accurately identifies the concept.

In the nineteenth century, New York City began to experience traffic jams. The horse-drawn vehicles were making street traffic dangerous. *How did William Eno solve this problem?*

throws a ball. You might want to scrutinize the serves of more-skilled players to see if they confirm your hypothesis. You'll also want to test the hypothesis in your own game to see if the two aspects of the hypothesis—that good servers toss the ball high and that they swing the racket like a baseball player throws a ball—improve your serve.

Even though your concept formation is on track and your tennis serve improves, chances are you'll still be somewhat dissatisfied. With a difficult concept (such as the mechanics of a good serve), you may need an expert—a professional tennis coach—to help you. The pro's concept is likely to include many more features than the ones you discovered, as well as complex rules related to those features. For example, the pro might tell you that tossing the ball high helps, but that it works much better if you rotate the grip on your racket counterclockwise. In general, concepts with more features and more complicated rules are more difficult to learn. Part of being an expert in any field is grasping the complicated rules of difficult concepts.

Although psychologists have learned much about concept formation, some experts believe that most of the research on which this knowledge is based is too artificial. Eleanor Rosch (1973) argues that real-life concepts are much less precise than the concepts studied in university research laboratories. Real-life concepts have "fuzzy boundaries" (that is, it often is unclear exactly which features are critical to the concept). Rosch contends that some members of a concept category are more typical than others. Think of your concept of a football player: perhaps muscular, large, and stressed out by combining sports and academics. Football players who match this description are said to *prototypical*—they fit the prototype of a football player. However, some football players are thin, and some do well academically. Some are even women. These individuals are not prototypical, but they are still football players. Thus, members of a concept category can vary considerably and still have the characteristics that make them members of a particular category.

Cultural experiences affect concept formation. This can have important implications for testing and education. For example, inner-city children might be at a disadvantage when reading textbooks that focus on suburban experiences rather than urban life. People perform better when asked questions that are consistent with their cultural experiences (Segall & others, 1990). For example, it might take you a while to learn the concepts

According to Bransford and Stein's IDEAL problem-solving method, the five steps shown here produce effective problem solving. How can the IDEAL method be applied to the problem of littering?

IDEAL

| Identifying problems | Defining and representing problems | Exploring possible strategies | Acting on the strategies | Looking back and evaluating the effects |

involved in a Japanese tea ceremony or in the proper care of camels. However, living in Japan and the Middle East, respectively, would facilitate your formation of these concepts.

Problem Solving

It is impossible to solve problems without using concepts. Think about driving, something many of us do every day. Signs and traffic signals every few blocks tell us to stop, yield, or proceed. Most of the symbols that keep traffic moving so smoothly are the brainchild of William Eno, the "father of traffic safety." Eno, born in New York City in 1858, became concerned about the horrendous traffic jams in the city. Horse-drawn vehicles were making street traffic dangerous. Eno published a paper about the urgency of traffic reform. His proposed solutions to the problem created new concepts, such as stop signs, one-way street, and pedestrian islands, which continue to be an important part of traffic safety today.

Like William Eno, we face many problems in the course of our everyday lives. These include trying to figure out the fastest way to get across town, planning how to get enough money to buy a CD player, working a jigsaw puzzle, or estimating how much money we owe in taxes.

problem solving

An attempt to find an appropriate way of attaining a goal when the goal is not readily available.

Problem solving *is an attempt to find an appropriate way of attaining a goal when the goal is not readily available.* Whatever the problem, we want to come up with the fastest and best solution possible. Next, we look at several problem-solving approaches, starting with the IDEAL method created by two cognitive psychologists.

The IDEAL Method. John Bransford and Barry Stein (1984) developed a problem-solving method with a catchy title: IDEAL, which stands for I (Identify the problem), D (Define and present the problem), E (Explore possible strategies), A (Act on the strategies), and L (Look back and evaluate the effects of your activities) (see figure 7.3). Let's go through this method for solving problems step by step.

Identifying Problems. Before a problem can be solved, it first needs to be recognized. Take another civic problem, that of litter. Many communities are becoming increasingly unhappy with the amount of refuse dumped along their roadsides. As the trash accumulates, someone in the community recognizes the problem and says that something has to be done about it.

Defining Problems.   The second step is to define the problem as carefully as possible. When community officials take a close look at the kinds of refuse that are beginning to pile up, they begin to notice patterns. Fast-food refuse, aluminum cans, and paper casually tossed out of car windows seem to account for most of it. The officials also note that the problem seems worse after a weekend than during the week.

> *A problem well-stated is a problem half-solved.*
> —CHARLES KETTERING, *American Business Executive, 20th Century*

Exploring Alternative Approaches.   The next step in solving problems involves coming up with several possible strategies. For example, communities across the globe have tried out different strategies to reduce littering. In Singapore, people who litter are harshly dealt with. Even spitting on the streets warrants a public flogging. Such severe consequences would probably not be well received in the United States. However, penalizing offenders in a milder fashion is one viable alternative. They could be sentenced to recycling duty or required to pay stiff fines. But litterers can be hard to catch in the act. Another strategy successfully adopted by several communities is to place a premium on the return of aluminum cans and returnable bottles. This strategy might cut back on a substantial part of the litter problem. Each proposed solution must be evaluated carefully so that the proposal with the greatest potential is selected and implemented.

Acting on a Plan.   We won't really know about the effectiveness of the solution until we act on it and find out if it actually works. The more carefully we have considered the consequences of implementing the plan, the more likely the solution will be effective. For example, communities that offer premiums for recyclables may have anticipated that a number of citizens would begin to collect cans and bottles as a way to make money.

Looking at the Effects.   The final stage in the IDEAL method involves evaluating the effectiveness of the solution. It helps to have some clear criteria in mind about what effects will be the most satisfying. For example, at what point will a recycling program be considered a success? When the refuse is reduced by 50 percent? When the rate of accumulation slows? When no one litters any more? In the case of public problems and solutions, people may have different standards regarding what they consider to be successful.

Algorithms and Heuristics.   Other approaches are also used to solve problems. Two kinds of procedures that are helpful are algorithms and heuristics. **Algorithms** *are step-by-step procedures that guarantee an answer to a problem.* When you solve a multiplication problem, you are using an algorithm—you learned this algorithm as part of your schooling. When you follow the directions for putting together a lawn chair, you are using an algorithm.

Although we can solve some problems by using algorithms, we are usually forced to rely on heuristics. **Heuristics** *are rules of thumb that can suggest a solution to a problem but do not ensure that it will work.* Let's say you're heading to a friend's house and you've never been there before. You are driving around in an unfamiliar part of town, and after a while you realize you're lost. If you know your destination is north, you might use the heuristic of turning onto a road that heads in that direction. This procedure might work, but it also might fail—the road might end or turn off to the east.

Other familiar heuristics include *dividing a problem into subproblems* and *working backward.* Completing your college degree is a good example of dividing a problem into subproblems. You make steady progress toward getting your degree, semester by semester, course by course, test by test. Working backward is also a useful problem-solving heuristic in college. When you have to write a research paper, identify the due date on your master calendar. Then plan the stages of completion accordingly; working backward from when it is due. For example, your final draft should be done a few days before the deadline, the first draft two weeks before, the research one month before, and so on.

algorithms
Procedures that guarantee an answer to a problem.

heuristics
Rules of thumb that can suggest a solution to a problem but do not ensure that it will work.

Sometimes problem-solving strategies fail. We will explore several ways that faulty strategies can interfere with your effectiveness.

Each of us occasionally gets into the mental rut of solving problems by using a particular strategy. A **learning set** *is a strategy an individual tends to use to solve problems.* Learning sets often serve us efficiently. Without them, we would waste time looking for the solution to a problem we already know. You may have encountered a problem with learning sets in your college classes. Let's say several of your professors base their exams primarily on lecture materials. You pore over your lecture notes and ace the exams, so you follow the same strategy for your psychology class and spend very little time studying the textbook. When you see the first exam in this class, you learn that the old strategy is inappropriate—this exam has a number of questions based only on the text.

The following puzzle is often used to demonstrate the concept of a learning set. It's called the nine-dot problem. Take out a piece of paper and copy the arrangement of the dots:

● ● ●

● ● ●

● ● ●

Without lifting your pencil, connect the dots using only four straight lines. Most people have difficulty—and lots just give up on—finding a solution to the nine-dot problem. Part of the difficulty is that we have a learning set that tells us to think of the nine-dot configuration as a square. We consider the outer dots as the boundary and do not extend the lines beyond them, yet the solutions to the nine-dot problem, shown at the end of the chapter, require going outside the square.

If you've ever used a shoe to hammer a nail, you've overcome what's called "functional fixedness" to solve a problem. The concept of **functional fixedness,** *the inability to solve a problem because it is viewed only in terms of usual functions,* is similar to the concept of learning set. If the problem to be solved involves usual functions, then it can easily be solved, but, if the problem involves something new and different, solving the problem will be trickier. An example of a problem that requires overcoming functional fixedness involves what is called the Maier String Problem (Maier, 1931) (see figure 7.4). The problem is to figure out how to tie two strings together when they can't be reached at the same time. If you hold one and then move it toward the other, you cannot reach the second one. It seems as though you are stuck, but there is a pair of pliers on a table. Can you solve the problem?

The solution is to use the pliers as a weight and tie them to the end of the string (see figure 7.5). Swing this string back and forth like a pendulum. Then let go of the "weight"

learning set

A strategy that an individual tends to use to solve problems.

functional fixedness

The inability to solve a problem because it is viewed only in terms of usual functions.

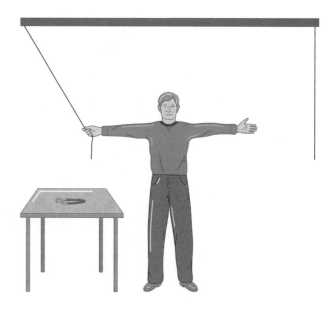

$\mathscr{F}$IGURE 7.4

Maier String Problem

How can you tie the two strings together if you cannot reach them both at the same time?

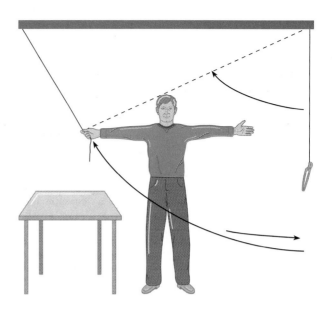

FIGURE 7.5

Solution to the Maier String Problem

Use the pliers as a weight to create a pendulum motion that brings the second string closer.

and grasp the stationary string. Finally, reach out and grab the swinging string. Your past experience with pliers makes this a difficult problem to solve. To solve the problem, you need to find a unique use for the pliers, in this case as a weight to create a pendulum.

Two heuristic strategies can produce faulty reasoning. Amos Tversky and Richard Kahneman (1974) hypothesized that we often take cognitive shortcuts that prevent us from having all the data we need to solve a problem. When we use the **availability heuristic,** *we judge the probability of an event by the ease with which prior occurrences come to mind.* For example, when you buy a plane ticket, you might be more apprehensive if you make your purchase the day after an airliner crashed. Your actual risk of going down in flames is the same as it was before the crash, but the vividness of the crash and your proximity to it make you feel more vulnerable.

The **representativeness heuristic** *is the strategy of judging the probability of an event based on how well it matches a prototype.* Consider the following description of an individual's dinner companion: skilled at carpentry, proficient at wrestling, owns a pet snake, knows motorcycle repair, and has been arrested for beating someone with a chain. Is it more likely that he is a member of a motorcycle gang or is a salesman? Most people say "motorcycle gang." They probably are wrong. Why? Because they failed to take into account the size of the population from which the person was drawn. There are far more salesmen in the world than motorcycle gang members. The relative size of both groups increases the probability that the dinner companion is a salesman.

Reasoning

What exactly is reasoning? **Reasoning** *is the mental activity of transforming information to reach conclusions.* Examples of this transformation of information to reach conclusions are found in inductive reasoning and deductive reasoning, as well as other forms of reasoning we will discuss.

> *I think, therefore I am.*
> —RENÉ DESCARTES, *French Philosopher and Mathematician, 17th Century*

Inductive Versus Deductive Reasoning. **Inductive reasoning** *is reasoning from the specific to the general. That is, it involves drawing conclusions about all members of a category based on observing only some members.* Any time a psychologist studies a small number of individuals, such as 20 college freshmen, and draws a conclusion about a large number of individuals, such as all college students, inductive reasoning is being used. In your college courses you might be asked to draw general conclusions from a specific case. For example,

availability heuristic

Judging the probability of an event by the ease with which prior occurrences come to mind.

representativeness heuristic

Judging the probability of an event by how well it matches a prototype.

reasoning

The mental activity of transforming information to reach conclusions.

inductive reasoning

Reasoning from the specific to the general; drawing conclusions about all members of a category based on observing only some of the members.

you might have to speculate about the general nature of T. S. Eliot's poetry after reading only one of his poems, such as *The Wasteland*. Or you might have to decide whether a link in one culture between poverty and increased violence also applies to other cultures.

Analogies draw on inductive reasoning. An **analogy** *is a type of formal reasoning that is always made up of four parts. The relation between the first two parts is the same as the relation between the other two.* Consider this example: "Beethoven is to music as Picasso is to ___." To answer correctly (fill in the word *art*), you must use inductive reasoning. You have to induce the relation between Beethoven and music (the former created the latter) and apply this to Picasso (what did Picasso create?). If you took the SAT or ACT test, you probably were asked to supply correct words for some analogies.

Analogies can be helpful in solving problems, especially when they are visually represented. Benjamin Franklin noticed that a pointed object drew a stronger spark than a blunt object when both were in the vicinity of an electrified body. Originally he believed that this was an unimportant observation. Then he realized that pointed rods of iron could be used to protect buildings and ships from lightning. The pointed rod attracts the lightning, deflecting it from buildings and ships. Wilhelm Kekulé discovered the ringlike structure of the benzene molecule in organic chemistry only after he visualized a snake biting its tail and realized that the benzene molecule had an analogous structure (see figure 7.6). In many ways, analogies make the strange familiar and the familiar strange.

In contrast, **deductive reasoning** *is reasoning from the general to the specific. It involves working with general statements to derive a specific conclusion.* Solving puzzles and riddles often requires deductive reasoning. It may be easier to remember the characteristics of deduction if you think about Sherlock Holmes, the master British detective. No matter how tough the problem, Holmes always deduced the right solution. For example, in a typical case he sorted through an assortment of general clues to narrow in on the one correct solution to a murder.

Some aspects of college may make you feel like a detective using deductive reasoning. You may have to memorize some general mathematical rules and use them to solve a specific math problem. When you use the library to retrieve new information, you often have to start with some general categories before you hone in on the specific reference you need.

Working out any complex problem often involves using a combination of inductive and deductive reasoning. For example, a psychologist might draw on a theory of how children develop to predict that 6-year-olds will succeed on a task but 4-year-olds will fail. To test this prediction, the psychologist conducts an experiment on a sample of twenty 6-year-olds and twenty 4-year-olds. Theorizing and making predictions about a specific case involve deductive reasoning. Actually conducting a research study and applying the findings to children in general involves inductive reasoning.

Much of what we have been talking about so far in our discussion of reasoning focuses on formal reasoning and logic. As we see next, many of life's circumstances also require reasoning, but reasoning of a more informal nature that is commonly referred to as "critical thinking."

Critical Thinking

Much of our everyday reasoning differs in character from formal reasoning. You can't turn to a textbook on logic to figure out where to go to college or decide which person to become friends with. Many of life's challenging problems that you will face do not have

analogy

A type of formal reasoning that is always made up of four parts. The relation between the first two parts is the same as the relation between the last two.

deductive reasoning

Reasoning from the general to the specific; working with abstract statements (premises) and deriving a conclusion.

$\mathcal{F}$IGURE 7.6

Use of Analogy in Problem Solving

The benzene ring *(a)* is one of the most important structures in organic chemistry. It was discovered by Wilhelm Kekulé after he imagined how its structure might be analogous to a snake biting its tail *(b)*.

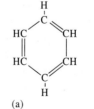

(a)

(b)

an "answer key." These problems frequently have fuzzy boundaries, incomplete data, and a sense of urgency that do not compare with the crisp, self-contained problems typical of formal reasoning.

Critical thinking is currently of considerable interest to both psychologists and educators (Halonen, 1995; Langer, 1997). However, critical thinking is not an entirely new idea. Educator John Dewey (1933) was working with a similar idea when he advocated teaching students to "think reflectively." Although today's definitions of **critical thinking** vary, they have in common the notions of *grasping the deeper meaning of problems, exploring different approaches and perspectives, asking relevant questions, and making accurate inferences.*

Today, educators at all levels embrace the idea that students should be taught to think more critically. However, there is little agreement on how this should be done. Robert J. Sternberg (1985) thinks that schools focus too much on formal reasoning and not enough on everyday reasoning. He recommends that teachers provide students with guided practice so they can learn to do the following:

- Learn to recognize when problems exist.
    (How bad must a problem be before I take action?)
- Define problems more precisely.
    (What specific information do I need before I take action?)
- Cope with poorly structured problems.
    (How can I restructure the problem to get a better handle on it?)
- Deal with problems that are not self-contained.
    (Which college should I go to if I also want to start a family?)
- Address problems with no single right answer or any clear-cut criteria.
    (Which career will be most rewarding for me?)
- Manage risky personal issues.
    (Should I have the surgery my doctor recommends, or should I wait?)

Many educators have reshaped their curricula to incorporate opportunities for students to think critically. However, many educators approach critical thinking in different ways. For example, English teachers often focus on developing students' ability to critically analyze literature. Biology teachers frequently encourage students to use critical thinking to design and execute experiments. Next, we will explore the nature of critical thinking in psychology.

Thinking Critically About Behavior.   Like educators, psychologists don't completely agree on what critical thinking is. However, most critical thinking approaches in psychology do focus on trying to make sense out of behavior, evaluating the accuracy of claims about behavior, and making wise personal choices.

Suppose your best friend tells you that his grade point average has improved by a whole grade since the term began because he began listening to Beethoven while studying. He encourages you to buy a collection of Beethoven CDs and listen to them regularly to improve your grades. Should you rush out and buy the Beethoven CDs? Or should you ask some penetrating questions that help you determine whether this strategy works?

Inferences are an important aspect of critical thinking in psychology. For example, your friend made an **inference,** *a conclusion drawn from premises* (in this case from an observation about behavior), that listening to Beethoven is the critical factor that caused his grades to improve. He also inferred that because the Beethoven strategy worked for him, it will also work for you. But aren't there other factors that might have led to his improved grades? He might be taking an easier schedule this term. His parents might have set up a reward system for higher grades. He might have started managing his time better so that he has more time for studying. All of these factors are plausible alternatives for the cause-and-effect claim your friend is promoting.

critical thinking

Grasping the deeper meaning of problems, keeping an open mind about different approaches and perspectives, and deciding for oneself what to believe or do.

inference

A conclusion drawn from a premise or premises.

One goal of this book is to help you learn to think more critically about psychological issues. In the section at the front of this book called "Learning to Learn in Psychology," we described critical thinking as an important outcome for this course. At the end of each chapter, we also have included critical thinking exercises.

Critical Thinking Pitfalls.   Just how rational are we? If we look at ourselves objectively, we can probably come up with numerous instances in which we could have benefited from better critical thinking. Following are some common pitfalls in critical thinking about behavior (Levy, 1997):

- *Substituting labels or names for explanations of behavior.* For example, if Trudy has problems sleeping through the night, her behavior is labeled "insomnia." When asked why she has trouble sleeping, she says, "It's because I have insomnia." However, insomnia is not an explanation: it is not the *cause* of her inability to sleep, it is simply the *fact* that she is unable to sleep. The *causes* of her insomnia might be factors such as drinking too much coffee at night or stress in her life.
- *Confusing correlation and causation.* When two events regularly occur together, it is easy to mistakenly believe that one causes the other. For example, Paul ate a greasy cheeseburger at noon and starts to feel queasy about 2 P.M. He assumes that the queasy feeling is caused by the greasy burger. Yet, the next day he is in the grips of the flu bug. So it likely was the flu virus, not the burger, that caused him to feel ill the previous day.
- *Explaining behavior with a single cause.* Most of us have a tendency to explain behavior as having a single, compelling cause. However, a better strategy is to think of most behavior as caused by multiple factors. Consider Elaine, the valedictorian of her class. When asked how she achieved this status, Elaine said, "Because my mother was such a positive force in my life." Although her mother likely contributed to Elaine's academic success, many other factors also likely were at work, such as good teachers, peer pressure, and high personal standards for success.
- *Resisting coincidence as an explanation.* Suppose an old friend from high school phones you out of the blue at the exact moment you are reminiscing about her. Especially if you haven't thought about that person in a while, you might entertain the possibility of having some special powers. But extraordinary events do happen by chance. We often find it easier to explain spooky occurrences as evidence of extrasensory perception rather than accept the fact that two events can occur together by chance alone.
- *Ignoring evidence that conflicts with our beliefs.* Suppose you want to buy a new car and you have your eye on a particular model. Rather than conduct an extensive study of the pluses and minuses of the many different models you could buy, you commit the problem of **confirmation bias** *when you examine only the evidence that supports what you already believe.* In this case you gather only favorable data on the model that you want to purchase and ignore the rest. If you buy the car and start to discover things going wrong, you might still cling to the belief that the car model is superior, despite all your troubles. The **belief perseverance effect** *occurs when we cling to our beliefs even in the face of evidence that says we should let go of them.*
- *Taking too much credit for confirming predictions after the fact.* As any good Monday-morning quarterback knows, it is easy to point out what should have been done when the game is over. We commit the error of **hindsight bias** *when we produce cogent explanations or predictions post hoc (after the fact).* For example, your sister's marriage breaks up after several years of struggle. You might be tempted to take her aside and disclose, "I knew this would happen when you married him!" This is not a good idea for several reasons. It overstates your competence in making predictions and you will regret that you expressed your hindsight if they ever reunite.

confirmation bias

Examining only the evidence that supports what we already believe.

belief perseverance effect

Clinging to our beliefs even in the face of evidence that says we should let go of them.

hindsight bias

Producing cogent explanations or predictions post hoc (after the fact).

Keep these traps in mind when you face critical thinking situations. Next we explore another type of thinking: thinking creatively.

Creativity

Most of use would like to be considered creative. However, by the time we have reached college, many of us relinquish becoming creative as a personal goal. Unless we have discovered some obvious talent, such as acting, art, or music, we may believe that our lives aren't very creative.

Psychologists take issue with such a narrow definition of creativity. They define **creativity** *as the ability to think in novel ways and come up with unique solutions to problems.* Defined this broadly, nearly everyone is capable of showing some creativity. Possibly people are more creative than they give themselves credit for.

One reason individuals tend to give up on being creative is the kind of education they receive as they grow up. Most education focuses on developing **convergent thinking,** *which produces one correct answer.* This is the kind of thinking required on most tests we have taken in school and on standardized intelligence tests. Few educational experiences encourage **divergent thinking,** *which produces many answers to the same question.* Divergent thinking is more characteristic of creative individuals (Guilford, 1967). Some tasks attempt to measure creative thinking. For example, how would you answer this question: "What image comes to mind when you hear the phrase 'sitting alone in a dark room'?" (Barron, 1989). Responses such as "the sound of a violin with no strings" and "patience" are considered creative because they are novel. Responses such as "lonely" and "bored" are rated as less creative because they are common responses.

Besides the ability to come up with novel solutions to situations, what other characteristics do creative individuals have? Following are five such characteristics (Perkins, 1984):

- *Commitment to a personal aesthetic or style.* Creative people are motivated to bring order, simplicity, and meaning to chaos. They have a high tolerance for ambiguity and thrive on untangling messy situations. In science, the core challenge often involves sorting through a maze of ambiguities to come up with a novel but simple solution.
- *Excellence in problem-finding skills.* Creative people enjoy planning solutions. They generate lots of options before deciding on their preferred course. A student once asked Nobel laureate chemist Linus Pauling how he came up with so many good ideas. Pauling's response: "I developed a huge number of ideas and threw away the bad ones."
- *Willingness to take risks.* Failure is always possible when you pursue creative solutions. Creative people accept failures and mistakes as givens. They often learn from their failures and use this information to find a more creative solution in the future. Consider famous actress Katharine Hepburn. Early in her career she was having little success finding acting roles. She worked hard, persisted in seeking more acting roles, and eventually bought her own film properties. Her creative success depended on her ability not to be devoured by the pressures of her early failures and on her courage to strike out in new directions.
- *Enthusiasm for getting feedback.* Creative people not only criticize their own works, they also actively seek criticism from others. Contrary to the popular image, creative people are not self-absorbed loners. They seek advice from others and test their ideas in the real world.
- *Finding joy in intrinsic rather than extrinsic rewards.* Creative people are motivated to produce something for the joy of creating, not for grades, money, or compliments. Their motivation is the satisfaction generated by the work itself. Competition for prizes and formal evaluations can undermine intrinsic motivation and creativity (Amabile, Phillips, & Collins, 1993).

You might have noticed that intelligence was not listed as a characteristic of creativity. Although most creative people are intelligent, the reverse is not necessarily true. Many highly intelligent people (as measured by IQ tests) are not very creative.

creativity
The ability to think in novel ways and to come up with unique solutions to problems.

convergent thinking
Thinking that produces one correct answer and is characteristic of the kind of thinking on standardized intelligence tests.

divergent thinking
Thinking that produces many answers to the same question and is characteristic of creativity.

If you don't consider yourself a very creative person, are there ways you can become more creative? The answer is yes, according to Mihaly Csikszentmihalyi (pronounced ME-high CHICK-sent-me-high-ee) (1995). He interviewed ninety leading figures in the sciences, arts, government, business, and education about their creativity. Figure 7.7 portrays three of these individuals and describes how their creative works emerge. Csikszentmihalyi applied the concept of *flow*—the enjoyment we experience when we are engaged in mental and physical challenges that absorb us—to creativity. He believes that anyone is capable of achieving flow in creativity. For some suggestions on how to do this, read Improving Personal and Cognitive Skills ("Going With the Flow").

Now that we have a good grasp of what thinking is and how to do it, we turn our attention to language. Much of our thinking involves language.

Mark Strand, U.S. poet laureate. Strand says his most creative moments come when he loses a sense of time and becomes totally absorbed in what he is doing. The absorbed state comes and goes—he can't stay in it for an entire day. When he gets an intriguing idea, he focuses intensely on it and transforms it into a visual image.

Nina Holton, a leading contemporary sculptor. Holton turns wild germs of ideas into playful, stunning sculptures. She says that when she is introduced to people they sometimes say, "It must be so exciting and wonderful to be a sculptor." Holton loves her work, but she agrees with Thomas Edison that creativity is about 10 percent inspiration and 90 percent hard work.

Jonas Salk, inventor of the polio vaccine. He gets his best ideas late at night when he suddenly wakes up. He spends about 5 minutes visualizing problems he had thought about during the day. Then he begins to see an unfolding, as if a poem, painting, story, or concept is about to take form. Salk also believes that many creative ideas are generated through conversations with others who have open, curious minds and positive attitudes.

𝓕IGURE 7.7

How Creative Works Emerge

*I*mproving Personal and Cognitive Skills

Going With the Flow

Based on in-depth interviews with some of the world's most creative people in a number of fields, Mihaly Czikszentmihalyi (1995) provided this advice for learning to lead a more creative life:

*   *Be surprised by something every day.*
    The surprise might involve something you see, hear, taste, or read about. Become totally absorbed in a book or a lecture. Swim widely and deeply in your life, and be open to discovering unexpected things.
*   *Surprise at least one person every day.*
    Much of life is too predictable and patterned. Ask someone a question you normally would not ask. Invite someone to go to a show or a museum you never have visited. Throw someone a "curve ball."
*   *Keep track of what surprises you.*
    Keep a diary, notes, or lab records to ensure that you will remember what surprised you. Each evening record the most surprising event of the day and your most surprising reaction. After a few weeks, you might detect a pattern of interest that is emerging in your notes, one that merits further exploration.
*   *Wake up in the morning with a "mission."*
    Creative people regularly wake up ready to tackle the world. It's not because they are cheerful, enthusiastic types. Rather, they have something meaningful to accomplish and can't wait to get started.
*   *Take charge of your schedule.*
    Figure out which time of day you are at your creative best. Some of us are more creative at night, others in the morning. Carve out time for creative thinking when you are at your best.
*   *Search for alternative solutions.*
    Examine problems from as many angles as possible. Creative people experiment and play with possibilities. They search through alternative solutions until they find the one that works best.

*R*eview

The Cognitive Revolution and Thinking

The cognitive revolution occurred in the last half-century. The computer played an important role in this revolution, stimulating the view of the mind as an information-processing system. Nonetheless, computers can do some things better than humans, and vice versa. Artificial intelligence (AI) is the science of creating machines capable of performing activities that require intelligence when they are done by people. Expert systems, computer-based systems for assessing knowledge and making decisions in advanced skill areas, have been applied to many domains.

A concept is used to group objects, events, and characteristics. Concepts help us to generalize, improve our memory, keep us from constantly having to relearn, have informational value, and improve our association skills. Psychologists have studied the ability to detect why an object is included in a particular concept. Developing hypotheses about concepts is an important aspect of thinking. Natural concepts have fuzzy boundaries (it is unclear which features are critical to the concept), and some members are better examples of a natural concept than others.

Problem solving is an attempt to find an appropriate way of attaining a goal when the goal is not readily available. Bransford and Stein developed the IDEAL method of solving problems, which includes these steps: I (Identifying problems), D (Defining problems), E (Exploring alternative approaches), A (Acting on a plan), and L (Looking at the effects). Algorithms and heuristics are two strategies that usually improve problem solving. Some faulty problem-solving strategies involve learning sets, functional fixedness, the availability heuristic, and the representativeness heuristic.

Reasoning is the mental activity of transforming information to reach conclusions. Inductive reasoning is reasoning from the specific to the general. Analogies draw on inductive reasoning. Deductive reasoning is reasoning from the general to the specific.

Critical thinking focuses on grasping the deeper meaning of problems, keeping an open mind about different approaches and perspectives, and deciding what to believe or do. Critical thinking in psychology often involves trying to make sense out of behavior, evaluating the accuracy of claims about behavior, and making wise personal choices. Among the traps people face in learning to think critically are substituting labels for explanations of behavior, confusing correlation and causation, explaining behavior with a single cause, resisting coincidence as an explanation, ignoring evidence that conflicts with our beliefs, and taking too much credit for confirming predictions after the fact.

Creativity is the ability to think in novel ways and come up with unique solutions to problems. Convergent thinking is thinking that produces one correct answer. Divergent thinking, which is more creative, produces many answers to the same question. In addition to seeking novel solutions to problems, creative people are committed to a personal or aesthetic style, excel at finding problems, are willing to take risks, are enthusiastic about getting feedback, and are intrinsically motivated. Czikszentmihalyi has applied the concept of flow to creativity.

LANGUAGE

In 1799 a nude boy was observed running through the woods in France. The boy was captured when he was 11 years old. It was believed that he had lived in isolation in the woods for at least 6 years. He was called the Wild Boy of Aveyron (Lane, 1976). When the boy was found, he made no effort to communicate. Even after a number of years, he never learned to communicate effectively. Sadly, a modern-day wild child named Genie, who had been raised in silent isolation in cruel conditions by her parents, was found in Los Angeles in 1970. Despite intensive intervention, Genie never acquired more than a primitive form of language. Both cases raise questions about the contributions of biology and environment to language, topics that we will explore in depth later. First, though, we need to define what language is.

What Is Language?

language

A system of symbols used to communicate with others; in humans, characterized by organizational rules and infinite generativity.

infinite generativity

A person's ability to produce an endless number of meaningful sentences using a finite set of words and rules, which makes language a highly creative enterprise.

Language *is a form of communication, both spoken and written, that is based on a system of symbols.* Think about how important language is in our everyday lives. We need language to speak to others, listen to others, read, and write. Our language enables us to describe past events in detail and to plan for the future. Language lets us pass down information from one generation to the next and to create a rich cultural heritage.

All human languages have some common characteristics. These include infinite generativity and organizational rules. **Infinite generativity** *is the ability to produce an endless number of meaningful sentences using a finite set of words and rules.* This quality makes language a highly creative enterprise. Language is characterized by a number of organizational rules that include phonology, morphology, syntax, and semantics, which we will discuss next.

> *Children pick up words as pigeons pick up peas.*
> —JOHN RAY, *English Naturalist, 17th Century*

phonology

The study of language's sound system.

Language is made up of basic sounds, or phonemes. **Phonology** *is the study of a language's sound system.* Phonological rules ensure that certain sound sequences occur (for example, *sp, ba,* or *ar*) and others do not (for example, *zx* or *qp*). A good example of a phoneme in the English language is /k/, the sound represented by the letter *k* in the word *ski* and the letter *c* in the word *cat*. Although the /k/ sound is slightly different in these two words, the variation is not distinguished, and the /k/ sound is described as a single phoneme. In some languages, such as Arabic, this kind of variation represents separate phonemes.

"If you don't mind my asking, how much does a sentence diagrammer pull down a year?"

© Bob Thaves.

morphology

The rules of combining morphemes, which are the smallest meaningful strings of sounds that contain no smaller meaningful parts.

syntax

The ways words are combined to form acceptable phrases and sentences.

semantics

The meanings of words and sentences.

Morphology *refers to the rules for combining morphemes, which are meaningful strings of sounds that contain no smaller meaningful parts.* Every word in the English language is made up of one or more morphemes. Some words consist of a single morpheme (for example, *help*), whereas others are made up of more than one morpheme (for example, *helper,* which has two morphemes, *help* + *-er,* with the morpheme *-er* meaning "one who," in this case "one who helps"). However, not all morphemes are words (for example, *pre-,* *-tion,* and *-ing*). Just as the rules that govern phonemes ensure that certain sound sequences occur, the rules that govern morphemes ensure that certain strings of sounds occur in particular sequences. For example, we would not reorder *helper* to *erhelp.*

Syntax *involves the way words are combined to form acceptable phrases and sentences.* If someone says to you, "Bob slugged Tom," and "Bob was slugged by Tom," you know who did the slugging and who was slugged in each case because you share the same syntactic understanding of sentence structure. You also understand that the sentence "You didn't stay, did you?" is a grammatical sentence but that "You didn't stay, didn't you?" is unacceptable and ambiguous.

Semantics *refers to the meaning of words and sentences.* Every word has a set of semantic features. *Girl* and *woman,* for example, share many of the same semantic features as the word *female,* but differ semantically in regard to age. Words have semantic restrictions on how they can be used in sentences. The sentence "The bicycle talked the boy into buying a candy bar" is syntactically correct but semantically incorrect. The sentence violates our semantic knowledge that bicycles do not talk.

How Language Develops

Most individuals in the United States acquire a vocabulary of nearly 10,000 words in a complex language by the time they are adults. How does this development take place?

Early Development.   Before babies ever say their first words, at the age of 10 to 13 months, they babble. Babbling—endlessly repeating sounds and syllables such as *goo-goo* and *ga-ga*—begins at about the age of 3 to 6 months and is determined by biological readiness, not reinforcement or the ability to hear (Locke & others, 1991). Even deaf babies babble for a time (Lenneberg, Rebelsky, & Nichols, 1965). Babbling probably allows the baby to exercise its vocal chords and helps develop articulation.

A child's first words name important people *(dada),* familiar animals *(kitty),* vehicles *(car),* toys *(ball),* food *(milk),* body parts *(eye),* clothes *(hat),* household items *(clock),* or greetings *(bye).* These were babies' first words 50 years ago and they are babies' first words today (Clark, 1983). The **holophrase hypothesis** *is the concept that single words can be used to imply complete sentences, and that infants' first words characteristically are holophrastic.* For example, the demand "Milk!" might mean "I'm hungry and want to eat *now.*"

By the time children reach the age of 18 to 24 months, they usually utter two-word statements. They quickly grasp the importance of expressing concepts and the role that language plays in communicating with others. To convey meaning in two-word statements, the child relies heavily on gesture, tone, and context. The wealth of meaning children can communicate with two words includes the following (Slobin, 1972).

holophrase hypothesis

The concept that a single word can be used to imply a complete sentence, and that infants' first words characteristically are holophrastic.

Identification: See doggie.

Location: Book there.

Repetition: More milk.

Nonexistence: Allgone thing.

Negation: Not wolf.

Possession: My candy.

Attribution: Big car.

Agent-action: Mama walk.

Action-direct-object: Hit you.

Action-indirect-object: Give papa.

Action-instrument: Cut knife.

Question: Where ball?

telegraphic speech

The use of short and precise words to communicate; characteristic of young children's two- and three-word utterances.

These examples are from children whose first languages were English, German, Russian, Finnish, Turkish, and Samoan. Although these two-word sentences omit many parts of speech, they are remarkably succinct in conveying many messages. In fact, a child's first combination of words has this economical quality in every language. **Telegraphic speech** *is the use of short and precise words to communicate; it is characteristic of young children's two- or three-word combinations.* When we send a telegram, we try to be short and precise, excluding any unnecessary words. As a result, articles, auxiliary verbs, and other connectives usually are omitted. Of course telegraphic speech is not limited to two-word phrases. "Mommy give ice cream" and "Mommy give Tommy ice cream" also are examples of telegraphic speech. As children leave the two-word stage, they move rather quickly into three-, four-, and five-word combinations.

As we have just seen, language unfolds in a sequence. At every point in development, the child's linguistic interaction with parents and others obeys certain principles (Budwig, 1995). Not only is this development strongly influenced by the child's biological wiring, but the language environment is more complex than behaviorists such as Skinner imagined.

Is There a Critical Period for Learning Language? Almost all children learn one or more languages during their early years of development, so it is difficult to determine whether there is a critical period for language development. In the 1960s, Erik Lenneberg (1967) proposed a biological theory of language acquisition. He said that language is a maturational process and that there is a critical period, between about 18 months of age and puberty, during which a first language must be acquired. Central to Lenneberg's thesis is the idea that language develops rapidly and with ease during the preschool years as a result of maturation. Lenneberg provided support for the critical-period concept from studies of several atypical populations, including children and adults with left-hemisphere brain damage, deaf children, and children with mental retardation (Tager-Flusberg, 1994). The children's brains had plasticity, and the children recovered their language skills but the adults did not. Lenneberg believed that adults had already passed the critical period during which plasticity of brain functioning allows reassignment and relearning of language skills.

The stunted language development of a modern "wild child" also supports the idea of a critical period for language acquisition. In 1970 a California social worker made a routine visit to the home of a partially blind woman who had applied for public assistance. The social worker discovered that the woman and her husband had kept their 13-year-old daughter Genie locked away from the world. Kept in almost total isolation during childhood, Genie could not speak or stand erect. She was forced to sit naked all day on a child's potty seat, restrained by a harness her father had made—she could move only her hands and feet. At night she was placed in a kind of straitjacket and caged in a crib with wire mesh sides and a cover. Whenever Genie made a noise, her father beat her. He never communicated with her in words but growled and barked at her.

Genie spent a number of years in extensive rehabilitation programs, such as speech and physical therapy (Curtiss, 1977; Rymer, 1993). She eventually learned to

Genie *(above)*. What were her experiences like, and what do they tell us about language acquisition?

walk upright with a jerky motion and to use the toilet. Genie also learned to recognize many words and to speak in rudimentary sentences. At first she spoke in one-word utterances. Later she was able to string together two-word combinations, such as "big teeth," "little marble," and "two hand." Consistent with the language development of most children, three-word combinations followed — for example, "small two cup." Unlike normal children, however, Genie did not learn how to ask questions and she doesn't understand grammar. Genie is not able to distinguish between pronouns or passive and active verbs. Four years after she began stringing words together, her speech still sounded like a garbled telegram. As an adult she speaks in short, mangled sentences, such as "Father hit leg," "Big wood," and "Genie hurt."

Second-language acquisition represents another independent source of evidence for the critical-period concept. Young children who are exposed to more than one language have little difficulty acquiring both languages and eventually speaking each with little or no interference from the other. By late childhood, children exposed to a new language have more difficulty learning it. At some point in late childhood or adolescence (as yet not pinpointed), there is a critical-period cutoff for speaking a new language without an accent (Obler, 1993).

Biological, Environmental, and Cultural Influences

Is the ability to generate rules for language, and then use them to create an infinite number of words, learned and influenced by the environment and cultural factors, or is it the product of biological facts and biological evolution?

Biological Influences. Estimates vary as to how long ago humans acquired language — from about 20,000 to 70,000 years ago. In evolutionary time, then, language is a very recent acquisition. A number of experts believe that biological evolution undeniably shaped humans into linguistic creatures (Chomsky, 1957). The brain, nervous system, and vocal apparatus of our predecessors changed over hundreds of thousands of years. Physically equipped to do so, *Homo sapiens* went beyond grunting and shrieking to develop abstract speech. Evolutionary forces may have pushed humans to develop abstract reasoning and to create an efficient system for communicating with others (Crick, 1977). For example, early humans probably developed complex plans and strategies for hunting. If the hunters could verbally signal one another about changes in strategies for hunting big game, the hunt much more likely would be successful. Language clearly gave humans an enormous edge over other animals and increased the chances of survival.

The strongest evidence for the biological basis of language is that children all over the world acquire language milestones at about the same time developmentally and in about the same order, despite vast variations in the language input they receive. For example, in some cultures adults never talk to infants under 1 year of age, yet these infants still acquire language. Also, there is no other convincing way to explain how quickly children learn language than through biological foundations.

Environmental Influences. We do not learn language in a social vacuum. Most children are steeped in language at a very early age. And children's earliest exposures to language are usually through their parents. Roger Brown (1973) wondered whether parental reinforcement was responsible for children learning to speak in grammatically correct ways as behavioral theorists would predict. After spending many hours observing parents and their young children, he found that parents sometimes smiled and praised their children for correct sentences, but they also reinforced many ungrammatical sentences. Brown concluded that learning grammar is not based on reinforcement.

What are some of the ways in which environment does contribute to language development? Imitation is one important candidate. A child who is slow to develop her language ability can be helped if her parents speak to her carefully in grammatically correct sentences.

One intriguing environmental factor that contributes to a young child's language acquisition is called **motherese,** *the way parents and other adults often talk to babies in a*

motherese
Talking to babies in a higher-pitched voice than normal and with simple words and sentences.

higher-pitched voice than normal and with simple words and sentences. Most people automatically shift into motherese as soon as they start talking to a baby—usually without being aware they're doing so. We speak in motherese, it seems, to capture the infant's attention and maintain communication. To read further about how to talk with babies and toddlers, see Applications in Psychology.

Children differ in their ability to acquire language, and this variation cannot be readily explained by differences in environmental input alone. For children who are slow in developing language skills, opportunities to talk and be talked with are important. But remember that encouragement of language development is the key, not drill and practice. Language development is not a simple matter of imitation and reinforcement, a fact acknowledged even by most behaviorists today.

$\mathscr{A}$pplications in Psychology

How to Talk With Babies and Toddlers

In *Growing Up With Language,* linguist Naomi Baron (1992) provides a number of helpful ideas about ways that parents can facilitate their child's language development. A summary of her ideas follows:

Infants

* *Be an active conversational partner.*
  Initiate conversation with the infant. If the infant is in a daylong child-care program, ensure that the baby get adequate language stimulation from adults.
* *Talk as if the infant understands what you are saying.*
  Adults can generate positive self-fulfilling prophecies by addressing their young children as if they understand what is being said. The process may take 4 to 5 years, but children gradually rise to match the language model presented to them.
* *Use a language style with which you feel comfortable.*
  Don't worry about how you sound to other adults when you talk with a child. Your effect, not your content, is more important when talking with an infant. Use whatever type of baby talk you feel comfortable with.

Toddlers

* *Continue to be an active conversational partner.*
  Engaging toddlers in conversation, even one-sided conversation, is the most important thing an adult can do to nourish a child linguistically.
* *Remember to listen.*
  Since toddlers' speech is often slow and laborious, parents are often tempted to supply words and thoughts for them. Be patient. Let toddlers express themselves, no matter how painstaking the process is or how great a hurry you are in.
* *Use a language style with which you are comfortable, but consider ways of expanding the child's language abilities and horizons.* For example, using long sentences need not be problematic; don't be afraid to use ungrammatical language to imitate the toddlers' novel forms (such as "No eat"); use rhymes; ask questions that encourage answers

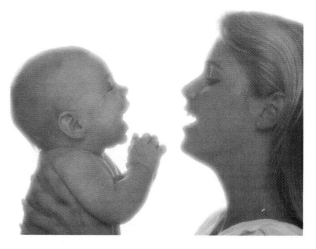

It is unquestionably a good idea for parents to talk to their babies right from the start. The best language teaching occurs when the talking is begun before the infant becomes capable of its first intelligible speech.

other than "Yes"; actively repeat, expand, and recast the child's utterances; introduce new topics; and use humor in your conversation.

* *Adjust to a child's idiosyncrasies instead of working against them.*
  Many toddlers have difficulty pronouncing words and making themselves understood. Whenever possible, make toddlers feel that they are being understood.
* *Avoid sexual stereotypes.*
  Don't let the toddler's sex unwittingly determine your amount or style of conversation. Many American mothers are more linguistically supportive of girls than of boys, and many fathers talk less with their children than mothers do. Active and cognitively enriching initiatives from both mothers and fathers benefit both boys and girls.
* *Resist making normative comparisons.*
  Be aware of the ages at which a child reaches specific milestones (first word, first fifty words, first grammatical combination), but be careful not to measure this development rigidly against children of neighbors or friends. Such social comparisons can bring about unnecessary anxiety.

Cultural Influences. Take a moment and reflect on these questions: How did the culture in which you grew up influence your language? What role does language play in academic achievement?

linguistic relativity hypothesis
The view that culture shapes language, which further determines the structure of thinking and shapes our basic ideas.

The Linguistic Relativity Hypothesis. Linguist Benjamin Whorf claimed that language determines the way we think. Whorf's (1956) **linguistic relativity hypothesis** *states that culture shapes language, which further determines the structure of thinking and shapes our basic ideas.* The Inuit in Alaska, for instance, have a dozen or more words to describe the various textures, colors, and physical states of snow; the Hopi Indians have no words for past and future; and Arabs have 6,000 words for camels.

Our cultural experiences for a particular concept shape a catalog of names that can be either rich or poor. For example, if the "camel" part of your mental library of names is the product of years of experience with camels, you probably see and think about this desert animal in finer gradations than does someone who has no experience with camels. In this way, language acts like a window that filters the amount and nature of information passed on for further processing.

Critics of Whorf's theory say that words merely reflect, rather than cause, the way we think. The Inuits' adaptability and livelihood in Alaska depend on their capacity to recognize various conditions of snow and ice. Recent criticism of the linguistic relativity hypothesis argues that the Inuits have no more words for snow and ice than do people living in the continental United States. Even though you don't know the words for the different defensive alignments in football, just like you don't have words for all the different conditions of snow and ice, you might still be able to perceive these differences.

What is the nature of linguistic relativity?

Rosch (1973) found just that. She studied the effect of language on color perception among the Dani in New Guinea. The Dani have only two words for color—one that approximates white and one that approximates black. If the linguistic relativity hypothesis were correct, the Dani would lack the ability to tell the difference among such colors as green, blue, red, yellow, and purple. However, Rosch found that the Dani perceive colors just as we perceive them when they were successful at a color matching task. As we know from chapter 3, color perception is biologically determined by receptors in the retinas in the eyes. Whorf's linguistic relativity hypothesis missed the mark, but researchers agree that although language does not determine thought, it can influence it.

Language's Role in Achievement and School. Octavio's Mexican parents moved to the United States a year before Octavio was born. They do not speak English fluently and have always spoken to Octavio in Spanish. At 6 years of age, Octavio has just entered the first grade at an elementary school in San Antonio, Texas, and he speaks no English. What is the best way to teach Octavio? How much easier would elementary school be for Octavio if his parents had been able to speak to him in Spanish *and* English when he was an infant?

Well over 6 million children in the United States come from homes in which English is not the primary language. Often, like Octavio, they live in a community in which a language other than English is the main means of communication. These children face a more difficult task than most of us: They must master the native tongue of their family to communicate effectively at home and they must also master English to make their way in the larger society. The number of bilingual children is expanding at such a rapid rate in the U.S. (some experts predict a tripling of their number early in the twenty-first century) that they constitute an important subgroup of language learners that society must deal with. Although the education of such children in the public schools has a long history, only recently has a national policy evolved to guarantee high-quality language experience for them.

bilingual education

Programs for students with limited proficiency in English that instruct students in their own language part of the time while they learn English.

Bilingual education *refers to programs for students with limited proficiency in English that instruct students in their own language part of the time while they learn English.* The rationale for bilingual education was provided by the U.S. Commission on Civil Rights (1975): Lack of English proficiency is the main reason language minority students do poorly in school; bilingual education should keep students from falling far behind in a subject while they are learning English. Bilingual programs vary extensively in content and quality. At a minimum, they include instruction in English as a second language for students with limited English proficiency. Bilingual programs often include some instruction in Spanish as well. The largest number of bilingual programs in the United States are Spanish, so our examples refer to Spanish, although the principles also apply to bilingual programs in other languages. Bilingual programs differ in the extent to which Latino culture is taught to all students. Some bilingual programs teach Spanish to all students, regardless of whether their primary language is Spanish.

The National Association for the Education of Young Children (NAEYC) has made a number of excellent recommendations for teaching and interacting with linguistically and culturally diverse children. Following is the consensus of their team of experts about working with linguistically and culturally diverse children (NAEYC, 1996):

- Recognize that all children are cognitively, linguistically, and emotionally connected to the language and culture of their home.
- Acknowledge that children can demonstrate their knowledge and capacity in many ways. Whatever language children speak, they should be able to demonstrate their capabilities and also feel appreciated and valued.
- Understand that without comprehensible input, second-language learning can be difficult. It takes time to become competent in any language. Although verbal proficiency in a second language can be attained in 2 or 3 years, the skills needed to understand academic content through reading and writing can take 4 or more years. Children who do not become proficient in their second language after 2 or 3 years often are not proficient in their first language either.

What are some good strategies for working with groups of children who are linguistically and culturally diverse?

- Model appropriate use of English and provide the child with opportunities to use newly acquired vocabulary and language. The teacher also can learn a few words in the child's first language to show respect for the child's culture.
- Actively involve parents and families in the child's learning. Parents and families should be invited to engage in language-learning activities with their children. Encourage parents and help them become knowledgeable about the value for children of knowing more than one language. Provide parents with strategies to support and maintain home-language learning.
- Recognize that children can and will acquire the use of English even when their home language is used and respected. Bilingualism does not interfere with proficiency in either language or cognitive development (Hakuta & Garcia, 1989).

One final point about bilingualism deserves attention. The United States is one of the few countries in the world in which most students graduate from high school knowing only their own language. For example, in Russia, schools have ten grades, called forms, which correspond roughly to the twelve grades in American schools. Children begin school at age 7. In the third form, Russian students begin learning English. Because of the emphasis on teaching English in their schools, most Russian citizens today under the age of 35 speak at least some English (Cameron, 1988).

Let's now turn from one controversial issue, the effects of bilingualism on language development, to another controversial issue, whether animals have language.

Do Animals Have Language?

Many animal species do have complex and ingenious ways to signal danger and to communicate about basic needs such as food and sex. For example, in one species of firefly the female has learned to imitate the flashing signal of another species to lure the aliens into her territory. Then she eats them. But is this language in the human sense? And what about higher animals, such as apes? Is ape language similar to human language? Can we teach language to apes?

Some researchers believe that apes can learn language. One celebrity in this field is a chimp named Washoe, who was adopted when she was about 10 months old (Gardner & Gardner, 1971). Since apes do not have the vocal apparatus to speak, the researchers tried to teach Washoe the American Sign Language, which is one of the sign languages of the deaf. Washoe used sign language during everyday activities, such as meals, play, and car rides. In 2 years, Washoe learned 38 different signs, and by the age of 5 she had a vocabulary of 160 signs. Washoe learned how to put signs together in novel ways, such as "You drink" and "You me tickle." A number of other efforts to teach language to chimps have had similar results (Premack, 1986).

The debate about chimpanzees' ability to use language focuses on two key issues: Can apes understand the meaning of symbols; that is, can they comprehend that one thing stands for another? And can apes learn syntax; that is, can they learn the mechanics and rules that give human language its creative productivity? The first of these issues may have been settled recently by Sue Savage-Rumbaugh and her colleagues (1993). The researchers found strong evidence that two chimps named Sherman and Austin can understand symbols (see figure 7.8). For example, if Sherman or Austin is sitting in a room, and a symbol for an object is displayed on a screen, he will go into another room, find the object, and bring it back. If the object is not there, he will come back empty-handed (Cowley, 1988). The two chimps can play a game in which one chimp points to a symbol for food (M & Ms), and the other chimp selects the food from a tray, then they both eat it. These observations are clear evidence that chimps can understand symbols (Rumbaugh & others, 1991).

However, there still is no strong evidence that chimps can learn syntax. Perhaps other animals can. Ron Schusterman has worked with a sea lion named Rocky, teaching him to follow commands such as "Ball fetch" and "Disc ball fetch." The first command means that Rocky should take a disc to a ball in his tank. The second command means that

FIGURE 7.8

Sue Savage-Rumbaugh with a Chimp in Front of a Board with Language Based Symbols

The Rumbaughs (Sue and Duane) of the Yerkes Primate Center and Georgia State University have studied the basic question of whether chimps understand symbols. Their research evidence suggests chimps can understand symbols.

"I HOPE WE GET TO COMMUNICATE WITH THEM. I'D JUST LIKE TO TELL THEM WE HAVE NO INTEREST IN COMMUNICATING WITH THEM."

Rocky should take the ball to the disc. Although Rocky and other sea lions make some errors in decoding these complex commands, they perform at levels much better than chance, indicating that they have learned rules that link the ordering of symbols to abstract meanings. Such rules are either syntax or something close to it.

The debate over whether or not animals can use language to express thoughts is far from resolved. Researchers do agree that animals can communicate with each other and that some can be trained to manipulate language based symbols. While such accomplishments may be remarkable, they fall far short of human language with its infinite number of novel phrases to convey the richness and subtleties of meaning that are the foundation of human relationships.

Our thinking and language skills set us apart from other life forms on this planet. Through our thinking and language, we have mastered our world and adapted effectively to its challenges. We will continue our investigation of thinking and language as we explore individual differences in mental functioning by studying the nature of intelligence.

eview

Language

Language involves a system of symbols we use to communicate with each other. The system is governed by rules yet allows infinite generativity. Some of the mechanics of language include phonology, morphology, syntax, and semantics.

One-word utterances occur at about 10 to 13 months of age; the holophrase hypothesis has been applied to this. By 18 to 24 months, most infants use two-word combinations. This is often referred to as telegraphic speech. Based on the effects of brain injury on language at different points in development, Lenneberg argued that a critical period for language acquisition ends at puberty. The experiences of Genie and other such children also suggest that the early childhood years are a critical period in language development. And the facts about second-language acquisition, especially the timetable for learning to speak a second language with-

out an accent, provide evidence for a critical period.

Biological evolution shaped humans into linguistic creatures. The strongest evidence for the biological basis of language is that children all over the world reach language milestones at about the same age and in about the same order, despite vast differences in the language input they receive. Cultural evolution spurred the need to communicate as humans worked together for survival.

Reinforcement and imitation probably facilitate language development but might not play a critical role. Adults universally seem to adopt motherese when speaking to children. An interactionist view emphasizes the contributions of both biology and experience in language—that is, children are already biologically prepared to learn language when they and their caregivers interact.

Whorf's controversial linguistic relativity hypothesis states that language determines the structure of thinking. Thoughts and ideas are associated with words, and different languages promote different ways of thinking. Language does not determine thought, but it does influence it. One critical variable in understanding language's role in achievement and school is whether the child speaks the language in which the classes are taught and, if so, how well. National debate rages about the best way to teach children whose native language is not English. There is great diversity in bilingual programs.

Although animals can communicate about basic drives, it is unclear whether animals have all the properties of human language. Chimpanzees, however, can be taught to use symbols.

INTELLIGENCE

The primary components of intelligence are close to the mental processes we have already discussed in this chapter—thinking and language. The difference between how we discussed thinking and language and how we will discuss intelligence lies in the concept of individual differences in assessment. **Individual differences** *are the consistent, stable ways people are different from each other.* We can talk about individual differences in personality or in any other domain of psychology, but it is in the area of intelligence that psychologists give the most attention to individual differences. For example, an intelligence test informs you whether you can logically reason better than most others who have taken the test. Before we discuss intelligence tests, though, we need to examine what intelligence is and how tests are constructed.

The Nature of Intelligence

Intelligence is one of our most highly prized possessions, yet its concept is something that even the most intelligent people have failed to agree on. Unlike such characteristics as height, weight, and age, intelligence cannot be directly measured. It's a bit like size, which is a more abstract notion than height or weight. We can only estimate size from a set of empirical measures of height and weight. Similarly, we can only estimate a person's intelligence. We cannot peel back a scalp and observe intellectual processes in action. We can study these processes indirectly by evaluating a person's intelligent acts (Kail & Pellegrino, 1985). For the most part, psychologists rely on intelligence tests to provide an estimate of these mental abilities.

Many psychologists and laypeople equate intelligence with verbal ability and problem-solving skills. Others prefer to define it as a person's ability to learn from and adapt to the experiences of everyday life. Let's combine the two and settle on the following definition of **intelligence:** *verbal ability, problem-solving skills, and the ability to learn from and adapt to the experiences of everyday life.*

Although we have just defined general intelligence, keep in mind that the way intelligence is expressed in behavior may vary from culture to culture (Lonner, 1990). For example, in most Western cultures, people are considered intelligent if they are both smart (have considerable knowledge and can solve verbal problems) and fast (can process information quickly). On the other hand, in the Buganda culture in Uganda, people who are wise, slow in thought, and say the socially correct thing are considered intelligent (Wober, 1974).

Single Versus Multiple Models of Intelligence. Chances are that because you are taking college courses, someone has labeled you as "smart." You might even know estimates of your intelligence based on intelligence tests that you took in school or in a psychologist's office. Some of those tests produce an overall score to express how smart you are relative to others who have taken the same test. However, a nagging problem for psychologists is whether or not it is reasonable to measure intelligence in a general way and express it as a single score.

The first person to introduce the concept that intelligence can be expressed by an overall score was Alfred Binet. In 1904, the French Ministry of Education asked him to devise a screening device that could identify children who had difficulty learning in school. He created the concept of **mental age (MA),** *an individual's level of mental development relative to others.* He compared the performance of children suspected of having mental retardation with normally functioning children of the same age using the 30-item test he developed. Children with average mental abilities scored consistent with their chronological age (CA). Bright children's MAs were higher than their CAs, while children with low intelligence had MAs below their CAs.

The term **intelligence quotient (IQ)** *was devised in 1912 by William Stern. IQ consists of a person's mental age divided by chronological age, multiplied by 100:*

$$IQ = MA/CA \times 100$$

individual differences

The consistent, stable ways people differ from each other.

intelligence

Verbal ability, problem-solving skills, and the ability to learn from and adapt to the experiences of everyday life.

mental age (MA)

An individual's level of mental development relative to others.

intelligence quotient (IQ)

Devised in 1912 by William Stern; a person's mental age divided by chronological age, multiplied by 100.

If mental age is the same as chronological age, then the person's IQ is 100; if mental age is above chronological age, then IQ is more than 100; if mental age is below chronological age, then IQ is less than 100. Scores noticeably above 100 are considered above average, and scores noticeably below 100 are considered below average. For example, a 6-year-old child with a mental age of 8 would have an IQ of 133, whereas a 6-year-old child with a mental age of 5 would have an IQ of 83.

Charles Spearman (1927) agreed with Binet and Stern that there is a general form of intelligence. Spearman referred to this as *g*, which he said unifies a person's intellectual profile. Spearman also proposed that intelligence has specific forms as well, which he referred to as *s*. His theory became known as the **two-factor theory,** *which states that intelligence has both general* (g) *and specific* (s) *forms.*

A decade later, L. L. Thurstone (1938) rejected the notion of general intelligence and proposed the **multiple-factor theory,** *which states that intelligence consists of seven primary abilities: verbal comprehension, number ability, word fluency, spatial visualization, associative memory, reasoning, and perceptual speed.* Thurstone argued that a person could be competent in one area of intelligence (such as verbal comprehension) and far less competent in another (such as perceptual speed).

Intelligence tests developed in the 1940s and 1950s, such as the Wechsler Scales (which we will profile shortly), continued to promote the idea that intelligence has both general and specific forms. More recently, there has been a flurry of interest in conceptualizing the specific forms of intelligence. Two theories that adopt this view—Sternberg's and Gardner's—are profiled next.

Sternberg's Triarchic Theory. Robert J. Sternberg recalls being terrified of taking IQ tests as a child. He literally froze, he says, when the time came to take such tests. Even as an adult, Sternberg stings with humiliation when he recalls being in sixth grade and taking an IQ test with the fifth graders. Sternberg finally overcame his anxieties about IQ tests and not only performed much better on them, but at age 13 he even devised his own IQ test and began assessing his classmates—until the school psychologist found out and scolded him. In fact, Sternberg became so fascinated with the topic that he made it a lifelong pursuit.

The **triarchic theory of intelligence** *is Sternberg's (1986) theory that intelligence has three factors: componential, experiential, and contextual.* To illustrate these three types of intelligence, we will consider three separate individuals: Ann, who scores high on traditional intelligence tests like the Wechsler Scales and is a star analytical thinker; Juan, who

two-factor theory

Spearman's theory that individuals have both general intelligence, which he called *g,* and a number of specific intelligences, which he called *s.*

multiple-factor theory

L. L. Thurstone's theory that intelligence consists of seven primary mental abilities: verbal comprehension, number ability, word fluency, spatial visualization, associative memory, reasoning, and perceptual speed.

triarchic theory

Sternberg's theory that intelligence consists of componential intelligence, experiential intelligence, and contextual intelligence.

"You're wise, but you lack tree smarts."

does not have the best test scores but is insightful and creative; and Art, a street-smart person who has learned to deal in practical ways with his world, although his scores on traditional intelligence tests are low.

Sternberg calls Ann's analytical thinking and abstract reasoning componential intelligence. It is the closest to what we call intelligence in this chapter and what is commonly measured by intelligence tests. Juan's insightful and creative thinking is called experiential intelligence by Sternberg. Art's street smarts and practical knowledge are called contextual intelligence by Sternberg (see figure 7.9).

In Sternberg's view of componential intelligence, the basic unit in intelligence is a component, simply defined as a basic unit of information processing. Sternberg believes that such components include the ability to acquire or store information, to retain or retrieve information, to transfer information, to plan, to make decisions, to solve problems, and to translate thoughts into performance. Notice the similarity of these components to the description of memory in chapter 6 and the description of thinking earlier in this chapter.

The second part of Sternberg's model focuses on experience. According to Sternberg, intelligent people have the ability to solve new problems quickly, but they also learn how to solve familiar problems in an automatic, rote way so their minds are free to handle other problems that require insight and creativity.

The third part of the model involves practical intelligence—such as how to get out of trouble, how to replace a fuse, and how to get along with people. Sternberg describes this practical, or contextual, intelligence as all of the important information about getting along in the real world that we are not taught in school. He believes that contextual intelligence is sometimes more important than "book knowledge."

Gardner's Frames of Intelligence.   Howard Gardner (1983) also objected to the notion of a unitary IQ score. However, Gardner's approach to intelligence was based on studying case histories in which either substantial deficits or impressive abilities existed. He was able to define seven frames of intelligence that corresponded to these case studies. Gardner identified *spatial skills, bodily awareness (movement skills), mathematics, artistic abilities, verbal abilities, interpersonal abilities, and interpersonal abilities (insightful skills for analyzing oneself)* as frames in which we can have strengths or weaknesses.

> *Everyone is ignorant, only on different subjects.*
> —WILL ROGERS, *American Writer and Humorist, 20th Century*

Let's explore one frame of intelligence proposed by Gardner. He suggested that many individuals demonstrate deficits in arithmetic skills. Although they are far more rare, there are also individuals who show extraordinary calculation skills. For example, some individuals can identify, as a function of their calculation skills on what day of the week a specific day well in the future will fall. Others can perform complex calculations without pencil or paper. Gardner argued that some individuals who measure in the mentally retarded range on a standard IQ test might show a contrasting splinter skill in the area of calculation. This outcome was the focus of the fascinating film *Rain Man,* in which the autistic main character was able to do a variety of calculations. These skills included the ability to help his brother successfully gamble in Las Vegas by keeping track of the cards that already had been played.

Sternberg's and Gardner's approaches have not yet led to the development of widely accepted ways of measuring these multiple forms of intelligence. In the next section, we will explore the complicated procedures involved in measuring intelligence.

Measuring Intelligence

The first evidence of formal tests comes from China. In 2200 B.C. the emperor Ta Yü conducted a series of three oral "competency tests" for government officials. Based on the results, the officials either were promoted or fired. Variations on these early exams have been causing anxiety for employees and students ever since. Test developers in this century have been on a continuing quest to produce tests that are more useful and fair.

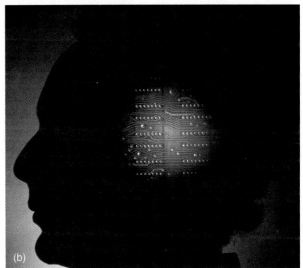

*F*IGURE 7.9

Sternberg's Triarchic Model of Intelligence

(a) Componential intelligence is the closest to what is commonly measured on intelligence tests and is reflected in the ability to process information as we read. *(b)* Photographer Mieke Maas showed experiential intelligence in creating this unique image of a printed circuit board inside an individual's head. Experiential intelligence involves creativity and insight. *(c)* Contextual intelligence refers to practical knowledge, especially "street smarts."

Dustin Hoffman's portrayal in *Rain Man* depicted how a man with autism and cognitive deficits could accomplish remarkable feats of counting and mathematics. Such skills are described as *savant skills.* They support the idea that intelligence can be expressed in multiple abilities.

reliability

A measure of whether a test performs in a consistent manner.

test-retest reliability

Consistency of results when a person is given the same test on two different occasions.

inter-rater reliability

The extent to which two raters score a test the same.

validity

The extent to which a test measures what it is purported to measure.

content validity

The extent to which a test covers broadly the content it is purported to cover.

criterion validity

A test's ability to predict other measures, or criteria, of an attribute.

Criteria for Test Design.   Any good test must meet three criteria—it must be reliable, it must be valid, and it must be standardized.

Reliability *is a measure of whether the test performs in a consistent manner.* With a reliable test, scores should not fluctuate significantly as a result of chance factors, such as how much sleep the test taker got the night before, who the examiner is, or the temperature in the testing room. One method of assessing reliability is **test-retest reliability,** *comparing one person's test results from two different test sessions to determine the consistency of the test.* For example, on a reliable test, a college student scores in the same range on the test in September as in February. One drawback of evaluating test-retest reliability is that people sometimes do better the second time they take the test because they are familiar with it.

Another challenge to a test's reliability is **inter-rater reliability,** *the extent to which two raters score a test the same.* A well-designed test should produce essentially the same score from two different raters who score the same test performance. As you can imagine, coming up with equivalent scores is challenging if the test is poorly designed to begin with or the scorers are not properly trained.

Even if a test produces reliable results, it will not be a good test unless it is valid. **Validity** *is the extent to which a test measures what it is intended to measure.* For example, would measuring the circumference of the head be a good way to predict intelligence? Clearly, it would not. Head measurements will produce a *reliable* result, but head size is not a *valid* measure of intelligence. Let's look at test validity in a little more detail.

Content validity *is the extent to which the test covers broadly the content it purports to cover.* For example, if your instructor for this class plans a comprehensive final exam, it will probably cover topics from each of the chapters rather than just two or three chapters. If an intelligence test purports to measure both verbal ability and problem-solving ability, the test should include a liberal sampling of each. The test does not have high content validity if it asks you to define several vocabulary items (one measure of verbal ability) and does not require you to use reason in solving a number of problems.

Criterion validity *is a test's ability to predict other measures, or criteria, of an attribute.* For example, rather than rely solely on the results of one intelligence test to assess a person's intelligence, a psychologist might also ask that person's employer how he or she performs at work. The employer's perception is another criterion for assessing intelligence. Using more than one measure—such as administering a different intelligence test, soliciting an employer's perception of intelligence, or observing a person's problem-solving ability—is a good strategy for establishing criterion validity.

Good tests are not only reliable and valid, but they also are standardized. **Standardization** *involves developing uniform procedures for administering and scoring a test, and it also involves developing norms for the test.* Uniform testing procedures require that the testing environment be as similar as possible for everyone who takes the test. For example, the test directions and the amount of time allowed to complete the test should be uniform. **Norms** *are established standards of performance for a test. Norms are developed by giving the test to a large group of people who represent the target population. This allows the researcher to determine the distribution of test scores. Norms inform us which scores are considered high, low, or average.* For example, a score of 120 on an intelligence test has little meaning alone. The score takes on meaning when we compare it with other scores. If only 20 percent of the standardized group scores above 120, then we can interpret that score as high, rather than average or low.

Although there has been some effort in recent years to standardize intelligence tests for African Americans and Latinos, little has been done to standardize tests for people from other ethnic minorities. Psychologists need to ensure that the tests are standardized for a person's particular ethnic group and to put the test results in an appropriate cultural context. Otherwise they must use caution interpreting the test's results (Murphy & Davidshofer, 1998; Saklofske & Zeidner, 1995).

Contemporary Intelligence Tests. Psychologists have several options to choose from when they want to measure intelligence. Two of the most popular choices are the Stanford-Binet test and the Wechsler scales.

The Stanford-Binet Tests. The Binet test has been revised many times to incorporate advances in the understanding of intelligence and intelligence testing. These revisions are called the Stanford-Binet tests (Stanford University is where the revisions were done). Many of the revisions were carried out by Lewis Terman, who applied Stern's IQ concept to the test, developed extensive norms, and provided detailed, clear instructions for each problem on the test.

In an extensive effort to standardize the Stanford-Binet test, it has been given to thousands of children and adults of different ages, selected at random from various parts of the United States. By administering the test to large numbers of people and recording the results, researchers have found that intelligence measured by the Stanford-Binet approximates a normal distribution (see figure 7.10). A **normal distribution** *is symmetrical, with a majority of cases falling in the middle of the possible range of scores and few scores appearing toward the extremes of the range.*

The Wechsler Scales. Besides the Stanford-Binet, the other widely used intelligence tests are the Wechsler scales, developed by David Wechsler. They include the Wechsler Adult Intelligence Scale–Revised (WAIS-R); the Wechsler Intelligence Scale for Children–Revised (WISC-R), to test children between the ages of 6 and 16; and the Wechsler Preschool and Primary Scale of Intelligence (WPPSI), to test children from the ages of 4 to 6½.

Not only do the Wechsler scales provide an overall IQ score, but the items are grouped according to 11 subscales, 6 of which are verbal and 5 nonverbal. This allows an examiner to obtain separate verbal and nonverbal IQ scores and to see quickly the areas of mental performance in which a tested individual is below average, average, or above average. The inclusion of a number of nonverbal subscales makes the Wechsler test more representative of verbal and nonverbal intelligence; the Stanford-Binet test includes some nonverbal items but not as many as the Wechsler scales. Several of the Wechsler subscales are shown in figure 7.11.

Variations in Cognitive Ability

Intelligence tests have been used to diagnose mental retardation, learning disabilities, and intellectual giftedness. At times, intelligence tests also have been misused for this purpose. Keep this in mind as we explore the nature of mental retardation, learning differences, and giftedness.

---

standardization

The development of uniform procedures for administering and scoring a test; also the development of norms for the test.

norms

Established standards of performance for a test.

normal distribution

A symmetrical distribution in which a majority of cases fall in the middle of the possible range of scores and few scores fall in the extremes of the range.

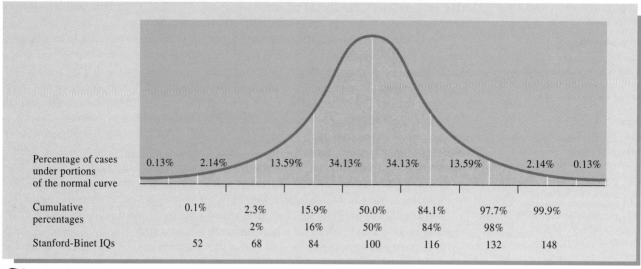

Percentage of cases under portions of the normal curve	0.13%	2.14%	13.59%	34.13%	34.13%	13.59%	2.14%	0.13%
Cumulative percentages	0.1%	2.3%	15.9%	50.0%	84.1%	97.7%	99.9%	
		2%	16%	50%	84%	98%		
Stanford-Binet IQs	52	68	84	100	116	132	148	

ℱIGURE 7.10

The Normal Curve and Stanford-Binet IQ Scores

The distribution of IQ scores approximates a normal curve. Most of the population falls in the middle range of scores. Notice that extremely high and extremely low scores are very rare. Slightly more than two-thirds of the scores fall between 84 and 116. Only about 1 in 50 individuals has an IQ of more than 132 and only about 1 in 50 individuals has a IQ of less than 68.

mental retardation

A condition of limited mental ability in which an individual has a low IQ, usually below 70 on a traditional intelligence test, and has difficulty adapting to everyday life.

Mental Retardation. The most distinctive feature of mental retardation is inadequate intellectual functioning. Long before formal tests were developed to assess intelligence, the mentally retarded were identified by a lack of age-appropriate skills in learning and caring for themselves. Once intelligence tests were developed, numbers were assigned to indicate degree of mental retardation. It is not unusual to find that of two retarded people with the same low IQ, one is married, employed, and involved in the community and the other requires constant supervision in an institution. These differences in social competence led psychologists to include deficits in adaptive behavior in their definition of mental retardation. **Mental retardation** *is a condition of limited mental ability in which an individual has a low IQ, usually below 70 on a traditional intelligence test, and has difficulty adapting to everyday life.* About 5 million Americans fit this definition of mental retardation.

There are several classifications of mental retardation. About 89 percent of the mentally retarded fall into the mild category, with IQs of 55 to 70. About 6 percent are classified as moderately retarded, with IQs of 40 to 54; these people can attain a second-grade level of skills and may be able to support themselves as adults through some types of labor. About 3.5 percent of the mentally retarded are in the severe category, with IQs of 25 to 39; these individuals learn to talk and engage in very simple tasks but require extensive supervision. Less than 1 percent have IQs below 25; they fall into the profoundly mentally retarded classification and are in need of constant supervision.

Mental retardation can have an organic cause, or it can be social and cultural in origin. **Organic retardation** *is mental retardation caused by a genetic disorder or by brain damage;* organic *refers to the tissues or organs of the body, so there is some physical damage in organic retardation.* Down syndrome, one form of mental retardation, occurs when an extra chromosome is present in an individual's genetic makeup. It is not known why the extra chromosome is present, but it may involve the health or age of the female ovum or male sperm. Most people who suffer from organic retardation have IQs that range between 0 and 50.

Cultural-familial retardation *is a mental deficit in which no evidence of organic brain damage can be found; individuals' IQs range from 50 to 70.* Psychologists suspect that such mental deficits result from the normal variation that distributes people among the range of IQ scores above 50, combined with growing up in a below-average intellectual environment. As children, those who are familially retarded can be detected in schools, where they often fail, need tangible rewards (candy rather than praise), and are highly sensitive to what others—both peers and adults—want from them. However, as adults

organic retardation

Mental retardation caused by a genetic disorder or by brain damage. *Organic* refers to the tissues or organs of the body, so there is some physical damage in organic retardation.

cultural-familial retardation

A mental deficit in which no evidence of organic brain damage can be found; these individuals' IQs range from 50 to 70.

VERBAL SUBSCALES

SIMILARITIES

An individual must think logically and abstractly to answer a number of questions about how things might be similar.

For example, "In what ways are boats and trains the same?"

COMPREHENSION

This subscale is designed to measure an individual's judgment and common sense.

For example, "Why do individuals buy automobile insurance?"

PERFORMANCE SUBSCALES

PICTURE ARRANGEMENT

A series of pictures out of sequence is shown to an individual, who is asked to place them in their proper order to tell an appropriate story. This subscale evaluates how individuals integrate information to make it logical and meaningful.

For example, "The pictures below need to be placed in an appropriate order to tell a story."

BLOCK DESIGN

An individual must assemble a set of multicolored blocks to match designs that the examiner shows. Visual-motor coordination, perceptual organization, and the ability to visualize spatially are assessed.

For example, "Use the four blocks on the left to make the pattern at the right."

Remember that the Wechsler includes 11 subscales, 6 verbal and 5 nonverbal. Four of the subscales are shown here.

*F*IGURE 7.11

Sample Subscales of the Wechsler Adult Intelligence Scale–Revised

Simulated items similar to those in the Wechsler Intelligence Scales for Adults and Children. Copyright 1949, 1955, 1974, 1981, 1991 by The Psychological Corporation. Reproduced by permission.

the familially retarded are usually invisible, perhaps because adult settings don't tax their cognitive skills as sorely. It may also be that the familially retarded increase their intelligence as they move toward adulthood.

learning difference

Problematic development in specific academic skills that does not reflect overall intellectual ability.

Learning Differences. Perhaps as many as one in ten of all Americans suffers academically from a **learning difference,** *a problematic development in specific academic skills that does not reflect overall intellectual ability.* Learning differences are distinct from

This mother is caring for her infant and her child with Down syndrome *(right)*. What causes a child to develop Down syndrome?

dyslexia

A learning difference that negatively influences the quality and rate of reading.

intelligence. Some individuals who have a learning difference even have IQ scores in the genius range. Famous Americans who have gone public with their learning differences include actors Tom Cruise and Tracy Gold.

There are many kinds of learning differences. **Dyslexia** *is a learning difference that negatively influences the ability to read.* People with dyslexia, such as Jay Leno, describe frustration from strings of letters (words and sentences) that are hard to decipher. These individuals might perform poorly in school, especially when called on by teachers. Because of their anxieties about poor performance and their slower learning rate, students with dyslexia often have wounded self-esteem. They are sometimes accused of "not trying" or "being lazy" by those who fail to understand their struggles. Other learning differences involve deficits in performing arithmetic calculations (dyscalculia), problematic writing skills, and difficulties in articulating or expressing speech. See the Self-Assessment to see whether you might have a learning difference that could be impeding your success in college.

The field of learning disabilities is relatively new. However, some tests have been developed to determine whether an individual has a learning difference. Historically, psychologists interpreted a large difference between performance and verbal subscales on the Wechsler scales as possibly indicating a learning disability. More recent testing techniques address the specific forms of learning differences. Individuals who have a verified learning difference as determined by a qualified examiner might be entitled to special support through the Education for All Handicapped Children Act of 1975.

Learning differences do not automatically predict academic failure. Successful students with learning differences often use compensating strategies to assist them in areas that are influenced by their differences. For example, students with dyslexia might find it easier to learn concepts by listening to audiotape versions of text than by reading text. They might also find classes easier to cope with if they audiotape professors' lectures rather than rely on written notes. Switching to auditory learning methods circumvents the need to rely on skills in which they routinely fare poorly. Students with expressive problems can invest in spell-checking devices or recruit proofreaders to compensate for their limitations in recognizing misspelled words.

$\mathcal{S}$elf-Assessment

Do You Have a Learning Difference?

Despite the fact that your intelligence test results might place you in the average or above-average range for intellectual ability, you might have a learning difference or disability if any of the following characterize you. Place a checkmark beside any of the items that are true of you.

_____ Difficulties in reading comprehension (processing and retaining the meaning of written words)

_____ Difficulties with math, including basic mathematics and quantitative reasoning

_____ Problems in written and oral expression, including spelling, written composition, listening, speaking, vocabulary skills, and related abilities

_____ Underdeveloped or uneven cognitive learning strategies

_____ Difficulties in concentrating, which might include distractibility, hyperactivity, or attention disorder

_____ Poor spatial orientation and difficulties in ideas related to directions (e.g., discerning right vs. left; north vs. south)

_____ Inadequate time concepts (including chronic lateness and confusion about personal responsibility related to time)

_____ Difficulties in making relationships and comparisons (e.g., discerning lightweight vs. heavy)

_____ Poor gross or fine motor coordination

_____ Problems in interpreting subtleties in social interaction

_____ Difficulties in following directions as well as in following the flow of class discussion

_____ Perceptual disturbance (e.g., letter reversals)

_____ Diminished auditory or visual memory

_____ Experience of accusations from teachers that you are "being lazy," despite working hard and putting in a lot of time in your studies

If you placed checkmarks beside many of the above items, you might consider going to the study skills center at your college. The professionals there can conduct a more thorough assessment of your learning situation.

gifted

Having above-average intelligence (an IQ of 120 or higher) and/or superior talent for something.

Giftedness.   There have always been people whose abilities and accomplishments outshine others'—the whiz kid in class, the star athlete, the natural musician. People who are **gifted** _have above-average intelligence (an IQ of 120 or higher) and/or superior talent for something._ When it comes to programs for the gifted, most school systems select children who have intellectual superiority and academic aptitude. Children who are talented in the visual and performing arts (arts, drama, dance), athletics, or other special aptitudes tend to be overlooked.

Ellen Winner (1996) recently described three characteristics of children who are gifted, whether in art, music, or academic domains:

1. _Precocity._ Gifted children are precocious. They begin to master an area earlier than their peers. Learning in their domain is more effortless than for ordinary children. Most gifted children are precocious because they have a high inborn ability in a particular domain or domains.

2. _Marching to their own drummers._ Gifted children learn in a qualitatively different way than ordinary children. One way they march to a different drummer is that they need minimal help from adults to learn. They often resist explicit instruction. They also often make discoveries on their own and solve problems in unique ways.

3. _A passion to master._ Gifted children are driven to understand the domain in which they have high ability. They display an intense, obsessive interest and an ability to focus their motivation. They are not children who need to be pushed by parents. They motivate themselves, says Winner.

Ten-year-old Alexandria Nechita recently burst on to the child prodigy scene. She paints quickly and impulsively on large canvases. Her paintings—in the modernist tradition—sell for up to $80,000 each. Alexandria colored in coloring books for hours when she was only 2 years old. She had no interest in dolls or friends. Once she started school she would resume painting as soon as she got home in the evening. And she continues to paint—relentlessly and passionately. It is, she says, what she loves to do.

Lewis Terman (1925) has followed the lives of approximately 1,500 children whose Stanford-Binet IQs averaged 150 into adulthood. The study will not be complete until the year 2010. Terman has found that this remarkable group is an accomplished lot: Of the 800 males, 78 have obtained doctorates (they include two past presidents of the

Alexandria Nechita has a passion for painting, preferring it to all other activities. Her early artistic success confirms her status as a child prodigy.

American Psychological Association), 48 have earned M.D.s, and 85 have been granted law degrees. Most of these figures are 10 to 30 times higher than those found among the 800 men of the same age chosen randomly as a comparison group. These findings challenge the commonly held belief that the intellectually gifted are emotionally disturbed or socially maladjusted.

Many of the highly gifted women in Terman's study questioned their intelligence and concluded that their cognitive skills had waned in adulthood. Studies of gifted women today reveal that they have a stronger confidence in their cognitive skills and intellectual abilities than the gifted women in Terman's study had (Tomlinson-Keasey, 1990).

Until recently, giftedness and emotional distress were thought to go hand in hand. English novelist Virginia Woolf suffered from severe depression, for example, and eventually committed suicide. Sir Isaac Newton, Vincent van Gogh, Ann Sexton, Socrates, and Sylvia Plath all had emotional problems. However, these are the exception rather than the rule. In general, no relation between giftedness and mental disorder has been found. A number of recent studies support the conclusion that gifted people tend to be more mature, have fewer emotional problems than others, and grow up in a positive family climate (Feldman & Piirto, 1995).

Culture and Ethnicity

Are there cultural and ethnic differences in intelligence? How does adaptation affect the role culture plays in understanding intelligence? Are standard intelligence tests biased? If so, can we develop tests that are fair?

The Heredity-Environment Controversy.   Arthur Jensen (1969) sparked lively and at times hostile debate when he stated his theory that intelligence is primarily inherited and that environment and culture play only a minimal role in intelligence. In one of his most provocative statements, Jensen claimed that genetics account for clear-cut differences in the average intelligence among races, nationalities, and social classes. When Jensen published an article in the *Harvard Educational Review* stating that lower intelligence probably is the reason why African Americans do not perform as well in school as Whites, he was called naive and racist. He received hate mail by the bushel, and police had to escort him to his classes at the University of California at Berkeley.

Jensen reviewed the research on intelligence, much of which involved comparisons of identical and fraternal twins. Remember that identical twins' have exactly the same genetic makeup. If intelligence is genetically determined, Jensen reasoned, identical twins' IQs should be similar. Fraternal twins and ordinary siblings are less similar genetically, so their IQs should be less similar. Jensen found support for his argument. The studies on intelligence in identical twins that Jensen examined showed an average correlation between their IQs of .82, a very high positive association. Investigations of fraternal twins, however, produced an average correlation of .50, a moderately high positive correlation. Note the substantial difference of .32. To show that genetic factors are more important than environmental factors, Jensen compared identical twins reared together with those reared apart. The correlation for those reared together was .89, and for those reared apart it was .78, a difference of .11. Jensen argued that if environmental factors were more important than genetic factors, siblings reared apart, who experienced different environments, should have IQs that differed more than .11. Jensen places heredity's influence on intelligence at about 80 percent. To read further about the role of heredity in intelligence, turn to Sociocultural Worlds.

Sociocultural Worlds

The Bell Curve Controversy

In *The Bell Curve: Intelligence and Class Structure in Modern Life,* Richard Hernstein and Charles Murray (1994) argued that America is rapidly evolving a huge underclass of intellectually deprived individuals whose cognitive abilities will never match the future needs of most employers. The authors believe that this underclass, a large proportion of which is African American, may be doomed by their shortcomings to welfare dependency, poverty, crime, and lives void of any hope of ever reaching the American dream.

Hernstein and Murray believe that IQ can be quantitatively measured and that IQ test scores vary across ethnic groups. They point out that in the United States, Asian Americans score several points higher than Whites, while African Americans score about 15 points lower than Whites. They also argue that these IQ differences are at least partly due to heredity. The authors say that government money spent on education programs such as Project Head Start is wasted, helping only the government's bloated bureaucracy.

Why do Hernstein and Murray call their book *The Bell Curve?* The term *bell curve* refers to the shape of a normal distribution graph (discussed earlier in this chapter), which looks like a bell, bulging in the middle and thinning out at the edges. The normal distribution graph is used to represent large numbers of people who are sorted according to some shared characteristic, such as weight, exposure to asbestos, taste in clothes, or IQ.

Hernstein and Murray often refer to bell curves to make a point: that predictions about any individual based exclusively on the person's IQ are virtually useless. It is only when weak

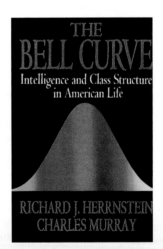

correlations between intelligence and job success are applied to large groups of people that they have predictive value. Within such large groups, say Hernstein and Murray, the pervasive influence of IQ on human society becomes apparent (Browne, 1994).

Significant criticisms have been leveled at *The Bell Curve.* Experts on intelligence generally agree with Hernstein and Murray that African Americans score lower than Whites on IQ tests. However, many of these experts raise serious questions about the ability of IQ tests to accurately measure a person's intelligence. Among the criticisms of IQ tests is that the tests are culturally biased against African Americans and Latinos. In 1971, the Supreme Court endorsed such criticisms and ruled that tests of general intelligence, in contrast to tests that solely measure fitness for a particular job, are discriminatory and cannot be administered as a condition of employment.

A final criticism is that most investigations of heredity and environment do not include environments that differ radically. Thus, it is not surprising that many genetic studies show environment to be a fairly weak influence (Fraser, 1995).

Today, most researchers agree that genetics do not determine intelligence to the extent Jensen envisioned (Ceci, 1996). For most people, this means that modifying their environment can change their IQ scores considerably (Campbell & Ramey, 1993). It also means that programs designed to enrich a person's environment can have a considerable impact, improving school achievement and the acquisition of skills needed for employability. While genetic endowment may always influence a person's intellectual ability, the environmental influences and opportunities we provide children and adults do make a difference.

Keep in mind, though, that environmental influences are complex (Neisser & others, 1996). Growing up with all the "advantages," for example, does not necessarily guarantee success. Children from wealthy families may have easy access to excellent schools, books, travel, and tutoring, but they may take such opportunities for granted and fail to develop the motivation to learn and to achieve. In the same way, "poor" or "disadvantaged" does not automatically equal "doomed."

Cultural and Ethnic Comparisons.   In the United States, children from African American and Latino families score below children from White families on standardized intelligence tests. On the average, African American schoolchildren score 10 to 15 points lower on standardized intelligence tests than White schoolchildren do (Anastasi, 1988). We are talking about average scores, though. Estimates also indicate that 15 to 25 percent of all African American schoolchildren score higher than half of all White schoolchildren, and many Whites score lower than most African Americans do. This is because the distributions of the scores for African Americans and Whites overlap.

How extensively are ethnic differences in intelligence influenced by heredity and environment? The evidence in support of a genetic interpretation is suspect. For example, as African Americans have gained social, economic, and educational opportunities, the gap between African American and White children on standardized intelligence tests has begun to narrow. When children from disadvantaged African American families are adopted into more advantaged middle-class families, their scores on intelligence tests more closely resemble national averages for middle-class children than averages for lower-class children (Scarr, 1991). This comparison also presumes the acceptance of the definition of intelligence used for standardized intelligence tests. If intelligence is measured in a manner inconsistent with a child's own culture, the child is likely to have a lower score.

Culture, Intelligence, and Adaptation.   People adapt to their environment, and what's appropriate in one environment night not be appropriate in another. As mentioned earlier in the chapter, intelligence is expressed differently in different cultures. In one study, the researcher asked members of the Kpelle in Liberia (located on the western coast of Africa) to sort twenty objects (Glick, 1975). The Kpelle did not sort the objects into the "appropriate" categories the researcher had predicted, such as food in one group, tools in another, and so forth. Instead, they sorted the objects into functional groups, such as a knife with an apple and a potato with a hoe. Surprised by the answers, the researcher asked the Kpelle to explain their reasoning. The Kpelle responded that that was the way a wise person would group things. When the researcher asked how a fool would classify the object, the Kpelle answered that four neat piles of food in one category, four tools in another category, and so on was the "fool's way." The Kpelle were not lacking in intelligence; the researcher lacked an understanding of the Kpelle culture. The Kpelle sorted the items in ways that were adaptive for their culture.

Another example of human adaptability involves spatial ability. One study showed that people who live in hunter-gatherer societies score higher on spatial ability tests than do people from industrialized societies (Berry, 1971). People who must hunt to eat depend on the spatial skills for survival.

Few of us will ever have firsthand experience with hunter-gatherer societies, but many of us know people who are adaptable, savvy, and successful yet do not score correspondingly high on intelligence tests. Canadian cross-cultural psychologist John Berry (1983) has an explanation for this gap between intelligence exhibited in one's own culture and intelligence displayed in a formal testing situation. He describes people as being embedded in four levels of environmental contexts. Level 1, the ecological context, is an individual's natural habitat. Level 2, the experiential context, is the pattern of recurring experiences from which the individual regularly learns. Level 3, the performance context, is the limited set of circumstances in which the individual's natural behavior is observed. Level 4, the experimental context, is the set of environmental circumstances under which test scores are actually generated (Berry's model is presented in figure 7.12).

When the experimental context differs considerably from the ecological or experiential context, Berry says, the individuals being tested are at a disadvantage. Presumably, the greater the difference, the greater the disadvantage. However, relations among contexts change. If an individual has been given the same test previously, some of the gap between the experiential and experimental contexts closes, resulting in higher test scores.

Cultural Bias and Culture-Fair Tests. Many of the early intelligence tests were culturally biased, favoring people from urban rather than rural environments, middle-class rather than lower-class people, and White rather than African Americans (Miller-Jones, 1989). For example, a question on an early test asked what should be done if you find a 3-year-old child in the street. The correct answer was "Call the police"; however, children from inner-city families who perceive the police as adversaries are unlikely to choose this answer. Similarly, children from rural areas might not choose this answer if there is no police force nearby. Such questions clearly do not measure the knowledge necessary to adapt to one's environment or to be "intelligent" in an inner-city neighborhood or in rural America (Scarr, 1984). Also, members of minority groups often do not speak English or might speak nonstandard English. Consequently, they may be at a disadvantage in trying to understand verbal questions framed in standard English, even if the content of the test is appropriate.

Cultures also vary in the way they define intelligence. Most European Americans, for example, think of intelligence in terms of technical skills, but people in Kenya consider responsible participation in family and social life an integral part of intelligence. Similarly, an intelligent person in Uganda is someone who knows what to do and then follows through with appropriate action. Intelligence to the Iatmul people of Papua, New Guinea, involves the ability to remember the names of 10,000 to 20,000 clans, and the islanders in the widely dispersed Caroline Islands incorporate the talent of navigating by the stars into their definition of intelligence.

An example of possible cultural bias in intelligence tests can be seen in the case study of Gregory Ochoa. When Gregory was a high school student, he and his classmates took

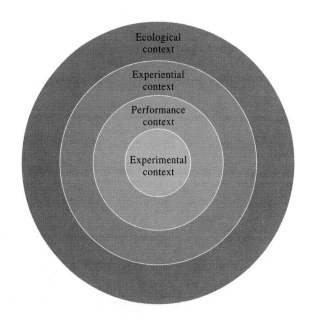

$\mathcal{F}$IGURE 7.12

Berry's Model of the Contexts of Intelligence

In this model of the intelligence, there is much more to consider than the actual context in which a test is being administered (the experimental context). In addition, it is also important to consider three other contextual levels—the performance context, experiential context, and ecological context.

an IQ test. When Gregory looked at the test questions, he understood only a few words, because he did not speak English very well and spoke Spanish at home. Several weeks later, Gregory was placed in a special class for students with mental retardation. Many of the students in the class, it turns out, had last names such as Ramirez and Gonzales. Gregory lost interest in school, dropped out, and eventually joined the Navy. In the Navy, Gregory took high school courses and earned enough credits to attend college later. He graduated from San Jose City College as an honors student, continued his education, and became a professor of social work at the University of Washington in Seattle.

As a result of such cases, researchers have tried to develop tests that accurately reflect a person's intelligence. **Culture-fair tests** *are intelligence tests that are intended not to be culturally biased.* Two types of culture-fair tests have been devised. The first includes questions that are familiar to people from all socioeconomic and ethnic backgrounds. For example, a child might be asked how a bird and a dog are different, on the assumption that virtually all children are familiar with birds and dogs. The second type of culture-fair test excludes all verbal questions. Figure 7.13 shows a sample question from the Raven Progressive Matrices Test. Even though such tests are designed to be culture-fair, people with more education still score higher on them than those with less education do.

One test that takes into account the socioeconomic background of children is the SOMPA, which stands for System of Multicultural Pluralistic Assessment (Mercer & Lewis, 1978). This test can be given to children from 5 to 11 years of age and was especially designed for children from low-income families. Instead of relying on a single test, SOMPA is based on information from four areas of a child's life: (1) verbal and nonverbal intelligence, assessed by the WISC-R; (2) social and economic background, obtained through a 1-hour parent interview; (3) social adjustment to school, determined through a questionnaire that parents complete; and (4) physical health, assessed by a medical examination.

Most researchers agree that traditional intelligence tests are probably culturally biased. However, efforts to develop culture-fair tests so far have yielded unsatisfactory results. The construction of culture-fair tests does not guarantee culture-fairness, but it does attempt to minimize errors derived from differences in cultural contexts.

culture-fair tests

Intelligence tests that are intended to not be culturally biased.

"YOU CAN'T BUILD A HUT, YOU DON'T KNOW HOW TO FIND EDIBLE ROOTS AND YOU KNOW NOTHING ABOUT PREDICTING THE WEATHER. IN OTHER WORDS, YOU DO TERRIBLY ON OUR I.Q. TEST."

© 1994 by Sidney Harris—"You Want Proof? . . ." W. H. Freeman and Company

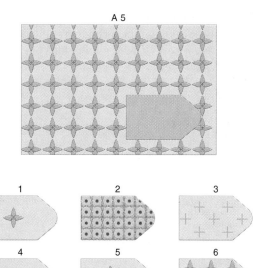

FIGURE 7.13

Sample Item from the Raven Progressive Matrices Test

Psychologists present a matrix arrangement of symbols, such as the one at the top of this figure, and ask the person to be tested to complete the matrix by selecting the appropriate missing symbol from a group of symbols. *Figure A5 from the Raven Standard Progressive Matrices. Copyright © J. C. Raven Limited. Reprinted by permission.*

The Use and Misuse of Intelligence Tests

Psychological tests are tools. Like all tools, their effectiveness depends on the knowledge, skill, and integrity of the user. A hammer can be used to build a beautiful kitchen cabinet or it can be used as a weapon of assault. Like a hammer, psychological tests can be used for positive purposes or they can be badly abused. It is important for both the test constructor and the test examiner to be familiar with the current state of scientific knowledge about intelligence and intelligence tests.

Even though they have limitations, tests of intelligence are among psychology's most widely used tools. To be effective, though, intelligence tests must be viewed realistically. They should not be thought of as unchanging indicators of intelligence. They should be used in conjunction with other information about an individual, not relied on as the sole indicator of intelligence. For example, an intelligence test should not solely determine whether a child is placed in a special education or gifted class. The child's developmental history, medical background, performance in school, social competencies, and family experiences should be taken into account too.

The single number provided by many IQ tests can easily lead to stereotypes and expectations about an individual. Many people do not know how to interpret the results of intelligence tests and sweeping generalizations are too often made on the basis of an IQ score. For example, imagine that you are a teacher in the teacher's lounge the day after school has started in the fall. You mention a student—Johnny Jones—and a fellow teacher remarks that she had Johnny in class last year; she comments that he was a real dunce and points out that his IQ is 78. You cannot help but remember this information, and it might lead you to think that Johnny Jones is not very bright so it is useless to spend much time teaching him. In this way, IQ scores are misused and stereotypes are formed (Rosenthal & Jacobsen, 1968).

Ability tests can help a teacher divide children into homogeneous groups of children who function at roughly the same level in math or reading so they can be taught the same concepts together. However, when children are placed in tracks, such as "advanced," "intermediate," and "low," extreme caution needs to be taken. Periodic assessment of the groups is needed, especially with the "low" group. Ability tests measure *current* performance, and maturational changes or enriched environmental experiences may advance a child's intelligence, requiring that he or she be moved to a higher group.

Despite their limitations, when used judiciously by a competent examiner, intelligence tests provide valuable information about individuals. There are not many alternatives to these tests. Subjective judgments about individuals simply reintroduce the bias the tests were designed to eliminate.

In this chapter, we have discussed many facets of thinking, language, and intelligence, including some ideas about how children's language develops and the nature of children's intelligence. In the next chapter, we will turn our attention exclusively to how we develop as human beings.

eview

Intelligence

Intelligence consists of verbal ability, problem-solving skills, and the ability to learn from and adapt to the experiences of everyday life. In the study of intelligence, extensive attention is given to individual differences and the assessment of intelligence. The way intelligence is expressed in behavior may vary from one culture to another.

Psychologists debate whether intelligence is a general ability or a number of specific abilities. Spearman's two-factor theory and Thurstone's multiple-factor theory state that a number of specific factors are involved. Sternberg's triarchic theory states that intelligence consists of three factors: componential, experiential, and contextual. Gardner proposed that there are seven factors in intelligence.

Three important criteria for tests are reliability, validity, and standardization. Reliability is whether a test produces consistent results; two types are test-retest reliability and inter-rater reliability. Validity is the extent to which a test measures what it is intended to measure. Two kinds of validity are content and criterion. Standardization involves uniform procedures for administering and scoring a test, as well as norms.

Binet developed the first intelligence test and the concept of mental age; Stern developed the concept of IQ. The Binet has been standardized and revised a number of times. The many revisions are called the Stanford-Binet tests. The test approximates a normal distribution. Besides the Stanford-Binet, the most widely used intelligence tests are the Wechsler scales. They include the WAIS-R, WISC-R, and WPPSI. These tests provide an overall IQ, verbal and performance IQs, and information about 11 subscales.

An individual with mental retardation has a low IQ, usually below 70 on a traditional IQ test, and has difficulty adapting to everyday life. There are several classifications of mental retardation. The two main types of retardation are organic and cultural-familial. A learning difference negatively influences the development of specific academic skills that does not reflect overall intellectual ability. Dyslexia is one kind of learning difference. A gifted individual has above-average intelligence (an IQ of 120 or more) and/or superior talent for something. Gifted disadvantaged children are of special concern.

In the late 1960s, Jensen argued that intelligence is approximately 80 percent heredi-

tary and that genetic differences exist in the average intelligence of ethnic groups and social classes. Intelligence is influenced by heredity, but not as strongly as Jensen believed. The environments we provide children and adults make a difference. There are cultural and ethnic differences on intelligence tests, but the evidence suggests they are not genetically based. In recent decades, the gap between African Americans and Whites on intelligence test scores has diminished as African Americans have experienced more socioeconomic opportunities. To understand intelligence within a given culture, the adaptive requirements of the culture must be known. Early intelligence tests favored White, middle-class, urban individuals. Current tests try to reduce this bias. Culture-fair tests are an alternative to traditional tests; most psychologists believe they cannot completely replace the traditional tests.

Despite their limitations, when used by a judicious examiner, intelligence tests are valuable tools for determining individual differences in intelligence. The tests should be used in conjunction with other information about the individual. IQ scores can produce unfortunate stereotypes and expectations about intelligence.

Overview

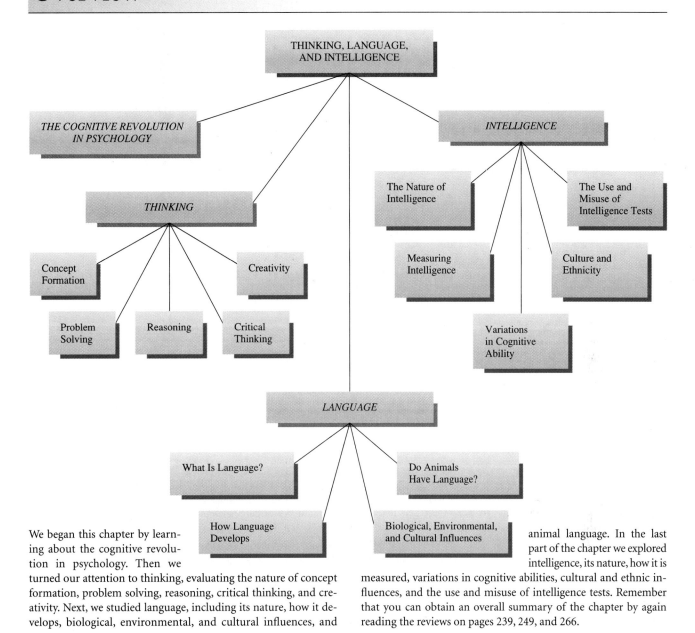

THINKING, LANGUAGE, AND INTELLIGENCE

THE COGNITIVE REVOLUTION IN PSYCHOLOGY

INTELLIGENCE

THINKING

The Nature of Intelligence

The Use and Misuse of Intelligence Tests

Concept Formation

Creativity

Measuring Intelligence

Culture and Ethnicity

Problem Solving

Reasoning

Critical Thinking

Variations in Cognitive Ability

LANGUAGE

What Is Language?

Do Animals Have Language?

How Language Develops

Biological, Environmental, and Cultural Influences

We began this chapter by learning about the cognitive revolution in psychology. Then we turned our attention to thinking, evaluating the nature of concept formation, problem solving, reasoning, critical thinking, and creativity. Next, we studied language, including its nature, how it develops, biological, environmental, and cultural influences, and animal language. In the last part of the chapter we explored intelligence, its nature, how it is measured, variations in cognitive abilities, cultural and ethnic influences, and the use and misuse of intelligence tests. Remember that you can obtain an overall summary of the chapter by again reading the reviews on pages 239, 249, and 266.

Key Terms

artificial intelligence (AI) 227
expert systems 227
concepts 228
problem solving 230
algorithms 231
heuristics 231
learning set 232
functional fixedness 232
availability heuristic 233

representativeness heuristic 233
reasoning 233
inductive reasoning 233
analogy 234
deductive reasoning 234
critical thinking 235
inference 235
confirmation bias 236
belief perseverance effect 236

hindsight bias 236
creativity 237
convergent thinking 238
divergent thinking 239
language 240
infinite generativity 240
phonology 240
morphology 241
syntax 241
semantics 241

holophrase hypothesis 241
telegraphic speech 242
motherese 243
linguistic relativity hypothesis 245
bilingual education 246
individual differences 250
intelligence 250
mental age (MA) 250
intelligence quotient (IQ) 250

Solution to Nine-Dot Problem

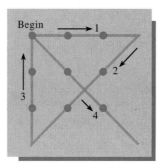

Thinking It Over

Exercises in . . .

. . . Critical Thinking

Review the list of critical thinking pitfalls described on page 000. Try to come up with some personal examples that illustrate as many of the pitfalls as you can. Keep these personal examples in mind as you plan how to become a better critical thinker.

. . . Creative Thinking

The hallmark of a good creative thinker is being able to create images, symbols, or comparisons that help others understand their own experiences. See if you can generate vivid images and comparisons that help illustrate your frame of mind by keeping track of how you are feeling as the day progresses. For example, when you get up, do you feel like an energetic 3-year-old ready to play or like a zombie drained of life forces? Compile a list of ten comparisons or images that show your creativity.

. . . Active Learning

Make plans with a classmate to visit a day-care center. Contact the director of the center and say that you are taking a psychology class and want to spend an hour or two observing children with regard to language development. Record examples you observe of the different stages of language development described in this chapter. Also, make some notes about how rich or impoverished the language environment of the children is. Base your judgments of the language environment on Naomi Baron's recommendations, which are described in the Applications box on page 244.

. . . Reflective Learning

Now that you have read about how psychologists view intelligence, do a candid evaluation of how important it is to you to be thought of as intelligent by others. Also, reflect on whether your ideas about intelligence have changed as a result of reading this chapter. Further, do you want to know your IQ if you don't already know it? If you do know it, do you wish you did not?

Resources for Psychology and Improving Humankind

Association for Children and Adults with Learning Disabilities (ACLD)

4156 Library Road
Pittsburgh, PA 15234
412-341-1515

This organization provides free information and referrals to anyone. It publishes a newsletter, *ACLD Newsbriefs,* and also distributes books.

Canadian Down Syndrome Society/Société canadienne de syndrome de Down

12837 76th Avenue, #206
Surrey, BC V3W 2V3
604-599-6009

The Society works to improve the lives of Canadians with Down syndrome and to educate the public about Down syndrome.

***Choosing Books for Kids* (1986)**

by Joanne Oppenheim, Barbara Brenner, and Betty Boegehold
New York: Ballantine

This is an excellent book on how to choose the right book for the right child at the right time.

Council of Canadians with Disabilities

294 Portage Avenue, #926
Winnipeg, MB R3C 0B9
204-947-0303

This national advocacy organization for people with disabilities publishes the newsletter *A Voice of Our Own.*

***Growing Up With Language* (1992)**

by Naomi Baron
Reading, MA: Addison-Wesley

This book does an excellent job of conveying the appropriate role of parents in children's language development. The author focuses on three representative children and their families, exploring how children put their first words together, how they struggle to understand meaning, and how they come to use language as a creative tool. She shows parents how their own attitudes about language are extremely important in the child's language development.

***The Ideal Problem Solver* (1984)**

by John Bransford and Barry Stein
New York: W. H. Freeman

This book discusses hundreds of fascinating problems and ways to solve them effectively.

Literacy Volunteers of America

5795 Widewaters Parkway
Syracuse, NY 13214
315-445-8000

This group trains and aids individuals and organizations to tutor adults in basic literacy and conversational English. Training materials and services are available.

National Association for Gifted Children

1155 15th Street
Washington, DC 20005
202-785-4268

This is an association of academicians, educators, and librarians. The organization's goal is to improve the education of gifted children. They provide periodic reports on the education of gifted children and publish the journal *Gifted Children Quarterly.*

National Down Syndrome Congress

1800 Dempster Street
Park Ridge IL 60068-1146
800-232-NDSC

This organization promotes the well-being of individuals with Down syndrome. They publish a newsletter and maintain a library of books about mental retardation.

National Organization on Disability

910 Sixteenth Street, NW
Washington, DC 20006
202-293-5960

This organization acts as a clearinghouse for information about many forms of disability, including mental retardation.

***The New York Times Parents' Guide to the Best Books for Children* (1991)**

by Eden Lipson
New York: Random House

This revised and updated edition includes book recommendations for children of all ages. More than 1,700 titles are evaluated. The six sections are organized according to reading level: Wordless, picture, story, early reading, middle reading, and young adult. Each entry provides the essential information needed to become acquainted with the book's content and find it in a local library or bookstore. More than 55 indexes make it easy to match the right book to the right child. This is an extensive, thorough, competent guide to selecting children's books.

Odyssey: A Curriculum for Thinking (1986)

by M. J. Adams (Coordinator)
Watertown, MA: Mastery Education Corporation

This comprehensive program attempts to improve adolescent decision making in a number of circumstances. The program consists of about a hundred 45-minute lessons, and a teacher's manual describes topics such as verbal reasoning, problem solving, decision making, and inventive thinking.

The Orton Dyslexia Society, Inc.

80 Fifth Avenue, Room 903
New York, NY 10011
212-691-1930

This nonprofit organization is concerned with the many children and adults who experience difficulty in learning such skills as speaking, reading, writing, spelling, and mathematics.

Special Olympics International

13150 New York Ave, NW, Suite 500
Washington DC 20005

This international organization is dedicated to sponsoring year-round sports training and athletic competition in a variety of Olympic-type events for mentally retarded children and adults.

Testing and Your Child (1992)

by Virginia McCullough
New York: Plume

Written for parents, this comprehensive guide provides details about 150 of the most common educational, psychological, and medical tests, focusing on everything from intelligence to giftedness to achievement to personality.

Internet Resources

http://ai.iit.nrc.ca/misc.html
Institute for Information Technology provides resources on artificial intelligence.

http://casper.beckman.uiuc.edu/~c-tsai4/cogsci/
Learn about all aspects of cognitive science.

http://www.calstatela.edu/faculty/nthomas/index.htm
A resource on imagination, cognition, and consciousness.

http://www.june29.com/HLP/
The Human Language Page provides comprehensive links to language concerns.

http://cogsci.ucsd.edu/~maglio/completion.html
Participate in a psycholinguistics study on-line.

http://where.com/scott.net/asl/
Explore American Sign Language.

http://www.brain.com/iq/
The BrainTainment Center offers links for IQ testing.

http://www.miracle.com/mensa-international/
Find out if you can join the "top 2% society" for intelligence.

http://thearc.org/welcome.html
Home page for the Association of Retarded Citizens.

http://thearc.org/welcome.html
Explore resources for dyslexia at this site.

8

Human Development

In every child who is born, under no matter what circumstances, and of no matter what parents, the potentiality of the human race is born again.

—JAMES AGEE
American Writer, 20th Century

PREVIEW

As the twenty-first century approaches, children's well-being is one of our most important concerns. Development does not end with childhood, though, and intriguing questions are being raised about how much people can continue to change even when they are old. In this chapter we will explore the following topics: the nature of development, development during the childhood years, adolescence, late adulthood and aging, and death and dying. To begin our discussion of development, we describe the story of Jessica Dubroff, who was a child pilot at just 7 years of age. Jessica's story raises some provocative issues regarding the best way to parent children.

The Story of Jessica Dubroff: Child Pilot

In 1996, Jessica Dubroff began takeoff in a cold rain, piloting her single-engine Cessna airplane. She died when the airplane then nose-dived onto a highway. Seven-year-old Jessica was only 4 feet, 2 inches tall and weighed just 55 pounds. What was she doing flying an airplane? She was attempting to become the youngest person ever to fly across the continent.

Jessica had been propelled on by overzealous parents, by media drawn to a natural human-interest story, and by a Federal Aviation Administration that looked the other way. Jessica's feet did not even reach the rudder pedals. Overnight, in death, Jessica became the poster child of parental and media exploitation. Some thought she had been granted too much freedom and had not been allowed to be a child.

Jessica's parents seemed determined to give their daughter independence from the beginning. She was delivered in a birthing tub without the benefit of a doctor or midwife. Her parents' philosophy was that real life is the best tutor, experience the best preparation for life. As a result, they kept Jessica and her brother (age 9) and sister

Some critics argue that Jessica Dubroff was not allowed to be a child. *Was she given too much freedom and choice? Did her parents act irresponsibly?*

(age 3) at home and did not file a home-schooling plan with local authorities. Jessica had no dolls, only tools. Instead of studying grammar, she did chores and sought what her mother called "mastery." Her parents gave her few, if any, boundaries.

Jessica became interested in flying after her parents gave her an airplane ride for her sixth birthday, only 23 months before her fatal crash. During the media blitz surrounding Jessica's cross-country flight, her father admitted that the flight had been his idea but claimed that he had presented it to Jessica as a choice. He became Jessica's press agent, courting television, radio, and newspapers to publicize her flight.

After the crash, television viewers saw Jessica's mother say that if she had it to do over again, she would do nothing differently. She also commented that she had done everything she could to ensure that Jessica would have freedom and choice. However, the general consensus among child developmentalists is that children should be given freedom and choice *within the bounds of responsibility* (Stengel, 1996).

Jessica's story is rare and tragic, but the dangers of overachieving, of growing up too soon, of intensely focusing on a single activity, often show up in many different ways. The child actor grows up without an education, the tennis star loses touch with childhood friends, the figure skater takes part in a plot to club an opponent. Child athletes might ruin their bodies: ballerinas develop anorexia, teenage football players take steroids. Too many children live overscheduled lives, moving from one lesson to the next. They are being robbed of the time and the variety of experiences they need to develop coping skills to deal with life's realities.

A vicious cycle has been set in motion. Parents who live vicariously through their children produce children who grow up feeling they have missed out on childhood, a time when play and its unstructured freedom should be prominent. Children should be allowed to have a well-rounded life, one that's not focused on achievement in a single domain. ❖

WHAT IS DEVELOPMENT?

Each of us develops partly like all other individuals, partly like some other individuals, and partly like no other individual. Most of the time, our attention is captured by a person's uniqueness—like Madonna's outrageousness, Will Smith's magnetic appeal, or Pete

Sampras's tennis prowess. But psychologists who study life-span development are interested in our shared, as well as our unique, characteristics. As humans, we have all traveled common paths. Each of us—Madonna, Will Smith, Pete Sampras, artist Georgia O'Keeffe, Martin Luther King, Jr., yourself—walked at about 1 year of age, engaged in fantasy play as a young child, sought more independence as an adolescent, and worked at some occupation as a young adult. Each of us, if we live long enough, will experience hearing problems and deaths of family members.

When we speak of **development,** we mean *a pattern of movement or change that begins at conception and continues throughout the life span.* Most development involves growth, although it also consists of decay (as in death). The pattern of change is complex because it is the product of several processes—biological, cognitive, and socioemotional.

Biological, Cognitive, and Socioemotional Processes

Biological processes *involve changes in the individual's physical nature.* Genes inherited from parents, the development of the brain, height and weight gains, changes in motor skills, the hormonal changes of puberty, and cardiovascular decline all reflect the role of biological processes in development.

Cognitive processes *involve changes in the individual's thought, intelligence, and language.* Watching a colorful mobile swinging above the crib, putting together a two-word sentence, memorizing a poem, imagining what it would be like to be a movie star, and solving a crossword puzzle all reflect the role of cognitive processes in development.

Socioemotional processes *involve changes in the individual's relationships with other people, changes in emotions, and changes in personality.* An infant's smile in response to her mother's touch, a young boy's aggressive attack on a playmate, a girl's development of assertiveness, an adolescent's joy at the senior prom, and the affection of an elderly couple all reflect the role of the socioemotional processes in development.

Remember as you read about biological, cognitive, and socioemotional processes that they are intricately interwoven (Santrock, 1999). You will read about how socioemotional processes shape cognitive processes, how cognitive processes promote or restrict socioemotional processes, and how biological processes influence cognitive processes. Although it is helpful to study the different processes in separate sections of the chapter, keep in mind that you are studying the development of an integrated individual with a mind and body that are interdependent (see figure 8.1).

development

The pattern of movement or change that begins at conception and continues through the life span.

biological processes

Processes that involve changes in an individual's physical nature.

cognitive processes

Processes that involve changes in an individual's thought, intelligence, and language.

socioemotional processes

Processes that involve changes in an individual's relationships with other people, changes in emotions, and changes in personality.

$\mathcal{F}$IGURE 8.1

Changes in Development Are the Result of Biological, Cognitive, and Socioemotional Processes

These processes are interwoven as individuals develop.

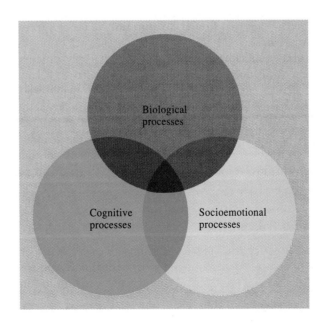

Maturation and Experience (Nature and Nurture)

We can think of development as produced not only by the interplay of biological, cognitive, and socioemotional processes, but also by the interplay of maturation and experience. **Maturation** *is the orderly sequence of changes dictated by each person's genetic blueprint.* Just as a sunflower grows in an orderly way—unless defeated by an unfriendly environment—so does the human grow in an orderly way, according to the maturational view. The range of environments can be vast, but, the maturational approach argues, the genetic blueprint produces commonalities in our growth and development. We walk before we talk, speak one word before two words, grow rapidly in infancy and less so in early childhood, experience a rush of sexual hormones in puberty after a lull in childhood, reach the peak of our physical strength in late adolescence and early adulthood and then decline, and so on. The maturationists acknowledge that extreme environments—those that are psychologically barren or hostile—can depress development, but they believe basic growth tendencies are genetically wired into the human.

By contrast, other psychologists emphasize the importance of experiences in life-span development. Experiences run the gamut from the individual's biological environment (nutrition, medical care, drugs, and physical accidents) to the social environment (family, peers, schools, community, media, and culture).

The debate about whether development is primarily influenced by maturation or by experience has been a part of psychology since its beginning. This debate is often referred to as the **nature/nurture controversy.** Nature *refers to an organism's biological inheritance,* nurture *to environmental experiences. The "nature" proponents claim biological inheritance is the most important influence on development. The "nurture" proponents claim that environmental experiences are the most important.*

Continuity and Discontinuity

Think for a moment about who you are. Did you become this person gradually, like the slow, cumulative growth of a seedling into a giant oak? Or did you experience sudden, distinct changes in your development, the way a caterpillar changes into a butterfly? For the most part, developmental psychologists who emphasize experience have described development as a gradual, continuous process; those who emphasize maturation have described development as a series of distinct stages (see figure 8.2).

The view that stresses **continuity of development** argues that *development involves gradual, cumulative change from conception to death.* A child's first word, while seemingly an abrupt, discrete event, is actually the result of months of growth and practice. Similarly, while puberty might seem to happen overnight, it is actually a gradual process that occurs over several years.

The view that stresses **discontinuity of development** argues that *development involves distinct stages in the life span.* In this view, each of us passes through a sequence of stages that are qualitatively, rather than quantitatively, different. As a caterpillar changes into a butterfly, it does not become more caterpillar; it becomes a different kind of organism. Its development is discontinuous. Similarly, a child who earlier could think only in concrete terms becomes capable of thinking abstractly about the world. This is a qualitative, discontinuous change in development, not a continuous, quantitative change.

In addition to scientific issues like whether development is due mainly to maturation or experience, or is more continuous or discontinuous, the field of life-span development involves applied issues. Among the most important current applied issues are those involving social policy.

Social Policy

Social policy *is a national government's course of action designed to influence the welfare of its citizens.* A current trend is to conduct developmental research that produces knowledge that will lead to wise and effective decision making about social policy (McCall &

$\mathcal{F}$IGURE 8.2

Continuity and Discontinuity in Development

Is human development more like a seedling's gradually growing into a giant oak or a caterpillar's suddenly becoming a butterfly?

others, 1998; Zill, 1996). When more than 20 percent of all children and more than half of all ethnic minority children are being raised in poverty, when children and young adolescents are giving birth, when the use and abuse of drugs is widespread, when the specter of AIDS is present, and when the provision of health care for the elderly is inadequate, our nation needs revised social policy.

If our American way of life fails the child, it fails us all.
—PEARL BUCK, *American author, 20th century*

Among the groups that have worked to improve the lives of the world's children are UNICEF in New York and the Children's Defense Fund in Washington, D.C. Marian Wright Edelman, president of the Children's Defense Fund, has been a tireless advocate of children's rights. Especially troubling to Edelman (1992, 1997) are the indicators of societal neglect that place the United States at or near the bottom of industrialized nations in the treatment of children. Edelman says that parenting and nurturing the next generation of children is our society's most important function and that we need to take it more seriously than we have in the past. Sociocultural Worlds provides some rather stunning comparisons of American children with children in other countries, underscoring the need for improved social policy for children.

Standing up for children is the most important mission in the world. If Rosa Parks can sit down for freedom, you can stand up for children.
—MARIAN WRIGHT EDELMAN, *Lawyer and Humanitarian, 20th century*

Sociocultural Worlds

Caring for Children Around the World

According to the Children's Defense Fund, a nonprofit group that works on behalf of children's rights, the United States does not compare well with other countries when it comes to caring for children. Although we have the resources to care properly for children, we would get an F for performance on many key markers for children's well-being. Consider the following:

- More than 20 percent of all children and more than half of all ethnic minority children are being raised in poverty.
- United States' 1-year-olds have lower immunization rates against polio than 1-year-olds in 14 other countries. Polio immunization rates for non-White infants in the United States rank behind 48 other countries, including Albania, Colombia, and Jamaica.
- The United States' overall infant mortality rate lags behind 18 other countries. Our non-White infant mortality rate ranks 13th compared to other nations' overall rates. An African American child born in inner-city Boston has less chance of surviving the first year of life than does a child born in Panama, North or South Korea, or Uruguay.
- In a study of 8 industrialized nations (the United States, Switzerland, Sweden, Norway, former West Germany, Canada, England, and Australia), the United States had the highest poverty rate.
- The United States has the highest adolescent pregnancy rate of any industrialized Western nation.
- The United States and South Africa are the only industrialized countries that do not provide child care and universal health coverage to families.

- The United States invests a smaller portion of its gross national product (GNP) in child health than do 18 other industrialized nations. It invests a smaller portion of its GNP in education than do 6 other industrialized countries.

Marian Wright Edelman (1995), president of the Children's Defense Fund, condemns our national social policies toward children and argues that the United States needs to devote more attention to caring for its children—too many American children from every socioeconomic and ethnic group are deprived of the opportunity to reach their full potential.

Marian Wright Edelman, president of the Children's Defense Fund (shown here interacting with a young child), has been a tireless advocate of children's rights and has been instrumental in calling attention to the needs of children.

CHILD DEVELOPMENT

Imagine . . . at one time you were an organism floating around in a sea of fluid in your mother's womb. Many special things have taken place in your development since you were born. But as nineteenth-century poet and essayist Samuel Taylor Coleridge remarked, "The history of man for nine months preceding his birth probably is far more interesting and contains more stunning events than all the years that follow."

Prenatal Development

Within a matter of hours after fertilization, a human egg divides, becomes a system of cells, and continues this growth of cells at an astonishing rate. In a mere 9 months, a squalling bundle of energy has its grandmother's nose, its father's eyes, and its mother's abundant hair.

A baby is the most complicated object made by unskilled labor.

—ANONYMOUS

conception (fertilization)
Union of an egg and a sperm.

zygote
A fertilized egg.

The Course of Prenatal Development. *Conception, also called fertilization, occurs when a single sperm cell from the male penetrates the female's ovum (egg). A **zygote** is a fertilized*

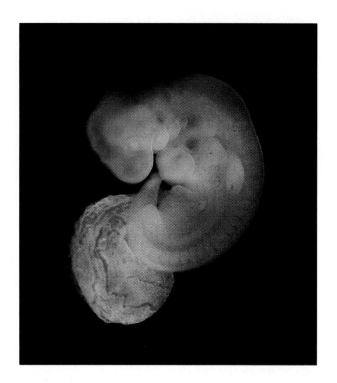

$\mathcal{F}$IGURE 8.3

Embryo at 4 Weeks

At about 4 weeks, an embryo is about 0.2 inch in length. The head, eyes, and ears begin to show. The head and neck are half the body length; the shoulders will be located where the whitish arm buds are attached.

germinal period

The period of prenatal development that takes place in the first 2 weeks after conception.

embryonic period

The period of prenatal development that occurs from 3 to 8 weeks after conception.

fetal period

The prenatal period of development that begins 2 months after conception and lasts for 7 months, on the average.

egg. It receives one-half of its chromosomes from the mother, the other half from the father. The zygote begins as a single cell. The **germinal period** *is the first 2 weeks after conception.* After 1 week and many cell divisions, the zygote is made up of 100 to 150 cells. At the end of 2 weeks, the mass of cells attaches to the uterine wall.

> *What web is this*
> *Or will be, is, and was?*
> —JORGE LUIS BORGES, *Argentinian Poet and Essayist, 20th century*

During the **embryonic period,** *2 to 8 weeks after conception,* some remarkable developments unfold (see figure 8.3). Before most women even know they are pregnant, the rate of cell differentiation intensifies, support systems for the cells form, and organs appear. In the third week, the neural tube that eventually becomes the spinal cord is forming. At about 21 days, eyes being to appear, and by 24 days, the cells of the heart begin to differentiate. During the fourth week, arm and leg buds emerge. At 5 to 8 weeks, arms and legs become more differentiated, the face starts to form, and the intestinal tract appears. All of this is happening in an organism that, by 8 weeks, weighs only $\frac{1}{30}$ ounce and is just over 1.5 inches long (see figure 8.4).

The **fetal period** *begins 2 months after conception and lasts, on the average, for 7 months.* Growth and development continue their dramatic course, and organs mature to the point where life can be sustained outside the womb. At 4 months after conception, the fetus is about 6 inches long and weighs 4 to 7 ounces. Prenatal reflexes become more apparent, and the mother feels the fetus move for the first time (see figure 8.5). At 6 months after conception, the eyes and eyelids are completely formed, a fine layer of hair covers the fetus, the grasping reflex appears, and irregular breathing begins. By 7 to 9 months, the fetus is much longer and weighs considerably more. In addition, the functioning of various organs steps up.

Challenges to Prenatal Development.   As these massive changes take place during prenatal development, some pregnant women tiptoe about in the belief that everything they do has a direct effect on the unborn child. Others behave more casually, assuming their experiences have little impact. The truth lies somewhere between these extremes. Although it floats in a comfortable, well-protected environment, the fetus is not totally immune to the larger environment surrounding the mother. Many substances in this environment can affect the development of the fetus.

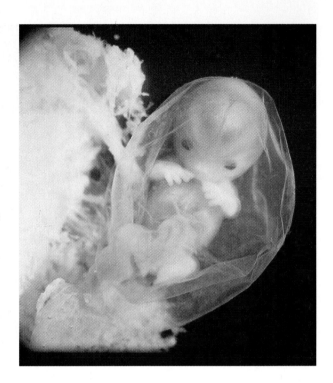

𝓕IGURE 8.4

Embryo at 8 Weeks

At 8 weeks and 4 centimeters (1.6 inches), the developing individual is no longer an embryo, but a fetus. Everything that will be found in the fully developed human being has now been differentiated. The fetal stage is a period of growth and perfection of detail. The heart has been beating for a month, and the muscles have just begun their first exercises. Two of the mother-to-be's menstrual periods have now been skipped. Ideally, at about this time, the mother-to-be goes to a doctor or clinic for prenatal care.

teratogen

(The word comes from the Greek word *tera,* meaning "monster.") Any agent that causes a birth defect.

fetal alcohol syndrome (FAS)

A cluster of abnormalities that appear in the offspring of mothers who drink alcohol heavily during pregnancy.

A **teratogen** *(from the Greek word* tera, *meaning "monster") is any agent that causes a birth defect.* Rarely do specific teratogens, such as drugs, link up with specific birth defects, such as leg malformation. However, one example of this linkage is the drug *thalidomide.* During the late 1950s, several hundred women took thalidomide early in pregnancy to prevent morning sickness and insomnia. Tragically, babies born to these mothers had arms and legs that had not developed beyond stumps.

Heavy drinking by pregnant women can also be devastating to offspring. **Fetal alcohol syndrome (FAS)** *is a cluster of abnormalities that appear in the offspring of mothers*

𝓕IGURE 8.5

Fetus at 4½ Months

At 4½ months, the fetus is about 18 cm (just over 7 inches). When the thumb comes close to the mouth, the head may turn, and lips and tongue begin their sucking motions—a reflex for survival.

She has her father's eyes and her mother's smile. She also has AIDS.

Reduce your risk of getting or giving the AIDS virus.

DON'T SHOOT DRUGS.
IF YOU MUST SHOOT DRUGS, DON'T SHARE YOUR WORKS.
HAVE SAFE SEX OR NONE AT ALL.
IF YOU THINK YOU HAVE THE AIDS VIRUS, DON'T GET PREGNANT.
IT'S YOUR CHOICE. IT COULD BE YOUR CHILD'S LIFE.

EarthTide, Inc. Baltimore
Call: (301)-225-9635

who drink alcohol heavily during pregnancy. The abnormalities include facial deformities and defective limbs, face, and heart. Most of these children are below average in intelligence, and some are mentally retarded. Even moderate drinking during pregnancy is associated with developmental deficits. In one study, infants whose mothers drank moderately during pregnancy (for example, one to two drinks a day) were less attentive and alert, with the effects still present at 4 years of age (Streissguth & others, 1984).

With the increased use of cocaine in the United States, there is growing concern about its effects on the embryos, fetuses, and infants of pregnant cocaine users (Lester, Freier, & LaGasse, 1995). The most consistent finding is that infants born to cocaine abusers have reduced birthweight and length (Chasnoff & others, 1989). There are increased frequencies of congenital abnormalities in the offspring of cocaine users during pregnancy. However, other factors in the drug addict's lifestyle, such as malnutrition and other substance abuse, may be responsible for the congenital abnormalities. For example, cocaine users are more likely to smoke cigarettes and marijuana, drink alcohol, and take amphetamines than are cocaine nonusers. Researchers struggle to distinguish these potential influences from the effects of cocaine itself. Obtaining valid information about the frequency and type of drug use by mothers is also complicated, since many mothers fear prosecution or loss of custody because of their drug use.

The importance of a woman's health to the health of her offspring is clearly exemplified when the mother has human immunodeficiency virus (HIV), the virus that causes acquired immunodeficiency syndrome, or AIDS. As the number of women infected with HIV increases, more infants are born infected with HIV (Cohen & others, 1996).

AIDS is currently the sixth leading cause of death for children 1 to 4 years of age in the United States. From 15 to 30 percent of infants born to HIV-infected women are infected with the virus. This results in approximately 1,500 to 2,000 children born with HIV annually in the United States.

Developmentalists don't just let complications like AIDS, cocaine, and other drugs go uncountered. A number of programs have been developed to intervene in lives of these infants, many of whom are born prematurely. For example, Tiffany Field (1995) has

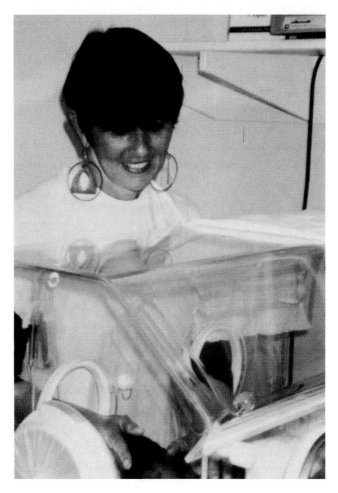

Shown here is Dr. Tiffany Field massaging a newborn infant. Dr. Field's
research has clearly demonstrated the power of massage in improving the
developmental outcome of at-risk infants.

shown that regular massage of preterm babies has a number of positive outcomes such
as weight gain and increased alertness. Let's now turn our attention to further aspects of
development after birth.

Physical Development

A newborn is not an empty-headed organism. It comes into the world already equipped
with several genetically "wired" reflexes. For example, a newborn has no fear of water,
naturally holding its breath and contracting its throat to keep water out. Some of the
reflexes we possess as newborns persist throughout our lives—coughing, blinking, and
yawning, for example. Others disappear in the months following birth as higher brain
functions mature and we develop voluntary control over many behaviors. One of the most
dramatic reflexes of a newborn is the Moro reflex. When a newborn is roughly handled,
hears a loud noise, sees a bright light, or feels a sudden change of position, it becomes
startled, arches its back, and throws back its head. At the same time, the newborn flings
its arms and legs out and then rapidly closes them to the center of its body as if falling.
The Moro reflex disappears by 3 to 4 months of age.

The infant's physical development in the first 2 years of life is dramatic. At birth, the
newborn (neonate) has a gigantic head (relative to the rest of the body) that flops around
uncontrollably. In the span of 12 months, the infant becomes capable of sitting anywhere,
standing, stooping, climbing, and often walking.

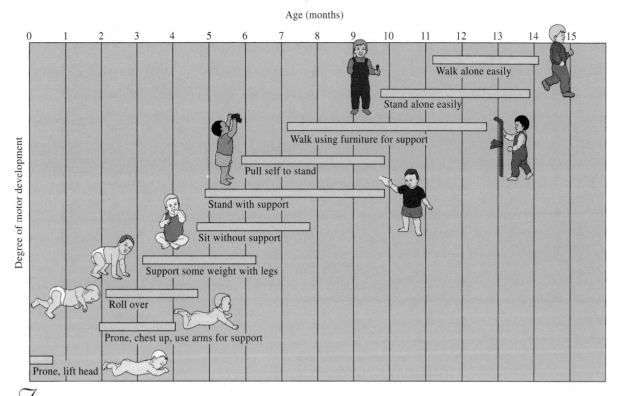

Age (months)

Degree of motor development

Walk alone easily

Stand alone easily

Walk using furniture for support

Pull self to stand

Stand with support

Sit without support

Support some weight with legs

Roll over

Prone, chest up, use arms for support

Prone, lift head

$\mathcal{F}$IGURE 8.6

Developmental Accomplishments in Gross Motor Skills During the First 15 Months

Figure 8.6 shows the average ages at which a number of motor milestones occur in infancy. During the second year, growth decelerates, but rapid increases in such activities as running and climbing take place.

A baby is an angel whose wings decrease as his legs increase.

—FRENCH PROVERB

As an infant walks, talks, runs, shakes a rattle, smiles, and frowns, changes in its brain are occurring. Consider that the infant began life as a single cell and 9 months later was born with a brain and nervous system that contained approximately 100 billion nerve cells. Indeed, at birth the infant has virtually all of the nerve cells (neurons) it is going to have in its entire life. However, at birth and in early infancy, the connectedness of these neurons is impoverished. As the infant ages from birth to 2 years, the interconnection of neurons increases dramatically as the dendrites (the receiving parts) of the neurons branch out (see figure 8.7).

Children's physical growth begins to slow down after infancy, otherwise we would be a species of giants. As they move through the preschool years, children are beginning to be able to make their bodies do what they want them to do. This gives them a greater sense of self-control. In the elementary school years, motor development becomes smoother and more coordinated.

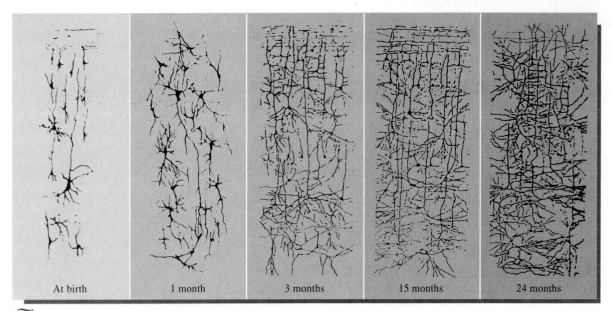

$\mathcal{F}$IGURE 8.7

The Development of Dendritic Spreading

Note the increase in connectedness between neurons over the course of the first 2 years of life.

| At birth | 1 month | 3 months | 15 months | 24 months |

Cognitive Development

Although physical development slows noticeably after the age of 2, children's minds continue to change and develop throughout childhood. The person most responsible for our understanding of children's cognitive development is the famous Swiss developmental psychologist Jean Piaget, whose work we turn to next.

Piaget's Theory. Piaget (1896–1980) stressed that children do not just passively receive information from their environment; they actively construct their own cognitive world. Two processes underlie a child's mental construction of the world—organization and adaptation. To make sense of our world, we organize our experiences. For example, we

eview

What Development Is, Prenatal Development, and Children's Physical Development

Development is a pattern of movement or change that occurs throughout the life span. Development involves the interplay of biological, cognitive, and socioemotional processes. Development is influenced by the interaction of maturation and experience. The debate over the role of maturation and experience is another version of the nature-nurture controversy. Development may be described as either continuous (gradual, cumulative change) or discontinuous (an abrupt sequence of stages). Whether development is determined more by earlier experiences or

more by later experiences is a hotly debated issue. Social policy is a national government's course of action designed to influence the welfare of its citizens. Improved social policy related to children is needed to help all children reach their potential. Social policy issues also involve the elderly and such matters as quality of health care and its affordability.

Conception occurs when a sperm unites with an ovum. The fertilized egg is a zygote. The first 2 weeks after conception is the germinal period, 2 to 8 weeks is the embryonic period, and 2 to 9 months

is the fetal period. Teratogens are agents that cause birth defects. Drugs and maternal diseases also cause health complications for newborns.

An infant comes into the world equipped with a number of reflexes. Physical development in the first 2 years is dramatic, with infants achieving a number of milestones. In the childhood years physical development slows down, although motor development becomes smoother and more coordinated.

Jean Piaget, the famous Swiss developmental psychologist, changed the way we think about the development of children's minds. For Piaget, a child's mental development is a continuous creation of increasingly complex forms.

assimilation

The incorporation of new information into existing knowledge.

accommodation

Changing behavior in order to adjust to new information.

sensorimotor thought

The first Piagetian stage, lasting from birth to about 2 years of age. In this stage, infants construct an understanding of the world by coordinating sensory experiences (such as seeing and hearing) with physical (motor) actions.

object permanence

The Piagetian term for one of an infant's most important accomplishments: understanding that objects and events continue to exist even when they cannot directly be seen, heard, or touched.

separate important ideas from less important ones. We connect one idea to another. However, not only do we organize our observations and experiences, but we also *adapt* our thinking to include those new ideas. Piaget (1960) believed we adapt in two ways: through assimilation and accommodation.

Assimilation *occurs when individuals incorporate new information into their existing knowledge.* **Accommodation** *occurs when individuals make some changes in behavior to adjust to new information.* Imagine giving a hammer and some nails to a 5-year-old and then asking her to hang a picture on the wall. She has never used a hammer, but from experience and observation she realizes that a hammer is an object to be held, that to hit the nail she must swing the hammer by the handle, and that she probably will need to swing it a number of times. Recognizing each of these things, she fits her behavior into information she already has (assimilation). However, the hammer is heavy, so she holds it near the top. She swings too hard and the nail bends, so she adjusts the pressure of her strikes. These adjustments reveal her ability to alter slightly her conception of the world (accommodation).

Piaget thought that even young infants are capable of assimilation and accommodation. Newborns reflexively suck everything that touches their lips (assimilation), but after several months they come to a new understanding of their world. Some objects, such as fingers and the mother's breast, can be sucked but others, such as fuzzy blankets, won't be as satisfying (accommodation).

Piaget also believed that we go through four stages in understanding the world. Each of the stages is age related and consists of distinct ways of thinking. Remember, it is the *different way* of understanding the world that makes one stage more advanced than another; knowing *more* information does not make the child's thinking more advanced, in Piaget's view. This is what Piaget meant when he said that the child's cognition is *qualitatively* different in one stage compared to another. Let's turn now to Piaget's first three stages: sensorimotor thought, preoperational thought, and concrete operational thought.

Sensorimotor Thought. **Sensorimotor thought** *is the first Piagetian stage of development, lasting from birth to about 2 years of age, corresponding to the period of infancy. In this stage, the infant constructs an understanding of the world by coordinating sensory experiences (such as seeing and hearing) with physical (motor) actions—hence the term* sensorimotor. At the beginning of this stage, the newborn engages with its environment with little more than reflexive patterns; at the end of the stage, the 2-year-old has complex sensorimotor patterns and is beginning to use primitive symbols in thinking.

We live in a world of objects. Imagine yourself as a 5-month-old infant and how you might experience the world. You are in a playpen filled with toys. One of the toys, a monkey, falls out of your grasp and rolls behind a larger toy, a hippopotamus. Would you know the monkey is behind the hippopotamus, or would you think it is completely gone? Piaget believed that "out of sight" literally was "out of mind" for young infants; at 5 months of age, then, you would not have reached for the monkey when it fell behind the hippopotamus. By 8 months of age, though, the infant begins to understand that out of sight is not out of mind; at this point, you probably would have reached behind the hippopotamus to search for the monkey, coordinating your senses with your movements.

Object permanence *is Piaget's term for one of the infant's most important accomplishments: understanding that objects and events continue to exist even when they cannot directly be seen, heard, or touched.* The most common way to study object permanence is to show an infant an interesting toy and then cover the toy with a sheet or a blanket. If infants understand that the toy still exists, they try to uncover it (see figure 8.8). Object permanence continues to develop throughout the sensorimotor period. For example, when infants initially understand that objects exist even when out of sight, they look for them only briefly. By the end of the sensorimotor period, infants engage in a more prolonged and sophisticated search for an object.

Preoperational Thought. Possibly because young children are not very concerned about reality, their drawings are fanciful and inventive. Suns are blue, skies are yellow, and cars

---

Child Development

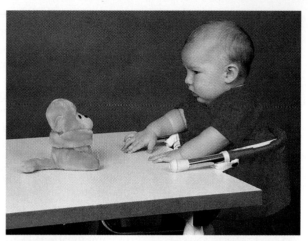

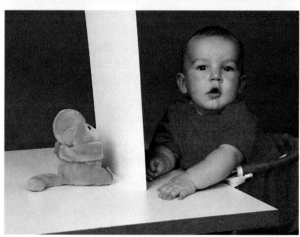

$\mathcal{F}$IGURE 8.8

Object Permanence

Piaget thought that object permanence was one of infancy's landmark cognitive accomplishments. For this 5-month-old boy, "out-of-sight" is literally out of mind. The infant looks at the toy monkey *(top)*, but, when his view of the toy is blocked *(bottom)*, he does not search for it. Eventually, he will search for the hidden toy monkey, reflecting the presence of object permanence.

float on clouds in their symbolic, imaginative world. In the elementary school years, the child's drawings become more realistic, neat, and precise. Suns are yellow, skies are blue, and cars travel on roads.

Preschool children begin to represent their world with words, images, and drawings. Symbolic thoughts go beyond simple connections of sensorimotor information and physical action. While preschool children can symbolically represent the world, they still cannot perform operations. **Operations,** *in Piaget's theory, are mental representations that are reversible.* Preschool children have difficulty understanding that reversing an action brings about the original conditions from which the action began. This sounds rather complicated, but stay with us. The following two examples will help you to understand Piaget's concept of reversibility. The preschool child may know that $4 + 2 = 6$ but not understand that the reverse, $6 - 2 = 4$, is true. Or let's say a preschooler walks to his friend's house each day but always gets a ride home. If you asked him to walk home one day he would probably reply that he didn't know the way since he had never walked home before. **Preoperational thought** *is the term Piaget gave to the 2- to 7-year-old child's understanding of the world. Children at this stage of reasoning cannot understand such logical operations as the reversibility of mental representations.*

A well-known test of whether a child can think "operationally" is to present a child with two identical beakers, A and B, filled with liquid to the same height (see figure 8.9). Next to them is a third beaker, C. Beaker C is tall and thin, while beakers A and B are wide and short. The liquid is poured from B into C, and the child is asked whether the amounts in A and C are the same. The 4-year-old child invariably says that the amount of liquid in the tall, thin beaker (C) is greater than that in the short, fat beaker (A). The 8-year-old child consistently says the amounts are the same. The 4-year-old child, a preoperational thinker, cannot mentally reverse the pouring action; that is, she cannot imagine the liquid going back from container C to container B. Piaget said that children such

operations

In Piaget's theory, mental representations that are reversible; internalized sets of actions that allow the child to do mentally what was done physically before.

preoperational thought

The term Piaget gave to the 2- to 7-year-old child's understanding of the world. Children at this stage of reasoning cannot understand such logical operations as the reversibility of mental representations.

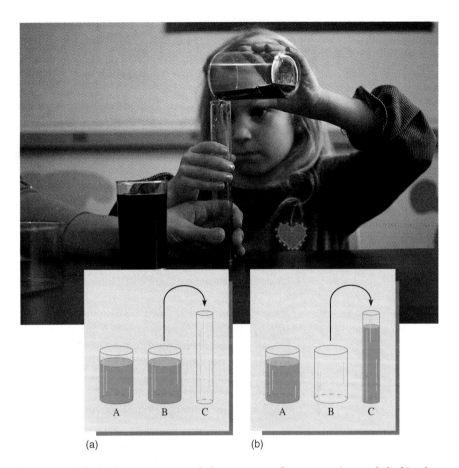

FIGURE 8.9

Piaget's Conservation Task

The beaker test is a well-known Piagetian test to determine whether a child can think operationally—that is, can mentally reverse actions and show conservation of the substance. *(a)* Two identical beakers are presented to the child. Then, the experimenter pours the liquid from B into C, which is taller and thinner than A or B. *(b)* The child is asked if these beakers (A and C) have the same amount of liquid. The preoperational child says no. When asked to point to the beaker that has more liquid, the preoperational child points to the tall, thin beaker.

(a)   (b)

conservation

A belief in the permanence of certain attributes of objects or situations in spite of superficial changes.

egocentrism

A salient feature of preoperational thought; the inability to distinguish between one's own perspective and someone else's perspective.

concrete operational thought

The term Piaget gave to the 7- to 11-year-old child's understanding of the world. At this stage of thought children can use operations. Logical reasoning replaces intuitive thought as long as the principles are applied to concrete examples.

as this 4-year-old girl have not grasped the concept of **conservation,** *a belief in the permanence of certain attributes of objects or situations in spite of superficial changes.*

The child's thought in the preoperational stage also is egocentric. By **egocentrism,** *Piaget meant the inability to distinguish between one's own perspective and someone else's perspective.* The following telephone conversation between 4-year-old Mary, who is at home, and her father, who is at work, typifies Mary's egocentric thought:

Father: Mary, is mommy there?

Mary: (silently nods)

Father: Mary, may I speak to mommy?

Mary: (nods again silently)

Piaget also called preoperational thought *intuitive,* because when he asked children why they knew something, they often did not give logical answers, but offered personal insights or guesses instead. Yet, as Piaget observed, young children seem so sure that they know something, even though they do not use logical reasoning to arrive at the answer. Young children also have an insatiable desire to know their world, and they ask a lot of questions.

"Why does a lady have to be married to have a baby?"

"Who was the mother when everybody was the baby?"

"Why do leaves fall?"

"Why does the sun shine?"

Concrete Operational Thought. **Concrete operational thought** *is the term Piaget gave to the 7- to 11-year-old child's understanding of the world. At this stage of thought children can use operations. Logical reasoning replaces intuitive thought as long as the principles are applied to concrete examples.* For instance, the concrete operational thinker cannot imagine the steps necessary to complete an algebraic equation, which is too abstract at this stage of children's development.

Earlier we described a beaker task that was too difficult for a child who had not yet reached the stage of operational thought. Another well-known task to demonstrate Piaget's concrete operational thought involves two equal amounts of clay. The experimenter shows the child two identical balls of clay and then rolls one ball into a long, thin shape. The other is retained in its original ball shape. The child is then asked if there is more clay in the ball or in the long, thin piece of clay. By the time children reach 7 to 8 years of age, most answer that the amount of clay is the same. To solve this problem correctly, children have to imagine that the clay ball is rolled out into a long, thin strip and then returned to its original round shape—imagination that involves a reversible mental action. Concrete operations allow the child to coordinate several characteristics rather than focusing on a single property of an object. In the clay example, the preoperational child is likely to focus on height *or* width. The child who has reached the stage of concrete operational thought coordinates information about both dimensions.

Many of the concrete operations identified by Piaget focus on the way children think about the properties of objects. One important skill at this stage of reasoning is the ability to classify or divide things into different sets or subsets and to consider their interrelations. To study an example of children's classification skills, see figure 8.10.

formal operational thought

Piaget's fourth stage of cognitive development, which appears between 11 and 15 years of age. Formal operational thought is abstract, idealistic, and logical.

Formal Operational Thought. **Formal operational thought** *is Piaget's name for the fourth stage of cognitive development, which appears between 11 and 15 years of age. Formal operational thought is abstract, idealistic, and logical.* Unlike elementary school children, adolescents are no longer limited to actual concrete experience as the anchor of thought. They can conceive make-believe situations, hypothetical possibilities, or purely abstract propositions. Thought also becomes more idealistic. Adolescents often compare themselves and others to ideal standards. And they think about what an ideal world would be

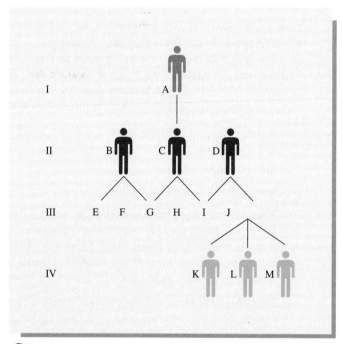

$\mathcal{F}$IGURE 8.10

Classification: An Important Ability in Concrete Operational Thought

One way to determine whether children possess classification skills is to see if they understand a family tree of four generations (Furth & Wachs, 1975). This family tree suggests that the grandfather (A) has three sons (B, C, and D), each of whom has two sons (E through J), and that one of these sons (J) has three sons (K, L, and M). A child who comprehends the classification system can move up and down a level (vertically), across a level (horizontally), and up and down and across a level (obliquely) within the system. For example, a child who grasps concrete operational thought understands that person J can be, at the same time, a father, brother, and grandson. A preoperational child cannot perform this classification and says that a father cannot fulfill these other roles.

like, wondering if they couldn't carve out a better world than the one the adult generation has handed to them.

At the same time adolescents think more abstractly and idealistically, they also think more logically. Adolescents begin to think more like a scientist thinks, devising plans to solve problems and systematically testing solutions. This type of problem solving has an imposing name. **Hypothetical-deductive reasoning** *is Piaget's name for adolescents' ability to develop hypotheses, or best hunches, about ways to solve problems, such as an algebraic equation. They then systematically deduce, or conclude, which is the best path to follow to solve the problem.* By contrast, children are more likely to solve problems in a trial-and-error fashion.

Piagetian Contributions and Criticisms.   We owe to Piaget the present field of cognitive development. We owe to him a long list of masterful concepts that have enduring power and fascination. These include the concepts of object permanence, conservation, assimilation, and accommodation. We also owe to Piaget the currently accepted vision of children as active, constructive thinkers who manufacture their own development (Flavell, 1992; Lourenco & Machado, 1996).

Piaget's theory has not gone unchallenged, however. Questions are raised about the following areas: estimates of the child's competence at different developmental levels; stages; training of children to reason at higher levels; and culture and education.

Some cognitive abilities emerge earlier than Piaget thought, and their subsequent development is more prolonged than he believed. Some aspects of object permanence emerge much earlier in infancy than Piaget believed. Even 2-year-olds are nonegocentric in some contexts—as when they realize that another person will not see an object they see if the person is blindfolded or is looking in a different direction. Young children are not as "pre" this and "pre" that (precausal, preoperational, and so on) as Piaget thought (Flavell, 1992). Some aspects of formal operational thinking that involve abstract reasoning do not consistently emerge in early adolescence as Piaget envisioned. And adults often reason in far more irrational ways than Piaget believed (Siegler, 1995). In sum, recent trends highlight the cognitive competencies of infants and young children and the cognitive shortcomings of adolescents and adults.

Most contemporary developmentalists agree that children's cognitive development is not as grand-stage-like as Piaget thought. **Neo-Piagetians** *are developmentalists who have elaborated on Piaget's theory, believing children's cognitive development is more specific in many respects than he thought* (Case, 1992). Neo-Piagetians don't believe that all of Piaget's ideas should be junked. However, they argue that a more accurate vision of the child's

Researchers have found that the infant's cognitive development is more advanced than Piaget believed.

cognitive development involves fewer references to grand stages and more emphasis on the roles of strategies, skills, how fast and automatically children can process information, the task-specific nature of children's cognition, and the importance of dividing cognitive problems into smaller, more precise steps.

Culture and education also exert stronger influences on children's development than Piaget believed. The age at which individuals acquire conservation skills is associated to some extent with the degree to which their culture provides relevant practice. And in many developing countries, formal operational thought is rare. The theory of children's cognitive development that we will explore next places more importance on culture than Piaget did.

Vygotsky's Theory of Cognitive Development. Children's cognitive development does not occur in a social vacuum. Lev Vygotsky (1896–1934), a Russian psychologist, recognized this important point about children's minds more than half a century ago. Vygotsky's theory is increasingly receiving attention as we move toward the close of the twentieth century (Steward, 1995).

One of Vygotsky's (1962) most important concepts is that of the **zone of proximal development (ZPD),** *which refers to tasks that are too difficult for children to master alone but that can be mastered with the guidance and assistance of adults or more-skilled children.* Thus, the lower limit of the ZPD is the level of problem solving reached by a child working independently. The upper limit is the level of additional responsibility the child can accept with the assistance of an able instructor (see figure 8.11). Vygotsky's emphasis on the ZPD underscored his belief in the importance of social influences on cognitive development. The practical teaching involved in ZPD begins toward the zone's upper limit, where the child is able to reach the goal only through close collaboration with an instructor. With continued instruction and practice, the child depends less and less on explanations, hints, and demonstrations, until she masters the skills necessary to perform the task alone. Once the goal is achieved, it can become the foundation for a new ZPD.

Many researchers who work in the field of culture and development are comfortable with Vygotsky's theory, which focuses on sociocultural contexts. Vygotsky emphasized how the development of higher mental processes, such as reasoning, involve learning to use the inventions of society, such as language and mathematical systems. He also stressed the importance of teachers and role models in children's mental development. Vygotsky's emphasis on the importance of social interaction and culture in children's cognitive development contrasts with Piaget's description of the child as a solitary young scientist.

Piaget once observed that children's cognitive development is a continuous creation of increasingly complex forms. As we will see next, this observation applies to children's socioemotional development as well.

zone of proximal development (ZPD)

Tasks that are too difficult for children to master alone but that can be mastered with the guidance and assistance of adults or more-skilled children.

𝓕IGURE 8.11

Vygotsky's Zone of Proximal Development

Vygotsky's zone of proximal development has a lower limit and an upper limit. Tasks in the ZPD are too difficult for the child to perform alone. They require assistance from an adult or a skilled child. As children experience the verbal instruction or demonstration, they organize the information in their existing mental structures so they can eventually perform the skill or task alone. *What implications does the ZPD have for school design?*

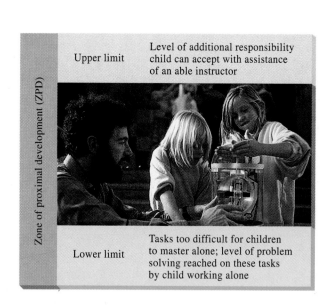

Upper limit — Level of additional responsibility child can accept with assistance of an able instructor

Zone of proximal development (ZPD)

Lower limit — Tasks too difficult for children to master alone; level of problem solving reached on these tasks by child working alone

Socioemotional Development

As children grow and develop, they are socialized by and socialize others—parents, siblings, peers, and teachers, for example. Their small world widens as they discover new refuges and new challenges. To begin, we will examine Erik Erikson's masterpiece on how we develop.

Erikson's Theory of Socioemotional Development.   Erik Erikson (1902–1994) spent his childhood and adolescence in Europe. After working as a psychoanalyst under Freud's direction, Erikson came to the United States in 1933. He became a United States citizen and taught at Harvard University.

Erikson recognized Freud's contributions to our understanding of human development, but he broke rank with some of Freud's basic tenets. In contrast to Freud's psychosexual stages, for instance, Erikson (1950, 1968) argues that we develop in *psychosocial stages*. In addition, Freud believed that our basic personality is shaped in the first 5 years of life, but Erikson emphasizes developmental change throughout the life span. In Erikson's view, everyone must pass through eight stages of development on the way to maturity and wisdom. The first four of these stages occur in childhood, the last four in adolescence and adulthood (see figure 8.12). Each stage is precipitated by a "crisis" that requires a person to grapple with a unique developmental task. For Erikson, this crisis is not a catastrophe, but a turning point of increased vulnerability or enhanced potential. The more successfully people resolve the crises, the more competent they are likely to become.

Let's now explore Erikson's first four stages—those that involve childhood—in greater detail. We will discuss Erikson's last four stages later in the chapter when we study adolescence and adulthood.

Trust versus mistrust, *which occurs during the baby's first year, is Erikson's first psychosocial stage. Trust is built when an infant's basic needs—such as comfort, food, and warmth—are met.* Trust in infancy sets the stage of a life-long expectation that the world will be a good and pleasant place to live.

Erikson's second stage of development, **autonomy versus shame and doubt,** *occurs around the age of 2. After developing trust, infants begin to discover that their behavior is their own. They start to assert their sense of independence or autonomy; they realize their will.* If infants are overly restrained or punished too harshly, they are likely to develop a sense of shame and doubt.

Initiative versus guilt, *Erikson's third stage of development, occurs during the preschool years. As preschool children encounter a widening social world, they are challenged more than they were as infants. Active, purposeful behavior is needed to cope with these challenges.* Children are asked to assume responsibility for their bodies, their behavior, their toys, and their pets. Developing a sense of responsibility increases initiative. Uncomfortable guilt feelings may arise, though, if the child is irresponsible and is made to feel too anxious. Erikson has a positive outlook on this stage. He believes most guilt is quickly compensated for by a sense of accomplishment.

Sometime during the elementary school years children go through Erikson's fourth developmental stage, **industry versus inferiority.** *Children's initiative brings them into contact with a wealth of new experiences. As they move into middle and late childhood, they direct their energy toward mastering knowledge and intellectual skills.* With their expansive imaginations, children at this stage are thirsty to learn. The danger in the elementary school years is a sense of inferiority—feeling incompetent and inadequate. Erikson believes teachers have a special responsibility to help children develop a sense of competence and achievement. They should "mildly but firmly coerce children into the adventure of finding out that one can learn to accomplish things which one would never have thought of by oneself" (Erikson, 1968).

Attachment.   Erikson (1968) believes that the caregiver's responsive and sensitive behavior toward the infant during its first year provides an important foundation for later development. A number of contemporary developmental psychologists who study the process of "attachment" during infancy agree. Attachment usually refers to a strong relationship between two people in which each person does a number of things to continue

---

trust versus mistrust

Erikson's first psychosocial stage, experienced in the first year of life. Trust is built when an infant's basic needs—such as needs for comfort, food, and warmth—are met.

autonomy versus shame and doubt

Erikson's second psychosocial stage, occurring from about 1 to 3 years of age. After developing trust, infants begin to discover that their behavior is their own. They start to assert their sense of independence, or autonomy; they realize their will.

initiative versus guilt

Erikson's third stage of development, occurring during the preschool years. As preschool children encounter a widening social world, they are challenged more than they were as infants. Active, purposeful behavior is needed to cope with these challenges.

industry versus inferiority

Erikson's fourth stage of development, occurring during the elementary school years. In this stage, children's initiative brings them into contact with a wealth of new experiences. As they move into middle and late childhood, they direct their energy toward mastering knowledge and intellectual skills.

Erikson's stages	Developmental period	Characteristics
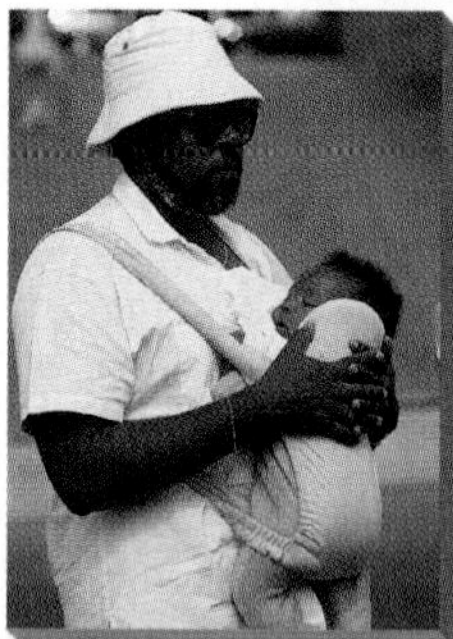 Trust versus mistrust	Infancy (first year)	A sense of trust requires a feeling of physical comfort and a minimal amount of fear about the future. Infants' basic needs are met by responsive, sensitive caregivers.
 Autonomy versus shame and doubt	Infancy (second year)	After gaining trust in their caregivers, infants start to discover that they have a will of their own. They assert their sense of autonomy, or independence. They realize their will. If infants are restrained too much or punished too harshly, they are likely to develop a sense of shame and doubt.
 Initiative versus guilt	Early childhood (preschool years, ages 3–5)	As preschool children encounter a widening social world, they are challenged more and need to develop more purposeful behavior to cope with these challenges. Children are now asked to assume more responsibility. Uncomfortable guilt feelings may arise, though, if the children are irresponsible and are made to feel too anxious.
 Industry versus inferiority	Middle and late childhood (elementary school years, 6 years–puberty)	At no other time are children more enthusiastic than at the end of early childhood's period of expansive imagination. As children move into the elementary school years, they direct their energy toward mastering knowledge and intellectual skills. The danger at this stage involves feeling incompetent and unproductive.

𝓕IGURE 8.12

Erikson's Eight Stages of Human Development

attachment

A close emotional bond between the infant and its caregiver.

the relationship. Many types of people are attached: relatives, lovers, a teacher and a student. In the language of developmental psychology, **attachment** *is the close emotional bond between the infant and its caregiver.*

Theories about infant attachment abound (Rubin & Pietromonaco, 1998). Freud believed that the infant becomes attached to the person or object that provides oral satisfaction. For most infants, this is the mother, since she is most likely to feed the infant.

But researchers have questioned the importance of feeding in attachment. Harry Harlow and Robert Zimmerman (1959) evaluated whether feeding or contact comfort was more important to infant attachment. The researchers separated infant monkeys from their mothers at birth and placed them in cages where they had access to two artificial "mothers." One of the mothers was made of wire, the other of cloth. Half of the infant

Erikson's stages	Developmental period	Characteristics	
Identity versus identity confusion	Adolescence (10 to 20 years)	Individuals are faced with finding out who they are, what they are all about, and where they are going in life. An important dimension is the exploration of alternative solutions to roles. Career exploration is important.	
Intimacy versus isolation	Early adulthood (20s, 30s)	Individuals face the developmental task of forming intimate relationships with others. Erikson described intimacy as finding oneself yet losing oneself in	
Generativity versus stagnation	Middle adulthood (40s, 50s)	A chief concern is to assist the younger generation in developing and leading useful lives.	
Integrity versus despair	Late adulthood (60s –)	Individuals look back and evaluate what they have done with their lives. The retrospective glances can either be positive (integrity) or negative (despair).	

monkeys were fed by the wire mother, half by the cloth mother. The infant monkeys nestled close to the cloth mother and spent little time on the wire one, even when it was the wire mother that gave milk. This study clearly demonstrates that contact comfort, not feeding, is the crucial element in the attachment process (see figure 8.13).

In a famous study, Konrad Lorenz (1965) illustrated attachment behavior in geese. Lorenz separated the eggs laid by one goose into two groups. He returned one group to the goose to be hatched; the other group was hatched in an incubator. The goslings in the first group performed as predicted; they followed their mother as soon as they hatched. But those in the second group, who first saw Lorenz after hatching, followed him everywhere as if he were their mother. Lorenz marked the goslings and then placed both groups under a box. Mother goose and "mother" Lorenz stood aside as the box was lifted.

$\mathscr{F}$IGURE 8.13

Harlow's Classic "Contact Comfort" Study

Regardless of whether they were fed by a wire mother or by a cloth mother, the infant monkeys overwhelmingly preferred to be in contact with the cloth mother, demonstrating the importance of contact comfort in attachment. *What implications does this research have for child-care practices?*

imprinting

The tendency of an infant animal to form an attachment to the first moving object it sees or hears.

Each group of goslings went directly to its "mother" (see figure 8.14). Lorenz called this process **imprinting,** *the tendency of an infant animal to form an attachment to the first moving object it sees and/or hears.*

For goslings, the critical period for imprinting is the first 36 hours after birth. There also appears to be a longer, more flexible "sensitive" period for attachment in human infants. A number of developmental psychologists believe that attachment to the caregiver in humans during the *first year* provides an important foundation for later devel-

$\mathscr{F}$IGURE 8.14

Imprinting

Konrad Lorenz, a pioneering student of animal behavior, is followed through the water by three imprinted greylag geese. Lorenz described imprinting as rapid, innate learning within a critical period that involves attachment to the first moving object seen. For goslings the critical period is the first 36 hours after birth.

opment. This view has been especially emphasized by John Bowlby (1969, 1989) and Mary Ainsworth (1979). Bowlby believes the infant and the mother instinctively form an attachment. He believes the newborn is innately equipped to elicit the mother's attachment behavior; it cries, clings, smiles, and coos. Later the infant crawls, walks, and follows the mother. The infant's goal is to keep the mother nearby. Research on attachment supports Bowlby's view that the infant's attachment to its caregiver intensifies at about 6 to 7 months (Schaffer & Emerson, 1964).

Some babies have a more positive attachment experience than others. Mary Ainsworth (1979) believes that the difference depends on how sensitive the caregiver is to the infant's signals. Ainsworth says that in **secure attachment** *infants use the caregiver, usually the mother, as a secure base from which to explore the environment.* Infants who are securely attached are more likely to have mothers who are more sensitive, accepting, and expressive of affection toward them than those who are insecurely attached (Waters & others, 1995).

The securely attached infant moves freely away from the mother but also keeps tabs on her location by periodically glancing at her. The securely attached infant responds positively to being picked up by others, and when put back down, happily moves away to play. An insecurely attached infant, in contrast, avoids the mother or is ambivalent toward her. The insecurely attached infant fears strangers and is upset by minor, everyday sensations.

Many researchers, such as Ainsworth and Bowlby, believe secure attachment during the infant's first year provides an important foundation for psychological development later in life (Bretherton, 1996; Sroufe, 1996). For example, in one study, researchers found that infants who were securely attached to their mothers were less frustrated and happier at 2 years of age than their insecurely attached counterparts (Matas, Arend, & Sroufe, 1978).

Not all developmentalists believe that a secure attachment in infancy is the only path to competence in life. Some developmentalists believe that too much emphasis is placed on the importance of the attachment bond in infancy (Young & Shahinfar, 1995). Jerome Kagan (1992), for example, believes that infants are highly resilient and adaptive. He argues that they are evolutionarily equipped to stay on a positive developmental course even in the face of wide variations in parenting. Kagan and others stress that genetic and temperament characteristics play more important roles in a child's social competence than the attachment theorists, such as Bowlby and Ainsworth, acknowledge (DiBiase, 1993). For example, infants may have inherited a low tolerance for stress; this, rather than an insecure attachment bond, may be responsible for their inability to get along with peers.

Another criticism of attachment theory is that it ignores the diversity of socializing agents and contexts that exist in an infant's world (Thompson, 1991). In some cultures, infants show attachments to many people. In the Hausa culture in Nigeria, both grandmothers and siblings provide a significant amount of care to infants (Super, 1980). Infants in agricultural societies tend to form attachments to older siblings, who are assigned a major responsibility for younger siblings' care. The attachments formed by infants in group care in Israeli kibbutzim provide another challenge to the singular attachment thesis.

Researchers recognize the importance of competent, nurturant caregivers in an infant's development. At issue, though, is whether or not secure attachment, especially to a single caregiver, is critical.

Parenting Styles. Even though many children spend a great deal of time in childcare situations away from the home, parents are still the main caregivers for the vast majority of the world's children. And parents have always wondered what is the best way to rear their children. "Spare the rod and spoil the child." "Children are to be seen and not heard." There was a time when parents took those adages seriously. But our attitudes toward children—and parenting techniques—have changed.

Diana Baumrind (1971, 1991) believes parents interact with their children in one of four basic ways. She classifies these parenting styles as authoritarian, authoritative, neglectful, and indulgent.

Authoritarian parenting *is a restrictive, punitive style in which the parents exhort the child to follow their directions and to respect work and effort. The authoritarian parent firmly*

---

secure attachment

Securely attached infants use the caregiver, usually the mother, as a secure base from which to explore the environment. Ainsworth believes that secure attachment in the first year of life provides an important foundation for psychological development later in life.

authoritarian parenting

A restrictive, punitive style in which the parent exhorts the child to follow the parent's directions and to respect work and effort. The authoritarian parent places firm limits and controls on the child and allows little verbal exchange.

limits and controls the child, with little verbal exchange. Authoritarian parenting is associated with children's social incompetence. In a difference of opinion about how to do something, for example, the authoritarian parent might say, "You do it my way or else.... There will be no discussion!" Children of authoritarian parents often are anxious about social comparison, fail to initiate activity, and have poor communication skills.

Authoritative parenting *encourages children to be independent but still places limits and controls on their behavior. Extensive verbal give-and-take is allowed and parents are warm and nurturant toward the child.* Authoritative parenting is associated with children's social competence. An authoritative parent might put his arm around the child in a comforting way and say, "You know you should not have done that; let's talk about how you can handle the situation better next time." Children whose parents are authoritative tend to be socially competent, self-reliant, and socially responsible.

Neglectful parenting *is a style in which parents are uninvolved in their child's life. This style is associated with the child's social incompetence, especially a lack of self-control.* This parent cannot give an affirmative answer to the question "It's 10 P.M. Do you know where your child is?" Children have a strong need for their parents to care about them. Children whose parents are neglectful might develop a sense that other aspects of the parents' lives are more important than they are. Children whose parents are neglectful tend to show poor self-control and do not handle independence well.

Indulgent parenting *is a style in which parents are involved with their children but place few demands or restrictions on them. Indulgent parenting is associated with children's social incompetence, especially a lack of self-control.* Such parents let their children do what they want, and the result is the children never learn to control their own behavior and always expect to get their way. Some parents deliberately rear their children in this way because they believe the combination of warm involvement with few restraints will produce a creative, confident child. One boy whose parents deliberately reared him in an indulgent manner moved his parents out of their bedroom suite and took it over for himself. He is almost 18 years old and still has not learned to control his behavior; when he can't get something he wants, he throws temper tantrums. As you might expect, he is not very popular with his peers. Children whose parents are indulgent never learn respect for others and have difficulty controlling their behavior. To read about some strategies for developing good parenting skills, see Improving Personal and Cognitive Skills ("Being a Competent Parent").

authoritative parenting
A style in which parents encourage children to be independent but still places limits and controls on their actions. Extensive verbal give-and-take is allowed, and parents are warm and nurturant toward the child.

neglectful parenting
A style of parenting in which parents are very uninvolved in the child's life; it is associated with children's social incompetence, especially a lack of self-control.

indulgent parenting
A style of parenting in which parents are very involved with their children but place few demands or controls on them; it is associated with children's social incompetence, especially a lack of self-control.

*I*mproving Personal and Cognitive Skills

Being a Competent Parent

Following are some strategies for learning to be a competent parent:

- *Learn more about child development.*
  Take a course or read a good book on child development. Several good books are profiled at the end of this chapter in the resources section.
- *Consider the child's developmental level.*
  Competent parents adapt to changes in their children. For example, using reasoning will be more effective with school-age children than with toddlers.
- *Practice authoritative parenting.*
  An authoritative parent is nurturing, engages the child verbally, and exercises gentle control. This style helps children to develop self-control more effectively than authoritarian, neglectful, and indulgent styles.

- *Use good communication skills.*
  Be a good listener. Talk *with* children, not *at* them.
- *Provide appropriate role models.*
  Regardless of a family's constellation (single-parent, opposite-sex parents, same-sex parents), children need exposure to both female and male role models. If adults in the family refuse these responsibilities or cannot provide these models, recruit some friends who will accept the honor.
- *Save time for yourself.*
  Don't become so highly involved with your children that you forget to reserve some special time for yourself and your own interests. You must replenish your resources if you intend to stay a nurturing parent.

Parenting is a very important profession, but no test of fitness for it is ever imposed in the interest of children.

GEORGE BERNARD SHAW, *Irish Playwright, 20th Century*

Cultural, Social Class, and Ethnic Variations Among Families. In the broadest sense, good parents everywhere seem to share a common approach to child rearing. One study examined the behavior of parents in 186 cultures around the world and found that most parents use a warm and controlling style, one that is neither permissive nor restrictive, in dealing with their children (Rohner & Rohner, 1981). Good parents seem to know instinctively that children do best when they are guided by love and at least some moderate parental control.

Despite such commonalities, researchers have also found telling differences in parenting across social classes and cultures (Harkness & Super, 1995). For example, there is wide variation in some child-rearing practices among social classes in the United States and most Western cultures (Hoff-Ginsburg & Tardif, 1995). Working-class and low-income parents, for instance, often place a high value on "external characteristics," such as obedience and neatness. Middle-class families, on the other hand, seem to prize "internal characteristics," such as self-control and the ability to delay gratification. Middle-class parents also are more likely to explain things, to use reasoning to accompany their discipline, to ask their children questions, and to praise them. In contrast, parents in low-income and working-class households are more likely to discipline their children with physical punishment and to criticize their children (Kohn, 1977).

Ethnic minority families differ from White American families in their size, structure and composition, reliance on kinship networks, and level of income and education (Garcia & others, 1995). Large and extended families are more common among ethnic minority groups than among White Americans. For example, more than 30 percent of Latino American families consist of five or more individuals. African American and Latino American children interact more with grandparents, aunts, uncles, cousins, and more distant relatives than do White American children. Single-parent families are more common among African Americans and Latino Americans than among White Americans. In comparison with two-parent households, single parents often have more limited resources of time, money, and energy. This shortage of resources may prompt them to encourage early autonomy among their children and adolescents. Also, ethnic minority parents are less well educated and engage in less joint decision making than do White American parents, and ethnic minority children are more likely to come from low-income families than are White American children (Committee for Economic Development, 1987). Although impoverished families often raise competent children, poor parents may have a diminished capacity for supportive and involved parenting (McLoyd, 1993).

Are there ways that communities and families can help protect ethnic minority children from harm and injustice? Yes, the community and family can filter out destructive racist messages. Parents can be competent role models and provide encouragement and support to their children. Also, the extended family in many ethnic minority families is an important buffer against stress.

eview

Children's Cognitive and Socioemotional Development

Jean Piaget, a famous Swiss psychologist, developed an important theory of children's minds, according to which a child constructs an understanding of the world through organization and adaptation. Adaptation consists of assimilation and accommodation. Piaget identified four stages of cognitive development: sensorimotor, preoperational, concrete operational, and formal operational. Sensorimotor thought lasts from birth to about 2 years of age and involves the coordination of sensorimotor action. Object permanence is an important accomplishment in the sensorimotor stage. A key aspect of cognitive development is being able to perform operations, mental representations that are reversible. The preoperational child (2 to 7 years) cannot do this. Preoperational thought is more symbolic than sensorimotor thought, it lacks conservation skills, it is egocentric, and it is intuitive rather than logical. A concrete operational child (7 to 11 years) can engage in operations, shows conservation skills, reasons logically but only in concrete circumstances, does not think abstractly, and has classification skills. Piaget stated that formal operational thought begins between 11 and 15 years of age. Formal operational thought is abstract and idealistic, but includes planning and logical analysis.

Piaget was a genius at observing children. He showed us some important things to look for and mapped out some general cognitive changes that occur during children's development. Criticisms of Piaget's views focus on such matters as estimates of children's competence, stages (neo-Piagetians offer more-precise views and information-processing explanations), and culture and education.

In Vygotsky's view, cognitive skills develop through social interaction embedded in a cultural backdrop. Vygotsky emphasized the importance of the zone of proximal development (ZPD), which refers to tasks too difficult for children to master alone but that can be mastered with the guidance and assistance of adults or more highly skilled children. Vygotsky's view is receiving increased attention.

Erik Erikson's theory emphasizes development throughout the human life span. Erikson says that individuals go through eight psychosocial stages, guided by the epigenetic principle. Erikson's four childhood stages are trust versus mistrust (first year), autonomy versus shame and doubt (second year), initiative versus guilt (3–5 years), and industry versus inferiority (6 years–puberty), identity versus identity confusion (adolescence), intimacy versus isolation (twenties, thirties), generativity versus stagnation (forties,

fifties), and integrity versus despair (sixties onward).

Attachment is a close bond between an infant and a caregiver. A number of attachment theories exist. Feeding does not seem to be critical in attachment, but contact comfort, familiarity, and the caregiver's sensitivity and responsiveness are. Many developmental psychologists, especially Bowlby and Ainsworth, believe that attachment in the first year provides an important foundation for later development. Ainsworth argues that secure attachment is critical for competent social development; others do not.

Baumrind's parenting strategies—authoritarian, authoritative, neglectful, and indulgent—are widely used classifications. Socially competent children are more likely to have authoritative parents. Although there are cross-cultural variations in families, authoritative parenting is the most common childrearing style around the world. Working-class and low-income parents place a higher value on "external characteristics," middle-class parents a higher value on "internal characteristics." However, there are variations in any social class, especially among ethnic groups. Chinese American, African American, and Mexican American families all have a strong tradition of the extended family.

ADOLESCENCE

Twentieth-century poet-essayist Roger Allen once remarked, "In case you are worried about what's going to become of the younger generation, it's going to grow up and start worrying about the younger generation." Virtually every society has worried about its younger generation, but it was not until the beginning of the twentieth century that the scientific study of adolescence began.

Historical Beginnings and the Nature of Adolescence

storm-and-stress view

G. Stanley Hall's view that adolescence is a turbulent time charged with conflict and mood swings.

In 1904, psychologist G. Stanley Hall wrote the first scientific book on adolescence. Hall referred to the adolescent years as a time of "storm and stress." The **storm-and-stress view** *is Hall's concept that adolescence is a turbulent time charged with conflict and mood swings.* Thoughts, feelings, and actions oscillate between conceit and humility, good and temptation, happiness and sadness. The adolescent may be nasty to a peer one moment and kind the next moment. At one time the adolescent may want to be alone, yet seconds later seek companionship.

During most of the twentieth century, American adolescents have been described as abnormal and deviant. In addition to Hall, Freud described adolescents as sexually driven and conflicted. And media portrayals of adolescents—from *Rebel Without a Cause* in the late 1950s to *Boyz 'N' the Hood* in the 1990s—showed adolescents as rebellious, conflicted, faddish, delinquent, and self-centered.

Adults probably forget their own adolescence. Most adults can with a little effort recall things they did that stretched—even shocked—the patience of their own parents. In matters of taste and manners, young people of every generation have seemed radical, unnerving, and different to adults—different in how they look, how they behave, the music they enjoy. But it is an enormous error to confuse the adolescent's enthusiasm for trying on new identities and enjoying moderate amounts of outrageous behavior with hostility toward parental and societal standards. Acting out and boundary testing are time-honored ways in which adolescents move toward accepting, rather than rejecting, parental values.

It does little good, and can do considerable disservice, to think of adolescence as a time of rebellion, crisis, pathology, and deviation. It's far more accurate to view adolescence as a time of evaluation, a time of decision making, a time of commitment as young people carve out their place in the world. How competent they will become often depends on their access to a range of legitimate opportunities and long-term support from adults who deeply care about them.

As we move toward the close of the twentieth century, experts on adolescence are trying to dispel the myth that adolescents are a sorry lot. That stereotype is usually based on a small group of highly visible adolescents. A study by Daniel Offer and his colleagues (1988) showed that the vast majority of adolescents are competent human beings who are not experiencing deep emotional turmoil. He sampled the self-images of adolescents around the world—in the United States, Australia, Bangladesh, Hungary, Israel, Japan, Taiwan, Turkey, and West Germany—and found that three out of four had a positive self-image. They were moving toward adulthood in generally healthy ways, happy most of the time, enjoying life, valuing work and school, having positive feelings about their family and friends, expressing confidence in their sexual selves, and believing they have the ability to cope with life's stresses—not exactly in the throes of storm and stress.

At the same time, adolescents have not experienced an improvement in health over the past 30 years, largely as a result of a new group of dangers called the "new morbidity." These include problems such as accidents, suicide, homicide, substance abuse, sexual diseases including AIDS, delinquency, and emotional difficulties.

Our discussion underscores an important point about adolescents: They do not make up a homogeneous group. The majority of adolescents negotiate the lengthy path to adult maturity successfully, but too large a group does not. Ethnic, cultural, gender, socioeconomic, age, and lifestyle differences influence the actual life trajectory of every adolescent. Different portrayals of adolescents emerge, depending on the particular group of adolescents being described (Brooks-Gunn, 1996; Feldman & Elliott, 1990). The complex relationships among physical, cognitive, and socioemotional development that influence rates of health and emotional problems make it important for us to understand these aspects of adolescent development. Let's examine physical development first.

Physical Development

Imagine a toddler displaying all the features of puberty—a 3-year-old girl with fully developed breasts or a boy just slightly older with a deep male voice. We would see this by the year 2250 if the age of puberty were to continue to decrease at its present pace. Menarche (first menstruation) has declined from 14.2 years in 1900 to about 12.45 years today. Age of menarche has been declining an average of about 4 months a decade for the last century. We are unlikely, though, to see pubescent toddlers in the future because what happened in the last century is special. That something special is a higher level of nutrition and health. A lower age of menarche is associated with higher standards of living (Petersen, 1979).

Menarche is one event that characterizes puberty, but there are others as well. **Puberty** *is a period of rapid skeletal and sexual maturation that occurs mainly in early adolescence.* However, it is not a single, sudden event. We know when a young person is going through puberty, but pinpointing its beginning and its end is difficult. Except for

puberty
A period of rapid skeletal and sexual maturation that occurs in early adolescence.

From *Penguin Dreams and Stranger Things* by Berke Breathed. Copyright © 1985 by The Washington Post Company. By permission of Little, Brown and Company.

menarche, which occurs rather late in puberty, no single marker heralds puberty. For boys, the first whisker or pubic hair could mark its appearance, but both may go unnoticed.

Hormonal changes characterize pubertal development. Hormones are powerful chemical substances secreted by the endocrine glands and carried through the body in the bloodstream. The concentrations of certain hormones increase dramatically during puberty (Dorn & Lucas, 1995). **Testosterone** *is a hormone associated in boys with the development of genitals, an increase in height, and a change in voice.* **Estradiol** *is a hormone associated in girls with breast, uterine, and skeletal development.* These hormonal and body changes occur on the average about 2 years earlier in females (10½ years) than in males (12½ years).

Some individuals enter puberty early, others late. A special concern is that early maturation places girls at risk for a number of developmental problems. These include drug use, delinquency, adolescent pregnancy, and school-related problems (Brooks-Gunn, 1996). Less negative effects of early maturation have been found for boys, although early-maturing boys have a less positive identity development when they reach adulthood than late-maturing boys (Peskin, 1967). One of the problems for both girls and boys who are early-maturing is that they often get more positive attention for their physical development than for their cognitive development. Another problem is that they are introduced to adult temptations, such as sex and drugs, before they are able to effectively handle them.

Cognitive Development

As we noted earlier, cognitive development continues long after infancy and childhood. Adolescents undergo some significant cognitive changes. What are they? For one thing, there is the fascinating development of adolescent egocentrism. Before we discuss this concept, though, let's review Piaget's thoughts on how adolescents think.

Piaget's Ideas About Adolescent Cognition. Piaget believed that adolescents enter a new stage of cognitive development at about 11 to 15 years of age. He called this stage *formal operational thought.* The three main characteristics of formal operational thought are that it is abstract, idealistic, and logical. Adolescents think more abstractly than children. Formal operational thinkers can solve problems that require an understanding of abstract concepts, such as algebraic equations. Adolescents often think about what is possible. For example, they think about ideal characteristics of themselves, others, and the world. And adolescents begin to think more like scientists. They devise plans to solve problems and systematically test solutions. Piaget gave this type of thinking an imposing name: *hypothetical-deductive reasoning.*

Adolescent Egocentrism. Adolescent thought, especially in early adolescence, is also egocentric. **Adolescent egocentrism** *involves the belief that others are as preoccupied with the adolescent as she herself is, the belief that one is unique, and the belief that one is indestruc-*

testosterone

A hormone associated in boys with development of the genitals, an increase in height, and a change of voice.

estradiol

A hormone associated in girls with breast, uterine, and skeletal development.

adolescent egocentrism

The adolescent's belief that others are as preoccupied with the adolescent as she is herself, that she is unique, and that she is indestructible.

Adolescence is a time of evaluation, decision making, and commitment as adolescents seek to find out who they are and carve out a place for themselves in the world.

tible (Elkind, 1978). Attention-getting behavior, so common in adolescence, reflects egocentrism and the desire to be onstage, noticed, and visible. Imagine the eighth-grade boy who feels as if all eyes are riveted on his tiny facial blemish. Imagine also the sense of uniqueness felt by the following adolescent girl: "My mother has no idea about how much pain I'm going through. She has never been hurt like I have. Why did Bob break up with me?" And imagine the sense of indestructibility of two adolescent males drag racing down a city street. This sense of indestructibility can contribute to drug use and suicide attempts.

> *In youth, we clothe ourselves with rainbows, and go brave as the zodiac.*
> RALPH WALDO EMERSON, *American Poet and Essayist, 19th Century*

Moral Development. Another aspect of cognitive development that changes in adolescence is moral development. Lawrence Kohlberg (1986) created eleven stories and asked children, adolescents, and adults some questions about the stories. One of the stories goes like this:

> In Europe a woman was near death from a special kind of cancer. There was one drug that the doctors thought might save her. It was a form of radium that a druggist in the same town had recently discovered. The drug was expensive to make, but the druggist was charging ten times what the drug cost him to make. He paid $200 for the radium and charged $2,000 for a small dose of the drug. The sick woman's husband, Heinz, went to everyone he knew to borrow the money, but he could get together only $1,000. He told the druggist that his wife was dying and asked him to sell it cheaper or let him pay later. But the druggist said, "No. I discovered the drug, and I am going to make money from it." Desperate, Heinz broke into the man's store to steal the drug for his wife (Kohlberg, 1969).

After reading the story, the interviewee answers a series of questions about the moral dilemma. Should Heinz have done that? Was it right or wrong? Why? Is it a husband's duty to steal the drug for his wife if he can get it in no other way? Would a good husband do it? Did the druggist have the right to charge that much when there was no law actually setting a limit on the price? Why?

Based on answers that people gave to questions about this and other moral dilemmas, Kohlberg proposed the existence of three levels of moral development, with each level characterized by two stages. A key concept in understanding moral development,

internalization
The developmental change from behavior that is externally controlled to behavior that is controlled by internal, self-generated standards and principals.

preconventional level
Kohlberg's lowest level of moral thinking, in which an individual shows no internalization of moral values—moral thinking is based on punishments (stage 1) or rewards (stage 2) that come from the external world.

conventional level
Kohlberg's second level of moral thinking, in which an individual shows an intermediate level of internalization. The individual abides by certain standards (internal), but they are the standards of others (external), such as parents' standards (stage 3) or society's laws (stage 4).

postconventional level
Kohlberg's highest level of moral thinking; moral development is completely internalized and not based on others' standards. An individual recognizes alternative moral courses, explores the options, and then develops a personal moral code. The code is among the principles generally accepted by the community (stage 5) or it is more individualized (stage 6).

justice perspective
A theory of moral development that focuses on the rights of the individual; individuals independently make moral decisions. Kohlberg's theory is a justice perspective.

care perspective
In Carol Gilligan's theory of moral development, the care perspective focuses on people in terms of their connectedness with others, interpersonal communication, relationships with others, and concern for others.

especially Kohlberg's theory, is **internalization,** *the developmental change from behavior that is externally controlled to behavior that is controlled by internal, self-generated standards and principles.*

1. The **preconventional level** *is Kohlberg's lowest level of moral thinking, in which the individual shows no internalization of moral values—moral thinking is based on punishments (stage 1) or rewards (stage 2) that come from the external world.* In regard to the story about Heinz and the druggist, at stage 1 an individual might say he should not steal the drug because he might get caught and be put in jail. At stage 2, a person might say he should not steal the drug because the druggist needs to make a profit.

2. The **conventional level** *is Kohlberg's second level of moral thinking, in which the individual has an intermediate level of internalization. The individual abides by certain standards (internal), but they are the standards of others (external), such as parents (stage 3) or the laws of society (stage 4).* At stage 3, an individual might say that Heinz should steal the drug for his wife because that is what society expects a good husband would do; at stage 4, an individual might say that it is natural to want to save his wife but that it still is always wrong to steal.

3. The **postconventional level** *is Kohlberg's highest level of moral thinking; moral development is completely internalized and not based on others' standards. The individual recognizes alternative moral courses, explores the options, and then develops a personal moral code. The code is among the principles generally accepted by the community (stage 5) or it is more individualized (stage 6).* At stage 5, an individual might say that the law was not set up for these circumstances so Heinz can steal the drug; it is not really right, but he is justified in doing it. At stage 6, the individual is faced with the decision of whether to consider the other people who need the drug just as badly as his wife. Heinz should consider the value of all lives involved.

Kohlberg believed these levels and stages occur in a sequence and are age-related. Some evidence for Kohlberg's theory has been found, although few people reach stages 5 and 6 (Colby & others, 1983). Kohlberg thought moral development occurs through maturation of thought, the mutual give-and-take of peer relations, and opportunities for role taking. Parent-child relationships do not contribute to moral thought in Kohlberg's view because they are too dominated by their parents' moral values, with little opportunity for the youth to experiment with alternative moral values.

Kohlberg's provocative view continues to generate considerable research on moral development, but critics challenge his theory. One criticism of Kohlberg's view is that moral reasons are often a shelter for immoral behavior. When bank embezzlers and presidents are asked about their moral reasoning, it may be advanced, even at Kohlberg's postconventional level, but when their own behavior is examined it may be filled with cheating, lying, and stealing. The cheaters, liars, and thieves may know what is right and what is wrong, but still do what is wrong.

A second major criticism of Kohlberg's view is that it does not adequately reflect relationships and concerns for others. The **justice perspective** *is a theory of moral development that focuses on the rights of the individual; individuals stand alone and independently make moral decisions. Kohlberg's theory is a justice perspective.* By contrast, the **care perspective** *is Carol Gilligan's (1982) theory of moral development that sees people in terms of their connectedness with others and focuses on interpersonal communication, relationships with others, and concern for others.* According to Gilligan, Kohlberg greatly underplayed the care perspective in moral development. She believes this may have happened because he was a male, most of his research was with males rather than females, and he used male responses as a model for his theory.

Gilligan (1996) also believes that girls reach a critical juncture in their development when they reach adolescence. Gilligan says that at the edge of adolescence, at about 11 or 12 years of age, girls become aware that their intense interest in intimacy is not prized by the male-dominated culture, even though society values females as caring and altruistic. The dilemma, says Gilligan, is that girls are presented with a choice that makes them

Carol Gilligan *(center)* is shown with some of the students she has interviewed about the importance of relationships in a female's development. According to Gilligan, the sense of relationships and connectedness is at the heart of female development.

appear either selfish (if they become independent and self-sufficient) or selfless (if they remain responsive to others). Gilligan states that as young adolescent girls experience this dilemma, they increasingly "silence" their distinctive voices. They become less confident and more tentative in offering their opinions, which often persists into adulthood. Some researchers believe this self-doubt and ambivalence too often translates into depression and eating disorders among adolescent girls.

A third criticism of Kohlberg's view is that it is culturally biased (Miller, 1995). One review of research on moral development in 27 countries found that moral reasoning appears to be more culture-specific than Kohlberg envisioned and that Kohlberg's scoring system does not recognize higher-level moral reasoning in certain cultural groups (Snarey, 1987). Kohlberg did not recognize values such as communal equity and collective happiness in Israel, the unity and sacredness of all life forms in India, or the relation of the individual to the community in New Guinea as examples of higher-level moral reasoning. Kohlberg's system would not score these values at the highest level of moral reasoning because they do not emphasize the individual's rights and abstract principles of justice. In summary, moral reasoning is shaped more by the values and beliefs of a culture than Kohlberg acknowledged.

Socioemotional Development

Mark Twain, reflecting on his youth commented, "When I was a boy of 14 my father was so ignorant I could hardly stand to have the man around. But when I got to be 21, I was astonished how much he learnt in seven years." Let's explore the world of parent-adolescent relationships Twain spoke about.

Parent-Adolescent Relationships.　　There are many myths about parent-adolescent relationships, including the following: (1) Adolescents detach themselves from parents and move into an isolated world of peers. (2) Throughout adolescence, parent-adolescent relationships are intense, filled with conflict, and highly stressful.

Adolescents do not simply move away from parental influence into a decision-making world all their own. As adolescents move toward becoming more autonomous, it is healthy for them to continue to be attached to their parents. Just as they did in infancy and childhood, parents continue to provide an important support system that helps the adolescent explore a wider, more complex social world full of uncertainties, challenges, and stresses (Santrock, 1998).

Conflict with parents does increase in adolescence, but it does not reach the tumultuous proportions described by G. Stanley Hall, and it is not uniformly intense throughout adolescence (Holmbeck, 1996, 1998). Rather, much of the conflict involves the everyday events of family life, such as keeping a bedroom clean, dressing neatly, getting home by a certain hour, not talking on the phone forever, and so on. Such conflicts with parents are more common in early adolescence, especially during the apex of pubertal change, than in late adolescence.

In sum, the old model of parent-adolescent relationships suggested that as adolescents mature they detach themselves from parents and move into a world of autonomy apart from parents. The old model suggested that parent-adolescent conflict is intense and stressful throughout adolescence. The new model emphasizes that parents serve as important attachment figures and support systems as adolescents explore a wider, more complex social world (Cohen & Beckwith, 1996). The new model also emphasizes that in the majority of families, parent-adolescent conflict is moderate rather than severe, and that the everyday negotiations and minor disputes can serve the positive developmental function of helping the adolescent make the transition from childhood dependency to adult independence (see figure 8.15).

Peers.　　Imagine you are back in junior or senior high school: friends, cliques, parties, and clubs probably come to mind. During adolescence, especially early adolescence, we conform more than we did in childhood. Conformity to peers, especially their antisocial standards, often peaks around the eighth or ninth grade, a time when teenagers might join a peer in stealing hubcaps from a car, drawing graffiti on a wall, or harassing a teacher (Berndt & Perry, 1990).

Dating also takes on added importance during adolescence. As Dick Cavett (1974) remembers, the thought of an upcoming dance or sock hop was absolute agony: "I knew I'd never get a date. There seemed to be only this limited set of girls I could and should be seen with, and they were all taken by the jocks." Adolescents spend considerable time either dating or thinking about dating, which has gone far beyond its original courtship function to a form of recreation, a source of status and achievement, and a setting for learning about close relationships. Dating is but one of a number of circumstances that

*F*IGURE 8.15

Old and New Models of Parent-Adolescent Relationships

Old model of parent-adolescent relationships

- Autonomy, detachment from parents; parent and peer worlds isolated

- Intense conflict throughout adolescence; stormy and stressful on a daily basis

New model of parent-adolescent relationships

- Autonomy, but attachment to parents; adolescent-parent and adolescent-peer worlds interconnected

- Moderate conflict promotes growth; conflict greater in early adolescence signal the development of an identity in adolescence that is different from the identity formed in childhood.

Our discussion of adolescents' socioemotional development so far has taken us through families and peers—two of the most important social contexts in the adolescent's development. Experiences in these as well as other settings such as schools, influence one of the most dramatic changes in the adolescent's life—identity development.

identity versus identity confusion

The fifth of Erikson's stages of human development, occurring primarily in the adolescent years. Identity development involves finding out who we are, what we are all about, and where we are headed in life.

Identity Development.   **Identity versus identity confusion** *is the fifth of Erikson's (1968) stages of human development, occurring primarily in the adolescent years. The development of identity involves finding out who we are, what we are all about, and where we are headed in life.* Seeking an identity is about trying on one face after another, trying to find one's own.

During adolescence, individuals enter what Erikson calls a "psychological moratorium"—a gap between the security of childhood and the autonomy of adulthood. In their search for identity, adolescents experiment with different roles. Those who successfully explore a number of alternatives emerge with a new sense of self that is both refreshing and acceptable; those who do not successfully resolve the identity crisis are confused, suffering what Erikson called identity confusion. This confusion takes one of two courses: Individuals withdraw, isolating themselves from peers and family, or they lose themselves in the crowd. Adolescents want to decide freely for themselves such matters as what careers they will pursue, whether they will go to college, and whether they will marry. In other words, they want to free themselves from the shackles of their parents and other adults and make their own choices. At the same time, many adolescents have a deep fear of making the wrong decision and of failing. But as adolescents pursue their identity and their thoughts become more abstract and logical, they reason in more sophisticated ways. They are better able to judge what is morally right and wrong and become capable decision makers.

> *"Who are you?" Said the caterpillar. Alice replied rather shyly, "I—I hardly know, sir, just at present—at least I know who I was when I got up this morning, but I must have changed several times since then."*
>
> LEWIS CARROLL, *English Writer, 19th Century*

Identity is a self-portrait composed of many pieces, including these:

- The career and work path that a person wants to follow (career or vocational identity)
- Whether a person is conservative, liberal, or middle-of-the-road and how politically active a person is (political identity)
- A person's spiritual beliefs and the importance of church, synagogue, or other place of worship (religious identity)
- Whether a person is single, married, divorced, and so on (relationship identity)
- The extent to which a person is motivated to achieve and is intellectual (achievement, intellectual identity)
- Whether a person is heterosexual, homosexual, or bisexual (sexual identity)
- Whether a person shows traditional gender characteristics (masculine or feminine) or a blend of those characteristics (androgynous)
- Which part of the world or country a person is from and how intensely the person identifies with her or his cultural and ethnic heritage (ethnic/cultural identity)
- The kinds of things a person likes to do, which can include sports, music, hobbies, and so on (interests)
- A person's personality characteristics, such as being introverted or extroverted, hostile or friendly, anxious or calm, and the like (personality)
- How an individual integrates disability or health limitations into a fulfilling lifestyle (physical identity)

Identity Statuses.   James Marcia (1980) believes that two aspects of identity are important in determining a person's identity status: exploration and commitment. *Exploration* occurs when a person explores various options. This might include evaluating several career paths or interests. *Commitment* involves making a decision about which identity path to follow and making a personal investment in attaining the identity. In Marcia's view, the extent of a person's exploration and commitment gives rise to one of four identity statuses:

- *Identity confusion.* This occurs when a person has not yet explored meaningful alternatives and also has not made a commitment. Many young adolescents have an identity confusion status. For example, they have not yet begun to explore different career options.
- *Identity foreclosure.* This happens when someone makes a commitment to an identity before adequately exploring various options. For example, an adolescent might say that she wants to be a doctor because that is what her parents want her to be, rather than explore career options and then deciding to be a doctor on her own.
- *Identity moratorium.* This occurs when a person is exploring alternative paths but has not yet made a commitment. Many college students are in a moratorium status with regard to many areas of identity development. For example, a student might be exploring different majors or careers in depth but not have decided which major or career path to adopt.
- *Identity achievement.* A person achieves identity when she or he has explored alternative paths and makes a commitment. For example, a person might have examined a number of careers over an extended period of time and finally decided on a specific career path.

Is an identity something that is cast in stone once you achieve it? No, people's lives can change and so can their identities. Marcia says that people go through what he calls "MAMA" cycles (*Moratorium, Achievement, Moratorium, Achievement*). A person's first identity is just that: a first. It is not and should not be a person's last. As people go through their adult years, they are likely to go back and forth between identity achievement and moratorium (Marcia, 1998).

As we saw earlier, identity development involves many different domains of life. The Self-Assessment lists these domains and gives you an opportunity to evaluate your identity status with respect to them. For some suggestions on developing a positive identity, see Improving Personal and Cognitive Skills.

$\mathcal{S}$elf-Assessment

Exploring Your Identity

Think deeply about your exploration and commitment in the areas listed below. For each area, check whether your identity status is diffused, foreclosed, moratorium, or achieved.

IDENTITY STATUS

IDENTITY COMPONENT	Diffused	Foreclosed	Moratorium	Achieved
Vocational (career) identity				
Political identity				
Religious identity				
Relationship identity				
Achievement, intellectual identity				
Sexual identity				
Gender identity				
Ethnic/cultural identity				
Interests				
Personality				
Physical identity				

If you checked "Diffused" or "Foreclosed" for any areas, take some time to think about what you need to do to move into a moratorium identity status in those areas.

$\mathcal{I}$mproving Personal and Cognitive Skills

Developing a Positive Identity

Following are some strategies for developing a positive identity:

- *Be aware that identity is complex and takes a long time to develop.*
Your identity is complex and made up of many components. One of your main identity tasks is to integrate all of these parts into a meaningful whole. Your identity does not spring forth in a sudden burst of insight. It is achieved in bits and pieces over your lifetime.
- *Make the most of your college years.*
For many people, the college years are an important time for identity development. Why? Because college is a setting where exploration and different views are encouraged. Your views likely will be challenged by instructors and classmates, and this can expand your identity.
- *Examine whether your identity is yours or your parents'.*
Some college students have foreclosed on a particular identity without adequately considering alternatives. This especially occurs when individuals accept their parents' views without deeply questioning whether they want to be clones of their parents. Individuals might come back to adopt an identity similar to that of their parents, but along the way identity moves forward when different paths are evaluated.
- *Expect your identity to change.*
Even for people who think they have achieved the identity they want, their identities will change at some point in the future. Your identity will stay with you the rest of your life, but it won't be cast in stone. You will change and your world will change, especially if you explore new opportunities and challenges.

Identity, Culture, and Ethnicity. Erikson is especially sensitive to the role of culture in identity development. He points out that, throughout the world, ethnic minority groups have struggled to maintain their cultural identities while blending into the dominant culture (Erikson, 1968). Erikson says that this struggle for an inclusive identity, or identity within the larger culture, has been the driving force in the founding of churches, empires, and revolutions throughout history.

For ethnic minority individuals, adolescence is often a special juncture in their development (McLoyd & Steinberg, 1998). Although children are aware of some ethnic and cultural differences, most ethnic minority individuals consciously confront their ethnicity for the first time in adolescence. Compared with children, adolescents are more able to interpret ethnic and cultural information, to reflect on the past, and to speculate about the future (Harter, 1990). As they cognitively mature, ethnic minority adolescents become acutely aware of the evaluations of their ethnic groups by the majority White culture (Ogbu, 1989). As one researcher commented, the young African American child may learn that Black is beautiful, but conclude as an adolescent that White is powerful.

"Do you have any idea who I am?"

These Congolese Kota boys painted their faces as part of a rite of passage to adulthood. *What kinds of rites of passage do American adolescents have?*

rites of passage
Ceremonies or rituals that mark an individual's transition from one status to another.

Rites of Passage.　Culture is an important contributor to identity. Culture can influence identity development through the presence or absence of **rites of passage,** *ceremonies or rituals that mark an individual's transition from one status to another.* In some cultures, rites of passage mark a clear distinction between childhood and adulthood. Their absence in most industrialized cultures tends to leave many young people unsure whether or not they have reached adult status. Perhaps high school graduation ceremonies come closest to being a rite of passage for adolescents in today's industrialized world (Fasick, 1988). Even so, many high school graduates continue to live with their parents, are economically dependent on them, and are undecided about their career and lifestyle.

The Challenges of Adolescence

In every culture, adolescents face a number of challenges they must cope with effectively. In American culture, these challenges are interrelated. For example, heavy substance abuse is related to early sexual activity, lower grades, dropping out of school, and delinquency. Early initiation of sexual activity is associated with the use of cigarettes and alcohol, use of marijuana and other illicit drugs, lower grades, dropping out of school and delinquency. Delinquency is related to early sexual activity, early pregnancy, substance abuse, and dropping out of school. As many as 10 percent of the adolescent population in the United States have serious multiple-problem behaviors (such as dropping out of school or being behind in their grade level, using heavy drugs, regularly using cigarettes and marijuana, and being sexually active but not using contraception). Many, but not all, of these very high-risk youth "do it all." Another 15 percent of adolescents participate in many of these same behaviors but with slightly lower frequency and less deleterious consequences. These high-risk youth often engage in two- or three-problem behaviors (Dryfoos, 1992).

In addition to understanding that many adolescents engage in multiple-problem behaviors, it also is important to develop programs that reduce adolescent problems. In a recent review of the programs that have been successful in preventing or reducing

$\mathscr{A}$pplications in Psychology

Improving the Lives of Adolescents

Today's adolescents face greater risks to their health than ever before. Drug and alcohol abuse, depression, violence, pregnancy, sexually transmitted diseases, and school-related problems place far too many of today's adolescents at risk for not reaching their full potential. Recent estimates suggest that as many as one-fourth of American adolescents are in the high-risk category (Dryfoos, 1992).

Adolescent expert Ruby Takanishi (1993) described the importance of improving the opportunity side of the adolescent risk-opportunity equation. The new strategy is to move away from focusing on remediation of single problems, such as drug abuse or delinquency or adolescent pregnancy, to the promotion of adolescent health or a cluster of health-

enhancing behaviors. This approach recognizes that targeting only one problem behavior, such as drug abuse, may overlook its link to other problems, such as school failure or delinquency.

Just giving information to adolescents is not sufficient to improve their health and well-being. Like people at other points in the human life span, adolescents have to be motivated to use information, skills, and services.

Networks of support from families, peers, and caring adults are crucial for improving the lives of at-risk youth. And social policymakers need to target improved economic opportunities for youth and their families.

Each of us who comes in contact with adolescents—as adults, parents, youth workers, professionals, and educators—can help to make a difference in improving their health and well-being.

Programs for helping at-risk adolescents currently involve intensive individualized attention and communitywide multiagency collaboration.

adolescent problems, adolescent researcher Joy Dryfoos (1990, 1992) described the common components of these successful programs. The two most successful common components were these:

1. *Intensive individualized attention.* In successful programs, each high-risk child is attached to a responsible adult who gives the child attention and deals with the child's specific needs. This theme occurred in a number of different programs. In a successful substance-abuse program, a student assistance counselor was available full-time for individual counseling and referral for treatment.

2. *Communitywide multiagency collaborative approaches.* The basic philosophy of communitywide programs is that a number of different programs and services have to be in place. In one successful substance abuse program a communitywide health promotion campaign was implemented that used local media and community education in concert with a substance-abuse curriculum in the schools. Further information about improving adolescents' lives is presented in Applications in Psychology.

Although many of today's adolescents are privileged, wielding unprecedented economic power, many have little access to resources or opportunity (Burt, Resnick & Novick, 1998). They simultaneously move through what seems like an endless preparation for life. Each generation of adolescents is the fragile cable by which the best and worst of their parents' generation is transmitted to the present. In the end, there are only two lasting gifts adults can leave youth—one being roots, the other wings.

Adolescence

G. Stanley Hall is the father of the scientific study of adolescence. In the early 1900s he proposed the storm-and-stress view. However, adolescence is more appropriately viewed as a time of decision making and commitment rather than a time of rebellion and crisis. Adolescents are not a homogeneous group, and different portrayals of adolescence emerge based on the opportunities and support given to adolescents.

Puberty is a rapid change to maturation that occurs during early adolescence. Its onset has begun earlier in recent years. Hormonal changes are prominent, and the average boy enters puberty 2 years later than the average girl. Early maturation can place girls at risk for a number of problems.

Piaget believed that formal operational thought develops at 11 to 15 years of age. Its three main characteristics are that it is abstract, idealistic, and logical. Elkind

stated that adolescent egocentrism is common. Kohlberg proposed a cognitive developmental theory of moral development that has three (two-stage) levels: (1) preconventional, (2) conventional, and (3) post-conventional. The three levels vary in the degree to which moral development is internalized. Among his critics, Gilligan believes Kohlberg underrepresented the care perspective.

The old model of parent-adolescent relations emphasized autonomy and detachment from parents, as well as intense, stressful conflict throughout adolescence. The new model emphasizes both attachment and autonomy, with parents acting as support systems and attachment figures for adolescents; the new model also stresses that moderate, rather than severe, parent-adolescent conflict is common and that it can serve a positive developmental function. Adolescents spend

increased time with peers, and conformity to antisocial peer standards peaks in eighth or ninth grade.

Erikson believes that adolescence is characterized by identity versus identity confusion, the fifth stage in his eight-stage theory. Adolescents enter a psychological moratorium between childhood dependency and adult independence, seeking to discover who they are and where they are going in life. Marcia proposed that exploration and commitment determine four identity statuses: diffused, foreclosed, moratorium, and achieved. Rites of passage occur in primitive cultures but are mostly absent in most industrialized countries. Many at-risk adolescents have more than one problem. The two most successful prevention/intervention strategies for helping at-risk adolescents are (1) intensive, individualized attention, and (2) communitywide, multiagency collaboration.

ADULT DEVELOPMENT AND AGING

When does an adolescent become an adult? It's not easy to pin down just when we enter adulthood. In one recent study, on the average, 21-year-olds said that they became adults when they were 18 to 19 years old (Scheer, 1996). Factors they said contributed to their adult status included graduating from high school, becoming more financially independent, being more responsible, and making more independent decisions.

Periods of Adult Development

Just as the years from conception to adulthood are characterized by certain periods, so too are the adult years. Adult development is commonly divided into three periods: early, middle, and late. *Early adulthood* begins in the late teens or early twenties and ends in the late thirties or early forties. It is a time when individuals establish personal and economic independence, pursue a career, and seek intimacy with one or more persons. *Middle adulthood* occurs in the forties and fifties. It is a time of concern for transmitting something meaningful to the next generation, as well as career satisfaction, responsibility, and adjustment to physical decline. *Late adulthood* begins in the sixties and lasts until the person dies. It is a time of adjustment to decreased strength and health, retirement, reduced income, learning how to age successfully, and engaging in a life review.

Notice that approximate age ranges identify the periods of adult development and that the age ranges overlap. Psychologists are more certain about the periods of childhood than the periods of adulthood. Most of us would agree that a 1-year-old child is in the period of infancy and that a 4-year-old child is in the period of early childhood. However, the periods of adulthood are much broader. There is less agreement on whether or not a 41-year-old is in middle adulthood. Not only are the criteria and age bands for adult periods less clear-cut than for childhood, but as prominent life-span theorist Bernice Neugarten (1986) argues, we are rapidly becoming an age-irrelevant society. She points out that we are already familiar with the 28-year-old mayor, the 30-year-old college president, the 35-year-old grandmother, and the 65-year-old father of a preschooler.

Neugarten believes that most adult themes appear and reappear throughout the adult years. Issues of intimacy and freedom that haunt a couple throughout a relationship in early adulthood may be just as salient in later adulthood. The pressure of time, reformulating goals, and coping with success and failure are not the exclusive properties of adults at any particular age. Keeping in mind that the age bands of adult periods are fuzzy, let's now see what physical, cognitive, and socioemotional changes take place during the adult years.

Physical Development

Actress Bette Midler said that after 30, a body has a mind of its own. Comedian Bob Hope once remarked that middle age is when your age starts to show around your middle. How do we age physically as we go through the adult years?

Early and Middle Adulthood. Not only do we reach our peak performance during early adulthood, but we also are the healthiest then. Few young adults have chronic health problems. They have fewer colds and respiratory problems than they had as children. However, young adults rarely recognize that bad eating habits, heavy drinking, and smoking in early adulthood can impair their health as they age. Despite warnings on packages and in advertisements that cigarettes are hazardous to health, individuals increase their use of cigarettes as they enter early adulthood (Johnston, O'Malley, & Bachman, 1992). They also increase their use of alcohol, marijuana, amphetamines, barbiturates, and hallucinogens.

As we enter middle adulthood, we are more acutely concerned about our health status. We experience a general decline in physical fitness throughout middle adulthood and some deterioration in health. The three greatest health concerns at this age are heart disease, cancer, and weight. Cancer related to smoking often surfaces for the first time in middle adulthood.

The *Harvard Medical School Newsletter* reports that about 20 million Americans are on a "serious" diet at any particular moment. Being overweight is a critical health problem, especially in middle adulthood. For individuals who are 30 percent or more overweight, the probability of dying in middle adulthood increases by 40 percent. Obesity also increases the probability an individual will suffer other ailments, including hypertension and digestive disorders.

Because U.S. culture stresses a youthful appearance, physical deterioration—graying hair, wrinkling skin, and a sagging body—in middle adulthood is difficult to handle. Many middle-aged adults dye their hair and join weight reduction programs; some even undergo cosmetic surgery to look young. In one study, the middle-aged women focused more attention on their facial attractiveness than did the older or younger women. Middle-aged women also perceived that the signs of aging had a more detrimental effect on their appearance (Novak, 1977).

For women, middle age also means that menopause will occur. **Menopause** *is the time in middle age, usually in the late forties or early fifties, when a woman's menstrual periods cease completely.* The average age at which women have their last period is 52. A small percentage of women—10 percent—undergo menopause before 40. There is a dramatic decline in the production of estrogen by the ovaries. Estrogen decline produces some uncomfortable symptoms in some menopausal women—"hot flashes," nausea, fatigue, and rapid heartbeat, for example. Some menopausal women report depression and irritability, but in some instances these feelings are related to other circumstances in the women's life, such as becoming divorced, losing a job, caring for a sick parent, and so on (Dickson, 1990).

Research investigations reveal that menopause does not produce psychological problems or physical problems for the majority of women (McKinlay & McKinlay, 1984). Menopause overall is not the negative experience for most women it was once thought to be. The loss of fertility is an important marker for women—it means that they have to make final decisions about having children. Women in their thirties who have never had children sometimes speak about being "up against the biological clock" because they cannot much longer postpone questions about having children (Blechman & Brownell, 1987), although new frontiers in fertility technology may change this limitation.

Estrogen replacement therapy is increasingly recommended for women who are making the transition to menopause. The American Geriatrics Association's recent recommendations for middle-aged women include these (Bidikov & Meier, 1997):

- Taking estrogen to reduce the risk of osteoporosis (loss of bone tissue), coronary disease, and menopausal symptoms (hot flashes and sweating)
- Being aware of the increased risk of breast cancer linked to estrogen replacement therapy
- Actively participating in the decision about using estrogen replacement; some women are also choosing herbal therapy as a less risky alternative for menopausal symptoms

Do men go through anything like the menopause that women experience? Men do experience sex-related hormone declines in their fifties and sixties, but the decline is usually gradual and not as precipitous as women's estrogen decline.

Late Adulthood and Aging. The life span—the upper boundary of life, the maximum number of years an individual can live—has remained virtually unchanged since the beginning of recorded history. What has changed is life expectancy—the number of years that will probably be lived by the average person born in a particular year. Even though improvements in medicine, nutrition, exercise, and lifestyle have given us, on the average, 30 additional years of life since 1900, few of us will live to be 100. To determine your chances of living to be 100, see the Self-Assessment.

Osborn Segerberg (1982) interviewed 1,200 centenarians about many aspects of their life. Here is a bit of what life looks like through their eyes:

- Mary Butler said that finding something to laugh about every day is important. She believes a good laugh is better than a dose of medicine anytime.
- Elza Wynn concluded that he has been able to live so long because he made up his mind to live. He was thinking about dying when he was 77, but decided he would wait awhile.

menopause

The time in middle age, usually in the late forties or early fifties, when a woman's menstrual periods cease completely.

$\mathcal{S}$elf-Assessment

Can You Live to Be 100?

The following test gives you a rough guide for predicting your longevity. The basic life expectancy for males is age 73 and for females 80. Write down your basic life expectancy. If you are in your fifties or sixties, you should add ten years to the basic figure because you have already proved yourself to be a durable individual. If you are over age sixty and active, you can even add another two years.

Basic Life Expectancy

Decide how each item below applies to you and add or subtract the appropriate number of years from your basic life expectancy.

1. Family history
   Add five years if two or more of your grandparents lived to 80 or beyond. _____
   Subtract four years if any parent, grandparent, sister, or brother died of heart attack or stroke before 50. _____
   Subtract two years if anyone died from these diseases before 60. _____
   Subtract three years for each case of diabetes, thyroid disorder, breast cancer, cancer of the digestive system, asthma, or chronic bronchitis among parents or grandparents. _____

2. Marital status
   If you are married, add four years. _____
   If you are over twenty-five and not married, subtract one year for every unwedded decade. _____

3. Economic status
   Add two years if your family income is over $60,000 per year. _____
   Subtract three years if you have been poor for the greater part of your life. _____

4. Physique
   Subtract one year for every ten pounds you are overweight. _____
   For each inch your girth measurement exceeds your chest measurement deduct two years. _____
   Add three years if you are over forty and not overweight. _____

5. Exercise
   Add three years if you exercise regularly and moderately (jogging three times a week). _____
   Add five years if you exercise regularly and vigorously (long-distance running three times a week). _____
   Subtract three years if your job is sedentary. _____
   Add three years if your job is active. _____

6. Alcohol
   Add two years if you are a light drinker (one to three drinks a day). _____
   Subtract five to ten years if you are a heavy drinker (more than four drinks per day). _____

7. Smoking
   Subtract eight years if you smoke two or more packs of cigarettes per day. _____
   Subtract two years if you smoke one to two packs per day. _____
   Subtract two years if you smoke less than one pack. _____
   Subtract two years if you regularly smoke a pipe or cigars. _____

8. Disposition
   Add two years if you are a reasoned, practical person. _____
   Subtract two years if you are aggressive, intense, and competitive. _____
   Add one to five years if you are basically happy and content with life. _____
   Subtract one to five years if you are often unhappy, worried, and often feel guilty. _____

9. Education
   Subtract two years if you have less than a high school education. _____
   Add one year if you attended four years of school beyond high school. _____
   Add three years if you attended five or more years beyond high school. _____

10. Environment
    Add four years if you have lived most of your life in a rural environment. _____
    Subtract two years if you have lived most of your life in an urban environment. _____

11. Sleep
    Subtract five years if you sleep more than nine hours a day. _____

12. Temperature
    Add two years if your home's thermostat is set at no more than 68° F. _____

13. Health care
    Add three years if you have regular medical checkups and regular dental care. _____
    Subtract two years if you are frequently ill. _____

Your Life Expectancy Total _____

Frenchwoman Jeanne Louise Calment, pictured here at age 120, claimed the title of oldest person alive, until her death in 1997. Greater ages have been claimed, but scientists say the maximum human life span is about 120 years.

Alzheimer's disease

A degenerative, irreversible brain disorder that impairs memory and social behavior.

- Billy Red Fox believes that being active and not worrying are important keys to living to be 100. At 95, he switched jobs to become a public relations representative. Even at 100, Billy travels 11 months of the year making public appearances and talking to civic clubs.
- Rebecca Miller says that the spirit of independence and self-reliance is the story of her life. Her spirit shines through her bright eyes. An avid reader throughout her life, she still reads with the aid of a magnifying glass.
- Duran Baez remarried at 50 and went on to have 15 more children. At 100 years of age, he was asked, "Do you have any ambition you have not yet realized?" Duran replied, "No." He said that he had lived the kind of life he expected, raising a good family, never doing any harm to anybody, staying honest all his life, and finding out that people really do like him. Duran says, "That's enough for the time being."

Even if we are remarkably healthy through our adult years, we begin to age at some point. What are the biological explanations of aging? Virtually all biological theories of aging and life span assign an important role to genes (Schneider & others, 1996). Research demonstrates that the body's cells can divide only a limited number of times; cells from embryonic tissue can divide about 100 times, for example (Hayflick, 1977). Based on the rate at which cells divide, biologists place the upper limit of the human life span at about 120 years. To read about some helpful ways to cope with aging, see Improving Personal and Cognitive Skills ("How to Die Young as Late in Life as Possible").

In old age, arteries become more resistant to the flow of blood, and heart output—about 5 quarts a minute at age 50—drops about 1 percent a year after age 50. The increased resistance of the blood vessels results in elevated heart rate and blood pressure, which are related to heart disease. Even in a healthy older person, blood pressure that was 100/75 at age 25 will probably be 160/90 at age 70.

As we age in late adulthood, the probability that we will have a disease or become seriously ill increases. For example, a majority of individuals who are alive at age 80 have some physical impairment. Alzheimer's disease is of special concern (Butters, Delis, & Lucas, 1995). **Alzheimer's disease** *is a degenerative, irreversible brain disorder that impairs memory and social behavior.* More than 2 million people over the age of 65 have Alzheimer's disease.

$\mathcal{I}$mproving Personal and Cognitive Skills

How to Die Young as Late in Life as Possible

Gerontologists have discovered a number of factors that are associated with living a long life. Of course, the goal of many people is not just to live a long life, but, as one discussant at an American Psychological Association convention said, "How to die young as late in life as possible" (Brody, 1994). Following are the best strategies for longevity we know today:

- *Exercise regularly.*
  Being physically fit is positively related to a number of positive physical and mental health outcomes.
- *Consistently maintain a healthy weight.*
  Strive to maintain a reasonable, manageable, consistent weight for your body build.
- *Have positive close relationships.*
  Happily married adults live longer than unhappy single adults. So do people with good social support systems, such as close friends.

- *Don't abuse drugs.*
  Heavy drinkers do not live as long as moderate drinkers or those who do not drink at all.
- *Don't smoke.*
  A sure way to die early is to smoke.
- *Become well educated.*
  Individuals with college degrees and beyond live longer than their non-college-educated counterparts.
- *Keep your mind alive.*
  Be curious, seek intellectual challenges, and pursue enjoyable interests throughout your life.
- *Get good health care.*
  Obtain the best health care available and have regular medical checkups.
- *Cope effectively with stress.*
  Highly aggressive, intense people who are "wired" all the time don't live as long as calm people who cope effectively with stress. Mentally healthy, happy people live longer than mentally unhealthy, unhappy people.

Cognitive Development

Think back to when you were a young adolescent, maybe taking an algebra class or writing a paper. How have you changed cognitively since then?

Early and Middle Adulthood.   Piaget believed that adults do not change at all, cognitively, after adolescence. In his view, a person with a Ph.D. in physics thinks no differently than a young adolescent, who supposedly has reached the level of formal operational thinking. According to Piaget, the physicist and the young adolescent both use logical thought to develop alternatives for solving a problem, then they deduce the correct solution from the alternatives; the only difference is that the physicist has more knowledge in a specific domain (physics).

Was Piaget right? One problem with Piaget's view is that some adolescents and adults never reach the developmental stage of formal operational thinking. And other psychologists think that we do change cognitively as we become adults. For example, the absolutist nature of adolescent logic and youth's buoyant optimism diminish in early adulthood (Labouvie-Vief, 1986). Competent young adults are less caught up in idealism and tend to think logically and to adapt to life as circumstances demand. Less clear is whether our mental skills, especially memory, actually decline with age.

Putting together the pieces of the research puzzle on cognition, memory appears to decline more often when long-term rather than short-term memory is involved. For example, middle-aged individuals can remember a phone number they heard 30 seconds ago, but they probably won't remember the number as efficiently the next day. Memory is also more likely to decline when organization and imagery are not used. In addition, memory tends to decline when the information to be recalled is recently acquired or when the information is not used often. For example, middle-aged adults probably won't remember the rules to a new game after only a lesson or two, and they are unlikely to know the new fall television schedule after its first week. And finally, memory tends to decline if recall rather than recognition is required. Middle-aged individuals can more efficiently select a phone number they heard yesterday if they are shown a list of phone numbers (recognition) rather than having to simply recall the number off the tops of their heads. Memory in middle adulthood also declines if the individual's health is poor (Rybash, Roodin, & Hoyer, 1998).

Late Adulthood and Aging.   At the age of 70, John Rock introduced the birth control pill. At age 76, Anna Mary Robertson Moses, better known as Grandma Moses, took up painting and became internationally famous. And when Pablo Casals reached 95 years of age, a reporter called him the greatest cellist who ever lived but asked why he still practiced 6 hours a day. Casals replied, "Because I feel like I am making progress."

> *Age only matters when you are aging. Now that I have reached a great age, I might as well be twenty.*
>
> PABLO PICASSO, *Spanish Artist, 20th Century*

The issue of intellectual decline through the adult years is a provocative one. David Wechsler (1972) concluded that the decline is simply part of the general aging process we all go through. But the issue seems more complex (Birren & others, 1996). Remember that we do not have just one type of intelligence; intelligence comes in different forms. Older adults do not score as high on intelligence tests as young adults when speed of processing is involved and this undoubtedly harms their performance on school-related tasks and traditional measures of intelligence. But when we consider general knowledge and wisdom, older adults often outperform younger adults.

Recently, Paul Baltes and his colleagues (Baltes, 1996; Baltes, Lindenberger, & Staudinger, 1998) further clarified the distinction between those aspects of the aging mind that show decline and those that do not, or even show some improvement. He makes a distinction between "cognitive mechanics" and "cognitive pragmatics." Using computer language as an analogy, **cognitive mechanics** *are the hardware of the mind and reflect the*

cognitive mechanics
The hardware of the mind, reflecting the neurophysiological architecture of the brain as developed through evolution. At the operational level, cognitive mechanics involve speed and accuracy of the processes involving sensory input, visual and motor memory, discrimination, comparison, and categorization.

Older adults might not be as quick with their thoughts as younger adults, but they might have more wisdom. This elderly woman shares the wisdom of her experiences with a classroom of children.

cognitive pragmatics

The culture-based "software" of the mind. At the operational level, cognitive pragmatics include reading and writing skills, language comprehension, educational qualifications, professional skills, and also the type of knowledge about the self and life skills that help us master or cope with life.

neurophysiological architecture of the brain as developed through evolution. At the operational level, cognitive mechanics involve speed and accuracy of the processes involving sensory input, visual and motor memory, discrimination, comparison, and categorization. Because of the strong influence of biology, heredity, and health on cognitive mechanics, their decline with aging is likely. Conversely, **cognitive pragmatics** *refer to the culture-based "software" of the mind. At the operational level, cognitive pragmatics include reading and writing skills, language comprehension, educational qualifications, professional skills, and also the type of knowledge about the self and life skills that help us to master or cope with life.* Because of culture's strong influence on cognitive pragmatics, their improvement into old age is possible.

Socioemotional Development

As both Sigmund Freud and the Russian novelist Leo Tolstoy observed, adulthood is a time for work and a time for love. For some of us, though, finding our place in society and committing ourselves to a stable relationship take longer than we would have imagined.

Early and Middle Adulthood.   Careers and work, lifestyles, and marriage are some of the themes of early and middle adulthood for many people.

Careers and Work.   Career interests continue to be an important aspect of life for many middle-aged adults. A popular notion about midlife is that it is a time when people carefully examine their career, evaluate what they have accomplished, and seriously consider a change. However, only about 10 percent of Americans change careers in midlife. And only some do so because they seek greater fulfillment; others do so because they get laid off or fired.

Lifestyles.   Until about 1930, the legitimate endpoint of social development in young adulthood was considered to be joining in a stable marriage. Since then, however, we have seen the emergence of the desire for individual fulfillment begin to compete with the cultural "given" of marriage. Fewer adults are opting for marriage to achieve their intimacy goals.

What factors have contributed to the decline of marriage in the United States? Some heterosexual couples simply do not choose to make their relationship formal by marrying. Some have discovered that marriage produces financial liabilities that living together unmarried avoids. For example, married couples might pay more in taxes or might have to sacrifice some social security benefits. For couples who do marry, relationships appear to be more fragile and intense than earlier in the century. Idealistic expectations about marriage probably contribute to dissatisfaction in marriage—one spouse might expect the other to be simultaneously a lover, a friend, a confidant, a counselor, a breadwinner, and a parent (Notarius, 1996). Many myths about marriage contribute to these unrealistic expectations (Rice, 1996). Currently the average duration of marriage in the United States is slightly more than 9 years. Although the divorce rate has begun to slow since the 1970s, it still remains alarmingly high (Hernandez, 1988).

Many myths also are associated with being single, ranging from "the swinging single" to "the desperately lonely, suicidal single." Most singles are somewhere between these two extremes. The pluses of being single include time to make decisions about one's life, time to develop personal resources to meet goals, freedom to make autonomous decisions and pursue one's own schedule and interests, opportunities to explore new places and try out new things, and privacy. Common problems of single adults include a lack of intimate relationships with others, loneliness, and finding a niche in a marriage-oriented society. Some single adults would rather remain single; others would rather be married.

Gay and lesbian couples face even more complicated choices. Most states refuse to accept homosexual marriage as a legitimate legal contract. In addition, most employers do not offer partner benefits to individuals in committed homosexual relationships, so most of these partnerships experience financial pressures during health crises that married couples don't face. For homosexual couples who choose to become parents, their lives become filled with complex negotiations with medical systems, adoption agencies, and the like.

Stage Theories of Adult Personality Development. Psychologists have proposed different theories about adult development. Most theories address themes of work and love, career and intimacy. One set of theories proposes that adult development unfolds in stages.

Erikson's eight stages of the human life span include one stage for early adulthood and one stage for middle adulthood. Erikson believes that only after identity is well developed can true intimacy occur. **Intimacy versus isolation** *is Erikson's sixth stage of development, occurring mainly in early adulthood. Intimacy is the ability to develop close, loving relationships.* Intimacy helps us to form our identity because, in Erikson's words, "We are what we love." If intimacy does not develop, Erikson argues that a deep sense of isolation and impersonal feelings overcome the individual.

intimacy versus isolation
Erikson's sixth stage of development, occurring mainly in early adulthood. Intimacy is the ability to develop close, loving relationships.

generativity versus stagnation
Erikson's seventh stage of development, occurring mainly in middle adulthood. Middle-aged adults need to help the younger generation lead useful lives.

Generativity versus stagnation *is Erikson's seventh stage of development, occurring mainly in middle adulthood. Middle-aged adults need to assist the younger generation in leading useful lives.* Competent child rearing is one way to achieve generativity. However, adults can also satisfy this need through guardianship or a close relationship with the children of friends and relatives. The positive side of this stage—generativity—reflects an ability to positively shape the next generation. The negative side—stagnation—leaves the individual with a feeling of having done nothing for the next generation. As Erikson (1968) put it, "Generations will depend on the ability of all procreating individuals to face their children."

In *The Seasons of a Man's Life,* Daniel Levinson (1978) also described adult development as a series of stages. He extensively interviewed middle-aged male hourly workers, academic biologists, business executives, and novelists and concluded that developmental tasks must be mastered at a number of different points in adulthood (see figure 8.16).

In early adulthood, the two major tasks are exploring the possibilities for adult living and developing a stable life structure. The twenties represent the novice phase of adult development. By the end of a boy's teens, a transition from dependence to independence should occur. This transition is marked by a dream—an image of the kind of life the young man wants, especially in terms of marriage and a career. The novice phase is a time of experimenting and testing the dream in the real world.

Men actually determine their goals by the age of 28 to 33. During the thirties, a man usually works to develop his family life and career. In the late thirties, he enters a phase of becoming his own man (BOOM, becoming one's own man, as Levinson calls it). By age 40, he reaches a stable point in his career; outgrows his earlier, more tenuous status as an adult; and now looks forward to the kind of life he will lead as a middle-aged adult.

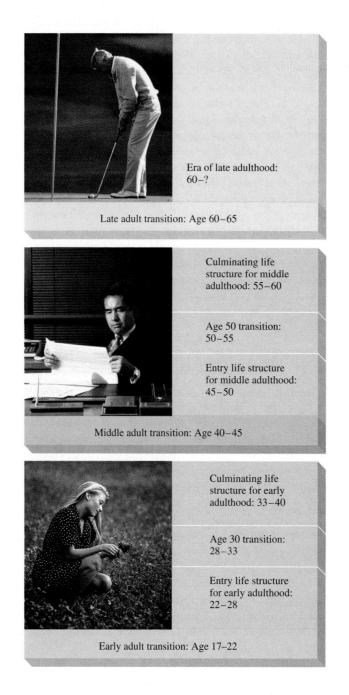

Era of late adulthood:
60–?

Late adult transition: Age 60–65

Culminating life
structure for middle
adulthood: 55–60

Age 50 transition:
50–55

Entry life structure
for middle adulthood:
45–50

Middle adult transition: Age 40–45

Culminating life
structure for early
adulthood: 33–40

Age 30 transition:
28–33

Entry life structure
for early adulthood:
22–28

Early adult transition: Age 17–22

𝓕IGURE 8.16
Levinson's Periods of Adult
Development

In Levinson's view, the change to middle adulthood lasts about 5 years and requires that adults come to grips with four major conflicts that have existed since adolescence: (1) being young versus being old; (2) being destructive versus being constructive; (3) being masculine versus being feminine; and (4) being attached to others versus being separated from them. The success of the midlife transition depends on how effectively they can reduce these polarities and accept each of them as a part of their being. Levinson's original subjects were all males, but more recently he reported that these midlife issues hold for females as well.

> *Middle age is such a foggy place.*
>
> ROGER ROSENBLATT, *American Writer, 20th Century*

"Goodbye, Alice, I've got to get this California thing out of my system."
Leo Cullum © 1984 from The New Yorker Collection. All Rights Reserved.

Erikson and Levinson emphasize that we go through a number of adult stages of development. In evaluating these stage theories, several points need to be kept in mind. First, the research on which they are based is not empirically sound. Much of it involves clinical observations rather than rigorous, controlled observations. Second, the perspectives tend to describe the stages as crises, especially in the case of the midlife stage. Research on middle-aged adults reveals that few adults experience midlife in the tumultuous way described by the stage-crisis views. Individuals vary extensively in how they cope with and perceive midlife (Vaillant, 1977).

Life Events and Cohort Effects. Life events rather than stages may be responsible for changes in our adult lives. Events such as marriage, divorce, the death of a spouse, a job promotion, and being fired from a job involve varying degrees of stress and influence our development as adults (Holmes & Rahe, 1967). However, we also need to know about the many factors that mediate the influence of life events on adult development. These include physical health, intelligence, personality, family support, and income, for example (Hultsch & Plemons, 1979). In addition, we need to know how people perceive the life events and how they cope with the stress involved. For instance, one person may perceive a divorce as highly stressful. Another person may perceive the same life event as a challenge. We also need to consider the person's life stage and circumstances. Divorce may be more stressful for an individual in his fifties who has been married for many years, for example, than for someone in her twenties who has been married only a few years. Individuals may cope with divorce more effectively in the 1990s than people did in the 1890s because divorce has become more commonplace and accepted in today's society.

An increasing number of developmental psychologists stress that changing social expectations influence how different **cohorts**—*groups of individuals born in the same year or time period*—move through the life span. For example, people born during the Depression may have a different outlook on life than those born during the optimistic 1950s.

Continuity and Discontinuity. William James (1890/1950) said that our basic personality is like plaster, set by the time we are 30. James believed that our bodies and attitudes may change through the adult years but the basic core of our personality remains the same. Some contemporary researchers, such as Paul Costa (1988; Costa & McRae, 1995), also believe that traits such as how extraverted we are, how well-adjusted we are, and our openness to new experiences do not change much during our adult lives. Costa says that a person who is shy and quiet at age 25 will basically be that same shy and quiet person

cohorts

Groups of individuals born in the same year or time period.

at age 50. Yet other psychologists are enthusiastic about our capacity for change as adults. They argue that too much importance is attached to personality change in childhood and not enough to change in adulthood.

A more moderate view of the stability-change issue comes from the architects of the California Longitudinal Study, which now spans more than 50 years (Eichorn & others, 1981). These researchers believe some stability exists over the long course of adult development, but that adults are more capable of changing than Costa thinks. For example, a person who is shy and introverted at age 25 may not be completely extraverted at age 50 but may be less introverted than at 25. This person may have married someone who encouraged him to be more outgoing and supported his efforts to socialize. Perhaps he changed jobs at age 30 and became a salesman, placing him in a situation where he was required to develop his social skills.

Late Adulthood and Aging.   Although we may be in the evening of our lives in late adulthood, we are not meant to live out our remaining years passively. **Activity theory** *states that the more active and involved older people are, the more satisfied they are and the more likely they will stay healthy.* Researchers have found that older people who go to church, attend meetings, take trips, and exercise are happier than those who simply sit at home. Predictably, better health and higher income are also related to older adults' life satisfaction.

The elderly often face painful discrimination. A new word in our vocabulary is **ageism,** *which is prejudice against people because of their age, in particular prejudice against older people.* Older adults might be branded with a number of stereotypes—such as being feebleminded, boring, ugly, parasitic. As a result they might be treated like children and described as cute and adorable. And far worse, they often are not hired for new jobs or are forced out of existing ones, they might be shunned, or they might even be edged out of their own families. The elderly who are poor or who are from ethnic minority backgrounds face special hardships, such as inadequate health care and housing.

Life-span developmentalist Paul Baltes and his colleagues (Baltes, Lindenberger, & Staudinger, 1998) believe that successful aging is related to three main factors: selection, optimization, and compensation. *Selection* is based on the concept that in old age there is a reduced capacity and loss of functioning, which mandates a reduction of performance in most domains of life. *Optimization* suggests that it is possible to maintain performance in some areas by practice and the use of new technologies. *Compensation* becomes relevant when life tasks require a level of capacity beyond the current level of the older adult's performance potential. Older adults especially need to compensate in circumstances with high mental or physical demands, such as when thinking about and memorizing new material, reacting quickly when driving a car, or running fast (Dixon & Backman, 1995). Illness in old age makes the need for compensation obvious.

Our aging society and older persons' status in this society raise policy issues about the well-being of older adults. Of special concern is the escalating cost of quality health care and older persons' access to health care. Advocacy groups that promote the well-being of the elderly include the American Association of Retired Persons (AARP) and the Gray Panthers. Maggie Kuhn *(above),* founder of the Gray Panthers, has actively sought to improve society's image of the elderly, obtain better living conditions for the elderly, and gain political clout. The Gray Panthers—with more than 80,000 members—pressures Congress on everything from health insurance to housing costs for the elderly.

activity theory

The theory that the more active and involved older people are, the more satisfied they will be with their lives and the more likely they will stay healthy.

ageism

Prejudice against people based on their age; in particular, prejudice against older people.

Consider the late Arthur Rubinstein, who was interviewed when he was 80 years old. Rubinstein said that three factors were responsible for his ability to maintain his status as an admired concert pianist into old age. First, he mastered the weaknesses of old age by reducing the scope of his repertoire and playing fewer pieces (an example of selection). Second, he spent more time at practice than earlier in his life (an example of optimization). And third, he used special strategies such as slowing down before fast segments, thus creating the image of faster playing than was objectively true (an example of compensation).

"Life is lived forward, but understood backwards," said the Danish philosopher Søren Kierkegaard. This is truer of late adulthood than of any other life period. Kierkegaard's words reflect Erikson's final stage of development through the life span. Erikson called this eighth stage **integrity versus despair**. *Occurring mainly in late adulthood, it is a time of looking back at what we have done with our lives.* If the older person has developed a positive outlook in each of the preceding periods of development, the retrospective glances and reminiscences will reveal a life well spent, and the individual will feel satisfied (integrity). But if the older adult has a negative outlook on life, the retrospective glances may produce doubt, gloom, and despair about the value of one's life.

integrity versus despair
Erikson's eighth stage of development, occurring mainly in late adulthood. This is a time of looking back at what we have done with our lives.

DEATH AND DYING

"I'd like to know what this show is all about before it's out," wrote the twentieth-century Dutch poet and inventor Piet Hein. Death may come at any time, but it is during late adulthood that we realize our days are literally numbered. Societies throughout history have had philosophical or religious beliefs about death. And most have some form of ritual to mark the passing from life to death. Some cultures hold a ceremonial meal accompanied by festivities. In others, mourners wear a black armband. Figure 8.17 shows two rituals that reveal cultural variations in dealing with death.

$\mathcal{F}$IGURE 8.17

Cultural Variations in Death

(a) A New Orleans street funeral is in progress. *(b)* A deceased person's belongings are left on a mountainside in Tibet.

In most cultures, death is not viewed as the end of existence—although the biological body dies, the spirit lives on. This belief is held by many Americans. Reincarnation, the belief that the soul is reborn in a new human body, is an important aspect of Hindu and Buddhist religions. Cultures often differ in their perception of death and their reaction to death. In the Gond culture of India, death is believed to be caused by magic and demons; Gonds react to death with anger. In the Tanala culture of Madagascar, death is thought to be caused by natural forces. The members of the Tanala culture peacefully react to death.

Elisabeth Kübler-Ross (1974) says that we go through five stages in facing death: denial and isolation, anger, bargaining, depression, and acceptance. Initially, the individual responds, "No, it can't be me. It's not possible." But denial is only a temporary defense. When the individual recognizes that denial no longer can be maintained, she often becomes angry and resentful. Now the individual's question becomes, "Why me?" Anger often is displaced onto physicians, nurses, family members, and even God. In the third stage, the dying person develops the hope that death can somehow be postponed or delayed. The individual now says, "Yes, me, but. . . ." The dying person bargains and negotiates, often with God, offering a reformed life dedicated to God and the service of others for a few more months of life.

As the dying individual comes to accept the certainty of her death, she often enters a period of preparatory grief, becoming silent, refusing visitors, and spending much of the time crying or grieving. This behavior is a normal effort to disconnect the self from all love objects. Kübler-Ross describes the final stage, characterized by peace and acceptance of one's fate, as the end of the struggle, the final resting stage before death.

Not everyone goes through the stages in the sequence Kübler-Ross proposed. Indeed, Kübler-Ross herself says she has been misread, pointing out that she never believed every individual copes with death in a specific sequence. But she does maintain that the optimal way to cope with death is through the stages she has outlined.

But some individuals struggle until the very end, angrily hanging onto their lives. They follow the encouragement of Dylan Thomas: "Do not go gentle into that good night. Old age should burn and rave at close of day . . . rage, rage against the dying of the light." In these instances, acceptance of death never comes. People die in different ways and experience different feelings and emotions in the process: hope, fear, curiosity, envy, apathy, relief, even anticipation. They often move rapidly from one mood to another and in some instances two moods may be present simultaneously.

Those left behind after the death of an intimate partner suffer profound grief and often endure financial loss, loneliness, increased physical illness, and increased psychological disorders including depression (DeSpelder & Strickland, 1996). But how they cope with the crisis varies considerably. Widows outnumber widowers by the ratio of 5 to 1 because women live longer than men, because women tend to marry men older than themselves, and because a widowed man is more likely to remarry. Widowed women are probably the poorest group in America, despite the myth of huge insurance settlements. Many are also lonely, and the poorer and less educated they are, the lonelier they tend to be. The bereaved are at increased risk for many health problems, including death. For both widows and widowers, social support helps them to adjust to the death of a spouse.

In closing our discussion of development through the human life span, think for a moment about Erik Erikson's words, "In the end, the power behind development is life."

*R*eview

Adult Development and Aging

Adult development can be divided into three periods—early adulthood (twenties, thirties), middle adulthood (forties, fifties), and late adulthood (sixties and up). However, Neugarten argues that age has become less effective as a predictor of human behavior in recent years.

Our physical skills usually peak in early adulthood, when it becomes easy to develop bad health habits. In middle adulthood, most individuals experience a decline in physical fitness, some deterioration in health, and an increased interest in health matters. Life expectancy has increased dramatically, but the life span has remained virtually unchanged for centuries. Virtually all biological theories of aging assign an important role to genes. Based on the rate at which cells divide, the upper limit on the human life span is about 120 years. As we grow old, the chances of becoming seriously ill

increase. Alzheimer's disease is a degenerative brain disorder that impairs memory and social behavior.

Some psychologists argue that cognition becomes more pragmatic in early adulthood. Cognitive skills are strong in early adulthood. In middle adulthood, memory might decline, but strategies such as organization can reduce its decline. There is extensive debate about how extensive intellectual decline is in late adulthood. As we age, the speed of processing information declines but wisdom can increase. Baltes recently proposed a distinction between cognitive mechanics (biologically based cognition) and cognitive pragmatics (experientially based cognition).

Careers and work are important dimensions of early and middle adulthood. Adults must choose the type of lifestyle they want to follow—single, married, or divorced, for example. One set of

personality theories proposes that adult development unfolds in stages (Erikson, Levinson). Other theorists emphasize life events and cohort effects. The stage theorists exaggerated the prevalence of a midlife crisis. There is both continuity and discontinuity in adult personality development. Everything we know about late adulthood suggests that an active lifestyle is preferable to disengagement. Baltes believes that successful aging involves selection, optimization, and compensation. Erikson believes that the final issue in the life span to be negotiated is integrity versus despair, which involves a life review.

Death can come at any point in the life span, but in late adulthood we know it is near. Most societies have rituals that deal with death, although cultures vary in their orientation toward death. Kübler-Ross proposed five stages of coping with death.

Overview

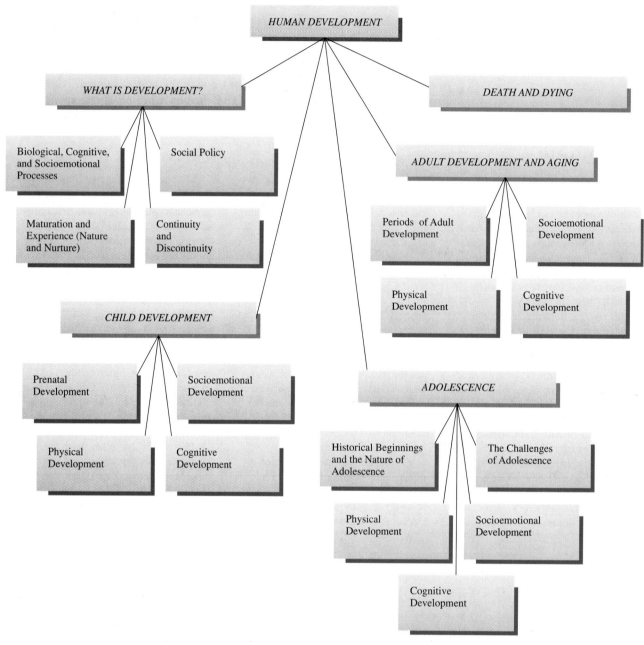

HUMAN DEVELOPMENT

WHAT IS DEVELOPMENT?

DEATH AND DYING

Biological, Cognitive, and Socioemotional Processes

Social Policy

Maturation and Experience (Nature and Nurture)

Continuity and Discontinuity

ADULT DEVELOPMENT AND AGING

Periods of Adult Development

Socioemotional Development

Physical Development

Cognitive Development

CHILD DEVELOPMENT

Prenatal Development

Socioemotional Development

Physical Development

Cognitive Development

ADOLESCENCE

Historical Beginnings and the Nature of Adolescence

The Challenges of Adolescence

Physical Development

Socioemotional Development

Cognitive Development

We began this chapter by exploring the nature of development, biological, cognitive, and socioemotional processes, maturation and experience (nature and nurture), continuity and discontinuity, and social policy. Then we studied children's development, adolescent development, and adult development in aging. Discussions of physical, cognitive, and socioemotional development were examined in each developmental period. To begin our coverage of children's development, we explored prenatal development and

birth. To begin our discussion of adolescence, we evaluated its historical beginnings. To begin the section on adult development and aging, we outlined the three main adult developmental periods—early, middle, and late. We also read about death and dying.

Don't forget that you can obtain an overall summary of the chapter by again studying the reviews on pages 284, 298, 310, and 323.

Key Terms

Think It Over

Exercises in . . .

. . . Critical Thinking

First Lady Hillary Clinton wrote a book called *It Takes a Village* in which she proposed that society should take wider responsibility for raising the country's children. Many people embraced the notion that we need to be doing more to give children a better start in life. Others see this position as a violation of parental rights and responsibilities. Review the information provided in this chapter on the status of children in America and then develop an argument that you think would be persuasive about what we should be doing as a society for the welfare of children.

. . . Creative Thinking

Create a list of questions that you can pose to a preoperational child to see how that child thinks the world operates. Consider asking about holiday rituals, family relations, how airplanes and cars work, or any other notion that can tap the child's understanding of the physical world. Videotape your interview and then analyze it to see how well the child illustrates preoperational thinking. (If the child is special to you, offer a copy of the tape to the child's caregiver as a thank-you).

. . . Active Learning

Convene a discussion among individuals of different generations to explore how their attitudes and views are similar or different. Try to get at least one older adult, one middle-aged adult, and one adolescent in the group discussion.

. . . Reflective Thinking

Project yourself into the future. Imagine that you have been working hard for 25 years at the job for which you are currently preparing, and that you have just been notified that you will be given an early retirement option so that the company can save some money. Write a journal entry about how you imagine yourself facing this challenge. How would you resolve this dilemma? Be sure to identify the values that underlie your decisions.

Resources for Psychology and Improving Humankind

Baby Steps (1994)

by Claire Kopp
New York: W. H. Freeman

Baby Steps is a guide to physical, cognitive, and socioemotional development in the first 2 years of life.

The Carnegie Council on Adolescent Development

2400 N Street, NW
Washington, DC 20037
202-429-7979

The Carnegie Council on Adolescent Development is a program of the Carnegie Foundation of New York. Its goal is to improve the health and well-being of adolescents. The council has generated a number of task forces to improve education, reduce adolescent pregnancy, and reduce alcohol and drug use among adolescents.

Child Development, Developmental Psychology, Journal of Research on Adolescence, and Journal of Gerontology

These are leading research journals in human development and they publish a wide array of articles on biological, cognitive, and socioemotional dimensions of development.

Child Poverty Action Group

22 Wellesley Street, East
Toronto ON M4Y 1G3 Canada
416-922-3126

Among its other advocacy initiatives, this group sponsors a toll-free help line for children in trouble.

Foster Grandparent Program

ACTION, The National Volunteer Association
Washington, DC
202-634-9108

This program matches older Americans with special-needs children. Older adult volunteers work in many different settings, ranging from Head Start programs to foster-care homes. ACTION also runs the Senior Companion Program, which matches older adults with frail elderly persons. A special goal of this program is to help the homebound elderly gain the confidence needed for independent living.

Handbook of Parenting, Vols. 1–4 (1995)

by Mark Bornstein (ed.)
Hillsdale NJ: Erlbaum

These four volumes provide a wealth of information on a wide variety of parenting issues. Leading researchers discuss such topics as divorce, adoption, gifted children, ethnicity, day care, moral development, and poverty.

How to Save the Children (1992)

by Amy Hatkoff and Karen Klopp
New York: Simon & Schuster

This innovative resource guide is filled with practical ideas about how volunteerism can help to counter the effects of poverty and neglect on America's children.

How to Survive the Loss of a Love (1991)

by Melba Colgrove, Harold Bloomfield, and Peter McWilliams
Los Angeles, CA: Prelude Press

This book provides messages about how to cope with the loss of a loved one. The authors address loss through death as well as other types of loss, such as divorce, rape, loss of long-term goals, and loss through aging.

The Measure of Our Success: A Letter to My Children and Yours (1992)

by Marian Wright Edelman
Boston: Beacon Press

Edelman's book stimulates thought about what kind of nation we want to be, what kind of values mean the most to us, and what we can do to improve the health and well-being of our nation's children and parents.

National Association for the Education of Young Children (NAEYC)

1834 Connecticut Avenue, NW
Washington, DC 20009-5786
202-232-8777
800-424-2460

NAEYC is a large organization that serves as an important advocacy group for young children, has developed guidelines for a number of dimensions of early childhood education, and publishes the excellent journal *Young Children*.

The National Council on Aging

1331 F Street, NW
Washington, DC 20005
202-347-8800

This organization is dedicated to increasing the well-being of older Americans. The council publishes a number of materials about aging and services available to older Americans.

Older Women's League (OWL)

666 11th Street NW, Suite 700
Washington, DC 20001
202-783-6686

The Older Women's League is for women of any age who support issues of concern to midlife and older women, including access to jobs and pensions for older women and maintaining self-sufficiency. The League publishes *Owl Observer*.

Touchpoints (1992)

by T. Berry Brazelton
Reading, MA: Addison-Wesley

Touchpoints is respected pediatrician T. Berry Brazelton's most recent book. Brazelton focuses on the concerns and questions that parents have about the child's feelings, behavior, and development from pregnancy to first grade.

Internet Resources

http://www.efn.org/~djz/birth/birthindex.html
On-line resource for pregnancy and birth concerns.

http://www.netaxs.com:80/~iris/infoweb/baby.html
Great links on baby care.

http://www.attach-bond.com/
Explore all kinds of attachment concerns at this site.

http://idealist.com/children/
The Child Development Website reviews classic psychology theories of development.

http://www.sunnyhill.bc.ca/Lalonde/JPS/biography/biog.html
A life history of Jean Piaget.

You and Your Adolescent (1990)

by Laurence Steinberg and Ann Levine
New York: HarperPerennial

This is an excellent book for parents of adolescents. It serves the dual purpose of educating parents about how adolescents develop and giving them valuable parenting strategies for coping with teenagers.

http://www.personal.psu.edu/faculty/n/x/nxd10/family3.htm
Links on how to survive being in a family.

http://www.personal.psu.edu/faculty/n/x/nxd10/adolesce.htm
A resource page created by college students on managing adolescence.

http://www.iog.wayne.edu/apadiv20/newslet.htm
APA's Division 20 on Adulthood and Aging publishes its newsletter.

http://www.iog.wayne.edu/apadiv20/newslet.htm
Comprehensive links about near-death experiences.

http://www.wic.org/bio/eross.htm
A biography of death and dying specialist Elisabeth Kübler-Ross.

9

Motivation and Emotion

The passions are at once temptors and chastisers. As temptors, they come with garlands of flowers on brows of youth; as chastisers, they appear with wreaths of snakes on the forehead of deformity. They are angels of light in their delusion; they are fiends of torment in their inflictions.

—HENRY GILES
American Educator and Geneticist, 20th Century

When you are motivated badly enough to get something, you will probably expend the energy and effort to get it. In this chapter, we will explore many aspects of motivation, evaluating why people do what they do. Among the areas of motivation we will read about are hunger, sex, competence, and achievement. We also will examine the complex and fascinating world of emotions.

The Story of Terry Fox: A Runner's Courage and Values

A young Canadian, Terry Fox, completed one of the greatest long-distance runs in history. Averaging a marathon (26.2 miles) a day for 5 months, he ran 3,359 miles across Canada. What makes his feat truly remarkable is that Terry Fox had lost his leg to cancer and ran this great distance with a prosthetic limb.

What motivated Terry Fox to make his run? When he was hospitalized with cancer, he decided that if he survived he would do something to generate funds for cancer research. Many people feel overwhelmed by a cancer diagnosis and resign themselves to a lesser quality of life while they wait for the disease to run its course. But Terry Fox found a compelling reason to live. He concluded that his purpose in life was to go beyond himself and make a positive difference in the world, and he felt renewed by his second chance.

On the way to his goal of completing his run across Canada, Terry encountered unforeseen hurdles: severe headwinds, heavy rain, snow, and icy roads. These challenges took a toll. After his first month of running, Fox was averaging only eight miles a day, far less than what he needed to average in order to complete his run before the harshest Canadian weather set in. Fox reached down inside himself to muster more motivation and energy to succeed. He kept going, picking up his pace in the second month, and was back on track to reach his goal.

Fox's accomplishments are all the more impressive when we consider that prior to his cancer diagnosis, he was only an average athlete and had a shy, introverted

Terry Fox completed one of the greatest long-distance runs in history. *What was his motivation?*

motivation

Why people behave, think, and feel the way they do. Motivated behavior is energized and directed.

motives

What energize and direct behavior toward solving a problem or achieving a goal.

intrinsic motivation

Motivation based on your own internal desires and needs.

extrinsic motivation

Motivation based on positive or negative external incentives.

personality. However, once his motivation kicked in, he completed one of the most meaningful runs in history. He learned to shed some of his shyness and began to give impassioned speeches to thousands of people in an effort to persuade them to donate to cancer research. Fox's contributions go far beyond the funds he raised. His example stands as a testimonial to what motivation can accomplish even in the face of great adversity. ❖

PERSPECTIVES ON MOTIVATION

Every why hath a wherefore.

—WILLIAM SHAKESPEARE, *English Playwright, 17th Century*

Why do you get so hungry? Why do you show interest in sex? Why do you study the way you do? Why do you strive to create change in your life? The answer lies in the nature of motivation. **Motivations** *are the factors that help explain why people behave, think, and feel the way they do.* **Motives** *are specific forces (such as hunger, sex, achievement) that energize and direct behavior toward solving a problem or achieving a goal.*

Motives differ in kind. For example, if you are hungry, you will probably put this book down and get something to eat. If you are sexually motivated, you might go to a party and flirt with someone you think is attractive. If you are strongly motivated to achieve, you might study in the library until midnight. When you are motivated, you get food, go to a party, stay at the library.

Motives differ in other ways as well. Motives differ in intensity. We can speak of an individual's being more or less hungry or more or less motivated to have sex, or of one person being more motivated to achieve than another person.

Motives differ in their origins. Some motives, such as the motive to sleep or to satisfy thirst, are clearly innate. Biologically based motives are active from birth and are responsible for survival (see table 9.1 for a list of biologically based motives). In contrast, learning and experience are likely to be stronger factors in social motives, such as the need to achieve. Some motives, such as sex, clearly combine biological and social influences.

A related distinction is whether actions are internally or externally motivated. This distinction is often referred to as intrinsic versus extrinsic motivation. For example, do you study hard because you have high standards for the quality of your work (intrinsic motivation) or because you want to achieve good grades so you can get into graduate or medical school (extrinsic motivation)? **Intrinsic motivation** *refers to motives based on your own internal desires and needs;* **extrinsic motivation** *refers to positive or negative external incentives that influence behavior.*

𝒯ABLE 9.1

Physiological Motives

What needs must be met to ensure our survival	How long can we last without meeting the need?
Breathing	4–5 minutes
Bladder and bowel relief	Depends on intake
Sleep	72–96 hours
Water	4–5 days
Food	20 days
Shelter	Depends on setting

Finally, motives differ in the degree to which you are conscious of them. For example, you rarely pay conscious attention to your biological need to breathe unless you find that your oxygen supply is threatened. Some motives for your own behavior might not be clear to you even after you have analyzed your actions. Other motives, such as hunger, vividly command attention. You might not be able to pay conscious attention to anything else until your hunger is satisfied.

Contemporary perspectives in psychology differ in the ways they explain motivation. We turn to a systematic exploration of these perspectives next, beginning with the evolutionary approach.

The Evolutionary Perspective

The role of unlearned behaviors and instincts plays a prominent role in explaining motivation from the evolutionary perspective. We will explore instinct theory and ethology as evolutionary approaches in motivation.

instinct

An innate, biological determinant of behavior.

Instinct Theory.   Early in this century, psychologists were interested in explanations of motivation based on **instinct,** *an innate, biological determinant of behavior.* Influenced by Darwin's evolutionary theory, American psychologist William McDougall (1908) argued that all behavior is determined by instincts. He said we have instincts for acquisitiveness, curiosity, gregariousness, pugnacity, and self-assertion, among others.

It was not long before a number of psychologists had created copious lists of instincts. Psychologists thought that perhaps we have one instinct for physical aggression, one for assertive behavior, and yet another for competitive behavior. Instinct theory, though, did not really explain anything. The "wherefore" behind Shakespeare's why was not adequately explored. An instinct was invariably inferred from the behavior it was intended to explain. For example, if a person was aggressive, it was inferred that he had an instinct for aggression. If another person was sociable, it was inferred that she had an instinct for sociability. However, instinct theory did call attention to the idea that some of our motivation is unlearned and involves physiological factors. This idea is important in our understanding of motivation today, but instinct theory itself landed in psychology's dustbin many years ago.

ethology

The study of the biological basis of behavior in natural habitats.

Ethology.   Although psychologists rejected the biological concept of instinct many years ago, biology's role in motivation continues to be strong. You might remember our discussion of Konrad Lorenz's classic study of imprinting in chapter 8. Recall how the goslings became attached to Lorenz because he was the first moving object they saw shortly after they were born. Lorenz interpreted the goslings' behavior as evidence of rapid, innate learning within a critical time period. Lorenz's field is **ethology,** *the study of the biological basis of behavior in natural habitats.* Ethology is sometimes referred to as modern instinct theory, although Lorenz and other ethologists have carefully avoided using the term *instinct* because of the tainted name it got earlier in psychology's history. Ethology emerged as an important field because of the work of European zoologists, such as Lorenz, in the 1930s, who argued that behaviorism had gone too far in promoting the role of environmental experiences in motivation.

Like behaviorists, ethologists are careful observers of behavior. Unlike many behaviorists, though, ethologists believe that laboratories are not good settings for observing behavior. They observe behavior in its natural surroundings instead, believing that behavior cannot be completely understood unless it is examined in the context in which it evolved. For example, ethologists have observed many species of animals in the wild, discovering their powerful motivation to stake out their own territory and band together to fight off any intruders (Lorenz, 1966).

Ethological theory reminds us of our biological origins and raises the issue of how strongly we are motivated by our biological makeup versus our experiences in life. Are we motivated to hurt someone else because we were born that way or because of our interactions with people who hit and yell, for example? As you can see, even though classical instinct theory is no longer viable, the issue regarding whether motivation is innate or learned, biologically or experientially based, is still alive.

Drive Reduction Theory

If you do not have an instinct for sex, maybe you have a need or a drive for it. A **drive** *is a psychological state that occurs because of a physiological need.* A **need** *is a deprivation that energizes the drive to eliminate or reduce the deprivation.* You might have a need for water, for food, or for sex. The need for food, for example, arouses your hunger drive. This motivates you to do something—to go out for a hamburger, for example—to reduce the drive and satisfy the need. As a drive becomes stronger, we are motivated to reduce it. This explanation is known as **drive reduction theory,** *which states that a physiological need creates an aroused state (drive) that motivates the organism to satisfy the need.*

Usually needs and drives are closely associated in time. For example, when your body needs food, your hunger drive will probably be aroused. An hour after you have eaten a Big Mac, you might still be hungry (thus, you need food), but your hunger drive might have subsided. From this example, you can sense that *drive* pertains to a psychological state, *need* pertains to a physiological state.

The goal of drive reduction is **homeostasis,** *the body's tendency to maintain an equilibrium, or steady state.* Hundreds of biological states in the body must be maintained within a certain range: temperature, blood sugar level, potassium and sodium levels, oxygen level, and so on. When you dive into an icy swimming pool, your body heats up. When you walk out of an air-conditioned room into the heat of a summer day, your body cools down. These changes occur automatically in an attempt to restore your body to its optimal state of functioning.

Homeostasis is achieved in the body much like a thermostat in a house keeps the temperature constant. For example, assume the thermostat in your house is set at 68 degrees. The furnace heats the house until a temperature of 68 degrees is reached, then the furnace shuts off. Without a source of heat, the temperature in the house eventually falls below 68 degrees. The thermostat detects this and turns the furnace back on again. The cycle is repeated so that the temperature is maintained within narrow limits.

The body's physiological makeup—relfexes, brain structures, body organs, and hormones—also plays an important role in understanding motivation. Later in this chapter we will discuss these physiological mechanisms in our discussion of hunger, which is just one of many physiological drives that govern our behavior.

The Psychoanalytic Perspective

William McDougall, in his advocacy for instinct theory, found an intellectual ally in Sigmund Freud (1917), who proposed that behavior is instinctually based. Freud believed that sex and aggression are especially powerful in motivating behavior, and he based his theories about personality development on this motivational construct.

One major legacy of Freud's theorizing about motivation is the belief that we are largely unaware of why we behave the way we do. Psychoanalytic theorists argue that few of us know why we love someone, why we eat so much, why we are so aggressive, or why we are so shy. Although Freud's perspective is no longer as powerful a paradigm as it once was, psychologists continue to debate the role of conscious versus unconscious thought in understanding motivation. (Much more detail about psychoanalytic theory appears in chapter 10).

The Behavioral Perspective

In the behavioral perspective, external factors such as incentives, play a key role in determining a person's motivation. **Incentives** *are positive or negative stimuli or events that motivate an individual's behavior.* For example, a yearly income of more than $100,000 is a positive incentive for becoming a physician; the threat of an intruder is a negative incentive for purchasing a security system for your home. By identifying the concept of incentive, psychologists expanded their definition of the why of behavior to include both internal factors (physiological needs and psychological drives) and external factors (incentives). In sum, behaviorists believe external factors and environmental contexts strongly influence a person's motivation.

The Cognitive Perspective

Consider your motivation to do well in this class. Your confidence in your ability to do well and your expectation for success may help you relax, concentrate better, and study more effectively. If you think too much about not doing well in the class and fear that you will fail, you may become too anxious and not perform as well. Your ability to consciously control your behavior and resist the temptation to party too much and to avoid studying will improve your achievement, too. So will your ability to use your information-processing abilities of attention, memory, and problem solving as you study for and take tests.

One of the most important recent trends in motivation is the increased interest in conscious, *self-generated goals.* The belief is that these goals influence a person's ongoing thought, behavior, and emotional reactions (Emmons, 1996). Albert Bandura (1991, 1997) believes that cognitive factors such as plans and self-efficacy (the belief that one can master a situation and produce positive outcomes) play powerful roles in motivation. If individuals have low self-efficacy, they might not even try to pursue a goal. A plan can motivate a person's behavior for days, weeks, months, and even years. For instance, if a college student decides she wants to become a marine biologist, she might map out an educational plan that encompasses the next decade of her life.

The Humanistic Perspective

Is getting an A in this class more important to you than eating? If the person of your dreams were to tell you that you are marvelous, would that motivate you to throw yourself in front of a car for that person's safety? According to humanist Abraham Maslow (1954, 1971), our "basic" needs must be satisfied before our "higher" needs can be. The **hierarchy of motives** *is Maslow's concept that all individuals have specific needs that must be satisfied in the following sequence: physiological needs, safety needs, the need for love and belongingness, the need for esteem, cognitive needs, aesthetic needs, and the need for self-actualization* (see figure 9.1). According to this hierarchy, people must satisfy their need for food before they can achieve and must satisfy their need for safety before their need for love.

It is the need for self-actualization that Maslow has described in the greatest detail. **Self-actualization,** *the highest and most elusive of Maslow's needs, is the motivation to develop one's full potential as a human being.* According to Maslow, self-actualization is possible only after the other needs in the hierarchy are met. Maslow cautions that most people stop maturing after they have developed a high level of self-esteem and, thus, do not become self-actualized. Many of Maslow's writings focus on how people can reach the elusive motivational state of self-actualization. We will discuss much more about Maslow's theory in chapter 10.

The idea that human motives are hierarchically arranged is an appealing one. Maslow's theory stimulates us to think about the ordering of motives in our own lives. However, the ordering of needs is somewhat subjective. Some people seek greatness in a career in order to achieve self-esteem, for example, while putting their needs for love and belongingness on hold.

The Sociocultural Perspective

Environmental and sociocultural influences play an important role in motivation. For example, Maslow's hierarchy seems to be a comprehensive explanation and organization of the motives that influence behavior. Although Maslow's theory works well in explaining motivations in Western cultures, how well would his hierarchy work to explain motives in other cultures? A different priority of motives appears to work better for Chinese culture (Nevis, 1983). In contrast to Western self-actualization in which individuals realize their full, self-directed potential, Chinese self-actualization occurs by fulfilling the obligation to serve society. Lower-order needs in the hierarchy are also different. Belonging might take greater precedence than physiological or safety needs in Chinese culture. This comparison demonstrates that we must always exercise caution in applying Western theories to non-Western cultures.

---

hierarchy of motives

Maslow's concept that all individuals have five main needs that must be satisfied, in the following sequence: physiological, safety, love and belongingness, self-esteem, and self-actualization.

self-actualization

The highest and most elusive of Maslow's needs; the motivation to develop to one's full potential as a human being.

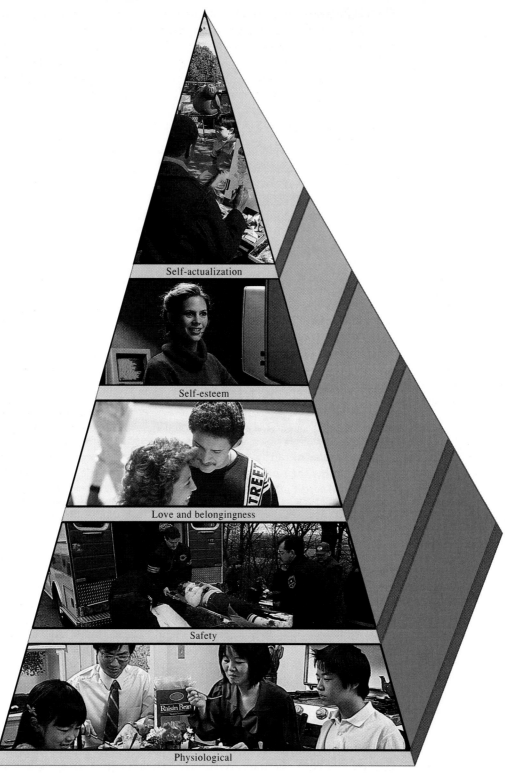

$\mathcal{F}$IGURE 9.1

Maslow's Hierarchy of Motives

Abraham Maslow developed the hierarchy of human motives to show how we have to satisfy certain basic needs before we can satisfy higher needs. The diagram shows lower-level needs toward the base of the pyramid, higher-level needs toward the peak. The lowest needs (those that must be satisfied first) are physiological—hunger, thirst, and sleep, for example. The next needs that must be satisfied are safety needs, which ensure our survival—we have to protect ourselves from crime and war, for example. Then we must satisfy love and belongingness needs—we need the security, affection, and attention of others, for example. Near the top of Maslow's hierarchy are self-esteem needs—we need to feel good about ourselves as we learn skills, pursue a profession, and deal with people, for example. Finally, at the top of the pyramid and the highest needs are self-actualization needs—reaching our full potential as human beings. Included among self-actualization needs are the motivations for truth, goodness, beauty, wholeness, and justice.

Social motives are especially influenced by sociocultural factors. Consider achievement. To understand achievement, we need to examine how parents and children interact, how children compare their performances with those of their peers, what role models children select, and the culture's standard for achievement. All of these variables influence a child's efforts. We will take a closer look at achievement motivation later in this chapter.

Even biological motives have sociocultural underpinnings. For example, you wouldn't choose to satisfy your hunger at a baseball game by dragging along a fancy, eight-course dinner. For most baseball fans, a hot dog from a vendor is the only acceptable way to address hunger pangs at the ballpark. Next we will explore selected motives, beginning with hunger.

Review

Perspectives on Motivation

Motivations are the factors that help explain why people behave, think, and feel the way they do. Motives are specific forces (such as hunger, sex, achievement) that energize and direct behavior toward solving a problem or achieving a goal. Motives differ in kind and intensity. Motives can be primarily biological or learned in origin and internally versus externally driven. Motives vary in the degree to which we are consciously aware of them.

The role of evolutionary factors in motivation is explored in instinct theory and ethology. Instinct theory flourished early in the twentieth century, but instincts do not entirely explain motivation. Ethology is the study of the biological basis of behavior in natural habitats.

According to drive reduction theory, a physiological need creates an aroused state (drive) that motivates the organism to satisfy the need. Homeostasis is an important motivational process promoted by drive reduction theory. The body's physiological makeup—including reflexes, brain structures, organs, and hormones—also plays an important role in contemporary theories of motivation.

In the behavioral perspective, external factors and environmental contexts play powerful roles in motivation. Incentives are positive or negative stimuli or events that motivate an individual's behavior. More recently, cognitively oriented behaviorists have introduced concepts such as those of self-efficacy and plans to explain

a person's motivation. According to Freud's psychoanalytic theory, instincts (especially sex and aggression) are the motivational forces underlying human behavior. In Freud's theory, individuals are largely unaware of what motivates them. The contemporary view of motivation also emphasizes the importance of cognitive factors. In the cognitive perspective, people are aware and rational. Maslow's hierarchy of motives reflects the humanistic perspective. Maslow believed that some motives need to be satisfied before others; self-actualization is the highest motive in Maslow's hierarchy. And as is true of so much human behavior, environmental and sociocultural factors play an important role in motivation.

SELECTED MOTIVES

In this portion of the chapter, we will explore different types of motives. First we will study hunger, which has strong biological underpinnings. Second, we will examine the motive of sex, a bridge between biological and social motives. And third, we will evaluate the cognitive/social motives of competence and achievement.

Hunger

Imagine that you live in a small village in a nonindustrialized country. You are very poor and have little food to eat. Hunger continuously gnaws at everyone in your village. Now imagine yourself as the typical American, eating not only breakfast, lunch, and dinner, but snacking along the way—and maybe even raiding the refrigerator at midnight.

Food is an important aspect of life in any culture. Whether we have very little or large amounts of food available to us, hunger influences our behavior. What mechanisms explain why we get hungry?

Physiological Factors.   You are sitting in class and it is 2 P.M. You were so busy today that you skipped lunch. As the professor lectures, your stomach starts to growl. For many of us, a growling stomach is one of the main signs that we are hungry. Psychologists have wondered for many years about the role of peripheral factors—such as the stomach, liver, and blood chemistry—in hunger.

Peripheral Factors. In 1912 Walter Cannon and A. L. Washburn conducted an experiment that revealed a close association between stomach contractions and hunger (see figure 9.2). As part of the procedure, a partially inflated balloon was passed through a tube inserted in Washburn's mouth and pushed down into his stomach. A machine that measures air pressure was connected to the balloon to monitor Washburn's stomach contractions. Every time Washburn reported hunger pangs, his stomach was also contracting. This finding, which was confirmed in subsequent experiments with other volunteers, led the two to believe that gastric activity is *the* basis for hunger.

Stomach signals are not the only factors that affect hunger, however. People who have had their stomachs surgically removed still get hunger pangs. Stomach contractions can be a signal for hunger, but the stomach also can send signals that stop hunger. We all know that a full stomach can decrease our appetite. In fact, the stomach actually tells the brain not only how full it is, but also how much nutrient is in the stomach load. That is why a stomach full of rich food stops your hunger faster than a stomach full of water (Deutsch & Gonzales, 1980). The same stomach hormone (called cholecystokinin, or CCK) that helps start the digestion of food reaches your brain through the bloodstream and signals you to stop eating.

Blood sugar (or glucose) is an important factor in hunger, probably because the brain is critically dependent on sugar for energy. One set of sugar receptors is located in the brain itself, and these receptors trigger hunger when sugar levels get too low. Another set of sugar receptors is in the liver, which is the organ that stores excess sugar and releases it into the blood when needed. The sugar receptors in the liver signal the brain via the vagus nerve; this signal can also make you hungry (Novlin & other, 1983). Another important factor in blood sugar control is the hormone insulin, which causes excess sugar in the blood to be stored in the cells as fats and carbohydrates. Insulin injections cause profound hunger because they drastically lower blood sugar.

Psychologist Judith Rodin (1984) has further clarified the role of insulin and glucose in understanding hunger and eating behavior. She points out that when we eat complex carbohydrates, such as cereals, bread, and pasta, insulin levels go up but then fall off gradually. When we consume simple sugars, such as candy bars and soft drinks, insulin levels rise and then fall off sharply—the familiar "sugar low." Glucose levels in the blood are affected by these complex carbohydrates and simple sugars in similar ways. The consequence is that we are more likely to eat again within several hours if we have just eaten simple sugars than we are if we have just eaten complex carbohydrates. Also, the food we eat at one meal often influences how much we will eat at our next meal. Thus, consuming doughnuts and candy bars, in addition to providing no nutritional value, sets up an ongoing sequence of what and how much we probably will crave the next time we eat.

Brain Processes. So far we have been talking about peripheral factors in hunger. However, the brain is also involved in hunger. The brain's **ventromedial hypothalamus (VMH)** *is a region of the hypothalamus that plays an important role in controlling hunger.* When a rat's

ventromedial hypothalamus (VMH)

A region of the hypothalamus that plays an important role in controlling hunger.

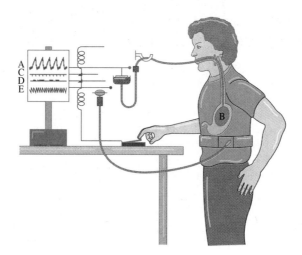

$\mathcal{F}$IGURE 9.2

Cannon and Washburn's Classic Experiment on Hunger

Notice the letters *A, B, C, D,* and *E* in the drawing. *A* is the record of the increases and decreases in the volume of the balloon in the subject's stomach, *B.* Number of minutes elapsed is shown in *C.* The subject's indication of feeling hungry is recorded at *D. E* is a reading of the movements of the abdominal wall to ensure that such movements are not the cause of changes in stomach volume.

VMH is surgically destroyed, it immediately becomes hyperphagic (that is, it eats too much) and rapidly becomes obese (Brobeck, Tepperman, & Long, 1943). Researchers thought that the VMH was a "satiety center" and its destruction left animals unable to fully satisfy their hunger. The picture now emerging, however, suggests that the destruction causes a hormonal disorder (remember that the hypothalamus is the master control center for many hormones). After the VMH is destroyed, a rat's body cells act as if they are starving, constantly converting all nutrients from the blood into fat and never releasing them. That is the main reason the animals become obese (see figure 9.3). One of the fascinating aspects of this condition is that the animals stop gaining weight once they reach a certain weight, suggesting that hormones and body cells control the body's overall "set point" for body weight. **Set point** *refers to the weight maintained when no effort is made to gain or lose weight.*

To summarize, the brain monitors both blood sugar levels and the condition of the stomach, then integrates this information (and probably other information as well) in the process of regulating hunger. Hypothalamic regions, especially the VMH, are involved in integrating information about hunger.

Your internal physiological world is very much involved in your feelings of hunger. In addition to the physiological processes, some external and cognitive factors are involved.

External Cues. Psychologists are interested in how environmental cues might stimulate hunger. You may know someone who seems incapable of walking past an ice cream shop without stopping to eat a huge hot fudge sundae.

Stanley Schachter (1971) believes that one of the main differences between obese and normal-weight individuals is their attention to environmental cues. From his perspective, people of normal weight attend to internal cues for signals of when to eat—for example, when blood sugar level is low or hunger pangs are sensed in the stomach. In contrast, an obese person responds to such external cues as signals of when to eat—how food tastes, looks, and smells, for example.

set point
The weight maintained when no effort is made to gain or lose weight.

𝓕IGURE 9.3

The Role of the Ventromedial Hypothalamus (VMH) in the Obesity of Rats

(a) A hyperphagic rat gained three times its body weight after a lesion (surgical destruction) had been made in its VMH. *(b)* This graph displays the weight gain by a group of rats in which lesions had been made in the VMH (hyperphagic) and by a group of rats in which no lesions had been made (control). *Examine the graph. At what point does it look like the set point kicks in for the hyperphagic rat? It is at about 1 month—notice the leveling off of the weight gain in the graph.*

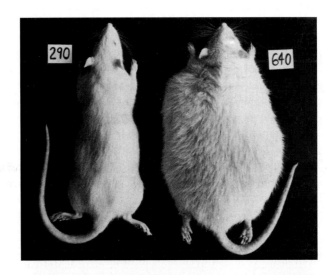

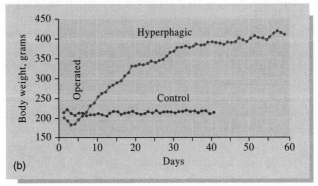

Self-Control and Exercise. Rodin (1984) points out that, not too long ago, we believed that obesity was caused by such factors as unhappiness or responses to external food cues. According to Rodin, a number of biological, cognitive, and social factors are more important. We already discussed the important biological factors, including the roles of complex carbohydrates and simple sugars in insulin and glucose levels. In regard to external cues, Rodin says that, although obese persons are more responsive to external food cues than normal-weight persons are, there are individuals at all weight levels who respond more to external than to internal stimuli. Many persons who respond to external cues also have the conscious ability to control their behavior and keep environmental food cues from externally controlling their eating patterns (Stunkard, 1989).

Rodin believes that, not only is conscious self-control of eating patterns important in weight control, but so is exercise. No matter what your genetic background, aerobic exercise increases your metabolic rate, which helps you burn calories. Much more information about dieting, eating behavior, and exercise appears in our discussion of health in chapter 11.

> *I've been on a constant diet for the last two decades. I've lost a total of 789 pounds. By all accounts, I should be hanging from a charm bracelet.*
>
> ERMA BOMBECK, *American Humorist, 20th Century*

Sex

We do not need sex for everyday survival the way we need food and water, but we do need it for the survival of the species. We begin our fascinating inquiry into sexual motivation by considering hormonal and cultural factors in sexual responsiveness.

Sexual Responsiveness. Both biological and psychological factors are involved in our sexual arousal. Human sexual behavior is influenced by the presence of hormones in the bloodstream. Hormones are among the most powerful, yet subtle, chemical in nature. All of the hormones are controlled by the pituitary gland, which is located in the brain. **Estrogens** *are the main class of sex hormones in females* while **androgens** *(of which testosterone is the most important) are the main class of sex hormones in males.*

estrogens
The main class of female sex hormones.

androgens
The main class of male sex hormones.

At puberty, males experience a dramatic increase in testosterone levels, with a resultant increase in sexual thoughts and fantasies, masturbation, and nocturnal emissions. Indeed, in male adolescents, the higher the blood levels of testosterone, the more the adolescent is preoccupied with sexual thoughts and engages in sexual activities. Throughout the year, the male's testes secrete androgens in fairly consistent amounts. Because of the consistent levels, males are hormonally ready to be stimulated to engage in sexual behavior at any time. As a man ages, his testosterone level gradually declines; this is usually accompanied by a decline in sexual interest and activity.

At puberty, females' ovaries begin to produce the female sex hormones called estrogen. Unlike androgen, estrogen is not constantly produced. Rather, estrogen levels vary over an approximately month-long cycle. Estrogen levels are highest when the female is ovulating (releasing an egg from one of her ovaries), which is midway through the menstrual cycle. It is at this time that a female is most likely to become pregnant. In many nonhuman animals, this high-estrogen period is the only time that females are receptive to male initiatives to mate. Although the strength of sexual interest in females varies with estrogen levels, human females are capable of being interested in sexual involvement throughout the menstrual cycle. Indeed, only a minimal level of estrogen seems to be required to sustain sexual desire in women. Thus, as we move from the lower to the higher animals, hormonal control over behavior is less dominant, although still important, in sexual arousal. For humans, both sociocultural and cognitive factors play more-important roles. Still, estrogen does have some influence on women's sexuality. Although post-menopausal women have a significant drop in estrogen, they are still sexually active. If given estrogen, they experience an increased interest in sex and report that sexual activity is more pleasurable.

There are individual differences in what turns people on. One woman might be thrilled to having her ears nibbled; another might find it annoying. Most of us think of kissing as highly stimulating, but in a vast majority of tribal societies kissing is either unheard of or thought to be disgusting.

Cultural and Gender Influences on Arousal. What "turns people on" is influenced not only by their individual preferences, but also by their sociocultural background and cognitive interpretations. The range of sexual values across cultures is extensive. Some cultures consider sexual pleasures as "normal" or "desirable" while other cultures view sexual pleasures as "weird" or "abnormal." Consider the people who live on the small island of Ines Beag off the coast of Ireland. They are among the most sexually repressed people in the world. They know nothing about tongue kissing or hand stimulation of the penis, and nudity is detested. For both females and males, premarital sex is out of the question. Men avoid most sexual experiences because they believe that sexual intercourse reduces their energy level and is bad for their health. Under these repressive conditions, sexual intercourse occurs only at night and takes place as quickly as possible as the husband opens his nightclothes under the covers and the wife raises her nightgown. As you might suspect, female orgasm is rare in this culture (Messinger, 1971).

By contrast, consider the Mangaian culture in the South Pacific. In Mangaia, young boys are taught about masturbation and are encouraged to engage in it as much as they like. At age 13, the boys undergo a ritual that initiates them into sexual manhood. First their elders instruct them about sexual strategies, including how to aid their female partner in having orgasms. Then, 2 weeks later, the boy has intercourse with an experienced woman who helps him hold back ejaculation until she can achieve orgasm with him. By the end of adolescence, Mangaians have sex virtually every day. Mangaian women report a high frequency of orgasm.

Obviously, a society's attitudes about appropriate sexual behavior influence the sexual behavior of young people in the society and the type of sexual education they are given. See (Baldwin & Baldwin, 1998) Sociocultural Worlds to learn about the sexual attitudes and behavior of youth in Holland and Sweden.

Men and women differ in the role that visual stimulation plays in sexual arousal. Men are more aroused by what they see. Perhaps this fact helps to explain why erotic magazines and X-rated movies are more directed toward males than toward females (Money, 1986). More than through visual stimulation, women become sexually aroused through tender, loving touches that are coupled with verbal expressions of love. Moreover, men can become aroused quickly, while women's arousal typically builds gradually.

> *Whoever named it necking was a poor judge of anatomy.*
> —GROUCHO MARX, *American Comedian, 20th Century.*

human sexual response pattern

A cycle of four phases—excitement, plateau, orgasm, and resolution—identified by Masters and Johnson.

The Human Sexual Response Cycle. How do humans respond physiologically during sexual activity? To answer this question, gynecologist William Masters and his colleague Virginia Johnson (1966) carefully observed and measured the physiological responses of 382 female and 312 male volunteers as they masturbated or had sexual intercourse. The **human sexual response pattern** *consists of four phases—excitement, plateau, orgasm, and resolution—as identified by Masters and Johnson* (see figure 9.4). The *excitement phase* begins erotic responsiveness; it lasts from several minutes to several hours, depending on the nature of the sex play involved. Engorgement of blood vessels and increased blood flow in genital areas and muscle tension characterize the excitement phase. The most obvious signs of response in this phase are lubrication of the vagina and partial erection of the penis.

The second phase of the human sexual response, call the *plateau phase,* is a continuation and heightening of the arousal begun in the excitement phase. The increases in breathing, pulse rate, and blood pressure that occurred during the excitement phase become more intense, penile erection and vaginal lubrication are more complete, and orgasm is closer.

The third phase of the human sexual response cycle is *orgasm.* How long does orgasm last? Some individuals sense that time is standing still when it takes place, but orgasm lasts for only about 3 to 15 seconds. Orgasm involves an explosive discharge of neuromuscular tension and an intense pleasurable feeling. However, not all orgasms are exactly alike. For example, females show three different patterns in the orgasm phase, as shown

Sociocultural Worlds

Sex Education and Attitudes Among Youth in Holland and Sweden

In Holland and Sweden, sex does not carry the mystery and conflict it does in American society. Holland does not have a mandated sex education program, but adolescents can obtain contraceptive counseling at government-sponsored clinics for a small fee. The Dutch media also have played an important role in educating the public about sex through frequent broadcasts focused on birth control, abortion, and related matters. Most Dutch adolescents do not consider having sex without birth control.

Swedish adolescents are sexually active at an earlier age than are American adolescents, and they are exposed to even more explicit sex on television. However, the Swedish National Board of Education has developed a curriculum that ensures that every child in the country, beginning at age 7, will experience a thorough grounding in reproductive biology and, by the age of 10 or 12, will have been introduced to information about various forms of contraception. Teachers are expected to handle the subject of sex whenever it becomes relevant, regardless of the subject they are teaching. The idea is to take some of the drama and mystery out of sex so that familiarity will make students less vulnerable to unwanted pregnancy and sexually transmitted diseases (Wallis, 1985). American society is not nearly so open about sex education.

Sex is much more demystified and less dramatized in Sweden than in the United States, and adolescent pregnancy rates are much lower in Sweden than in the United States.

in figure 4: (a) multiple orgasms, (b) no orgasm, and (c) excitement rapidly leading to orgasm, bypassing the plateau phase; the third pattern most clearly corresponds to the male pattern in intensity and resolution.

Following orgasm, the individual enters the *resolution phase,* in which blood vessels return to their normal state. One difference between males and females in this phase is that females may be stimulated to orgasm again without delay. Males enter a refractory period, lasting anywhere from several minutes to an entire day, in which they cannot have another orgasm. The length of the refractory period increases as men age.

Sexual Attitudes and Behavior. Describing sexual practices in America has always been challenging. Alfred Kinsey and his colleagues (Kinsey, Pomeroy, & Martin, 1948) shocked the nation by reporting that his survey of American's sexual practices revealed that, among other observations, half of American men had engaged in extramarital affairs. However, Kinsey's results were not representative since he recruited volunteers wherever he could find them, including hitchhikers who passed through town, fraternity men, and even mental patients. Despite the study's flaws, the Kinsey data were widely circulated and many people felt that they must be leading a more conservative sexual life than others.

Subsequent large-scale magazine surveys confirmed the trend toward permissive sexuality (for example, in a *Playboy* magazine poll of its readers; Hunt, 1974). In these surveys, Americans were portrayed as engaging in virtually unending copulation. However, most magazine polls are skewed because of the background of the readers who complete the surveys. For example, surveys in *Playboy* and *Cosmopolitan* might appeal to subscribers who want to use the survey to brag about their sexual exploits.

Not until 1994 were more accurate data obtained from a well-designed, comprehensive study of American's sexual patterns. Robert Michael and his colleagues interviewed

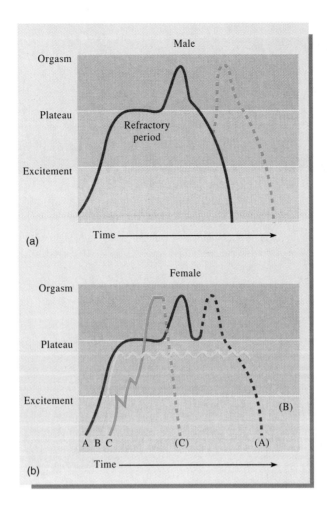

$\mathcal{F}$IGURE 9.4

Male and Female Human Sexual Response Patterns

(a) This diagram shows the excitement, plateau, orgasm, and resolution phases of the human male sexual response pattern. Notice that males enter a refractory period, which lasts from several minutes up to a day, in which they cannot have another orgasm. *(b)* This diagram shows the excitement, plateau, orgasm, and resolution phases of the human female sexual response pattern. Notice that female sexual responses follow one of three basic patterns. Pattern *A* somewhat resembles the male pattern, except that pattern *A* includes the possibility of multiple orgasms (the second peak in pattern *A*) without falling below the plateau level. Pattern *B* represents nonorgasmic arousal. Pattern *C* represents intense female orgasm, which resembles the male pattern in its intensity and rapid resolution.

nearly 3,500 people from 18 to 50 years of age who were randomly selected, a sharp contrast from earlier samples that were based on unrepresentative groups of volunteers.

Among the key findings from the 1994 survey:

- Americans tend to fall into three categories: One-third have sex twice a week or more, one-third a few times a month, and one-third a few times a year or not at all.
- Married couples have sex the most and also are the most likely to have orgasms when they do. Figure 9.5 portrays the frequency of sex for married and noncohabiting individuals in the past year.
- Most Americans do not engage in kinky sexual acts. When asked about their favorite sexual acts, the vast majority (96 percent) said that vaginal sex was "very" or "somewhat" appealing. Oral sex was in third place, after an activity that many have not labeled a sexual act—watching a partner undress.
- Adultery is clearly the exception rather than the rule. Nearly 75 percent of the married men and 85 percent of the married women indicated that they have never been unfaithful.
- Men think about sex far more than women do—54 percent of the men said they think about it every day or several times a day, whereas 67 percent of the women said they think about it only a few times a week or a few times a month.

In sum, one of the most powerful messages in the 1994 survey was that Americans' sexual lives are more conservative than previously believed. Although 17 percent of the men and 3 percent of the women said they have had sex with at least 21 partners, the overall impression from the survey was that sexual behavior is ruled by marriage and monogamy for most Americans.

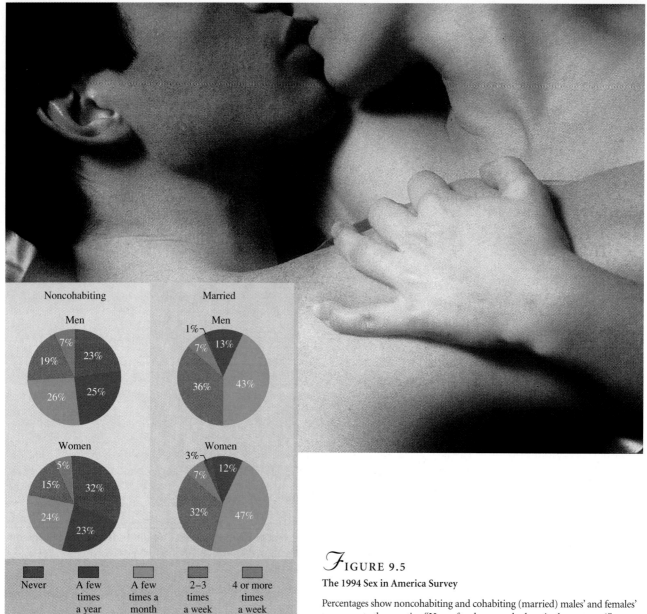

Noncohabiting

Men

23%
25%
26%
19%
7%

Women

32%
23%
24%
15%
5%

Married

Men

1%
13%
43%
36%
7%

Women

3%
12%
47%
32%
7%

| ■ Never | ■ A few times a year | A few times a month | 2–3 times a week | 4 or more times a week |

𝓕IGURE 9.5

The 1994 Sex in America Survey

Percentages show noncohabiting and cohabiting (married) males' and females' responses to the question "How often have you had sex in the past year?"

sexual script

A stereotyped pattern of role prescriptions for how individuals should behave sexually.

traditional religious script

A sexual script in which sex is acceptable only within marriage; both premarital and extramarital sex are taboo, especially for women. In this script, sex is for reproduction and sometimes for affection.

romantic script

A sexual script in which sex is synonymous with love. In this script, if people develop a relationship and fall in love, it is acceptable for them to have sex, whether married or not.

Whether we are conservative or permissive in our sexual practices may be related to the kind of sexual script we accept. A **sexual script** *is a stereotyped pattern of role prescriptions for how an individual should behave sexually.*

Two well-known sexual scripts are the traditional religious script and the romantic script. In the **traditional religious script,** *sex is accepted only within marriage. Extramarital sex is taboo, especially for women. In this sexual script, sex means reproduction and sometimes affection. In the* **romantic script,** *sex is synonymous with love. According to the romantic script, if we develop a relationship with someone and fall in love, it is acceptable to have sex with the person whether we are married or not.* In the twentieth century in America, the romantic sexual script has become increasingly popular.

Females and males have often been socialized to follow different sexual scripts (King, 1996). Differences in female and male sexual scripts can cause problems for individuals as they work out their sexual identities and seek sexual fulfillment. Females learn to link sexual intercourse with love more than males do. Females might rationalize their sexual behavior by telling themselves that they were swept away by love. Far more females than males have intercourse only with partners they love and would like to marry. Other reasons females offer for having sexual intercourse include giving in to the male's desire for pleasure, gambling that sex is a way to get a boyfriend or husband, curiosity, and sexual desire unrelated to loving and caring. The male sexual script emphasizes sexual conquest; higher status tends to accrue to males who can claim substantial sexual activity. For males, sex and love often are not as intertwined as they are for females.

Although it has become increasingly acceptable for females to engage in premarital sex, a **double standard,** *a belief that many sexual activities are acceptable for males but not for females,* still exists in many areas of sexuality. The double standard can harm women because it encourages them to deny their sexuality and do minimal planning to ensure that their sexual activities are safe. Further, the double standard encourages males to dismiss or devalue their female partner's values and feelings. It also puts pressure on males to be as sexually active as possible.

Homosexual Attitudes and Behavior.　Until the end of the nineteenth century, it was generally believed that people were either heterosexual or homosexual. Today, it is more accepted to view sexual orientation as occurring along a continuum from exclusively heterosexual to exclusively homosexual rather than as an either/or proposition. Kinsey and his associates (1948) described this continuum along a 6-point scale, with a 0 signifying exclusive heterosexuality and 6 indicating exclusive homosexuality (see figure 9.6). Some individuals are also **bisexual,** *being sexually attracted to people of both sexes.* In Kinsey's research, approximately 1 percent of individuals reported being bisexual (1.2 percent of males and .7 percent of females) and about 2 to 5 percent of individuals reported being homosexual (4.7 percent of males and 1.8 percent of females). In the recent Sex in America survey, only 2.7 percent of the men and 1.3 percent of the women reported having had homosexual sex in the past year (Michael & others, 1994).

Many people think of heterosexual and homosexual behavior as distinct patterns of behavior that are easy to define and are fixed decisions. In fact, preference for a sexual partner of the same or opposite sex is not always a fixed decision, made once in life and adhered to forever (Hershberger, 1998). For example, an individual, especially a male, might engage in homosexual experimentation in adolescence but not as an adult.

Why are some individuals homosexual and others heterosexual? Speculation about this question has been extensive, but no firm answers are available. Homosexual and heterosexual males and females have similar physiological responses during sexual arousal and seem to be aroused by the same types of tactile stimulation. Investigators find no differences between homosexuals and heterosexuals in a wide range of attitudes, behaviors, and adjustments (Bell, Weinberg, & Mammersmith, 1981). Recognizing that homosexuality is not a form of mental illness, the American Psychiatric Association discontinued its classification of homosexuality as a disorder, except in those cases where the individuals themselves consider the sexual orientation to be abnormal.

double standard

A belief that many sexual activities are acceptable for males but not females.

bisexual

Being sexually attracted to people of both sexes.

$\mathcal{F}$IGURE 9.6

The Continuum of Sexual Orientation

The continuum ranges from exclusive heterosexuality, which Kinsey and associates (1948) rated as 0, to exclusive homosexuality (6). People who are about equally attracted to both sexes (ratings 2 to 4) are bisexual.

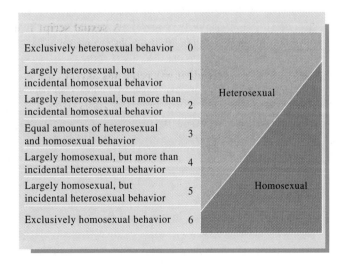

Exclusively heterosexual behavior	0
Largely heterosexual, but incidental homosexual behavior	1
Largely heterosexual, but more than incidental homosexual behavior	2
Equal amounts of heterosexual and homosexual behavior	3
Largely homosexual, but more than incidental heterosexual behavior	4
Largely homosexual, but incidental heterosexual behavior	5
Exclusively homosexual behavior	6

Heterosexual

Homosexual

An individual's sexual orientation—heterosexual, homosexual, or bisexual—is most likely determined by a combination of genetic, hormonal, cognitive, and environmental factors (Whitman, Diamond, & Martin, 1993). Most experts on homosexuality believe that no one factor alone causes homosexuality and that the relative weight of each factor may vary from one individual to the next. In effect, no one knows exactly what causes an individual to be homosexual. Scientists have a clearer picture of what does not cause homosexuality. For example, children raised by gay or lesbian parents or couples are no more likely to be homosexual than are children raised by heterosexual parents (Patterson, 1996). There also is no evidence that male homosexuality is caused by a dominant mother or a weak father, or that female homosexuality is caused by girls choosing male role models. One of the biological factors believed to be involved in homosexuality is prenatal hormone conditions (Gladue, 1994). In the second to fifth months after conception, the exposure of the fetus to hormone levels characteristic of females may cause the individual (male or female) to be attracted to males. If this critical prenatal period hypothesis turns out to be correct, it would explain why researchers and clinicians have found that a homosexual orientation is difficult to modify.

Sex-Related Problems.   In this section, we will explore various kinds of problems related to sexuality. These problems include **psychosexual disorders,** *which are sexual problems caused mainly by psychological problems,* as well as situations in which sex is used to cause harm (such as rape and sexual harassment).

Psychosexual Dysfunctions.   Myths about males and females would have us believe that many women are "frigid" and uninterested in sexual pleasure, while most men can hardly get enough. Both myths conceal the facts, revealed through the accumulating experiences of sex therapy clinics (Crooks & Bauer, 1996). The facts are that both women and men have similar desires for sexual pleasure, but both sexes may experience psychological problems that interfere with the attainment of pleasure. **Psychosexual dysfunctions** *are disorders that involve impairments in the sexual response cycle, either in the desire for gratification or in the ability to achieve it.* In disorders associated with the desire phase, both men and women show little or no sexual drive or interest. In disorders associated with the excitement phase, men may not be able to maintain an erection. In disorders associated with the orgasmic phase, both women and men reach orgasm too quickly or not at all. Premature ejaculation in men occurs when the time between the beginning of sexual stimulation and ejaculation is unsatisfactorily brief. Many women do not routinely experience orgasm in sexual intercourse, a pattern so common it can hardly be called dysfunctional. Inhibited male orgasm does occur, but it is much less common than inhibited female orgasm.

The treatment of psychosexual dysfunctions has undergone nothing short of a revolution in recent years. Once thought of as extremely difficult therapeutic challenges, most cases of psychosexual dysfunction now yield to techniques tailored to improve sexual functioning (Bhugra & de Silva, 1998; LaPera & Nicastro, 1996).

Attempts to treat psychosexual dysfunctions through traditional forms of psychotherapy, as if the dysfunctions were personality disorders, have not been very successful; however, treatments that focus directly on each sexual dysfunction have reached success rates of 90 percent or more (McConaghy, 1993). For example, the success rate of a treatment that encourages women to enjoy their bodies and engage in self-stimulation to orgasm, with a vibrator if necessary, approaches 100 percent (Anderson, 1983). Some of these women subsequently transfer their newly developed sexual responsiveness to interactions with partners. Success rates also approach 100 percent in the treatment of premature ejaculation, but considerably lower success rates occur in the treatment of males who cannot maintain an erection.

Incest.   **Incest** *is sex between close relatives, which is virtually universally taboo.* By far the most common form of incest is brother–sister sex, followed by father–daughter sex. Mother–son incest is rare. Same-sex incest, usually father–son, is also rare. Incest is psy-

psychosexual disorders

Sexual problems caused mainly by psychological factors.

psychosexual dysfunctions

Disorders that involve impairments in the sexual response cycle, either in the desire for gratification or in the ability to achieve it.

incest

Sex between close relatives, which is virtually universally taboo.

chologically harmful, not only for immediate family relationships, but also for the future relationships of a child involved in incest. A biological hazard of incest is that an offspring that results from incest has a strong likelihood of being mentally retarded.

Paraphilias. **Paraphilias** *are psychosexual disorders in which the source of an individual's sexual satisfaction is an unusual object, ritual, or situation.* Many sexual patterns deviate from what we consider to be "normal." These abnormal patterns of sexual arousal from unusual sources include fetishism, transvestism, transsexualism, exhibitionism, voyeurism, sadism, masochism, and pedophilia (Doctor's, Neff, 1998).

Fetishism *is a psychosexual disorder in which an individual relies on inanimate objects or a specific body part for sexual gratification.* Even though an individual may have a sexual preference—for example, a man's preference for women with long legs or a woman's preference for men with beards, most of us are attracted to someone because of a wide range of personal factors. Some individuals are obsessed with certain objects—fur, women's underpants, stockings—that arouse them. Most fetishists are male.

Transvestism *is a psychosexual disorder in which an individual obtains sexual gratification by dressing up as a member of the opposite sex.* Most transvestites view themselves as heterosexual and lead quiet, conventional lives, cross-dressing usually only in the privacy of their homes. A transvestite might cross-dress only during sex with his or her spouse.

Transsexualism *is a psychosexual disorder in which an individual has an overwhelming desire to become a member of the opposite sex.* The individual's gender identity is at odds with the anatomical facts, and he or she may undergo surgery to change sex.

Exhibitionism and voyeurism are the two sex practices that often come to the attention of the police. **Exhibitionism** *is a psychosexual disorder in which individuals expose their sexual anatomy to others to obtain sexual gratification.* **Voyeurism** *is a psychosexual disorder in which individuals derive sexual gratification by observing the sex organs or sex acts of others, often from a secret vantage point.* Both exhibitionism and voyeurism provide substitute gratification and a sense of power to otherwise sexually anxious individuals, especially males. In many instances, voyeurs are sexually inhibited.

Aggressive sexual fantasies are not uncommon, and, in the course of sexual activity, a slight amount of force can be involved. However, in normal sexual activity, force is not extensive and does not harm the sexual partner or oneself. In contrast, **sadism** *is a psychosexual disorder in which individuals derive sexual gratification from inflicting pain on others.* The word *sadism,* comes from the novels of the Marquis de Sade (1740–1814), who wrote about erotic scenes in which women were whipped. **Masochism** *is a psychosexual disorder in which individuals derive sexual gratification from being subjected to a physical pain, inflicted by others or themselves.* The word *masochism* comes from the novels of Austrian writer Leopold von Sacher-Masoch (1836–1895), whose male characters became sexually excited and gratified when they were physically abused by women. It is not unusual for a sadist and a masochist to pair up to satisfy each other' sexual wishes; such relationships are called sadomasochistic.

Pedophilia *is a psychosexual disorder in which the sex object is a child and the intimacy usually involves manipulation of the child's genitals.* A pedophile covertly or overtly masturbates while talking to children, manipulates the child's sex organs, or has the child engage in sexual behavior. Most pedophiles are men, usually in their thirties or forties. Like exhibitionists, they often have puritanical ideas about sex. The target of a male pedophile often is a girl he knows well, such as a relative, neighbor, or family friend.

Rape. **Rape** *is forcible sexual intercourse with a person who does not give consent.* Legal definitions of rape differ from state to state. For example, in some states, husbands are not prohibited from forcing their wives to have intercourse, although this has been challenged in several states. Because of difficulties involved in reporting rape, the actual incidence is not easily determined. It appears that rape occurs most often in large cities, where it has been reported that 8 of every 10,000 women 12 years and older are raped each year. Nearly 200,000 rapes are reported each year in the United States.

paraphilias
Psychosexual disorders in which the source of an individual's sexual satisfaction is an unusual object, ritual, or situation.

fetishism
Psychosexual disorder in which an individual relies on inanimate objects or a specific body part for sexual gratification.

transvestism
Psychosexual disorder in which an individual obtains sexual gratification by dressing up as a member of the opposite sex.

transsexualism
A psychosexual disorder in which an individual has an overwhelming desire to become a member of the opposite sex.

exhibitionism
A psychosexual disorder in which individuals obtain sexual gratification from exposing their sexual anatomy to others.

voyeurism
A psychosexual disorder in which individuals obtain sexual gratification from observing the sex organs or sex acts of others, often from a secret vantage point.

sadism
A psychosexual disorder in which individuals obtain sexual gratification from inflicting pain on others.

masochism
A psychosexual disorder in which individuals obtain sexual gratification from being subjected to pain, inflicted by others or themselves.

pedophilia
A psychosexual disorder in which the sex object is a child and the intimacy usually involves manipulation of the child's genitals.

rape
Forcible sexual intercourse with a person who does not give consent.

Why is rape so pervasive in the American culture? Feminist writers believe males are socialized to be sexually aggressive, to regard women as inferior beings, and to view their own pleasure as the most important objective. Researchers have found the following common characteristics among rapists: aggression enhances the offender's sense of power or masculinity; rapists are angry at women generally; and they want to hurt and humiliate the victim (Browne & Williams, 1993).

An increasing concern is **date or acquaintance rape,** *which is coercive sexual activity directed at someone with whom the individual is at least casually acquainted.* Date rape is an increasing problem on college campuses (Rosen & Stith, 1995). As many as two-thirds of college males admit to fondling females against their will and one-half admit to forced sexual activity.

Rape is a traumatic experience for the victim and those close to her (Koss & Boeschen, 1998). The rape victim initially feels shock and numbness, and is often acutely disorganized. Some women show their distress through words and tears, others show more internalized suffering. As victims strive to get their lives back to normal, they may experience depression, fear, and anxiety for months or years. Sexual dysfunctions, such as reduced sexual desire and an inability to reach orgasm, occur in 50 percent of rape victims (Sprei & Courtois, 1988). Many rape victims make changes in their lifestyle—such as moving to a new apartment or refusing to go out at night. A woman's recovery depends on both her coping abilities and her psychological adjustments prior to the assault. Social support from parents, boyfriend or husband, and others close to her are important factors in recovery, as is the availability of professional counseling, which sometimes is obtained through a rape crisis center (Allison & Wrightsman, 1993). For some recommendations on reducing rape, see Improving Personal and Cognitive Skills ("Taking Action for a Rape-Free Culture").

Although most victims of rape are women, male rape does occur. Men in prisons are especially vulnerable to rape, usually by heterosexual males who use rape as a means of establishing their dominance and power. Though it might seem impossible for a man to be raped by a woman, a man's erection is not completely under his voluntary control, and some cases of male rape by women have been reported (Sarrel & Masters, 1982). Although male victims account for fewer than 5 percent of all rapes, the trauma that males suffer is just as great as that experienced by females.

Sexual Harassment.   Women encounter sexual harassment in many different forms—from sexist remarks and covert physical contact (patting, brushing against their bodies) to blatant propositions and sexual assaults (Paludi, 1995). Literally millions of women experience such sexual harassment each year in work and educational settings (Paludi, in press). Sexual harassment can result in serious psychological consequences for the victim.

date or acquaintance rape

Coercive sexual activity directed at someone with whom the perpetrator is at least casually acquainted.

$\mathcal{I}$mproving Personal and Cognitive Skills

Taking Action for a Rape-Free Culture

Following are some recommendations for men from men about rape (Men Stopping Men Rape, 1997):

• Understand that without mutual agreement, sex becomes rape.

• Be sensitive to expectations. Don't project your sexual feelings onto your partner by just assuming that she or he feels the same way you do. Also, establishing consent at one point does not reduce the need to reestablish consent later.

• Take no for an answer. Too often men ignore it when a woman says no, assuming that she means maybe or even yes. Accept what women say. If they say no, it means no, and respect that.

• Recognize and intervene to stop sexual assault. Assault can occur anyplace: at a party, on the street, at the workplace. Be aware of women being assaulted physically or verbally and intervene with comments or questions. Physically intervene if necessary. It is important to ask the woman if she wants help.

• Stop being violent. No disagreement needs to produce violent behavior. There are many alternatives, such as talking about the problem, accepting a compromise, and taking a "time-out" to cool down.

Sexual harassment is a manifestation of power and domination of one person over another. The elimination of such exploitation requires the development of work and academic environments that are compatible with the needs of women workers and students, providing them with equal opportunities to develop a career and obtain an education in a climate free of sexual harassment (Marks & Nelson, 1993).

We have seen that environmental influences play a key role in understanding the motives of hunger and sex. But just as the environment influences us, so we, too, can influence our environment. Next, we will explore the motivation involved in adapting to and mastering our environment.

Hunger and Sex

In hunger, the brain monitors both blood sugar levels and the condition of the stomach (interest in the stomach was stimulated by Canon's research), then integrates this information. Hypothalamic regions are important in hunger, especially VMH. Schachter stressed that environmental cues are involved in the control of eating, but Rodin argues that conscious self-control and exercise are more important than external cues in understanding hunger and eating behavior.

Biological, psychological, and sociocultural factors are involved in sexual arousal. Hormones are important biological factors. Androgens are the main class of sex hormones in males, and estrogens are the main class in females. Hormonal control of sexual behavior is stronger in nonhuman animals than in humans. Masters and Johnson mapped out the human sexual response cycle, which consists of four phases: excitement, plateau, orgasm, and resolution.

In the 1994 Sex in America survey, Americans' sexual lives were portrayed as being more conservative than in previous surveys. Sexual scripts are stereotyped patterns of how people should behave sexually, and they often are different for males and females. Today, it generally is accepted to view sexual orientation along a continuum from being exclusively heterosexual to being exclusively homosexual. An individual's sexual orientation is likely determined by a combination of genetic, hormonal, cognitive, and environmental factors.

Psychosexual dysfunctions involve impairments in the sexual response cycle. Significant advancements in the treatment of these dysfunctions have occurred in recent years. Incest is virtually universally taboo. Paraphilias are psychosexual disorders in which the source of sexual pleasure is an unusual object, ritual, or situation. Paraphilias include fetishism, transvestism, transsexualism, exhibitionism, voyeurism, sadism, masochism, and pedophilia.

Unfortunately, some individuals force others to engage in sexual activity against their will. Rape is forcible sexual intercourse with a person who does not give consent. Rape usually produces traumatic reactions in its victims. Sexual harassment occurs when one person uses his or her power over another individual in a sexual manner.

Competence

We are a species motivated to gain mastery over our world, to explore unknown environments with enthusiasm and curiosity, and to achieve. In the 1950s, psychologists recognized that motivation involves much more than the reduction of biological needs. **Competence motivation** *is the motivation to deal effectively with the environment, to be adept at what we attempt, to process information efficiently, and to make the world a better place.* R. W. White (1959) said we do these things not because they serve biological needs, but because we have an internal motivation to interact effectively with our environment.

Among the research White used to support his concept of competence motivation were experiments that showed that organisms are motivated to seek stimulation rather than to reduce a need. For example, monkeys solved simple problems just for the opportunity to watch a toy train (Butler, 1953) (see figure 9.7). Rats consistently chose a complex maze with a number of pathways over a simple maze with few pathways. A series of experiments suggested that college students could not tolerate sensory deprivation for more than 2 to 3 days (Bexton, Heron, & Scott, 1954). These students developed a strong motivation to quit the experiment, even though they were getting paid to participate in it. They became bored, restless, and irritable. Even when you have looked forward to a day off, you probably can sit around for only so long doing nothing. Sooner or later you get bored. Competence motivation fuels our curiosity and involvement with the world.

competence motivation

The motivation to deal effectively with the environment, to be adept at what we attempt, and to make the world a better place.

Motivation for Novel Stimulation

This monkey showed a motivation for novel stimulation and was willing to work just so he could unlock the window and watch a toy train go around in a circle.

> *Even if you are on the right track, you will get run over if you just sit there.*
> —WILL ROGERS, *American Writer and Humorist, 20th Century*

Although spending days in isolation can be stressful, might shorter periods of environmental restriction be beneficial? Researchers have found that lying in a water immersion tank (which restricts environmental stimulation) for about twenty 1-hour sessions can reduce blood pressure, chronic pain, and stress (Suedfield & Coren, 1989). In our fast-paced modern world, then, sometimes it makes good sense to restrict our environmental stimulation for short periods of time.

Achievement

achievement motivation (need for achievement)

The desire to accomplish something, to reach a standard of excellence, and to expend effort to excel.

Some people do not merely feel compelled to be competent. They are instead highly motivated to succeed (Eccles, Wigfield & Schiefele, 1998). They spend considerable effort striving to excel. Other people are not as motivated to succeed and don't work as hard to achieve. These two types of individuals vary in their **achievement motivation,** or **need for achievement,** *the desire to accomplish something, to reach a standard of excellence, and to expend effort to excel.* Borrowing from Henry Murray's (1938) theory and measurement of personality, psychologist David McClelland (1955) assessed achievement by showing individuals ambiguous pictures that were likely to stimulate achievement-related responses. The individuals were asked to tell a story about the picture, and their comments were scored according to how strongly they reflected achievement. Researchers have found that individuals whose stories reflect high achievement motivation have a stronger hope for success than fear of failure, are moderate rather than high or low risk takers, and persist with effort when tasks become difficult (Atkinson & Raynor, 1974).

> *Whatever you can do, or dream you can, begin it. Boldness has genius, power and magic in it.*
> —JOHANN WOLFGANG VON GOETHE, *German Poet and Playwright, 19th Century*

McClelland (1978) also wondered if you could boost achievement behavior by increasing achievement motivation. To find out, he trained the businessmen in a village in India to become more achievement oriented, encouraging them to increase their hope for success, reduce their fear of failure, take moderate risks, and persist with a great deal of effort when tasks become difficult. Compared to village businessmen in a nearby town, the village businessmen who were trained by McClelland started more new businesses and employed more new people in the 2 years after the training.

Cognitive Factors in Achievement.   Since the time of McClelland's early theory and research, explanations of achievement have increasingly become more cognitive. Contemporary views of achievement often emphasize such cognitive factors as attributions, intrinsic motivation, goal setting, and planning.

Formulating Achievement Attributions.   **Attribution theory** *states that individuals are motivated to discover the underlying causes of behavior as part of the effort to make sense out of the behavior.* In a way, attribution theorists say, people are like intuitive scientists, seeking the cause behind what happens.

The reasons individuals behave the way they do can be classified in a number of ways, but one basic distinction stands out above all others—the distinction between internal causes, such as the actor's personality traits or motives, and external causes, which are environmental, situational factors such as rewards or task difficulty (Heider, 1958). If college students do not do well on a test, do they attribute it to the teacher's plotting against them and making the test too difficult (external cause) or to their not studying hard enough (internal cause)? The answer to such a question influences how people feel about themselves. If students believe that their performance is the teachers' fault, they will not feel as bad as when they do poorly because they do not spend enough time studying.

An extremely important aspect of internal causes for achievement is *effort* (Brophy, 1998). Unlike many causes of success, effort is under a person's control and amenable to change. The importance of effort in achievement is recognized even by children. In one study, third- to sixth-grade students felt that effort was the most effective strategy for good school performance (Skinner, Wellborn, & Connell, 1990).

Intrinsic and Extrinsic Motivation.   Earlier in this chapter we mentioned that whether motivation is internal (intrinsic) or external (extrinsic) is a key aspect of understanding motivation. This is especially true in the area of achievement.

Almost every boss, parent, or teacher has wondered whether or not to offer a reward to someone who does well (extrinsic motivation), or whether to let the individual's internal, self-determined motivation operate (intrinsic motivation). If someone is producing shoddy work, seems bored, or has a negative attitude, offering incentives may improve his or her motivation. But there are times when external rewards can diminish achievement motivation. One study showed that, of students who already had a strong interest in art, those who did not expect a reward spent more time drawing than did their counterparts who knew they would be rewarded for drawing (Lepper, Greene, & Nisbett, 1973).

Is it reasonable to draw from this study the generalization that extrinsic rewards always decrease intrinsic motivation? The undermining effects of extrinsic rewards appear to be linked to three factors (Reeve, 1996): expectation of being rewarded, salience of the reward, and tangibility of the reward. If people engage in a task with an expectation that a reward will follow, they will be less likely to develop intrinsic motivation for the task. A reward's *salience* is how prominent the role of the reward is in the activity. If the reward generates too much interest, intrinsic interest in the task also is undermined. Finally, tangible rewards, those that can be seen, felt, or tasted, can undercut intrinsic motivation, while praise and encouragement often do not.

Goal Setting and Planning.   Goal setting and planning are critical aspects of achievement that often work in concert. When people set goals, they need to plan how to reach the goals. Goals help individuals to reach their dreams, increase their self-discipline, and maintain interest. To determine how goal-oriented you are, complete the Self-Assessment. And to read about some good strategies for setting goals see Improving Personal and Cognitive Skills ("Strategies for Setting Goals").

attribution theory
The theory that individuals are motivated to discover the underlying causes of behavior as part of their effort to make sense out of the behavior.

Self-Assessment

How Goal-Directed Are You?

To find out how goal-directed you are, mark the answer that best describes your behavior in each of these situations:

	Almost always like me	Like me most of the time	Not like me most of the time	Hardly ever like me
1. When I am faced with small tasks that need attention, I attend to them right away.				
2. When I am involved in a project or task that is important to me, I take some time to clarify my objectives.				
3. I'm good at not getting bogged down in inconsequential details.				
4. When I write down a list of things to do on a given day, I manage to get all of them done.				
5. My planning keeps me from saying or doing things I might regret afterward.				
6. I can accurately project when projects will get done.				
7. I develop both long-term and short-term goals for important things in my life.				
8. My responsibilities don't overwhelm me.				
9. Give me a deadline and I will meet it.				
10. When I am under pressure, I still plan my days and weeks in a clear, logical manner.				

Scoring

Give yourself 4 points for each time you answered "Almost always like me," 3 points for "Like me most of the time," 2 points for "Not like me most of the time," and 1 point for "Hardly ever like me."

Total Score: ____

Interpretation

35–40 points: You are without question a goal-directed person. You organize your life and do a good job of planning. In some cases, though, you might be organizing your life to an extreme. Don't forget to smell the roses and take at least some time to enjoy your college life.

25–34 points: You are above average in being goal-directed, although your goal-directed behavior might vary with the situation or activity. Think more about setting goals in all of the important areas of your life.

15–24 points: You need to work on becoming more goal-directed. You likely are not reaching your full potential because you are not very goal-directed.

14 points or below: You might consider yourself a spontaneous or free-spirited person, but you are jeopardizing your college success by not being goal-directed. You likely are easily distracted and probably procrastinate too much. Make a serious commitment to becoming more goal-directed.

SOURCE: Adapted from Skinner, K. (1997). *How goal-directd are you?* Dallas, TX: Southern Methodist University Press.

Currently, there is a great deal of interest in studying people's self-generated goals (Emmons, 1997). Some examples of such goals are "personal projects," "life tasks," and "personal strivings" (Emmons & Kaiser, 1995). Personal projects can range from trivial pursuits (such as letting a bad haircut grow out) to life goals (such as becoming a good parent). Life tasks are problems individuals are currently working on. They usually focus on normal life transitions such as going to college, getting married, and entering an occupation. Many college students say that their life tasks revolve around academic achieve-

Improving Personal and Cognitive Skills

Strategies for Setting Goals

Following are some helpful strategies in setting goals:

- *Set goals that are challenging, reasonable, and specific.*
  When people set challenging goals, they commit to improving themselves. A good strategy is to be realistic but to stretch to achieve something meaningful. Another good strategy is to set concrete, specific goals. A fuzzy goal is "I want to be successful." A more specific goal is "I want to make dean's list."
- *Develop both long-term and short-term goals.*
  Some long-term goals, like getting into medical school or becoming an engineer, take years to reach. Other goals are more short-term, such as studying 10 hours this weekend. Your short-term goals are steps along the journey to your long-term goals.

- *Become a systematic planner.*
  To plan effectively, you need to be organized. This means getting your life in order and setting priorities. Good planning means not showing up for a class to find yourself facing a test you did not know about. Good planning also means that you hand in papers on time. And it means that you don't have to cram for tests.
- *Live your life one day at a time.*
  David McNally, the author of *Even Eagles Need a Push* (1990) advises that when you set goals and plan, be sure to remember that you live your life one day at a time. Make your commitments in bite-size chunks. A house is built one brick at a time, a cathedral one stone at a time. The artist paints one stroke at a time. The student studies one hour at a time.

ment and social concerns (Cantor & Langston, 1989). Personal strivings represent what an individual is typically trying to do. For example, someone might say that she typically tries to do well in school.

Not only are cognitive factors, such as attribution, intrinsic motivation, and self-generation of goals important in understanding achievement, so are the sociocultural contexts in which we live.

Cultural, Ethnic, and Socioeconomic Variations in Achievement. People in the United States are often more achievement oriented than people in many other countries. One study of 104 societies revealed that the parents in nonindustrialized countries placed a lower value on their children's achievement and independence and a higher value on obedience and cooperation than did the parents in industrialized countries (Barry, Child, & Bacon, 1959). In comparisons between Anglo-American children and Mexican and Latino children, the Anglo-American children were more competitive and less cooperative. For example, one study found that Anglo-American children are more likely to keep other children from gaining when they could not realize those gains themselves (Kagan & Madsen, 1972). Another study showed that Mexican children are more family oriented, whereas Anglo-American children tend to be more concerned about themselves (Holtzmann, 1982).

Until recently, researchers studying achievement focused almost exclusively on White males, and when achievement in ethnic minority groups has been studied, the cultural differences have too often been viewed against standards of achievements for White males. As a result, many researchers have reached the conclusion that ethnic minorities are somehow deficient when it comes to achievement (Gibbs & Huang, 1989).

In addition, most studies on ethnic minorities do not take into account socioeconomic status. Socioeconomic status (also called SES) is determined by a combination of occupation, education, and income. When both ethnicity and social class are taken into account in the same study, social class tends to be a far better predictor of achievement than is ethnicity (Graham, 1986). For example, middle-class individuals, regardless of their ethnic background, have higher aspirations and expectations for success, and they recognize the importance of effort more than their lower-class counterparts do. Sandra Graham (1990), for example, has found that middle-class African American children do not fit the stereotypes of either deviant or special populations. They, like their middle-class White counterparts, have high expectations for their own achievement and understand that failure is often due to lack of effort rather than to lack of luck.

UCLA psychologist Sandra Graham is shown here talking with a group of young boys about motivation. Dr. Graham has conducted important research showing that middle-class African American children—like their White counterparts—have high achievement expectations and understand that their failure is often due to lack of effort rather than to lack of luck.

It's also an indisputable fact that many people from ethnic minority backgrounds face educational, career, and social barriers (Huston, McLoyd, & Coll, 1994; Swanson, 1995). The Civil Rights Acts of 1964 and 1991 have made some progress in chipping away at these barriers, but much more needs to be done. We do not have all of the answers to the problems of poverty and racism in this country, but, as the Reverend Jesse Jackson commented, perhaps we have begun to ask some of the right questions.

Review

Competence motivation is the motivation to deal effectively with the environment, to be adept at what one attempts, to process information efficiently, and to make the world a better place. This concept recognizes that motivation is much more than simply reducing physiological needs. We studied two aspects of competence motivation.

Achievement motivation (need for achievement) is the desire to accomplish something, to reach a standard of excellence, to expend effort to excel. Cognitive factors in achievement are highlighted in attribution theory, intrinsic motivation, and goal-setting/planning.

Intrinsic motivation is the desire to be competent and to do something for its own sake. Extrinsic motivation is externally determined by rewards and punishments. In many instances, individuals' achievement motivation is influenced by both internal and external factors.

Effort is especially important in intrinsic motivation. Goal setting and planning go hand in hand in achieving. Goals help individuals to reach their dreams, increase their self-discipline, and maintain their interest. Goal-directed individuals set challenging, reasonable, and specific goals, establish long-term and short-term goals, and plan systematically.

Individuals in the United States are more achievement oriented than individuals in most other cultures are. A special concern is the achievement of individuals from various ethnic groups. Too often ethnic differences are interpreted as "deficits" by middle-class, White standards. When researchers examine both ethnicity and social class in the same study, social class is often a much better predictor of achievement. Middle-class individuals fare better than their lower-class counterparts in a variety of achievement situations.

EMOTION

Motivation and emotion are closely linked. Think about sex, which often is associated with joy; about aggression, which usually is associated with anger; and about achievement, which is associated with pride, joy, and anxiety. The terms *motivation* and *emotion* both come from the Latin word *movere,* which means "to move." Both motivation and emotion spur us into action.

Defining and Classifying Emotion

Just as with motivation, there are different kinds and intensities of emotions. A person can be not only motivated to eat rather than have sex, but more or less hungry, or more or less interested in having sex. Similarly, a person can be happy or angry, and can be fairly happy or ecstatic, annoyed or fuming.

Defining emotion is difficult because it is not always easy to tell when a person is in an emotional state. Are you in an emotional state when your heart beats fast, your palms sweat, and your stomach churns? when you think about how much you are in love with someone? when you smile or grimace? The body, the mind, and the face play important roles in understanding emotion. Psychologists debate how critical each is in determining whether we are in an emotional state (Evans, 1989). For our purposes, we will define **emotion** as *feeling, or affect, that involves a mixture of physiological arousal (fast heart rate, for example), conscious experience (thinking about being in love with someone, for example), and behavior (smiling and grimacing, for example).*

> *Blossoms are scattered by the wind and the wind cares nothing, but the blossoms of the heart no wind can touch.*
>
> —YOSHIDA KENKO, *Japanese Author, 20th Century*

When we think about emotions, a few dramatic feelings, such as rage, fear, and glorious joy, usually spring to mind. But emotions can be subtle as well—the feeling a mother has when she holds her baby, the mild irritation of boredom, the uneasiness of living in the nuclear age. And the kinds of emotions we can experience are legion. There are more than 200 words for emotions in the English language. How have psychologists handled the complex task of classifying emotions?

Wheel Models. A number of psychologists use wheel diagrams to classify the emotions we experience. One such model was proposed by Robert Plutchik (1980), who believes that emotions have four dimensions: (1) they are positive or negative; (2) they are primary or mixed; (3) many are polar opposites; and (4) they vary in intensity. Ecstasy and enthusiasm are positive emotions; grief and anger are negative emotions. For example, think about your ecstasy when you get an unexpected A on a test, or your enthusiasm about the football game this weekend—these are positive emotions. In contrast, think about negative emotions, such as your grief when someone close to you dies or your anger when someone verbally attacks you. Positive emotions enhance self-esteem; negative emotions lower self-esteem. Positive emotions improve our relationships with others; negative emotions often depress the quality of those relationships.

Plutchik believes that emotions are like colors. Just as every color of the spectrum can be produced by mixing the primary colors, so can every emotion be produced by mixing what he calls "primary emotions." Plutchik describes anger, disgust, sadness, surprise, fear, acceptance, joy, and anticipation as the primary emotions. As shown in figure 9.8, Plutchik developed the emotion wheel to illustrate how mixtures of primary emotions that are adjacent to each other can generate other emotions. For example, combining sadness and surprise produces disappointment. Jealousy is a combination of love and anger. Some emotions are opposite. These include love and remorse, optimism and disappointment. Plutchik argues that people cannot experience emotions that are polar opposites simultaneously. That is, you cannot feel sad at the same time you feel happy. Imagine just getting a test back in class. As you scan the paper for your grade, your emotional response is happy or sad, not both.

Two-Dimensional Approach. The two-dimensional approach to classifying emotions argues that there are two broad dimensions of emotional experience: positive affectivity and negative affectivity. **Positive affectivity (PA)** *refers to the range of positive emotion, from high energy, enthusiasm, and excitement to being calm, quiet, and withdrawn. Joy or happiness involves positive affectivity.* **Negative affectivity (NA)** *refers to emotions that are negatively toned, such as anxiety, anger, guilt, and sadness.* PA and NA are independent dimensions, in that a person can be high along both dimensions at the same time (for example, in a high energy state and enthusiastic, yet angry).

Positive Affectivity: Happiness. Our positive affectivity is influenced by how aroused we are. Early in this century, two psychologists described the role of arousal in performance.

emotion
Feeling, or affect, that involves a mixture of arousal (fast heartbeat, for example), conscious experience (thinking about being in love with someone, for example), and overt behavior (smiling or grimacing, for example).

positive affectivity (PA)
The range of positive emotion, from high energy, enthusiasm, and excitement to being calm, quiet, and withdrawn. Joy and happiness involve positive affectivity.

negative affectivity (NA)
Emotions that are negatively toned, such as anxiety, anger, guilt, and sadness.

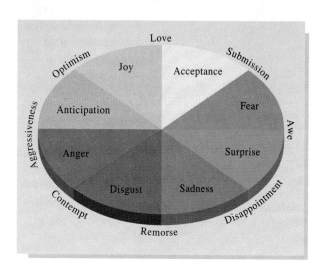

Figure 9.8

Plutchik's Wheel of Emotions

This diagram shows the eight primary emotions and "dyads" that result from mixtures of adjacent primaries. For example, a combination of the primary emotions of fear and surprise produces awe. Joy mixed with acceptance leads to love. *Reprinted with permission from Psychology Today Magazine. Copyright © 1980 (Sussex Publishers, Inc.)*

u-curve hypothesis

The generalization that performance is best under conditions of moderate, rather than low or high, arousal.

What is now known as the **u-curve hypothesis** *states that performance is best under conditions of moderate rather than low or high arousal.* At the low end of arousal, you might be too lethargic to perform tasks well; at the high end, you may not be able to concentrate. Think about how aroused you were the last time you took a test. If your arousal was too high, your performance probably suffered.

Moderate arousal often serves us best in tackling life's tasks, but there are times when low or high arousal produces optimal performance. For well-learned or simple tasks (signing your name, pushing a button on request), arousal can be quite high without impairing performance. By contrast, when learning a task (such as how to play tennis) or doing something complex (such as solving an algebraic equation), much lower arousal is preferred. Figure 9.9 projects how arousal might influence easy, moderate, and difficult tasks. As tasks become more difficult, the ability to be alert and attentive, but relaxed, is critical to optimal performance.

In addition to arousal level, an important dimension of positive affectivity is happiness. Happiness is one of the most elusive emotions we seek. Like other emotions, its intensity varies. Sometimes we are incredibly happy, at other times only a little happy. You might be overwhelmed with happiness if you get the highest grade on the next test in this class but only slightly happy if you get a B or a low A.

Psychologists' interest in happiness focuses on positive ways we experience our lives, including cognitive judgments of our well-being. That is, psychologists want to know what makes you happy and how you perceive your happiness. Many years ago, French philosopher Jean-Jacques Rousseau described the subjective nature of happiness this way: "Happiness is a good bank account, a good cook, and a good digestion."

Figure 9.9

Arousal and Performance: The u-curve hypothesis

The Yerkes-Dodson u-curve hypothesis law states that optimal performance occurs under moderate arousal. However, for new or difficult tasks, low arousal may be best; for well-learned, easy tasks, high arousal can facilitate performance.

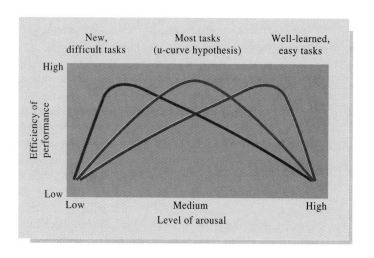

"My life is O.K., but it's no jeans ad."
Richard Cline © 1988 from The New Yorker
Collection. All Rights Reserved.

In a review of research on happiness, being a good cook and good digestion were not on the list of factors that contribute to our happiness, but these four factors were (Myers, 1992):

- Self-esteem—happy people like themselves
- Optimism—happy people are hope-filled
- Extroversion—happy people are outgoing
- Personal control—happy people believe that they choose their own destinies

Some factors that many people believe are involved in happiness, such as age and gender, actually are not.

But what about Rousseau's "good bank account"? Can we buy happiness? One study tried to find out if lottery winners are happier than people who have not received a windfall of money (Brickman, Coates & Janoff-Bulman, 1978). Twenty-two major lottery winners were compared with twenty-two people living in the same area of the city. The general happiness of the two groups did not differ when they were asked about the past, present, and the future. The people who hadn't won a lottery actually were happier doing life's mundane things such as watching television, buying clothes, and talking with a friend.

Winning a lottery does not appear to be the key to happiness. What is important, though, is having enough money to buy life's necessities. Extremely wealthy people are not happier than people who can purchase the necessities. People in wealthy countries are not happier than people in poor countries. The message is clear: If you believe money buys happiness, think again (Diener, 1984).

Mihaly Csikszentmihalyi (1990) has been studying the optimal experiences of emotion—those times when people report feelings of deep enjoyment and happiness—for more than two decades. According to Csikszentmihalyi, optimal experiences include what the sailor feels when the wind ships through her hair the boat lunges through the waves—sails, hull, wind, and sea harmoniously vibrating in the sailor's body. Optimal experience is what an artist feels when the colors on a canvas begin to establish a magnetic relation with each other, and a new *thing* begins to take shape in front of the astonished creator. Optimal experience of emotions also is the feeling a father has when his child responds to his smile for the first time. Such events do not occur only when external conditions are favorable, however; people who have survived concentration camps or have lived through near-fatal dangers often recall that in the midst of their ordeal they experienced extraordinarily rich epiphanies of emotion in response to such simple events as hearing the song of a bird in the forest, completing a difficult task, or sharing a crust of bread with a friend.

Flow, *according to Csikszentmihalyi, involves optimal experiences in life that are most likely to occur when people develop a sense of mastery. Flow involves a state of concentration in which an individual becomes absorbed while engaging in an activity.* Flow can be controlled and should not be left to chance. We can develop flow by setting challenges for ourselves—tasks that are neither too difficult nor too simple for our abilities. With such goals, we learn to order the information that enters consciousness and thereby the quality of our lives. See Applications in Psychology for further insights about Csikszentmihalyi's work.

Negative Affectivity: Anger. Remember that negative affectivity includes all moods or emotions that are negatively toned, such as anger, anxiety, guilt, and sadness. To illustrate the nature of negative affectivity, we will focus on one emotion—anger.

Anger is a powerful emotion. It has a strong impact not only on our social relationships, but also on the person experiencing the emotion (Lazarus, 1991). We can easily recount obvious examples of anger that often harm not only others but the angry individual as well—unrestrained and recurrent violence toward others, verbal and physical abuse of children, perpetual bitterness, the tendency to carry a "chip on the shoulder" in which a person over-interprets others' actions as demeaning, and the inability to inhibit the expression of anger.

What makes people angry? People often get angry when they think they are not being treated fairly or when their expectations are violated. One researcher asked people to remember or keep records of their anger experiences (Averill, 1983). Most of the people said they became at least mildly angry several times a week; some said they became mildly angry several times a day. In many instances, the people said they got angry because they

flow

According to Csikszentmihalyi, optimal experiences in life that are most likely to occur when a person develops a sense of mastery. Flow involves a state of concentration in which an individual becomes absorbed in an activity.

$\mathcal{A}$pplications in Psychology

Flow

In the course of his research, Csikszent-mihalyi (1990) tried to understand as precisely as possible how people felt when they most enjoyed themselves, and why. He began by studying several hundred "experts"—artists, athletes, musicians, chess masters, and surgeons—who seemed to spend their time in activities they preferred. From their accounts of what it felt like to do what they were doing, he developed a theory of optimal experience based on the concept of flow. Following the study of these several hundred "experts" Csikszentmihalyi and many colleagues around the world interviewed people from different walks of life. Optimal experiences were described in virtually the same way by females and males; young people and old people; and people in many different cities, countries, and cultures—Korea, Thailand, India, Tokyo, Navajo, Italy, and Chicago.

Csikszentmihalyi says that flow is the way people describe their state of mind and feeling when their consciousness is harmoniously ordered and they want to pursue whatever they are doing for its own sake. In reviewing some of the activities that consistently produce flow—such as sports, games, art, and hobbies—it becomes easier to understand what makes people happy. But we cannot rely completely on games and art for our happiness in life. To achieve control over what happens to our thoughts and feelings, we can draw on an almost infinite range of opportunities for enjoyment—the use of physical energy and sensory skills ranging from athletics to music to yoga, as well as the development of symbolic skills such as poetry, philosophy, or math, he says. Since most of us spend the largest part of our lives working and interacting with others, especially family members, it is important for us to transform jobs into flow-producing activities and to think of ways of making relations with parents, spouses, children, and friends more enjoyable.

Many of our lives are also punctured by tragedy, and even the most fortunate of us are subjected to stressors of many kinds. Yet such blows and stressors do not necessarily diminish a person's happiness, because it is how people respond to and cope with stress that determines whether they will profit from misfortune or be miserable. Thus, people who experience flow develop effective coping skills and manage to enjoy life despite adversities.

Csikszentmihalyi believes that the last step in achieving flow is joining all of life's experiences into a meaningful pattern. For example, it is not unusual for famous athletes to be deeply committed to their sport and to gain pleasure from playing but off the playing field to be morose and hostile. Picasso enjoyed painting, but as soon as he lay down his brushes he turned into a rather unpleasant man. Bobby Fischer, the chess genius, appeared to be helplessly inept except when his mind was on chess. These and many other examples remind us that having achieved flow in one activity does not guarantee that it will be carried over to the rest of life. However, when people can join all of their experiences into a meaningful pattern, they feel in control of their life and think that it makes sense. The fact that they are not slim, rich, or powerful no longer matters. The tide of rising expectations is silenced, and unfulfilled needs no longer trouble them. Even humdrum experiences become enjoyable.

perceived that a friend or a loved one performed a misdeed. They especially got angry when they perceived the other persons' behavior as unjustified, avoidable, and willful.

Doesn't getting angry sometimes make us feel better and possibly help us cope better with our challenging lives? Just as *catharsis* (releasing anger or aggressive energy by directly or vicariously engaging in anger) doesn't reduce aggression over the long term, but rather usually increases it, so it also is with anger. As Carol Tavris (1989) commented in her book *Anger: The Misunderstood Emotion,* one of the main results of the ventilationist approach to anger is to raise the noise level of society, not reduce anger or solve our problems. To read about some strategies for managing anger effectively, see Improving Personal and Cognitive Skills.

$\mathcal{I}$mproving Personal and Cognitive Skills

Managing Your Anger

Every person gets angry at one time or another. How can we control our anger so it does not become destructive? Following are some good strategies (Tavris, 1989):

1. When your anger starts to boil and your body is getting aroused, work on lowering the arousal by waiting. Emotional arousal will usually simmer down if you just wait long enough.
2. Cope with the anger in ways that involve neither being chronically angry over every little bothersome annoyance nor passively sulking, which simply rehearses your reasons for being angry.
3. Form a self-help group with others who have been through similar experiences with anger. The other people will likely know what you are feeling and together you might come up with some good solutions to anger problems.
4. Take action to help others, which can put your own miseries in perspective, as exemplified in the actions of the women who organized Mothers Against Drunk Drivers, or any number of people who work to change conditions so that others will not suffer what they did.
5. Seek ways of breaking out of your usual perspective. Some people have been rehearsing their "story" for years, repeating over and over the reasons for their anger. Retelling the story from other participants' points of view often helps individuals to find routes to empathy.

Let not the sun go down on your wrath.
—EPHESIANS 4:26

$\mathcal{R}$eview

Defining and Classifying Emotion

Emotions are feelings that involve a mixture of physiological arousal, conscious experience, and overt behavior. A number of psychologists have classified emotions by placing them on a wheel. One such model was proposed by Plutchik, who believes that emotions are positive or negative, are primary or mixed, are bipolar opposites, and vary in intensity. The two-dimensional approach argues there are two broad dimensions of emotional experience: Positive affectivity and negative affectivity. Positive affectivity refers to the range of positive emotion from high energy, enthusiasm, and excitement to calm, quiet, and withdrawn. Joy or happiness involves positive affectivity. Negative affectivity refers to emotions that are negatively toned such as anxiety, anger, guilt, and sadness.

Our positive affectivity is influenced by how aroused we are. The u-curve hypothesis addressed the issue of arousal and performance, emphasizing maximum performance under moderate arousal. However, task difficulty needs to be considered when determining optimal arousal. Happiness is an important dimension of positive affectivity. Self-esteem, a good marriage or love relationship, social contacts, regular exercise, the ability to sleep well, and religious faith are all related to happiness. Positive emotions such as happiness are more likely to increase generosity, eagerness, expansiveness, and free-flowing use of one's resources than negative emotions like sadness. People are the happiest when they develop a sense of mastery over their lives. In developing a sense of mastery, people often experience flow, a state of concentration that individuals reach when they become absorbed in an activity.

We examined anger as a representative of negative affectivity. Anger is a powerful emotion that not only has a strong influence on social relationships, but also on the person experiencing anger. Most psychologists consider catharsis to be an ineffective way of coping with anger. Strategies for reducing anger include: waiting, not being chronically angry over every little annoyance or passively sulking, forming a self-help group with others who have been through similar experiences with anger, taking action to help others, and seeking ways of breaking out of a usual perspective.

Theories of Emotion

As you drive down a highway, the fog thickens. Suddenly you see a pile of cars in front of you. Your mind temporarily freezes, your muscles tighten, your stomach becomes queasy, and your heart feels like it is going to pound out of your chest. You immediately slam on the brakes and try to veer away from the pile of cars. Tires screech, windshield glass flies, metal smashes, then all is quiet. After a few seconds, you realize you are alive. You find that you can walk out of the car. Your fear turns to relief, as you sense your luck in not being hurt. In a couple of seconds, the relief turns to anger. You loudly ask who caused the accident. In this situation, what triggered your emotion? Was it your body? Your mind? Extensive debate characterizes whether the mind or the body is primarily responsible for our experience of emotion (Izard, Schultz & Levinson, 1998).

We will begin our investigation of the mind-body debate in emotion by examining the dominant theories.

The James-Lange Theory.   In the automobile crash, common sense tells you that you are trembling because of your fear and anxiety. But William James (1890/1950) and Carl Lange (1922) said emotion works in the opposite way. The **James-Lange theory** *states that emotion results from physiological states triggered by stimuli in the environment.* That is, according to the James-Lange theory, you saw the pile of cars, tried to avoid it, then crashed. Subsequently, you noticed your heart was almost beating out of your body and your hands were trembling. Now your feelings of anxiety and fear follow your body's reactions. In sum, you perceive a stimulus in the environment, your body responds, and then you interpret the body's reaction as emotion. In one of James's own examples, you perceive you have lost your fortune, you cry, and then interpret the crying as feeling sad. This goes against the commonsense sequence of losing your fortune, feeling sorry, and then crying.

The Cannon-Bard Theory.   Walter Cannon (1927) objected to the James-Lange theory. To understand his objection, consider the car crash once again. Seeing the pileup of cars causes the hypothalamus of your brain to do two things simultaneously: First it stimulates your autonomic nervous system to produce the physiological changes involved in emotion (increased heart rate, rapid breathing, for example); second, it sends messages to your cerebral cortex, where the experience of emotion is perceived. Philip Bard (1934) supported this theory, and so it became known as the **Cannon-Bard theory,** *the theory that emotion and physiological reactions occur simultaneously.* Figure 9.10 shows how the James-Lange and Cannon-Bard theories differ. A pivotal difference between these theories concerns the nature of physiological changes associated with emotion. Whereas the James-Lange camp emphasized biological activity throughout the body (such as a racing heart, a tightening of the stomach, and trembling muscles), the Cannon-Bard camp focused more on what was happening in the brain. Since the original formulations of the theories, psychological and medical researchers have found evidence that the components of both theories are true.

Cognitive Theories of Emotion.   Does emotion depend on the tides of the mind? Are we happy only when we think we are happy? Cognitive theories of emotion share an important point: Emotion always has a cognitive component. Thinking is said to be responsible for feelings of love and hate, joy and sadness. While giving cognitive processes the main credit for emotion, the cognitive theories also recognize the role of the brain and body in emotion (Mandler, 1984). That is, the hypothalamus and autonomic nervous system make connections with the peripheral areas of the body when emotion is experienced. According to cognitive theorists, both body and thought are involved in emotion.

Schachter and Singer's View: The Cognitive Interpretation of Arousal.   Stanley Schachter and Jerome Singer (1962) developed a theory of emotion that gives cognition a strong role. They agree that emotional events produce internal, physiological arousal. As we sense the arousal, we look to the external world for an explanation of why we are aroused. We interpret the external cues present and then label the emotion. For example, if you feel good after someone has made a pleasant comment to you, you might label the emotion "happy." If you feel bad after you have done something wrong, you might label the feeling "guilty." Schachter and Singer believe much of our arousal is diffuse and not tied to specific emotions. Because the arousal is not instinctive, its meaning is easily misinterpreted.

To test their theory of emotion, Schachter and Singer (1962) injected subjects with epinephrine, a drug that produces high arousal. After volunteer subjects were given the drug, they observed someone else behave in either a euphoric way (shooting crumpled paper at a wastebasket) or an angry way (stomping out of the room). As predicted, the euphoric and angry behavior influenced the subjects' cognitive interpretation of

James-Lange theory

The theory that emotion results from physiological states triggered by stimuli in the environment.

Cannon-Bard theory

The theory that emotion and physiological states occur simultaneously.

James-Lange theory

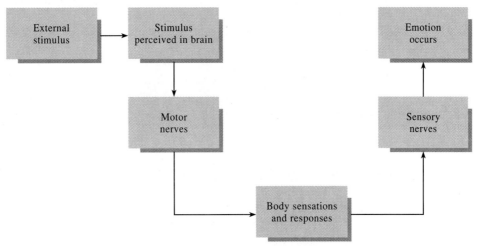

Emotion takes place after
physiological reactions.

Cannon-Bard theory

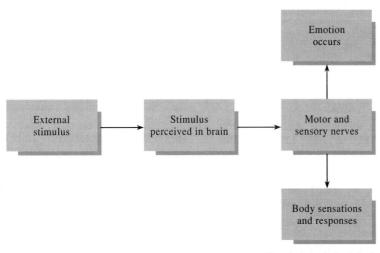

Emotions and physiological
reactions occur simultaneously.

𝓕IGURE 9.10

James-Lange and Cannon-Bard Theories of Emotion

their own arousal. When they were with a happy person, they rated themselves as happy; when they were with an angry person, they said they were angry. But this effect was found only when the subjects were not told about the true effects of the injection. When subjects were told that the drug would increase their heart rate and make them jittery, they said the reason for their own arousal was the drug, not the other person's behavior.

Psychologists have had difficulty replicating the Schachter and Singer experiment but, in general, research supports the belief that misinterpreted arousal intensifies emotional experiences (Leventhal & Tomarken, 1986). An intriguing study substantiates this belief. It went like this: An attractive woman approached men while they were crossing the Capilano River Bridge in British Columbia. Only those without a female companion were approached. The woman asked the men to make up a brief story for a project she was doing on creativity (Dutton & Aron, 1974). By the way, the Capilano River Bridge sways precariously more than 200 feet above rapids and rocks (see figure 9.11). The female interviewer made the same request of other men crossing a much safer, lower

FIGURE 9.11

Capilano River Bridge Experiment: Misinterpreted Arousal Intensifies Emotional Experiences

The precarious Capilano River Bridge in British Columbia is shown at left; the experiment is shown in progress at right. An attractive woman approached men while they were crossing the 200-foot-high bridge; she asked them to make up a story to help her out. She also made the same request on a lower, much safer bridge. The men on the Capilano River Bridge told sexier stores, probably because they were aroused by the fear or excitement of being up so high on a swaying bridge. Apparently they interpreted their arousal as sexual attraction for the female interviewer.

bridge. The men on the Capilano River Bridge told more sexually oriented stories and rated the female interviewer more attractive then men on the lower, less frightening bridge did.

The Primacy Debate: Cognition or Emotion? Richard Lazarus (1984, 1991) believes cognitive activity is a precondition for emotion. He says we cognitively appraise ourselves and our social circumstances. These appraisals, which include values, goals, commitments, beliefs, and expectations, determine our emotions. People may feel happy because they have a deep religious commitment, angry because they did not get the raise they anticipated, or fearful because they expect to fail an exam.

Robert Zajonc (1984; Murphy & Zajonc, 1993) disagrees with Lazarus. Emotions are primary, he says, and our thoughts are a result of them. Who is right? Both likely are correct. Lazarus refers mainly to a cluster of related events that occur over a period of time, whereas Zajonc describes single events or a simple preference for one stimulus over another. Lazarus speaks about love over the course of months and years, a sense of value to the community, and plans for retirement; Zajonc talks about a car accident, an encounter with a snake, and liking ice cream better than spinach. Some of our emotional reactions, such as a shriek on detecting a snake, are virtually instantaneous and probably don't involve cognitive appraisal. Other emotional circumstances, especially those that occur over a long period of time, such as a depressed mood or anger toward a friend, are more likely to involve cognitive appraisal.

Distinguishing Emotions

Is there a difference in the way our bodies respond when we are feeling angry, compared to when we are feeling nervous? In other words, are there specific physiological reactions for each emotion we experience? To answer these questions, we need to understand the basic nature of the autonomic nervous system.

The Physiology of Emotion. Although fear and anger can sometimes be distinguished using a sophisticated monitoring apparatus, most day-to-day moods cannot be distinguished by autonomic nervous system (ANS) activity (see chapter 2 for a portrayal of the autonomic nervous system). Recently researchers have begun to focus on the role of different types of brain activity as a function of mood. For example, Richard Davidson and his colleagues (1990) have found that sad moods are related to brain-wave activity in the left frontal region of the brain, while positive moods provoke right frontal region activity. Also, emotional states associated with fear and anxiety result in increased neurotransmitter activity in the temporal lobes of the cortex (Scioli & Averill, 1998).

Different types of drugs that selectively alter specific neurotransmitters in the brain are effective in exaggerating or modulating many mood states. For example, certain antidepressant medications reduce the massive fear associated with some panic attacks. Other drugs, such as alcohol, also can elevate a person's mood.

In sum, emotions affect our physiological states, and vice versa. William James was partially correct in arguing that different emotions occasionally produce unique patterns of autonomic nervous system activity. He probably overestimated the effects of the specific changes, however. Walter Cannon was partially correct in noting that the brain plays a pivotal role in dictating emotional experiences. However, Cannon failed to appreciate that different emotions can trigger completely different brain regions, which, by themselves, might or might not influence autonomic nervous system activity.

The Polygraph and Lie Detection. You have been asked to think about your emotional states in the face of an automobile crash. Now put yourself in the situation of lying to someone. Because body changes predictably accompany emotional states, scientists reasoned that a machine might be able to determine if a person is lying. The **polygraph** *is a machine that is used to try to determine if someone is lying by monitoring changes in the body—heart rate, breathing, and electrodermal response (an index that detects skin resistance to passage of a weak electric current)—thought to be influenced by emotional states.* In a typical polygraph test, an individual is asked a number of neutral questions and several key, not so neutral, questions. If the individual's heart rate, breathing, and electrodermal response increase substantially when the key questions are asked, the individual is assumed to be lying. (Figure 9.12 shows a polygraph testing situation.)

The polygraph has been widely used, especially in business, to screen new employees for honesty and to reveal employee theft. Following President Reagan's directive in 1983, the government increased its use of the polygraph to discover which individuals were leaking information to the media. Congressional hearings followed, and psychologists were called to testify about the polygraph's effectiveness (Saxe, Dougherty & Cross, 1985). Testimony focused on how a standard lie detector situation does not exist. Inferring truth or deception based on physiological assessment of emotions requires a number of strategies. The complexity of the lie detector situation was brought out in testimony. Although the degree of arousal in response to a series of questions is measured through simple physiological changes, no unique physiological response to deception has been revealed (Lykken, 1985). Heart rate and breathing can increase for reasons other than lying, making interpretation of the physiological indicators of arousal complex.

Accurately identifying truth or deception rests on the skill of the examiner and the skill of the individual being examined. Individuals intent on lying can take

*F*IGURE 9.12

Polygraph Testing

A polygraph is supposed to tell whether someone is lying by monitoring changes in the body believed to be influenced by emotional states. Controversy has swirled about the polygraph's use. Because of the polygraph's inaccuracy, Congress passed the Employee Polygraph Protection Act of 1988, restricting the use of the polygraph in nongovernment settings.

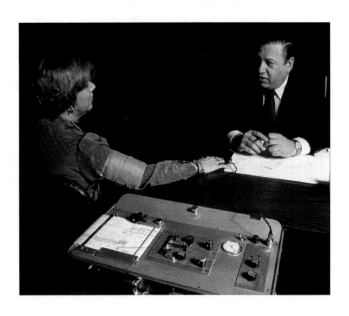

countermeasures to avoid detection. Drugs, such as tranquilizers that have a calming effect on the individual, are difficult to detect unless a test is conducted to reveal their use. Sometimes, though, the mere presence of the polygraph and the subject's belief that it is accurate at detecting deception triggers confession. Police might use the polygraph in this way to get a criminal to confess. In such cases, the polygraph has served a positive purpose, but in too many instances it has been misused and misrepresented. Experts argue that the polygraph errs about one-third of the time, especially because it cannot distinguish between such feelings as anxiety and guilt (Lykken, 1985). The testimony of psychologists that lie detectors are not always accurate led to the Employee Polygraph Protection Act of 1988, which restricts most nongovernment polygraph testing.

> *A lie can travel half way around the world while the truth is putting on its shoes.*
> —MARK TWAIN, *American Writer and Humorist, 19th Century*

Sociocultural Influences on Emotion

The complete experience of emotion depends not only on the body's responses and the mind's perceptions but also on the society's customs (Roseman & others, 1995).

The Universality of Emotional Expressions. In *The Expression of the Emotions in Man and Animals,* Charles Darwin (1872/1965) argued that the facial expressions of human beings are innate, are the same in all cultures around the world, and evolved from the emotions of animals. Darwin compared the similarity of human snarls of anger with the growls of dogs and the hisses of cats. He compared the giggling of chimpanzees, when they are tickled under their arms, with human laughter.

Today psychologists still believe that emotions, especially facial expressions of emotion, have strong biological ties (Sherer & Wallbott, 1994). For example, children who are blind from birth and have never observed the smile or frown on another person's face, still smile or frown in the same way that children with normal vision do.

The universality of facial expressions and the ability of people from different cultures to label accurately the emotion that lies behind a facial expression has been extensively researched. Paul Ekman's (1980, 1993) careful observations revealed that our many faces of emotion do not vary significantly from one culture to another. For example, Ekman and his colleague photographed people expressing such emotions as happiness, fear, surprise, disgust, and grief. When they showed the photographs to people from the United States, Chile, Japan, Brazil, and Borneo (an Indonesian island in the western Pacific Ocean), each person tended to label the faces with the same emotions (Ekman & Friesen, 1968). Another study focused on the way the Fore tribe, an isolated, Stone Age culture in New Guinea, matched descriptions of emotions with facial expressions (Ekman & Friesen, 1971). Before Ekman's visit, most of the Fore had never seen a Caucasian face. Ekman showed them photographs of American faces expressing such emotions as fear, happiness, anger, and surprise. Then he read stories about people in emotional situations. The Fore were able to match the descriptions of emotions to the facial expressions in the photographs. The similarity of facial expressions of emotions between people in New Guinea and people in the United States is shown in figure 9.13.

Variations in Emotional Expression. Whereas facial expressions of basic emotions appear to be universal across cultures, display rules for emotion are not culturally universal. **Display rules** *are sociocultural standards that determine when, where, and how emotions should be expressed.* For example, although happiness is a universally expressed emotion, when, where, and how it is displayed may vary from one culture to another. The same is true for other emotions, such as fear, sadness, and anger. For example, members of the Utku culture in Alaska discourage anger by cultivating acceptance and by dissociating themselves from any display of anger (Briggs, 1970). If a trip is hampered by an unexpected snowstorm, the Utku do not become frustrated but accept the presence of

display rules
Sociocultural standards that determine when, where, and how emotions should be expressed.

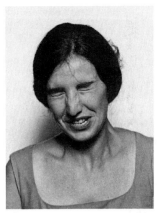

$\mathcal{F}$IGURE 9.13

Emotional Expressions in the United States and New Guinea

At left is a woman from the United States and, on the right, two men from the Fore tribe in New Guinea. Notice the similarity in the expression of disgust and happiness. Psychologists believe that the facial expression of emotion is virtually the same in all cultures.

the snowstorm and build an igloo. Most of us would not act as mildly in the face of sub-zero weather and barriers to our travel.

Many nonverbal signals of emotion, though, vary from one culture to another. For example, male-to-male kissing is commonplace in some cultures, such as Yemen (in the Middle East), but uncommon in other cultures, such as the United States. The "thumb up" sign, which means either everything is "OK" or the desire to hitch a ride in most cultures, is an insult in Greece, similar to a raised third finger in the United States (Morris & others, 1979).

Think for a moment about how display rules for emotion influence your own behavior. Can you think of a time when you felt an emotion strongly but did not show this to others who were around you at the time? Why did you not show the emotion? How did you hide your emotion?

Gender Influences. Unless you've been isolated on a mountaintop away from people, television, magazines, and newspapers, you probably know the master stereotype about gender and emotion: She is emotional, he is not. This stereotype is a powerful and pervasive image in our culture (Shields, 1991).

Is this stereotype supported when researchers study the nature of emotional experiences in females and males? Researchers have found that females and males are often more alike in the way they experience emotion than the master stereotype would lead us to believe. Females and males often use the same facial expressions, adopt the same language, and describe their emotional experiences similarly when they keep diaries about their life experiences. Thus, the master stereotype that females are emotional and males are not is simply that—a stereotype. Given the complexity and vast territory of emotion, we should not be surprised that this stereotype is not supported. For many emotional experiences, researchers do not find differences between females and males. Both sexes are equally likely to experience love, jealousy, anxiety in new social situations, anger when they are insulted, grief when close relationships end, and embarrassment when they make mistakes in public (Tavris & Wade, 1984).

When we go beyond the master stereotype and consider some specific emotional experiences, the context in which emotion is displayed, and certain beliefs about emotion, gender does matter in understanding emotion (Shields, 1991). Consider anger. Men are more likely to show anger toward strangers, especially other men, when they feel they have been challenged, and men are more likely to turn their anger into aggressive action than women are (Tavris, 1989).

Emotional differences between females and males are more likely to occur in contexts that highlight social roles and relationships. For example, females are more likely than males to give accounts of emotion that include interpersonal relationships (Saarni,

In the Middle Eastern country of Yemen, male-male mouth-to-mouth kissing is commonplace. In Western European countries, cheek-to-cheek kissing is a commonplace practice for males, but in the United States it is very uncommon.

1988). And females are more likely than males to express fear and sadness, especially when communicating with their friends and family.

Beliefs about emotion play an important role in understanding how gender and emotion work in our culture. We often use beliefs about emotion to define the difference between what is masculine and feminine, male and female (Shields, 1991). For example, in one study, men were more likely to agree with the belief that men should conceal their feelings, but when reporting their own behavior, more women than men reported greater inhibition of emotional expression. Sex differences in self-reports tend to be consistent with emotion stereotypes, as if individuals compare themselves to a cultural standard when generating a response—"I must be emotional, after all I'm a woman," or "I must be inexpressive, after all I'm a man."

At this point, we have evaluated many areas of emotion. As you will see next, one final topic on emotion has generated a great deal of interest recently.

Emotional Intelligence

emotional intelligence

Emotional self-understanding, managing your own emotions, reading others' emotions, and handling relationships well.

In his book *Emotional Intelligence* (1995), Daniel Goleman argues that when it comes to predicting a person's competence, IQ as measured by standard IQ tests might matter less than what he calls "emotional intelligence." Goleman says that **emotional intelligence** *involves emotional self-awareness, managing emotions, reading emotions, and handling relationships.* In Goleman's view, emotional self-awareness is especially important because it allows us to exercise some self-control. The idea is not to repress feelings, but become aware of them so that we can cope effectively. No emotional intelligence test has been devised along the lines of IQ tests, but the Self-Assessment will provide you with some insights about the makeup of your own emotional intelligence.

The personal costs of deficits in emotional intelligence can range from problems in marriage and parenting to poor health. Lack of emotional intelligence can sabotage the intellect and ruin careers. The good news, says Goleman, is that emotional intelligence is not fixed at birth and can be nurtured and strengthened.

Goleman's ideas mesh with those of Robert Sternberg and Howard Gardner that were presented in chapter 7. Recall that Sternberg and Gardner believe that intelligence involves far more than traditional intellectual skills like reasoning and memory. They, like Goleman, argue that being intelligent also means having good social and emotional skills.

This concludes our discussion of motivation and emotion. Earlier in the chapter when we examined motivation, we described a number of perspectives on motivation that included psychoanalytic, behavioral, and humanistic views. In the next chapter, "Personality," you will read further about these views.

$\mathcal{S}$elf-Assessment

How Emotionally Intelligent Are You?

Goleman describes four important domains of emotional intelligence: emotional self-awareness, managing emotions, reading emotions, and handling relationships. Score each of the following items from 1 (Very much unlike me) to 5 (Very much like me):

	1	2	3	4	5

Emotional Self-Awareness

1. I am good at recognizing my emotions.
2. I am good at understanding the causes of my feelings.
3. I am good at separating my feelings from my actions.

Managing Emotions

4. I am good at tolerating frustration.
5. I am good at managing my anger.
6. I have positive feelings about myself.
7. I am good at coping with stress.
8. My emotions don't interfere with my ability to focus and accomplish my goals.
9. I have good self-control and am not impulsive.

Reading Emotions

10. I am good at taking other people's perspectives.
11. I show empathy and sensitivity to others' feelings.
12. I am good at listening to what other people are saying.

Handling Relationships

13. I am good at analyzing and understanding relationships.
14. I am good at solving problems in relationships.
15. I am assertive (rather than passive, manipulative, or aggressive) in relationships.
16. I have one or more good close friendships.
17. I am good at sharing and cooperating.

Scoring and Interpretation

Add up your score for all 17 items: Total Emotional Intelligence Score: _____
If you scored from 75 to 85, you are very emotionally intelligent. You likely are excellent at understanding your own emotions, managing your emotions, reading others' emotions, and handling relationships. If you scored from 65 to 74, you have good emotional intelligence, but there probably are some areas that you still need to work on. Look at the items you scored 3 or below to see where you need to improve. If you scored from 45 to 54, you have only average emotional intelligence. Give some serious thought to working on your emotional life. Examine your emotional weaknesses and work on improving them. If you scored 44 or below, you have weak emotional intelligence. Your lack of emotional intelligence is likely interfering with your competence. If your emotional intelligence scores are in the average or weak range, consider talking with a counselor at your college about ways you can improve it.

Theories of Emotion, Distinguishing Emotion, Sociocultural Influences, and Emotional Intelligence

In the James-Lange theory, we initially perceive a stimulus, our body responds, and then we experience the emotion. In the Cannon-Bard theory, emotion and physiological reactions occur simultaneously. Whereas the James-Lange theory emphasizes biological activity throughout the body, the Cannon-Bard theory focuses more on what is happening in the brain.

Cognitive theories argue that emotion always has a cognitive component and that, in most instances, cognition directs emotion. In Schachter and Singer's view, people cognitively interpret their arousal. Emotional events produce emotional arousal. Arousal is often diffuse, so we look to the external world to interpret it. We label the emotion based on environmental cues. Lazarus believes that cognition always directs emotion; Zajonc says emotion is dominant. Both are probably right.

Can emotions be distinguished on the basis of their physiological nature? Emo-

tions affect our physiological states, and vice versa. James was partially correct in arguing that different emotions occasionally produce unique patterns of autonomic nervous system (ANS) activity. He probably overestimated the effects of specific changes. Cannon was partially correct in noting that the brain plays a pivotal role in dictating emotional experiences. However, Cannon failed to appreciate that different emotions can trigger different brain regions, which in themselves might not influence ANS activity. Polygraphs are based on the principle of arousal in emotion. The polygraph situation is complex, and psychologists are skeptical about its validity. One of the polygraph's most beneficial functions is to induce confession. Nonverbal leakage can occur when we communicate with others.

Emotions often involve social contexts and relationships. Most psychologists believe that facial expressions of basic emo-

tions are universal across all cultures. However, display rules for emotion often vary from one culture to another. Display rules include rules for nonverbal signals in body movements, posture, and gesture. The master stereotype of gender and emotion is that females are emotional, males are not. This is a stereotype; understanding emotion and gender is much more complex. When we go beyond the master stereotype and consider some specific aspects of emotional experiences, the context in which emotion is displayed, and certain beliefs about emotion, gender does matter in understanding emotion. Female/male differences in emotion are more likely to occur in contexts that highlight social roles and relationships.

Emotional intelligence involves emotional self-understanding, managing your emotions, reading others' emotions, and handling relationships.

Overview

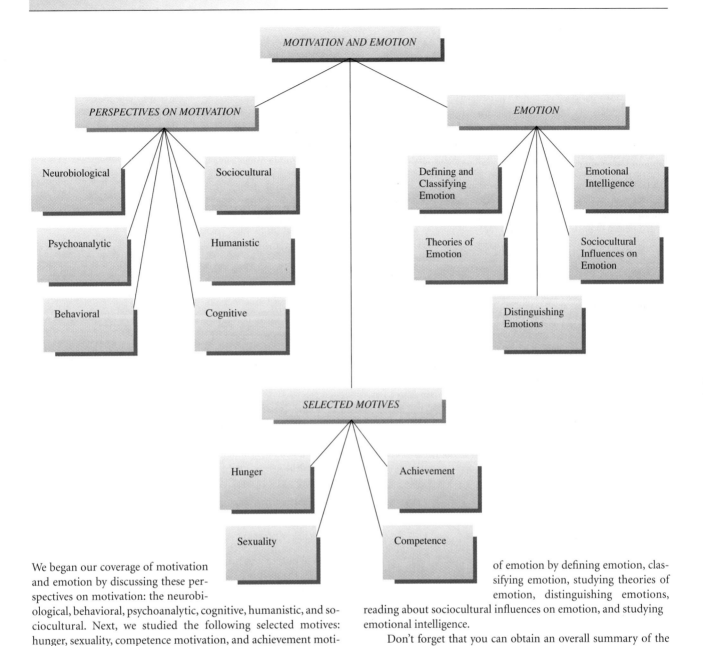

We began our coverage of motivation and emotion by discussing these perspectives on motivation: the neurobiological, behavioral, psychoanalytic, cognitive, humanistic, and sociocultural. Next, we studied the following selected motives: hunger, sexuality, competence motivation, and achievement motivation. In the final section of the chapter we evaluated the nature of emotion by defining emotion, classifying emotion, studying theories of emotion, distinguishing emotions, reading about sociocultural influences on emotion, and studying emotional intelligence.

Don't forget that you can obtain an overall summary of the chapter by again reading the in-chapter reviews on pages 335, 347, 352, 357 and 366.

Key Terms

motivations   330
motives   330
intrinsic motivation   331
extrinsic motivation   331
instinct   331
ethology   332
drive   332
need   332
drive reduction theory   332
homeostasis   332
incentives   333
hierarchy of motives   335
self-actualization   335
ventromedial hypothalamus
   (VMH)   337

set point   338
estrogens   339
androgens   339
human sexual response
   pattern   341
sexual script   342
traditional religious script
   343
romantic script   343
double standard   344
bisexual   344
psychosexual disorders   345
psychosexual dysfunctions
   345
incest   345

paraphilias   346
fetishism   346
transvestism   346
transsexualism   346
exhibitionism   346
voyeurism   346
sadism   346
masochism   346
pedophilia   346
rape   346
date or acquaintance
   rape   347
competence motivation   348
achievement motivation (need
   for achievement)   349

attribution theory   350
emotion   354
positive affectivity (PA)   355
negative affectivity (NA)   355
u-curve hypothesis   355
flow   356
James-Lange theory   359
Cannon-Bard theory   359
polygraph   362
display rules   364
emotional intelligence   365

Thinking It Over

Exercises in . . .

. . . Critical Thinking

People differ in how much they are motivated to seek power. Some people get "drunk on power" and it becomes a motive that consumes their life. Think of someone you know or have heard of who is highly motivated by power. How would each of the perspectives on motivation we described earlier in this chapter explain this person's power motive?

Evolutionary:

Drive reduction:

Psychoanalytic:

Behavioral:

Cognitive:

Humanistic:

Sociocultural:

. . . Creative Thinking

Advertisers often exploit Maslow's hierarchy of needs to help sell their products. Select any object in your home. Develop an ad campaign in which you appeal to the different levels in Maslow's hierar-

chy to try to sell that object. For example, how can you sell toothpaste that appeals to such varying needs as safety and belongingness?

. . . Active Learning

Go to the library and track down a description of sexual attitudes and behaviors in another culture. How do they compare with the sexual attitudes and behavior in your own culture as outlined in Robert Michael's 1994 study on sexual attitudes and behaviors discussed earlier in this chapter?

. . . Reflective Learning

Think about the last time you became extremely angry. Compare how you handled your anger with the strategies recommended in the Improving Personal and Cognitive Skills box "Managing Your Anger." Are there new strategies you can use that can help you keep from becoming unraveled by your emotions?

Resources for Psychology and Improving Humankind

The Dance of Anger (1985)

by Harriet Lerner
New York: HarperPerennial

The Dance of Anger is written mainly for women about the anger in their lives, both their own anger and the anger of people they live with, especially men. Lerner describes styles of anger that don't work for women and motivates women to cope with anger in more positive ways.

Emotional Intelligence (1995)

by Daniel Goleman
New York: Basic Books

Goleman argues that emotional intelligence is just as important as intellectual intelligence. The book includes many insights about how we can live more emotionally healthy lives.

Even Eagles Need a Push (1990)

by David McNalley
New York: Dell

This is an excellent book to get you motivated. A number of exercises and stories serve to get you energized and directed.

Flow (1990)

by Mihaly Csikszentmihalyi
New York: Harper & Row

Flow is about the optimal experiencing of life. Csikszentmihalyi has been investigating the concept of flow for more than two decades. Earlier in the chapter we discussed the author's view of what flow is, namely a deep happiness people feel when they have a sense of mastering something.

National Gay and Lesbian Task Force (NGLTF)

1734 14th Street, NW
Washington, DC 20009-3409
202-332-6483

This is the oldest national gay and lesbian civil rights advocacy organization; it lobbies, provides grassroots organizing, publishes materials, and offers referrals.

The New Male Sexuality (1992)

by Bernie Zilbergeld
New York: Bantam

The New Male Sexuality is a very up-to-date, comprehensive book about male sexuality.

Why We Eat What We Eat (1996)

edited by Elizabeth Capaldi
Washington, DC: American Psychological Association

Experts cut through popular myths about eating to present the latest research on how eating patterns develop. Topics include the development of food preferences and aversions, how eating patterns develop in childhood, how biology affects eating behavior, and how social contexts influence eating patterns.

Telling Lies: Clues to Deceit in the Marketplace, Politics, and Marriage (1985)

by Paul Ekman
New York: W. W. Norton

Ekman explains how to read facial expressions and gestures to determine whether people are lying.

For Yourself (1975)

by Lonnie Barbach
New York: Signet

For Yourself provides advice for women about how to achieve sexual fulfillment. Barbach addresses the worries that often distress nonorgasmic women and tells them how to achieve orgasm. Barbach attacks the negative cultural attitudes that say women should not enjoy sex.

Internet Resources

http://www.sexuality.org/
Society for Human Sexuality runs a popular home page for Web-surfers over 18.

http://www.clark.net/pub/sluggo/anger.htm
Slugnet offers anger management tips with the motto, "Why count to ten when you can break something right away?"

http://newciv.org/GIB/BOV/BV-366.HTML
A list of psychology-based resources about being happy.

http://www.biology.demon.co.uk/Biology/mod1/thermo/homeo.htm
Learn about how homeostasis works in maintaining a constant temperature.

http://www.trauma-pages.com/
Explore what happens to motivation following trauma.

http://www.carleton.ca/~tpychyl/
Visit this Web site when you need help on overcoming procrastination.

http://www.psych101.com/hum/maslow.html
Read about the life of a founding father of humanistic psychology, Abraham Maslow.

10

Personality

Every person cries out to be read differently.

—SIMONE WEIL
French Philosopher, 20th Century

P R E V I E W

*I*n this chapter we will explore the complex nature of personality through the frameworks that psychologists have developed to capture the ways individuals differ. Historically, five main perspectives have dominated the field: trait, psychoanalytic, behavioral, cognitive, and humanistic. We will explore each perspective to gain important insights about what makes people tick. The chapter concludes with an exploration of how personality theories have produced distinctive strategies for assessing personality.

❖

The Story of Mark Twain: A Visit to the Publisher

*I*n the fall of 1890, Mark Twain decided to visit his publisher, George Putnam. According to Twain, the book clerk took one look at his unimposing clothes and formed some negative impressions about him that prompted the clerk to inform Twain somewhat harshly that Mr. Putnam "wasn't in." Twain knew it was a falsehood, so he decided to transact some unusual business with the clerk. He asked for a preferred volume, which the clerk retrieved. The clerk announced a price of three dollars for the transaction.

Then Twain identified himself as a publisher and requested that the clerk allow him the typical publisher's discount of 60 percent. The clerk appeared to be unmoved. Next Twain claimed that he was also an author and requested the discount of 30 percent reserved for authors. Twain observed that the clerk lost the color from his face. Finally Twain claimed that he also maintained his membership in the human species and suggested that the typical discount for such membership was 10 percent. Without a word, the severe-looking clerk deliberated for a moment and announced that he would have to refund fifteen cents to Twain because the publisher also offered a discount to seriously shy people.

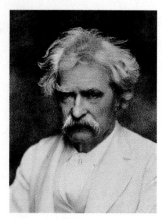

Author Mark Twain's encounter with a bookseller illustrates how personality theories explain his tendency to play pranks on others.

personality
Enduring, distinctive thoughts, emotions, and behaviors that characterize the way an individual adapts to the world.

This story about one of the legendary characters in American literature illustrates several principles related to the key ideas in this chapter on personality. It suggests how challenging it can be to judge other people accurately. Informally, we take into account how they look, how they dress, and how they behave. It is easy to be wrong, as both Twain and the clerk so deftly illustrated. The clerk misjudged Twain's character and vocation due to his unimpressive dress, and Twain misjudged the clerk as humorless due to his severe manner.

However, personality psychologists generally are not content with the superficial judgments that most of us make in our day-to-day dealings with people. Instead, they would ask many questions about Twain and his wry sense of humor and his tendency to play pranks. Had Twain always been a prankster? Was his teasing a result of his experiences in his early childhood? Was he rewarded for his teasing attitudes? Did he need to tease other people to live up to his full potential? How did Twain's style reflect the values of the society in which he was raised? ❖

THE NATURE OF PERSONALITY

Capturing your uniqueness as a person is not an easy task. Most of us believe that we have some enduring personality patterns. Psychologists define **personality** *as enduring, distinctive thoughts, emotions, and behaviors that characterize the way a person interacts with the world.*

The term *personality* has many informal uses in our culture that are distinct from what psychologists study when they conduct research on personality (Peterson, 1988). For example, we refer to Christy as having a "great personality." In this sense, we positively evaluate something about her that goes beyond looks, possessions, intelligence, or status. She makes us feel good to be around her. On the other hand, we might describe one of Christy's classmates as having "no personality." This negative evaluation suggests that there is little about the classmate that makes him attractive: no passions, no weird hobby or unusual ability, and little skill in engaging and keeping our attention. Celebrities are often referred to as "personalities." Whoopi Goldberg, Eddie Murphy, and David Letterman are well known not just for what they do, but for how they do it. They play roles in our culture that become identified with the personality characteristics they bring to the roles.

Psychologists recognize that personality descriptions identify the essential characteristics of individuals and allow us to observe subtle differences among us. Personality (*personality*) does not exist apart from the person, but it does involve social contexts. Think about personality as a blueprint or a map—a representation of the essential features that endear us to or alienate us from others.

Personality Theories

The diversity of theories makes understanding personality a challenge (Feist & Feist, 1998). Just when you think one theory has the correct explanation of personality, another theory will make you rethink your earlier conclusion. To keep from getting frustrated, remember that personality is a complex, multifaceted topic and no single theory has been able to account for all its aspects; each theory has contributed an important piece to the personality puzzle. In fact, many pieces of information in different personality theories are *complementary* rather than contradictory. Together they let us see the total landscape of personality in all its richness.

We will explore these theories of personality: trait, psychoanalytic, behavioral, cognitive social learning, and humanistic.

Trait Theories

traits
Broad dispositions that lead to characteristic responses.

As you saw in the story of Mark Twain that introduced this chapter, it is easy to misjudge others' personality characteristics. However, personality theorists scrutinize patterns of behavior to identify personality **traits,** *broad dispositions that lead to characteristic*

Many celebrities, such as Whoopi Goldberg, are called "personalities." They are well known, not just for what they do, but also for how they do it. Whoopi Goldberg's outgoing personality is a property of Whoopi Goldberg and is related to how she functions in the world. Of course, it is not just celebrities who have a personality. Each of us has a personality that is our property and is related to how we function in the world.

trait theories

Theories that propose that people have broad dispositions that are reflected in the basic ways they behave, such as whether they are outgoing, friendly, dominant, or assertive.

somatotype theory

Sheldon's theory that precise charts reveal distinct body types, which in turn are associated with certain personality characteristics.

endomorph

Sheldon's term for a soft, round, large-stomached person who is relaxed, gregarious, and food loving.

mesomorph

Sheldon's term for a strong, athletic, and muscular person who is energetic, assertive, and courageous.

ectomorph

Sheldon's term for a tall, thin, fragile person who is fearful, introverted, and restrained.

responses. **Trait theories** *propose that people have broad dispositions that are reflected in the basic ways they behave, such as whether they are outgoing and friendly or withdrawn and moody.* Different explanations based on traits or types have emerged over time, and have met with varying levels of acceptance, popularity, and durability. Although trait theorists sometimes differ on which traits make up personality, they all agree that traits are the fundamental building blocks of personality (Johnson, 1997; Wiggins, 1997). Some early trait approaches were called "type" theories.

Personality Type Theories. Sheldon (1954) developed **somatotype theory**, *a personality theory according to which a person's body shape and personality type are related.* Sheldon argued that people come in three basic types (see figure 10.1). **Endomorph** *was Sheldon's term for a soft, round, large-stomached person who is relaxed, gregarious, and food-loving.* A **mesomorph** *is a strong, athletic, and muscular person who is energetic, assertive, and courageous.* An **ectomorph** *is a thin, fragile-looking person who is fearful, introverted, and restrained.*

Intuitively appealing as it was, somatotyping ran aground (although Sheldon's terminology still shows up in discussions related to body shape). For starters, although Sheldon did attempt to conduct research to support his theories, his work was riddled with experimenter bias and other design problems that rendered his explanations suspect. Subsequent controlled research revealed no significant relation between body type and personality (Cortes & Gatti, 1970). Many people simply do not fit neatly into his categories, which ignore the diversity and complexity of human characteristics. Thus, somatotype theory is not considered scientifically valid. Such early attempts to explain personality demonstrate that appealing ideas do not always survive scientific scrutiny.

Endomorph
Chef Paul Prudhomme

Mesomorph
Actor Sylvester Stallone

Ectomorph
Singer Mariah Carey

$\mathcal{F}$IGURE 10.1

Sheldon's Body Types

Although these famous individuals fit the body types described by Sheldon, their personalities might not fit Sheldon's predictions.

Early Trait Approaches. Gordon Allport (1937) was one of the earliest architects of the trait approach. One of his interests was in trying to establish the range of traits that make up personality, which was a herculean task. In one of his efforts, he counted almost 18,000 dictionary words that could be used to describe people (Allport & Odbert, 1936). Allport suggested that a reasonable research strategy would be to find overarching categories that reduce the vast number of words necessary to describe personality traits. In the 1940s and 1950s, researchers began to show interest in how traits can be clustered around a smaller number of factors. For example, Raymond Cattell (1943) selected sixteen personality factors and constructed a personality questionnaire based on his theory that those sixteen personality factors were stable.

Even fewer factors were proposed by Hans Eysenck (1947). By analyzing the personality test results of large numbers of people, Eysenck found evidence for only two dimensions of personality: stability versus instability, and introversion versus extraversion (see figure 10.2). **Introversion** *is a tendency to be reserved, independent, and quiet.* **Extraversion** *is a tendency to be sociable, active, and fun-seeking.* Eysenck also discovered that the dimensions themselves can be related. For instance, an *introverted stable* personality is careful, even-tempered, and calm. An *extraverted unstable* personality is aggressive, excitable, and impulsive. To evaluate your introversion/extraversion tendencies, complete the Self-Assessment.

The Five-Factor Model. Many of today's trait psychologists are encouraged by growing evidence for not two, but five, basic dimensions of personality (Costa & McRae, 1995; McRae & Costa, 1997). These are sometimes referred to as "the big five." According to the **five-factor model,** *personality consists of five main factors: neuroticism, extraversion, openness to experience, agreeableness, and conscientiousness.* Each of these "big five" factors is a category, representing a continuum:

- *Neuroticism* is the degree to which an individual demonstrates emotional maladjustment and instability. Persons high on this trait (high N) are inclined to poor adjustment and psychological problems, including anxiety, anger, depression, self-consciousness, impulsivity, and vulnerability. Persons low on this trait (low N) are better adapted, are more realistic, and tolerate frustration better than persons high on this trait.
- *Extraversion* is the amount and intensity of preferred interpersonal interactions. Extraverts (high E) tend to be high-spirited and energetic, while introverts (low E) tend to be more reserved and passive.

introversion

A tendency to be reserved, independent, and quiet.

extraversion

A tendency to be sociable, active, and fun-seeking.

five-factor model

A model that bases personality on five main factors: neuroticism, extraversion, openness to experience, agreeableness, and conscientiousness.

Self-Assessment

Introversion/Extraversion

Instructions

For each of the following 20 questions, answer either *yes* (if it is generally true for you) or *no* (if it is generally not true for you).

1. Do you often long for excitement?
2. Are you usually carefree?
3. Do you stop and think things over before doing anything?
4. Would you do almost anything for a dare?
5. Do you often do things on the spur of the moment?
6. Generally, do you prefer reading to meeting people?
7. Do you prefer to have few but special friends?
8. When people shout at you do you shout back?
9. Do other people think of you as very lively?
10. Are you mostly quiet when you are with people?
11. If there is something you want to know about, would you rather look it up in a book than talk to someone about it?
12. Do you like the kind of work that you need to pay close attention to?
13. Do you hate being with a crowd who plays jokes on one another?
14. Do you like doing things in which you have to act quickly?
15. Are you slow and unhurried in the way you move?
16. Do you like talking to people so much that you never miss a chance of talking to a stranger?

17. Would you be unhappy if you could not see lots of people most of the time?
18. Do you find it hard to enjoy yourself at a lively party?
19. Would you say that you were fairly self-confident?
20. Do you like playing pranks on others?

Scoring

To arrive at your score for extraversion, give one point for each of the following items answered *yes:* #1, 2, 4, 5, 8, 9, 14, 16, 17, 19, and 20. Then give yourself one point for each of the following items answered *no:* #3, 6, 7, 10, 11, 12, 13, 15, 18. Add up all the points to arrive at a total score.

Interpretation

Your total score should be between 0 and 20. If your scores are very high (15–20), you are the "life of the party." You clearly prefer being with others to being alone. If your scores are very low (1–5), you are a loner. You find greater pleasure in solitary activities. If you are somewhere in between (6–14), you are flexible in how you prefer to spend your time. You can take pleasure in the company of others (especially if your score is in the higher range) but still manage to appreciate solitude.

- *Openness to experience* is the degree to which a person actively seeks out and appreciates experiences for their own sake. On one end of the continuum, open (high O) individuals show curiosity, imagination, and some unconventionality in their values. They tend to experience emotions more vividly. Low O persons tend to be more conventional, conservative, and rigid in their beliefs and have diminished emotional responsiveness.

$\mathscr{F}$IGURE 10.2

Eysenck's Dimensions of Personality

On the basis of his factor analytic studies, Eysenck concluded that personality consists of two basic dimensions: (1) stability-instability and (2) introversion-extraversion.

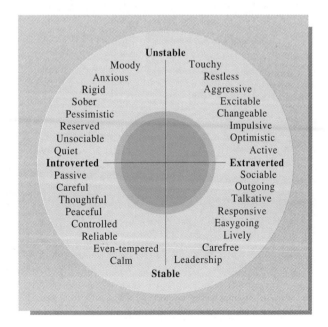

- *Agreeableness* is the degree to which a person compassionately connects with others. Agreeable (high A) individuals tend to be good-natured, trusting, and helpful. Antagonistic (low A) individuals tend to be suspicious, irritable, and vengeful.
- *Conscientiousness* is the degree of organization, self-control, and persistence a person shows in pursuing goals. Conscientious (high C) people tend to be hardworking, ambitious, and driving. Nonconscientious (low C) people tend to be shiftless, negligent, and pleasure-seeking.

Recently researchers have studied the five-factor model in different cultures (McRae & Costa, 1997). For instance, an analysis of German, Portuguese, Hebrew, Chinese, Korean, and Japanese languages revealed concepts that were similar to the American concepts of the "big five" factors.

Of course, not everyone heralds the big five as the ultimate solution in personality research. Trait models are helpful for describing behavior but fall short when it comes to explaining behavior. As research continues, time will tell whether the big five model will remain a robust explanation or follow the early type models and become merely a historical curiosity.

Culture and Personality Traits. In America, "the squeaky wheel gets the grease." In Japan, "the nail that stands out gets pounded down." Such aphorisms suggest that people in Japan and America have very different views of personality (Markus & Kitayama, 1991).

In cross-cultural research, the search for basic traits has been extended to characteristics that are common to whole nations. In recent years, the most elaborate search for traits common to members of a particular culture has focused on the concept of individualism versus collectivism (Diener & others, 1995). **Individualism** *involves giving priority to personal goals rather than to group goals; it emphasizes values that serve the self, such as*

individualism

Gives priority to personal goals rather than to group goals; an emphasis on values that serve the self, such as feeling good, personal achievement and distinction, and independence.

Many Eastern cultures, such as that of Japan, have a strong emphasis on connectedness with others and group behavior. In such collectivistic cultures, individuals are under considerable pressure to conform and to work for the common good.

An emphasis on values that serve the group by subordinating personal goals to preserve group integrity, the interdependence of members, and harmonious relationships.

feeling good, personal achievement and distinction, and independence. **Collectivism** *emphasizes values that serve the group by subordinating personal goals to preserve group integrity, the interdependence of members, and harmonious relationships.* Cross-cultural psychologists describe the cultures in many non-Western countries, such as Russia, Japan, and India, as more collectivistic than individualistic (Triandis, 1994, 1997). To read about how collectivists and individualists can interact more effectively, see Applications in Psychology.

As with other attempts to explain personality, the individualism/collectivism dichotomy also has its detractors. They argue that describing entire nations of people as having a basic personality obscures the extensive diversity and individual variation that characterizes any nation's people. Also, certain values, such as wisdom, mature love, and tolerance, serve both individual and collective interests (Schwartz, 1990). We are unlikely to find significant differences in some values and behaviors when we make cross-cultural comparisons between individualistic and collectivistic cultures.

Evaluating Trait Explanations.   Contemporary trait theorists have made headway in establishing trait approaches as a legitimate and well-respected means of describing individual differences. They emphasize identifying the stable and consistent patterns demonstrated by individuals across situations. Although trait approaches historically favored the biological basis of personality, more recently theorists have incorporated the influences of culture and environment on trait development.

Trait theory has spurred a large amount of research and is primarily responsible for the growth and acceptance of psychological testing. However, trait theorists accept the premise that individuals have enough self-awareness to be competent at judging their own characteristics. For example, they pay less attention to the idea that behavior can be motivated unconsciously.

Trait theory still is a rather limited source for explaining why people do what they do. For example, we can speculate about how Mark Twain might have fared if his personality were analyzed according to the five-factor model. Twain was a bit of a paradox. He sometimes claimed to dislike and disrespect other people, and yet he thrived in his prolific publishing career, his international travel, and lecture appearances. He probably would be rated as low in neuroticism and high in extraversion, openness, and conscientiousness. However his tendency to be a prankster might pose a problem. He could look

*A*pplications in Psychology

How Collectivists and Individualists Can Interact More Effectively

If you come from a collectivistic culture and you are about to interact with someone from an individualistic culture, are there ways you can communicate with the other person more effectively? Similarly, if you are from an individualistic culture and are about to interact with someone from a collectivistic culture, are there ways you can communicate with the person more effectively? Cross-cultural psychologists Harry Triandis, Richard Brislin, and C. Harry Hui (1988) think so. Some of their recommendations follow. First are the suggestions for collectivists interacting with individualists:

- Compliment the person more than you are used to doing in your culture.
- Avoid feeling threatened if the individualist acts competitively.

- Talk about your accomplishments. You don't have to be as modest as in your own culture. At the same time, it is not a good idea to boast.
- Recognize that individualists don't value allegiance to the group as much as you do.

If you are an individualist, the following are good strategies for communicating more effectively with a collectivist:

- Learn to pay more attention to group membership.
- Place more emphasis on cooperation than on competition.
- If you must criticize, do so carefully and only in private situations. Never criticize someone in public because it will cause them to "lose face."
- Cultivate long-term relationships. Be patient. People in collectivistic cultures like dealing with "old friends."

*I*mproving Personal and Cognitive Skills

Justice and the Use of Trait Labels

The practice of using trait labels to describe others can help us make sense of the world. However, sometimes the labels lead us to make premature judgments about people. We assign a trait to a person and then move on. Even if the person's behavior changes, too often we keep the label we initially used to describe the person. The following are some ways we can avoid the risks of inappropriate trait labeling and improve our judgments of others:

1. *Reserve judgment, especially when we are inclined to ascribe negative traits.*
   Learn not to have "knee-jerk" reactions about people. Wait until you have more data about them. One episode of a person's behavior can lead to very misleading trait judgments about the person.
2. *Focus on specific behaviors rather than on trait labels when describing a person.*
   Marriage therapists help couples learn to focus on specific behaviors that are upsetting to them rather than describe

their partner's behavior in terms of generalizing trait labels. For example, the person might be encouraged to say, "It upsets me a lot when you don't come home on time" rather than "You are inconsiderate" or "You are insecure."

3. *Consider the context in which the behavior occurs.*
   Many behaviors are influenced by the situation. When you think of someone as mean, think about the specific circumstances (such as too little sleep or financial worries) that might bring out this negative personality characteristic.
4. *Don't expect people to always be consistent.*
   People don't always behave the same way day after day, month after month, year after year. Circumstances in their lives can change, and they might become more mature or change in other ways. After a time, a trait label that once might have seemed appropriate (such as *antagonistic*) might no longer seem to fit the person.

disagreeable physically, so he might have used pranks and teasing as a way of staying connected to others. These contradictions would have confounded his scoring on agreeableness. Despite these descriptions, trait theory does give us a deep understanding of the influences on Twain's personality.

In our everyday interactions with others, we often describe others in terms of one or more traits. But we need to be cautious about relying on trait terms to describe a person (see Improving Personal and Cognitive Skills). Next we turn to a dramatically different approach to explaining personality—psychoanalytic theory.

The Nature of Personality and Trait Theories

Personality refers to our enduring thoughts, emotions, and behaviors that characterize the way we interact with the world. Different personality theories emphasize different features of personality.

Different explanations of types and traits have emerged over time. Sheldon's heavily criticized somatotype theory, linking body shape and personality, has largely been abandoned. Allport was an early architect of the trait approach.

Eysenck identified two dimensions—extraversion versus introversion and stability versus instability—that he believed were the foundation of all personality characteristics. The five-factor model of personality emerged in the 1980s and stimulated new interest in explaining personality in terms of traits. The "big five" factors are neuroticism, extraversion, openness to experience, agreeableness, and conscientiousness.

Culture also influences personality traits. Cultures promote either collectivistic or individualistic values that shape individual behavior. Not all cultures emphasize understanding the self. Trait approaches are intended to provide a comprehensive way to describe individual differences but do not foster a deep understanding of personality.

Psychoanalytic Theories

While Americans were busy mapping and measuring personality traits, the explorations of personality in Europe were very different. Beginning with the controversial theories of Sigmund Freud, psychoanalytic approaches sought to understand personality at a deeper level. Psychoanalytic theorists generally proposed that behavior is merely a surface characteristic of a complex of forces. They argued that to understand a person's personality, we must explore the influences of unconscious factors on behavior and discover the symbolic meanings of behavior. Let's examine Freud's background and ideas more fully.

Freud's Theory.   Loved and hated, respected and despised—Sigmund Freud, whether right or wrong in his views, was one of the most influential and controversial thinkers of the twentieth century. Freud was a medical doctor who specialized in nervous conditions. His psychoanalytic theory originated from his work with anxiety-ridden, neurotic patients.

To better understand Freud's theory let's consider Freud's personal background, including the society in which he was born, lived, and worked. Freud was born in Vienna, Austria, in 1856. An eldest child, he was regarded as a genius by his brothers and sisters and doted on by his mother. Later we will see that one aspect of Freud's theory is its assumption that young boys are sexually attracted to their mothers. It is possible that Freud derived this belief from his own romantic attachment to his mother, who was beautiful and about 20 years younger than Freud's father.

Victorian morality flourished in turn-of-the-century Vienna. Male and female roles were clearly distinguished, with women playing a subservient role to men. Human sexuality was barely acknowledged, so Freud's enthusiasm for sex as a force that shaped personality was not popularly received by most of the professional community. When Freud began publishing his observations, many found his ideas brilliant; others found them and Freud himself to be outrageous.

Freud spent most of his life in Vienna, working with his patients, discussing his insights with his followers, and publishing his extensive theories. Near the end of his life, he escaped Nazi anti-Semitism by fleeing to London. He died in 1939 at the age of 83 after multiple surgeries for cancer of the jaw perhaps linked to his intense cigar-smoking habit. Freud lived long enough to see his work recognized as revolutionizing the way we think about personality as well as how patients with psychological disorders are treated.

The Role of the Unconscious.   Freud rebelled against the idea that human behavior is entirely rational. According to Freud, we are not aware of most of the forces at work in shaping our behavior—most of the influences on our behavior are unconscious, driven by sexual and aggressive impulses.

Freud envisioned the mind as something like a huge iceberg, with the massive part below the surface of the water being the unconscious part. Freud said that each of our lives is filled with tension and conflict; to reduce this tension and conflict, we keep information locked in the unconscious mind. For Freud, the unconscious mind holds the key to understanding behavior. Freud believed that even trivial behaviors have special significance when the unconscious forces behind them are revealed. A twitch, a doodle, a joke, a smile, each may have an unconscious reason for appearing. They often slip into our lives without our awareness. For example, Allison is kissing and hugging Tyler, whom she is to marry in several weeks. She says, "Oh, *Jeff,* I love you so much." Tyler pushes her away and says, "Why did you call me Jeff? I thought you didn't think about him anymore. We need to have a talk!" You probably can think of times when such *Freudian slips* have tumbled out of your own mouth.

The Structure of Personality.   Freud (1917) believed that personality has three structures: the id, the ego, and the superego.

The **id** *is the Freudian structure of personality that consists of instincts, which are the individual's reservoir of psychic energy.* In Freud's view, the id is unconscious; it has no contact with reality. The id works according to the **pleasure principle,** *the Freudian concept that the id always seeks pleasure and avoids pain.*

---

id
The Freudian structure of personality that consists of instincts, which are the person's reservoir of psychic energy.

pleasure principle
The Freudian concept that the id always seeks pleasure and avoids pain.

Sigmund Freud, the father of psychoanalysis.

ego

The Freudian structure of personality that deals with the demands of reality; the ego is called the executive branch of personality because it makes rational decisions.

reality principle

The Freudian concept that the ego tries to make the pursuit of individual pleasure conform to the norms of society.

defense mechanisms

The psychoanalytic term for unconscious methods of dealing with conflict; the ego distorts reality, thereby protecting itself from anxiety.

superego

The Freudian structure of personality that is the moral branch of personality. The superego takes into account whether something is right or wrong.

erogenous zones

Those parts of the body at each stage of development that, according to Freud's theory, have especially strong pleasure-giving qualities.

fixation

The psychoanalytic defense mechanism that occurs when the individual remains locked in an earlier developmental stage because her or his needs are under- or overgratified.

oral stage

The term Freud used to describe development during the first 18 months of life, when the infant's pleasure centers on the mouth.

It would be a dangerous and scary world if our personalities were all id. As young children mature, for example, they learn they cannot slug other children in the face. They also learn they have to use the toilet instead of their diaper. As children experience the demands and constraints of reality, a new structure of personality is formed—the **ego**, *the Freudian structure of personality that deals with the demands of reality. The ego is called the executive branch of personality because it makes rational decisions.* Whereas the id is completely unconscious, the ego is partly conscious. It houses our higher mental functions—reasoning, problem solving, and decision making, for example. The ego abides by the **reality principle,** *the Freudian concept that the ego tries to make the pursuit of individual pleasure conform to the norms of society.* Few of us are cold-blooded killers or wild wheeler-dealers; we take into account the obstacles to our satisfaction that exist in our world. We recognize that our sexual and aggressive impulses cannot go unrestrained. The ego helps us test reality, to see how far we can go without getting into trouble and hurting ourselves.

The ego uses a number of strategies to resolve conflicts between the impulses of the id and the constraints of the superego. Through **defense mechanisms,** *the ego deals with conflict by distorting reality. This protects the ego from anxiety.* Table 10.1 describes some common defense mechanisms. As you read the table, reflect on whether you or people you know use these. Defense mechanisms are unconscious—when we use them, we are not aware that we are. In moderation or as a temporary measure, using defense mechanisms is not necessarily unhealthy. Sometimes therapists might work to strengthen clients' defense mechanisms to make them less vulnerable to anxiety. Problems arise when defense mechanisms dominate a person's behavior, preventing the person from facing life's demands directly.

The id and ego have no morality. They do not take into account whether something is right or wrong. In contrast, the **superego** *is the Freudian structure of personality that is the moral branch of personality. The superego takes into account whether something is right or wrong.* The superego is what we often refer to as the "conscience." The superego considers only whether the id's sexual and aggressive impulses can be satisfied in moral terms. You probably are beginning to sense that both the id and the superego make life rough for the ego. Your ego might say, "I will have sex only occasionally and be sure to use an effective form of protection against pregnancy and sexually transmitted diseases." However, your id is saying, "I want to be satisfied; sex feels so good." Your superego is also at work: "I feel guilty about having sex."

Remember many psychoanalysts consider personality to be like an iceberg; most of our personality exists below the level of awareness, just as the massive part of an iceberg is beneath the surface of the water. Figure 10.3 illustrates this analogy and the extent of the unconscious part of our mind.

The Development of Personality. As Freud listened to, probed, and analyzed his patients, he became convinced that their problems were the result of experiences early in life. Freud believed that we go through five stages of psychosexual development and that, at each stage of development, we experience pleasure in one part of the body more than others. **Erogenous zones** *are those parts of the body that, at each stage of development, according to Freud's theory, have especially strong pleasure-giving qualities.*

Freud thought that adult personality is determined by the way we resolve conflicts among these early sources of pleasure—the mouth, the anus, and then the genitals—and the demands of reality. When these conflicts are not resolved, the individual may become fixated at a particular stage of development. **Fixation** *is the psychoanalytic defense mechanism that occurs when the individual remains locked in an earlier developmental stage because her or his needs are under- or overgratified.* For example, a parent may wean a child too early, be too strict in toilet training, punish the child for masturbation, or "smother" the child with too much attention. We will return to the idea of fixation and how it may show up in an adult's personality, but first we need to learn more about the early stages of personality development.

Oral stage *is the term Freud used to describe development during the first 18 months of life, in which the infant's pleasure centers on the mouth.* Chewing, sucking, and biting are chief sources of pleasure, and they help reduce tension.

How Defense Mechanisms Reduce Anxiety

Defense Mechanism	How It Works	Example
Repression	The ego pushes unacceptable id impulses and traumatic memories out of conscious awareness and into the unconscious mind.	Betty was traumatized in childhood by her sister's death. She can't recall the funeral even though her relatives assure her that she was present.
Denial	The ego rejects realities that are too anxiety-provoking and stores them in the unconscious.	Dean felt completely numb when the doctor interpreted his test results and told him he had cancer.
Rationalization	The ego replaces an unacceptable motive with a more suitable cover story or excuse.	Ron's bid to run for student senate is unsuccessful. He rationalizes his loss by saying he must not have wanted it or he would have campaigned more vigorously.
Displacement	The ego shifts unacceptable feelings from one object to another, more suitable object.	Trudy is harassed by her boss at work, but rather than risk her job, she waits and unloads on her husband at home.
Sublimation	The ego replaces an unacceptable impulse with a socially approved course of action.	Cynthia has strong sexual urges that she expresses by becoming an artist who paints nudes.
Projection	The ego attributes our own shortcomings, problems, and faults to others.	Shawn, a real manipulator at work, complains that his fellow employees manipulate at work to get ahead.
Reaction formation	The ego transforms an unacceptable impulse into an opposite impulse.	Toni is fascinated by the horrors related to war, but becomes a crusading peace activist.
Regression	The ego facilitates a return to a form of behavior that reduced anxiety during an earlier developmental period.	Newlyweds Darren and Charlotte run home to their mothers every time they have a big argument.

F IGURE 10.3

Conscious and Unconscious Processes: The Iceberg Analogy

This rather odd-looking diagram illustrates the psychodynamic belief that most of the important personality processes occur below the level of conscious awareness. In examining people's conscious thoughts and their behaviors, we can see some reflections of the ego and the superego. Whereas the ego and superego are partly conscious and partly unconscious, the primitive id is the unconscious, totally submerged part of the iceberg.

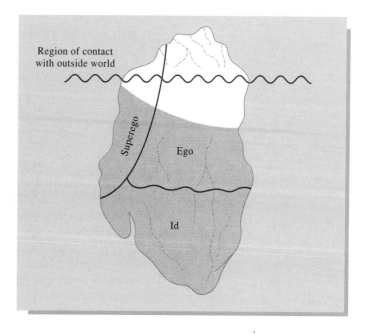

anal stage

Freud's second stage of development, occurring between 1½ and 3 years of age, in which the child's greatest pleasure involves the anus or the elimination functions associated with it.

phallic stage

Freud's third stage of development, which occurs between the ages of 3 and 6. During the phallic stage, pleasure focuses on the genitals as the child discovers that self-stimulation is enjoyable.

Oedipus complex

In Freud's theory, the young child's developing an intense desire to replace the parent of the same sex and to enjoy the affections of the opposite-sex parent.

latency stage

The fourth Freudian stage of development, occurring approximately between 6 years of age and puberty; the child represses all interest in sexuality and develops social and intellectual skills.

genital stage

The fifth Freudian stage of development, occurring from puberty on; the time of sexual reawakening; the source of sexual pleasure now becomes someone outside of the family.

The **anal stage** *is Freud's second stage of development, occurring between 1½ and 3 years of age, in which the child's greatest pleasure involves the anus or the elimination functions associated with it.* In Freud's view, the exercise of anal muscles reduces tension and provides pleasure.

The **phallic stage,** *Freud's third stage of development, occurs between the ages of 3 and 6; its name comes from the Latin word* phallus, *which means "penis." During the phallic stage, pleasure focuses on the genitals as the child discovers that self-stimulation is enjoyable.* In Freud's view, the phallic stage has a special importance in personality development because this period triggers the Oedipus complex. This name comes from an ancient Greek play by Sophocles, in which Oedipus, the son of the king of Thebes, unknowingly kills his father and marries his mother. The **Oedipus complex,** *in Freud's theory, is the young child's developing an intense desire to replace the parent of the same sex and to enjoy the affections of the opposite-sex parent.* As discussed in Sociocultural Worlds, the Oedipus complex, like many other aspects of Freud's theory, was not as universal as Freud believed; his concept was heavily influenced by the sociohistorical, cultural context of turn-of-the-century Vienna.

At about 5 to 6 years of age, children recognize that their same-sex parent might punish them for their incestuous wishes. To reduce this conflict, the child represses lustful feelings and identifies with the same-sex parent, striving to be like him or her. If the conflict is not resolved, the individual may become fixated at the phallic stage.

The **latency stage** *is the fourth Freudian stage of development, occurring approximately between 6 years of age and puberty; the child represses all interest in sexuality and develops social and intellectual skills.* This activity channels much of the child's energy into emotionally safe areas and aids the child in forgetting the highly stressful conflicts of the phallic stage.

The **genital stage** *is the fifth and final Freudian stage of development, occurring from puberty on. The genital stage is the time of sexual reawakening; the source of sexual pleasure now becomes someone outside of the family.* Freud believed that unresolved conflicts with parents reemerge during adolescence. Once the conflicts are resolved, Freud believed, the individual becomes capable of developing a mature love relationship and of functioning independently as an adult. Figure 10.4 summarizes Freud's psychosexual stages.

Psychoanalytic Revisionists and Dissenters.   Freud was among the first theorists to explore many new and uncharted regions of personality and is credited with founding psychoanalysis. As others joined him in this new medical frontier, neo-Freudians discovered that they had to update and revise Freud's ideas. Although they honored many of his concepts, they rejected some aspects of Freudian theory altogether. In particular, Freud's critics have said his ideas about sexuality, early experience, social factors, and the unconscious mind were misguided (Adler, 1927; Erikson, 1968; Fromm, 1947; Horney, 1945; Jung, 1917; Sullivan, 1953). The critics stressed several points:

- Sexuality is not the pervasive underlying force behind personality that Freud believed it to be.
- The first 5 years of life are not as powerful in shaping adult personality as Freud thought; later experiences deserve more attention than they have been given.
- The ego and conscious thought processes play more dominant roles in our personality than Freud gave them credit for; we are not wed forever to the id and its instinctual, unconscious clutches. The ego has a line of development separate from the id; viewed in this way, achievement, thinking, and reasoning are not always tied to sexual impulses, as Freud thought.
- Sociocultural factors are much more important than Freud believed. Freud placed more emphasis on the biological basis of personality by stressing the id's dominance.

Let's examine three theories by dissenters and revisionists of Freud's theory in greater detail—the theories of Karen Horney, Carl Jung, and Alfred Adler.

Horney's Sociocultural Modification.   Although she agreed with much of Freud's theory of personality development, Karen Horney (1885–1952) rejected the classical psychoanalytic concept that anatomy determines behavior in favor of an approach that emphasizes

Sociocultural Worlds

Freud's Theory of the Oedipus Complex: Culturally and Gender Biased

The Oedipus complex is one of Freud's most influential concepts pertaining to the importance of early psychosexual relationships for later personality development. Freud developed his theory during the Victorian era of the late 1800s, when sexual interests, especially those of females, were repressed. According to Freud, the phallic stage begins for a girl when she realizes she has no penis. He also believed that she recognizes the superiority of the penis to her anatomy and, thus, develops *penis envy*. Blaming her mother for her lack of a penis, the girl renounces her love for her mother and becomes intensely attached to her father. Because her desire for having a penis can never be satisfied directly, Freud speculated that the young girl yearns for a penis substitute, preferably by bearing a male child. Freud believed that this challenge is never fully resolved but merely dissipates over time as the girl begins to identify with—to take on the values and feminine behavior of—her mother. As a result, Freud assumed that women do not develop as strong a conscience (superego) as men.

Many psychologists believe that Freud placed far too much emphasis on biology's role in personality development. Freud concluded, for example, that boys are likely to develop a dominant, powerful personality because they have a penis; without a penis, girls are predisposed to become submissive and weak. In basing his view of male/female differences in personality

development on anatomical differences, Freud ignored the enormous impact of culture and experience.

More than half a century ago, English anthropologist Bronislaw Malinowski (1927) observed the family dynamics of the Trobriand Islanders of the Western Pacific and found that the Oedipus complex is not universal. In the Trobriand Islands, the biological father is not the head of the household; that role is reserved for the mother's brother, who acts as a disciplinarian. In Freud's view, this family constellation should make no difference in the Oedipus complex; the young boy should still vie for his mother's love and perceive his father as a hated rival. However, Malinowski found no such conflict between fathers and sons in the Trobriand Islanders. However, he did observe that the young boys feared and directed negative feelings toward their maternal uncles, the disciplinary figures. Malinowski's findings undermined claims of universality for Freud's Oedipus complex theory, because it showed that the sexual relations within the family do not create conflict and fear for a child.

One contemporary feminist scholar says that Freud's reliance on a male-centered perspective of Oedipus misses a crucial theme presented in Sophocles' trilogy that better explains relations between men and women (Kaschak, 1992). In another of Sophocles' plays, Antigone (Oedipus's daughter through his incestuous marriage to his own mother) loses her life defending the honor of her dead brother, to whom she had been devoted.

Oral stage   Anal stage   Phallic stage   Latency stage   Genital stage

𝓕IGURE 10.4

Freudian Psychosexual Stages

Freud said we go through five stages of psychosexual development. In the oral stage, pleasure centers around the mouth. In the anal stage, pleasure focuses on the anus—the nature of toilet training is important here. In the phallic stage, pleasure involves the genitals—the opposite-sex parent becomes a love object. In the latency stage, a child represses sexual urges—same-sex friendship is prominent. In the genital stage, sexual reawakening takes place—the source of pleasure now becomes someone outside the family.

Carl Jung, a Swiss psychoanalytic theorist.

collective unconscious

In Jung's theory, the impersonal, deepest layer of the unconscious mind, which is shared by all human beings because of their common ancestral past.

archetypes

Primordial influences in every individual's collective unconscious that filter our perceptions and experiences.

individual psychology

The name Adler gave to his theory to emphasize the uniqueness of every individual.

$\mathcal{F}$IGURE 10.5

Mandalas

Because mandalas have been used to represent the self in so many different cultures and historical periods, Carl Jung believed that they are an archetype for the self.

the importance of sociocultural factors in development. She cautioned that such ideas as penis envy are only hypotheses. She insisted that these hypotheses should be supported with observable data before they are accepted as fact.

Horney pointed out that previous research about how women function was limited by the fact that those who described women, who influenced and represented the culture, and who determined the standards for suitable growth and development were men. She countered the notion of penis envy with the hypothesis that both sexes envy the attributes of the other and that men covet women's reproductive capacities. She also argued that women who feel penis envy are desirous only of the status that men have in most societies, not of their anatomy (Westkott, 1986).

Horney also believed that the need for security, not for sex or aggression, is the prime motive in human existence. Horney reasoned that a person whose needs for security have been met should be able to develop his or her capacities to the fullest extent. She also suggested that people usually develop one of three strategies in their effort to cope with anxiety. First, individuals may *move toward* people, seeking love and support. Second, individuals may *move away* from people, becoming more independent. Third, individuals may *move against* people, becoming competitive and domineering. A secure individual uses these three ways of coping in moderation and balance, whereas an insecure individual often uses one or more of these strategies in an exaggerated fashion, becoming too dependent, to independent, or too aggressive.

Psychologists continue to revise psychoanalytic theory. Nancy Chodorow's (1978, 1989) feminist revision of psychoanalytic theory, for example, emphasizes that many more women than men define themselves in terms of their relationships, that many men use denial as a defense mechanism in regard to their relationships with others, and that emotions tend to play a more prominent role in women's lives.

> *Psychoanalysis is the creation of a male genius, and almost all those who have developed these ideas have been men. It is only right and reasonable that they should evolve more easily a masculine psychology and understand more of the development of men than of women.*
> —KAREN HORNEY, *American Psychotherapist, 20th Century*

Jung's Depth Psychology.   Freud's contemporary, Carl Jung (1875–1961), shared an interest in the unconscious; however, he believed that Freud underplayed the unconscious mind's role in personality. Jung suspected that the roots of personality go back to the dawn of human existence. The **collective unconscious** *is the impersonal, deepest layer of the unconscious mind, which is shared by all human beings because of their common ancestral past.* These common experiences have made a deep, permanent impression on the human mind. **Archetypes** *are the primordial influences in every individual's collective unconscious that filter our perceptions and experiences.* Jung's psychoanalytic theory is often referred to as "depth psychology" because archetypes reside deep within the unconscious mind, far deeper than what Freud described as our personal unconscious.

Two common archetypes are *anima* (woman) and *animus* (man). Jung believed that each of us has a passive, "feminine" side and an assertive, "masculine" side. We also have an archetype for self, which often is expressed in art. For example, the mandala, a figure within a circle, has been used so often that Jung took it to represent the self (see figure 10.5). Another archetype is the shadow, our darker self, which is evil and immoral. The shadow appears in many evil and immoral figures—Satan, Dracula, Mr. Hyde (of Jekyll and Hyde), and Darth Vader (of the *Star Wars* movies) (Peterson 1988).

> *I have never seen a greater monster of miracle in the world than myself.*
> —MICHEL DEMONTAIGNE, *French Essayist, 16th Century*

Adler's Individual Psychology.   Alfred Adler (1870–1937) was another contemporary of Freud. **Individual psychology** *is the name Adler gave to his theory to emphasize the unique-*

ness of every individual. Unlike Freud's belief in the power of the unconscious mind, Adler argued that we have the conscious ability to monitor and direct our lives. He also believed social factors are more important in shaping our personality than sexual motivation (Silverman & Corsini, 1984). Adler's emphasis on individual psychology is captured in the Self-Assessment, where you can evaluate your need to be unique.

Adler thought that everyone strives for superiority. Adler's concept of **striving for superiority** *emphasizes the human motivation to adapt, improve, and master the environment.* Striving for superiority is our response to feelings of inferiority that we all experience as infants and young children when we interact with people who are bigger and more powerful. We strive to overcome these feelings of inferiority because they are uncomfortable. **Compensation** *is Adler's term for the individual's attempt to overcome imagined or real inferiorities or weaknesses by developing one's abilities.* Adler believed that compensation was normal, and he said we often make up for a weakness in one ability by excelling in a different ability. For example, one person may be a mediocre student but compensate for this by excelling in athletics. **Overcompensation** *is Adler's term for the individual's attempt to deny rather than acknowledge a real situation, or the exaggerated effort to conceal a weakness.* Adler described two patterns of overcompensation. **Inferiority complex** *is the name Adler gave to exaggerated feelings of inadequacy.* **Superiority complex** *is his concept for exaggerated self-importance designed to mask feelings of inferiority.*

Adler highlighted the importance of <u>birth order</u> in explaining an individual's personality. Birth order refers to your sibling location in a family—whether you are firstborn, lastborn, or middle-born, for example. As you might imagine, Adler thought that firstborns more often feel a sense of superiority, lastborn's a sense of inferiority. Researchers have found that firstborn's are more adult- and achievement-oriented, but also have more guilt and anxiety than later-borns (Stanhope & Corter, 1993)

Keep in mind, though, that it is easy to fall into the trap of thinking that an individual's entire personality is determined by birth order. That just is not so. You may have heard someone say, "He's that way because he is a firstborn," or "She's that way because she is a middle child." Many psychologists believe that birth order has been overdramatized as a predictor of behavior in this manner. In addition to birth order per se, it also is important to consider the sex of the individual, age spacing of siblings, parenting practices, the individual's temperament (shy or outgoing, for example), heredity, cognition, and many other factors when predicting behavior (Santrock, 1999). That's good news, right? It would be disconcerting if we thought that regardless of all the effort we put into our lives we are still destined to have a particular personality because of our location in a particular sibling order.

In sum, Adler's theory emphasizes that people strive toward a positive being, create their own goals, and are influenced by family experiences, especially those generated by birth order. In Adler's view, people become better adapted by developing social interests and reducing feelings of inferiority. Like Jung, Adler has a number of disciples today.

Evaluation of Psychoanalytic Theories. Although psychoanalytic theories have diverged over time, they do share some core principles. Psychoanalytic theorists assert that personality is determined by biological forces, early life experiences, and, to a lesser degree, current experiences. The test of time has been withstood by two basic principles of psychoanalytic theory: that early experiences do influence personality development, and that personality can be better understood by examining it developmentally.

Psychoanalysts also recognize that behavior is not all rational and that we are not fully aware of our own motives. Unconscious motives lie behind some of our most puzzling behavior. Adjustment is not always an easy task; the individual's inner world often conflicts with outer demands of reality. Psychoanalytic theorists emphasize conflicts, anxiety, sexual impulse, and negative forces in our lives. These approaches have been criticized for painting too bleak a picture of human nature.

The main concepts of psychoanalytic theories have been difficult to test; they are largely matters of inference and interpretation. Researchers have not, for example, successfully investigated such key concepts as repression in the laboratory. Much of the data used to support psychoanalytic theories have come from clinicians' subjective

$\mathcal{S}$elf-Assessment

Need for Uniqueness

Instructions

The following statements concern your perceptions about yourself in a variety of situations. Your task is to indicate the strength of your agreement with each statement, utilizing a scale in which 1 denotes strong disagreement, 5 denotes strong agreement, and 2, 3, and 4, represent intermediate judgments. In the blank preceding each statement, place your number from 1 to 5. *There are no "right" or "wrong" answers, so select the number that most clearly reflects your feeling about each statement.*

_____ 1. When I am in a group of strangers, I am not reluctant to express my opinion openly.

_____ 2. I find that criticism affects my self-esteem.

_____ 3. I sometimes hesitate to use my own ideas for fear they might be impractical.

_____ 4. I think society should let reason lead it to new customs and throw aside old habits or mere traditions.

_____ 5. People frequently succeed in changing my mind.

_____ 6. I find it sometimes amusing to upset the dignity of teachers, judges, and "cultured" people.

_____ 7. I like wearing a uniform because it makes me proud to be a member of the organization it represents.

_____ 8. People have sometimes called me "stuck-up."

_____ 9. Others' disagreements make me uncomfortable.

_____ 10. I do not always need to live by the rules and standards of society.

_____ 11. I am unable to express my feelings if they result in undesirable consequences.

_____ 12. Being a success in one's career means making a contribution that no one else has made.

_____ 13. It bothers me if people think I am being too unconventional.

_____ 14. I always try to follow rules.

_____ 15. If I disagree with a superior on his or her views, I usually do not keep it to myself.

_____ 16. I speak up in meetings in order to oppose those whom I feel are wrong.

_____ 17. Feeling "different" in a crowd of people makes me feel uncomfortable.

_____ 18. If I must die, let it be an unusual death rather than an ordinary death in bed.

_____ 19. I would rather be just like everyone else than be called a "freak."

_____ 20. I must admit I find it hard to work under strict rules and regulations.

_____ 21. I would rather be known for always trying new ideas than for employing well-trusted methods.

_____ 22. It is better always to agree with the opinions of others than to be considered a disagreeable person.

_____ 23. I do not like to say unusual things to people.

_____ 24. I tend to express my opinions publicly, regardless of what others say.

_____ 25. As a rule, I strongly defend my own opinions.

_____ 26. I do not like to go my own way.

_____ 27. When I am with a group of people, I agree with their ideas so that no arguments will arise.

_____ 28. I tend to keep quiet in the presence of persons of higher rank, experience, etc.

_____ 29. I have been quite independent and free from family rule.

_____ 30. Whenever I take part in group activities, I am somewhat of a nonconformist.

_____ 31. In most things in life, I believe in playing it safe rather than taking a gamble.

_____ 32. It is better to break rules than always to conform with an impersonal society.

Scoring

Reverse score on items 2, 3, 5, 7, 9, 11, 13, 14, 17, 19, 22, 23, 26, 27, 28, and 31. On these items, a 5 = 1, 4 = 2, 3 = 3, 2 = 4, and 1 = 5. Then add the score for all 32 items.

Interpretation

Possible scores on this assessment range from 160 to 32. For 1,400 students at the University of Kansas and Purdue University who took this Self-Assessment, a score of 100 was the 50th percentile. Compare your score to their outcome. If your score is above 100, being a distinctive individual is important to you. The *higher* you score, the greater is your *need for uniqueness*. Scores below 100 suggest this might not be an important need for you. The *lower* you score, the less is your need to be different from others. Remember, the scale does not necessarily tell you how different from others you truly are, but only how important this need is to you.

evaluations of clients; it is easy for clinicians to find what they expect to find because of the theories to which they subscribe. Other data come from patients' recollections of the distant past (especially those from early childhood) and are of dubious accuracy. Also, critics believe that psychoanalytic theories place too much weight on the ability of these early experiences within the family to shape personality, and that we retain the capacity for change and adaptation throughout our lives.

Some psychologists object that Freud overemphasized the role of sexuality in personality and that Freud and Jung placed too much faith in the unconscious mind's ability to control behavior. Others object that the Freudian perspectives provide models of people that are too negative and pessimistic. We are not born into the world with only a bundle of sexual and aggressive instincts. The demands of reality do not always conflict with our biological needs.

Many psychoanalytic theories of personality, especially Freud's, have a male bias. Although Horney's theory helped correct this bias, psychoanalytic theory continues to be revised today.

How effectively can psychoanalytic theory explain Mark Twain's personality? Psychoanalytic theory would focus on many aspects of Twain's behavior. For some examples: It would say that Twain sublimated his aggressive and sexual impulses into creative writing. As with Freud, Twain's constant cigar-puffing might suggest fixation at the oral stage of development; Twain's sarcasm is further "evidence" for this fixation. A psychoanalytic theorist might suspect problematic weaning in Twain's early childhood.

At this point, you should have a sense of what personality is and a basic understanding of the themes of psychoanalytic theories. Next, we will explore three views of personality that are very different from the psychoanalytic theories.

 *R*eview

Psychoanalytic Theories

Freud was one of the most influential thinkers in the twentieth century. He was a medical doctor who believed that most of the mind is unconscious. Freud said that personality has three structures: id, ego, and superego. The id is the reservoir of psychic energy that tries to satisfy our basic needs; it is unconscious and operates according to the pleasure principle. The ego tries to provide pleasure by operating within the boundaries of reality. The superego is the moral branch of personality. The conflicting demands of personality structures produce anxiety; defense mechanisms protect the ego and reduce this anxiety. Repression, the most pervasive defense mechanism, pushes unacceptable impulses from the id back into the unconscious mind. Other defense mechanisms include rationalization, displacement, sublimation, projection, reaction formation, and regression. Freud was convinced that problems develop because of childhood experiences. He said we go through five psychosexual stages of development: oral, anal, phallic, latency, and

genital. He believed that if our needs are under- or overgratified at a particular stage, we can become fixated at that stage. During the phallic stage, the Oedipus complex is a major source of conflict.

The psychoanalytic dissenters and revisionists have argued that Freud placed too much emphasis on sexuality and the first 5 years of life and too little emphasis on the ego and conscious thought processes, as well as sociocultural factors. Karen Horney rejected the classical psychoanalytic concept that anatomy determines behavior, advocated by Freud, in favor of a sociocultural approach. She especially emphasized that Freud's theory is male biased. Horney said that the need for security, not sex or aggression, is the prime motive in human existence. She also theorized that individuals usually develop one of three strategies to cope with anxiety—moving toward people, moving away from people, or moving against people. Today, through the efforts of such individuals as Nancy Chodorow, the male bias of psychoanalytic theory continues to be rectified. Jung

thought Freud underplayed the role of the unconscious mind. He developed the concept of the collective unconscious, and his theory is often called depth psychology. Alfred Adler's theory is called individual psychology; it stresses every individual's uniqueness. Adler said people are striving toward a positive being and that they create their own goals. Their adaptation is enhanced by developing social interests and reducing feelings of inferiority.

The strengths of the psychoanalytic theories include an emphasis on the past, the developmental course of personality, mental representations of the environment, the concept of the unconscious mind, an emphasis on conflict, and their influence on psychology as a discipline. Their weaknesses include the difficulty in testing the main concepts, a lack of empirical data and an overreliance on reports of the past, too much emphasis on sexuality and the unconscious mind, a negative view of human nature, too much power given to early experience, and a male bias.

Behavioral Theories

Tom is engaged to marry Ann. Both have extraverted personalities and enjoy being with each other. Psychoanalytic theorists would say that their personalities are derived from long-standing relationships with their parents, especially in their early childhood experiences. They also would argue that the reason for their mutual attraction is unconscious; they are unaware of how their biological heritage and early life experiences have been carried forward to influence their adult functioning.

Behaviorists would observe Tom and Ann and see something quite different. They would focus on Tom and Ann's experiences, especially their most recent ones, to understand the reason for their attraction. Tom rewards Ann's social and attentive behavior, and vice versa. Behaviorists would make no reference to the unconscious mind, Oedipal stirrings, or defense mechanisms.

Behaviorists believe psychology should examine only what can be directly observed and measured. At approximately the same time Freud was interpreting his patients' unconscious minds through their recollections of early childhood experiences, behaviorists such as John B. Watson were conducting detailed observations of behavior under controlled laboratory conditions. Out of the behavioral tradition grew the belief that personality is observable behavior, learned through experiences with the environment. The two versions of the behavioral approach today are the behavioral view of B. F. Skinner and social learning theories.

Skinner's Behaviorism.   B. F. Skinner concluded that personality is the individual's *behavior,* which is determined by the *external environment.* Skinner believed we do not have to resort to biological or cognitive processes to explain personality (behavior). Some psychologists say that including Skinner among personality theorists is like inviting a wolf to a party of lambs because he took the "person" out of personality (Phares, 1984).

Behaviorists counter that you cannot pinpoint where personality is or how it is determined. In Skinner's view, personality simply consists of the collection of the person's observed, overt behaviors; it does not include internal traits or thoughts. For example, observations of Sam reveal that his behavior is shy, achievement-oriented, and caring. In short, these behaviors *are* his personality. According to Skinner, Sam is this way because the rewards and punishments in Sam's environment have shaped him into a shy, achievement-oriented, and caring person. Because of interactions with family members, friends, teachers, and others, Sam has *learned* to behave in this fashion.

Behaviorists who support Skinner's view believe that consistency in behavior comes from consistency in environmental experiences. If Sam's shy, achievement-oriented, and caring behavior is consistently rewarded, his pattern of behavior likely will be consistent. However, Skinner stressed that our behavior always has the capacity for change if new learning experiences are encountered. For example, Sam's caring behavior might go unnoticed or unrewarded. If so, over time he might become rewarded more for selfish behavior. The issue of consistency in personality is an important one. We will return to it on several occasions later in the chapter.

Because behaviorists believe that personality is learned and often changes according to environmental experiences and situations, it follows that by rearranging experiences and situations the individual's personality can be changed. For the behaviorist, shy behavior can be changed into outgoing behavior; aggressive behavior can be turned into passive behavior; and lethargic, boring behavior can be shaped into enthusiastic, interesting behavior if the right contingencies are in place.

Evaluating the Behavioral Theories.   Skinner would be among the sharpest critics of using behaviorism to explore personality. He regarded the environment as the critical factor in understanding behavior and saw no need to invoke the contents of the "black box" of the human mind to explain or predict patterns of behavior. In Skinner's world, shifts in rewards and punishments modify behavior without relying on internal personality characteristics. One of the strengths of behaviorism is that it fosters an awareness of the importance of careful observation.

reductionistic

Explaining behavior too simply, in terms of only one or two factors; a criticism of behaviorism.

Critics of behaviorism suggest that behaviorism is too **reductionistic,** *explaining behavior too simply in terms of only one or two factors.* This mechanical approach to human behavior omits human qualities that can't be explained by reinforcement contingencies. Critics question whether it is possible to account for all behaviors in terms of rewards and punishments.

Why did Mark Twain write? According to behaviorists, he wrote because he received monetary rewards and abundant social attention when his work was published. Why did he leave his early career of riverboat navigation? Because the opportunities for rewards were insufficient. Why did he smoke cigars? Because of the powerful pleasure smoking provided. Why did he adopt a teasing approach with strangers? Because he found it fun to have the upper hand with people he didn't know well. Only by observing his behavior and conducting a careful analysis of the contingencies that produce increases or decreases in behavior would behaviorists feel satisfied with an explanation.

Cognitive Social Learning Theories

Some psychologists believe that behaviorists basically are right when they say that personality is learned and influenced strongly by environmental experiences. But they think Skinner went too far by ruling our cognition in understanding personality. We are not mindless robots, responding mechanically to events in the environment. Rather, we think, reason, imagine, plan, expect, interpret, believe, value, and compare. We even have the ability to control our own environments. **Cognitive social learning theory** *stresses the importance of cognition, behavior, and environment in determining personality.*

Ironically, it was disagreement with the trait and psychoanalytic approaches that launched the cognitive movement in personality theory. In his landmark book *Personality and Assessment,* Walter Mischel (1968) challenged both trait and psychoanalytic theories on their shared position that broad personality traits are consistent across situations and over time. Mischel believed that personality often changes according to a given situation. Mischel's view was called **situationism,** *which means that personality often varies considerably from one context to another.*

Suppose you want to assess the happiness of Amy, an introvert, and Jahmal, an extrovert. Trait theory leads you to expect that Jahmal will be happy and outgoing all the time; however, his ability to be quiet and reserved when he is studying in the library points to his capacity to evaluate and adapt to a situation that calls for a more subdued approach. On the other hand, timid Amy might become the life of the party when she is watching her favorite football team conquer its opponent during a Superbowl party with her friends. Considering both individual traits and influences in different settings improves our ability to predict others' behavior.

One outcome of the trait/situation controversy is that the link between traits and situations has been more precisely specified. For example, researchers have found that (1) the narrower and more limited a trait is, the more likely it is that the trait will predict behavior; (2) some people consistently demonstrate some traits and other people consistently demonstrate others; (3) personality traits exert a stronger influence on individual behavior when situational influences are less powerful; and (4) people choose some situations and avoid others—these choices are influenced by the degree to which the situation fits their personality traits (Ickes, Snyder, & Garcia, 1997). For example, if you are an "aggressive" person, you are more likely than a "passive" person to choose to go see a bullfight.

A second outcome of situationism was that learning theory had to adopt a more cognitive point of view to explain why individuals are capable of adapting to different contexts or sometimes behave differently in the same contexts. Mischel (1973) coined the term *cognitive social learning theory* to capture the distinctive quality of this new direction in personality research.

Mischel's main research area is **delay of gratification,** *the ability to defer immediate satisfaction for a more desirable future outcome.* One way we might learn to delay gratification is to represent goal objects in different ways. In one study, when young children mentally represented rewards in consummatory ways, such as focusing on dimensions of their taste (thinking how yummy, crunchy, and tasty pretzels are), they delayed gratification much less than young children who mentally represented the rewards in nonconsummatory ways (thinking about pretzels as sticks or tiny logs) (Mischel & Baker, 1975). This type of experiment illustrated that the way in which we mentally represent the outcomes of a situation influences our ability to delay gratification.

Delay of gratification is an important aspect of being productive and competent. Consider the following choices between getting satisfaction now or delaying gratification:

Albert Bandura *(top)* and Walter Mischel *(bottom)* crafted the contemporary version of social learning theory, which Mischel labeled "cognitive social learning theory." Bandura's research has focused on observational learning, Mischel's on how we delay gratification.

- Party and binge drink now (immediate gratification) or study hard to get good grades at the end of the term (delayed gratification)
- Cut classes to sleep, play, or pursue personal pleasures (immediate gratification) or go to class regularly to get a college degree (delayed gratification)
- Spend money now on trinkets (immediate gratification) or save money to take a vacation or buy a car later (delayed gratification)

In addition to Walter Mischel, Albert Bandura has been a powerful figure in crafting cognitive social learning theory. Bandura (1977, 1986) believes that we acquire an extensive amount of behavior through imitation. However, for imitation to take place, Bandura says, the cognitive processes of attention and memory must be in operation. Think about the last time you tried to learn a skill by observing a model. You had to attend to the skill, memorize it, model it, and then practice it to build it into your own repertoire. More recently, Bandura (1994, 1997, 1998) has explored the cognitive concept of **self-efficacy,** *the belief that one can master a situation and produce positive outcomes.* You will read more about cognitive-behavioral approaches to personality change in chapter 12.

Evaluating Cognitive Social Learning Theories. As was true for its predecessor, behavioral theory, cognitive social learning theory emphasizes environmental influences in the development of personality. However, cognitive social learning theory has overcome many of the criticisms that formerly plagued behaviorism. Cognitive social learning theory promotes a much richer understanding of behavior by incorporating cognition's influence on behavior, which explains its growing popularity. Cognitive approaches explain why one individual can show such different behaviors in different circumstances. They also provide effective ways to understand why behavior can be inconsistent over time.

Although it is less reductionistic, cognitive social learning theory is fragmented—it does not present one grand theory to account for personality. Instead, cognitive researchers tend to focus on explaining narrower ranges of behavior. They have been criticized for paying attention to change and perhaps missing the substantial contributions of enduring personality qualities. Some critics say that cognitive social learning theory still retains a mechanical quality that does not do justice to the rich dimensions of personality.

How would cognitive social learning theorists explain Mark Twain's personality? They would examine his wry sense of humor—particularly whether certain situations, such as an unresponsive lecture audience or a prickly book clerk's attitude, might more readily induce his playful sarcasm. They also would explore how Twain's role models influenced his overall development. They would speculate that he was able to postpone temptations effectively because his writing was so prolific. However, it is unlikely that they could come up with a unified cognitive explanation of Twain's unique personality.

Some psychologists, especially humanists, say that the creative, spontaneous, and human dimension of personality is still missing from the cognitive social learning theory. Next we turn our attention to the humanistic theories.

Humanistic Theories

Remember our example of the engaged couple, Tom and Ann, who were described as having warm, friendly personalities. Phenomenological and humanistic psychologists would say that Tom and Ann's warm, friendly personalities are a reflection of their inner selves; these psychologists would emphasize that a key to understanding their mutual attraction is their positive perceptions of each other. Tom and Ann are not viewed as controlling each other or each other's behavior; rather, each has determined a course of action and has freely chosen to marry. No recourse to biological instincts or unconscious thoughts as reasons for their attraction is necessary in the phenomenological and humanistic perspectives. This explanation represents a **phenomenological worldview,** *which stresses the importance of our perceptions of ourselves and of our world in understanding personality; this worldview emphasizes that, for each individual, reality is what that individual perceives.*

self-efficacy

The belief that one can master a situation and produce positive outcomes.

phenomenological worldview

A worldview that stresses the importance of our perceptions of ourselves and of our world in understanding personality.

Carl Rogers was a pioneer in the development of the humanistic perspective.

humanistic theory

The most widely adopted phenomenological approach to personality. It stresses a person's capacity for personal growth, freedom to choose one's own destiny, and positive qualities.

conditional positive regard

Rogers' term for making the bestowal of love or praise conditional on the individual's conforming to parental or social standards.

self-concept

An individual's overall perceptions of her or his abilities, behavior, and personality; a central theme for Rogers and other humanists.

unconditional positive regard

Rogers's term for accepting, valuing, and being positive toward another person regardless of the person's behavior.

Humanistic theory *is the most widely adopted phenomenological approach to personality. The humanistic perspective stresses a person's capacity for personal growth, freedom to choose one's own destiny, and positive qualities.* Humanistic psychologists believe that each of us has the ability to cope with stress, to control our lives, and to achieve what we desire. Each of us has the ability to break through and understand ourselves and our world.

You probably sense that the humanistic theories provide stark contrasts to the psychoanalytic theories, which are based on conflict, destructive drives, and little faith in human nature, and to the behavioral perspective, which, at worst, seems to reduce human beings to mere puppets on the strings of rewards and punishments. Carl Rogers and Abraham Maslow were two of the leading architects of the humanistic approach to personality.

Carl Rogers' Approach. Like Freud, Carl Rogers (1902–1987) began his inquiry into human nature with people who were troubled. In the knotted, anxious, and defensive verbal stream of his clients, Rogers (1961) examined the nature of their world that kept them from having positive self-concepts and reaching their full potential as human beings. He proposed several concepts to explain the humanistic point of view.

Our Conditioned, Controlling World. Rogers believed that most people have considerable difficulty accepting their own feeling, which are innately positive. As we grow up, people who are central to our lives condition us to move away from these positive feelings. Our parents, siblings, teachers, and peers place constraints and contingencies on our behavior; too often we hear such phrases as "Don't do that," "You didn't do that right," and "How can you be so stupid?" When we don't do something right, we often get punished; parents may even threaten to take away their love. **Conditional positive regard** *is Rogers' term for making the bestowal of love or praise conditional on the individual's conforming to parental or social standards.* The result is low self-esteem.

These constraints and negative feedback continue during our adult lives. The result tends to be that our relationships either carry the dark cloud of conflict or we conform to what others want. As we struggle to live up to society's standards, we distort and disvalue our true selves. By constantly acting according to other people's standards, we might even completely lose our sense of our self.

The Self. Through an individual's experiences with the world, a self emerges—the "I" or "me" of our existence. Rogers did not believe that all aspects of the self are conscious, but he did believe they are all accessible to consciousness. The self is a whole, consisting of one's self-perceptions (how attractive I am, how well I get along with others, how good an athlete I am) and the values we attach to these perceptions (good-bad, worthy-unworthy, for example). **Self-concept,** *a central theme for humanists, refers to individuals' overall perceptions of their abilities, behavior, and personality.* According to Rogers, a person who has a poor self-concept is likely to think, feel, and act negatively.

In discussing self-concept, Rogers distinguished between the *real* self—that is, the self as it really is as a result of our experiences—and the *ideal* self, which is the self we would like to be. The greater the discrepancy between the real self and the ideal self, said Rogers, the more maladjusted we will be. To improve our adjustment, we can develop more positive perceptions of our real self, not worry so much about what others want, and increase our positive experiences in the world. To evaluate whether you have positive or negative perceptions of yourself, complete the Self-Assessment. And for some strategies to elevate your self-esteem, see Improving Personal and Cognitive Skills.

Unconditional Positive Regard, Empathy, and Genuineness. Rogers stressed that we can help a person develop a more positive self-concept through unconditional positive regard, empathy, and genuineness. Rogers said that we need to be accepted by others, regardless of what we do. **Unconditional positive regard** *is Rogers' term for accepting, valuing, and being positive toward another person regardless of the person's behavior.* Rogers recognized that when a person's behavior is below acceptable standards, inappropriate, or even obnoxious, the person still needs the respect, comfort, and love of others. Rogers strongly believed that unconditional positive regard elevates a person's self-worth.

Self-Assessment

Self-Esteem

Instructions

The statements below have been used by people to describe themselves. Please read each one carefully, and circle the number that best describes how much of a problem each has been for you in the past month, including today. Use the following scale for your answers:

a = Strongly agree
b = Agree
c = Disagree
d = Strongly disagree

1. I feel that I'm a person of worth, at least on an equal basis with others.   a b c d
2. I feel that I have a number of good qualities.   a b c d
3. All in all, I am inclined to feel that I am a failure.   a b c d
4. I am able to do things as well as most people.   a b c d
5. I feel I do not have much to be proud of.   a b c d
6. I take a positive attitude toward myself.   a b c d
7. On the whole, I am satisfied with myself.   a b c d
8. I wish I could have more respect for myself.   a b c d
9. I certainly feel useless at times.   a b c d
10. At times I think I am no good at all.   a b c d

Scoring

For questions 1, 2, 4, 6, and 7, give yourself two points for a, one point for b, minus one point for c, and minus two points for d. For questions 3, 5, 8, 9, and 10, give yourself two points for d, one point for c, minus one point for b, and minus two points for a.

Interpretation

If you scored 16 to 20, you are fortunate. Your self-esteem is very high and you are likely to be able to bounce back readily from negative experiences. If you scored 11 to 15, your self-esteem is still fairly high, but there are probably some minor things you could do to enhance your self-esteem. A score from 6 to 10 suggests that there are some steps you could take to develop stronger self-esteem. If you scored 5 or less, you are really struggling to come to term with your own value. You might want to reexamine the statements you checked that earned minus two points and think through some activities that could help you rate yourself more positively.

The living self has one purpose only: to come into its own fullness of being, as a tree comes into full blossom, or a bird into spring beauty, or a tiger into lustre.
—D. H. LAWRENCE, *American Author, 20th Century*

The Fully Functioning Person. Rogers (1980) stressed the importance of becoming a fully functioning person—someone who is open to experience, is not very defensive, is aware of and sensitive to the self and the external world, and for the most part has a harmonious relationship with others. A discrepancy between the real self and the ideal self may occur, others may try to control us, and our world may have too little unconditional positive regard. However, Rogers believed that human beings are highly resilient and capable of becoming fully functioning.

Our self-actualizing tendency is reflected in Rogers' comparison of persons with a plant he once observed on the coastline of northern California. As Rogers looked out at the waves beating furiously against the jagged rocks and shooting mountains of spray into the air, he noticed the breakers pounding a sea palm (a kind of seaweed that looks like a 2- to 3-foot-high palm tree). The plant seemed fragile and top-heavy. The waves crashed against the plant, bending its slender trunk almost flat and whipping its leaves in a torrent of spray, yet the moment the wave passed the plant was erect, tough, and resilient again. It was incredible that the plant could take this incessant pounding hour after hour,

$\mathcal{I}$mproving Personal and Cognitive Skills

Raising Your Self-Esteem

The concept of self-esteem is important to the humanistic perspective. Following are some helpful strategies for increasing self-esteem (Bednar & Peterson, 1995):

- *Identify the causes of your low self-esteem.*
  This is critical to increasing self-esteem. Is your low self-esteem the result of low grades? the consequence of living with people who constantly criticize you? due to poor social relationships? Look at the different domains of your life and determine which areas are bringing your overall self-esteem down. These are the areas to work on.
- *Get emotional support and social approval.*
  Emotional support and social approval will increase your self-esteem. Sources of emotional support and social

approval include friends, family, classmates, a counselor, a mentor, or other people we come in contact with on a regular basis in our lives. When people are warm and friendly to us, are sensitive to our needs, and give us approval, our self-esteem benefits.
- *Set achievable goals.*
  Achievement increases self-esteem. Doing well in the areas of your life that are important to you will raise your self-esteem.
- *Learn to cope with life's challenges.*
  Self-esteem increases when people face their problems and devise coping strategies to tackle the difficulties. Coping effectively makes us feel good about ourselves. When we avoid coping with problems they can mount up and lower our self-esteem further.

week after week, possibly even year after year, all the time nourishing itself, maintaining its position, and growing. In this palmlike seaweed, Rogers saw the tenacity and forward thrust of life and the ability of a living thing to push into a hostile environment and not only hold its own but adapt, develop, and become itself. So is the potential with each of us, according to Rogers (1963).

Abraham Maslow's Approach. Another theorist who made self-actualization the centerpiece of his humanistic philosophy was Abraham Maslow (1908–1970). Maslow was one of the most powerful forces behind the humanistic movement in psychology. He called the humanistic approach the "third force" in psychology—that is, an important alternative to the psychoanalytic and behavioral forces. Maslow pointed out that psychoanalytic theories place too much emphasis on disordered individuals and their conflicts. Behaviorists ignore the person all together, he said.

Remember from chapter 9 that Maslow (1954) said we have a hierarchy of needs in which certain basic needs (physiological needs, and needs for safety, love and

A generation of ethnic awareness and pride appears to have advanced the self-esteem of members of ethnic minority groups.

belongingness, and self-esteem) have to be satisfied before we can satisfy the highest need, the need for self-actualization. Remember also that Maslow described *self-actualization* as a motivation to develop one's full potential as a human being. Maslow (1971) charted the human potential of creative, talented, and healthy people. Table 10.2 lists the characteristics Maslow found in self-actualized people.

$\mathcal{T}$ A B L E   1 0 . 2

Maslow's Characteristics of Self-Actualized Individuals

Realistic orientation

Self-acceptance and acceptance of others and the natural world as they are

Spontaneity

Problem-centered rather than self-centered

Air of detachment and need for privacy

Autonomous and independent

Fresh rather than stereotyped appreciation of people and things

Generally have had profound mystical or spiritual, through not necessarily religious, experiences

Identification with humankind and a strong social interest

Tendency to have strong intimate relationships with a few special, loved people rather than superficial relationships with many people

Democratic values and attitudes

No confusion of means with ends

Philosophical rather than hostile sense of humor

High degree of creativity

Resistance to cultural conformity

Transcendence of environment rather than always coping with it

SOURCE: A. H. Maslow, *The Farthest Reaches of Human Nature*, pp. 153–174. Copyright © 1971 Viking Press, NY.

Evaluating Humanistic Theories.   Humanistic theories have made psychologists aware that the way we perceive ourselves and the world around us is a key element of personality. Humanistic psychologists also have reminded us that we need to consider the whole person and the positive bent of human nature. Their emphasis on conscious experience has given us the view that personality contains untapped potential that can be developed to its fullest.

A weakness of humanistic theories is that its key concepts are difficult to test. Self-actualization, for example, is not easy to observe or measure, so psychologists are not certain how to study this concept empirically. Some humanists even scorn the experimental approach, preferring clinical interpretation as a data base. Verification of humanistic concepts has come mainly from clinical experiences rather than controlled, experimental studies. Some critics also believe that humanistic psychologists are too optimistic about human nature, overestimating the freedom and rationality of humans. Harsher critics say the humanists encourage self-love and narcissism.

What would humanists have to say about Mark Twain's personality? They might point to him as a model of someone who has maximized his potential. His astounding literary creations, which are still read and still generate controversy, are evidence of Twain's self-actualized behavior. Humanistic theorists might speculate that there would be little discrepancy between Twain's ideal self and his real self. Although Twain hardly was a model for expressing unconditional positive regard, he did exemplify a kind of optimism about the positive aspects of human nature through the innocence he expressed in some of his fictional characters. Humanists would also recognize his finely tuned sense of humor as an important way in which Twain exerted control over his environment.

But Twain's resilience diminished in the last decade of his life, as age and personal losses took their toll. The deaths of his wife and two of his daughters, alienation from a third daughter, and declining health led Twain to become withdrawn and depressed. He grumbled, when he moved to his last residence, "The country home I need is a cemetery" (Kaplan, 1965, p. 385). Humanistic approaches have some difficulty explaining dramatic negative changes in personality, such as Twain's changes from pranksterism to depression.

Comparing Personality Theories

The diversity of theories makes understanding personality a challenge. Just when you think one theory has the correct explanation of personality, another theory will make you rethink your earlier conclusion. To keep from getting frustrated, remember that personality is a complex, multifaceted topic and no single theory has been able to account for all its aspects; each theory has contributed an important piece to the personality puzzle. In fact, many pieces of information in different personality theories are *complementary* rather than contradictory. Together they let us see the total landscape of personality in all its richness.

We will compare several of the most important dimensions to help you review the theories presented in this chapter. We present a summary of these dimensions in table 10.3. The discrete presentation of the perspectives in the table might seem cryptic, so you may want to reread the explanations of each approach earlier in the chapter where you are

*T*ABLE 10.3
Comparing Personality Theories

Personality Dimensions	Trait Theories	Psychoanalytic Theories	Behavioral Theories	Cognitive Social Learning Theories	Humanistic Theories
Which contributes more, biological factors or experience?	Biology and experience	Biology followed by experience	Experience	Experience	Mainly experience
What drives personality?	Not relevant	Instincts; needs	Environmental factors	Environmental factors and cognitions	Self-actualization; needs
Is personality consistent or variable across situations?	Consistent	Consistent	Variable	Variable	Variable
How important is the unconscious mind in shaping behavior?	Not important	Very important	Not important	Not important	Not important
Are the theories pessimistic or optimistic about human nature?	Neutral	Pessimistic	Neutral	Optimistic	Optimistic

| Gordon Allport | Sigmund Freud | B. F. Skinner | Walter Mischel | Carl Rogers |

unclear. The table also helps to overcome the illusion that there is little overlap in the theories. A careful reading demonstrates both similarities and differences among the theories.

What Is the Relative Importance of Biological Factors Versus Experience?   Trait explanations originally were based on the idea that traits are biologically derived; however, later trait approaches acknowledge the power of experience and cultural influences in behavior. Freud's theory has a strong biogenetic foundation, although many psychoanalytic revisionists argue that he vastly underestimated the influence of experience and culture on behavior. Behavioral and cognitive social learning theories both see experience as a powerful influence on personality, Skinner being the strongest advocate. Like behaviorists, cognitive social learning theorists pay little attention to biological factors. Humanists are more inclined to stress environmental over biological variables, but they acknowledge that fulfilling basic physical needs is an essential aspect of a fulfilling life.

What Forces Drive Personality?   Trait psychologists generally do not explore motivating forces of personality; they explore and measure overt behaviors and traits. Instincts and needs drive personality, according to psychoanalytic theorists. Both behavioral and cognitive social learning theorists cite environmental factors as the driving force of personality patterns; however, the latter group also takes cognitive factors to be important. Humanists describe the desire to be self-actualizing or to fulfill human potential as the driving force.

How Consistent or Variable Is Personality Across Situations?   Both trait and psychoanalytic approaches tend to stress the uniformity of behaviors across situations. Behavioral and cognitive social learning theorists endorse the idea that personality can change when factors in the environment change. Cognitive social learning theorists, in particular, stress that individuals are sensitive to changing contexts. Personality traits can interact with situations to produce behavior. Humanists also suggest that humans have substantial power to choose their behavior, which allows for a greater variety of behavioral options.

How Important Is Unconscious Mind in Influencing Personality?   The unconscious mind is a major force, according to psychoanalytic theories. Humanists focus on conscious, purposeful behavior rather than the mysteries of the unconscious mind. Trait, behavioral, and cognitive social learning theories do not include the unconscious mind.

Is the Personality Theory Optimistic or Pessimistic About Human Nature?   Trait and behavioral approaches are neutral about the quality of human nature. Freud and some of his followers were decidedly pessimistic, although some neo-Freudians adopted a more positive stance in their later writings. Cognitive social learning theory and humanistic theory support a more optimistic view of humankind. Both stress the potential for positive contributions.

By now you should have a better understanding of personality, perhaps even *your* personality. But personality theory represents a scientific attempt to explain personality—so how do we go about observing and measuring personality?

eview

Behavioral, Social Learning, and Humanistic Theories, and Theory Comparisons

In Skinner's behaviorism, cognition is unimportant in understanding personality. Rather, personality is observed behavior, which is influenced by the rewards and punishments in the environment. Personality varies according to the situation, in the behavioral view.

In the 1970s, Mischel and Bandura crafted social learning theory's contemporary version, cognitive social learning theory, which stresses the importance of cognition, behavior, and environment in understanding personality.

Strengths of both behavioral and social learning theories include emphases on environmental determinants of behavior and a scientific climate for investigating personality, as well as the focus on cognitive processes and self-control in the social learning approach. The behavioral view has been criticized for taking the person out of personality and for ignoring cognition. These approaches have not given adequate attention to enduring individual differences and to personality as a whole.

The phenomenological worldview emphasizes our perceptions of ourselves and our world and centers on the belief that reality is what is perceived. Humanistic theory is the most widely known phenomenological approach. In Carl Rogers' approach, each of us is a victim of conditional positive regard. The result is that our real self is not valued. The self is the core of personality; it includes both the real and the ideal self. Rogers said we can help others develop a more positive self-concept in three ways: unconditional positive regard, empathy, and genuineness. Rogers also stressed that each of us has the innate, inner capacity to become a fully functioning person. Maslow called the humanistic movement the "third force" in psychology. Each of us has a self-actualizing tendency, according to Maslow. He distinguishes between deficiency needs and self-actualization needs, or metaneeds. The phenomenological and humanistic approaches sensitized psychologists to the importance of subjective experience, consciousness, self-concept, the whole person, and our innate, positive nature. Their weaknesses are the absence of an empirical orientation, a tendency to be too optimistic, and an inclination to encourage self-love.

Personality theories should be regarded as complementary rather than contradictory. However, all theories can be distinguished along several dimensions, including their views on the role of biological factors, the motivating forces of personality, the flexibility and consistency of personality patterns, the unconscious mind, and human nature.

PERSONALITY ASSESSMENT

"The line running this way indicates that you are a gregarious person, someone who really enjoys being around people. This division over here suggests that you are a risk taker; I bet you like to do things that are adventurous sometimes." These are the words you might hear from a palmist. Palmistry purports to "read" an individual's personality by interpreting precisely the irregularities and folds in the skin of the hand. For example, a large mound of Saturn, the portion of the palm directly below the third joint of the middle finger, ostensibly relates to wisdom, good fortune, and prudence.

Although palmists claim to provide a complete assessment of personality through reading lines in the hand, researchers debunk palmistry as quackery (Lanyon & Goodstein, 1987). Researchers argue that palmists give no reasonable explanation for their inferences about personality and point out that the hand's characteristics can change through age and even through exercise.

Even so, palmists manage to stay in business. They do so, in part, because they are keen observers—they respond to such cues as voice, general demeanor, and dress, which are more relevant signs of personality than the lines and folds on a person's palm. Palmists also are experts at offering general, trivial statements, such as "Although you usually are affectionate with others, sometimes you don't get along with people." This statement falls into the category of the **Barnum effect:** *if you make your descriptions broad enough, any person can fit them.* The effect was named after the famous showman P. T. Barnum, whose name still helps advertise the world's largest circus. Barnum used to lure gullible people with "Come one, come all—come and see a horse's tail where the head should be!" He would then show them a horse turned around in its stall.

In contrast, many psychologists use a number of scientifically developed tests and methods to evaluate personality, each assessing personality for different reasons (Butcher, 1995; Shrout & Fiske, 1995). Clinical and school psychologists assess personality to better understand an individual's psychological problems; they hope the assessment will improve their diagnosis and treatment of the individual. Industrial psychologists and

Barnum effect

If you make your descriptions broad enough, any person can fit them.

vocational counselors assess personality to aid the individual's selection of a career. Research psychologists assess personality to investigate the theories and dimensions of personality discussed so far in this chapter. For example, if a psychologist wants to investigate self-concept, a measure of self-concept is needed. Some psychologists do not use formal assessment techniques. They prefer to rely on clinical observation and their years of expertise in interpreting clinical behavior.

Before we explore some specific personality tests, two more important points need to be made about the nature of personality assessment. First, the kinds of tests chosen by psychologists frequently depend on the psychologist's theoretical bent. Second, most personality tests are designed to assess stable, enduring characteristics, free of situational influence.

> But the main thing is, does it hold good measure?
> —Robert Browning, *English Poet, 19th century*

Self-Report Tests

self-report tests

Tests that assess personality traits by asking individuals what their traits are; not designed to reveal unconscious personality characteristics.

Self-report tests *assess personality traits by asking what they are; these tests are not designed to reveal unconscious personality characteristics.* For example, self-report tests of personality include such items as the following:

I am easily embarrassed.

I love to go to parties.

I like to watch cartoons on TV.

Self-report tests are questionnaires that include a large number of such statements or questions. You respond with a limited number of choices (yes or no, true or false, agree or disagree, on a scale of 1 to 5, and so on). How do psychologists construct self-report tests of personality?

face validity

An assumption that the content of test items is a good indicator of what an individual's personality is like.

Constructing Self-Report Tests. Many of the early personality tests were based on **face validity,** *which is an assumption that the content of the test items is a good indicator of what an individual's personality is like.* For example, if I developed a test item that asks you to respond whether or not you are introverted and you answer, "I enjoy being with people," I accept your response as a straightforward indication that you are not introverted. Tests based on face validity assume that you are responding honestly and nondefensively, giving the examiner an accurate portrayal of your personality.

social desirability

A factor that can lead individuals to give answers that they believe are socially desirable, rather than what they really think or feel, in order to make themselves look better.

Not everyone responds honestly, however, especially when questions concern their own personality. Even if the individual is basically honest, she or he might be giving socially desirable answers. **Social desirability** *is a factor that can lead individuals to give answers that they believe are socially desirable, rather than what they really think or feel, in order to make themselves look better.* For example, if someone is basically a lazy person, she may not want you to know this and she may try to present herself in a more positive way; therefore, she would respond negatively to the following item: "I fritter away time too much." Because of such responses, psychologists realized they needed to go beyond face validity in constructing personality tests; they accomplished this by developing empirically keyed tests

empirically keyed tests

Tests that rely on the test items to predict a particular criterion. Unlike tests based on face validity, in which the content of the test items is supposed to be a good indicator of what a tested individual's personality is like, empirically keyed tests make no assumptions about the nature of the items.

Empirically keyed tests *rely on the test items to predict a particular criterion. Unlike tests based on face validity, in which the content of the items is supposed to be a good indicator of what a tested individual's personality is like, empirically keyed tests make no assumptions about the nature of the items.* Imagine we want to develop a test that will determine whether or not applicants for the position of police officer are likely to be competent at the job. We might ask a large number of questions of police officers, some of whom have excellent job records, others who have not performed as well. We would then use the questions that differentiate competent and incompetent police officers on our test to screen job applicants. If the item "I enjoy reading poetry" predicts success as a police officer, then we should include it on the test, even though it seems unrelated to police work. Next we will examine the most widely used empirically keyed personality test.

**Minnesota Multiphasic
Personality Inventory (MMPI)**
The self-report personality test
most widely used in clinical and
research settings.

The Minnesota Multiphasic Personality Inventory.   The **Minnesota Multiphasic Personality Inventory (MMPI)** *is the self-report personality test that is most widely used in clinical and research settings.* Psychologists originally developed the MMPI to improve the process of diagnosing individuals with mental disorders. A thousand statements were given to both people with mental disorders and apparently normal people. How often individuals agreed with each item was calculated; only the items that clearly differentiated the individuals with mental disorders from the normal individuals were retained. For example, a statement might be included on the depression scale of the MMPI if people diagnosed with a depressive disorder agreed with the statement significantly more than did normal individuals. This criterion keying allows us to include a statement with little face value, such as "I sometimes tease animals," on the depression scale, or any other scale, of the MMPI.

The MMPI eventually was streamlined to 566 items, including some repeated items, each of which can be answered *True, False,* or *Cannot say.* The items vary widely in content and include statements like the following:

I like to read magazines.

I never have trouble falling asleep.

People are out to get me.

A person's answers are grouped according to ten clinical categories, or scales, that measure such problems as depression, psychopathic deviation, schizophrenia, and social introversion.

The MMPI includes four validity scales in addition to the ten clinical scales. The validity scales were designed to indicate whether an individual is dishonest, careless, defensive, or evasive when answering the test items. For example, if an individual responds "False" to a number of items, such as "I get angry sometimes," it would be interpreted that she is trying to make herself look better than she really is. The rationale for the lie scale is that each of us gets angry at least some of the time, so the individual who responds "False" to many such items is faking her responses.

For the first time in its approximately 40-year history, the MMPI was revised in 1989. The revision added new content scales and deleted some statements, including all items pertaining to religion and most of the questions about sexual practices. The revised MMPI-2 has 567 items. Its basic clinical scales have not changed; however, content scales that relate to the broader professional interests of some clinicians and employers were added. In addition, cross-cultural research influenced the restructuring of the MMPI-2. The content scales focus on substance abuse, eating disorders, Type A behavior, repression, anger, cynicism, low self-esteem, family problems, and inability to function in a job.

Thousands of research studies and many books have documented the ability of the MMPI to improve the accuracy of diagnosis of mentally disturbed individuals. The MMPI has been used in more than 50 countries; more than 125 translations of the test are available.

However, cross-cultural psychologists don't automatically applaud the translation and use of the MMPI in other cultures. Mere translations without the development of norms specific to the culture might not produce a valid interpretation of personality. Cross-cultural psychologist Walter Lonner (1990) points out that the MMPI was developed by American psychologists and follows a Western view of mental health. Because it was standardized on a group of people in Minnesota, he recommends considerable caution when using the MMPI, as well as other personality tests, on people from other cultures.

The MMPI also contains some outdated stereotypes regarding gender. For example, if a woman responds on the MMPI that she likes hunting and fishing, she might be labeled abnormally masculine simply because more men report enjoying hunting and fishing.

Although the MMPI is used to assess normal functioning, critics suggest that this practice might not be appropriate or ethical. They believe that the MMPI is now being misused in business and education to predict which individual will make the best job candidate or which career an individual should pursue. Also, persons who are inadequately trained in psychological testing and diagnosis sometimes both give and interpret the MMPI, despite the fact that this is a clear violation of the code of ethics of the American Psychological Association. In these cases the MMPI is often used for purposes other than those for which it was originally designed.

The Five-Factor Personality Instruments.   The popularity of the five-factor model has encouraged the development and use of self-report strategies to define personality factors. The NEO Personality Inventory (Costa & McRae, 1985) and the NEO-PI-Revised (Costa, McRae, & Dye, 1991) assess the degree of neuroticism, extraversion, agreeableness, conscientiousness, and openness using self-report statements that call for agreement or disagreement. For example, the statement "I never seem to be able to get organized" contributes to the scoring of conscientiousness. The self-report inventories are increasingly being used in research and mental health settings.

Evaluating Self-Report Tests.   Adherents of the trait approach have strong faith in the utility of self-report tests. They point out that self-report tests have produced an improved understanding of the nature of personality traits than can be derived from, for example, projective tests. However, some critics (especially psychoanalysts) believe that self-report measures do not get at the core of personality and its unconscious determinants. Other critics (especially behaviorists) believe that self-report tests do not adequately capture the situational variations in personality and the ways in which personality changes as individuals interact with the environment.

Projective Tests

A **projective test** *presents individuals with an ambiguous stimulus and then asks them to describe it or tell a story about it. Projective tests are based on the assumption that the ambiguity of the stimulus allows individuals to project into it their feelings, desires, needs, and attitudes.* The test is especially designed to elicit an individual's unconscious feelings and conflicts, providing an assessment that goes deeper than the surface of personality. Projective tests attempt to get *inside* your mind to discover how you *really* feel and think, going beyond the way you overtly present yourself.

The Rorschach Inkblot Test.   The **Rorschach inkblot test,** *developed in 1921 by Swiss psychiatrist Hermann Rorschach, is the most well-known projective test; it uses individual perception of inkblots to determine personality.* The test consists of ten cards, half in black and white and half in color, which are shown to the individual one at a time (see figure 10.6). The psychologist asks the person to describe what she or he sees in each of the Rorschach inkblots. For example, an individual might say, "That looks like two people fighting." After the individual has responded to all ten inkblots, the examiner presents each of the inkblots again and inquires about the individual's earlier response. For example, the examiner might ask, "*Where* did you see the two people fighting?" and "*What* about the inkblot made the two people look like they were fighting?" Besides

projective tests

Tests that present individuals with an ambiguous stimulus and then ask them to describe it or tell a story about it. Projective tests are based on the assumption that the ambiguity of the stimulus allows individuals to project into it their feelings, desires, needs, and attitudes.

Rorschach inkblot test

The most well-known projective test, developed in 1921 by Swiss psychiatrist Hermann Rorschach, uses individuals' perceptions of inkblots to determine their personality.

*F*IGURE 10.6

Type of Stimulus Used in the Rorschach Inkblot Test

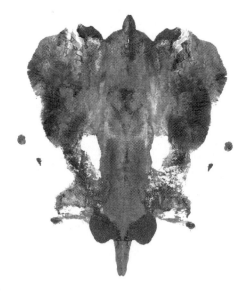

recording the responses, the examiner notes the individual's mannerisms, gestures, and attitudes.

How useful is the Rorschach test in assessing personality? The answer to this question depends on one's perspective. The Rorschach test enjoys widespread use in clinical circles; many clinicians swear by it. A recent survey revealed the Rorschach-based testimony was legally challenged in only 6 of nearly 8,000 court cases (Weiner, Exner, & Sciara, 1996). Many clinicians say that when the clinician is properly trained and the test accurately scored, the Rorschach provides insights about the unconscious mind that no other personality test can (Exner & Wiener, 1995). Clinicians use another practical safeguard in their testing strategies by conducting multiple tests and using the evidence that converges from all the tests as the basis for their conclusions. Thus, Rorschach interpretations are typically supported by other test findings.

However, from a scientific perspective, researchers are skeptical about the Rorschach test (Wood, Nezworski, & Stejskal, 1996). Their disenchantment stems from its failure to meet many criteria for reliability and validity (described in chapter 7). For example, if the Rorschach test were reliable, two different scorers working independently should agree on the personality characteristics of the individual taking the test. If the Rorschach were valid, the individual's personality should predict behavior outside of the testing situation; that is, it should predict whether an individual will attempt suicide, become severely depressed, cope successfully with stress, or get along well with others. Conclusions based on research evidence suggest that Rorschach does not meet the criteria for reliability or validity. Unfortunately, research evidence in support of using the Rorschach test is primarily in the form of unpublished studies. This has led to serious reservations about use of the Rorschach test in diagnosis and clinical practice.

Thematic Apperception Test (TAT)

An ambiguous projective test designed to elicit stories that reveal something about an individual's personality; developed by Henry Murray and Christiana Morgan in the 1930s.

The Thematic Apperception Test (TAT). The **Thematic Apperception Test (TAT),** *which was developed by Henry Murray and Christiana Morgan in the 1930s, is an ambiguous projective test designed to elicit stories that reveal something about an individual's personality.* The TAT consists of a series of pictures, each on an individual card (see figure 10.7). The person administering the TAT asks the subject to tell a story about each of the pictures, including the events leading up to the situation described, the characters' thoughts and feelings, and how the situation turns out. Psychologists assume that the person projects her own

*𝓕*IGURE 10.7

A Picture from the Thematic Apperception Test (TAT)

unconscious feelings and thoughts into the story she tells. In addition to being used as a projective test in clinical practice, the TAT is used in the research of achievement motivation. Several of the TAT cards stimulate the telling of achievement-related stories, which enables the researcher to determine the person's need for achievement (McClelland & others, 1953).

Other Projective Tests. Many other projective tests are used in clinical assessment. One test asks individuals to complete a sentence (for example, "I often feel . . ." "I would like to . . ."); another test asks the individual to draw a person; and another test presents a word, such as *fear* or *happy,* and asks the individual to say the first thing that comes to mind. Like the Rorschach, these projective tests have their detractors and advocates; the detractors often criticize the tests' low reliability and validity, and the advocates describe the tests' ability to reveal the underlying nature of the individual's personality better than more straightforward tests.

Behavioral Assessment

Behavioral assessment attempts to obtain more objective information about an individual's personality by directly observing the individual's behavior. Instead of removing situational influences from personality, as projective tests and self-report measures do, behavioral assessment assumes that personality cannot be evaluated apart from the environment.

Recall from chapter 5 that behavior modification is an attempt to apply learning principles to change maladaptive behavior. Behavioral assessment of personality emerged from this tradition. For example, recall that an observer often will make baseline observations of the frequency of the individual's behaviors. This might be accomplished under controlled laboratory conditions or in natural circumstances. The therapist then modifies one aspect of the environment, such as getting parents and the child's teacher to stop giving the child attention when he or she engages in aggressive behavior. After a specified period of time, the therapist observes the child again to determine if the changes in the environment were effective in reducing the child's maladaptive behavior.

Sometimes, though, direct observations are impractical. What does a psychologist with a behavioral orientation do to assess personality? She might ask individuals to make their own assessments of behavior, encouraging them to be sensitive to the circumstances that produced the behavior and the outcomes or consequences of the behavior.

The influence of social learning theory has increased the use of cognitive assessment in personality evaluation. The strategy is to discover what thoughts underlie behavior; that is, how do individuals think about their problems? What kinds of thoughts precede maladaptive behavior, occur during its manifestation, and follow it? Psychologists assess such cognitive processes as expectations, planning, and memory, possibly through interviews or questionnaires. For example, an interview might include questions that ask of individuals whether they exaggerate their faults and condemn themselves more than the situation warrants. A questionnaire might ask a person what her thoughts are after an upsetting event or assess the way she thinks during tension-filled moments.

Personality Assessment

Psychologists use a number of tests and measures to assess personality. These measures are often tied to a psychologist's theoretical orientation. Personality tests were basically designed to measure stable, enduring aspects of personality.

Self-report measures are designed to assess an individual's traits; the most widely used self-report measure is the MMPI, an empirically keyed test.

Projective tests use ambiguous stimuli to encourage individuals to project their personality into the stimuli. They are designed to assess the unconscious aspects of personality. The Rorschach is the most widely used projective test; its effectiveness is controversial.

Behavioral assessment tries to obtain more objective information about personality through the observation of behavior and its environmental ties. Cognitive assessment increasingly is being used as part of behavioral assessment.

Overview

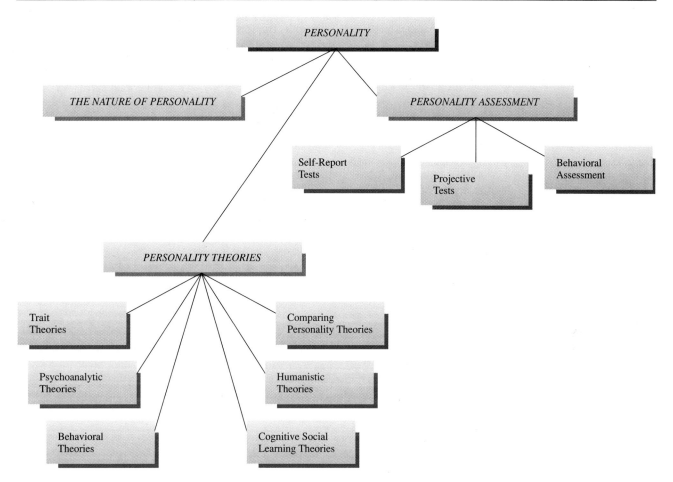

We began this chapter by exploring the definition of personality, in terms of both informal usage of the term and a more formal psychological definition. We spent considerable time exploring various personality theories—trait, psychoanalytic, behavioral, cognitive social learning, and humanistic. We also looked at ways to compare personality theories. We concluded by examining personality assessment through self-report tests, projective tests, and behavioral assessment. Remember that you can obtain an overall summary of the chapter again by studying the in-chapter reviews on pages 378, 387, 397, and 402.

Key Terms

personality 372
traits 372
trait theories 373
somatotype theory 373
endomorph 373
mesomorph 373
ectomorph 373
introversion 374
extraversion 374
five-factor model 374
individualism 376
collectivism 377
id 379
pleasure principle 379
ego 380
reality principle 380

defense mechanisms 380
superego 380
erogenous zones 380
fixation 380
oral stage 380
anal stage 382
phallic stage 382
Oedipus complex 382
latency stage 382
genital stage 382
collective unconscious 384
archetypes 384
individual psychology 384
striving for superiority 385
compensation 385
overcompensation 385

inferiority complex 385
superiority complex 385
reductionistic 388
cognitive social learning
    theory 389
situationism 389
delay of gratification 389
self-efficacy 390
phenomenological worldview
    390
humanistic theory 391
conditional positive regard
    391
self-concept 391
unconditional positive regard
    391

Barnum effect 397
self-report tests 398
face validity 398
social desirability 398
empirically keyed tests 398
Minnesota Multiphasic
    Personality Test (MMPI)
    399
projective tests 400
Rorschach inkblot test 400
Thematic Apperception Test
    (TAT) 401

Thinking It Over

Exercises . . .

. . . In Critical Thinking

Becoming a good critical thinker in psychology means developing the ability to use theories to explain behavior. Select a character from a movie you like. Try to explain how that character developed, according to each of these five personality theories: trait, psychoanalytic, behavioral, cognitive social learning, and humanistic.

When your analysis is complete, judge which approach seems to do the best job of explaining the character's personality.

. . . In Creative Thinking

Develop a creative method (a poem, a cartoon, a song) that will help you distinguish the characteristics of the different theories of personality we have discussed. Show your product to several classmates to get their feedback on how successful you were in helping them learn the characteristics of the theories.

. . . In Active Learning

Get a reading of your personality through a pseudoscientific method. For example, find a description of personality using a horoscope or go see a palmist. Examine the profile of your person-

ality generated by the pseudoscientific method. Might the Barnum effect be present? Be as critical as you can in debunking the pseudoscientific method's explanation of your personality.

. . . In Reflective Learning

Using the five-factor model of personality, rate yourself on the "big five" dimensions:

1.....2.....3.....4.....5.....6.....7.....8.....9.....10

Low end of scale   *High end of scale*

Emotionally stable _____ Neurotic

Introverted _____ Extraverted

Closed to Experience _____ Open to Experience

Antagonistic _____ Agreeable

Irresponsible _____ Conscientious

Reflect on how pleased or displeased you are with this rating of your personality.

Are there dimensions of your personality that are not included in these five traits?

Are there characteristics of your personality that you wish you could change?

Resources for Psychology and Improving Humankind

Control Your Depression (1992, rev. ed.)

by Peter Lewinsohn, Ricardo Muñoz, Mary Youngren, and Antonnete Zeiss
New York: Fireside

Control Your Depression tells you how to reduce your depression by learning self-control techniques, relaxation training, pleasant activities, planning ahead, modifying self-defeating thinking patterns, and other behavioral/cognitive strategies.

Gentle Roads to Survival (1991)

by Andre Auw
Lower Lake, CA: Aslan

In *Gentle Roads to Survival,* Auw presents a guide to making self-healing choices in difficult circumstances. Auw, a psychologist who was a close associate of Carl Rogers, tells you how to become a survivor.

Man and His Symbols (1964)

by Carl Jung
Garden City, NY: Doubleday

This book includes the writings of Jung and four of his disciples; Jung's ideas are applied to anthropology, literature, art, and dreams.

Man, the Manipulator (1972)

by Everett Shostrum
New York: Bantam

This paperback presents humanistic ideas about the route from manipulation to self-actualization. Many case studies are included.

Mental Measurements Yearbook (1992, 11th ed.)

edited by Jack Kramer and Jane Conoley
Lincoln: University of Nebraska Press

This voluminous resource provides details about a wide range of personality tests.

Personality (1992, 2nd ed.)

by Christopher Peterson
Fort Worth, TX: Harcourt Brace

This well-written textbook on personality includes many applications to real-world issues.

Personality Research, Methods, and Theory (1995)

Patrick Shrout and Susan Fiske (eds.)
Hillsdale, NJ: Erlbaum

This volume examines current thinking about what can be known about personality, how concepts related to personality can best be measured, and how to approach research problems in specific areas of personality. Topics include the big-five trait factors, cultural dimensions, and conceputalizing and measuring self-esteem.

Psychological Testing of Hispanics (1992)

by Kurt Geisinger
Washington, DC: American Psychological Association

This book addresses a number of issues related to the psychological testing of Hispanics, including testing in clinical settings and the workplace.

Internet Resources

http://austria-info.at/personen/freud/index.html
Learn all about Freud's contribution to the psychology of personality.

http://www.cgjung.com/cgjung/
A home page dedicated to the works of C. G. Jung.

http://www.wynja.com/personality/theorists.html
This Web page explores the relation between personality and consciousness.

http://www.ahpweb.org/aboutahp/whatis.html
Humanism from Maslow through the 21st Century.

http://www.centacs.com/tests.htm
See how psychologists test the five factors of personality.

http://www.psych.ucsb.edu/~kopeikin/121lec14.htm
Explore the evolution of psychological testing.

11

Abnormal Psychology

They cannot scare me with their empty spaces

Between stars—on stars where no human race is.

I have it in me so much nearer home

To scare myself with my own desert places.

—ROBERT FROST
American Poet, 20th Century

PREVIEW

*M*ental disorders know no social and economic boundaries. They find their way into the lives of the rich and famous and the poor and the unknown. In this chapter, we will study several mental disorders, including the depression that troubled the life of Ernest Hemingway. We begin by examining some basic questions about the nature of abnormal behavior, then turn our attention to the following mental disorders: anxiety, somatoform, dissociative, mood, schizophrenic, personality, and substance-use disorders. We also evaluate the legal aspects of mental disorders.

❖

The Story of Ernest Hemingway: Deterioration, Despair, and Death

*E*ven before his father's suicide, the American author Ernest Hemingway seemed obsessed by the theme of self-destruction. As a young boy he enjoyed reading Stevenson's "The Suicide Club." At one point in his adult life, Hemingway said he would rather go out in a blaze of light than have his body worn out by age and his illusions shattered.

Hemingway's suicidal thoughts sometimes coincided with his marital crises. Just before marrying his first wife, Hadley, Hemingway became apprehensive about his new responsibilities and alarmed her by the mention of suicide. Five years later, during a crisis with his second wife, Pauline, he calmly told her he would have committed suicide if their love affair had not been resolved happily. Hemingway was strangely comforted by morbid thoughts of death. When he was feeling down and out, Hemingway would think about death and various ways of dying; the best way he thought, unless he could arrange to die in his sleep, would be to go off an ocean liner at night.

Hemingway committed suicide in his sixties. His suicide made many people wonder why a man with such good looks, sporting skills, friends, women, wealth, fame, genius, and a Nobel Prize would kill himself. His actual life did not reflect the glamorous one others assigned to him. Rather, Hemingway had developed a combination of physical and mental disturbances. He had neglected his health for some years, and suffered from weight loss, skin disease, alcoholism, diabetes, hypertension, and impotence. His body in a shambles, he dreaded becoming an invalid and the slow death this would bring. Hospitalization, shock therapy, medication, and psychotherapy left his demons untouched. At this point, the severely depressed Hemingway was losing his memory and no longer could write. One month before his suicide, Hemingway said, "Staying healthy. Working good. Eating and drinking with friends. Enjoying myself in bed. I haven't any of them" (Meyer, 1985, p. 559). ❖

A depressed Hemingway shortly before his suicide.

DIMENSIONS OF ABNORMALITY

Hemingway's depression and suicide clearly constitute behavior that our culture regards as "abnormal." But what made his condition abnormal? What caused his decline? Although abnormal in our culture, would his suicide have been more acceptable in other contexts? These concerns lead us to larger questions about the nature of abnormal behavior in general: What causes abnormal behavior? How do we classify abnormal behavior? How prevalent is abnormality in our culture and others? Next we will consider each of these important questions.

Defining Abnormality

Distinguishing what is abnormal behavior from what is normal behavior is not an easy task. Many scholars have suggested that a variety of factors can define abnormality, including statistical prevalence, maladaptiveness and harmfulness, personal discomfort, and cultural norms.

Statistical Prevalence. Consider Albert Einstein, Charles Barkley, and Barbara Walters. We think of each of them as atypical. However, we don't think Einstein was abnormal because he was a genius, that Barkley is abnormal because of his mastery of basketball (although some might consider his temperamental outbursts a sign of abnormal behavior), or that Walters is abnormal because she is one of television's most talented and highly paid interviewers.

However, many forms of mental disorder are *statistically unusual occurrences* in the sense that the vast majority of individuals in a culture do not experience the problem. Most of us, unlike Hemingway, do not commit suicide as a way of solving problems. Most of us do not engage in extensive handwashing rituals or hear relentless self-critical voices inside our heads. Thus, one way psychologists categorize behaviors as abnormal is by how infrequently they occur among the general population.

Maladaptiveness and Harmfulness. Statistical rarity alone may be an insufficient criterion of abnormality. However, the second category—*maladaptiveness and harmfulness*—adds another dimension. Maladaptive behavior fails to promote the well-being, growth, and fulfillment of the person and might contribute to the misery or harm of others. Maladaptive and harmful behavior takes many forms, including depression, suicide, bizarre irrational beliefs, assaults on others, and drug addiction. These abnormal behaviors interfere with the ability to function effectively in the world.

At first glance, Hemingway's suicide appears to be maladaptive and harmful because it ended a brilliant writing career. However, we could challenge this inference. Hemingway's declining health and writing obstacles may have prevented him from living a fulfilling life. His depression may have impeded his ability to see other solutions to the problems he experienced.

Personal Discomfort. Hemingway's actions clearly fit the third criterion of abnormal behavior—*personal discomfort*. He communicated his despair in many ways throughout his life. As a criterion of abnormal behavior, personal discomfort need not be as severe as that experienced by Hemingway. Guilt, grief, strain, frustration, disappointment, anger, and fear can all serve as the foundation for experiences that become so intense that they no longer feel "within normal limits" of human experience.

Cultural Influences. Cultures develop *norms* about what behavior is acceptable and what behavior is not. We might consider the same behavior abnormal in one context and thoroughly acceptable in another. For example, many people in Western cultures believe that suicide is an unacceptable behavior. Thus, the norm or social custom is avoidance of suicide. In contrast, *hari-kiri* is a form of suicide that the Japanese culture encourages as an honorable alternative to shaming the family.

In some cultures, people go about their daily activities with few or no clothes on. If we were to see someone walking naked down a city street in the United States, we probably would consider such behavior inappropriate; we also might think that such norm-violating behavior signaled that the person was in mental distress.

Sometimes the definition of abnormality changes from one historical period to another. For example, early in this century, many Americans believed that masturbation was sinful and caused everything from warts to insanity. Today only a few people think of masturbation as wicked, and most people accept the practice as part of normal sexuality.

A final contextual example also poignantly demonstrates the fact that some individuals are empowered with the authority to label behaviors as "abnormal" and that other individuals are likely to be labeled. Prior to the Civil Way, authorities diagnosed slaves who attempted to escape as having drapetomania. This diagnosis categorized as mental illness a behavior that more likely was an adaptive response to severe life circumstances.

In sum, **abnormal behavior** is behavior that is maladaptive, harmful, statistically unusual, personally distressing, and/or designated abnormal by the culture.

> *Madness reveals the ungluing we all secretly fear: the mind taking off from the body, the possibility that that magnet that attaches us to a context in the world can lose its grip.*
>
> —MOLLY HASKELL, *American Author, 20th Century*

The Origins of Abnormal Behavior

What causes people to behave abnormally? Psychologists typically sort the causes of abnormal behavior into three categories: biological factors, psychological factors, and sociocultural factors.

The Biological Approach. Proponents of the biological approach believe that abnormal behavior is due to a physical malfunction in the body, especially the brain. If an individual behaves in an uncontrollable manner, is out of touch with reality, or is severely depressed, biological factors are the primary culprits. Today scientists and researchers who adopt the biological approach often focus on brain processes and genetic factors as the causes of abnormal behavior. In the biological approach, drug therapy is frequently used to treat abnormal behavior.

The **medical model,** *also called the disease model, was the forerunner of the biological approach; the medical model states that abnormality is a disease or illness precipitated by internal physical causes.* Within this perspective, abnormalities are called mental *illnesses* and the individuals afflicted are *patients* in *hospitals,* who are treated by psychiatrists and, to a lesser extent, psychologists.

The Psychological Approaches. Although the biological approach provides an important perspective for understanding abnormal behavior, many psychologists believe that the medical model underestimates the importance of psychological factors, such as emotional turmoil, inappropriate learning, distorted thoughts, and inadequate relationships. The theories of personality described in chapter 10—psychoanalytic, behavioral and

---

abnormal behavior
Behavior that is maladaptive, harmful, statistically unusual, personally distressing, and/or designated abnormal by the culture.

medical model
Also called the disease model; the forerunner of the biological approach. This model states that abnormal behavior is a disease or illness precipitated by internal physical causes.

social learning, and humanistic theories—provide insight into the nature of abnormal as well as normal behavior. Much more about the approaches to the treatment of abnormal behavior appears in the next chapter.

The Sociocultural Approach.   As you might expect, the sociocultural approach emphasizes how culture, ethnicity, gender, age, and other sociocultural elements influence abnormal behavior. Most experts on abnormal behavior agree that many psychological disorders are universal, appearing in most cultures (Al-Issa, 1982a; World Health Organization, 1975). However, the frequency and intensity of abnormal behavior vary across cultures. Variations in disorders are related to social, economic, technological, religious, and other features of cultures (Costin & Draguns, 1989).

Some disorders appear to be especially culture-bound. Al-Issa (1982a) described specific patterns illustrating how cultures influence abnormal behaviors. Certain exceptional patterns are *culturally approved* as opportunities to express expected but unusual behavior. Some cultures provide certain opportunities in which inebriation and sexual excesses are expected. The Mardi Gras celebrations of New Orleans are an example; another is the Greenland Eskimos' *Schimpfduelle*—ritualized insulting with song and drumming. Some abnormal patterns are *culturally tolerated*. For example, in the Highlands of New Guinea, young men under severe stress enact the "wild man" syndrome. The wild man shows agitation, destroys property, and threatens attack. Others in the culture subdue, sometimes pamper, and ultimately reintegrate the wild man into the culture. Finally, some patterns are *culturally suppressed* through adherence to strong cultural prohibitions. Abnormal behavior can surface in direct contrast to the cultural norm. For example, the severe aggression that sometimes appears in Japanese who have a mental disorder is likely due to the suppression promoted by the Japanese culture's nonviolent norms (Al-Issa, 1982a).

Prevalence Estimates

How prevalent are mental disorders in the United States today? In a survey of 18,571 people randomly selected from five U.S. cities—Hew Haven, Connecticut; Baltimore, Maryland; St. Louis, Missouri; Piedmont, North Carolina; and Los Angeles, California—more than 15 percent of the respondents had suffered from a mental disorder during the previous month (Robins & Regier, 1990). Only one-third of the individuals reporting mental disorders had received treatment in the previous 6 months.

Gender Prevalence.   For the 1-month incidence of mental disorders, the data were also analyzed separately for men and women. The women had a slightly higher overall rate of mental disturbances than the men (16.6 percent versus 15.4 percent). The women had higher rates of mood disorders (for example, depression) (9.7 percent versus 4.7 percent); the men had higher rates of substance-use disorders (6.3 percent versus 1.6 percent) and antisocial personality disorders (0.8 percent versus 0.2 percent).

Women tend to be diagnosed as having disorders that typify traditional stereotypes of females. In particular, women are more likely than men to suffer from anxiety disorders and depression, disorders with symptoms that are internalized, or turned inward. Conversely, men are socialized to direct their energy toward the outside world—that is, to externalize their feelings and thoughts—and are more likely to have disorders involving aggression and substance abuse.

Several explanations have been given as to why women are diagnosed and treated for mental disorders at a higher rate than men (Paludi, 1995). One possibility is that women do not have more mental disorders than men do, but that women are simply more likely to behave in ways that others label as mental disorders. For example, women have been taught to express their emotions, whereas men have been trained to control them. If women express feelings of sorrow and sadness, some individuals may conclude that women are more mentally disturbed than men are. Thus, the difference between the rates of mental disorders could involve the possibility that women more freely display and discuss their problems than men do.

A second explanation of the gender difference in the diagnosis of mental disorders focuses on women's inferior social position and the greater discrimination against women. Women are also more likely to experience certain trauma-inducing circumstances, such as incest, sexual harassment, rape, and marital abuse. Such abuse can increase women's emotional problems.

A third explanation of the gender difference in the diagnosis of mental disorders is that women are often placed in a "double-bind" situation in our society. For example, women can be labeled as mentally disordered for either overconforming or underconforming to feminine gender-role stereotypes. That is, a woman who is overdependent, overemotional, and irrational is overconforming to the traditional feminine gender-role stereotype. On the other hand, a woman who is independent, who values her career as much as or more than her family, who doesn't express emotions, and who acts in a worldly and self-confident manner is underconforming to feminine gender-role stereotypes. In either case, the woman might be labeled emotionally disordered. In sum, even though statistics show that women are more likely than men to have mental disorders, this gender difference may be the result of antifemale bias in American society.

Ethnic, Socioeconomic, and Contextual Factors.   In the United States, variations in mental disorders involve not only gender, but such factors as socioeconomic status, urbanization, neighborhood, and ethnicity (Kaplan & others, 1998). For example, people who live closest to the center of a city have the greatest risk of developing a mental disorder (Suinn, 1984). Ethnic minority status also heightens the risk of mental distress (Huang & Gibbs, 1989). In one study on hospitalization rates, persons with Spanish surnames were more likely to be admitted for mental health problems when they were in the minority than when they were the majority (Bloom, 1975).

Many ethnic minority individuals with mental disorders live in low-income neighborhoods. However, knowing that people from poor minority neighborhoods have high rates of disorder does not reveal *why* they have such rates. Does poverty cause pathology, or is poverty a form of pathology for narrowly trained diagnosticians who are unaware of what behaviors and self-protective beliefs are necessary to survive in harsh circumstances? Researchers who are sensitive to, and comfortable with, these cultural dynamics are vital to the search for answers to these questions.

Environmental settings don't need to be economically impoverished to produce adverse effects on mental health. Some individuals live in enriched contexts that they find to be spiritually impoverished. Even your own experience in college points to the effects of harsh environmental conditions. Think about how your own "normal" behaviors can shift during exams. You might feel overwhelmed with anxiety, negative thinking, and self-defeating impulses. If you are lucky, once exams are over your transient struggles with abnormal behavior diminish.

Interactionist Approaches.   When considering an individual's behavior, whether abnormal or normal, it is important to remember the complexity of human nature and the multiple influences on behavior. Neither the biological nor the psychological nor the sociocultural approach independently captures this complexity. Abnormal behavior is influenced by biological factors (brain processes and heredity, for example), by psychological factors (emotional turmoil and distorted thoughts, for example), and by sociocultural factors (poverty and gender, for example).

diathesis-stress model

Environmental stress and biogenetic disposition interact to produce abnormal behavior.

According to one interactionist approach, the **diathesis-stress model,** *environmental stress and biogenetic disposition interact to produce abnormal behavior* (Zubin & Spring, 1977). This approach suggests that some people are born with genetic predispositions toward abnormal behavior, but that the behavior will not develop unless these individuals encounter "necessary and sufficient" undermining environmental circumstances. The stronger a person's biological predisposition to abnormal behavior, the less severe the environmental circumstances necessary and sufficient to catalyze that behavior in the person. The weaker a person's biological predisposition to abnormal behavior, the more intense the environmental experiences must be for the behavior to arise in that person. Even though the exact nature of genetic, psychological, and environmental contributions usually cannot be specified, all of these factors interact to produce abnormal behavior, and a full explanation of abnormality would take all three kinds of factors into account.

Classifying Abnormal Behavior

Ever since human history began, people have suffered from diseases, sadness, and bizarre behavior. For almost as long, healers have tried to treat and cure them. The classification of mental disorders goes back to the ancient Egyptians and Greeks and has its roots in biology and medicine.

The first classification of mental disorders in the United States, based on the census data of 1840, used one category for all mental disorders. This one inclusive category included both the mentally retarded and the insane.

In the twentieth century, the American Psychiatric Association developed the major classification of mental disorders in the United States. The *Diagnostic and Statistical Manual of Mental Disorders (DSM)*, published in 1952, included better definitions of mental disorders than previous classification efforts. A revised edition, the *DSM-III*, produced with more systematic assistance from expert diagnosticians, appeared in 1968. A third edition, the *DSM-III*, was published in 1980, and a revision of that manual, the *DSM-III-R*, in 1987. Published in 1994, the current manual, the *DSM-IV*, emphasizes refined empirical support of diagnostic categories.

Advantages and Disadvantages of Diagnosis.　Before we discuss the most widely used system to classify mental disorders, we will explore the many benefits of classifying mental disorders. First, a classification system provides professionals with a shorthand system for understanding what the labels communicate about the disturbances. Second, a classification system permits psychologists to construct theories about the causes of particular disorders and design treatments for them. Third, a classification system can help psychologists to make predictions about disorders; it provides information about the likelihood that a disorder will occur, which individuals are most susceptible to the disorder, the progress of the disorder once it appears, and the treatment *prognosis* (likelihood of recovery) (Meehl, 1986).

For example, Kim notices that she becomes very moody and has a hard time concentrating as the days grow shorter in the fall. After consulting with a clinical psychologist, she discovers that her symptoms fit seasonal affective disorder, a mood problem that seems to be induced by reduced exposure to sunlight. Based on the diagnosis, the clinician can begin a treatment strategy that might involve therapy, mediation, or extended exposure to light. The clinician predicts that Kim's prognosis is good if she adheres to the prescribed treatment plan.

Advocates of the psychological and sociocultural approaches sometimes criticize the medical model and diagnostic practices because they believe that these encourage labeling processes that can be harmful. Some psychologists and psychiatrists believe that labeling individuals as "mentally ill" encourages them to perceive themselves as "sick" and to avoid assuming responsibility for coping with their problems (Szasz, 1977).

Although diagnosis and treatment details are confidential, many people fear the consequences if their diagnoses should become public knowledge. For example, one American vice-presidential candidate withdrew from his party's ticket when the public became aware that he had received treatment for depression earlier in his career. Clinicians fear that reliance on third-party payers, such as health insurance companies, and the use of computers to process mental health claims will add to the risk of breached confidentiality. This fear can discourage people who need mental health care from seeking treatment.

Using diagnostic procedures with members of ethnic minority groups can be especially problematic. In particular, studies have found that a client's ethnicity can adversely influence the assessment and diagnosis of mental disorders (Ramirez, 1989). For example, during diagnostic interviews, Native Americans might behave in ways that signal mental distress to a clinician unfamiliar with the Native American culture: Native Americans might be nonassertive, hesitant, and soft-spoken; they might exchange only limited eye contact; they might show discomfort and decreased performance on timed tasks; they might be reluctant to provide details about their personal lives; and they might have a group orientation rather than a self orientation (Hynd & Garcia, 1979).

Assessing mental disorders in ethnic minority individuals is further complicated by the well-documented findings of ethnic and social class biases in diagnosis (Snowden & Cheung, 1990). One study revealed that clinicians find fewer psychological disorders among people from affluent backgrounds than among poor people; in fact, people from the lowest socioeconomic backgrounds are diagnosed as having mental disorders at twice the expected rate and are labeled with the most severe diagnoses (Hollingshead & Redlich, 1958). For example, one study found that the highest rate of mental disorders is in poor African American urban communities (Gould, Wunsch-Hitzig, & Dohrenwend, 1981).

Using the *DSM-IV*. Continuing revisions of the *DSM* reflect advancements in knowledge about the classification of mental disorders. On the basis of research and clinical experience, the *DSM-IV* added, dropped, or revised categories, sometimes generating controversy among the diagnosticians who rely on the classification system.

For example, the *DSM-III* dropped two important categories that have some historic importance: neurosis and psychosis. **Neurotic disorders** *were defined as relatively mild mental disorders in which the individual has not lost contact with reality.* Individuals who are extremely anxious, troubled, and unhappy may still be able to carry out their everyday functions and have a clear perception of reality; these individuals would be classified as neurotic. **Psychotic disorders** *were defined as severe mental disorders in which the individual has lost contact with reality.* Psychotic individuals have such distorted thinking and perception that they live in a very different world from that of others. Psychotic individuals might hear voices that are not present or think they are famous individuals, such as Jesus Christ or Napoleon. The DSM classification system dropped the terms *neurotic* and *psychotic* because they were too broad and ill-defined to be diagnostic labels. Although the DSM system dropped the labels, clinicians still sometimes use them as a convenient way of referring to relatively mild or relatively severe mental disorders, respectively.

The **DSM-IV** *(Diagnostic and Statistical Manual of Mental Disorders, fourth edition) is the most recent major classification of mental disorders; it contains eighteen major classifications and descriptions of more than two hundred specific disorders.* One of the features of the DSM-IV is its **multiaxial system,** *which classifies individuals on the basis of five dimensions, or "axes," that include the individual's history and highest level of competent functioning in the last year.* This system ensures that the individual will not merely be assigned to a mental disorder category but instead will be characterized in terms of a number of clinical factors. Following is a description of each of the axes:

Axis I. Clinical Disorders: The primary classification or diagnosis of the disorder (for example, fear of people). This axis includes all disorders except for the personality disorders.

Axis II. Personality Disorders/Developmental Problems: Personality disorders, longstanding problems in relating to others (for example, long-standing antisocial personality disorder), or developmental problems affecting the adjustment of children and adolescents.

Axis III. General Medical Conditions: General medical conditions that might be relevant in understanding the mental disorder (for example, an individual's history of disease, such as a cardiovascular problem).

Axis IV. Psychosocial and Environmental Problems: Stressors in the individual's recent past that might have contributed to the mental problem (for example, divorce, death of parent, or loss of a job).

Avis V. Global Assessment of Functioning: The individual's current level of functioning, on a scale of 100 (superior) to 1 (inability to maintain safety). The scale takes into account chronicity of symptoms and overall adjustment.

What are some of the changes in the *DSM-IV?* More than two hundred mental health professionals contributed to the development of *DSM-IV.* They were a much more diverse group than their predecessors, who were mainly white male psychiatrists. More women,

---

neurotic disorders

Relatively mild mental disorders in which the individual has not lost contact with reality.

psychotic disorders

Severe mental disorders in which the individual has lost contact with reality.

DSM-IV

Diagnostic and Statistical Manual of Mental Disorders, fourth edition. The *DSM-IV* is the most recent major classification of mental disorders and contains eighteen major classifications and describes more than 200 specific disorders.

multiaxial system

A feature of the *DSM-IV* in which individuals are classified on the basis of five dimensions, or "axes," that include the individual's history and highest level of functioning in the last year.

ethnic minorities, and nonpsychiatrists, such as clinical psychologists, were involved in the construction of the *DSM-IV* (Nathan, 1994). This led to greater attention to the context of gender- and ethnicity-related diagnosis. For example, *DSM-IV* contains an appendix entitled "Guideline for Cultural Formation and Glossary of Culture-Related Syndromes" (Mezzich, Fabrega, & Kleinman, in-press). Also, the *DSM-IV*'s publication is accompanied by a number of sourcebooks that present the empirical base of the *DSM-IV*. Thus, the *DSM-IV* is based more on empirical data than its predecessors were. In previous versions of the *DSM,* the reasons for diagnostic changes were not always explicit, so the evidence that led to their formulation was never available for public evaluation.

The Controversy Surrounding the *DSM-IV*. The most controversial aspect of the *DSM-IV* continues an issue that has been present since publication of the first *DSM* in 1952. Although more nonpsychiatrists were responsible for drafting the *DSM-IV* than in previous editions, the *DSM-IV* still reflects a medical or disease model (Clark, Watson, & Reynolds, 1995). Classifying individuals based on their symptoms and using medical terminology continues the dominance of the psychiatric tradition of thinking about mental disorders in terms of illness and disease. This strategy implies an internal cause of disorders that is more or less independent of external or environmental factors (Adams & Cassidy, 1993). Thus, even though researchers have begun to illuminate the complex interaction of genetic, neurobiological, cognitive, and environmental factors in the *DSM* disorders, the *DSM-IV* continues to espouse a medical or disease model of mental disorders (Allen, 1998; First, Frances, & Pincus, 1995).

The *DSM-IV* also is controversial because it continues to label as mental disorders what are often thought of as everyday problems. For example, under learning or academic skills disorders, the *DSM-IV* includes the categories of reading disorder, mathematics disorder, and disorder of written expression. Under substance-related disorders, the *DSM-IV* includes the category of caffeine-use disorders. We don't usually think of these problems as mental disorders. Including them as mental disorders implies that such "normal behavior" should be treated as a mental disorder. But the developers of the *DSM* system argue that mental health providers have been treating many problems not included in earlier editions of the *DSM* and that the classification system should be more comprehensive. One practical reason that everyday problems in living were included in the *DSM-III-R* and the *DSM-IV* is so that more individuals can get their health insurance companies to pay for professional help. Most health insurance companies reimburse their clients only for disorders listed in the *DSM-IV* system.

The *DSM-IV* was developed by American mental health professionals. Most mental health professionals in other countries adopt the *Inrternational Classification of Disease (ICD)* guidelines established by the World Health Organization. The tenth edition of the *ICD (ICD-10)* was published in 1993. An effort was made to bring the *DSM-IV* into closer correspondence with the *ICD-10,* but substantial differences in categories still persist (Frances, Pincus, & Widiger, in press). Such differences ensure that American and non-American mental health professionals will continue to have problems communicating with each other.

Despite some resistance, psychologists usually adopt the *DSM-IV* to use in their practices, but psychiatrists are more satisfied with it. Even though the *DSM-IV* has its critics, it still is the most comprehensive classification system available.

Review

Dimensions of Abnormality

Abnormal behavior can be statistically unusual within a culture, maladaptive and harmful, personally distressful, and/or designated as abnormal by the culture. A number of views have been proposed about the origins of abnormal behavior. Proponents of the biological approach believe that abnormal behavior is due to a physical malfunction in the body, especially in the brain. The disease model, also called the medical model, was the forerunner of the biological approach; the medical model states that abnormality is a disease or illness precipitated by internal physical causes. Many psychologists believe that the medical model underestimates the importance of psychological factors in abnormal behavior. The sociocultural approach emphasizes how culture, ethnicity, gender, age, and other sociocultural elements influence abnormal behavior. Some disorders are especially culture-bound. Psychologists have made prevalence estimates, including estimates for gender, ethnicity, and economic status, of mental disorders. Many psychologists believe that an interactionist approach to mental disorders is a wise strategy. One interactionist approach is called the diathesis-stress model.

DSM stands for *Diagnostic and Statistical Manual of Mental Disorders.* The *DSM-II* included the categories of neurotic and psychotic behavior. Though some mental health professionals still use the terms *neurotic* and *psychotic,* they have been dropped from the *DSM* classification. Mental disorder classification systems have both advantages and disadvantages. The most recent version of the *DSM (DSM-IV)* was published in 1994. One of the *DSM-IV*'s features is its multiaxial system. The *DSM-IV* Task Force was made up of a much more diverse group of individuals than its predecessors were and the *DSM-IV* is more empirically based than earlier editions. The most controversial aspects of the *DSM-IV* continue to be the classification of individuals based on their symptoms and the use of medical terminology that perpetuates the medical or disease model of mental disorders. Critics also point out that some everyday problems should not be included as disorders. The *DSM-IV* and the *ICD-10 (International Classification of Disease)* are still not completely compatible.

DIAGNOSTIC CATEGORIES OF MENTAL DISORDERS

Let's now examine the major categories of diagnosis featured in the *DSM-IV.* Although this is not an exhaustive exploration of the multitude of categories, the review will suggest the general qualities of the most prominent mental disorders, which we will illustrate by mentioning case studies.

Anxiety Disorders

Anxiety is a diffuse, vague, highly unpleasant feeling of fear and apprehension. People with high levels of anxiety worry a lot. **Anxiety disorders** *are psychological disorders that include the following main features: motor tension (jumpiness, trembling, inability to relax), hyperactivity (dizziness, a racing heart, or perspiration), and apprehensive expectations and thoughts.* Five important types of anxiety disorders are reviewed in this section.

anxiety disorders

Psychological disorders that include the following main features: motor tension (jumpiness, trembling, inability to relax), hyperactivity (dizziness, racing heart, or perspiration), and apprehensive expectations and thoughts.

Generalized Anxiety Disorder.   Anna, who is 27 years old, had just arrived for her visit with the psychologist. She seemed very nervous and was wringing her hands, crossing and uncrossing her legs, and playing nervously with strands of her hair. She said her stomach felt like it was in knots, that her hands were cold, and that her neck muscles were so tight they hurt. She said that, lately, arguments with her husband had escalated. In recent weeks, Anna indicated, she had felt more and more nervous throughout the day, as if something bad were about to happen. If the doorbell sounded or the phone rang, her heart beat rapidly and her breathing quickened. When she was around people, she had a difficult time speaking. She began to isolate herself. Her husband became impatient with her, so she decided to see a psychologist (Goodstein & Calhoun, 1982).

generalized anxiety disorder

An anxiety disorder that consists of persistent anxiety for at least 1 month. An individual with this disorder is unable to specify the reasons for the anxiety.

Anna has a **generalized anxiety disorder,** *an anxiety disorder that consists of persistent anxiety for at least 1 month; an individual with a generalized anxiety disorder is unable to specify the reasons for the anxiety.* One study found that people with generalized anxiety disorder have higher degrees of muscle tension and hyperactivity than people with other types of anxiety disorders (Barlow & others, 1986). These individuals say they have been tense and anxious for over half their lives. To assess your anxiety tendencies, complete the Self-Assessment.

Self-Assessment

Burns Anxiety Inventory

Instructions

Place a check in the appropriate space to the right of each category to indicate how much this type of feeling bothered you in the last few days. Sample answers are shown.

	0 Not at all	1 Somewhat	2 Moderately	3 A lot
Category I: *Anxious Feelings*				
1. Anxiety, nervousness, worry, or fear			✓	
2. Feeling that things around you are strange or unreal		✓		
3. Feeling detached from part or all of your body		✓		
4. Sudden unexplained panic spells			✓	
5. Apprehension or sudden feeling of doom			✓	
6. Feeling tense, stressed, "uptight," or on edge		✓		
Category II: *Anxious Thoughts*				
7. Difficulty concentrating		✓		
8. Racing thoughts		✓		
9. Frightening fantasies or daydreams			✓	
10. Feeling that you are on the verge of losing control				✓
11. Fears of cracking up or going crazy				✓
12. Fears of fainting or passing out				✓
13. Fears of physical illness or heart attacks or dying				✓
14. Concerns about looking foolish or inadequate		✓		
15. Fears of being alone, isolated, or abandoned			✓	
16. Fears of criticism or disapproval	✓			
17. Fears that something terrible is about to happen			✓	
Category III: *Physical Symptoms*				
18. Skipping, racing, or pounding heart (palpitations)			✓	
19. Pain, pressure, or tightness in the chest			✓	
20. Tingling or numbness in the toes or fingers	✓			
21. Butterflies or discomfort in the stomach	✓			
22. Constipation or diarrhea	✓			
23. Restlessness or jumpiness			✓	
24. Tight, tense muscles		✓		
25. Sweating not brought on by heat or exercise	✓			
26. A lump in the throat	✓			
27. Trembling or shaking		✓		
28. Rubbery or "jelly" legs		✓		
29. Feeling dizzy, lightheaded, or off balance		✓		
30. Choking or smothering sensations or difficulty breathing			✓	
31. Headaches or pains in the neck or back	✓			
32. Hot flashes or cold chills	✓			
33. Feeling tired, weak, or easily exhausted	✓			

Total Score on Items 1–33: __42__

Scoring

Total Score	Degree of Anxiety
0–4	Relaxed with no anxiety
5–10	Normal but slightly nervous
11–20	Mild anxiety
21–30	Moderate anxiety
31–50	Severe anxiety
51–99	Extreme anxiety or panic

SOURCE: From *Ten Days to Self-Esteem* by David D. Burns, M.D. Copyright © 1993 by David D. Burns, M.D. By permission of William Morrow & Company, Inc. The Burns Anxiety Inventory, Copyright © 1984 by David D. Burns, M.D. Further reproduction requires written permission. Clinicians interested in obtaining a license to reproduce this test and other assessment devices for use in their practices may contact Dr. Burns at PO Box 1983, Lost Altos Hills, CA 94023 for more information.

panic disorder

A recurrent anxiety disorder that is marked by the sudden onset of apprehension or terror.

Panic Disorder.   **Panic disorder** *is a recurrent anxiety disorder marked by the sudden onset of intense apprehension or terror.* The individual often has a feeling of impending doom but might not feel anxious all the time. Anxiety attacks often strike without warning and produce severe palpitations, extreme shortness of breath, chest pains, trembling, sweating, dizziness, and a feeling of helplessness (McNally, 1998). Victims are seized by the fear that they will die, go crazy, or do something they cannot control.

What are some of the psychosocial factors involved in panic disorder? Most panic attacks are spontaneous; those that are not spontaneous are triggered by a variety of events. In many instances, a stressful life event has occurred in the past 6 months, most often a threatened or actual separation from a loved one or a change in job.

Phobic Disorders.   Agnes is a withdrawn 30-year-old who has been unable to go higher than the second floor of any building for more than a year. When she tries to overcome her fear of heights by going up to the third, fourth, or fifth floor, she becomes overwhelmed by anxiety. She remembers how it all began. One evening she was working alone and was seized by an urge to jump out of an eighth-story window. She was so frightened by her impulse that she hid behind a file cabinet for more than 2 hours until she calmed down enough to gather her belongings and go home. As she reached the first floor of the building, her heart was pounding, she was perspiring heavily. After several months, she gave up her position and became a lower-paid salesperson so she could work on the bottom floor of the store (Cameron, 1963).

phobic disorder

An anxiety disorder that occurs when an individual has an irrational, overwhelming, persistent fear of a particular object or situation; commonly called a phobia.

A **phobic disorder,** *commonly called a phobia, is an anxiety disorder in which an individual has an irrational, overwhelming, persistent fear of a particular object or situation.* Individuals with generalized anxiety disorder cannot pinpoint the cause of their nervous feelings; individuals with phobias can. A fear becomes a phobia when a situation is so dreaded that an individual goes to almost any length to avoid it; for example, Agnes quit her job to avoid being in high places. Some phobias are more debilitating than others. An individual with a fear of automobiles has a more difficult time functioning in our society than a person with a fear of snakes, for example.

Phobias come in many forms. Some of the most common phobias involve heights, open spaces, people, close spaces, dogs, dirt, the dark, and snakes (see table 11.1 to read about a number of phobias). Simple phobias are relatively common and are easier to treat through psychotherapy than complex phobias, such as agoraphobia, are. **Agoraphobia,** *the fear of entering unfamiliar situations, especially open or public spaces, is the most common type of phobic disorder.* It accounts for 50 to 80 percent of the phobic population, according to some estimates (Foa, Steketze, & Young, 1984). Women are far more likely than men to suffer from agoraphobia. One study found that 84 percent of the individuals being treated for agoraphobia are women, and almost 90 percent of those women are married (Al-Issa, 1982b).

agoraphobia

The fear of entering unfamiliar situations, especially open or public space; the most common phobic disorder.

𝒯 A B L E   1 1 . 1

Types of Common Phobias

Acrophobia	Fear of high places
Aereophobia	Fear of flying
Agoraphobia	Fear of open places
Arachnophobia	Fear of spiders
Claustrophobia	Fear of closed places
Hydrophobia	Fear of water
Mysophobia	Fear of dirt
Nyctophobia	Fear of darkness
Ophidiophobia	Fear of nonpoisonous snakes
Thanatophobia	Fear of death
Xenophobia	Fear of strangers

Agoraphobia is the fear of entering unfamiliar situations, especially open or public places. Individuals with agoraphobia try to avoid crowded situations. They fear that escape would be difficult or impossible if they become highly anxious in such crowded situations. Agoraphobic individuals also usually avoid standing in line and riding in vehicles, activities that intensify their feelings of vulnerability.

Psychologists have become increasingly interested in *social phobia,* the fear of social situations (Clum & Febbraro, 1998). Bashful or timid people often suffer from this phobia. Social phobia affects as many as 2 of every 100 Americans and tends to be evenly distributed between the sexes (Robins & others, 1984).

Why do people develop phobias? The answer often depends on the researcher's perspective. Psychoanalytic theorists, for example, say phobias develop as defense mechanisms to ward off threatening or unacceptable impulses—Agnes, for instance, hid behind a file cabinet because she feared she would jump out of an eighth-story window. Learning theorists, however, explain phobias differently; they say phobias are learned fears. In Agnes's case, she might have fallen out of a window when she was a little girl and, as a result, now associates falling with pain and fears high places. On the other hand, she may have heard about or seen other people who were afraid of high places. These last two examples are conditioning and observational learning explanations for Agnes's phobia. Cross-cultural psychologists point out that phobias also are influenced by cultural factors. Agoraphobia, for example, is much more common in the United States and Europe than in other areas of the world (Kleinman, 1988).

Neuroscientists are finding that biological factors, such as greater blood flow and metabolism in the right hemisphere of the brain than in the left, may also be involved in phobias. First-generation relatives of individuals suffering from agoraphobia and panic attacks have high rate of these disorders themselves, suggesting a possible genetic predisposition for phobias (d'Ansia, 1989).

Obsessive-Compulsive Disorders.   Bob is 27 years old and lives in a well-kept apartment. He has few friends and little social life. He was raised by a demanding mother and an aloof father. Bob is an accountant who spends long hours at work. He is a perfectionist. His demanding mother always nagged at him to improve himself, to keep the house spotless, and to be clean and neat, and she made Bob wash his hands whenever he touched his genitals. As a young adult, Bob finds himself ensnared in an exacting ritual in which he removes his clothes in a prearranged sequence and then endlessly scrubs every inch of his body from head to toe. He dresses himself in precisely the opposite way from which he takes off his clothes. If he deviates from this order, he *has* to start the sequence all over again. Sometimes Bob performs the cleansing ritual four or five times an evening. Even though he is aware that this ritual is absurd, he simply cannot stop (Meyer & Osborne, 1982).

Obsessive-compulsive disorder (OCD) *is an anxiety disorder in which an individual has anxiety-provoking thoughts that will not go away (obsession) and/or urges to perform repetitive, ritualistic behaviors to prevent or produce a future situation (compulsion).* Individuals with obsessive-compulsive disorder repeat and rehearse doubts and daily routines, sometimes hundreds of times a day. The basic difference between obsession and compulsion is the difference between thought and action. Obsessions can immobilize the person with horrifying yet irresistible thoughts of killing someone in a traffic accident, for instance, whereas compulsions can result in bloody hands from hours of washing away imaginary germs. Although obsessions and compulsions are different, a person afflicted with OCD might be caught in the relentless grip of both problems (Frost & Steketee, 1998).

> *There is nothing worse than taking something into your head that is a revolving wheel you can't control.*
>
> —UGO BETTI, *Italian Playwright, 20th Century*

The most common compulsions are excessive checking, cleansing, and counting. For example, Wesley believes that he has to check his apartment for gas leaks and make sure the windows are locked. His behavior is not compulsive if he does this once, but, if he goes back to check five or six times and then constantly worries that he may not have checked carefully enough once he has left the house, his behavior is compulsive. Most individuals do not enjoy their ritualistic behavior but feel anxious when they do not carry it out.

Post-Traumatic Stress Disorder. Margie sought help in therapy because she thought she was "losing her grip." Her boss continually complained that she wasn't paying attention to her work as a cashier. He would sometimes find her staring off into space when she should have been stocking shelves. When interrupted, she couldn't really explain what she was thinking about. She seemed irritable and easily upset. Until she was violently mugged while walking her dog in the park 2 months ago, Margie had been a model employee and a generally well adjusted person. Margie's behavior suggests that she might be a victim of post-traumatic stress disorder.

Post-traumatic stress disorder *is a mental disturbance that develops through exposure to a traumatic event (such a war), a severely oppressive situation (such as the holocaust), severe abuse (as in rape), a natural disaster (such as a flood or tornado), or an accidental disaster (such as a plane crash.) The disorder is characterized by anxiety symptoms that either immediately follow the trauma or are delayed by months or even years.* The symptoms vary but can include the following:

- "Flashbacks" in which the individual relives the event in nightmares, or in an awake but dissociative-like state
- Constructed ability to feel emotions, often reported as feeling numb, resulting in an inability to experience happiness, sexual desire, enjoyable interpersonal relationships
- Excessive arousal, resulting in an exaggerated startle response or an inability to sleep
- Difficulties with memory and concentration
- Feelings of apprehension, including nervous tremors
- Impulsive outbursts of behavior such as aggressiveness, or sudden changes in lifestyle

Not every individual exposed to the same disaster develops post-traumatic stress disorder, which occurs when the individual's usual coping abilities are overloaded (Jaycox & Foa, 1998; Solomon, 1993). For example, it is estimated that 15 to 20 percent of Vietnam veterans experienced post-traumatic stress disorder. Vietnam veterans who had some autonomy and decision-making authority, such as Green Berets, were less likely to develop the disorder than soldiers who had no control over where they would be sent or when, and who had no option but to follow orders.

Some experts consider females who have been sexually abused and assault victims to be the single largest group of post-traumatic stress disorder sufferers (Koss, 1990). This

obsessive-compulsive disorder (OCD)

An anxiety disorder in which the individual has anxiety-provoking thoughts that will not go away (obsession) and/or urges to perform repetitive, ritualistic behaviors to prevent or produce a future situation (compulsion).

post-traumatic stress disorder

A mental disorder that develops through exposure to any of several traumatic events, characterized by anxiety symptoms that may be apparent 1 month after the trauma or be delayed by months or even years until onset.

is not very surprising, since these victims had no autonomy nor decision making in the situation. Few women are prepared to deal with the traumatic circumstances and consequences of rape. Many victims of sexual assault receive mixed societal messages after the trauma about the degree of their responsibility, and many victims remain secretive about having been raped. All these factors increase their risk for post-traumatic stress disorder.

Somatoform Disorders

"Look, I am having trouble breathing. You don't believe me. Nobody believes me. There are times when I can't stop coughing. I'm losing weight. I know I have cancer. My father died of cancer when I was twelve." Herb has been to six cancer specialists in the last 2 years; none can find anything wrong with him. Each doctor has taken X rays and conducted excessive laboratory tests, but Herb's test results do not indicate any illnesses. Might some psychological factors be responsible for Herb's sense that he is physically ailing?

Somatoform disorders *are mental disorders in which psychological symptoms take a physical, or somatic, form, even though no physical causes can be found.* Although these symptoms are not caused physically, they are highly distressing for the individual; the symptoms are real, not faked. Two types of somatoform disorders are hypochondriasis and conversion disorder.

Hypochondriasis.   Carly seemed to be a classic hypochondriac. She always seemed to overreact to a missed heartbeat, shortness of breath, or a slight chest pain, fearing that something was wrong with her. **Hypochondriasis** *is a somatoform disorder in which the individual has a pervasive fear of illness and disease.* At the first indication of something being amiss in her body, Carly calls the doctor. When a physical examination reveals no problems, she usually does not believe the doctor. She often changes doctors, moving from one to another searching for a diagnosis that matches her own. Most hypochondriacs are pill enthusiasts; their medicine chests spill over with bottles of drugs they hope will cure their imagined maladies. Carly's pill collection was spectacular.

Hypochondriasis is a difficult category to diagnose accurately. It often occurs in conjunction with other mental disorders, such as depression (Escobar & Gara, 1998).

Conversion Disorder.   **Conversion disorder** *is a somatoform disorder in which an individual experiences genuine physical symptoms, even though no physiological problems can be found.* Conversion disorder received its name from psychoanalytic theory, which stressed that anxiety is "converted" into a physical symptom. A hypochondriac has no physical disability; an individual with a conversion disorder does have some loss of motor or sensory ability. Individuals with a conversion disorder may be unable to speak, may faint, or may even be deaf or blind.

Conversion disorder was more common in Freud's time than today. Freud was especially interested in this disorder, in which physical symptoms made no neurological sense. For example, individuals with *glove anesthesia* reported that their entire hand is numb from the tip of their fingers to a cutoff point at the wrist. As shown in figure 11.1, if these individuals were experiencing true physiological numbness, their symptoms would be very different. Like hypochondriasis, conversion disorder often appears in conjunction

somatoform disorders

Mental disorders in which the psychological symptoms take a physical, or somatic, form, even though no physical causes can be found.

hypochondriasis

A somatoform disorder in which the individual has a pervasive fear of illness and disease.

conversion disorder

A somatoform disorder in which an individual experiences genuine physical symptoms, even though no physiological problems can be found.

$\mathcal{F}$IGURE 11.1

Glove Anesthesia

A patient who complains of numbness in the hand might be diagnosed as suffering from conversion disorder if the area of the hand affected showed that a disorder of the nervous system was not responsible. The skin areas served by nerves in the arm are shown in *(a)*. Therefore, damage to a nerve in the arm tends to make only a portion of the hand numb (for example, the thumb and forefinger). The glove anesthesia shown in *(b)* could not result from damage to these nerves.

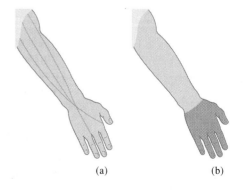

(a)   (b)

with other mental disturbances. During long-term evaluation, conversion disorder often becomes displaced by another mental or physical disorder.

Dissociative Disorders

dissociative disorders

Psychological disorders that involve a sudden loss of memory or change in identity.

Dissociative disorders *are psychological disorders that involve a sudden loss of memory or change in identity. Under extreme stress or shock, an individual's conscious awareness becomes dissociated (separated or split) from previous memories and thoughts.* Three kinds of dissociative disorders are amnesia, fugue, and multiple personality.

Amnesia and Fugue. In chapter 6, amnesia was described as the inability to recall important events. Amnesia can be caused by an injury to the head, for example. However, **psychogenic amnesia** *is a dissociative disorder involving memory loss caused by extensive psychological stress.* For example, a man showed up at a hospital and said he did not know who he was. After several days in the hospital, he awoke one morning and demanded to be released. Eventually he remembered that he had been involved in an automobile accident in which a pedestrian had been killed. The extreme stress of the accident and the fear that he might be held responsible had triggered the amnesia.

psychogenic amnesia

A dissociative disorder involving memory loss caused by extensive psychological stress.

Fugue, *which means "flight," is a dissociative disorder in which an individual not only develops amnesia but also unexpectedly travels away from home and assumes a new identity.* For example, one day a woman named Barbara vanished without a trace. Two weeks later, looking more like a teenager than a 31-year-old woman, with her hair in a ponytail and wearing bobby socks, Barbara was picked up by police in a nearby city. When her husband came to see her, Barbara asked, "Who are you?" She could not remember anything about the past 2 weeks of her life. During psychotherapy, she gradually began to recall her past. She had left home with enough money to buy a bus ticket to the town where she grew up as a child. She had spent days walking the streets and standing near a building where her father had worked. Later she had gone to a motel with a man; according to the motel manager, she had entertained a series of men over a 3-day period (Goldstein & Palmer, 1975).

fugue

A dissociative disorder in which an individual not only develops amnesia but also unexpectedly travels away from home and establishes a new identity (*fugue* means "flight").

Dissociative Identity Disorder **Dissociative identity disorder,** *formerly called multiple personality disorder, is the most dramatic but least common dissociative disorder; individuals suffering from this disorder have two or more distinct personalities,* or *selves,* like the fictional Dr. Jekyll and Mr. Hyde of Robert Louis Stevenson's short story. Each personality has its own memories, behaviors, and relationships; one personality dominates the individual at one point; another personality takes over at another time. The personalities might not be aware of each other, and the shift from one to the other can occur suddenly during distress.

dissociative identity disorder

Formerly called multiple personality disorder. The most dramatic but least common dissociative disorder; individuals with this disorder have two or more distinct personalities.

One of the most famous cases of multiple personality involves the "three faces of Eve," which in reality is only a portion of the dramatic life history of Chris Sizemore. Sizemore recalls that she had her first experience with dissociation when she was 2. For the next 44 years, she experienced a life filled with severe headaches and periods of amnesia. Around age 25 she was diagnosed with dissociative identity disorder. Her psychiatrists identified three alters functioning in her life and named them Eve Black, Eve White, and Jane (Thigpen & Cleckly, 1957).

Eve White was the original, dominant personality. She had no knowledge of her second personality, Eve Black, although Eve Black had been alternating with Eve White for a number of years. Eve White was bland, quiet, and serious—a rather dull personality. Eve Black, by contrast, was carefree, mischievous, and uninhibited. She "came out" at the most inappropriate times, leaving Eve White with hangovers, bills, and a reputation in local bars that she could not explain. During treatment, a third personality, Jane, emerged. More mature than the other two, Jane seemed to have developed as a result of therapy (see figure 11.2 for a portrayal of the three faces of Eve). However, Sizemore's personality didn't stabilize at that point. Alters continued to show up in trios, with one alter demonstrating characteristics of the wife and mother, another the party girl, and the third an intellectual. Of the 22 alters that appeared, 10 were poets, 7 artists, and 1 a tailor. According to Sizemore (1989), when her integrated personality emerged at age 47, she could paint and write but she couldn't sew.

$\mathcal{F}$IGURE 11.2

Multiple Personality: The Three Faces of Eve

Chris Sizemore, the subject of the book *Three Faces of Eve,* is shown with a work she painted and entitled *Three Faces in One.*

A summary of the research literature on dissociative identity disorder suggests that the most striking feature related to the disorder is an inordinately high rate of sexual or physical abuse during early childhood (Ludolph, 1982). Sexual abuse occurred in 56 percent of the reported cases, for example. Their mothers had been rejecting and depressed and their fathers distant, alcoholic, and abusive. Remember that, although fascinating, multiple personality disorder is rare. Until the 1980s, only about 300 cases had been reported (Suinn, 1984). In the past decade, however, hundreds more cases have been labeled "multiple personality disorder." Some argue that the increase represents a diagnostic fad. Others believe that it is not so rare but has been frequently misdiagnosed as schizophrenia. Improved techniques for assessing the physiological changes that occur when individuals change personalities increase the likelihood that more accurate rates can be determined (Braun, 1988).

Now that we have considered three major types of mental disorders—anxiety, somatoform, and dissociative—we will turn to a set of widespread disorders, the mood disorders.

Review

Anxiety Disorders, Somatoform Disorders, and Dissociative Disorders

Anxiety is a diffuse, vague, highly unpleasant feeling of fear and apprehension. The main features of anxiety disorders are motor tension, hyperactivity, and apprehensive expectations and thoughts. Generalized anxiety disorder consists of persistent anxiety for at least 1 month without being able to pinpoint the cause of the anxiety. Panic disorder involves recurrent panic attacks marked by a sudden onset of intense apprehension or terror. Phobic disorders, commonly called phobias, involve an irrational, overwhelming, persistent fear of an object or a situation. Phobias come in many forms; the most common is agoraphobia. Psychoanalytic and learning explanations of phobias have been given; sociocultural and biological factors also are involved. Obsessive-compulsive disorders consist of recurrent obsessions or compulsions. Obsessions are anxiety-provoking thoughts that won't go away. Compulsions are urges to perform repetitive, ritualistic behaviors that usually occur to prevent or produce a future situation. Post-traumatic stress disorder is a mental disorder that develops through exposure to a traumatic event, a severely oppressive situation, severe abuse, a natural disaster, or an accidental disaster. Anxiety symptoms may immediately follow the trauma or may be delayed months or even years.

Somatoform disorders develop when psychological symptoms take a physical, or somatic, form, even though no physical cause can be found. Two somatoform disorders are hypochondriasis and conversion disorder. Hypochondriasis is a pervasive fear of illness and disease. It rarely occurs alone; depression often accompanies hypochondriasis. Conversion disorder develops when an individual experiences genuine symptoms, even though no physiological problems can be found. Conversion disorder received its name from psychoanalytic theory, which stressed that anxiety is "converted" into a physical symptom. Some loss of motor or sensory ability occurs. The disorder was more common in Freud's time than today.

The dissociative disorders involve a sudden loss of memory or a change in identity. Under extreme stress or shock, the individual's conscious awareness becomes dissociated (separated or split) from previous memories and thoughts. Psychogenic amnesia involves memory loss caused by extensive psychological stress. Fugue involves a loss of memory, but individuals unexpectedly travel away from home or work, assume a new identity, and do not remember their old one. Dissociative identity disorder involves the presence of two or more distinct personalities in the same individual. The disorder is rare.

Mood Disorders

mood disorders

Psychological disorders characterized by wide emotional swings, ranging from deeply depressed to highly euphoric and agitated.

The **mood disorders** *are psychological disorders characterized by wide emotional swings, ranging from deeply depressed to highly euphoric and agitated.* Depression can occur alone, as in major depression, or it can alternate with mania, as in bipolar disorder (DeBattista, Solvason & Schatzberg, 1998). Depression is linked to the increasing rate of suicide. We will consider each of these disturbances in turn and then examine the causes of the mood disorders.

major depression

A mood disorder in which the individual is deeply unhappy, demoralized, self-derogatory, and bored with changes in appetite and sleep patterns, decreased energy, feelings of worthlessness, concentration problems, and guilt feelings that might prompt thoughts of suicide.

Major Depression. **Major depression** *is a mood disorder in which the individual is deeply unhappy, demoralized, self-derogatory, and bored. An individual with major depression shows changes in appetite and sleep patterns, decreased energy, feelings of worthlessness, problems concentrating, and guilt feelings that might prompt thoughts of suicide.* For example, Peter had been depressed for several months. Nothing cheered him up. His depression began when the girl he wanted to marry decided marriage was not for her, at least not with Peter. Peter's emotional state deteriorated to the point where he didn't leave his room for days at a time, he kept the shades drawn and the room dark, and he could hardly get out of bed in the morning. When he managed to leave his room, he had trouble maintaining a conversation and he usually felt exhausted. By the time Peter finally contacted his college counseling center, he had gone from being mildly depressed to being in the grips of major depression.

Although most people don't spiral into major depression, as Peter did, everyone feels "blue" sometimes. In our stress-filled world, people often use the term *depression* to describe brief bouts of normal sadness or discontent over life's problems Perhaps you haven't done well in a class or things aren't working out in your love life. You feel down in the dumps and say you are depressed. In most instances, though, your depression won't last as long or be as intense as Peter's; after a few hours, days, or weeks, you snap out of your gloomy state and begin to cope more effectively with depression.

For many individuals, however, depression is a lingering, exhausting experience that can sometimes be severe enough to weaken ties with reality. Depression is so widespread that it has been called the "common cold" of mental disorders; more than 250,000

Diagnostic Categories of Mental Disorders

individuals are hospitalized every year for the disorder. Students, professors, corporate executives, laborers—no one is immune to depression.

> *I was much too far out all my life*
> *And not waving but drowning.*
>
> —STEVIE SMITH, *American Writer, 20th Century*

A man's lifetime risk of developing major depression is approximately 10 percent. The risk is much greater for a woman—almost 25 percent. In fact, depression is the most common psychiatric diagnosis for African American and White women (Russo, 1985). To read further about women's depression, see Sociocultural Worlds.

In May 1988, the National Institute of Mental Health (NIMH) launched the public education phase of the first major program to communicate information about mood disorders (Regier & others, 1988). The inadequate care that results from a lack of understanding or a misunderstanding of depression is expensive and tragic. The annual cost of major depression to the nation is more than $16 billion. Given the existing range of psychological and pharmacological treatments, many individuals who go untreated suffer needlessly. To determine the degree to which depression is present in your life, complete the Self-Assessment.

bipolar disorder
A mood disorder characterized by extreme mood swings; an individual with this disorder might be depressed, manic, or both.

Bipolar Disorder. **Bipolar disorder** *is a mood disorder characterized by extreme mood swings; an individual with this disorder might be depressed, manic, or both.* We have

$\mathcal{S}$ociocultural Worlds

Women and Depression

Around the world, depression occurs more frequently among women than among men. The female-male ratio ranges from 2:1 to 3:1 in most industrialized countries (Nolen-Hoeksema, 1990). Three explanations of the sex difference in depression are the following: (1) women are more willing to seek help and, therefore, are more likely to be categorized as having depression; (2) biological differences may exist between females and males that predispose females to become more depressed than males; and (3) psychosocial factors—different rearing environments, different social roles, and less favorable economic and achievement opportunities, for example—may produce greater depression in women than men. Some psychologists have also theorized that alcoholism may mask, or act as a cover for, depression in men (Culbertson, 1991).

Among the psychosocial factors in women's depression that were proposed by the American Psychological Association's National Task Force on Women and Depression (McGrath & others, 1990) were the following:

- Women's depression is related to avoidant, passive, dependent behavior patterns; it is also related to focusing too much on depressed feelings instead of on action and mastery strategies.
- The rate of sexual and physical abuse of women is much higher than previously thought and is a major factor in women's depression. Depressive symptoms may be long-standing effects of post-traumatic stress syndrome for many women.

- Marriage often confers a greater protective buffer against stress for men than for women. In unhappy marriages, women are three times as likely as men to be depressed. Mothers of young children are especially vulnerable to stress and depression; the more children in the house, the more depression women report.
- Poverty is a pathway to depression and three out of every four people in poverty in the United States are women and children. Minority women, elderly women, chemically-dependent women, lesbians, and professional women are also high-risk groups for depression and merit special attention and support.

Careful diagnosis is critical in the treatment of women's depression. Diagnostic assessment for women, in particular, should include taking a history of sexual and physical violence; exploring prescription drug use; discovering past and current medical conditions; and doing a reproductive life history to determine how menstruation, birth control, pregnancy, childbirth, abortion, and menopause may have contributed to women's depression. According to the Women's Task Force, depression is misdiagnosed at least 30 to 50 percent of the time in women. Approximately 70 percent of the prescriptions for antidepressants are given to women, often with improper diagnosis and monitoring. Prescription drug misuse is a danger for many women.

Understanding the nature of women's depression is a complex undertaking and merits more attention. Perhaps the current effort to better understand women's depression will be successful and reduce women's pain and suffering from depression.

Self-Assessment

Are You Depressed?

Instructions

Below is a list of the ways you might have felt or behaved in the *last week*. Indicate what you felt by putting an X in the appropriate box for each item.

Items	Rarely or None of the Time (Less Than 1 Day)	Some or a Little of the Time (1–2 Days)	Occasionally or a Moderate Amount of the Time (3–4 Days)	Most or All of the Time (5–7 Days)
During the past week:				
1. I was bothered by things that usually don't bother me.	☐	☐	☐	☐
2. I did not feel like eating; my appetite was poor.	☐	☐	☐	☐
3. I felt that I could not shake off the blues even with help from my family and friends.	☐	☐	☐	☐
4. I felt that I was just as good as other people.	☐	☐	☐	☐
5. I had trouble keeping my mind on what I was doing.	☐	☐	☐	☐
6. I felt depressed.	☐	☐	☐	☐
7. I felt that everything I did was an effort.	☐	☐	☐	☐
8. I felt hopeful about the future.	☐	☐	☐	☐
9. I thought my life had been a failure.	☐	☐	☐	☐
10. I felt fearful.	☐	☐	☐	☐
11. My sleep was restless.	☐	☐	☐	☐
12. I was happy.	☐	☐	☐	☐
13. I talked less than usual.	☐	☐	☐	☐
14. I felt lonely.	☐	☐	☐	☐
15. People were unfriendly.	☐	☐	☐	☐
16. I enjoyed life.	☐	☐	☐	☐
17. I had crying spells.	☐	☐	☐	☐
18. I felt sad.	☐	☐	☐	☐
19. I felt that people disliked me.	☐	☐	☐	☐
20. I could not get going.	☐	☐	☐	☐

Scoring

For items 4, 8, 12, and 16, give yourself a 3 each time you checked rarely or none, 2 each time you checked some or a little, 1 each time you checked occasionally or moderate, and a 0 each time you checked most or all of the time. For the remaining items, give yourself a 0 each time you checked rarely or none, 1 each time you checked some or a little, 2 each time you checked occasionally or moderate, and 3 each time you checked most or all of the time. Total up your score for all 20 items.

Interpretation

If your score is around 7, then you are like the average male in terms of how much depression you have experienced in the last week. If your score is around 8 or 9 your score is similar to the average female. Scores less than the average for either males or females indicate that depression probably has not been a problem for you during the past week. If your score is 16 or more, you might benefit from professional help for the depression you are experiencing.

described the symptoms of depression. In contrast, someone who is manic experiences elation, exuberance, and tireless stamina. He or she may be humorous, scheming, restless, and irritable; have a tendency for excess; and be in almost constant motion.

Consider Charlene. She was alternately agitated and euphoric. She had experienced extreme mood swings since she was a child. At age 43, her family wanted to have her hospitalized. She claimed that she had discovered the "secret to life" and laughed heartily when anyone asked her to reveal the secret. Her energy seemed boundless. She often woke at 3 A.M. to do the daily vacuuming. Her family really started worrying when she could no longer control her spending. They found twenty-eight sets of coordinated towels and washcloths stashed under her bed. When she attempted to purchase three cars on the same day, her loan requests were rejected. She threatened suicide, and her family knew they needed help.

The lifetime risk of bipolar disorder is estimated at approximately 1 percent for both men and women (Weissman & Boyd, 1985). It is more common among divorced persons, although, in such cases, bipolar disorder may be a cause rather than a consequence of the divorce. Bipolar disorder also occurs more frequently in the close relatives of individuals with bipolar disorder than in the close relatives of depressed but non-bipolar-disordered individuals.

Suicide.   The rate of suicide has tripled since the 1950s in the United States. Each year about 25,000 people take their own lives. At about the age of 15, the suicide rate begins to rise rapidly. Suicide accounts for 12 percent of the mortality in the adolescent and young adult age group. Men are about three times more likely than women to succeed at committing suicide. This may be due to their choice of method for attempting it—shooting themselves, for example. By contrast, females more often select methods, such as sleeping pills, which do not immediately cause death. Although males successfully commit suicide more frequently, females attempt it more often.

Estimates indicate that 6 to 10 suicide attempts occur for every successful suicide in the general population. For adolescents, the figure is as high as 50 attempts for every life taken. As many as 2 in every 3 college students have thought about suicide on at least one occasion.

There is no simple answer to why people commit suicide. Biological factors appear to be involved. Suicide, as with major depression, tends to run in families. Immediate and highly stressful circumstances, such as the loss of a spouse or a job, flunking out of school, or an unwanted pregnancy, can lead people, especially those who are genetically predisposed, to attempt suicide. Also, drug-related suicide attempts are more common now than in the past.

However, earlier experiences, such as a long-standing history of family instability and unhappiness, can also play a role in attempted suicides. Studies of gifted men and women found several predictors of suicide, such as anxiety, conspicuous instability in work and relationships, depression, and alcoholism (Schneidman, 1971; Tomlinson-Keasey, Warren, & Elliot, 1986).

Not all individuals who attempt suicide are clinically depressed. For example, most suicides are committed by older white males who are divorced, in poor health, and unemployed. Substance abuse and having a terminal illness also are related to suicidal thoughts and behavior. In high-pressure cultures, such as Japan and the United States, suicide rates are much higher than in less achievement oriented cultures.

Psychologists do not have the complete answers for detecting suicide impulses or for preventing them. However, psychologists believe that the most effective intervention for preventing suicide comes from those who have had special training. For some valuable suggestions for communicating with someone you think may be contemplating suicide, see Improving Personal and Cognitive Skills.

Causes of Mood Disorders.   Explanations for mood disorders, such as Peter's depression and Charlene's bipolar disorder, come from psychoanalytic theory, cognitive and learning theories, biogenetic theories, and sociocultural theories.

Psychoanalytic Explanations.   In 1917 Sigmund Freud published a paper called "Mourning and Melancholia," in which he described his view of depression. Freud believed that depression is a turning inward of aggressive instincts. He theorized that a child's early attachment to a love object (usually the mother) contains a mixture of love and hate. When the child loses the love object or her dependency needs are frustrated, feelings of loss coexist with anger. Since the child cannot openly accept such angry feelings toward the individual she loves, the hostility is turned inward and experienced as depression. The unresolved mixture of anger and love is carried forward to adolescence and adulthood, where loss can bring back those early feelings of abandonment.

British psychiatrist John Bowlby (1980, 1989) agrees with Freud that childhood experiences are an important determinant of depression in adulthood. He believes that a combination of an insecure attachment to the mother, a lack of love and affection as a child, and the actual loss of a parent during childhood give rise to a negative cognitive set, or

*I*mproving Personal and Cognitive Skills

Managing Suicide Threats

The following are good strategies to follow when dealing with someone who is threatening suicide:

What to do:

1. Ask direct, straightforward questions in a calm manner. For example: "Are you thinking about hurting yourself?" Be a good listener.
2. Evaluate the seriousness of the suicide intent by asking questions about the person's feelings, relationships, and thoughts about the type of method to be used. If a gun, pills, rope, or other means is mentioned and a specific plan has been developed, the situation is dangerous. Stay with the person until help arrives.
3. Listen and be supportive. Emphasize that unbearable pain can be survived.

4. Encourage the person to get professional help and assist him or her in getting this help. If the person is willing, take the person to a mental health facility or hospital.

What not to do:

1. Don't ignore the warning signs.
2. Don't refuse to talk about suicide if the person wants to talk about it.
3. Don't react with horror, disapproval, or repulsion.
4. Don't offer false reassurances ("Everything will be all right") or make judgments ("You should be thankful for . . .").
5. Don't abandon the person after the crisis seems to have passed or after professional counseling has begun.

schema. The schema built up during childhood causes the individual to interpret later losses as yet other failures in one's effort to establish enduring and close positive relationships.

One longitudinal study of depression found that parents' lack of affection, high control, and aggressive achievement orientation in their children's early childhood are associated with depression among adolescent girls but not boys (Gjerde, 1985). This difference may be because depression generally occurs more often in girls than boys.

Cognitive and Learning Explanations. Individuals who are depressed rarely think positive thoughts. They interpret their lives in self-defeating ways and have negative expectations about the future. Psychotherapist Aaron Beck believes that such negative thoughts reflect schemas that shape the depressed individual's experiences (Beck, 1967). These habitual negative thoughts magnify and expand a depressed person's negative experiences. The depressed person may overgeneralize about a minor occurrence and think that he is worthless because a work assignment was turned in late, his son was arrested for shoplifting, or a friend made a negative comment about his hair. Beck believes that depressed people blame themselves far more than is warranted. For example, an athlete may accept complete blame for a team's loss when five or six other teammates, the opposing team, and other factors were involved.

Self-defeating and sad thoughts fit the clinical picture of the depressed individual. Whether these thoughts are the cause or the consequence of the depression, however, is controversial. Critics say that self-defeating thoughts are an outgrowth of biological and environmental conditions that produce depression.

Some years ago, in the interest of science, a researcher drowned two rats (Richter, 1957). The first rat was dropped into a tank of warm water; it swam around for 60 hours before it drowned. The second rat was handled differently. The researcher held the rat tightly in his hand until it quit struggling to get loose. Then the rat was dropped into the tank; it swam around for several minutes before it drowned. The researcher concluded that the second rat drowned more quickly because its previous experiences told it to give up hope; the rate had developed a sense of helplessness.

Learned helplessness *occurs when animals or humans are exposed to aversive stimulation, such as prolonged stress or pain, over which they have no control. The inability to avoid such aversive stimulation produces an apathetic state of helplessness.* Martin Seligman (1975) argued that learned helplessness is one reason many individuals become depressed. When individuals encounter stress and pain over which they have no control, they eventually feel helpless and depressed. Some researchers believe that the helplessness

learned helplessness
An apathetic state that occurs when animals or humans are exposed to aversive stimulation, such as prolonged stress or pain, over which they have no control.

characteristic of learned helplessness is often the result of a person's extremely negative, self-blaming attributions (Abramson, Metalsky, & Alloy, 1989).

Biogenetic Explanations. Biological explanations of depression involve genetic inheritance and chemical changes in the brain. In a large twin study conducted in Denmark, the identical twins were more likely to suffer from mood disorders than were the fraternal twins (Bertelson, 1979). If one identical twin developed a mood disorder, the other had a 70 percent chance of developing the disorder; a fraternal twin ran only a 13 percent risk. Another study revealed that biological relatives of an individual with a mood disorder are more likely to suffer from the disorder than are adopted relatives (Wender & others, 1986).

Remember from chapter 2 that neurotransmitters are chemical messengers that carry information from one neuron to the next. Two neurotransmitters involved in depression are norepinephrine and serotonin. Depressed individuals have decreased levels of norepinephrine, whereas individuals in a manic state have increased levels. Patients with unusually low serotonin levels are 10 times as likely to commit suicide than individuals with normal levels (Stanley & Stanley, 1989). The endocrine system also may be involved in depression—excessive secretion of cortisol from the adrenal gland occurs in depressed individuals, for example (Joyce, Donald, & Elder, 1987). More about the biological aspects of depression appears in the next chapter, where we will discuss the use of drugs to alleviate depression.

Sociocultural Explanations. Seligman (1989) speculated that the reason so many young American adults are prone to depression is that our society's emphasis on self, independence, and individualism, coupled with an erosion of connectedness to others, family, and religion, has spawned a widespread sense of hopelessness. Depressive disorders are found in virtually all cultures in the world, but their incidence, intensity, and components vary across cultures. A major difference in depression between Western and many non-Western cultures is the absence of guilt and self-deprecation in the non-Western cultures (Draguns, 1990).

Some cross-cultural psychologists believe that mourning rituals in many non-Western cultures reduce the risks of depression. For example, low depression rates in Taiwan may be related to the overt expression of grief that occurs in Chinese funeral celebrations (Tseng & Hsu, 1969). Ancestor worship in Japan also may act against depression because love objects are not considered to be lost through death (Yamamoto & others, 1969). The mourning practices of African Americans also may reduce depression by providing an opportunity for adequate grieving and by providing the bereaved with support rather than having to cope with death in isolation (Vitols, 1967).

Earlier in this chapter, you learned that women run a far greater risk of depression than men—at a ratio of 2:1. Researchers have shown that depression is especially high among single women who are the head of household and among young married women who work at unsatisfying, dead-end jobs (Russo, 1990). Such stressful circumstances, as well as others involving sexual abuse, sexual harassment, unwanted pregnancy, and powerlessness disproportionately affect women. These sociocultural factors may interact with biological and cognitive factors to increase women's rate of depression. A second possibility may be that men in mainstream American society obscure their depression with aggressive behavior that "acts out," or externalizes, their sad feelings. In cultures where alcohol abuse and aggression are rare, such as the culturally homogeneous Amish community (a religious sect in Pennsylvania), the rates of depression of women and men are virtually equal.

Separating the environmental, cognitive, biological, and sociocultural causes of depression is not easy (Beckman & Leber, 1995). Whether neurotransmitters, cognitive factors, environmental factors, or cross-cultural factors are cause or effect is still unknown. Like most behaviors we have discussed, depression is best viewed as complex and multiply determined (Kendall & Watson, 1989). To read further about the importance of becoming educated about depression, turn to Applications in Psychology.

Schizophrenic Disorders

Schizophrenia produces a bizarre set of symptoms and wreaks havoc on an individual's personality. **Schizophrenic disorders** *are severe psychological disorders characterized by distorted*

schizophrenic disorders
Severe psychological disorders characterized by distorted thoughts and perceptions, odd communication, inappropriate emotion, abnormal motor behavior, and social withdrawal.

$\mathscr{A}$pplications in Psychology

Becoming Educated About Depression

As we saw earlier in this chapter, depression is one of the most pervasive mental disorders. In the last several decades, important advances have been made in the treatment of depression. Different medications, several forms of psychotherapy, and the combination of medication and therapy have been successful in alleviating the debilitating symptoms of depression. As many as 80 percent of persons with depression are likely to show improvement if they are diagnosed and treated properly (Leshner, 1992).

Unfortunately, a survey by the National Institute of Mental Health revealed that only one-third of individuals with depression in the United States receive any professional help for their disorder. Approximately three-fourths of the depressed individuals said they would just live with their depression until the disorder passes. Some people with depression take the unwise course of self-treating their symptoms by abusing drugs or alcohol.

Why do so many people with depression go untreated? The reasons include the public's poor understanding of depression's nature and the probability of successful treatment; stigmatization of the disorder, which makes many depressed individuals unwilling to seek treatment and makes family members and associates perceive depressed individuals as lazy or having a flawed character; and the failure of many health professionals and physicians to recognize and diagnose

depression in clients, which is an essential step for appropriate referral or treatment.

To help remedy the dilemma of so many depressed individuals going undiagnosed and untreated, in 1986 the National Institute of Mental Health began a national campaign to educate the general public, as well as health professionals, about the nature of depression and its treatment. The campaign is called the NIMH Depression Awareness, Recognition, and Treatment (D/ART) program. As part of this campaign, NIMH has developed and distributed a wide array of educational materials and has worked with local and national groups to encourage better public and professional understanding of depression.

A recent thrust of the D/ART campaign is to focus on the workplace as a key site for recognizing depression and providing referral and treatment through employee assistance plans. Employers have been receptive to the D/ART workplace program because they recognize the extensive toll that depression takes in absenteeism and reduced productivity.

You can obtain more information about the nature, diagnosis, and treatment of depression by writing:

Depression/USA
Rockville, MD 20857

And other organizations involved in promoting a better understanding of depression and help for individuals with affective disorders are listed at the end of this chapter.

---

thoughts and perceptions, odd communication, inappropriate emotion, abnormal motor behavior, and social withdrawal. The term schizophrenia *comes from the Greek words* schizo, *meaning "split," and* phrenia, *meaning "mind." The individual's mind is split from reality, and his or her personality loses its unity.* Schizophrenia is not the same as multiple personality, which sometimes is called a "split personality." Schizophrenia involves the split of *the* personality from reality, not the coexistence of several personalities within one individual.

Characteristics of Schizophrenic Disorders.   Bob began to miss work. He spent his time watching his house from a rental car parked inconspicuously down the street and following his fellow employees as they left work to see where they went and what they did. He kept a little black book, in which he scribbled cryptic notes. When he went to the water cooler at work, he pretended to drink but, instead, looked carefully around the room to observe if anyone seemed guilty or frightened.

Bob's world seemed to be closing in on him. After an explosive scene at the office one day, he became very agitated. He left and never returned. By the time Bob arrived at home, he was in a rage. He could not sleep that night, and the next day he kept his children home from school; all day he kept the shades pulled on every window. The next night, he maintained his vigil. At 4 A.M., he armed himself and burst out of the house, firing shots in the air while daring his enemies to come out (McNeil, 1967).

Bob is a paranoid schizophrenic. About 1 in every 100 Americans will be diagnosed as having some form of schizophrenia in their lifetime (Gottesman, 1989). Schizophrenic disorders are serious, debilitating mental disorders, and about one-half of all mental hospital patients in the United States are schizophrenics. More now than in the past, schizophrenics live in society and periodically return for treatment at mental hospitals (Kane

& Barnes, 1995). Drug therapy, which will be discussed in the next chapter, is primarily responsible for fewer schizophrenics being hospitalized. About one-third of all schizophrenics get better, about one-third get worse, and another third stay about the same once they develop this severe mental disorder.

What symptoms do these individuals have? Many schizophrenics have *delusions,* or false beliefs—one individual may think he is Jesus Christ, another Napoleon, for example. The delusions are utterly implausible. One individual may think her thoughts are being broadcast over the radio; another may think that a double agent is controlling her every move. Schizophrenics also may hear, see, feel, smell, and taste things that are not there. These *hallucinations* often take the form of voices. The schizophrenic might think he hears two people talking about him, for example. On another occasion, he might say, "Hear that rumbling in the pipe? That is one of my men in there watching out for me."

Often schizophrenics do not make sense when they talk or write. Their language does not appear to follow any rules. For example, one schizophrenic might say, "Well, Rocky, babe, help is out, happening, but where, when, up, top, side, over, you know, out of the say, that's it. Sign off." Such speech has no meaning to the listener. These incoherent, loose word associations are called *word salad.* As shown in figure 11.3, schizophrenics' paintings also have a bizarre quality.

A schizophrenic's motor behavior may be bizarre, sometimes taking the form of an odd appearance, pacing, statuelike postures, or strange mannerisms. Some schizophrenics withdraw from their social world; they become so insulated from others that they seem totally absorbed in interior images and thoughts (Schiffman & Walker, 1998).

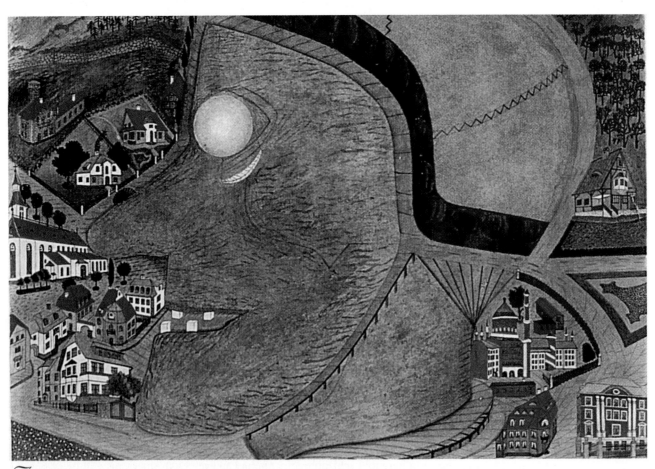

$\mathcal{F}$IGURE 11.3

A Painting by a Schizophrenic

This painting is named *Landscape* and it is by August Neter, a successful nineteenth-century electrical engineer until he became schizophrenic in 1907. He lost interest in his work as an engineer as his mind became disorganized.

disorganized schizophrenia

A schizophrenic disorder in which an individual has delusions and hallucinations that have little or no recognizable meaning.

catatonic schizophrenia

A schizophrenic disorder characterized by bizarre motor behavior, which sometimes takes the form of an immobile stupor.

paranoid schizophrenia

A schizophrenic disorder characterized by delusions of reference, grandeur, and persecution.

undifferentiated schizophrenia

A schizophrenic disorder characterized by disorganized behavior, hallucinations, delusions, and incoherence.

Forms of Schizophrenic Disorders. Schizophrenic disorders appear in four main forms: disorganized, catatonic, paranoid, and undifferentiated schizophrenia.

Disorganized schizophrenia *is a schizophrenic disorder in which an individual has delusions and hallucinations that have little or no recognizable meaning—hence, the label "disorganized."* A disorganized schizophrenic withdraws from human contact and might regress to silly, childlike gestures and behavior. Many of these individuals were isolated or maladjusted during adolescence.

Catatonic schizophrenia *is a schizophrenic disorder characterized by bizarre motor behavior, which sometimes takes the form of a completely immobile stupor* (see figure 11.4). Even in this stupor, catatonic schizophrenics are completely conscious of what is happening around them. An individual in a catatonic state sometimes shows *waxy flexibility;* for example, if the person's arm is raised and then allowed to fall, the arm stays in the new position.

Paranoid schizophrenia *is a schizophrenic disorder characterized by delusions of reference, grandeur, and persecution.* The delusions usually form a complex, elaborate system based on a complete misinterpretation of actual events. It is not unusual for schizophrenics to develop all three delusions in the following order. First, they sense they are special and have been singled out for attention (delusions of reference). Individuals with delusions of reference misinterpret chance events as being directly relevant to their own lives—a thunderstorm, for example, might be perceived as a personal message from God. Second, they believe that this special attention is the result of their admirable and special characteristics (delusions of grandeur). Individuals with delusions of grandeur think of themselves as exalted beings—the pope or the president, for example. Third, they think that others are so jealous and threatened by these characteristics that they spy and plot against them (delusions of persecution). Individuals with delusions of persecution think they are the target of a conspiracy—for example, recall Bob's situation described earlier.

Undifferentiated schizophrenia *is a schizophrenic disorder characterized by disorganized behavior, hallucinations, delusions, and incoherence.* This category of schizophrenia is used when an individual's symptoms either don't meet the criteria for the other types or they meet the criteria for more than one of the other types.

*F*IGURE 11.4

A Catatonic Schizophrenic

Disturbances in motor behavior are prominent symptoms in catatonic schizophrenia. Individuals may cease to move altogether, sometimes taking on bizarre postures.

Causes of Schizophrenia. Schizophrenic disorders may be caused by genetic and biological factors, as well as environmental and sociocultural factors.

Genetic Factors. If you have a relative with schizophrenia, what are the chances you will develop schizophrenia? It depends on how closely you are related. As genetic similarity increases, so does your risk of becoming schizophrenic (Sasaki & Kennedy, 1995). As shown in figure 11.5, an identical twin of a schizophrenic has a 46 percent chance of developing the disorder, a fraternal twin 14 percent, a sibling 10 percent, a nephew or niece 3 percent, and an unrelated individual in the general population 1 percent (Gottesman & Shields, 1982). Such data strongly suggest that genetic factors are involved in schizophrenia, although the precise nature of the genetic influence is unknown.

Neurobiological Factors. Many neuroscientists believe that imbalances in brain chemistry, including deficits in brain metabolism and a malfunctioning dopamine system cause schizophrenia (Goldberg, Berman, & Weinberger, 1995). Imaging techniques, such as the PET scan, clearly show deficits in brain metabolism. Do these deficits cause the disorder or are they simply symptoms of a disorder whose true origin lies deeper in the brain, in the genes, or in the environment? Whether the neurobiological factors are the cause or the effect, information about them improves our knowledge of schizophrenia's nature. We do know that schizophrenics produce too much of the neurotransmitter dopamine. More about the dopamine system appears in the next chapter, where we will discuss the use of drugs to block excess dopamine production.

> *This wretched brain gave way,*
> *And I became a wreck,*
> *At random driven,*
> *Without one glimpse of reason.*
>
> —THOMAS MOORE, *Irish Poet, 19th Century*

Environmental Factors. As scientists learn about schizophrenia's neurobiological basis, they must remember that schizophrenia, like all other behavior, does not occur in an environmental vacuum. Some researchers believe that environmental factors are important in schizophrenia (Goldstein, 1986); others believe that genetic factors outweigh environmental factors (Gottesman & Shields, 1982).

Sociocultural Factors. Disorders of thought and emotion are common to schizophrenia in all cultures, but the type and incidence of schizophrenic disorders may vary from cul-

*F*IGURE 11.5

Lifetime Risk of Becoming Schizophrenic According to Genetic Relatedness

As your genetic relatedness to an individual with schizophrenia increases, so does your risk of becoming schizophrenic.

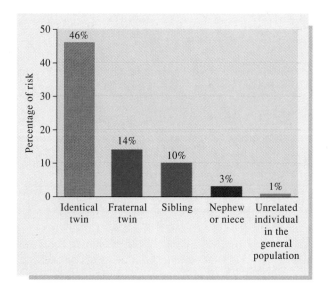

ture to culture. For example, one of the more puzzling results is that the admission rates to mental health facilities for schizophrenia are very high for Irish Catholics in the Republic of Ireland (Torrey & others, 1984) but not for Irish Catholics living elsewhere (Murphy, 1978). One reason for this difference could be that the diagnostic criteria used in the Republic of Ireland are different from those used elsewhere, but this is not likely to be the complete answer. There are many areas of the world where the incidence of schizophrenia is considerably higher or lower than the worldwide incidence of just under 1 percent.

Rates of schizophrenia also vary for different groups within a culture (Sartorius, 1992). For example, one study revealed that Blacks have higher rates of schizophrenia than Whites in both the United States and Great Britain (Bagley, 1984). In that study, Blacks had a significantly greater number of life crises that may have precipitated schizophrenic episodes. Also, the African Americans and African Britons who became schizophrenic had higher aspirations than those who did not. One explanation could be that their efforts to become assimilated into, and to achieve parity within, a mainstream society that is oppressively racist create considerable stress for them.

We have seen that the mood disorders and the schizophrenic disorders are complex and often debilitating. Next you will read about an intriguing set of disorders involving personality.

eview

Mood Disorders and Schizophrenic Disorders

The mood disorders are characterized by wide emotional swings, ranging from deeply depressed to highly euphoric and agitated. Depression can occur alone, as a major depression, or it can alternate with mania, as in bipolar disorder. Individuals with major depression are sad, demoralized, bored, and self-derogatory. They often do not feel well, lost stamina easily, have a poor appetite, and are listless and unmotivated. Depression is so widespread that it is called the "common cold" of mental disturbances.

Bipolar disorder is characterized by extreme mood swings; an individual with this disorder might be depressed, manic, or both. In the manic phase, individuals are exuberant, have tireless stamina, and have a tendency for excess. They also are restless, irritable, and in almost constant motion. The rate of suicide has increased dramatically in the United States. There is no simple answer to why individuals attempt suicide—immediate, earlier, biological, and cultural factors may be involved. Explanations of mood disorders come from psychoanalytic theory, cognitive and learning theories, biogenetic theories, and sociocultural theories.

Schizophrenic disorders are severe mental disorders characterized by distorted thoughts and perceptions, odd communication, inappropriate emotion, abnormal motor behavior, and social withdrawal. The individual's mind splits from reality, and the personality loses its unity. About 1 in 100 Americans becomes schizophrenic, and schizophrenia accounts for approximately one-half of all individuals in mental hospitals. Many schizophrenics have delusions, or false beliefs, and hallucinations. They often do not make sense when they talk or write. The schizophrenic's motor behavior may be bizarre, and the schizophrenic may withdraw from social relationships.

Schizophrenia appears in four main forms: disorganized, catatonic, paranoid, and undifferentiated. Proposed causes of schizophrenia include genetic and biological factors, as well as environmental factors. Many neuroscientists believe that imbalances in brain chemistry cause schizophrenia. Cognitive and emotional disorders of thought are common in schizophrenia in all cultures, but the type and incidence of schizophrenic disorders may vary cross-culturally and across social classes.

Personality Disorders

personality disorders

Psychological disorders that develop when personality traits become inflexible and, thus, maladaptive.

Personality disorders *are psychological disorders that develop when personality traits become inflexible and, thus, maladaptive.* Individuals with these maladaptive traits often do not recognize that they have a problem and might show little interest in changing. Personality disorders are notoriously difficult to treat therapeutically (Livesley, 1995).

Although there are eleven distinct personality disorder diagnoses described in the *DSM-IV,* clinicians think of the disorders as "clustered" around dominant characteristics. One cluster of personality disorders involves odd or eccentric behaviors. A second cluster emphasizes fear and anxiety. And a third cluster stresses dramatic, emotional, or erratic behaviors. We will describe one or more representative disorders from each of the clusters to illustrate their features. The complete list of personality disorders appears in table 11.2

$\mathcal{T}$ A B L E   1 1 . 2

Clusters and Characteristics of Individual Personality Disorders as Described in the *DSM-IV*

The Anxious, Fearful Cluster	
Avoidant	Heightened sensitivity, avoids new events
Dependent	Indecisive, overreliant on others
Obsessive-Compulsive	Overconscientious, rigid, perfectionistic
Passive-Aggressive	Procrastinates, "forgets" commitments
The Odd, Eccentric Cluster	
Paranoid	Guarded, overcautious, unforgiving
Schizoid	Isolated, emotionally inexpressive
Schizotypal	Peculiar behavior and appearance, detached
The Dramatic, Emotional, Erratic Cluster	
Antiosocial	Guiltless, law-breaking, exploitive
Borderline	Unstable, untrusting, fearful of being alone
Historic	Seductive, shallow, moody
Narcissistic	Shows entitlement and jealousy, self-absorbed

schizotypal personality disorder

A personality disorder in the odd, eccentric cluster. Individuals with this disorder appear to be in contact with reality, but many aspects of their behavior are distasteful, which leads to rejection or withdrawal from others.

The Schizotypal Personality Disorder.   The **schizotypal personality disorder** *is a personality disorder in the odd/eccentric cluster. Individuals with this disorder appear to be in contact with reality but many aspects of their behavior are distasteful, which leads to rejection or withdrawal from others.* Individuals are likely to be diagnosed with this label based on their eccentric patterns of behavior. Consider Bruce. Although he was able to hold a job, he associated little with his co-workers. He strongly preferred to spend his breaks and time away from work with a sketchpad designing new flags for countries of the world. His geographic and political knowledge was impressive, but it was painful for him to engage in conversations with others. In contrast, when constructing new flags, he hummed and talked to himself.

obsessive-compulsive personality disorder (OCD)

A personality disorder in the anxious, fearful cluster; anxious adjustment is the primary feature.

Obsessive-Compulsive Personality Disorder.   **Obsessive-compulsive personality disorder** *is in the anxious, fearful cluster of personality disorders. Anxious adjustment is its primary feature.* Individuals with this personality disorder tend to be exacting, precise, and orderly. They generate discomfort in others by requiring the same precision from others. They pay attention to each detail as a means of warding off anxiety. Individuals who show obsessive-compulsive style often are successfully adjusted to positions that require careful execution of details. For instance, Alex is a policeman in charge of preparing and maintaining evidence for trials. He repeatedly checks his files for completeness and order. Although well respected for the quality of his work by his fellow officers, he becomes enraged when they alter his meticulous organization. Note that obsessive-compulsive *personality* disorder is not the same thing as obsessive-compulsive disorder, which we discussed earlier in the chapter. The former involves a meticulous and demanding organizational style; the latter involves a series of ritualized activities to ward of anxious thoughts.

Borderline Personality Disorder.   **Borderline personality disorder** *is in the dramatic, emotional, erratic cluster of personality disorders.* Consider Pam, who never could manage to keep a college roommate. Each relationship would start off with a promise. Pam spoke enthusiastically about each new prospect as being "different from all the others." She bought them presents and almost courted their friendship. However, within a few weeks she would wildly criticize a new roommate for her poor hygiene, her preference for "low-life" acquaintances, and her impossible housekeeping skills. In desperation, she would threaten to kill herself if someone more caring and sensitive were not assigned to her immediately. Individuals with borderline tendencies often view the world as neatly divided into good and bad features. Their tolerance of frustration is very limited, as is their capacity to trust others. These individuals use manipulative, attention-seeking acts as a means of controlling others.

The Antisocial Personality Disorder. The **antisocial personality disorder** *is also in the dramatic, emotional, erratic cluster of personality disorders. It is the most problematic personality disorder for society. These individuals (who used to be called psychopaths or sociopaths) regularly violate the rights of others.* Individuals with antisocial personality disorder often resort to crime, violence, and delinquency. This disorder begins before the age of 15 and continues into adulthood; it is much more typical of males than of females. Consider Martin, who shows many of the behaviors typical of adults with antisocial personality. He cannot maintain a consistent work record. He steals, harasses others, rarely plans ahead, and fails to meet his financial obligations. He repeatedly gets into fights and shows little remorse when he has harmed someone. Tiffany also demonstrates many antisocial characteristics already in high school: truancy, school suspension, running away from home, stealing, vandalism, drug use, sexual acting-out, and violation of rules at home and school. Such behaviors are commonplace among young adults afflicted with antisocial personality disorder (Meyer, Wolverton & Deitsch, 1998).

Substance-Use Disorders

In chapter 4, we discussed a number of drugs and their effects on individuals. A problem associated with drug use is called a **substance-use disorder,** *which is characterized by one or more of the following features: (1) a pattern of pathological use that involves frequent intoxication, a need for daily use, and an inability to control use—in a sense, psychological dependence; (2) a significant impairment of social or occupational functioning attributed to the drug use; and (3) physical dependence that involves serious withdrawal problems.*

The use of many of the drugs described in chapter 4 can lead to a substance-use disorder. Alcohol, barbiturates, and opium derivatives all are capable of producing either physical or psychological dependence. Alcoholism is an especially widespread substance-use disorder; it has been estimated that 6 to 8 million Americans are alcoholics. Although substantial numbers of women abuse alcohol, more men than women are alcoholics. Among African Americans, the male-female alcoholic ratio is 3:2; among White Americans, the ratio is approximately 4:1 (Russo, 1990).

Many individuals are surprised to learn that substantial numbers of women are alcoholics or abusers of other drugs. Although most of the research on drug abuse has been directed toward males, studies have found that females are just as likely to be treated for drug-related problems in emergency rooms. Without a more intense research effort directed at female drug abusers, the unique facets of their drug abuse will go uncharted. For both male and female drug abusers, biogenetic, psychological, and sociocultural factors may all be involved.

LEGAL ASPECTS OF MENTAL DISORDERS

The legal status of individuals with mental disorders raises a number of controversial issues: What is involved in committing disordered and dangerous individuals to mental institutions? What is the status of using the insanity defense for capital crimes? How does "guilty but insane" differ from competence to stand trial? We will consider each of these issues in turn.

borderline personality disorder

A personality disorder in the dramatic, emotional, and erratic cluster; the person's behavior exhibits these characteristics.

antisocial personality disorder

A personality disorder in the dramatic, emotional, and erratic cluster; the most problematic personality disorder for society. Individuals with this disorder often resort to crime, violence, and delinquency.

substance-use disorder

A disorder characterized by one or more of the following features: (1) a pattern of pathological use that involves frequent intoxication, a need for daily use, and an inability to control use—in the sense of psychological dependence; (2) a significant impairment of social or occupational functioning attributed to drug use; and (3) physical dependence that involves serious withdrawal problems.

commitment

The process by which an individual becomes institutionalized in a mental hospital.

civil commitment

Commitment that transpires when a judge deems an individual to be a risk to self or others due to a mental disorder.

criminal commitment

Commitment that occurs when a mental disorder is implicated in the commission of a crime.

insanity

A legal term not a psychological one. A legally insane person is considered mentally disordered and incapable of being responsible for his or her actions.

insanity defense

A plea of "innocent by reason of insanity," used as a legal defense in criminal trials.

Two famous cases involving insanity pleas resulted in different outcomes. When Jeffrey Dahmer was tried for murder and cannibalism, his insanity defense was unsuccessful. In contrast, a jury found Lorena Bobbitt "innocent by reason of insanity" in her assault on her husband.

Commitment and Dangerousness

Having a mental disorder in itself is not adequate grounds for placing individuals in mental institutions against their will. However, the behavior of some mentally disordered individuals is so severe that they are a threat to themselves and/or to others, and they may need protective confinement. Although procedures vary somewhat from state to state, certain conditions usually must be present before the state can formally commit persons to a mental institution: The persons must have a mental disorder and must be dangerous either to themselves or to other people. Dangerousness judgments in the absence of criminal involvement may depend on a demonstrated inability to take care of one's daily physical needs.

Commitment, *the process by which an individual becomes institutionalized in a mental hospital,* can be voluntary or involuntary. Some individuals commit themselves, recognizing that their behavior is potentially dangerous or incompetent. However, the state commits others on an involuntary basis through judicial proceedings. **Civil commitment** *transpires when a judge deems an individual to be a risk to self or others as a function of mental disorder.* A civic commitment proceeding often involves psychiatric evaluation and a formal judicial hearing. The judge must conclude that the evidence is "clear and convincing," based on a 1979 precedent *(Addington v. Texas),* or they cannot order hospitalization.

Determining whether a mentally disordered individual is dangerous is not easy, even for mental health professionals. Nonetheless, there are times when professionals have to make dangerousness judgments. Recent court decisions have held mental health professionals liable when unconfined clients they were treating have caused harm to others. Legal precedents require therapists to warn potential victims if their patients threaten to kill someone (Faulkner, McFarland, & Bloom, 1989).

Criminal Responsibility

Criminal commitment *occurs when a mental disorder is implicated in the commission of a crime.* Procedures may ensure that the individual receives mental health care as an inpatient in a mental health hospital rather than imprisonment. Two areas in which psychologists make decisions about criminal responsibility include the insanity defense and the determination of competence to stand trial. We will examine each of these challenges in turn.

The Insanity Defense. **Insanity** *is a legal term, not a psychological term. A legally insane person is considered mentally disordered and incapable of being responsible for his or her actions.* The **insanity defense** *is a plea of "innocent by reason of insanity" used as a legal defense in criminal trials.* In our society, guilt implies responsibility and intent—to be guilty of a crime, an individual has to have knowingly and intentionally committed it. The jury determines whether the defendant is guilty, based on such legally defined criteria. Controversy swirls about the concept of insanity because of concerns that criminals will unfairly use this plea to avoid prosecution.

In recent years, two publicized cases employing the insanity defense have led to different outcomes. Jeffrey Dahmer's attorneys were unable to persuade the jury in 1992 that his murdering and ritualized cannibalism of fifteen young men resulted from insanity. The prosecution pointed to his skilled execution and coverup of the crimes as evidence that he was rational and should be held responsible. The jury found Dahmer guilty and sane at the time he committed the crimes and ordered him to serve fifteen life terms without parole. In 1994, Dahmer was murdered by another inmate.

In a contrasting example from 1994, Lorena Bobbitt's attorneys were successful in employing the insanity plea. Lorena Bobbitt claimed that she had suffered years of physical and sexual abuse from her husband, John. According to her defense attorneys, after one particularly abusive episode with her husband, she experienced an irresistible impulse. She waited for her husband to fall asleep. Then she cut off his penis, drove away from the house, and threw his penis out of the car window. Although her trial was controversial, the jury found her "guilty, but insane" at the time she committed the crime. After several weeks of confinement in a mental hospital, Lorena Bobbitt was able to return to the community although she has made other appearances in court related to assaultive behavior.

The appropriateness of the insanity plea remains highly controversial (Slovenko, 1995). Successful insanity defense is relatively rare because juries struggle with applying the legal criteria to complex situations. Some experts recommend changes in the defense, arguing that the courts should establish whether or not the defendant committed the crime, independently of establishing the defendant's sanity status (Steadman & others, 1989). Many states have moved to adopt this approach. In addition, the Supreme Court reviewed a case in 1994 that opened the opportunity for states to revisit their insanity plea practices.

competency

An individual's ability to understand and participate in a judicial proceeding.

Determining Competency. **Competency** *is an individual's ability to understand and participate in a judicial proceeding.* Competent individuals can consult with a lawyer and ask questions about the proceedings. Individuals whom the courts deem competent to stand trial may still plead that they were "guilty, but insane" at the time they committed the offenses. Individuals deemed incompetent to stand trial may be remanded to institutional care at the discretion of a judge who has evaluated the testimony of expert witnesses and other evidence pertinent to the individual's current state of mind (Thompson, 1998).

In this chapter we have examined the nature of abnormal psychology and the many disorders that individuals can develop. In the next chapter, we will explore the strategies that psychologists use to treat these disorders.

eview

Personality Disorders, Substance-Use Disorders, and the Legal Aspects of Disorders

Personality disorders are psychological disorders that develop when personality traits become inflexible and, thus, maladaptive. Individuals with a personality disorder often do not recognize that they have a problem and show little interest in changing their behavior. Three clusters of personality disorders are the anxious, fearful cluster; the odd, eccentric cluster; and the dramatic, emotional, erratic cluster. The schizotypal personality is in the odd, eccentric cluster; obsessive-compulsive personality disorder is in the anxious, fearful cluster; borderline personality disorder and antisocial personality disorder are in the dramatic, emotional, erratic cluster.

A substance-use disorder is characterized by one or more of the following features: (1) a pattern of pathological use that involves frequent intoxication, a need for daily use, and an inability to control use—in the sense of psychological dependence; (2) a significant impairment of social or occupational functioning, attributed to the drug use; and (3) physical dependence that involves serious withdrawal problems.

The legal status of individuals with mental disorders raises a number of controversial issues: commitment and dangerousness, criminal responsibility, the insanity defense, and determining competence.

Overview

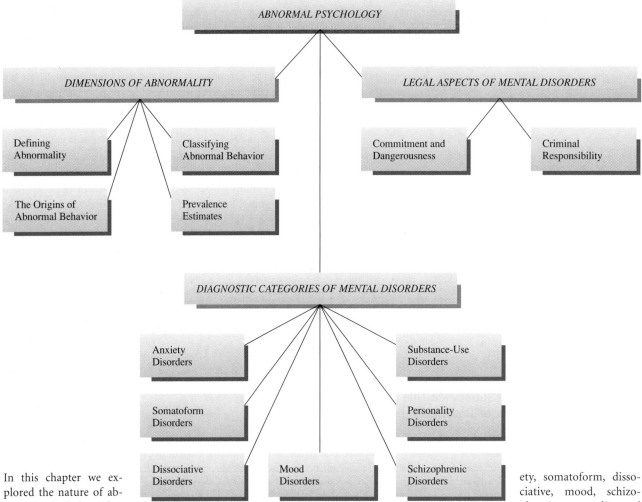

In this chapter we explored the nature of abnormal psychology, beginning with an evaluation of the dimensions of abnormality. We defined abnormality, studied the origins of abnormal behavior, read about prevalence estimates of disorders, and learned about how mental disorders are classified. Then we spent considerable time exploring the diagnostic categories of mental disorders: anxiety, somatoform, dissociative, mood, schizophrenic, personality, and substance-use. Next, we read about the legal aspects of mental disorders, especially the concepts of commitment and dangerousness, as well as criminal responsibility. Don't forget that you can obtain an overall summary of the chapter by again reading the in-chapter reviews on pages 415, 423, 433, and 437.

Key Terms

Thinking it Over

Exercises . . .

. . . In Critical Thinking

Regardless of the kind of problem a client brings into the therapist's office, some aspects of the first contact are often fairly standard. Try to generate a list of ten questions that you think a therapist wants to know the answers to before developing a treatment plan for the client. If possible, compare your list with others in your class. See if you and your classmates can agree on a protocol for establishing a relationship with the client and gathering important information.

. . . In Creative Thinking

Many therapists report that individuals with a personality disorder are among the hardest clinical populations to work with. Somewhat interestingly, if individuals with a personality disorder make the right choice in a partner and job (whose characteristics complement their own), they may not require therapy. Examine the list of personality disorders in table 11.2. For each disorder, what kind of partner and job match might reduce the adjustment problems of an individual with that personality disorder?

. . . In Active Learning

Visit a courtroom to witness a hearing that involves issues related to psychological disorders. This could be a competency hearing or a trial in which the results of personality tests are used to try to persuade the jury. Describe what you learned from the courtroom visit. (If visiting a courtroom is not practical, you may be able to watch some court activity on Court TV or other news specials related to trials in the news).

. . . In Reflective Learning

An increasing problem in treating clients in psychotherapy is security of records. When a therapist applies to an insurance company for payment, some aspects of the therapist's treatment, including diagnosis, become a part of the insurance company's database. How important is it for clients to have their records kept confidential? Could such exposure reduce your willingness to seek therapy? Is this type of record keeping inevitable when therapy costs are paid by an insurance company?

Resources for Psychology and Improving Humankind

Anxiety Disorders and Phobias: A Cognitive Perspective (1985)

by Aaron Beck and Gary Emery
New York: Basic Books

This book provides information about different types of anxiety and how people can change their thinking to overcome the anxiety that is overwhelming them.

Depression and Related Affective Disorders

Johns Hopkins Hospital Meyer 3–181
600 N. Wolfe Street
Baltimore, MD 21205
410-955-4647

This is an organization for individuals with affective disorders and their families, friends, and mental health professionals. The organization provides support, referrals, and educational programs and publishes a quarterly newsletter, *Smooth Sailing.*

Don't Panic (1986)

by Reid Wilson
New York: HarperPerennial

Wilson presents a self-help program for coping with panic attacks. You learn how to conquer panic attacks, especially through the use of self-monitoring, breathing exercises, focused thinking, mental imagery, and deep muscle relaxation.

Feeling Good (1980)

by David Burns
New York: Avon

Feeling Good is a cognitive therapy approach to coping with depression. Burns outlines the techniques people can use to identify and combat false assumptions that underlie their flawed negative thinking. Another good choice is Burns's *The Feeling Good Handbook,* which applies cognitive therapy to depression and other problems, including anxiety and those involving relationships.

International Society for the Study of Multiple Personality and Dissociation

5700 Old Orchard Road, 1st Floor
Skokie, IL 60077-1024
708-966-4322

This organization of mental health professionals and students promotes a greater understanding of dissociation.

National Foundation for Depressive Illness

P.O. Box 2257
New York, NY 10116
800-248-4344

This foundation provides information and education about recent medical advances in affective mood disorders; it also has a referral service.

National Mental Health Association

1021 Prince Street
Alexandria, VA 22314-2971
800-969-NMHA

This consumer advocacy organization is devoted to promoting mental health and improving the lives of individuals with a mental disorder. It publishes *NMHA Focus* four times a year, as well as pamphlets on mental health issues.

National Mental Health Consumers Association

P.O. Box 1166
Madison, WI 53701

This organization seeks to protect the rights of mental health clients in housing, employment, and public benefits; it encourages the creation of self-help groups and aids them in acquiring funding and networking with other organization.

Seeing Both Sides: Controversies in Abnormal Psychology (1995)

by Scott Lilienfeld
Pacific Grove, CA: Brooks/Cole

This book presents the pros and cons of nineteen controversial issues in abnormal psychology. The issues include whether psychotherapy is effective, whether psychiatric patients should be hospitalized against their will, and whether the diagnostic system is biased against females.

Youth Suicide National Center

204 E. 2nd Avenue, Suite 203
San Mateo, CA 94401
415-347-3961

This national clearinghouse develops and distributes educational materials on suicide and reviews current youth suicide prevention and support programs. Publication include *Suicide in Youth and What You Can Do About It* and *Helping Your Child Choose Life: A Parent's Guide to Youth Suicide.*

Internet Resources

http://wchat.on.ca/web/asarc/mpd.html
Explore the link between child abuse and multiple personality disorder.

http://www.clark.net/pub/pwalker/Health and Human Services/Substance Abuse/
A comprehensive site about substance abuse and other addiction problems.

http://www.long-beach.va.gov/ptsd/stress.html
A web site dedicated to understanding post-traumatic stress.

http://www.bowiestate.edu/departments/mckelvie/main.htm
A primer on ethical and legal issues in abnormal behavior.

http://www.cmhc.com/guide/dep2quiz.htm
On-line screening for depression.

http://www.med.nyu.edu/Psych/public.html
On-line screening instruments for a variety of mental health concerns.

http://www.iglou.com/fairlight/ocd/
A helpful site about obsessive-compulsive disorders.

http://www.moodswing.org/bdfaq.html
Frequently asked questions about bipolar disorder.

http://www.navicom.com/~patty/
A fascinating site devoted to borderline personality disorder.

http://www.uvm.edu/~cbcl/
A child behavior checklist for screening about behavior problems.

http://www.cmhc.com/guide/schizo.htm
Information for individuals with schizophrenia and their families.

12

Therapies

Nothing can be changed until it is faced.

—JAMES BALDWIN
American Novelist, 20th Century

PREVIEW

*M*any people today seek therapy. Some want to gain insight into themselves and improve their lives. Others may need help overcoming trauma, such as physical or sexual abuse in childhood. And others find themselves in the immobilizing grip of fears such as agoraphobia or the delusions of schizophrenia. Whatever the reason may be that people seek therapy, there are many different therapeutic approaches to help them—at last count there were more than 450. We will explore the most widely practiced therapies and give you an understanding for what it would be like to go to a therapist with a particular orientation. But before we study the scope of today's therapies, let's experience a therapeutic intervention for a troubled little girl.

❖

The Story of Amanda: Anguish on the Roof

*A*lthough Amanda weighed just under 40 pounds, the aura of despair she brought with her when she came to the clinical psychologist's office made her seem even smaller, even more fragile. Prior to her parents' divorce, she had been a vivacious 5-year-old. But once she heard the news that they were divorcing, said, she became transformed: moody, noncompliant, and untalkative. She sometimes sneaked into their rooms and stole or destroyed their things. Amanda also had trouble sleeping through the night. However, it was her refusal to talk that most concerned her parents. Desperate to get their little girl back, they sought help from a psychologist who specialized in children's issues.

Every time Amanda arrived for therapy, she enacted the same ritual. Without a word to the therapist, she went straight to the corner to the big doll house. She methodically emptied the house of its furnishings and put them into a big pile. Then she selected three dolls—a mother, a father, and a little girl—and placed them on the roof to play. First, they played. Then they danced. Then they fought. Inevitably someone fell from the roof and died "because no one would come to help." Sometimes it was the father, who often just happened to impale himself on his golf clubs. Sometimes it was the mother, mangled when she "fell" on the pile of family furniture. But most often it was the little girl no one would save.

The therapist had seen other children like Amanda cope with their losses in this way. She sat with Amanda while she played and sometimes narrated Amanda's actions. Occasionally she gently questioned Amanda about the motives that prompted the fight or the fall. However, for the most part the therapist carefully watched Amanda's expressive play and interpreted the possibilities to help her deal with the guilt and anger she felt about the breakup of her family. The therapist also conducted separate sessions with the parents to help them learn how to give Amanda high-quality attention, avoid drawing her into their relationship disputes, and set and maintain consistent boundaries to reduce her confusion.

As therapy progressed, Amanda's play became less frenetic and less violent. The members of Amanda's doll family stopped playing on the roof and were no longer sacrificed to her anger. Amanda built a second house out of blocks where the father could go live and began enacting other kinds of adjustment as the therapy came to a close. ❖

THE NATURE OF THERAPY

It would be difficult to pinpoint exactly when, historically, some people were first designated as healers to help others with disordered thoughts, emotions, and behavior. However, it is clear today that not only is therapy an acceptable avenue for resolving personal challenges and mental problems, it has become a thriving enterprise. Contemporary practitioners come from a variety of backgrounds and work with an astonishing array of problems with individuals, groups, and communities. We will first examine the historical underpinnings of modern psychotherapeutic interventions.

As we study the origins of modern therapy, keep in mind that our knowledge about the causes and treatment of disorder is far more sophisticated than that of our ancestors. By the same token, our descendants' knowledge may show many of our own beliefs and practices to be foolish or harmful. The shifts in perspective through the years regarding dysfunction, as well as the durability of some beliefs, underscore the importance of context in influencing judgments about what constitutes normal and disordered behavior.

Historial Viewpoint

In ancient societies, individuals believed that abnormal behavior had both mystical and organic origins. In many cultures, disordered behavior represented possession by a spirit residing in the afflicted person. When evil spirits were deemed responsible, the authorities imposed **trephining**, *a procedure that involves chipping a hole in the skull to allow the evil spirit to escape* (see figure 12.1). In some other cultures, behavior disorder was interpreted as a sign that nature was out of balance (Torrey, 1986). Such individuals might be granted special privilege, rather than treatment designed to bring them back within the bounds of expected behavior.

In the fourth century B.C., Hippocrates, a Greek physician, proposed that mental problems and disordered behavior resulted from brain damage or an imbalance of body chemicals. He prescribed rest, exercise, a bland diet, and abstinence from sex and alcohol as cures for depressed mood. Unfortunately, Hippocrates's theories lost their influence.

In the Middle Ages there was a resurgence of the belief that spiritual possession was the cause of disorder. Many of those who were identified as "different" probably suffered from neurological disorders, such as epilepsy or Tourette's syndrome, a disease that involves repetitive motor and vocal tics. Many of the unfortunates, whom the authorities deemed possessed by evil spirits, were labeled as witches. **Exorcism,** *a religious rite that involved prayer, starvation, beatings, and various forms of torture,* became a popular intervention to cast out the evil spirits. When exorcism involved particularly harsh practices,

trephining

A procedure, no longer used, that involved chipping a hole in the skull to allow evil spirits to escape.

exorcism

A religious rite used during the Middle Ages that was designed to remove evil spirits from a person; it involved prayer, starvation, beatings, and various forms of torture.

*F*IGURE 12.1

Trephining

The technique of trephining involved chipping a hole in the skull through which an evil spirit, believed to be the source of the person's abnormal behavior, might escape. The fact that some people actually survived the operation is shown by this skull. The bone had had time to heal considerably before the individual died.

the notion was to make the disordered individuals so physically uncomfortable that no evil spirit would remain in their bodies. If that didn't work, the only "cure" left was to destroy the body. From the fourteenth through the seventeenth century, 200,000 to 500,000 people thought to be witches were either hanged or burned at the stake.

During the Renaissance, *asylums* ("sanctuaries") were built to house the mentally disordered. Mentally disordered people were placed in an asylum to protect them from the exploitation they experienced on the streets. But the asylums were not much better; the mentally disordered often were chained to walls, caged, or fed sparingly.

Fortunately, reforms in asylum care began to change how the mentally disordered were treated. For example, physician Philippe Pinel (1745–1826) joined with a hospital staff worker, Jean Pussin, to initiate reforms at La Bicetre, an asylum in Paris. They believed that asylum patients were people who could not reason well because of their serious personal problems. They proposed that treating the mentally disordered like animals not only was inhumane but hindered their recovery. They began their reforms by improving the asylum's living conditions. Dungeons were replaced with bright-colored rooms. Staff members were encouraged to spend long hours talking with patients, listening to their problems and giving them advice. After Pinel left to assume a new position, his colleague Jean Pussin unchained large numbers of inmates, many of whom had not been outside the

Even after Pinel and others reformed mental institutions, some rather strange techniques were invented to control the most difficult mentally disabled individuals. The tranquilizing chair *(left)* and circulating swing *(right)* were used to calm mentally disabled individuals at the beginning of the nineteenth century. Fortunately, their use soon diminished.

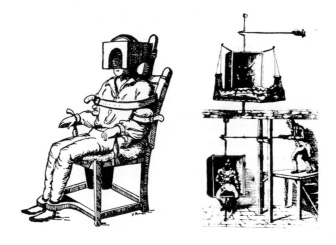

asylum for 30 or 40 years. Although Pinel has often been given credit for the unchaining of patients, as just mentioned, it actually was Pussin who carried this out.

Although Pinel's and Pussin's efforts led to reform, it was slow to come. Even as late as the nineteenth century in the United States, the mentally disordered were kept alongside criminals in prisons. Dorothea Dix, a nurse who had taken a position at a prison in the middle of the nineteenth century, was instrumental in getting the mentally disordered separated from criminals. She embarked on a state-to-state campaign to upgrade prisons and persuaded officials to use better judgment in deciding which individuals should be placed in prisons. State governments began building large asylums for the mentally disordered because of Dix's efforts, although the conditions in the asylums often were no better than in the prisons.

In the twentieth century, significant advances in how we view and treat the mentally disordered have taken place. The importance of humane treatment, concern for preventing mental disorders, and improved methods of therapy characterize the modern view.

Current Practice

Psychotherapy *is the process of working with individuals to reduce their emotional problems and improve their adjustment.* Mental health professionals help individuals recognize, define, and overcome personal and interpersonal difficulties. Psychotherapists use a number of strategies to accomplish these goals: talking, interpreting, listening, rewarding, and modeling, for example. Psychotherapy *does not* include biomedical treatment, such as drugs or surgery.

Orientations. The theories of personality discussed in chapter 10 are the basis for a number of important approaches to psychotherapy, which can generally be distinguished as *insight* or *action* therapies. **Insight therapy** *encourages insight into and awareness of oneself as the critical focus of therapy.* **Action therapy** *promotes direct changes in behavior; insight is not essential for change to occur.* Psychodynamic therapies, based on the psychoanalytic theories of Freud and those in his tradition, and humanistic therapies, based on the humanistic theories of Rogers and Maslow, among others, are considered to be insight therapies. Therapeutic applications of Skinner's behavioral principles constitute action therapies. Cognitive therapies have both insight-oriented and action-oriented components.

Most contemporary therapists do not use one form of therapy exclusively with their clients. The majority of today's therapists are **eclectic**—*they use a variety of approaches to therapy.* Often therapists tailor the therapeutic approach to their clients' needs. Even a therapist with a psychodynamic orientation might use humanistic approaches or a family therapist might use behavioral techniques, for example.

Practitioners and Settings. A variety of mental health professionals, including clinical psychologists, psychiatrists, and counselors, practice psychotherapy. Remember from chapter 1 that psychiatrists have a medical degree and can prescribe drugs for mental disabilities. Clinical psychologists, by contrast, are trained in graduate programs of psychology and use psychotherapy rather than drugs to treat mental problems, although many psychologists are beginning to advocate granting prescription privileges to appropriately trained psychologists. Table 12.1 describes the main types of mental health professionals, their degrees, the years of education required for the degrees, and the nature of the training.

Just as there is a variety of mental health professionals, there is a variety of settings in which therapy takes place. During the first half of this century, psychotherapists primarily practiced in mental hospitals, where individuals remained for months, even years. During the past several decades, psychologists have recognized that psychotherapy is not just for those who are so mentally disordered that they cannot live in society. Today people who seek counseling and psychotherapy may go to a community health center, to the outpatient facility of a hospital, or to the private office of a mental health practitioner.

psychotherapy

The process of working with individuals to reduce their emotional problems and improve their adjustment.

insight therapy

Therapy that encourages insight into and awareness of oneself as the critical focus of therapy.

action therapy

Therapy that promotes direct changes in behavior; insight is not essential for change to occur.

eclectic

Using a variety of approaches.

Main Types of Mental Health Professionals

Professional Type	Degree	Experience Beyond Bachelor's Degree	Nature of Training
Clinical psychologist and counseling psychologist	Ph.D., ED.d., or Psy.D.	5–7 years	Includes both clinical and research training. Involves a 1-year internship in a psychiatric hospital or mental health facility. Recently some universities have developed Psy.D. programs, which lead to a professional degree with stronger clinical than research emphasis. The Psy.D. training program takes about the same number of years as the clinical psychology Ph.D. program and also requires a 1-year internship.
Psychiatrist	M.D.	7–9 years	Four years of medical school, plus an internship and residency in psychiatry, are required. A psychiatry residency involves supervision in therapies, including psychotherapy and biomedical therapy.
Social worker	M.S.W., D.S.W., or Ph.D.	2–5 years	Graduate work in a school of social work that includes specialized clinical training in mental health facilities.
Psychiatric nurse	R.N., M.A., or Ph.D.	0–5 years	Graduate work in school of nursing, with special emphasis on care of mentally disabled individuals in hospital settings and mental health facilities.
Occupational therapist	B.S., M.A., or Ph.D.	0–5 years	Emphasis on occupational training, with focus on physically or psychologically handicapped individuals. Stresses getting individuals back into the mainstream of work.
Pastoral counselor	None to Ph.D. or D.D. (Doctor of Divinity)	0–5 years	Requires ministerial background and training in psychology. An internship in a mental health facility as a chaplain is recommended.
Counselor	M.A.	2 years	Graduate work in department of psychology or department of education, with specialized training in counseling techniques.

Note: The above listing refers to the mental health professionals who go through formal training at recognized academic and medical institutions. The government commonly licenses these professionals and certifies their skills. Professional organizations regulate their activities.

Access to Services. Psychotherapy usually is an expensive proposition. Even though reduced fees, and occasionally free services, can be arranged in public hospitals for those who are poor, many of the people who are most in need of psychotherapy do not get it. Psychotherapists have been criticized for preferring to work with "young, attractive, verbal, intelligent, and successful" clients (Called YAVISes) rather than "quiet, ugly, old, institutionalized, and different" clients (called QUOIDs). A national sample of clinical psychologists established that psychologists appear to be less willing to work with poorer and less-educated clients than with people from higher socioeconomic classes (Sutton & Kessler, 1986). This preference is attributed in part to the fact that disenfranchised individuals tend to have a poor *prognosis* (likelihood of improving from treatment). Such individuals might have difficulties keeping to the rigid appointment schedules required by most therapists, perhaps because their lives are chaotic. These problems hinder the development of a strong working alliance between client and therapist, which has adverse effects on prognosis.

Financial factors also promote a preference for working with clients from higher socioeconomic classes. YAVIS clients tend to seek mental health care from private practitioners in mental health agencies and use health insurance to pay for their care when their therapists can provide a diagnosis consistent with the *DSM-IV*. QUOID clients usually must rely on reduced-fee or cost-free programs provided by public agencies supported through private grants or government funding. Clinicians generally earn higher incomes by concentrating services with YAVIS clients rather than QUOID clients.

The challenge involved in paying for psychotherapeutic services has led to dramatic changes in mental health care delivery in recent years. Concerned by mounting mental health care costs that seemed to derive from protracted psychotherapy with questionable gains, health insurance companies began to seek new delivery systems. **Managed health care,** *a system in which external reviewers approve the type and length of treatment to justify insurance reimbursement,* has grown rapidly. Therapists whose clients participate in managed health care must confer with an external agent about their treatment goals and make systematic reports about client progress to secure continued insurance funding.

Many problems have surfaced with this practice (Fox, 1995). Although managed health care has promoted the development of more explicit and measurable treatment plans, the emphasis on cost management clearly favors short-term over long-term therapy methods. This emphasis can inappropriately shift some treatment to superficial interventions when the clinical problem requires more depth and more time than the health care managers allow. Both clients and therapists report discomfort with the potential violation of confidentiality and privacy when reporting therapy details to a third party. Some research suggests that the bureaucracy involved in setting up the watchdog system may absorb the savings that were supposed to be gained through the implementation of the system. Insurance reimbursement and managed health care will both be significantly affected by implementation of national health care mandate (Hoge, 1998).

Ethical Standards.   Those who seek treatment from qualified mental health care practitioners can feel some reassurance that their problems will be addressed professionally and ethically, based on the systems used in certifying practitioners. Licensing and certification practices require mental health care providers to know relevant state and professional ethical codes before their credentials are granted. Most of these codes require ethical practice as well as vigilance about unethical practice by others in the field. The codes typically address the importance of doing no harm to clients, protecting the privacy of clients, avoiding dual relationships with clients, and staying updated in contemporary practices. Violations of ethical codes can result in the loss of one's license to practice.

So far we have glimpsed the history and basic nature of psychotherapy as it is practiced today. Contemporary psychotherapies include a number of diverse approaches to working with people to reduce their problems and improve their adjustment. We begin our survey by discussing forms of individual psychotherapy.

eview

The Nature of Therapy

Historically, some of the first forms of therapy derived from the belief, in ancient societies, that abnormal behavior had both mystical and organic origins. Many early treatments of mental disabilities were inhumane. Asylums were built during the Renaissance. Pinel's efforts led to extensive reform. Dix's efforts helped to separate the mentally disabled from prisoners.

In contemporary practice, psychotherapy is the process of working with individuals to reduce their emotional problems

and improve their adjustment. Among the orientations of therapists are insight therapy, which encourages insight into and awareness of oneself (both psychoanalytic and humanistic therapies are insight therapies), and action therapy, which promotes direct changes in behavior for which insight is not essential (Skinner's behaviorism is an action therapy). Cognitive therapies have both insight and action components. Many therapists take an eclectic approach to therapy.

Practitioners include clinical psychologists, counseling psychologists, psychiatrists, and social workers. Psychotherapy takes place in a greater variety of settings today than in the past. Individuals of lower socioeconomic status are less likely to receive therapy than are individuals of higher socioeconomic status. Managed health care has increased dramatically in recent years, although not without problems. Psychotherapists are supposed to adhere to certain ethical standards.

INDIVIDUAL THERAPIES

Your image of individual therapy might be the stereotype of the client lying down on a couch while the therapist makes notes about the client's day-to-day experiences. In fact, few individual therapists follow this strategy. Most individual therapies take place face to face and are more conversational. We will explore four orientations of individual therapy: psychoanalytic, humanistic, behavioral, and cognitive.

Psychodynamic Therapies

psychodynamic therapies

Therapies that stress the importance of the unconscious mind, extensive therapist interpretation, and the role of infant and early childhood experiences.

The **psychodynamic therapies** *stress the importance of the unconscious mind, extensive interpretation by the therapist, and the role of infant and early childhood experiences.* Many psychodynamic approaches have grown out of Freud's psychoanalytic theory of personality. Today some therapists with a psychodynamic perspective show allegiance to Freud; others do not.

psychoanalysis

Freud's therapeutic technique for analyzing an individual's unconscious thought.

Freud's Psychoanalysis. **Psychoanalysis** *is Freud's therapeutic technique for analyzing an individual's unconscious thought.* Freud believed that clients' current problems could be traced to childhood experiences, many of which involved conflicts about sexuality. He also recognized that the early experiences were not readily available to the individual's conscious mind. Only through extensive questioning, probing, and analyzing was Freud able to put the pieces of the individual's personality together and help the individual become aware of how these early experiences were affecting present adult behavior. To reach the shadowy world of the unconscious, psychoanalytic therapists often use the therapeutic techniques of free association, catharsis, interpretation, dream analysis, transference, and resistance.

free association

The technique of encouraging individuals to say aloud whatever comes to mind, no matter how trivial or embarrassing.

In psychoanalysis the therapist uses **free association,** *the technique of encouraging individuals to say aloud whatever comes to mind, no matter how trivial or embarrassing.* When Freud detected that a client was resisting the spontaneous flow of thoughts, he probed further. He believed that the crux of the person's emotional problem probably lurked below this point of resistance. Freud thought that, when clients talked freely, their emotional feelings emerged. **Catharsis** *is the psychoanalytic term for clients' release of emotional tension when they relive an emotionally charged and conflicted experience.*

catharsis

The psychoanalytic term for clients' release of emotional tension when they relive an emotionally charged and conflicted experience.

Interpretation plays an important role in psychoanalysis. As the therapist interprets free associations and dreams, the client's statements and behavior are not taken at face value. To understand what is truly causing the client's conflicts, the therapist constantly searches for symbolic, hidden meanings in what the individual says and does. From time to time, the therapist suggests possible meanings of the client's statements and behavior.

dream analysis

The psychotherapeutic technique psychoanalysts use to interpret a client's dream. Psychoanalysts believe that dreams contain information about the individual's unconscious thoughts and conflicts.

Dream analysis *is the psychotherapeutic technique psychoanalysts use to interpret a client's dreams. Psychoanalysts believe that dreams contain information about the individual's unconscious thoughts and conflicts.* Freud distinguished between the dream's manifest and latent content. **Manifest content** *is the psychoanalytic term for the conscious, remembered aspects of a dream.* **Latent content** *is the psychoanalytic term for the unconscious, unremembered, symbolic aspects of a dream.* A psychoanalyst interprets a dream by analyzing its manifest content for disguised unconscious wishes and needs, especially those that are sexual and aggressive. For some examples of the sexual symbols psychoanalysts use to interpret dreams, turn to figure 12.2. Freud cautioned against overinterpreting, however. Once Freud was challenged about possibly having an oral fixation himself, symbolized by his relentless cigar smoking. In response, he quipped, "Sometimes a cigar is just a cigar."

manifest content

The psychoanalytic term for the conscious, remembered aspects of a dream.

latent content

The psychoanalytic term for the unconscious, unremembered, symbolic aspects of a dream.

Freud also believed that transference was an inevitable and essential aspect of the analyst-client relationship. **Transference** *is the psychoanalytic term for the client's relating to the analyst in ways that reproduce or relive important relationships in the client's life.* A client might interact with an analyst as if the analyst were a parent or lover, for example. When transference dominates therapy, the client's comments may become directed toward the analyst's personal life. Transference is often difficult to overcome in psychotherapy. However, transference can be used therapeutically as a model of how clients relate to important people in their lives.

transference

The psychoanalytic term for a client's relating to an analyst in ways that reproduce or relive important relationships in the client's life.

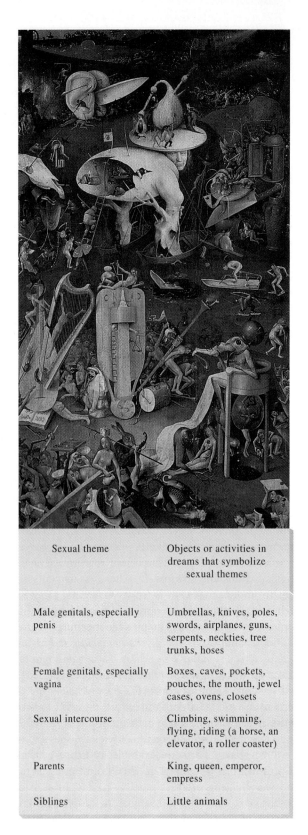

Sexual theme	Objects or activities in dreams that symbolize sexual themes
Male genitals, especially penis	Umbrellas, knives, poles, swords, airplanes, guns, serpents, neckties, tree trunks, hoses
Female genitals, especially vagina	Boxes, caves, pockets, pouches, the mouth, jewel cases, ovens, closets
Sexual intercourse	Climbing, swimming, flying, riding (a horse, an elevator, a roller coaster)
Parents	King, queen, emperor, empress
Siblings	Little animals

*F*IGURE 12.2

The Psychoanalyst's Interpretation of Sexual Symbolism in Dreams

resistance

The psychoanalytic term for a client's unconscious defense strategies that prevent the analyst from understanding the client's problems.

Resistance *is the psychoanalytic term for a client's unconscious defense strategies that prevent the analyst from understanding the client's problems.* Resistance occurs because it is painful to bring conflicts into conscious awareness. By resisting therapy, individuals do not have to face their problems. Showing up late or missing sessions, arguing with the psychoanalyst, or faking free associations are examples of resistance. Some clients go on

To encourage his patients to relax, Freud had them recline on the couch in his study while he sat in the chair on the left, out of their view.

endlessly about a trivial matter to avoid facing their conflicts. A major goal to the analyst is to break through this resistance.

> *Psychotherapy, unlike castor oil which will work no matter how you get it down, is useless when forced on an uncooperative patient.*
> —ABIGAIL VAN BUREN, *American Advice Columnist, 20th Century*

Current Psychodynamic Therapies. Although the face of psychodynamic therapy has changed extensively since its inception almost a century ago, many contemporary psychodynamic therapists still probe clients' unconscious thoughts about their earliest childhood experiences to provide clues to their clients' current problems (Wallerstein, 1992). Many contemporary psychodynamic therapists also try to help clients gain insight into their emotionally laden, repressed conflicts (Horowitz, 1998; Strupp, 1992).

However, only a small percentage of contemporary psychodynamic therapists rigorously follow Freud's guidelines. Many psychodynamic therapists still emphasize the importance of unconscious thought and early family experiences, but they also accord more power to the conscious mind and current relationships in understanding a client's problems. Clients rarely see their therapist several times a week. Now clients usually have weekly appointments.

> *Fortunately, analysis is not the only way to resolve inner conflicts. Life itself still remains a very effective therapist.*
> —KAREN HORNEY, *American psychotherapist, 20th Century*

Contemporary psychodynamic approaches emphasize the development of the self in social contexts (Erikson, 1968; Kohut, 1977; Mahler, 1979). In Heinz Kohut's view, early relationships with attachment figures, such as one's parents, are critical. As we develop, we do not relinquish these attachments; we continue to need them. Kohut's prescription for therapy involves getting the patient to identify and seek out appropriate relationships with others. He also wants patients to develop more realistic appraisals of relationships. Kohut believes that therapists need to interact with their clients in ways that are empathic and understanding. As we will see next, empathy and understanding are absolute cornerstones for humanistic therapists as they encourage their clients to further their sense of self.

humanistic psychotherapies

Therapies that encourage clients to understand themselves and to grow personally by emphasizing conscious thoughts rather than unconscious thoughts, the present rather than the past, and growth and fulfillment rather than curing illness.

Humanistic Therapies

In the **humanistic psychotherapies,** *clients are encouraged to understand themselves and to grow personally. In contrast to psychodynamic therapies, humanistic therapies emphasize conscious thoughts rather than unconscious thoughts, the present rather than the past, and growth and fulfillment rather than curing illness.* Two main forms of the humanistic psychotherapies are person-centered therapy and Gestalt therapy.

Fritz Perls was the founder of Gestalt therapy.

person-centered therapy

A form of humanistic therapy developed by Carl Rogers, in which the therapist provides a warm, supportive atmosphere to improve the client's self-concept and encourage the client to gain insight about problems.

genuineness

The Rogerian concept of the importance of the therapist's being genuine and not hiding behind a facade.

accurate empathy

Rogers's term for the therapist's ability to identify with the client.

active listening

Rogers's term for the ability to listen to another person with total attention to what the person says and means.

Gestalt therapy

A humanistic therapy developed by Fritz Perls, in which the therapist questions and challenges clients to help them become more aware of their feelings and face their problems.

Person-Centered Therapy.   **Person-centered therapy** *is a form of humanistic therapy developed by Carl Rogers in which the therapist provides a warm, supportive atmosphere to improve the client's self-concept and encourage the client to gain insight about problems.* Rogers's therapy was initially called client-centered therapy, but he rechristened it person-centered therapy to underscore his deep belief that everyone has the ability to grow (Rogers, 1961, 1980). The relationship between the therapist and the person is an important aspect of Rogers's therapy. The therapist must enter into an intensely personal relationship with the client, not as a physician diagnosing a disease but as one human being to another. Notice that Rogers referred to the "client" and then the "person" rather than the "patient." Rogers's approach demonstrates a strong individualistic bias that would fare best in cultures that stress the value of the individual.

Recall from chapter 10 that Rogers believed that each of us grows up in a world filled with *conditions of worth;* the positive regard we receive from others has strings attached. We usually do not receive love and praise unless we conform to the standards and demands of others. This causes us to be unhappy and have low self-esteem as adults; rarely do we think that we measure up to such standards or think that we are as good as others expect us to be.

To free the person from worry about the demands of society, the therapist creates a warm and caring environment. A Rogerian therapist tries to avoid disapproving of what a client says or does. Rogers believed this *unconditional positive regard* improved the person's self-esteem. The therapist's role is "nondirective"—that is, he or she does not try to lead the client to any particular revelation. The therapist is there to listen sympathetically to the client's problems and to encourage greater self-regard, independent self-appraisal, and decision making.

Rogers advocated other techniques in addition to using unconditional positive regard. **Genuineness** *is the Rogerian concept of the importance of the therapist's being genuine and not hiding behind a facade. Therapists must let clients know their feelings.* **Accurate empathy** *is Rogers's term for the therapist's ability to identify with the client.* Rogers believed that therapists must sense what it is like to be the client at any moment in the client-therapist relationship. **Active listening** *is Rogers's term for the ability to listen to another person with total attention to what that person says and means.* One way therapists improve active listening is by restating or paraphrasing what the client said. Clients report that this practice helps them feel supported in order to gain the courage to make changes they wish to make.

Gestalt Therapy.   **Gestalt therapy** *is a humanistic therapy, developed by Frederick (Fritz) Perls (1893–1970), in which the therapist questions and challenges clients to help them become more aware of their feelings and face their problems.* Perls was trained in Europe as a Freudian psychoanalyst, but as his career developed his ideas became noticeably different from Freud's. Perls agreed with Freud that psychological problems originate in unresolved past conflicts and that these conflicts need to be acknowledged and worked through. Also like Freud, Perls (1969) stressed that interpretation of dreams is an important aspect of therapy.

In other ways, however, Perls and Freud were miles apart. Perls believed that unresolved conflicts should be brought to bear on the here and now of the individual's life. The therapist *pushes* clients into deciding whether they will continue to allow the past to control their future or whether they will choose *right now* what they want to be in the future. To this end, Perls *confronted* individuals and encouraged them to actively control their lives and to be open about their feelings.

Gestalt therapists use a number of techniques to encourage individuals to be open about their feelings, to develop self-awareness, and to actively control their lives. The therapist sets examples, encourages congruence between verbal and nonverbal behavior, and uses role playing. To demonstrate an important point to a client, a Gestalt therapist might exaggerate a client's characteristic. To stimulate change, the therapist might openly confront the client.

Another technique of Gestalt therapy is role playing, by either the client, the therapist, or both. For example, if an individual is bothered by conflict with her mother, the therapist might play the role of the mother and reopen the quarrel. The therapist may encourage the individual to act out her hostile feelings toward her mother by yelling, swearing, or kicking the couch, for example. In this way, Gestalt therapists hope to help individuals better manage their feelings instead of letting their feelings control them.

As you probably noticed, a Gestalt therapist is much more directive than a person-centered therapist. By being more directive, the Gestalt therapist provides more interpretation and feedback. Nonetheless, both of these humanistic therapies encourage individuals to take responsibility for their feelings and actions, to understand their true selves, to develop a sense of freedom, and to look at what they are doing with their lives.

Now that we have studied the insight therapies, we will turn our attention to therapies that take a very different approach to working with individuals to reduce their problems and improve their adjustment—the behavior therapies.

eview

Psychodynamic and Humanistic Therapies

Psychodynamic therapies stress the importance of the unconscious mind, early family experiences, and extensive interpretation by the therapist. Psychoanalysis is Freud's technique for analyzing an individual's unconscious thought. Free association, catharsis, interpretation, dream analysis, transference, and resistance are techniques used in psychoanalytic therapy. Although psychodynamic therapy has changed, many contemporary psychodynamic therapists still probe the unconscious mind for early family experiences that might provide clues to the client's current problems. The development of the self in social contexts is an important theme in Kohut's contemporary approach.

In the humanistic therapies, clients are encouraged to understand themselves and to grow personally. The humanistic therapies emphasize conscious thoughts, the present, and growth and fulfillment. Person-centered therapy, developed by Rogers, emphasizes that the therapist should provide a warm and supportive atmosphere to improve the client's self-image and to encourage the client to gain insight into problems. The therapist replaces conditions of worth with unconditional positive regard and uses genuineness, accurate empathy, and active listening to raise the client's self-esteem. Gestalt therapy, developed by Fritz Perls, emphasizes that the therapist should question and challenge clients in order to help them become more aware of their feelings and face their problems. Gestalt therapy is more directive than is the nondirective approach of person-centered therapy.

Behavior Therapies

behavior therapies

Therapies that use principles of learning to reduce or eliminate maladaptive behavior.

Behavior therapies *use principles of learning to reduce or eliminate maladaptive behavior.* Behavior therapies are based on the behavioral theory of learning and personality described in chapters 5 and 10. Behavior therapists do not search for unconscious conflicts, like psychodynamic therapists, or encourage individuals to develop accurate perceptions of their feelings and self, like humanistic therapists. Insight and self-awareness are not the keys to helping individuals develop more adaptive behavior patterns, say the behavior therapists. The insight therapies—psychodynamic and humanistic—treat maladaptive symptoms as signs of underlying, internal problems. Behavior therapists, however, assume that the overt maladaptive symptoms are the problem. Individuals can become aware of why they are depressed and still be depressed, say the behavior therapists. A behavior therapist tries to eliminate the depressed symptoms or behaviors themselves rather than try to get individuals to gain insight or awareness about why they are depressed (O'Donahue & Krasner, 1995).

Behavior therapists initially based their interventions almost exclusively on the learning principles of classical and operant conditioning, but behavior therapies have become more diverse in recent years. As cognitive social learning theory grew in popularity and the cognitive approach became more prominent in psychology, behavior therapists increasingly included cognitive factors in their therapy.

Classical Conditioning Approaches.   In chapter 5, you learned how we acquire, or learn, some behaviors, especially fears, through classical conditioning and that these behaviors can be unlearned, or extinguished. If an individual has learned to fear snakes or heights through classical conditioning, perhaps the individual could unlearn the fear. Two procedures based on classical conditioning that are used in behavior therapy are systematic desensitization and aversive conditioning.

systematic desensitization

A method of behavior therapy that treats anxiety by associating deep relaxation with successive visualizations of increasingly intense anxiety-producing situations; this technique is based on classical conditioning.

Systematic Desensitization. **Systematic desensitization** *is a method of behavior therapy that treats anxiety by associating deep relaxation with successive visualization of increasingly intense anxiety-producing situations; this technique is based on classical conditioning.* (Wolpe, 1963). Consider the common fear of taking a test. Using systematic desensitization, a behavior therapist first asks the client which aspects of the fearful situation—in this case, taking a test—are the most and least frightening. Then, the behavior therapist arranges these circumstances in order from most to least frightening. An example of this type of desensitization hierarchy is shown in figure 12.3.

The next step is to teach individuals to relax. Behavior therapists teach clients to recognize the presence of muscular contractions, or tensions, in various parts of their bodies and then to contract and relax different muscles. Once individuals are relaxed, the therapist asks them to imagine the least fearful stimulus in the hierarchy. Subsequently the therapist moves up the list of items from least to most fearful while the clients remain relaxed. Eventually individuals are able to imagine the most fearful circumstance without being afraid. In this manner, individuals learn to relax while thinking about anxiety-provoking ideas.

Researchers have found that systematic desensitization is often an effective treatment for a number of phobias, such as fear of giving a speech, fear of heights, fear of flying, fear of dogs, and fear of snakes. If you were afraid of snakes, for instance, the therapist might initially have you watch someone handle a snake. Then the therapist would ask you to engage in increasingly more fearful behaviors—you might first just go into the same room with the snake, next you would approach the snake, subsequently you would touch the snake, and eventually you would play with the snake (Bandura, Blanchard, & Ritter, 1969).

aversive conditioning

An approach to behavior therapy that involves repeated pairings of an undesirable behavior with aversive stimuli to decrease the behavior's rewards so that the individual will stop doing it; this technique is based on classical conditioning.

Aversive Conditioning. **Aversive conditioning** *is an approach to behavior therapy that involves repeated pairings of an undesirable behavior with aversive stimuli to decrease the behavior's rewards so the individual will stop doing it; this technique is based on classical conditioning.* Aversive conditioning is used to teach people to avoid such behaviors as smoking, overeating, and drinking. Electric shocks, nausea-inducing substances, and verbal insults are some of the noxious stimuli used in aversive conditioning (Bernstein, 1991).

How would aversive conditioning be used to reduce a person's alcohol consumption? Prior to drinking an alcoholic beverage, a person consumes a mixture that induced nausea. In classical conditioning terminology, the alcoholic beverage is the conditioned stimulus and the nausea-inducing agent is the unconditioned stimulus. By repeatedly pairing alcohol with the nausea-inducing agent, alcohol becomes the conditioned stimulus that

1. On the way to the university on the day of an examination
2. In the process of answering an examination paper
3. Before the unopened doors of the examination room
4. Awaiting the distribution of examination papers
5. The examination paper lies face down before her
6. The night before an examination
7. One day before an examination
8. Two days before an examination
9. Three days before an examination
10. Four days before an examination
11. Five days before an examination
12. A week before an examination
13. Two weeks before an examination
14. A month before an examination

*F*IGURE 12.3

A Desensitization Hierarchy from Most to Least Feared Circumstances

"Leave us alone! I am a behavior therapist! I am helping my patient overcome a fear of heights!"

© 1990 by Sidney Harris.

elicits nausea, the conditioned response. As a consequence, alcohol is no longer associated with something pleasant but, rather, is associated with something highly unpleasant.

Operant Conditioning Approaches. Andy is a college student who has difficulty studying. He complains that he always starts to fall asleep when he goes to his desk to study. He has decided to see a therapist about how he might improve his studying because his grades are deteriorating. The behavior therapist's first recommendation is to replace his desk lamp's 40-watt bulb with a brighter one. The second recommendation is to turn his desk away from his bed. The third recommendation is to do only schoolwork at his desk; he is not allowed to write a letter, read a magazine, or daydream while at the desk. If he wants to do any of these other things, he must leave his desk.

To help Andy improve his study habits, the behavior therapist first evaluated Andy's responses to the stimuli in his room. Then the therapist gave Andy direct and precise suggestions about what to do. The therapist did not spend time analyzing his unconscious conflicts or encouraging him to "get in touch with his feelings." Rather, the therapist wanted to change Andy's responses to the environmental stimuli that were causing the problem.

When we discussed operant conditioning in chapter 5, we examined how an individual's behavior is controlled by its consequences. We also discussed *behavior modification,* which is often used by behavior therapists. The idea behind behavior modification is to replace unacceptable, maladaptive responses with acceptable, adaptive ones. Consequences are set up to ensure that acceptable responses are reinforced and unacceptable ones are not (Bergin & Garfield, 1994).

A **token economy** *is a behavior modification system in which behaviors are reinforced with tokens (such as poker chips) that can be exchanged later for desired rewards (such as candy, money, or going to a movie).* Behavior therapists have implemented token economies in a number of classrooms, institutions for the mentally retarded, homes for delinquents, and mental hospitals with schizophrenics.

In some instances, behavior modification works; in others it does not. One person may become so wedded to the tokens that, when they are removed, the positive behavior associated with the tokens disappears. Yet another person might continue the positive behavior after the tokens are removed. Some critics object to behavior modification because they believe such extensive control of another person's behavior unethically infringes on the individual's rights. However, as with the college student who could not study, maladaptive responses can be turned into adaptive ones through behavior modification.

The behavior therapies you have just read about do not include cognitive processes in their effort to modify the behavior of individuals with problems. As we will see next, cognitive therapy gives thought processes a more prominent role in helping individuals reduce their problems and improve their adjustment.

Cognitive Behavior Therapy. **Cognitive behavior therapy** *is an approach to behavior therapy that tries to help individuals behave more adaptively by modifying their thoughts. Cognitive behavior therapy stems from both cognitive psychology, with its emphasis on the effect of thoughts on behavior, and behaviorism, with its emphasis on behavior-change techniques.* Cognitive behavior therapists strive to change misconceptions, strengthen coping skills, increase self-control, and encourage constructive self-reflection (Meichenbaum, 1993).

token economy

A behavior modification system in which behaviors are reinforced with tokens (such as poker chips) that can be exchanged later for desired rewards (such as candy, money, or going to a movie).

cognitive behavior therapy

An approach to behavior therapy that tries to help individuals behave more adaptively by modifying their thoughts.

self-efficacy
The belief that one can master a situation and produce positive outcomes.

An important aspect of cognitive behavior therapy is **self-efficacy,** *the belief that one can master a situation and produce positive outcomes.* Self-efficacy is especially important in developing adaptive behavior according to social learning therapist Albert Bandura. Moreover, Bandura (1997) believes that self-efficacy is the key to successful therapy. At each step of the therapy process, people need to bolster their confidence by telling themselves, "I'm going to master this problem," "I can do it," "I'm improving; I'm getting better," and so on. As people gain confidence and engage in adaptive behavior, the successes become intrinsically motivating. Before long, individuals persist with considerable effort in their attempts to solve their problems because of the positive outcomes that were set in motion by self-efficacy.

self-instructional methods
Cognitive behavioral techniques aimed at teaching individuals to modify their own behavior.

Self-instructional methods *are cognitive behavior techniques aimed at teaching individuals to modify their own behavior* (Meichenbaum, 1977). Using self-instructional methods, cognitive behavior therapists try to get clients to change what they say to themselves. The therapist gives the client examples of constructive statements, known as "reinforcing self-statements," that the client can repeat in order to take positive steps to handle stress or meet a goal. The therapist also encourages the client to practice the statements through role playing and strengthens the client's newly acquired skills through reinforcements. To read about some strategies for talking to yourself in stressful circumstances, see Improving Personal and Cognitive Skills.

Cognitive Therapies

cognitive therapies
Therapies that emphasize that an individual's cognitions, or thoughts, are the main source of abnormal behavior; cognitive therapies attempt to change the individual's feelings and behaviors by changing her or his cognitions.

D., a 21-year-old single, undergraduate student has delusions that he is evil. He perceives himself as a failure in school and a failure to his parents. He is preoccupied with negative thoughts, dwells on his problems, and exaggerates his faults. Such thinking is common among depressed individuals, and suggests that cognitive therapy might be a viable approach to treat D.'s depression. The **cognitive therapies** *emphasize that the individual's cognitions or thoughts are the main source of abnormal behavior. Cognitive therapies attempt to change the individual's feelings and behaviors by changing cognitions.* Cognitive therapies differ from psychoanalytic therapies by focusing more on overt symptoms instead of deep-seated unconscious thoughts, by providing more structure to the individual's

*I*mproving Personal and Cognitive Skills
Changing What You Say to Yourself

Cognitive behavior therapy tries to get people to change what they say to themselves. Following is a series of statements people can use to help them prepare for stress, confront the stress, cope with feelings at critical moments, and reinforce themselves (Meichenbaum, Turk, & Burstein, 1975):

- **Preparing for Stress**

  What do I have to do?

  I'm going to map out a plan to deal with it.

  I'll just think about what I have to do.

  I won't worry. Worry doesn't help anything.

  I have a lot of different strategies to call on.

- **Confronting the Stress**

  I can meet the challenge.

  I'll just keep taking one step at a time.

I can handle it. I'll just relax, breathe deeply, and use one of the strategies.

I won't think about the pain. I'll focus on what I have to do.

- **Coping with Feelings at Critical Moments**

  What is it I have to do?

  I was supposed to expect the pain to increase. I just have to keep myself in control.

  When the pain comes, I'll just pause and keep focusing on what I have to do.

- **Reinforcing Self-Statements**

  Good, I did it.

  I handled it well.

  I knew I could do it.

  Wait until I tell other people how I did it!

thoughts, and by being less concerned about the origin of the problem. However, the cognitive therapies are less likely than the cognitive behavior therapies to use structured training sessions that require the individual to practice prescribed exercises. Instead the cognitive therapies are more likely to adhere to a conversational format. The cognitive therapies also are less interested than the cognitive behavior therapies in manipulating the environment to increase adaptive behavior.

In recent years many therapists have focused more strongly on the cognitive perspective in their practices (Mahoney, 1993). Two of the most important cognitive therapies are Albert Ellis's rational emotive therapy and Aaron Beck's cognitive therapy.

Rational-Emotive Therapy. *Rational-emotive therapy* *is based on Albert Ellis's assertion that individuals become psychologically disordered because of their beliefs, especially those that are irrational and self-defeating.* Ellis (1962, 1996) says that we usually talk to ourselves when we experience stress; too often the statements are irrational, making them more harmful than helpful.

Ellis abbreviated the therapy process into the letters *A, B, C, D, E*. Therapy usually starts at *C*, the individual's upsetting emotional Consequence; this might involve depression, anxiety, or a feeling of worthlessness. The individual often says that C was caused by A, the *Activating Experience*, such as a blowup in marital relations, loss of job, or failure in school. The therapist works with the individual to show that an intervening factor, B, the individual's *Belief System*, is actually responsible for why he moved from A to C. Then the therapist goes on to D, which stands for *Disputation*; at this point, the individual's irrational beliefs are disputed or contested by the therapist. Finally, E is reached, which stands for *Effects* or outcomes of the rational-emotive therapy, as when individuals put their changed beliefs to work. A summary of the A–E steps is presented in figure 12.4.

Beck's Cognitive Therapy. Aaron Beck (1976, 1993) developed a form of cognitive therapy to treat psychological dysfunctions, especially depression. He believes the most effective therapy with depressed individuals involves four phases: (1) The depressed clients are shown how to identify self-labels—that is, how they view themselves; (2) They are taught to notice when they are thinking distorted or irrational thoughts; (3) They learn how to substitute appropriate thoughts for inappropriate ones; (4) They are given feedback and motivating comments from the therapist to stimulate their use of these techniques.

Results from a large-scale study by the National Institute of Mental Health (NIMH) supports the belief that Beck's cognitive therapy is an effective treatment for depression (Mervis, 1986). Aaron Beck and his colleagues conducted this therapy with moderately to severely depressed individuals for 16 weeks at three different sites. The symptoms of depression were eliminated completely in more than 50 percent of the individuals receiving Beck's cognitive therapy, compared to only 29 percent in a comparison group (Clark & Beck, 1989).

A comparison group is an important feature in most psychological research. Without a comparison group the researchers in the NIMH study would have had no way of knowing if the symptoms of depression in the experimental group would have disappeared even without therapy. That is, it is possible that in any random sample of depressed individuals, more than 50 percent show a remission of symptoms over a 16-week period, regardless of whether or not they receive therapy. Because only 29 percent

*𝒻*IGURE 12.4
A–E Steps in Ellis's Rational Emotive Therapy

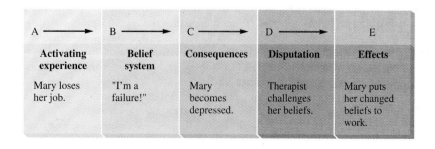

A ⟶	B ⟶	C ⟶	D ⟶	E
Activating experience	**Belief system**	**Consequences**	**Disputation**	**Effects**
Mary loses her job.	"I'm a failure!"	Mary becomes depressed.	Therapist challenges her beliefs.	Mary puts her changed beliefs to work.

$\mathcal{I}$mproving Personal and Cognitive Skills

Conquering Depression

Depression can almost always be helped. Following are some strategies for reducing depression and improving mood:

- *Cognitive restructuring.*
  Almost everyone who is depressed is very self-critical. They think or say things like, "I must be worthless, for all of those bad things to have happened to me." Cognitive restructuring involves evaluating your negative thoughts and learning to think in more positive, adaptive ways.
- *Improving interpersonal relationships.*
  Many people who are depressed have interpersonal relationships that are problematic. If people are in an abusive relationship or a relationship in which someone constantly criticizes them, it can be hard to recover from depression. Couples therapy or family therapy may help. So can a good friend.
- *Activity scheduling.*
  Activities can be connected to the way people feel. People who are depressed often are passive or inactive. A positive strategy for coping with depression is to become more involved in pleasurable activities. When we do activities

that are enjoyable or activities that accomplish something, we usually feel better. Examples of enjoyable activities are talking with a friend, listening to music, playing a computer game, building furniture, taking a walk, and going to a favorite sporting event, movie, symphony, and so on.
- *Exercise.*
  Researchers have found that exercise is an excellent antidote for depression. As we just mentioned, people who are depressed often are inactive. A regular exercise program can improve mood considerably.
- *Medication.*
  About two of every three people who are depressed can be helped to some degree by antidepressant medication. If you are depressed or know someone who is depressed, consultation with a physician or psychiatrist will inform you about different antidepressant medications.
- *Become more knowledgeable about depression and how to overcome it.*
  David Burns's *Feeling Good* and *The Feeling Good Workbook* (1980) are described in the resources section at the end of this chapter. They are excellent, easy-to-read books on what depression is and how to conquer it.

of the depressed individuals in the comparison group were free of their symptoms, the researchers had good reason to believe that the cognitive therapy—which produced more than a 50 percent remission of symptoms—was effective. To read further about strategies for reducing depression, see Improving Personal and Cognitive Skills.

At this point we have discussed four major approaches to therapy—psychodynamic, humanistic, behavioral, and cognitive. Next we will study "systems" approaches to therapy that focus on treatment in various kinds of group settings. Table 12.2 will help you keep the approaches straight in your mind.

$\mathcal{R}$eview

Behavior and Cognitive Therapies

Behavior therapies use principles of learning to reduce or eliminate maladaptive behavior. Behavior therapies are based on behavioral theories of learning and personality. Behavior therapists try to eliminate symptoms or behaviors rather than trying to get individuals to gain insight into their problems. Two classical conditioning procedures used in behavior therapy are systematic desensitization and aversive conditioning. Operant conditioning approaches emphasize modifying an individual's maladaptive responses to the environment. The idea behind behavior modification is to replace unacceptable,

maladaptive responses with acceptable, adaptive ones. Consequences are set up to ensure that acceptable responses are reinforced; unacceptable ones are not. A token economy is an example of behavior modification. Cognitive behavior therapy tries to help individuals behave more adaptively by modifying their thoughts. Cognitive behavior therapists strive to change misconceptions, strengthen coping skills, increase self-control, and encourage constructive self-talk.

Cognitive therapies include rational-emotive therapy and cognitive therapy. Rational-emotive therapy, developed by

Albert Ellis, is based on the idea that individuals become psychologically disabled because of their beliefs, especially those that are irrational and self-defeating; therapy is designed to change these beliefs. Aaron Beck developed a form of cognitive therapy to treat psychological disorders, especially depression. The therapy involves identifying self-labels, detecting irrational thoughts, substituting appropriate for inappropriate thoughts, and receiving feedback from the therapist to stimulate these cognitive changes.

TABLE 12.2

A Comparison of Psychotherapies

Dimension of therapy	Psychodynamic orientation	Humanistic orientation	Behavioral orientation	Cognitive orientation
Focus of treatment	Problem focus; symptoms represent deep-seated unresolved unconscious conflicts	Person focus; individuals fail to function at an optimal level of development	Problem focus; challenges come from maladaptive behavior patterns	Situation focus; difficulties arise from inappropriate cognition
Therapy objective	Insight into underlying unconscious conflicts	Insight into inherent potential for growth	Action by learning more adaptive behavior	Insight and action geared toward changing cognition
Nature of therapy and techniques	Psychoanalysis, including free association, dream analysis, resistance, and transference; therapist interprets heavily	Person-centered therapy, including unconditional positive regard, genuineness, accurate empathy, and active listening; Gestalt therapy including confrontation to encourage honest expression of feelings; self-appreciation emphasized	Observation of behavior and its controlling conditions; specific advice given about what should be done; therapies based on classical conditioning, operant conditioning; also includes cognitive behavior therapy (self-efficacy, self-instructional methods)	Conversation with client designed to get him or her to change irrational and self-defeating beliefs; therapies emphasizing self-efficacy and self-instruction

SYSTEMS INTERVENTIONS

A major issue in therapy is how it can be structured to reach more people and at less cost. One way to address this problem is for therapists to see clients in a group rather than individually. A second way is through community psychology approaches. These approaches have the advantage of working with individuals in the context of a larger system.

Group Therapies

Nine people make their way into a room, each looking tentatively at the others. Although each person has met the therapist during a diagnostic interview, no one knows any of the other clients. Some of the people seem reluctant, others enthusiastic. All are willing to follow the therapist's recommendation that group therapy might help each of them learn to cope better with their problems. As they sit down and wait for the session

Family systems therapy has become increasingly popular in recent years. In family systems therapy, the assumption is that psychological adjustment is related to patterns of interaction within the family unit.

to begin, one thinks, "Will they really understand me?" Another wonders, "Do the others have problems like mine?" Yet another thinks, "Can I stick my neck out with these people?"

Individual therapy is often expensive and time consuming. Freud believed that therapy is a long process and saw clients as often as three to five times a week for a number of years. Advocates of group therapy stress that individual therapy is limited because the client is seen outside the normal context of relationships, relationships that may hold the key to successful therapy. Many psychological problems develop in the context of interpersonal relationships—within one's family, marriage, or peer group, for example. By seeing individuals in the context of these important groups, therapy may be more successful (Fuhrman & Burlingame, 1995).

Group therapy is diversified. Some therapists practice psychodynamic, humanistic, behavior, or cognitive therapy. Others use group approaches that are not based on the major psychotherapeutic perspectives. Six features make group therapy an attractive format (Yalom, 1995):

1. *Information.* Individuals receive information about their problems from either the group leader or other group members.
2. *Universality.* Many individuals develop the sense that they are the only persons who have such frightening and unacceptable impulses. In the group, individuals observe that others also feel anguish and suffering.
3. *Altruism.* Group members support one another with advice and sympathy and learn that they have something to offer others.
4. *Corrective recapitulation of the family group.* A therapy group often resembles a family (and, in family therapy, the group *is* a family), with the leaders representing parents and the other members' siblings. In this "new" family, old wounds can be healed and new, more positive "family" ties made.
5. *Development of social skills.* Corrective feedback from peers can modify flaws in an individual's interpersonal skills. A self-centered individual might see that he is self-centered if five other group members inform him about his self-centeredness; in individual therapy, he may not believe the therapist.
6. *Interpersonal learning.* The group can serve as a training ground for practicing new behaviors and relationships. For example, a hostile woman might learn that she can get along better with others by not behaving so aggressively.

Family and Couple Therapy.   "A friend loves you for your intelligence, a mistress for your charm, but your family's love is unreasoning; you were born into it and are of its flesh and blood. Nevertheless, it can irritate you more than any group of people in the world," commented French biographer André Maurois. His statement suggests that the family may be the source of an individual's problems. **Family therapy** *is group therapy with family members.* **Couple therapy** *is group therapy with married or unmarried couples whose major problem is their relationship.* These approaches stress that, although one person may have some abnormal symptoms, the symptoms are a function of family or couple relationships (Barker, 1998; Combrink-Graham, 1998; Lebow & Gurman, 1995). Psychodynamic, humanistic, or behavior therapies may be used in family or couple therapy, but the main form of family therapy is family systems therapy.

Family systems therapy *is a form of therapy based on the assumption that psychological adjustment is related to patterns of interaction within the family unit.* Families who do not function well foster abnormal behavior on the part of one or more of their members (Minuchin, 1985; Satir, 1964). Four of the most widely used family systems therapy techniques are these:

1. *Validation.* The therapist expresses an understanding and acceptance of each family member's feelings and beliefs and, thus, validates the person. When the therapist talks with each family member, she finds something positive to say.
2. *Reframing.* The therapist teaches families to reframe problems; problems are cast as a family problem, not an individual's problem. For example, the family therapist reframes the problems of a delinquent adolescent in terms of how each family mem-

family therapy
Group therapy with family members.

couple therapy
Group therapy with married or unmarried couples whose major problem is their relationship.

family systems therapy
A form of therapy based on the assumption that psychological adjustment is related to patterns of interaction within the family unit.

ber contributed to the situation. The father's lack of attention to his son and marital conflict may be involved.

3. *Structural change.* The family systems therapist tries to *restructure* the coalitions in a family. In a mother-son coalition, the therapist might suggest that the father take a stronger disciplinarian role to relieve the mother of some of the burden. Restructuring might be as simple as suggesting that parents explore satisfying ways to be together; the therapist may recommend that, once a week, the parents go out for a quiet dinner together, for example.

4. *Detriangulation.* In some families, one member is the scapegoat for two other members who are in conflict but pretend not to be. For example, in the triangle of two parents and one child, the parents may insist that their marriage is fine but find themselves in subtle conflict over how to handle the child. The therapist tries to disentangle, or *detriangulate,* this situation by shifting attention away from the child and toward the conflict between the parents.

Although many of the principles of family therapy can be applied to most families, cross-cultural psychologists caution against transferring a Western view of family dynamics to other cultures. Unique sociohistorical, cultural circumstances experienced by different ethnic minority groups also require certain considerations. To read about some of the considerations regarding family therapy in African American families, see Sociocultural Worlds.

Couple therapy proceeds in much the same way as family therapy. Conflict in marriages and in relationships between unmarried individuals frequently involves poor communication. In some instances, communication has broken down entirely. The therapist

$\mathcal{S}$ociocultural Worlds

Family Therapy with African Americans

Family therapists who work with African American families are often called on to fulfill various roles, such as educator, director, advocate, problem solver, and role model. As a therapist takes on these roles, he or she must recognize that the clients are members of a community, as well as individuals or members of families (Aponte, 1979). The following case study illustrates some of the multiple roles and the community orientation that a therapist must be aware of in working with African American families (Grevious, 1985).

Mrs. B. entered family therapy because her 11-year-old son Todd was disruptive in school and falling behind in his work. She complained of feeling overwhelmed and not being able to cope with the situation. The therapist conducted a home visit and observed that the family lived in a run-down building in a poor neighborhood. Even so, the therapist found that Mrs. B.'s apartment was immaculate, work and sleep space had been set aside for Todd. It was obvious from the well-worn Bible on the coffee table and the religious paintings and calendars on the walls that Mrs. B. had strong religious convictions. The therapist discovered that Mrs. B.'s strong-willed mother recently had moved into the apartment after an incapacitating leg operation. The grandmother's diabetes created additional stress in the home. Despite her illness, the grandmother tried to exercise considerable control over Mrs. B. and Todd, causing a power struggle in the family. The therapist also learned that Mrs. B. had recently stopped attending church. After the

therapist encouraged her to attend church again, Mrs. B.'s spirits improved considerably. In addition, the grandmother joined a senior citizens program, which transported her to the center three times a week and to church two Sundays a month. These increased community activities for the grandmother had a positive impact on the family.

Family therapists who see African American clients also believe that it is important to provide concrete advice or assistance (Foley, 1975). If the problem is a parent-child relationship, for example, a family therapist might recommend that the parents participate in a parent training program, rather than conduct insight therapy. Also, therapists may occasionally need to educate African American families about social service programs and the difficulties they might encounter in gaining access to those programs.

A family therapist who works with African American families also needs to emphasize their strengths, such as pride in being African American, the extended family, and religion, as well as take into consideration their vulnerabilities, such as the impact of racism, discrimination, and victimization (Boyd-Franklin, 1989). Therapists might need to advocate for African American clients whose strain lies in trying to adjust to demands that might be unfair or discriminatory. In addition, therapists need to recognize that there will be diversity of experience among African American families. More about therapy with African Americans and other ethnic minorities appears later in the chapter

tries to improve the communication between the partners. In some cases, she will focus on the roles partners play: one may be "strong," the other "weak"; one may be "responsible," the other "spoiled," for example. Couple therapy addresses diverse problems such as jealousy, sexual messages, delayed childbearing, infidelity, gender roles, two-career families, divorce, and remarriage (Sullivan & Christensen, 1998). Now we turn our attention to other forms of group therapy—personal growth and self-help groups.

Systems approaches do not always have to be conducted by trained therapists to be effective. Personal growth groups and encounter groups use the power of peers as the therapy agent.

Personal Growth Groups. A number of group therapies in recent years have focused on people whose lives are lacking in intimacy, intensity, and accomplishment. **Personal growth groups** *have their roots in the humanistic therapies; they emphasize personal growth and increased openness and honesty in interpersonal relations.*

An **encounter group** *is a personal growth group designed to promote self-understanding through candid group interaction.* For example, one member of an assembled group thinks he is better than everyone else. After several minutes of listening to the guy's insufferable bragging, one group member says, "Look, jerk, nobody here likes you; I would like to sell you for what you think you are worth and buy you for what you are actually worth!" Other members of the group might also criticize the braggart. Outside of an encounter group, most people probably would not confront someone about bragging; in an encounter group, they may feel free to express their true feelings about each other.

Encounter groups improve the psychological adjustment of some individuals, but not others. For example, in one study, the majority of college students who were members of an encounter group felt better about themselves and got along better with others than did their counterparts who were not involved in an encounter group (Lieberman, Yalom, & Miles, 1973). However, 8 percent of the participants in the encounter group felt that the experience was harmful. For the most part, they blamed the group leader for intensifying their problems; they said the leader's remarks were so personally devastating that they could not handle them.

Self-Help Groups. Although encounter groups are not as popular today as they were in the 1970s, they were the forerunners of today's self-help groups. **Self-help groups** *are voluntary organizations of individuals who get together on a regular basis to discuss topics of common interest. The group leader and members give support to help individuals with their problems.* Self-help groups are so-called because they are conducted without a professional therapist. Self-help groups play an important role in our nation's mental health—approximately 6.25 million people participate in such groups each year.

In addition to reaching so many people in need of help, these groups are important because they use community resources and are relatively inexpensive (Gottlieb, 1998). They also serve people who are less likely to receive help otherwise, such as less-educated middle-aged adults, homemakers, and blue-collar workers.

Founded in 1930 by a reformed alcoholic, Alcoholics Anonymous (AA) is one of the best-known self-help groups. Mental health professionals often recommend AA for their alcoholic clients. Weight Watchers and TOPS (Take Off Pounds Sensibly) are also self-help groups. There are myriad self-help groups, such as Parents Without Partners, lesbian and gay support groups, cocaine-abuse support groups, and child-abuse support groups.

You may be wondering how a group of people with the same problem can come together and do one another any good. You might be asking yourself why they don't just help themselves and eliminate the need for the group. In fact, seeing that others share the same burden makes people feel less isolated, less like freaks of nature; it increases a psychological sense of community or belonging; and it can give hope where there might have been none before (Levine & Perkins, 1987).

Self-help groups also provide an ideology, or set of beliefs, that members can use as a guide. These groups provide members with a sympathetic audience for confession, sharing, and emotional release. The social support, role modeling, and sharing of concrete strategies for solving problems that unfold in self-help groups add to their effectiveness.

---

personal growth groups

Groups that have their roots in the humanistic therapies; they emphasize personal growth and increased openness and honesty in interpersonal relations.

encounter group

A personal-growth group designed to promote self-understanding through candid group interaction.

self-help groups

Voluntary organizations of individuals who get together on a regular basis to discuss topics of common interest. The group leader and members give support to help individuals with their problems.

For instance, a woman who has been raped may not believe a male counselor who tells her that, with time, she will be able to put back together the pieces of her life and work through much of the psychological pain. However, the same message from another rape survivor—someone who has had to work through the same feelings of rage, fear, and violation—may be more believable.

Many individuals feel uncomfortable with formal methods of therapy or support. Instead, they might turn to friends, relatives, religious leaders, or designated officials of the community to assist them in solving problems. In the next section, we will explore the nature of community psychology, which often focuses on prevention as well as treatment.

Community Psychology

The community psychology movement was born in the early 1960s, when it became apparent to mental health practitioners, including clinical psychologists, that our mental health care system was woefully inadequate. The system was not reaching the poor. Many of those who could afford help often did not seek therapy because of its social stigma. As a result, deinstitutionalization became a major thrust of the community psychology movement. **Deinstitutinalization** *is the movement to transfer the treatment of mental disabilities from inpatient mental institutions to community-based facilities that stress outpatient care.* New drugs for treating the severely mentally disabled, such as schizophrenics, meant that large numbers of people could be released from mental institutions and treated in community-based centers (Lamb, 1998).

In 1963 Congress passed the Community Mental Health Center Act, which provided funds for establishing one facility for every 50,000 individuals in the nation. The centers were designed to meet two basic goals—to provide community-based mental health services and to commit resources that help *prevent* disorders as well as treat them. Outpatient care is one of the important services that community mental health centers provide. Individuals can attend therapy sessions at a center and still keep their jobs and live with their families. Another important innovation that grew out of the community psychology movement is called outreach services. Rather than expecting people with mental or emotional problems to make an appointment at a mental health center, mental health care workers in this program go to community locations, such as storefront clinics, where they

deinstitutionalization
The movement to transfer the treatment of mental disabilities from inpatient medical institutions to community-based facilities that stress outpatient care.

The increased use of drug therapy in mental institutions facilitated the transfer of many mental patients back to the community. The architects of deinstitutionalization believed that these individuals could be given medication to keep them stabilized until they could find continuing care. However, many residents of mental health institutions have no families or homes to go to and community mental health facilities are not adequately equipped to deal with the severe cases. Many individuals who are discharged from state mental hospitals join the ranks of "the homeless." Of course, though, not all homeless people are former mental patients. Controversy continues about whether individuals should be discharged so readily from state mental institutions, which usually struggle with underfunding and staff shortages.

are accessible and needed most. Many community-based mental health services stay open 24 hours a day, often handling such emergencies as suicide attempts and drug overdoses.

The philosophy of community-based services also includes training teachers, ministers, family physicians, and others who directly interact with community members to offer lay counseling and various workshops, such as assertiveness training or coping with stress. This broadens mental health resources, allowing more people to receive help in settings where they are more likely to be comfortable than in traditional mental health centers (Orford, 1992).

In principle, community-based mental health systems should work well. In practice, the systems are severely underfunded, overenrolled, and sometimes hopelessly bureaucratic. Despite these problems, community psychologists continue to work on many levels to improve community systems (Seidman & French, 1998).

primary prevention

A community psychology concept, borrowed from the public health field, denoting efforts to reduce the number of new cases of mental disorders.

Primary Prevention. **Primary prevention** *is a community psychology concept, borrowed from the public health field, that describes efforts to reduce the number of new cases of mental disorders.* By definition, primary prevention programs are offered to populations completely free of a disorder. Like immunization in public health, primary prevention programs try to identify and "inoculate" people against the development of mental disorders. Primary prevention programs tend to follow one of three strategies: community-wide, milestone, or high-risk (Bloom, 1985).

In the *community-wide* approach, programs are available to everyone in a given geographic area. In Washington, D.C., the program "Beautiful Babies Right from the Start," for example, provides free prenatal care and well-baby care for the baby's first 18 months to women and their infants in the poorest communities. This program attempts to prevent pregnant women from engaging in harmful behaviors, such as substance abuse or poor nutrition, that put infants at risk for premature birth, low birthweight, and such disorders as hyperactivity, impaired memory, and disorganized thinking. In the *milestone* approach, the target group is every person in a population who reaches a certain hurdle, or critical life transition, such as being fired, becoming a parent for the first time, or gong away to college. Counseling for fired employees and orientation programs for college students are two examples of milestone programs. In a *high-risk* program, the focus is on specific groups of people whose chances of developing mental disorders are extremely high, such as children of alcoholics, children with chronic illnesses, and ethnic minority children.

secondary prevention

A prevention method involving screening for early detection of problems and early intervention; a community psychology concept.

Secondary Prevention. **Secondary prevention** *is a community psychology concept in which screening for early detection of problems, as well as early intervention, is carried out.* A major goal of secondary prevention programs is to reach large numbers of potential clients. These programs often use *paraprofessionals,* volunteers without formal mental health training who work closely with psychologists, to meet this goal. One approach to secondary prevention involves teaching coping skills to people under high levels of stress, the bereaved, the newly employed, and prospective parents. Another type involves screening groups of individuals, such as schoolchildren, to find those who show early signs of problems and provide them with mental health services.

tertiary prevention

A community psychology concept denoting efforts to reduce the long-term consequences of mental health disorders that were not prevented or arrested early in the course of the disorders.

Tertiary Prevention. **Tertiary prevention** *is a community psychology concept that describes efforts to reduce the long-term consequences of mental health disorders that were not prevented or arrested early in the course of the disorders.* Tertiary prevention programs are geared toward people who once required long-term care or hospitalization and provide services that can reduce the probability they will become so debilitated again. Halfway houses (community residences for individuals who no longer require institutionalization but who still need some support in readjusting to the community) are an example of tertiary prevention. Such programs seek to increase individuals coping skills by reducing their social isolation, by increasing their social skills, and by developing educational strategies tailored to their needs.

Community psychology has successfully reached large numbers of mentally and emotionally distressed people, not only through prevention but also through intervention

empowerment

Helping individuals develop skills they need to improve their adaptation and circumstances.

(Levine, Toro, & Perkins, 1993). Unfortunately, strong cutbacks in federal funding of community mental health centers in the 1980s have diminished their effectiveness and stalled their expansion.

Because programs such as outreach services may be the only mental health care available to those who are poor or who are from ethnic minority backgrounds, community psychology approaches are especially important (Marin, 1993). Remember from our earlier comments that psychotherapy has been more available to the wealthy. An explicit value of community psychology is to assist people who are disenfranchised from society to gain access to comparable forms of support. **Empowerment** *refers to helping individuals develop skills they need to improve their adaptation and circumstances.*

eview

Systems Interventions

Some approaches have the advantage of working with individuals in the context of a larger system. These therapies include group therapies, family and couple therapy, and community psychology.

Group therapies emphasize that social relationships hold the key to successful therapy; therefore, therapy involving group interactions may be more beneficial than individual therapy. Family therapy and couple therapy, as well as personal growth groups, are common. Community psychology was born in the early 1960s. Deinstitutionalization, in which the treatment of mental disorders is transferred from inpatient mental institutions to outpatient community mental health facilities, has been especially important in community psychology. As a result, mental health services are more accessible to individuals from low-income and ethnic minority backgrounds. Three community psychology approaches are primarily prevention, secondary prevention, and tertiary prevention. Empowerment—providing assistance so that individuals can gain more control over their lives—is a key concept in community psychology.

IS PSYCHOTHERAPY EFFECTIVE?

Do individuals who go through therapy get better? Are some approaches more effective than others, or is the situation similar to that of the Dodo in *Alice's Adventures in Wonderland?* Dodo was asked to judge the winner of a race; he decided, "Everybody has won and all must have prizes." How would we evaluate the effectiveness of psychotherapy? Would we take the client's word, or the therapist's word? What would be our criteria for effectiveness? Would it be "feeling good," "adaptive behavior," "improved interpersonal relationships," "autonomous decision making," or "more positive self-concept," for example? During the past several decades, an extensive amount of thought and research has addressed these questions.

Outcome Research on the Effectiveness of Psychotherapy

Four decades ago, Hans Eysenck (1952) shocked the pundits in the field of psychotherapy by concluding that treatment is ineffective. Eysenck analyzed 24 studies of psychotherapy and found that approximately two-thirds of the individuals with neurotic symptoms improved. Sounds impressive so far. But Eysenck also found that a similar percentage of neurotic individuals on waiting lists to see a psychotherapist also showed marked improvement even though they were not given any psychotherapy at all.

Critics of Eysenck's findings suggested that there were many irregularities in how he analyzed his data and drew conclusions. Even so, Eysenck's pronouncement prompted a flurry of research on psychotherapy's effectiveness. Hundreds of studies on the outcome of psychotherapy have now been conducted (Sanderson, 1995; Wampold & others, 1997).

One strategy for analyzing these diverse studies is called **meta-analysis**, *in which the researcher statistically combines the results of many different studies.* In one meta-analysis of psychotherapy research, 475 studies were statistically combined (Smith, Glass, & Miller, 1980). Only those studies in which a therapy group had been compared with

meta-analysis

A research strategy that involves statistically combining the results of many different studies.

an untreated control group were compared. The results were much kinder to psychotherapy effectiveness than Eysenck's earlier results: On 88 percent of the measures, individuals who received therapy improved more than those who did not. This meta-analysis documents that psychotherapy is effective in general, but it does not inform us about the specific ways in which different therapies might be effective.

People who are thinking about seeing a psychotherapist not only want to know whether psychotherapy in general is effective, but they would especially like to know which form of psychotherapy is effective for their particular problem. In the meta-analysis conducted by Mary Lee Smith and her colleagues (Smith, Glass, & Miller, 1980) comparisons of different types of psychotherapy were also made. For example, behavior therapies were compared with insight therapies (psychodynamic, humanistic). Both the behavior and insight therapies were superior to no treatment at all, but they did not differ from each other in effectiveness. While no particular therapy was the best in the study by Smith and her colleagues, some therapies do seem to be more effective in treating some disorders than others. The behavior therapies have been most successful in treating specific behavioral problems, such as phobias and sexual dysfunctions. (Bowers & Clum, 1988). The cognitive therapies have been most successful in treating depression (Clark & Beck, 1989). Also, many therapies have their maximum benefit early in treatment with less improvement occurring as the individual remains in therapy (Karasu, 1986).

One large-scale survey of *Consumer Reports* magazine readers found the following (Seligman, 1995):

- Treatment by a mental health professional was usually effective. Most of the respondents improved as a result of mental health treatment.
- Long-term therapy was more effective than short-term therapy.
- Psychologists, psychiatrists, and social workers were the most effective, all being more effective than marriage counselors. Family doctors were just as effective as mental health professionals in the short term, but were worse in the long term.
- No specific type of therapy (such as behavioral, psychoanalytic, cognitive) was better than any other for any problem.

Keep in mind that this is a biased sample, composed of *Consumer Reports* magazine readers, who are more educated and more likely to benefit from therapy than a random sample. Also, this information involved self-report, was retrospective, and did not include assessment or diagnosis by mental health professionals. Nonetheless, at least for this large sample (about 7,000 individuals), psychotherapy, especially long-term psychotherapy, benefited individuals (Seligman & Rosenhan, 1998).

The informed consumer needs to be aware of some evidence that in certain cases psychotherapy can actually be harmful. For example, people who have a low tolerance of anxiety, low motivation, and strong signs of psychological deterioration may worsen as therapy progresses. Characteristics of the therapist also have been related to a worsening of the client's status as therapy progresses. Therapists who are aggressive, who try to get clients to disclose personal information too quickly, and who are impatient with the process of change may exacerbate their clients' problems (Suinn, 1984). Therapist bias can be harmful when the therapist does not understand ethnic, religious, gender, or other cultural differences, but instead pressures such clients to conform to White, middle-class norms. Finally, therapists who engage in sex with a client harm the client; such behavior is absolutely unethical.

While incompetent and unethical therapists do exist, there are many impeccable therapists who successfully help their clients. Like jazz musicians, psychotherapists must be capable of improvising, gracefully. As psychologist Jerome Frank put it, "Successful therapy is not just a scientific process, it is a healing art as well."

Common Themes and Specificity in Psychotherapy

After carefully studying the nature of psychotherapy for more than 25 years, Jerome Frank (1982) concluded that effective psychotherapies have the common elements of expectations, mastery, and emotional arousal. By inspiring an expectation of help, the therapist motivates the client to continue coming to therapy. These expectations are powerful morale builders and symptom relievers in themselves. The therapist also increases the client's sense of mastery and competence. For example, clients begin to feel that they can cope effectively with their world. Therapy also arouses the individual's emotions, essential to motivating behavioral change, according to Frank.

The therapeutic relationship is another important ingredient in successful psychotherapy (Strupp, 1995). A relationship in which the client has confidence and trust in the therapist is essential to effective psychotherapy. In one study, the most common ingredient in the success of different psychotherapies was the therapist's supportiveness of the client (Wallerstein, 1989). The client and therapist engage in a "healing ritual," which requires the active participation of both the client and the therapist. As part of this ritual, the client gains hope and becomes less alienated.

But while psychotherapies have common themes, some critics worry about carrying this commonality too far. Specificity in psychotherapy still needs careful attention—we need to understand "*what* treatment is most effective for *this* individual with *that* specific problem, and under *which* set of circumstances" *within* the cultural context (Paul, 1967). At this time, however, we do not know which approach works best in which situation with which therapist. Some therapists are better trained than others, some are more sensitive to a person's feelings, some are more introverted, and some are more conservative. Because of the myriad ways we differ as human beings, the ideal "fit" of therapist and client is difficult to pinpoint scientifically.

Given the variety of therapist characteristics, it can be challenging to find the right therapist to help you with your concerns. To read about guidelines for seeking professional help, see Applications in Psychology. Then complete the Self-Assessment to evaluate whether you could benefit from seeing a competent therapist.

One other dimension that influences the match between a therapist and a client is the degree to which their sociocultural characteristics are in sync. Only in the last two decades have many psychologists become sensitive to therapy's sociocultural dimensions. Let's explore how gender, ethnicity, socioeconomic status, and culture influence treatment effectiveness.

Gender Issues in Treatment Effectiveness

One of the by-products of changing gender roles for women and men is a rethinking of approaches to psychotherapy. In some instances, the development of abnormal behavior and lack of effective psychotherapy may be due to traditional gender conditioning (Worell & Robinson, 1993). Our discussion of gender and therapy focuses on three areas: autonomy and relatedness in therapy, consciousness-raising groups, and feminist therapies, each of which we examine in turn.

Increased interest has focused on gender roles in psychotherapy. *Might female psychotherapists be more likely to encourage autonomy and relatedness, rather than autonomy alone, as psychotherapy goals?*

Applications in Psychology

Guidelines for Seeking Professional Help

How do you find a competent, qualified therapist? This question is not as easy to answer as it might seem. We may face many of the same problems when we try to find a "good" medical doctor, accountant, or dentist; however, the way most people go about finding these other professional services might not be the best way of selecting a therapist. Asking a friend for a good therapist ignores the fact that some approaches to therapy work better with some problems than others. Also, every therapeutic relationship is different, so one person's experience in therapy is not translatable to another person's.

Here are some general suggestions when looking for a therapist:

1. *Seek recommendations from those who are knowledgeable about therapy.* The psychology faculty on your campus—your professors as well as psychologists in student services—may be able to help you shorten your search by recommending someone with a good track record related to your concern.

2. *Identify the professional's credentials.* Although all different types of mental health professionals may be competent, psychologists, psychiatrists, and social workers all differ in their approach to therapy, based on differences in training: Psychologists tend to be focused on the person's emotions and behaviors; psychiatrists are trained as medical doctors, so their perspective is likely to involve physical aspects of psychological problems; and social workers will be inclined to take a person's entire family and social situation into account. Regardless of the exact profession, some minimal credentials should be considered important. All states have licensing regulations for professionals who provide public services. Thus, a therapist should be licensed or certified by a state in order to practice. In addition, in some cases it may be important for a professional to have some advanced, specialized training in a certain area. For example, if a person is seeking help with a specific problem, like drug abuse, alcohol abuse, or a sexual problem, the therapist should have some training in that area. You should ask about the professional's credentials either before or during a first visit.

3. *Be a thoughtful and careful consumer of mental health services.* With any services, the more informed you are about the services provided, the better decision you can make about whether or not they are the right services for you. Calling around and asking specific questions about approaches and specializations is one way to become informed about the services offered by therapists. Consider how important it may be that the therapist is of your same or opposite sex, whether it is important that they have experience with your specific difficulty, as well as other specific characteristics. You may also want to learn more about their theoretical orientation to therapy as described in this chapter. Most professionals are quite comfortable talking about their background and training. Your confidence and trust in the professional is an important part of how well therapy will work for you.

4. *When staring therapy, give it some time before making a judgment of how useful it is.* Making changes is very difficult. Expecting too much too soon can result in premature dissatisfaction and disappointment. Because a large part of therapy involves the development of a relationship with the therapist, it may take several meetings to really know if things are going well. One suggestion is to give it four to six weekly meetings. If it does not seem like things are going the way you would like, it is a good idea to discuss your progress with the therapist and ask what you should expect with regard to making progress. Setting specific goals with specific time expectations can be helpful. If your goals are not being met, you might consider a new therapist.

These general guidelines should be used when first looking for a therapist. Remember that people should continually evaluate their own progress throughout therapy and when they feel dissatisfied with how it is going, they should discuss this with their therapist. Therapy is like other services: when dissatisfied you can always look for another therapist. Don't think that just because one therapist has not been helpful none will be. All therapists and therapeutic relationships are different. Finding the right therapist is one of the most important factors in therapy success (Kalichman, 1994).

> *Freud is the father of psychoanalysis. It had no mother.*
> —GERMAINE GREER, *Feminist Author, 20th Century*

Autonomy and relatedness are central issues to an understanding of gender conditioning. For many years autonomy was championed as an important characteristic for maturity. As a result, autonomy was the unquestioned goal of many psychotherapies, relatedness was not. Thomas Szasz (1965), for example, claimed that the basic goal of psychotherapy is to foster autonomy, independence, and freedom. The humanistic therapies—those of Rogers, Maslow, and Perls—argued that to become psychologically

$\mathcal{S}$elf-Assessment

When Should You Go to Therapy?

Instructions

There are no hard-and-fast rules about when people should seek therapy for help with their personal problems. However, complete the checklist below to see whether the challenges you face could be helped by a competent therapist.

	Often	Sometimes	Not at all
I feel sad or blue for no particular reason.			
I hear voices that tell me what I should do.			
I feel so anxious that it is hard for me to function.			
I have trouble concentrating sufficiently to get any work done.			
I feel impulses that encourage me to act in ways I know I shouldn't.			
I alienate other people when I really don't want to.			
I feel frightened by things that I know shouldn't be so fear-provoking.			
I seem to get sick more often than most of my friends.			
I can't seem to remember certain periods in my life very well.			
I feel so good that I almost feel superhuman.			
I worry that people around me might be planning to hurt me.			
I smell strange smells that no one else seems to be able to smell.			

Scoring Interpretation

If your life doesn't feel very satisfying and you answered "often" to any of the items listed, consider talking it over with a qualified therapist. Some items on the assessment warrant a therapist's attention even if you mark the item "sometimes." For example, hearing voices and smelling strange smells are problematic enough that even minor experiences of this type suggest a professional evaluation might be in order. Crippling anxiety, compelling impulses, loss of memories for certain periods of your life, and worries that others intend to do you harm also can be helped by good therapy. Of course, you can also use feedback from people who care about you, to make this decision. If people you love are telling you something is wrong, act on their concern. A good therapist can make life easier for you and them.

healthy, an individual has to become self-actualized through self-determination and fulfillment of needs, independent of social constraints or personal commitments.

But therapists are taking a new look at autonomy as the ideal goal of therapy for females. Should therapy with females focus more on the way most females have been socialized and place more emphasis on relationships? Can females, even with psychotherapy, achieve autonomy in a male-dominated society? Are conventional ways of thinking about autonomy and relatedness appropriate for capturing the complexity of human experience? Would psychotherapy for females, as well as for males, be improved if its goals were more androgynous in nature, stressing better psychological functioning in *both* autonomy and relatedness?

Because traditional therapy often has not adequately addressed the specific concerns of women in a sexist society, several nontraditional approaches have arisen. These nontraditional therapies emphasize the importance of helping people break free from traditional gender roles and stereotypes. The nontraditional therapies avoid language that labels one sex as more socially desirable or valuable.

Feminist therapists, both male and female, believe that traditional psychotherapy continues to carry considerable gender bias, and that women clients cannot realize their full potential without becoming aware of society's sexism. The goals of feminist therapists are no different from other therapist's goals. Feminist therapists make no effort to turn clients into feminists, but want the female client to be fully aware of how the nature of the female role in the American society can contribute to the development of a mental disorder. Feminist therapists believe women must become aware of the effects of social oppression on their own lives if they are to achieve their mental health goals.

Gender is not the only sociocultural domain that influences therapy outcomes. Next, we will evaluate ethnicity and socioeconomic status as sociocultural factors in therapy success.

Ethnicity and Socioeconomic Status in Treatment Effectiveness

For far too long, psychotherapists were concerned almost exclusively with helping middle- and upper-class individuals cope with their problems while ignoring the needs of people who were poor or from ethnic minority backgrounds (Murray, 1998).

Orientation of Ethnic Minority Individuals to Therapy.   As part of their history of being ignored by psychotherapists, ethnic minority individuals have developed a preference for discussing problems with parents, friends, and relatives rather than mental health professionals. Another reason why they turn to family and friends when they are in emotional or mental distress is that there are so few ethnic minority psychotherapists (Sue, Ivey, & Pedersen, 1996). For example, in one study, African American college students were more likely to use the college's mental health facilities if an African American clinician or counselor were available than if only White counselors were available (Thompson & Cimbolic, 1978). However, therapy can be effective when the therapist and client are from different cultural backgrounds if the therapist has excellent clinical skills and is culturally sensitive. Researchers have also found that Asian Americans, African Americans, Latinos, and Native Americans terminate psychotherapy after an initial session at a much higher rate than do White Americans (Sue, Allen, & Conway, 1978). The social stigma of being a "mental patient," fear of hospitalization, conflict between their own belief system and the beliefs of modern mental health practitioners, and the availability of an alternate healer, are additional reasons ethnic minority individuals terminate therapy early.

Psychotherapy involves interpersonal interaction and communication. Verbal and nonverbal messages need to be accurately sent and received. Although, as we indicated earlier, very effective therapy can take place when the client and therapist are from different sociocultural backgrounds, barriers to communication can develop in such circumstances that can destroy and undermine the effectiveness of psychotherapy (Atkinson & Hackett, 1998; Atkinson, Morten & Sue, 1998; Parham, 1996).

Some Thoughts About Improvements in Therapy for Ethnic Minority Individuals.
Therapists might need to adapt their preferred treatment styles when working with ethnic minority individuals (Sue & others, 1998). For example, some therapists recommend that, when working with Latinos, therapists should reframe problems as being medical rather than psychological, to reduce resistance. The assumption is that many Latinos will be more receptive to a medical orientation than to a psychological orientation. Some therapists recommend that, when working with African Americans, therapists use externally focused, action-oriented therapy rather than internally focused, intrapsychic therapy.

Such recommendations, however, raise some important questions. For example, is it possible for therapists to effectively change their therapy orientation to work with ethnic minority groups? A psychoanalytic therapist might find it difficult to use the externally focused, action-oriented therapy recommended for African Americans. By using a specific approach, supposedly based on the client's cultural background, how does the therapist deal with diversity and individual differences in an ethnic or cultural group? Because of the problems raised by such questions, we cannot just say, "Know the cultural background of the client or use this approach with that particular ethnic or cultural group."

According to Stanley Sue (1991), what we can say is that when they see ethnic minority clients, therapists should emphasize two processes, at least in initial therapy sessions: (1) credibility, and (2) giving. **Credibility** *refers to a therapist's believability.* **Giving** *refers to clients' receiving some kind of benefit from treatment early in the therapy process.* Two factors are important in increasing credibility: ascribed status and achieved status. Ascribed status is one's position or role defined by others or cultural norms. In some cultures, the young are subordinate to the old, those who are naive abide by those in authority, and females have less power than males. Credibility must also be achieved. The therapist can achieve credibility by doing something that the client perceives as being helpful or competent. Lack of ascribed credibility may be the main reason ethnic minority individuals tend to steer clear of therapy; lack of achieved credibility may be the main reason ethnic minority individuals terminate therapy once it has begun as well as problems with rapport.

credibility

A therapist's believability.

giving

The client's receiving some kind of benefit from treatment early in the therapy process.

(a)

(b)

(c)

What might be the most effective psychotherapy with *(a)* a man from impoverished circumstances in rural Appalachia, *(b)* an Asian American businessman, and *(c)* an African American female construction worker?

In terms of giving, clients may wonder how talking to a therapist will alleviate their problems. Therapists need to help ethnic minority clients see the relationship between therapy and why it will help a person get better (Caldwell, 1996). It is important for the therapist to make this association in the first session. Many ethnic minority clients do not understand Western psychotherapy. The first session should not be just an assessment session, but rather the therapist should find out about the client, give some recommendations for treatment, and say something concrete to the client so the client will leave the first session saying, "I got something out of it that I think will help me and I want to come back again."

As can be seen in the preceding discussion, many people might be more comfortable seeking treatments that have a biological rationale. In the next section, we will evaluate interventions that involve biomedical therapies. For the most part, these approaches are the domain of psychiatrists, who often use one or more of the forms of psychotherapy we have discussed so far in conjunction with medical intervention.

BIOMEDICAL THERAPIES

Physicians have regularly been the person families turn to when a family member no longer can function adequately. As medical science progressed, the tools physicians used to combat "mental illness" became more sophisticated than recommendations to get rest or a change of scenery.

biomedical therapies

Treatments to reduce or eliminate the symptoms of psychological disorders by altering the way an individual's body functions. Drug therapy is the most common form.

Biomedical therapies *are treatments to reduce or eliminate the symptoms of psychological disorders by altering the way an individual's body functions. Drug therapy is the most common form of biomedical therapy. Much less widely used biomedical therapies are electroconvulsive therapy and psychosurgery.* Psychologists and other mental health professionals may provide psychotherapy in conjunction with the biomedical therapy administered by psychiatrists and medical doctors.

Drug Therapy

Although medicine and herbs have long been used to alleviate symptoms of emotional distress, it was not until the twentieth century that drug treatments began to revolutionize mental health care. Psychotherapeutic drugs are mainly used for three diagnostic categories: anxiety, depression, and schizophrenia. Let's explore the effectiveness of drugs in these areas, beginning with drugs to treat anxiety.

antianxiety drugs

Drugs that are commonly known as tranquilizers and reduce anxiety by making individuals less excitable and more tranquil.

Antianxiety Drugs. **Antianxiety drugs** *are commonly known as tranquilizers. These drugs reduce anxiety by making individuals less excitable and more calm.* Benzodiazepines are the antianxiety drugs that offer the greatest relief for anxiety symptoms. They work by binding to the receptor sites of neurotransmitters that become overactive during anxiety. The most frequently prescribed benzodiazepines include Xanax, Valium, and Librium.

Why are antianxiety drugs so widely used? Many individuals experience stress, anxiety, or an inability to sleep well. Family physicians or psychiatrists prescribe these drugs to improve our ability to cope with these situations more effectively. The relaxed feelings brought on by antianxiety drugs bring welcome relief to many individuals who are experiencing high levels of anxiety and stress in their lives.

antidepressant drugs

Drugs that regulate mood. The three main classes of antidepressant drugs are tricyclics, such as Elavil; MAO inhibitors, such as Nardil; and SSRI inhibitors, such as Prozac.

Antidepressant Drugs. **Antidepressant drugs** *regulate mood. The three main classes of antidepressant drugs are tricyclics, such as Elavil; SSRI drugs, such as Prozac; and MAO inhibitors, such as Nardil.* The *tricyclics,* so called because of their three-ringed molecular structure, probably work because they increase the level of certain neurotransmitters, especially norepinephrine and serotonin. The tricyclics reduce the symptoms of depression in approximately 60 to 70 percent of cases. The tricyclics are not effective in improving mood until 2 to 4 weeks after the individual begins taking them. And the tricyclics sometimes have adverse side effects—restlessness, faintness, and trembling, for example. The most prominent of the selective serotonin reuptake inhibiting (SSRI) type of antidepressant drug is Prozac. SSRI drugs work by interfering with the reabsorption of serotonin in the brain. Prozac is most frequently prescribed for dysthymia, a mild to moderate form of clinical depression, but it has also successfully treated anxiety, obsession, and shyness. Although many individuals report that they feel fully themselves when taking Prozac, the drug can be disinhibiting and dangerous for some individuals, who report an increase in suicidal feelings and aggressive impulses. The MAO inhibitors are not as widely used as the tricyclics because they are more toxic, require more dietary restrictions, and usually have less-potent therapeutic effects. Nonetheless, some severely depressed individuals who do not respond to the tricyclics do respond to the MAO inhibitors.

lithium

A drug that is widely used to treat bipolar disorder.

Lithium *is a drug that is widely used to treat bipolar disorder* (recall that this disorder involves wide mood swings of depression and mania). The amount of lithium that circulates in the bloodstream needs to be carefully monitored because its effective dosage is precariously close to toxic levels. Memory impairment is also associated with lithium use.

As with schizophrenia, the effective treatment of the affective disorders can involve a combination of drug therapy and psychotherapy. One study showed that the combination of tricyclics and interpersonal psychotherapy produced a lower than normal relapse rate for depressed clients (10 percent versus 22 percent) (Frank & Kupfer, 1986).

antipsychotic drugs

Powerful drugs that diminish agitated behavior, reduce tension, decrease hallucinations and delusions, improve social behavior, and produce better sleep patterns in severely mentally disabled individuals, especially schizophrenics.

Antipsychotic Drugs. **Antipsychotic drugs** *are powerful drugs that diminish agitated behavior, reduce tension, decrease hallucinations and delusions, improve social behavior, and produce better sleep patterns in individuals who have a severe mental disorder, especially schizophrenics.* Before antipsychotic drugs were developed in 1950, few, if any, interventions brought relief from the torment of psychotic symptoms. Once the effectiveness of the medications was apparent, the medical community abandoned more intrusive interventions, such as brain surgery and electroconvulsive shock, for schizophrenia.

The *neuroleptics* are the most widely used class of antipsychotic drugs. Neuroleptics vary in their potency. Low-potency neuroleptics include Thorazine and Mellaril. High-potency neuroleptics include Haldol and Prolixin. The most widely used explanation for the effectiveness of neuroleptics is their ability to block the dopamine system's action in the brain (Rebec, 1996). Schizophrenics have too much of the neurochemical messenger dopamine. Numerous well-controlled investigations reveal that when used in sufficient doses, the neuroleptics reduce a variety of schizophrenic symptoms, at least in the short term (Holcomb & others, 1996).

The neuroleptics do not cure schizophrenia, and they can have severe side effects. The neuroleptics treat the symptoms of schizophrenia, not its causes. If an individual stops taking the drug, the symptoms return. Neuroleptic drugs have substantially reduced the length of hospital stays for schizophrenics. Although schizophrenics are able to return to the community because drug therapy keeps their symptoms from reappearing, most have difficulty coping with the demands of society and most are chronically unemployed.

tardive dyskinesia

A major side effect of the neuroleptic drugs; a neurological disorder characterized by grotesque, involuntary movements of the facial muscles and mouth, as well as extensive twitching of the neck, arms, and legs.

Tardive dyskinesia *is a major side effect of the neuroleptic drugs; it is a neurological disorder characterized by grotesque, involuntary movements of the facial muscles and mouth as well as extensive twitching of the neck, arms, and legs.* As many as 20 percent of schizophrenics taking neuroleptics develop this disorder. Elderly women are especially vulnerable. Long-term neuroleptic therapy also is associated with increased depression and anxiety. Schizophrenics who take neuroleptics for many years report that they feel miserable most of the time, for example. Nonetheless, for the majority of schizophrenics, the benefits of neuroleptic treatment outweigh its risk and discomforts. Strategies to increase the effectiveness of the neuroleptics involve administering lower dosages over time rather than a large initial dose and combining drug therapy with psychotherapy.

The drug Clozaril was introduced in the 1990s. It shows promise for reducing schizophrenia's symptoms without the side effects of the neuroleptics. Clozaril blocks serotonin reuptake to produce its sedating effects. However, for a small proportion of schizophrenics, Clozaril has a toxic effect on white blood cells, which requires regular blood testing.

The small percentage of schizophrenics who are able to hold jobs suggests that drugs alone will not make them contributing members of society. Vocational, family, and social-skills training are needed in conjunction with drug therapy to facilitate improved psychological functioning and adaptation to society.

The use of psychotherapeutic drugs is the most widely practiced biomedical therapy. However, as we see next, in extreme circumstances, electroconvulsive therapy and even psychosurgery may be used.

Electroconvulsive Therapy

electroconvulsive therapy (ECT)
Commonly called shock treatment, a type of therapy sometimes used to treat severely depressed individuals by causing brain seizures similar to those caused by epilepsy.

"Then something bent down and took hold of me and shook me like the end of the world. Wee-ee-ee-ee-ee, it shrilled, through an air crackling with blue light, and with each flash a great jolt drubbed me until I thought my bones would break and the sap fly out of me like a split plant." Such images as this description from Sylvia Plath's (1971) auto-biographic novel, *The Bell Jar,* have shaped the public's view of **electroconvulsive therapy (ECT)**. *Commonly called "shock treatment," ECT is sometimes used to treat severely depressed individuals. The goal of ECT is to cause a seizure in the brain much like what happens spontaneously in some forms of epilepsy.* A small electric current, lasting for 1 second or less, passes through two electrodes placed on the individual's head. The current excites neural tissue, stimulating a seizure that last for approximately 1 minute.

ECT has been used for more than 40 years. In earlier years, it often was used indiscriminately, sometimes even as a punishment for patients. ECT is still used on as many as 60,000 individuals a year, mainly to treat major depression. Adverse side effects may include memory loss or other cognitive impairment. Today ECT is given mainly to individuals who have not responded to drug therapy or psychotherapy.

ECT sounds as if it would entail intolerable pain, but the manner in which it is administered today involves little discomfort. The patient is given anesthesia and muscle relaxants before the current is applied; this allows the individual to sleep through the procedure, it minimizes convulsions, and it reduces the risk of physical injury. The individual awakens shortly afterward with no conscious memory of the treatment.

The following example reveals how ECT, used as a last resort, can be effective in reducing depression (Sackheim, 1985). Diane is a 36-year-old teacher and mother. She has been in psychotherapy for several years. Prior to entering the hospital, she had taken tricyclics with unsuccessful results. In the first 6 months of her hospital stay, doctors tried various drugs to reduce her depression; none worked. She slept poorly, lost her appetite, and showed no interest even in reading newspaper headlines. Obsessed with the idea that she had ruined her children's lives, she repeatedly threatened suicide. With her consent, doctors began ECT; after

Electroconvulsive therapy (ECT), commonly called "shock therapy," causes a seizure in the brain. ECT is still given to as many as 60,000 people a year, mainly to treat major depression.

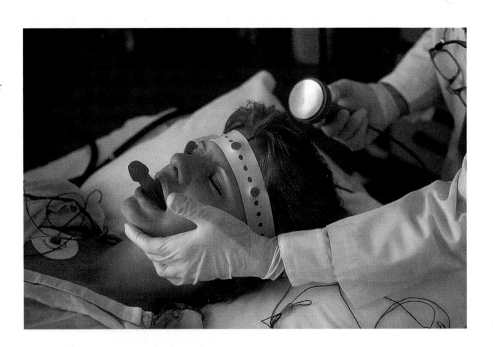

five treatments, Diane returned to her family and job. Not all cases of ECT turn out as positively, however; and even when ECT works, no one knows why it works (Kramer, 1987).

Psychosurgery

psychosurgery

A biomedical therapy that involves the removal or destruction of brain tissue to improve the person's psychological adjustment.

One biomedical treatment is even more extreme than ECT. **Psychosurgery** *is a biomedical therapy that involves the removal or destruction of brain tissue to improve the individual's psychological adjustment.* The effects of psychosurgery are irreversible.

In the 1930s, Portuguese physician Egas Moniz developed a procedure known as a *prefrontal lobotomy.* In this procedure, a surgical instrument is inserted into the brain and rotated, severing fibers that connect the frontal lobe, important in higher thought processes, and the thalamus, important in emotion. Moniz theorized that, by severing the connections between these brain structures, the symptoms of severe mental disorders could be alleviated. Prefrontal lobotomies were conducted on thousands of patients from the 1930s through the 1950s. Moniz was even awarded the Nobel Prize for his work. However, although some patients may have benefited from the lobotomies, many were left in vegetablelike states because of the massive assaults on their brains.

These crude lobotomies are no longer performed. Since the 1960s, psychosurgery has become more precise. When psychosurgery is now performed, a small lesion is made in the amygdala or another part of the limbic system. Today only several hundred patients per year undergo psychosurgery; it is used as a last resort and with extreme caution.

In this chapter we have studied many different strategies for helping people who have a psychological disorder. In the next chapter, we continue our attempt to provide answers to how people's mental problems can be prevented and treated.

 *R*eview

The Effectiveness of Psychotherapy and Biomedical Therapies

Psychotherapy in general is effective, but no single treatment is more effective than others. Behavioral therapies are often most successful in treating specific behavioral problems, such as phobias; cognitive therapy is often most successful in treating depression. Common themes in successful therapies include expectations, a sense of mastery, emotional arousal, and a confiding relationship. We still need to examine further which therapy works best with which individual in which setting with which therapist.

Historically the goal of therapy has been autonomy, but questions are raised about this as an ideal goal of therapy,

especially for females. The goals of psychotherapy should include more attention to relatedness. One nontraditional, gender-related therapy is feminist therapy. For too long people from ethnic minority and low socioeconomic status backgrounds were ignored by psychotherapists. Credibility and giving are two important therapy processes with ethnic minority clients.

Biomedical therapies are designed to reduce or eliminate the symptoms of psychological disorders by altering the way an individual's body functions. Drug therapy is the most common biomedical therapy. Drug therapy may be effective when

other therapies have failed, as in reducing the symptoms of schizophrenia. Three major classes of psychotherapeutic drugs are antianxiety, antidepressant, and antipsychotic.

Electroconvulsive therapy, commonly called "shock treatment," creates a seizure in the brain; its most common use is as a last resort in treating severe depression. Psychosurgery is an irreversible procedure; brain tissue is destroyed in an effort to improve psychological adjustment. Today's psychosurgery is more precise than the early prefrontal lobotomies. Psychosurgery is used only as a last resort.

Overview

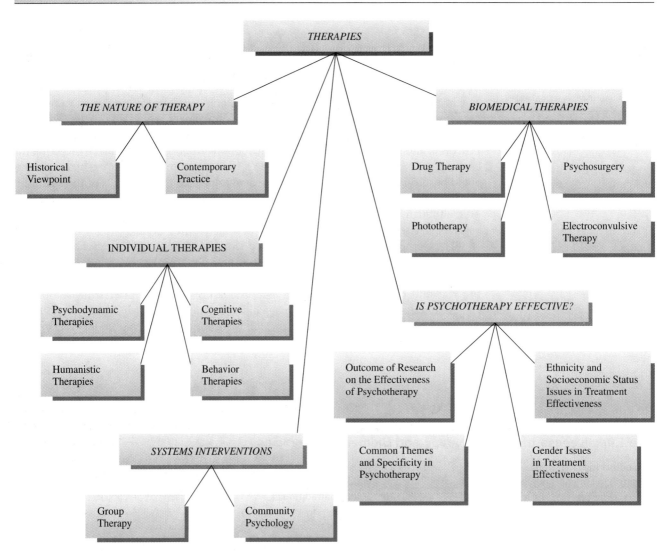

We began this chapter by exploring the nature of psychotherapy, both historically and in terms of contemporary practice. We spent considerable time examining the individual therapies—psychodynamic, humanistic, behavioral, and cognitive. Then we studied systems interventions—group therapy and community psychology. We read about whether therapy is effective, considering outcome research, themes and specificity, and gender, ethnicity, and social class issues. Our coverage of biomedical therapies focused on drug therapy, phototherapy, electroconvulsive therapy, and psychosurgery. Don't forget that you can obtain an overall summary of this chapter by again reading the in-chapter reviews on pages 448, 453, 458, 465, and 475.

Key Terms

trephining   444
exorcism   444
psychotherapy   446
insight therapy   446
action therapy   446
eclectic   446
managed health care   448
psychodynamic
   therapies   449
psychoanalysis   449
free association   449
catharsis   449
dream analysis   449
manifest content   449
latent content   449
transference   449

resistance   450
humanistic psychotherapies
   451
person-centered therapy   452
genuineness   452
accurate empathy   452
active listening   452
Gestalt therapy   452
behavior therapies   453
systematic desensitization
   454
aversive conditioning   454
token economy   455
cognitive behavior therapy
   455
self-efficacy   456

self-instructional methods
   456
cognitive therapies   456
rational-emotive therapy   457
family therapy   460
couple therapy   460
family systems therapy   460
personal growth groups   462
encounter group   462
self-help groups   462
deinstitutionalization   463
primary prevention   464
secondary prevention   464
tertiary prevention   464
empowerment   465
meta-analysis   465

credibility   471
giving   471
biomedical therapies   472
antianxiety drugs   472
antidepressant drugs   472
lithium   473
antipsychotic drugs   473
tardive dyskinesia   473
electroconvulsive therapy
   (ECT)   474
psychosurgery   475

Thinking It Over

Exercises...

...In Critical Thinking

Select a person whose personality problems have brought the person to the attention of the public. This might be a famous criminal, politician, movie star, athlete, or other public figure. Identify three therapy approaches that might help the person improve his or her adjustment and cope more effectively. Select the alternative you think is best and justify why you think it is a good choice for that person.

...In Creative Thinking

Imagine that you are a therapist and that you are assigned to see an individual from a background that is completely different from yours. What are some creative ways you can gather information about the client's heritage to function more effectively with this client?

...In Active Learning

Visit the mental health facilities on your campus. Try to arrange a 15-minute interview with someone who practices psychotherapy to find out about the nature of her or his work. Generate at least ten questions ahead of time to increase the probability that your interview will be productive. What conclusions can you draw about the kind of people who likely are good at being a psychotherapist? How do you think you would fare as a client?

...In Reflective Learning

Under what circumstances (what kinds of problems) would you feel more comfortable participating in a group therapy approach? What kinds of problems would you not want to address in a group format? How likely is it that you would participate in therapy of any kind? Explain.

Resources for Psychology and Improving Humankind

Case Approach to Counseling and Psychotherapy (1996, 4th ed.)

by Gerald Corey
Pacific Grove, CA: Brooks/Cole

A central client, Ruth, becomes the focus for the application of nine different therapies, including psychoanalytic, Adlerian, person-centered, Gestalt, cognitive-behavior, and family systems.

The Compleat Therapist (1991)

by Jeffrey Kottler
New York: Jossey-Bass

Kottler reveals the techniques all good therapists have in common and combines the most effective healing therapies into one framework. These characteristics include the therapist's personality, skillful thinking processes, communication skills, and intimate and trusting relationships. This book gives excellent insight into the characteristics of therapists that help clients improve regardless of the therapist's theoretical orientation.

The Consumer's Guide to Psychotherapy (1992)

by Jack Engler and Danile Goleman
New York: Simon & Schuster

This is a comprehensive manual on psychotherapy for consumers. Among the questions the authors ask and evaluate are:

- How do I decide if I need therapy?
- Which therapy approach is best for me?
- How do I find the right therapist?
- What questions should I ask during the first session?
- How can I afford therapy?
- How can I tell if therapy is really working?
- How do I know when to end therapy?

The book is based on the clinical opinions of almost 1,000 therapists nationwide. Included are case studies and listings of mental health organizations, as well as therapist referral sources.

Counseling American Minorities (1999, 6th Ed.)

by Donald Atkinson, George Morten, and Derald Sue
Burr Ridge, IL: McGraw-Hill

This book provides valuable information about counseling and psychotherapy with individuals from ethnic minority backgrounds. Entire sections are devoted to the American Indian client, the Asian American client, the African American client, and the Latino client. You might also want to read *Psychotherapy and Counseling with Minorities* (New York: Pergamon, 1991) by Manuel Ramirez.

Current Psychotherapies (1989, 2nd ed.)

edited by Ray Corsini
Itasca, IL: Peacock

Therapists from various schools of psychotherapy describe their approaches.

Five Therapists and One Client (1991)

by Raymond Corsini and contributors
Itasca, IL: Peacock

Therapists who have five distinctive approaches to helping clients describe their conceptual orientation, therapy techniques, and demonstrate how they would likely work with the same fictitious client. The imaginary client is a relatively normal individual with unusual and persistent problems—a common client for psychotherapists in private practice. Four clear-cut systems of psychotherapy were selected: Alfred Adler's individual therapy, Carl Rogers's person-centered therapy, Albert Ellis's rational-emotive therapy, and behavior therapy. Finally, a fifth therapy approach—eclectic therapy—was chosen. How therapists from these five different approaches would handle the same client serves as the core of the book, helping you to see distinctive ways therapists with different orientations conduct psychotherapy.

Gestalt Therapy Verbatim (1969)

by Fritz Perls
Lafayette, CA: Real People Press

Fritz Perls, the founder of Gestalt therapy, lays out the main ideas of his approach in vivid detail.

Great Cases in Psychotherapy (1979)

by D. Wedding and R. Corsini
Itasca, IL: Peacock

A complete description of a number of well-known cases in psychotherapy, including clients of Sigmund Freud, Fritz Perls, Alfred Adler, Carl Jung, and Carl Rogers.

National Alliance of the Mentally Ill

2101 Wilson Road, Suite 302
Arlington, VA 22201
703-524-7600

This is an alliance of self-help/advocacy groups concerned with severe and chronically mentally disordered individuals. The objective is to provide emotional support and practical guidance to families. The Alliance has resource materials available and publishes a monthly newsletter, *NAMI Advocate*.

Internet Resources

http://www.behavior.net/
Participate in on-line discussions about various therapy forms.

http://www.erols.com/leopold/webdoc7.htm
Consider a career in creative arts therapy.

http://www.azstarnet.com/~lehrman/
Explore eastern methods for making personal changes at this site.

http://www.webmart.net/~hkngfam/index.htm
Freudian Slips offers a comprehensive guide to therapeutic forms.

http://www.webmart.net/~hkngfam/index.htm
The White Buffalo society offers treatment based on principles from Native American traditions.

http://www.poey.demon.co.uk/linksj.htm
Explore family therapy interventions at this site.

http://www.pinkpractice.co.uk/
"The Pink Practice" provides mental health support to the lesbian, gay, and bisexual community.

http://www.healthguide.com/Therapy/sysdesens.stm
A guide for managing anxiety using systematic desensitization.

13

Health, Stress, and Coping

OUTLINE

BOXES

Look to your health and if you have it value it next to a

good conscience. . . . Health is a blessing we mortals can

achieve.

—Izaak Walton
English Writer, 17th Century

This chapter is about the role psychology plays in understanding health, stress, and coping. We will examine how people can cope more effectively with stress and live healthier lives. You will learn about both effective and ineffective coping strategies. Before we tackle health, stress, and coping, we will examine the historical and contemporary approaches to understanding health concerns. To begin, we will examine the life of Mort, an air traffic controller, and ask you to respond to some items that can reveal your vulnerability to stress.

❖

The Story of Mort: Overwhelmed by Stress

Mort, age 52, has worked as an air traffic controller for the past 15 years. An excitable person, he compares the job to being in a cage. During peak air traffic, the tension is almost unbearable. In these frenzied moments, Mort's emotions are a mixture of rage, fear, and anxiety. Unfortunately, the tension also spills over into his family life. In his own words, "When I go home, my nerves are hopping. I take it out on the nearest person." Two years ago, Mort's wife, Sally, told him that if he could not calm his emotions and handle stress more effectively, she would leave him. She suggested that he change to a less upsetting job, but he ignored her advice. His intense emotional behavior continued, and she left him. Last week the roof fell in on Mort. That Sunday evening, the computer that monitors air traffic temporarily went down and Mort had a heart attack. Quadruple bypass surgery saved his life.

Yesterday his doctor talked with him about the stress in his life and what could be done to reduce it. Mort rarely gets enough sleep, weighs too much but frequently skips meals, never exercises, smokes two packs of cigarettes a day, and drinks two or three scotches every evening (more on weekends). He professes no religious interests. He rarely dates since his divorce and has no relatives living within 50 miles. He has only one friend and does not feel very close to him. Mort says that he never has enough time to do the things he wants to do and rarely has quiet time to himself during the day. He has fun only about once every 2 weeks.

The doctor gave Mort a test, shown in the Self-Assessment, to reveal his vulnerability to stress. Mort scored 68 on the stress test, indicating he is seriously vulnerable to stress and close to the extremely vulnerable range. Stress is inevitable in our lives, so it is important to understand what factors are involved in managing stress and in maintaining a healthy lifestyle. How do *you* fare on the stress test? ❖

RELATING HEALTH AND PSYCHOLOGY

The link between health and psychological factors is easy to make. You may have noticed in your own life that when you are feeling healthy, life is great. When you are "under the weather" from illness or "under the gun" from stress, other aspects of your life—the quality of your work, the smoothness of your relationships, your ability to study—are all likely to suffer. This connection was first observed many centuries ago.

> *The body never lies.*
>
> —MARTHA GRAHAM, *Dancer, 20th Century*

Historical Background

Good health requires good habits. This was recognized as early as 2600 B.C. by Asian physicians and around 500 B.C. by Greek physicians. Unlike other early cultures, these cultures did not blame the gods for illness. Nor did they think that magic would cure illness. Instead, they realized that people have some control over their health. In these two cultures, the physician's role was to guide and assist the patient in restoring a natural and emotional balance in life.

Despite the wisdom of this integrated viewpoint, this belief did not persist during much of the history that followed. Later ideas about health and illness were based more on superstition and folklore, and old treatment methods seem primitive and foolish by

$\mathcal{S}$elf-Assessment

Stress Test

Rate yourself on each item, using a scale of 1–5:
1 = almost always
2 = often
3 = sometimes
4 = seldom
5 = never

1. I eat at least one hot, balanced meal a day.
2. I get 7 to 8 hours of sleep at least four nights a week.
3. I give and receive affection regularly.
4. I have at least one relative within 50 miles whom I can rely on.
5. I exercise to the point of perspiration at least twice a week.
6. I smoke less than half a pack of cigarettes a day.
7. I take fewer than five alcoholic drinks a week.
8. I am the appropriate weight for my height.
9. I have an income adequate to meet my basic expenses.
10. I get strength from my religious beliefs.
11. I regularly attend church.
12. I have a network of friends and acquaintances.
13. I have one or more friends to confide in about personal matters.
14. I am in good health (including eyesight, hearing, teeth).
15. I am able to speak openly about my feelings when angry or worried.
16. I have regular conversations with the people I live with about domestic problems (e.g., chores, money, and daily living issues).
17. I do something for fun at least once a week.
18. I am able to organize my time effectively.
19. I drink fewer than three cups of coffee (or tea or cola drinks) a day.
20. I take quiet time for myself during the day.

Total:

To get your total score, add up the figures and subtract 20. Any number over 30 indicates a vulnerability to stress. You are seriously vulnerable if your score is between 50 and 75 and extremely vulnerable if it is over 75.

today's standards. For example, it used to be common to apply leeches for a variety of illnesses—a treatment that might have hastened many a sick person's demise. Although western medical practice became more sophisticated over time, it still maintained a dualistic approach of viewing the mind and body as independent.

As we approach the twenty-first century, once again we recognize the power of lifestyles and psychological states in promoting health. We are returning to the ancient view that the ultimate responsibility for influencing health rests with the individuals themselves. Without negating the importance of our genetic predispositions and the power of viruses and bacteria, we have come to believe that our daily behavioral choices and our general attitude about life play a significant role in the quality of our health. In addition, we affirm this belief using extensive research strategies in a variety of contexts. Psychologists and other health-related scientists generate evidence to support many of the relationships that the ancient Asians and early Greeks originally suspected.

Current Approaches

Several specialized fields have emerged, primarily in the disciplines of psychology and biology, to explore how health and psychology relate. We will examine each specialty area in turn.

Health psychology *is a multidimensional approach to health that emphasizes psychological factors, lifestyle, and the nature of the health-care delivery system.* To underscore the increasing interest in health, the American Psychological Association created a new division, Health Psychology, in 1978. **Behavioral medicine,** *a field closely related to health psychology, attempts to combine medical and behavioral knowledge to reduce illness and promote health.* The interests of health psychologists and behavioral medicine researchers are broad: They include examining decisions about adherence to medical recommendations, evaluating the effectiveness of media campaigns in reducing smoking, identifying the psychological factors that affect weight loss, and exploring the role of exercise in reducing stress.

Psychoneuroimmunology *is the field that explores connections among psychological factors (such as attitudes and emotions), the nervous system, and the immune system.* The immune system keeps us healthy by recognizing and destroying foreign materials such as bacteria, viruses, and tumors. The machinery of the immune system consists of billions of white blood cells located in the lymph system. Stress levels appear to influence the efficiency of the white blood cells in keeping the system clean of foreign viruses or bacteria.

Researchers are beginning to uncover connections between psychological factors and the immune system (Anderson, Kiecolt, & Glaser, 1994). For example, Sandra Levy (1985) explored the immune system's activity when cancer spread to the lymph nodes of women treated for breast cancer. Levy found that women who became angry and agitated about their disease had stronger immune systems than women who passively accepted the disease and adjusted to their condition. Levy believes that accepting the disease reflects a feeling of helplessness; in contrast, anger indicates that patients believe they can fight the disease. Beliefs about control, she says, might affect the immune system. Psychologists increasingly believe that directly confronting problems, seeking solutions, getting answers, sharing concerns, and taking an active role in treatment are wise strategies that help cancer patients cope more effectively and might have physical benefits (Weisman, 1989).

In summary, the specialty areas of health psychology, behavioral medicine, and psychoneuroimmunology provide scientific evidence that psychological factors play a role in health and illness. Before we examine the effects of stress in greater detail, let's explore the challenges of promoting health.

PROMOTING HEALTH

We can do a great deal to promote better health by establishing healthy habits and evaluating and changing our behaviors that interfere with good health. Regular exercise and good nutrition are essential ingredients to a healthier lifestyle. Not overeating and not smoking are important in improving the quality of a person's health. And making sound sexual decisions adds to life's quality.

health psychology

A multidimensional approach to health that emphasizes psychological factors, lifestyle, and the nature of the health-care delivery system.

behavioral medicine

A field closely related to health psychology that attempts to combine medical and behavioral knowledge to reduce illness and promote health.

psychoneuroimmunology

The field that explores the connections among psychological factors (such as attitudes and emotions), the nervous system, and the immune system.

THE FAR SIDE   By GARY LARSON

"One!"

THE FAR SIDE © 1982. Reprinted by permission of Chronicle Features, San Francisco, Calif.

aerobic exercise

Sustained exercise—jogging, swimming, or cycling, for example—that stimulates heart and lung activity.

Regular Exercise

In 1961, President John F. Kennedy offered the following message: "We are underexercised as a nation. We look instead of play. We ride instead of walk. Our existence deprives us of the minimum of physical activity essential for healthy living." Without question, people are jogging, cycling, and aerobically exercising more today than in 1961, but far too many of us are still couch potatoes. **Aerobic exercise** *is sustained exercise—jogging, swimming, or cycling, for example—that stimulates heart and lung activity.*

The main focus of exercise's effects on health has involved preventing heart disease. Most health experts recommend that you should try to raise your heart rate to 60 percent of your maximum heart rate. Your maximum heart rate is calculated as 220 minus your age multiplied by 0.6, so if you are 20, you should aim for an exercise heart rate of 120 ($220 - 20 = 200 \times 0.6 = 120$). If you are 45, you should aim for an exercise heart rate of 105 ($220 - 45 = 175 \times 0.6 = 105$).

People in some occupations get more vigorous exercise than those in others. For example, longshoremen have about half the risk of fatal heart attacks as co-workers like crane drivers and clerks who have physically less demanding jobs. Further, elaborate studies of 17,000 male alumni of Harvard University found that those who exercised strenuously on a regular basis had a lower risk of heart disease and were more likely to still be

Moderate or intense exercise benefits physical and mental health.

alive in their middle adulthood years (Lee, Hsieh, & Paffenbarger, 1995; Paffenbarger & others, 1986).

Many experts recommend that adults should engage in 30 minutes or more of moderate-intensity physical activity on most, preferably all, days of the week; however, only about one-fifth of adults are active at these recommended levels of physical activity. Examples of the physical activities that qualify as moderate or vigorous are listed in table 13.1.

Researchers have found that exercise benefits not only physical health, but mental health as well. In particular, exercise improves self-concept and reduces anxiety and depression (Ossip-Klein & others, 1989). In sum, moderate or intense exercise benefits our physical *and* mental health. To read about getting motivated to exercise, see Improving Personal and Cognitive Skills.

TABLE 13.1
Moderate and Vigorous Physical Activities

Moderate	Vigorous
Walking, briskly (3–4 mph)	Walking, briskly uphill or with a load
Cycling for pleasure or transportation (≤10 mph)	Cycling, fast or racing (>10 mph)
Swimming, moderate effort	Swimming, fast treading crawl
Conditioning exercise, general calisthenics	Conditioning exercise, stair ergometer, ski machine
Racket sports, table tennis	Racket sports, singles tennis
Golf, pulling cart or carrying clubs	Golf, practice at driving range
Fishing, standing/ casting	Fishing in stream
Canoeing, leisurely (2.0–3.9 mph)	Canoeing, rapidly (≥4 mph)
Home care, general cleaning	Moving furniture
Mowing lawn, power mower	Mowing lawn, hand mower
Home repair, painting	Fix-up projects

Proper Nutriton

We are a nation obsessed with food. We spend an extraordinary amount of time thinking about, gobbling up, and avoiding food. In chapter 9, we discussed the nature of hunger. Here we will explore prevailing standards for proper nutrition as well as problems related to eating, such as obesity, dieting, and eating disorders.

Nutritional Standards.   Despite the growing variety of choices Americans can make in the grocery store, many of us are unhealthy eaters. We take in too much sugar and not enough foods that are high in vitamins, minerals, and fiber. We eat too much fast food and too few well-balanced meals. These choices increase fat and cholesterol intake, both of which are implicated as long-term health risks.

Evidence for the negative effects of poor nutritional choices comes from both animal and cross-cultural research. For example, mice fed a high-fat diet are more likely to develop breast cancer than mice fed a low-fat diet. And a cross-cultural study of women found a strong positive correlation between fat consumption and death rates from breast cancer (Cohen, 1987) (see figure 13.1).

*I*mproving Personal and Cognitive Skills

Motivating Yourself to Exercise

Following are some helpful strategies for finding a place for exercise in your life:

- *Make exercise a high priority in your life.*

Find time in your regular schedule for exercise. If exercise is not important enough to you to be on your regular schedule, you probably aren't spending enough time in exercise. Regular exercise by college students is related to their good health.

- *Reduce TV time.*

Heavy TV viewing by college students is linked to their poor health (Astin, 1993). Replace some of your TV time with exercise time.

- *Chart your progress.*

Systematically recording your exercise workouts will help you chart your progress. This strategy is especially helpful in getting people to maintain their exercise program over a long period of time.

- *Get rid of excuses.*

People make up all kinds of excuses for not exercising. A typical excuse is, "I just don't have enough time."

- *Imagine the alternative.*

Ask yourself whether you are too busy to take care of your own health. What will your life be like if you lose your health?

- *Learn more about exercise.*

The more you know about exercise, the more you are likely to start an exercise program and continue it. Read the resources section at the end of the chapter for a good book on exercise.

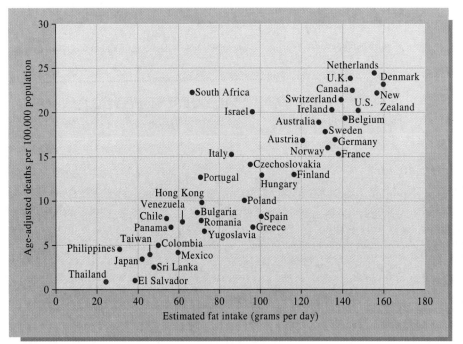

*F*IGURE 13.1

Cross-Cultural Comparisons of Diet and Cancer

In countries in which individuals have a low daily intake of fat, the rate of breast cancer is low (in Thailand, for example). In countries in which individuals have a high daily intake of fat, the rate of breast cancer is high (in the Netherlands, for example). *From "Diet and Cancer" by Leonard A. Cohen. Copyright © 1987 by Scientific American, Inc. All rights reserved.*

One of the most telling comparisons to link fat intake and cancer is between the United States and Japan. Both countries have similar levels of industrialization and education, as well as high medical standards. Although the overall cancer rates of the two countries are similar, cancers of the breast, colon, and prostrate are common in the United States but rare in Japan. By contrast, cancer of the stomach is common in Japan but rare in the United States. Within two generations, Japanese immigrants to Hawaii and California have breast cancer rates that are significantly higher than those in Japan and that approach those of Americans. Many researchers believe that the high fat intake of Americans and the low fat intake of the Japanese are implicated in the countries' different cancer rates.

American nutritional standards have changed over time, and this has added to our confusion about which foods we should eat. Only a few decades ago, eggs and dairy foods were promoted as virtually ideal food sources. Now we know that some dairy products, such as whole milk, eggs, and butter, should generally be avoided and replaced with low-fat substitutes. Today, nutritionists believe that proper nutrition goes beyond just specifying an adequate calorie range; it should also involve carefully selecting foods that provide appropriate nutrients with their calories. A sound nutritional plan provides the nutrients we need—fat, carbohydrates, protein, vitamins, minerals, and water—in the proper amounts.

Several health goals can be accomplished through a sound nutritional plan. Not only does a well-balanced diet provide more energy, but healthy selections lower blood pressure, cancer risk, and even tooth decay. If you think that you need to make some nutritional changes, the recommendations in Improving Personal and Cognitive Skills may help.

Next, we will explore the negative effects of what happens when nutritional strategies fail, beginning with obesity.

Obesity. Estimates indicate that 31 percent of men and 24 percent of women in the United States are overweight, with 12 percent of both sexes severely overweight (National Academy of Sciences Research Council, 1989). The economic costs of obesity are estimated at $39 billion per year, or more than 5 percent of all health costs. The staggering cost figures stem from obesity's association with diabetes, hypertension, cardiovascular diseases, and some cancers (Friedman & Brownell, 1998; Thompson, 1996).

Many scientists believe heredity plays an important role in obesity. Animals can be inbred to develop a propensity for obesity (Blundell, 1984). Further, identical human

*I*mproving Personal and Cognitive Skills

Eating Right

What are some strategies for improving your nutritional choices? They include the following:

- *Don't eat more calories than you need on a regular basis.*
  A standard calorie count for women, children, and men over 50 is 2,000 per day. Other individuals, especially those who are physically active, require more—up to 2,500.
- *Cut back on fat in your diet.*
  Less than 30% of your calorie intake should come from fat. Limit cholesterol to 300 milligrams a day.
- *Increase fruits and vegetables.*
  Each day, eat five or more fruits or vegetables. Especially eat green and yellow vegetables, as well as citrus fruits, because they are vitamin-rich.

- *Increase starches and other complex carbohydrates.*
  These include breads, cereals, and legumes (beans), which promote regularity.
- *Eat moderate amounts of protein each day.*
  Too little protein can lead to anemia, or iron loss in the blood. Too much protein probably means you are taking in too many calories.
- *Avoid supplementing your diet with vitamins that exceed recommended daily allowances (RDAs).*
  Most people can get the vitamins they need through a well-balanced diet. Consuming handfuls of vitamin supplements has not been demonstrated to have health benefits, and it can be expensive.
- *Drink lots of water.*
  Your body needs lots of water to function optimally. One good idea is to drink water instead of carbonated beverages, which provide no nutritional value.

set point

The weight maintained when no effort is made to gain or lose weight.

basal metabolism rate (BMR)

The minimal amount of energy an individual uses in a resting state.

twins have similar weights, even when they are reared apart. Estimates of variance in body mass that can be explained by heredity range from 25 percent to 70 percent.

The amount of stored fat in your body is an important factor in your **set point,** *the weight maintained when no effort is made to gain or lose weight.* Fat is stored in adipose cells. When these cells are filled, you do not get hungry. When people gain weight—because of genetic predisposition, early childhood eating patterns, or adult overeating—the number of fat cells increases, and they might not be able to get rid of them. A normal-weight individual has 30 to 40 billion fat cells. An obese individual has 80 to 120 billion fat cells. When individuals go on a diet, their fat cells might shrink but they do not go away.

Another factor in weight is **basal metabolism rate (BMR),** *the minimal amount of energy an individual uses in a resting state.* BMR varies with age and sex. Rates decline precipitously during adolescence and then more gradually during adulthood; they also are slightly higher for males than for females. Many individuals gradually increase their weight over a period of many years. To some degree the weight gain may be due to a declining basal metabolism rate. The declining BMR underscores the importance of reducing our food intake as we grow older if we want to maintain our weight.

In addition to hereditary and biological factors, environmental factors are involved in weight and shape in important ways. The human gustatory system and taste preferences developed at a time when reliable sources of food were scarce. Our earliest ancestors probably developed a preference for sweets, since ripe fruit, which is a concentrated source of sugar (and thus calories), was so accessible. Today many people still have a "sweet tooth" but unlike our ancestors' ripe fruit, which contained sugar *plus* vitamins and minerals, the soft drinks and candy bars we snack on today too often fill us with empty calories.

Strong evidence of the environment's influence is the doubling of the rate of obesity in the United States since 1900, likely due to greater availability of food (especially food high in fat), energy-saving devices, and declining physical activity. The obesity rate also increased more than 50 percent from the 1960s to 1980. Obesity is six times more frequent among low-income women than among upper-income women, and more common among Americans than among Europeans.

Dieting. Many divergent interests are involved in the topic of dieting. They include the public, health professionals, policy makers, the media, and the powerful diet and food industries. On the one side are societal norms that promote a very lean, aesthetic body. This ideal is supported by an industry valued at more than $30 billion a year in diet books, programs, videos, foods, and pills. On the other side are health professionals and a growing minority of the press. Although they recognize the alarmingly high rate of obesity, they are frustrated by high relapse rates. They also are increasingly concerned that chronic dieting can have negative effects on health (Brownell & Rodin, 1994).

> *Eat, drink, and be merry, for tomorrow ye shall diet.*
> —LEWIS HENRY, *American Writer, 20th Century*

Dieting is a pervasive concern of many Americans. In a large-scale national survey, 52 percent of women and 37 percent of men reported that they were overweight (Horm & Anderson, 1993). The population is not uniform, and clearly not everyone should go on a diet. A 10 percent reduction in body weight might produce striking benefits for an older, obese, hypertensive man but be unhealthy for an adolescent female who is not overweight. The pressure to be thin, and thus diet, is greatest among young women, yet they do not have the highest risk of obesity.

Although many Americans regularly embark on a diet, few are successful in keeping weight off long-term (McFarlane, Polivy & Herman, 1998). Some critics argue that all diets fail (Wooley & Garner, 1991). However, there is evidence that some individuals who go on diets do lose weight and maintain the loss (Brownell & Cohen, 1995). How often this occurs and whether some diet programs are better than others are still open questions.

Something important that we do know about losing weight is that the most effective programs include an exercise component. Exercise not only burns up calories but continues to raise the metabolic rate for several hours *after* the exercise. Also, exercise lowers a person's set point for weight, which makes it easier to maintain a lower weight (Bennett & Gurin, 1982).

Even when diets do produce weight loss, they can place the dieter at risk for other health problems. One main concern focuses on weight cycling (commonly referred to as "yo-yo dieting," in which the individual engages in a recurring cycle of dieting and weight gain) (Wadden & others, 1996). Researchers have found a link between frequent changes in weight and chronic disease (Brownell and Rodin, in press). Also, liquid diets and other very-low-calorie strategies are related to gall bladder damage.

With these problems in mind, when overweight people diet and maintain their weight loss, they do become less depressed and reduce their risk for a number of health-impairing disorders (Christensen, 1996). Next, we will explore problems that occur at the other end of the weight spectrum—when people become so thin that their health becomes impaired.

Anorexia Nervosa and Bulimia.   Eighteen-year-old Gina gradually eliminated foods from her diet to the point at which she subsisted by eating *only* applesauce and eggnog. She spent hours observing her body, wrapping her fingers around her waist to see if it was getting any thinner. She fantasized about becoming a beautiful fashion model and wearing designer bathing suits. However, even when she dropped 85 pounds, Gina still felt fat. She continued to lose weight, eventually emaciating herself. She was hospitalized and treated for **anorexia nervosa,** *an eating disorder that involves the relentless pursuit of thinness through starvation.* Anorexia nervosa can eventually lead to death, as it did for popular singer Karen Carpenter and gymnast Christy Henrich.

Most anorexics are White adolescent or young adult females from well-educated, middle- and upper-income families. They have distorted body images, perceiving themselves as overweight even when they are skeletal. Numerous causes of anorexia nervosa have been proposed (Mussell & Mitchell, 1998). One is the current fashion image of thinness, reflected in the saying "You can't be too rich or too thin." Many anorexics grow up in families with high achievement demands that they are unable to meet. For instance, unable to control their grades, they turn to something they can control: their weight.

Bulimia *is an eating disorder in which the individual consistently follows a binge-and-purge eating pattern.* The bulimic goes on an eating binge and then purges by self-induced vomiting or using a laxative. Sometimes the binges alternate with fasting, at other times

anorexia nervosa
An eating disorder that involves the relentless pursuit of thinness through starvation.

bulimia
An eating disorder in which the individual consistently follows a binge-and-purge eating pattern.

Because they tend to adopt severe weight-loss strategies, athletes and dancers appear to be especially vulnerable to anorexia nervosa. Gymnast Christy Henrich weighed only 47 pounds when she died. Her self-starvation was sparked by unfavorable comments about her weight from a competition judge.

with normal eating. Like anorexia nervosa, bulimia is primarily a female disorder. Bulimia has become prevalent among traditional-age college women.

Anorexics can control their eating, but bulimics cannot. Depression is a common characteristic of bulimics. Bulimia can produce gastric and chemical imbalance in the body. Many of the causes proposed for anorexia nervosa are also offered for bulimia (Fairburn, 1995).

In our coverage of nutrition and eating problems, we have seen that many people have difficulty maintaining a healthy weight. Next, we will explore another area in which people have difficulty in self-control.

Freedom from Smoking

Shifts toward promoting health are most obvious in the area of smoking prevention. Nearly a decade after the surgeon general warned that cigarettes are responsible for major health problems, the tobacco industry is under siege with lawsuits—from consumers whose health has been impaired, and from states that have to foot much of the bill for smoking-related illness. Such massive litigation has prompted tobacco companies to begin negotiations with legal authorities to figure out a way to stem the tide of lawsuits and limit their liability for health-related damages.

Converging evidence from a number of studies underscores the dangers of smoking or being around those who do (Millis, 1998). For example, smoking is linked to 30 percent of cancer deaths, 21 percent of heart disease deaths, and 82 percent of chronic pulmonary disease deaths. Secondhand smoke is implicated in as many as 9,000 lung cancer deaths a year (Sandler & others, 1989). Children of smokers are at special risk for respiratory and middle-ear diseases.

Fewer people smoke today than in the past, and almost half of all living adults who ever smoked have quit. The prevalence of smoking in men has dropped from over 50 percent in 1965 to about 25 percent today. However, more than 50 million Americans still smoke cigarettes today. And recently cigar smoking, with risks similar to those of cigarette smoking, has increased.

Most adult smokers would like to quit, but their addiction to nicotine often turns their efforts into dismal failure. Nicotine, the active drug in cigarettes, is a stimulant that increases the smoker's energy and alertness, a pleasurable and reinforcing experience (Payne & others, 1996). Nicotine also stimulates neurotransmitters that have a calming or pain-reducing effect. However, smoking not only works as a positive reinforcer, it also works as a negative reinforcer by ending a smoker's painful craving for nicotine. A smoker gets relief from this aversive state simply by smoking another cigarette. The immediate gratification of smoking is extremely hard to overcome even for adults who recognize that smoking is "suicide in slow motion."

How can smokers quit? Four methods can be effective in helping smokers abandon their habit: nicotine substitution, stimulus control, aversive conditioning, and going "cold turkey."

Nicotine Substitutes. Nicotine gum and the nicotine patch work on the principle of supplying small amounts of nicotine to diminish the intensity of withdrawal. Nicotine gum, now available without a prescription, is a drug that smokers can take orally when they get the urge to smoke. The nicotine

THE FAR SIDE By GARY LARSON

The real reason dinosaurs became extinct

patch is a nonprescription adhesive pad that delivers a steady dose of nicotine to the individual. The dose is gradually reduced over an 8- to 12-week period. Success rates for the nicotine patch have been encouraging.

Stimulus Control.　This behavior modification technique sensitizes the smoker to social cues associated with smoking. For example, the individual might associate a morning cup of coffee or a social drink with smoking. Stimulus control strategies help the smoker to avoid these cues or learn to substitute other behaviors for smoking. This approach has met with mixed results.

Aversive Conditioning.　Imagine smoking as many cigarettes as possible until the ashtray overflows and the smell of stale cigarettes feels like it is permanently embedded in your fingertips. The concept behind aversive conditioning is to smoke until you feel nauseous, with the hope that this feeling will condition you to the point that you won't want to smoke anymore. Sometimes this works, sometimes it doesn't.

Going "Cold Turkey."　Some people have success by simply stopping smoking without making any major changes in their lifestyle. They decide they are going to quit and they do. Lighter smokers usually have more success with this approach than heavier smokers.

> *I'm glad I don't have to explain to a man from Mars why each day I set fire to dozens of little pieces of paper, and then put them in my mouth.*
> —MIGNON MCLAUGHLIN, *Humorist and Writer, 20th Century*

Sound Sexual Decision-Making

In this section, we will explore the importance of making healthy decisions in your sex life. To begin, let's see how sexually knowledgeable Americans are.

Sexual Knowledge.　How much do we really know about sex? According to June Reinisch (1990), director of the Kinsey Institute, the United States is a nation whose citizens know more about how their automobiles function than about how their bodies function sexually. Reinisch directed a national assessment of approximately 2,000 adults' sexual knowledge. Almost two-thirds did not know that most erection problems begin with physical, not psychological, problems. Fifty percent did not know that oil-based lubricants should not be used with condoms or diaphragms because some can produce holes in them in less than a minute.

One conclusion we can draw from Reinisch's national survey is that there is a great deal we do not know. But what might be even more problematic are the unfounded sexual myths that we believe. American adolescents believe a distressing amount of misinformation and myths about sex. In one study, a majority of adolescents believed that pregnancy risk is greatest during menstruation (Zelnick & Kanter, 1977). To read about other myths and misunderstandings about sexuality, see Applications in Psychology. These examples underscore the serious need to improve our sexual awareness and knowledge, which can help to reduce unwanted pregnancies and promote sexual self-protection.

Contraception.　Most couples in the United States want to control whether and when they will conceive a child. For them it is important to have accurate knowledge about contraception.

Inadequate knowledge about contraception, coupled with inconsistent use of effective contraceptive methods, has resulted in this country's having the dubious distinction of having the highest adolescent pregnancy rate in the industrialized world (Coleman, 1995). Although the rate of use among teenagers is improving, many still do not use contraception. Moreover, a majority of adolescents do not use contraception during their first sexual intercourse experience (Hofferth, 1990). Seventy percent of females who become sexually active before the age of 15 have unprotected first intercourse; the percentage drops to about 50 percent for those who become active around the age of 18 or 19.

Applications in Psychology

The Value of Sexual Skepticism

As we navigate the sometimes murky waters of sexuality, we encounter many myths. Because misinformation about sex is so widespread, adopting a skeptical attitude about sexual claims makes good sense.

Following are some myths that a group of psychology students claimed to have believed until they encountered disconfirming evidence:

- You can get pregnant most easily if you make love in water.
- If women don't achieve an orgasm during sex, then they won't get pregnant.
- A woman can prevent pregnancy by jumping up and down after sex.
- You can't get pregnant the first time you have intercourse.
- Women can't achieve orgasm without direct stimulation of the G-spot.
- The size of a man's penis determines how satisfying sex will be.
- The size of a man's penis corresponds to the size of his nose (foot, thumb).
- Simultaneous orgasm is the only acceptable form of satisfaction.
- Breast-feeding prevents pregnancy.
- If men can't ejaculate after a certain threshold of stimulation has been reached, they'll become sick.

Some of these myths are abandoned after experience provides (sometimes painful) disconfirmation. How can adolescents and adults learn to navigate the precarious waters of sexuality with a minimum of misinformation to make informed choices about their behavior? The following specific strategies can help protect you.

1. *Regard cause-and-effect claims about sexuality with suspicion.* Nature encourages behavior that will help living

organisms reproduce. Pregnancy requires contact of an egg and sperm. Measures that don't directly prevent that contact are not likely to be effective against pregnancy.

2. *Remember your own mortality.* It is relatively easy, especially in moments of passion, to abandon good judgment about self-protection. In such moments we tend to think of ourselves as immune to the laws of nature ("It won't happen to me"; "Just this once and never again"). Many carefree lovers end up very care-ridden by the biological consequences of impulsive unprotected sex.

3. *Evaluate the risk if the claim appears to be untrue.* Taking risks is part of life. However, sexual risk-taking in the absence of knowledge can result in dramatic life-changing outcomes. Where the risk is too great, restraint is the wiser course.

4. *Assess whether the source of the claims is trustworthy and astute.* Sometimes people promote myths as a strategy for getting into a sexual relationship. Claims made by a person in the hopes of achieving intimacy could be manipulative; you need to establish whether you can trust a person you are considering becoming intimate with. People also sometimes pass along misguided sexual lore, with an intention not to take advantage but only to inform—but end up only misinforming. You need to establish whether the person you are discussing sexual lore with is likely to be well informed.

5. *Ask for evidence to support claims that are risk-promoting.* Always require evidence in support of any claim about a cause-and-effect relationship in behavior. This is imperative regarding claims that are relevant to the risks you might be taking by engaging in sexual activity. Questions to keep in mind include the following: *How did you learn about that? How much confidence do you have in the claim? What if you are wrong?*

Age also influences the choice of contraceptive method. Older adolescents and young adults are more likely to rely on the pill or diaphragm; younger adolescents are more likely to use a condom or withdrawal (Hofferth, 1990). Even adults in stable relationships sometimes do not use adequate contraception, perhaps feeling that some contraceptives, such as condoms, interrupt the spontaneity of sex, or they might overestimate the effectiveness of some of the unreliable methods.

No method of contraception is best for everyone. When choosing a method of contraception, couples need to consider such factors as their physical and emotional concerns, the method's effectiveness, the nature of their relationship, their values and beliefs, and the method's convenience. Calculations of the effectiveness of a contraceptive method often are based on the failure rates during the first year of use. It is estimated that if no contraceptive method were used, about 90 percent of women would become pregnant in their first year of being (heterosexually) sexually active (Hatcher & others, 1988).

Sexually Transmitted Diseases.   **Sexually transmitted diseases (STDS)** *are diseases that are contracted primarily through sex—intercourse as well as oral-genital and anal-genital sex.* The following are some of the most common STDs:

- *Gonorrhea.* Gonorrhea is a bacterial infection that is commonly called "the clap." Early symptoms of gonorrhea are more common in men than women. In men these symptoms are a foul-smelling, cloudy discharge from the penis, and burning sensations during urination. A yellow-green discharge can occur in women but might go unnoticed. If not treated quickly, gonorrhea can produce sterility in both women and men. Antibiotics can effectively treat gonorrhea.
- *Syphilis.* Syphilis also is caused by bacteria. It is less common than gonorrhea but potentially far more dangerous. The first syphilis symptom usually is a *chancre* (a painless sore) that appears about 3 weeks after infection. For women, the sore usually appears on the inner vaginal wall or cervix; for men, on the penis. Syphilis can be treated effectively with penicillin in its early stages, but untreated it eventually leads to death.
- *Chlamydia.* This STD is caused by bacteria, but the STD acts like a virus, growing only within the body's cells. Chlamydia is the most common bacterial STD in the United States. An estimated 3 to 5 million women, men, and infants develop a chlamydial infection each year. The STD is transmitted primarily through sexual contact. Chlamydia comes in several forms. In many instances, chlamydia initially produces few or no symptoms. However, one form of chlamydia, *pelvic inflammatory disease (PID),* can produce disrupted menstrual cycles, chronic pelvic pain, and fever. PID can leave some women sterile. Chlamydia can be treated effectively with antibiotics.
- *Genital herpes.* This STD is caused by a virus and infects 10 to 20 million Americans. About 3 of 4 individuals exposed to an infected partner will develop herpes. The most common herpes symptoms are one or more small, painful red bumps in the genital region. For women, this occurs on the labia; for men, on the penis. Not long after their initial appearance, the red bumps turn into blisters filled with highly infectious fluid. Drugs such as Zovirax and Acyclovir can reduce herpes symptoms, but there is no known cure for herpes.
- *AIDS.* No single STD has had a greater impact on sexual behavior, or created more fear in the last decade, than AIDS. **AIDS** *is a sexually transmitted disease that is caused by the human immunodeficiency virus (HIV), which destroys the body's immune system.* A person who has contracted HIV is vulnerable to germs that a normal immune system could destroy.

Although 90 percent of U.S. AIDS cases continue to occur among homosexual males and intravenous drug users, a disproportionate increase among female sexual partners of bisexual males or intravenous drug users has been recently noted. In 1997, 25 percent of AIDS patients were female (Centers for Disease Control, 1998). This increase suggests that the risk of AIDS is increasing among heterosexuals who have multiple sex partners.

Experts say that AIDS can be transmitted only by (Kalichman, 1995):

- sexual contact
- sharing hypodermic needles
- blood transfusion (which in the last few years has been tightly monitored)
- other direct contact of cuts or mucous membranes with blood and sexual fluids

Remember that it is not who you are, but what you do, that puts you at risk for getting HIV. *Anyone* who is sexually active or uses intravenous drugs is at risk. No one is immune. Once an individual is infected, the prognosis is likely illness and death. The only safe behavior is abstinence from sex, which is not perceived as an option by most individuals. Beyond abstinence, there is only safer behavior, such as sexual behavior without exchange of semen, vaginal fluids, or blood, and sexual intercourse with a condom.

Just asking a date about his or her sexual behavior does not guarantee protection from AIDS and other sexually transmitted diseases. For example, in one investigation, 655 college students were asked to answer questions about lying and sexual behavior (Cochran

$\mathcal{I}$mproving Personal and Cognitive Skills

Protecting Against STDs

What are some good strategies for protecting against STDs? They include these:

- *Know your and your partner's risk status.*

Anyone who has had previous sexual activity with another person may have contracted an STD without being aware of it. Spend time getting to know a prospective partner before you have sex. Use this time to inform the other person about your STD status and inquire about that person's STD status. Remember that many people lie about their STD status.

- *Obtain medical examinations.*

Many experts recommend that couples who want to begin a sexual relationship have a medical checkup to rule out

STDs before they engage in sex. If cost is an issue, contact your campus health service or public health clinic.

- *Do not have unprotected sex.*

When correctly used, condoms help prevent many STDs from being transmitted. Condoms are most effective in preventing gonorrhea, syphilis, chlamydia, and AIDS. They are less effective against herpes.

- *Avoid sex with multiple partners.*

One of the best predictors of getting an STD is having sex with multiple partners. Having more than one sex partner elevates the likelihood that you will encounter an infected partner.

Relating Health and Psychology: Promoting Health

Health psychology is a multidimensional approach to health that emphasizes psychological factors, lifestyle, and the nature of the health-care delivery system. Closely related to health psychology is the field of behavioral medicine, which combines medical and behavioral knowledge to reduce illness and promote health. Psychoneuroimmunology explores the connections among psychological factors, the nervous system, and the immune system. Researchers have found that our emotions and attitudes are connected to our immune system.

Both moderate and intense exercise produce important physical and mental health benefits. Effective nutritional

strategies include eating balanced, low-fat meals, although cultures vary in the types of nutrition they promote. Understanding obesity focuses on heredity, set point, basal metabolism rate, and environmental factors. Exercise is an important component of successful weight-loss programs. Smoking is a factor in many deaths in the United States. Many people try to stop smoking but find it extremely difficult because smoking is immediately pleasurable, reinforcing, and addictive.

Many Americans have limited knowledge about sexuality. Many sexually active heterosexuals do not use adequate contraception. Sexually transmitted diseases (STDs) are diseases that are contracted

mainly through sexual contact. Gonorrhea, syphilis, chlamydia, herpes, and AIDS are STDs. AIDS is caused by HIV (human immunodeficiency virus), which destroys the body's immune system. HIV is contracted through sexual contact or sharing of needles.

Seven of the ten leading causes of death in the United States, such as heart disease, stroke, and cancer, are associated with unhealthy behavioral styles. A number of health goals have been proposed for the year 2000. Cultural factors influence coronary problems and cancer. Gender and ethnicity play roles in life expectancy and health.

& Mays, 1990). Of the 422 respondents who said they were sexually active, 34 percent of the men and 10 percent of the women said they had lied so their partner would have sex with them. Much higher percentages—47 percent of the men and 60 percent of the women—said they had been lied to by a potential sexual partner. When asked what aspects of their past they would be most likely to lie about, more than 40 percent of the men and women said they would understate the number of their sexual partners. Twenty percent of the men, but only 4 percent of the women, said they would lie about their results from an AIDS blood test.

To read about some good strategies for protecting against AIDS and other STDs, see Improving Personal and Cognitive Skills. As we learn next, prevention is a critical dimension of promoting health.

Prevention Issues

Being healthy involves far more than simply going to a doctor when you get sick and being treated for disease. We are becoming increasingly aware that our behavior determines whether we will develop a serious illness and when we will die (Lenfant, 1995). Seven of the ten leading causes of death in the United States are associated with the *absence* of healthy behaviors. Diseases such as influenza, polio, and rubella no longer are major causes of death. More deaths now are caused by heart disease (36 percent of all deaths), cancer (22 percent), and stroke (17 percent).

Personal habits and lifestyle play key roles in resisting disease and thriving under stress. These findings lead health psychologists, behavioral medicine specialists, and public health professionals to predict the next major step in improving the general health of the American population will be primarily behavioral, not medical. The federal government and the Society for Public Health Education have set health objectives for the year 2000 (Schwartz & Eriksen, 1989). Among them are the following:

- To develop preventive services targeting diseases and such problems as cancer, heart disease, stroke, unintended pregnancy (especially among adolescents), and AIDS.
- To promote health, including behavior modification and health education; stronger programs are urged for dealing with smoking, alcohol and drug abuse, nutrition, physical fitness, and mental health.
- To work toward cleaner air and water.
- To improve workplace safety, including reducing exposure to toxic chemicals.
- To meet the health needs of special populations, such as gaining a better understanding of disease prevention in African American and Latino populations. Minority groups suffer disproportionately from cancer, heart disease, diabetes, and other major diseases.

America's health-care costs have soared and are moving toward the $1 trillion mark annually. Health experts hope to make a dent in these costs by encouraging people to live healthier lives. Many corporations have begun to recognize that health promotion for their employees is cost effective. Businesses are increasingly examining their employees' health behavior and the workplace environment as they recognize the role health plays in productive work. Smoke-free work environments, onsite exercise programs, bonuses to quit smoking and lose weight, and company-sponsored athletic events are increasingly found in American businesses.

Gender and ethnicity play roles in life expectancy and health. According to psychologist Bonnie Strickland (1989), males are at greater risk than females for death at every age in the life span. The cause of death also varies for men and women. For example, four times more men than women die as a result of homicide, and twice as many men as women die as a result of respiratory cancer, suicide, pulmonary disease, accidents, cirrhosis of the liver, and heart disease.

African Americans have a higher mortality rate than Whites for thirteen of the fifteen leading causes of death (Winett, King, & Altman, 1989). Also, of all ethnic minority women, African American women are the most vulnerable to health problems. For example, African American women, compared with White American women, are three times more likely to have high blood pressure, are twice as likely to die from cardiovascular disease, have a 35 percent higher death rate for diabetes, are four times more likely to be a victim of homicide.

Not only are there cross-cultural and ethnic variations in health, but women and men experience health and the health-care system differently (Stanton & Gallant, 1995). Women's physical complaints are too often dismissed as trivial or interpreted as emotional rather than physical. Most medical research has been conducted with men by men. Frequently the results are generalized to women without sufficient justification (Rabinowitz & Sechzur, 1993). Women's health advocates press for greater inclusion of women in the medical profession and as subjects in medical studies in hope that bias against women will be reduced. They also promote increased attention to health issues that are of special concern to women, such as unintended or unwanted pregnancy, breast and reproductive disorders, and the influence of poverty on health.

UNDERSTANDING STRESS

We live in a world that includes many stressful circumstances. According to the American Academy of Family Physicians, two-thirds of all office visits to family doctors are for stress-related symptoms. Stress is also believed to be a major contributor to coronary heart disease, cancer, lung problems, accidental injuries, cirrhosis of the liver, and suicide, six of the leading causes of death in the United States. In 1989 two of the five best-selling drugs in the United States were an antianxiety drug (Xanax) and an ulcer medication (Zantac). No one really knows whether we experience more stress than our parents or grandparents did at our age, but it seems as if we do.

Stress is one of those terms that is not easy to define. Initially the word *stress* was borrowed from physics. Humans, it was thought, are in some ways similar to physical objects, such as metals, that resist moderate outside forces but lose their resilience at a point of greater pressure. However, unlike metal, human beings can think, reason, and experience a myriad of social and environmental circumstances that make defining stress more complex in psychology than in physics (Hobfoll, 1989).

Although psychologists debate whether stress is the threatening events in our world or our response to those demands, we will define stress broadly. **Stress** *is the response of individuals to the circumstances and events, called stressors, that threaten them and tax their coping abilities.* To understand stress, we need to know about the related biological, personality, cognitive, environmental, and sociocultural factors (see figure 13.2).

Biological Factors

When you are under stress, what happens to your body? As it readies itself to handle the assault of stress, a number of physiological changes take place.

The Nervous System. Many scientists now believe there are two main pathways in the nervous system that connect the brain and endocrine system in response to stress. The first pathway is through the autonomic nervous system (ANS). Your central nervous system perceives a stressor and then the sympathetic part of the ANS releases the stress hormones *epinephrine* (adrenaline) and *norepinephrine* (noradrenaline) from nerve endings in the inner portion of the adrenal glands. A surge of adrenaline not only elevates blood pressure, but has been linked to sudden death through heart disease. The autonomic nervous system changes in response to stress have also been linked

stress

The response of individuals to the circumstances and events, called stressors, that threaten them and tax their coping abilities.

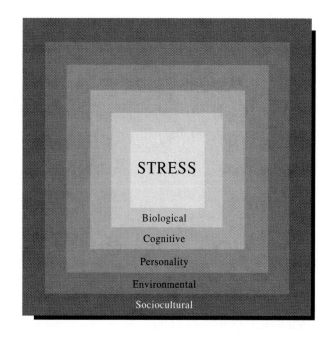

$\mathcal{F}$IGURE 13.2

Factors Involved in Stress

Among the most important factors involved in understanding stress are biological factors (such as our body's response to stress); cognitive factors (such as whether we appraise an event as threatening or challenging); personality factors (such as how we handle anger or whether we trust others); environmental factors (such as the frustrating stressors we experience in our world); and sociocultural factors (such as frustration caused by limited opportunity).

to stomach problems, such as ulcers. The second pathway is used when the cerebral cortex perceives a stressor and the information is routed through the hypothalamus and pituitary gland to the outer part of the adrenal gland, where the hormone *cortisol* is released.

The General Adaptation Syndrome. According to the Austrian-born founder of stress research, the late Hans Selye (1974, 1983), stress simply is the wear and tear on the body due to the demands placed on it. Any number of environmental events or stimuli will produce the same stress response in the body. Selye observed patients with different problems: the death of someone close, loss of income, arrest for embezzlement. Regardless of which problem the patient had, similar symptoms appeared: loss of appetite, muscular weakness, and decreased interest in the world.

general adaptation syndrome (GAS)

Selye's concept of the common effects on the body when demands are placed on it. The GAS consists of three stages: alarm, resistance, and exhaustion.

General adaptation syndrome (GAS) *is Selye's term for the common effects on the body when demands are placed on it. The GAS consists of three stages: alarm, resistance, and exhaustion.* First, in the *alarm stage,* the body enters a temporary state of shock, a time when resistance to illness and stress fall below normal limits. In trying to cope with the initial effects of stress, the body quickly releases hormones, which, in a short time, adversely affect the immune system's functioning. It is during this time that the individual is prone to infections from illness and injury. Fortunately, the alarm stage passes rather quickly as the body begins to build up its resistance. In the *resistance stage,* a number of glands throughout the body begin to manufacture different hormones that protect the individual in many ways. During this stage, the body's immune system can fight off infection with remarkable efficiency. Similarly, hormones that reduce inflammation normally associated with injury are present at high levels. If the all-out effort to combat stress fails and the stress persists, the individual moves into the *exhaustion stage.* Now the wear and tear on the body takes its toll—the person may collapse in a state of exhaustion and vulnerability to disease increases. Figure 13.3 provides an illustration of Selye's general adaptation syndrome.

eustress

Selye's term for the positive features of stress.

Not all stress is bad, though. **Eustress** *is Selye's term for the positive features of stress.* Competing in an athletic event, writing an essay, or pursuing someone who is attractive requires the body to expend energy. Selye does not say we should avoid these fulfilling experiences in life, but he does emphasize that we should minimize their wear and tear on our bodies.

One of the main criticisms of Selye's view is that human beings do not always react to stress in the uniform way he proposed. There is much more to understanding stress in humans than knowing their physical reactions to it. We also need to know about their physical makeup, their perceptions, their personalities, and the contexts in which the stressors occur (Seiffge-Krenke, 1995).

*F*IGURE 13.3

Selye's General Adaptation Syndrome

The general adaptation syndrome (GAS) is the typical series of responses individuals have to stress: alarm, resistance, and exhaustion.

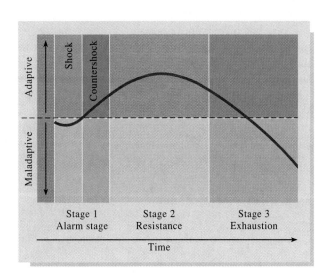

Cognitive Factors

Most of us think of stress as environmental events that place demands on our lives, such as losing one's notes from a class, being yelled at by a friend, failing a test, or being in a car wreck. While there are some common ways we all experience stress, not everyone perceives the same events as stressful. For example, one person may perceive an upcoming job interview as threatening, while another person may perceive it as challenging. One person may perceive a D grade on a paper as threatening, another person may perceive the same grade as challenging. To some degree, then, what is stressful depends on how people cognitively appraise and interpret events. This view has been championed by Richard Lazarus (1993, 1996, 1998). **Cognitive appraisal** *is Lazarus's term to describe individuals' interpretation of events in their lives as harmful, threatening, or challenging, and their determination of whether they have the resources to effectively cope with the event.*

In Lazarus's view, events are appraised in two steps: primary appraisal and secondary appraisal. In *primary appraisal,* individuals interpret whether an event involves *harm* or loss that has already occurred, a *threat* of some future danger, or a *challenge* to be overcome. *Harm* is the individual's appraisal of the damage the event has already inflicted. For example, if you overslept yesterday and missed an exam, the harm has already been done. *Threat* is the individual's appraisal of potential future damage an event may bring. For example, missing the exam may lower the instructor's opinion of you and increase the probability you will get a low grade in the course at the end of the semester. *Challenge* is the individual's appraisal of the potential to overcome the adverse circumstances of an event and ultimately to profit from it. For example, a student may use missing the exam as an opportunity to become acquainted with the instructor and actually benefit from what initially appeared to be a hopelessly bad circumstance.

> *The ultimate measure of a man is not where he stands in moments of comfort and convenience, but where he stands at times of challenge and controversy.*
> —MARTIN LUTHER KING, JR., *American Clergyman and Civil Rights Leader, 20th Century*

After individuals cognitively appraise an event for its harm, threat, or challenge, Lazarus says that they subsequently engage in secondary appraisal. In *secondary appraisal,* individuals evaluate their resources and determine how effectively they can be used to cope with the event. This appraisal is called *secondary* because it comes after primary appraisal and depends on the degree to which the event has been appraised as harmful, threatening, or challenging. Coping involves a wide range of potential strategies, skills, and abilities for effectively managing stressful events. In the example of missing an exam, if you learn that a makeup will be given 2 days later, you may not experience much stress since you already have studied for the exam and have several additional days to study for it. But if the instructor says that you have to write a lengthy paper for missing the test, you may cognitively appraise your situation and determine that this additional requirement places considerable demands on your time and wonder whether you will be able to meet the requirement. In this case, your secondary appraisal indicates a more stressful situation than simply having to take a makeup test several days later (Sears, Peplau, & Taylor, 1996).

Lazarus believes an individual's experience of stress is a balance of primary and secondary appraisal. When harm and threat are high, and challenge and resources are low, stress is likely to be high; when harm and threat are low, and challenge and resources are high, stress is more likely to be low.

Personality Factors

Do you have certain personality characteristics that make you more vulnerable to stress? Do other characteristics help you cope with stress? First, we will examine one personal-

cognitive appraisal

Lazarus's concept of individuals' interpretation of events in their lives as harmful, threatening, or challenging, and their determination of whether they have the resources to effectively cope with the event.

TYPE Z BEHAVIOR

...ity pattern that makes people more vulnerable to stress (Type A behavioral pattern) and then explore another pattern that helps them cope with stress (hardiness).

Type A Behavior Pattern. In the late 1950s a secretary for two California cardiologists, Meyer Friedman and Ray Rosenman, observed that the chairs in their waiting rooms were tattered and worn, but only on the front edge. The cardiologists had noticed the impatience of their cardiac patients, who often arrived exactly on time for an appointment and were in a great hurry to leave. Subsequently they conducted a study of 3,000 healthy men between the ages of 35 and 59 over a period of 8 years (Friedman & Rosenman, 1974). During the 8 years, one group of men had twice as many heart attacks or other forms of heart disease as anyone else. And autopsies of the men who died revealed that this same group had coronary arteries that were more obstructed than other men. Friedman and Rosenman described the coronary-disease group as characterized by **Type A behavior pattern,** *a cluster of characteristics—being excessively competitive, hard-driven, impatient, and hostile—thought to be related to the incidence of heart disease.*

However, further research on the link between Type A behavior and coronary disease indicates that the association is not as strong as Friedman and Rosenman believed (Williams, 1989). Researchers have examined the different components of Type A behavior, such as hostility, to determine a more precise link with coronary risk (Friedman, 1998). People who are hostile or consistently turn anger inward, it turns out, are more likely to develop heart disease. Such people have been labeled "hot reactors," meaning they have intense physiological reactions to stress—their hearts race, their breathing quickens, and their muscles tense up—which could lead to heart disease. Redford Williams (1989), a leading researcher in charting the behavioral and psychological dimensions of heart disease, believes each of us has the ability to control our anger and develop more trust in others, which he believes will reduce the risk for heart disease.

Hardiness. **Hardiness** *is a personality style characterized by a sense of commitment (rather than alienation), control (rather than powerlessness), and a perception of problems as challenges (rather than threats)* (Maddi, 1998). In the Chicago Stress Project, male business managers 32 to 65 years of age were studied over a 5-year period. During the 5 years, most of the managers experienced stressful events, such as divorce, job transfers, the death of a close friend, inferior performance evaluations at work, and working at a job with an unpleasant boss. In one study, managers who developed an illness (ranging from the flu to a heart attack) were compared with those who did not (Kobasa, Maddi, & Kahn, 1982). The latter group was more likely to have a hardy personality. Another study investigated whether or not hardiness along with exercise and social support buffered stress and reduced illness in executives' lives (Kobasa & others, 1985). When all three factors were present in an executive's life, the level of illness dropped dramatically. This suggests the power of multiple buffers of stress, rather than a single buffer, in maintaining health. Still at issue, however, is the significance of the various components of hardiness.

Type A behavior pattern

A cluster of characteristics—being excessively competitive, hard-driven, impatient, and hostile—thought to be related to the incidence of heart disease.

hardiness

A personality style characterized by a sense of commitment (rather than alienation), control (rather than powerlessness), and a perception of problems as challenges (rather than threats).

Review

Biological, Cognitive, and Personality Factors in Stress

Stress is the way we respond to circumstances that threaten us and tax our coping abilities. Many scientists now believe there are two pathways through the nervous system that connect the brain with the endocrine system in response to stress. One route is through the autonomic system, the other is through the hypothalamus and pituitary. Selye's general adaptation syndrome (GAS) describes the common effects of stress on the body. Stress is described as the wear and tear on the body due to the demands placed on it, according to Selye. This involves three stages—alarm, resistance, and exhaus-

tion. Not all stress is bad; Selye calls good stress eustress. Critics argue that humans do not always respond as uniformly as Selye envisioned and that we also need to know about such factors as an individual's coping strategies.

Lazarus believes that stress depends on how individuals cognitively appraise and interpret events. Cognitive appraisal is Lazarus's term for individuals' interpretation of events in their lives as harmful, threatening, or challenging (primary appraisal) and their determination of whether they have the resources to cope effectively with the event (secondary appraisal).

Personality factors that are related to stress include Type A behavior and hardiness. The Type A behavior pattern refers to a cluster of characteristics—being excessively competitive, hard-driven, impatient, and hostile—thought to be related to heart disease. The Type A pattern is controversial, with some researchers arguing that only specific components of the cluster, such as hostility, are associated with heart disease. Hardiness is a personality style characterized by commitment, control, and a perception of problems as challenges rather then threats. Hardiness buffers stress and is related to reduced illness.

Environmental Factors

Many circumstances, large and small, can produce stress in our lives. In some instances, cataclysmic events such as war, an automobile accident, a fire, or the death of a loved one produce stress. In others, the everyday pounding of being overloaded with work, of being frustrated in an unhappy relationship, or of living in poverty produce stress. What makes some situations stressful and others less so?

overload

The occurrence of stimuli so intense that the person cannot cope with them.

Overload, Conflict, and Frustration.   Overload *happens when stimuli become so intense that we can no longer cope with them.* For example, persistent high levels of noise overload our adaptability. Overload can occur with work as well. How often have you said to yourself, "There are not enough hours in the day to do all I have to do." In today's computer age, we are especially faced with information overload. It is easy to develop the stressful feeling that we don't know as much about a topic as we should, even if we are a so-called expert.

burnout

A hopeless, helpless feeling brought about by relentless work-related stress. Burnout leaves its sufferers in a state of physical and emotional exhaustion that includes chronic fatigue and low energy.

Today the buzzword for overload is **burnout,** *a hopeless, helpless feeling brought about by relentless work-related stress. Burnout leaves its sufferers in a state of physical and emotional exhaustion that includes chronic fatigue and low energy.* Burnout usually occurs not because of one or two traumatic events but because of a gradual accumulation of heavy, work-related stress (Leiter & Maslach, 1998). Burnout is most likely to occur among individuals who deal with others in highly emotional situations (such as nurses and social workers) but have only limited control over altering their clients'/patients' outcomes.

On a number of college campuses, burnout, reaching a rate of 25 percent at some schools, is the most frequent reason students leave school before earning their degrees. Dropping out of college for a term or two used to be considered a sign of weakness. Now it is more accepted and is sometimes called "stopping out" because the student fully intends to return; counselors may actually encourage some students who feel overwhelmed with stress to take a break from college. Before recommending "stopping out" though, most counselors first suggest that the student examine ways to reduce overload and possible coping strategies that would allow the student to remain in school. The simple strategy of taking a reduced or better-balanced class load sometimes works, for example. Most college counseling services have professionals who can effectively work with students to alleviate the sense of being overloaded and overwhelmed by life.

Stimuli not only overload us, but they also can be a source of conflict. Conflict occurs when we must decide between two or more incompatible stimuli. Three major types of conflict are approach/approach, avoidance/avoidance, and approach/avoidance. The

approach/approach conflict

A conflict in which the individual must choose between two attractive stimuli or circumstances.

avoidance/avoidance conflict

A conflict in which the individual must choose between two unattractive stimuli or circumstances.

approach/avoidance conflict

A conflict involving a single stimulus or circumstance that has both positive and negative characteristics.

frustration

Any situation in which a person cannot reach a desired goal.

approach/approach conflict *is a conflict in which the individual must choose between two attractive stimuli or circumstances.* Should you go to a movie or watch a video at home? Do you buy a Corvette or a Porsche? The approach/approach conflict is the least stressful of the three types of conflict because either choice leads to a positive result, even though choosing one over the other means you miss out on the positive experience of the other.

The **avoidance/avoidance conflict** *is a conflict in which the individual must choose between two unattractive stimuli or circumstances.* Will you go to the dentist to have a bad tooth pulled or endure the toothache? Do you go through the stress of giving an oral presentation in class or not show up and get a zero? You want to avoid both, but in each case, you must choose one. Obviously these conflicts are more stressful than having the luxury of having two enticing choices. In many instances, we delay our decision about the avoidance/avoidance conflict until the last possible moment, perhaps in hopes that other options will present themselves.

The **approach/avoidance conflict** *is a conflict involving a single stimulus or circumstance that has both positive and negative characteristics.* Let's say you really like the person you are going with and are thinking about getting married. On the one hand, you are attracted by the steady affection and love that marriage might bring, but, on the other hand, marriage is a commitment you might not feel ready to make. You look at a menu and face a dilemma—the double chocolate delight would be sumptuous, but is it worth the extra pound of weight? Our world is full of approach/avoidance conflicts and they can be highly stressful. In these circumstances, we often vacillate before deciding (Miller, 1959).

Frustration is another circumstance that produces stress. **Frustration** *refers to any situation in which a person cannot reach a desired goal.* If we want something and cannot have it, we feel frustrated. Our world is full of frustrations that build up to make our life more stressful—not having enough money to buy the car we want, not getting promoted at work, not getting an A average, being delayed for an important appointment by traffic, and being rejected by a friend. Failures and losses are especially frustrating—not getting grades that are high enough to get into medical school or losing someone we are closely attached to through death, for example. Sometimes the frustrations we experience are major life events, as in the cases of divorce and death. At other times, the accumulation of daily hassles may make us feel as though we're being nibbled to death by ducks.

Life Events and Daily Hassles.   Think about your life. What events have created the most stress for you? A change in financial status, getting fired at work, a divorce, the death of someone you loved, a personal injury? And what about the everyday circumstances of your life? What hassles you the most? Not having enough time to study, arguing with your significant other, not getting enough credit for the work you do at your job?

Researchers have proposed that significant life events are a major source of stress and loosely have linked such life events with illnesses. The effects of individual life events, such as a tornado or volcanic eruption, can be evaluated, or the effects of *clusters* of events can be studied. Thomas Holmes and Richard Rahe (1967) devised a scale to measure clusters of life events and their possible impact on illness in the context of the United States. Their widely used Social Readjustment Rating Scale includes events ranging from the death of a spouse (100 stress points) to minor violations of the law (11 stress points). To evaluate the life events you have experienced in the last year, complete the Self-Assessment.

People who experience clusters of stressful life events, such as divorce, being fired from a job, or sexual difficulties, are more likely to become ill (Maddi, 1989). However, the ability to predict illness from life events alone is modest. Total scores on life-events scales such as the Social Readjustment Rating Scale are frequently ineffective at predicting future health problems. A life-events checklist tells us nothing about a person's physiological makeup, constitutional strengths and weaknesses, ability to cope with stressful circumstances, support systems, or the nature of the social relationships involved—all of which are important in understanding how stress is related to illness. A divorce, for example, might be less stressful than a marriage filled with day-to-day tension. In addition the Holmes-Rahe scale includes positive events, such as marital reconciliation and gaining a new family member, which can also

Self-Assessment

Life Events

Instructions

Below are listed events that commonly occur in the life of a college student. Place a check in the space provided for each of those events that have happened to you during the *last 12 months*. After you have checked off the events, total the point values in parentheses for each marked item.

(100) _____ Death of a close family member
(80) _____ Jail term
(63) _____ Final year or first year in college
(60) _____ Pregnancy (yours or caused by you)
(53) _____ Severe personal illness or injury
(50) _____ Marriage
(45) _____ Any interpersonal problems
(40) _____ Financial difficulties
(40) _____ Death of a close friend
(40) _____ Arguments with your roommate (more than every other day)
(40) _____ Major disagreements with your family
(30) _____ Major change in personal habits
(30) _____ Change in living environment
(30) _____ Beginning or ending a job
(25) _____ Problems with your boss or professor
(25) _____ Outstanding personal achievement
(25) _____ Failure in some course
(20) _____ Final exams
(20) _____ Increased or decreased dating
(20) _____ Change in working conditions
(20) _____ Change in your major
(18) _____ Change in your sleeping habits
(15) _____ Several-day vacation
(15) _____ Change in eating habits
(15) _____ Family reunion
(15) _____ Change in recreational activities
(15) _____ Minor illness or injury
(11) _____ Minor violations of the law
_____ Total

Scoring

The total of your life stress units might correlate with the frequency of serious illness you experienced in the last year. If your units added up to 300 or more, you have an 80 percent chance of having a significant illness within a year. Between 299 and 150, your chance of significant illness decreases to 50 percent. If you scored 149 or less, your risk of significant illness drops to 30 percent.

SOURCE: Girdano, D. and Everly, G. S. (1979) *Controlling Stress and Tension: A Holistic Approach.* Prentice-Hall, Englewood Cliffs: New Jersey, 1979, pp. 56–57.

create stressors that must be faced. However, the changes that result from positive events are not as difficult to cope with as the changes that result from negative events.

Psychologists increasingly consider the nature of daily hassles and daily uplifts to gain better insight about the nature of stress (Lazarus & Folkman, 1984). It might be that the primary sources of stress are not life's major events but, rather, our daily experiences. Enduring a boring but tense job or marriage and living in poverty do not show up on scales of major life events; yet the everyday tension involved in these living conditions adds up to a highly stressful life and in some cases psychological disturbance or illness.

How about your own life? What are the biggest hassles? One study showed that the most frequent daily hassles of college students were wasting time, being lonely, and worrying about meeting high achievement standards (Kanner & others, 1981). In fact, the fear of failing in our success-oriented world often plays a role in college students' depression. College students also found that the small things in life—having fun, laughing, going to movies, getting along well with friends, and completing a task—were their main sources of feeling uplifted.

Critics of the daily-hassles approach argue that some of the same problems with life-events scales occur when assessing daily hassles (Dohrenwend & Shrout, 1985). For example, knowing about a person's daily hassles tells us nothing about the body's resilience to stress, the person's coping ability or strategies, or how that person perceives stress.

Sociocultural Factors

Sociocultural factors influence the stressors individuals are likely to encounter, whether events are perceived as stressful or not, and the expectations individuals have about how stressors should be confronted. Among the sociocultural factors that influence stress are acculturation, socioeconomic status, and gender.

Acculturation and Acculturative Stress.   Cultural subgroups in the United States can find contacts with mainstream society stressful. **Acculturation** *refers to cultural change that results from continuous, firsthand contact between two distinctive cultural groups.* **Acculturative stress** *refers to the negative consequences of acculturation.*

Canadian cross-cultural psychologist John Berry (1980) believes that a person facing acculturation can adapt to the pressures of change in four different ways—through assimilation, integration, separation, or marginalization. These four outcomes depend on how the individual answers two important questions: (1) Is my cultural identity of value and should I retain it? (2) Do I want to seek positive relations with the larger, dominant culture?

Assimilation *occurs when individuals relinquish their cultural identity and move into the larger society.* The nondominant group may be absorbed into an established "mainstream," or many groups may merge to form a new society (what is often called a "melting pot"). By contrast, **integration** *implies the maintenance of cultural integrity as well as the movement to become an integral part of the larger culture.* In this circumstance, a number of ethnic groups all cooperate within a larger social system ("a mosaic"). **Separation** *refers to self-imposed withdrawal from the larger culture.* If imposed by the larger society, however, separation becomes *segregation.* People might maintain their traditional way of life because they desire an independent existence (as in the case of "separatist" movements) or the dominant culture might exercise its power to exclude the other culture (as in the circumstances of slavery and apartheid).

Finally, there also is an option that involves a considerable amount of confusion and anxiety because the essential features of one's culture are lost but do not become replaced by those of the larger society. **Marginalization** *refers to the process in which groups are put out of cultural and psychological contact with both their traditional society and the larger, dominant society.* Marginalization often involves feelings of alienation and a loss of identity. Marginalization does not mean that a group has no culture but indicates that this culture may be disorganized and unsupportive of the acculturating individual.

As you see, separation and marginalization, especially, are the least adaptive responses to acculturation. While separation can have benefits under certain circumstances, it may be especially stressful for individuals who seek separation while most members of their group seek assimilation. Integration and assimilation are healthier adaptations to acculturative pressures. But assimilation means some cultural loss, so it may be more stressful than integration, where selective involvement in the two cultural systems may provide the supportive base for effective coping. To read further about acculturation, see Sociocultural Worlds.

Socioeconomic Status.   Poverty imposes considerable stress on individuals and families (Hoff-Ginsburg & Tardif, 1995). Chronic conditions such as inadequate housing, dangerous neighborhoods, burdensome responsibilities, and economic uncertainties are potent stressors in the lives of the poor. Ethnic minority families are disproportionately among the poor. For example, Puerto Rican families headed by women are 15 times more likely to live in poverty than are families headed by White men. Similarly, families headed by African American women are ten times more likely to live in poverty than families headed by White men (National Advisory Council on Economic Opportunity, 1980). Many people who become poor during their lives remain so for only 1 or 2 years. However, African Americans and female heads of household are especially at risk for persistent poverty. The average poor African American child experiences poverty that will last almost 20 years (Wilson & Neckerman, 1986).

Poverty is also related to threatening and uncontrollable life events. For example, poor women are more likely to experience crime and violence than middle-class women are (Bell & others, 1981). And poverty undermines sources of social support that play a

---

acculturation

Cultural change that results from continuous, firsthand contact between two distinctive cultural groups.

acculturative stress

The negative consequences of acculturation.

assimilation

Individuals' relinquishing their cultural identity and moving into the larger society.

integration

Maintenance of cultural integrity as well as movement to become an integral part of the larger culture.

separation

Self-imposed withdrawal from the larger culture.

marginalization

The process in which groups are put out of cultural and psychological contact with both their traditional society and the larger, dominant society.

Sociocultural Worlds

The Acculturative Stress of Ethnic Minority Individuals

As upwardly mobile ethnic minority families have attempted to penetrate historically all-White neighborhoods, interracial tensions often mount (Huang & Gibbs, 1989). Although many Americans think of racial tensions and prejudice largely as Black/White issues, this no longer is the case. Racial tensions and hostility often emerge among the various ethnic minorities as each struggles for housing and employment opportunities, seeking a fair share of these limited markets. Clashes become inevitable as Latino family markets spring up in African American urban neighborhoods; as Vietnamese extended families displace Puerto Rican apartment dwellers; as the increasing enrollment of Asian students on college campuses is perceived as a threat to affirmative action policies by other ethnic minority students.

Although the dominant White society has on many occasions tried to enslave or dispossess entire populations, these ethnic minority groups have survived and flourished. In the face of severe stress and oppression, these groups have shown remarkable resilience and adaptation by developing their own communities and social structures—such as African American churches, Vietnamese American mutual assistance associations, Chinese American family associations, Japanese-language schools, American Indian "bands" and tribal associations, and Mexican American kin systems. In addition, they have learned to negotiate with the dominant White culture. They essentially have mastered two cultures and developed impressive strategies for adapting to life in America. The resilience and adaptation of ethnic minority groups can teach us much about coping and survival in the face of overwhelming adversity.

This Chinese American family association has helped its members cope with acculturative stress.

role in buffering the effects of stress. Poverty is related to marital unhappiness and to having spouses who are unlikely to serve as confidants (Brown, Bhrolochain, & Harris, 1975). Further, poverty means having to depend on many overburdened and often unresponsive bureaucratic systems for financial, housing, and health assistance that may contribute to a poor person's feelings of powerlessness.

Gender. Another sociocultural factor that plays a role in stress is gender. In the United States men and women differ in their longevity. Although men appear to have lower morbidity (fewer illness problems), they die younger than women. Life expectancy for men is 72 years; women can expect to live on the average of 79 years. Men and women tend to succumb to the same illnesses. Heart disease is the primary killer for both sexes.

Researchers are especially interested in how women's stress and health are affected by working outside of the home in demanding careers (Rodin & Ickovics, 1990). In almost all studies, employed women are healthier than nonemployed women (LaCroix & Haynes, 1987). Researchers have found that women who stay at home and who perceive their lives as stressful and unhappy, who feel extremely vulnerable, and who engage in little physical activity are especially as risk for health problems (Verbrugge, 1989).

The nature and quality of a woman's experiences within a role are important considerations in understanding stress and health (Revenson & McFarlane, 1998). For example, roles with time constraints, irregular schedules, and little autonomy can jeopardize health. Therefore, women clerical workers, in particular, are more prone to health problems than other working women are (Haynes & Feinleib, 1980). In fact, contrary to the cultural belief that a high-powered career is more stressful to a woman's well-being, it seems that the more authority and autonomy a woman has on the job, the greater her sense of well-being (Baruch, Barnett, & Rivers, 1985).

Earlier in our discussion of social class and stress, we found that poverty is associated with increased stress and poorer health. Women are disproportionately among the poor. What's more, poor women face the double jeopardy of poverty and sexism. For example, women are paid less than men and are often denied opportunities to work because of their sex. The term **feminization of poverty** *refers to the fact that far more women than men live in poverty. Women's low incomes, divorce, and the resolution of divorce cases by the judicial system are the likely causes of the feminization of poverty.* Approximately one of every two marriages today will end in a divorce, meaning that far more women today than in the past must support themselves and, in many cases, one or more children as well. Further, women today are far less likely to receive alimony, or spousal support, than in the past. Even when alimony or child-support payments are awarded to a woman, they are poorly enforced.

As we saw in our discussion of socioeconomic status, ethnic minority women have especially high rates of poverty. These women face the extremely stressful triple jeopardy of poverty, racism, and sexism. Researchers must turn their attention to the mental health risks that accompany poverty and to ways that poor people, especially women, can cope more effectively with stress.

At this point, we have discussed the biological, cognitive, personality, environmental, and sociocultural factors involved in stress. Next, we will see that it also is extremely important to understand how to cope with stress.

feminization of poverty

The fact that, increasingly, far more women than men live in poverty. Women's low incomes, divorce, and the way the judicial system typically resolves divorce cases are the likely causes of the feminization of poverty.

Vonnie McLoyd (*right*) has conducted a number of important investigations of the roles of poverty, ethnicity, and unemployment in children's and adolescents' development. She has found that economic stressors often diminish children's and adolescents' belief in the utility of education and their achievement strivings.

Review

Environmental and Sociocultural Factors in Stress

Overload, conflict, and frustration can lead to stress. Stress can be produced because stimuli become so intense and prolonged that we cannot cope. Three types of conflict are approach/approach, avoidance/avoidance, and approach/avoidance. Frustration occurs when we cannot reach a goal. Stress also may be produced by major life events or daily hassles. Life-events lists tell us nothing about how individuals cope with stress, their body strengths and weaknesses, and other important dimensions of stress. Daily hassles provide a more focused look, but their evaluation should include information about a person's coping ability and physical characteristics.

Acculturation is cultural change that results from continuous, firsthand contact between two cultural groups. Acculturative stress is the negative consequences of acculturation. Four outcomes characterize an acculturating individual: assimilation, integration, segregation, and marginalization. The resilience and adaptation of ethnic minority groups can teach us much about coping and survival in the face of overwhelming adversity. Poverty imposes considerable stress on individuals. Chronic conditions, such as inadequate housing, dangerous neighborhoods, burdensome responsibilities, and economic uncertainties, are potent stressors in the

lives of the poor. The incidence of poverty is especially high in ethnic minority families.

Gender is also a sociocultural determinant of stress. Of special interest is how the increased participation by women in the workforce has influenced their stress and health. Employment is associated with increased health among women. Stressful roles with little autonomy and authority, such as being a clerical worker, often decrease women's health. Special concerns are the feminization of poverty and poverty among ethnic minority women.

COPING STRATEGIES

Coping is an extremely important aspect of successful adjustment and effective living. Just what do we mean by coping? **Coping** *involves managing taxing circumstances, expending effort to solve life's problems, and seeking to master or reduce stress.* A stressful circumstance can be rendered considerably less stressful when a person successfully copes with it. What are some effective ways to cope with stress?

Problem-Focused Coping

In our discussion of stress earlier in the chapter, we described Richard Lazarus's view that cognitive appraisal—interpreting events as harmful, threatening, or challenging, and determining whether one has the resources to effectively cope with the event—is critical to coping. Lazarus also believes that two general types of coping efforts can be distinguished. **Problem-focused coping** *is Lazarus's term for the cognitive strategy of squarely facing one's troubles and trying to solve them.* For example, if you are having trouble with a class, you might go to the study skills center at your college or university and enter a training program to learn how to study more effectively. You have faced your problem and attempted to do something about it. **Emotion-focused coping** *is Lazarus's term for responding to stress in an emotional manner, especially using defensive appraisal.* Emotion-focused coping involves using the defense mechanisms. In emotion-focused coping, we might avoid something, rationalize what has happened to us, deny it is occurring, laugh it off, or call on our religious faith for support. If you use emotion-focused coping, you might avoid going to the class. You might say the class doesn't matter, deny that you are having a problem, laugh and joke about it with your friends, or pray that you will do better. In one study, depressed people used coping strategies to avoid facing their problems more than people who were not depressed (Ebata & Moos, 1989).

Avoidance strategies *are responses that individuals use to keep stressful circumstances out of awareness so they do not have to deal with them.* Everything we know about coping suggests that avoidance strategies are extremely harmful to individuals' adjustment.

Optimism and Positive Thinking

It is important to be optimistic rather than pessimistic. In one study, college students initially were identified as optimists or pessimists (Peterson & Stunkard, 1986). Then their

coping

Managing taxing circumstances, expending effort to solve life's problems, and seeking to master or reduce stress.

problem-focused coping

Lazarus's term for the cognitive strategy of squarely facing one's own troubles and trying to solve them.

emotion-focused coping

Lazarus's term for responding to stress in an emotional manner, especially using defensive appraisal.

avoidance strategies

Responses that individuals use to keep stressful circumstances out of their awareness so they do not have to deal with them.

health was monitored over the next year. The pessimistic students had twice as many infections and visits to the doctor's office as the optimists.

Can pessimists develop a more optimistic outlook? Martin Seligman (1991) believes they can. He believes the key to becoming more optimistic is to challenge self-defeating thoughts. This strategy can also help people who are inclined to wallow in self-pity when bad circumstances arise. Albert Ellis (1996) thinks that a good strategy for becoming more optimistic is to dispute negative thoughts. Pessimists tend to use absolute, all-encompassing terms to describe their defeats. They often use words like *never* and *always.* They might say, "I will never be able to get all of this work done" or "I always come up short." Ellis tells people to talk back to negative thoughts in a self-confident, positive way that eradicates self-blame and negative feelings.

By thinking positively, people put themselves in a good mood and improve their self-esteem. Thinking positively also gives people the sense that they are controlling their environment rather than letting it control them (Taylor, 1998). Negative thinking increases the likelihood that people will get angry, feel guilty, and magnify their mistakes.

A good coping strategy, then, is to say positive things to yourself. Uncountered negative thinking has a way of becoming a self-fulfilling prophecy—if you tell your-self that you can't do something, you probably won't do it. How can you monitor your self-talk? At random times during the day, ask yourself, "What am I saying to my-self right now?" If you expect that an impending experience will be stressful, reflect on how you are talking to yourself about it as you anticipate the experience. Table 13.2 presents some examples of how positive self-statements can be used to replace negative ones.

$\mathcal{T}$ A B L E   1 3 . 2

Examples of Positive Self-Statements That Can Replace Negative Self-Statements in Coping with Stressful Situations

Situation	Negative self-statement	Example
Having a long, difficult assignment due the next day	"I'll never get this work done by tomorrow."	"If I work real hard I may be able to get it all done for tomorrow." "This is going to be tough but it is still possible to do it." "Finishing this assignment for tomorrow will be a real challenge." "If I don't get it finished, I'll just have to ask the teacher for an extension."
Losing one's job	"I'll never get another job."	"I'll just have to look harder for another job." "There will be rough times ahead, but I've dealt with rough times before." "Hey, maybe my next job will be a better deal altogether." "There are agencies that can probably help me get some kind of job."
Moving away from friends and family	"My whole life is left behind."	"I'll miss everyone, but it doesn't mean we can't stay in touch." "Just think of all the new people I'm going to meet." "I guess it will be kind of exciting moving to a new home." "Now I'll have two places to call home."
Breaking up with a person you love	"I have nothing to live for. He/she was all I had."	"I really thought our relationship would work, but it's not the end of the world." "Maybe we can try again in the future." "I'll just have to try to keep myself busy and not let it bother me." "If I met him (her), there is no reason I won't meet someone else someday."
Not getting into graduate school	"I guess I'm really dumb. I don't know what I'll do."	"I'll just have to reapply next year." "There are things I can do with my life other than going to grad school." "I guess a lot of good students get turned down. It's just so unbelievably competitive." "Perhaps there are a few other programs that I could apply to."
Having to participate in a class discussion	"Everyone else knows more than I do, so what's the use of saying anything?"	"I have as much to say as anyone else in the class." "My ideas may be different, but they're still valid." "It's OK to be a bit nervous; I'll relax as I start talking." "I might as well say something; how bad could it sound?"

Social Support

Our crowded, polluted, noisy, and achievement-oriented world can make us feel over-whelmed and isolated. Now more than ever, we may need support systems such as family members, friends, and co-workers to buffer stress. **Social support** *is information and feedback from others that one is loved and cared for, esteemed and valued, and included in a network of communication and mutual obligation.*

Researchers consistently have found that social support helps individuals cope with stress. For example, in one study depressed persons had fewer and less-supportive relationships with family members, friends, and co-workers than did people who were not depressed (Billings, Cronkite, & Moos, 1981). In another study, the prognosticators of cancer, mental illness, and suicide included a lack of closeness to one's parents and a negative attitude toward one's family (Thomas, 1983). Widows die at a rate that is 3 to 13 times higher than the rate for married women, for every known cause of death. Close, positive attachments to others, both family and friends, consistently show up as important buffers of stress.

Consider Robert, who had been laid off by an automobile manufacturer when it was about to fold, then a decade later by a truck manufacturer, and more recently by yet another automobile manufacturer. By all accounts you would expect Robert to be down in the dumps or possibly think that life had given him a bum deal. Yet he is one of the most well-adjusted individuals in the community. When asked his secret in the face of adversity and stress, he attributes his ability to cope to a wonderful family and some great friends. Far more important than Robert's trials and tribulations is the support he receives from others, which helps him to handle stress.

In thinking about ways to improve your coping, it is important for you to recognize the potential sources of social support in your own environment and learn how to effectively draw on these resources in times of stress (Rodriguez & Cohen, 1998 Taylor, 1991). Sometimes your coping can also be improved by joining community groups, interest groups, or informal social groups that meet regularly.

Assertive Behavior

There are four main ways people can deal with conflict in their lives: be aggressive, be manipulative, be passive, or be assertive. That is, faced with a conflict, a person can blow up, get down and dirty, cave in, or speak up.

Less-adaptive strategies either fail to solve conflict, alienate others, or both. For example, aggressive individuals run roughshod over others. They demand, are abrasive, and act in hostile ways. Aggressive people are often insensitive to others' rights and feelings. Manipulative people try to get what they want by making other people feel sorry for them or feel guilty. They don't take responsibility for meeting their own needs. Rather, manipulative individuals play the role of the victim or the martyr to get people to do things for them. Passive individuals are nonassertive and submissive. They let others run roughshod over them. Passive individuals don't express their feelings and don't let others know what they want.

In contrast, assertive individuals express their feelings, ask for what they want, and say no to something they don't want. When people act assertively, they act in their own best interests. They stand up for their legitimate rights and express their views openly. In the view of assertiveness experts Robert Alberti and Michael Emmons (1995), assertiveness builds equal relationships.

Of the four styles of dealing with conflict, acting assertively is by far the best coping strategy. To determine your style of coping with conflict, complete the Self-Assessment. And for some good strategies to become more assertive, see Improving Personal and Cognitive Skills.

Be fair with others, but then keep after them until they are fair with you.
—ALAN ALDA, *American Actor, 20th Century*

Self-Assessment

Coping with Conflict

Instructions

Think about the following situations one at a time. Check which response is most typical of the way you would behave in that situation:

1. You are being kept on the phone by a salesperson tying to sell you something you don't want. You
   a. place an order to have the excuse to get off the phone.
   b. say that something is burning on the stove and excuse yourself.
   c. show your irritation by hanging up on the salesperson in midsentence.
   d. state your intention not to buy the product and terminate the call.

2. You want to break off a relationship that is no longer working for you. You
   a. say nothing because you know the relationship will just wear out eventually.
   b. say that something is really wrong with you and that you are saving your partner from being hurt in the long run.
   c. just do not call ever again.
   d. explain your feelings but conclude by stating that you desire to end the relationship.

3. You are sitting in a movie and the people behind you are talking. You
   a. don't say anything because you hope the action of the movie will quiet them.
   b. report their noisiness to the theater manager.
   c. turn around and insult their upbringing that somehow omitted proper behavior in a theater.
   d. ask them to discontinue their conversation now that the movie has begun.

4. You are standing in line and someone cuts into line in front of you. You
   a. avoid eye contact but look disgruntled.
   b. look to see if you know anyone further up the line who will let you break in.
   c. confront the person in a loud voice, saying "Have you no manners at all?"
   d. ask the person to take their appropriate place at the end of the line in view of how long others have waited.

5. Your instructor is lecturing too softly to be heard. You
   a. take notes as best you can and borrow from someone else to make up for what you missed.
   b. start making noise deliberately to see if you can distract the professor.
   c. ask the professor, "Is there some reason you are speaking so we can't hear you?"
   d. Ask the professor to speak up because it is hard to hear.

6. You are expressing something that is important to you when another person interrupts. You
   a. wait patiently for that person to finish so you can get back to your thought.
   b. interrupt the interrupter to show what that experience feels like.
   c. tell the interrupter in no uncertain terms that you weren't done and hate to be interrupted when you are talking.
   d. wait for the interrupter to finish and then explain that you were interrupted and would like the opportunity to finish your idea.

7. Your friend owes you money and you could use it now. You
   a. find some other way to generate funds.
   b. hint to your friend about the amount of money someone else owes you to remind the person in a subtle way about the debt.
   c. demand the money and perhaps include some interest for the length of the loan.
   d. state that you have a financial need and would like to make arrangements to have your loan repaid.

8. You want to start a conversation at a party. You
   a. wait to see what others want to talk about first.
   b. complain about how quiet people are at the party.
   c. tell some jokes that you heard to get the crowd going.
   d. ask some questions of others to draw them out.

Scoring and Interpretation

Total the number of a, b, c, and d answers you gave to find the letter that reflects your dominant score. a answers are passive, b answers are manipulative, c answers are aggressive, and d answers are assertive. If the assertive style is not your dominant style, be sure to read the recommendations for how to become more assertive in Improving Personal and Cognitive Skills ("Becoming More Assertive").

SOURCE: After E. J. Bourne, (1995), *The Anxiety and Phobia Workbook* (rev. 2nd ed.). Oakland, CA: New Harbinger.

Improving Personal and Cognitive Skills

Becoming More Assertive

Following are some strategies for becoming more assertive (Bourne, 1995):

- *Set up a time for discussing what you want to discuss.*
  Talk with the other person to establish a mutually convenient time to talk. This step is omitted when you need to be assertive on the spot.
- *State the problem in terms of its consequences for you.*
  Outline your point of view clearly. This gives the other person a better sense of your position. Describe the problem as objectively as you can without blaming or judging the other person. For example, you might tell a roommate or family member, "I'm having a problem with the loud music you are playing. I'm studying for a test tomorrow and the music is so loud I can't concentrate."
- *Express your feelings.*
  Go ahead and express your feelings (openly but noncombatively). It lets the other person know how important the issue is to you. Suppressing your feelings prolongs the problem.

- *Make your request.*
  This is an important part of being assertive. Ask for what you want in a straightforward, direct way. Following are some guidelines for making assertive requests:

1. *Make sure your nonverbal behavior is assertive.* Maintain eye contact. Square your shoulders. Be calm and self-confident.
2. *Keep the request simple.* One or two easy-to-understand sentences will do. For example, "Please come with me to the counseling center to get help for our problems."
3. *Don't apologize for your request.* Be direct and say, "would you please. . . ." Don't say, "I know this is an imposition on you, but. . . ." If the other person criticizes you at this point, just restate the request directly, strongly, and confidently.
4. Describe the benefits to the person. With close friends or intimate partners, describing the benefits of cooperating with the request can be an honest offer of mutual give-and-take rather than manipulation.

Stress Management

Because many people have difficulty in managing stress themselves, psychologists have developed a variety of stress management programs that can be taught to individuals. We will study the nature of these stress management programs and evaluate some of the techniques that are used in them, such as meditation, relaxation, and biofeedback.

stress management programs

Programs that teach individuals how to appraise stressful events, how to develop skills for coping with stress, and how to put these skills to use.

Stress management programs *teach individuals how to appraise stressful events, how to develop skills for coping with stress, and how to put these skills into use in their everyday lives.* Stress management programs are often taught through workshops, which are increasingly offered in the workplace (Taylor, 1991). Aware of the high cost of lost productivity due to stress-related disorders, many organizations have become increasingly motivated to help their workers identify and cope with stressful circumstances in their lives. Some stress management programs are broad in scope, teaching a variety of techniques to handle stress; others are more narrow, teaching a specific technique, such as relaxation or assertiveness training (Dougall & Baum, 1998). Some stress management programs are also taught to individuals who are experiencing similar kinds of problems—such as migraine headache sufferers or individuals with chronically high blood pressure (Auerbach & Gramling, 1998). Colleges are increasingly developing stress management programs for students. If you are finding the experience of college extremely stressful and are having difficulty coping with taxing circumstances in your life, you might want to consider enrolling in a stress management program at your college or in your community. Let's now examine some of the techniques used in stress management programs.

meditation

A system of thought and form of practice that incorporates exercises to attain bodily or mental control and well-being, as well as enlightenment.

Meditation.   At one time, meditation was believed to have more in common with mysticism than with science. While meditation has become popular in the United States only in recent years, it has been an important part of life in Asia for centuries.

transcendental meditation (TM)

The most popular form of meditation in the United States. TM is derived from an ancient Indian technique and involves a mantra, which is a resonant sound or phrase that is repeated mentally or aloud to focus attention.

Meditation *is the system of thought and form of practice that incorporates exercises to attain bodily or mental control and well-being, as well as enlightenment.* The strategies of meditation vary but usually take one of two forms: either cleansing the mind to have new experiences or increasing concentration. **Transcendental meditation (TM)** *is the most* *popular form of meditation in the United States; it is derived from an ancient Indian technique and involves a mantra, which is a resonant sound or phrase that is repeated mentally or aloud to focus attention.* One widely used TM mantra is the phrase *Om mani padme hum.* By concentrating on this phrase, the individual replaces other thoughts with the syllables *Om mani padme hum.* In transcendental meditation the individual learns to associate a mantra with a special meaning, such as beauty, peace, or tranquillity.

As a physiological state, meditation shows qualities of both sleep and wakefulness, yet it is distinct from them. It resembles the hypnagogic state, which is the transition from wakefulness to sleep, but at the very least it is prolongation of that state.

Early research on meditation's effects on the body showed that oxygen consumption was lowered, heart rate slowed down, blood flow increased in the arms and forehead, and EEG patterns were predominantly of the alpha variety—regular and rhythmic (Wallance & Benson, 1972). Other researchers have found support for the positive physiological changes that result from meditation and believe that meditation is superior to relaxation in reducing body arousal and anxiety (Friedman, Meyers, & Benson, 1998).

Relaxation. Many researchers acknowledge meditation's positive physiological effects but believe that relaxation is just as effective (Holmes, 1987). To learn how to put more relaxation into your life, try out the following exercise.

How relaxed are you right now? Would you like to feel more tranquil and peaceful? If so, you can probably reach that feeling state by following some simple instructions. First, you need to find a quiet place to sit. Get a comfortable chair and sit quietly and upright in it. Let your chin rest comfortably on your chest, your arms in your lap. Close your eyes. Then pay attention to your breathing. Every time you inhale and every time you exhale, notice it and pay attention to the sensations of air flowing through your body, the feeling of your lungs filling and emptying. After you have done this for several breaths, begin to repeat silently to yourself a single word every time you breathe out. The word you choose does not have to mean anything. You can make the word up, you could use the word *one,* or you could try a word that is associated with the emotion you want to produce, such as *trust, love, patience,* or *happy.* Try several different words to see which one works best for you. At first, you will find that thoughts intrude and you are no longer attending to your breathing. Just return to your breathing and say the word each time you exhale. After you

Meditation has been an important dimension of Asians' lives for centuries.

have practiced this exercise for 10 to 15 minutes, twice a day, every day for 2 weeks, you will be ready for a shortened version. If you notice stressful thoughts or circumstances appearing, simply engage in the relaxation response on the spot for several minutes. If you are in public, you don't have to close your eyes, just fix your gaze on some nearby object, attend to your breathing, and say your word silently every time you exhale.

> *The time to relax is when you don't have time for it.*
> —SYDNEY J. HARRIS, *English-Born American Newspaper Columnist, 20th Century*

Audiotapes that induce the relaxation response are available in most bookstores. They usually include soothing background music along with instructions for how to do the relaxation response. These audiotapes can especially help induce a more relaxed state before you go to bed at night.

Biofeedback. For many years operant conditioning was believed to be the only effective means to deal with voluntary behaviors such as aggression, shyness, and achievement. Behavior modification helped people to reduce their aggression, to be more assertive and outgoing, and to get better grades, for example. Involuntary behaviors such as blood pressure, muscle tension, and pulse rate were thought to be outside the boundaries of operant conditioning and more appropriate for classical conditioning. Beginning in the 1960s, though, psychologist Neal Miller (1969) and others began to demonstrate that people can control internal behaviors. **Biofeedback** *is the process in which individuals' muscular or visceral activities are monitored by instruments and information from the instruments is given (fed back) to the individuals so they can learn to voluntarily control the physiological activities.*

How does biofeedback work? Let's consider the problem of reducing an individual's muscle tension. The individual's muscle tension is monitored and the level of tension is fed back to him. Often the feedback is in the form of an audible tone. As muscle tension rises, the tone becomes louder; as it drops, the tone becomes softer. The reinforcement in biofeedback is the raising and lowering of the tone (or in some cases, seeing a dot move up or down on a television screen) as the individual learns to control muscle tension.

biofeedback
The process in which individuals' muscular or visceral activities are monitored by instruments and information is given (fed back) to the individuals so they can learn to voluntarily control these activities.

Multiple Coping Strategies

Sometimes a single coping strategy won't make a big dent in your problems. In such cases, don't hesitate to use a variety of coping strategies. For example, if you have lost some confidence and are feeling anxious, you might use deep relaxation and positive self-talk and seek more social support.

eview

Coping Strategies

Coping involves managing taxing circumstances, expending effort to solve life's problems, and seeking to master or reduce stress. A stressful circumstance can be rendered considerably less stressful by successfully coping with it.

A good strategy is to engage in problem-focused coping rather than emotion-focused coping. Problem-focused coping involves squarely facing one's problems and trying to solve them. A bad strategy is to keep stressful circumstances out of awareness. Other good strategies are to establish an optimistic outlook and to think positively. Saying positive things to yourself can help. Yet another good coping strategy is to seek social support. There are four main ways people can deal with conflict in their lives: be aggressive, be manipulative, be passive, or be assertive. Being assertive is an excellent coping strategy; the other three are not.

Another coping strategy is to join a stress management program. These programs teach people how to appraise stressful events, develop skills for coping, and put these skills to work in the everyday world. Three techniques that might be used in stress management programs are meditation, relaxation, and biofeedback. Transcendental meditation (TM) is the most popular form of meditation practiced in the United States. Relaxation can have positive physiological effects. Biofeedback trains people to voluntarily control such bodily states as muscle tension. If a single coping strategy doesn't work, use multiple strategies.

Overview

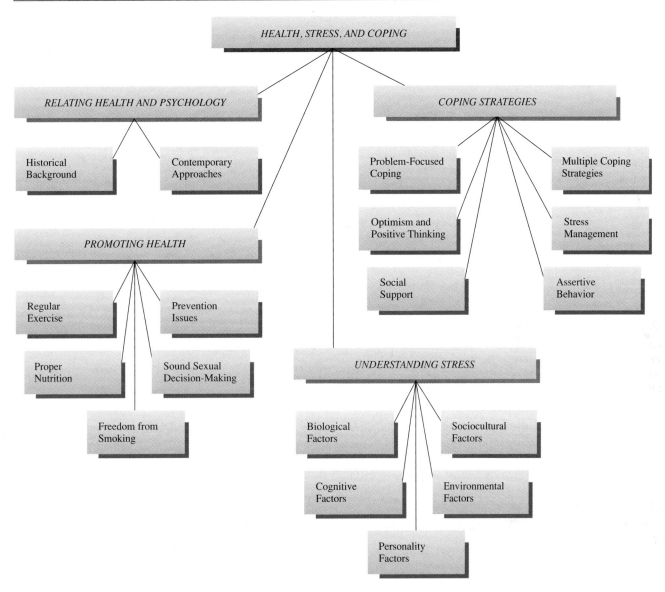

We began this chapter on health, stress, and coping by exploring the relation between health and psychology, including the historical background of the relation and contemporary perspectives. Then we turned our attention to promoting health—through regular exercise, proper nutrition, freedom from smoking, and prevention issues. Next, we sought to understand stress and its biological, cognitive, personality, environmental, and sociocultural factors.

Coping involves problem-focused coping, an optimistic outlook and thinking positively, social support, assertive behavior, stress management, and using multiple coping strategies.

Don't forget that you can obtain an overall summary of the chapter by again reading the in-chapter reviews on pages 494, 500, 506, and 512.

Key Terms

Thinking It Over

Exercises...

...In Critical Thinking

Find an advertisement for a weight-loss product. Then design a study that can help to establish the weight-loss product's effectiveness or ineffectiveness in helping people shed some pounds. What kinds of variables do you need to control? What will be your independent variable and your dependent variable? Who will be your subjects? How long will they be on the treatment program? Will you do a follow-up assessment to determine whether the subjects have maintained their weight loss over time?

...In Creative Thinking

Identify a social dilemma you have been experiencing lately that has caused you to feel frustrated with a friend's behavior. Describe the problem, especially the behaviors that bother you. As creatively as possible, come up with ways to respond to the problem that involve the four styles of coping with conflict: being passive, being manipulative, being aggressive, and being assertive.

...In Active Learning

Take a trip to the grocery store. Observe the way people line up to pay for their groceries. Do any of the people show behaviors that reflect the Type A behavior pattern? List some strategies that might help these Type A individuals to cope more effectively with stress.

...In Reflective Learning

Reflect on the meaning of your total score on the "Life Events" Self-Assessment. How much of your total score is based on stress and how much on eustress? How effectively did the Life Events Scale predict whether you became ill during the last year?

Resources for Psychology and Improving Humankind

AIDS Hotline
National AIDS Information Clearinghouse

P.O. Box 6003
Rockville, MD 20850
800-342-AIDS
800-344-SIDA (Spanish)
800-AIDS-TTY (Deaf)

The people answering this hotline will respond to any questions children, youth, or adults have about HIV infection or AIDS. Pamphlets and other materials on AIDS are available.

American Anorexia/Bulimia Association

418 E. 76th Street
New York, NY 10021
212-734-1114

This association acts as an information and referral service related to anorexia nervosa and bulimia and publishes the *American Anorexia/Bulimia Association Newsletter.*

Answering Your Questions About AIDS (1996)

by Seth Kalichman
Washington, DC: American Psychological Association

This collection of 350 of the most commonly asked questions about HIV infection and AIDS provides clear answers based on the latest medical and psychological research.

Body Traps (1992)

by Judith Rodin
New York: William Morrow

Body Traps focuses on the relation of a person's body to self-image and the destructive effects of society's standards on women's perceptions of their bodies. Rodin recommends strategies for avoiding body traps and developing more positive ways of relating to ourselves as we are.

Division of STD/HIV Prevention

National Center for Prevention Services
Centers for Disease Control and Prevention
Atlanta, GA 30333
404-639-2564

This organization offers very up-to-date information about preventing sexually transmitted diseases. This division administers a number of government programs for the prevention of STDs and HIV infection.

The LEARN Program for Weight Control (1988)

by Kelly Brownell
Dallas: American Health

This excellent book, written by a leading researcher, outlines an effective, healthy program for losing weight and maintaining the weight loss.

Learned Optimism (1990)

by Martin Seligman
New York: Pocket Books

Learned Optimism is one of the new breed of positive-thinking books, a breed that first began to appear in the late 1980s and has increased in number recently. Such books are based on psychological research and give specific strategies for optimistic thinking rather than earlier cheerleading books that were low on substance. Seligman's positive message is that since pessimism is learned, it can be unlearned. Included are self-tests to determine your levels of optimism, pessimism, and depression.

Letting Go of Stress

by Emmitt Miller
P.O. Box W
Stanford, CA 94305
1-800-TAPES

This excellent audiocassette can help you cope with stress by learning how to relax.

The New Aerobics (1970)

by Kenneth Cooper
New York: Bantam

The New Aerobics lays out Cooper's age-adjusted recommendations for aerobic exercise. Cooper's book is research based and easy to read, and if you are in only average or poor physical shape, Cooper's recommended program will reap physical and psychological benefits for you.

The New Aerobics for Women (1988)

by Kenneth Cooper and Mildred Cooper
New York: Bantam

This book tailors the concept of aerobic exercise to the capabilities and needs of women. It includes age-adjusted formulas for appropriate exercise that are tailored to a woman's lifestyle and current level of physical fitness.

The New Fit or Fat (1991, rev. ed.)

by Covert Bailey
Boston: Houghton Mifflin

The New Fit or Fat describes ways to become healthy by developing better diet and exercise routines. Bailey argues that the basic problem for overweight people is not losing weight, which fat people do periodically, but gaining weight, which fat people do more easily than those with a different body chemistry.

Recommended Music for Relaxation

Listening to soft music can create a relaxing feeling. The following instrumental music tapes are available in many music and book stores:

Spencer Bower: *Emerald Portraits*
Michael Jones: *After the Rain Pianoscapes*
David Lanz: *Nightfall*
George Winston: *Autumn December*

The Relaxation & Stress Workbook (1995, 4th Ed.)

by Martha Davis, Elizabeth Eshelman, and Matthew McKay
Oakland, CA: New Harbinger

This excellent workbook includes many exercises to help you learn relaxation techniques and improve your ability to cope with stress.

Internet Resources

http://education.indiana.edu/cas/adol/adol.html
Referrals to counseling and a description of a variety of issues that affect the mental well-being of young adults.

http://www.something-fishy.com/ed.htm
This comprehensive Web site links about anorexia, bulimia, overeating, and other disorders.

http://www.wellweb.com/preview/zpre.htm
Current medical research, tips on healthy lifestyles, and information on diseases and medications.

http://www.health.org
Prevention Online offers the latest information on research about substance use and addiction.

http://www.quitnet.org/quitnetta
The Massachusetts Tobacco Control Program operates this Web site that describes prevention strategies and current research on smoking.

14

Social Psychology

Man is by nature a social animal.

—ARISTOTLE

Greek Philosopher, 4th Century B.C.

*T*his chapter is about the fascinating worlds of people's social lives. We will study how people think about their social behavior and interaction with others, how people influence others and are influenced by them, and the nature of their social relationships with friends, lovers, and others. To begin, you will read the harrowing story of Marshall Herff Applewhite and the Heaven's Gate cult. As you read the story, think about why the cult members were so attracted to Applewhite and how he gained so much influence over them.

The Story of Marshall Herff Applewhite: Apostle to the "Level Above Human"

*A*lthough most people were quite taken with the celestial drama of the appearance of Hale-Bopp in 1997, very few suspected that a human drama would unfold in San Diego in connection with the comet. Under the leadership of Marshall Herff Applewhite, known as "Do" to the members of the Heaven's Gate cult, thirty-nine cult members swallowed pudding laced with barbiturates and washed it down with vodka. Then, they reclined on their beds so their spirits could escape their mortal "containers" and ascend to the "Level Above Human." Applewhite had convinced them that an enormous UFO was in Hale-Bopp's slipstream and that the comet's appearance meant it was time to go "home." The mass suicide was the largest in U.S. history.

Applewhite began recruiting followers to his blend of New Age mysticism and science-fiction fantasy in 1975. But it wasn't until he reached out on the Internet that his message found many sympathetic listeners. Twenty-one women and eighteen men ranging in age from 26 to 72 found Applewhite's message compelling enough to abandon their families and join in his austere lifestyle. Until the comet signaled the time

Marshall Herff Applewhite cheerfully explained the suicidal intentions of the Heaven's Gate cult in a videotape. His comforting charisma was often likened to the allure of Mr. Rogers, a TV idol of preschool children.

of their departure, Heaven's Gate supported itself by creating low-cost Web pages in a business venture called "Higher Source Contract Enterprises."

Members of Heaven's Gate wore baggy clothes and cropped their hair close to the head to deny gender distinctions. They avoided touching, to distance themselves even further from their earthly containers and from what they believed were lurid desires that contaminated their spirits. They paid their rent and other bills in cash to avoid government attention. They made bourbon pound and rum cakes for the outside world, but Applewhite did not allow them to indulge in the creations themselves. They also were required to do everything in pairs to prevent backsliding.

How did Applewhite manage to be so persuasive? Applewhite has been compared to TV's Mr. Rogers because of his comforting manner. Applewhite conveyed enthusiasm and a childlike innocence that stimulated his followers to believe he truly was a modern martyr. Building on the trust he had created with his cult, Applewhite conned them into thinking that he had a deadly cancer in order to further manipulate his followers' emotions. An autopsy revealed no presence of cancer.

Applewhite's personal background is strewn with troubles. At one point he asked to be hospitalized to rid himself of strange voices inside his head. He was arrested for car theft and overdosed on drugs. His struggle with personal demons seemed to subside when he met Bonnie Nettles, a nurse with interests in astrology and unusual religions. They struck up what was to become a long-term platonic friendship. The autopsies of Applewhite and several other male Heaven's Gate members revealed that they had been castrated to diminish their sexual drive.

The Heaven's Gate deaths occurred in three waves. Each victim had packed an overnight bag and had a five-dollar bill and some quarters in a pocket. Each wore new Nikes and was covered with a purple shroud (a cloth used to wrap a body for burial). The last two victims, who were found with bags on their heads, had carefully folded up the other bags used in the first two waves. In videotapes they made before their deaths, Heaven's Gate members expressed their joy in leaving Earth to move on to a higher life.

Applewhite was not the first charismatic leader to have such powerful influence over his followers. Later in the chapter you will read about other leaders who have gained enormous social influence over others. ❖

SOCIAL COGNITION

As we interact with our world, we are both actors and spectators, doing and perceiving, acting and thinking. Social psychologists are interested in how we perceive our social world and how we try to make sense of our own behavior and the behavior of others. They are also interested in how we form and change our attitudes. We will begin the study of social cognition by exploring the nature of social perception.

Social Perception

social perception

Judgment about the qualities of individuals, which involves how we form impressions of others, how we gain self-knowledge from perception of others, and how we present ourselves to others to influence their perceptions of us.

Social perception *is our judgment about the qualities of individuals, which involves how we form impressions of others, how we gain self-knowledge from our perception of others, and how we present ourselves to others to influence their perceptions of us.*

Impression Formation. Our evaluations of people often fall into broad categories— good or bad, happy or sad, introvert or extrovert, for example. If someone asked for your impression of your psychology professor, you might respond, "She is great." Then you might go on to describe your perception of her characteristics—for example, "She is charming, intelligent, witty, and sociable." These opinions represent inferences you make from the samples of her behavior you experience directly. From this description we can also infer that you have a positive impression of her.

As we form impressions of others, we organize the information in two important ways. Our impressions are both integrated and unified. Traits, actions, appearance, and all of the other information we obtain about a person are closely connected in memory, even though the information may have been obtained in an interrupted or random fashion. We might obtain some information today, more next week, some more in 2 months. During those 2 months, we interacted with many other people and developed impressions of them as well. Nonetheless, we integrate each relevant experience with a particular person and perceive it as unified, a continuous block of information.

Consider Peg. You meet her and she tells you that she is about to have her first baby. You make a mental note about her situation and form some impressions about her personality. These impressions will be distinctive no matter how many other people you meet. When you encounter Peg later, you notice that she looks tired and disheveled. You remember her pregnancy and now infer that new motherhood must be a tiring business. You integrate this new information to maintain a coherent impression of her.

Our first encounter with someone also often contributes to an enduring impression we form. **Primacy effect** *is the enduring quality of initial impressions.* One reason for the primacy effect is that we pay less attention to subsequent information about the individual (Anderson, 1965). The next time you want to impress someone, a wise strategy is to make sure that you put your best foot forward in your first encounter.

Social Comparison.   How many times have you asked yourself questions such as "Am I as smart as Jill?" "Is Bob better looking than I am?" or "Is my taste as good as Carmen's?" We gain self-knowledge from our own behavior; we also gain it from others through **social comparison,** *the process in which individuals evaluate their thoughts, feelings, behaviors, and abilities in relation to other people. Social comparison helps individuals to evaluate themselves, tells them what their distinctive characteristics are, and aids them in building an identity.*

Leon Festinger's (1954) theory of social comparison stresses that when objective norms are unavailable to evaluate our opinions and abilities, we compare ourselves with others. Festinger believed that we are more likely to compare ourselves with others who are similar to us than with those who are dissimilar to us. If we compare ourselves with someone who is very different from us, we will not be able to obtain an accurate appraisal of our own behavior and thoughts. This means that we will develop more accurate self-perceptions if we compare ourselves with people in communities similar to where we grew up and live, with people who have similar family backgrounds, and with people of the same sex, for example. Social comparison theory has been extended and modified over the years and continues to provide an important rationale for why we affiliate with others and how we come to know ourselves (Kenrick & others, 1993).

In contrast to Festinger's emphasis on the role of social comparison in evaluating one's abilities, recently researchers have focused more on the self-enhancing properties of downward comparisons (Banaji & Prentice, 1994). Individuals under threat (negative feedback, low self-esteem, depression, and illness, for example) try to improve their well-being by comparing themselves with someone less fortunate (Gibbons & McCoy, 1991).

Impression Management.   How do you present yourself to others? Do you try to act naturally and be yourself, or do you deliberately change your behavior to get other people to have a more favorable impression of

"Randall, my old college nemesis, I was hoping I'd find you here."

Copyright 1986, USA TODAY. Reprinted with permission.

primacy effect

The enduring quality of initial impressions.

social comparison

The process in which individuals evaluate their thoughts, feelings, behaviors, and abilities in relation to other people.

impression management

The process in which individuals strive to present themselves in a favorable light.

you? **Impression management** *is the process in which individuals strive to present themselves in a favorable light.* When we present ourselves to others, we usually try to make ourselves look better than we really are. Collectively we spend billions of dollars rearranging our faces, our bodies, our minds, and our social skills so that others will form a more favorable impression of us.

In situations where you want to influence the impressions you make on others, how can you go about doing this? Four recommended "impression-management" strategies follow:

1. *Use behavioral matching.* This simply means doing what the other person is doing. When you are with a modest person, behave in a modest way. When you are with a carefree person, behave in a carefree way.
2. *Conform to expectations in the situation.* Don't show up barefoot in your professor's office—save that look for the beach or frat house. Don't play a radio in the library, and don't read at a party.
3. *Show appreciation of others and make favorable comments about them.* People like to be complimented. Look for something good to say about the person you are communicating with, such as "I really like your watch. Where did you find it?"
4. *Use positive nonverbal cues.* We not only can influence what others think of us by our words but also by a number of nonverbal cues, such as nodding or smiling.

Keep in mind, though, that impression management techniques that work in one cultural setting may not work in another. In particular, appreciation and flattery are often culture-bound. For example, in some Eastern European countries, if one person expresses great admiration for another's watch, courtesy dictates that the watch should be given to the admirer! In the Native American culture of the Sioux, it's considered courteous to open a conversation with a compliment. Nonverbal cues also vary considerably from culture to culture. For example, the "okay" sign made by holding three fingers up with thumb and finger circled has a meaning in the West that is very different from its meaning in Japan, where the signal symbolizes money, and in South America, where it issues a sexual invitation (Keating, 1994).

Some people are more concerned about and aware of the impressions they make than others are. **Self-monitoring** *is individuals' attention to the impressions they make on others and the degree to which they fine-tune their performance accordingly.* Lawyers and actors are among the best self-monitors; salespeople, con artists, and politicians are not far behind. A former mayor of New York City, Fiorello LaGuardia, was so good at self-monitoring that, by watching silent films of his campaign speeches, it was possible to tell which ethnic group he was courting for votes.

Individuals who are very skilled at self-monitoring seek information about appropriate ways to present themselves and invest considerable time in trying to "read" and understand others (Simpson, 1995). Social psychologist Mark Snyder (1979) developed a scale to measure the extent to which an individual is a high or low self-monitor. To see how you fare in self-monitoring, complete the Self-Assessment.

The principle of self-monitoring stresses that individuals vary in how much they are tuned in to the impact they make on the external world. A theory of psychology that has become popular in recent years stresses that we seek to explain behavior in terms of internal or external factors. It is called attribution theory.

Attribution

Attribution theorists argue that we want to know why people do the things they do because the knowledge will enable us to cope more effectively with the situations that confront us. **Attribution theory** *states that individuals are motivated to discover the underlying causes of behavior as part of their interest in making sense out of the behavior.* In a way, attribution theorists say people are much like intuitive scientists, seeking the reason something happens.

We can classify the reasons individuals behave the way they do in a number of ways, but one basic distinction stands out above all the others—the distinction between internal causes, such as the actor's personality traits or motives, or external causes, which are

self-monitoring

Individuals' attention to the impressions they make on others and the degree to which they fine-tune their performance accordingly.

attribution theory

The theory that individuals are motivated to discover the underlying causes of behavior as part of their interest in making sense out of the behavior.

Self-Assessment

Self-Monitoring

Instructions

These statements concern personal reactions to a number of situations. No two statements are exactly alike, so consider each statement carefully before answering. If a statement is true or mostly true as applied to you, circle the T. If a statement is false or not usually true as applied to you, circle the F.

1. I find it hard to imitate the behavior of other people.   T   F
2. I guess I put on a show to impress or entertain people.   T   F
3. I would probably make a good actor.   T   F
4. I sometimes appear to others to be experiencing deeper emotions than I actually am.   T   F
5. In a group of people, I am rarely the center of attention.   T   F
6. In different situations and with different people, I often act like very different persons.   T   F
7. I can only argue for ideas I already believe.   T   F
8. In order to get along and be liked, I tend to be what people expect me to be.   T   F
9. I may deceive people by being friendly when I really dislike them.   T   F
10. I'm not always the person I appear to be.   T   F

Scoring

Give yourself one point for each of questions 1, 5, and 7 that you answered F. Give yourself one point for each of the remaining questions that you answered T. Add up your points. If you are a good judge of yourself and scored a 7 or above, you are probably a high self-monitoring individual. This means you are likely to pay careful attention to the impact you make on others and might even adjust your behavior based on these impressions. If you scored 3 or below, you are probably a low self-monitor. You are inclined to pay less attention to what others think of you and probably don't adjust your behavior accordingly.

---

environmental, situation factors (Heider, 1958). If you don't do well on a test, do you attribute it to the professor's plotting against you and making the test too difficult (external cause) or to your being too lazy to study hard enough (internal cause)? The answer to such a question influences how we feel about ourselves. If we believe our poor performance is the professor's fault (he gives unfair tests, for example), we don't feel as bad as when we make negative attributions about ourselves.

Our attributions are not always accurate. In a given situation the person who acts, or the actor, produces the behavior to be explained. Then the onlooker, or the observer, offers a causal explanation of the actor's behavior or experience. Actors often explain their own behavior with external causes, while observers often explain the actor's behavior with internal causes. The **fundamental attribution error** *states that observers overestimate the importance of traits and underestimate the importance of situations when they seek explanations of an actor's behavior* (Ross, 1977). For example, an observer might see that you are failing at your academic work and be inclined to perceive you as a lazy person (trait). By contrast, you, the actor, are inclined to look out into the world and explain your behavior as due to a vindictive teacher or an overloaded schedule (situational factors).

Because actors and observers often have different ideas about what causes behavior, many attributions are biased. Behavior is determined by a number of factors, so it is not surprising that our lives are full of squabbling and arguing about the causes of behavior. Attribution theory challenges us to consider multiple perspectives on disagreements in relationships, the courts, the Senate, and many other social arenas (Harvey, 1995).

Attitudes and Behavior

As Mark Twain said, "It is a difference of opinion that makes horses race." **Attitudes** *are beliefs and opinions that can predispose individuals to behave in certain ways.* We have attitudes about all sorts of things, and we live in a world in which we try to influence each other's attitudes.

fundamental attribution error

Observers' tendency to overestimate the importance of traits and underestimate the importance of situations when they seek explanations of an actor's behavior.

attitudes

Beliefs and opinions that can predispose individuals to behave in certain ways.

Think about your attitudes toward religion, politics, and sex. Now think about your behavior in these areas. Consider sex, for example. How liberal or conservative are your sexual attitudes? Does your behavior match your attitudes? Researchers have found that we have more accepting attitudes toward sexual practices than our behavior actually shows (Dreyer, 1982). As we study the relation of attitudes to behavior, two questions arise: How strongly do attitudes influence behavior? How strongly does behavior influence attitudes?

Predicting Behavior from Attitudes.   More than 60 years ago, Richard LaPiere (1934) toured the United States with a Chinese couple. LaPiere expected to encounter prejudice against the Asians. He thought they would be banned from restaurants and hotels, for example. Surprisingly, in more than 10,000 miles of travel, the threesome was rejected only once. It appeared, LaPiere thought, that there were few negative attitudes toward Asians in the United States. To see if this actually was the case, LaPiere wrote a letter to all 251 places he and his Asian friends had visited, asking the proprietors if they would provide food or lodging to Asians. More than half responded; of those, a resounding 90 percent said they absolutely would not allow Asians in their restaurant or motel. LaPiere's study documented a powerful lesson in understanding human behavior: what we say may be different from what we do.

The connection between attitudes and behaviors may vary with the situation. In the study of attitudes toward Asians in the 1930s, the Chinese who accompanied LaPiere were well dressed and carried expensive luggage; they might have inspired different attitudes if they had appeared in cheaper attire or if they had not been traveling in the company of a European male. To consider further situational influences on attitude-behavior connections, imagine asking someone about his attitude toward people who drive pickup trucks. Let's say he responds, "Totally classless." A month later the guy stops for a cup of coffee in a small West Texas town. A burly man in the next booth is talking with his buddies about the merits of pickup trucks. He turns to our friend and asks, "How do you like that green pickup truck sitting outside?" Needless to say, his response is not "totally classless." This example suggests that the demands of the situation can be powerful even when we hold strong beliefs. This is an important point that social psychologists refer to throughout their work on explaining social behavior.

Behavior's Influence on Attitudes.   Does *doing* change *believing*? If you quit drinking, will you have a more negative attitude toward drinking? If you take up an exercise program, are you more likely to extol the benefits of cardiovascular fitness when someone asks your attitude about exercise?

Changes in behavior can precede changes in attitudes (Bandura, 1989). Social psychologists offer two main explanations of behavior's influence on attitudes. The first is that people have a strong need for cognitive consistency; consequently, they might change their attitudes to make them more consistent with their behavior. The second is that our attitudes often are not completely clear, so we observe our behavior and make inferences about it to determine what our attitudes should be. Let's consider these two views in more detail.

cognitive dissonance

A concept developed by social psychologist Leon Festinger; an individual's motivation toward consistency and away from inconsistency.

Festinger's Cognitive Dissonance Theory.   **Cognitive dissonance,** *a concept developed by social psychologist Leon Festinger (1957), refers to an individual's motivation to reduce the discomfort (dissonance) caused by two inconsistent thoughts.* We might feel uneasy about a discrepancy that exists between our attitudes and our behavior. The absence of internal justification for the difference between what we believe and what we do creates dissonance. We can engage in a variety of actions to reduce the dissonance. For example, many people believe it is unhealthy to smoke yet can't seem to resist lighting up. This discrepancy between attitude and behavior creates discomfort. To reduce this dissonance, the smoker must either stop smoking or change his or her attitudes. "No one has proven smoking kills people" and "I'll have to die from something" are dissonance-reducing attitudes.

We often justify our behavior, as twentieth-century Irish playwright George Bernard Shaw did with his father's alcoholism: "If you cannot get rid of the family skeleton, you may as well make it dance." Shaw's justification helped him reduce the tension between his father's drinking problem and his attitude about it. Cognitive dissonance is about making our skeletons dance, about trying to reduce tension by cognitively justifying things that are unpleasant (Aronson, 1992).

Bem's Self-Perception Theory.   Not all social psychologists, however, are satisfied with cognitive dissonance as an explanation for the influence of behavior on attitudes. Daryl Bem, for example, believes that the cognitive dissonance view relies too heavily on internal factors, which are difficult to measure. Bem (1967) argues that we should move away from such nebulous concepts as "cognitions" and "psychological discomfort" and replace them with more behavioral terminology. **Self-perception theory** is Bem's theory of the *attitude-behavior connection; it stresses that individuals make inferences about their attitudes by perceiving their behavior.* For example, consider the remark "I am spending all of my time thinking about the test I have next week; I must be anxious," or "This is the third time I have gone to the student union in 2 days; I must be lonely." Bem believes we look to our own behavior when our attitudes are not completely clear. This means that when we have clear ideas about something, we are less likely to look to our behavior for clues about our attitudes; however, if we feel ambivalent about something or someone, our behavior is a good place to look to determine our attitude. Figure 14.1 compares cognitive dissonance and self-perception theories.

We just explored how social cognitions help us to perceive ourselves and others and to form attitudes. Social cognitions form the basis of the decisions we make about whether to pursue certain relationships. Next, we will examine many dimensions of social influence.

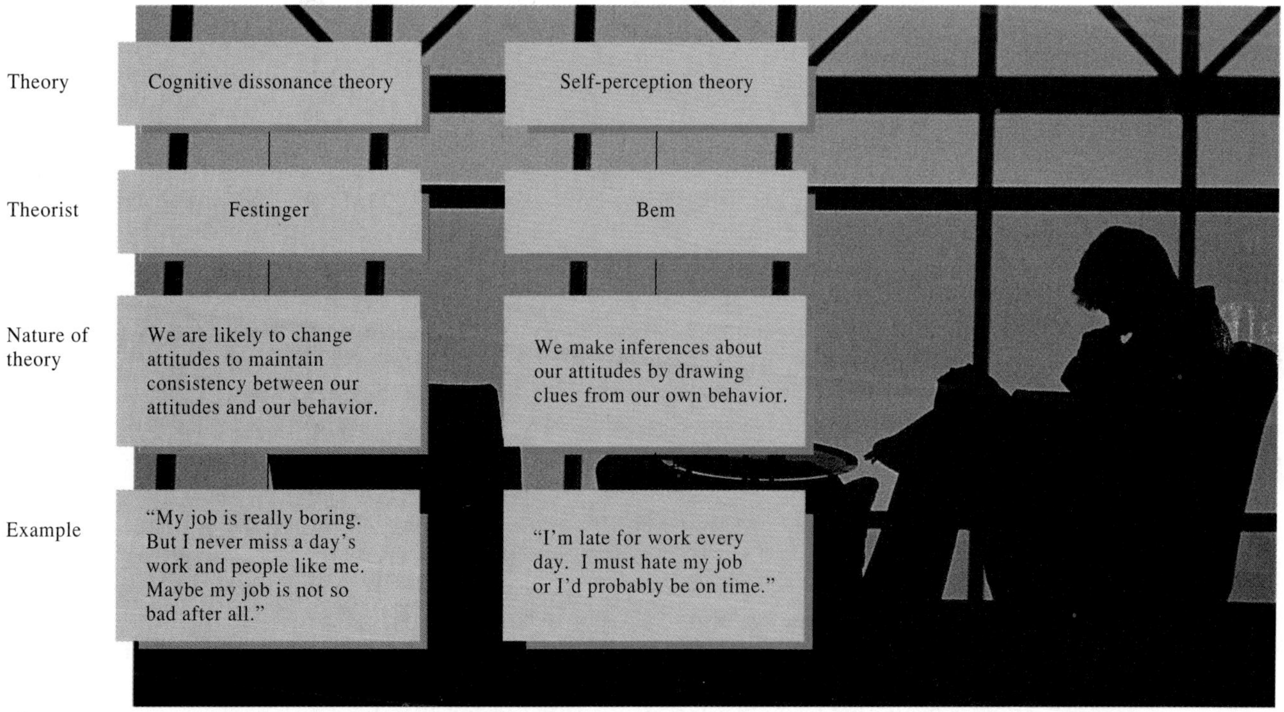

self-perception theory
Bem's theory of connections between attitudes and behavior; it stresses that individuals make inferences about their attitudes by perceiving their behavior.

Theory	Cognitive dissonance theory	Self-perception theory
Theorist	Festinger	Bem
Nature of theory	We are likely to change attitudes to maintain consistency between our attitudes and our behavior.	We make inferences about our attitudes by drawing clues from our own behavior.
Example	"My job is really boring. But I never miss a day's work and people like me. Maybe my job is not so bad after all."	"I'm late for work every day. I must hate my job or I'd probably be on time."

𝓕IGURE 14.1
Two Views of Behavior's Influence on Attitudes

Review

Social Perception, Attribution, and Attitudes and Behavior

Three important dimensions of social perception are developing impressions of others, making social comparisons, and presenting ourselves to others to influence their social perceptions. Our impressions are integrated and unified. First impressions are important and influence impressions at a later point. We evaluate ourselves by comparison with others. Festinger stressed that social comparison provides an important source of self-knowledge, especially when no other objective means is available; we are more likely to compare ourselves with others who are similar. We usually try to make ourselves look better than we really are. Four recommended impression management strategies are to (1) use behavioral matching, (2) conform to situational norms, (3) show apprecia-

tion of others and flatter them, and (4) use positive nonverbal cues. Self-monitoring involves individuals' awareness of the impressions they make on others and the degree to which they fine-tune their performance accordingly.

Attribution focuses on the motivation to infer causes of behavior in order to make sense out of the world. One of the most frequent and important ways we classify the causes of behavior is in terms of internal and external causes. Our attributions are not always accurate; the human mind has a built-in bias in making causal judgments. The fundamental attribution error involves overestimating the importance of traits and internal causes while underestimating the importance of situations and external causes. Actors are

more likely to choose external causes, observers internal causes. The observer may be in greater error. Attitudes are beliefs and opinions. Social psychologists are interested in how strongly attitudes predict behavior. Today it is believed that, when situational influences are weak, the attitude-behavior connection is strengthened. Cognitive dissonance theory, developed by Festinger, argues that, because we have a strong need for cognitive consistency, we change our attitudes to make them more consistent with our behavior so that dissonance is reduced. Bem developed a more behavioral approach, called self-perception theory; it stresses the importance of making inferences about our own behavior, especially when our attitudes are not clear.

SOCIAL INFLUENCE

> *In the scale of the destinies, brawn will never weigh as much as brain.*
> —JAMES RUSSELL LOWELL, *American Poet, 19th Century*

Both brawn and brain have been used to influence others but it is a person's brain power that most intrigues social psychologists who are interested in explaining how people influence others and how others influence them.

Interpersonal Influence

Social influence between two people comes in many forms. However, influence involves a change in attitude or a change in action that results from the efforts of another. We will examine two kinds of interpersonal influence: persuasion and obedience to authority.

Persuasion. We spend many hours of our lives trying to persuade people to do or believe various things. Politicians, for example, have full arsenals of speech writers and image consultants to ensure that their words and behavior are as persuasive as possible. Social psychologists believe that persuasion involves four key components: who conveys the message (the source), what medium is used (the channel), what the message is (the communication), and for whom the message is intended (the target).

> *No matter what side of an argument you're on, you always find some people on your side that you wish were on the other side.*
> —JASCHA HEIFETZ, *Russian American Musician, 20th Century*

The Communicator (Source). Suppose you are running for president of the student body. You tell students you are going to make life at your college better. Would they believe you? That would depend on several different factors.

Two factors involved in whether or not we believe someone are the *expertise* and the *credibility* of the communicator. Expertise depends on qualifications. If you had held other elective offices, students would be more likely to believe you have the expertise to be their president. We attribute credibility to experts, believing they are knowledgeable about the topics they address.

In addition to expertise and credibility, *trustworthiness* is an important quality of an effective communicator. This factor depends on whether what you say and how you say it is perceived as honest or dishonest. It was in Abraham Lincoln's best interest, then, to be called "Honest Abe"; being perceived as honest increased the power of his communication.

Social psychologists believe that *power, attractiveness, likableness,* and *similarity* are four important characteristics that add to a communicator's ability to change people's attitudes. In running for student body president, you will probably have more clout with students if you have been on the university president's student issues committee. Power may be an important characteristic for a communicator because it is associated with the ability to impose sanctions or control rewards and punishments (Kelley & Thibaut, 1978). In running for student body president, you are also more likely to get votes if students perceive you as attractive and similar to themselves. That's why you often see presidential candidates putting on miners' helmets in West Virginia, speaking a Spanish phrase in San Antonio, or riding a tractor in Iowa. The candidates are striving to show that they share common interests and an identity with their audience.

Similarity is also widely used in advertising. In commercials we might see a homemaker scrubbing the floor while advertising a new cleaner or a laborer laughing with his buddies at a bar while drinking beer. The creators of these commercials hope you will relate to these people because you perceive them as similar to yourself. Of course, many products are promoted by appealing to our personal ideals. To do this, attractive or famous individuals are used in advertisements. Elizabeth Taylor tries to persuade us to buy cologne, and Michael Jordan tries to persuade us to buy athletic shoes, for example.

Other factors that influence attitudes are the sex of the communicator and gender roles. To learn more about how gender might be a factor in attitudes about political candidates, turn to Sociocultural Worlds. As we will see next, the content of the message also is an important factor in influencing attitudes.

The Medium (Channel).   The communicator needs to be concerned about which medium to use to get a message across. Consider the difference between watching a presidential debate on television and reading about it in the newspaper. Television lets us see how the candidates deliver the message, what their appearance and mannerisms are like, and so on. Because it presents live images, television is considered the most powerful medium for changing attitudes. One study revealed that the winners of various political primaries were predicted by the amount of media exposure they had (Grush, 1980).

Television's power of persuasion is staggering. By the time the average American adolescent graduates from high school, he or she has watched 20,000 hours of television, far more than the number of hours spent in the classroom. Social scientists have studied television's influence on matters such as the impact of commercials on purchases, of mass media political campaigning on voting, of public service announcements on health, of broad-based ideological campaigns on lifestyles, and of television violence on aggression.

How strong is television's influence on an individual's attitudes and behavior? Some reviews of research conclude that there are few effects (Zeigler & Harmon, 1989). Other reviews conclude television has a more formidable effect (Clifford, Bunter, & McAleer, 1995).

The Message (Communication).   In exploring the message's role in persuasion, social psychologists examine whether positive or negative messages are more effective, as well as whether it is better to appeal to the rational or the emotional side of an argument.

Sociocultural Worlds

The Gender Gap in Politics

Some political analysts attributed the outcome of the 1996 presidential election to the voting power of "the soccer moms." Others suggested that the candidates' party platforms clearly demonstrated a difference in commitment to women's issues. Others suggested, less charitably, that the outcome was due to the difference in physical attractiveness between the candidates. Regardless of the specific cause, President Bill Clinton was elected in part because of Republican Robert Dole's failure to appeal to women voters—that is, he did not bridge "the gender gap."

Suffragettes in 1920 successfully campaigned for the right to vote guaranteed by the Nineteenth Amendment. However, women did not become a political force to reckon with until much later in the century. For example, it wasn't until 1984 that a woman—Geraldine Ferraro—was selected to fill the vice-presidential slot on the Democratic ticket. Although the Democrats did not win the 1984 election, Ferraro's selection was an important step for women in their efforts to achieve equality.

As more women have sought political office, the issue of gender has assumed a more important role in attitude change. Surveys reveal that, in today's political climate, we are more likely to vote for qualified female candidates, especially if they are running for lower political offices (Gallup, 1984). Discrimination still exists, though, especially in gubernatorial campaigns (Yankelovich, Skelly, & White, 1984).

The challenge is to determine for whom and under what circumstances gender makes the most difference. Social psychologist Carol Sigelman and her colleagues (1986) wanted to find out to what extent voters are influenced by a candidate's gender, physical attractiveness, and prestige in relation to the responsibility of the office being sought. The researchers gave college students information about six challengers to an incumbent in either a mayoral or county clerk's race. The challengers were men and women of high, moderate, or low physical attractiveness. The researchers found that the male, but not the female, voters discriminated against the female candidates. In addition, the men saw the women as less qualified, fewer of the men voted for the women, and the men rated the women lower overall. The males' antifemale bias was not offset by a preference for the women candidates by the female voters, however. The female voters tended to choose evenly between the male and female candidates. Also, attractiveness was less consistently an asset for the female candidates than it was for the males. Although it appears that less discrimination against female candidates occurs today than in past years, this research suggests that equality has not yet been reached.

Geraldine Ferraro campaigned as a vice-presidential candidate on the Mondale-Ferraro Democratic ticket in 1984. *What is gender's role in political attitudes?*

Negative appeals tend to play on our emotions, positive appeals on our logic. For example, how often have you seen politicians vow to run a clean campaign but, before long, start slinging dirt? A negative appeal may have contributed to George Bush's decisive presidential victory over democratic candidate Michael Dukakis. Bush succeeded in branding Dukakis with the "L" word *(liberal)* during the campaign. However, when Bush tried the same strategy with Bill Clinton in 1992, he failed because the sociopolitical context had changed and Clinton was more effective than Dukakis in combating Bush's assertion.

Emotional arguments also are more effective when the audience is scared. All other things being equal, the more frightened we are, the more we can be scared into changing our attitudes. Following the telecast of the vivid nuclear war film *The Day After,* more negative attitudes about the United States' massive nuclear arsenal surfaced (Schofield & Pavelchak, 1985, 1989). Advertisers also exploit our fears in order to promote sales. For example, you may have seen the Michelin tire ad that shows a baby riding inside a tire or the life insurance ad that shows a widow and her young children moving out of their home, which they lost because they did not have enough insurance. Fear appeals are most effective when they generate manageable anxiety, along with a method to reduce the anxiety (Leventhal, 1970). If the audience feels overwhelmed by anxiety, it might feel too helpless to take action.

Not all emotional appeals are negative. Music is widely used to make us feel good about commercial messages. When we watch such commercials, we might associate the pleasant feelings of the music with the product, even though the music itself does not provide any information about the product. Think about all of the "golden oldie" music advertisers adapt to selling contemporary products like toothpaste and shampoo.

In contrast to emotional appeals, rational approaches tend to work best when the audience is well informed. Editorials that lay out a logical foundation for an argument are easier to evaluate and feel less cluttered to the well informed than an emotional appeal. Knowledgeable consumers prefer logical evidence to emotional appeals.

Another aspect of the message involves the question of *when* to deliver it. Should you wait until the end of your presentation to make your strongest points or put your best foot forward at the beginning? In the **foot-in-the-door strategy,** *an individual presents a weaker point or makes a small request with which the listeners will probably comply in the beginning, saving the strongest point until the end.* In the words of social psychologist Robert Cialdini (1993), "Start small and build." For example, a sales pitch for a health spa might offer you 4 weeks' use of the facility for $10 and hope that, after the 4 weeks, you will pay $200 for a 1-year membership. In contrast, in the **door-in-the-face strategy,** *a communicator makes the strongest point or demand in the beginning, which the listeners probably will reject, then presents a weaker point or moderate "concessionary" demand toward the end.* For example, the salesperson for the health spa might initially offer you the 1-year membership for $200, which you turn down, then offer you a "bargain" 4-weeks-for-$10 package.

The Audience (Target). What are some characteristics of audiences that determine whether a message will be effective? This is a difficult question to answer because audience characteristics interact with what type of message is being conveyed and how complex it is. Thus, consumer psychologists often conduct extensive surveys to discover whether a new product will have appeal. You may have been stopped by a researcher while you were strolling through a mall to ask your opinions about a new product.

Two audience characteristics that are related to their persuadability are gender and intelligence. When their knowledge about a topic is not extensive, women are easier to persuade than men (Eagly, 1983). Also, individuals who have developed strong attitudes based on their life experiences are less likely to change their attitude. This might explain why highly intelligent people are often hard to persuade (Rhodes & Wood, 1992). They have thought through their positions more carefully and have more knowledge to combat attempts at persuasion.

So far in our discussion of social influence, we have explored a number of factors that affect whether we can persuade someone to accept our message or reject it. As we saw at the beginning of the chapter, Marshall Herff Applewhite was able to gain a powerful influence over his cult followers. The members of his Heaven's Gate cult obediently carried out his instructions to kill themselves. Next, we will further explore this intriguing aspect of human behavior we call obedience.

Obedience. **Obedience** *is behavior that complies with the explicit demands of an individual in authority.* Although many parents try to instill obedience in their children, obedience sometimes can be destructive, as it was in, for instance, the tragedy of Heaven's Gate, the massacre of Vietnamese civilians at My Lai, and the Nazi crimes against Jews and others in World War II.

The following demonstration, first performed by Stanley Milgram (1974) at Yale University, provides insight about obedience. As part of an experiment in psychology, imagine that you are asked to deliver a series of painful electric shocks to another person. You are told that the purpose of the study is to determine the effects of punishment on

foot-in-the-door strategy
A strategy in which an individual presents a weaker point or makes a small request with which listeners will probably comply in the beginning, saving the strongest point until the end.

door-in-the-face strategy
The technique in which a communicator makes the strongest point or demand in the beginning, which listeners will probably reject, then presents a weaker point or moderate, "concessionary" demand toward the end.

obedience
Behavior that complies with the explicit demands of an individual in authority.

(a) A 50-year-old man ("learner") is strapped into a chair. The experimenter makes it look as if a shock generator is being connected to his body through a number of electrodes. *(b)* The subject ("teacher") is given a sample 75-volt shock. *How far do you think you might have taken the shock in order to help science and assist the "learner" to learn?*

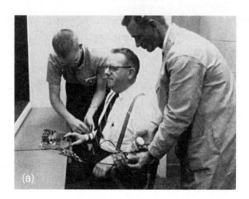

memory. Your role is to be the "teacher" and punish the mistakes made by a "learner"; each time the learner makes a mistake, your job is to increase the intensity of the shock by a certain amount. You are given a 75-volt shock to show you how it feels. You are then introduced to the "learner," a nice 50-year-old man who mumbles something about having a heart condition. He is strapped to a chair in the next room and communicates with you through an intercom. As the trials proceed, the "learner" quickly runs into trouble and is unable to give the correct answers. Should you shock him? The apparatus in front of you has thirty switches, ranging from 15 volts (light) to 375 volts (marked "danger") to 450 volts (marked "XXX"). As you raise the intensity of the shock, the "learner" says he's in pain. At 150 volts, he demands to have the experiment stopped. At 180 volts, he cries out that he can't stand it anymore. At 300 volts, he yells about his heart condition and pleads to be released. If you hesitate in shocking the learner, however, the experimenter tells you that you have no choice; the experiment must continue.

As you might imagine, in Milgram's study the "teachers" were uneasy about shocking the "learner." At 240 volts, one "teacher" responded, "Two hundred forty volts delivered: Aw, no. You mean I've got to keep going with that scale? No sir, I'm not going to kill that man—I'm not going to give him 450 volts!" (Milgram, 1965, p. 67). At the very high voltage, the "learner" quit responding. When the "teacher" asked the experimenter what to do, he simply instructed the "teacher" to continue the experiment and told him that it was his obligation to complete the job. Figure 14.2 shows the setting of the experiment. The 50-year-old "learner" actually was a phony subject (what researchers call a "confederate" of the experimenter). He was not being shocked at all. Of course, the "teachers" were unaware of this.

After the experiment was completed, the participants were told that the "learner" was not actually shocked. Even though they were debriefed and told that they really had not shocked anyone, a question lingers: Why did the real participants take the levels of shock so far in the face of feedback that they might have been harming the unfortunate learner? The "teachers" defended their actions in many ways. The attending experimenter had claimed full responsibility and persuasively encouraged them to continue for the benefit of science. They had made the commitment and felt compelled to follow through. Some attempted to minimize their actions by touching the shock lever as lightly as possible. Some reported feeling very anxious about the dilemma, and many laughed nervously as they complied with orders to administer stronger shocks. However, even when the teachers did not comply, by refusing to deliver the full range of shock, Milgram reported that not one of the teachers ever offered to provide the learner with any assistance or check to see if the learner was all right.

Was it ethical to impose such discomfort and even anguish on the participants in the research?

Milgram argued that we have learned a great deal about human nature from the experiments. He claimed that they tell us how far individuals will go in their obedience, even if it means being cruel to someone. The volunteers were interviewed later, and more than four of every five said that they were glad they had participated in the study; none said they were sorry they had participated. When Milgram conducted his studies on obedience, the ethical guidelines for research were not as stringent as they are today. The current ethical guidelines of the American Psychological Association stress that researchers should obtain informed consent from their volunteers. Deception should be used only for very important purposes. Individuals are supposed to feel as good about themselves when the experiment is over as they did when it began. Under today's guidelines, it is unlikely that the Milgram experiment would be conducted.

In subsequent studies, Milgram set up a storefront in Bridgeport, Connecticut, and recruited volunteers through newspaper ads. Milgram wanted to create a more natural environment for the experiment and to use a wider cross-section of volunteers. In these additional studies, close to two-thirds of the individuals still selected the highest level of shock for the "learner." In variations of the experiment, Milgram discovered some circumstances that encouraged disobedience: when an opportunity was given to see others disobey, when the authority figure was not perceived to be legitimate and was not close by, and when the victim was made to seem more human. To read about resisting social influence, see Applications in Psychology.

In our discussion of obedience, we focused on one person's power over another individual. Next, we enlarge our scope and study the nature of social relations in groups, including both positive and negative influences.

$\mathcal{A}$pplications in Psychology

Resisting Social Influence

If a man does not keep pace with his companions, perhaps it is because he hears a different drummer. Let him step to the music which he hears, however measured or far away.
—HENRY DAVID THOREAU

Most of us in this culture would prefer to think of ourselves as stepping to our own music, maybe even setting the rhythms for others, rather than trying to keep pace with our companions. However, society requires a certain degree of conformity if society is to function at all. For example, without conformity, traffic patterns in America would be nightmarish. As we go through our lives, we are both conformist and nonconformist. Sometimes conforming can be quite comfortable. For example, chances are good that you wear blue jeans during some part of your week as a result of conforming to some fashion standards. However, sometimes we are overwhelmed by the persuasion and influence of others. In some of those circumstances, we may need to resist and gain personal control over our lives.

Our individualistic culture prizes self-direction. It is important to remember that our relation to the social world is reciprocal; when others are attempting to exert undue social influence over us, we can recognize and resist this influence in the tradition espoused by Thoreau. We can also exert personal control over our actions and influence others in turn (Bandura, 1989, 1997). If you believe that someone in a position of authority is making an unjust request or asking you to do

something wrong, what choice of actions do you have? Your choices include:

- You can comply.
- You also can give the appearance of complying but secretly do otherwise.
- You can publicly dissent by showing doubts and disenchantment but still follow directives.
- You can openly disregard the orders and refuse to comply.
- You can challenge or confront the authority.
- You might get higher authorities to intervene or organize a group of people who agree with you to show the strength of your view.

In 1989 Chinese students led a massive demonstration against the Chinese government in Beijing. The students resisted the government's social influence by putting together resources to challenge the Chinese authorities; however, the government eventually prevailed after ordering the massacre of hundreds of students.

Review

Interpersonal Influence—Persuasion and Obedience

Persuasion involves the communicator (source), the medium (channel), the message (communication), and the audience (target). Communicators are most influential when they have expertise and credibility, trustworthiness, and power. Attractiveness and similarity also are important. Because it delivers live images, television may be the most powerful medium. Its persuasive capabilities are staggering, given the frequency of viewing. Experts debate television's influence. Another aspect of the message is when to deliver it. This involves the foot-in-the-door and door-in-the-face strategies. The less informed we are the more emotional appeals work. The more frightened we are, the more we will be influenced. Positive appeals can be persuasive, especially through the use of music. Although audience characteristics are hard to sort out, women and individuals who are less knowledgeable about the topic are easier to persuade.

Obedience is behavior that complies with the explicit demands of an authority. Milgram's classic experiment demonstrated the power of obedience. The subjects followed the experimenter's directions even though they perceived they were hurting someone. Milgram's experiment raises the question of ethics in psychological experimentation.

Influence in Groups

A student joining a fraternity, a jury deciding a criminal case, a company president delegating authority, a family reunion, a prejudiced remark about a minority group, conflicts among nations, arguments in the neighborhood, and attempts to reach peace—all of these circumstances reflect our lives as members of groups. Each of us belongs to many groups. Some we choose; others we do not. We choose to belong to a club, but we are born into a particular ethnic group, for example. Some group participation is very satisfying; other group experiences are frustrating and ineffective.

The Nature of Groups.   Group membership satisfies our personal needs, rewards us, provides information, raises our self-esteem, and gives us an identity. We might join a group because we think it will be enjoyable and exciting and satisfy our need for affiliation and companionship. We might join a group because we will receive rewards, either material or psychological. By taking a job with a company, we get paid to work for a group, but we also reap prestige and recognition. Groups are an important source of information. For example, as we listen to other members talk in a Weight Watchers group, we learn about their strategies for losing weight. As we sit in the audience at a real estate seminar, we learn how to buy property with no money down. Many of the groups of which you are a member—your family, a college, a club, a team—make you feel good, raise your self-esteem, and provide you with an identity.

Any group to which you belong has certain things in common with all other groups. All groups have their own **norms,** *rules that apply to all members of a group.* The city government requires each of its workers to wear socks, Mensa requires individuals to have a high IQ, Polar Bear Club members must complete a 15-minute swim in below-freezing temperatures. These are examples of norms.

Roles *are rules and expectations that govern certain positions in a group. Roles define how people should behave in a particular position in the group.* In a family, parents have certain roles, siblings have other roles, and a grandparent has yet another role. On a football team, many roles must be filled: center, guard, tackle, end, quarterback, halfback, and fullback, for example, and that only covers the offense. Roles and norms, then, tell us what is expected of the members of a group. They establish common principles of behavior that make groups more effective and productive. They make it easier to coordinate the action of the group, so that more resources can be brought to bear on a particular problem. This can improve the ability to complete tasks on time and accurately, especially compared to the efficiency of one person working alone.

However, group participation can have drawbacks. Conflicts can develop between group members. Coalitions can form that erode group unity. Further, agreed-upon roles and norms can lead to the expectation that the members of the group should all think and act in the same way. This can result in pressures to conform, which we will explore next.

norms

Rules that apply to the members of a group.

roles

Rules and expectations that govern certain positions in a group. Roles define how people should behave in a particular position in the group.

Conformity.   Conformity comes in many forms and affects many areas of our lives. Do you take up jogging because everyone else is doing it? Does fashion dictate that you let your hair grow long this year and cut it short the next? Would you take cocaine if pressured by others or would you resist? **Conformity** *occurs when individuals adopt the attitudes or behavior of others because of real or imagined pressure from others to do so.*

Conformity to rules and regulations result in people engaging in a number of behaviors that make society run more smoothly. For example, consider what would happen if most people did not conform to rules such as these: stopping at red lights, driving on the correct side of the road, not punching others in the face, going to school regularly, and so on. However, in the following experiments, researchers reveal how conformity pressures can sometimes make us act against our better judgment and even have dramatic, unfortunate consequences.

> *Every society honors its live conformists and its dead troublemakers.*
> —MIGNON MCLAUGHLIN, *American Writer, 20th Century*

Put yourself in the following situation. You are taken into a room, where you see five other people seated around a table. A person in a white lab coat enters the room and announces that you are about to participate in an experiment on perceptual accuracy. The group is shown two cards, the first having only a single vertical line on it, the second card with three vertical lines of varying length. You are told that the task is to determine which of the three lines on the second card is the same length as the line on the first card. You look at the cards and think "What a snap. It's so obvious which is longest." The other people in the room are actually associates of the experimenter (researchers often call such persons "confederates" of the experimenter); they've been hired to perform in ways the experimenter dictates (of course, you are not aware of this). On the first several trials, everyone agrees about which line matches the standard. Then, on the fourth trial, each of the others picks an incorrect line; you have a puzzled look on your face. As the last person to make a choice, you're in the dilemma of responding as your eyes tell you or conforming to what the others have said. How do you think you would answer?

Solomon Asch conducted this classic experiment on conformity in 1951 (see figure 14.3). He believed there would be little yielding to group pressure. To find out if this was so, Asch instructed his accomplices to respond incorrectly on 12 of the 18 trials. Although the majority of participants did not conform, to Asch's surprise, the volunteer participants conformed to the incorrect answers 35 percent of the time. The pressure to conform is strong. Even in a clear-cut situation, such as in the Asch experiment, we may conform to what others say and do. We don't want to be laughed at or have others be angry with us.

Put yourself in another situation. You have volunteered to participate in a psychology experiment. By the flip of a coin, half of the volunteers are designated as prisoners and half as guards in a mock prison; you are one of the fortunate ones because you will be a guard. How much would you and your fellow volunteers conform to the social roles of "guard" and "prisoner"? You are instructed to maintain law and order—to do a guard's job. You will make a fine guard, you think, because you are kind and respect the rights and dignity of others. In just a few hours, however, you find that your behavior, and that of the other "guards" and "prisoners," has changed; each of you has begun to conform to what you think are the expected social roles for guards and prisoners. Over the course of 6 days, you and the other guards begin to make the prisoners obey petty, meaningless rules and force them to perform tedious, useless, and sometimes humiliating tasks. What's more, you find yourself insulting the prisoners and keeping them "in line" with night sticks. Many of the prisoners begin acting like robots. They develop an intense hatred for you and the other guards and constantly think about ways to escape.

You may be thinking that this scenario stretches credibility. No one you know, and certainly not you, would behave in such an abusive way. However, psychologist Philip Zimbardo and his colleagues (1972) conducted just such an experiment with a group of normal, mature, stable, intelligent young men at Stanford University. In fact, the prison study was scheduled to last 2 weeks, but the behavior of the "guards" and "prisoners" changed so drastically that the experiment had to be stopped after 6 days. Although many

conformity
Individuals' adopting the attitudes or behavior of others because of real or imagined pressure from others to do so.

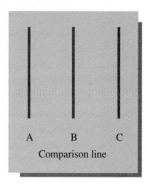

Standard line

A B C
Comparison line

$\mathcal{F}$IGURE 14.3

Asch's Conformity Experiment

The figures show the stimulus materials for the Asch conformity experiment on group influence. The photograph shows the dilemma for the subject *(seated in the middle)* after five confederates of the experimenter chose the incorrect line.

of the prisoners resisted the guards and asked questions initially, after a while they gave up and virtually stopped reacting. Five of the prisoners had to be released, four because of severe depression or anxiety and the fifth because he broke out in a rash all over his body; several of the guards became brutal with the prisoners. Figure 14.4 shows some of the circumstances in the prison study.

Groupthink.   Sometimes groups make rational decisions and come up with the best solution to a problem. Not always. Group members, especially leaders, often want to develop or maintain unanimity among group members. **Groupthink** *is the motivation of group members to maintain harmony and unanimity in decision making, suffocating differences of opinion in the process* (Janis, 1972). Groupthink evolves because members often boost each other's egos and increase each other's self-esteem by seeking conformity, especially in stressful circumstances. This motivation for harmony and unanimity may result in disastrous decisions and policy recommendations. For example, in the aftermath of the explosion of the *Challenger* shuttlecraft, many NASA team members admitted that they had harbored reservations about the craft's safety before it was launched. However, they suppressed their concerns in the face of the rest of the launch team's enthusiasm. When they failed to express their doubts, the momentum of the group took over. The *Chal-*

groupthink

The motivation of group members to maintain harmony and unanimity in decision making, suffocating differences of opinion in the process.

$\mathcal{F}$IGURE 14.4

Zimbardo's Prison Experiment

(a) A volunteer for a psychology experiment is picked up on campus—he had lost a coin flip and was designated a prisoner. *(b)* A student conforms to the hostile, abusive role of prison guard.

deindividuation

A state of reduced self-awareness, weakened self-restraints against impulsive actions, and apathy about negative social evaluation.

lenger explosion cost the lives of seven astronauts and damaged American confidence in the space program.

Leaders often lay the foundation for groupthink when they favor a solution and promote it within the group. Members of the group also tend to be cohesive and isolate themselves from qualified outsiders who could influence their decisions. Leaders can avoid groupthink by encouraging dissident opinions, by not presenting a favored plan at the outset, by appointing a "devil's advocate" to argue for unpopular opinions, and by having several independent groups work on the same problem.

Deindividuation. Group membership usually confers many advantages. However, some group processes are not only unpleasant but dangerous. As early as 1895, Gustav LeBon observed that a group can foster uninhibited behavior, ranging from wild celebrations to mob behavior. The brutal activities of the Ku Klux Klan, the wearing of erotic outfits in public during Mardi Gras wild times, and "good ol' boys" rolling a car on spring break in Fort Lauderdale might be due to **deindividuation,** *a state of reduced self-awareness, weakened self-restraints against impulsive actions, and apathy about negative social evaluation.*

One explanation of deindividuation is that the group offers anonymity. We might act in an uninhibited manner in a group because we believe that authority figures and victims are less likely to discover that we are the culprits. Losing the boundaries of the self is characteristic of participation in cults.

Cults. Heaven's Gate was hardly America's first experience with cults. David Koresh's Branch Davidians also met with a grisly end when their compound in Waco, Texas, went up in flames in 1993. The Reverend James Jones ordered his followers in the People's Temple to kill themselves by drinking cyanide-laced Kool-Aid in 1978, resulting in the deaths of more than 900 people. Apparently most members of these groups were devoted to their leaders' philosophies, philosophies that often seem irrational to outsiders.

Cults are religious groups that isolate themselves from the outside world and practice severe lifestyles as part of their worship. They represent a unique combination of some of the social psychology concepts we have studied so far. For example, individuals who are targeted for cult membership are gradually introduced to the demands and sacrifices of cult life (Zimbardo & Leippe 1991). A casual contact might lead to a coffee date and then a more extended visit with the larger group. Once the basic principles of the cult seem acceptable, the member is required to conform to stringent group norms. For example, some of the male Heaven's Gate members were castrated to rid themselves of sexual drives. Resistance to cult requirements fades as personal boundaries weaken. The deindividualized members then submerge themselves in the group's more powerful identity in exchange for the rewards promised by the cult's leader, such as loving acceptance in the present or salvation in the future. Cult leaders reinforce their positions of power through other tactics as well (Galanter, 1989). They weaken members' resistance by making meals and sleep unpredictable. They define solutions to complex problems in simplistic but appealing ways, often selling their beliefs with charismatic performances. Finally, they do not tolerate deviations from narrowly defined norms, which reinforces the power of groupthink to suppress resistance among group members.

We can become deindividuated in groups. Examples of situations in which people can lose their individual identity include *(a)* at Ku Klux Klan rallies, *(b)* at Mardi Gras, and *(c)* in national patriotism crowds.

Certain individuals in the minority have played important roles in history. Martin Luther King, Jr., helped African Americans gain important rights.

Fortunately, not all leadership comes to the tragic ends that unfolded in these cults. Next, we will explore other dimensions of leadership in group relations.

Leadership. What made Churchill a great leader? Was it his personality, the situation he was thrust into, or some combination of the two?

> *I am certainly not one of those who needs to be prodded. In fact, if anything, I am the prod.*
>
> —WINSTON CHURCHILL, *British Prime Minister, 20th Century*

great person theory
The theory that individuals with certain traits are best suited for leadership positions.

The **great person theory** *says that some individuals have certain traits that make them best suited for leadership positions.* Leaders are commonly thought to be assertive, cooperative, decisive, dominant, energetic, self-confident, tolerant of stress, willing to assume responsibility, diplomatic and tactful, and persuasive. Although we can list traits and skills possessed by leaders, a large number of research studies conclude that we cannot predict who will become a leader solely from an individual's personality characteristics.

situational theory of leadership
The theory that the needs of a group change from time to time and that a person who emerges as leader in one circumstance will not necessarily be the person who becomes a leader in another circumstance.

Is it the situation, then, that produces leaders? According to the **situational theory of leadership,** *the needs of a group change from time to time, and a person who emerges as a leader in one circumstance will not necessarily be the person who becomes a leader in another circumstance.* Many psychologists believe that a combination of personality characteristics and skills and situational influences determines who will become a leader. Not only did the situational pressures of World War II contribute to Churchill's becoming a leader; so did his personality traits of assertiveness, decisiveness, energy, and willingness to assume responsibility.

Majority-Minority Influence. Think about the groups in which you have been a member. Who had the most influence, the majority or the minority? In most groups—whether a jury, family, or corporate meeting—the majority holds sway over the minority. The majority exerts both normative and informational pressure on the group. Its adherents set the group's norms; those who do not go along may be rejected. The majority also has a greater opportunity to provide information that will influence decision making.

In most cases, the majority wins, but there are occasions when the minority has its day. How can the minority swing the majority? The minority cannot win through normative influence because it is outnumbered. It must do its work through *informational pressure*. If the minority presents its views consistently, confidently, and nondefensively, then the majority is more likely to listen to the minority's view. The minority position might have to be repeated several times in order to create sufficient impact.

In group situations, some individuals are able to command the attention of others and thus have a better opportunity to shape and direct subsequent social outcomes. To achieve such a high social impact, they have to distinguish themselves in various ways from the rest of the group. They have to make themselves noticed by others—by the opinions they express, the jokes they tell, or by their nonverbal style. They may be the first ones to raise a new idea, to disagree with a prevailing point of view, or to propose a creative alternative solution to a problem. People who have a high social impact often are characterized by their willingness to be different.

Certain individuals in a minority can play a crucial role. Individuals with a history of taking minority stands can trigger others to dissent, showing them that disagreement is possible and that the minority stand might be the best course. Such is the ground for some of history's greatest moments. When Abraham Lincoln spoke out against slavery, the majority view was racist and was tearing the country apart. A century later Rosa Parks refused to ride in the back of a bus. Her minority influence catalyzed the modern civil rights movement.

Although the scale is smaller, the triumph might be the same for a gang member who influences the gang's decision not to vandalize, the woman executive who persuades her male colleagues to adopt a less sexist advertising strategy, or the ethnic minority student who expresses his views in a majority White classroom.

> *Life shrinks or expands in proportion to one's courage.*
> —ANAIS NIN, *French Novelist, 20th Century*

 eview

Group Relations

Groups satisfy our personal needs, reward us, provide us with information, raise our self-esteem, and improve our identity. Groups involve norms and roles. In some cases, groups have drawbacks, especially when conflicts and coalitions emerge.

Conformity involves change in an individual's behavior because of real or imagined pressure to do so. Two experiments demonstrate conformity's power in our lives: Asch's study on judgments of line length and Zimbardo's study of social roles in a mock prison.

Groupthink is the motivation of group members to maintain harmony and unanimity in decision making, suffocating differences of opinion in the process. Deindividuation is the loss of identity as an individual and the development of group identity. Deindividuation promotes anonymity. A loss of self also is encouraged in cults, which are religious groups that isolate themselves from the outside world and practice severe lifestyles as part of their worship.

Both the great person theory, which emphasizes personality traits and skills, and situational factors have been proposed to explain why certain people become leaders. Personality and situational factors likely combine to determine who will become a leader.

In the study of the majority and the minority, the majority usually has the most influence. However, there are times when the minority has its day, most often being effective through informational pressure.

INTERPERSONAL RELATIONSHIPS

> *No love, no friendship can cross the path of our destiny without leaving some mark on it forever.*
> —FRANCOIS MAURIAC, *French Writer, 20th Century*

Social psychologists have long been fascinated by the social cognitions, affect, and behaviors that comprise interpersonal relationships. To begin our inquiry into interpersonal relationships, we will explore what attracts us to certain people.

Attraction

Birds of a feather do indeed flock together. *Familiarity,* having spent time together or in close proximity, is an essential condition for a close relationship to develop. Usually friends and lovers have been around each other for a long time; they may have grown up together, gone to high school or college together, worked together, or gone to the same social events. Once we have been exposed to someone for a period of time, what is it that makes the relationship breed friendship and even love?

One of the strongest lessons from studies of close relationships is the importance of *similarity,* sharing preferences and outlooks. Our friends, as well as our lovers, are much more like us than unlike us. We and the people we are closely involved with have similar attitudes, behaviors, and other characteristics, such as taste in clothes, intelligence, personality, political attitudes, other friends, values, lifestyle, physical attractiveness, and so on.

consensual validation

A concept that provides an explanation of why people are attracted to others who are similar to them. Our own attitudes and behavior are supported when someone else's attitudes and behavior are similar to ours—their attitudes and behavior validate ours.

Consensual validation *provides an explanation of why people are attracted to others who are similar to them. Our own attitudes and behavior are supported when someone else's attitudes and behavior are similar to ours—their attitudes and behavior validate ours.* People tend to shy away from the unknown. We may tend, instead, to prefer people whose attitudes and behavior we can predict. And similarity implies that we will enjoy doing things with the other person, which often requires a partner who likes the same things and has similar attitudes.

How important is *physical attraction* in an interpersonal relationship? Many advertising agencies have us believe it is the most important factor in establishing and maintaining a relationship. However, heterosexual men and women differ on the importance they place on good looks when they seek an intimate partner. Women tend to rate as most important such traits as considerateness, honesty, dependability, kindness, and understanding; men prefer good looks, cooking skills, and frugality (Buss & Barnes, 1986).

Despite the priority that men say they give to a woman's physical appearance, in some cases women who are very attractive draw fewer romantic overtures. Sometimes men pursue women who are more likely to respond to their romantic actions. And attractive women might trust men less because they fear that men want them only for their looks.

Complicating research conclusions about the role of physical attraction in relationships are the changing standards for what is deemed attractive. The criteria for beauty can differ, not just *across* cultures, but over time *within* cultures as well (Lamb & others, 1993). In the 1940s, the ideal female beauty in the United States was typified by the well-rounded figure of Marilyn Monroe. As a result of the American preoccupation with health, Monroe's 135 pound, 5-foot-5-inch physique is regarded as overweight by today's standards. In the 1980s and 1990s, the ideal physique for both men and women is neither pleasingly plump nor extremely slender.

The force of similarity also operates at a physical level. We usually seek out someone at our own level of attractiveness in both physical characteristics and social attributes. Most of us come away with a reasonably good chance of finding a "good match." Research indicates that this **matching hypothesis**—*that although we might prefer a more attractive person in the abstract, in the real world we end up choosing someone who is close to our own level of attractiveness*—holds up (Kalick & Hamilton, 1986).

matching hypotheses

The hypothesis that while we may prefer a more attractive person in the abstract, in the real world we end up choosing someone who is close to our own level of attractiveness.

Several additional points help to clarify the role of physical beauty and attraction in our close relationships. Much of the research has focused on initial or short-term encounters; researchers have not often evaluated attraction over the course of months and years. As relationships endure, physical attraction probably assumes less importance. Rocky Dennis, as portrayed in the movie *Mask,* is a case in point. His peers and even his mother initially wanted to avoid Rocky, whose face was severely distorted, but over the course of his childhood and adolescent years, the avoidance turned into attraction and love as people got to know him. As Rocky's story demonstrates, familiarity can overcome even severe initial negative reactions to a person.

> *Ask a toad what is beauty . . . he will answer that it is a female with two great round eyes coming out of her little head, a large flat mouth, a yellow belly and a brown back.*
>
> —VOLTAIRE, *French Philosopher, 18th Century*

Once attraction initiates a relationship, other opportunities exist to deepen the relationship to friendship and love. We begin with friendship.

Friendship

> *One friend in life is much, two are many, and three hardly possible.*
> —HENRY ADAMS, *American Historian, 19th/20th Centuries*

friendship
A form of close relationship that involves enjoyment, acceptance, trust, intimacy, respect, mutual assistance, understanding, and spontaneity.

As suggested by Henry Adams, true friendship is hard to come by. **Friendship** *is a form of close relationship that involves enjoyment, acceptance, trust, intimacy, respect, mutual assistance, understanding, and spontaneity.* We like to spend time with our friends, and we accept their friendship without trying to change them. We assume our friends will act in our best interest and believe that they make good judgments. We help and support our friends and they return the assistance. When we share experiences and deep personal matters with a friend, we believe that the friend will understand our perspective. We feel free to be ourselves around our friends (Davis, 1985). One study of more than 40,000 individuals revealed that many of these characteristics are considered the qualities of a best friend (Parlee, 1979).

Gender plays a role in self-disclosure and friendships. These gender differences appear in same-sex friendships and the miscommunications between men and women in close relationships. Women tend to hone their self-disclosure skills and learn to trust the relationship-enhancing qualities of self-disclosure in their same-sex peer/friendship relationships. In peer/friendship relationships that emphasize competition and challenge, males often avoid revealing weaknesses and at times associate self-disclosure with loss of control and with vulnerability. Thus, females and males not only reveal different preferences for and patterns of self-disclosure but also interpret the meaning and purpose of self-disclosure differently.

Friendships are an important dimension of our close relationships. *What are the common characteristics of friendship?*

Romantic Love

romantic love

Also called passionate love or eros; a type of love with strong components of sexuality and infatuation; it often predominates in the early part of a love relationship.

Romantic love *is also called passionate love or eros; it has strong components of sexuality and infatuation, and it often predominates in the early part of a love relationship.* Poets, playwrights, and musicians through the ages have lauded the fiery passion of romantic love—and lamented the searing pain when it fails. Think for a moment about songs and books that hit the top of the charts. Chances are they're about love. Well-known love researcher Ellen Berscheid (1988) says that it is romantic love we mean when we say that we are "in love" with someone. It is romantic love she believes we need to understand if we are to learn what love is all about.

In our culture, romantic love is the main reason we get married. In 1967, a famous study showed that men maintained that they would not get married if they were not "in love." Women either were undecided or said that they would get married even if they did not love their prospective husband (Kephart, 1967). In the 1980s, women and men tended to agree that they would not get married unless they were "in love." And more than half of today's men and women say that not being "in love" is sufficient reason to dissolve a marriage (Berscheid, Snyder, & Omoto, 1989).

> *I flee who chases me, and chase who flees me.*
> —OVID, *Roman Poet, 1st Century A.D.*

Romantic love is especially important among college students. One study of unattached college men and women found that more than half identified a romantic partner, rather than a parent, sibling, or friend, as their closest relationship (Berscheid, Snyder, & Omoto, 1989). We are referring to romantic love when we say, "I am *in love,*" not just "I *love.*"

Romantic love includes a complex intermingling of different emotions—fear, anger, sexual desire, joy, and jealousy, for example. Obviously, some of these emotions are a source of anguish. One study found that romantic loves were more likely than friends to be the cause of depression (Berscheid & Fei, 1977).

Although Berscheid admits this is an inadequate answer, she concluded that romantic love is about 90 percent sexual desire. Berscheid (1988) believes sexual desire is vastly neglected in the study of romantic love. As she puts it, "To discuss romantic love without also prominently mentioning the role sexual arousal and desire plays in it is very much like printing a recipe for tiger soup that leaves out the main ingredient."

> *Love is purely a creation of the human imagination . . . the most important example of how the imagination continually outruns the creature it inhabits.*
> —KATHERINE ANNE PORTER, *American Writer, 20th Century*

Companionate Love

affectionate love

Also called companionate love; a type of love that occurs when an individual desires to have the other person near and has a deep, caring affection for the person.

Love is more than just passion (Hatfield & Rapson, 1998). **Affectionate love,** *also called companionate love, is the type of love that occurs when individuals desire to have the other person near and have a deep, caring affection for the person.*

There is a growing belief that the early stages of love have more romantic ingredients, but as love matures, passion tends to give way to affection. Phillip Shaver (1986) describes the initial phase of romantic love as a time that is fueled by a mixture of sexual attraction and gratification, a reduced sense of loneliness, uncertainty about the security of developing another attachment, and excitement from exploring the novelty of another human being. With time, he says, sexual attraction wanes, attachment anxieties either lessen or produce conflict and withdrawal, novelty is replaced with familiarity, and lovers either find themselves securely attached in a deeply caring relationship or distressed—feeling bored, disappointed, lonely, or hostile, for example. In the latter case, one or both partners might eventually seek another close relationship.

When two lovers go beyond their preoccupation with novelty, unpredictability, and the urgency of sexual attraction, they are more likely to detect deficiencies in each other's caring. This may be the point in a relationship when women, who often are better caregivers than men, sense that the relationship has problems. Wives are almost twice as likely as husbands to initiate a divorce, for example (National Center for Health Statistics, 1989).

So far we have discussed two forms of love: romantic (or passionate) and affectionate (or companionate). Robert J. Sternberg (1988) described a third form of love, consummate love, which he said is the strongest, fullest type of love. Sternberg proposed the **triangular theory of love:** *that love includes three dimensions—passion, intimacy, and commitment* (see figure 14.5). Couples must share all three dimensions to experience consummate love.

Passion, as described earlier, is physical and sexual attraction to another. Intimacy is the emotional feelings of warmth, closeness, and sharing in a relationship. Commitment is our cognitive appraisal of the relationship and our intent to maintain the relationship even in the face of problems. If passion is the only ingredient (with intimacy and commitment low or absent), we are merely *infatuated.* This might happen in an affair or a fling in which there is little intimacy and even less commitment. A relationship marked by intimacy and commitment but low or lacking in passion is called *affectionate love,* a pattern often found among couples who have been married for many years. If passion and commitment are present but intimacy is not, Sternberg calls the relationship *fatuous love,* as when one person worships another from a distance. To determine your type of love complete the Self-Assessment. For some suggestions on how to create a positive relationship with a partner, See Improving Personal and Cognitive Skills.

> *We are who we love.*
> —ERIK ERIKSON, *European-Born American Psychotherapist, 20th Century*

Not all of us experience the passion, intimacy, and commitment of love, and not all of us have many, or even one, close friend in whom we can confide. Understanding our social relationships also involves exploring feelings of loneliness.

triangular theory of love

Sternberg's theory that love comes in three main forms: passion, intimacy, and commitment.

$\mathcal{F}$IGURE 14.5

Sternberg's Triangle of Love

Sternberg says that the experience we call love is shaped by three dimensions: passion, intimacy, and commitment. Various combinations of these three dimensions produce particular types of love. *Which types of love have you experienced?*

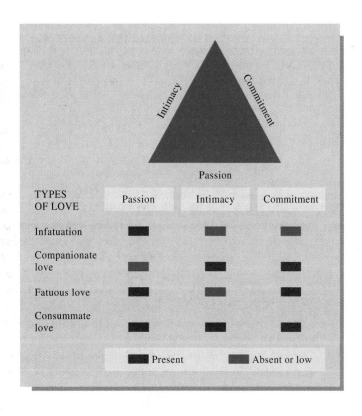

Self-Assessment

The Type of Love You Have

Instructions

Imagine the blank spaces filled in with the name of one person you love or care about deeply. Then rate each of the items from 1 to 9, where 1=not all, 5=moderately, and 9=extremely.

_____ 1. I actively support _____'s well being.
_____ 2. I have a warm relationship with _____.
_____ 3. I can count on _____ in times of need.
_____ 4. _____ is able to count on me in times of need.
_____ 5. I am willing to share myself and my possessions with _____.
_____ 6. I receive considerable emotional support from _____.
_____ 7. I give considerable emotional support to _____.
_____ 8. I communicate well with _____.
_____ 9. I value _____ greatly in my life.
_____ 10. I feel close to _____.
_____ 11. I have a comfortable relationship with _____.
_____ 12. I feel that I really understand _____.
_____ 13. I feel that _____ really understands me.
_____ 14. I feel that I can really trust _____.
_____ 15. I share deeply personal information about myself with _____.
_____ 16. Just seeing _____ excites me.
_____ 17. I find myself thinking about _____ frequently during the day.
_____ 18. My relationship with _____ is very romantic.
_____ 19. I find _____ to be very personally attractive.
_____ 20. I idealize _____.
_____ 21. I cannot imagine another person making me as happy as _____.
_____ 22. I would rather be with _____ than anyone.
_____ 23. There is nothing more important to me than my relationship with _____.
_____ 24. I especially like physical contact with _____.
_____ 25. There is something special about my relationship with _____.
_____ 26. I adore _____.
_____ 27. I cannot imagine my life without _____.
_____ 28. My relationship with _____ is passionate.
_____ 29. When I see romantic movies and read romantic books I think of _____.
_____ 30. I fantasize about _____.

_____ 31. I know that I care about _____.
_____ 32. I am committed to maintaining my relationship with _____.
_____ 33. Because of my commitment to _____, I would not let other people come between us.
_____ 34. I have confidence in the stability of my relationship with _____.
_____ 35. I could not let anything get in the way of my commitment to _____.
_____ 36. I expect my love for _____ to last for the rest of my life.
_____ 37. I will always feel a strong responsibility for _____.
_____ 38. I view my commitment to _____ as a solid one.
_____ 39. I cannot imagine ending my relationship with _____.
_____ 40. I am certain of my love for _____.
_____ 41. I view my relationship with _____ as permanent.
_____ 42. I view my relationship with _____ as a good decision.
_____ 43. I feel a sense of responsibility toward _____.
_____ 44. I plan to continue my relationship with _____.
_____ 45. Even when _____ is hard to deal with, I remain committed to our relationship.

Scoring and Interpretation

The first 15 items reflect intimacy, 16 to 30 measure passion, and 31 to 45 evaluate commitment. Add your total score for each of the three areas: 1–15 (intimacy), 16–30 (passion), and 31–45 (commitment). You can compare your scores with the average scores of a group of men and women (average age=31) who were either married or in a close relationship.

Intimacy	Passion	Commitment	Percentile
93	73	85	15
102	85	96	30
111	98	108	50
120	110	120	70
129	123	131	85

The fourth column (percentile) shows the percentage of the adults who scored at that level or above. Thus, if your intimacy score is 122, you have more intimacy than 70 percent of the adults who have taken this self-assessment.

SOURCE: R. Sternberg, "The Triangular Love Scale," From *The Triangle of Love*," (1988). New York: Basic Books.

Loneliness

Some of us are lonely. We might think that no one knows us very well. We might feel isolated and sense that we do not have anyone we can turn to in times of need or stress. Our society's emphasis on self-fulfillment and achievement, the importance we attach to commitment in relationships, and a decline in stable close relationships are among the reasons loneliness is common today (de Jong-Gierveld, 1987).

Loneliness is associated with a person's gender, attachment history, self-esteem, and social skills (Lau & Gruen, 1992). Both men and women who lack female companions

$\mathcal{I}$mproving Personal and Cognitive Skills

Building a Positive Partner Relationship

What are some good strategies for developing a positive relationship with a partner? They include the following (Sternberg, 1988):

- *Don't take your relationship for granted.*
  If you or your partner takes your relationship for granted, the relationship can run into trouble. Nourish the relationship and give it high priority along with your studies and/or work.
- *Develop a positive identity.*
  Too many people seek in a partner what they lack in themselves. When both partners have positive self-esteem and identities, the relationship benefits.
- *Share your life with your partner.*
  Don't isolate yourself from your partner. Take time to discuss your day with your partner. Look for activities you can share. Remember to ask about your partner's activities so that you aren't too self-focused.
- *Be open with your partner.*
  It is easy to lie or to hold back the truth when communi-

cating with your partner. However, once omissions, distortions, and lies start, they often multiply and can destroy a relationship. Eventually, the relationship can become like an empty shell as it loses depth and trust.

- *See things from your partner's point of view.*
  It is easy to want to get more than you give. Ask yourself how your partner perceives you. This helps you develop the empathy and understanding that are important in a positive close relationship.
- *Read a good book on improving close relationships.*
  A good one is *Getting the Love You Want* by Harville Hendrix (1988), which is profiled at the end of the chapter in the resources section.
- *Talk with a professional.*
  If your relationship runs into trouble, you can't seem to get the problems resolved, and you want to continue the relationship, consider seeing a counseling or clinical psychologist. Your college likely has counseling services available for students seeking help for their relationship problems.

have a greater risk of being lonely. Lonely people often have a history of poor relationships with their parents. Early experiences of rejection and loss (as when a parent dies) can cause a lasting feeling of being alone. Lonely people often have low self-esteem and tend to blame themselves more than they deserve for their inadequacies. Also, lonely people usually have poor social skills. For example, they show inappropriate self-disclosure, self-attention at the expense of attention to a partner, or an inability to develop comfortable intimacy.

When traditional-age students leave the familiar world of their hometown and family to enter college, they may feel especially lonely. Many college freshmen feel anxious about meeting new people and developing a new social life. One student commented:

My first year here at the university has been pretty lonely. I wasn't lonely at all in high school. I lived in a fairly small town—I knew everyone and everyone knew me. I was a member of several clubs and played on the basketball team. It's not that way at the university. It is a big place and I've felt like a stranger on so many occasions. I'm starting to get used to my life here and in the past few months I've been making myself meet people and get to know them, but it has not been easy.

As this comment illustrates, freshmen rarely take their high school popularity and social standing into the college environment. There may be a dozen high school basketball stars, National Merit scholars, and former student council presidents in a single dormitory wing. Especially if students attend college away from home, they face the task of forming new social relationships.

In one study, 2 weeks after the school year began, 75 percent of 354 college freshmen felt lonely at least part of the time since arriving on campus (Cutrona, 1982). More than 40 percent said their loneliness was moderate to severe in intensity. Students who were the most optimistic and had the highest self-esteem were more likely to overcome their loneliness by the end of their freshman year. Loneliness is not reserved only for traditional-age college freshmen, though. Upperclassmen and nontraditional-age students are often lonely as well.

Males and females attribute their loneliness to different sources. Men are more likely to blame themselves, and women are more likely to blame external factors. Men initiate relationships, whereas women are traditionally socialized to wait, then respond. Perhaps men blame themselves because they feel they should do something about their loneliness, whereas women wonder why no one calls.

If you think that you are not in tune with people around you, and if you can't find companionship when you want it, you probably are lonely (Perlman & Peplau, 1998). If you recently have left an important relationship, you might feel lonely until you rebuild your social network. For some suggestions on how to deal with loneliness, see Improving Personal and Cognitive Skills.

> *Where you used to be, there is a hole in the world, which I find myself constantly walking around in the daytime, and falling into at night.*
> —EDNA ST. VINCENT MILLAY, *American Poet, 20th Century*

Yet another aspect of close relationships is the special bond that develops when one person helps another. In the next section, we will explore why human beings are motivated to help others.

Altruism

altruism
An unselfish interest in helping someone else.

Altruism *is an unselfish interest in helping another person.* We often hear or read about acts of generosity and courage, such as rock concerts and other fund-raisers to help AIDS victims, the taxi driver who risks his life to save a woman in a dark alley, and volunteers who pull a baby from an abandoned well. You might have placed some of your hard-earned cash in the palm of a homeless person or perhaps cared for a wounded cat. How do psychologists account for such acts of human altruism?

Evolutionary psychologists emphasize that some types of altruism help our prospects for the survival of our genes and our opportunity to reproduce (Buss, 1995). For example, natural selection favors parents who care for their children and improve their probability of surviving. A parent feeding its young is performing a biological altruistic act because the young's chance of survival is increased. So is a mother bird who performs a distraction ritual to lure predators away from the eggs in her nest. She is willing to sacrifice herself so that three or four of her young offspring will have the chance to survive, thus

*I*mproving Personal and Cognitive Skills

Overcoming Loneliness

If you are lonely, how can you become better connected with others? Following are some strategies:

- *Participate in activities that you can do with others.*
Join organizations or volunteer your time for a cause you believe in. You likely will get to know others whose views are similar to yours. Going to just one social gathering can help you develop social contacts. When you go, introduce yourself to others and start a conversation. Another strategy is to sit next to new people in your classes or find someone to study with.
- *Draw a diagram of your social network.*
List whether the people in the diagram meet your social needs. If not, pencil in the people you would like to get to know.
- *Engage in positive behaviors when you meet new people.*
You will improve your chances of developing enduring

relationships if you engage in certain behaviors when you meet new people. Be nice, considerate, honest, trustworthy, and cooperative. Have a positive attitude, be supportive of the other person, and make positive comments about him or her.
- *Be aware of the early warning signs of loneliness.*
People often feel bored or alienated before loneliness becomes pervasive. Head off loneliness by becoming involved in new social activities.
- *See a counselor or read a book.*
If you can't get rid of your loneliness on your own, you might want to contact the counseling services at your college. The counselor can talk with you about strategies for reducing your loneliness. You also might want to read a good book on loneliness. A good one is *Intimate Connections* by David Burns (1985), which is described at the end of this chapter in the resources section.

Friends of Ian O'Gorman *(being held aloft)* demonstrated an unusual degree of altruism when eleven of them shaved their heads prior to the chemotherapy that would cause Ian to lose his hair. Ian had non-Hodgkins lymphoma, and his chemotherapy protocol enhanced his chances of survival. The idea was originally Taylor Herber's. He claimed he would shave his head as a joke but then decided to do it because it would be less traumatizing for his best friend, who was likely to lose his hair as a side effect of chemotherapy. Others joined the cause as soon as they heard. His friends were relieved that the girls, who wanted to join in support, never followed through, since they believed Ian wouldn't want to be "followed around by a bunch of bald girls." The boys committed to future shaved heads if Ian's illness required more chemotherapy.

preserving her genes. Individuals also often show more empathy toward other relatives in relation to their genetic closeness. In the case of a natural disaster, people's uppermost concern is their family (Cunningham, 1986).

Evolutionary psychologists believe that benefits can accrue to individuals who form cooperative reciprocal relationships (Trivers, 1971). By being good to someone now, individuals increase the likelihood that they will receive a benefit from the other person in the future. Through this reciprocal process, both gain something beyond what they could have by acting alone.

Reciprocity and exchange are important aspects of altruism. Humans everywhere give to and receive from others. For example, sales representatives rely on the principle of reciprocity when they offer you free samples during your grocery shopping trip. They give you a sample of ice cream in exchange for your attention and possible purchase of the product. Reciprocity is a fundamental tenet of major religion in the world—including Judaism, Christianity, Buddhism, and Islam. Reciprocity encourages us to do unto others as we would have them do unto us. Certain sentiments are involved in reciprocity: In Western contexts, for instance, trust is probably the most important principle over the long run; guilt occurs if we do not reciprocate, and anger results if someone else does not reciprocate.

social exchange theory

The theory that individuals should benefit those who benefit them, or that, for a benefit received, an equivalent benefit should be returned at some point.

Social exchange theory *states that individuals should benefit those who benefit them, or for a benefit received, an equivalent benefit should be returned at some point.* Many examples of altruism do involve social exchanges. We exchange gifts, cards, and tips for competent service, for example. It sounds cold and calculating to describe altruism in terms of costs and benefits, but that is exactly what social exchange theory does.

Not all altruism is motivated by reciprocity and social exchange, but

"All I'm saying is, giving a little something to the arts might help our image."

egoism
An attitude in which one does something beneficial for another person in order to ensure reciprocity; to present oneself as powerful, competent, or caring; or to avoid social or self-censure for failing to live up to normative expectations.

this view alerts us to the importance of considering interactions between oneself and others to understand altruism. And not all seemingly altruistic behavior is unselfish. Some psychologists even argue that true altruism has never been demonstrated, while others argue that a distinction between altruism and egoism is possible (Batson & others, 1986). **Egoism** *is involved when person A gives to person B to ensure reciprocity; to gain self-esteem; to present oneself as powerful, competent, or caring; or to avoid social and self censure for failing to live up to normative expectations.* By contrast, altruism occurs when person A gives to person B with the ultimate goal of benefiting person B. Any benefits that come to person A are unintended.

Describing individuals as having altruistic or egoistic motives implies that person variables are important in understanding altruistic behavior. Altruistic behavior is determined by both person and situational variables. A person's ability to empathize with the needy or to feel a sense of responsibility for another's welfare affects altruistic motivations. The stronger these personality dispositions, the less we would expect situational variables to influence whether giving, kindness, or helping occur.

But as with any human behavior, characteristics of the situation influence the strength of altruistic motivation. Some of these characteristics include the degree of need shown by the other individual, the needy person's responsibility for his plight, the cost of assisting the needy person, and the extent to which reciprocity is expected.

One of the most widely studied aspects of altruism is bystander intervention. Why does one person help a stranger in distress while another won't lift a finger? It often depends on the circumstances. More than 20 years ago a young woman named Kitty Genovese cried out repeatedly as she was brutally murdered. She was attacked at about 3 A.M. in a respectable area of New York City. The murderer left and returned to attack her again three times; he finally put an end to Kitty's life as she crawled to her apartment door and screamed for help. It took the slayer about 30 minutes to kill Kitty. Thirty-eight neighbors watched the gory scene and heard Kitty Genovese's screams. No one helped or even called the police.

bystander effect
The effect of others' presence on a person's giving help; individuals who observe an emergency help less when someone, another observer, is present than when they are a lone observer.

diffusion of responsibility
The tendency to feel less responsible and to act less responsibly in the presence of others.

The **bystander effect** *occurs when someone who observes an emergency helps less when alone than when other potential helpers are present.* The bystander effect helps to explain the apparent cold-blooded indifference to Kitty Genovese's murder. Social psychologists John Darley and Bibb Latané (1968) documented the bystander effect in a number of criminal and medical emergencies. Most of the bystander intervention studies show that when alone, a person will help 75 percent of the time, but when another bystander is present, the figure drops to 50 percent. **Diffusion of responsibility,** *the tendency to feel less responsible and to act less responsibly in the presence of others,* is one explanation of why bystanders fail to act. When a situation is sufficiently ambiguous, we might tend to look to the behavior of others for clues about what to do. People may think that someone else will call the police or that since no one is helping, possibly the person does not need help.

Many other aspects of the situation influence whether the individual will intervene and come to the aid of the person in distress. Bystander intervention is less likely to occur in the following situations (Shotland, 1985):

- When the intervention might lead to personal harm, retaliation by the criminal, or days in court testifying
- When helping takes time
- When a situation is ambiguous
- When the individuals struggling or fighting are married or related
- When a victim is perceived as being drunk rather than disabled
- When the bystander and the victim don't come from the same ethnic group
- When bystanders have no prior history of victimization themselves, have witnessed few crimes and intervention efforts, or have not had training in first aid, rescue, or police tactics

In the next chapter, we will explore the challenges involved in interacting with individuals from diverse groups. Our increasing contact with people from other countries, as well as the increasing diversity of America's population, suggests that an important agenda for psychology is to study this sociocultural diversity.

Review

Interpersonal Relations

Familiarity precedes a close relationship. We like to associate with people who are similar to us.

Friendship is an important aspect of close relationships that is characterized by enjoyment, acceptance, trust, and other features. Females in general engage in more intimate self-disclosure than males do.

Romantic love is involved when we say we are "in love"; this includes passion, sexuality, and a mixture of emotions, not all of which are positive. Affectionate (companionate) love is more important as relationships mature. Shaver proposed a developmental model of love, and Sternberg proposed a triangular model. Sternberg believes that affectionate love is made up of intimacy and commitment, which along with romantic love constitute the three facets of his model of love.

Loneliness is associated with many factors, including a poor attachment history with parents and low self-esteem. It is important to remember the distinction between being alone and being lonely.

Altruism is an unselfish interest in helping another person. Examples of human altruism are plentiful. Evolutionary psychologists stress that altruism involves increasing the prospects for survival as well as reproduction. Reciprocity and social exchange are often involved, although not always. Motivation can be altruistic or egoistic. Psychologists have studied both person and situation variables involved in altruism. Extensive research has been conducted on bystander interventions.

Overview

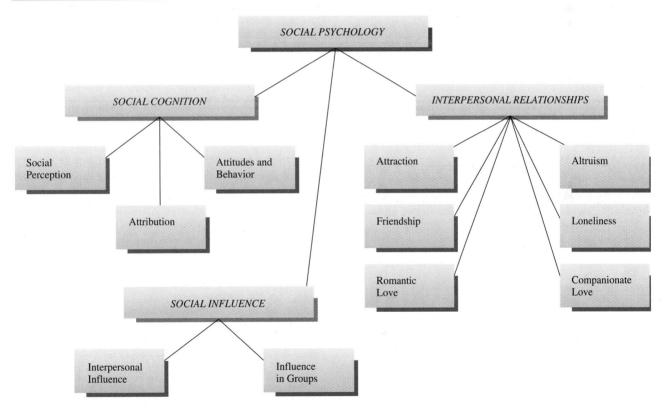

We began this chapter by studying the nature of social cognition, including social perception, attribution, and attitudes and behavior. Our coverage of social influence emphasized interpersonal influence (persuasion, obedience, and altruism) and influence in groups (the nature of groups, conformity, groupthink, deindividuation, and leadership). Then, we explored the nature of interpersonal relationships, including attraction, friendship, romantic love, companionate love, loneliness, and altruism.

Don't forget that you can obtain a more detailed summary of the chapter by again reading the in-chapter reviews on pages 524, 530, 535, and 545.

Key Terms

Thinking It Over

Exercises...

...In Critical Thinking

Stanley Milgram's research on obedience is controversial. Many people believe that it was unethical. Others think the research was justified because of what we learned from it about obedience. Suppose a researcher on your campus wanted to replicate, or redo, the Milgram study with students who did not know Milgram's results. Outline the reasons why you would support the new research study or disapprove of it.

...In Creative Thinking

Brainstorm with a group about some creative alternatives for developing new relationships on campus. Remember that the point of brainstorming is to generate as many alternatives as possible. Once you have developed a long list, go through each alternative systematically and evaluate its potential for success in helping new students on campus become less lonely.

...In Active Learning

One way to test out the power of a social norm is to break it. Without doing something so dramatic that it lands you in jail or seriously compromises your relationships, select a behavior that people practice without question and do something different that will surprise them. For example, face the rear when you are in an elevator. How do people react to you? What attributions do they make about your behavior? As observers, do they explain your behavior (the actor's) in negative trait terms, as the fundamental attribution error would predict?

...In Reflective Learning

Think about a time when you were placed in a compromising situation in which others were trying to influence you against your wishes. Examine the options listed in Applications in Psychology ("Resisting Social Influence") and determine how many applied to your personal dilemma. Were you pleased with the outcome? If you were in a similar situation now, how would you respond?

Resources for Psychology and Improving Humankind

Contact:The First Four Minutes (1972)

by L. Zunin and N. Zunin
New York: Ballantine

This book focuses on first impressions, arguing that the first 4 minutes are crucial to our long-term impressions of others. It includes information about nonverbal communication and how to cope with rejection.

Getting the Love You Want (1988)

by Harvill Hendrix
New York: Henry Holt

Getting the Love You Want is a guide for couples to help them improve their relationship. The book is based on Hendrix's couples workshop techniques, which are designed to help couples construct a conscious marriage, a relationship based on awareness of unresolved childhood needs and conflicts that cause individuals to select a particular spouse.

Influence (1993, rev. ed.)

by Robert Cialdini
New York: Quill

This highly acclaimed book by a well-known social psychologist explores how influence works in today's marketplace. Cialdini provides valuable suggestions for persuading other people and understanding how others try to persuade us. He also discusses how power works, the role of reciprocity in influence, the importance of commitment and consistency, how to say no, scarcity, relationships with others, advertising, sales techniques, and instant influence.

Intimate Connections (1985)

by David Burns
New York: William Morrow

This book describes how to overcome loneliness. Burns believes lonely individuals need to change their patterns of perception. He tells you how to make social connections and develop closer relationships with others. Checklists, daily mood logs, and self-assessments are found throughout the book.

A Lifetime of Relationships (1996)

by Nelly Vanzetti and Steve Duck
Pacific Grove, CA: Brooks/Cole

The authors address relationships across the lifespan. Among the topics covered are social support, parent-infant relationships, courtship and marriage, the transition to parenthood, and midlife friendship patterns.

Shyness (1987)

by Philip Zimbardo
Reading, MA: Addison-Wesley

According to Zimbardo, shyness is a widespread social problem that affects as many as four out of every five people at one time or another in their lives. He explores how and why people become shy and examines the roles that parents, teachers, spouses, and culture play in creating shy individuals.

Social Psychology: Handbook of Basic Principles (1996)

Edited by E. Tory Higgins & Arie Kruglanski
New York: Guilford Press

This handbook provides excellent reviews of many areas of social psychological theory and research. Especially noteworthy are the research reviews on many emerging topics such as social hypothesis testing and social goal-setting.

Understanding Group Behavior (1996, Vols.1 and 2)

by Erich Witte and James Davis
Hillsdale, NJ: Erlbaum

These books provide up-to-date coverage of current research on many different facets of group behavior. Topics discussed include issues involving task-oriented small groups, interpersonal relations in groups, jury decision making, minority opinions, social identity, and effective teamwork.

Internet Resources

http://cac.psu.edu/~arm3/social.html
A compendium for social psychology resources.

http://www.laurentian.ca/www/psyc/Modeling.html
Explore decision-making processes through multimedia.

http://swix.ch/clan/ks/CPSP1.htm
A "jumping off place" for social psychologists operated by a Zurich graduate student.

http://artsci.wustl.edu/~msahrend/SC.html
A Web site that explores social cognition and personality attraction.

http://www.usi.edu/libarts/socio/socpsy/socpsy.htm
Comprehensive references on social psychology from a sociology department.

http://www.wesleyan.edu/spn/
Over 3000 references to social psychology resources.

15

Human Commonality and Diversity

Consider the flowers of a garden: Though differing in kind, color, form, and shape, yet, inasmuch as they are refreshed by the waters of one spring, revived by the breath of one wind, invigorated by the rays of one sun, this diversity increases their charm and adds to their beauty. . . . How unpleasing to the eye if all the flowers and plants, the leaves and blossoms, the fruits, the branches, and the trees of that garden were all of the same shape and color! Diversity of hues, form, and shape enriches and adorns the garden and heightens its effect.

—'ABDU'L BAHA
Persian Baha'i Religious Leader, 19th/20th Century

Ours is a diverse, multicultural world that sometimes seems to bristle with human differences. Around the globe, we live in diverse climates, speak diverse languages, and practice diverse rituals and customs. Not only is our world diverse as a whole; the groups that make up our world are diverse, because they are made up of a great diversity of individuals. But despite all of our differences, we have a lot in common. In this chapter, we will explore both the commonalities and the diversities in various sociocultural dimensions, including culture, ethnicity, gender, and religion.

The Story of Tiger Woods: The Cablinasian Golf Pro

Tiger Woods did not just break into professional golf, he took it by storm. At age 21, Woods became the youngest champion of the famed Masters tournament in Augusta, Georgia. He has been golfing since the age of 3, and his love for the game is apparent in the self-assured smile that regularly beams from his face.

Tiger also is the first African American to win the Masters, in a sport with a checkered history in accepting African American athletes. In the days after the Masters, his ethnicity drew as much interest as his athletic prowess. In an interview with Oprah Winfrey, Woods said that he made up the term *Cablinasian* when he was a young boy, in response to frequent inquiries about his ethnicity, because he did not want to ignore any aspect of his heritage (his mother's ethnic heritage is Thai and Chinese, and his father's is Native American, African American, and White).

Woods's proclamation that he wanted to protect all aspects of his identity brought new attention to the issue of "mixed-race" heritage in America and the fault lines in how we think about race and ethnicity. Traditional classifications of race and ethnicity do not clearly delineate our specific, complicated racial and ethnic heritages. The

Golfer Tiger Woods's mixed racial heritage has contributed to skepticism about the traditional narrow classification of many people in terms of a single ethnic background.

U.S. Congress is debating whether to add the category "mixed race" to the national census in the year 2000.

Embracing a multiracial option can be hard for many Americans. Historically, anyone with a Black ancestor has been regarded as Black, or African American. This comes from a policy in the days of slavery known as the "one-drop rule"—that is, one drop of "Black blood" in your genetic heritage sealed your fate as human property.

The fight against racial prejudice and discrimination has been long and difficult in the United States. For this reason, some African Americans are disappointed that Tiger Woods does not identify his African American roots more forthrightly. However, Woods's popularity on the golf circuit suggests that people from many ethnic backgrounds not only cheer for him but identify with him. In actuality, many Americans have a mixed racial heritage. Formally adopting a category such as "mixed race" might stimulate us all to appreciate our similarities and cope more effectively with our differences. ❖

CULTURE AND ETHNICITY

Our world seems to have become smaller and more interactive through dramatic improvements in communications and travel. One consequence of living on a "shrinking globe" is that it has become critical to learn to live peaceably with others. And this requires understanding, tolerating, and appreciating what we have in common and how we differ (Singelis, 1998). The study of culture and ethnicity reveals many commonalities, along with diversity, in human behavior.

The Nature of Culture and Ethnicity

culture

The behavior patterns, beliefs, and all other products of a particular group of people that are passed on from generation to generation.

ethnicity

A group and individual characteristic based on cultural heritage, nationality, race, religion, and language.

cross-cultural studies

Studies that compare a culture with one or more other cultures and provide information about the degree to which people have characteristics that are similar, or universal, across cultures, and to what degree their behavior, thoughts, and feelings are culture specific.

ethnicity studies

The study of universal and distinctive behaviors across ethnic groups.

mainstream culture

A dominant set of values and expectations.

We first introduced the terms *culture* and *ethnicity* in chapter 1. **Culture** *refers to the behavior patterns, beliefs, and all other products of a particular group of people that are passed on from generation to generation.* **Ethnicity** *is based on cultural heritage, nationality, race, religion, and language.* Psychologists who study culture and ethnicity are interested in comparing what happens in one culture or ethnic group with what happens in another. **Cross-cultural studies** *compare two or more cultures to discover behavioral similarities and differences among cultures.* **Ethnicity studies** *focus on both universal and distinctive behaviors across ethnic groups.*

> We are all in this together—by ourselves.
> —LILY TOMLIN, *American Actor and Comedienne, 20th Century*

The richness of American culture can be found in any large U.S. city. In complex cultures, there is likely to be a **mainstream culture,** *a dominant set of values and expectations.* However, neighborhoods tend to cluster in terms of ethnic heritage. Some groups are ethnically *homogeneous*—their members have extremely similar ethnic heritage. Chinatown in San Francisco and Amish communities in the East and Midwest represent ethnically homogeneous groups. Other groups are ethnically *heterogeneous*—their members have a great variety of ethnic heritages.

Because all human beings are so alike physiologically, we all have many activities in common, no matter what our culture or ethnicity. For example, we all must spend parts of our day eating, sleeping, and working to survive, although we differ in how we do these things. (You might want to reread the Sociocultural Worlds box "Race and Ethnicity" in chapter 2 for some more details on our physiological commonalities.)

Cross-cultural expert Richard Brislin (1993) notes that diverse cultures will have commonalities simply by virtue of their being cultures. For instance, a culture's identity is transmitted from generation to generation; parents, teachers, community leaders, and cultural leaders bear the heaviest responsibility for this transmission. Whether the transmission occurs in an American elementary classroom, between teacher and child, or in an African tribe, between tribal elder and child, all cultures communicate their expectations about the ideals, values, assumptions, and so on that should guide individual behavior.

According to Brislin, many cultural and ethnic practices become invisible, or "second nature," to members of the culture, who might not notice many features of their culture or ethnicity until they encounter an outsider from another group or culture with different ideals and assumptions. Think about experiences you have had where you have not shared the dominant cultural or ethnic background of the majority of a group. Some of the behaviors you see in that group might not have made sense to you at first because you did not share the same cultural background.

We all tend to harbor protective attitudes toward our own culture and ethnic practices. Donald Campbell and his colleagues (Brewer & Campbell, 1976; Campbell & LeVine, 1968) found that people in all cultures have a tendency to

- believe that what happens in their culture is "natural" and "correct" and what happens in other cultures is "unnatural" and "incorrect,"
- perceive their cultural customs as universally valid, that is, "what is good for us is good for everyone,"
- behave in ways that favor their cultural group,
- feel proud of their cultural group, and
- feel hostile toward other cultural groups.

In fact, many cultures define the word *human* in terms of their own characteristics. The ancient Greeks distinguished between those who spoke Greek and those whose language sounded like "barber," a repetitive chatter; they called those who did not speak Greek *barbarians.* Similarly, the ancient Chinese labeled themselves the "the central kingdom." In many languages, the word for "human" is the same as the name of the tribe, suggesting that people from foreign cultures are not perceived as fully human.

Individualism and Collectivism.   Some cross-cultural research emphasizes the search for basic traits common to a whole nation. In recent years, the most elaborate search for traits has focused on the dichotomy between individualism and collectivism (Hofstede, 1980; Triandis, 1994; Triandis, Chen, & Chan, 1998). **Individualism** *involves giving priority to personal goals rather than to group goals; it emphasizes values that serve the self, such as feeling good, personal distinction and achievement, and independence.* **Collectivism** *emphasizes values that serve the group by subordinating personal goals to preserve group integrity, interdependence of the members, and harmonious relationships.* Many Western cultures, such as the United States, Canada, Great Britain, and the Netherlands, are described as individualistic; many Eastern cultures, such as China, Japan, India, and Thailand, are described as collectivistic.

Many of psychology's basic tenets have been developed in individualistic cultures like the United States. Consider the flurry of *self-* terms in psychology that have an individualistic focus: for example, *self-actualization, self-awareness, self-efficacy, self-reinforcement, self-criticism, self-serving, selfishness,* and *self-doubt* (Lonner, 1988; Rumpel, 1988).

Critics of the Western notion of psychology point out that human beings have always lived in groups, whether large or small, and have always needed one another for survival. They argue that the Western emphasis on individualism may undermine our basic species need for relatedness (Kagitcibasi, 1995). Some social scientists believe that many problems in Western cultures are intensified by the Western cultural emphasis on individualism. Individualistic cultures have higher rates than collectivistic cultures for suicide, drug abuse, crime, teenage pregnancy, divorce, child abuse, and mental disorders. Some critics believe that that pendulum might have swung too far toward individualism in many Western cultures. Regardless of their cultural background, people need a positive sense of *self* and *connectedness to others* to develop fully as human beings.

Some psychologists criticize the individualism/collectivism dichotomy. They argue that describing an entire nation of people as having a basic personality obscures the diversity and individual variation that characterize any nation's people. Also, certain values characterize both individual and collective interests, such as wisdom, mature love, and tolerance (Schwartz & Sagiv, 1995). Thus, individuals can possess *both* individualistic and collectivistic qualities (Gaines & Reed, 1995).

individualism

Giving priority to personal goals rather than to group goals; an outlook that emphasizes values that serve the self, such as feeling good, personal distinction and independence.

collectivism

Giving priority to values that serve the group by subordinating personal goals to preserve group integrity, interdependence of group members, and harmonious relationships.

Cultures vary in their pace of life. In France *(left)*, people often take leisurely lunches that include extended conversation that is not related to work. In the United States *(right)*, people often grab their lunch on the run in a fast-food restaurant, then hurry back to work.

Work and Achievement.   The Unites States is an achievement-oriented culture with a strong work ethic. We tend to define ourselves by our occupations. Most of us will spend more hours with co-workers than with our families. Some of us become work-obsessed, forsaking other kinds of pleasure to fulfill work obligations. In contrast, some cultures take great pride in their ability to find time to play. In France, Italy, Spain, and many other countries, leisurely lunch periods are filled with good food and extended conversation that is not work related. In Spain and Italy, the lunch often is followed by an afternoon nap before returning to work. By contrast, in the United States many people rush through their lunch period, grabbing food on the run and spurning leisurely conversation. And afternoon naps are definitely not on their schedules.

Even though the United States is an achievement-oriented culture, it might not be as achievement-oriented as some other cultures, and it might pursue achievement differently than some other achievement-oriented cultures. Recent comparisons of American children with children from Japan and China revealed that the Japanese and Chinese were better at math, spent more time working on math in school, and did more math homework than their American counterparts (Stevenson, 1995). Americans go about their achievement more independently, whereas Asians are more likely to work with others to seek group goals.

Stereotyping, Prejudice, and Ethnocentrism

Understanding the antagonisms that can develop between groups requires knowledge about stereotyping, prejudice, and ethnocentrism. These factors are involved in development of discrimination against groups (Jones, 1997).

stereotype

A generalization about a group's characteristics that does not consider any variation from one individual to another.

Stereotyping.   A **stereotype** *is a generalization about a group's characteristics that does not take into account any variation from one individual to the next.* Think about your image of a dedicated accountant. Most of us describe such a person as quiet, boring, unsociable, and so on. Rarely would we come up with a mental image of this person as extraverted, the life of the party, or artistic. Characterizing all accountants as boring is a clear example of a stereotype. Another stereotype is to describe all Italians as excitable. Researchers have found that we are less likely to detect variations among individuals who belong to "other" groups than those who belong to "our" group. For example, Whites are more likely to stereotype African Americans than other Whites during eyewitness identification (Brigham, 1986).

Stereotypes can be acquired through direct experience or imitation. In terms of direct experience, suppose that you lose your job to someone with freckles. To rationalize your job loss, you might form the generalization that all people with freckles are ruthless competitors. Or you might derive such a prejudice from imitation—perhaps you heard your parents describe freckles as "devil marks" when you were growing up. Stereotypes can lead to prejudice.

prejudice

An unjustified, usually negative, attitude toward an individual based on the individual's membership in a group.

Prejudice.   You probably feel that you know what prejudice is. And like most people, you probably don't think of yourself as prejudiced. In fact, each of us is prejudiced. **Prejudice** *is an unjustified attitude toward an individual based on the individual's membership in a group. Most prejudice involves negative attitudes.* The group against which the person is prejudiced can be made up of people of a particular race, sex, age, religion, nation, or other detectable characteristic (Gaines & Reed, 1995; Hecht, 1998).

> *Sometimes it's like a hair across your cheek. You can't see it. You can't find it with your fingers, but you keep brushing at it because the feel of it is irritation.*
> —MARIAN ANDERSON, *American Opera Singer, 20th Century*

To see how easy it is for a stereotype to grow into prejudice, consider the demonstration in a third-grade classroom portrayed in the film *Eye of the Storm* (1970). As shown in this film, Jane Elliot told her students that scientific research had documented that blue-eyed children are smarter than brown-eyed children. She offered a plausible reason why this finding might be true and then offered special privileges to blue-eyed children while ridiculing brown-eyed children. She soon discovered that an in-group and an out-group had formed, each making negative comments about the other. Out-group children became passive or uncooperative during class activities. Blue-eyed children refused to play with their brown-eyed "inferiors." Before things got too out of control, Elliot told the students that she had misinterpreted the findings. She claimed that the scientists actually had found that brown-eyed children were smarter. Again, she offered a justification and resumed giving out differential treatment, this time favoring the brown-eyed children. The same type of outcome occurred again. She concluded the experiment and told the children about her deceptions. Then she gave the children a frank talk about the stereotypes they had formed and the prejudices that had followed. However, seen from hindsight, there were some serious ethical faults in Elliot's technique, because she didn't protect her students against psychological harm. Her strategy for demonstrating how discrimination develops would never be approved by research oversight committees today, despite the vividness of the demonstration.

discrimination

The enactment of prejudices to limit opportunities to an out-group or extend privileges to an in-group.

Discrimination *occurs when individuals enact their prejudices to limit opportunities available to an out-group or extend privileges to an in-group based solely on their group membership.* The horrific consequences of prejudice and its enactment through discrimination are apparent throughout human history. The population of North American Indians dropped from an estimated 3 million in the seventeenth century to about 600,000 today because of brutal slayings by European immigrants. More than 6 million Jews, as well as members of other groups, were murdered by the Nazis in the 1940s under the justification of "purifying" the European racial stock. Only a fraction of the world's surviving Jews remain in Europe today.

Whites' racial prejudice against African Americans has characterized much of America's history. When Africans were brought to America as slaves, their enslavers described them as property and treated them in subhuman ways. In the first half of the twentieth century, most African Americans lived in the South and were still largely segregated by law—restaurants, movie theaters, and buses had separate areas for Whites and African Americans. Even with the downfall of segregation, much higher portions of African Americans than Whites live below the poverty line today.

African Americans and Native Americans are not the only ethnic minority groups that have been subjected to prejudice in the United States. Many Latinos also live below the poverty line and have low educational achievement and low-paying jobs. Lesbians and gays have historically been subjected to considerable prejudice from the heterosexual majority. This prejudice has been so intense that most homosexuals stayed "in the closet" until recently, not revealing their sexual orientation for fear of prejudice and discrimination. In fact, virtually every minority group has been the victim of prejudice at one time or another. Discrimination and prejudice are fueled by the natural positive bias we feel toward those who are like us, a topic we explore next.

ethnocentrism

The tendency to favor one's own group over other groups.

Ethnocentrism. **Ethnocentrism** *is the tendency to favor one's own group over other groups.* Ethnocentrism's positive side is that it fosters a sense of pride in our group that fulfills the human urge to attain and maintain a positive self-image. As we approach the end of the twentieth century, group pride has mushroomed. Black Pride, Latino Pride, Gay Pride. The Scots grow more Scottish, the Irish more Irish.

There is something paradoxical, though, about such pride. Most members of a group will attest that the group does not discriminate against others. As the American radical Stokeley Carmichael said in 1966, "I'm for the Negro. I'm not against anything." Too often members of groups stress differences with others rather than solely emphasizing pride in their own group.

However, in-group pride does not always reflect ethnocentrism. What might be occurring in some in-group/out-group considerations is in-group/out-group bias, the tendency to view members of one's own group as having heterogeneous and desirable qualities *and* to view the members of other groups as having homogeneous and undesirable qualities. Members of socioeconomically and/or sociopolitically oppressed minority groups (such as women, African Americans, Latinos, and gays and lesbians) often assert in-group pride as a necessary counter to the many overt and covert messages transmitted by society that denigrate them simply by virtue of their group membership (Gaines & Reed, 1995).

social identity theory

The theory that when individuals are assigned to a group, they invariably think of the group as an in-group for them. This occurs because individuals want to have a positive self-image. Social identity theory helps to explain prejudice and conflict between groups.

Henry Tajfel (1978) proposed **social identity theory,** *which states that when individuals are assigned to a group, they invariably think of the group as an in-group for them. This occurs because individuals want to have a positive self-image. Social identity theory helps explain prejudice and conflict between groups.* Tajfel is one of an increasingly small group of European Jews who survived World War II. His goal was to explain the extreme violence and prejudice his group experienced.

Self-image consists of both a personal identity and many different social identities. Tajfel argues that individuals can improve their self-image by enhancing either their personal or their social identity. Tajfel believes our social identity is especially important. When we compare the social identity of our group with the social identity of another group, we often maximize the distinctiveness of the two groups.

Racism

racism

The belief that members of another race or ethnic group are inferior.

For some people, virtually every member of an out-group is inferior. **Racism** *is the belief that the members of another race or ethnic group are inferior.* Many racists believe that members of another race or ethnic group are inferior in a host of characteristics, from morals to intelligence, simply because they were born into that particular out-group (Eberhardt & Fiske, 1998).

We live in a society that has discriminated against virtually every ethnic minority group—Asians, Latinos, eastern and southern Europeans—as they arrived on our shores. However, slavery and the system of segregation that followed it are unique to African Americans. Some psychologists argue that, as a result, African Americans have had more difficulty achieving equality than any other ethnic minority group (Sears, Peplau, & Taylor, 1997).

In many parts of the world today, it is unfashionable to express intense racism openly, although in some countries intense racism openly rears its ugly head (Brislin, 1993). Consider the recent "ethnic cleansing" in Bosnia, where Serbs and Croats act on centuries-old hatred related to geographic, familial, and political loyalties. In Africa, countries such as Rwanda and Burundi have experienced civil turmoil as new tribal chiefs have attempted to create social orders favorable to their rule.

In the United States, intense racism heated up when African American athlete and movie actor O. J. Simpson was found not guilty in the murders of his ex-wife Nicole and her friend, Ron Goldman, both of whom were White. A majority of African Americans agreed with the verdict and thought that the trial had exposed the discriminatory practices of the Los Angeles police department. A majority of White Americans thought the mostly African American jury was unable to overcome its racial bias and convict a guilty Simpson.

Another challenge regarding ethnicity is *unconscious racism.* A person who is unconsciously racist claims not to be prejudiced but acts in ways that reveal racist bias. When

Group members often show considerable pride in their group identity, as reflected in *(a)* African Americans' celebration of Martin Luther King Day, *(b)* Mexican Americans' celebration of Cinco de Mayo, *(c)* Native Americans' celebration of their heritage, and *(d)* Polish Americans' celebration of their cultural background.

such people find their beliefs put to the test, they discover that they are uncomfortable with members of groups against whom they thought they harbored no prejudice.

Today, most Whites show more accepting attitudes toward African Americans than even a decade or two ago (Sears & Funk, 1991). The vast majority of Whites support African Americans' right to hold public office and to have access to public accommodations, fair housing, and so forth. However, occasional incidents like O. J. Simpson's murder trial still spark conflict and hatred between African Americans and Whites. And often there is resistance to programs that could help African Americans reach full equality, such as affirmative action and school desegregation (Bobocel & others, 1998). For example, in one study of students at 390 colleges and universities, more than half of the African Americans and almost one-fourth of the Asian Americans (but only 6 percent of the Whites) said that they felt excluded from school activities (Hurtado, Dey, & Trevino, 1994). In fact, many states have, like California, discontinued affirmative action practices in state university admissions.

> If we lacked imagination enough to foresee something better, life would indeed be a tragedy.
> —LAURENCE J. PETER, *Contemporary American Management Consultant*

According to Asian American psychologist Stanley Sue (1990), proponents of equal opportunity want to eliminate discrimination. Their goal is to abolish racial or ethnic bias, intentional patterns of segregation, and discriminatory admissions or selection criteria. However, even if discrimination is eliminated, there is no guarantee that equal outcomes will be achieved. Realizing this, advocates of equal outcomes believe it is important to have special programs and affirmative action to narrow the gap between ethnic minority groups and Whites. In their view, color-blind policies that are applied to ethnic groups already showing negative disparities with Whites only serve to maintain differential achievements. In Sue's view, the dilemma here is apparent—advocates of equal opportunity run the risk of perpetuating unequal outcomes. The controversy has unfortunately been turned into one of discrimination. That is, if it is unfair to discriminate against ethnic minority groups, should we now discriminate in reverse against the majority group? A more meaningful question is, what kind of society do we want? According to Sue, the goal of our society should be to maximize the potential of every individual, irrespective of color, ethnic group, or sex.

Most people in most cultures want to participate fully in society, but they don't necessarily agree on how to accomplish that goal. People are often caught between conflicting values of assimilation and pluralism (Sue, 1990).

Assimilation *refers to the absorption of an ethnic minority group into the dominant group, which often means the loss of some or all of the behavior and values of the ethnic minority group.* Those who advocate assimilation usually exhort ethnic minority groups

assimilation

The absorption of an ethnic minority group into the dominant group, which often means the loss of some or all of the behavior and values of the ethnic minority group.

The treatment of African Americans by White police officers has been a source of racial conflict for many years in the United States. In this videotape segment, Rodney King is being beaten by Los Angeles policemen. His beating was perceived by many African Americans as one more event in the long-standing police brutality toward African Americans. By contrast, many police officers explained the beating as a consequence of the high crime rate among urban African American males.

pluralism
The coexistence of distinct ethnic and cultural groups in the same society.

to become more American. By contrast, **pluralism** *refers to the coexistence of distinct ethnic and cultural groups in the same society.* Those who advocate pluralism usually promote cultural differences, urging that those differences be maintained and appreciated. Because the mainstream way of life was considered superior for so many years, assimilation was thought to be the best course for American society. Although assimilation still has many supporters, many people now believe that pluralism is the best approach.

Improving Interethnic Relations

> *I have a dream that my four little children will one day live in a nation where they will be judged not by the color of their skin but by the content of their character.*
> —MARTIN LUTHER KING, *American Religious and Civil Rights Leader, 20th Century*

How might we possibly reach the world Martin Luther King envisioned—a world without prejudice and racism? Beginning with Gordon Allport's classic study of prejudice in 1954, researchers have consistently found that contact itself does not improve relations with people from other ethnic backgrounds. What does improve interethnic relations?

Superordinate Goals.   Years ago social psychologist Muzafer Sherif and his colleagues (1961) fueled "we/they" competition between two groups of 11-year-old boys at a summer camp called Robbers Cave in Oklahoma. In the first week one group hardly knew the other group existed. One group became known as the Rattlers (a tough and cussing group whose shirts were emblazoned with a snake insignia) and the other was known as the Eagles.

Near the end of the first week each group learned of the other's existence. It took little time for "we/they" talk to surface ("They had better not be on our ball field." "Did you see the way one of them was sneaking around?"). Sherif, who disguised himself as a janitor so he could unobtrusively observe the Rattlers and Eagles, arranged for the two groups to compete in baseball, touch football, and tug-of-war. Counselors manipulated and judged events so the teams were close. Each team perceived the other to be unfair. Raids, burning the other group's flag, and fights resulted. The Rattlers and Eagles further derided one another as they held their noses in the air as they passed each other. Rattlers described all Rattlers as brave, tough, and friendly, and called all Eagles sneaky and smart alecks. The Eagles reciprocated by labeling the Rattlers crybabies.

After we/they competition transformed the Rattlers and Eagles into opposing "armies," Sherif devised ways to reduce hatred between the groups. He tried noncompetitive contact but that didn't work. Only when both groups were required to work cooperatively to solve a problem did the Rattlers and Eagles develop a positive relationship. Sherif created superordinate tasks that required the efforts of both groups: working together to repair the only water supply to the camp, pooling their money to rent a movie, and cooperating to pull the camp truck out of a ditch.

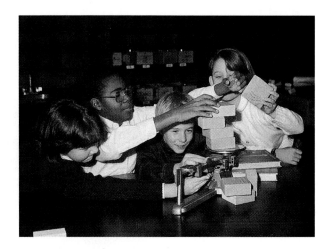

According to Elliot Aronson, jigsaw classrooms reduce ethnic conflict. *How does the jigsaw classroom work?*

Might Sherif's idea—that of creating cooperation between groups rather than competition—be applied to ethnic groups? When the schools of Austin, Texas, were desegregated through extensive busing, increased racial tension among African Americans, Mexican Americans, and Whites resulted in violence in the schools. The superintendent consulted Eliot Aronson, a prominent social psychologist, who was at the University of Texas in Austin at the time. Aronson (1986) thought it was more important to prevent ethnic hostility than to control it. He observed a number of elementary school classrooms in Austin and saw how fierce the competition was between children of unequal status.

Aronson stressed that the reward structure of the classrooms needed to be changed from a setting of unequal competition to one of cooperation among equals, without making any curriculum changes. To accomplish this, he put together the *jigsaw classroom*. The jigsaw classroom works by creating a situation where all of the students have to pull together to get the "big picture." Let's say we have a class of 30 students, some White, some African American, and some Latino. The academic goal is to learn about the life of Joseph Pulitzer. The class might be broken up into five study groups of six students each, with the groups being as equal as possible in terms of ethnic composition and academic achievement level. Learning about Pulitzer's life becomes a class project divided into six parts, with one part given to each member of the six-person group. The components might be paragraphs from Pulitzer's biography, such as how the Pulitzer family came to the United States, Pulitzer's childhood, his early work, and so on. The parts are like the pieces of a jigsaw puzzle. They have to be together to form the complete puzzle.

Each student has an allotted time to study her or his part. Then the group meets and each member tries to teach her or his part to the group. After an hour or so each student is tested on the life of Pulitzer. Each student must learn the entire lesson; learning depends on the cooperation and effort of other members. Aronson believes that this type of learning increases students' interdependence through cooperatively teaching a common goal.

The strategy of emphasizing cooperation rather than competition and the jigsaw approach have been widely used in classrooms in the United States. A number of studies reveal that this type of cooperative learning is associated with increased self-esteem, better academic performance, friendships among classmates, and improved interethnic perceptions (Slavin, 1989).

It is not easy to get groups who do not like each other to cooperate. The air of distrust and hostility is hard to overcome. Creating superordinate goals that require cooperation of both groups is one viable strategy, as evidenced in Sherif's and Aronson's work. Other strategies involve disseminating positive information about the "other " and reducing the potential threat of each group.

Intimate Contact.   We indicated earlier that contact by itself does not improve interethnic relations. However, one form of contact—intimate contact—can (Brislin, 1993). Intimate contact in this context does not mean sexual relations. Rather it involves sharing one's personal worries, troubles, successes, failures, personal ambitions, and coping

Intimate personal contact that involves sharing doubts, hopes, problems, ambitions, and much more is one way to improve interethnic relations.

strategies. When people reveal personal information about themselves, they are more likely to be perceived as an individual rather than as a member of a category. And, the sharing of personal information often produces the discovery that others previously considered as "them" or the out-group have many of the same feelings, hopes, and concerns, which can help to break down in-group/out-group, we/they barriers.

In one interethnic contact, African American and White residents in an integrated housing project were studied (Deutsch & Collins, 1951). The residents lived in small apartments, and the housing project included shared facilities, such as laundry rooms and playgrounds for children, which allowed for interethnic contact. Whites found it more enjoyable to talk with African Americans than to stare at the walls while their laundry was being cleaned, and African American and White parents began to converse with each other as they watched their children play. The young African American and White children played with each other regardless of skin color. Initially the conversations focused on such nonintimate matters as the quality of the washing machines and the weather, but

$\mathcal{I}$mproving Personal and Cognitive Skills

Developing Positive Relations with Diverse Others

Here are some suggestions for how you can develop more positive relations with people who come from backgrounds different from your own:

- *Engage in cooperative activities.*
  People from diverse backgrounds who engage in cooperative activities to attain a goal improve their attitudes toward each other. Get together with one or more diverse others to form a study group.
- *Increase intimate contact.*
  Contact with diverse others alone does not increase liking. However, when we get to know diverse others intimately and share worries, hopes, and coping strategies, our intercultural liking, respect, and trust increase.
- *Search your soul.*
  What kind of person do you want to be? What are your values? Make being sensitive to diverse others a part of your value system.

- *Do some perspective taking.*
  Think about how diverse others experience their world, Putting yourself in someone else's shoes can help you develop empathy for the person and understand their views.
- *Improve your intercultural communication skills.*
  Appreciate the richness of diversity as an asset rather than a barrier to intercultural communication. Learn how to show respect for the other person's culture in all of your communication.
- *Increase your knowledge of diverse others.*
  In many cases, we really don't know that much about the people we are prejudiced against. Read about people from different ethnic and cultural groups. Take a college course on cultural issues. Read a good book on ethnicity and culture. One good one is Richard Brislin's (1993) *Understanding Culture's Influence on Behavior,* which is profiled at the end of this chapter in the resources section.

Applications in Psychology

Improving the Lives of African American and Latino Youth

Many ethnic minority youth lack opportunities to reach their full potential. Consider the following:

- One African American teenager in every three, and one Latino teenager in every four, lives with an unemployed parent.
- An African American female teenager is more than twice as likely as her White counterpart to have a baby.
- Sixteen- and 17-year-old Latina girls are four times more likely than their White peers to be behind in school.
- Fifteen- to 19-year-old African American males are nine times more likely than their White counterparts to be homicide victims.

Marian Wright Edelman (1997), founder and head of the Children's Defense Fund, has much to say about the problems of youth who grow up in poverty. She believes that we are at a crucial moral moment in history at which we need to decide what legacy we will send to the future through our children. Edelman argues that we need a new ethic of caring, an ethic that says that what truly is important is the future of children and youth. As Rosa Parks said, "If I can sit down for freedom, you can stand up for children."

One effective program for ethnic minority youth is the Children's Aid Society in New York City (Simons, Finlay, & Yang, 1991). The organization has three youth development centers that serve Harlem's mostly African American and Latino communities. The adolescents are mainly from single-parent homes without health insurance. Most of the families are on public assistance. In fifteen 2-hour discussions, family life and sex-education courses cover pregnancy prevention, gender roles, social roles, and intimacy for the adolescents. The adolescents' parents also participate in a course on how to talk with adolescents about sex and how to prevent child abuse. Adolescents participate in a sport program that emphasizes self-control. A theater program of weekly workshops with actors and actresses from Harlem's National Black Theater is also part of the program. The workshops address motivation and appropriate self-expression by examining such questions as "How do you express anger?" and "How can you ask a question in class?" Career awareness and job preparation classes are available through the Job Club.

Funding for the program comes from the New York State Department of Social Services, foundations, corporations, and individuals. The cost per adolescent is about $1,750 and the program serves more than 300 youth. Our nation needs more programs like this that provide youth with the opportunity to look to the future in positive ways.

We are not just citizens of the United States or Canada. We are citizens of the world, by increasing our understanding of the behavior and values of cultures around the world, we hope that we can interact with people from other cultures more effectively and make this planet a more hospitable, peaceful place in which to live.

eventually they moved on to more personal matters. The Whites and the African Americans discovered that they shared a number of similar concerns, such as jobs and work, the quality of schools for their children, taxes, and so on. The African Americans' and Whites' revelation that they shared many of the same concerns and problems helped to diminish in-group/out-group thoughts and feelings. Sharing intimate information and becoming friendly with someone from another ethnic group helps to make people more tolerant and less prejudiced toward the other ethnic group.

To read further about how to develop positive relations with people from diverse backgrounds, see Improving Personal and Cognitive Skills. For some strategies for improving the lives of ethnic minority adolescents, read Applications in Psychology.

> *Prejudices, it is well known, are more difficult to eradicate from the heart whose soil has never been loosened or fertilized by education; they grow there, firm as weeds among stones.*
>
> —CHARLOTTE BRONTË, *English Novelist, 19th Century*

Review

Culture and Ethnicity

Culture refers to the behavior patterns, beliefs, and all other products of a particular group of people that are passed on from generation to generation. *Ethnicity* refers to cultural heritage, national characteristics, race, religion, and language. Complex cultures usually have a dominant set of cultural values expressed in the cultural mainstream. Cultural and ethnic groups can be heterogeneous or homogeneous. We share common properties that encourage similar kinds of activities related to survival, regardless of our cultural and ethnic traditions. Cross-cultural studies compare cultures to discover whether behavior is culture-universal or culture-specific. Cultures can be classified as individualistic (emphasis on personal goals and the self) or collectivistic

(emphasis on the group and harmonious relationships). Many Western cultures are described as individualistic, many Eastern cultures as collectivistic.

A stereotype is a generalization about a group's characteristics that does not take into account any variation from one member of the group to the next. Prejudice is an unjustified attitude (usually negative) toward an individual based on the individual's membership in a group. Stereotyping and prejudice can lead to discrimination. Ethnocentrism is the tendency to favor one's own group over other groups. One theory devised to explain ethnocentrism is Tajfel's social identity theory, which states that when individuals are assigned to a group they invariably see that group as an in-group for them. This

occurs because they want to have a positive self-image.

Racism is a belief that the members of a race or ethnic group are inferior. Intense racism is less prevalent today than it once was, but it still rears its ugly head from time to time. Unconscious racism also is present in some contexts.

Two ways that interethnic relations can be improved are through the development of superordinate goals and through intimate contact. Sherif's Robber's Cave study and Aronson's jigsaw classroom documented how superordinate goals that create cooperation rather than competition can improve interethnic relations. Intimate contact—sharing one's personal worries, hopes, and coping strategies—also can improve interethnic relations.

Misunderstanding, prejudice, and discrimination are not restricted to cultural and ethnic groups. These social dynamics also characterize our gender relations.

GENDER

As females and males, human beings are involved in the existence and continuation of life. As females and males, we are different yet similar. Psychologists increasingly recognize that gender—our sociocultural worlds as females and males—is an important aspect of human behavior. What exactly does gender mean? Many psychologists use the term **gender** *to define the sociocultural dimension of being male or female.*

gender
The sociocultural dimension of being female or male.

> *We need every human gift and cannot afford to neglect any gift because of artificial barriers of sex or race or class or national origin.*
> —MARGARET MEAD, *American Anthropologist, 20th Century*

Developing Gender Identity

To understand how we develop a specific gender identity, we need to consider biological, social, and cognitive influences on gender.

Biological Influences. It was not until the 1920s that researchers confirmed the existence of human sex chromosomes, the genetic material that determines our sex. Humans normally have 46 chromosomes arranged in pairs. The 23rd pair may have two X-shaped chromosomes, to produce a female, or it may have both an X-shaped and a Y-shaped chromosomes to produce a male (see figure 15.1).

In the first few weeks of gestation, female and male embryos look alike. Male sex organs start to differentiate from female sex organs when a Y chromosome in the male embryo triggers secretions of **androgen,** *the main class of male sex hormones.* Low levels of androgen in a female embryo allow the normal development of female sex organs.

androgen
The main class of male sex hormones.

Although rare, an imbalance in this system of hormone secretion can occur during fetal development. If there is insufficient androgen in the male embryo or an excess of androgen in the female embryo, the result is an individual with both male and female sex

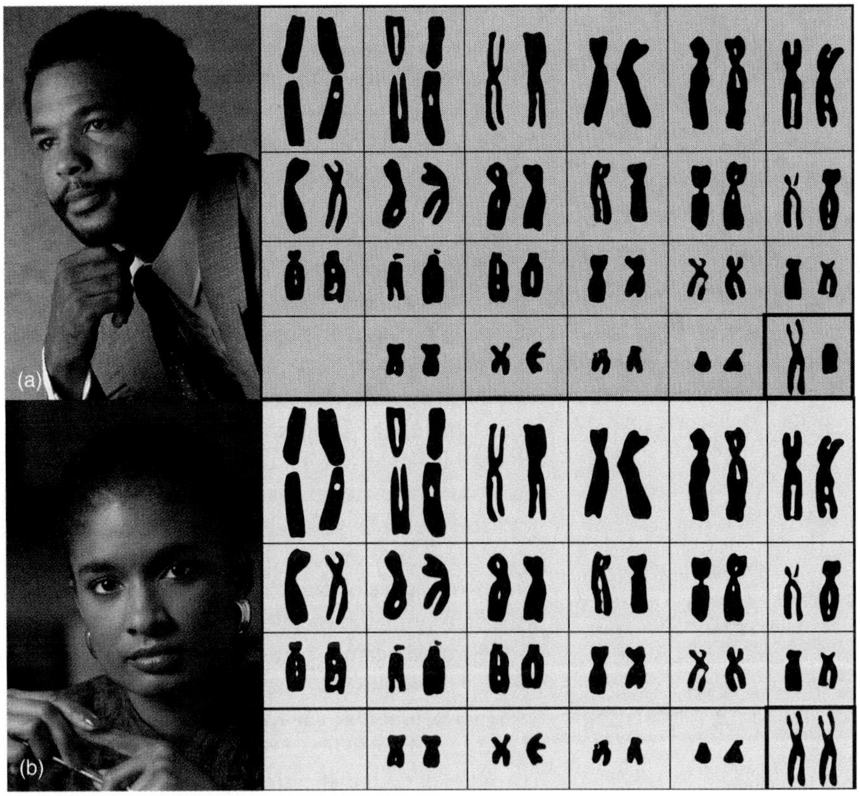

FIGURE 15.1

The Genetic Difference Between Males and Females

(a) The chromosome structure of a male. *(b)* The chromosome structure of a female. The 23rd pair is shown in the bottom right box of each set. Notice that the Y chromosome of the male is smaller than the X chromosome. To obtain such a picture of chromosomes, a cell is removed from the individual's body, usually from inside the mouth, and the chromosomes are photographed under magnification.

estrogen

The main class of female sex hormones.

organs, a hermaphrodite. When genetically female (XX chromosomes) infants are born with masculine-looking genitals, surgery can achieve a genital/genetic match. At puberty, production of **estrogen,** *the main class of female sex hormones,* influences both physical development and behavior. However, even prior to puberty, these females often behave in a more aggressive, "tomboyish" manner than most girls. They also dress and play in ways that are more characteristic of boys than girls (Ehrhardt, 1987).

Is the behavior of these surgically corrected girls due to their prenatal hormones? Or is it the result of their social experiences? Experiments with different animal species reveal that when male hormones are injected into female embryos the females develop masculine physical traits and behave more aggressively (Hines, 1982). However, as we move from animals to humans, hormones exert less control over behavior. Perhaps, because these girls looked more masculine, they were treated more like boys and so adopted their tomboyish ways.

On the other hand, some recent disclosures of case studies involving surgical accidents shed some light on the power of prenatal hormones in determining gender. In one unusual case, a male child's penis was accidentally amputated in surgery. The parents were advised to raise the child as a female with the help of hormone supplements. The child's interests remained traditionally masculine and the individual opted for a masculine lifestyle as an adult, including roles as a husband and adoptive father. Such results support the idea that gender differentiation already is taking place *in utero.*

Prenatal hormones might or might not influence gender behavior, but psychoanalytic theorists such as Sigmund Freud and Erik Erikson argued that an individual's genitals do play a pivotal role. Freud said that human behavior and history are directly influenced by sexual drives and suggested that gender and sexual behavior are essentially unlearned and instinctual. Erikson (1968) went even further: He argued that because of genital structure, females are more inclusive and passive, and males more intrusive and aggressive. Critics of this central idea—that "anatomy is destiny"—contend that Freud does not give enough credit to experience and that women and men are more free to choose their behavior than Freud admits.

Sex hormone levels may be related to some cognitive abilities in females and males, especially spatial ability. For example, girls whose glands overproduce testosterone have spatial abilities more similar to those of the average boy than to those of the average girl (Hines, 1990). Boys whose glands underproduce testosterone, and thus are late maturing, have spatial abilities more similar to those of the average girl than to those of the average boy (Kimura, 1989).

Sex hormones also are related to aggression. Violent male criminals have above-average levels of testosterone (Dabbs & others, 1987), and professional football players have higher levels of testosterone than ministers do (Dabbs & Morris, 1990). However, these comparisons are correlations; we can't be certain whether testosterone influences occupational direction, occupational direction influences testosterone, or both. However, some answers have been suggested by animal studies. Researchers have been able to increase the aggressiveness of animals in different species by giving them testosterone.

Social Influences. In our culture, adults discriminate between the sexes shortly after the infant's birth. The "pink and blue" treatment may be applied to boys and girls before they leave the hospital. Soon afterward, differences in hairstyles, clothes, and toys become obvious. Adults and peers reward these differences throughout development. And girls and boys learn gender roles through imitation or observational learning by watching what other people say and do. In recent years, the idea that parents are the critical agents in gender-role development has come under fire. Culture, schools, peers, the media, and other family members also influence gender behavior (Maccoby, 1993). Yet it is important to guard against swinging too far in this direction, because—especially in the early years of development—parents are important influences on gender development.

Two prominent theories address the way children acquire masculine and feminine attitudes and behaviors from their parents: identification theory and social learning theory of gender. **Identification theory** *stems from Freud's view that the preschool child develops a sexual attraction to the parent of the opposite sex. At about the age of 5 or 6, Freud theorized, the child renounces this attraction because of anxious feelings and identifies with the same-sex parent, unconsciously adopting this parent's behavior.* Today, however, many experts do not believe that sexual attraction is involved in children's gender development. Children become masculine or feminine much earlier than 5 or 6 years of age, even when the same-sex parent is absent from the family.

The **social learning theory of gender** *argues that children learn maleness and femaleness by observing and imitating masculine and feminine behavior, as well as through rewards and punishments for what is considered appropriate and inappropriate gender behavior.* For example, parents teach gender behavior when they praise their daughters for playing with dolls or when they reproach their sons for crying.

While parents provide children with the first models of gender roles, children also learn from observing other adults in the neighborhood and on television. As children get older, peers become increasingly important influences. For example, when children play in ways that our culture says are sex-appropriate, they tend to be rewarded by their peers. Those who engage in activities that are considered inappropriate tend to be criticized or abandoned by their peers. Children show a clear preference for same-sex peers (Maccoby, 1990). After watching elementary school children repeatedly play in same-sex groups, two researchers characterized the playground as "gender school" (Luria & Herzog, 1985).

Cognitive Influences. Critics of the social learning view argue that gender roles are not as passively acquired as it suggests. Two cognitive theories—cognitive developmental theory and gender schema theory—stress that individuals actively construct their gender worlds.

Cognitive Developmental Theory. According to the **cognitive developmental theory of gender,** *children's gender typing occurs after they have developed a concept of gender. Once they consistently conceive of themselves as female or male, children often organize their world on the basis of gender.* Initially developed by psychologist Lawrence Kohlberg (1966), this theory argues that gender development proceeds in the following way: "I am a girl, I want to do girl things; therefore, the opportunity to do girl things is rewarding." Having acquired the ability to categorize, children strive toward consistency in the use of categories and behavior.

identification theory

A theory that stems from Freud's view that preschool children develop a sexual attraction to the opposite-sex parent, then at 5 to 6 years of age, renounce the attraction because of anxious feelings, subsequently identifying with the same-sex parent and unconsciously adopting the same-sex parent's behavior.

social learning theory of gender

The idea that children's gender development occurs through observation and imitation of gender-related behavior, as well as through the rewards and punishments children experience for gender-appropriate and gender-inappropriate behaviors.

cognitive developmental theory of gender

The theory that children's gender typing occurs after they have developed a concept of gender and that, once they begin to consistently conceive of themselves as male or female, children often organize their world on the basis of gender.

Two-year-olds can apply the labels *girl* and *boy* correctly to themselves and others, but their concept of gender is simple and concrete. Preschool children rely on physical features such as dress and hairstyle to decide who falls in which category. Girls are people with long hair, while boys are people who never wear dresses. Many preschool children believe that people can change their own gender at will by getting a haircut or a new outfit. They do not yet have the cognitive machinery to think of gender as adults do. According to Kohlberg, all the reinforcement in the world won't modify that fact. However, by the concrete operational stage (the third stage in Piaget's theory, entered at about 6 to 7 years of age), children understand gender constancy—that a male is still a male regardless of whether he wears pants or a skirt, or his hair short or long (Tavris & Wade, 1984). When their concept of gender constancy is clearly established, children are then motivated to become a competent or "proper" boy or girl. Consequently, she or he finds female or male activities rewarding and imitates the behavior of same-sex models.

Gender Schema Theory.   A cognitive **schema** *is a mental framework that organizes and guides an individual's perceptions. A* **gender schema** *organizes the world in terms of female and male.* **Gender schema theory** *states that an individual's attention and behavior are guided by an internal motivation to conform to gender-based sociocultural standards and stereotypes.* Gender schema theorists suggest that "gender typing" occurs when individuals are ready to encode and organize information along the lines of what is considered appropriate or typical for males and females in a society. Whereas Kohlberg's cognitive developmental theory argues that a particular cognitive prerequisite—gender constancy—is necessary for gender typing, gender schema theory states that a general readiness to respond to and categorize information on the basis of culturally defined gender roles is the key ingredient that fuels children's gender-typing activities.

Regardless of the factors that influence gender behavior, the consequences of gender have become an area of intense focus and research in the last several decades. Next, we will explore the myths and realities of how females and males are similar or different.

Gender Comparisons

There is a growing consensus in gender research that differences between the sexes have often been exaggerated (Hyde & Plant, 1995). It is not unusual to find statements such as the following: "While only 32 percent of females were found to . . . , fully 37 percent of the males were. . . ." This difference of 5 percent likely is a very small difference, and might or might not even be statistically significant or capable of being replicated in a separate study (Denmark & Paludi, 1993). And generalizations that claim that males

schema

A mental framework that organizes and guides an individual's perceptions.

gender schema

A cognitive structure that organizes the world in terms of female and male.

gender schema theory

The theory that children's attention and behavior are guided by an internal motivation to conform to gender-based, sociocultural standards and stereotypes.

"So according to the stereotype, you can put two and two together, but I can read the handwriting on the wall."

outperform females, such as "Males outperform females in math," do not mean that all males outperform all females. Rather, such a statement means, in the case of our example, that the average math achievement scores for males at certain ages are higher than the average math achievement scores for females at those ages. The math achievement scores of females and males overlap considerably, so that although an *average* difference might favor males, many females have higher math achievement than many males. Further, there is a tendency to think of differences between females and males as biologically based. Remember that when differences occur, they might be socioculturally based.

> *There is more difference within the sexes than between them.*
> —IVY COMPTON-BURNETT, *English Novelist, 20th Century*

Let's now examine some of the differences between the sexes, keeping in mind that (a) the differences are averages—not *all* females versus *all* males; (b) even when differences are reported, there is considerable overlap between the sexes; and (c) the differences may be due primarily to biological factors, sociocultural factors, or both (Caplan & Caplan, 1994). First, we examine physiological and biological differences, and then we turn to cognitive and social differences.

Physical/Biological. From conception on, females survive better than males, and females are less likely than males to develop physical or mental disorders. Estrogen strengthens the immune system, making females more resistant to infection, for example. Female hormones also signal the liver to produce more "good" cholesterol, which makes their blood vessels more elastic than males'. Testosterone triggers the production of low-density lipoprotein, which clogs blood vessels. Males have twice the risk of coronary disease as females. Higher levels of stress hormones cause faster clotting in males, but also higher blood pressure than in females. Adult females have about twice the body fat of their male counterparts, most of it concentrated around breasts and hips. In males, fat is more likely to go to the abdomen. On the average, males grow to be 10 percent taller than females. Male hormones promote the growth of long bones; female hormones stop such growth at puberty.

Similarity was the rule rather than the exception in a recent study of metabolic activity in the brains of females and males (Gur & others, 1995). The exceptions involved areas of the brain that involve emotional expression and physical expression (which are more active in females). Overall, though, there are many physical differences between females and males. Are there as many cognitive differences?

Cognitive. According to a classic review of gender differences in 1974, Eleanor Maccoby and Carol Jacklin concluded that males have better math skills and better visuospatial ability (the kind of skills an architect needs to design a building's angles and dimensions), while females have better verbal abilities. More recently, Maccoby (1987) revised her conclusion about several gender dimensions. She said that the accumulation of research evidence now suggests that differences in verbal ability between females and males have virtually disappeared, but that the math and visuospatial differences still exist. Another recent analysis also found that the spatial difference favors males (Voyer, Voyer, & Bryden, 1995).

Some experts in the gender area, such as Janet Shibley Hyde (1993), believe that the cognitive differences between females and males have been exaggerated. For example, Hyde argues that there is considerable overlap in the distributions of females' and males' scores on math tasks. Figure 15.2 shows that although males outperform females on math tasks, their scores overlap substantially with females' scores. Thus, while the *average* difference favors males, many females have higher scores on math tasks than most males do.

For some areas of achievement, gender differences are so large they can best be described as nonoverlapping. For example, no major league baseball players are female, and 96 percent of all registered nurses are female. In contrast, many measures of achievement-related behaviors do not reveal gender differences. For example, girls show just as much persistence at tasks. The question of whether males and females differ in their expectations for success at various achievement tasks is not yet settled.

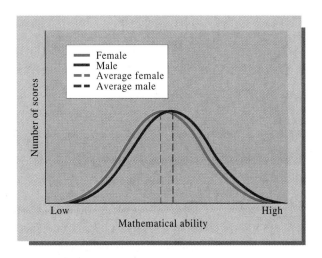

FIGURE 15.2

Mathematics Performance of Males and Females

Notice that, although the average male mathematics score is higher than the average female score, the overlap between the sexes is substantial. Not all males have better mathematics performance than all females—the substantial overlap indicates that, although the average score of males is higher, many females outperform most males on such tasks.

Socioemotional. Females and males also differ in their social connectedness. Boys often define themselves apart from their caregivers and peers, while girls emphasize their social ties. As adults, females often become more caring, supporting, and empathic, while males become more independent, self-reliant, and unexpressive. Most males are more active and aggressive than most females (Maccoby & Jacklin, 1974). The consistent difference in aggression often appears in children's development as early as 2 years of age.

Deborah Tannen (1990) analyzed the talk of women and men. She reported that a common complaint that wives have about their husbands is "He doesn't listen to me anymore." Another is "He doesn't talk to me anymore." Lack of communication, while high on women's lists of reasons for divorce, is much less often mentioned by men.

Tannen distinguishes rapport talk from report talk. **Rapport talk** *is the language of conversation. It is a way of establishing connections and negotiating relationships. Women prefer to engage in rapport talk.* Women enjoy private speaking more, and men's lack of interest in rapport talk bothers many women. By contrast, **report talk** *is talk that is designed to give information, which includes public speaking. Men prefer to engage in report talk.* Men hold center stage through such verbal performances as telling stories and jokes. They learn to use talk as a way of getting and keeping attention.

Males are more likely to help in contexts in which a perceived danger is present and they feel competent to help (Eagly & Crowley, 1986). For example, males are more likely than females to help a person who is stranded by the roadside with a flat tire; automobile problems are an area about which many males feel a sense of competence. By contrast, when the context involves volunteering time to help a child with a personal problem, females are more likely to help than males are, because there is little danger present and females feel more competent at nurturing. In many cultures, girls show more caregiving behavior than boys do. However, in the few cultures where they both care for younger siblings on a regular basis, girls and boys are similar in their tendencies to nurture (Whiting, 1989).

Context is also relevant to gender differences in the display of emotions (Shields, 1991). Consider anger. Males are more likely to show anger toward strangers, especially other males, when they think they have been challenged. Males also are more likely than females to turn their anger into aggressive action, especially when such action is endorsed in that particular culture (Tavris & Wade, 1984).

We find contextual variations in specific situations not only within a particular culture, but also across cultures. Many Western cultures, such as the United States, have become more flexible about gender behavior. However, in many cultures around the world, traditional gender roles guide the behavior of males and females. Consider China and Egypt. In these cultures, it is still widely accepted for males to engage in dominant behavior and females to behave in subordinate ways. In such ways, sociocultural contexts determine what is considered to be gender-appropriate and gender-inappropriate socioemotional behavior.

rapport talk

The language of conversation. It is a way of establishing connections and negotiating relationships. Women prefer to engage in rapport talk.

report talk

Talk that is designed to give information, which includes public speaking. Men prefer to engage in report talk.

In the culture of the Wodaabe, a nomadic group in Niger, Africa, men—not women—compete in beauty contest's to enhance their appeal as potential mates. They apply makeup to enhance their features, adopt colorful and appealing attire, and even have talent competitions. The mating rituals involve dancing and eyeball-rolling. The Wodaabe place great value on being able to role the eyes in and out independently because they link strength of the eye muscles to the ability to make strong marriages. Such contests might sound familiar to us even if the gender and context are different.

> *Women and men. Men and women. It'll never work.*
> —ERICA JONG, *Contemporary American Author*

Not all psychologists agree that differences between females and males are rare or small. Alice Eagly (1996) says that such a belief arose from a feminist commitment to similarity between the sexes as a route to political equality, and from piecemeal and inadequate interpretations of relevant empirical research. Many feminists express a fear that differences between females and males will be interpreted as deficiencies in females and as biologically based, which could promote the old stereotypes that portray women as inferior to men (Unger & Crawford, 1992). According to Eagly, contemporary psychology has produced a large body of research that reveals that behavior is sex differentiated to varying extents.

Evolutionary psychologist David Buss (1996) argues that men and women differ psychologically in those domains in which they have faced different adaptive problems across their evolutionary history. In all other domains, predicts Buss, the sexes will be found to be psychologically similar. He cites males' superiority in the cognitive domain of spatial rotation. This ability is essential for hunting, in which the trajectory of a projectile must anticipate the trajectory of a prey animal as each moves through space and time. Buss also cites a sex difference in casual sex, with men engaging in this behavior more than women do. In one study, men said that ideally they would like to have more than eighteen sex partners in their lifetime, whereas women stated that ideally they would like to have only four or five (Buss & Schmitt, 1993). In another study, 75 percent of the men but none of the women approached by an attractive stranger of the opposite sex consented to a request for sex (Clark & Hatfield, 1989). Such sex differences, says Buss, are exactly the type predicted by evolutionary psychology, because multiple sexual liasons improve the likelihood of males' passing on their genes. A woman's contribution to the gene pool is improved by securing resources for her offspring, which is promoted more effectively by a monogamous relationship.

In sum, controversy swirls about the issue of whether sex differences are rare and small or common and large, and this is evidence that negotiating the science and politics of gender is not an easy task. Next, we will explore how gender roles have changed, especially in American culture.

Gender Expectations and Stereotypes

Expectations regarding females' and males' behavior vary from culture to culture and over time. First we will discuss traditional Western gender roles, and then we will turn our attention to recent changes in Western gender roles.

Traditional Gender Roles.   Not long ago, it was an accepted Western notion that boys should grow up to be masculine and that girls should grow up to be feminine, that boys are made of frogs and snails and puppy dogs' tails, and that girls are made of sugar and spice and all that's nice. Today, diversity characterizes gender roles and the feedback individuals receive from their culture. A girl's mother might promote femininity, the girl might be close friends with a tomboy, and the girl's teachers at school might encourage her assertiveness.

In the past, the well-adjusted male was expected to be independent, aggressive, and power oriented. The well-adjusted female was expected to be dependent, nurturant, and uninterested in power. Further, masculine characteristics were considered to be healthy and good by society; female characteristics were considered to be undesirable. A classic study in the early 1970s summarized the traits and behaviors that college students believed were characteristic of males and those they believed were characteristic of females (Broverman & others, 1972). The traits clustered into two groups that were labeled "instrumental" and "expressive." The instrumental traits paralleled the male's purposeful, competent entry into the outside world to gain goods for his family; the expressive traits paralleled the female's responsibility to be warm and emotional in the home.

gender stereotypes
Broad categories, exaggerated generalizations, and/or false beliefs about females and males.

Gender stereotypes *are broad categories, exaggerated generalizations, and/or false beliefs about males and females.* The world is extremely complex, and the use of stereotypes is one way we simplify this complexity. If we simply assign a label, such as *soft*, to someone, we then have much less to consider when we think about that person. But once labels are assigned, they are remarkably difficult to abandon—even in the face of contradictory evidence.

Many stereotypes are so general they are very ambiguous—"feminine" and "masculine," for instance. Diverse behaviors can be called on to support each stereotype, such as playing with dolls and wearing lipstick for "feminine" and scoring a touchdown and growing facial hair for "masculine." Stereotypes are sometimes modified in the face of cultural change: During the reign of Louis XIV, for example, French noblemen wore satin breeches, cosmetics, and high heels; as our country expanded westward, however, men were rugged, clothed in leather, and often dirty. In contrast, however, many stereotypes about women and about people of color have not changed despite profound sociohistorical changes. Stereotypes also fluctuate according to socioeconomic circumstances. For example, a lower socioeconomic group might be more likely than higher socioeconomic groups to include "rough and tough" as part of a masculine stereotype.

Stereotyping of females and males is pervasive, according to a far-ranging study of college students in thirty countries (Williams & Best, 1982). Men are widely believed to

Self-Assessment

Are You Androgynous?

Instructions

The items below are from the Bem Sex-Role Inventory. To find out whether you score as androgynous, rate yourself on each item, on a scale from 1 (never or almost never true) to 7 (always or almost always true).

1. self-reliant	1	2	3	4	5	6	7
2. yielding	1	2	3	4	5	6	7
3. helpful	1	2	3	4	5	6	7
4. defends own beliefs	1	2	3	4	5	6	7
5. cheerful	1	2	3	4	5	6	7
6. moody	1	2	3	4	5	6	7
7. independent	1	2	3	4	5	6	7
8. shy	1	2	3	4	5	6	7
9. conscientious	1	2	3	4	5	6	7
10. athletic	1	2	3	4	5	6	7
11. affectionate	1	2	3	4	5	6	7
12. theatrical	1	2	3	4	5	6	7
13. assertive	1	2	3	4	5	6	7
14. flatterable	1	2	3	4	5	6	7
15. happy	1	2	3	4	5	6	7
16. strong personality	1	2	3	4	5	6	7
17. loyal	1	2	3	4	5	6	7
18. unpredictable	1	2	3	4	5	6	7
19. forceful	1	2	3	4	5	6	7
20. feminine	1	2	3	4	5	6	7
21. reliable	1	2	3	4	5	6	7
22. analytical	1	2	3	4	5	6	7
23. sympathetic	1	2	3	4	5	6	7
24. jealous	1	2	3	4	5	6	7
25. has leadership abilities	1	2	3	4	5	6	7
26. sensitive to the needs of others	1	2	3	4	5	6	7
27. truthful	1	2	3	4	5	6	7
28. willing to take risks	1	2	3	4	5	6	7
29. understanding	1	2	3	4	5	6	7

be dominant, independent, aggressive, achievement-oriented, and enduring, while women are widely believed to be nurturant, affiliative, less confident, and more helpful in times of distress.

In a more recent investigation, women and men in developed countries perceived themselves as more similar to one another than women and men who lived in less developed countries (Williams & Best, 1989). This makes sense. In the more highly developed countries, women are more likely to attend college and have careers; and as sexual equality increases, stereotypes between women and men probably will diminish. Women are more likely than men to perceive similarity between the sexes.

> *If you are going to generalize about women, you will find yourself up to here in exceptions.*
>
> —DOLORES HITCHENS, *American Mystery Writer, 20th Century*

Even though stereotypes are often inaccurate, labels themselves can have significant consequences. A man who becomes labeled "feminine," for instance, can experience significant social difficulty in both work and social situations. A woman labeled "masculine" might be excluded from social events, not asked to parties, or passed over for certain jobs, such as teaching young children, that are seen as requiring "feminine skills."

30. secretive	1	2	3	4	5	6	7
31. makes decisions easily	1	2	3	4	5	6	7
32. compassionate	1	2	3	4	5	6	7
33. sincere	1	2	3	4	5	6	7
34. self-sufficient	1	2	3	4	5	6	7
35. eager to soothe hurt feelings	1	2	3	4	5	6	7
36. conceited	1	2	3	4	5	6	7
37. dominant	1	2	3	4	5	6	7
38. soft-spoken	1	2	3	4	5	6	7
39. likable	1	2	3	4	5	6	7
40. masculine	1	2	3	4	5	6	7
41. warm	1	2	3	4	5	6	7
42. solemn	1	2	3	4	5	6	7
43. willing to take a stand	1	2	3	4	5	6	7
44. tender	1	2	3	4	5	6	7
45. friendly	1	2	3	4	5	6	7
46. aggressive	1	2	3	4	5	6	7
47. gullible	1	2	3	4	5	6	7
48. inefficient	1	2	3	4	5	6	7
49. acts as a leader	1	2	3	4	5	6	7
50. childlike	1	2	3	4	5	6	7
51. adaptable	1	2	3	4	5	6	7
52. individualistic	1	2	3	4	5	6	7
53. does not use harsh language	1	2	3	4	5	6	7
54. unsystematic	1	2	3	4	5	6	7
55. competitive	1	2	3	4	5	6	7
56. loves children	1	2	3	4	5	6	7
57. tactful	1	2	3	4	5	6	7
58. ambitious	1	2	3	4	5	6	7
59. gentle	1	2	3	4	5	6	7
60. conventional	1	2	3	4	5	6	7

Scoring and Interpretation

(a) Add up your ratings for items 1, 4, 7, 10, 13, 16, 19, 22, 25, 28, 31, 34, 37, 40, 43, 46, 49, 55, and 58. Divide the total by 20. That is your masculinity score.

(b) Add up your ratings for items 2, 5, 8, 11, 14, 17, 20, 23, 26, 29, 32, 35, 38, 41, 44, 47, 50, 53, 56, and 59. Divide the total by 20. That is your femininity score.

(c) If your masculinity score is above 4.9 (the approximate median for the masculinity scale) and your femininity score is above 4.9 (the approximate femininity median) then you would be classified as androgynous on Bem's scale.

sexism

Prejudice and discrimination against an individual because of her or his sex.

Sexism. *Sexism is prejudice and discrimination against an individual because of her or his sex.* A person who says that women cannot be competent lawyers is expressing sexism; so is a person who says that men cannot be competent nursery school teachers. Prejudice and discrimination against women have a long history, and they continue.

Stereotypes harm females more than males because the characteristics assigned to males are more valued than those assigned to females (Doyle & Paludi, 1998). Females receive less attention in schools, are less visible in leading roles on television, are rarely depicted as competent, dominant characters in children's books, are paid less than males even when they have more education, and are underrepresented in decision-making roles throughout our society, from corporate executive suites to Congress.

Sexism can be obvious, as when a chemistry professor tells a female premed student that women belong in the home (Matlin, 1993). Sexism can also be more subtle, as when the word *girl* is used to refer to a mature woman. In one recent analysis, an attempt was made to distinguish between old-fashioned and modern sexism (Swim & others, 1995). *Old-fashioned sexism* is characterized by endorsement of traditional gender roles, differential treatment for men and women, and a stereotype that females are less competent than males. Like modern racism, *modern sexism* is characterized by the denial that there is still discrimination, antagonism toward women's demands, and lack of support for policies designed to help women (for example, in education and work).

Androgyny. In the 1970s, as both males and females became dissatisfied with the burdens imposed by their strictly stereotyped roles, alternatives to "masculinity" and "femininity" were explored. Instead of thinking of masculinity and femininity as a continuum, with more of one meaning less of the other, it was proposed that individuals could show both expressive and instrumental traits. This thinking led to the development of the concept of **androgyny**, *the presence of a high degree of desirable masculine and feminine characteristics in the same individual* (Bem, 1977; Spence & Helmreich, 1978). The androgynous individual might be a male who is assertive (masculine) and nurturant (feminine), or a female who is dominant (masculine) and sensitive to others' feelings (feminine).

Measures have been developed to assess androgyny. One of the most widely used gender measures, the Bem Sex-Role Inventory, was constructed by a leading early proponent of androgyny, Sandra Bem. To see what the items on Bem's measure are like, complete the Self-Assessment. Based on their responses to the items in the Bem sex-role inventory, individuals are classified as having one of four gender-role orientations: masculine, feminine, androgynous, or undifferentiated (see figure 15.3). The androgynous individual is simply a female or a male who has a high degree of both feminine (expressive) and

androgyny

The presence of desirable feminine and masculine characteristics in the same individual.

*F*IGURE 15.3
Gender-Role Classification

masculine (instrumental) traits. No new characteristics are used to describe the androgynous individual. A feminine individual is high on feminine (expressive) traits and low on masculine (instrumental) traits; a masculine individual shows the reverse of these traits. An undifferentiated person is not high on feminine or masculine traits.

Androgynous women and men, according to Bem, are more flexible and more mentally healthy than either masculine and feminine individuals, while undifferentiated individuals are the least competent. To some degree, though, context influences which gender role is most adaptive. In close relationships, a feminine or androgynous gender role may be more desirable because of the expressive nature of close relationships. However, a masculine or androgynous gender role may be more desirable in academic and work settings because of their demands for action and assertiveness. And the culture in which individuals live also plays an important role in determining what is adaptive. On the one hand, increasing numbers of children in the United States and other modernized countries such as Sweden are being raised to behave in androgynous ways. But traditional gender roles continue to dominate the cultures of many countries around the world.

Gender-Role Transcendence. Although the concept of androgyny was an improvement over exclusive notions of femininity and masculinity, it has turned out to be less of a panacea than many of its early proponents envisioned (Paludi, 1995). Some theorists, such as Joseph Pleck (1979), believe the idea of androgyny should be replaced with **gender-role transcendence,** *the belief that when an individual's competence is at issue, it should be conceptualized not on the basis of femininity, masculinity, or androgyny, but rather on a person basis.* Thus, rather than merging gender roles or stereotyping people as "feminine" or "masculine," Pleck believes we should begin to think about people as people. However, both the concepts of androgyny and gender-role transcendence draw attention away from women's unique needs and the power imbalance between women and men in most cultures (Hare-Mustin & Maracek, 1988). Shortly, we will see that a major focus of the feminist agenda is to reduce that imbalance of power.

Women's Issues. **Feminists** *are individuals who believe that women and men should have the same rights.* Many feminist scholars believe that psychology has portrayed human behavior with a "male dominant" theme (Paludi, 1998). They also believe that sexism is still rampant in society. As Jean Baker Miller (1986) wrote in *Toward a New Psychology of Women,*

> In the last decade it has become clearer that if women are trying to define and create a full personhood, we are engaged in a huge undertaking. We see that this attempt means building a new way of living which encompasses all realms of life, from global economic, social and political levels to the most intimate personal relationships. (p. xi)

Feminist scholars are putting greater emphasis on women's life experiences and development (including girls and women as authorities about their own experiences), or as Harvard psychologist Carol Gilligan (1996) advocates, listening to women's voices and studying women's ways of knowing; women's career and family roles; abuse of women and rape; and women's experiences of connectedness and self-determination.

Miller (1976, 1986) has been an important voice in stimulating the examination of psychological issues from a female perspective. She believes that the study of women's psychological development opens up paths to a better understanding of all psychological development, male or female. She also concludes that when researchers examine what women have been doing in life, a large part of it is active participation in the development of others. In Miller's view, women often try to interact with others in ways that will foster the other person's development along many dimensions—emotionally, intellectually, and socially.

Most feminist thinkers believe it is important for women to not only maintain their competency in relationships but to be self-motivated, too (Donelson, 1998). Miller believes that through increased self-determination, coupled with already developed relationship skills, many women will gain greater power in the American culture. And as feminist scholar Harriet Lerner (1989) concludes in her book *The Dance of Intimacy,* it is important for women to bring to their relationships nothing less than a strong, assertive, independent, and authentic self. She believes competent relationships are those in which

gender-role transcendence
The belief that when an individual's competence is at issue, it should be conceptualized not on the basis of femininity, masculinity, or androgyny, but rather on a person basis.

feminist
A person who believes that women and men should have the same rights.

the separate "I-ness" of both persons can be appreciated and enhanced while still staying emotionally connected to each other.

Not only is a distinct female voice an important dimension of the feminist perspective on gender, but so is the effort to reduce and eventually end prejudice and discrimination against women (Kirk & Oka Zawa-Rey, 1998). While women have broken through many male bastions in the last several decades, feminists argue that much work is left to be done. Feminists today believe that too many people passively accept traditional gender roles and believe that discrimination no longer exists in politics, work, family, and education. They encourage individuals to question these assumptions, and they especially strive to get females to evaluate the gender circumstances of their lives. Feminists hope that whether you are male or female, you will become more conscious of gender issues, of female and male roles, and of fairness and sensitivity in female-male interactions and relationships. To read about some of the inequities that women around the world continue to experience in the 1990s, turn to Sociocultural Worlds.

A special concern involves ethnic minority women, or *women of color*. Too many women of color have experienced both racism and sexism. African American women are underrepresented in all areas of psychology and other academic disciplines. Our society needs to commit to providing women of color with the opportunities they deserve.

Men's Issues.   The male of the species—what is he really like? What are his concerns?

Male Role Strain.   According to Joseph Pleck's (1981, 1995) *role-strain* view, male roles are contradictory and inconsistent. Men not only experience stress when they violate men's roles, they also are harmed when they *do* act in accord with expectations for men's roles (Levant, 1996). The following are some of the areas where men's roles can cause considerable strain (Levant & Brooks, 1997; Philpot & others, 1997):

- *Health.* Men live 8 to 10 years less than women do. They have higher rates of stress-related disorders, alcoholism, car accidents, and suicide. Men are more likely than women to be the victims of homicide. In sum, the male role is hazardous to men's health.
- *Male-female relationships.* Too often, the male's role involves images that men should be dominant, powerful, and aggressive and should control women. Also, the male role has involved looking at women in terms of their bodies rather than their minds and feelings. Earlier, we described Deborah Tannen's (1990) concept that men show too little interest in rapport talk and relationships. And the male role has included the view that women should not be considered equal to men in work, earnings, and many other aspects of life. Too often these dimensions of the male role have produced men who have denigrated women, been violent toward women, and been unwilling to have equal relationships with women.
- *Male-male relationships.* Too many men have had too little interaction with their fathers, especially fathers who are positive role models. Nurturing and being sensitive to others have been considered aspects of the female role, and not the male role. And the male role emphasizes competition rather than cooperation. All of these aspects of the male role have left men with inadequate positive, emotional connections with other males.

To reconstruct their masculinity in more positive ways, Ron Levant (1995) believes, every man should (1) reexamine his beliefs about manhood, (2) separate out the valuable aspects of the male role, and (3) get rid of those parts of the masculine role that are destructive. All of this involves becoming more "emotionally intelligent"—that is, becoming more emotionally self-aware, managing emotions more effectively, reading emotions better (one's own emotions and others'), and being motivated to improve close relationships.

Males of Color and White Males.   Although it is useful to speak of "the male experience," it is important to consider variations in male experiences. An increasing number of men

Sociocultural Worlds

Women's Struggle for Equality: An International Journey

What are the political, economic, educational and psychosocial conditions of women around the world? Frances Culbertson (1991), as president of the section of the American Psychological Association on the Clinical Psychology of Women, summarized these conditions.

Women and Politics

In politics, women too often are treated as burdens rather than assets. Especially in developing countries, women marry early and have many children quickly, in many cases before their undernourished bodies have an opportunity to mature. These women have little access to education, work, health care, and family planning. Some experts on women's issues believe these needs would have a better chance of being met if women were more strongly represented at the decision-making and managerial levels of governments and international organizations. For example, in 1990, less than 10 percent of the members of national legislatures were women, and for every 100 ministerial level positions around the world, only 5 were filled by women (Sadik, 1991).

Women and Employment

Women's work around the world is more limiting and narrower than that of men (Monagle, 1990). Bank tellers and secretaries are most often women. Domestic workers in North America and in Central and South America are most often women. Around the world, jobs defined as women's work carry low pay, low status, and little security. Two authors described many of these circumstances as "job ghettos" (Seager & Olson, 1986). In 1990, the only countries in the world that had maternity leave and guaranteed jobs on the basis of national law were Brazil, Chile, Mexico, Finland, Sweden, Switzerland, Germany, Italy, Egypt, Syria, and Russia. Among the major countries without these provisions was the United States.

Women and Education

Canada, the United States, and Russia have the highest percentages of educated women (Seager & Olson, 1986). The countries with the fewest women being educated are in Africa, where in some areas women are given no education at all. In developing countries, 67 percent of women and 50 percent of men over the age of 25 have never been to school. In 1985, 80 million more boys than girls were in primary and secondary educational settings around the world.

Women and Psychosocial Issues

Women around the world experience violence, often from someone close to them. In Canada, 10 percent of women reported they had been beaten by the man they lived with in their home. In the United States almost 2 million women are beaten in their homes each year (Seager & Olson, 1986). In a survey, "The New Woman Ethics Report," wife abuse was listed as number one among the fifteen most pressing concerns facing society today (Johnson, 1990). Beating women continues to be accepted and expected in too many countries. While most countries around the world now have battered women's shelters, the remedy is still usually too little, too late.

In an investigation of depression in high-income countries, women were twice as likely as men to be diagnosed as being depressed (Nolen-Hoeksema, 1990). In the United States, from adolescence through adulthood, females are more likely than males to be depressed (McGrath & others, 1990). Many sociocultural inequities and experiences contribute to the greater incidence of depression in females than in males.

In many cultures, sex is not supposed to be pleasurable for women. For example, in the Near East and Africa, a sizable number of women are given clitorectomies, the surgical removal of the clitoris, to reduce their sexual pleasure. Many women are the victims of date rape and stranger rape. Many people—both men and women—expect women to assume total responsibility for contraception.

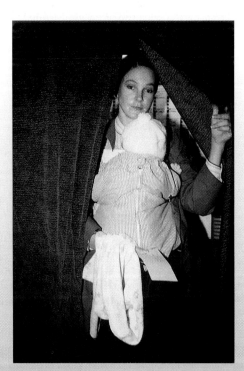

Around the world women too often are treated as burdens rather than assets in the political process. Few women have leadership positions in government. Some experts on women's issues believe that if women are to gain more access to work, education, health care, and family planning, they need to be more strongly represented at the decision-making and managerial levels of government and business.

$\mathcal{I}$mproving Personal and Cognitive Skills

Improving Women's and Men's Lives

Both women and men feel hampered by gender stereotypes and expectations. Here are a few suggestions for how we can all improve some of those aspects of our lives that have traditionally been governed by gender stereotypes and expectations.

Ways Women Can Improve Their Lives

- *Develop your own standards.*
  Decide for yourself what kinds of goals you will have and what kinds of work you will devote your abilities and energy to. In particular, don't fall into the trap of evaluating yourself and your life by men's standards for women (which stereotypically focus on women's physical characteristics and whether a woman's behavior satisfies men's egos).
- *Value your relationship skills.*
  Emotionally, intellectually, and socially, women tend to be good at communicating with, being sensitive to, and helping others. Value these characteristics in yourself. These are skills everyone must learn, if we are going to live peaceably together in our rapidly "shrinking" world.
- *Work on your self-development.*
  Actively create for yourself a strong, positive identity. Become more self-motivated. Examine your own needs and how they can be fulfilled. Because of traditional female conditioning, many women are not good at honoring their own needs or creating a strong identity for themselves.

Ways Men Can Improve Their Lives

- *Make relationship skills a high priority in your life.*
  Recognize that having good friends and social support

might even help you live longer. Work on being a good listener.
- *Become better attuned to your emotional makeup.*
  Learn to sense, identify, and articulate your feelings. Because of traditional masculine conditioning, many men are not good at recognizing and understanding their feelings.
- *Learn to be less aggressive.*
  Traditional masculine conditioning teaches males that they have to be "tough" and "virile," and this promotes aggression. Learn to be assertive rather than aggressive.
- *Take seriously the role of being a father.*
  Children need their fathers to participate in their rearing. Children benefit from having two competent, nurturant, loving, and sensitive parents. Far too many men have neglected this important, rewarding role.

How We All Can Contribute to Better Understanding Between Women and Men

- *Resist sexist humor.*
  Sexist jokes are disrespectful, partly simply because they are based on gender stereotypes. Women and men are all individuals, and we won't learn to understand one another until we learn to see (and respect) one another for who we really are.
- *Don't tolerate sexual harassment or discrimination.*
  Be vigilant about recognizing inappropriate and harmful uses of power. If you are sexually harassed or discriminated against, report it. If you find yourself sexually harassing or discriminating against someone, stop that behavior and rectify any harm you've done.

are becoming responsible fathers, sharing household duties with women, and relinquishing their power motives. And men's experiences vary according to their ethnicity and culture. For example, many African American males grow up in poverty, surrounded by violence.

White males have concerns of their own. For instance, many White males feel strain from current cultural practices that promote greater diversity in the workplace, fearing that they will be discriminated against in entry-level jobs and laid off due to diversity-driven initiatives.

What is the future of the women's and men's movements? Perhaps at some point they can work together toward an "androgynous" or "gender-role transcendent" movement that allows females and males to express themselves as human beings, thus freeing themselves from the constraints and rigidity of traditional gender roles. For some suggestions on how women's lives and men's lives can be improved, see Improving Personal and Cognitive Skills.

eview

Gender

Gender is the sociocultural dimension of being female or male. Biological influences on gender include the genetic material that determines our sex (such as X and Y chromosomes) and hormones (androgens and estrogens). Social influences on gender come from culture, family, peers, school, and the media. Identification theory and social learning theory emphasize the role of parents as models for gender behavior. Two theories—cognitive developmental theory and gender schema theory—argue that cognitive factors are important in gender development.

There is concern that some differences between females and males have been exaggerated and that differences are too often mistakenly explained in terms of biological causes. There are a number of physical/biological differences between males and females, but cognitive differences are either small or nonexistent. With regard to socioemotional factors, males are more aggressive and females place more emphasis on social relationships.

Gender stereotypes are broad categories, exaggerated generalizations, and/or false beliefs about males and females. Gender stereotyping is extensive. Some gender stereotypes involve prejudice and discrimination—this is called sexism.

Earlier in this century, competent males were described as masculine (independent, dominant, and so on) and competent females were described as feminine (dependent, submissive, and so on). In the 1970s arose the concept of androgyny—that competent individuals have both desirable masculine and desirable feminine characteristics. Some experts believe that too much attention has been given to androgyny. They argue that a stronger emphasis should be given to gender-role transcendence.

Feminist scholars believe that psychology has portrayed human behavior with a male-dominant theme. They also believe that sexism is rampant. Most feminist scholars say it is important for females to retain their competence and interest in relationships, but also to direct more effort into self-development. A special concern involves ethnic minority women, or women of color. Men have been successful at achieving, but the male role involves considerable strain. It is possible to talk about "the male experience," but there is diversity among males.

So far we have explored the influences that culture, ethnicity, and gender have in producing diverse behavior. Next, we turn to another defining influence in diversity: religion.

RELIGION

Religion plays an important role in the lives of many people. Just how extensive and diverse is religious influence?

Religion enlightens, terrifies, subdues; it gives faith, inflicts remorse, inspires revolutions, and inflames devotion.
—HENRY NEWMAN, *English Churchman and Writer, 19th Century*

The Nature and Scope of Religious Influence

Billions of people around the world guide their lives by the beliefs of Judaism, Christianity, Islam, and Buddhism (Hood, 1995). Of the world's 5.5 billion people, about two-thirds are involved in religion or are affected by religion in important ways. In one survey, 98 percent of the population in India, 88 percent in Italy, 72 percent in France, and 63 percent in Scandinavia said that they believe in God (Gallup, 1988).

In a recent national poll in the United States, 95 percent said they believe in God or a universal spirit ("Spiritual America," 1994). About 60 percent said that they attend religions services. Only 9 percent professed to having no religion at all. About three-fourths of Americans say that they pray or engage in some form of religions ritual (*Religion in America*, 1993).

The religious need of the human mind remains alive, never more so.
—CHARLOTTE PERKINS GILMAN, *American Feminist Writer, 19th Century*

Women consistently show more interest in religion than men do (Miller & Hoffman, 1995). More women than men participate in organized religion (such as going to worship services) and personal religion (such as praying), say that they believe in a higher power or presence, and say that religion is important in their lives.

Religious interest is widespread around the world. Of the world's 5.5 billion people, approximately two-thirds either are involved in a religion or have been affected by religion in important ways. The large photograph shows worshipers at the Makka (Mecca) mosque in Saudi Arabia. *(top left inset)* A Jewish rabbi reads prayer. *(top right inset)* Temple of the Thousand Buddhas in Bangkok, Thailand. *(bottom left inset)* Children at the San Fernando Catholic Christmas service in San Antonio, Texas. *(bottom right inset)* A congregation singing at an American Protestant church.

Despite the widespread practice of religion, it is a challenge to try to define religion. There is great diversity in religious practices around the world, and each religion has its own unique history.

One approach to defining religion is to explore the function of religion in people's lives. Religion addresses the fundamental questions of life (Batson & others, 1993), including these:

- What should I accomplish with my life?
- What will happen when I die?
- What is the meaning of life?

religion

A belief system that individuals use to morally and spiritually guide their behavior.

But religion goes beyond pondering life's most complex questions. **Religion** *is a belief system that individuals use to morally and spiritually guide their behavior.* A person's religion is multifaceted and includes beliefs, practices, feelings, knowledge, and outcomes.

A person's religion involves their *beliefs.* For example, one person believes that Jesus was the Messiah and rose from the dead, another person believes that the Messiah has not yet come, and still another practices religious traditions that are not founded upon the concept of a Messiah, such as Buddhist devotion to the Dharma.

A person's religion includes *practice,* which refers to the religious rituals the person engages in. Religious practice can include singing, chanting, scripture reading, going to confession, or bowing to a stone. Whether you are Jewish and pray at the Wailing Wall or celebrate the passing of life at an Irish wake, you are engaging in the rituals of religious practice.

Religious experiences involve a rich range of *feelings,* or emotions. These feelings can range from the joy felt in conducting one's life according to certain religious principles to the fear and guilt that can be precipitated by violating religious doctrines.

A person's religion includes *knowledge.* Religious knowledge refers to what people know about their own religion. Although it is possible to practice faith "blindly," most religions have educational components to help people build their religious commitment.

A person's religion also includes *outcomes.* Religious outcomes involve the impact that religion has on an individual's everyday life. For example, Gallup polls consistently report that people who practice religion on a regular basis are more likely to commit time to charitable work serving the poor or sick than are people who never attend any kind of religious service. Another outcome focuses on the possibility of religious persecution. History is filled with examples of people who have been persecuted for their religious beliefs—or lack thereof. For example, the famous seventeenth-century Italian astronomer Galileo was harassed and threatened when he espoused scientific beliefs about the solar system that did not support the beliefs of the Catholic Church.

Most religions outline acceptable behaviors for living a moral life. Some individuals might believe firmly in the doctrines of the religion yet not always put their beliefs into practice. When people's actions do not coincide with their professed religious beliefs, we say that they are *hypocritical.*

Religious Orientation

intrinsic religious orientation
Religious motives that lie within the person; living the religion.

extrinsic religious orientation
Personal motives that lie outside the religion itself; using religion for some nonreligious ends.

Psychologists who study religion distinguish between intrinsic and extrinsic religious orientations (Paloutzian, 1996). An **intrinsic religious orientation** *involves internal religious motives within the person.* By contrast, an **extrinsic religious orientation** *involves external motives outside of the religion, using the religion for nonreligious ends.*

Social psychologist Gordon Allport (1966) said that intrinsically motivated people *live* their religion and that extrinsics *use* it. One person who lived her religion was Mother Teresa of Calcutta, India, who ministered to the poor and sick. Her work expanded to five continents and she was awarded the Nobel Peace Price for her altruistic efforts. In contrast, some religious figures, such as Jim and Tammy Faye Baker, have been accused of using their public role in religion for their personal profit. However, not all extrinsic religious motivation is negative. For example, young people might use religious gatherings to search for potential life partners.

Developing Religious Commitment

Whether intrinsic or extrinsic, how does religious commitment develop? According to religion expert James Fowler (1981), religious commitment can be a lifelong process. Fowler proposed that individuals go through six stages as they explore life's meaning, whether as part of an organized religion or independent from it:

- *Stage 1: Intuitive-projective faith* (early childhood). Young children create their own images of good and evil. Right and wrong are seen in terms of consequences to the self. Fantasy and reality are the same thing.
- *Stage 2: Mythical-lyrical faith* (elementary school years). Religious stories are interpreted more literally. God is perceived as being much like a parent figure who rewards the good and punishes the bad. What is right is often seen in terms of fair exchange.
- *Stage 3: Synthetic-conventional faith* (early adolescence). Young adolescents start to think about religion in more abstract ways but still conform to the religious beliefs taught to them by others. At this stage, they have not adequately explored alternative ideologies.
- *Stage 4: Individualistic-reflective faith* (late adolescence, transition to adulthood). In late adolescence, individuals are for the first time becoming capable of taking full

responsibility for their religious beliefs. They explore questions such as "Is the religious doctrine that was taught to me as I was growing up really what I want, or are there other beliefs that might fit me better?"

- *Stage 5: Conjunctive faith* (middle adulthood). This stage is fueled by confronting the reality that one's life is finite. With this awareness, individuals become more understanding of opposing viewpoints on religion.
- *Stage 6: Universalizing faith* (middle and late adulthood). Individuals transcend specific belief systems and achieve a sense of unity with all being.

Fowler believes there is a sequential order to these stages. That is, people have to go through stage 1 before stage 2, and so on. He also says that very few people ever reach stages 5 and 6. Critics of Fowler's view cite the lack of research evidence for the theory and argue that there is more individual variation in the development of religious faith than Fowler's view suggests.

Varieties of Religious Experience

Religion sets the stage for many kinds of experience. In this section, we will explore mystical experience, conversion, and spiritual well-being.

Mystical Experience and Conversion.   As many as one-third of the U.S. population report that they have had profound religious experiences, and almost one-half say they feel a presence or power in their lives that is distinct from themselves (Gallup & Jones, 1989). What accounts for these experiences? Both personal characteristics, referred to as *dispositional factors,* and environmental circumstances, referred to as *situational factors,* contribute. For example, people classified as intrinsically motivated are more likely to report profound religious experiences than are people who are extrinsically motivated (Hood, 1995). Situational factors that contribute to mystical experiences include becoming immersed in a religious ritual, using hallucinogens, being immersed in water, and being deprived of sensory experiences. Preparing mentally for a religious experience also can trigger the spiritual effect being sought.

In some situations, mystical experience can lead to **religious conversion,** *a change from having no beliefs to accepting a religious belief system, or a change from one belief system to another.* An early view of conversion suggested that people are often coerced into accepting a new faith. This view of conversion has been replaced by the view that people actively seek answers by exploring and selecting a new religious system that can help relieve tension in their lives. Once they recognize the potential of the new way of life, they develop closer bonds with people in the new faith and disconnect from others.

Spiritual Well-Being.   A long-standing stereotype is that religion is a crutch for the weak. However, researchers in the psychology of religion have found that many religious individuals are competent. In one study, individuals with intrinsic religious motivation reported a greater sense of competence and control, as well as less worry and guilt, than did individuals with extrinsic religious motivation (Ventis, 1995); the intrinsics also reported fewer physical illnesses. And in one longitudinal study, competent middle-aged men and women were more likely than less competent middle-aged individuals to have a religious affiliation (Clausen, 1993). In addition, people who report sustained levels of happiness are more likely to say they have a meaningful religious faith than people who are not happy over a long period of time (Myers & Diener, 1995).

> *I pray, work hard, and leave the rest to God.*
> —Florence Griffith Joyner, *U.S. Olympic Track Star, 20th Century*

To evaluate the role of spiritual well-being in your life, complete the Self-Assessment. Next we will explore one final topic in the psychology of religion: the connection between religious belief and prejudice.

religious conversion

A change from having no religious beliefs to accepting a religious system, or changing from one belief system to another.

Self-Assessment

Spiritual Well-Being

Instructions

For each of the following statements, assign a score from 1 to 6 according to how strongly you agree or disagree with it.

	Strongly Agree					Strongly Disagree
1. I don't find much satisfaction in prayer or meditation.	1	2	3	4	5	6
2. I don't know who I am, where I came from, or where I am going.	1	2	3	4	5	6
3. My spiritual life makes me feel loved and connected.	1	2	3	4	5	6
4. I think that life is a positive experience.	1	2	3	4	5	6
5. I feel disconnected from a spiritual force in my daily situations.	1	2	3	4	5	6
6. I feel unsettled about my future.	1	2	3	4	5	6
7. My spiritual life offers me personally meaningful relationships.	1	2	3	4	5	6
8. I feel very fulfilled and satisfied with life.	1	2	3	4	5	6
9. I don't get much personal strength and support from my spiritual practices.	1	2	3	4	5	6
10. I feel a sense of well-being about the direction my life is headed in.	1	2	3	4	5	6
11. I believe that my spiritual practices help me deal with my problems.	1	2	3	4	5	6
12. I don't enjoy much about life.	1	2	3	4	5	6
13. I don't have a personally satisfying spiritual relationship.	1	2	3	4	5	6
14. I feel good about my future.	1	2	3	4	5	6
15. My religious practices help me not to feel lonely.	1	2	3	4	5	6
16. I think that life is full of conflict and unhappiness.	1	2	3	4	5	6
17. I feel most fulfilled when I'm in close spiritual communion.	1	2	3	4	5	6
18. Life doesn't have much meaning.	1	2	3	4	5	6
19. My spiritual relationships contribute to my sense of well-being.	1	2	3	4	5	6
20. I believe there is some real purpose for my life.	1	2	3	4	5	6

Scoring and Interpretation

The spiritual well-being scales measure two main areas: (1) religious well-being and (2) existential well-being. The religious scale refers to religion and one's relationship to spirituality, the existential scale to meaning in life and questions about the nature of one's existence. To obtain your spiritual well-being score, add up your responses to items 1, 5, 9, and 13; reverse the scores for items 3, 7, 11, 15, 17, and 19 (that is change the 1 to a 6, the 2 to a 5, the 3 to a 4, and so on). Com-bine these two subtotals to get your overall spiritual well-being score.

To obtain your existential well-being score, add up your responses to items 2, 6, 12, 16, and 18; reverse the scores for items 4, 8, 10, 14, and 20. Combine these two subtotals to obtain your overall existential well-being score.

Your overall scores on each of these two scales can range from 10 to 60. On each of the scales, a score of 40 or higher reflects well-being (religious or existential).

Religion and Prejudice. Common sense suggests that people whose religious doctrines promote "brotherly love" probably are not very prejudiced. Ironically, social psychologist Gordon Allport identified what he called the *grand paradox:* People who attend church are more prejudiced than nonchurchgoers (Allport & Ross, 1967). However, when he examined this connection more closely, he discovered that the link varied according to regularity of church attendance. Regular churchgoers, who were more likely to have an intrinsic religious orientation, were relatively low in prejudice toward ethnic groups, while sporadic attenders, who were more likely to have an extrinsic religious orientation, were more prejudiced.

Review

Diversity in Religion

Religion plays an important role in the lives of many people. About two-thirds of the world's population say that religion is important in their lives. About three-fourths of Americans say that they pray or perform other religious rituals.

Religion involves a belief system that individuals use for spiritual and moral guidance. This system has a number of components, including belief, practice, feeling, knowledge, and outcomes.

People with an intrinsic religious motivation have an internal motivation for religion; those with an extrinsic religious motivation have an external motivation for religion. Some experts say that intrinsically motivated individuals live their religion and that those who are extrinsically motivated use their religion.

Our religious commitments can change as we develop through our lives. James Fowler proposed a six-stage developmental model that begins with the intuitive faith of young children and ends with a universalizing faith in middle/late adulthood.

Both dispositional and situational factors are involved in reports of mystical experience. In today's view, religious conversion is an active search for a belief system that will reduce tension in the individual's life. Intrinsically motivated religious individuals report greater spiritual well-being, more sustained levels of happiness, and less physical illness than their extrinsic counterparts. Gordon Allport documented the grand paradox: People who attend church are more prejudiced than those who are nonchurchgoers. However, when he studied this link more closely it was related to the regularity of church attendance.

Overview

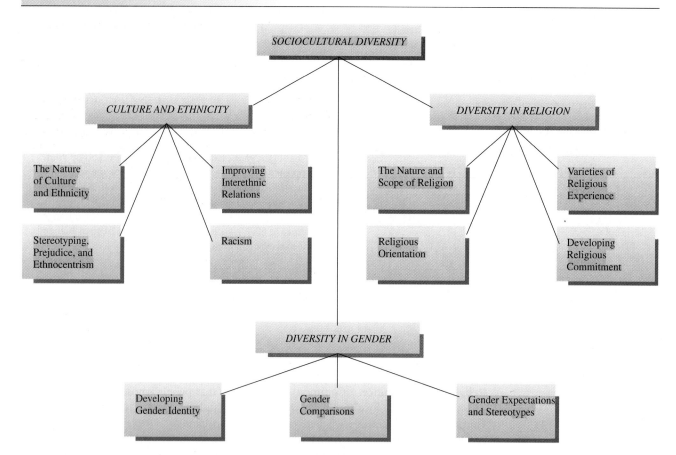

We began this chapter on sociocultural diversity by exploring these aspects of culture and ethnicity: their nature, stereotyping, prejudice, and ethnocentrism, racism, and improving interethnic relations. Our coverage of gender focused on developing gender identity, gender comparisons, and gender expectations and stereotypes. We studied these aspects of religion: the nature of religion, the scope of religious influence, religious orientation, developing religious commitment, and varieties of religious experience.

Don't forget that you can obtain an overall summary of the chapter by again studying the in-chapter reviews on pages 560, 575, and 580.

Key Terms

Thinking It Over

Exercises...

...In Critical Thinking

Identify a contemporary conflict that involves ethnicity or race. It can be a neighborhood, national, or global conflict. How many concepts listed in the "Key Terms" section of this chapter can be applied to explain how this conflict originated and is being maintained? Do any of these concepts suggest ways the conflict might be resolved?

...In Creative Thinking

Get together with some other students and brainstorm to come up with some creative ways to reduce gender conflicts on your campus. Invent a slogan or logo that illustrates your conflict reduction strategy.

...In Active Learning

Investigate cultural, ethnic, and religious diversity on your campus. Find out how many countries are represented in the student body and identify them. Do the same for ethnic groups and religions. How diverse is your campus?

...In Reflective Learning

Think about some period of your life when you were handicapped by someone stereotyping you. For example, you might be a short person and recognize that there are characteristic ways that people deal with you that might grow out of their stereotypes about short people. Describe the experience of others' making judgments about you based on characteristics that you cannot control. Consider whether there are stereotypes you harbor that influence your treatment of others.

Resources for Psychology and Improving Humankind

American Association of University Women

1111 Sixteenth Street
Washington, DC 20036

This organization promotes education and equity for girls and women. It provides sabbaticals for public school teachers to learn how to more effectively teach girls and supports community projects to foster equal opportunities for females.

American Psychological Association, Division 36: Psychology of Religion

American Psychological Association
Office of Divisional Affairs
750 First Street, NE
Washington, DC 20002-4242

This organization is the foremost professional society for psychologists in the field of psychology of religion. The division publishes a quarterly newsletter and has a student membership category.

Association of Black Psychologists

P.O. Box 55999
Washington, DC 20040-5999
202-722-0808

This organization of professional psychologists and others in associated disciplines publishes the *Resource Manual for Black Psychology Students* and a number of other brochures and bulletins related to African American psychology.

Campus Outreach Opportunity League (COOL)

University of Minnesota
386 McNeal Hall
St. Paul, MN 55108-1011
612-624-3018

COOL promotes and supports student involvement in community service. It has a network of more than six hundred colleges and universities. Its goal is to help students address such issues as homelessness, hunger, illiteracy, and cultural diversity. If you are interested in starting or strengthening a community service program on your campus, COOL staff members will help you develop your strategy.

Canada Ethnocultural Council/ Conseil ethnoculturel du Canada

251 Laurier Ave. West, #100
Ottawa, ON K1P 5J6
613-230-3867

A coalition of 38 national organizations representing over 2000 ethnic groups across Canada. They publish the magazine *Ethno Canada,* support legislation, and sponsor conferences and research on multicultural issues.

Center for Community Change

1000 Wisconsin Avenue, NW
Washington, DC 20007
202-342-0519

The objective of this center is to provide information and technical assistance to low-income and minority-based organizations to increase the effectiveness of their programs.

Culture and Social Behavior (1994)

by Harry Triandis
New York: McGraw-Hill

This insightful book by one of cross-cultural psychology's leading figures, Harry Triandis, aims to unveil how culture influences people's social behavior. Among the topics given considerable coverage are how to study cultures, how to analyze subjective culture, culture and communication, cultural influences on aggression, helping, dominance, and conformity, dealing with diversity in intercultural relations, and intercultural training.

International Association of Cross-Cultural Psychologists

c/o Jeff Lewis
Pitzer College
1050 N. Mills Avenue
Claremont, CA 91711

This organization of professionals and students interested in cross-cultural psychology publishes the *Journal of Cross-Cultural Psychology* and *Cross-Cultural Psychology Bulletin.*

Invitation to the Psychology of Religion (1996, 2nd ed.)

by Raymond Paloutzian
Needham Heights, MA: Allyn & Bacon

This book provides a broad overview of topics in the psychology of religion, including religious development, conversion, religious experience, attitudes and behavior, and mental health.

The Mismeasure of Woman (1992)

by Carol Tavris
New York: Touchstone

The Mismeasure of Woman explores many aspects of women's lives that have been misrepresented. This is an excellent book on gender stereotyping, similarities and differences between the sexes, and how women should be measured by their own standards, not men's.

National Urban League

The Equal Opportunity Building
500 East 62nd Street
New York, NY 10021
212-310-9000

The National Urban League is an influential social service and civil rights organization with more than 30,000 volunteers working to obtain equal opportunities for African Americans and other ethnic minority groups. If you are interested in helping, contact the affiliate where you live or the National Urban League at the address listed above.

National Women of Color Association

Department of Women's Studies
336 North Hall
University of Wisconsin, LaCrosse
LaCrosse, WI 54601
608-785-8357

This association is a fellowship of women of color, including but not limited to ethnic minority groups in the United States. Research information about women of color is available, and a newsletter is published.

The New Male (1980)

by Herb Goldberg
New York: Signet

Goldberg elaborates on ways that males can combine some of the strengths of their masculinity—such as assertiveness and independence—with increased exploration of the inner self, emotions, and close relationships with others to become more complete, better adjusted males.

Resource Center for Women

445 Sherman Avenue
Palo Alto, CA 94306
415-324-1710

This center provides information and guidance for women so that they can make informed decisions about the direction of their lives. It publishes *Career Connections*.

Teaching a Psychology of People: Resources for Gender and Sociocultural Awareness (1988)

edited by P. A. Berman and K. Quina
Washington, DC: American Psychological Association

This book includes a variety of chapters by psychologists interested in the roles of ethnicity and culture in understanding behavior and mental processes.

Internet Resources

http://latino.sscnet.ucla.edu/diversity1.html
These pages provide comprehensive links to topics of interest to multicultural constituents.

http://www3.arcade.uiowa.edu/gw/comm/GenderMedia/tvfilm.html
This site, maintained by the University of Iowa, explores how gender is treated in popular culture media.

http://www.planetout.com
A worldwide online community for gay, lesbian and bisexual people.

http://www.ubp.com
The Universal Black Pages offers resources, news, and lists of organizations for Black students.

http://www.latinolink.com
Latinolink offers helpful information, chat forums, and bulletin boards of interest to Latino and Hispanic students.

http://www.mit.edu:8001/afs/athena.mit.edu/user/i/r/irie/www/aar.html
This site is designed for issues related to Asian-American students.

http://galaxy.einet.net/GJ/disabilities.html
This page provides a comprehensive resource individuals with disabilities.

http://www.academic.info.net/religindex.html
Comprehensive Web site comparing the world's religions.

http://www.bcpl.net/~sandyste/school.psych.html
Society for Cross-Cultural Research Web site.

16

Applied Psychology

What's wrong with this world is that it is not finished

yet. We need to put our signature on it and say,

"It works."

—William Faulkner
American Novelist, 20th Century

P sychology has spawned an amazing array of practical applications. In this chapter we will study the following fields of applied psychology: industrial/organizational (I/O) psychology, environmental psychology, forensic psychology (psychology and the law), sport psychology, and educational psychology. One area of I/O psychology is called human factors psychology, and we open this chapter with the story of an unpleasant episode experienced by the first American astronaut, Alan Shepard. This episode could have been avoided if NASA had consulted a human factors psychologist when they were preparing for Shepard's space flight. These psychologists study the design of machines and environments to find their best fit with the human beings who will be using them.

The Story of Astronaut Alan Shepard: Sitting on Top of a Rocket

T he date is May 5, 1961. Alan Shepard, the first American to be put into space, awaits his moment in history inside his tiny Mercury capsule. He is just going to go up and come back down. He isn't even going to orbit Earth. The whole trip is supposed to last only 15 minutes, so why bother equipping his spacesuit with a device that would allow him to urinate safely, right? However, after Shepard is strapped into his seat, delay after delay occurs. He communicates to mission control that he needs to urinate. Mission control tells him to hang in there, launch is about to occur.

Think about this situation. You are the first astronaut to sit on top of a rocket—a potential bomb. Wouldn't you be just a little nervous? Shepard radios down that he can't hold it much longer. NASA begins to worry because the "window" for launch

How would attention to human factors by NASA personnel have benefited Alan Shepard when he became the first person in space?

applied psychology
The field that uses psychological principles to improve the lives of human beings and solve human problems.

requires perfect timing. They tell Shepard that he can't get out of the capsule now. And besides, the hatch is bolted shut, so charges would have to be ignited to blow off the door. Finally, Shepard radios NASA that he can't wait any longer. So what does NASA do? They tell him to go ahead and wet his pants.

Shepard is wired from head to toe, electronically connected to all sorts of technical equipment. When he follows NASA's instructions and wets his pants, instruments start short-circuiting all over the place. We'll skip the disgusting details except for this: In the cockpit on the launchpad, Shepard's head was lower than his feet! With all the time and money NASA spent planning the mission, you'd think they would have considered something as basic as an astronaut's need to urinate! ❖

WHAT IS APPLIED PSYCHOLOGY?

In the second half of the twentieth century, we have witnessed a surge of interest in applied psychology. **Applied psychology** *is the field that uses psychological principles to improve the lives of human beings and solve human problems.* Like all psychologists, applied psychologists are trained in the basic science of psychology. Their unique contributions result from their application of psychological concepts to problems of human behavior (Aamodt, 1996). In the first half of the twentieth century, most psychologists taught at universities and engaged in basic research. However, today about two-thirds of psychologists work in applied settings, such as business, industry, clinics, hospitals, schools, community agencies, or government (see figure 16.1).

Applied psychology is at work when

- an *industrial psychologist* advises a corporation about improvements in the selection of employees
- an *organizational psychologist* develops a plan for company restructuring that can facilitate communication and productivity
- an *engineering (or human factors) psychologist* designs a piece of equipment that helps workers perform their jobs more effectively
- a *forensic psychologist* conducts research on witness testimony and serves as a consultant to an attorney
- a *sport psychologist* works with professional athletes to improve their confidence and reduce their performance anxiety

*F*IGURE 16.1
Settings in Which Psychologists Work

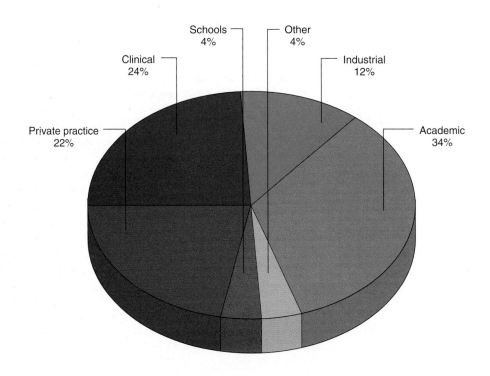

- an *educational psychologist* gives psychological tests to a child who is having problems in school and consults with his teachers and parents about ways to improve his academic performance

INDUSTRIAL/ORGANIZATIONAL PSYCHOLOGY

Work is what most of us will do at least half of our waking hours for more than 40 years of our lives. **Industrial/organizational (I/O) psychology** *is the branch of psychology that focuses on the workplace—both its workers and the organization that employs them—to make work more enjoyable and productive.* I/O psychology is commonly partitioned into industrial psychology, organizational psychology, and human factors (engineering) psychology.

Industrial Psychology

Industrial psychology *is the subdivision of I/O psychology that involves personnel and human resource management. This includes job analysis, selection of employees, performance appraisal, and training.* Industrial psychology is increasingly referred to as *personnel psychology*. Let's explore each of these dimensions of industrial psychology.

Job Analysis.   Virtually all personnel functions stem from job analysis, which helps determine which candidates to hire as well as how to train and evaluate them. By carefully conducting a job analysis and then using the results to guide personnel decisions, industrial psychologists increase the likelihood that they will give all job applicants (regardless of race, religion, national origin, sex, and so on) equal employment opportunities.

The important steps in conducting a job analysis include these:

1. Identify the job's component tasks and behaviors. For example, some of the component tasks of a sales job with a medical equipment company might be communication with doctors and nurses, working long hours, coping with stressful circumstances, and learning at a high level of competence.
2. Specify the skills, abilities, and knowledge needed to carry out the tasks and behaviors. Standardized tests are often used as part of this step.
3. Based on the first two steps, generate a job description that can be used for hiring and training.

Selection of Employees.   Industrial psychologists use many different selection tools to pick the right person for the right job. Among the most widely used personnel selection tools are application forms, psychological tests, interviews, and work sample tests.

Psychological tests used by industrial psychologists include general aptitude tests (such as IQ tests), specific aptitude tests (such as those designed to assess mechanical ability, clerical ability, or spatial relations), personality tests (such as the Minnesota Multiphasic Personality Inventory [MMPI], and vocational inventories (like the Strong Interest Inventory).

Currently, there is considerable interest in whether psychological tests based on the "big five" factors (emotional stability, extraversion, openness, agreeableness, and conscientiousness) that were discussed in chapter 10 can predict job success. The two measures that most often are used to assess the big five factors as predictors of job success are the Revised NEO Personality Inventory developed by Paul Costa and Robert McRae (1992), and the Hogan Personality Inventory (HPI), created by Robert Hogan (1986). The jury is still out on how successfully these "big five" measures can predict job success. Researchers have recently found that the HPI does predict such job performance criteria as supervisor ratings and training course success (Wiggins & Trapnell, 1997).

Interviews are often given special weight in hiring decisions (Barber & others, 1994). Interviewers can be especially good at evaluating a candidate's interpersonal and communication skills. Interviews that are structured and focus on specifics rather than generalities are the most successful at selecting employees who eventually perform well. To read about some good strategies to use when interviewing for a job, see Improving Personal and Cognitive Skills.

industrial/organizational (I/O) psychology

The branch of psychology that focuses on the workplace—both its workers and the organization that employs them—to make work more enjoyable and productive.

industrial psychology

The subdivision of I/O psychology that involves personnel and human resource management. This includes job analysis, selection of employees, performance appraisal, and training.

Improving Personal and Cognitive Skills

Knock 'Em Dead in an Interview

Martin Yate (1999) recommends some good strategies for handling a job interview:

- *Be prepared to give detailed examples of your past experiences.*
  Employers figure that your past performance is a good predictor of what you will do if they hire you. Make a list of your best past experiences, work- and non-work-related, and be prepared to describe them.
- *Put together a great resume.*
  If you don't have a resume, make one. Employers use resumes to decide whether they want to interview you in the first place. Make sure the resume is very organized. Write it clearly and don't use jargon.
- *Do your homework before the interview.*
  Don't just "wing" the interview. Find out as much about the prospective employer as possible. Employers are impressed by applicants who have taken the time to learn about their company.
- *Try to figure out what questions you will be asked and practice answering them.*
  Some typical interview questions are these:
  "What are your greatest strengths?"
  "Why should I hire you?"
  "What motivates you?"

Also, be prepared for some zingers like these:
"What is your greatest weakness?"
"Tell me something you did that you are not proud of."

- *Put together some questions of your own.*
  Ask some detailed questions about the nature of the job, the people you will be working with, what the expectations for the job are, and so on.
- *Always stay cool.*
  No matter how stressful the interview is, be polite and mannerly.
- *Show your interest in the job, if you want it.*
  At the end of the interview, decide whether you want the job. If you do want it, clearly express your interest in it. If the job is not offered at that point, ask when the two of you can talk again.
- *Send a follow-up letter.*
  Type up a letter immediately after the interview if the job interests you. Make it short, less than a page. Mail it within a day after the interview. If you don't hear anything within a week, call the organization and ask about the job's status.

Performance Appraisal. A performance appraisal involves a systematic description of an employee's strengths and weaknesses. *Systematic* is a key word here because performance appraisal can be biased if it is not systematic. Performance appraisal is an emotion-laden topic. Few of us relish being corrected, no matter how much truth the criticism holds and no matter how tactfully the criticism is delivered. However, industrial psychologists can develop appropriate performance criteria that can be used to reinforce effective work behavior and provide incentives to set new goals for future performance.

Training. More than 90 percent of the private corporations in the United States conduct some form of employee training. Training is often used to bring newly hired employees up to a level where they can function competently in the job. As technological advances continue, training will be necessary to prevent worker obsolescence. Industrial psychologists can determine how employers' needs will change and design retraining strategies to keep the workforce responsive to such changes (Nichols, McHugh, & McHugh, 1996).

Performance appraisal, like all other personnel practices, is subject to legal constraints. It is illegal to discriminate against an employee on the basis of race, color, creed, national origin, or sex. One way to minimize the potential for illegal discrimination is to base performance appraisals on actual job behaviors (*He failed to reach his production quotas in 10 out of 12 months*) rather than vague, global judgments (*She is a cold person who hurts the company's image*).

Organizational Psychology

organizational psychology
The subfield of I/O psychology that examines the social and group influences in an organization.

Organizational psychology *is the subfield of I/O psychology that examines the social and group influences in an organization.* Organizational psychologists deal with such issues as changes in the nature of the workforce, changes in the company's organizational structure, diversification of a product line, changes in workers' schedules, and modification of workspace. Among organizational psychology's areas of study are job satisfaction, motivation, communication, and changes in the organization.

Job Satisfaction.   Imagine what type of job you will have 15 years from now. What will it take for the job to satisfy you? Many factors are involved in job satisfaction, including organizational factors such as pay, promotion opportunities, and rewards intrinsic to the work itself. Job satisfaction also includes group factors such as how much you like your coworkers and supervisor (Robbins, 1996).

Organizational psychologists know that it is important for workers to be satisfied with their job, because those who are dissatisfied miss more work and are more likely to seek employment elsewhere. Also, job satisfaction is related to age. Job satisfaction increases steadily through an individual's work life, on the average—from age 20 to at least age 60 (Rhodes, 1983). Satisfaction probably increases with age because as we get older we get paid more, have higher-status positions, and have more job security. Organizational psychologists advise management about how these and other factors affect workers' job satisfaction.

Motivation.   An important task in the work world is to figure out how to motivate employees to do their best work possible. Organizational psychologists often use behavior modification strategies to improve worker productivity and morale. The reinforcements or incentives they typically recommend include bonuses, awards, time off, promotions, and praise. For example, an organizational psychologist might suggest that the company designate someone as "employee of the month." Recently, some organizational psychologists have recommended that their companies consider flextime arrangements for employees, a strategy that serves some employees' needs without increasing the employer's costs.

Another aspect of motivation that interests organizational psychologists is whether workers are more productive and happy when they work individually or in groups. Historically, Americans have worked individually. By contrast, employees in many Eastern countries, such as China, Japan, and Korea, have traditionally worked as teams. To read further about the team-oriented Japanese style of management that is often used in the United States, see Sociocultural Worlds. Interestingly, though, because of changes in productivity and labor-market conditions in the last decade, Japanese firms have increasingly studied how American businesses work.

Communication.   The field of business recognizes the growing importance of communication (Lussier, 1996). Surveys of major corporations suggest that effective communication is the main reason executives get promoted. Yet there are 25 million people in the workforce who cannot read or write. Another 35 million have reading skills that are so weak they cannot even read the simplest of written instructions. AT&T spends $6 million a year on getting its workers to have minimal reading skills.

A leading authority on managerial behavior, William Haney (1986), believes that a common problem occurs when communicators miss each other's meanings. Consider the following humorous examples of cloudy communication:

- A Peruvian manager received a cable from his boss in the United States. The cable read: "Send me factory and office head count broken down by sex." The reply went like this: "249 in factory, 30 in office, 3 on sick leave, none broken down by sex—our problem is with alcohol."
- Sign over a greasy-spoon diner: Eat Here and Get Gas.

Sociocultural Worlds

Nenko Management in Japan

In the past several decades, Americans have become very interested in the Japanese style of management called Nenko, which emphasizes group decision making by consensus. Approximately 30 percent of Japan's manufacturing companies practice Nenko. This management approach consists of three basic strategies: articulate a unique company philosophy, engage employees in extensive socialization, and view the organization as an internal labor market (Havatny & Pucik, 1981; Oh, 1976).

Employees are hired soon after they graduate and generally remain in Nenko organizations throughout their careers. Nenko companies go to great lengths to establish a "family" atmosphere. Employees not only work together, they often live together in company housing, vacation at company resorts, and socialize at company centers. Young employees are selected on the basis of not only their technical qualifications but also the ease with which they can be assimilated, or "fit" into the organization.

Employees dedicate their service and loyalty to the company. In their first several years of work, employees rotate into different jobs at the same level in an organization so they can learn various aspects of the business and get to know their co-workers. This strategy helps socialize employees to the company's culture and philosophy. Their early salaries are meager, but they receive other forms of economic subsidy from the company to support them until their salaries grow.

Nenko organizations use a number of specific techniques to support their objectives (Havatny & Pucik, 1981). Employers assign tasks to work teams, not to individuals; managers evaluate group performance rather than individual performance. They base individual salary appraisals on the quality of group performance. Not surprisingly, Japanese workers usually develop a strong group identity. Subtle pressures encourage Nenko workers to seek friendships in the organization. Managers spend considerable time talking with employees about personal concerns, providing housing assistance, suggesting recreational activities, and sometimes even assisting in arranging marriage. Such strategies help the firm's management convey its concern for the employee's welfare; in return, employees become committed to the organization.

However, the Nenko approach has its critics. The approach blatantly discriminates against women, who are considered only temporary employees and are paid at substantially lower rates. Nenko employees retire at age 55. If they stay on the job longer, their pay is also cut dramatically (Oh, 1976). Employment in a Nenko company is difficult to secure and depends on the appropriateness of the candidate's educational track, which might begin as early as preschool. Critics suggest that

Nenko promotes conformity at the expense of individual creativity. They also argue that Nenko might not be the real cause of Japan's economic success, since it is found only in the major Japanese firms: many small companies cannot afford the luxury of hiring employees for life. Critics argue that Japan's meteoric economic rise also has been fueled by postwar reconstruction, a close alliance between government and business, a strong sense of nationalism and a strong cultural tradition of duty, obedience, and discipline (Steers, 1988).

Nenko advocates argue that its basic strategies can help American organizations improve their performance. The approach has been successfully applied in some American firms, such as Rockwell International, an aerospace firm, and Eli Lilly, a pharmaceutical company. Despite the criticisms, Nenko will have considerable value for certain firms, although others might function more effectively using different management approaches (Lincoln & Kalleberg, 1990). This may be especially true of companies that operate in individualistic cultural contexts, which focus on individual achievement, rather than collectivist contexts, which foster collaboration and group pride. As we approach the twenty-first century, global economic interdependence will emphasize three features of successful workers (Brislin, 1993): (1) awareness of impending changes and the cultural contexts in which they occur; (2) awareness of knowledge that will help them adapt; and (3) skill in dealing with conflicts and emotional confrontations in resolving problems among diverse peoples.

In Japan—a collectivistic culture—the management style emphasizes group and consensual decision making, and Japanese management engages employees in extensive socialization.

- "Wanted: Man to handle dynamite. Must travel unexpectedly."
- "For sale: Large Great Dane. Registered pedigree. Will eat anything. Especially fond of children."

One of communication's great lessons is to be *clear and concise.* The Lord's Prayer is 56 words, the Gettysburg Address is 266 words. The Pentagon produced sixteen single-spaced pages of specifications for a simple plastic whistle used by military police and drill sergeants. Government officials say they have simplified the tax code, yet volumes of incomprehensible tax rulings fill libraries.

Communication is one of the keys to any successful relationship—whether between marital partners, parents and children, management and workers, or simply between workers. When communication is inefficient or breaks down, so does the quality of the organization.

In a recent survey of its members by the National Association of College Employers (Collins, 1996), communication skills were at the top of employers' lists of important employee skills. Indeed, the top three items on the employers' wish list all involved communication skills: (1) oral communication skills, (2) interpersonal skills, and (3) teamwork skills. According to the survey, employers also want candidates to be proficient in their field, have leadership and analytical skills, and be flexible. Organizational psychologists can offer on-site training to improve these skills or consult directly with employees who are considered to be deficient in these areas. To read about some strategies for becoming a good communicator, see Improving Personal and Cognitive Skills.

The Changing Places and Faces of Organizations.   What jobs will be more plentiful in the future? What will the workplace be like as we move into the twenty-first century? Expect changes in jobs, the organization, and the worker.

Tomorrow's Jobs.   The long-term shift from goods-producing to service-producing employment will continue. By the year 2000, nearly 4 of 5 jobs will be in industries that provide services, such as banking, insurance, health care, education, data processing, and management consulting. Jobs that require the most education and training will be the fastest growing and highest paying. The Self-Assessment gives you an opportunity to determine whether your career interests are in areas with the fastest-growing jobs.

*I*mproving Personal and Cognitive Skills

Becoming a Skilled Communicator

Following are some strategies for effective communication:

- *Talk "with" not "to" the other person.*
  Don't hog conversations. Making a speech to another person is not having a conversation.
- *Be an active listener.*
  Pay careful attention to the person who is talking. This shows the person that you are interested in what he or she has to say. Maintain good eye contact with the person, at least in mainstream American culture.
- *Use "I" rather than "you" messages.*
  Examples of "you" messages: *"You* always are so critical" and *"You* let me down." "You" messages communicate that the speaker is qualified to judge the listener. "I" messages

are less provocative. For example, you might say, *"I'm* angry about being criticized so much" and *"I'm* disappointed that I didn't get more support." "I" statements express your feelings without judging the other person.
- *Use positive nonverbal behavior.*
  Realize that communication has both verbal and nonverbal channels. Whether you smile or frown, for instance, communicates just as much as the words you say.
- *Know the barriers to effective communication.*
  Some barriers to effective communication include criticizing ("It's your fault"), name-calling or putting down the other person ("You idiot"), ordering ("Go get that pizza right now!"), and threatening or trying to control the other person ("If you don't clean up your desk, I'm not going to help you with your report").

$\mathcal{S}$elf-Assessment

Do Your Career Interests Match the Fastest-Growing Jobs?

Instructions

The occupations listed below are the fastest growing in the United States. They are arranged by education level. The first column has occupations that are growing at the fastest rate of increase.

The second column has occupations that are growing the fastest numerically. Place a check next to any occupations that interest you, then evaluate how seriously you might be considering a career in these fastest-growing areas.

Occupations growing at the fastest (percentage) rates | Occupations having the biggest increases in total number of jobs

First-professional degree

☐ Chiropractors ☐ Lawyers
☐ Lawyers ☐ Physicians
☐ Physicians ☐ Clergy
☐ Clergy ☐ Chiropractors
☐ Podiatrists ☐ Dentists

Doctoral degree

☐ Medical scientists ☐ College and university faculty
☐ Biological scientists ☐ Biological scientists
☐ College and university faculty ☐ Medical scientists
☐ Mathematicians and all other mathematical scientists ☐ Mathematicians and all other mathematical scientists

Master's degree

☐ Operations research analysts ☐ Management analysts
☐ Speech-language pathologists and audiologists ☐ Counselors
☐ Management analysts ☐ Speech-language pathologists and audiologists
☐ Counselors ☐ Psychologists
☐ Urban and regional planners ☐ Operations research analysts

Work experience plus bachelor's degree

☐ Engineering, mathematics, and natural science managers ☐ General managers and top executives
☐ Marketing, advertising, and public relations managers ☐ Financial managers
☐ Artists and commercial artists ☐ Marketing, advertising, and public relations managers
☐ Financial managers ☐ Engineering, mathematics, and natural science managers
☐ Education administrators ☐ Education administrators

Bachelor's degree

☐ Systems analysts ☐ Systems analysts
☐ Computer engineers ☐ Teachers, secondary school
☐ Occupational therapists ☐ Teachers, elementary school
☐ Physical therapists ☐ Teachers, special education
☐ Special education teachers ☐ Social workers

Associate degree

☐ Paralegals ☐ Registered nurses
☐ Medical records technicians ☐ Paralegals
☐ Dental hygienists ☐ Radiologic technologists and technicians
☐ Respiratory therapists ☐ Dental hygienists
☐ Radiologic technologists and technicians ☐ Medical records technicians

SOURCE: *Occupational Outlook Handbook*, 1996–1997, table 1, p. 7.

Employers especially recommend that students do the following during their college years:

- Get work-related experience
- Be involved in some extracurricular activities on or off campus
- Get good grades
- Develop good computer skills

Students can get positive work experiences during college by participating in cooperative education programs, internships, or part-time or summer work relevant to their field of study.

Changing Organizations.   Organizations themselves also will change. Many companies are "downsizing" to improve profits. Mergers and acquisitions also displace workers with increasing regularity. In addition, more businesses are expanding their international operations. This means that the success of many companies increasingly will depend on the ability of employees to communicate effectively with people from diverse backgrounds.

Many jobs also are becoming more complex and cognitively demanding. As knowledge increases, technically trained workers, such as engineers, face a "half-life" of 5 years. That is, half of what engineers know in any given year will be obsolete 5 years later because of rapid technological advances. This means that continuing education and retraining of workers will increase.

Millions of workers center their lives on the workplace. Heads of organizations realize that the workplace is an important setting for promoting health and well-being. Consequently, many companies have established programs to help workers balance work and family and promote health through fitness centers and stress management programs.

Gender and Ethnicity.   In the year 2000, workers will be more culturally diverse. One-third of all new entrants into the labor force will be ethnic minorities. Larger numbers of women will enter the workforce, putting increased pressure on society to help balance the demands of work and family (Schein & others, 1996).

In the 1980s there emerged the concept of the "glass ceiling," a subtle barrier that is virtually transparent yet prevents women and ethnic minorities from moving up the management ladder (Morrison & von Glinow, 1990). Today women fill nearly one-third of all management positions, an improvement of almost 20 percent since 1972. However, only 2 percent of all senior executives are women. The picture for ethnic minorities is even more dismal. Only one African American heads a Fortune 1000 company.

Many organizational psychologists believe that the workplace needs to adjust to accommodate women and ethnic minorities. Eastman Kodak and Dupont are two companies that have implemented programs to help managers diversify their workforce and reduce discrimination. The companies invested in special recruiting initiatives and offer

Many organizational psychologists believe that the workplace needs to adjust to better accommodate women and ethnic minorities. One training strategy of some corporations is to provide support groups for recruiting women and ethnic minorities and socializing them about the culture of the organization. *Can you think of other strategies?*

Diane Keaton (*above*) lost her job when she couldn't find a way to juggle her career and family roles and still give her child adequate care and attention in the movie *Baby Boom.* Some individuals are turning down higher-paying jobs to take jobs with more flexibility. The increased trend toward flexibility appears in *The Corporate Reference Guide to Work-Family Programs* that was released in 1991—of the 188 Fortune 1000 companies surveyed, 77 percent reported that they have instituted flexible scheduling, and 48 percent offer job sharing.

ongoing diversity sensitivity training to promote effective collaboration. One value of such programs is that issues are brought out in the open, allowing individuals to express their perspectives on diversity issues.

Support groups can help increase the number of women and ethnic minorities in management. For example, in Washington, D.C., the Executive Leadership Council is made up of fifty African American managers who recruit and hire ethnic minorities. Such support groups provide career guidance and psychological support for women and ethnic minorities who seek management positions.

The future is not entirely bleak for women, because they are advancing the fastest in "cutting-edge" industries like computers, finance, and advertising. The reasons for this rapid advancement are that (1) there was no time to establish old rules, or the old rules that favored males don't apply because the "game" has changed so much, and (2) the types of jobs now being created are different. American women have filled two-third of the millions of new jobs in the information and service industries in the last two decades. This type of work is not done on an assembly line and can't be managed as if it were. Historically, management has been masculine in orientation, with an emphasis on independence and power. Leadership in the information and services industries has often not followed this masculine orientation. Rather, it often has emphasized a facilitative role for leaders that involves building worker loyalty and developing positive relationships.

So far, we have seen how I/O psychologists are involved in personnel and human resource management, as well as improving human relations in organizations. As you will see next, there is yet another aspect of work where psychologists make contributions.

Human Factors Psychology

human factors psychology
The subdivision of I/O psychology that focuses on the design of machines that workers use to perform their jobs, and the environment in which humans function, to make it safer and more efficient.

Human factors psychology *is the subdivision of I/O psychology that focuses on the design of machines that workers use to perform their jobs, and the environment in which humans function, to make it safer and more efficient.* For example, your driving behavior is influenced by I/O psychologists who assisted in designing the instrument panel so that knobs and controls are easy to use and visual displays can be easily read.

Human factors psychologists spend considerable time determining the most appropriate displays to use (Payne, Lang, & Blackwell, 1995). One of the initial decisions they have to make is which sensory modality to use. Typically, displays are visual. However, depending on the situation and the information that needs to be monitored, auditory and tactile displays might be used. Consider the routine operation of a car. You get visual feedback about the speed at which you are driving, the temperature of the engine, and the oil pressure. You might hear a beeping sound if a door is not completely closed. You might latch your seatbelt just to escape the annoying sound of a buzzer. Or consider

What are some of the important considerations that human factors psychologists give attention to in work performance?

airplane design. The landing flap controls on many airplanes are shaped like the landing flaps themselves, so that pilots can manage the controls without looking at them. Figure 16.2 shows a number of shape-coded controls. All of these designs take into account how to provide information without interfering with the task.

An important human factors concern is how consistently controls are designed from one machine to the next. In World War II, the United States was losing more planes to human error than to enemy fire. The arrangement of displays and controls in the cockpits of different aircraft were inconsistent. When pilots who had learned to fly one particular type of plane were assigned to fly a different type of plane, they were confronted with a different cockpit layout. For example, the lever used to raise the wheels in a new plane might be in the same place as the lever to operate the flaps in the old one. This is the equivalent of switching the clutch and the brake pedal in you car—imagine the problems this would cause you. Fortunately, manufacturers standardized the positions for most controls in recent years. For instance, the light switches are located in similar places on most cars. And human factors psychologists are involved in designing and standardizing the most effective displays and keyboards for computers.

𝓕IGURE 16.2

Shape-Coded Controls

Controls need to be clearly coded to assure their correct and rapid identification. One way to accomplish this is to shape code the controls. Each knob on a console might be a recognizably different shape, which allows for rapid visual identification of the correct control. It also allows tactual identification in the dark or when the operator's eyes must focus somewhere else. An effective way of shape coding controls is to design the control so that its shape represents or symbolizes its function.

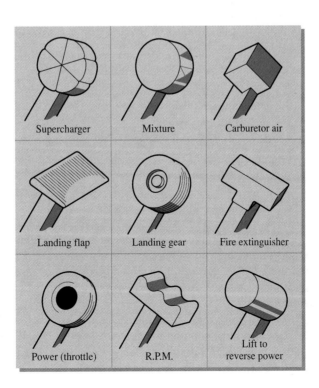

I/O psychologists are specialists in the business environment. As you will see next, the physical setting of business is but one of many environments that interest environmental psychologists.

*R*eview

The Nature of Applied Psychology and Industrial/Organizational Psychology

Applied psychology is the field that uses psychological principles to improve the lives of human beings and solve human problems. Among the areas of applied psychology are industrial/organizational psychology, environmental psychology, forensic psychology, sport psychology, and educational psychology.

Industrial/organizational (I/O) psychology is the branch of applied psychology that focuses on the workplace—both its workers and the organization that

employs them. Industrial psychology is the subdivision of I/O psychology that involves personnel and human resource management. This includes job analysis, selection of employees, performance appraisal, and training.

Organizational psychology is the subfield of I/O psychology that examines the social and group influences in an organization. Organizational psychology's areas of study include job satisfaction, motivation, communication, and changes in the orga-

nization. Changes in organizations include more jobs in service-related industries and an increasingly diverse labor force.

Human factors psychology is the subdivision of I/O psychology that focuses on the design of machines that workers use to perform their jobs and the environment in which humans function, to make it safer and more efficient. Human factors psychologists spend considerable time determining the most appropriate displays to use.

ENVIRONMENTAL PSYCHOLOGY

Environmental psychology explores the physical setting of all other areas discussed in this book, including perception, cognition, learning, development, personality, abnormal behavior, and social relations. Whether we are looking, thinking, learning, talking to a friend, working, or walking in the woods, we do it in a physical setting. Everything we do is in either a built or a natural environment. **Environmental psychology** *is the study of transactions between people and the physical environment.*

environmental psychology

The study of transactions between people and the physical environment.

> We shape our buildings and afterwards our buildings shape us.
> —Winston Churchill, *English Statesman and Writer, 20th Century*

The topics that environmental psychologists study include these:

- How different building and room arrangements influence behavior
- The characteristics of preferred landscapes
- Strategies for navigating in various environmental arrangements
- The psychological impact of pollution
- How crowding affects behavior
- The effects of noise and light on behavior

Let's examine several of these topics, beginning with a look at how noise affects behavior.

Noise

Noise is a significant environmental influence on behavior. Usually noise has little effect on us when it is at a low volume or when we are doing simple, routine tasks. However, under some conditions noise can annoy us and disrupt our behavior (Nivison & Endresen, 1993). For example, noise at irregular intervals annoys us more than noise at predictable intervals. Also, noise is especially bothersome when we can't do anything to control it.

Too often in today's urban environments we don't have control over noise. This was the case with some children living in a New York City high-rise apartment building right next to a busy highway (Cohen, Glass, & Singer, 1973). Children who lived on the bottom floors (and were exposed to a high level of noise) did considerably worse on reading tests than children living on the upper floors did (who were exposed too a much lower level of noise). In another study, children who lived in the air corridor of the Los Angeles International Airport were compared with children who lived in a quieter neighborhood away from the air corridor (Cohen & others, 1981). Every day, more than 300 jets roared over the children in the air corridor. The children in this high-noise air corridor had higher blood pressure and were more easily distracted on tasks than their counterparts who lived in the low-noise neighborhood.

Density and Crowding

Human beings continue to populate the earth in ever increasing numbers. The result is that many parts of our planet have become very densely populated. In one recent study, the strongest and most consistent predictor of whether a person would help someone else in thirty-six U.S. cities was population density (Levine & others, 1994). The lower the population density, the more likely people were to help a blind person, return a dropped pen, or give to United Way.

Nonetheless, some cultures have to live with high density. Hong Kong's density is about four times that of downtown Toronto. However, Hong Kong's crime rate is about one-fourth of Toronto's and Toronto has a low crime rate by North American standards. After centuries of living together in close proximity, the Chinese have learned to interact with each other without raising tensions.

In many cases, though, density can harm a person's health, increase aggression, and poison social interactions (Gifford, 1987). As density increases in prisons, discipline problems and death rates go up (Paulus, McCain, & Cox, 1981). At colleges, students who live in densely populated dorms (ones with long corridors that have common bathrooms and

The Favella slum in Rio de Janeiro. Residential crowding is one of the many topics that environmental psychologists study. *How are density and crowding related?*

lounge facilities) are more socially withdrawn and perceive themselves as having less control than students in less crowded dorms (with smaller suites and private bathrooms) (Baum & Valins, 1977).

Environmental psychologists make a distinction between density and crowding (Veitch & Arkkelin, 1995). **Density** *refers to the number of people per unit area.* **Crowding** *is the psychological experience that others are too close.* Usually, when density (the objective measure) is high, crowding (the psychological measure) also is high. However, density and crowding do not always go hand in hand. Many people don't think it is a good party unless the guests are all crammed in together. By contrast, sometimes people feel crowded when density is low, as when we must ride fifty floors in a large, otherwise empty elevator with someone we detest.

> *The thing that in the subway is called congestion is highly esteemed in the night club as intimacy.*
>
> —SIMEON STRUNSKY, *Russian-Born American Author, 20th Century*

An important aspect of understanding crowding is how much control people perceive themselves as having over the situation they are in. The less control they perceive themselves as having, the more stressful they find their densely packed surroundings. For example, if we think that we can leave the crowded conditions at any point, we feel less stress than if we think we can't leave.

Environmental Damage

In the twentieth century, our planet's natural resources are decreasing and the planet has become more polluted. Tropical and temperate rain forests are being depleted. And too often we act if our planet were a huge garbage pail—as if we could endlessly dump toxic wastes and litter into without harming it. How can we get people to treat the planet better?

<div class="sidebar">

density

The number of people per unit area.

crowding

The psychological experience that others are too close.

Our planet's natural resources are diminishing as the built environment takes over more of the natural environment's space. *What are some strategies for getting people to engage in less environmentally damaging behavior?*

</div>

Most people agree that people should not pollute the environment and squander its resources. However, their behavior does not always match their professed beliefs. So, one strategy is to arouse awareness of cognitive dissonance in people by getting them to understand that they are not practicing what they are preaching. For example, some people say that they should not throw trash out the window of a car but do it anyway. Getting these people to be aware that their professed beliefs and their actions don't match up may help. Another strategy is try to get people to understand that their environment-damaging behavior is not socially acceptable. That is, get them to become aware that a large majority of the people believe that what they are doing is wrong.

As a society, we have become increasingly interested in environmental issues. However, nothing in recent years matches our fascination for legal matters. Next, we explore the intriguing psychological aspects of the legal system.

eview

Environmental Psychology

Environmental psychology is the study of transactions between people and the physical environment. Environmental psychology explores the physical setting of all other topics discussed in this book, ranging from perception to social relations.

One area of study in environmental psychology is noise, which is unwanted sound. Noise affects our behavior negatively when we are engaging in complex tasks, when it occurs at irregular intervals, and when we perceive that we cannot control it. Too often in today's urban environments, people perceive themselves as powerless to control noise.

Density is the objective measure of how many people are in a unit area. In many cases, high density can harm a person's health, increase aggression, and poison social interactions. Crowding is the psychological experience that others are too close to us. Usually, density and crowding are closely related, but not always. As with noise, perceived control is an important factor in understanding crowding.

An important concern of many environmental psychologists is how to change environmentally damaging behavior. Two strategies are to increase awareness of cognitive dissonance between professed beliefs and behavior, and to get people to understand that their environmentally damaging behavior is not acceptable to the vast majority of people.

FORENSIC PSYCHOLOGY

forensic psychology

The area of psychology that applies psychological concepts to the legal system.

The field of **forensic psychology** *applies psychological concepts to the legal system.* In the trials of O. J. Simpson, Timothy McVeigh, and less famous suspects, the research and knowledge of forensic psychologists is at work in many ways. Social and cognitive psychologists increasingly conduct research on topics related to psychology and the law. And forensic psychologists increasingly are hired by legal teams to provide input about many aspects of a trial. In chapter 6, we discussed eyewitness identification, one of forensic psychology's many domains, in an Applications in Psychology box. Following are some of the other activities of forensic psychologists:

- Conducting research on the role of defendants' characteristics in determining conviction
- Providing input about which potential jurors to select
- Analyzing the nonverbal behavior of jurors to assess their attitude toward the defendant
- Conducting research with mock juries to see what factors influence juries' decisions
- Testifying as expert witnesses

Let's explore these areas of forensic psychology further: characteristics of defendants and juries; the jury in action; and psychologists as expert witnesses.

Characteristics of Defendants and Juries

Just because they have certain characteristics some defendants are more likely to be acquitted in a trial than others. In the United States, with other factors being equal, low-income, poorly educated, ethnic minority persons are more likely to be convicted than are higher-income, better educated White persons. Unattractive defendants are more likely to be convicted than attractive ones (Nemeth, 1981). Also, low-income individuals are more likely to be given harsh sentences than are higher-income persons. Another inequity in the legal system is that defendants who have very high incomes can hire expensive legal experts who have high rates of success in getting clients acquitted. Defendants from low-income backgrounds do not have this access. As a consequence, a disproportionate percentage of prison inmates are low-income persons.

Jury members with certain characteristics are more likely to convict defendants and recommend harsher sentencing. Jurors who are White, older, better educated, higher in social status, and politically conservative fit this profile.

> *A jury consists of twelve persons chosen to decide who has the best lawyer.*
> —ROBERT FROST, *American Poet, 20th Century*

The match between the juror and the defendant plays a role in whether the juror will vote for conviction and harsher sentencing. Whites are more likely to be kinder to Whites, African Americans to African Americans, and so on. More-affluent jurors are more likely to give affluent defendants a break, just as jurors from low-income backgrounds are less likely to convict poor people. Forensic psychologists counsel attorneys about which potential jurors should be challenged during what is called *voir dire* (jury selection).

The Jury System in Action

The jury system has a long tradition in American law, and every person has a right to be tried by a jury. In recent years, the jury system has been in the media spotlight, especially in cases like the O. J. Simpson trial. Of the millions of Americans who watched the Simpson trial on television, many formed strong opinions about whether the jurors' verdict of not guilty was fair or biased. Few people argue that the jury system should be abolished, but it is not a perfect system. According to psychological research, there are many reasons why juries might not always reach the right verdict (Aronson, Wison, & Akert, 1997). As we see next, these reasons include the media and pretrial publicity.

The Media and Pretrial Publicity. The media play an important role in trials. They usually get most of their information from the police and the district attorney, who want to convict the defendant. Not surprisingly, these sources give the media the strongest possible indication that the defendant is guilty, and this is the information that the media gives the public. Researchers have found that the more information people get about a case from the media, the more likely they are to believe that the defendant is guilty (Otto, Penrod, & Dexter, 1994).

Lawyers usually ask potential jurors if they have heard anything about the case and, if so, whether they believe that they can still render a fair verdict. Judges can instruct juries to disregard what they have heard in the media. And in some cases, judges isolate juries until the trial is over. The best situation is to have jurors who have heard nothing about the case, but in high-profile cases, such as those of O. J. Simpson, Timothy McVeigh, and Theodore Kaczynski, that is virtually impossible.

Making Judgments and Decisions. Forensic psychologists conduct research to try to determine which factors influence the verdict in a trial. Many jurors form opinions early about whether a defendant is innocent or guilty. They often make this judgment before they hear all of the evidence.

Once jurors begin their deliberations, they try to reach a consensus by discussing, arguing, and bargaining. In the O. J. Simpson criminal trial, one juror voted guilty but quickly changed her mind. This is a common tendency in jury deliberations. As we saw

According to many legal analysts, the turning point in the murder trial was when the gloves appeared not to fit O. J. Simpson.

in chapter 14, pressures to conform can be strong. Most jurors can eventually bring dissenting jurors to their side.

Even if dissenting jurors seldom can sway the majority about a defendant's guilt or innocence, they might be able to change the majority's view of the degree of guilt. For example, if a jury decision is guilty, several dissenting jurors might be able to persuade the majority to vote for second-degree instead of first-degree murder. Forensic psychologists are often called on after a verdict is made public to help explain the group dynamics behind the decision.

Psychologists as Expert Witnesses

Psychologists serve as expert witnesses in the courtroom. Legal topics about which psychologists might testify include these (Nietzel & Dillehay, 1986):

*   *Insanity defense.* Psychologists regularly evaluate a defendant's mental condition at the time of the alleged offense. They also might judge the degree to which the defendant is responsible for the crime.
*   *Competency to stand trial.* Psychologists testify to whether a defendant has an adequate understanding of the legal proceedings.
*   *Civil commitment.* Psychologists decide whether a defendant with a mental disorder presents an immediate danger or threat of danger to self or others. This type of evaluation can influence whether the person is deemed to require treatment or not.
*   *Psychological damages in civil cases.* Psychologists make judgments about what psychological damages an individual has suffered because of another's harmful conduct.
*   *Negligence and product liability.* Psychologists testify about how environmental and perceptual factors affect a person's use of a product or ability to take precautions in its use.
*   *Class action suits.* Psychologists judge whether people are being discriminated against in schools and the workplace because of their sex, race, age, and so on.
*   *Guardianship and conservatorship.* Psychologists evaluate whether a person has the mental ability to make decisions about her or his living conditions.
*   *Child custody.* Psychologists recommend which parent to award custody to, or whether joint custody is desirable.

As can be seen, psychologists serve as expert witnesses about a wide range of matters involving human behavior.

eview

Forensic Psychology

Forensic psychology applies psychological concepts to the legal system. Social psychologists and cognitive psychologists conduct research on psychology and the law. Also, forensic psychologists are increasingly hired by legal teams to provide input about many aspects of a trial.

Characteristics of defendants and jurors affect jury decision making. Defendants from low-income, poorly educated, ethnic minority backgrounds, as well as unattractive defendants, are more likely to be convicted. White, older, better educated, higher social status, and politi-

cally conservative jurors are more likely to vote for conviction and harsher sentencing. The match between the juror and the defendant plays a role in whether the juror votes for conviction: The greater the similarity, the less likely a vote of conviction.

The media play a prominent role in trials. The more information people get from the media, the more likely they are to say a defendant is guilty, probably because the media get much of their information from the police and the district attorney. Many jurors form early

judgments about the defendant's guilt or innocence, before all of the evidence is presented. The pressures to conform are strong in jury deliberation, and the majority of jurors usually can bring the minority of jurors to their side.

Psychologists increasingly serve as expert witnesses in the courtroom. They testify about the insanity defense, competency to stand trial, civil commitment, psychological damages in civil cases, negligence and product liability, class action suits, guardianship, and child custody.

Next, we move away from competition in the courtroom to competition in another arena: sports. Sport psychology is a growing specialty in the field of psychology.

SPORT PSYCHOLOGY

Consider the following situations:

- A pro basketball player has lost confidence in his shooting and is in a bad slump.
- A college tennis player becomes overwhelmed with anxiety when a match gets close. Her game starts to deteriorate.
- An amateur golfer is getting ready to play in the club championship, but her putting game is erratic.

What do the pro basketball player, college tennis player, and amateur golfer have in common? Their performance probably would benefit from working with a sport psychologist. **Sport psychology** *is the field that applies psychology's principles to improving sport performance and the enjoyment of sport participation.*

Sport psychology is a relatively new field but is rapidly gaining acceptance. At the 1996 Olympics, more than twenty sport psychologists worked with U.S. athletes and coaches (Murray, 1996). To help athletes maximize their talents, sport psychologists help athletes to

- set goals,
- use mental imagery to enhance performance, and
- practice stress-relieving techniques.

They also help coaches to

- motivate athletes,
- reduce anxiety in their players, and
- communicate more effectively with their athletes.

Improving Sport Performance

Sport psychologists call on a number of techniques to help athletes improve their performance (Pargman, 1998). Many of these techniques come from the field of clinical psychology (especially the cognitive and behavioral therapies) and are adapted to the achievement demands that athletes face. These techniques are often based on the realization that, to do their best, athletes need to concentrate on the task. They need to manage their performance anxiety and keep their emotions in check. Some of the effective techniques they can use to do this are (Singer, 1996):

- *Emphasize the process rather than the outcome.* Legendary Green Bay Packers football coach Vince Lombardi once remarked that "winning isn't everything, it is the *only* thing." Today, however, sport psychologists say that the win-at-all-costs philosophy is not a good one. Too often, athletes focus on winning and losing rather than on the task at hand. Sport psychologists encourage athletes to immerse themselves in what they are doing and not worry so much about the outcome.
- *Use deep breathing and muscle relaxation.* Some athletes get very nervous. As the competition is about to begin, their minds race, their hearts feel like they are about to leap out of their chests, and they perspire profusely. In such cases, sport psychologists often use some form of deep breathing or muscle relaxation technique to help the athletes calm down and concentrate better. In chapter 9, we outlined a series of steps individuals can go through to relax. Indeed, sport psychologists use many of the strategies for coping with stress that we described in chapter 9, such as cognitive restructuring and positive self-talk, and tailor them to improving athletes' performance.
- *Use cognitive restructuring and positive self-talk.* A common problem for athletes in a slump is that they think and say negative things to themselves. A sport psychologist might get them to cognitively restructure their thoughts and words in a more positive direction. Sometimes athletes will exaggerate their recent failures and not look at the big picture. For example, for a baseball player who has been in a hitting slump for 3 weeks, a sport psychologist would get the player to think more about his overall successful batting average for the entire year to help rebuild his confidence.

sport psychology
The field that applies psychology's principles to improving sport performance and the enjoyment of sport participation.

Basketball star Michael Jordan *(left)* and tennis star Martina Hinges *(right)* both are athletes who excel in professional sports. *In addition to their outstanding physical skills, what psychological skills likely help them achieve such high levels of performance under pressure?*

- *Use visualization.* Visualization involves getting an athlete to imagine a positive situation and outcome. The sport psychologist might work with a golfer to visualize the golf ball going in the hole after it is putted, the tennis player to visualize how smooth and fluid her strokes are, and the place kicker in football to visualize the ball going through the goal posts. Sport psychologists sometimes review video clips of the athlete's performances, select only the best performances, and have the athlete watch those clips as part of developing positive visualization.

Enjoying Sport Participation

When athletes don't enjoy the practice and the play of their sport, they can lose their motivation. Tara Scanlan (1996) surveyed more than 2,000 children who were participating in sport and conducted in-depth interviews with many elite athletes to discover what inspires their commitment to a sport. Most of the athletes, regardless of their competition level, told her that enjoyment fueled their motivation and commitment.

Too often parents push their children into sports that the children do not enjoy. The overwhelming anxiety and burnout that some children experience when pushed too hard too early in their lives is a concern of sport psychologists. They seek to help athletes, young and old, to enjoy sport and to use sport as a way of improving the quality of their lives.

eview

Sport Psychology

Sport psychology is the field that applies psychology's principles to improving sport performance and enjoying sport participation. Sport psychology is a relatively new field, but it is rapidly gaining acceptance.

Sport psychologists use a number of techniques to improve sport performance.

These include emphasizing the process rather than the outcome, using deep breathing and muscle relaxation, using cognitive restructuring and positive self-talk, and using visualization.

A special interest of sport psychologists is to help people enjoy their partici-

pation in sports, which includes being vigilant about how hard young athletes are being pushed.

One of the most dramatic differences between secondary schools in the United States and secondary schools in other countries is the extensive emphasis on sport in U.S. schools (Thomas, 1988). Indeed, the United States is the only country in the world in which sports are an integral part of the public school curriculum. Next, we will explore another specialty in the field of psychology, one that focuses on applying psychology to education.

EDUCATIONAL PSYCHOLOGY

Educational psychology *is the field that applies psychological concepts to teaching and learning.* Educational psychologists conduct research, consult with school administrators, and counsel teachers about how to make students' educational experiences more productive and enjoyable. They also might work directly with students to improve their adjustment in school. We will explore several topics that concern educational psychologists: socioeconomic status, ethnicity, and schools; exceptional learners; and learner-centered psychological principles.

Socioeconomic Status, Ethnicity, and Schools

Educational psychologists are on the "front line" in advocating for educational experiences that are equitable for all students regardless of their socioeconomic or ethnic background. Criticisms have been leveled that schools do a much better job of educating children from White, middle-class backgrounds than they do of educating children from ethnic minority, low-income backgrounds. The critics point out that schools have not effectively educated low-income and ethnic minority children to overcome the barriers that block their achievement (Edelman, 1997).

Children from low-income and ethnic minority backgrounds do have more difficulties in school than their middle-class White counterparts. African American and Latino students are much less likely than White or Asian American students to be enrolled in academic, college preparatory programs, and they are much more likely to be enrolled in remedial and special education programs. And completing high school, or even college, has brought less attractive job opportunities for African American and Latino youth than for White youth.

James Comer *(left)* is shown with some of the inner-city African American children who attend a school that became a better learning environment because of Comer's intervention. Comer is convinced that a strong, familylike atmosphere is a key to improving the quality of inner-city schools.

One person who is trying to do something about the poor quality of education for inner-city children is James Comer (1988, 1993). He believes everyone with a stake in a school should have a say in how it is run. Comer is especially concerned about the lack of parental support and involvement in the education of low-income and ethnic minority children. Consequently, his educational model involves creating a family-like environment that provides considerable support for children. He also wants administrators and teachers to make parents feel more comfortable in coming to their children's schools.

The social and academic achievement of children from low-income and ethnic minority backgrounds benefits when schools have

- positive, strong expectations for achievement,
- teachers who are sensitive to sociocultural diversity, and
- positive links with the community,

and when parents have

- positive involvement in their children's education, and
- high expectations for their children's achievement.

Exceptional Learners

exceptional learners

Students who require additional services to meet their individual needs.

Educational psychologists are instrumental not only in designing programs for children with special needs but also in identifying students who might benefit from such programs. **Exceptional learners** *are students who require additional services to meet their individual needs.* Exceptional learners include students with physical and health problems, a learning disability, mental retardation, communication problems, and behavioral problems. Exceptional learners also include students who are gifted and talented.

More than a decade ago it was considered appropriate to educate exceptional learners outside the regular classroom. The trend today is to include all students in the regular classroom as much as possible. This used to be called mainstreaming. However, the contemporary term is **inclusion,** *which means educating exceptional learners in regular classrooms.*

inclusion

Educating exceptional learners in the regular classroom.

Some of the education of exceptional learners might take place in a resource room in addition to the regular classroom. The resource room is an instructional classroom for exceptional learners and the trained resource professionals who work with them.

Learner-Centered Psychological Principles

In the 1990s, working groups of the Educational Psychology Division of the American Psychological Association crafted a number of principles they believe represent the best way for learning to take place (Presidential Task Force on Psychology and Education, 1993; Work Group of the American Psychological Association's Board of Affairs, 1995). These "learner-centered psychological principles" move the focus of learning away from the teacher and toward the student (Lambert & McCombs, 1998). Following are a number of these learner-centered principles (Santrock, in press).

- *The nature of learning.* Learning benefits when it is done naturally, involves personally meaningful goals, and is actively constructed. Learning consists of academic knowledge, cognitive skills and strategies, socioemotional skills, and motor skills. These recommendations are compatible with one of this book's main themes (skills), the discussion of Piaget's and Vygotsky's theories in chapter 8 ("Human Development"), and our coverage of the construction of memory and strategies in chapter 6 ("Memory").
- *Goals of learning.* Student learning improves when students set goals and plan. Teachers can help students learn how to set long-term and short-term goals, develop plans to reach these goals, and monitor their progress toward the goals, and they can help students monitor their progress. This recommendation is consistent with our discussion of goal setting, planning, and achievement in chapter 9 ("Motivation and Emotion").

Applications in Psychology

Schools for Thought

Too often students emerge from instruction with only a fragile understanding of the material. For example, in science, students might be able to repeat various scientific principles that they have been taught but run into difficulties when they have to explain everyday scientific phenomena. Similarly, in math, students might be able to plug numbers into formulas but when confronted with variations of these problems be unable to solve them. Thus, many students acquire enough information to pass tests in school but do not develop a deep understanding of concepts.

A program designed to encourage students to think more deeply and solve real-world problems is called "Schools for Thought" (Lamon & others, 1996). It involves a combination of three innovative educational projects: (1) the Jasper Project, (2) Fostering a Community of Learners, and (3) Computer Supported Intentional Learning Environments.

The Jasper Project was developed by the Cognition and Technology Group at Vanderbilt (1997). It consists of twelve videodisc-based adventures that are designed to improve the mathematical thinking of students in grades 5 and up, as well as help students make connections with other disciplines, including science, history, and social studies. The adventures focus on a number of real-world problems that need to be solved. The Jasper adventures end with challenges that motivate students to generate new problems to solve. The Jasper Project encourages collaborative problem-solving among students: Groups of students share their problem-solving strategies and present their strategies to the class, discussing strengths and weaknesses of their approaches. Figure 16.A

portrays two of the Jasper adventures. In addition to the math adventures, the Cognition and Technology Group at Vanderbilt also recently has created videodisc-based adventures in science and literacy.

Ann Brown and Joe Campione (Brown, in press; Brown & Campione, 1996) have developed a program called Fostering a Community of Learners that focuses on literacy development and biology. It is appropriate for 6- to 12-year-old students. Reflection and discussion are key dimensions of the program. Constructive commentary, questioning, querying, and criticism are the mode rather than the exception. Three strategies encourage reflection and discussion: (1) Using adults as role models: Visiting experts and classroom teachers introduce the big ideas at the beginning of a unit, modeling how to think reflectively and deeply, as well as continually asking students to justify their opinions and then support them with evidence; (2) Children teaching children: Cross-age teaching is used, with older students working with younger students face-to-face and via e-mail; reciprocal teaching is also used, with students taking turns leading a discussion group; (3) On-line computer consultation: Experts provide coaching and advice, as well as commentary about what it means to learn and understand, through e-mail. A culture of learning, negotiating, sharing, and producing work that is displayed to others is at the heart of Fostering a Community of Learners. This approach has much in common with what educational expert Jerome Bruner (1996) recently recommended for improving the culture of education.

Computer-Supported Intentional Learning Environments (CSILE) provides problem-focused computer learning opportunities for students (Scardamalian & Bereiter, 1994). A typical CSILE classroom has eight linked computers, and classrooms are connected to form a communal base for the

- *The construction of knowledge and thinking.* Successful learners link and integrate new information with existing knowledge in meaningful ways instead of keeping the new information isolated. Because of students' unique experiences and the mind's active construction of knowledge, students organize information in individualized ways. Students benefit when teachers help them develop shared understanding of important knowledge and skills. Successful learners use a range of competent thinking strategies, including thinking reflectively, deeply, and creatively. These recommendations are related to our discussion of thinking in chapter 7 ("Thinking, Language, and Intelligence").
- *Contexts of learning.* Learning is influenced by the contexts in which it occurs. These contexts include such environmental factors as instruction, culture, and technology. Learning occurs best in a supportive context. Because students live in an increasingly diverse world, it is important to provide opportunities for them to experience and learn about diversity. These recommendations fit with one of this book's main themes

entire school. Students are encouraged to enter their views and questions, compare perspectives, and reflect on joint understanding of ideas. Students work both collaboratively and individually. Students can attach a graphic note, such as a picture or a diagram, to another student's entry. However, only the original author of the note can edit or delete the notes. Authors are informed when a comment has been attached to one of their notes.

As indicated earlier, these three programs have been combined in the Schools for Thought project that is currently being implemented in a number of schools. The following are some of the principles of Schools for Thought (Lamon & others, 1996):

- Stress the importance of thinking about real-world problems and integrating information across subject areas such as geography, geology, science, history, language arts, and reading. Many problems to be solved have a community focus.

- Emphasize the importance of many students' having many opportunities to plan and orchestrate their own learning, as well as to work collaboratively with other students.
- Use technology to break the isolation of the traditional classroom. Students are encouraged to communicate electronically with a community of learners beyond the classroom's walls.
- Use structure. These are not just freewheeling discovery environments. Teachers and community experts function as guides to keep learning focused on key principles in the domains being studied, such as math, science, social sciences, or the language arts.

The following Web site gives periodic updates about the Schools for Thought project: http://peabody.vanderbilt.edu/projects/funded/sft/general.

"Blueprint for Success"

Christina and Marcus, two students from Trenton, visit an architectural firm on Career Day. While learning about the work of architects, Christina and Marcus hear about a vacant lot being donated in their neighborhood for a playground. This is exciting news because there is no place in their downtown neighborhood for children to play. Recently, several students have been hurt playing in the street. The challenge is for students to help Christina and Marcus design a playground and ballfield for the lot.

"The Big Splash"

Jasper's young friend Chris wants to help his school raise money to buy a new camera for the school TV station. His idea is to have a dunking booth in which teachers would be dunked when students hit a target. He must develop a business plan for the school principal in order to obtain a loan for his project. The overall problem centers on developing this business plan, including the use of a statistical survey to help him decide if this idea would be profitable.

𝓕IGURE 16. A
Problem-Solving Adventures in the Jasper Series

(contexts) and our discussion of diversity in chapter 15 ("Human Commonality and Diversity").

- *Motivational and emotional influences on learning.* The depth and breadth of information processed, and what is learned and remembered, are influenced by personal expectations of success and failure, the motivation to learn, and emotions. Student learning benefits when teachers have high expectations for students and students are intrinsically (self-, internally) motivated. Intrinsic motivation increases when learning involves real-world tasks and contexts. Being a competent learner requires extended, persistent effort. Intense negative feelings such as anxiety, fear, and worry, interfere with learning. These recommendations connect with one of this book's main themes (applications) and our coverage in chapter 9 ("Motivation and Emotion").

To read about an educational approach that reflects many of these learner-centered psychological principles, see Applications in Psychology.

Review

Educational Psychology

Criticisms have been raised that schools do a better job of educating White and middle-class children than they do of educating ethnic minority and lower-class children. African American and Latino children do have more academic difficulties. Comer's approach is to give schools a more family-like environment for ethnic minority, lower-class children. These children improve their social and academic achievement when their schools and parents have strong positive expectations that the children will have high levels of achievement.

Exceptional learners are students who require additional services to meet their educational needs. The trend is toward inclusion, which means educating exceptional learners in regular school classrooms.

Learner-centered psychological principles include the nature of learning (learning benefits when it is done naturally, involves personally meaningful goals, and is actively constructed), goals of learning (learning improves when students set goals and plan), construction of knowledge and thinking (successful learners link and integrate new information with existing knowledge; successful learners think reflectively, deeply, and creatively), contexts of learning (learning benefits when contexts such as instruction, culture, and technology are taken into account), and motivational and emotional influences (learning benefits when there are high expectations, intrinsic motivation, real-world tasks, and effort, and when negative emotions are absent).

This is a good time to reflect on what you have learned about psychology this term and to consider whether you might be interested in a career in psychology. You have seen that psychology is a multifaceted field and that there are many different ways to be a psychologist. You have observed that psychologists' work ranges from research and teaching to psychotherapy to applications in many subfields including I/O psychology, environmental psychology, forensic psychology, sport psychology, and educational psychology. To get a better sense of whether a career in psychology is in your future, complete the Self-Assessment.

Self-Assessment

Is Psychology in Your Future?

Instructions

Students who are successful as psychology majors have a profile that is related to the questions below. Answer true or false to each item.

		True	*False*
1.	I often think about what makes people do what they do.	_____	_____
2.	I like reading about new findings that scientists have discovered doing behavioral research.	_____	_____
3.	I am often skeptical when someone tries to persuade me about behavioral claims, unless there is scientific evidence to back up the claim.	_____	_____
4.	I like the prospect of measuring behavior and doing statistics to determine meaningful differences.	_____	_____
5.	I can usually come up with multiple explanations to account for behavior.	_____	_____
6.	I appreciate the physiological underpinnings of behavior.	_____	_____
7.	I think I could come up with ideas to research to help explain behaviors I am curious about.	_____	_____
8.	I am often approached by others who want me to listen to their problems and share my ideas about what to do.	_____	_____
9.	I don't get especially frustrated if I can't get answers to my questions.	_____	_____
10.	I am usually careful with details.	_____	_____
11.	I enjoy writing and speaking about things I am learning.	_____	_____
12.	I like to solve puzzles.	_____	_____
13.	I recognize why it is important to uphold ethical standards in research and therapy.	_____	_____
14.	I feel comfortable that psychology can provide me with an education that will lead to a good job.	_____	_____

Scoring and Interpretation

If you answered "true" to a majority of the items, psychology is a major that likely matches up well with your interests. Although the items are not a perfect predictor of whether you will enjoy majoring in and pursuing a career in psychology, they can give you an indication of whether you might benefit from finding out more about what psychologists do and what is involved in becoming a psychologist. Your psychology professor or a career counselor at your college likely can inform you about the best way to pursue a career in psychology.

Overview

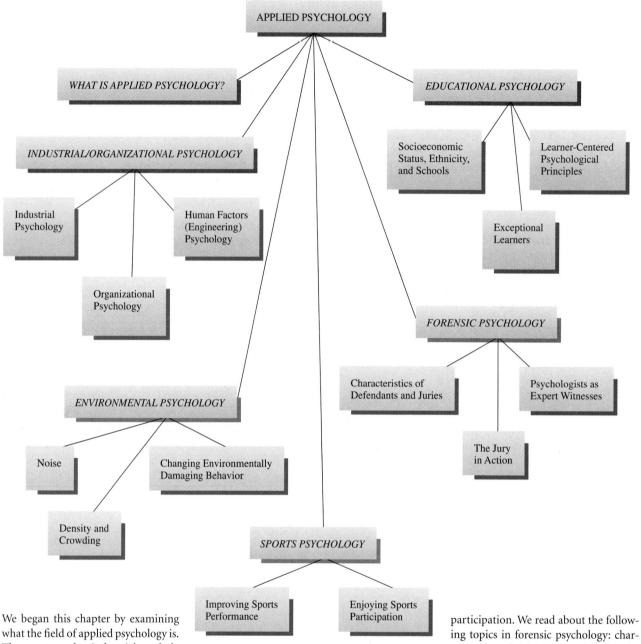

We began this chapter by examining what the field of applied psychology is. Then we turned to industrial psychology/organizational (I/O) psychology, evaluating its three main areas: industrial, organizational, and human factors (engineering) psychology. Our coverage of environmental psychology focused on noise, density and crowding, and changing environmentally damaging behavior. We also discussed sport psychology and its emphasis on improving sport performance and enjoying sport participation. We read about the following topics in forensic psychology: characteristics of defendants and juries, the jury in action, and psychologists as expert witnesses. And we explored these topics in educational psychology: socioeconomic status, ethnicity, and schools; exceptional learners; and learner-centered psychological principles. Don't forget that you can obtain an overall summary of the chapter by again studying the five in-chapter reviews on pages 596, 599, 601, 603, and 608.

Key Terms

applied psychology 586
industrial/organizational (I/O) psychology 587
industrial psychology 587
organizational psychology 589

human factors psychology 594
environmental psychology 596
density 598

crowding 598
forensic psychology 599
sport psychology 602
educational psychology 604
exceptional learners 605

inclusion 605

Thinking It Over

Exercises...

...In Critical Thinking

Many people believe that psychologists have overstepped their bounds when they offer expertise in jury selection. These critics argue that psychologists help lawyers "stack" the jury to benefit their client. Others say that psychologists should be used in this manner to give defendants every possible chance of having a fair trial. Develop arguments for one side or the other. Try to find someone in your class who favors the opposing side and discuss your positions with each other.

...In Creative Thinking

Project yourself into the career that you hope to pursue at the end of your college studies. Imagine an interview situation in which you are auditioning for the perfect entry-level position in this field. Speculate about the kinds of questions an interviewer is likely to ask you to gauge your interests, attitudes, and talents for the position. If you have the opportunity, share your ideas with someone working in this field to obtain feedback about how on-target your ideas are.

...In Active Thinking

Go to a public place and observe how the built environment influences behavior. How do people know what to do in this space? Are there signs that guide action? Does a person need special training to be able to navigate the space? How much do noise and crowding influence the behavior in the setting? It might help to pretend that you are a traveler from a foreign country who is encountering this space for the first time. What do you see?

. . . In Reflective Learning

Not everyone is a born athlete. Even if you are exceptionally skilled in sports, you probably have avoided some sports because you don't feel competent in those areas. Think about the sport activities that you prefer versus those that you avoid. Then identify the kinds of self-talk you engage in when you are trying both kinds of sports. To what degree do you engage in negative self-talk, regardless of how much you enjoy what you are doing? Are there tips that sport psychologists offer that could improve your enjoyment of the activity?

Resources for Psychology and Improving Humankind

Exploring Sports and Exercise Physiology (1996)

edited by Judy Raalte and Britton Brewer
Washington, DC: American Psychological Association

This book profiles a number of areas of sport psychology, including how to use imagery to improve performance, how to set goals, and the type of education needed to become a sport psychologist.

The Jasper Project (1997)

The Cognition and Technology Group at Vanderbilt Mahwah; NJ: Erlbaum.

This innovative videodisc-based project is designed to improve students' mathematical thinking skills.

Knock 'Em Dead (1999)

by Martin Yate
Holbrook, MA: Bob Adams

Knock 'Em Dead is an annually updated guide to job interviewing. *Knock 'Em Dead* is subtitled "With Great Answers to Interview Questions." Yate tells you the best answers to many key questions you are likely to be asked in a job interview.

National Directory of Citizen Volunteer Environmental Monitoring Programs (1990)

By Virginia Lee and Eleanor Ely
Rhode Island Sea Grant
University of Rhode Island
Narragansett, RI 02882
401-379-6842

This is a comprehensive registry of state and national programs. The directory is free.

National Response Center

1-800-424-8802

Call this number to report oil spills or the release of other hazardous matter.

The Nature Conservancy

1815 N. Lynn Street
Arlington, VA 22209
703-841-5300

This is a private nonprofit organization committed to finding, purchasing, protecting, and maintaining rare species' habitats around the world. Call or write the organization's headquarters for the list of state offices or for information about volunteering to work on a nature preserve.

Rainforest Action Network (RAN)

450 Broadway
San Francisco, CA 94111
415-398-4404

RAN is a national organization dedicated to saving the world's tropical rain forests and the human rights of those living in and near them. RAN publishes a monthly and a quarterly newsletter.

Professional Psychology (1980, June)

This entire issue of this applied psychology journal is devoted to providing an overview of the field of industrial/organizational psychology.

Reaching Potentials, Vols. 1 and 2 (1992, 1996)

edited by Sue Bredekamp and Teresa Rosegrant
Washington, DC: National Association for the Education of Young Children

These volumes provide excellent guidelines for developmentally appropriate education for young children.

The Seven Habits of Highly Effective People (1989)

by Stephen Covey
New York: Simon & Schuster

The Seven Habits of Highly Effective People tells you how to harness your potential to achieve your goals. Covey argues that to become a quality leader in an organization, you must first become a quality-oriented individual. To reach this status you have to identify the underlying principles that are important in your life and then evaluate whether you are living up to those standards.

We the Jury: The Jury System and the Ideal of Democracy (1995)

by J. Abramson
New York: Basic Books.

This book examines the jury system in considerable detail. Topics discussed include how juries reach verdicts and when an individual juror will conform to the opinion of the majority of the jurors.

Internet Resources

http://www.wesleyan.edu/spn/
References to assorted sites on sport psychology.

http://spot.colorado.edu/~collinsj/
Read about sport psychology organizations.

http://www.enhanced-performance.com/nideffer/articles.html
How to prevent "choking" during sports competitions.

http://www.usernomics.com/hf.html
This site serves as a good jumping off place for information on human factors.

http://sorrel.humboldt.edu/~campbell/iolinks.htm
Examine sources related to psychology in the workplace.

http://ualvm.ua.edu/~jhooper/landmark.html
A summary of landmark cases related to psychology.

http://www.ozemail.com.au/~dwillsh/
Comprehensive forensic references including material on serial killers.

http://www.bcpl.net/~sandyste/school psych.html
School psychology resources for students, parents, and teachers.

http://www.bcpl.net/~sandyste/school psych.html
"Plugging In" offers advice on using educational technology.

Appendix

Analyzing the Data

OUTLINE

with Don Hockenbury

The essence of life is statistical improbability on a colossal scale.

—RICHARD DAWKINS

American Biologist, 20th Century

COMMUNICATING WITH DATA

Gross national product. Grade point average. Dow Jones Industrial Average. Earned-run average. Whether you realize it or not, statistics weave in and out of our life on a daily basis. For example, high schools, colleges, and universities use statistics to track student demographics, such as the number of students attending college, student grade point averages, and the tally of students who drop out. Advertisers use statistics to persuade you to buy their products by telling you that other consumers prefer their products "by a margin of five to one." Weather reports indicate that the temperature is "ten degrees above the average for this time of year." Statistics are also widely used in sports, such as football, baseball, and basketball. Crime statistics and statistics about homeless people are just two examples of many patterns of data the federal government tracks and reports. In short, statistics are so much a part of our lives that an understanding of basic statistics is essential if you want to be an informed citizen. Communicating effectively with numbers has become a survival skill in our culture.

Psychologists use statistics to communicate about data they collect in order to describe behavior patterns and evaluate research hypotheses. You will remember that psychologists often design research with a quantitative bias. They develop research strategies in which they operationalize and measure behavior. Researchers subject these measurements to statistical analysis to determine whether their hypotheses are sound.

The purpose of this appendix is to help you make sense out of some basic statistical concepts that are used in everyday life as well as in scientific research. **Statistics** *are mathematical methods used to describe, summarize, and draw conclusions about data.* We will address two basic categories of statistics. Our primary focus will be on **descriptive statistics,** *mathematical procedures used to describe and summarize data in a meaningful fashion.* In contrast, **inferential statistics,** *complex mathematical methods used to draw conclusions about data,* will be addressed only briefly in this appendix.

DESCRIPTIVE STATISTICS

Psychologists use descriptive statistics to describe the characteristics of either a single variable or a relationship or *interaction* between two variables. This is important in most psychological studies, because if we were simply to report all the individual scores, it would

statistics

Mathematical methods used to describe, summarize, and draw conclusions about data.

descriptive statistics

Mathematical procedures used to describe and summarize samples of data in a meaningful fashion.

inferential statistics

Complex mathematical methods used to draw conclusions about data that have been collected.

"Tonight, we're going to let the statistics speak for themselves."
Drawing by Koren; © 1974 The New Yorker Magazine, Inc.

be virtually impossible to interpret the meaning of the results. Descriptive statistics allow us to avoid this situation by employing several measures that reveal the overall characteristics of the data. Descriptive statistics can be reported as numerical representations or graphic representations. Let's look at these practices.

Descriptive Statistics for One Variable

Data regarding one variable can be communicated in several ways. We can examine the raw data or we can organize the data numerically in a frequency distribution. We can create graphs—histograms or frequency polygons—that represent the data. We can also characterize single-variable data using numerical estimates called measures of central tendency and measures of variability.

Suppose that we are interested in number of siblings (brothers and sisters) as the primary variable. (Recently some educational researchers have found some interesting connections between number of siblings and aspects of academic performance, but we will return to this relationship when we examine descriptive statistics for two variables later in the chapter.) Let's start with an example from an imaginary introductory psychology class. All 20 students in this class answer a short questionnaire, which asks for the number of brothers and sisters they have, among other data of interest. We will use the sibling information to illustrate the way descriptive statistics can communicate about a set of data.

Raw Data.   Following are the number of siblings each member of the class indicated:

6	4	3	8
6	2	0	2
1	2	3	0
2	3	2	1
3	2	2	8

What kinds of conclusions can you derive by looking at this raw data on siblings? It is difficult to draw any general conclusions about the overall tendencies of the group, because raw data are overwhelming. It would be even more difficult if our sample size were 500 or 1,000 students in the class instead of just 20. We need to organize the data in a more meaningful way using descriptive statistics.

frequency distribution

A listing of scores from lowest to highest with the number of times each score appears in a sample.

Frequency Distribution.   The first step in organizing the data is developing a **frequency distribution,** *a listing of scores from lowest to highest, with the number of times each score appears in a sample.* Figure A.1a shows the frequency distribution for our data on number of siblings. The column on the left lists the possible responses (number of siblings), and the column on the right shows how often that response was given. Although the frequency distribution offers an advantage over raw data, interpreting the data can still be problematic, particularly when numbers of categories of data are large. Researchers generate graphic representations of the data to make interpretation easier.

histogram

A graph of a frequency distribution, in which vertical bars represent the frequency of scores per category or class.

Graphic Representations.   A **histogram** *is frequency distribution in graphic form, in which vertical bars represent the frequency of scores per category or class.* Figure A.1b shows a histogram for our data on sibling numbers. A histogram is often called a *bar graph* or, occasionally, a *block diagram.* The news media frequently use histograms to provide visual impact about research findings. Researchers are likely to use histograms when the number of categories of the variable (that is, number of bars) is small and will not be hard to interpret.

As you examine the histograms, you can see its correspondence with the frequency distribution. The value or score is represented on the horizontal axis (x axis) of the histogram. The frequency of responses at each value is represented on the vertical axis (y axis). Both representations identify seven students who have two siblings and no students who have five siblings.

frequency polygon

Basically the same as a histogram except that the data are represented with lines instead of bars.

A **frequency polygon** *is similar to the histogram except that we represent the data with lines rather than bars.* Figure A.1c shows a frequency polygon for the data on number of siblings. Researchers use frequency polygons when either the sample size is very large or

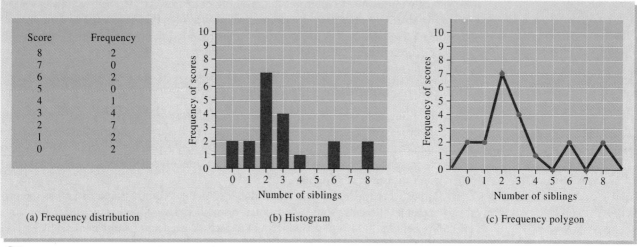

Score	Frequency
8	2
7	0
6	2
5	0
4	1
3	4
2	7
1	2
0	2

(a) Frequency distribution

(b) Histogram

(c) Frequency polygon

𝓕IGURE A.1

Frequency Distribution, Histogram, and Frequency Polygon

These data are from a hypothetical survey on number of siblings reported by 20 students in your psychology class. *(a)* A frequency distribution lists the scores from lowest to highest, with the number of times each score appears. *(b)* A histogram depicts the frequency distribution in graphic form, with vertical bars representing the frequency of scores. *(c)* A frequency polygon is basically the same as a histogram except that the data are represented with lines rather than bars. *Which of these formats do you find easiest to interpret?*

the number of categories within the variable would make it challenging to interpret the data from a histogram. As shown in the histogram and the frequency polygon, the *x* axis indicates the score values, and the *y* axis indicates how often each score occurs in the set of data.

One frequency polygon that has been of considerable interest to psychologists is the **normal distribution** *(also called a bell-shaped curve), which is a symmetrical distribution with a majority of cases falling in the middle of the possible range of scores and few scores appearing toward the extremes of the range.* Many naturally occurring phenomena, such as height, weight, athletic ability, and some aspects of human intelligence, follow or closely approximate a normal distribution. Because of its important role in data interpretation, we will return to the normal curve later in the appendix.

Although histograms and frequency polygons can help graphically represent a group of scores, you may want to communicate about your group of scores using a numerical estimate, either a measure of central tendency, a measure of variability, or both. Let's look at these two measures.

Measures of Central Tendency. If you want to describe an "average" value for a set of scores, you would use one of the measures of central tendency. In essence, a **measure of central tendency** *is a single number that tells you the overall characteristics of a set of data.* There are three measures of central tendency: the mean, the median, and the mode.

The **mean** *is the numerical average for a group of scores or values.* The mean is calculated by adding all the scores and then dividing by the number of scores. To compute the mean for the data collected on number of siblings, we add all the scores, equaling 60, then divide by the total number of scores, 20. This gives us a mean of 3 siblings. This procedure is shown on the left side of figure A.2.

The **median** *is the score that falls exactly in the middle of a distribution of scores after they have been arranged (ranked) in order.* When you have an odd number of scores (say, five or seven scores), the median is the score with the same number of scores above it as below it after all the scores have been ranked. For example, suppose you ask your five closest college friends how many courses they are currently taking. You arrange the responses in order from lowest to highest and get the following scores: 1, 2, 4, 5, 7. The median is represented by the middle value in the ranked order, or 4 classes. When you have an even number of scores (8, 10, or 20 scores, for example), you simply add the middle 2 scores and divide by 2 to arrive at the median. In our example using number

normal distribution

A symmetrical distribution with a majority of cases falling in the middle of the possible range of scores and few scores appearing toward the extremes of the range.

measure of central tendency

A single number that tells you the overall characteristics of a set of data.

mean

The numerical average for a group of scores or values.

median

The score that falls exactly in the middle of a distribution of scores after they have been arranged (ranked) from highest to lowest.

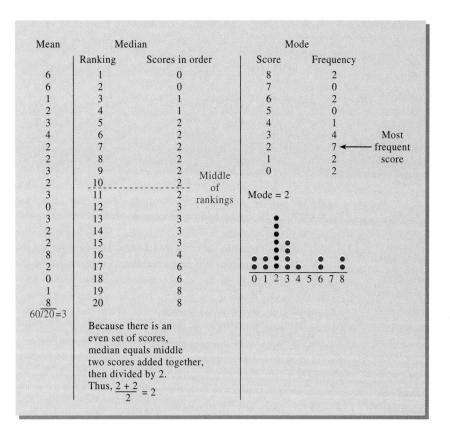

Mean		Median		Mode	
	Ranking	Scores in order		Score	Frequency
6	1	0		8	2
6	2	0		7	0
1	3	1		6	2
2	4	1		5	0
3	5	2		4	1
4	6	2		3	4
2	7	2		2	7 ← Most frequent score
2	8	2		1	2
3	9	2		0	2
2	10	2	Middle of rankings		
3	11	2		Mode = 2	
0	12	3			
3	13	3			
2	14	3			
2	15	3			
8	16	4			
2	17	6			
0	18	6			
1	19	8			
8	20	8			

60/20 = 3

Because there is an even set of scores, median equals middle two scores added together, then divided by 2. Thus, $\frac{2 + 2}{2} = 2$

0 1 2 3 4 5 6 7 8

FIGURE A.2

Mean, Median, and Mode

These data are from a hypothetical survey on number of siblings reported by 20 students in your psychology class. The mean is the numerical average for a group of scores; it is calculated by adding all the scores and then dividing by the number of scores. The median is the score that falls exactly in the middle of a distribution of scores after they have been ranked from highest to lowest. When there is an even number of scores, as there is here, you add the middle two scores and divide by 2 to calculate the median. The mode is the score that appears most often.

mode

The score that occurs most often.

measures of variability (measures of dispersion)

Measures of how much the scores in a sample vary from one another.

range

The distance between the highest and the lowest score.

of siblings, we have an even number of scores (20), so the median is the 10th and 11th scores added together and divided by 2, or (2 + 2)/2. Thus, the median number of siblings for our set of 20 responses is 2, as shown in figure A.2. One important characteristic of the mean is that it is unaffected by one or a few extreme scores.

The **mode** *is the score that occurs most often.* The mode can be determined very easily by looking at a frequency distribution, histogram, or frequency polygon. In our present example, the mode is 2, which is the number of siblings indicated most often by the members of your psychology class. Although the mode is the least used measure of central tendency, it has descriptive value because, unlike the mean and the median, there can be two or more modes. Consider the following 15 scores on a 10-point surprise quiz: 9, 3, 8, 5, 9, 3, 6, 9, 4, 10, 2, 3, 3, 9, 7. The quiz scores 9 and 3 each appear four times. No other score in this example appears as often or more often. Thus, this set of scores has two modes, or a *bimodal distribution*. It is, in fact, possible to have several modes, or a *multimodal distribution*. It also is possible to have no mode at all.

Depending on the research question being investigated, the mode may actually provide more meaningful information than either the mean or the median. For example, developers of a program to help people stop smoking would benefit more from knowing that the "modal" age of the greatest number of people who smoke is either 22 *or* 58 than from knowing that the mean age of smokers is 37. By knowing that smoking behavior is distributed bimodally in the population, they can more appropriately target their program to young adults and older adults rather than to middle-aged adults.

Measures of Variability. Along with obtaining the overall or central characteristics for a sample, we can also ask *how much the scores in a sample vary from one another. These measures are called* **measures of variability** *or* **measures of dispersion.** The two measures of variability are called the range and the standard deviation.

The **range** *is the numerical difference between the highest and the lowest scores.* The range for our data on number of siblings would be 8 (high score) minus 0 (low score), for a range of 8. Generally speaking, the range is a rather simplistic estimate of variability, or dispersion, for a group of scores. More important, because the range involves only

standard deviation

A measure of how much the scores vary, on the average, around the mean of a sample.

two scores, it can produce a misleading index of variability; thus, the range is rarely used as a measure of variability. The most commonly used measure of variability is the standard deviation.

The **standard deviation** *is a measure of how much the scores vary on the average around the mean of a sample.* It indicates how closely scores are clustered around the mean. The smaller the standard deviation, the less variability from the mean and vice versa. The mathematical steps involved in calculating a standard deviation are presented in figure A.3.

Researchers often present the mean and standard deviation of a set of scores on a single variable together. This practice communicates the average and the range of scores in conventional terms that allow scientists and psychologists to infer a great deal about the nature of the original data. In addition, these measures are less cumbersome and more efficient than graphic representations.

The Properties of the Normal Distribution. As we saw earlier, frequency polygons for many types of data produce a normal distribution. For example, the normal distribution of

Scores	Score minus mean (x)	Difference squared (x^2)
0	−3	9
0	−3	9
1	−2	4
1	−2	4
2	−1	1
2	−1	1
2	−1	1
2	−1	1
2	−1	1
2	−1	1
2	−1	1
3	0	0
3	0	0
3	0	0
3	0	0
4	1	1
6	3	9
6	3	9
8	5	25
8	5	25

Mean = 60/20 = 3 $\qquad$ $\Sigma x^2 = 102$

$$\text{Standard deviation} = \sqrt{\frac{\Sigma x^2}{N}} = \sqrt{\frac{102}{20}} = \sqrt{5.1} = 2.26$$

$\mathcal{F}$IGURE A.3

Computing the Standard Deviation

The standard deviation is a measure of how much the scores vary, on the average, around the mean of a sample. In this figure, you can see how the standard deviation was calculated for the data gathered from a hypothetical survey on number of siblings reported by 20 students in your psychology class. In computing a standard deviation, four steps have to be followed:

1. Calculate the mean of the scores.
2. From each score, subtract the mean and then square that difference. (Squaring the scores will eliminate any negative signs that result from subtracting the mean.)
3. Add the squares and then divide by the number of scores.
4. Calculate the square root of the value obtained in step 3. This is the standard deviation.

The formula for these four steps is

$$\textbf{Standard deviation} = \sqrt{\frac{\Sigma x^2}{N}}$$

where x = the individual score minus the mean, N = the number of scores, and Σ = the sum of.

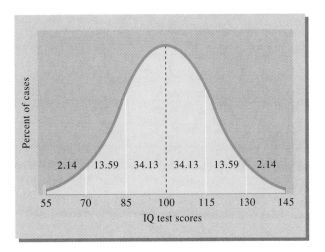

IQ scores as measured by the Wechsler Adult Intelligence Scale is shown in figure A.4. This figure illustrates several important characteristics of the normal distribution. For example, it is perfectly symmetrical. The same numbers of scores lie above the mean as below it. Because of this perfect symmetry, the mean, median, and mode are identical in a normal distribution. The bell shape illustrates that the most common scores are near the middle. The scores become less frequent and more extreme the farther away from the middle they appear.

The normal distribution incorporates information about both the mean and the standard deviation. Notice that the mean estimate of intelligence (IQ) in figure A.4 is 100 and the standard deviation is 15 IQ points. As shown in figure A.5, the area on the normal curve that is one standard deviation above the mean and one standard deviation below the mean represents 68.26 percent of the scores. At two standard deviations above and below the mean, we can account for 95.42 percent of the scores. Finally, three standard deviations above and below the mean contain 99.74 percent of the scores. If we apply this information to estimating intelligence in the population in figure A.4, we can see that 68 percent of the population has an IQ between 85 and 115, 95 percent of the population has an IQ between 70 and 130, and 99 percent of the population has an IQ between 55 and 145.

Descriptive Statistics for Two Variables

Up to this point, we've focused on descriptive statistics used to describe only one variable. Often the goal of research is to describe the relationship between two variables. This information can be represented graphically in scatter plots as well as numerically using the correlation coefficient.

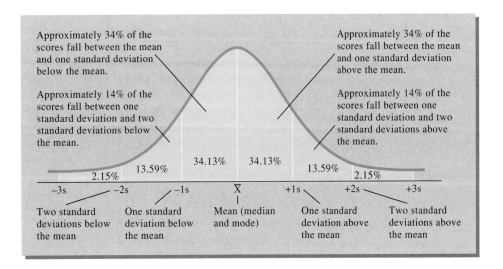

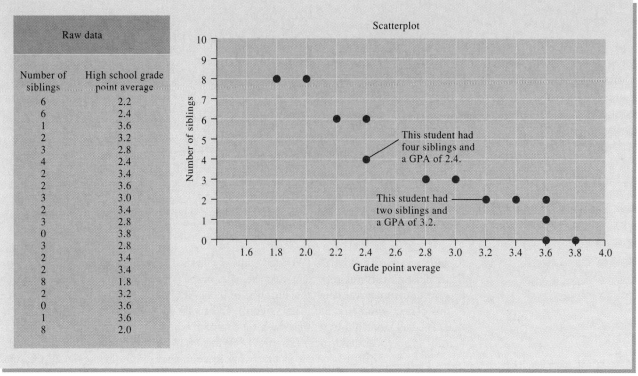

Raw data	
Number of siblings	High school grade point average
6	2.2
6	2.4
1	3.6
2	3.2
3	2.8
4	2.4
2	3.4
2	3.6
3	3.0
2	3.4
3	2.8
0	3.8
3	2.8
2	3.4
2	3.4
8	1.8
2	3.2
0	3.6
1	3.6
8	2.0

$\mathcal{F}$IGURE A.6

Descriptive Measures for Two Variables

This scatter plot depicts the possible relationship between number of siblings and grade point average. Each dot on the scatter plot represents one pair of scores as reported by each member of your class in a hypothetical survey. The raw data from that survey are shown on the left.

scatter plot

A graph on which pairs of scores are represented.

Scatter Plots. Let's return to the example of the information we collected on your classmates. In addition to number of siblings, we also asked them to report their high school grade point averages. The raw data we collected are shown on the left side of figure A.6. Also shown is a scatter plot of those scores. A **scatter plot** *is a graph on which pairs of scores are represented*. In this case, we are looking at the possible relationship between number of siblings and academic performance. The possible scores for one variable—number of siblings—are indicated on the *y* axis, and the scores for the second variable—grade point average—are indicated on the *x* axis. Each dot on the scatter plot represents one pair of scores as reported by each member of your class. As you can see, there seems to be a distinct pattern to our scatter plot—that is, as the number of siblings increases, high school GPA decreases. Tentatively, at least, there appears to be an association between these two variables.

Let's look at some other examples. Assume that we have collected data to determine the relationship between how much weight students carry around in their backpacks on campus and their estimates of fatigue on a "1 to 10" scale. For example, Mary carries 12 pounds of books and complains about being tired ("about an 8"). Terri carries very few books with her and rarely feels tired ("about a 1"). We have gathered these two types of data on each student in the class. Each point on the scatter plot represents the data reported for one student. Where the point cuts off the *x* axis represents the "pounds per backpack." Where the point cuts off the *y* axis is the "fatigue rating on a scale of 1 to 10." The clustering of the points on the scatter diagram and the general direction of the slope of the points tells us about the direction of the relationship. For example, patterns of dots that slope upward from left to right indicate a positive relationship between the two factors. Lines that slope downward from left to right indicate a negative relationship between the two factors. Examples of scatter plots with different slopes showing positive and negative correlations appear in figure A.7.

An example of a scatter plot for a negative relationship can be illustrated by looking at another aspect of the classroom—yawning during lecture. Suppose we collect data

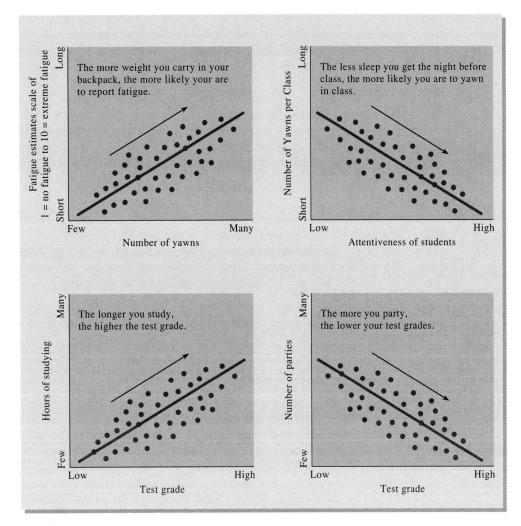

$\mathscr{F}$IGURE A.7

Scatter Plots Showing Positive and Negative Correlations

Which of these scatter plots show positive correlations and which show negative correlations? Graphs A and C show positive correlations. A positive correlation occurs when two factors vary in the same direction. Graphs B and D show negative correlations. A negative correlation occurs when two factors vary in opposite directions.

from members of the psychology class on how much sleep they got the night before the class and then ask them to keep track of the number of times they yawn during the class. For example, Paul couldn't stop yawning. During the 50-minute class, he counted 25 yawns and revealed he had only 3 hours of sleep the night before. Dirk slept soundly for 8 hours the night before and didn't recall yawning even once. Hours of sleep each student reports (the variable on the y axis) and the number of times each student yawns in class the next day (the x-axis variable) are plotted using one data point on a scatter diagram with a resulting pattern sloping downward from left to right. The diagram suggests a negative relationship between the two variables. Hours of sleep and yawning behavior are negatively related.

The Correlation Coefficient.   Just as we found measures of central tendency and measures of variability to be more precise than frequency distributions or histograms in describing one variable, it would be helpful if we had a type of measurement that is more precise than a scatter plot to describe the relationship between two variables. In such cases, we could compute a correlation coefficient.

A **correlation coefficient** *is a numerical value that expresses the degree of relationship between two variables.* There are two parts to a correlation coefficient: the number or value of the coefficient and the sign (positive or negative). The correlation coefficient ranges from $+1.00$ to -1.00 and tells you about the nature of the relationship between the two factors.

The strength of the relationship between two variables depends on the numerical value of the coefficient. You need to think about the range of the correlation coefficient as being different from an integer number line ($\ldots -3, -2, -1, 0, 1, 2, 3, \ldots$). In other words, negative numbers are not less than positive numbers. A correlation coefficient of $+.65$ is just as strong as a correlation of minus -65. The rule is simple: The closer the number is to 1.00, the stronger the correlation. Conversely, the closer the number is to .00, the weaker the relationship. A correlation of .00 indicates that no relationship at all exists between two sets of variables. (See table A.1.)

$\mathscr{T}$ A B L E A . 1
Guidelines for Interpreting the Strength of the Correlation Coefficient

1.00	Perfect relationship; the two factors always occur together
.76–.99	Very strong relationship; the two factors occur together very often
.51–.75	Strong relationship; the two factors occur together frequently
.26–.50	Moderate relationship; the two factors occur together occasionally
.01–.25	Weak relationship; the two factors seldom occur together
.00	No relationship; the two factors never occur together

The plus and minus signs of the correlation coefficient tell you nothing about the strength of the correlation. Instead, these valences indicate the direction of the relationship between the two variables. A **positive correlation** *is a relationship in which the two factors vary in the same direction.* Both variables tend to go up together *or* both factors tend to go down together. Either situation represents a positive relationship, in that both factors vary together. A **negative correlation** *is a relationship in which the two factors vary in opposite directions.* As one factor increases, the other factor decreases. The plus or minus sign tells you nothing about the strength of correlation. Thus, a correlation of $+.15$ indicates a weak positive correlation, and a $-.74$ indicates a strong negative correlation. A correlation of $-.87$ is stronger than a correlation of $+.45$.

Returning to our collected data on backpack weight and fatigue ratings, an alternative to plotting a scatter diagram is calculating the correlation coefficient between these two variables. In this instance, we find a correlation coefficient (represented by the letter r) of $+.77$. The number tells us that these two factors happen together frequently. The positive sign indicates that the two factors vary in the same direction, or *covary*. In simpler language, the more weight you haul in your backpack, the more likely you are to report fatigue. Note that this is not a perfect correlation ($+1.00$). Some students might be weightlifters who can haul a lot of supplies and books without reporting any fatigue. Other students might feel taxed by carrying even one or two books. But overall, the high positive correlation suggests that fatigue reports and backpack weight are very strongly related.

Suppose that when we calculate the correlation coefficient between hours of sleep and number of classroom yawns, we get $r = -.57$. The correlation confirms the relationship illustrated in the scatter diagram. Yawning in class appears to be strongly negatively correlated with the hours of sleep obtained the night before. The *more* sleep you get, the *less* yawning you will do. The *more* yawning you do in class, the *less* sleep we could predict you got from the night before class.

Now return to our original example examining the relation between number of siblings and high school grade point average. The correlation between these two variables is $-.95$. How would you interpret this correlation? This means that the relationship between grade point and sibling number is negative and very strong. We interpret the number .95 to represent a very strong relation between the two variables. The negative sign demonstrates an *inverse* relationship. Thus, students with fewer siblings tend to have higher grade point averages, whereas students with many siblings appear to have worse grades.

We must exercise caution when interpreting correlation coefficients. For example, could we conclude that if you are an only child, you will get a 4.0 GPA? Are you destined to make poor grades if you grew up in a large family? Of course not. Individual performances cannot be precisely determined using correlation coefficients. Correlation coefficients are population parameters and do not correspond precisely to individual values and prediction. At best, we can make only general predictions based on the trends in the data.

Another interpretive problem is that *correlation does not necessarily indicate causality.* Although researchers frequently use correlation coefficients to analyze the relationship between two variables, the general public frequently misinterprets the findings. Causality means that one factor makes, produces, or creates change in a second factor. Correlation means that two factors *seem* to be related, associated, or connected such that, as one factor changes, the other factor seems to change. Correlation implies potential causality that may or may not actually be there. Even though two factors are strongly or even perfectly correlated, in reality a third factor may be responsible for the changes observed. Thus, in our hypothetical example showing a very strong negative correlation between number of siblings and GPA, the changes observed in these two variables could be due to a third factor. For example, perhaps children who grow up in larger families have a greater tendency to hold part-time jobs after school, thereby limiting the amount of time they can study, or children who grow up in small families may be more likely to have their own rooms, thereby allowing them more uninterrupted study time. In any case, the point remains the same: correlation only potentially indicates a causal relationship.

Correlation methods permit research in situations that cannot be experimentally manipulated, such as natural disasters like the 1993 earthquake in Los Angeles.

Look at the terms in bold type in the following headlines:

Researchers **Link** Coffee Consumption to Cancer of Pancreas

Scientists Find **Connection** Between Ear Hair and Heart Attacks

Psychologists Discover **Relation** Between Marital Status and Health

Researchers Identify **Association** Between Loneliness and Social Skills

Parental Discipline **Tied** to Personality Disorders in Children

All of the words in bold type are synonymous with correlation, not causality. The general public, however, tends to equate such terms as *connection* or *association* with causality. As you read about the findings of psychological studies, or findings in other sciences, guard against making the same interpretation. Remember, correlation means only that two factors seem to occur together.

Student number	Number of siblings (X variable)	Score minus mean (3.0)	Difference squared	High school GPA (Y variable)	Score minus mean (3.0)	Difference squared	x multiplied by y
N	X	x	x^2	Y	y	y^2	xy
1	6	3	9	2.2	−.8	.64	−2.4
2	6	3	9	2.4	−.6	.36	−1.8
3	1	−2	4	3.6	.6	.36	−1.2
4	2	−1	1	3.2	.2	.04	−0.2
5	3	0	0	2.8	−.2	.04	0.0
6	4	1	1	2.4	−.6	.36	−0.6
7	2	−1	1	3.4	.4	.16	−0.4
8	2	−1	1	3.6	.6	.36	−0.6
9	3	0	0	3.0	0.0	.00	0.0
10	2	−1	1	3.4	.4	.16	−0.4
11	3	0	0	2.8	−.2	.04	0.0
12	0	−3	9	3.8	.8	.64	−2.4
13	3	0	0	2.8	−.2	.04	0.0
14	2	−1	1	3.4	.4	.16	−0.4
15	2	−1	1	3.4	.4	.16	−0.4
16	8	5	25	1.8	−1.2	1.44	−6.0
17	2	−1	1	3.2	.2	.04	−0.2
18	0	−3	9	3.6	.6	.36	−1.8
19	1	−2	4	3.6	.6	.36	−1.2
20	8	5	25	2.0	−1.0	1.00	−5.0
	N = 20	Mean = 3.0	$\Sigma x^2 = 102$	Mean = 3.0		$\Sigma y^2 = 6.72$	$\Sigma xy = -25.00$

$$r = \frac{\Sigma xy}{\sqrt{\Sigma x^2 \times \Sigma y^2}} = \frac{-25.00}{\sqrt{(102)(6.72)}} = \frac{-25.00}{\sqrt{685.44}} = \frac{-25.00}{26.18} = -.95$$

ℱIGURE A.8

Computation of a Correlation Coefficient

These data are from a hypothetical survey on number of siblings and high school GPA reported by 20 students in your psychology class. The correlation coefficient of −.95 indicates a very strong negative relationship between number of siblings and high school GPA. The following formula is used to calculate a correlation coefficient:

$$\mathbf{r} = \frac{\Sigma xy}{\sqrt{\Sigma x^2 \times \Sigma y^2}}$$

where x is the difference between each X variable minus the mean; y is the difference between each Y variable minus the mean; Σxy is the sum of the cross products (each x score multiplied by its corresponding y score); Σx^2 is the sum of the squares of the x scores; and $\Sigma y2$ is the sum of the squares of the y scores. This figure contains the calculation of the correlation coefficient of −.95. From our previous discussion, we know that this is a very strong association indicating that, as number of siblings increases, grade point average decreases. What exactly does this mean? How are we supposed to interpret this hypothetical finding? Does this mean that, if you are an only child, you will have a 4.0 GPA? Does this mean that, if you grew up in a large family, you are destined to make poor grades?

Thus, the correlation coefficient is a very useful and important statistical tool for psychological as well as other kinds of research. The correlational method is especially helpful in situations in which variables cannot be manipulated and measured. It may be unethical to conduct an experiment because it poses either a physical or a psychological danger to the subjects. For instance, it would be unethical to carry out an experiment in which expectant mothers are directed to smoke varying number of cigarettes to see how cigarette smoke affects the babys' birthweights. Some factors simply cannot be manipulated experimentally, such as the effects of the 1993 earthquake in Los Angeles or the childhood backgrounds of people who are abusive parents. In these situations, psychologists might collect data using systematic *observation* of subjects rather than systematic *manipulation* in the experimental method. Systematic observation techniques include case studies, naturalistic observation, interviews, questionnaires, and standardized tests. All of these approaches can produce measurements that can be related and interpreted using correlational coefficients. The mathematical steps involved in computing a correlation coefficient are shown in figure A.8.

INFERENTIAL STATISTICS

As you've seen in the previous section, correlational studies cannot establish causality. How, then, can a researcher provide compelling evidence for a causal relationship between two variables? As you may recall from chapter 1, psychologists use the experimental method to examine cause-and-effect hypotheses about variables. They use inferential statistics to interpret their findings.

Experimental Design

In the experimental method, researchers hold all variables constant and then systematically manipulate the factor that they think produces change (the independent variable). They measure the variable believed to be affected by these manipulations (the dependent variable). If the researchers have held all factors constant except for their manipulation of the independent variable, then any changes observed in the dependent variable can be attributed to the independent variable; changes in the independent variable *caused* changes to occur in the dependent variable. This is the most compelling evidence of causality that science can provide, assuming that the experiment was carefully designed and controlled to avoid such experimental pitfalls as experimenter bias, subject bias, situational bias, or invalid scores. Furthermore, experimental evidence of causality is even more compelling if the research can be *replicated*, or repeated, by other researchers using different subjects.

Suppose we decide to design some interventions for college students who are struggling in their courses. We wish to design an experimental study to test whether the interventions (the cause) that we have in mind will have the desired outcome (the effect) of improving college grades. We recruit participants for the study and randomly assign them to one of three situations: intervention 1 (improved nutrition), intervention 2 (required study periods), or the control group (no intervention). We hypothesize that required study periods are more effective in enhancing grade point average than is improved nutrition or no intervention. After we collect the data, we have to interpret whether the data support or disconfirm the hypothesis.

Psychologists usually get a preliminary idea about whether their data support the hypothesis by scrutinizing the means for each group. Figure A.9 depicts a histogram of these artificial data. Note that the independent variable (type of intervention) occupies the *x* axis. The dependent variable (grade point average) is represented on the *y* axis. At first glance, the data appear to support the original hypothesis. However, how large do those differences have to be before we can conclude confidently that the differences are meaningful? Inferential statistics can help answer that question.

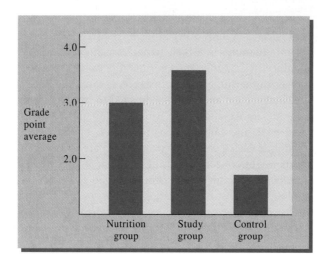

IGURE A.9

Histogram Contrasting the
Fictionalized Mean Grade Point
Averages Derived in an Experi-
ment in Which Two Intervention
Strategies Were Employed to
Improve Grades

Hypothesis Testing

There are many kinds of inferential statistics. Depending on the characteristics of the data and the number of groups being compared, psychologists apply different tests. In our experiment on improving grade point averages, we would use the t-test or analysis of variance, although there are other inferential procedures.

Inferential statistics are complex mathematical methods used to draw conclusions about data that have been collected. More specifically, inferential statistics are used to indicate whether or not data sufficiently support or confirm a research hypothesis. To accomplish this, inferential statistics rely on statements of probability and statistical significance, two important concepts that we will examine briefly.

Although it is beyond the scope of this appendix to explore these different measures of inferential statistics in detail, the logic behind inferential statistics is relatively simple. Measures of inferential statistics yield a statement of probability about the differences observed between two or more groups; this probability statement tells what the odds are that the observed differences were due simply to chance. If an inferential statistical measure tells you that the odds are less than 5 out of 100 (or .05) that the differences are due to chance, the results are considered statistically significant. In statistical terminology, this is referred to as the *.05 level of statistical significance,* or the *.05 confidence level.* Put another way, **statistical significance** *means that the differences observed between two groups are so large that it is highly unlikely those differences are due merely to chance.*

The .05 level of statistical significance is considered the minimum level of probability that scientists will accept for concluding that the differences observed are real, thereby supporting a hypothesis. Some researchers prefer to use more rigorous levels of statistical significance, such as the .01 level of statistical significance (1 out of 100) or the .001 level of statistical significance (1 out of 1,000). Regardless of which level of statistical significance used, by knowing that a research result is statistically significant, you can be reasonably confident that the finding is not due simply to chance. Of course, replication of the study, with similar significant results, can increase your confidence in the finding even further.

However, a statistically significant difference does not always translate into a difference that has meaning in everyday life. Before assuming that a finding is significant both statistically and in everyday terms, it's wise to look at the actual differences involved. Sometimes the differences are so small as to be inconsequential. For example, in comparisons of average scores for males and females on the math section of the Scholastic Aptitude Test, the difference is statistically significant, with males performing better than females (Benbow & Stanley, 1983). In reality, however, the average difference is only a few points. Caution, therefore, should be exercised in the practical interpretation of statistically significant findings.

statistical significance

The idea that the differences observed between two groups are sufficiently large that it is highly unlikely that they are due merely to chance.

Overview

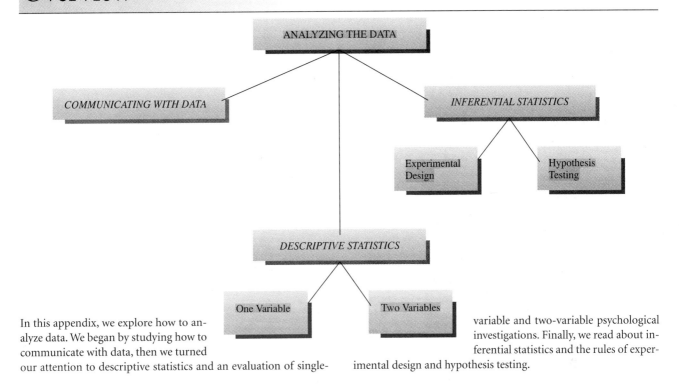

In this appendix, we explore how to analyze data. We began by studying how to communicate with data, then we turned our attention to descriptive statistics and an evaluation of single-variable and two-variable psychological investigations. Finally, we read about inferential statistics and the rules of experimental design and hypothesis testing.

Key Terms

Glossary

A

abnormal behavior Behavior that is maladaptive, harmful, statistically unusual, personally distressing, and/or designated abnormal by the culture. 409

absolute threshold The minimum amount of sensory energy that we can detect 50 percent of the time. 76

accommodation The action of the lens of the eye to increase or decrease its curvature. 83

accommodation Changing behavior in order to adjust to new information. 285

acculturation Cultural change that results from continuous, firsthand contact between two distinctive cultural groups. 503

acculturative stress The negative consequences of acculturation. 503

accurate empathy Rogers's term for the therapist's ability to identify with the client. 452

achievement motivation (need for achievement) The desire to accomplish something, to reach a standard of excellence, and to expend effort to excel. 348

action potential The brief wave of electrical charge that sweeps down the axon. 47

action therapy Therapy that promotes direct changes in behavior; insight is not essential for change to occur. 446

activation-synthesis view The view that dreams have no inherent meaning but, rather, reflect the brain's efforts to make sense out of or find meaning in the neural activity that takes place during REM sleep. In this view, the brain has considerable random activity during REM sleep, and dreams are an attempt to synthesize the chaos. 136

active listening Rogers's term for the ability to listen to another person with total attention to what the person says and means. 452

activity theory The theory that the more active and involved older people are, the more satisfied they will be with their lives and the more likely they will stay healthy. 320

acupuncture A technique in which thin needles are inserted at specific points in the body to produce effects such as local anesthesia. 95

addiction Physical dependence on a drug. 140

additive mixture The mixing of light beams from different parts of the color spectrum. 86

adolescent egocentrism The adolescent's belief that others are as preoccupied with the adolescent as she is herself, that she is unique, and that she is indestructible. 300

aerobic exercise Sustained exercise—jogging, swimming, or cycling, for example—that stimulates heart and lung activity. 484

affectionate love Also called companionate love; a type of love that occurs when an individual desires to have the other person near and has a deep, caring affection for the person. 538

afferent nerves Sensory nerves that carry information to the brain. 43

afterimages Sensations that remain after a stimulus is removed. 89

ageism Prejudice against people based on their age; in particular, prejudice against older people. 320

agoraphobia The fear of entering unfamiliar situations, especially open or public space; the most common phobic disorder. 417

algorithms Procedures that guarantee an answer to a problem. 231

AIDS A sexually transmitted disease that is caused by the human immunodeficiency virus (HIV), which destroys the body's immune system. 493

all-or-none principle The principle that once the electrical impulse reaches a certain level of intensity, it fires and moves all the way down the axon, remaining at the same strength throughout its travel. 47

alpha waves The EEG pattern of individuals who are in a relaxed or drowsy state. 127

altered state of consciousness A mental state that is noticeably different from normal awareness. Drugs, meditation, traumas, fatigue, hypnosis, and sensory deprivation produce altered states of consciousness. 123

altruism An unselfish interest in helping someone else. 542

Alzheimer's disease A degenerative, irreversible brain disorder that impairs memory and social behavior. 314

amnesia The loss of memory. 213

amplitude Measured in decibels (dB), the amount of pressure produced by a sound wave relative to a standard. 90, 125

amygdala A limbic system structure that is involved in emotion and the discrimination of objects that are important in the organism's survival. These include appropriate food, mates, and social rivals. 54

anal stage Freud's second stage of development, occurring between 1½ and 3 years of age, in which the child's greatest pleasure involves the anus or the elimination functions associated with it. 382

analogy A type of formal reasoning that is always made up of four parts. The relation between the first two parts is the same as the relation between the last two. 234

androgens The main class of male sex hormones. 338, 560

androgyny The presence of desirable feminine and masculine characteristics in the same individual. 570

anorexia nervosa An eating disorder that involves the relentless pursuit of thinness through starvation. 489

anterograde amnesia A memory disorder in which the individual cannot form memories of new information or events. 213

antianxiety drugs Drugs that are commonly known as tranquilizers and reduce anxiety by making individuals less excitable and more tranquil. 472

antidepressant drugs Drugs that regulate mood. The three main classes of antidepressant drugs are tricyclics, such as Elavil; MAO inhibitors, such as Nardil; and SSR inhibitors, such as Prozac. 472

antipsychotic drugs Powerful drugs that diminish agitated behavior, reduce tension, decrease hallucinations and delusions, improve social behavior, and produce better sleep patterns in severely mentally disabled individuals, especially schizophrenics. 473

antisocial personality disorder A personality disorder in the dramatic, emotional, and erratic cluster; the most problematic personality disorder for society. Individuals with this disorder often resort to crime, violence, and delinquency. 435

anxiety disorders Psychological disorders that include the following main features: motor tension (jumpiness, trembling, inability to relax), hyperactivity (dizziness, racing heart, or perspiration), and apprehensive expectations and thoughts. 415

aphasia An inability to recognize or express language. 60

apparent movement The illusion of movement that occurs when we perceive a stationary object as moving. 106

applied psychology The field that uses psychological principles to improve the lives of human beings and solve human problems. 586

approach/approach conflict A conflict in which the individual must choose between two attractive stimuli or circumstances. 501

approach/avoidance conflict A conflict involving a single stimulus or circumstance that has both positive and negative characteristics. 501

archetypes Primordial influences in every individual's collective unconscious that filter our perceptions and experiences. 384

artificial intelligence (AI) The science of creating machines capable of performing activities that require intelligence when they are done by people. 227

assimilation The incorporation of new information into existing knowledge. 285

assimilation Individuals' relinquishing their cultural identity and moving into the larger society. 503

association cortex Areas of the brain that are involved in our highest intellectual functions, such as problem solving and thinking; also called association areas. 55

astrology A pseudopsychology that uses the position of the stars and planets at the time of a person's birth to describe, explain, and predict the person's behavior. 27

attachment A close emotional bond between the infant and its caregiver. 292

attitudes Beliefs and opinions that can predispose individuals to behave in certain ways. 521

attribution theory The theory that individuals are motivated to discover the underlying causes of behavior as part of their interest in making sense out of the behavior. 520

auditory nerve The nerve that carries neural impulses to the brain's auditory areas. 93

authoritarian parenting A restrictive, punitive style in which the parent exhorts the child to follow the parent's directions and to respect work and effort. The authoritarian parent places firm limits and controls on the child and allows little verbal exchange. Authoritarian parenting is associated with children's social incompetence. 295

authoritative parenting A style in which parents encourage children to be independent but still places limits and controls on their actions. Extensive verbal give-and-take is allowed, and parents are warm and nurturant toward the child. Authoritative parenting is associated with children's social competence. 296

automatic processes A form of consciousness that requires minimal attention and does not interfere with other ongoing activities. 123

automatic processing A process of encoding information in memory that does not require capacity, resources, or effort. 200

autonomic nervous system The division of the peripheral nervous system that takes messages to and from the body's internal organs, monitoring such processes as breathing, heart rate, and digestion. 43

autonomy versus shame and doubt Erikson's second psychosocial stage, occurring from about 1 to 3 years of age. After developing trust, infants begin to discover that their behavior is their own. They start to assert their sense of independence, or autonomy; they realize their will. 291

availability heuristic Judging the probability of an event by the ease with which prior occurrences come to mind. 233

aversive conditioning An approach to behavior therapy that involves repeated pairings of an undesirable behavior with aversive stimuli to decrease the behavior's rewards so that the individual will stop doing it; this technique is based on classical conditioning. 454

avoidance/avoidance conflict A conflict in which the individual must choose between two unattractive stimuli or circumstances. 501

avoidance strategies Responses that individuals use to keep stressful circumstances out of their awareness so they do not have to deal with them. 506

axon The part of the neuron that carries information away from the cell body to other cells. 45

B

barbiturates Depressant drugs, such as Nembutal and Seconal, that induce sleep or reduce anxiety. 144

Barnum effect If you make your descriptions broad enough, any person can fit them. 397

basal ganglia Small groups of neurons in the midbrain that help with high-level integrative functions. 50

basal metabolism rate (BMR) The minimal amount of energy an individual uses in a resting state. 488

baseline A basis for comparison that depicts behavior in the absence of the manipulated factor. 22

basilar membrane A membrane that is housed inside the cochlea and runs its entire length. 93

behavior Everything that organisms can do that can be directly observed. 5

behavior modification The application of operant conditioning principles to change human behavior. 172

behavior therapies Therapies that use principles of learning to reduce or eliminate maladaptive behavior. 453

behavioral medicine A field closely related to health psychology that attempts to combine medical and behavioral knowledge to reduce illness and promote health. 483

behavioral perspective A perspective that emphasizes the scientific study of observable behavioral responses and their environmental determinants. 8

belief perseverance effect Clinging to our beliefs even in the face of evidence that says we should let go of them. 236

beta waves The EEG pattern for high-frequency electrical activity in the brain, characteristic of periods of concentration. 127

bilingual education Programs for students with limited proficiency in English that instruct students in their own language part of the time while they learn English. 246

binocular cues Depth cues that are based on both eyes working together. 105

biofeedback The process in which individuals' muscular or visceral activities are monitored by instruments and information is given (fed back) to the individuals so they can learn to voluntarily control these activities. 512

biological processes Processes that involve changes in an individual's physical nature. 275

biomedical therapies Treatments to reduce or eliminate the symptoms of psychological disorders by altering the way an individual's body functions. Drug therapy is the most common form. 472

bipolar disorder A mood disorder characterized by extreme mood swings; an individual with this disorder might be depressed, manic, or both. 424

bisexual Being sexually attracted to people of both sexes. 343

blind spot The area of the retina where the optic nerve leaves the eye on its way to the brain. 84

borderline personality disorder A personality disorder in the dramatic, emotional, and erratic cluster; the person's behavior exhibits these characteristics. 435

brain implant The implantation of healthy tissue into a damaged brain. 64

brightness A characteristic of color based on its intensity. 86

brightness constancy Recognition that an object retains the same degree of brightness even when different amounts of light fall on it. 108

bulimia An eating disorder in which the individual consistently follows a binge-and-purge eating pattern. 489

burnout A hopeless, helpless feeling brought about by relentless work-related stress. Burnout leaves its sufferers in a state of physical and emotional exhaustion that includes chronic fatigue and low energy. 500

bystander effect The effect of others' presence on a person's giving help; individuals who observe an emergency help less when someone, another observer, is present than when they are a lone observer. 544

C

Cannon-Bard theory The theory that emotion and physiological states occur simultaneously. 358

care perspective In Carol Gilligan's theory of moral development, the care perspective focuses on people in terms of their connectedness with others, interpersonal communication, relationships with others, and concern for others. 302

carpentered-world hypothesis The hypothesis that people who live in cultures in which straight lines, right angles, and rectangles predominate should be more susceptible to illusions, such as the Müller-Lyer illusion, involving straight lines, right angles, and rectangles than are people who live in noncarpentered cultures. 111

case study An in-depth look at one individual. This method is used mainly by clinical psychologists when the unique aspects of a person's life cannot be duplicated for either practical or ethical reasons. 20

catatonic schizophrenia A schizophrenic disorder characterized by bizarre motor behavior, which sometimes takes the form of an immobile stupor. 431

catharsis The psychoanalytic term for clients' release of emotional tension when they relive an emotionally charged and conflicted experience. 449

cell body The part of the neuron that contains the nucleus, which directs the manufacture of the substances the neuron uses for its growth and maintenance. 45

central nervous system (CNS) The brain and spinal cord. 42

cerebellum A part of the brain that extends from the rear of the hindbrain and is located above the medulla; it consists of two rounded structures thought to play important roles in motor control. 50

cerebral cortex (cerebrum) The most recently evolved part of the brain; covering the rest of the brain like a cap, it is the largest part of the brain and makes up about 80 percent of its volume. 54

chaining An operant conditioning technique used to teach a complex sequence, or chain, of behaviors. The procedure begins by shaping the final response in the sequence, then working backward until a chain of behaviors is learned. 168

chromosomes Threadlike structures, located in the nucleus of each human cell, that come in 23 pairs, one member of each pair coming from each parent. 38

chunking The grouping or "packing," of information into higher-order units that can be remembered as single units. Chunking expands working memory by making large amounts of information more manageable. 194

circadian rhythm A daily behavioral or physiological cycle, such as the 24-hour sleep/wake cycle. 125

civil commitment Commitment that transpires when a judge deems an individual to be a risk to self or others due to a mental disorder. 436

clairvoyance The ability to perceive remote events that are not in sight. 113

classical conditioning A form of learning in which a neutral stimulus becomes associated with a meaningful stimulus and acquires the capacity to elicit a similar response. 153

cochlea A long, tubular, fluid-filled structure in the inner ear that is coiled up like a snail. 93

cognitive appraisal Lazarus's concept of individuals' interpretation of events in their lives as harmful, threatening, or challenging, and their determination of whether they have the resources to cope effectively with the event. 498

cognitive behavior therapy An approach to behavior therapy that tries to help individuals behave more adaptively by modifying their thoughts. 455

cognitive developmental theory of gender The theory that children's gender typing occurs after they have developed a concept of gender and that, once they begin to consistently conceive of themselves as male or female, children often organize their world on the basis of gender. 562

cognitive dissonance A concept developed by social psychologist Leon Festinger; an individual's motivation toward consistency and away from inconsistency. 522

cognitive map An organism's mental representation of the structure of physical space. 180

cognitive mechanics The hardware of the mind, reflecting the neurophysiological architecture of the brain as developed through evolution. At the operational level, cognitive mechanics involve speed and accuracy of the processes involving sensory input, visual and motor memory, discrimination, comparison, and categorization. 315

cognitive perspective A perspective that emphasizes the mental processes involved in knowing: how we direct our attention, how we perceive, how we remember, and how we think and solve problems. 10

cognitive pragmatics The culture-based "software" of the mind. At the operational level, cognitive pragmatics include reading and writing skills, language comprehension, educational qualifications, professional skills, and also the type of knowledge about the self and life skills that help us master or cope with life. 316

cognitive processes Processes that involve changes in an individual's thought, intelligence, and language. 275

cognitive social learning theory The contemporary version of social learning theory that stresses the importance of cognition, behavior, and environment. 389

cognitive therapies Therapies that emphasize that an individual's cognitions, or thoughts, are the main source of abnormal behavior; cognitive therapies attempt to change the individual's feelings and behaviors by changing her or his cognitions. 456

cohorts Groups of individuals born in the same year or time period. 319

collective unconscious In Jung's theory, the impersonal, deepest layer of the unconscious mind, which is shared by all human beings because of their common ancestral past. 384

collectivism An emphasis on values that serve the group by subordinating personal goals to preserve group integrity, the interdependence of members, and harmonious relationships.   377, 551

color blindness   Defective color vision   88

commitment   The process by which an individual becomes institutionalized in a mental hospital.   436

compensation   Adler's term for the individual's attempt to overcome imagined or real inferiorities or weaknesses by developing her or his abilities.   385

competence motivation   The motivation to deal effectively with the environment, to be adept at what we attempt, and to make the world a better place.   347

competency   An individual's ability to understand and participate in a judicial proceeding.   437

complex sounds   Sounds in which numerous frequencies of sound blend together.   91

computer-assisted axial tomography (CAT scan)   A three-dimensional imaging technique in which pictures obtained by passing X rays through the head are assembled by a computer into a composite image.   66

conception (fertilization)   Union of an egg and a sperm.   278

concepts   Categories used to group objects, events, and characteristics on the basis of common properties.   228

concrete operational thought   The term Piaget gave to the 7- to 11-year-old child's understanding of the world. At this stage of thought children can use operations. Logical reasoning replaces intuitive thought as long as the principles are applied to concrete examples.   287

conditional positive regard   Rogers's term for making the bestowal of love or praise conditional on the individual's conforming to parental or social standards.   391

conditioned response (CR)   The learned response to the conditioned stimulus that occurs after CS-US association.   154

conditioned stimulus (CS)   A previously neutral stimulus that elicits the conditioned response after being paired with the unconditioned stimulus.   154

cones   Receptors for color perception.   83

confirmation bias   Examining only the evidence that supports what we already believe.   236

conformity   Individuals' adopting the attitudes or behavior of others because of real or imagined pressure from others to do so.   531

consciousness   Awareness of external and internal stimuli or events.   122

consensual validation   A concept that provides an explanation of why people are attracted to others who are similar to them. Our own attitudes and behavior are supported when someone else's attitudes and

behavior are similar to ours—their attitudes and behavior validate ours.   536

conservation   A belief in the permanence of certain attributes of objects or situations in spite of superficial changes.   287

contemporary model of working memory   Baddeley's model that emphasizes that long-term memory often precedes working memory and that working memory uses long-term memory in flexible ways.   198

content validity   The extent to which a test covers broadly the content it is purported to cover.   255

context   The historical, economic, social, and cultural factors that influence mental processes and behavior.   6

continuity of development   The view that development involves gradual, cumulative change from conception to death.   276

contour   A location at which a sudden change of brightness occurs.   103

control group   The comparison group in an experiment; it is treated in every way like the experimental group except for the manipulated factor.   22

controlled processes   The most alert states of consciousness, in which individuals actively focus their efforts toward a goal.   123

conventional level   Kohlberg's second level of moral thinking, in which an individual shows an intermediate level of internalization. The individual abides by certain standards (internal), but they are the standards of others (external), such as parents' standards (stage 3) or society's laws (stage 4).   302

convergence   A binocular cue for depth perception in which the eyes turn inward as an object gets closer. When eyes converge or diverge, information is sent to the brain, which interprets the information about the inward (object is closer) or outward (object is further away) eye movement.   106

convergent thinking   Thinking that produces one correct answer and is characteristic of the kind of thinking on standardized intelligence tests.   237

conversion disorder   A somatoform disorder in which an individual experiences genuine physical symptoms, even though no physiological problems can be found.   420

coping   Managing taxing circumstances, expending effort to solve life's problems, and seeking to master or reduce stress.   506

cornea   A clear membrane just in front of the eye; its function is to bend the light falling on the surface of the eye just enough to focus it at the back of the eye.   83

corpus callosum   A large bundle of axons that connects the brain's two hemispheres.   55

correlation coefficient   A numerical value that expresses the degree of relationship between two variables.   622

correlational method   A method in which the goal is to describe the strength of the relation between two or more events or characteristics.   20

counterconditioning   A classical conditioning procedure for weakening a conditioned response of fear by associating the fear-provoking stimulus with a new response that is incompatible with the fear.   158

couple therapy   Group therapy with married or unmarried couples whose major problem is their relationship.   460

crack   An intensified form of cocaine that consists of chips of pure cocaine that are usually smoked.   144

creativity   The ability to think in novel ways and to come up with unique solutions to problems.   237

credibility   A therapist's believability.   471

criminal commitment   Commitment that occurs when a mental disorder is implicated in the commission of a crime.   436

criterion validity   A test's ability to predict other measures, or criteria, of an attribute.   255

critical thinking   Grasping the deeper meaning of problems, keeping an open mind about different approaches and perspectives, and deciding for oneself what to believe or do.   235

cross-cultural studies   Studies that compare a culture with one or more other cultures and provide information about the degree to which people have characteristics that are similar, or universal, across cultures, and to what degree their behavior, thoughts, and feelings are culture specific.   550

crowding   The psychological experience that others are too close.   598

cue-dependent forgetting   Forgetting information because of failure to use effective retrieval cues.   210

cultural-familial retardation   A mental deficit in which no evidence of organic brain damage can be found; these individuals' IQs range from 50 to 70. Psychologists suspect that such mental deficits result from the normal variation that distributes people along the range of intelligence scores above 50, combined with growing up in a below-average intellectual environment.   258

culture-fair tests   Intelligence tests that are intended to not be culturally biased.   265

culture specificity hypotheses   The hypothesis that cultural experiences determine what is socially relevant in a person's life, and, therefore, what the person is most likely to remember.   216

culture   The behavior patterns, beliefs, and other products of a particular group of people; these include the values, work patterns, music, dress, diet, and rituals that are passed on from generation to generation. 11, 550

D

data Information that is obtained from systematic observation. 17

date or acquaintance rape Coercive sexual activity directed at someone with whom the perpetrator is at least casually acquainted. 346

daydreaming A form of consciousness that involves a low level of conscious effort. 123

debriefing Informing research participants about the complete nature of the study as soon as possible after the research is over. 24

decay theory The theory that when something new is learned, a neurochemical "memory trace" is formed, but over time this trace tends to disintegrate. 212

deception Intentionally misleading a participant about the purpose of a research study. 24

declarative memory The conscious recollection of information, such as specific facts or events, and, at least in humans, information that can be verbally communicated. Declarative memory has been called "knowing that" and, more recently, "explicit memory." 196

deductive reasoning Reasoning from the general to the specific; working with abstract statements (premises) and deriving a conclusion. 234

defense mechanisms The psychoanalytic term for unconscious methods of dealing with conflict; the ego distorts reality, thereby protecting itself from anxiety 380

deindividuation A state of reduced self-awareness, weakened self-restraints against impulsive actions, and apathy about negative social evaluation. 533

deinstitutionalization The movement to transfer the treatment of mental disabilities from inpatient medical institutions to community-based facilities that stress outpatient care. 463

delay of gratification The ability to defer immediate satisfaction for a more desirable future outcome. 389

delta waves The EEG pattern characteristic of deepening sleep and progressive muscle relaxation. 127

dendrite The receiving part of the neuron, serving the important function of collecting information and orienting it toward the cell body. 45

density The number of people per unit area. 598

deoxyribonucleic acid (DNA) A complex molecule that contains genetic information. 38

dependent variable The factor that is measured in an experiment. It can change as the independent variable is manipulated. The

label *dependent* is used because this variable depends on what happens to the subjects in the experiment. 22

depth perception The ability to perceive objects three-dimensionally. 105

descriptive method Systematic and objective description of behavior. 20

descriptive statistics Mathematical procedures used to describe and summarize samples of data in a meaningful fashion. 614

development The pattern of movement or change that begins at conception and continues through the life span. 275

diathesis-stress model A model according to which environmental stress and biogenetic disposition interact to produce abnormal behavior. 411

dichromats People with only two kinds of cones; they do not have normal color vision. 89

difference threshold Also called the just noticeable difference (jnd); the smallest difference in stimulation required to discriminate one stimulus from another 50 percent of the time. 76

diffusion of responsibility The tendency to feel less responsible and to act less responsibly in the presence of others. 544

discontinuity of development The view that development involves distinct stages in the life span. 276

discrimination In classical conditioning, the process of learning to respond to certain stimuli and not to others. 155

discrimination The enactment of prejudices to limit opportunities to an out-group or extend privileges to an in-group. 553

discriminative stimuli Stimuli that signal that a response will be reinforced. 172

disorganized schizophrenia A schizophrenic disorder in which an individual has delusions and hallucinations that have little or no recognizable meaning—hence the label *disorganized*. 431

display rules Sociocultural standards that determine when, where, and how emotions should be expressed. 362

dissociative disorders Psychological disorders that involve a sudden loss of memory or change in identity. Under extreme stress or shock, an individual's conscious awareness becomes dissociated (separated or split) from previous memories and thoughts. 421

dissociative identity disorder Formerly called multiple personality disorder. The most dramatic but least common dissociative disorder; individuals with this disorder have two or more distinct personalities. 421

divergent thinking Thinking that produces many answers to the same question and is characteristic of creativity. 237

dominant-recessive genes principle The principle that if one gene of a pair is dominant and the other is recessive, the dominant gene exerts its effect, overriding the potential influence of the recessive gene. A recessive gene exerts its influence only if both genes of the pair are recessive. 39

door-in-the-face strategy The technique in which a communicator makes the strongest point or demand in the beginning, which listeners will probably reject, then presents a weaker point or moderate, "concessionary" demand toward the end. 527

dopamine A brain neurotransmitter that is related to movement, attention, learning, and mental health. 48

double-blind study A study in which neither the subjects nor the experimenters know which subjects are in the experimental group and which are in the control group until the results are calculated. 24

double standard A belief that many sexual activities are acceptable for males but not females. 343

dream analysis The psychotherapeutic technique psychoanalysts use to interpret a client's dreams. Psychoanalysts believe that dreams contain information about the individual's unconscious thoughts and conflicts. 449

drive An aroused state that occurs because of a physiological need. 332

drive reduction theory The theory that a physiological need creates an aroused state (drive) that motivates the organism to satisfy the need. 332

DSM-IV *Diagnostic and Statistical Manual of Mental Disorders*, fourth edition. The *DSM-IV* is the most recent major classification of mental disorders and contains eighteen major classifications and describes more than 200 specific disorders. 413

dyslexia A learning difference that negatively influences the quality and rate of reading. 259

E

echoic memory The auditory sensory registers in which information is retained for up to several seconds. 193

eclectic Using a variety of approaches. 446

ecological theory A relatively recent view of sleep that is based on the theory of evolution. It argues that the main purpose of sleep is to prevent animals from wasting their energy and harming themselves during the parts of the day or night to which they have not adapted. 130

ectomorph Sheldon's term for a tall, thin, fragile person who is fearful, introverted, and restrained. 373

educational psychology The field that applies psychological concepts to teaching and learning. 604

efferent nerves Motor nerves that carry the brain's output. 43

effortful processing Processing that requires capacity or resources to encode information in memory. 200

ego The Freudian structure of personality that deals with the demands of reality; the ego is called the executive branch of personality because it makes rational decisions. 380

egocentrism A salient feature of preoperational thought; the inability to distinguish between one's own perspective and someone else's perspective. 287

egoism An attitude in which one does something beneficial for another person in order to ensure reciprocity; to present oneself as powerful, competent, or caring; or to avoid social or self-censure for failing to live up to normative expectations. 544

eidetic memory Also called photographic memory; a form of memory involving especially vivid details. The small number of individuals who have eidetic memory can recall significantly more details of visual information than most of us can. 194

elaboration The extensiveness of information processing at any given depth in memory. 201

electroconvulsive therapy (ECT) Commonly called shock treatment, a type of therapy sometimes used to treat severely depressed individuals by causing brain seizures similar to those caused by epilepsy. 474

electroencephalograph (EEG) An instrument that records the electrical activity of the brain; electrodes placed on an individual's scalp record brain-wave activity, which is reproduced on a chart known as an electroencephalogram. 66

embryonic period The period of prenatal development that occurs from 3 to 8 weeks after conception. 279

emotion Feeling, or affect, that involves a mixture of arousal (fast heartbeat, for example), conscious experience (thinking about being in love with someone, for example), and overt behavior (smiling or grimacing, for example). 353

emotion-focused coping Lazarus's term for responding to stress in an emotional manner, especially using defensive appraisal. 506

emotional intelligence Emotional self-understanding, managing your own emotions, reading others' emotions, and handling relationships well. 364

empirically keyed tests Tests that rely on the test items to predict a particular criterion. 398

empowerment Helping individuals develop skills they need to improve their adaptation and circumstances. 465

encoding The transformation of information in, and/or transfer of information into, a memory system. 199

encounter group A personal-growth group designed to promote self-understanding through candid group interaction. 462

endocrine system The hypothalamus and other endocrine glands that release their chemical products directly into the bloodstream. 53

endomorph Sheldon's term for a soft, round, large-stomached person who is relaxed, gregarious, and food loving. 373

endorphins Natural opiates that are brain neurotransmitters; they are involved in pleasure and the control of pain. 48

environment All of the surrounding conditions and influences that affect the development of living things. 36

environmental psychology The study of transactions between people and the physical environment. 596

episodic memory The retention of information about the where and when of life's happenings. 196

erogenous zones Those parts of the body at each stage of development that, according to Freud's theory, have especially strong pleasure-giving qualities. 380

estradiol A hormone associated in girls with breast, uterine, and skeletal development. 300

estrogens The main class of female sex hormones. 338

ethnic identity Identification based on membership in an ethnic group. 11

ethnicity A characteristic based on cultural heritage, nationality, race, religion, and language. 11, 550

ethnicity studies The study of universal and distinctive behaviors across ethnic groups. 550

ethnocentrism The tendency to favor one's own group over other groups. 554

ethology The study of the biological basis of behavior in natural habitats. 331

eustress Selye's term for the positive features of stress. 497

evolutionary perspective A perspective that emphasizes the importance of adaptation, reproduction, and "survival of the fittest." 10

evolutionary psychology A contemporary perspective that emphasizes the roles of evolution and psychological mechanisms in adaptive behavior. 41

exceptional learners Students who require additional services to meet their individual needs. 605

exhibitionism A psychosexual disorder in which individuals obtain sexual gratification from exposing their sexual anatomy to others. 345

exorcism A religious rite used during the Middle Ages that was designed to remove evil spirits from a person; it involved prayer, starvation, beatings, and various forms of torture. 444

experiment A carefully regulated procedure in which one or more factors believed to influence the behavior being studied are manipulated and all other factors are held constant. 22

experimental group The group whose experience is being manipulated in an experiment. 22

experimental method Provides the deepest explanation of all methods and allows psychologists to determine behavior's causes. (See also experiment) 21

experimenter bias The researcher's expectations influence the outcome of the research. 23

expert systems Computer-based systems for assessing knowledge and making decisions in advanced skill areas. 227

extinction In *classical conditioning*, the weakening of the conditioned response in the absence of the unconditioned stimulus. 157

extinction In *operant conditioning*, a decrease in the tendency to perform a behavior that no longer receives either positive or negative reinforcement. 171

extrasensory perception Perception that occurs without the use of known sensory processes. 113

extraversion A tendency to be sociable, active, and fun-seeking; one of the main personality traits according to Eysenck. 374

extrinsic motivation Motivation based on positive or negative external incentives. 330

extrinsic religious orientation Personal motives that lie outside the religion itself; using religion for some nonreligious ends. 577

F

face validity An assumption that the content of test items is a good indicator of what an individual's personality is like. 398

family systems therapy A form of therapy based on the assumption that psychological adjustment is related to patterns of interaction within the family unit. 460

family therapy Group therapy with family members. 460

feminist A person who believes that women and men should have the same rights. 571

feminization of poverty The fact that, increasingly, far more women than men live in poverty. Women's low incomes, divorce, and the way the judicial system typically resolves divorce cases are the likely causes of the feminization of poverty. 505

fetal alcohol syndrome (FAS) A cluster of abnormalities that appear in the offspring of mothers who drink alcohol heavily during pregnancy. 280

fetal period The prenatal period of development that begins 2 months after conception and lasts for 7 months, on the average. 279

fetishism Psychosexual disorder in which an individual relies on inanimate objects or a specific body part for sexual gratification. 345

figure-ground relationship The principle by which we organize the perceptual field into stimuli that stand out (figure) and those that are left over (ground). 103

five-factor model A model that bases personality on five main factors: neuroticism, extraversion, openness to experience, agreeableness, and conscientiousness. 374

fixation The psychoanalytic defense mechanism that occurs when the individual remains locked in an earlier developmental stage because her or his needs are under- or overgratified. 380

fixed action patterns Behaviors that are driven by genetic inheritance and are species-specific. 153

fixed-interval schedule Reinforcement of the first appropriate response after a fixed amount of time has elapsed. 170

fixed-ratio schedule Reinforcement of a behavior after a set number of responses. 170

flow According to Csikszentmihalyi, optimal experiences in life that are most likely to occur when a person develops a sense of mastery. Flow involves a state of concentration in which an individual becomes absorbed in an activity. 355

foot-in-the-door strategy A strategy in which an individual presents a weaker point or makes a small request with which listeners will probably comply in the beginning, saving the strongest point until the end. 527

forebrain The region of the brain that governs its highest functions; among its important structures are the thalamus, the hypothalamus and endocrine system, the limbic system, and the cerebral cortex. 50

forensic psychology The area of psychology that applies psychological concepts to the legal system. 599

formal operational thought Piaget's fourth stage of cognitive development, which appears between 11 and 15 years of age. Formal operational thought is abstract, idealistic, and logical. 288

fovea A minute area in the center of the retina where vision is at its best. 83

free association The technique of encouraging individuals to say aloud whatever comes to mind, no matter how trivial or embarrassing. 449

frequency With respect to sound waves, the number of cycles (full wavelengths) that pass through a point in a given time. 90, 125

frequency distribution A listing of scores from lowest to highest with the number of times each score appears in a sample. 615

frequency polygon Basically the same as a histogram except that the data are represented with lines instead of bars. 615

frequency theory The theory of hearing that states that the perception of a sound's frequency is due to how often the auditory nerve fires. 93

friendship A form of close relationship that involves enjoyment, acceptance, trust, intimacy, respect, mutual assistance, understanding, and spontaneity. 537

frontal lobe The portion of the cerebral cortex that is behind the forehead and is involved in the control of voluntary muscles and in intelligence. 54

frustration Any situation in which a person cannot reach a desired goal. 501

fugue A dissociative disorder in which an individual not only develops amnesia but also unexpectedly travels away from home and establishes a new identity (fugue means "flight"). 421

functional fixedness The inability to solve a problem because it is viewed only in terms of usual functions. 232

functionalism An approach to psychology that emphasizes the functions of the mind and behavior in adapting to the environment. 7

fundamental attribution error Observers' tendency to overestimate the importance of traits and underestimate the importance of situations when they seek explanations of an actor's behavior. 521

G

gate-control theory The theory that the spinal column contains a neural gate that can be opened (allowing the perception of pain) or closed (blocking the perception of pain). 95

gender schema A cognitive structure that organizes the world in terms of female and male. 563

gender schema theory The theory that children's attention and behavior are guided by an internal motivation to conform to gender-based, sociocultural standards and stereotypes. 563

gender stereotypes Broad categories, exaggerated generalizations, and/or false beliefs about females and males. 567

gender-role transcendence The belief that when an individual's competence is at issue, it should be conceptualized not on the basis of femininity, masculinity, or androgyny, but rather on a person basis. 571

gender The sociocultural dimension of being female or male. 11, 560

general adaptation syndrome (GAS) Selye's concept of the common effects on the body when demands are placed on it. The GAS consists of three stages: alarm, resistance, and exhaustion. 497

generalization In *classical conditioning*, the tendency of a new stimulus that is similar to the original conditioned stimulus to elicit a response that is similar to the conditioned response. 155

generalization In *operant conditioning*, giving the same response to similar stimuli. 171

generalized anxiety disorder An anxiety disorder that consists of persistent anxiety for at least 1 month. An individual with this disorder is unable to specify the reasons for the anxiety. 415

generativity versus stagnation Erikson's seventh stage of development, occurring mainly in middle adulthood. Middle-aged adults need to help the younger generation lead useful lives. 317

genes Short segments of DNA that are the units of hereditary information. Genes act as blueprints for cells to reproduce themselves through cell division called mitosis and manufacture the proteins that maintain life. 38

genital stage The fifth Freudian stage of development, occurring from puberty on; the time of sexual reawakening; the source of sexual pleasure now becomes someone outside of the family. 382

genuineness The Rogerian concept of the importance of the therapist's being genuine and not hiding behind a facade. 452

germinal period The period of prenatal development that takes place in the first 2 weeks after conception. 279

Gestalt psychology An approach that states that people naturally organize their perceptions according to certain patterns. *Gestalt* is a German word that means "configuration" or "form." One of Gestalt psychology's main principles is that the whole is not equal to the sum of its parts. 104

Gestalt therapy A humanistic therapy developed by Fritz Perls, in which the therapist questions and challenges clients to help them become more aware of their feelings and face their problems. 452

gifted Having above-average intelligence (an IQ of 120 or higher) and/or superior talent for something. 259

giving The client's receiving some kind of benefit from treatment early in the therapy process. 471

graphology A pseudopsychology that uses handwriting analysis to describe, explain, and predict behavior. 28

great person theory The theory that individuals with certain traits are best suited for leadership positions. 534

groupthink The motivation of group members to maintain harmony and unanimity in decision making, suffocating differences of opinion in the process. 532

H

hallucinogens Psychoactive drugs that modify a person's perceptual experiences and produce hallucinatory visual images. Hallucinogens are also called psychedelic ("mind altering") drugs. 145

hardiness A personality style characterized by a sense of commitment (rather than alienation), control (rather than powerlessness), and a perception of problems as challenges (rather than threats). 499

health psychology A multidimensional approach to health that emphasizes psychological factors, lifestyle, and the nature of the health-care delivery system. 483

heuristics Rules of thumb that can suggest a solution to a problem but do not ensure that it will work. 231

hidden observer A part of the person that is aware of what is happening during hypnosis yet remains passive. 138

hierarchy of motives Maslow's concept that all individuals have five main needs that must be satisfied, in the following sequence: physiological, safety, love and belongingness, self-esteem, and self-actualization. 333

hindbrain The lowest portion of the brain, located at the skull's rear. It consists of the spinal cord, the lower brain stem (pons and medulla), and the cerebellum. 50

hippocampus A limbic system structure that has a special role in the storage of memories. 54

histogram A graph of a frequency distribution, in which vertical bars represent the frequency of scores per category or class. 615

holophrase hypothesis The concept that a single word can be used to imply a complete sentence, and that infants' first words characteristically are holophrastic. 241

homeostasis The body's tendency to maintain an equilibrium or steady state. 332

hormones Chemical messengers manufactured by the endocrine glands. 53

hue A characteristic of color based on its wavelength content. 86

human factors psychology The subdivision of I/O psychology that focuses on the design of machines that workers use to perform their jobs, and the environment in which humans function, to make it safer and more efficient. 594

human sexual response cycle A cycle of four phases—excitement, plateau, orgasm, and resolution—identified by Masters and Johnson. 339

humanistic perspective A perspective that emphasizes a person's capacity for personal growth, freedom to choose a destiny, and positive qualities. 9

humanistic psychotherapies Therapies that encourage clients to understand themselves and to grow personally. Humanistic therapies emphasize conscious thoughts rather than unconscious thoughts, the present rather than the past, and growth and fulfillment rather than curing illness. 451

humanistic theory The most widely adopted phenomenological approach to personality. It stresses a person's capacity for personal growth, freedom to choose one's own destiny, and positive qualities. 391

hypnosis A psychological state of altered attention and awareness in which the individual is unusually receptive to suggestions. 137

hypochondriasis A somatoform disorder in which the individual has a pervasive fear of illness and disease. 420

hypothalamus An area just below the thalamus that monitors three enjoyable activities—eating, drinking, and sex; it also helps to direct the endocrine system through the pituitary gland; and it is involved in emotion, stress, and reward. 51

hypotheses Assumptions that can be tested to determine their accuracy. 17

hypothetical-deductive reasoning Piaget's name for adolescents' cognitive ability to develop hypotheses, or best guesses, about how to solve problems, such as algebraic equations. 289

I

iconic memory The visual sensory registers, in which information is retained for about 1/4 second. 193

id The Freudian structure of personality that consists of instincts, which are the person's reservoir of psychic energy. 379

identification theory A theory that stems from Freud's view that preschool children develop a sexual attraction to the opposite-sex parent, then at 5 to 6 years of age, renounce the attraction because of anxious feelings, subsequently identifying with the same-sex parent and unconsciously adopting the same-sex parent's behavior. 562

identity versus identity confusion The fifth of Erikson's stages of human development, occurring primarily in the adolescent years. Identity development involves finding out who we are, what we are all about, and where we are headed in life. 305

impression management The process in which individuals strive to present themselves in a favorable light. 520

imprinting The tendency of an infant animal to form an attachment to the first moving object it sees or hears. 294

incentives Positive or negative stimuli or events that motivate a person's behavior. 332

incest Sex between close relatives, which is virtually universally taboo. 344

inclusion Educating exceptional learners in the regular classroom. 605

independent variable The manipulated, influential, experimental factor. The label *independent* is used because this variable can be changed independently of other factors. 22

individual differences The consistent, stable ways people differ from each other. 250

individual psychology The name Adler gave to his theory to emphasize the uniqueness of every individual. 384

individualism Gives priority to personal goals rather than to group goals; an emphasis on values that serve the self, such as feeling good, personal achievement and distinction, and independence. 376, 551

inductive reasoning Reasoning from the specific to the general; drawing conclusions about all members of a category based on observing only some of the members. 233

indulgent parenting A style of parenting in which parents are very involved with their children but place few demands or controls on them; it is associated with children's social incompetence, especially a lack of self-control. 296

industrial psychology The subdivision of I/O psychology that involves personnel and human resource management. This includes job analysis, selection of employees, performance appraisal, and training. 587

industrial/organizational (I/O) psychology The branch of psychology that focuses on the workplace—both its workers and the organization that employs them—to make work more enjoyable and productive. 587

industry versus inferiority Erikson's fourth stage of development, occurring during the elementary school years. In this stage, children's initiative brings them into contact with a wealth of new experiences. As they move into middle and late childhood, they direct their energy toward mastering knowledge and intellectual skills. With their expansive imaginations, children at this stage are eager to learn. 291

inference A conclusion drawn from a premise or premises (such as an observation about behavior). 235

inferential statistics Complex mathematical methods used to draw conclusions about data that have been collected. 614

inferiority complex The name Adler gave to exaggerated feelings of inadequacy. 385

infinite generativity A person's ability to produce an endless number of meaningful sentences using a finite set of words and rules, which makes language a highly creative enterprise. 240

information theory The contemporary explanation of how classical conditioning works: The key to understanding classical conditioning is the information the organism obtains from the situation. 160

informed consent Participants in a research study are informed of what their participation involves as well as whether any risk is present, and have the right to withdraw from the study at any time. 24

initiative versus guilt Erikson's third stage of development, occurring during the preschool years. As preschool children encounter a widening social world, they are challenged more than they were as infants. Children in this stage are asked to assume responsibility for their bodies, their behavior, their toys, and their pets. 291

inner ear The oval window, cochlea, and organ of Corti. 93

insanity A legal term, not a psychological one. A legally insane person is considered mentally disordered and incapable of being responsible for his or her actions. 436

insanity defense A plea of "innocent by reason of insanity," used as a legal defense in criminal trials. 436

insight learning A form of problem solving in which an organism develops a sudden understanding of a problem's solution. 183

insight therapy Therapy that encourages insight into and awareness of oneself as the critical focus of therapy. 446

insomnia A common sleep problem; the inability to sleep. 131

instinct An innate, biological determinant of behavior. 331

instinctive drift The tendency of animals to revert to instinctive behavior that interferes with learning. 183

integration Maintenance of cultural integrity as well as movement to become an integral part of the larger culture. 503

integrity versus despair Erikson's eighth stage of development, occurring mainly in late adulthood. This is a time of looking back at what we have done with our lives. 321

intelligence Verbal ability, problem-solving skills, and the ability to learn from and adapt to the experiences of everyday life. 250

intelligence quotient (IQ) Devised in 1912 by William Stern; a person's mental age divided by chronological age, multiplied by 100. 251

interference theory The theory that we forget not because memories are actually lost from storage, but because other information gets in the way of retrieval of what we want to remember. 210

internalization The developmental change from behavior that is externally controlled to behavior that is controlled by internal, self-generated standards and principles. 302

interneurons Central nervous system neurons that mediate sensory input and motor output. Interneurons make up most of the brain. 44

interview A measure researchers use that involves asking questions to find out about a person's experiences and attitudes. 19

intimacy versus isolation Erikson's sixth stage of development, occurring mainly in early adulthood. Intimacy is the ability to develop close, loving relationships. 317

intrinsic motivation Motivation based on your own internal desires and needs. 330

intrinsic religious orientation Religious motives that lie within the person; living the religion. 577

introversion A tendency to be reserved, independent, and quiet; one of the main personality traits according to Eysenck. 374

ions Electrically charged particles that include sodium (NA^+), chloride (Cl^-), and potassium (K^+). The neuron creates electrical signals by moving these charged ions back and forth through its membrane; the waves of electricity that are created sweep along the membrane.

iris The colored part of the eye, which can range from light blue to dark brown. 82

J

James-Lange theory The theory that emotion results from physiological states triggered by stimuli in the environment. 358

justice perspective A theory of moral development that focuses on the rights of the individual; individuals independently make moral decisions. Kohlberg's theory is a justice perspective. 302

K

kinesthetic senses Senses that provide information about movement, posture, and orientation. 97

L

laboratory A controlled setting where many of the complex factors of the "real world" have been removed. 18

language A system of symbols used to communicate with others; in humans, characterized by organizational rules and infinite generativity. 240

latency stage The fourth Freudian stage of development, occurring approximately between 6 years of age and puberty; the child represses all interest in sexuality and develops social and intellectual skills. 382

latent content The psychoanalytic term for the unconscious, unremembered, symbolic aspects of a dream. 449

latent learning Changes in behavior that occur without direct experience. 160

law of effect Developed by Robert Thorndike, this law states that behaviors followed by positive outcomes are strengthened, whereas behaviors followed by negative outcomes are weakened. 162

learned helplessness A response that occurs when animals or humans are exposed to aversive stimulation, such as prolonged stress or pain, over which they have no control. The inability to avoid such aversive stimulation produces an apathetic state of helplessness. 427

learning A relatively permanent change in behavior that occurs through experience. 153

learning difference Problematic development in specific academic skills that does not reflect overall intellectual ability. 258

learning set A strategy that an individual tends to use to solve problems. 232

lens of the eye The transparent and somewhat flexible ball-like entity filled with a gelatinous material; its function is to bend the light falling on the surface of the eye just enough to focus it at the back of the eye. 83

levels of processing theory Craik and Lockhart's theory that memory processing occurs on a continuum from shallow to deep; in this theory, deeper processing produces better memory. 200

light A form of electromagnetic energy that can be described in terms of wavelengths. 81

limbic system A loosely connected network of structures under the cerebral cortex that plays an important role in memory and emotion. 54

linguistic relativity hypothesis The view that culture shapes language, which further determines the structure of thinking and shapes our basic ideas. 244

lithium A drug that is widely used to treat bipolar disorder. 473

long-term memory A type of memory that holds huge amounts of information for a long period of time, relatively permanently. 195

loudness The perception of a sound wave's amplitude. 90

lucid dreams A class of dreams in which a person "wakes up" mentally but remains in the sensory landscape of the dream world. 136

M

magnetic resonance imaging (MRI) An imaging technique that involves creating a magnetic field around a person's body and using radio waves to construct images of the person's tissues (such as brain tissues) and biochemical activity.   67

mainstream culture   A dominant set of values and expectations.   550

maintenance rehearsal   The conscious repetition of information that increases the length of time the information stays in working memory.   194

major depression   A mood disorder in which the individual is deeply unhappy, demoralized, self-derogatory, and bored. An individual with a major depression shows changes in appetite and sleep patterns, decreased energy, feelings of worthlessness, concentration problems, and guilt feelings that might prompt thoughts of suicide.   423

managed health care   A system in which external reviewers approve the type and length of treatment to justify insurance reimbursement.   448

manifest content   The psychoanalytic term for the conscious, remembered aspects of a dream.   449

marginalization   The process in which groups are put out of cultural and psychological contact with both their traditional society and the larger, dominant society.   503

masochism   A psychosexual disorder in which individuals obtain sexual gratification from being subjected to pain, inflicted by others or themselves.   345

matching hypothesis   The hypothesis that while we may prefer a more attractive person in the abstract, in the real world we end up choosing someone who is close to our own level of attractiveness.   536

maturation   The orderly sequence of changes dictated by each person's genetic blueprint.   276

mean   The numerical average for a group of scores or values.   616

measure of central tendency   A single number that tells you the overall characteristics of a set of data.   616

measures of variability (measures of dispersion)   Measures of how much the scores in a sample vary from one another.   617

median   The score that falls exactly in the middle of a distribution of scores after they have been arranged (ranked) from highest to lowest.   616

medical model   Also called the disease model; the forerunner of the biological approach. This model states that abnormal behavior is a disease or illness precipitated by internal physical causes.   409

meditation   A system of thought and form of practice that incorporates exercises to attain bodily or mental control and well-being, as well as enlightenment.   510

medulla   A part of the brain that begins where the spinal cord enters the skull; it helps to control breathing and regulates a portion of the reflexes that allow us to maintain an upright posture.   50

memory   The retention of information over time. Psychologists study how information is initially placed, or encoded, into memory; how it is retained, or stored, after being encoded; and how it is found, or retrieved, for a certain purpose later.   192

memory processes   The encoding of new information into memory, the representation of information, and the retrieval of what was previously stored.   199

memory span   The number of digits an individual can report back in order following a single presentation of them.   193

menopause   The time in middle age, usually in the late forties or early fifties, when a woman's menstrual periods cease completely.   312

mental age (MA)   An individual's level of mental development relative to others.   251

mental processes   Thoughts, feelings, and motives that each person experiences privately but that cannot be observed directly.   6

mental retardation   A condition of limited mental ability in which an individual has a low IQ, usually below 70 on a traditional intelligence test, and has difficulty adapting to everyday life.   257

mentor   A role model who acts as an advisor, coach, and confidant.   176

mesomorph   Sheldon's term for a strong, athletic, and muscular person who is energetic, assertive, and courageous.   373

meta-analysis   A research strategy that involves statistically combining the results of many different studies.   465

method of introspection   The process in which specially trained people systematically observe and analyze their own mental experience.   7

method of loci   A mnemonic strategy in which information is associated with a well-known sequence of activities or locations.   219

midbrain   An area between the hindbrain and the forebrain where many nerve fiber systems ascend and descend to connect lower and higher portions of the brain; in particular, the midbrain relays information between the brain and the eyes and ears.   50

middle ear   An area of the ear with these four main parts: eardrum, hammer, anvil, and stirrup.   92

Minnesota Multiphasic Personality Inventory (MMPI)   The self-report personality test most widely used in clinical and research settings.   399

mnemonics   Techniques for making memory more efficient.   219

mode   The score that occurs most often.   617

monocular cues   Depth cues based on each eye working independently.   105

mood disorders   Psychological disorders characterized by wide emotional swings, ranging from deeply depressed to highly euphoric and agitated. Depression can occur alone, as in major depression, or it can alternate with mania, as in bipolar disorder.   423

morphology   The rules of combining morphemes, which are the smallest meaningful strings of sounds that contain no smaller meaningful parts.   241

motherese   Talking to babies in a higher-pitched voice than normal and with simple words and sentences.   244

motivation   Why people behave, think, and feel the way they do. Motivated behavior is energized and directed.   330

motives   What energize and direct behavior toward solving a problem or achieving a goal.   330

movement aftereffects   An illusion of movement that occurs when we watch continuous movement in one direction and then look at a stationary surface, which then appears to move in the opposite direction.   106

multiaxial system   A feature of the *DSM-IV* in which individuals are classified on the basis of five dimensions, or "axes," that include the individual's history and highest level of functioning in the last year. This system ensures that the individual will not merely be assigned to a mental disorder category, but instead will be characterized by a number of clinical factors.   413

multiple-factor theory   L. L. Thurstone's theory that intelligence consists of seven primary mental abilities: verbal comprehension, number ability, word fluency, spatial visualization, associative memory, reasoning, and perceptual speed.   251

myelin sheath   A layer of fat cells that encases most axons; it insulates the axon and helps nerve impulses travel faster.   45

N

narcolepsy   The overpowering urge to fall asleep.   132

natural selection   The evolutionary process that favors the individuals within a species that are best adapted to survive and reproduce in their particular environment.   41

nature   A term often used to describe an organism's biological inheritance.   36

nature/nurture controversy   *Nature* refers to an organism's biological inheritance, *nurture* to environmental experiences. The "nature" proponents claim biological inheritance is the most important influence on development, the "nurture" proponents claim that environmental experiences are the most important.   276

need   A deprivation that energizes the drive to eliminate or reduce the deprivation.   332

negative affectivity (NA)   Emotions that are negatively toned, such as anxiety, anger, guilt, and sadness.   353

negative correlation   A relationship in which the two factors vary in opposite directions.   622

negative reinforcement   Reinforcement in which the frequency of a response increases because the response either removes a stimulus or involves avoiding the stimulus.   164

neglectful parenting   A style of parenting in which parents are very uninvolved in the child's life; it is associated with children's social incompetence, especially a lack of self-control.   296

neo-Piagetians   Developmentalists who have elaborated on Piaget's theory, believing that children's cognitive development is more specific in many respects than Piaget thought.   289

neurobiological perspective   A perspective that emphasizes that the brain and nervous system play central roles in understanding behavior, thought, and emotion.   10

neurons   Nerve cells, the basic units of the nervous system.   42

neurotic disorders   Relatively mild mental disorders in which the individual has not lost contact with reality.   413

neurotransmitters   Chemical substances that carry information across the synaptic gap to the next neuron.   47

night terror   A state characterized by sudden arousal from sleep and intense fear, usually accompanied by a number of physiological reactions.   122

nightmare   A frightening dream that awakens the sleeper from REM sleep.   132

nonstate view   The view that hypnotic behavior is similar to other forms of social behavior and can be explained without appealing to special processes. Hypnotic behavior is purposeful, goal-directed action that is best understood by the way subjects interpret their situation and how they try to present themselves.   139

normal distribution   A symmetrical distribution with a majority of cases falling in the middle of the possible range of scores and few scores appearing toward the extremes of the range. Also called a bell-shaped curve.   256, 616

norms   Established standards of performance for a test. Norms are established by giving the test to a large group of people who represent the target population. This allows the researcher to determine the distribution of test scores. Norms tell us which scores are high, low, or average.   255

norms   Rules that apply to the members of a group.   530

nurture   A term often used to describe an organism's environmental experiences.   36

O

obedience   Behavior that complies with the explicit demands of an individual in authority.   527

object permanence   The Piagetian term for one of an infant's most important accomplishments: understanding that objects and events continue to exist even when they cannot directly be seen, heard, or touched.   285

observational learning   Learning that occurs when a person observes and imitates someone else's behavior; also called imitation or modeling.   174

obsessive-compulsive disorder (OCD)   An anxiety disorder in which the individual has anxiety-provoking thoughts that will not go away (obsession) and/or urges to perform repetitive, ritualistic behaviors to prevent or produce a future situation (compulsion).   419

obsessive-compulsive personality disorder (OCD)   A personality disorder in the anxious, fearful cluster; anxious adjustment is the primary feature.   434

occipital lobe   The portion of the cerebral cortex at the back of the head that is involved in vision.   54

Oedipus complex   In Freud's theory, the young child's developing an intense desire to replace the parent of the same sex and to enjoy the affections of the opposite-sex parent.   382

olfactory epithelium   Tissue located at the top of the nasal cavity that contains a sheet of receptor cells for smell.   100

operant conditioning (instrumental conditioning)   A form of learning in which the consequences of behavior produce changes in the probability of the behavior's occurrence.   161

operations   In Piaget's theory, mental representations that are reversible; internalized sets of actions that allow the child to do mentally what was done physically before.   286

opiates   Opium and its derivatives, which depress the central nervous system's activity.   144

opponent-process theory   The theory that cells in the visual system respond to red-green and blue-yellow colors; a given cell might be excited by red and inhibited by green, while another cell might be excited by yellow and inhibited by blue.   89

oral stage   The term Freud used to describe development during the first 18 months of life, when the infant's pleasure centers on the mouth.   380

organ of Corti   A part of the ear that runs the length of the cochlea and sits on the basilar membrane. It contains the ear's sensory receptors, which change the energy of sound waves into nerve impulses that can be processed by the brain.   93

organic retardation   Mental retardation caused by a genetic disorder or by brain damage. Organic refers to the tissues or organs of the body, so there is some physical damage in organic retardation.   258

organizational psychology   The subfield of I/O psychology that examines the social and group influences in an organization.   589

outer ear   The pinna and the external auditory canal.   91

overcompensation   Adler's term for the individual's attempt to deny rather than acknowledge a real situation, or the individual's exaggerated efforts to conceal a weakness.   385

overload   The occurrence of stimuli so intense that the person cannot cope with them.   500

P

pain threshold   The stimulation level at which pain is first perceived.   95

panic disorder   A recurrent anxiety disorder that is marked by the sudden onset of apprehension or terror.   417

papillae   Bumps on the surface of the tongue that contain taste buds, which are the receptors for taste.   100

paranoid schizophrenia   A schizophrenic disorder characterized by delusions of reference, grandeur, and persecution.   431

paraphilias   Psychosexual disorders in which the source of an individual's sexual satisfaction is an unusual object, ritual, or situation.   345

parasympathetic nervous system   The division of the autonomic nervous system that calms the body.   43

parietal lobe   The portion of the cerebral cortex at the top of the head and toward the rear; it is involved in processing bodily sensations.   54

partial reinforcement   Intermittent reinforcement; responses are not reinforced every time they occur.   169

pedophilia   A psychosexual disorder in which the sex object is a child and the intimacy usually involves manipulation of the child's genitals.   345

pegword method   A mnemonic strategy that involves using a set of mental pegwords associated with numbers.   219

perception   The brain's process of organizing and interpreting sensory information to give it meaning.   75

perceptual set Expectations that influence how perceptual elements will be interpreted. 103

peripheral nervous system A network of nerves that connects the brain and spinal cord to other parts of the body. Takes information to and from the brain and spinal cord and carries out the commands of the CNS to execute various muscular and glandular activities. 42

person-centered therapy A form of humanistic therapy developed by Carl Rogers, in which the therapist provides a warm, supportive atmosphere to improve the client's self-concept and encourage the client to gain insight about problems. 452

personal growth groups Groups that have their roots in the humanistic therapies; they emphasize personal growth and increased openness and honesty in interpersonal relations. 462

personality Enduring, distinctive thoughts, emotions, and behaviors that characterize the way an individual adapts to the world. 372

personality disorders Psychological disorders that develop when personality traits become inflexible and, thus, maladaptive. 433

phallic stage Freud's third stage of development, which occurs between the ages of 3 and 6; its name comes from the Latin word *phallus,* which means "penis." During the phallic stage, pleasure focuses on the genitals as the child discovers that self-stimulation is enjoyable. 382

phenomenological worldview A worldview that stresses the importance of our perceptions of ourselves and of our world in understanding personality. This view emphasizes that, for each individual, reality is what that person perceives. 390

phobias Irrational fears. 158

phobic disorder An anxiety disorder that occurs when an individual has an irrational, overwhelming, persistent fear of a particular object or situation; commonly called a phobia. 417

phonology The study of language's sound system. 240

phrenology Gall's pseudoscientific idea that the bumps on the skull are associated with personality and intelligence. 61

pitch The perceptual interpretation of sound's frequency. 90

pituitary gland An important endocrine gland that sits at the base of the skull and is about the size of a pea; this gland controls growth and regulates other glands. 53

place theory The theory of hearing that states that each frequency produces vibrations at a particular spot on the basilar membrane. 93

placebo effect Subjects' expectations, rather than the experimental treatment, produce the desired outcomes. 23

plasticity The brain's capacity to modify and reorganize itself following damage. 64

pleasure principle The Freudian concept that the id always seeks pleasure and avoids pain. 379

pluralism The coexistence of distinct ethnic and cultural groups in the same society. 556

polygraph A machine that is used to try to determine if someone is lying, by monitoring changes in the body—heart rate, breathing, and electrodermal response (an index that detects skin resistance to passage of a weak electric current)—thought to be influenced by emotional states. 361

pons A bridge in the hindbrain that contains several clusters of fibers involved in sleep and arousal. 50

population The complete group of organisms from which the sample is selected. 18

positive affectivity (PA) The range of positive emotion, from high energy, enthusiasm, and excitement to being calm, quiet, and withdrawn. Joy and happiness involve positive affectivity. 353

positive correlation A relationship in which the two factors vary in the same direction. 622

positive reinforcement Reinforcement in which the frequency of a response increases because the response is followed by a stimulus. 163

positron-emission tomography (PET scan) An imaging technology that measures the amount of specially treated glucose in various areas of the brain, then sends this information to a computer. 66

postconventional level Kohlberg's highest level of moral thinking; moral development is completely internalized and not based on others' standards. An individual recognizes alternative moral courses, explores the options, and then develops a personal moral code. The code is among the principles generally accepted by the community (stage 5) or it is more individualized (stage 6). 302

posthypnotic amnesia The subject's inability to remember what took place during hypnosis, induced by the hypnotist's suggestions. 137

posthypnotic suggestion A suggestion, made by the hypnotist while the subject is in a hypnotic state, that the subject carries out after emerging from the hypnotic state. 137

post-traumatic stress disorder A mental disorder that develops through exposure to any of several traumatic events, such as war, the Holocaust, severe abuse as in rape, natural disasters such as floods and tornados, and

accidental disasters such as plane crashes. The disorder is characterized by anxiety symptoms that may be apparent 1 month after the trauma or be delayed by months or even years until onset. 419

precognition Knowing events before they occur. 113

preconventional level Kohlberg's lowest level of moral thinking, in which an individual shows no internalization of moral values—moral thinking is based on punishments (stage 1) or rewards (stage 2) that come from the external world. 302

prejudice An unjustified, usually negative, attitude toward an individual based on the individual's membership in a group. 553

preoperational thought The term Piaget gave to the 2- to 7-year-old child's understanding of the world. Children at this stage of reasoning cannot understand such logical operations as the reversibility of mental representations. 286

preparedness The species-specific biological predisposition to learn in certain ways but not in others. 183

primacy effect Superior recall for items at the beginning of a list. 208

primacy effect The enduring quality of initial impressions. 519

primary prevention A community psychology concept, borrowed from the public health field, denoting efforts to reduce the number of new cases of mental disorders. 464

primary reinforcement The use of reinforcers that are innately satisfying (that is, they do not require any learning on the organism's part to make them pleasurable). 168

proactive interference Interference that occurs when material that was learned earlier disrupts the recall of material learned later. 210

problem-focused coping Lazarus's term for the cognitive strategy of squarely facing one's own troubles and trying to solve them. 506

problem solving An attempt to find an appropriate way of attaining a goal when the goal is not readily available. 230

procedural memory Knowledge in the form of skills and cognitive operations about how to do something. Procedural memory has been called "knowing how" and, more recently, "implicit memory." 196

projective tests Tests that present individuals with an ambiguous stimulus and then ask them to describe it or tell a story about it. Projective tests are based on the assumption that the ambiguity of the stimulus allows individuals to project into it their feelings, desires, needs, and attitudes. 400

pseudopsychology A nonscientific system that resembles psychology but lacks scientific support. 28

psychiatry   A branch of medicine practiced by physicians with an M.D. degree who specialize in abnormal psychology and therapy. 13

psychoactive drugs   Substances that act on the nervous system to alter our states of consciousness, modify our perceptions, and change our moods. 139

psychoanalysis   Freud's therapeutic technique for analyzing an individual's unconscious thought. 449

psychoanalytic perspective   A perspective that emphasizes unconscious thought, conflict between biological instincts and society's demands, and early family experiences. 9

psychodynamic therapies   Therapies that stress the importance of the unconscious mind, extensive therapist interpretation, and the role of infant and early childhood experiences. 449

psychogenic amnesia   A dissociative disorder involving memory loss caused by extensive psychological stress. 421

psychokinesis   Closely associated with ESP; the mind-over-matter phenomenon of being able to move objects without touching them, such as mentally getting a chair to rise off the floor or shattering a glass merely by staring at it. 113

psychological dependence   The need to take a drug to cope with problems and stress. 140

psychology   The scientific study of behavior and mental processes in context. 5

psychoneuroimmunology   The field that explores the connections among psychological factors (such as attitudes and emotions), the nervous system, and the immune system. 483

psychophysics   The formal study of psychological reactions to physical stimuli. 75

psychosexual disorders   Sexual problems caused mainly by psychological factors. 344

psychosexual dysfunctions   Disorders that involve impairments in the sexual response cycle, either in the desire for gratification or in the ability to achieve it. 344

psychosurgery   A biomedical therapy that involves the removal or destruction of brain tissue to improve the person's psychological adjustment. 475

psychotherapy   The process of working with individuals to reduce their emotional problems and improve their adjustment. 446

psychotic disorders   Severe mental disorders in which the individual has lost contact with reality. 413

puberty   A period of rapid skeletal and sexual maturation that occurs in early adolescence. 299

punishment   A consequence that decreases the probability that a behavior will occur. 164

pupil   The opening, which appears black, in the center of the iris. 82

Q

questionnaires (or surveys)   Measures similar to interviews except that the respondents read the questions and mark their answers on paper rather than verbally responding to the interviewer. 19

R

racism   The belief that members of another race or ethnic group are inferior. 554

random assignment   Assignment of subjects to experimental and control groups by chance. This practice reduces the likelihood that the experiment's results will be due to any preexisting differences between the groups. 22

random sample   A sample obtained by a method that gives every member of the population an equal chance of being selected for study. 18

range   The distance between the highest and the lowest score. 617

rape   Forcible sexual intercourse with a person who does not give consent. 345

rapport talk   The language of conversation. It is a way of establishing connections and negotiating relationships. Women prefer to engage in rapport talk. 565

rational-emotive therapy   Therapy based on Albert Ellis's assertion that people become psychologically disordered because of their beliefs, especially those that are irrational and self-defeating. 457

reality principle   The Freudian concept that the ego tries to make the pursuit of individual pleasure conform to the norms of society. 380

reasoning   The mental activity of transforming information to reach conclusions. 233

recall   A memory measure in which the individual must retrieve previously learned information, as on an essay test. 209

recency effect   Superior recall for items at the end of a list. 208

recognition   A memory measure in which the individual only has to identify (recognize) learned items, as on a multiple-choice test. 209

reductionistic   Explaining behavior too simply, in terms of only one or two factors; a criticism of behaviorism. 388

reflexes   Automatic stimulus-response connections that are "hardwired" into the brain. 153

reinforcement (reward)   A consequence that increases the probability that a behavior will occur. 163

reliability   A measure of whether a test performs in a consistent manner. 254

religion   A belief system that individuals use to morally and spiritually guide their behavior. 576

religious conversion   A change from having no religious beliefs to accepting a religious system, or changing from one belief system to another. 578

REM sleep   A periodic stage of sleep during which dreaming occurs. 128

repair theory   The theory that sleep restores, replenishes, and rebuilds our brains and bodies, which are somehow worn out by the day's waking activities. 130

replication   Repeating research strategies to confirm original findings. 24

report talk   Talk that is designed to give information, which includes public speaking. Men prefer to engage in report talk. 565

representativeness heuristic   Judging the probability of an event by how well it matches a prototype. 233

resistance   The psychoanalytic term for a client's unconscious defense strategies that prevent the analyst from understanding the client's problems. 450

resting potential   The stable, negative charge of an inactive neuron. 45

reticular formation   A diffuse collection of neurons involved in stereotyped patterns of behavior such as walking, sleeping, or turning to attend to a sudden noise. 50

retina   The light-sensitive surface in the back of the eye that houses light receptors called rods and cones. 83

retinal or binocular disparity   Perception in which the individual sees a single scene even though the images on the eyes are slightly different. 106

retroactive interference   Interference that occurs when material learned later disrupts the recall of material learned earlier. 210

retrograde amnesia   A memory disorder that involves memory loss for a segment of the past but not for new events. 213

rites of passage   Ceremonies or rituals that mark an individual's transition from one status to another. 308

rods   Receptors in the retina that are exquisitely sensitive to light but are not very useful for color vision. 83

roles   Rules and expectations that govern certain positions in a group. Roles define how people should behave in a particular position in the group. 530

romantic love   Also called passionate love or Eros; a type of love with strong components of sexuality and infatuation; it often predominates in the early part of a love relationship. 538

romantic script   A sexual script in which sex is synonymous with love. In this script, if people develop a relationship and fall in love, it is acceptable for them to have sex, whether married or not.   342

Rorschach inkblot test   The most well-known projective test, developed in 1921 by Swiss psychiatrist Hermann Rorschach. It uses individuals' perceptions of inkblots to determine their personality.   400

S

sadism   A psychosexual disorder in which individuals obtain sexual gratification from inflicting pain on others.   345

sample   The group of organisms (human or animal) being studied.   18

saturation   A characteristic of color based on its purity.   86

scatter plot   A graph on which pairs of scores are represented.   620

schedules of reinforcement   Timetables that determine when a response will be reinforced.   169

schema   A mental framework that organizes and guides an individual's perceptions.   205, 563

schizophrenic disorders   Severe psychological disorders characterized by distorted thoughts and perceptions, odd communication, inappropriate emotion, abnormal motor behavior, and social withdrawal.   428

schizotypal personality disorder.   A personality disorder in the odd, eccentric cluster. Individuals with this disorder appear to be in contact with reality, but many aspects of their behavior are distasteful, which leads to rejection or withdrawal from others.   434

science of psychology   The science that uses systematic methods to observe, describe, explain, and predict human behavior.   6

scientific method   A strategy designed to obtain accurate information. It includes these steps: Identify and analyze a problem, develop tentative explanations, collect data, draw conclusions, and confirm or revise theory.   17

sclera   The white outer part of the eye, which helps to maintain the shape of the eye and to protect it from injury.   82

script   A schema for an event.   207

secondary prevention   A prevention method involving screening for early detection of problems and early intervention; a community psychology concept.   464

secondary reinforcement   Reinforcement that acquires its positive value through experience; secondary reinforcers are learned, or conditioned, reinforcers.   168

secure attachment   Securely attached infants use the caregiver, usually the mother, as a secure base from which to explore the environment. Ainsworth believes that secure attachment in the first year of life provides an important foundation for psychological development later in life.   295

selective attention   The focusing of attention on a narrow band of information.   200

self-actualization   The highest and most elusive of Maslow's needs; the motivation to develop to one's full potential as a human being.   333

self-concept   An individual's overall perceptions of her or his abilities, behavior, and personality; a central theme for Rogers and other humanists.   391

self-efficacy   The belief that one can master a situation and produce positive outcomes. 390, 456

self-efficacy   The expectation that one can master a situation and produce positive outcomes.   180

self-help groups   Voluntary organizations of individuals who get together on a regular basis to discuss topics of common interest. The group leader and members give support to help individuals with their problems. Self-help groups are so-called because they are conducted without a professional therapist. 462

self-instructional methods   Cognitive behavioral techniques aimed at teaching individuals to modify their own behavior.   456

self-monitoring   Individuals' attention to the impressions they make on others and the degree to which they fine-tune their performance accordingly.   520

self-perception theory   Bem's theory of connections between attitudes and behavior; it stresses that individuals make inferences about their attitudes by perceiving their behavior.   523

self-report tests   Tests that assess personality traits by asking individuals what their traits are; not designed to reveal unconscious personality characteristics.   398

semantic memory   A person's general knowledge about the world. It includes a person's fields of expertise, general academic knowledge of the sort learned in school, and "everyday" knowledge about meanings of words, famous individuals, important places, and common things.   196

semantics   The meanings of words and sentences.   241

semicircular canals   Canals in the inner ear that contain the sensory receptors that detect body motion, such as tilting of the head or body.   97

sensation   The process of detecting and encoding stimulus energy in the world.   75

sensation seeking   Behavior motivated by the need for varied, novel, and complex sensations and experiences.   79

sensorimotor thought   The first Piagetian stage, lasting from birth to about 2 years of age. In this stage, infants construct an understanding of the world by coordinating sensory experiences (such as seeing and

hearing) with physical (motor) actions—hence the term *sensorimotor*.   285

sensory adaptation   Diminished sensitivity to prolonged exposure to a stimulus.   79

sensory deprivation   The absence of normal external stimulation for extended periods of time.   80

sensory memory   Memory that holds information from the world in its original sensory form for only an instant, not much longer than the brief time for which one is exposed to the visual, auditory, and other sensations.   192

separation   Self-imposed withdrawal from the larger culture.   503

serial position effect   The effect of an item's position in a list on our recall of it; in particular, recall is superior for items at the beginning and at the end of a list.   208

serotonin   A brain neurotransmitter that is involved in the regulation of sleep, mood, arousal, and pain.   48

set point   The weight maintained when no effort is made to gain or lose weight.   337, 488

sexism   Prejudice and discrimination against an individual because of her or his sex.   569

sexual script   A stereotyped pattern of role prescriptions for how individuals should behave sexually.   342

sexually transmitted diseases (STDS)   Diseases that are contracted primarily through sex—intercourse as well as oral-genital and anal-genital sex.   493

shape constancy   Recognition that an object remains the same shape even though its orientation to us changes.   107

shaping   The process of rewarding approximations of desired behavior.   167

signal detection theory   The theory that no absolute threshold exists—but that, rather, sensitivity to sensory stimuli depends on the strength of the sensory stimulus, the respondent's sensory abilities, and a variety of psychological and contextual factors.   77

situational theory of leadership   The theory that the needs of a group change from time to time and that a person who emerges as leader in one circumstance will not necessarily be the person who becomes a leader in another circumstance.   534

situationism   Mischel's view that a person's personality often varies from one context to another.   389

size constancy   Recognition that an object remains the same size even though the retinal image of the object changes.   107

skepticism   The tendency to doubt the validity of claims in the absence of evidence.   26

sleep apnea   A sleep disorder in which individuals stop breathing because their windpipe fails to open or brain processes involved in respiration fail to work properly. 132

sleep spindles Brief bursts of higher-frequency brain waves during sleep 127

social comparison The process in which individuals evaluate their thoughts, feelings, behaviors, and abilities in relation to other people. 519

social desirability The tendency of participants to tell the interviewer what they think is socially acceptable or desirable rather than what they truly feel or think. 19, 398

social exchange theory The theory that individuals should benefit those who benefit them, or that, for a benefit received, an equivalent benefit should be returned at some point. 543

social identity theory The theory that when individuals are assigned to a group, they invariably think of the group as an in-group for them. This occurs because individuals want to have a positive self-image. Social identity theory helps to explain prejudice and conflict between groups. 554

social learning theory of gender The idea that children's gender development occurs through observation and imitation of gender-related behavior, as well as through the rewards and punishments children experience for gender-appropriate and gender-inappropriate behaviors. 562

social perception Judgment about the qualities of individuals, which involves how we form impressions of others, how we gain self-knowledge from perception of others, and how we present ourselves to others to influence their perceptions of us. 518

social policy A national government's course of action designed to influence the welfare of its citizens. 276

social support Information and feedback from others that one is loved and cared for, esteemed and valued, and included in a network of communication and mutual obligation. 508

sociocultural perspective A perspective that emphasizes that culture, ethnicity, and gender, among other sociocultural contexts, are essential to understanding behavior. 10

socioemotional processes Processes that involve changes in an individual's relationships with other people, changes in emotions, and changes in personality. 275

somatic nervous system A division of the peripheral nervous system consisting of sensory nerves that convey information from the skin and muscles to the central nervous system about such matters as pain and temperature, and motor nerves, which tell muscles when to act. 42

somatoform disorders Mental disorders in which the psychological symptoms take a physical, or somatic, form, even though no physical causes can be found. 420

somatotype theory Sheldon's theory that precise charts reveal distinct body types, which in turn are associated with certain personality characteristics. 373

somnambulism Sleepwalking; it occurs during the deepest stages of sleep. 131

sounds Vibrations of air that are processed by the auditory (hearing) system; also called sound waves. 90

S-O-R model A model of learning that gives some importance to cognitive factors. *S* stands for stimulus, *O* for organism, and *R* for response. 179

special process theory Hilgard's theory that hypnotic behavior involves a special cognitive state that is different from normal cognitive states during nonhypnotic behavior, and that hypnotic responses are involuntary and involve a hidden observer. 138

spontaneous recovery The process in classical conditioning by which a conditioned response can appear again after a time delay without further conditioning. 157

sport psychology The field that applies psychology's principles to improving sport performance and the enjoyment of sport participation. 602

standard deviation A measure of how much the scores vary, on the average, around the mean of a sample. 618

standardization The development of uniform procedures for administering and scoring a test; also the development of norms for the test. 255

standardized tests Tests that require people to answer a series of written or oral questions. The tests have two distinct characteristics. First, an individual's score is totaled to produce a single overall score. Second, the individual's score is compared to the scores of large numbers of other similar people to determine how the individual responded relative to others. 19

statistical significance The idea that the differences observed between two groups are sufficiently large that it is highly unlikely that they are due merely to chance. 626

stereotype A generalization about a group's characteristics that does not consider any variation from one individual to another. 552

stimulants Psychoactive drugs that increase the central nervous system's activity. 144

stimulus substitution Pavlov's theory of how classical conditioning works: The nervous system is structured in such a way that the CS and US bond together and eventually the CS substitutes for the US. 160

storm-and-stress view G. Stanley Hall's view that adolescence is a turbulent time charged with conflict and mood swings. 298

stream of consciousness A continuous flow of changing sensations, images, thoughts, and feelings. 122

stress The response of individuals to the circumstances and events, called stressors, that threaten them and tax their coping abilities. 496

stress management programs Programs that teach individuals how to appraise stressful events, how to develop skills for coping with stress, and how to put these skills to use. 510

striving for superiority The human motivation to adapt to, improve, and master the environment. 385

stroboscopic motion The illusion of movement created when the image of an object is flashed on and off in rapid succession at slightly different places on the retina. 106

structuralism An approach to psychology that emphasizes classifying sensations in order to discover the mind's structures. 7

subliminal perception Perception of stimuli below the threshold of awareness. 78

substance-use disorder A disorder characterized by one or more of the following features: (1) a pattern of pathological use that involves frequent intoxication, a need for daily use, and an inability to control use—in the sense of psychological dependence; (2) a significant impairment of social or occupational functioning attributed to drug use; and (3) physical dependence that involves serious withdrawal problems. 435

subtractive mixture The mixing of pigments rather than of beams of light. 87

superconducting quantum interference device (SQUID) A brain-scanning device that senses tiny changes in magnetic fields. 67

superego The Freudian structure of personality that is the moral branch of personality. The superego takes into account whether something is right or wrong. 380

superiority complex Adler's concept of exaggerated self-importance that is designed to mask feelings of inferiority. 385

sympathetic nervous system The division of the autonomic nervous system that arouses the body. 43

synapses Tiny gaps between neurons. Most synapses are between the axon of one neuron and the dendrites or cell body of another neuron. 47

syntax The ways words are combined to form acceptable phrases and sentences. 241

systematic desensitization A method of behavior therapy that treats anxiety by associating deep relaxation with successive visualizations of increasingly intense anxiety-producing situations; this technique is based on classical conditioning. 454

T

tardive dyskinesia   A major side effect of the neuroleptic drugs; a neurological disorder characterized by grotesque, involuntary movements of the facial muscles and mouth, as well as extensive twitching of the neck, arms, and legs.   473

taste aversion   The conditioned avoidance of ingesting substances that cause nausea or other unpleasant reactions.   184

telegraphic speech   The use of short and precise words to communicate; characteristic of young children's two- and three-word utterances.   242

telepathy   The transfer of thought from one person to another.   113

temporal lobe   The portion of the cerebral cortex that is just above the ears and is involved in hearing.   54

teratogen   (The word comes from the Greek word *tera*, meaning "monster.") Any agent that causes a birth defect. The field of study that investigates the causes of birth defects is called teratology.   280

tertiary prevention   A community psychology concept denoting efforts to reduce the long-term consequences of mental health disorders that were not prevented or arrested early in the course of the disorders.   464

test-retest reliability   Consistency of results when a person is given the same test on two different occasions.   254

testosterone   A hormone associated in boys with development of the genitals, an increase in height, and a change of voice.   300

thalamus   An area at the top of the brain stem in the central core of the brain; it serves as an important relay station functioning much like a telephone switchboard between the diverse areas of the cortex and the reticular formation.   50

theory   A coherent set of ideas that helps to explain data and make predictions.   17

Thematic Apperception Test (TAT)   An ambiguous projective test designed to elicit stories that reveal something about an individual's personality; developed by Henry Murray and Christiana Morgan in the 1930s.   401

theta waves   Low-frequency and low-amplitude EEG patterns that characterize stage 1 sleep.   127

timbre   The tone color or perceptual quality of a sound.   91

tip-of-the-tongue phenomenon, or TOT state   A type of effortful retrieval that occurs when people are confident they know something but just can't quite seem to pull it out of memory.   208

token economy   A behavior modification system in which behaviors are reinforced with tokens (such as poker chips) that can be exchanged later for desired rewards (such as candy, money, or going to a movie).   455

tolerance   The state in which a greater amount of a drug is needed to produce the same effect.   140

traditional information-processing model   Atkinson and Shiffrin's model according to which memory involves a sequence of three stages—sensory registers, short-term (working) memory, and long-term memory.   197

traditional religious script   A sexual script in which sex is acceptable only within marriage; both premarital and extramarital sex are taboo, especially for women. In this script, sex is for reproduction and sometimes for affection.   342

trait theories   Theories that propose that people have broad dispositions that are reflected in the basic ways they behave, such as whether they are outgoing and friendly or whether they are dominant and assertive.   373

traits   Broad dispositions that lead to characteristic responses.   372

tranquilizers   Depressant drugs, such as Valium and Xanax, that reduce anxiety and induce relaxation.   144

transcendental meditation (TM)   The most popular form of meditation in the United States. TM is derived from an ancient Indian technique and involves a mantra, which is a resonant sound or phrase that is repeated mentally or aloud to focus attention.   510

transference   The psychoanalytic term for a client's relating to an analyst in ways that reproduce or relive important relationships in the client's life.   449

transsexualism   A psychosexual disorder in which an individual has an overwhelming desire to become a member of the opposite sex.   345

transvestism   Psychosexual disorder in which an individual obtains sexual gratification by dressing up as a member of the opposite sex.   345

trephining   A procedure, no longer used, that involved chipping a hole in the skull to allow evil spirits to escape.   444

triangular theory of love   Sternberg's theory that love comes in three main forms: passion, intimacy, and commitment.   539

triarchic theory   Sternberg's theory that intelligence consists of componential intelligence, experiential intelligence, and contextual intelligence.   251

trichromatic theory   The theory that color perception is based on the existence of three types of receptors, each of which is maximally sensitive to different, but overlapping, ranges of wavelengths.   88

trichromats   People with normal color vision; they have three kinds of cone receptors.   89

trust versus mistrust   Erikson's first psychosocial stage, experienced in the first year of life. Trust is built when an infant's basic needs—such as needs for comfort, food, and warmth—are met.   291

two-factor theory   Spearman's theory that individuals have both general intelligence, which he called *g*, and a number of specific intelligences, which he called *s*.   251

Type A behavior pattern   A cluster of characteristics—being excessively competitive, hard-driven, impatient, and hostile—thought to be related to the incidence of heart disease.   499

U

unconditional positive regard   Rogers's term for accepting, valuing, and being positive toward another person regardless of the person's behavior.   391

unconditioned response (UR)   An unlearned response that is automatically associated with the unconditioned stimulus.   153

unconditioned stimulus (US)   A stimulus that produces a response without prior learning.   153

unconscious thought   Freud's concept of a reservoir of unacceptable wishes, feelings, and thoughts that are beyond conscious awareness.   122

undifferentiated schizophrenia   A schizophrenic disorder characterized by disorganized behavior, hallucinations, delusions, and incoherence.   431

V

validity   The extent to which a test measures what it is purported to measure.   255

variable-interval schedule   Reinforcement of a response after a variable amount of time has elapsed.   170

variable-ratio schedule   A timetable in which responses are rewarded an average number of times, but on an unpredictable basis.   170

ventromedial hypothalamus (VMH)   A region of the hypothalamus that plays an important role in controlling hunger.   336

vestibular sense   The sense that provides information about balance and movement.   97

visual illusion   An illusion that occurs when two objects produce exactly the same retinal image but are perceived as different images.   109

volley theory   The theory of hearing that states that high frequencies can be signaled by teams of neurons that fire at different offset times to create an overall firing rate that could signal a very high frequency.   93

voyeurism   A psychosexual disorder in which individuals obtain sexual gratification from observing the sex organs or sex acts of others, often from a secret vantage point.   345

wavelength The distance from the peak of one wave to the peak of the next. 81

Weber's law The principle that two stimuli must differ by a constant proportion (rather than a constant amount) for their difference to be detected. 76

withdrawal An addict's undesirable intense pain and craving for an addictive drug when the drug is withdrawn. 140

working memory Also sometimes called short-term memory, this is a limited-capacity memory system in which information is retained for as long as 30 seconds, unless the information is rehearsed, in which case it can be retained longer. 193

Yerkes-Dodson law The generalization that performance is best under conditions of moderate, rather than low or high, arousal. 354

zone of proximal development (ZPD) Tasks that are too difficult for children to master alone but that can be mastered with the guidance and assistance of adults or more-skilled children. 290

zygote A fertilized egg. 278

References

A

Aamodt, M. G. (1996). *Applied industrial/organizational psychology* (2nd ed.). Pacific Grove, CA: Brooks/Cole.

Abramson, L. Y., Metalsky, G. I., & Alloy, L. B. (1989). Hopelessness depression: A theory-based subtype of depression. *Psychological Review, 96,* 358–372.

Adams, H. E., & Cassidy, J. F. (1993). The classification of abnormal behavior: An overview. In P. B. Sutker & H. E. Adams (Eds.), *Comprehensive textbook of psychopathology* (2nd ed.). New York: Plenum Press.

Adler, A. (1927). *The theory and practice of individual psychology.* New York: Harcourt, Brace, & World.

Adler, T. (1991, January). Seeing double? Controversial twins study is widely reported, debated. *APA Monitor, 22,* 1, 8.

Ainsworth, M. D. S. (1979). Infant-mother attachment. *American Psychologist, 34,* 932–937.

Al-Issa, I. (1982a). Does culture make a difference in psychopathology? In I. Al-Issa (Ed.), *Culture and psychopathology.* Baltimore: University Park Press.

Al-Issa, I. (1982b). Sex differences in psychopathology. In I. Al-Issa (Ed.), *Culture and psychopathology.* Baltimore: University Park Press.

Albee, G. W. (1988). Foreword. In P. A. Bronstein & K. Quina (Eds.), *Teaching a psychology of people: Resources for gender and sociocultural awareness.* Washington, DC: American Psychological Association.

Alberti, R., & Emmons, M. (1995). *Your perfect right* (7th ed.). San Luis Obispo, CA: Impact.

Allen, J. B. (1998). DSM-IV. In H. S. Friedman (Ed.), *Encyclopedia of mental health (vol. 1).* San Diego: Academic Press.

Allison, J. A., & Wrightsman, L. S. (1993). *Rape: The misunderstood crime.* Newbury Park, CA: Sage.

Allport, G. W. (1966). The religious context of prejudice. *Journal for the Scientific Study of Religion, 5,* 447–457.

Allport, G. (1954). *The roots of prejudice.* Cambridge, MA: Addison-Wesley.

Allport, G. (1937). *Personality: A psychological interpretation.* New York: Holt.

Allport, G. W., & Odbert, H. S. (1936). Trait names: A psycholexical study. *Psychological Monographs, 47* (whole no. 211).

Allport, G. W., & Ross, J. M. (1967). Personal religious orientation and prejudice. *Journal of Personality and Social Psychology, 5,* 432–443.

Alvarez, R., & Lopez, M. (1996). Effects of elements or compound preexposure on conditioned taste aversion as a function of retention interval. *Animal Learning and Behavior, 23,* 391–399.

Amabile, T. M., Phillips, E. D., & Collins, M. A. (1993, August). *Creativity by contract: Social influences on the creativity of professional artists.* Paper presented at the meeting of the American Psychological Association, Toronto.

Amoore, J. E. (1970). *Molecular basis of odor.* Springfield, IL: Charles C Thomas.

Anastasi, A. (1988). *Psychological testing* (6th ed.). New York: Macmillan.

Anderson, B. L. (1983). Primary orgasmic dysfunction: Diagnostic considerations and a review of treatment. *Psychological Bulletin, 93,* 105–136.

Anderson, B. L., Kiecolt, J.K., & Glaser, R. (1994). A biobehavioral model of cancer stress and disease course. *American Psychologist, 49,* 389–404.

Anderson, N. H. (1965). Primary effects in personality impression formation using a generalized order effect paradigm. *Journal of Personality and Social Psychology, 2,* 1–9.

Aponte, H. (1979). Family therapy and the community. In M. S. Gibbs, J. R. Lachenmeyer, & J. Sigel (Eds.), *Community psychology: Theoretical and empirical approaches.* New York: Gardner Press, 1979.

Aronson, E. (1992). *The social animal* (6th ed.). New York: W. H. Freeman.

Aronson, E. (1986, August). *Teaching students things they think they already know all about: The case of prejudice and desegregation.* Paper presented at the meeting of the American Psychological Association, Washington, DC.

Aronson, E., Wilson, T. D., & Akert, R. M. (1977). *Social psychology* (2nd ed.). New York: Longman.

Asch, S. E. (1951). Effects of group pressure on the modification and distortion of judgments. In H. S. Guetzkow (Ed.), *Group leadership and men.* Pittsburgh: Carnegie University Press.

Ashe, J. H., & Aramakis, V. B. (1998) Brain development and plasticity. In H. S. Friedman (Ed.), *Encyclopedia of mental health (vol. 1).* San Diego: Academic Press.

Astin, A. W. (1993). *What matters in college.* San Francisco: Jossey-Bass.

Atkinson, D. R., & Hackett, G. (1998). *Counseling diverse population (2nd Ed.),* Burr Ridge, IL: McGraw-Hill.

Atkinson, D. R., Morten, G., & Sue, D.W. (1998). *Counseling American minorities (5th Ed.).* Burr Ridge, IL: McGraw-Hill.

Atkinson, D. R., Morten, G., & Sue, D. W. (1999). *Counseling American minorities: A cross-cultural perspective* (6th ed.). Dubuque, IA: McGraw-Hill.

Atkinson, J. W., & Raynor, I. O. (1974). *Motivation and achievement.* Washington, DC: V. H. Winston.

Atkinson, R. C., & Shiffrin, R. M. (1968). Human Memory: A proposed system and its control processes. In K. W. Spence & J. T. Spence (Eds.), *The psychology of learning and motivation* (Vol. 2). San Diego: Academic Press.

Auerbach, S. M., & Gramling, S. E. (1998). *Stress management.* Upper Saddle River, NJ: Prentice-Hall.

Averill, J. R. (1983). Studies on anger and aggression: Implications for theories of emotion. *American Psychologist, 38,* 1145–1160.

Azar, B. (1996, January). Damaged area of brain can reorganize itself. *APA Monitor, 27,* 18–19.

B

Baars, B. J. (1989). *A cognitive theory of consciousness.* New York: Cambridge University Press.

Baddeley, A. (1993). Working memory and conscious awareness. In A. F. Collins, S. E. Gathercole, M. A. Conway, & P. E. Morris (Eds.), *Theories of memory.* Hillsdale, NJ: Erlbaum.

Baddeley, A. (1990) *Human memory: Theory and practice.* Boston: Allyn & Bacon.

Bagley, C. (1984). The social aetiology of schizophrenia in immigrant groups. In J. E. Mezzich & C. E. Berganza (Eds.), *Culture and psychopathology.* New York: Columbia University Press.

Bahrick, H. P., Bahrick, P. O., & Wittlinger, R. P. (1975). Fifty years of memory for names and faces: A cross-sectional approach. *Journal of Experimental Psychology: General, 104,* 54–75.

Baldwin, J. D., & Baldwin, J. I. (1998). Sexual behavior. In H. S. Friedman (Ed.), *Encyclopedia of mental health (vol. 3).* San Diego: Academic Press.

Ball, W., & Tronick, E. (1971). Infant responses to impending collision: Optical and real. *Science, 171,* 818–820.

Baltes, P. B. (1996, August). *On the incomplete architecture of human ontogenesis.* Invited award address presented at the meeting of the American Psychological Association, Toronto.

Baltes, P. B., Linderberger, U., & Staudinger, U. M. (1998). Life-span theory in developmental psychology. In R. M. Lerner (Ed.), *Theoretical models of human development. Vol. 1: Handbook of Child Psychology* (5th ed.), New York: Wiley.

Banaji, M., & Prentice, D. A. (1994). The self in social contexts. *Annual Review of Psychology, 45,* 297–332.

Bandura, A. (1998). Self-efficacy, In H. S. Friedman (Ed.), *Encyclopedia of mental health (vol. 3).* San Diego: Academic Press.

Bandura, A. (1997). *Self-efficacy: The exercise of self-control.* New York: W. H. Freeman.

Bandura, A. (1997). *Self-efficacy.* Upper Saddle River, NJ: Prentice Hall.

Bandura, A. (1994). Social cognitive theory of mass communication. In J. Bryant & D. Zillman (Eds.), *Media effects.* Hillsdale, NJ: Erlbaum.

Bandura, A. (1991). Self-efficacy: Impact of self-beliefs on adolescent life paths. In R. M. Lerner, A. C. Petersen, & J. Brooks-Gunn (Eds.), *Encyclopedia of adolescence* (Vol. 2). New York: Garland.

Bandura, A. (1989). Social cognitive theory. In R. Vasta (Ed.), *Six theories of child development: Revised formulations and current issues.* Greenwich, CT: JAI Press.

Bandura, A. (1986). Social foundations of thought and action. Englewood Cliffs, NJ: Prentice Hall.

Bandura, A. (1977). *Self-efficacy: The exercise of self-control.* New York: W. H. Freeman.

Bandura, A. (1977). *Self-efficacy: The exercise of self-control.* W. H. Freeman.

Bandura, A. (1977), *Social learning theory.* Englewood Cliffs, NJ: Prentice Hall.

Bandura, A. (1965). Influence of models' reinforcement contingencies on the acquisition of imitative responses. *Journal of Personality and Social Psychology, 1,* 589–595.

Bandura, A., Blanchard, E. B., & Ritter, B. (1969). Relative efficacy of desensitization and modeling approaches for inducing behavioral, affective, and attitudinal changes. *Journal of Personality and Social Psychology, 13,* 173–199.

Barber, A. E., Hollenbeck, J. R., Tower, S. L., & Phillips, J. M. (1994). The effects of interview focus on recruitment effectiveness: A field experiment. *Journal of Applied Psychology, 79,* 886–896.

Bard, P. (1934). Emotion. In C. Murchison (Ed.), *Handbook of general experimental psychology.* Worcester, MA: Clark University Press.

Barker, P. (1998). Family therapy, In H. S. Friedman (Ed.), *Encyclopedia of mental health (vol. 1).* San Diego: Academic Press.

Barlow, D. H., Blanchard, E. B., Vermilyea, J. A., Vermilyea, B. B., & Dimardo, P. A. (1986). Generalized anxiety and generalized anxiety disorder: Description and reconceptualization. *American Journal of Psychiatry, 143,* 40–44.

Baron, N. (1992). *Growing up with language.* Reading, MA: Addison-Wesley.

Barron, F. (1989, April). The birth of a notion. Exercises to tap you creative potential. *Omni,* pp. 112–119.

Barry, H., Child, I. L., & Bacon, M. K. (1959). Relation of child training to subsistence economy. *American Anthropologist, 61,* 51–63.

Bartlett, F. C. (1932). *Remembering.* Cambridge, England: Cambridge University Press.

Bartley, S. H. (1969). *Principles of perception.* New York: Harper & Row.

Bartoshuk, L. (1994, June). *Clinical studies as aids in teaching taste.* Paper presented at the meeting of the American Psychological Association, Washington, DC.

Baruch, G. K., Biener, I., & Barnett, R. C. (1987). Women and gender in research on work and family. *American Psychologist, 42,* 130–136.

Batson, C. D., Bolen, M. H., Cross, J. A., & Jeuringer-Benefiel, H. E. (1986). Where is the altruism in the altruistic personality? *Journal of Personality and Social Psychology, 50,* 212–220.

Batson, C. D., Schoenrade, P., & Ventis, W. L. (1993). *Religion and the individual.* New York: Oxford University Press.

Baum, A. & Valins, S. (1977). *Architecture and social behavior: Psychological studies of social density.* Mahwah, NJ: Erlbaum.

Baumrind, D. (1991). Parenting styles and adolescent development. In J. Brooks-Gunn, R. Lerner, & A. C. Petersen (Eds.), *The encyclopedia of adolescence.* New York: Garland.

Baumrind, D. (1971). Current patterns of parental authority. *Developmental Psychology Monographs, 4* (1, Pt. 2).

Beck, A. (1976). *Cognitive therapies and the emotional disorders.* New York: International Universities Press.

Beck, A. T. (1993). Cognitive therapy: Past, present, and future. *Journal of Consulting and Clinical Psychology, 61,* 194–198.

Beck, A.T. (1967). *Depression.* New York: Harper & Row.

Beckman, F. E. & Leber, W. R. (Eds.). (1995). *Handbook of depression* (2nd ed.) New York: Guilford Press.

Bednar, R. L., & Peterson, S. R. (1995). *Self-esteem* (2nd ed.). Washington, DC: American Psychological Association.

Bell, A. P., Weinberg, M. S., & Mammersmith, S. K. (1981). *Sexual preference: Its development in men and women.* New York: Simon & Schuster.

Belle, D., Longfellow, C., Makosky, V., Saunder, E., & Zelkowitz, P. (1981). Income, mothers' mental health, and family functioning in a low-income population. In American Academy of Nursing (Ed.), *The impact of changing resources on health policy.* Kansas City: American Nurses Association.

Bem, D. J. (1967). Self-perception. An alternative interpretation of cognitive dissonance phenomena. *Psychological Review, 74,* 183–200.

Bem, S. L. (1977). On the utility of alternative procedures for assessing psychological androgyny. *Journal of Consulting and Clinical Psychology, 45,* 196–205.

Benbadis, S. R., Wolgamuth, B. R., Perry, M. C., & Dudley, S. D. (1995). Dreams and rapid eye movement sleep in the multiple sleep latency test. *Sleep, 18,* 105–108.

Benbow, C. P., & Stanley, J. C. (1983). Sex differences in mathematical reasoning ability: More facts. *Science, 222,* 1029–1031.

Bennett, M. E., & others (1993). Identifying young substance-abusers: the Rutgers Collegiate Substance Abuse Screening Test. *Journal of Studies on Alcohol, 54,* 522–527.

Bennett, W. I., & Gurin, J. (1982). *The dieter's dilemma: Eating less and weighing more.* New York: Basic Books.

Berger, S. M. (1971). Observer perseverance as related to a model's success: A social comparison analysis. *Journal of Personality and Social Psychology, 19,* 341–350.

Bergin, A. E., & Garfield, S. L. (1994). *Handbook of psychotherapy and behavior change.* New York: Wiley.

Berndt, T. J., & Perry, T. B. (1990). Distinctive features and effects of early adolescent friendships. In R. Montemayor (Ed.), *Advances in adolescent research.* Greenwich, CT: JAI.

Bernstein, I. L. (1991). Aversion conditioning in response to cancer and cancer treatment. *Clinical Psychology Review, 11,* 185–191.

Berry, J. W. (1983). Textured contexts: Systems and situations in cross-cultural psychology. In S. H. Irvine & J. W. Berry (Eds.), *Human assessment and cultural factors.* New York: Plenum.

Berry, J. W. (1980). Acculturation as varieties of adaptation. In A. Padilla (Ed.), *Acculturation: Theory, model, and some new findings.* Washington, DC: American Association for the Advancement of Science.

Berry, J. W. (1971). Ecological and cultural factors in spatial perceptual development. *Canadian Journal of Behavioral Science, 3,* 324–336.

Berscheid, E. (1988). Some comments on love's anatomy: Or, whatever happened to an old-fashioned lust? In R. J. Sternberg & M. L. Barnes (Eds.). *Anatomy of love.* New Haven, CT: Yale University Press.

Berscheid, E., & Fei, J. (1977). Sexual jealousy and romantic love. In G. Clinton & G. Smith (Eds.), *Sexual jealousy.* Englewood Cliffs, NJ: Prentice Hall.

Berscheid, E., Snyder, M., & Omoto, A. M. (1989). Issues in studying close relationships: Conceptualizing and measuring closeness. In C. Hendrick (Ed.), *Close relationships.* Newbury Park, CA: Sage.

Bertelson, A. (1979). A Danish twin study of manic-depressive disorders. In M. Schous & E. Stromgren (Eds.), *Origin, prevention, and treatment of affective disorders.* Orlando, FL: Academic Press.

Bexton, W. H., Heron, W., & Scott, T. H. (1954). Effects of decreased variation in the sensory environment. *Canadian Journal of Psychology, 8,* 70–76.

Bhugra, D., & de Silva, P. (1998). Sexual dysfunction therapy. In H. S. Friedman (Ed.), *Encyclopedia of mental health (vol. 3).* San Diego: Academic Press.

Bidikov, I., & Meier, D. E. (1997). Clinical decision-making with the woman after menopause. *Geriatrics, 52* (3), 28–35.

Billings, A. G., & Moos, R. H. (1981). The role of coping responses and social resources in attenuating the stress of life events. *Journal of Behavioral Medicine, 4,* 157–189.

Birren, J. E., Schaie, K. W., Abeles, R. P., & Salthouse, T. J. (Eds.) (1996). *Handbook of the psychology of aging* (4th ed.). San Diego: Academic Press.

Blackmore, S. (1987). A report of a visit to Carl Sargent's laboratory. *Journal of the Society for Psychical Research, 54,* 186–198.

Blechman, E. A., & Brownell, K, D, (Eds.). (1987). *Handbook of behavioral medicine for women.* Elmsford, NY: Pergamon.

Bloom, B. (1975). *Changing patterns of psychiatric care.* New York: Human Science Press.

Bloom, B. L. (1985). *Community mental health: A general introduction* (2nd ed.). Monterey, CA: Brooks/Cole.

Blundell, J. E. (1984). Systems and interactions: An approach to the pharmacology of feeding. In A. J. Stunkard & E. Stellar (Eds.), *Eating and its disorders.* New York: Raven Press.

Bobocel, D. R., Hing, L. S., Davey, L. M., & Zanna, M. P. (1998). The concern for justice and reactions to affirmative action. In R. Cropanzano (Ed.), *Justice in the workplace—II.* Mahwah, NJ: Erlbaum.

Bogatz, G., & Ball, S. (1972). *Reading with television: An evaluation of the Electric Company.* Princeton, NJ: Educational Testing Service.

Bolles, R. C. (1993). *The story of psychology: A thematic history.* Pacific Grove, CA: Brooks/Cole.

Bouchard, T. J., Heston, L., Eckert, E., Keyes, M., & Resnick, S. (1981). The Minnesota Study of Twins Reared Apart: Project description and sample results in the developmental domain. *Twin Research, 3,* 227–233.

Bourguignon, E., & Evascu, T. (1977). Altered states of consciousness within a general evolutionary perspective: A holocultural analysis. *Behavior Science Research, 12,* 199–216.

Bourne, L. J. (1995). *The anxiety and phobia workbook.* Oakland, CA: New Harbinger.

Bower, G. H., Clark, M., Winenz, D., & Lesgold, A. (1969). Hierarchical retrieval schemes in recall of categorized word lists. *Journal of Verbal Learning and Verbal Behavior, 3,* 323–343.

Bowers, K. S. (August, 1992). *The problem of consciousness.* Paper presented at the meeting of the American Psychological Association, Washington, DC.

Bowers, T. G., & Clum, G. A. (1988). Relative contribution of specific and nonspecific treatment effects: Meta-analysis of placebo-controlled behavior therapy research. *Psychological Bulletin, 103,* 315–323.

Bowlby, J. (1989). *Secure attachment.* New York: Basic Books.

Bowlby, J. (1980). Attachment and loss. In *Loss, sadness, and depression* (Vol. 3). New York: Basic Books.

Bowlby, J. (1969). *Attachment and loss* (Vol. 1). London: Hogarth Press.

Boyd-Franklin, N. (1989). *Black families in therapy.* New York: Guilford.

Bransford, J. D., & Stein, B. S. (1984). *The ideal problem solver.* New York: W. H. Freeman.

Braun, B. G. (1988). *The treatment of multiple personality disorder.* Washington, DC: American Psychiatric Press.

Breland, K. & Breland, M. (1961). The misbehavior of organisms. *American Psychologist, 16,* 681–684.

Bretherton, I. (1996). Attachment theory and research in historical and personal context. *Contemporary Psychology, 41,* 236–237.

Brewer, M. B., & Campbell, D. T. (1976). *Ethnocentrism and intergroup attitudes.* New York: Wiley.

Brickman, P., Coates, D., & Janoff-Bulman, R. J. (1978). Lottery winners and accident victims: Is happiness relative? *Journal of Personality and Social Psychology, 36,* 917–927.

Briggs, J. L. (1970). *Never in anger.* Cambridge, MA: Harvard University Press.

Brigham, J. C. (1986). Race and eyewitness identifications. In S. Worschel & W. G. Austin (Eds.), *Psychology of intergroup relations.* Chicago: Nelson-Hall.

Brigham, J. C., Maas, A., Snyder, L. D., & Spalding, K. (1982). Accuracy of eyewitness identification in a field setting. *Journal of Personality and Social Psychology, 41,* 683–691.

Brislin, R. (1993). *Understanding culture's influence on behavior.* Fort Worth, TX: Harcourt Brace.

Brobeck, J. R., Tepperman, T., & Long, C. N. (1943). Experimental hypothalamic hyperphagia in the albino rat. *Yale Journal of Biological Medicine, 15,* 831–853.

Brody, J. (1994, August). *How to die young as late in life as possible.* Paper presented at the meeting of the American Psychological Association, Toronto.

Bronfenbrenner, U., & Morris, P. A. (1998). The ecology of developmental process. In W. Damon (Ed.), *Handbook of child psychology (5th Ed., Vol. 1).* New York: Wiley.

Bronstein, P. A., & Quina, K. (1988). Perspectives on gender balance and cultural diversity in the teaching of psychology. In P. A. Bronstein & K. Quina (Eds.), *Teaching a psychology of people: Resources for gender and sociocultural awareness.* Washington, DC: American Psychological Association.

Brophy, J. (1998). *Motivation.* Burr Ridge, IL: McGraw-Hill.

Brooks-Gunn, J. (1966, March). *The uniqueness of the early adolescent transition.* Paper presented at the meeting of the Society for Research on Adolescence, Boston.

Broverman, I., Vogel, S., Broverman, D., Clarkson, F., & Rosenkranz, P. (1972). Sexrole stereotypes: A current appraisal. *Journal of Social Issues, 28,* 59–78.

Brown, A. L. (in press). Transforming schools into communities of thinking and learning. *American Psychologist.*

Brown, A. L., & Compione, J. C. (1996). Psychological learning theory and the design of innovative environments. In L. Schauble & R. Glaser (Eds.), *Innovations in learning.* Mahwah, NJ: Erlbaum.

Brown, E., Deffenbacher, K., & Sturgill, W. (1977). Memory for faces and the circumstances of encounter. *Journal of Applied Psychology, 6,* 311–318.

Brown, G., Bhrolchain, M., & Harris, T. (1975). Social class and psychiatric disturbance among women in an urban population. *Sociology, 9,* 225–254.

Brown, R. (1973). *A first language: The early stages.* Cambridge, MA: Harvard University Press.

Browne, A., & Williams, K. R. (1993). Gender, intimacy, and lethal violence: Trends from 1976 through 1987. *Gender and Society, 7,* 78–98.

Browne, M. W. (1994, October 16). What is intelligence, and who has it? *New York Times Book Review,* pp. 2–3, 41–42.

Brownell, K. D., & Cohen, L. R. (1995). Adherence to dietary regimens. *Behavioral Medicine, 20,* 226–242.

Brownell, K. D., & Rodin, J. (1994). The dieting maelstrom: Is it possible and advisable to lose weight? *American Psychologist, 9,* 781–791.

Brownell, K.D., & Rodin, J. (in press). Medical, metabolic, and psychological effects of weight cycling and weight variability. *Archives of Internal Medicine.*

Bruner, J. S. (1996). *The culture of education.* Cambridge, MA: Harvard University Press.

Budwig, N. (1995). *A developmental-functionalist approach to child language.* Hillsdale, NJ: Erlbaum.

Burgess, K. (1968). The behavior and training of a killer whale *(Orcinus orca)* at San Diego Sea World. *International Zoo Yearbook, 8,* 202–205.

Burns, D. (1985). *Intimate connections.* New York: William Morrow.

Burns, D. (1980). *Feeling good.* New York: Avon.

Burt, M. R., Resnick, G., & Novick, E. R. (1998). *Building supportive communities for at-risk adolescents.* Washington, DC: American Psychological Association.

Buss, C. M., & Barnes, M. (1986). Preferences in human mate selection. *Journal of personality and Social Psychology, 50,* 559–570.

Buss, D. M. (1996). The evolutionary psychology of human social strategies. In E. T. Higgins & A. W. Kruglanski (Eds.), *Social psychology: Handbook of basic principles.* New York: Guilford Press.

Buss, D. M. (1995). Evolutionary psychology: A new paradigm for psychological science. *Psychological Inquiry. 6.* 1–30.

Buss, D. M., & Schmitt, D. P. (1993). Sexual strategies theory: An evolutionary perspective on human mating. *Psychological Review, 100,* 204–232.

Butcher, J. N. (Ed.). (1995). *Clinical personality assessment.* New York: Oxford University Press.

Butler, R. A. (1953). Discrimination learning by rhesus monkeys to visual-exploration motivation. *Journal of Comparative and Physiological Psychology, 46,* 95–98.

Butters, N., Delis, D., & Lucas, J. (1995). Clinical assessment of memory disorders in amnesia and dementia. *Annual Review of Psychology, 46,* Palo Alto, CA: Annual Reviews.

C

Caldwell, C. H. (1996). Predisposing, enabling, and need factors related to help-seeking in Black women. In H. W. Neighbors & J. S. Jackson (Eds.), *Mental health in Black America.* Newbury Park, CA: Sage.

Cameron, D. (1988, February). Soviet schools. *NEA Today,* p. 15.

Cameron, N. (1963). *Personality development and psychopathology.* Boston: Houghton Mifflin.

Campbell, D. T., & LeVine, R. A. (1968). Ethnocentrism and intergroup relations. In R. Abelson & others (Eds.), *Theories of cognitive consistency: A sourcebook.* Chicago: Rand McNally.

Campbell, F. A., & Ramey, C. T. (1993, March). *Mid-adolescent outcomes for high risk students: An examination of the continuing effects of early intervention.* Paper presented at the biennial meeting of the Society for Research in Child Development, New Orleans.

Cannon, W. B. (1927). The James-Lange theory of emotions: A critical examination and an alternative theory. *American Journal of Psychology, 39,* 106–124.

Cannon, W. B., & Washburn, A. (1912). An explanation of hunger. *American Journal of Physiology, 29,* 441–454.

Canter, M. B., Bennett, B. E., Jones, S. E., & Nagy, T. F. (1994). *Ethics for psychologists.* Washington DC: American Psychological Association.

Cantor, N., & Langston, C.A. (1989). Ups and downs of life tasks in a life transition. In L. A. Pervin (Ed.), *Goal concepts in personality and social psychology* (pp.127–167). Hillsdale, NJ: Erlbaum.

Caplan, P. J., & Caplan, J. B. (1994). *Thinking critically about research on sex and gender.* New York: McGraw-Hill.

Carskadon, M. (1993, January 12) The great American sleep debt: Commentary. *Washington Post,* p. WH9.

Cartwright, R. D. (1989). Dreams and their meaning. In M. H. Dryger, T. Roth, & W. C. Dement (Eds.), *Principles and practice of sleep medicine.* San Diego: Harcourt Brace Jovanovich.

Cartwright, R. D. (1978, December). Happy endings for our dreams. *Psychology Today,* pp. 66–74.

Case, R. (Ed.). (1992). *The mind's staircase: Exploring the conceptual underpinnings of children's thought and knowledge.* Hillsdale, NJ: Erlbaum.

Cattell, R. B. (1943). The description of personality II. Basic traits resolved into cluster. *Journal of Abnormal and Social Psychology. 38,* 476–507.

Cavett, D. (1974). *Cavett.* San Diego: Harcourt Brace Jovanovich.

Ceci, S. (1996). Review of *Child Development* (8th ed.) by John W. Santrock. (Madison, WI: Brown & Benchmark).

Ceci, S. J., & Bruck, M. (1998). Children's testimony. In W. Damon (Ed.), *Handbook of child psychology (5th Ed., Vol. 4).* New York: Wiley.

Centers for Disease Control and Prevention. (1995, March). *Statistical report: AIDS in women.* Atlanta: Author.

Cervantes, R. C. (1987). Hispanics in psychology. In P. J. Woods & C. S. Wilkinson (Eds.), *Is psychology the major for you?* Washington, DC: American Psychological Association.

Chance, P. (1988). *Learning and behavior.* Belmont, CA: Wadsworth.

Chance, P. (1979). *Learning and behavior.* Belmont, CA: Wadsworth.

Chasnoff, L. J., Griffith, D. R., MacGregor, S., Dirkes, K., & Burns, K. A. (1989). Temporal patterns of cocaine use in pregnancy. *Journal of the American Medical Association, 261,* 1741–1744.

Chodorow, N. J. (1989). *Feminism and psychoanalytic theory.* New Haven, CT: Yale University Press.

Chodorow, N. J. (1978). *The reproduction of mothering.* Berkeley: University of California Press.

Chomsky, N. (1975). *Reflections on language.* New York: Pantheon.

Chomsky, N. (1957). *Syntactic structure.* The Hague: Mouton.

Christensen, L. (1996). *Diet-behavior relationships.* Washington, DC: American Psychological Association.

Church, A. T., & Lonner, W. J. (1998). The cross-cultural perspective in the study of personality. *Journal of Cross-Cultural Psychology, 29,* 32-62.

Cialdini, R. B. (1993). *Infulence: Science and practice* (3rd ed.). New York: Harper-Collins.

Clark, D. A., & Beck, A. T. (1989). Cognitive theory and therapy of anxiety and depression. In P. C. Kendall & D. Watson (Eds.), *Anxiety and depression.* San Diego: Academic Press.

Clark, E. V. (1983). Meanings and concepts. In P. H. Mussen (Ed.), *Handbook of child psychology* (4th ed., Vol. 3). New York: Wiley.

Clark, L. A., Watson, D., & Reynolds, S. (1995). Diagnosis and classification in psychopathology. *Annual Review of Psychology,* Vol. 46. Palo Alto, CA: Annual Reviews.

Clark, R. D., & Hatfield, E. (1989). Gender differences in receptivity to sexual offers. *Journal of Psychology and Human Sexuality, 2,* 39–55.

Clausen, J. A. (1993). *America lives.* New York: Free Press.

Clifford, B. R., Bunter, B., & McAleer, I. L. (1995). *Television and children.* Hillsdale, NJ: Erlbaum.

Clum, G. A., & Febbraro, G. A. R. (1998). Phobic disorders, In H. S. Friedman (Ed.), *Encyclopedia of mental health (vol. 3).* San Diego: Academic Press.

Cochran, S. D., & Mays, V. M. (1990). Sex, lies, and HIV. *New England Journal of Medicine, 322* (11), 774–775.

Cognition and Technology Group at Vanderbilt. (1997). *The Jasper Project.* Mahwah, NJ: Erlbaum.

Cohen, H. J., Grosz, J., Ayooh, K., & Schoen, S. (1996). Early intervention for children with

HIV infections. In M. J. Guralnick (Ed.), *The effectiveness of early intervention.* Baltimore: Paul H. Brookes.

Cohen, L. A. (1987, November). Diet and cancer. *Scientific American,* pp. 128–137.

Cohen, S., & Beckwith, L. (1996, March). *Mental health and attachment relationships.*

Cohen, S., Evans, G. W., Krantz, D. S., Stokols, D., & Kelly, S. (1981). Aircraft noise and children: Longitudinal and cross-sectional evidence on adaptation to noise and the effectiveness of noise abatement. *Journal of Personality and Social Psychology, 40,* 331–345.

Cohen, S., Glass, D. C., & Singer, J. E. (1973). Apartment noise, auditory discrimination, and reading ability in children. *Journal of Experimental Psychology, 9,* 407–422.

Colby, A., Kohlberg, L., Gibbs, J., & Leiberman, M. (1983). A longitudinal study of moral judgment. *Monographs of the Society for Research in Child Development* (Serial No. 201).

Coleman, J. (1995, March). *Adolescent sexual knowledge: Implications for health and health risks.* Paper presented at the meeting of the Society for Research in Child Development, Indianapolis,

Collins, M. (1996, winter). The job outlook for '96 grads. *Journal of Career Planning,* 51–54.

Combrinck-Graham, L. (1998). Family systems. In H. S. Friedman (Ed.), *Encyclopedia of mental health (vol. 1).* San Diego: Academic Press.

Comer, J. P. (1993). *African-American parents and child development: An agenda for school success.* Paper presented at the biennial meeting of the Society for Research on Child Development, New Orleans.

Comer, J. P. (1988). Educating poor minority children. *Scientific American, 259,* 42–46.

Committee for Economic Development. (1987). Children in need: Investment strategies for the educationally disadvantaged. Washington, DC: Author.

Condry, J. C. (1989). *The psychology of television.* Hillsdale, NJ: Erlbaum.

Coren, S., & Girus, J. S. (1972). Illusion decrement in intersecting line figures. *Psychonomic Science, 26,* 108–110.

Coren, S., & Ward, I. M. (1989). *Sensation and perception.* San Diego: Harcourt Brace Jovanovich.

Cortes, J. B., & Gatti, F. M. (1970, April). Physique and propensity. *Psychology Today,* pp. 42–44.

Costa, P. T. (1988, August). *Personality, continuity and the changes of adult life.* Paper presented at the American Psychological Association, Atlanta.

Costa, P. T., & McRae, R. R. (1995). Solid ground in the wetlands of personality: A reply to Block. *Psychological Bulletin, 117,* 216–220.

Costa, P. T., & McRae, R. R. (1992). *Revised NEO personality inventory.* Odessa, FL: Psychological Assessment Resources.

Costa, P. T., Jr., & McRae, R. R. (1985). *The NEO Personality Inventory Manual.* Odessa, FL: Psychology Assessment Resource.

Costa, P. T., Jr., & McRae, R. R., & Dye, P. A. (1991). Facet scales for agreeableness and conscientiousness: A revision of the NEO Inventory. *Personality and Individual Differences, 12,* 887–898.

Costin, F., & Draguns, J. G. (1989). *Abnormal Psychology.* New York: Wiley.

Cotton, N. (1979). The familial incidence of alcoholism: A review. *Journal of Studies on Alcohol, 40,* 89–116.

Cowley, G. (1988, May 23). The wisdom of animals. *Newsweek,* pp. 52–58.

Craik, F. I. M., & Lockhart, R. S. (1972). Levels of processing: A framework for memory research. *Journal of Verbal Learning and Verbal Behavior, 11,* 671–684.

Craik, F. I. M., & Tulving, E. (1975). Depth of processing and retention of words in episodic memory. *Journal of Experimental Psychology: General, 104,* 268–294.

Crick, M. (1977). *Explorations in language and meaning: Toward a scientific anthropology.* New York: Halsted Press.

Crooks, R., & Bauer, K. (1996). *Our sexuality* (6th ed.). Pacific Grove, CA: Brooks/Cole.

Csikszentmihalyi, M. (1995). *Creativity.* New York: HarperCollins.

Csikszentimihalyi, M. (1990). *Flow.* New York: Harper & Row.

Culbertson, F. M. (1991, August). *Mental health of women: An international journey.* Paper presented at the meeting of the American Psychological Association, San Francisco.

Cunningham, M. R. (1986). Measuring the physical in physical attractiveness: Quasi-experiments on the sociobiology of female facial beauty. *Journal of Personality and Social Psychology, 50,* 925–935.

Curtiss, S. (1977). *Genie.* New York: Academic Press.

Cutrona, C. E. (1982). Transition to college: Loneliness and the process of social adjustment. In L. A. Peplau & D. Perlman (Eds.), *Loneliness: A sourcebook of current theory, research and therapy.* New York: Wiley.

D

d'Ansia, G. I. D. (1989). Familial analysis of panic disorder and agoraphobia. *Journal of Affective Disorders, 17,* 1–8.

Dabbs, J. M., Jr., & Morris, R. (1990). Testosterone, social class, and antisocial behavior in a sample of 4,462 men. *Psychological Science, 1,* 209–211.

Dabbs, J. M., Jr., Frady, R. L., Carr, T. S., & Besch. N. F. (1987). Saliva, testosterone, and criminal violence in young adult prison inmates. *Psychosomatic Medicine, 49,* 174–182.

Dallenbach, K. M. (1927). The temperature spots and end-organs. *American Journal of Psychology, 52,* 331–347.

Darley, J. M., & Latané, B. (1968). Bystander intervention in emergencies: Diffusion of responsibility. *Journal of Personality and Social Psychology, 8,* 337–383.

Darwin, C. (1872/1965). *The expression of the emotions in man and animals.* Chicago: University of Chicago Press.

Darwin, C. (1859). *On the origin of species.* London: John Murray.

Davidson, R. J., Ekman, P., Saron, C.D., Senulis, J. A., & Friesen, W. V. (1990). Approach-withdrawal and cerebral asymmetry: Emotional expression and brain physiology. *Journal of Personality and Social Psychology, 58,* 330–341.

Dawkins, M. S. (1990). From an animal's point of view. *Behavioral and Brain Sciences, 13,* 1–8.

DeBattista, C., Solvason, H. B., & Schatzberg, A. F. (1998). Mood disorders. In H. S. Friedman (Ed.), *Encyclopedia of mental health (Vol. 2).* San Diego: Academic Press.

DeJong-Gierveld, J. (1987). Developing and testing a model of loneliness. *Journal of Personality and Social Psychology, 53,* 119–128.

Dement, W. (1993, January 12). The great American sleep debt: Commentary. *Washington Post,* p. WH9.

Denmark, F. L. (1998). Women and psychology: An international perspective. *American Psychologist, 53,* 465-473.

DeSpelder, L. A., & Strickland, A. L. (1996). *The last dance* (4th ed.). Mountain View, CA: Mayfield.

Deutsch, J. A., & Gonzales, M. F. (1980). Gastric nutrient content signals satiety. *Behavioral and Neural Biology, 30,* 113–116.

Deutsch, M., & Collins, M. (1951). *Interracial housing: A psychological evaluation of a social experiment.* Minneapolis: University of Minnesota Press.

Dewey, J. (1993). *How we think: A restatement of the relation of reflective thinking to the educative process.* Lexington, MA: D. C. Heath.

DiBiase, R. (1993, March). *Attachment, temperament, and ego development in adolescence.* Paper presented at the biennial meeting of the Society for Research in Child Development, New Orleans.

Dickson, G. L. (1990). A feminist post-structuralist analysis of the knowledge of menopause. *Advances in Nursing Science, 12,* 15–31.

Diener, E. (1984). Subjective well-being. *Psychological Bulletin, 95,* 542–575.

Dixon, R. A., & Backman, L. (1995). Concept of compensation. In R.A. Dixon & L. Backman (Eds.), *Compensating for psychological deficits and declines.* Hillsdale, NJ: Erlbaum.

Doctor, R. M., & Neff, B. (1998). Sexual Disorders. In H. S. Friedman (ed.), *Encyclopedia of mental health (vol. 3).* San Diego: Academic Press.

Dohrenwend, B. S., & Shrout, P. E. (1985). "Hassles" in the conceptualization and measurement of life stress variables. *American Psychologist, 40,* 780–785.

Dolnick, E. (1988, December). The right (left) stuff. *Omni,* p. 45.

Donelson, F. E., (1998). *Women's experiences.* Mountain View, CA: Mayfield.

Dorn, L. D., & Lucas, F. L. (1995, March). *Do hormone-behavior relations vary depending upon the endocrine and psychological status of the adolescent?* Paper presented at the meeting of the Society for Research in Child Development, Indianapolis.

Dougall, A. L., & Baum, A. (1998). Stress. In H. S. Friedman (Ed.), *Encyclopedia of mental health (vol. 3)*. San Diego: Academic Press.

Doyle, J. A., & Paludi, M. A. (1998). *Sex and gender (4th Ed.)*. Burr Ridge, IL: McGraw-Hill.

Draguns, J. G. (1990). Applications of cross-cultural psychology in the field of mental health. In R. W. Brislin (Ed.), *Applied cross-cultural psychology*. Newbury Park, CA: Sage.

Dreyer, P. H. (1982). Sexuality during adolescence. In B. B. Wolman (Ed.), *Handbook of developmental psychology*. Englewood Cliffs, NJ: Prentice Hall.

Dryfoos, J. G. (1992, March). *Integrating services for adolescents: The community schools.* Paper presented at the meeting of the Society for Research on Adolescence, Washington, DC.

Dryfoos, J. G. (1990). *Adolescents at risk: Prevalence and prevention.* New York: Oxford University Press.

Dunnett, S. B. (1989). Neural transplantation: Normal brain function and repair after damage. *Psychologist, 1*, 4–8.

Dutton, D., & Aron, A. (1974). Some evidence for heightened sexual attraction uinder conditions of high anxiety. *Journal of Personality and Social Psychology, 30*, 510–517.

E

Eagly, A. (1983). Gender and social influence: A social psychological analysis. *American Psychologist, 38*, 971–981.

Eagly, A. H. (1996). Differences between women and men. *American Psychologist, 51*, 158–159.

Eagly, A. H., & Crowley, M. (1986). Gender and helping behavior: A meta-analytic review of the social psychological literature. *Psychological Bulletin, 100*, 283–308.

Ebata, A. T., & Moos, R. H. (1989, April). *Coping and adjustment in four groups of adolescents.* Paper presented at the biennial meeting of the Society for Research in Child Development, Kansas City.

Eberhardt, J. L., & Fiske, S. T. (1998). *Racism.* Newbury Parke: Sage.

Eccles, J. S., Wigfield, A., & Schiefele, U. (1998). Motivation to succeed. In W. Damon (Ed.), *Handbook of child psychology (vol. 3)*. New York: Wiley.

Edelman, M. W. (1997, April). *Families, children, and social policy.* Invited address presented at the meeting of the Society for Research in Child Development, Washington, DC.

Edelman, M. W. (1992). *The measure of our success: A letter to my children and yours.* Boston: Beacon Press.

Efron, R. (in press). *The decline and fall of hemispheric specialization.* Hillsdale, NJ: Erlbaum.

Ehrhardt, A. A. (1987). A transactional perspective on the development of gender differences. In J. M. Reinisch, L. A. Rosenblum, & S. A. Sanders (Eds.), *Masculinity/femininity: Basic perspectives.* New York: Oxford University Press.

Eich, E. (1990, June). *Searching for mood dependent memory.* Paper presented at the meeting of the American Psychological Society, Dallas.

Eichorn, D. H., Clausen, J. A., Haan, N., Honzik. M. P., & Mussen, P. H. (Eds.). (1981). *Present and past in middle life.* New York: Academic Press.

Ekman, P. (1993). Facial expressions and emotion. *American Psychologist, 48*, 384–392.

Ekman, P. (1980). *The face of man.* New York: Garland STPM.

Ekman, P., & Friesen, W. V. (1971). Constants across cultures in the face and emotion. *Journal of Personality and Social Psychology, 17*, 124–129.

Ekman, P., & Friesen, W. V. (1968). The repertoire of nonverbal behavior—Categories, origins, usage and coding. *Semiotica, 1.* 49–98.

Elkind, D. (1978). Understanding the young adolescent. *Adolescence, 13*, 127–134.

Ellis, A. (1996). A rational emotive behavior therapist's perspective on Ruth. In G. Corey (Ed.), *Case approach to counseling and psychotherapy.* Pacific Grove, CA: Brooks/Cole.

Ellis, A. (1962). *Reason and emotion in psychotherapy.* New York: Lyle Stuart.

Ellis, A., & Velton, E. (1992). *When AA doesn't work for you: Rational steps to quitting alcohol.* Fort Lee, NJ: Barricade Books.

Ellis, H. C. (1987). Recent developments in human memory. In V. P. Makosky (Ed.), *The G. Stanley Hall Lecture Series.* Washington, DC: American Psychological Association.

Ellis, H. C., & Hunt, R. R. (1999). *Fundamentals of cognitive psychology (6th Ed.).* Burr Ridge, IL: McGraw-Hill.

Ellis, H. C., Thomas, R. L., & Rodriguez, I. A. (1984). Emotional mood states and memory: Elaborative encoding, semantic processing, and cognitive effort. *Journal of Experimental Psychology: Learning, Memory, and Cognition, 10*, 470–482.

Emmons, R. A. (1996). Motives and life goals. In S. Briggs, R. Hogan, & W. Jones (Eds.), *Handbook of personality psychology.* Orlando: Academic Press.

Emmons, R. A. (1977). Motives and goals, In R. Hogan, J. Johnson, & S. Briggs (Eds.), *Handbook of personality psychology.* San Diego: Academic Press.

Emmons, R. A., Kaiser, H. A. (1995). Goal orientation and emotional well-being: Linking goals and affect through the self. In L. L. Martin & A. Tesser (Eds.), *Striving and feeling.* Hillsdale, NJ: Erlbaum.

Erikson, E. H. (1968). *Identity: Youth and crisis.* New York: W. W. Norton.

Erikson, E. H. (1950). *Childhood and society.* New York: W. W. Norton.

Escobar, J. I., & Gara, M. A. (1998). Somatization and hypochondriasis. In H. S. Friedman (Ed.), *Encyclopedia of mental health (vol. 3)*. San Diego: Academic Press.

Evans, P. (1989). *Motivation and emotion.* New York: Routledge.

Exner, J. E., & Weiner, I. B. (1995). *The Rorschach, Vol. 3.* New York: Wiley.

Eysenck, H. J. (1952). The effects of psychotherapy: An evaluation. *Journal of Consulting Psychology, 16*, 319–324.

Eysenck, H. J. (1947). *Dimensions of personality.* London: Routledge & Kegan Paul.

F

Fairburn, C. G. (1995). *Overcoming binge eating.* New York: Guilford.

Fasick, F. A. (1988). Patterns of formal education in high school as rites of passage. *Adolescence, 23*, 457–468.

Faulkner, L. R., McFarland, B. H., & Bloom, J. D. (1989). An empirical study of emergency commitment. *American Journal of Psychiatry, 146*, 182–186.

Feist, J., & Feist, G. J. (1998). *Personality theories (4th Ed.).* Burr Ridge, IL: McGraw-Hill.

Feldman, D. H., & Piirto, J. (1995). Parenting talented children. In M. H. Bornstein (Ed.), *Handbook of parenting*, Vol. 1. Hillsdale, NJ: Erlbaum.

Feldman, S. S., & Elliot, G. R. (1990). Progress and promise of research on normal adolescent development. In S. S. Feldman & G. Elliott (Ed.). *At the threshold: The developing adolescent.* Cambridge, MA: Harvard University Press.

Festinger, L. (1957). *A theory of cognitive dissonance.* Evanston, IL: Row Peterson.

Festinger, L. (1954). A theory of social comparison processes. *Human Relations, 7*, 117–140.

Field, T. (1995). Cocaine exposure and intervention in early development. In M. Lewis & M. Bendersky (Eds.), *Mothers, babies, and cocaine.* Hillsdale, NJ: Erlbaum.

Fiez, J. A., Raife, E. A., Balota, D. A., Schwarz, J. P., Raichle, M. E., & Petersen, S. E. (1996). A positron emission tomography study of the short-term maintenance of verbal information. *Journal of Neuroscience, 16*, 808–822.

First, M. B., Frances, A., & Pincus, H. A. (1995). *DSM-IV handbook for differential diagnosis.* Washington, DC: American Psychiatric Press.

Fischer, J., & Gochros, H. L. (1975). *Planned behavior change.* New York: Free Press.

Fivush, R. (1995, March). *The development of narrative remembering: Implications for the recovered memory debate.* Paper presented at the meeting of the Society for Research in Child Development, Indianapolis.

Flavell, J. H. (1992). Cognitive development: Past, present, and future. *Developmental Psychology, 28*, 998–1005.

Foa, E. B., Steketze, G., & Young, M. C. (1984). Agoraphobia. *Clinical Psychology Review, 4,* 431–457.

Foley, V. (1975). Family therapy with black disadvantaged families: Some observations on roles, communications, and techniques. *Journal of Marriage and Family Counseling, 1,* 29–38.

Fowler, C. A., Wolford, G., Slade, R., & Tassinary, L. (1981). Lexical access with and without awareness. *Journal of Experimental Psychology: General, 110,* 341–362.

Fowler, J. W. (1981). *States of faith: The psychology of human development and the quest for faith.* New York: HarperCollins.

Fox, J. L. (1984). The brain's dynamic way of keeping in touch. *Science, 225,* 820–821.

Fox, R. E. (1995). The rape of psychotherapy. *Professional Psychology, 26,* 147–155.

Frank, E., & Kupfer, D. J. (1986). Psychotherapeutic approaches to treatment of recurrent unipolar depression: Work in progress. *Psychopharmacolgy Bulletin, 22,* 558–565.

Frank, J. D. (1982). Therapeutic components shared by all psychotherapies. In J. H. Harvey & M. M. Parks (Eds.), *Psychotherapy research and behavior change.* Washington, DC: American Psychological Association.

Fraser, S. (Ed.). (1995). *The bell curve wars: Race, intelligence, and the future of America.* New York: Basic Books.

Freud, S. (1900/1953). The interpretation of dreams. In J. Strachey (Ed.), *The standard edition of the complete psychological works of Sigmund Freud.* London: Hogarth Press.

Freud, S. (1917). *A general introduction to psychoanalysis.* New York: Washington Square Press.

Friedman, H. S. (1998). Heart disease: Psychological factors. In H. S. Friedman (Ed.), *Encyclopedia of mental health (vol. 2).* San Diego: Academic Press.

Friedman, M., & Rosenman, R. (1974). *Type A behavior and your heart.* New York: Knopf.

Friedman, M. A., & Brownell, K. D. (1998). Obesity. In H. S. Friedman (Ed.), *Encyclopedia of mental health (vol. 3).* San Diego: Academic Press.

Friedman, R., Myers, P., & Benson, H. (1998). Meditation and the relaxation response. In H. S. Friedman (Ed.), *Encyclopedia of mental health (vol. 2).* San Diego: Academic Press.

Fromm, E. (1947). *Man for himself.* New York: Holt Rinehart.

Frost, R. O., & Steketee, G. (1998). Obsessive-compulsive disorder. In H. S. Friedman (Ed.), *Encyclopedia of mental health (vol. 3).* San Diego: Academic Press.

Fuhrman, A., & Burlingame, G. M. (1995). *Handbook of group psychotherapy.* New York: Wiley.

Furmoto, L. (1989). The new history of psychology. In I. S. Cohen (Ed.), *The G. Stanley Hall lecture series* (Vol. 9). Wahington, DC: American Psychological Association.

Furmoto, L., & Scarborough, E. (1986). Placing women in the history of psychology. *American Psychologist, 41,* 35–42.

Furth, H. G., & Wachs, H. (1975). *Thinking goes to school.* New York: Oxford University Press.

G

Gage, F. H., & Bjorklund, A. (1986). Cholinergic septal grafts into the hippocampal formation improve spatial learning and memory in aged rats by an atropine-sensitive mechanism. *Journal of Neuroscience, 6,* 2837–2847.

Gaines, S. O., & Reed, E. S. (1995). Prejudice: from Allport to Dubois. *American Psychologist, 50,* 96–103.

Galanter, M. (1989). *Cults: Faith, healing, and coercion.* New York: Oxford University Press.

Gallup, G. (1988). *The Gallup poll.* New York: Random House.

Gallup, G. (1984, August–September). *Gallup Report,* Nos. 228 and 229, 2–9.

Gallup, G. H., Jr., & Jones, S. (1989). *100 questions and answers: Religion in America.* Princeton, NJ: Princeton Religion Research Center.

Garcia, C. T., Coll, E. C., Meyer, E. C., & Brillon, L. (1995). Ethnic and minority parenting. In M. H. Bornstien (Ed.), *Handbook of parenting,* Vol. 2. Hillsdale, NJ: Erlbaum.

Gardner, B. T., & Gardner, R. A. (1971). Two-way communication with an infant chimpanzee. In A. Schrier & F. Stollnitz (Eds.), *Behavior of nonhuman primates* (Vol. 4). New York: Academic Press.

Gardner, H. (1985). *The mind's new science.* New York: Basic Books.

Gardner, H. (1983). *Frames of mind.* New York: Basic Books.

Garraghty, P. E. (1996, June). *Neuroplasticity: From mechanisms to behavior.* Paper presented at the meeting of the American Psychological Society, San Francisco.

Gary, C. R., & Gummerman, K. (1975). The enigmatic eidetic image: A critical examination of methods, data, and theories. *Psychological Bulletin, 82,* 383–407.

Gazzaniga, M. S. (1986). *The social brain.* New York: Plemun.

Geschwind, N., & Behan, P. (1982). Left-handedness: Association with immune disease, migraine, and developmental learning disorder. *Proceedings of the National Academy of Sciences, 79,* 5097–5100.

Gibbons, F. X., & McCoy, S. B. (1991). Self-esteem, similarity, and reactions to active versus passive downward comparison. *Journal of Personality and Social Psychology, 60,* 414–424.

Gibbs, J. T., & Huang, L. N. (Eds.). (1989). *Children of color.* San Francisco: Jossey-Bass.

Gibson, E. J., & Walk, R. D. (1960). The "visual cliff." *Scientific American, 202,* 64–71.

Gifford, R. (1987). *Environmental psychology: Principles and practice.* Boston: Allyn & Bacon.

Gilligan, C. (1996). The centrality of relationships in psychological development: A puzzle, some evidence, and a theory. In G. G.

Noam & K. W. Fischer (Eds.), *Development and vulnerability in close relationships.* Hillsdale, NJ: Erlbaum.

Gilligan, C. (1982). *In a different voice.* Cambridge, MA: Harvard University Press.

Gjerde, P. (1985, April). *Adolescent depression and parental socialization patterns: A prospective study.* Paper presented at the biennial meeting of the Society for Research in Child Development, Toronto.

Gladue, B. A. (1994). The biopsychology of sexual orientation. *Current Direction in Psychological Science, 3,* 150–154.

Glick, J. (1975). Cognitive development in cross-cultural perspective. In F. Horowitz (Ed.), *Review of child development research* (Vol.4). Chicago: University of Chicago Press.

Godden, D. R., & Baddeley, A. D. (1975). Context-dependent memory in two natural environments: On land and under water. *British Journal of Psychology, 66,* 325–331.

Goldberg, T. E., Berman, K. F., & Weinberger, D. R. (1995). Neuropsychology and neurophysiology of schizophrenia. *Current Opinion in Psychiatry, 8,* 34–40.

Goldstein, E. B. (1996). *Sensation and perception* (4th ed.). Pacific Grove, CA: Brooks/Cole.

Goldstein, E. B. (1994). *Sensation and perception* (4th ed.). Belmont, CA: Wadsworth.

Goldstein, M. J. (1986, August). *Psychosocial factors in the course and onset of schizophrenia.* Paper presented at the meeting of the American Psychological Association, Washington, DC.

Goldstein, M. J., & Palmer, J. O. (1975). *The experience of anxiety.* New York: Oxford University Press.

Goleman, D. (1995). *Emotional intelligence.* New York: Bantam Books.

Goodstein, L. D., & Calhoun, J. F. (1982). *Understanding abnormal behavior.* Reading. MA: Addison-Wesley.

Goodwin, D. W. (1988). *Is alcoholism hereditary?* (2nd ed.). New York: Ballantine.

Gopaul-McNicol, S., & Brice-Baker, J. (1998). *Cross-cultural practice.* New York: Wiley.

Gottesman, I. I. (1989). Vital statistics, demography, and schizophrenia. *Schizophrenia Bulletin, 15,* 5–8.

Gottesman, I. I., & Shields, J. (1982). *The schizophrenic puzzle.* New York: Cambridge University Press.

Gottlieb, B. H. (1998). Support groups. In H. S. Friedman (Ed.), *Encyclopedia of mental health (vol. 3).* San Diego: Academic Press.

Gottlieb, G., Wahlsten, D., & Lickliter. R. (1998). The significance of biology for human development: A developmental psychobiological systems view. In W. Damon (Ed.), *Handbook of child psychology* (5th ed., Vol. 1). New York: Wiley.

Gould, M., Wunsch-Hitzig, R., & Dohrenwend, B. S. (1981). Estimating the prevalence of childhood psychopathology. *Journal of American Academy of Child Psychiatry, 20,* 462–476.

Graham, S. (1990). Motivation in Afro-Americans. In G. L. Berry & J. K. Asamen (Eds.), *Black students: Psychosocial issues and academic achievement.* Newbury Park, CA: Sage.

Graham, S. (1986, August). *Can attribution theory tell us something about motivation in Blacks?* Paper presented at the meeting of the American Psychological Association, Washington, DC.

Gray, C. R. & Gummerman, K. (1975). The enigmatic eidetic image: A critical examination of methods, data, and theories. *Psychological Bulletin, 82,* 383–407.

Graziano, W. J. (1995). Evolutionary psychology: Old music, but now on CDs? *Psychological Inquiry, 6,* 41–44.

Green, P. (1995, March). *Sesame Street: More than a television show.* Paper presented at the meeting of the Society for Research in Child Development, Indianapolis.

Greenough, W. T. (1997, April 21). Commentary in article, "Politics of biology." *U.S. News & World Report,* p. 79.

Greenough, W. T., Wallace, C. S., Alcantara, A. A., Anderson, B. J., Hawrylak, Sirevaag, A. M., Weiler, I. J., & Withers, G. S. (1997, August), *The development of the brain.* Paper presented at the meeting of the American Psychological Association, Chicago.

Greenwald, A. G. (1996, June 29). *Unconscious cognition and subliminal influence.* Paper presented at the Third Annual Institute of the Teaching of Psychology, American Psychological Society, San Francisco.

Gregory, R. L. (1978). *Eye and brain: The psychology of seeing* (3rd ed.). New York: McGraw-Hill.

Grevious, C. (1985). The role of the family therapist with low-income black families. *Family Therapy, 12,* 115–122.

Grush, J. E. (1980). Impact of candidate expenditures, regionality, and prior outcomes on the 1976 Democratic presidential primaries. *Journal of Personality and Social Psychology, 38,* 337–347.

Guilford, J. P. (1967). *The structure of intellect.* New York: McGraw-Hill.

Gur, R. C., Mozley, L. H., Mozley, P. D., Resnick, S. M., Karp, J. S., Alavi, A., Arnold, S. E., & Gur, R. E. (1995). Sex differences in regional cerebral glucose metabolism during a resting state. *Science, 267,* 528–531.

H

Haier, R. J. (1998). Brain scanning/neuroimaging. In H. S. Friedman (Ed.), *Encyclopedia of mental health (vol. 1).* San Diego: Academic Press.

Hakuta, K., & Garcia, E. E. (1989). Bilingualism and education. *American Psychologist, 44,* 374–379.

Hall, G. S. (1904). *Adolescence* (Vols. 1 & 2). Englewood Cliffs, NJ: Prentice Hall.

Halonen, J. (1995). Demystifying critical thinking. *Teaching of Psychology, 22,* 75–81.

Haney, W. V. (1986). *Communication and interpersonal relations: Text and cases.* Homewood, IL: Irwin.

Hare-Muston, R., & Marecek, J. (1988). The meaning of difference: Gender theory, postmodernism and psychology. *American Psychologist, 43,* 455–464.

Harkness, S., & Super, C. M. (1995). Culture and parenting. In M. H. Bornstein (Ed.), *Handbook of parenting,* Vol. 2. Hillsdale, NJ: Erlbaum.

Harlow, H. F., & Zimmerman, R. R. (1959). Affectional responses in the infant monkey. *Science, 130,* 421–432.

Harris, R. F., Wolf, N. M., & Baer, D. M. (1964). Effects of adult social reinforcement on child behavior. *Young Children, 20,* 8–17.

Harris, R. J., Schoen, L. M., & Hensley, D. L., (1992). A cross-cultural study of story memory. *Journal of Cross-Cultural Psychology, 23,* 133–147.

Harter, S. (1990). Self and identity development. In S. S. Feldman & G. R. Elliott (Eds.), *At the threshold: The developing adolescent.* Cambridge, MA: Harvard University Press.

Harvey, J. H. (1995). *Odyssey of the heart.* New York: W. H. Freeman.

Hasher, L., & Zacks, R. T. (1979). Automatic and effortful processes in memory. *Journal of Experimental Psychology: General, 108,* 356–388.

Hatcher, R., & others. (1988). *Contraceptive technology, 1988–1989* (14th ed.). New York: Irvington.

Hatfield, E., & Rapson, R. L. (1998). Love and intimacy. In H. S. Friedman (Ed.), *Encyclopedia of mental health (vol. 2).* San Diego: Academic Press.

Hatvany, N., & Pucik, V. (1981). An integrated management system: Lessons from the Japanese experience. *Academy of Management Review., 6,* 469–480.

Hayflick, L. (1977). The cellular basis for biological aging. In C. E. Finch & L. Hayflick (Eds.), *Handbook of the biology of aging.* New York: Van Nostrand.

Haynes, G. S., & Feinleib, M. (1980). Women, work and coronary heart disease: Prospective findings from the Framingham Heart Study. *American Journal of Public Health, 70,* 130–141.

Hecht, M. L. (1998). *Communicating prejudice.* Newbury Park: Sage.

Heider, F. (1958). *The psychology of interpersonal relations.* New York: Wiley.

Hellige, J. B. (1990). Hemispheric asymmetry. *Annual Review of Psychology, 41.* Palo Alto, CA: Annual Reviews.

Hernandez, D. J. (1988). Demographic trends and the living arrangements of children. In E. M. Hetherington & J. D. Arasteh (Eds.), *Impact of divorce, single-parenting, and step-parenting on children.* Hillsdale, NJ: Erlbaum.

Hernstein, R. J., & Murray C. (1994). *The bell curve: Intelligence and class structure in modern life.* New York: Free Press.

Heron, B. (1957). The pathology of boredom. *Scientific American, 196,* 52–56.

Hershberger, S. L. (1998). Homosexuality. In H. S. Friedman (Ed.), *Encyclopedia of mental health (vol. 2).* San Diego: Academic Press.

Herzog, H. A. (1995). Discussing animal rights and animal research in the classroom. In M. E. Ware & D. E. Johnson (Eds.), *Demonstrations and activities in teaching of psychology* (Vol. 1). Hillsdale, NJ: Erlbaum.

Hilgard, E. R. (1977). *Divided consciousness: Multiple controls in human thought and action.* New York: Wiley.

Hilgard, E. R. (1965). *Hypnotic suggestibility.* New York: Harcourt Brace.

Hines, M. (1990). Gonadal hormones and human cognitive development. In J. Balthazart (Ed.), *Hormones, brain, and behavior in vertebrates.* Basel: Karger.

Hines, M. (1982). Prenatal gonadal hormones and sex differences in human behavior. *Psychological Bulletin, 92,* 56–80.

Hines, T. (1988). *Pseudoscience and the paranormal.* Buffalo, NY: Prometheus Books.

Ho, M. K. (1992). *Minority children and adolescents in therapy.* Newbury Park, CA: Sage.

Hoagwood, K., Jensin, P., & Fischer, C. (Eds.) (1996). *Ethical issues in mental health research with children and adolescents.* Hillsdale, NJ: Erlbaum.

Hobfoll, S. E. (1989). Conversation of resources: A new attempt at conceptualizing stress. *American Psychologist, 44,* 513–524.

Hobson, J. A. (1992). A new model of brain-mind state: Activation level, input source, and mode of processing. In J. S. Antrobus & M. Bertini (Eds.), *The neuropsychology of sleep and dreaming.* Hillsdale, NJ: Erlbaum.

Hoff-Ginsburg, E., & Tardif, T. (1995). Socioeconomic status and parenting. In M. H. Bornstein (Ed.), *Handbook of parenting,* (Vol. 1). Hillsdale, NJ: Erlbaum.

Hofferth, S. L. (1990). Trends in adolescent sexual activity, contraception, and pregnancy in the United States. In J. Bancroft & J. M. Reinisch (Eds.), *Adolescence and puberty.* New York: Oxford University Press.

Hofstede, G. (1980). *Culture's consequences: International differences in work-related values.* Newbury Park, CA: Sage.

Hogan, J. (1986). *Hogan Personality Inventory manual.* Minneapolis: National Computer Systems.

Hoge, M. A. (1998). Managed care. In H. S. Friedman (Ed.), *Encyclopedia of mental health (vol. 2).* San Diego: Academic Press.

Holcomb, H. H., Cascella, N. G., Thaker, G. K., Medoff, D. R., Dannals, R. F., & Tamminga, C. A. (1996). Functional sites of neuroleptic drug action in the human brain. *American Journal of Psychiatry, 153,* 41–49.

Hollingshead, A. B., & Redlich, F. C. (1958). *Social class and mental illness.* New York: Wiley.

Holmbeck, G. (1998). Adolescence. In H. S. Friedman (Ed.), *Encyclopedia of mental health (vol. 1).* San Diego: Academic Press.

Holmbeck, G. N. (1996). A model of family relational transformations during the transition to adolescence: Parent-adolescent conflict and adaptation. In J. A. Graber, J. Brooks-Gunn & A. C. Petersen (Eds.), *Transition through adolescence.* Hillsdale. NJ: Erlbaum.

Holmes, D. (1987). The influence of meditation versus rest on physiological arousal: A second examination. In M. A. West (Ed.), *The psychology of meditation.* Oxford, England: Clarendon Press.

Holmes, T. H., & Rahe, R. H. (1967). The social readjustment rating scale. *Journal of Psychosomatic Research, 11,* 213–218.

Holtzmann, W. (1982). Cross-cultural comparisons of personality development in Mexico and the United States. In D. Wagner & H. W. Stevenson (Eds.), *Cultural perspectives on child development.* San Francisco: W. H. Freeman.

Hood, R. W., Jr. (1995). *Handbook of religious experience.* Birmingham, AL: Religious Education Press.

Hooper, J., & Teresi, D. (1993). *The 3-pound universe.* New York: Tarcher.

Horm, J., & Anderson, K. (1993). Who in America is trying to lose weight? *Annals of Internal Medicine, 119,* 672–676.

Horney, K. (1945). *Our inner conflicts.* New York: Norton.

Horowitz, M. J. (1998). Psychoanalysis. In H. S. Friedman (Ed.), *Encyclopedia of mental health (vol. 3).* San Diego: Academic Press.

Howard, R. W. (1995). *Learning and memory.* Westport, CT: Praeger.

Huang, L. N., & Gibbs, J. T. (1989). Future directions: Implications for research, training, and practice. In J. T. Gibbs & L. N. Huang (Eds.), *Children of color.* San Francisco: Jossey-Bass.

Hubel, D. H., & Wiesel, T. N. (1965). Receptive fields and functional architecture in two nonstriate visual areas (18 and 19) of the cat. *Journal of Neurophysiology, 28,* 229–289.

Hultsch, D. F., & Plemons, J. K. (1979). Life events and life-span development. In P. B. Baltes & O. G. Brim (Eds.), *Life-span development and behavior.* New York: Academic Press.

Hunt, M. (1974). *Sexual behavior in the 1970s.* Chicago: Playboy.

Hurtado, S., Dey, E. L., & Trevino, J. G. (1994). *Exclusion or self-segregation? Interaction across racial/ethnic groups on college campuses.* Paper presented at the American Educational Research Association annual meeting, New York City.

Hurvich, L. M., & Jameson, D. (1969). Human color perception. *American Scientist, 57,* 143–166.

Huston, A. C., McLoyd, V. C., & Coll, C. G. (1994). Children and poverty: Issues in contemporary research. *Child Development, 65,* 275–282.

Hyde, J. S. (1993). Meta-analysis and the psychology of women. In F. L. Denmark & M. A. Paludi (Eds.), *Handbook on the psychology of women.* Westport, CT: Greenwood.

Hyde, J. S., & Plant, E. A. (1995). Magnitude of psychological gender differences: Another side to the story. *American Psychologist, 50,* 159–161.

Hynd, G. W., & Garcia, W. I. (1979). Intellectual assessment of the Native American student. *School Psychology Digest, 8,* 446–454.

I

Ickes, W., Snyder, M., & Garcia S. (1997). Personality influences on the choice of situations. In R. Hogan, J. Johnson, & S. Briggs (Eds.), *Handbook of personality.* San Diego: Academic Press.

Izard, C. E., Schultz, D., & Levinson, K. L. (1998). Emotions and mental health. In H. S. Friedman (Ed.), *Encyclopedia of mental health (vol. 2).* San Diego: Academic Press.

J

James, W. (1890/1950). *The principles of psychology.* New York: Dover.

Jameson, D., & Hurvich, L. (1989). Essay concerning color constancy. *Annual Review of Psychology, 40.*

Janis, I. (1972). *Victims of groupthink: A psychological study of foreign-policy decisions and fiascos.* Boston: Houghton Mifflin.

Jaycox, L. H., & Foa, E. B. (1998). Posttraumatic stress. In H. S. Friedman (Ed.), *Encyclopedia of mental health (vol. 3).* San Diego: Academic Press.

Jensen, A. R. (1969). How much can we boost IQ and scholastic achievement? *Harvard Educational Review, 39,* 1–23.

Johnson, C. (1990, May). The new woman's ethics report. *New Woman,* p. 6.

Johnson, J. A. (1997). Units of analysis for the description and explanation of personality. In R. Hogan, J. Johnson, & S. Briggs (Eds.), *Handbook of personality psychology.* San Diego: Academic Press.

Johnson, M. A. (1998). The neural basis of cognitive development. In W. Damon (Ed.), *Handbook of child psychology (5th Ed., Vol. 2).* New York: Wiley.

Johnston, L. D., O'Malley, P. M., & Bachman, J. G. (1996a). *National survey results on drug use from the Monitoring the Future Study: Vol. 1. Secondary school students.* Ann Harbor, MI: University of Michigan, Institute of Social Research.

Johnston, L., O'Malley, P., & Bachman, G. (1996b) *National survey results on drug use from the Monitoring the Future Study: Vol. 2. College Students.* Ann Harbor, MI: University of Michigan, Institute of Social Research.

Johnston, L. D., O'Malley, P. M., & Bachman, J. G. (1992, January 25). *The 1991 survey of drug use by American high school and college students.* Ann Arbor: University of Michigan, Institute of Social Research.

Jones, B. E. (1989). Basic mechanisms of sleep-wake states. In M. H. Dryger, T. Roth, & W. C. Dement (Eds.), *Principles and practice of sleep medicine.* San Diego : Harcourt Brace Jovanovich.

Jones, J. M. (1997). *Prejudice and racism (2nd Ed.).* Burr Ridge, IL: McGraw-Hill.

Jones, J. M. (1994). The African American: A duality dilemma? In W. J. Lonner & R. Malpass (Eds.), *Psychology and culture.* Needham Heights, MA: Allyn & Bacon.

Jones, J. M. (1990, August). *Psychological approaches to race: What have they been and what should they be?* Paper presented at the meeting of the American Psychological Association, Boston.

Jones, J. M. (1987). Blacks in psychology. In P. J. Woods & C. S. Wilkinson (Eds.), *Is psychology the major for you?* Washington, DC: American Psychological Association.

Jones, M. C. (1924). A laboratory study of fear: The case of Peter. *Journal of Genetic Psychology, 31,* 308–315.

Joyce, P. R., Donald, R. N., & Elder, P. N. (1987). Individual differences in plasma cortisol changes during manta and depression. *Journal of Affective Disorders, 12,* 1–6.

Jung, C. G. (1917). *Analytic psychology.* New York: Moffat, Yard.

K

Kagan, J. (1992). Yesterday's promises, tomorrow's promises. *Developmental Psychology, 28,* 990–997.

Kagan, S., & Madsen, M. C. (1972). Experimental analysis of cooperation and competition of Anglo-American and Mexican children. *Developmental Psychology, 6,* 49–59.

Kagitcibasi, C., & Berry, J. W. (1989). Cross-cultural psychology: Current research and trends. *Annual Review of Psychology, 40.* Palo Alto, CA: Annual Reviews.

Kail, R., & Pellegrino, J. W. (1985). *Human intelligence.* New York: W. H. Freeman.

Kalichman, S. (1994). Guidelines for seeking professional help. In J. Simons, S. Kalichman, & J. W. Santrock, *Human adjustment.* Dubuque, IA: Brown & Benchmark.

Kalichman, S. C. (1995). *Understanding AIDS.* Washington, DC: American Psychological Association.

Kalick, S. M., & Hamilton, T. E. (1986). The matching hypothesis reexamined. *Journal of Personality and Social Psychology, 51,* 673–682.

Kandel, E. R., & Schwartz, J. H. (1982). Molecular biology of learning: Modulation of transmitter release. *Science, 218,* 433–443.

Kane, J. M., & Barnes, T. R. E. (1995). Schizophrenia research: Challenges and opportunities. *Current Opinion in Psychiatry, 8,* 19–20.

Kanner, A. D., Coyne, J. C., Schaefer, C., & Lazarus, R. S. (1981). Comparisons of two modes of stress measurement. Daily hassles and uplifts versus major life event. *Journal of Behavioral Medicine, 4,* 1–39.

Kaplan, J. S., Change, D., Abe-Kim, J., & Takeuchi, D. (1998). Ethnicity and mental health. In H. S. Friedman (Ed.), *Encyclopedia of mental health (vol. 2).* San Diego: Academic Press.

Karasu, T. B. (1986). The psychotherapies: Benefits and limitations. *American Journal of Psychotherapy, 15,* 324–342.

Kaschak, E. (1992). *Engendered lives: A new psychology of women's lives.* New York: Basic Books.

Katicibasi, C. (1995). Is psychology relevant to global human development issues? Experiences from Turkey. *American Psychologist, 50,* 293–300.

Kazdin, A. (Ed.) (1998). *Methodological issues and strategies in clinical research (2nd Ed.).* Washington, DC: American Psychological Association.

Keating, C. F. (1994). World without words: Messages from face and body. In W. J. Lonner & R. Malpass, *Psychology and culture.* Needham Heights, MA: Allyn & Bacon.

Kelley, H. H., & Thibaut, J. (1978). *Interpersonal relations: A theory of interdependence.* New York: Wiley.

Kendall, P. C., & Watson, D. (Ed.). (1989). *Anxiety and depression.* San Diego: Academic Press.

Kenrick, D. T., Montello, D. R., Gutierres, S. E., & Trost, M. R. (1993). Effects of physical attractiveness on affect and perceptual judgments: When social comparison overrides social reinforcement. *Personality and Social Psychology Bulletin, 19,* 195–199.

Kephart, W. M. (1967). Some correlates of romantic love. *Journal of Marriage and the Family, 29,* 470–474.

Kiecolt-Glaser, J. K., Malarkey, W. B., Chee, M., Newton, T., Cacioppo, J. T., Mao, H. Y., & Glaser, R. (1993, August). *Negative behavior during marital conflict is associated with immunological down-regulation.* Paper presented at the meeting of the American Psychological Association, Toronto.

Kimble, G. A. (1984). Psychology's two cultures. *American Psychologist, 39,* 833–839.

Kimble, G. A. (1961). *Hilgard and Marquis's conditioning and learning.* New York: Appleton-Century-Crofts.

Kimmel, E. B. (1992). Women's contributions to psychology. *Contemporary Psychology, 37,* 201–202.

Kimura, D. (1989, November). How sex hormones boost—or cut—intellectual ability. *Psychology Today,* pp. 62–66.

King, B. M. (1996). *Human sexuality today* (2nd ed.). Upper Saddle River, NJ: Prentice Hall.

Kinsey, A. C., Pomeroy, W. B., & Martin, E. E. (1948). *Sexual behavior in the human male.* Philadelphia: Saunders.

Kirk, G., & Okazawa-Rey, M. (Eds.)(1998). *Women's lives.* Mountain View, CA: Mayfield.

Kleinman, A. (1988). *Rethinking psychiatry.* New York: Macmillan.

Kobasa, N., Maddi, S., & Kahn, S. (1982). Hardiness and health. A prospective study. *Journal of Personality and Social Psychology, 42,* 168–177.

Kobasa, S. C., Maddi, S. R., Puccetti, M. C., & Zola, M. (1985). Relative effectiveness of hardiness, exercises, and social support as

resources against illness. *Journal of Psychosomatic Research, 29,* 525–553.

Kohlberg, L. (1986). A current statement on some theoretical issues. In S. Modgil & C. Modgil (Eds.), *Lawrence Kohlberg.* Philadelphia: Falmer Press.

Kohlberg, L. (1969). Stage and sequence: The cognitive-developmental approach to socialization. In D. A. Goslin (Ed.), *Handbook of socialization theory and research* (p. 379). Chicago: Rand McNally.

Kohlberg, L. (1966). A cognitive-developmental analysis of children's sex-role concepts and attitudes. In E. E. Maccoby (Ed.), *The development of sex differences.* Palo Alto, CA: Stanford University Press.

Kohler, W. (1925). *The mentality of apes.* New York: Harcourt Brace Jovanovich.

Kohn, M. L. (1977). *Class and conformity: A study in values* (2nd ed.). Chicago : University of Chicago Press.

Kohut, H. (1977). *The restoration of the self.* New York: International Universities Press.

Kolb, B. (1989). Brain development, plasticity, and behavior. *American Psychologist, 44,* 1203–1212.

Kolb, B., Whishaw, I.Q. & Cioe, J. (1998). Brain. In H.S. Friedman (Ed.), *Encyclopedia of mental health (vol. 1).* San Diego: Academic Press.

Kolb, D. (1983). *Experiential learning.* Englewood Cliffs, NJ: Prentice Hall.

Koocher, G. P., & Keith-Spiegel, P. (1996). *Ethics in psychology.* New York: Oxford University Press.

Kornetsky, C. (1986, August). *Effects of opiates and stimulants on brain stimulation: Implications for abuse.* Paper presented at the meeting of the American Psychological Association, Washington DC.

Koss, M., & Boeschen, L. (1998). Rape. In H. S. Friedman (Ed.), *Encyclopedia of mental health (vol. 3).* San Diego: Academic Press.

Koss, M. P. (1990). The women's mental health research agenda: Violence against women. *American Psychologist, 45,* 374–384.

Kramer, B. A. (1987). Electroconvulsive therapy use in geriatric depression. *Journal of Nervous and Mental Disease, 175,* 233–235.

Kübler-Ross, E. (1974). *Questions and answers on death and dying.* New York: Macmillan.

Kutchinsky, B. (1992). The child sexual abuse panic. *Nordisk Sexoligi, 10,* 30–42.

L

LaBerge, S. P. (1992). *Physiological studies of lucid dreaming.* Hillsdale, NJ: Erlbaum.

Labouvie-Vief, G. (1986, August). *Modes of knowing and life-span cognition.* Paper presented at the meeting of the American Psychological Association, Washington, DC.

LaCroix, A. Z., & Haynes, S. G. (1987). Gender differences in the health effects of workplace roles. In R. C. Barnett, L Biener, & G. K. Baruch (Eds.), *Gender and stress.* New York: Free Press.

Laguerre, M. S. (1981). Haitian Americans. In A. Harwood (Ed.), *Ethnicity and medical*

care. Cambridge, MA: Harvard University Press.

Lamb, C. S., Jackson, L. A., Cassiday, P. B., & Priest, D. J. (1993). Body figure preferences of men and women: A comparison of two generations. *Sex Roles, 28,* 345–358.

Lamb, H. R. (1998). Mental hospitals and deinstitutionalization. In H. S. Friedman (Ed.), *Encyclopedia of mental health (vol. 2).* San Diego: Academic Press.

Lambert, N. M., & McCombs, B. L. (1998). *How students learn: Reforming schools through learner-centered education.* Washington, DC: American Psychological Association.

Lamon, M., Secules, T., Petrosino, A. J., Hackett, R., Bransford, J. D., & Goldman, S. R. (1996). *The challenge in science and mathematics education.* Washington, DC: American Psychological Association.

Lamon, M., Secules, T., Petrosino, A. J., Hackett, R., Bransford, J. D., & Goldman, S. R. (1996). Schools for Thought. In L. Schauble & R. Glaser (Eds.), *Innovations in learning.* Mahwah, NJ: Erlbaum.

Lane, H. (1976). *The wild boy of Aveyron.* Cambridge, MA: Harvard University Press.

Lange, C. G. (1922). *The emotions.* Baltimore: Williams & Wilkins.

Langer, E. (1997). *The power of mindful learning.* New York, New York: Addison-Wesley/Longman.

Lanyon, R. I., & Goodstein, L. D. (1982). *Personality and assessment* (2nd ed.). New York: Wiley.

LaPera, G., & Nicastro, A. (1996). A new treatment for premature ejaculation: The rehabilitation of the pelvic floor. *Journal of Sex and Marital Therapy, 22,* 22–26.

LaPiere, R. (1934). Attitudes versus actions. *Social Forces, 13,* 230–237.

Lashley, K. S. (1950). In search of the engram. In *Symposium of the Society for Experimental Biology* (Vol. 4). New York: Cambridge University Press.

Lau, S., & Gruen, G. E. (1992). The social stigma of loneliness: Effect of target person's and perceiver's sex. *Personality and Social Psychology Bulletin, 18,* 182–189.

Lazarus, A. A. (1996). A multimodal behavior therapist's perspective on truth. In G. Corey (Ed.), *Case approach to counseling and psychotherapy* (4th ed.). Pacific Grove, CA: Brooks/Cole.

Lazarus, R. S. (1998). *Fifty years of the research and theory of R. S. Lazarus.* Mahwah, NJ: Erlbaum.

Lazarus, R. S. (1993). Coping theory and research: Past, present, and future. *Psychosomatic Medicine, 55,* 234–247.

Lazarus, R. S. (1991). *Emotion and adaptation.* New York: Oxford University Press.

Lazarus, R. S. (1984). On the primacy of cognition. *American Psychologist, 39,* 124–129.

Lazarus, R. S., & Folkman, N. (1984). *Stress appraisal and coping.* New York: Springer.

Lebow, J. L., & Gurman, A. S. (1995). Research assessing couple and family therapy. *Annual*

Review of Psychology, Vol. 46. Palo Alto, CA: Annual Reviews.

Lee, I., Hsieh, C., & Paffenbarger, R. S. (1995). Exercise intensity and longevity in men. *Journal of the American Medical Association, 273*, 1179–1184.

Lee, T. F. (1991). *The human genome project: Cracking the genetic code of life.* New York: Plenum Press.

Leiter, M. P., & Maslach, C. (1998). Burnout. In H. S. Friedman (Ed.), *Encyclopedia of mental health.* San Diego: Academic Press.

Lenfant, C. (1995). Improving the health of America's youth: The NHLBI perspective. *Journal of Health Education, 26*, 6–8.

Lenneberg, E. (1967). *The biological foundations of language.* New York: Wiley.

Lenneberg, E. H., Rebelsky, F. G., & Nichols, I. A. (1965). The vocalization of infants born to deaf and hearing parents. *Human Development, 8*, 23–37.

Lepper, M., Greene, D., & Nisbett, R. E. (1973). Undermining children's intrinsic interest with extrinsic rewards. *Journal of Personality and Social Psychology, 28*, 129–137.

Lerner, H. G. (1989). *The dance of intimacy.* New York: Harper & Row.

Leshner, A. I. (1992, July). Winning the war against clinical depression. *USA Today*, pp. 86–87.

Lester, B. M., Freier, K., & LaGasse, L. (1995). Prenatal cocaine exposure and child outcome: What do we really know? In M. Lewis & M. Bendersky (Eds.), *Mothers, babies, and cocaine.* Hillsdale, NJ: Erlbaum.

Levant, R. F. (1996). The male code and parenting: A psychoeducational approach. In M. P. Andronico (Ed.), *Men in groups.* Washington, DC: American Psychological Association.

Levant, R. F. (1995). *Masculinity reconstructed: Changing rules of manhood.* New York: Dutton.

Levant, R. F. & Brooks, G. R. (1997). *Men and sex: New psychological perspectives.* New York: Wiley.

Leventhal, H. (1970). Findings and theory in the study of fear communications. In L. Berkowitz (ed.), *Advances in experimental social psychology* (Vol. 5). New York: Academic Press.

Leventhal, H., & Tomarken, A. J. (1986). Emotion: Today's problems. *Annual Review of Psychology, 37*, 565–610.

Levine, M., & Perkins, D. V. (1987). *Principles of community psychology.* New York: Oxford University Press.

Levine, M., Toro, P. A., & Perkins, D. V. (1993). Social and community intervention. *Annual Review of Psychology, 44*, 525–558.

Levine, R. V., Martinez, T. S., Brase, G., & Sorenson, K. (1994). Helping in 36 U.S. cities. *Journal of Personality and Social Psychology, 67*, 69–82.

Levinson, D. (1978). *The seasons of a man's life.* New York: Knopf.

Levy, D. (1997). *Tools for critical thinking.* Boston: Allyn & Bacon.

Levy, S. M. (1985). *Behavior and cancer.* San Francisco: Jossey-Bass.

Lewin, R. (1988). Brain graft puzzles. *Science, 240.* 879.

Lewinsohn, P. M. (1987). The Coping with Depression course. In R. F. Muñoz (Ed.), *Depression prevention.* New York: Hemisphere.

Lewinsohn, P., Muñoz, R., Youngren, M., & Zeiss, A. (1992). *Control your depression* (rev. ed.). New York: Fireside.

Lieberman, M. A., Yalom, I., D., & Miles, M. B. (1973). *Encounter groups: First facts.* New York: Basic Books.

Liebert, R. M., & Sprafkin, J. (1988). *The early window* (3rd ed.). New York: Pergamon.

Lincoln, J. R., & Kalleberg, A. L. (1990). *Culture, control, and commitment: A study of work organization and work attitudes in the United States and Japan.* New York: Cambridge University Press.

Livesley, W. J. (Ed.). (1995). *The DSM-IV personality disorders.* New York: Guilford.

Locke, J. L., Bekken, K. E., Wein, D,. & Ruzecki, V. (1991, April). *Neuropsychology of babbling: Laterality effects in the production of rhythmic manual activity.* Paper presented at the Society for Research in Child Development meeting, Seattle.

Loftus, E. F. (1993a). Psychologists in the eyewitness world. *American Psychologist, 48*, 550–552.

Loftus, E. F. (1993b). The reality of repressed memories. *American Psychologist, 48*, 518–537.

Loftus, E. F. (1980). *Memory.* Reading, MA: Addison-Wesley.

Loftus, E. F. (1975). Spreading activation within semantic categories: Comments on Rosch's "Cognitive representations of semantic categories." *Journal of Experimental Psychology, 104*, 234–240.

Long, P. (1986, January). Medical mesmerism. *Psychology Today*, pp. 28–29.

Lonner, W. J. (1990). An overview of cross-cultural testing and assessment. In R. W. Brislin (Ed.), *Applies cross-cultural psychology*, Newbury Park, CA: Sage.

Lonner, W. J. (1988, October). *The introductory psychology text and cross-cultural psychology: A survey of cross-cultural psychologists.* Bellingham: Western Washington University, Center for Cross-Cultural Research.

Lorenz, K. Z. (1966). *On aggression.* San Diego: Harcourt Brace Jovanovich.

Lorenz, K. Z. (1965). *Evolution and modification of behavior.* Chicago: University of Chicago Press.

Lourenco, O., & Machado, A. (1996). In defense of Piaget's theory: A reply to 10 common criticisms. *Psychological Review, 103*, 143–164.

Ludolph, P. (1982, August). *A reanalysis of the literature on multiple personality.* Paper presented at the American Psychological Association, Washington, DC.

Luria, A. & Herzog, E. (1995, April). *Gender segregation across and within settings.* Paper presented at the biennial meeting of the Society for Research in Child Development, Toronto,

Luria, A. R. (1968). *The mind of a mnemonist.* New York: Basic Books.

Lussier, R. (1996). *Human relations in organizations* (3rd ed.). Burr Ridge IL: Irwin.

Lykken, D. T. (1985). The probity of the polygraph. In S. M. Kassin & L. S. Wrightman (Eds.), *The psychology of evidence and trial procedure.* Beverly Hills, CA: Sage.

Lynch, G. (1990, June). *The many shapes of memory and the several forms of synaptic plasticity.* Paper presented at the meeting of the American Psychological Society, Dallas.

M

Maccoby, E. E. (1993, March). *Trends and issues in the study of gender role development.* Paper presented at the biennial meeting of the Society for Research in Child Development, New Orleans.

Maccoby, E. E. (1990, June). *Gender and relationships: A developmental account.* Paper presented at the meeting of the American Psychological Society, Dallas.

Maccoby, E. E. (1987, November). Interview with Elizabeth Hall: All in the family. *Psychology Today*, pp. 54–60.

Maccoby, E. E., & Jacklin, C. N. (1974). *The psychology of sex differences.* Palo Alto, CA: Stanford University Press.

Maddi, S. (1998). Hardiness. In H. S. Friedman (Ed.), *Encyclopedia of mental health (vol. 2).* San Diego: Academic Press.

Maddi, S. (1989). *Theories of personality* (5th ed.). Homewood, IL: Dorsey.

Mader, S. (1999). *Biology* (6th ed.). Burr Ridge, IL: McGraw-Hill.

Mader, S. S. (1997). *Human biology* (4th ed.). Dubuque, IA: Wm. C. Brown.

Mahler, M. (1979). *Separation-individuation.* New York: Jason Aronson.

Mahoney, M. J. (1993). Introduction to special section: Theoretical developments in the cognitive psychotherapies. *Journal of Consulting and Clinical Psychology, 61*, 187–193.

Maier, N. R. F. (1931). Reasoning in humans. *Journal of Comparative Psychology, 12*, 181–194.

Malinowski, B. (1927). *Sex and repression in savage society.* New York: Humanities Press.

Mandler, G. (1984). *Mind and body.* New York: Norton.

Mandler, G. (1980). Recognizing: The judgment of previous occurrence. *Psychological Review, 87*, 252–271.

Marcia, J. E. (1998). Optimal development from an Eriksonian perspective. In H. S. Friedman (Ed.), *Encyclopedia of mental health (vol. 3).* San Diego: Academic Press.

Marcia, J. E. (1980). Ego identity development. In J. Adelson (Ed.), *Handbook of adolescent psychology.* New York: Wiley.

Marin, G. (1993). Defining culturally appropriate community intervention: Hispanics as a case study. *Journal of Community Psychology*, 149–161.

Marks, M. A., & Nelson E. S. Sexual harassment on campus: Effects of professor gender on perception of sexually harassing behaviors. *Sex Roles, 28,* 207–218.

Markus, H. R., & Kitayama, S. (1991). Culture and the self: Implications for cognition, emotion, and motivation. *Psychological Review, 98,* 224–253.

Martin, G. L. & Pear, J. (1996). *Behavior modification* (5th ed.). Upper Saddle River, NJ: Prentice Hall.

Martin, G. & Pear, J. (1988). *Behavior modification: What it is and how to do it* (3rd ed.). Englewood Cliffs, NJ: Prentice Hall.

Maslow, A. H. (1971). *The farther reaches of human mature.* New York: Viking.

Maslow, A. H. (1954). *Motivation and personality.* New York: Harper & Row.

Masters, W. H., & Johnson, V. E. (1966). *Human sexual response.* Boston: Little, Brown.

Matas, L., Arend, R. A., & Sroufe, L. A. (1978). Continuity in adaptation: Quality of attachment and later competence. *Child Development, 49,* 547–556.

Matlin, M. W. (1993). *The psychology of women* (2nd ed.). Fort Worth, TX: Harcourt Brace.

Matlin, M. W. (1988). *Perception* (2nd ed.) Boston: Allyn & Bacon.

Matlin, M. W. (1983). *Perception.* Boston: Allyn & Bacon.

Maultsby, M. C., & Wirga, M. (1998). Behavior therapy. In H. S. Friedman (Ed.), *Encyclopedia of mental health (vol. 1).* San Diego: Academic Press.

McCall, R. B., Green, B. L., Strauss, M. S., & Groark, C. J. (1998). Issues in community-based research and program evaluation. In W. Damon (Ed.), *Handbook of child psychology (5th Ed., Vol. 4).* New York: Wiley.

McCarley, R. W. (1989). The biology of dreaming sleep. In M. H. Dryger, T. Roth, & W. C. Dement (Eds.), *Principles and practice of sleep medicine.* San Diego: Harcourt Brace Jovanovich.

McClelland, D. C. (1978). Managing motivation to expand human freedom. *American Psychologist, 33,* 201–210.

McClelland, D. C. (1955). Some social consequences of achievement motivation. In M. R. Jones (Ed.), *Nebraska Symposium on Motivation.* Lincoln: University of Nebraska Press.

McClelland, D. C., Atkinson, J. W., Clark. R., & Lowell, E. L. (1953). *The achievement motive.* New York: Appleton-Century-Crofts.

McConaghy, N. (1993). *Sexual Behavior: Problems and management.* New York: Plenum.

McDougall, W. (1908). *Social psychology.* New York: G. Putnam & Sons.

McFarlane, T., Polivy, J., & Herman, C. P. (1998). Dieting. In H. S. Friedman (Ed.), *Encyclopedia of mental health (vol. 1).* San Diego: Academic Press.

McGrath, E., Keita, G. P., Strickland, B., & Russo, N. F. (1990). *Women and depression: Risk factors and treatment issues.* Washington, DC: American Psychological Association.

McGue, M., & Bouchard, T. J. (1989). Genetic and environmental determinants of information processing and special mental abilities. In R. J. Sternberg (Ed.), *Advances in the psychology of human intelligence.* Hillsdale, NJ: Erlbaum.

McGue, M., & Carmichael, C. M. (1995). Life-span developmental psychology: A behavioral genetic perspective. In L. F. Dilalla & S. M. C. Dollinger (Eds.), *Assessment of biological mechanisms across the life span.* Hillsdale, NJ: Erlbaum.

McKinlay, S. M., & McKinlay, J. B. (1984). *Health status and health care utilization by menopausal women.* Unpublished manuscript, Cambridge Research Center, American Institutes for Research, Cambridge, MA.

McLoyd, V. (1993, March). *Direct and indirect effects of economic hardship on socioemotional functioning in African-America adolescents.* Paper presented at the biennial meeting of the Society for Research in Child Development, New Orleans.

McLoyd, V. C. (1998). Children in poverty. In W. Damon (Ed.), *Handbook of child psychology (5th Ed., vol. 4).* New York: Wiley.

McLoyd, V. C., & Steinberg, L. (1998). *Studying minority adolescents.* Mahwah, NJ: Erlbaum.

McNally, D. (1990). *Even eagles need a push.* New York: Dell.

McNally, R. J. (1998). Panic Attacks. In H. S. Friedman (Ed.), *Encyclopedia of mental health (vol. 3).* San Diego: Academic Press.

McNeil, E. B. (1967). *The quiet furies.* Englewood Cliffs, NJ: Prentic Hall.

McRae, R. R., & Costa, P. T. (1997). Conception of correlates of openness to experience. In R. Hogan, J. Johnson, & S. Briggs (Eds.), *Handbook of personality psychology.* San Diego: Academic Press.

McShane, D. A. (1987). American Indians and Alaska natives in psychology. In P. J. Woods & C. S. Wilkinson (Eds.), *Is psychology the major for you?* Washington, DC: American Psychological Association.

Meehl, P. E. (1986). Diagnostic taxa as open concepts. In T. Millon & G. I. Klerman (Eds.), *Contemporary directions in psychopathology.* New York: Guilford Press.

Meichenbaum, D. (1993). Changing conceptions of cognitive behavior modification: Retrospect and prospect. *Journal of Consulting and Clinical Psychology. 61,* 202–204.

Meichenbaum, D. (1977). *Cognitive-behavior modification. An integrative approach.* New York: Plenum Press.

Meichenbaum, D., Turk, D., & Burstein, S. (1975). The nature of coping with stress. In I. Sarason & C. Spielberger (Eds.), *Stress and anxiety.* Washington, DC: Hemisphere.

Melzack, R., & Wall, P. D. (1983). *The challenge of pain.* New York: Basic Books.

Melzack, R., & Wall, P. D. (1965). Pain mechanisms: A new theory. *Science, 150,* 971–979.

Meltzoff, J. (1998). *Critical thinking about research.* Washington, DC: American Psychological Association.

Men Stopping Men Rape. (1997). *Taking action for a rape-free culture.* Madison, WI: Men Stopping Men Rape.

Mercer, J. R. & Lewis, J. F. (1978). *System of multicultural pluralistic assessment.* New York: Psychological Corporation.

Mervis, J. (1986, July). NIMH data point to cf fective treatment. *APA Monitor.*

Messinger, J. C. (1971). Sex and repression in an Irish folk community. In D. S. Marshall & R. C. Suggs (Eds.), *Human sexual behavior: Variations in the ethnic spectrum.* New York: Basic Books.

Meyer, J. (1985). *Hemingway.* New York: Harper & Row.

Meyer, R. G. (1998). Personality disorders. In H. S. Friedman (Ed.), *Encyclopedia of mental health (vol. 3).* San Diego: Academic Press.

Meyer, R. G., & Osborne, Y. V. H. (1982). *Case studies in abnormal behavior.* Boston: Allyn & Bacon.

Meyer, R. G., Wolverton, D., & Deitsch, S. E. (1998). Antisocial personality disorder. In H. S. Friedman (Ed.), *Encyclopedia of mental health (vol. 1).* San Diego: Academic Press.

Mezzich, J. E., Fabrega, H., & Kleinman, A. (in press). On enhancing the cultural sensitivity of *DSM-IV Journal of Nervous and Mental Disease.*

Michael, R., Gagnon, J., Laumann, E., & Kolata, G. (1994). *Sex in America.* Boston: Little, Brown.

Miechenbaum, D. (1977). *Cognitive-behavior modification. An integrative approach.* New York: Plenum Press.

Milgram, S. (1974). *Obedience to authority.* New York: Harper & Row.

Milgram, S. (1965). Some conditions of obedience and disobedience to authority. *Human Relations, 18,* 56–76.

Miller, A. S., & Hoffman, J. P. (1995). Risk and religion: An explanation of gender differences in religiosity. *Journal for the Scientific Study of Religion, 34,* 63–75.

Miller, G. A. (1956). The magical number seven, plus or minus two: Some limits on our capacity for information processing. *Psychological Review, 48,* 337–442.

Miller, J. B. (1986). *Toward a new psychology of women* (2nd ed.). Boston: Beacon Press.

Miller, J. G. (1995, March). *Culture, context, and personal agency: The cultural grounding of self and morality.* Paper presented at the meeting of the Society for Research in Child Development, Indianapolis.

Miller, N. E. (1985). The value of behavioral research on animals. *American Psychologist, 40,* 432–440.

Miller, N. E. (1969). Learning of visceral glandular responses. *Science, 163,* 434–445.

Miller, N. E. (1959). Liberalization of basic S-R concepts: Extension to conflict behavior, motivation, and social learning. In S. Koch (Ed.), *Psychology: A study of science.* New York: McGraw-Hill.

Miller-Jones, D. (1989). Culture and testing. *American Psychologist, 44,* 360–366.

Millis, R. M. (1998). Smoking. In H. S. Friedman (Ed.), *Encyclopedia of mental health (vol. 3)*. San Diego: Academic Press.

Minuchin, P. (1985). Families and individual development: Provocations from the field of family therapy. *Child Development, 56*, 289–302.

Mischel, W. (1973). Toward a cognitive social learning reconceptualization of personality. *Psychological Review, 80*, 252–283.

Mischel, W. (1968). *Personality and assessment.* New York: Wiley.

Mischel, W., & Baker, N. (1975). Cognitive transformations of reward objects through instructions. *Journal of Personality and Social Psychology, 31*, 254–261.

Mishkin, M., & Appenzellar, T. (1987). The anatomy of memory. *Scientific American, 256*, 80–89.

Mistry, J., & Rogoff, B. (1994). Remembering in cultural context. In W. J. Lonner & R. Malpass (Eds.), *Psychology and culture.* Boston: Allyn & Bacon.

Monagle, K. (1990, October). Women around the world. *New Woman*, pp. 195–197.

Money, J. (1986). *Lovemaps: Clinical concepts of sexual/erotic health and pathology, paraphilia, and gender transposition in childhood, adolescence, and maturity.* New York: Irvington.

Monk, T. H. (1989). Circadian rhythms in subjective activation, mood, and performance efficiency. In M. H. Dryger, T. Roth, & W. C. Dement (Eds.), *Principles and practice of sleep medicine.* San Diego: Harcourt Brace Jovanovich.

Monnier, M., & Hosli, L. (1965). Humoral regulation of sleep and wakefulness by hypnogenic and activation dialyzable factors. *Progress in Brain Research, 18*, 118–123.

Montague, A. (1971). *Touching: The human significance of the skin.* New York: Columbia University Press.

Moore, T. E. (1995). Subliminal self-help auditory tapes: An empirical test of perceptual consequences. *Canadian Journal of Behavioural Science, 27*, 9–20.

Morehouse, R. E., Farley, F. H., & Youngquist, J. V. (1990). Type T personality and the Jungian classification system. *Journal of Personality Assessment, 54*, 231–235.

Morris, D., Collett, P., Marsh, P., & O'Shaugnessy, M. (1979). *Gestures.* New York: Stein & Day.

Moses, J., Steptoe, A., Mathews, A., & Edwards, S. (1989). The effects of exercise training on mental well-being in the normal population: A controlled trial. *Journal of Psychosomatic Research, 33*, 47–61.

Murphy, H. B. (1978). Cultural factors in the genesis of schizophrenia. In E. Rosenthal & S. S. Kety (Eds.), *The transmission of schizophrenia.* Elmsford, NY: Pergamon.

Murphy, K. R., & Davidshofer, C. O. (1998). *Psychological testing (4th Ed.).* Upper Saddle River, NJ: Prentice-Hall.

Murphy, S. T., & Zajonc, R. B. (1993). Affect, cognition, and awareness: Affective priming with optimal and suboptimal stimulus exposures. *Journal of Personality and Social Psychology, 64*, 723–739.

Murray, B. (1996, July). Psychology sails into Olympic world. *APA Monitor, 27*, p. 6.

Murray, C. B. (1998). Racism and mental health. In H. S. Friedman (Ed.), *Encyclopedia of mental health (vol. 3)*. San Diego: Academic Press.

Murray, H. A. (1938). *Explorations in personality.* New York: Oxford University Press.

Mussell, M. P., & Mitchell, J. E. (1998). Anorexia nervosa and bulimia nervosa. In H. S. Friedman (Ed.), *Encyclopedia of mental health (vol. 1)*. San Diego: Academic Press.

Myers, D. (1992). *The pursuit of happiness.* New York: William Morrow.

Myers, D. G., & Diener, E. (1995). Who is happy? *Psychological Science, 6*, 10–19.

N

Nagashi, C. T. (1998). Behavioral genetics. In H. S. Friedman (Ed.), *Encyclopedia of mental health (vol. 1)*. San Diego: Academic Press.

Nash, J. M. (1997, February 3). Fertile minds. *Time*, pp. 50–54.

Nathan, P. E. (1994). DSM-IV: Empirical, accessible, not yet ideal. *Journal of Clinical Psychology, 50*, 103–109.

National Academy of Sciences, National Research Council. (1989). *Diet and health: Implication for reducing chronic disease risk.* Washington, DC: National Academy Press.

National Advisory Council on Economic Opportunity. (1980). *Critical choices for the '80s.* Washington, DC: U.S. Government Printing Office.

National Association for the Education of Young Children. (1996). NAEYC position statement: Responding to linguistic and cultural diversity—Recommendations for effective early childhood education. *Young Children, 51*, 4–12.

National Center for Health Statistics. (1989, June). *Statistics on marriage and divorce.* Washington, DC: U.S. Government Printing Office.

Neisser, U., Boodoo, G., Bouchard, T. J., Boykin, A. W., Brody, N., Ceci, S. J., Halpern, D. F., Loehlin, J. C., Perloff, R., Sternberg, R. J., & Urbina, S. (1996) Intelligence: Knowns & unknowns. *American Psychologist, 51*, 77–101.

Nemeth, C. J. (1981). Jury trials: Psychology and law. In L. Berkowitz (Ed.), *Advances in experimental social psychology* (Vol. 14). San Diego: Academic Press.

Neugarten, B. L. (1986) The aging society. In A. Pifer & L. Bronte (Eds.), *Our aging society: Paradox and promise.* New York: W. W. Norton.

Nevis, E. C. (1983). Using an American perspective in understanding another culture: Toward a hierarchy of needs for the Peoples Republic of China. *Journal of Applied Psychology, 19*, 256.

Nichols, W. G., McHugh, J. M., & McHugh, S. M. (1996). *Understanding business* (4th ed.). Burr Ridge, IL: Irwin.

Nicholson, A. N., Bradley, C. M., & Pasco, P. A. (1989). Medications: Effect on sleep and wakefulness. In M. H. Dryger, T. Roth & W. C. Dement (Eds.), *Principles and practice of sleep medicine.* San Diego: Harcourt Brace Jovanovich.

Nietzel, M. T., & Dillehay, R. C. (1986). *Psychological consultation in the courtroom.* Boston: Allyn & Bacon.

Nivison, M. E., & Endresen, I. M. (1993). An analysis of relationships among environmental noise, annoyance and sensitivity to noise, and the consequences for health and sleep. *Journal of Behavioral Medicine, 16*, 257–276.

Nolen-Hoeksema, S. (1998). *Abnormal psychology.* Burr Ridge, IL: McGraw-Hill.

Nolen-Hoeksema, S. (1990). *Sex differences in depression.* Stanford, CA: Stanford University Press.

Notarius, C. I. (1996). Marriage: Will I be happy or sad? In N. Vanzetti & S. Duck (Eds.), *A lifetime of relationships.* Pacific Grove, CA: Brooks/Cole.

Novak, C. A. (1977). Does youthfulness equal attractiveness? In L. E. Troll, J. Israel, & K. Israel (Eds.), *Looking ahead: A woman's guide to the problems and joys of growing older.* Englewood Cliffs, NJ: Prentice Hall.

Novlin, D., Robinson, B. A., Culbreth, L. A., & Tordoff, M. G. (1983). Is there a role for the liver in the control of food intake? *American Journal of Clinical Nutrition, 9*, 233–246.

O

O'Donahue, W., & Krasner, L. (Eds.). (1995). *Theories of behavior therapy.* Washington, DC: American Psychological Association.

Obler, L. K. (1993). Language beyond childhood. In J. B. Gleason (Ed.), *The development of language* (3rd ed.). New York: Macmillan.

Offer, D., Ostrov, E., Howard, K. I., & Atkinson, R. (1988). *The teenage world: Adolescents' self-image in ten countries.* New York: Plenum.

Ogbu, J. U. (1989, April). *Academic socialization of Black children: An inoculation against future failure?* Paper presented at the meeting of the Society for Research in Child Development, Kansas City.

Oh, T. K. (1976). Japanese management: A critical review. *Academy of Management Review, 1*, 14–25.

Olds, J. M. (1958). Self-stimulation experiments and differentiated reward systems. In H. H. Jasper, L. D. Proctor, R. S. Knighton, W. C. Noshay, R. T. Costello (Eds.). *Reticular formation of the brain.* Boston: Little, Brown.

Olds, J. M., & Milner, P. M. (1954). Positive reinforcement produced by electrical stimulation of the septal area and other areas of the rat brain. *Journal of Comparative and Physiological Psychology, 47*, 419–427.

Ones, D. S., Mount, M. K., Barrick, M. R., & Hunter, J. E. (1994). Personality and job performance: A critique of the Tett, Jackson, and Rothstein (1991) meta-analysis. *Personnel Psychology, 47,* 147–156.

Orford, J. (1992). *Community psychology: Theory and practice.* New York: Wiley.

Ossip-Klein, D. J., Doyne, E. J. Bowman, E. D., Osborn, K. M., McDougall-Wilson, I. B. & Neimeyer, R. A. (1989). Effects of running or weight lifting on self-concept in clinically depressed women. *Journal of Consulting and Clinical Psychology, 57,* 158–161.

Otto, A. L., Penrod, S. D., & Dexter, H. R. (1994). The biasing impact of pretrial publicity on juror judgments. *Law and Human Behavior, 18,* 453–469.

P

Paffenbarger, R. S., Hyde, R. T., Wong, A. L. & Hsieh, C. (1986). Physical activity, all-cause mortality, and longevity of college alumni. *New England Journal of Medicine, 314,* 605–612.

Paivio, A. (1986). *Mental representations: A dual coding approach.* New York: Oxford University Press.

Paivio, A. (1971). *Imagery and verbal processes.* New York: Holt, Rinehart & Winston.

Paloutzian, R. F. (1996). *Invitation to the psychology of religion* (2nd ed.). Needham Heights, MA: Allyn & Bacon.

Paludi, M. A. (1998). *The psychology of women.* Upper Saddle River, NJ: Prentice-Hall.

Paludi, M. A. (1995). *The psychology of women* (2nd ed.). Madison, WI: Brown & Benchmark.

Paludi, M. A. (in press). *Ivory power: Sexual harassment on campus.* Albany, NY: SUNY Press.

Pargman, D. (1998). *Understanding sport behavior.* Upper Saddle River, NJ: Prentice-Hall.

Parham, T. (1996). Multicultural counseling theory and African-American populations, In D. W. Sue (Ed.), *Theory of multicultural counseling and therapy.* Pacific Grove, CA: Brooks/Cole.

Parlee, M. B. (1979, April). The friendship bond: PT's survey report on friendship in America. *Psychology Today,* pp. 43–54, 113.

Patterson, C. J. (1996, August). *Children of lesbian and gay parents: Research, law, and policy.* Paper presented at the meeting of the American Psychological Association, Toronto.

Paul, G. L. (1967). Strategy of outcome research in psychotherapy. *Journal of Consulting Psychology, 31,* 109–119.

Paulus, P. B., McCain, G., & Cox, V. (1981). Prison standards: Some pertinent data on crowding. *Federal Probation, 15,* 48–54.

Pavlov, I. P. (1927). *Conditioned reflexes* (F. V. Anrep, Trans, and Ed.). New York: Dover.

Payne, D. G., Lang, V. A., & Blackwell, J. M. (1995). Mixed versus pure display format in integration and nonintegration visual display. *Human factors, 37,* 507–527.

Payne, T. J., Smith, P. O., Sturges, L. V., & Holleran, S. A. (1996). Reactivity to smoking cues: Mediating roles of nicotine and duration of deprivation. *Addictive Behaviors, 21,* 139–154.

Penfield, W. (1947). Some observations in the cerebral cortex of man. *Proceedings of the Royal Society, 134,* 349.

Perkins, D. N. (1984, September), Creativity by design. *Educational Leadership,* pp. 18–25.

Perlman, D., & Peplau, L. A. (1998). Loneliness. In H. S. Friedman (Ed.), *Encyclopedia of mental health (vol. 2).* San Diego: Academic Press.

Perls, E. (1969). *Gestalt therapy verbatim.* Lafayette, CA: Real People Press.

Persinger, M. A., & Krippner, S. (in press). Experimental dream telepathy-clairvoyance and geomagnetic activity. *Journal of the American Society for Psychical Research.*

Pert, A. B., & Snyder, S. H. (1973). Opiate receptor: Demonstration in a nervous tissue. *Science, 179.* 1011.

Peskin, H. (1967). Pubertal onset and ego functioning. *Journal of Abnormal Psychology, 72,* 45–56.

Petersen, A. C. (1979, January). Can puberty come any faster? *Psychology Today,* pp. 45–46.

Peterson, C. (1988) *Personality.* San Diego: Harcourt Brace Jovanovich.

Peterson, C., & Stunkard, A. J. (1986). *Personal control and health promotion.* Unpublished manuscript, Department of Psychology, University of Michigan, Ann Arbor.

Phares, E. J. (1984). *Personality.* Columbus, OH: Merrill.

Philpot, C. L., Brooks, G. R., Lusterman, D., & Nutt, R. L. (1997). *Bridging separate gender worlds.* Washington, DC: American Psychological Association.

Piaget, J. (1960). *The child's conception of the world.* Totowa, NJ: Littlefield.

Pinker, S. (1997). *How the mind works.* New York: Norton.

Plath, S. (1971). *The bell jar.* New York: Harper & Row.

Pleck, J. (1995). The gender role strain paradigm: An update. In R. F. Levant & W. S. Pollack (Eds.), *A new psychology of men.* New York: Basic Books.

Pleck, J. H. (1981). *The myth of masculinity.* Beverly Hills, CA: Sage.

Pleck, J. H. (1979). Men's family work: three perspectives and some new data. *Family Coordinator, 28,* 481–488.

Plutchik, R. (1980). *Emotion: A psychoevolutionary synthesis.* New York: Harper & Row.

Pollock, V. E., Schneider, L. S., Gabrielli, W. F., & Goodwin, D. W. (1987). Sex of parent and sex of offspring in the transmission of alcoholism: A meta-analysis. *Journal of Nervous and Mental Disease, 173,* 668–673.

Pouissant, A. F. (1972, February). Blaxploitation movies—Cheap thrills that degrade Blacks. *Psychology Today,* pp. 22–33.

Pratkanis, A. R., & Greenwald, A. G. (1988). Recent perspectives on unconscious processing: Still no marketing applications. *Psychology and Marketing, 5,* 337–353.

Premack, D. (1986). *Gavagi! The future history of the ape language controversy.* Cambridge, MA: MIT Press.

Presidential Task Force on Psychology and Education. (1993). *Working draft report on learner-centered psychological principles.* Washington, DC: American Psychological Association.

Price-Williams, D., Gordon, W., Ramirez, M. (1969). Skill and conservation: A study of pottery-making children. *Developmental Psychology, 1,* 796.

Pylyshyn, Z. W. (1973). What the mind's eye tells the mind's brain: A critique of mental imagery. *Psychological Bulletin, 80,* 1–24.

R

Rabinowitz, V. C., & Sechzur, J. (1993). Feminist methodologies. In F. L. Denmark & M. A. Paludi (Eds.), *Handbook of the psychology of women.* Westport, CT: Greenwood.

Ramirez, O. (1989). Mexican American children and adolescents. In J. T. Gibbs & L. N. Huang (Eds.), *Children of color.* San Francisco: Jossey-Bass.

Randi, J. (1980). *Flim-flam!* New York: Lippincott.

Rebec, G. V. (1996, June). *Neurochemical and behavioral insights into the mechanisms of action of stimulant drugs.* Paper presented at the meeting of the American Psychological Society, San Francisco.

Regier, D. A., Hirschfeld, R. M. A., Goodwin, F. K., Burke, J. D., Lazar, J. B., & Judd, L. L. (1988). The NIMH Depression Awareness, Recognition, and Treatment Program: Structure, aims, and scientific basis. *American Journal of Psychiatry, 145,* 1351–1357.

Reinisch, J. M. (1990). *The Kinsey Institute new report on sex: What you must know to be sexually literate.* New York: St. Martin's Press.

Religion in America. (1993). Princeton, NJ: Princeton Religion Research Center.

Rescorla, R. A. (1988). Pavlovian conditioning: It's not what you think it is. *American Psychologist, 43,* 151–160.

Rescorla, R. A., & Wagner, A. R. (1972). A theory of Pavlovian conditioning: Variations in the effectiveness of reinforcement and nonreinforcement. In A. Black & W. F. Prokasy (Eds.), *Classical conditioning II: Current theory and research.* New York: Appleton-Century-Crofts.

Restak, R. M. (1988). *The mind.* New York: Bantam.

Revenson, T. A., & McFarlane, T. A. (1998). Women's health. In H. S. Friedman (Ed.), *Encyclopedia of mental health (vol. 3).* San Diego: Academic Press.

Revitch, E., & Schlesinger, L. B. (1978). Murder: Evaluation, classification, and prediction. In I. L. Kutash, S. B. Kutash, & L. B. Schlesinger (Eds.), *Violence.* San Francisco: Jossey-Bass.

Rhodes, N., & Wood, W. (1992). Self-esteem and intelligence affect influenceability: The mediating role of message reception. *Psychological Bulletin, 111,* 156–171.

Rhodes, S. R. (1983). Age-related differences in work attitudes and behavior: A review and conceptual analysis. *Psychological Bulletin, 93,* 328–367.

Rice, F. P. (1996). *Intimate relationships, marriages, and families* (3rd ed.). Mountain View, CA: Mayfield.

Richter, C. P. (1975). On the phenomenon of sudden death in animals and man. *Psychosomatic Medicine, 19,* 191–198.

Robbins, S. P. (1996). *Organizational behavior* (7th ed.). Upper Saddle River, NJ: Prentice Hall.

Robins, L., & Regier, D. A. (Eds.). (1990). *Psychiatric disorders in America.* New York: Macmillan.

Robins, L. N., Helzer, J. F., Weissman, M. M., Orvashcel, H., Gruenberg, F., Burke, J. D., & Regier, D. A. (1984). Lifetime prevalence of specific psychiatric disorders in three sites. *Archives of General Psychiatry, 41,* 949–958.

Rodgers, C. D., Paterson, D. H., Cunningham, D. A., Noble, E. G., Pettigrew, F. P., Myles, W. S., & Taylor, A. W. (1995). Sleep deprivation: Effects on work capacity, self-paced walking, contractile properties, and perceived exertion. *Sleep, 18,* 30–38.

Rodin, J., & Ickovics, J. R. (1990). Women's health: Review and research agenda as we approach the 21st century. *American Psychologist, 45,* 1018–1034.

Rodin, J. (1984, December). Interview: A sense of control. *Psychology Today,* pp. 38–45.

Rodriguez, M. S., & Cohen, S. (1998). Social support. In H. S. Friedman (Ed.), *Encyclopedia of mental health (vol. 3).* San Diego: Academic Press.

Rogers, C. R. (1980). *A way of being.* Boston: Houghton-Mifflin.

Rogers, C. R. (1961). *On becoming a person.* Boston: Houghton-Mifflin.

Rogers, S. (1992–1993, winter).How a publicity blitz created the myth of subliminal advertising. *Public Relations Quarterly, 37,* 12–17.

Rohner, R. P., & Rohner, E. C. (1981). Parental acceptance-rejection and parental control: Cross-cultural codes. *Ethnology, 20,* 245–260.

Root, M. P. (Ed.). (1992). *Racially mixed people in America.* Newbury Park, CA: Sage.

Rosch, E. H. (1973). On the internal structure of perceptual and semantic categories. In T. E. Moore (Ed.), *Cognition and the acquisition of language.* New York: Academic Press.

Rose, R. J. (1995). Genetics and human behavior. *Annual Review of Psychology,* Vol. 46. Palo Alto, CA: Annual Reviews.

Roseman, I. J., Dhawan, N., Rettek, S. I., Naidu, R. K., & Thapa, K. (1995). Cultural differences and cross-cultural similarities in appraisals and emotional responses. *Journal of Cross-Cultural Psychology, 26,* 23–48.

Rosen, K. H., & Stith, S. M. (1995). Women terminating abusive dating relationships: A qualitative study. *Journal of Personal and Social Relationships, 12,* 155–160.

Rosenthal, R. (1994). Interpersonal expectancy effects: A 30-year-perspective. *Current Dimensions in Psychological Science, 3,* 176–179.

Rosenthal, R. (1966). *Experimenter effects in behavioral research.* New York: Appleton-Century-Crofts.

Rosenthal, R., & Jacobsen, L. (1968). *Pygmalian in the classroom.* New York: Holt, Rinehart & Winston.

Rosnow, R. L. (1995). Teaching research ethnics through role-play and discussion. In M. E. Ware & D. E. Johnson (Eds.), *Demonstrations and activities in teaching of psychology* (Vol. 1). Hillsdale, NJ: Erlbaum.

Ross, L. (1977). The intuitive psychologist and his shortcomings: Distortions in the attribution process. In L. Berkowitz (Ed.), *Advances in experimental social psychology* (Vol. 10). New York: Academic Press.

Rubin, L., & Pietromonaco, P. R. (1998). In H. S. Friedman (Ed.), *Encyclopedia of mental health (vol. 1).* San Diego: Academic Press.

Rumbaugh, D. M., Hopkins, W. D., Washburn, D. A., & Savage-Rumbaugh, E. S. (1991). Comparative perspectives of brain, cognition, and language. In N. A. Krasnegor, D. M. Rumbaugh, M. Studdert-Kennedy, & R. L. Schiefelbusch (Eds.), *Biological and behavioral determinants of language development.* Hillsdale, NJ: Erlbaum.

Rumpel, E. (1988, August). *A systematic analysis of the cultural content of introductory psychology textbooks.* Unpublished master's thesis, Western Washington University, Bellingham.

Russo, N. F. (1990). Overview: Forging research priorities for women's mental health. *American Psychologist, 45,* 368–374.

Russo, N. F. (1985). PSQ: A scientific voice in feminist psychology. *Psychology of Women Quarterly, 19,* 1–3.

Rybash, J. M., Roodin, P. A., & Hoyer, W. J. (1998). *Adult development and aging* (4th ed.). Burr Ridge, IL: McGraw-Hill.

Rymer, R. (1993). *Genie.* New York: Harper-Collins.

S

Saarni, C. (1988). Children's understanding of the interpersonal consequences of dissemblance of nonverbal emotional-expressive behavior. *Journal of Nonverbal Behavior, 12,* 275–294.

Sackheim, H.A. (1985, June). The case for ECT. *Psychology Today,* pp. 37–40.

Sacks, O. (1993, May 10). To see and not see. *New Yorker,* pp. 59–66+.

Sadik, N. (1991, March–April). Success in development depends on women. *Popline.* New York: World Population News Service.

Sagan, C. (1980). *Cosmos.* New York: Random House.

Saklofske, D. H., & Zeidner, M. (Eds.). (1995). *International handbook of personality and intelligence.* New York: Plenum.

Sanderson, W. C. (1995, March). Which therapies are proven effective? *APA Monitor,* p. 4.

Sandler, D. P., Comstock, G. W., Helsing, K. J., & Shore, D. L. (1989). Deaths from all causes in non-smokers who lived with smokers. *American Journal of Public Health, 79,* 163–167.

Santrock, J. W. (2000). *Educational psychology.* Burr Ridge, IL: McGraw-Hill.

Santrock, J. W. (1999). *Life-span development* (7th ed.). Burr Ridge IL: McGraw-Hill.

Santrock, J. W. (1998). *Adolescence (7th Ed.).* Burr Ridge, IL: McGraw-Hill.

Santrock, J. W. (1998). *Child development* (8th ed.). Burr Ridge, IL: McGraw-Hill.

Sargent, C. (1987). Skeptical fairytales from Bristol. *Journal of the Society for Psychical Research, 54.*

Sarrel, P., & Masters, W. (1982). Sexual molestation of men by women. *Archives of Human Sexuality, 11,* 117–131.

Sasaki, T., & Kennedy, J. L. (1995). Genetics of psychosis. *Current Opinion in Psychiatry, 8,* 25–28.

Satir, V. (1964). *Conjoint family therapy.* Palo Alto, CA: Science and Behavior Books.

Satorius, N. (1992). Commentary on prognosis for schizophrenia in the third world. *Culture, Medicine, and Psychiatry, 16,* 81–84.

Savage-Rumbaugh, E. S., Murphy, J., Sevick, R. A., Brakke. K. E., Williams, S. L., & Rumbaugh, D. (1993). Language comprehension in ape and child. *Monographs of the Society for Research in Child Development, 58* (3–4, Serial No. 233).

Saxe, L., Dougherty, D., & Cross, T. (1985). The validity of polygraph testing: Scientific analysis and public controversy. *American Psychologist, 40,* 335–366.

Scanlan, T. (1996, July). Commentary in "Dedication wanes when the fun ends." *APA Monitor, 27,* p. 22.

Scardamalia, M., & Bereiter, C. (1994). Computer support for knowledge-building communities. *Journal of Learning Sciences, 3,* 265–283.

Scarr, S. (1991, April). *Developmental theories for the 1990s.* Presidential address, biennial meeting of the Society for Research in Child Development, Seattle.

Scarr, S. (1984, May). [Interview.] *Psychology Today,* pp. 59–63.

Schachter, S. (1971) Some extraordinary facts about obese humans and rats. *American Psychologist, 26,* 129–144.

Schachter, S., & Singer, J. E. (1962). Cognitive, social, and physiological determinants of emotional state. *Psychological Review, 69,* 379–399.

Schaffer, H. R., & Emerson, P. E. (1964). The development of social attachments in infancy. *Monographs of the Society for Research in Child Development, 2913,* Serial No. 941.

Schank, R., & Abelson, R. (1977). *Scripts, plans, goals, and understanding.* Hillsdale, NJ: Erlbaum.

Scheer, S. D. (1996, March). *Adolescent to adult transitions: Social status and cognitive factors.* Paper presented at the meeting of the Society for Research on Adolescence, Boston.

Schein, V. E., Mueller, R., Lituchy, T., & Liu, J. (1996). Think manager—think male? A global phenomenon? *Journal of Organizational Behavior, 17,* 33–42.

Schiffman, J., & Walker, E. (1998). Schizophrenia. In H. S. Friedman (Ed.), *Encyclopedia of mental health (vol. 3).* San Diego: Academic Press.

Schneider, E. L., Rowe, J. W., Johnson, T., Holbrook, N., & Morrison, J. (Eds.). (1996). *Handbook of the biology of aging* (4th ed.). Orlando, FL: Academic Press.

Schneider, W., & Bjorklund, D. F. (1998). Memory. In W. Damon (Ed.), *Handbook of child psychology (5th Ed., Vol. 2).* New York: Wiley.

Schneidman, E. S. (1971). Suicide among the gifted. *Suicide and Life-Threatening Behavior, 1,* 23–45.

Schofield, J. W., & Pavelchak, M. A. (1989). Fallout from *The Day After:* Impact of a TV film on attitudes related to nuclear war. *Journal of Applied Social Psychology, 19,* 433–448.

Schofield, J. W., & Pavelchak, M. A. (1985). The day after: The impact of media event. *American Psychologist, 40,* 542–548.

Schultz, D., & Schultz, S. E. (1998). *Psychology and work today.* Upper Saddle River, NJ: Prentice-Hall.

Schwartz, R., & Ericksen, M. (1989). Statement of the Society for Public Health Education on the national health promotion disease prevention objectives for the year 2000. *Health Education Quarterly, 16,* 3–7.

Schwartz, S. H. (1990). Individualism—collectivism. *Journal of Cross-cultural Psychology, 21,* 139–157.

Schwartz, S. H., & Sagiv, L. (1995). Identifying culture-specifics in the content and structure of values. *Journal of Cross-Cultural Psychology, 26,* 92–116.

Scioli, A., & Averill, J. R. (1998). Emotion and cognition. In H. S. Friedman (Ed.), *Encyclopedia of mental health (vol. 2).* San Diego: Academic Press.

Seager J., & Olson, A. (Eds.). (1986). *Women of the world; An international atlas.* New York: Simon & Schuster.

Sears, D. O., & Funk, C. (1991). The role of self-interest in social and political attitudes. In M. Zann (Ed.), *Advances in experimental social psychology* (Vol.24). San Diego: Academic Press.

Sears, D. O., Peplau, L. A., & Taylor S. E. (1997). *Social psychology* (9th ed.). Englewood cliffs, NJ: Prentice Hall.

Sears, D. O., Peplau, L. A., & Taylor, S. E. (1996). *Social psychology* (9th ed.). Englewood Cliffs, NJ: Prentice Hall.

Segall, M. H., Campbell, D. T., & Herskovits, M. J. (1963). Cultural differences in the perception of geometric illusions. *Science, 193,* 769–771.

Segall, M. H., Dasen, P. R., Berry, J. W., & Poortinga, Y. H. (1990). *Human behavior in global perspective.* New York: Pergamon.

Segerberg, O. (1982). *Living to be 100: 1200 who did and how they did it.* New York: Scribner's.

Seidman, E., & French, S. E. (1998). Community mental health. In H. S. Friedman (Ed.), *Encyclopedia of mental health (vol. 1).* San Diego: Academic Press.

Seidemann, E., Meilijson, I., Abeles, M., Bergman, H., & Vaadia, E. (1996). Simultaneously recorded single units in the frontal cortex go through sequences of discrete and stable states in monkeys performing a delayed localization task. *Journal of Neuroscience, 16,* 752–768.

Seiffge-Krenke, I. (1995). *Stress, coping, and relationships in adolescence.* Hillsdale, NJ: Erlbaum.

Seligman, M. E. P. (1995). The effectiveness of psychotherapy: The *Consumer Reports* study. *American Psychologist, 50,* 965–974.

Seligman, M. E. P. (1991). *Learned optimism.* New York: Knopf.

Seligman, M. E. P. (1989). Why is there so much depression today? The waxing of the individual and the waning of the common. In *The G. Stanley Hall Lecture Series.* Washington, DC: American Psychological Association.

Seligman, M. E. P. (1975). *Helplessness: On depression, development and death.* San Francisco: W. H. Freeman.

Seligman, M. E. P. (1970). On the generality of the laws of learning. *Psychological review, 77,* 406–418.

Seligman, M. E. P., & Rosenhan, D. L. (1998). *Abnormality.* New York: Norton.

Selye, H. (1983). The stress concept. Past, present, and future. In C. I. Cooper (Ed.), *Stress research.* New York: Wiley.

Selye, H. (1974). *Stress without distress.* Philadelphia: W. B. Saunders.

Shanks, D. R. (1991). Categorization by a connectionist network. *Journal of Experimental Psychology: Learning, Memory, and Cognition, 17,* 433–443.

Shaver, P. (1986, August). *Being lonely, falling in love: Perspectives from attachment theory.* Paper presented at the meeting of the American Psychological Association, Washington, DC.

Sheldon, W. H. (1954). *Atlas of men.* New York: Harper.

Shepard, R. N. (1967). Recognition memory for words, sentences, and pictures. *Journal of Verbal Learning and Behavior, 6,* 156–163.

Sher, K. J. (1993). Children of alcoholics and the intergenerational transmission of alcoholism: A biopsychosocial perspective. In J. S. Baer, G. A. Marlatt, & R. J. McMahon (Eds.), *Addictive behaviors across the life span.* Newbury Park, CA: Sage.

Sher, K. J. (1991). *Children of alcoholics: A critical appraisal of theory and research.* Chicago: University of Chicago Press.

Sherer, K., & Wallbott, H. (1994). Evidence for the universality and cultural variation of different emotion response patterning. *Journal of Personality and Social Psychology. 66,* 310–328.

Sherif, M., Harvey, O. J., White, B. J., Hood, W. R., & Sherif, C. W. (1961). *Intergroup cooperation and competition: The Robbers Cave experiment.* Norman, OK: University of Oklahoma Press.

Shweder, R. A., Goodnow, J., Hatano, G., LeVine, R. A., Markus, H., & Miller, P. A. (1998). The cultural psychology of development. In W. Damon (Ed.), *Handbook of child psychology (5th Ed., Vol. 1).* New York: Wiley.

Shields, S. A. (1991). Gender in the psychology of emotion: A selective research review. In K. T. Strongman (Ed.), *International Review of Studies on Emotion* (Vol. 1). New York: Wiley.

Shotland, R. L. (1985, June). When bystanders just stand by. *Psychology Today,* pp. 50–55.

Shrout, P. E., & Fiske, S. T. (Eds.). (1995). *Personality research, methods, and theory.* Hillsdale, NJ: Erlbaum.

Siegler, R. S. (1995, March). *Nothing is; everything becomes.* Paper presented at the meeting of the Society for Research in Child Development, Indianapolis.

Siffre, M. (1975). Six months alone in a cave. *National Geographic, 147,* 426–435.

Sigelman, C. K., Thomas, D. B., Sigelman, L., & Ribich, F. D. (1986). Gender, physical attractiveness, and electability: An experimental investigation of vote biases. *Journal of Applied Social Psychology, 16,* 229–248.

Silverman, N. N., & Corsini, R. J. (1984). Is it true what they say about Adler's individual psychology? *Teaching of Psychology, 11,* 188–189.

Simon, H. A. (1990). Invariants in human behavior. *Annual Review of Psychology, 41.*

Simons, J. M., Finlay, B., & Yang, A. (1991). *The adolescent and young adult fact book.* Washington, DC: Children's Defense Fund.

Simpson, J. A. (1995). Self-monitoring and commitment to dating relationships: A classroom demonstration. In M. E. Ware & D. E. Johnson (Eds.), *Demonstrations and activities in teaching of psychology.* Hillsdale, NJ: Erlbaum.

Singelis, T. M. (1998). *Teaching about culture, ethnicity, and diversity.* Newbury Park, CA: Sage.

Singer, R. N. (1996, July). Commentary in "Dedication wanes when the fun ends." *APA Monitor, 27,* p. 22.

Sizemore, C. C. (1989). *A mind of my own.* New York: William Morrow.

Skinner, B. F. (1990). Can psychology be a science of mind? *American Psychologist, 45,* 1206–1210.

Skinner, B. F. (1971). *Beyond freedom and dignity.* New York: Knopf.

Skinner, B. F. (1961). Teaching machines. *Scientific American, 205*, 90–102.

Skinner, B. F. (1948). *Walden two.* New York: Macmillian.

Skinner, B. F. (1938). *The behavior of organisms: An experimental analysis.* New York: Appleton-Century-Crofts.

Slavin, R. (1989). Cooperative learning and student achievement. In R. Slavin (Ed.), *School and classroom organization.* Hillsdale, NJ: Erlbaum.

Slobin, D. (1972, July). Children and language: They learn the same all around the world. *Psychology Today*, pp. 71–76.

Slovenko, R. (1995). *Psychiatry and criminal culpability.* New York: Wiley.

Smith, M. L., Glass, G. N., & Miller, R. L. (1980). *The benefit of psychotherapy.* Baltimore: John Hopkins University Press.

Snarey, R. (1987, June). A question of morality. *Psychology Today*, pp. 6–8.

Snowden, D. A. (1995). *An epidemiological study of aging in a select population and its relationship to Alzheimer's disease.* Unpublished manuscript, Sanders Brown Center on Aging, Lexington, KY.

Snowden, L. R. & Cheung, F. K. (1990). Use of inpatient mental health services by members of ethnic minority groups. *American Psychologist, 45*, 347–355.

Sobell, L. C., & Sobell, M. (in press). Timeline follow-back: A technique for assessing self-reported ethanol consumption. In J. Allen & R. Z. Litten (Eds.), *Techniques to assess alcohol consumption.* Totowa, NJ: Humana.

Sobell, M. B., & Sobell, L. C. (1992). Hitting the wrong nail on the head: Comment to Peele. *Addictive Behaviors, 17*, 75–77.

Solomon, R. (1964). Punishment, *American Psychologist, 19*, 239–253.

Solomon, Z. (1993). *Combat stress reaction.* New York: Plenum.

Spanos, N. P. (1988). Misconceptions about influenceability research and sociocognitive approaches to hypnosis. *Behavioral and Brain Sciences, 11*, 714–716.

Spearman, C. E. (1927). *The abilities of man.* New York: Macmillan.

Spence, J. T., & Helmreich, R. (1978). *Masculinity and femininity: Their psychological dimensions.* Austin: University of Texas Press.

Sperling, G. (1960). The information available in brief visual presentations. *Psychological Monographs, 74* (Whole No. 11).

Sperry, R. W. (1974). Lateral specialization in surgically separated hemispheres. In F. O. Schmitt & F. G. Worden (Eds.), *The neurosciences: Third study program.* Cambridge, MA: MIT Press.

Sperry, R. W. (1968). Hemisphere deconnection and unity in conscious awareness. *American Psychologist, 23*, 723–733.

Spiritual America. (1994, April 4). *U.S. News and World Report*, pp. 48–59.

Sprie, J. E., & Courtois, C. A. (1988). The treatment of women's sexual dysfunctions arising from sexual assault. In R. A. Brown & J. R. Fields (Eds.), *Treatment of sexual problems in individual and couples therapy.* Great Neck. NY: PMA.

Squire, L. (1990, June). *Memory and brain systems.* Paper presented at the meeting of the American Psychological Society, Dallas.

Squire, L. (1987). *Memory and brain.* New York: Oxford University Press.

Squire, L. R. (1992). Memory and the hippocampus: A synthesis from findings with rats, monkeys, and humans. *Psychological Review, 99*, 195–231.

Sroufe, L. A. (1996). *Emotional development.* New York: Cambridge.

Stanhope, L., & Corter, C. (1993, March). *The mother's role in the transition to siblinghood.* Paper presented at the biennial meeting of the Society for Research in Child Development, New Orleans.

Stanley, B., & Stanley, M. (1989). Biochemical studies in suicide victims: Current findings and future implications. *Suicide and Life-Threatening Behavior. 19*, 30–42.

Stanovich, D. (1992). *How to think straight about psychology* (3rd ed.). New York: HarperCollins.

Stanton, A. L., & Gallant, S. J. (Eds.). (1995). *The psychology of women's health.* Washington, DC: American Psychological Association.

Steadman, H. J., Callahan, L. A., Robbins, P. C., & Morrissey, J. P. (1989). Maintenance of an insanity defense under Montana's "abolition" of the insanity defense. *American Journal of Psychiatry, 146*, 357–360.

Steers, R. M. (1988). *Introduction to organizational behavior* (2nd ed.). Glenview, IL: Scott, Foresman.

Stengel, R. (1996, April 22). "Fly til I Die." *Time*, pp. 34–40.

Stengel, R. (1992, March 16). Midnight's Mayor. *Time Magazine*, pp. 42–43.

Sternberg, R. J. (1988). *The triangle of love.* New York: Basic Books.

Sternberg, R. J. (1986). *Intelligence applied.* San Diego: Harcourt Brace Jovanovich.

Sternberg, R. J. (1985, December). Teaching critical thinking. Part 2: Possible solutions. *Phi Delta Kappan*, 277–280.

Stevenson, H. W. (1995). Mathematics achievement of American students: First in the world by the year 2000? In C. A. Nelson (Ed.), *Basic and applied perspectives on learning, cognition, and development.* Minneapolis: University of Minnesota Press.

Steward, P. (1995). *Beginning writers in the zone of proximal development.* Hillsdale, NJ: Erlbaum.

Streissguth, A. P., Martin, D. C., Sandman, B. M., Kirchner, G. L., & Darby, B. L. (1984). Intrauterine alcohol and nicotine exposure: Attention and reaction time in four-year-old children. *Developmental Psychology, 20*, 533–543.

Strickland, B. (1998). Sex-related differences in health and illness. *Psychology of Women Quarterly, 12*, 382–399.

Strupp, H. H. (1995). The psychotherapist's skills revised. *Clinical Psychology: Science and Practice, 2*; 70–74.

Strupp, H. H. (1992). The future of psychodynamic psychotherapy. *Psychotherapy, 29*, 21–28.

Stunkard, A. J. (1989). Perspectives on human obesity. In A. J. Stunkard & A. Baum (Eds.), *Perspectives on behavioral medicine: Eating, sleeping, and sex.* Hillsdale, NJ: Erlbaum.

Sue, D. W., Carter, R. T., Casas, J. M., Fouad, N. A., Ivey, A. E., Jensen, M., Lafromoise, T., Manese, J. E., Ponterotto, J. E., & Vazquez-Nutall, E. (1998). *Multicultural counseling experiences.* Newbury Park, CA: Sage.

Sue, D. W., Ivey, A. E., & Petersen, P. (1996). Research, practice, and training implications of multicultural counseling theory. In D. W. Sue (Ed.), *Theory of multicultural counseling and therapy.* Pacific Grove, CA: Brooks/Cole.

Sue, S. (1991, August). *Ethnicity and culture in psychological research and practice.* Paper presented at the meeting of the American Psychological Association, Boston.

Sue, S. (1990, August). *Ethnicity and culture in psychological research and practice.* Paper presented at the meeting of the American Psychological Association, Boston.

Sue, S., Allen, D., & Conaway, L. (1978). The responsiveness and equality of mental health care to Chicanos and Native Americans. *American Journal of Community Psychology, 6*, 137–146.

Suedfeld, P., & Coren S. (1989). Perceptual isolation, sensory deprivation, and rest: Moving introductory psychology tests out of the 1950s. *Canadian Psychology, 30*, 17–29.

Suinn, R. M. (1987). Asian Americans in psychology. In P. J. Woods & C. S. Wilkinson (Eds.), *Is psychology the major for you?* Washington, DC: American Psychological Association.

Suinn, R. M. (1984). *Fundamentals of abnormal psychology.* Chicago: Nelson-Hall.

Sullivan, H. S. (1953). *The interpersonal theory of psychiatry.* New York: W. W. Norton.

Sullivan, K. T., & Christensen, A. (1998). Couples therapy. In H. S. Friedman (Ed.), *Encyclopedia of mental health (vol. 1).* San Diego: Academic Press.

Super, C. M. (1980). Cross-cultural research on infancy. In H. C. Triandis & A. Heron (Eds.), *Handbook of cross-cultural psychology. Vol. 4: Developmental psychology.* Boston: Allyn & Bacon.

Sutton, R. G., & Kessler, M. (1986). National study of the effects of clients' socioeconomic status on clinical psychologists' professional judgments. *Journal of Consulting and Clinical Psychology, 54*, 275–276.

Swanson, D. P. (1995, March). *The effects of racial identity and socioeconomic status on academic outcomes for adolescents.* Paper presented at the meeting of the Society for Research in Child Development, Indianapolis, IN.

Swim, J. K., Aikin, K.J., Hall, W. S., & Hunter, B. A. (1995). Sexism and racism: Old-fashioned and modern prejudices. *Journal of Personality and Social Psychology, 68,* 199–214.

Synder, M. (1979). Self-monitoring processes. In L. Berkowitz (Ed.), *Advances in experimental social psychology* (Vol. 12). New York: Academic Press.

Syvalahti, E. K. (1985). Drug treatment of insomnia. *Annals of Clinical Research, 17,* 265–272.

Szasz, I. (1977). *Psychiatric slavers: When confinement and coercion masquerade as cure.* New York: Free Press.

Szasz, T. (1965). *The ethics of psychoanalysis.* New York: Basic Books.

T

Tager-Flusberg, H. (1994). (Ed.). *Constraints on language acquisition.* Hillsdale, NJ: Erlbaum.

Tajfel, H. (1978). The achievement of group differentiation. In H. Tajfel (Ed.), *Differentiation between social groups: Studies in the social psychology of intergroup relations.* London: Academic Press.

Takanishi, R. (1993). The opportunities of adolescence—research, interventions, and policy. *American Psychologist, 48,* 85–87.

Tannen, D. (1990). *You just don't understand: Women and men in conversation.* New York: Ballantine.

Tavris, C. (1992). *The mismeasure of woman.* New York: Touchstone.

Tavris, C. (1989). *Anger: The misunderstood emotion* (2nd ed.). New York: Touchstone.

Tavris, C., & Wade, C. (1984). *The longest war: Sex differences in perspective* (2nd ed.). San Diego: Harcourt Brace Jovanovich.

Taylor, S. (1998). Positive illusions. In H.S. Friedman (Ed.), *Encyclopedia of mental health (vol. 3).* San Diego: Academic Press.

Taylor, S. E. (1991). *Health psychology* (2nd ed.). New York: McGraw-Hill.

Teachman, J. D., & Polonko, K. A. (1990). Cohabitation and marital stability in the United States. *Social Forces, 69,* 207–220.

Terman, L. (1925). *Genetic studies of genius. Vol. 1: Mental and physical traits of a thousand gifted children.* Stanford, CA: Stanford University Press.

Thigpen, C. H., & Cleckley, H. M. (1957). *Three faces of Eve.* New York: McGraw-Hill.

Thomas, C. B. (1983). Unpublished manuscript, Johns Hopkins University, Baltimore.

Thomas, G. (Ed.). (1988). *World education encyclopedia.* New York: Facts on File.

Thompson, C. P., Herrmann, D. J., Read, J. D., Bruce, D., Payne, D. G., & Toglia, M. P. (1998). *Eyewitness memory.* Mahwah, NJ: Erlbaum.

Thompson, J. K. (Ed.) (1996). *Body image, eating disorders, and obesity.* Washington, DC: American Psychological Association.

Thompson, R. A. (1998). Legal dimensions of mental health. In H. S. Friedman (Ed.), *Encyclopedia of mental health (Vol. 2).* San Diego: Academic Press.

Thompson, R. A. (1991). Construction and reconstruction of early attachments: Taking perspective on attachment theory and research. In D. P. Keating & H. G. Rosen (Eds.), *Constructivist perspectives on atypical development.* Hillsdale, NJ: Erlbaum.

Thompson, R. A., & Cimbolic, P. (1978). Black students' counselor preference and attitudes toward counseling center use. *Journal of Counseling Psychology, 25,* 570–575.

Thurstone, L. L. (1938). *Primary mental abilities.* Chicago: University of Chicago Press.

Tolman, E. C. (1948). Cognitive maps in rats and men. *Psychological Review, 55,* 189–208.

Tolman, E. C. (1932). *Purposive behavior in animals and man.* New York: Appleton-Century-Crofts.

Tomlinson-Keasey, C. (1990). The working lives of Terman's gifted women. In H. W. Grossman & N. L. Chester (Eds.), *The experience and meaning of work in women's lives.* Hillsdale, NJ: Erlbaum.

Tomlinson-Keasey, C., Warren, L. W., & Elliott, J. F. (1986). Suicide among gifted women. A prospective study. *Journal of Abnormal Psychology, 95,* 123–130.

Torrey, E. F., & others. (1984). Endemic psychosis in western Ireland. *American Journal of Psychiatry, 141,* 966–970.

Torrey, E. T. (1986). *Witch doctors and psychiatrists: The common roots of psychotherapy and its future.* New York: Harper & Row.

Triandis, H. (1994). *Culture and social behavior.* New York: McGraw-Hill.

Triandis, H. C. (1997). Cross-cultural perspectives on personality. In R. Hogan, J. Johnson, & S. Briggs (Eds.), *Handbook of personality psychology.* San Diego: Academic Press.

Triandis, H. C. (1994). Culture and social behavior. In W. J. Lonner & R. Malpass (Eds.), *Psychology and culture.* Needham Heights, MA: Allyn & Bacon.

Triandis, H. C., Brislin, R., & Hui, C. H. (1988). Cross cultural training across the individualism-collectivism divide. *International Journal of Intercultural Relations, 12,* 269–289.

Triandis, H. C., Chen, X. P., Chan, D. K. (1998). Scenarios for the measurement of collectivism and individualism. *Journal of Cross-Cultural Psychology, 29,* 275–289.

Trimble, J. E., & Fleming, C. (1989). Client, counselor, and community characteristics. In P. Pedersen, J. Draguns, W. Lonner, & J. Trimble (Eds.), *Counseling across cultures* (3rd ed.). Honolulu: University of Hawaii Press.

Trivers, R. (1971). The evolution of reciprocal altruism. *Quarterly Review of Biology, 46,* 35–57.

Tseng, W., & Hsu, J. (1969). Chinese culture, personality formation, and mental illness. *International Journal of Social Psychiatry, 16,* 5–14.

Tulving, E. (1989). Remembering and knowing the past. *American Scientist, 77,* 361–367.

Tulving, E. (1972). Episode and semantic memory. In E. Tulving, & W. Donaldson (Eds.), *Origins of memory.* San Diego: Academic Press.

Turnbull, C. (1961). Some observations regarding the experiences and behavior of the Bambuti Pygmies. *American Journal of Psychology, 74,* 304–308.

Tversky, A., & Kahneman, D. (1974). Judgment under uncertainty: Heuristics and biases. *Science, 185,* 1124–1131.

U

U.S. Commission on Civil Rights (1975). *A better chance to learn: Bilingual bicultural education.* Washington, DC: U.S. Government Printing Office.

Unger, R., & Crawford, M. (1996). *Women and gender: A feminist psychology* (2nd ed.). New York: McGraw-Hill.

V

Vaillant, G. E. (1977). *Adaptation to life.* Boston: Little, Brown.

Vadum, A. C., & Rankin, N. O. (1998). *Psychological research.* Burr Ridge, IL: McGraw-Hill.

Van den Berghe, P. L. (1978). *Race and racism: A comparative perspective.* New York: Wiley.

Veitch, R., & Arkkelin, D. (1995). *Environmental psychology.* Upper Saddle River, NJ: Prentice Hall.

Ventis, W. L. (1995). The relationships between religion and mental health. *Journal of Social Issues, 51,* 171–192.

Verbrugge, L. M. (1989). The twain meet: Empirical explanations of sex differences in health and mortality. *Journal of Health and Social Behavior, 30,* 282–304.

Vitols, M. (1967). *Patterns of mental disturbance in the Negro.* Unpublished manuscript, Cherry Hospital, Goldsboro, NC.

Von Békésy, G. (1960). Vibratory patterns of the basilar membrane. In E. G. Wever (Ed.), *Experiments in hearing.* New York: McGraw-Hill.

Voyer, D., Voyer, S., & Bryden, M. P. (1995). Magnitude of sex differences in spatial abilities: A meta-analysis and consideration of critical variables. *Psychological Bulletin, 117,* 250–270.

Vygotsky, L. S. (1962). *Thought and language.* Cambridge, MA: MIT Press.

W

Wadden, T. A., Foster, G. D., Stunkard, A. J., & Conill, A. M. (1996). Effects of weight cycling on the resting energy expenditure and body composition of obese women. *Eating Disorders, 19,* 5–12.

Wagman, M. (1995). *The science of cognition.* Westport, CT: Praeger.

Wald, G., & Brown, P. K. (1965). Human color vision and color blindness. *Cold Spring*

Harbor Symposia on Quantitative Biology,
30, 345–359.

Wallace, R. K., & Benson, H. (1972). The physiology of meditation. *Scientific American,*
226, 85–90.

Wallerstein, R. (1992). *The common ground of psychoanalysis.* Northvale, NJ: Jason Aronson.

Wallerstein, R. S. (1989). The psychotherapy research project of the Menninger Foundation: An overview. *Journal of Consulting and Clinical Psychology, 57,* 195–205.

Wallis, C. (1985, December 9). Children having children. *Time,* pp. 78–88.

Wampold, B. E., Mondin, G. W., Moody, M., Stich, F., Benson, K., & Ahn, H. (1997). A meta-analysis of outcome studies comparing bona fide psychotherapies: Empirically, "All must have prizes." *Psychological Bulletin, 122,* 203–215.

Ward, C. (1994). Culture and altered states of consciousness. In W. J. Lonner & R. Malpass (Eds.). *Psychology and culture.* Needham Heights, MA: Allyn & Bacon.

Ward, C. (Ed.). (1989). *Altered states of consciousness and mental health: A cross-cultural perspective.* Newbury Park, CA: Sage.

Warden, C. J., & Jackson, T. A. (1935). Imitative behavior in the rhesus monkey. *Journal of Genetic Psychology, 46,* 103–125.

Wasserman, G. S. (1978). *Color vision: An historical introduction.* New York: Wiley.

Waters, E., Merrick, S. K., Albersheim, L. J., & Treboux, E. (1995, March). *Attachment security from infancy to early adulthood: A 20-year longitudinal study.* Paper presented at the meeting of the Society for Research in Child Development, Indianapolis.

Watson, D. L., & Tharp, R. R. (1996). *Self-directed behavior* (7th ed.). Pacific Grove, CA: Brooks/Cole.

Watson, J. B. (1928). *Psychological care of the infant and child.* New York: Norton.

Watson, J. B. (1913). Psychology as the behaviorist views it. *Psychological Review, 20,* 158–177.

Watson, J. B., & Raynor, R. (1920). Emotional reactions. *Journal of Experimental Psychology, 3,* 1–14.

Webb, W. B. (1978). Sleep and dreams. *Annual Review of Psychology.*

Wechsler, D. (1972). "Hold" and "Don't Hold" test. In S. M. Chown (Eds.). *Human aging.* New York: Penguin.

Weimer, W. B. (1974). Overview of a cognitive conspiracy. In W. B. Weimer & D. S. Palermo (Eds.). *Cognition and the symbolic processes.* Hillsdale, NJ: Erlbaum.

Weiner, I. B., Exner, J. E., & Sciara, A. (1996). Is the Rorschach welcome in the courtroom? *Journal of Personality Assessment, 67,* 422–424.

Weinstein, S. (1968). Intensive and extensive aspects of tactile sensitivity as a function of body part, sex, and laterality. In D. R. Kenshalo (Ed.), *The skin senses.* Springfield, IL: Charles C Thomas.

Weisenberg, M. (1982). Cultural and ethnic factors in reaction to pain. In I. Al-Issa (Ed.), *Culture and psychopathology.* Baltimore: University Park Press.

Weisman, A. D. (1989). Vulnerability and the psychological disturbances of cancer patients. *Psychosomatics, 30,* 80–85.

Weissman, M. M., & Boyd, J. H. (1985). Affective disorders: Epidemiology. In H. I. Kaplan & B. J. Sadock (Eds.), *Comprehensive textbook of psychiatry/IV.* Baltimore: Williams & Wilkins.

Wender, P. H., Kety, S. S., Rosenthal, D., Schulsinger, F., Ortmann J., & Lunds, I. (1986). Psychiatric disorder in the biological and adoptive families of adopted individuals with affective disorders. *Archives of General Psychiatry, 43,* 923–929.

Westkott, M. (1986). *The feminist legacy of Karen Horney.* New Haven, CT: Yale University Press.

White, R. W. (1959). Motivation reconsidered: The concept of competence. *Psychological Review, 66,* 297–333.

Whiting, B. B. (1989, April). *Culture and interpersonal behavior.* Paper presented at the biennial meeting of the Society for Research in Child Development, Kansas City.

Whitley, B. E. (1996). *Principles of research in behavioral science.* Mountain View, CA: Mayfield.

Whitman, F. L., Diamond, M., & Martin, J. (1993). Homosexual orientation in twins: A report of 61 pairs and three triplet sets. *Archives of Sexual Behavior, 22,* 187–198.

Whorf, B. L. (1956). *Language, thought, and creativity.* New York: Wiley.

Wiggins, J. S. (1997). In defense of traits. In R. Hogan, J. Johnson, & S. Briggs (Eds.), *Handbook of personality psychology.*

Wiggins, J. S., & Trapness, P. D. (1997). Personality structure: The return of the big five. In R. Hogan, J. Johnson, & S. Briggs (Eds.), *Handbook of personality research.* San Diego: Academic Press.

Williams, J. E., & Best, D. L. (1989). *Sex and psyche: Self-concept viewed cross-culturally.* Newbury Park, CA: Sage.

Williams, J. E., & Best, D. L. (1982). *Measuring sex stereotypes: A thirty nation study.* Newbury Park, CA: Sage.

Williams, M. E., & Condry, J. (1989, April). *Minority portrayals and cross-racial interaction television.* Paper presented at the biennial meeting of the Society for Research in Child Development, Kansas City.

Williams, R. B. (1989). Biological mechanisms mediating the relationship between behavior and coronary prone behavior. In A. W. Siegman & T. Dembrowski (Eds.), *In search of coronary-prone behavior: Beyond Type A.* Hillsdale, NJ: Erlbaum.

Wilson, W. J., & Neckerman, K. M. (1986). Poverty and family structure: The widening gap between evidence and public policy issues. In S. Danziger & D. Weinberg (Eds.), *Fighting poverty.* Cambridge, MA: Harvard University Press.

Winner, E. (1996). *Gifted children: Myths and realities.* New York: Basic Books.

Winnett, R. A., King, A. C., & Altman, D. G. (1989). *Health psychology and public health: An integrative approach.* New York: Pergamon.

Wise, R. A., & Rompre, P. P. (1989). Brain dopamine and reward. *Annual Review of Psychology, 40.*

Wober, M. (1966). Sensotypes. *Journal of Social Psychology, 70,* 181–189.

Wolpe, J. (1963). Behavior therapy in complex neurotic states. *British Journal of Psychiatry, 110,* 28–34.

Wong, H. Z. (1982). Asian and Pacific Americans. In L. Snowden (Ed.), *Reaching the underserved: Mental health needs of neglected populations.* Beverly Hills, CA: Sage.

Wooley, S. C., & Garner, D. M. (1991). Obesity treatment: The high cost of false hope. *Journal of the American Dietetic Association, 91,* 1248–1251.

Worell, J., & Robinson, D. (1993). Feminist counseling therapy for the 21st century. *Counseling Psychologist, 21,* 92–96.

Work Group of the American Psychological Association's Board of Affairs. (1995). *Working draft report on learner-centered psychological principles.* Washington, DC: American Psychological Association.

World Health Organization. (1975). *Schizophrenia: A multi-national study.* Geneva: World health Organization.

Wright, J. C. (1995, March). *Effects of viewing Sesame Street: The longitudinal study of media and time use.* Paper presented at the meeting of the Society for Research in Child Development, Indianapolis.

Y

Yalom, I. D. (Eds.). (1995). *The theory and practice of group psychotherapy* (4th ed.). New York: Basic Books.

Yamamoto, J., Okonogi, K., Iwasaki, T., & Yoshimura, S. (1969). Mourning in Japan. *American Journal of Psychiatry, 125,* 1660–1665.

Yankelovich, D., Skelly, F. & White, A. (1984). *Sex stereotypes and candidacy for high level political office.* New York: Yankelovich, Skelly, & White.

Yarmey, A. D. (1998). Person identification in showups and lineups. In C. P. Thompson & others (eds.), *Eyewitness memory.* Mahwah, NJ: Erlbaum.

Yarmey, A. D. (1973). I recognize your face but I can't remember your name: Further evidence on the tip of the tongue phenomenon. *Memory and Cognition, 1,* 287–290.

Yate, M. (1999). *Knock 'em dead.* Holbrook, MA: Bob Adams.

Young, S. K., & Shahinfar, A. (1995, March). *The contributions of maternal sensitivity and child temperament to attachment status at 14 months.* Paper presented at the meeting of the Society for Research in Child Development, Indianapolis.

Yuill, N., Oakhill, J., & Parkin, A. (1989). Working memory, comprehension ability and the resolution of text anomaly. *British Journal of Psychology, 80,* 351–361.

Z

Zajonc, R. B. (1984). On the primacy of affect. *American Psychologist, 39,* 117–123.

Zeigler, L. H., & Harmon, W. (1989). More bad news about the news. *Public Opinion, 12,* 50–52.

Zelnik, M., & Kantner, J. F. (1977). Sexual and contraceptive experiences of young unmarried women in the United States, 1976 and 1971. *Family Planning Perspectives, 9,* 55–71.

Ziegert, K. A. (1983). The Wedesih prohibition of corporal punishment: A preliminary report. *Journal of Marriage and the Family, 45,* 917–926.

Zill, N. (1996). National surveys as data sources for public policy research on poor children. In P. L. Chase-Lansdale & J. Brooks-Gunn (Eds.), *Escape from poverty.* New York: Cambridge University Press.

Zimbardo, P., Haney, C., Banks, W., & Jaffe, D. (1972). *The psychology of imprisonment: Privation, power, and pathology.* Unpublished manuscript, Stanford University, Stanford, CA.

Zimbardo, P. G., & Leippe, M. R. (1991). *The psychology of attitude change and social influence.* New York: McGraw-Hill.

Zorick, F. (1989). Overview of insomnia. In M. H. Dryger, T. Roth, & W. C. Dement (Eds.), *Principles and practice of sleep medicine.* San Diego: Harcourt Brace Jovanovich.

Zubin, J., & Spring, B. (1977). Vulnerability—A new view of schizophrenia. *Journal of Abnormal Psychology, 86,* 103–126.

Zuckerman, M. (1979). *Sensation seeking: Beyond the optimal level of arousal.* Hillsdale, NJ: Erlbaum.

Credits

9.6, From Alfred C. Kinsey, et al., *Sexual Behavior in the Human Male,* Copyright © 1948 The Kinsey Institute. Reprinted by permission of The Kinsey Institute for Research in Sex, Gender and Reproduction, Inc. Page 351, After Skinner, K. (1997). *How Goal Directed Are You?* Dallas, TX: Southern Methodist University. Fig. 9.7, Reprinted with permission from Psychology Today magazine, Copyright © 1980 (Sussex Publishers, Inc.).

Chapter 10

Fig. 10.1, From *Psychology: A Scientific Study of Human Behavior* by L.S. Wrightsman, C.K. Sigelman, and F.H. Sanford. Copyright © 1979, 1975, 1970, 1965, 1961 Brooks/Cole Publishing Company, Pacific Grove, CA 93950, a division of International Thomson Publishing, Inc. By permission of the publisher. Page 375, From G. Wilson, "Introversion/Extraversion" in *Dimensions of Personality,* edited by H. London and J.E. Exner. Copyright © 1978 John Wiley & Sons, Inc. Reprinted by permission of John Wiley & Sons, Inc. Page 386, From C.R. Snyder and H.L. Fromkin, *Uniqueness: The Human Pursuit of Difference.* Copyright © 1980 Plenum Publishing Corporation. Reprinted by permission. Fig. 10.2, M. Rosenberg, *Society and the Adolescent Self-Image,* Princeton University Press, 1965. Fig. 10.2, From Dr. Hans J. Eysenck, London, England. Reprinted by permission.

Chapter 11

Fig. 11.1, From Bootzin, et al., *Abnormal Psychology* Copyright © 1972 McGraw-Hill, Inc. Reproduced with permission of The McGraw-Hill Companies. Page 425, Reprinted from *Behavioral Research and Therapy,* vol. 3, J. Greer, "The Development of a Scale to Measure Fear," pages 45-53. Copyright © 1965, with permission from Elsevier Science. Fig. 11.2, From I. I. Gottesman and J. Shields, *The Schizophrenic Puzzle.* Copyright © 1992 Cambridge University Press. Reprinted with permission of Cambridge University Press.

Chapter 13

Page 482, "Vulnerability Scale" from the Stress Audit, developed by Lyle H. Miller and Alma Dell Smith. Copyright © 1987, Biobehaviorial Associates, Brookline, Mass. Reprinted with permission. Page 485, From Pate and others, *Journal of the American Medical Association,* 1995; 273:404. Fig. 13.1, From "Diet and Cancer" by Leonard A. Cohen. Copyright © 1987 by Scientific American, Inc. Used by permission of Slim Films. All Rights Reserved. Fig. 13.3, From H. Selye, *The Stress of Life,* Copyright © 1976 McGraw-Hill, Inc. Reproduced with permission of The McGraw-Hill Companies. Page 502, Reprinted from *Journal of Psychosomatic Research,* 11: 203-218. T.H. Holmes and R.H. Rahe, "The Social Readjustment Rating Scale," Copyright © 1967 with permission from Elsevier Science. Page 507, From *Contemporary Behavior Therapy,* by M.D. Spiegler and D.C. Guevremont. Copyright © 1993 Brooks/Cole Publishing Company, Pacific Grove, CA 93950, a division of International

Thomson Publishing Inc. By permission of the publisher. Page 509, After Bourne, E. J. (1995) *The Anxiety and Phobia Workbook.* New Harbinger Publications, Oakland, CA 94605 www.newharbinger.com.

Chapter 14

Page 521, From M. Snyder, *Journal of Personality and Social Psychology,* 30: 526-537. Copyright © 1974 by the American Psychological Association. Reprinted with permission of The McGraw-Hill Companies. Fig. 14.3, Data from R.J. Sternberg, *The Triangle of Love,* Basic Books, Inc., 1988. Page 540, Sternberg, R. (1988). "The Triangular Love Scale." From *The Triangle of Love.* New York: Basic Books. Fig. 14.4, Source: S.E. Asch, "Studies of Independence and Conformity: A Minority of One Against a Unanimous Majority" in *Psychological Monographs,* 90 (whole no. 416), American Psychological Association, 1956.

Chapter 15

Fig. 15.1, From *Psychology: A Scientific Study of Human Behavior* by L.S. Wrightsman, C.K. Sigelman, and F.H. Sanford. Copyright © 1979, 1975, 1970, 1965, 1961 Brooks/Cole Publishing Company, Pacific Grove, CA 93950, a division of Thomson Publishing Inc. By permission of the publisher. Page 579, From *Stress to Well-Being* by Craig W. Ellison and Raymond F. Paloutzian, Word Publishing, Nashville, Tennessee. All rights reserved.

Chapter 16

Page 592, Source: *Occupational Outlook Handbook,* 1996-1997, Table 1, p. 7., published by the U.S. Government.

Appendix

Fig. A.1, From *Psychology: Themes and Variations,* by Wayne Weiten. Copyright © 1998, 1995, 1992, 1989 Brooks/Cole Publishing Company, Pacific Grove, CA 93950, a division of International Thomson Publishing Inc. By permission of the publisher.

PHOTOGRAPHS

Chapter 1

Opener: © Mark Richards/ Photo Edit; p.4 (left): © Seana O'Sullivan/ Sygma; (right): AP/Wide World; F1.1: Archives of the History of American Psychology, University of Akron, Ohio; p. 12: © David Frazier; b,c, (both): © David Young Wolff/ Photo Edit: d: David Frazier; p.11: © Robert Fried/ Stock Boston; F1.2 (far left, down) a, b, (both): Bettmann Archive; c: Courtesy of Ruth Howard; d: UPI/Bettmann News Photos; e: Center for the Study of the Person; f: Courtesy of Sandra Bem; F1.2 (left, down) a,b, (both): Bettmann Archive; c: © Jane Reed; d: Bettmann Archive; e: Courtesy of Albert Bandura; f: Courtesy of Eleanor Maccoby; F1.2 (right, down) a,b, (both): Archives of the History of American Psychology, University of Akron, Ohio; c: Courtesy of Keith and Mamie Clark; d: Bettmann Archive; e: Courtesy of Roger Sperry; f: Courtesy of Judith Rodin; F1.2 (far right, down) a:

Archives of the History of American Psychology, University of Akron, Ohio; b,c,d (all): Bettmann Archive; e: Courtesy of John Berry, photo by Monica Hart; f: UPI/Bettmann News Photos; F1.3: © Rob Atkins/ The Image Bank, Chicago

Chapter 2

Opener: © Scott Camazine/ Photo Researchers; p.36: © Enrico Ferorelli; p.37 (large): Courtesy of United Nations; (top left): Courtesy of United Nations; (top middle): © Jim Shaffer; (top right): © Gio Barto/ The Image Bank, Dallas; (bottom left): Courtesy of United Nations; (bottom right): © Harvey Loyd/ The Stock Market; F2.1: Regents of the University of California; F2.2a: © Four by Five; F2.3a: © Elyse Lewin/ The Image Bank, Dallas; F2.3b: © Four By Five; F2.6a: © Lennart Nilsson; F2.9a: © Lennart Nilsson; F2.10a: © Hank Morgan/ Photo Researchers; F2.11a: John Wiley, California Institute of Technology, Estate of James Olds; F2.17: Courtesy of the National Library of Medicine; p.58: Courtesy of Jerre Levy; p.59: Courtesy of Steven and Cindi Binder; F2.19 (top left): Bettmann Archive; (top right): © Picture Group; (bottom left): Courtesy of NASA; (Bottom right): Bettmann Archive; p.64: © Rex USA, Ltd.; F2.A (both): © James Balog/ Tony Stone Images; F2.21 (left, middle): © Hank Morgan/ Photo Researchers; (right): © Dan McCoy/Rainbow

Chapter 3

Opener: © Eric Meola/ Image Bank; p.77: © Jim Pickerell/ Tony Stone Images; p.78: © Shooting Star; F3.2 (left): © Helmut Gritscher/ Peter Arnold; (right): © Douglas B. Nelson/ Peter Arnold; F3.5: © Morris Karol; F3.6a: © Burton McNeely/ The Image Bank, Dallas; F3.7: Courtesy of MacBeth, division of Koll Morgen; F3.8 (both): Fritz Goro/ Life Magazine, © 1944 Time, Inc.; F3.13 (left): © J. P. Laffont/ Sygma; (right): © Peabody Museum of Salem, photograph by Mark Sexton; F3.14a: © Lennart Nilsson; F3.14b: © Lou Jones/The Image Bank; F3.17: © 1953 M. C. Escher/Cordon Art; F3.18: © Asahi Shimbun; F3.20: © The National Gallery of Art; F3.22: © Scala/Art Resource; F3.24: © Lawrence Migdale; F3.28 (left): © Herman Eisenbeiss/ Photo Researchers; (right): © Emilio Marcado/ Jeroboam; F3.30: © Enrico Ferorelli; p.112: © R. Joedecke/ The Image Bank; F3.32: © Psychology Today; p.115: © Dana Fineman/ Sygma;

Chapter 4

Opener: © David Hiser/The Image Bank; p.124: © Dean/ The Image Works; b (inset): © Joel Gordon; F4.1a: © Steve Dunwell/The Image Bank; b: © David Young Wolff/ Photo Edit; c: © David Frazier Photo Library; d: © Randy Duchaine/ Stock Market; e: © Luis Castaneda/ The Image Bank; f: Caesar Paredes/ The Stock Market; g: © Barry Christenson/ Stock Boston; F4.4: From Dreamstage Scientific Catalog, © 1977 J. Alan Hobson & Hoffman La Roche; p.134 (left): © Scala/Art Resource; p.135: © James Wilson/ Woodfin Camp; p.138: Bettmann Archive; F4.6: © Mark Peterson/ SABA

Name Index

Doyle, J. A., 569
Doyne, E. J., 485
Draguns, J. G., 410, 428
Dreyer, P. H., 522
Dryfoos, J., 309, 310
Dudley, S. D., 128
Dunnett, S. B., 64
Dutton, D., 359
Dye, P. A., 400

E

Eagly, A. H., 527, 565, 566
Ebata, A. T., 506
Eberhardt, J. L., 554
Eccles, J. S., 348
Eckert, E., 36
Edelman, M. W., 277, 278, 559, 604
Edwards, S., 4
Ehrhardt, A. A., 561
Eich, E., 209
Eichorn, D. H., 320
Ekman, P., 360, 362
Elder, P. N., 428
Elkind, D., 301
Elliott, G. R., 299
Ellis, A., 143, 457, 507
Ellis, H. C., 10, 200, 219
Ellis, J. C., 202
Emerson, P. E., 295
Emmons, M., 508
Emmons, R. A., 333, 350
Endresen, I. M., 596
Eriksen, M., 495
Erikson, E. H., 291, 305, 307, 317, 382,
    451, 561
Escobar, J. I., 420
Evans, G. W., 597
Evascu, T., 123
Everly, G. S., 502
Exner, J. E., 401
Eysenck, H., 374, 465

F

Fabrega, H., 414
Fairburn, C. G., 490
Faulkner, L. R., 436
Febbraro, G. A. R., 418
Fei, J., 538
Feinleib, M., 505
Feist, G. J., 372
Feist, J., 372
Feldman, D. H., 261
Feldman, S. S., 299
Festinger, L., 519, 522
Field, T., 281
Fiez, J. A., 67
Finlay, B., 559
First, M. B., 414
Fischer, J., 168
Fisher, C., 24
Fiske, S. T., 397, 554
Fivush, R., 206
Flavell, J. H., 289
Fleming, C., 12
Foa, E. B., 417, 419
Foley, V., 461
Folkman, N., 502
Foster, G. D., 489

Fouad, N. A., 470
Fowler, C. A., 79
Fowler, J., 577
Fox, J. L., 64
Fox, R. E., 448
Frady, R. L., 562
Frances, A., 414
Frank, E., 473
Frank, J., 466
Fraser, S., 262
Freier, K., 281
French, S. E., 464
Freud, S., 122, 134, 332, 379, 426
Friedman, H. S., 499
Friedman, M., 499
Friedman, M. A., 487
Friedman, R., 511
Friesen, W. V., 360, 362
Frost, R. O., 419
Fuhrman, A., 460
Funk, C., 555
Furth, H. G., 288
Furumoto, L., 15

G

Gabrielli, W. F., 141
Gage, F. H., 66
Gagnon, J., 340, 343
Gaines, S. O., 551, 553, 554
Galanter, M., 533
Gallant, S. J., 495
Gallup, G. H., Jr., 526, 575, 578
Gara, M. A., 420
Garcia, C. T., 297
Garcia, E. E., 247
Garcia, S., 389
Garcia, W. I., 413
Gardner, B. T., 249
Gardner, H., 226, 253
Gardner, R. A., 249
Garfield, S. L., 455
Garner, D. M., 488
Garraghty, P. E., 64
Gatti, F. M., 373
Gazzaniga, M. S., 57
Geschwind, N., 60
Gibbons, F. X., 519
Gibbs, J. T., 302, 411, 504
Gibson, E., 110, 112
Gibson, J. J., 94
Gifford, R., 597
Gilligan, C., 302, 571
Girdano, D., 502
Girus, J. S., 110
Gjerde, P., 427
Gladue, B. A., 344
Glaser, R., 4, 483
Glass, D. C., 596
Glass, G. N., 465, 466
Glick, J., 263
Gochros, H. L., 168
Godden, D. R., 209
Goldberg, T. E., 432
Goldman, S. R., 606
Goldstein, E. B., 75, 93
Goldstein, M. J., 421, 432
Goleman, D., 364

Gonzales, M. F., 336
Goodnow, J., 11
Goodstein, L. D., 397, 415
Goodwin, D. W., 141
Goodwin, F. K., 424
Gopaul-McNicol, S., 6
Gordon, W., 186
Gottesman, I. I., 429, 432
Goldberg, T. E., 432
Gottlieb, B. H., 462
Gottlieb, G., 38
Gould, M., 413
Gramling, S. E., 510
Gray, C. R., 194
Graziano, W. J., 42
Green, B. L., 276
Green, P., 152
Greene, D., 349
Greenough, W. T., 38
Greenwald, A. G., 78, 79
Gregory, R. P., 111
Grevious, C., 461
Griffith, D. R., 281
Groark, C. J., 276
Grosz, J., 281
Gruen, G. E., 540
Gruenberg, F., 418
Grush, J. E., 525
Guilford, J. P., 237
Gummerman, K., 194
Gur, R. C., 61, 564
Gurin, J., 489
Gurman, A. S., 460
Gutierres, S. E., 519

H

Haan, N., 320
Hackett, G., 470
Hackett, R., 606
Haier, R. J., 66
Hakuta, K., 247
Hall, W. S., 569
Halonen, J., 235
Halpern, D. F., 261
Hamilton, T. E., 536
Haney, C., 24, 531
Haney, W., 589
Hare-Mustin, R., 571
Harkness, S., 297
Harlow, H., 292
Harmon, W., 525
Harris, R. F., 172
Harris, R. J., 207
Harris, T., 504
Harter, S., 307
Harvey, J. H., 521
Harvey, O. J., 556
Hasher, L., 200
Hatano, G., 11
Hatcher, R., 492
Hatfield, E., 538, 567
Havatny, N., 590
Hayflick, L., 314
Haynes, S. G., 505
Hecht, M. L., 553
Heider, F., 349, 521
Hellige, J. B., 59
Helmreich, R., 570
Helsing, K. J., 490

Helzer, J. F., 418
Hendrix, H., 541
Hensley, D. L., 207
Herman, C. P., 488
Hernandez, D. J., 317
Hernstein, R. J., 262
Heron, B., 80
Heron, W., 347
Herrmann, D. J., 206
Hershberger, S. L., 343
Herskovits, M. J., 112
Herzog, E., 562
Herzog, H. A., 25
Heston, L., 36
Hilgard, E. R., 138
Hines, M., 561, 562
Hines, T., 28, 116
Hing, L. S., 555
Hirschfeld, R. M. A., 424
Ho, M. K., 12
Hoagwood, K., 24
Hobfoll, S. E., 496
Hobson, J. A., 130
Hoff-Ginsburg, E., 297, 503
Hofferth, S. L., 491, 492
Hoffman, J. P., 575
Hofstede, G., 551
Hogan, R., 587
Hoge, M. A., 448
Holbrook, N., 314
Holcomb, H. H., 473
Hollenbeck, J. R., 587
Holleran, S. A., 490
Holmbeck, G. N., 304
Holmes, D., 511
Holmes, T. H., 319, 501
Honzik, M. P., 320
Hood, R. W., Jr., 124, 575, 578
Hood, W. R., 556
Hooper, J., 136
Hopkins, W. D., 249
Horm, J., 488
Horney, K., 382
Horowitz, M. J., 451
Hosli, L., 130
Howard, K. I., 299
Howard, R. W., 153
Hoyer, W. J., 315
Hsieh, C., 485
Hsu, J., 428
Huang, L. N., 411, 504
Huble, D., 85
Hui, C. H., 377
Hultsch, D. F., 319
Hunt, M., 340
Hunt, R. R., 10
Hunter, B. A., 569
Hurtado, S., 555
Hurvich, L. M., 89
Hyde, J. S., 563, 564
Hyde, R. T., 485
Hynd, G. W., 413

I

Ickes, W., 389
Ickovics, J. R., 505

Ivey, A. E., 470
Iwasaki, T., 428
Izard, C. E., 358

J

Jacklin, C. N., 564, 565
Jackson, L. A., 536
Jackson, T. A., 179
Jacobsen, L., 266
Jaffe, D., 24, 531
James, W., 122, 146, 319, 358
Jameson, D., 89
Janis, I., 532
Jaycox, L. H., 419
Jensen, A., 261
Jensen, M., 470
Jensen, P., 24
Johnson, C., 573
Johnson, J. A., 373
Johnson, M. A., 215
Johnson, T., 314
Johnson, V., 339
Johnston, L. D., 141, 145, 311
Jones, B., 130
Jones, J. M., 12, 15, 37, 552
Jones, M. C., 158
Jones, S., 578
Jones, S. E., 24
Joyce, P. R., 428
Judd, L. L., 424
Jung, C., 382

K

Kagan, J., 295
Kagitcibasi, C., 113, 551
Kahn, S., 499
Kahneman, R., 233
Kail, R., 250
Kaiser, H. A., 350
Kalichman, S. C., 468, 493
Kalick, S. M., 536
Kalleberg, A. L., 590
Kandel, E., 214
Kane, J. M., 429
Kanner, A. D., 502
Kanter, J. F., 491
Kaplan, J. S., 411
Karasu, T. B., 466
Karp, J. S., 61, 564
Kazdin, A., 26
Keating, C. F., 520
Keita, G. P., 424, 573
Keith-Spiegel, P., 24
Keller, K., 183
Kelley, H. H., 525
Kelly, S., 597
Kendall, P. C., 428
Kennedy, J. L., 432
Kenrick, D. T., 519
Kephart, W. M., 538
Kessler, M., 447
Kety, S. S., 428
Keyes, M., 36
Kiecolt, J. K., 483
Kiecolt-Glaser, J. K., 4
Kimble, G. A., 7

Kimmel, E. B., 15
Kimura, D., 562
King, A. C., 495
King, B. M., 342
Kinsey, A. C., 340, 343
Kirchner, G. L., 281
Kirk, G., 572
Kitayama, S., 376
Kleinman, A., 414, 418
Kobasa, N., 499
Kobasa, S. C., 499
Kohlberg, L., 301, 302, 562
Kohler, W., 181
Kohn, M. L., 297
Kohut, H., 451
Kolata, G., 340, 343
Kolb, B., 48, 64
Koocher, G. P., 24
Kornetsky, C., 53
Koss, M. P., 346, 419
Kramer, B. A., 475
Krantz, D. S., 597
Krasner, L., 453
Krippner, S., 113
Kübler-Ross, E., 322
Kupfer, D. J., 473
Kutchinsky, B., 212

L

LaBerge, S., 136
Labouvie-Vief, G., 315
LaCroix, A. Z., 505
Lafromoise, T., 470
LaGasse, L., 281
Laguerre, M. S., 96
Lamb, H. R., 463
Lamb, S. C., 536
Lambert, N. W., 605
Lamon, M., 606
Lane, H., 240
Lang, L. V., 594
Lange, C., 358
Langer, E., 102, 235
Lanyon, R. I., 397
LaPera, G., 344
LaPiere, R., 522
Lashley, K., 214
Latane, B., 544
Lau, S., 540
Laumann, E., 340, 343
Lazar, J. B., 424
Lazarus, R. S., 360, 498, 502
Leber, W. R., 428
Lebow, J. L., 460
Lee, I., 485
Lee, T. F., 41
Leiberman, M., 302
Leippe, M. R., 533
Leiter, M. P., 500
Lenfant, C., 495
Lenneberg, E. H., 241
Lepper, M., 349
Lerner, H., 571
Lesgold, A., 202
Leshner, A. I., 429
Lester, B. M., 281

Levant, R. F., 572
Leventhal, H., 359, 527
Levine, M., 462, 465
LeVine, R. A., 11, 551
Levine, R. V., 597
Levinson, D., 317
Levinson, K. L., 358
Levy, D., 236
Levy, S., 483
Lewinsohn, P., 17, 173
Lewis, J. F., 265
Lickliter, R., 38
Lieberman, M. A., 462
Liebert, R. M., 152
Lincoln, J. R., 590
Lindenberger, U., 315, 320
Lituchy, T., 593
Liu, J., 593
Livesley, W. J., 433
Locke, J. L., 241
Lockhart, R. S., 194, 200
Loehlin, J. C., 261
Loftus, E. F., 206, 212, 217
Long, C. N., 337
Long, P., 137
Lonner, W. J., 5, 250, 399, 551
Lopez, M., 184
Lorenz, K., 293, 331
Lourenco, O., 289
Lowell, E. I., 402
Lucas, F. L., 300
Lucas, J., 314
Ludolph, P., 422
Lunds, I., 428
Luria, A., 191, 562
Lussier, R., 589
Lusterman, D., 572
Lykken, D. T., 361, 362
Lynch, G., 214

M

Maas, A., 206
Maccoby, E. E., 562, 564, 565
MacGregor, S., 281
Machado, A., 289
Maddi, S. R., 499, 501
Mader, S., 36, 38
Mahler, M., 451
Mahoney, M. J., 457
Maier, N. R. F., 232
Malarkey, W. B., 4
Mammersmith, S. K., 343, 503
Mandler, G., 203, 358
Manese, J. E., 470
Mao, H. Y., 4
Maracek, J., 571
Marcia, J. E., 305, 306
Marin, G., 465
Marks, M. A., 347
Markus, H. R., 11, 376
Marsh, P., 363
Martin, D. C., 281
Martin, E. E., 340, 343
Martin, G. L., 167, 171
Martin, J., 344
Martinez, T. S., 597

Maslach, C., 500
Maslow, A. H., 9, 333, 393, 394
Masters, W., 339, 346
Matas, L., 295
Matlin, M. W., 100, 569
Matthews, A., 4
Maultsby, M. C., 453
Mays, V. M., 494
McAleer, I. L., 525
McCain, G., 597
McCall, R. B., 276
McCarley, R. W., 128, 136
McClelland, D. C., 348, 402
McCombs, B. L., 605
McConaghy, N., 344
McCoy, S. B., 519
McDougall, W., 331
McDougall-Wilson, I. B., 485
McFarland, B. H., 436
McFarlane, T. A., 488, 505
McGrath, E., 424, 573
McGue, M., 36, 40
McHugh, J. M., 588
McHugh, S. M., 588
McKinlay, J. B., 312
McKinlay, S. M., 312
McLoyd, V. C., 12, 297, 307
McNally, R. J., 417
McNeil, E. B., 429
McRae, R. R., 319, 374, 376, 400, 587
McShane, D. A., 15
Medoff, D. R., 473
Meehl, P. E., 412
Meichenbaum, D., 455, 456
Meier, D. E., 312
Meilijson, I., 66
Meltzoff, J., 18
Melzack, R., 95
Mercer, J. R., 265
Merrick, S. K., 295
Mervis, J., 457
Messinger, J. C., 339
Metalsky, G. I., 428
Meyer, E. C., 297
Meyer, J., 408
Meyer, R. G., 419, 433, 435
Meyers, P., 511
Mezzich, J. E., 414
Michael, R., 340, 343
Miles, M. B., 462
Milgram, S., 24, 527, 528
Miller, A. S., 575
Miller, G. A., 193, 501
Miller, J. B., 571
Miller, J. G., 303
Miller, N., 25, 512
Miller, P. A., 11
Miller, R. L., 465, 466
Miller-Jones, D., 264
Millis, R. M., 490
Milner, P., 52
Minuchin, P., 460
Mischel, W., 389
Mishkin, M., 215
Mistry, J., 216
Mitchell, J. E., 489

Mondin, G. W., 465
Money, J., 339
Monk, T. H., 125
Monnier, M., 130
Montague, A., 94
Montello, D. R., 519
Moody, M., 465
Moore, T. E., 79
Moos, R. H., 506, 508
Morris, D., 363
Morris, P. A., 10
Morris, R., 562
Morrison, A. M., 593
Morrison, J., 314
Morrissey, J. P., 437
Morten, G., 37, 470
Moses, J., 4
Mosley, P. D., 61
Mozley, L. H., 61, 564
Mozley, P. D., 564
Mueller, R., 593
Muñoz, R., 17
Murphy, H. B., 433
Murphy, J., 249
Murphy, K. R., 255
Murphy, S. T., 360
Murray, B., 602
Murray, C. B., 262, 470
Murray, H., 348
Mussell, M. P., 489
Mussen, P. H., 320
Myers, D. G., 578
Myles, W. S., 130

N

Nagashi, C. T., 36
Nagy, T. F., 24
Naidu, R. K., 362
Nash, J. M., 59
Nathan, P. E., 414
National Academy of Sciences Research Council, 487
National Advisory Council on Economic Opportunity, 503
National Association for the Education of Young Children (NAEYC), 247
National Center for Health Statistics, 539
Neckerman, K. M., 503
Neff, B., 345
Neimeyer, R. A., 485
Neisser, U., 261
Nelson, E. S., 347
Nemeth, C. J., 600
Neugarten, B., 311
Nevis, E. C., 333
Newton, T., 4
Nicastro, A., 344
Nichols, I. A., 241
Nichols, W. G., 588
Nicholson, A. N., 131
Nietzel, M. T., 601
Nisbett, R. E., 349
Nivison, M. E., 596
Noble, E. G., 130
Nolen-Hoeksema, S., 424, 573
Notarius, C. I., 317

Novak, C. A., 312
Novick, E. R., 310
Novlin, D., 336
Nutt, R. L., 572

O

Oakhill, J., 195
Obler, L. K., 243
Odbert, H. S., 374
O'Donahue, W., 453
Offer, D., 299
Oh, T. K., 590
Okazawa-Rey, M., 572
Okonogi, K., 428
Olds, J., 52
Olson, A., 573
O'Malley, P. M., 141, 145, 311
Omoto, A. M., 538
Orford, J., 464
Ortmann, J., 428
Orvashcel, H., 418
Osborn, K. M., 485
Osborne, Y. V. H., 419
O'Shaugnessy, M., 363
Ossip-Klein, D. J., 485
Ostrov, E., 299
Otto, A. L., 600

P

Paffenbarger, R. S., 485
Paivio, A., 203
Palmer, J. O., 421
Paloutzian, R. F., 124, 577
Paludi, M. A., 11, 42, 346, 410, 563, 569, 571
Pargman, D., 602
Parham, T., 470
Parkin, A., 195
Parlee, M. B., 537
Pasco, P. A., 131
Paterson, D. H., 130
Patterson, C. J., 344
Paul, G. L., 467
Paulus, P. B., 597
Pavelchak, M. A., 526
Payne, D. G., 206, 594
Payne, T. J., 490
Pear, J., 167, 171
Pedersen, P., 470
Pellegrino, J. W., 250
Penfield, W., 54
Penrod, S. D., 600
Peplau, L. A., 498, 542, 554
Perkins, D. N., 237
Perkins, D. V., 462, 465
Perlman, D., 542
Perloff, R., 261
Perls, F., 452
Perry, M. C., 128
Perry, T. B., 304
Persinger, M. A., 113
Pert, A. B., 48
Peskin, H., 300
Petersen, A. C., 299
Petersen, S. E., 67
Peterson, C., 372, 384, 506
Peterson, S. R., 393
Pettigrew, F. P., 130
Phillips, E. D., 237

Phillips, J. M., 587
Philpot, C. L., 572
Piaget, J., 285
Pietromonaco, P. R., 292
Piirto, J., 261
Pincus, H. A., 414
Pinker, S., 42
Plant, E. A., 563
Plat, S., 474
Pleck, J., 571, 572
Plemons, J. K., 319
Polivy, J., 488
Pollock, V. E., 141
Polonko, K. A., 5
Pomeroy, W. B., 340
Pomeroy, W. M., 343
Ponterotto, J. E., 470
Poortinga, Y. H., 111, 229
Pouissant, A. F., 177
Pratkanis, A. R., 78
Premack, D., 249
Prentice, D. A., 519
Presidential Task Force on Psychology and
    Education, 605
Price-Williams, D., 186
Priest, D. J., 536
Puccetti, M. C., 499
Pucik, V., 590
Pylyshyn, Z. W., 203

Q

Quina, K., 15

R

Rabinowitz, V. C., 495
Rahe, R. H., 319, 501
Raichle, M. E., 67
Raife, E. A., 67
Ramey, C. T., 261
Ramirez, M., 186
Ramirez, O., 412
Randi, J., 114
Rankin, N. O., 24
Rapson, R. L., 538
Rayner, R., 158
Raynor, I. O., 348
Read, J. D., 206
Rebec, G. V., 473
Rebelsky, F. G., 241
Reed, E. S., 551, 553, 554
Reiger, D. A., 410, 418, 424
Reinisch, J., 491
Rescorla, R. A., 159, 160
Resnick, G., 310
Resnick, S. M., 36, 61, 564
Restak, R. M., 95, 122, 226
Rettek, S. I., 362
Revenson, T. A., 505
Revitch, E., 20
Reynolds, S., 414
Rhodes, N., 527
Rhodes, S. R., 589
Rice, F. P., 317
Richter, C. P., 427
Ritter, B., 454
Robbins, P. C., 437
Robbins, S. P., 589
Robins, L. N., 410, 418

Robinson, B. A., 336
Robinson, D., 467
Rodgers, C. D., 130
Rodin, J., 336, 338, 488, 505
Rodriguez, I. A., 200
Rodriquez, M. S., 508
Rogers, C. A., 392, 393
Rogers, C. R., 9, 452
Rogers, S., 78
Rogoff, B., 216
Rohner, E. C., 297
Rohner, R. P., 297
Rompre, P. P., 53
Roodin, P. A., 315
Root, M. P., 37
Rosch, E. H., 229, 245
Rose, R. J., 39
Roseman, I. J., 362
Rosen, K. H., 346
Rosenhan, D. L., 466
Rosenkranz, P., 567
Rosenman, R., 499
Rosenthal, D., 428
Rosenthal, R., 24, 266
Rosnow, R. L., 24
Ross, J. M., 579
Ross, L., 521
Rowe, J. W., 314
Rubin, L., 292
Rumbaugh, D. M., 249
Rumpel, E., 551
Russo, N. F., 424, 428, 435, 573
Ruzecki, V., 241
Rybash, J. M., 315
Rymer, R., 243

S

Saarni, C., 363
Sackheim, H. A., 474
Sacks, O., 73
Sadik, N., 573
Sagan, C., 41
Sagiv, L., 551
Saklofske, D. H., 255
Salthouse, T. J., 315
Sanderson, W. C., 465
Sandler, D. P., 490
Sandman, B. M., 281
Santrock, J. W., 165, 275, 304, 385, 605
Sargent, C., 115
Saron, C. D., 360
Sarrel, P., 346
Sartorius, N., 433
Sasaki, T., 432
Satir, V., 460
Savage-Rumbaugh, E. S., 249
Saxe, L., 361
Scanlan, T., 603
Scarborough, E., 15
Scardamalian, M., 606
Scarr, S., 262, 264
Schachter, S., 337, 358
Schaefer, C., 502
Schaffer, H. R., 295
Schaie, K. W., 315
Schatzberg, A. F., 423
Scheer, S. D., 310
Schein, V. E., 593

Schiefele, U., 348
Schiffman, J., 430
Schlesinger, L. B., 20
Schmitt, D. P., 567
Schneider, E. L., 314
Schneider, L. S., 141
Schneider, W., 208
Schoen, L. M., 207
Schoen, S., 281
Schoenrade, P., 576
Schofield, J. W., 526
Schulsinger, F., 428
Schultz, D., 5, 358
Schultz, S. E., 5
Schwartz, J., 214
Schwartz, R., 495
Schwartz, S. H., 377, 551
Schwarz, J. P., 67
Sciara, A., 401
Scioli, A., 360
Scott, T. H., 347
Seager, J., 573
Sears, D. O., 498, 554, 555
Sechzur, J., 495
Secules Petrosino, A. J., 606
Segall, M. H., 111, 112, 229
Segerberg, O., 312
Seidemann, E., 66
Seidman, E., 464
Seiffge-Krenke, I., 497
Seligman, M. E. P., 183, 427, 428, 466, 507
Selye, H., 497
Senulis, J. A., 360
Sevick, R. A., 249
Shahinfar, A., 295
Shanks, D. R., 204
Sheldon, W. H., 373
Shepard, R. N., 206
Sher, K. J., 142
Sherer, K., 362
Sherif, C. W., 556
Sherif, M., 556
Shields, J., 432
Shields, S. A., 363, 364
Shiffrin, R. M., 197, 208
Shore, D. L., 490
Shotland, R. L., 544
Shrout, P. E., 397, 502
Shweder, R. A., 11
Siegler, R. S., 289
Siffre, M., 125
Silverman, N. N., 385
Simon, H. A., 10
Simons, J. M., 559
Simpson, J. A., 520
Singelis, T. M., 550
Singer, J. E., 358, 596
Singer, R. N., 602
Sirevaag, A. M., 38
Sizemore, C. C., 421
Skelly, F., 526
Skinner, B. F., 9, 122, 161, 162, 170, 173
Skinner, K., 350
Slade, R., 79
Slavin, R., 557
Slobin, D., 241
Slovenko, R., 437
Smith, M. L., 465, 466

Smith, P. O., 490
Snarey, R., 303
Snowden, D. A., 65
Snowden, L. R., 413
Snyder, L. D., 206
Snyder, M., 389, 520, 538
Snyder, S. H., 48
Sobell, L. C., 143
Sobell, M., 143
Solomon, R., 164
Solomon, Z., 419
Solvason, H. B., 423
Sorenson, K., 597
Spalding, K., 206
Spanos, N. P., 139
Spearman, C., 251
Spence, J. T., 570
Sperry, R., 57
Sprafkin, J., 152
Sprei, J. E., 346
Spring, B., 411
Squire, L. R., 10, 195, 214
Sroufe, L. A., 295
Stanhope, L., 385
Stanley, B., 428
Stanley, M., 428
Stanovich, D., 26
Stanton, A. L., 495
Staudinger, U. M., 315, 320
Steadman, H. J., 437
Steers, R. M., 590
Stein, B., 230
Steinberg, L., 307
Steketee, G., 417, 419
Stengel, R., 225, 274
Steptoe, A., 4
Sternberg, R. J., 235, 251, 261, 539, 540, 541
Stevenson, H. W., 552
Steward, P., 290
Stich, F., 465
Stith, S. M., 346
Stokols, D., 597
Strauss, M. S., 276
Streissguth, A. P., 281
Strickland, A. L., 323
Strickland, B., 424, 495, 573
Strupp, H. H., 451, 467
Stunkard, A. J., 338, 489, 506
Sturges, L. V., 490
Sturgill, W., 209
Sue, D. W., 37, 470
Sue, S., 471, 555
Suefield, P., 81, 348
Suinn, R. M., 15, 411, 422, 466
Sullivan, H. S., 382
Sullivan, K. T., 462
Super, C. M., 295, 297
Sutton, R. G., 447
Swim, J. K., 569
Syvalahti, E. K., 131
Szasz, T., 412, 468

T

Tager-Flusberg, H., 242
Tajfel, H., 554
Takanishi, R., 309
Takeuchi, D., 411
Tamminga, C. A., 473

Tannen, D., 565, 572
Tardif, T., 297, 503
Tassinary, L., 79
Tavris, C., 60, 363
Taylor, A. W., 130
Taylor, S. E., 498, 507, 508, 510, 554
Teachman, J. D., 5
Tepperman, T., 337
Teresi, D., 136
Terman, L., 260
Thaker, G. K., 473
Thapa, K., 362
Tharp, R. R., 181
Thibaut, J., 525
Thigpen, C. H., 421
Thomas, C. B., 508
Thomas, R. L., 200
Thompson, C. P., 206
Thompson, J. K., 487
Thompson, R. A., 295, 437, 470
Thurstone, L. L., 251
Toglia, M. P., 206
Tolman, E. C., 160, 180
Tomarken, A. J., 359
Tomlinson-Keasey, C., 261
Tordoff, M. G., 336
Toro, P. A., 465
Torrey, E. F., 433
Torrey, E. T., 444
Tower, S. L., 587
Trapnell, P. D., 587
Travis, C., 563, 565
Treboux, E., 295
Trevino, J. G., 555
Triandis, H. C., 377, 551
Trimble, J. E., 12
Trivers, R., 543
Tronick, E., 110
Trost, M. R., 519
Tseng, W., 428
Tulving, E., 196, 197
Tulving, F., 201
Turk, D., 456
Turnbull, C., 112
Tversky, A., 233

U

Unger, R., 566
Urbina, S., 261
U.S. Commission on Civil Rights, 246

V

Vaadia, E., 66
Vadum, A. C., 24
Vaillant, G. E., 319
Valins, S., 598
Van den Bergh, P. L., 37
Vazquez-Nutall, E., 470
Veitch, R., 598
Velton, E., 143
Ventis, W. L., 576, 578
Verbrugge, L. M., 505
Vermilyea, B. B., 415
Vermilyea, J. A., 415
Vitols, M., 428
Vogel, S., 567
Von Békésy, G., 93
von Glinow, M. A., 593

Voyer, D., 564
Voyer, S., 564
Vygotsky, L., 290

W

Wachs, H., 288
Wadden, T. A., 489
Wade, C., 363, 563, 565
Wagman, M., 227
Wagner, A. R., 160
Wahlsten, D., 38
Wald, G., 88
Walk, R., 110, 112
Walker, E., 430
Wall, P., 95
Wallace, C. S., 38
Wallance, R. K., 511
Wallbott, H., 362
Wallerstein, R. S., 451, 467
Wampold, B. E., 465
Ward, C., 123, 125
Warden, C. J., 179
Washburn, A. L., 336
Washburn, D. A., 249
Wasserman, G. S., 87
Waters, E., 295
Watson, D. L., 181, 414, 428
Watson, J. B., 8, 122, 158, 185
Webb, W. B., 128, 130
Wechsler, D., 315
Weiler, I. J., 38
Weimer, W. B., 226
Wein, D., 241
Weinberg, M. S., 343, 503
Weinberger, D. R., 432
Weiner, I. B., 401
Weinstein, S., 94
Weisenberg, M., 96

Weisman, A. D., 483
Weissman, M. M., 418, 426
Wender, P. H., 428
Westkott, M., 384
Whishaw, I. W., 48
White, A., 526
White, B. J., 556
White, R. W., 347
Whiting, B. B., 565
Whitley, B. E., 24
Whitman, F. L., 344
Whorf, B., 244
Wiesel, T., 85
Wigfield, A., 348
Wiggins, J. S., 373, 587
Williams, J. E., 567, 568
Williams, K. R., 346
Williams, M. E., 177
Williams, R. B., 499
Williams, S. L., 249
Wilson, W. J., 503
Winett, R. A., 495
Winner, E., 260
Winzenz, D., 202
Wirga, M., 453
Wise, R. A., 53
Wison, T. D., 600
Withers, G. S., 38
Wittlinger, R. P., 195
Wober, M., 111, 251
Wolf, N. M., 172
Wolford, G., 79
Wolgamuth, B. R., 128
Wolpe, J., 454
Wolverton, D., 435
Wong, A. L., 485
Wong, H. Z., 12
Wood, W., 527

Wooley, S. C., 488
Worell, J., 467
World Health Organization, 410
Wright, J. C., 152
Wrightsman, L. S., 346
Wunsch-Hitzig, R., 413

Y

Yalom, I. D., 460, 462
Yamamoto, J., 428
Yang, A., 559
Yankelovich, D., 526
Yarmey, A. D., 206, 208
Yate, M., 588
Yoshimura, S., 428
Young, M. C., 417
Young, S. K., 295
Youngren, M., 17
Yuill, N., 195

Z

Zacks, R. T., 200
Zajonc, R. B., 360
Zanna, M. P., 555
Zeidner, M., 255
Zeigler, L. H., 525
Zeiss, A., 17
Zelnick, M., 491
Ziegert, K. A., 185
Zill, N., 277
Zimbardo, P. G., 24, 531, 533
Zimmerman, R., 292
Zola, M., 499
Zorick, F., 131
Zubin, J., 411
Zuckerman, M., 79

Subject Index

Animal magnetism, 137, 138
Animals
 attachment theories related to, 292–295
 dreaming of, 136
 fixed action patterns, 153
 instinctive drift, 183–184
 language learning by, 247–249
 in research, 25
Anorexia nervosa, 489
Anterograde amnesia, 213
Antidepressants, 472–473
 MAO inhibitors, 472, 473
 selective serotonin reuptake inhibitors
  (SSRIs), 472–473
 tricyclic antidepressants, 472
Antipsychotic drugs, 473
 side effects, 473
Antisocial personality disorder, 435
Anxiety, self-assessment, 416
Anxiety disorders, 415–420
 antianxiety drugs, 472
 definition of, 415
 generalized anxiety disorder, 415
 obsessive-compulsive disorders,
  418–419
 panic disorder, 417
 phobic disorders, 417–418
 post-traumatic stress disorder, 419–420
Aphasia, 60
Apparent movement, 106
Applied psychology
 educational psychology, 604–608
 environmental psychology, 596–598
 forensic psychology, 599–601
 human factors (engineering) psychology,
  594–595
 industrial psychology, 587–588
 organizational psychology, 589–594
 sport psychology, 602–604
 study of, 586
Approach/approach conflict, 501
Approach/avoidance conflict, 501
Archetypes, 384
Aristotle, 6
Arousal, and performance, 354
Artificial intelligence, 227
Asian American Psychological Association,
 15
Asian Americans, 12
 intelligence test scores, 261
Assertive behavior
 elements of, 508–509
 increasing assertive behavior, 510
Assimilation
 of ethnic minorities, 503, 555
 in Piaget's theory, 285
Association of Black Psychologists, 15
Association cortex, 55
Astrology, 27–28
Asylums, 445
Attachment, 291–295
 critical period, 294
 definition of, 292
 Freud's theory, 292
 Harlow's experiment, 292–293
 imprinting, 293–294
 secure attachment, 295
 sociocultural view, 295

Attention
 and learning, 175
 and memory, 200, 220
 nature of, 200
 selective attention, 200
Attitudes, 521–523
 behavior's influence on, 522
 cognitive dissonance, 522–523
 definition of, 521
 prediction of behavior from, 522
 self-perception theory, 523
Attraction, 536–537
 and consensual validation, 536
 matching hypothesis, 536
 and physical attractiveness, 536
Attribution theory, 520–521
 achievement, 349
 basis of, 520
 fundamental attribution error, 521
Auditory nerve, 93–94
Auditory system, 90–94
 ear, structures of, 91–93
 frequency theory, 93
 neural-auditory processing, 93–94
 place theory, 93
 and sound, 90–91
 volley theory, 93
Authoritarian parenting, 295–296
Authoritative parenting, 296
Automatic processes, consciousness,
 123, 126
Automatic processing, memory, 200
Autonomic nervous system, functions of, 43
Availability heuristic, and faulty problem
 solving, 233
Aversive conditioning, 454–455, 491
Avoidance/avoidance conflict, 501
Avoidance strategies, 506
Axon, 45

B

Babbling, 241
Bacon, Francis, 7
Balance, vestibular sense, 97–98
Barbiturates, 144
Barnum effect, 397
Basal ganglia, 50
Basal metabolism rate (BMR), 488
Baseline, 22
Basilar membrane, 93
Beck Depression Inventory, 20
Beck's cognitive therapy, 457–458
Behavior
 definition of, 5
 predicting from attitudes, 522
Behavioral assessment, of personality, 402
Behavioral medicine, study of, 483
Behavioral methods, 453–455
 aversive conditioning, 454–455
 basis of, 453
 behavior modification, 172–173
 cigarette smoking cessation, 490–491
 cognitive behavior therapy, 455–456
 pain management, 98
 response cost, 165
 systematic desensitization, 454
 time out, 165
 token economy, 455

Behavioral theories, 387–389
 classical conditioning, 153–161
 evaluation of, 388–389
 history of, 8–9
 motivation, 332
 operant conditioning, 161–174
 personality development, 387–388
 phobia, 418
Behavior claims, evaluating validity of, 26–27
Behavior modification, 172–173
 definition of, 172
 examples of use, 172–173
Belief perserverence effect, and faulty critical
 thinking, 236
Bell curve concept, intelligence, 261
Bem Sex-Role Inventory, 568–570
Beta waves, sleep, 127
Bilingualism, 246–247
 bilingual education, 246–247
 interacting with linguistically diverse
  children, 246–247
Binge drinking, 141
Binocular cues, depth perception, 105
Biofeedback, for stress management, 512
Biological factors
 aggression, 562
 aging, 314
 development, 275
 emotion, 360–361
 gender differences, 564
 gender identity, 560–562
 hunger, 335–337
 language development, 243–244
 learning, 183–184
 memory, 214–216
 mental disorders, 409
 mood disorders, 428
 phobias, 418
 puberty, 300, 338
 stress, 496–497
 See also Evolutionary perspective
Bipolar disorder, 424–426
 lithium, 473
Birth order, 385
Bisexuality, 343
Blindness, recovery from, 73–74, 111, 113
Blind spot, 84, 85
Blood sugar levels, and hunger, 336
Body weight
 and basal metabolism rate (BMR), 488
 set point, 337, 488
Borderline personality disorder, 434–435
Brain, 49–67
 auditory processing, 93–94
 brain implants, 64–65
 cerebral cortex, 54–55
 forebrain, 50–55
 gender differences, 59–61
 hemispheric specialization, 57–59
 hindbrain, 50
 and hunger, 336–337
 hypothalamus, 51–54
 limbic system, 54
 localization/integration of function,
  61–62
 and memory, 214–216
 midbrain, 50
 plasticity of, 64

Dreams, 133–137
  activation-synthesis view, 136
  of animals, 136
  colors in, 136
  as entertainment, 135
  Freud's theory, 134–135, 449
  lucid dreams, 136
  problem solving in, 135
  remembering dreams, 136
  and REM sleep, 128–129
Drive, definition of, 332
Drive reduction theory, of motivation, 332
Drug therapy, 472–474
  antianxiety drugs, 472
  antidepressant drugs, 472–473
  antipsychotic drugs, 473
  lithium, 473
Drug use
  and addiction, 140
  and altered states of consciousness, 123
  drug abuse self-assessment, 141
  psychological dependence, 140
  and tolerance, 140
  and withdrawal, 140
Dubroff, Jessica, 273–274
Dyslexia, 258

E

Ear, structures of, 91–93
Eating disorders, 487–490
  anorexia nervosa, 489
  bulimia, 489–490
  obesity, 487–488
Echoic memory, 193
Eclectic psychotherapy, 446
Ecological theory, sleep, 130
Ectomorph, 373
Educational psychology, 604–608
  ethnic minorities, 604–605
  exceptional learners, 605
  learner-centered psychological principles, 605–607
  study of, 604
Efferent nerves, 43
Effortful processing, memory, 200
Ego, 379–380
Egocentrism
  adolescence, 300–301
  children, 287
Egoism, meaning of, 544
Eidetic (photographic) memory, 194
Elaboration, memory, 201–202
Electroconvulsive therapy (ECT), 474–475
Electroencephalograph (EEG), 66
  sleep patterns, 125–128
Embryonic period, 279
Emotion, 352–364
  anger, 355–357
  biological factors, 360–361
  Cannon-Bard theory, 358
  cognitive theories, 358–360
  definition of, 353
  and display rules, 362–363
  flow, 355, 356
  gender differences, 363–364
  happiness, 353, 354–355
  James-Lange theory, 358
  negative affectivity, 353, 355–357

and polygraph, 361–362
positive affectivity, 353, 354
sociocultural view, 362–363
U-curve hypothesis, 354
universality of facial expression of, 362
wheel models of, 353, 354
Emotional appeals, and persuasion, 526–527
Emotional intelligence, 364
  definition of, 364
  self-assessment for, 366
Emotion-focused coping, 506
Emotions
  gender differences, 565
  and hypothalamus, 51–54
  and limbic system, 54
Empirically keyed tests, 398
Employee selection, tests/interviews for, 587
Empowerment, 465
Encoding, in memory, 199–204
Encounter groups, 461
Endocrine system
  and depression, 428
  function of, 53
  and hypothalamus, 53
Endomorph, 373
Endorphins
  and drug use, 144
  functions of, 48
Environment, meaning of, 36
Environmental factors
  language development, 243–244
  schizophrenic disorders, 432
  See also Nature-nurture issue
Environmental psychology, 596–598
  density/crowding, 597–598
  noise, 596–597
  pollution of environment, 598–599
  topics in, 596
Epinephrine, 496
Episodic memory, 196
Erikson's theory, 291–293
  gender identity, 561
  generativity *versus* stagnation, 293, 317
  identity development, 305, 307
  identity *versus* identity confusion, 293
  identity *versus* identity confusion, 305
  identity statuses, 305–306
  industry *versus* inferiority, 291, 292
  initiative *versus* guilt, 291, 292
  integrity *versus* despair, 293, 321
  intimacy *versus* isolation, 293, 317
  trust *versus* mistrust, 291, 292
Erogenous zones, 380
Estradiol, 300
Estrogen, 338, 561
  decline in menopause, 312
  estrogen replacement therapy, and menopause, 312
Ethics
  in psychological research, 24–25
  and psychotherapy, 448
Ethnic identity, definition of, 11
Ethnicity, definition of, 11, 550
Ethnicity studies
  focus of, 550
  See also Sociocultural view
Ethnic minorities
  and achievement, 351

in American culture, 12
assimilation of, 503, 555
discrimination against, 553
in educational setting, 604–605
and health, 495
in history of psychology, 15
and identity development, 307
improvement programs for, 559
improving interethnic relations, 556–560
and intelligence, 261–264
and mental disorders, 411
and pluralism, 556
and psychotherapy, 470–472
and racism, 554–555
role models for, 177
and stress, 503
in workplace, 593–594
See also specific ethnic groups
Ethnocentrism, meaning of, 554
Ethological theory, motivation, 331
Ethology, study of, 331
Eustress, 497
Evolutionary perspective
  altruism, 542–543
  gender differences, 566
  history of, 10
  language development, 243–244
  motivation, 331
  natural selection, 41
  sleep, 130
Evolutionary psychology, 41–42
  study of, 41
  topics in, 42
Exceptional learners, 605
Exercise, 484–485
  aerobic exercise, 484
  benefits of, 485
  finding time for, 486
  types of, 485
Exhibitionism, 345
Exorcism, 444
Expectations, and learning, 180
Experimental group, 22
Experimental method, 21–24
  double-blind study, 24
  experimenter bias, 23–24
  groups in, 22
  placebo effect, 23
  random assignment in, 22
  replication, 24
  variables in, 22
Experimental psychology, study of, 13
Experimenter bias, 23–24
Expert systems, 227
Expert witnesses, psychologists as, 601
Extinction
  classical conditioning, 157
  operant conditioning, 171
Extrasensory perception, 113–116
  clairvoyance, 113
  experiments related to, 115–116
  versus magic tricks, 114–115
  precognition, 113
  psychokinesis, 113–114
  telepathy, 113, 115–116
Extraversion
  definition of, 374
  self-assessment for, 375

Extrinsic motivation, 330–331
    and achievement, 349
Extrinsic religious orientation, 577
Eye, parts of, 82–84
Eyewitness testimony, 206

F

Facial expression, and emotions, 362
Family therapy, 460
    and African Americans, 461
    family systems therapy, 460–461
Fechner, Gustav, 75, 76
Feminist psychology
    on Freud's theory, 382–384, 470
    on gender differences theory, 566
    on psychology of women, 571–572
Feminization of poverty, 505
Fetal alcohol syndrome, 280–281
Fetal period, 279
Fetishism, 345
Figure-ground relationship, 103–105
Five-factor model, of personality, 374–376
Five-factor personality instruments, 400
Fixation, 380
Fixed action patterns, 153
Fixed-interval schedule, 170
Fixed-ratio schedule, 170
Flow, 355, 356
    definition of, 355
Foot-in-the-door strategy, 527
Forebrain, 50–55
Forensic psychology, 599–601
    activities of, 599
    defendant/jury characteristics, 600
    expert witnesses, 601
    jury decision-making, 600–601
    study of, 15, 599
Forgetting, 103
    amnesia, 213
    cue-dependent forgetting, 210
    decay theory, 212
    and interference, 210–212
Formal operational thought, 288–289, 300
    hypothetical-deductive reasoning,
        289
Fostering a Community of Learners, 606
Fovea, 83–84
Fox, Terry, 329–330
Frames of intelligence model, 252
Frequency
    EEG wave, 125–126
    sound, 90
Frequency distribution, 615
Frequency polygon, 615–616
Frequency theory, of hearing, 93
Freud's theory, 379–383
    anal stage, 382
    attachment, 292
    conversion disorder, 420
    critique of, 382–383
    defense mechanisms, 380
    depression, 426
    dreams, 134–135, 449
    erogenous zones, 380
    fixation, 380
    and gender bias, 383, 384
    gender identity, 561
    genital stage, 382

id/ego/superego, 379–380
    latency stage, 382
    motivation, 332
    Oedipus complex, 382
    oral stage, 380
    phallic stage, 382
    of phobia, 418
    pleasure principle, 379–380
    psychoanalysis, 449–450
    reality principle, 380
    revisionists, 382, 384–385
    unconscious thought, 122, 379
    and Victorian morality, 379
Friendship, 537
    definition of, 537
    gender differences, 537
Frontal lobe, 54
Frustration, and stress, 501
Fugue, 421
Fully functioning person, 392–393
Functional fixedness, and faulty problem
        solving, 232–233
Functionalism, 7

G

Gage, Phineas T., 58
Gall, Franz Joseph, 61
Gate-control theory, pain, 95, 97
Gender
    definition of, 11, 560
    feminist perspective on, 571–572
    men's issues, 572, 574
    and sexism, 569
Gender differences, 563–567
    achievement, 564
    aggression, 562
    biological factors, 564
    brain, 59–61
    communication style, 565
    depression, 424, 573
    emotions, 363–364, 565
    evolutionary view, 566
    feminist view of, 566
    friendship, 537
    health, 495
    helping behavior, 565
    life expectancy, 504
    loneliness, 541–542
    math and verbal abilities, 564
    mental disorders, 410–411
    moral development, 302–303
    religious interest, 575
    sexual behavior, 566–567
    sexual scripts, 342–343
    suicide, 426
Gender identity, 560–563
    biological factors, 560–562
    cognitive developmental theory, 562–563
    gender schema theory, 563
    identification theory, 562
    social learning theory, 562
Gender roles
    androgyny, 568–571
    gender-role transcendence, 571
    gender stereotypes, 567–568
    traditional roles, 567
Gender schema, meaning of, 563
Gender schema theory, 563

General adaptation syndrome (GAS), 497
Generalization
    classical conditioning, 155
    operant conditioning, 171–172
Generalized anxiety disorder, 415
Generativity versus stagnation, 293, 317
Genes, 38–40
    dominant-recessive genes principle,
        39–40
Genetic factors
    intelligence, 261–262
    obesity, 487–488
    phobias, 418
    schizophrenic disorders, 432
    suicide, 426
Genetics, 38–41
    chromosomes, 38
    genes, 38–40
Genie, isolation and language learning,
        242–243
Genital herpes, 493
Genital stage, 382
Genuineness, 452
Germinal period, 279
Gestalt psychology, principles of, 104–105
Gestalt therapy, 452–453
Giftedness, 259–260
    characteristics of, 259
    definition of, 259
    longitudinal study of, 259–260
Giving, in therapy, 471
Goal setting
    and achievement, 349–351
    self-assessment for goal-direction, 359
Gonorrhea, 493
Graphology, 28
Great person theory, 534
Grief, 322–323
    and mourning rituals, 428
Group conflict
    discrimination, 553
    prejudice, 553
    racism, 554–556
    stereotyping, 552
Groups, 530–535
    characteristics of, 530
    and conformity, 531–532
    and deindividuation, 533–534
    and groupthink, 532–533
    leadership, 534
    minority/majority influence, 534–535
    norms in, 530
    roles in, 530
    social identity theory, 554
Group therapies, 459–463
    couple therapy, 460
    encounter groups, 461
    family systems therapy, 460–461
    family therapy, 460
    personal growth groups, 461
    positive features of, 460
    self-help groups, 461–462
Groupthink, 532–533

H

Habituation, sensory adaptation, 79
Hallucinations, in schizophrenia, 430
Hallucinogens, 145–146

Happiness, 353, 354–355
    factors involved in, 355
    and flow, 355, 356
Haptic system
    kinesthetic sense, 97
    pain, 94–97
    temperature, 94
    touch, 94
    vestibular sense, 97–98
Hardiness, meaning of, 499
Health
    cigarette smoking cessation, 490–491
    and ethnic minorities, 495
    and exercise, 484–485
    gender differences, 495
    and nutrition, 485–490
    and prevention, 495
    psychological fields of study related
        to, 483
    and sexual safety, 491–494
Health psychology, study of, 483
Hearing. *See* Auditory system
Heart disease, and Type A behavior
    pattern, 499
Heaven's Gate, 517–518
Helping behavior
    altruism, 542–544
    gender differences, 565
Hemispheric specialization, 57–59
    misconceptions about, 58–59
Heredity-environment controversy. *See* Nature-
    nurture issue
Heredity. *See* Genetics; Nature-nurture issue
Heroin, 144
Heuristics
    availability heuristic, 233
    and faulty problem solving, 233
    for problem solving, 231
    representativeness heuristic, 233
Hidden observer theory, hypnosis, 138
Hierarchy, meaning of, 202–203
Hierarchy of motives theory, 333–334
Hindbrain, 50
Hindsight bias, and faulty critical thinking,
    236
Hippocampus, 54
Hippocrates, 444
Histogram, 615
History of psychology
    ancient China, 6
    ancient Greeks, 6–7
    behaviorism, 8–9
    cognitive perspective, 10
    ethnic minorities in, 15
    evolutionary perspective, 10
    functionalism, 7
    humanistic perspective, 9
    important pioneers/theorists in, 14
    introspection, 7
    neurobiological perspective, 10
    psychoanalytic perspective, 9
    sociocultural perspective, 10–11
    structuralism, 7
    therapy, origins of, 444–446
    women in, 15
Hogan Personality Inventory (HPI), 587
Holophrase hypothesis, language development,
    241–242

Homeostasis, 332
Homosexuality, 343–344
    partners, difficulties of, 317
    theories of cause, 343–344
Horizontal-vertical illusion, 109, 110
Hormones
    and aggression, 562
    function of, 53
    and gender identity, 560–562
    and puberty, 300, 338
Horney's theory, 382–384
Howard, Ruth, 15
Hue, 86
Human factors (engineering) psychology,
    594–595
    study of, 594
    tasks in, 594–595
Human Genome Project, 40
Humanistic psychotherapies, 451–453
    Gestalt therapy, 452–453
    person-centered therapy, 452
Humanistic theories
    evaluation of, 394–395
    history of, 9
    Maslow's theory, 393–394
    motivation, 333
    of personality development, 390–395
    phenomenological worldview, 390
    Roger's theory, 391–393
Humanistic therapies
    Gestalt therapy, 452–453
    person-centered therapy, 452
Human sexual response, stages in,
    339–340
Hunger, 335–338
    and brain, 336–337
    external cues, 337
    obesity, 338
    physiological processes in, 335–336
Hypnosis, 137–139
    definition of, 137
    hidden observer theory, 138
    individual susceptibility to, 138
    nonstate view, 139
    posthypnotic amnesia, 137
    posthypnotic suggestion, 137
    special processes theory, 138
    uses of, 139
Hypochondriasis, 420
Hypothalamus, 51–54, 337
Hypotheses, meaning of, 17
Hypothesis testing, 626
Hypothetical-deductive reasoning, 289

I

Iconic memory, 193
Id, 379–380
IDEAL method, problem solving, 230–231
Identification theory, 562
Identity
    components of, 305
    ethnic identity, 11, 307
Identity development, 305–308
    Erikson's theory, 293, 305
    and ethnic minorities, 307
    self-assessment, 306
Identity *versus* identity confusion, 293, 305
Illusions. *See* Visual illusions

Imagery
    in memory, 203
    memory technique, 219
Implicit memory, 196
Impression formation, 518–519
Impression management, 519–520
    and self-monitoring, 520
    strategies for, 520
Imprinting, 293–294, 331
Incentives, and motivation, 332
Incest, 344–345
Independent variable, 22
Individual differences, definition of, 250
Individualism
    definition of, 375–376, 551
    interaction with collectivist, 377
Individual psychology, 384–385
    birth order, 385
    striving for superiority, 385
Inductive reasoning, 233–234
Indulgent parenting, 296
Industrial psychology, 587–588
    employee selection, 587
    job analysis, 587
    performance appraisal, 588
    study of, 15, 587
    training, 588
Industry *versus* inferiority, 291, 292
Infant development, 282–283
    cognitive development, 285
    physical development, 282–283
    socioemotional development, 291–294
Infants, taste preferences, 100
Inference, 235–236
Inferential statistics, 614, 625–626
    experimental design, 625
    hypothesis testing, 626
    statistical significance, 626
Inferiority complex, 385
Infinite generativity, of language, 240
Information-processing model, memory,
    197–198
Information theory, of classical conditioning,
    160–161
Informed consent, and psychological research,
    24
Initiative *versus* guilt, 291, 292
Inner ear, 93
Insanity, definition of, 436
Insanity defense, 436–438
    competency, 437
    meaning of, 436
Insight learning, 181–183
    definition of, 183
Insight therapy, 446
Insomnia, 131
Instinctive drift, 183–184
Instinct theory, motivation, 331
Integrity *versus* despair, 293, 321
Intelligence
    definition of, 250
    and ethnic minorities, 262
    frames of intelligence model, 252
    giftedness, 259–260
    learning differences, 257–258
    mental retardation, 256–257
    multiple-factor theory, 251
    nature-nurture issue, 261–264

information-processing model, 197–198
and limbic system, 54
long-term memory, 195
memory span, 193–194
neurobiological origins, 214–216
procedural memory, 196
repressed memories, 212
semantic memory, 196–197
sensory memory, 192–193
sociocultural view, 216
working memory, 193–195
working-memory model, 198–199
Memory problems
amnesia, 212–213
repression, 213
Memory processes
attention, 200
automatic and effortful processing, 200
cue-dependent forgetting, 210
cues, 209
decay theory, 212
elaboration, 201–202
encoding, 199–204
imagery, 203
interference theory, 210–212
levels of processing theory, 200–201
network theories, 204
organization, 202–203
primacy and recency effect, 208
recall, 209–210
recognition, 209
representation, 204–208
retrieval, 208–213
schema theories, 204–206
and scripts, 207–208
serial position effect, 208
tip-of-the-tongue phenomenon, 208
Memory techniques
for academic learning, 218–220
attention, 220
chunking, 194
general strategies, 216–217
imagery, 219
maintenance rehearsal, 194
method of loci, 219
mnemonics, 219
pegword method, 219
remembering names, 217–218
Menarche, 299
Menopause
and estrogen replacement therapy, 312
signs of, 312
Men's issues
improving lives, guidelines for, 574
reconstructing masculinity, 572, 574
role strain, 572
Mental age, 251
Mental disorders
anxiety disorders, 415–420
biological view, 409
and commitment, 436
and criminal responsibility, 436–437
*Diagnostic and Statistical Manual of
Mental Disorders-IV*, 412–414
diathesis-stress model, 411–412
dimensions of, 408–409
dissociative disorders, 421–422
and ethnic minorities, 411

gender differences, 410–411
*International Classification of Disease
(ICD)*, 414
mood disorders, 423–428
personality disorders, 433–434
psychological view, 409–410
schizophrenic disorders, 428–433
sociocultural view, 409, 410
and socioeconomic status, 411
somatoform disorders, 420–421
Mental processes, definition of, 5
Mental retardation, 256–257
classifications of, 257–258
cultural-familial retardation, 256–257
definition of, 256
organic retardation, 256
Mentors
for ethnic minorities, 177
and observational learning, 176
Mesomorph, 373
Meta-analysis, meaning of, 465
Method of loci, 219
Midbrain, 50
Middle ear, 92
Milgram experiment, on obedience,
527–529
Mindlessness, 103
Minnesota Multiphasic Personality Inventory
(MMPI), 19–20, 399, 587
Minnesota Study of Twins Reared Apart, 36
Mnemonics, types of, 219
Mode, 617
Monocular cues, depth perception, 105–106
Mood disorders, 423–428
biological factors, 428
bipolar disorder, 424–426
cognitive theories, 427–428
major depression, 423–424
psychoanalytic theories of, 426–427
sociocultural view, 428
and suicide, 426
Moon illusion, 110, 111
Moral development, 301–303
care perspective, 302–303
gender differences, 302–303
justice perspective, 302
Kohlberg's theory, 301–302
sociocultural view, 303
Morphine, 144
Morphology, 241
Motherese, and language development,
243–244
Motion perception, 106
and illusions of motion, 106
movement aftereffects, 106, 108
Motivation
behavioral theory, 332
cognitive theory, 333
definition of, 330
drive reduction theory, 332
of employees, 589
ethological theory, 331
Freud's theory, 332
hierarchy of motives theory, 333–334
humanistic perspective, 333
and incentives, 332
instinct theory, 331
intrinsic and extrinsic, 330–331

relationship to emotion, 352
sociocultural view, 333
Motives
achievement, 348–352
competence, 347–348
definition of, 330
hunger, 335–338
sex, 338–346
Motor development, infancy, 283
Movement aftereffects, 106, 108
Müller-Lyer illusion, 109–110
Multiaxial system, DSM-VI, 413
Multiple-factor theory, intelligence, 251
Myelin sheath, 45

N

Narcolepsy, 132
Native Americans, 12
discrimination against, 553
Natural selection, elements of, 41
Nature, meaning of, 36
Nature-nurture issue
alcoholism, 141–143
definition of, 276
elements of, 36, 38
intelligence, 261–264
meaning of, 7
perception, 110–111
Need, definition of, 332
Negative affectivity, 353, 355–357
Negative reinforcement, 164
Neglectful parenting, 296
Nembutal, 144
NEO Personality Inventory/NEO-PI-Revised,
400, 587
Neo-Piagetians, 289–290
Nerves, afferent and efferent, 43
Nervous system
nerve impulse, 45, 47
neural transmission, 43–44
neurotransmitters, 47–48
organization of, 42–43
stress response, 496–497
Network theories, memory, 204
Neurobiological perspective, history of, 10
Neurons
function of, 42
impulses of, 45–47
interneurons, 44
resting and action potentials, 45, 47
structure of, 44–45
synapses, 47
Neuroscience, study of, 13
Neurotic disorders, meaning of, 413
Neuroticism, 374
Neurotransmitters, 47–48
dopamine, 48
endorphins, 48
functions of, 47–48
serotonin, 48
Newborn, reflexes, 279
Nicotine, 144
Nightmares, 132
Night terrors, 121–122, 132
Noise, effects on performance,
596–597
Nonstate view, hypnosis, 139

Piaget's theory, 284–290
    accommodation in, 285
    adult development, 315
    assimilation in, 285
    concrete operational thought, 287–288
    contributions of, 289
    critique of, 289–290
    formal operational thought, 288–289, 300
    neo-Piagetians, 289–290
    object permanence, 285
    operations in, 286
    preoperational thought, 285–287
    sensorimotor thought, 285
Pinel, Philippe, 445–446
Pitch, sound, 90
Pituitary gland, functions of, 53–54
Placebo effect, 23
Place theory, of hearing, 93
Plasticity, of brain, 64
Pluralism, 556
Politics, gender gap in, 526, 573
Polygraph, 361–362
    validity of, 362
Pons, 50
Ponzo illusion, 109–110
Population, meaning of, 18
Positive affectivity, 353, 354
Positive reinforcement, 163
Positron-emission tomography (PET scan), 66–67
Postconventional level, moral development, 302
Posthypnotic amnesia, 137
Posthypnotic suggestion, 137
Post-traumatic stress disorder, 419–420
    causes of, 420
    signs of, 419
Poverty
    feminization of poverty, 505
    and stress, 503–504
Precognition, 113
Preconventional level, moral development, 302
Prefrontal lobotomy, 475
Prejudice
    classical conditioning of, 159
    meaning of, 553
    and religious orientation, 579
Prenatal development, 278–282
    and AIDS, 281
    central nervous system, 49
    cocaine effects, 281
    fetal alcohol syndrome, 280–281
    periods of, 279
    sex differentiation, 40, 560–561
    and teratogens, 280
Preoperational thought, 285–287
    conservation in, 287
    egocentrism in, 287
    operations in, 286
Preparedness, and learning, 183
Primacy effect, 519
    memory, 208
Primary prevention, 464
Primary reinforcement, 168–169
Primates, language learning by, 249
Proactive interference, memory, 210–211

Problem-focused coping, 506
Problem solving, 230–233
    algorithms, 231
    definition of, 230
    in dreams, 135
    faulty strategies, 232–233
    heuristics, 231
    IDEAL method, 230–231
Procedural memory, 196
Projection, 381
Projective tests, 400–402
Pseudopsychology, 28
Pseudoscience
    astrology, 27–28
    graphology, 28
Psychiatry, study of, 13
Psychoactive drugs, 139–146
    actions of, 139–140
    alcohol, 140–143
    barbiturates, 144
    hallucinogens, 145–146
    marijuana, 145
    opiates, 144
    reasons for use, 140
    stimulant drugs, 144
    and substance-use disorder, 435
    tolerance/addiction/dependence, 140
    tranquilizers, 144
Psychoanalysis, 449–450
    dream analysis, 449
    free association, 449
    interpretation, 449
    resistance, 450–451
    transference, 449
Psychoanalytic theories, 379–387
    evaluation of, 385–387
    Freud's theory, 379–383
    history of, 9
    Horney's theory, 382–384
    individual psychology, 384–385
    Jung's theory, 384
    of mood disorders, 426–427
    See also Erikson's theory; Freud's theory
Psychodynamic therapies, 449–451
    contemporary approaches, 451
    Freud's psychoanalysis, 449–450
Psychogenic amnesia, 421
Psychokinesis, 113–114
Psychological dependence, on drugs, 140
Psychological tests. See Personality assessment
Psychology
    areas of specialization in, 13–15
    definition of, 5
    education/training in, 16
    elements of, 5–6
    and everyday life, 4–5
    history of. See History of psychology
    versus pseudoscience, 27–29
    as science, 6
Psychology of women, study of, 15
Psychoneuroimmunology, study of, 483
Psychophysics, 75–79
    absolute threshold, 76–77
    difference threshold, 76
    signal detection theory, 77–78
    subliminal perception, 78–79
Psychosexual dysfunction, 344
Psychosurgery, 475

Psychotherapy, 446–448
    action therapy, 446
    client profiles, 447–448
    common themes in, 466–467
    eclectic, 446
    ethical standards, 448
    and ethnic minorities, 470–472
    gender issues, 467–470
    insight therapy, 446
    and managed health care coverage, 448
    mental health professional in practice, 446
    outcome research on, 465–466
    settings for, 446
    and therapeutic relationship, 467
Psychotic disorders, meaning of, 413
Puberty, 299–300
    hormones in, 300, 338
    and sexual behavior, 338
Punishment
    of children, 185
    definition of, 164
    versus negative reinforcement, 165–166
    operant conditioning, 164–166
Pupil, eye, 82–83
Pussin, Jean, 445–446

Q

Questionnaires, for data collection, 19

R

Race
    categories of, 37
    meaning of, 37
    stereotypes about, 37
Racism, 554–556
Random assignment, 22
Random sample, 18
Range, 617–618
Rape, 345–346
    aftereffects, 346, 419–420
    date rape, 346
    prevention guidelines for men, 346
    recovery from, 346
Rapid eye movement (REM) sleep, 127–130
Rapport talk, 565
Rational-emotive therapy, 457
    alcoholism treatment, 143
Rationalization, 381
Rational Recovery (RR), 143
Raven Progressive Matrices Test, 264, 265
Reaction formation, 381
Reality principle, 380
Reasoning, 233–234
    by analogy, 234
    deductive reasoning, 234
    inductive reasoning, 233–234
Recall, 209–210
Recency effect, memory, 208
Recognition, memory measure, 209
Reductionism, 388
Reflexes
    definition of, 153
    newborn, 279
Regression, 381
Reinforcement, 163–164
    negative reinforcement, 164
    and observational learning, 175
    positive reinforcement, 163

primary reinforcement, 168–169
secondary reinforcement, 168–169
token reinforcement, 169
Relaxation methods, for stress management, 511–512
Reliability of test, 254
inter-rater reliability, 254
test-retest reliability, 254
Religion
and altered states of consciousness, 124
commitment, stages in development, 577–578
definition of, 576
elements of, 576–577
gender differences, 575
intrinsic/extrinsic religious orientation, 577
and prejudice, 579
religious conversion, 578
spiritual well-being, 578–579
Repair theory, sleep, 130
Replication, 24
Report talk, 565
Representation, memory process, 204–208
Representativeness heuristic, and faulty problem solving, 233
Repression, 381
nature of, 213
repressed memories of child abuse, 212
Research in psychology
case study, 20
correlational method, 20–21
data collection measures, 19–20
descriptive methods, 20
direct observation, 19
ethical issues, 24–25
experimental method, 21–24
interviews/questionnaires, 19
questionnaires, 19
research subjects, selection of, 18
setting for, 18–19
standardized tests, 19–20
Resistance, 450–451
Response cost, 165
Resting potential, 45
Restricted environmental stimulation therapy (REST), 80–81
Reticular formation, 50
Retinal/binocular disparity, 106
Retrieval, memory process, 208–213
Retroactive interference, memory, 210–211
Retrograde amnesia, 213
Rites of passage, 308
Ritual possession, 123, 125
Robbers Cave experiment, 556–557
Rods, 83–84
Rogers's theory, 391–393
conditional and unconditional positive regard, 391
fully functioning person, 392–393
person-centered therapy, 452
self-concept in, 391
Role models
for ethnic minorities, 177
and observational learning, 176
Roles, definition of, 530
Role strain, 572
Romantic love, 538

Romantic script, on sex, 342–343
Rorschach Inkblot Test, 400–401

S

Sadism, 345
Sample
meaning of, 18
random sample, 18
Sanchez, George, 15
Saturation of color, 86
Scatter plot, 620–621
Schedules of reinforcement, 169–170
fixed-interval schedule, 170
fixed-ratio schedule, 170
partial reinforcement, 169
variable-interval schedule, 170
variable-ratio schedule, 170
Schema, definition of, 205, 563
Schema theories
gender schema theory, 563
memory, 204–206
Schizophrenic disorders, 428–433
antipsychotic drugs, 473
and brain, 48, 432
catatonic schizophrenia, 431
characteristics of, 428–430
disorganized schizophrenia, 431
environmental factors, 432
genetic factors, 432
paranoid schizophrenia, 431
sociocultural view, 432–433
undifferentiated schizophrenia, 431
Schizotypal personality disorder, 434
School/educational psychology, study of, 15
See also Educational psychology
Schools
improving interethnic relations, 557
Schools for Thought program, 606–607
Scientific method, steps in, 17
Sclera, 82
Script
definition of, 207
and memory, 207–208
sexual scripts, 342–243
Seconal, 144
Secondary prevention, 464
Secondary reinforcement, 168–169
Secular Organization for Sobriety (SOS), 143
Secure attachment, 295
Selective attention, 200
Selective serotonin reuptake inhibitors (SSRIs), 472–473
Self-actualization, 334
characteristics of, 394
meaning of, 333, 394
Self-concept, definition of, 391
Self-control problems, and operant conditioning, 167
Self-efficacy
and cognitive behavior therapy, 456
development of, 181
and learning, 180
meaning of, 180, 390
Self-esteem
increasing, strategies for, 393
self-assessment, 392

Self-fulfilling prophesy, 507
Self-help groups, 461–462
for alcoholism, 143
Self-instruction methods, 456
Self-monitoring, 520
self-assessment for, 521
Self-perception theory, 523
Self-report tests
empirically keyed tests, 398
and honest responses, 398
of personality, 398–400
Semantic memory, 196–197
Semantics, 241
Semicircular canals, and vestibular sense, 97–98
Sensation
auditory system, 90–94
definition of, 75
and hypothalamus, 52–54
kinesthetic senses, 97
pain, 94–97
psychophysics, concepts in, 75–79
sensation seeking, 79
sensory adaptation, 79
sensory deprivation, 79–81
smell, 100–101
taste, 100
temperature, 94
touch, 94
vestibular sense, 97–98
visual system, 81–89
Sensation seeking
meaning of, 79
self-assessment for, 80
Sensorimotor thought, 285
object permanence in, 285
Sensory deprivation, 79–81
effects of, 80
therapeutic use of, 80–81
Sensory memory, 192–193
Separation, of ethnic minorities, 503
Serial position effect, memory, 208
Serotonin, functions of, 48
Set point, 337, 488
Sex-determination, and chromosomes, 40
Sex education, sociocultural view, 340
Sexism, forms of, 569
Sexual behavior, 338–346
and Americans, 340–342
bisexuality, 343
and contraception, 491–492
double standard, 343
gender differences, 566–567
homosexuality, 343–344
human sexual response, 339–340
and puberty, 338
sexual scripts, 342–243
sociocultural view, 339
Sexual harassment, 346
Sexual knowledge, 491
common misconceptions about sex, 492
Sexually transmitted diseases (STD)
AIDS, 493–494
chlamydia, 493
genital herpes, 493
gonorrhea, 493
protective measures, 494
syphilis, 493

Structuralism, 7
Sublimation, 381
Subliminal perception, 78–79
Substance-use disorders, 435
Subtractive mixture, of color, 87
Suicide
    gender differences, 426
    genetic factors, 426
    sociocultural view, 426
    threats, steps to take, 427
Superconducting quantum interference device
    (SQUID), 67
Superego, 379–380
Superiority complex, 385
Synapses, 47
Syntax, 241
Syphilis, 493
Systematic desensitization, 454
System of Multicultural Pluralistic Assessment
    (SOMPA), 264

T

Tardive dyskinesia, 473
Taste
    categories of, 100–101
    sensation of, 100
Taste aversion, learning of, 184
Ta Yu, 6
Telegraphic speech, 242
Telepathy, 113, 115–116
Television viewing, and observational learning,
    151–152
Temperature, sensation of, 94
Temporal lobe, 54
Teratogens, and prenatal development, 280
Tertiary prevention, 464–465
Test design, 254–255
    norms, 255
    reliability, 254–255
    standardization, 255
    validity, 255
Testosterone, 300
    and aggression, 562
Test-retest reliability, 254
Thalamus, 50–51
Thematic Apperception Test (TAT), 401–402
Theory
    meaning of, 17
    revising theory, 17
Therapy
    behavior therapies, 453–455
    cognitive therapies, 453–458
    community psychology, 463–465
    drug therapy, 472–474
    electroconvulsive therapy (ECT), 474–475
    group therapies, 459–463
    guidelines for seeking therapy, 468
    historical view, 444–446
    humanistic psychotherapies, 451–453
    psychodynamic therapies, 449–451
    psychosurgery, 475
    psychotherapy, 446–448
    self-assessment for, 469

Theta waves, sleep, 127
Thinking
    concept formation, 228–230
    convergent thinking, 237
    creative thinking, 237–238
    critical thinking, 234–237
    divergent thinking, 237
    problem solving, 230–233
    reasoning, 233–234
Thorndike, E. L., 162
Timbre, sound, 91
Time out, 165
Tip-of-the-tongue phenomenon, 208
Titchener, Edward Bradford, 7
Token economy, 455
Token reinforcer, 169
Tolerance, and drug use, 140
Tongue, and taste, 100
Touch, sensation of, 94
Traditional religious script, on sex, 342
Training, new employees, 588
Traits, definition of, 372
Trait theories, 372–378
    evaluation of, 377
    five-factor model, 374–376
    introversion/extraversion, 374
    and labeling problem, 378
    sociocultural view, 376–377
    somatotype theory, 373
Tranquilizers, 144
Transcendental meditation, for stress
    management, 510–511
Transference, 449
Transvestism, 345
Trephining, 444
Triangular theory of love, 539
Triarchic theory, intelligence, 251–252
Trichromatic theory, color vision, 88
Trichromats, 89
Trust *versus* mistrust, 291, 292
Twin studies
    alcoholism, 141–142
    heredity *versus* environment, 35–36
    intelligence, 261
Type A behavior pattern, and heart disease, 499

U

U-curve hypothesis, emotion, 354
Unconditional positive regard, 391
Unconditioned response (UR), 153–154, 156
Unconditioned stimulus (US), 153, 156, 158
Unconscious thought, meaning of, 122, 379
Undifferentiated schizophrenia, 431
UNICEF, 277

V

Validity of test, 254–255
    content validity, 254
    criterion validity, 254–255
Valium, 144
Variable-interval schedule, 170
Variable-ratio schedule, 170
Variables, in experimental method, 22

Ventromedial hypothalamus, and hunger,
    336–337
Verbal ability, gender differences, 564
Vestibular sense, 97–98
Visual cliff, 110
Visual illusions, 109–111
    devil's tuning fork, 110, 111
    horizontal-vertical illusion, 109, 110
    moon illusion, 110, 111
    Müller-Lyer illusion, 109–110
    Ponzo illusion, 109–110
Visual system, 81–89
    accommodation, 83
    blind spot, 84, 85
    color vision, 83, 85–89
    eye, parts of, 82–84
    and light, 81–82
    neural-visual processing, 84–85
    rods and cones, 83–84
Volley theory, of hearing, 93
Voyeurism, 345
Vygotsky's theory, cognitive development, 290

W

Walker, Alice, 4, 9, 10, 11
Washburn, Margaret, 15
Watson, John, 8
Wavelength, light, 81–82
Weber, E. H., 76
Weber's law, 76
Wechsler scales, of intelligence, 255
Wish fulfillment, in dreams, 134–135
Withdrawal, from drugs, 140
Women
    and depression, 424, 573
    education for, 573
    and employment level, 573
    gifted women, 261
    in history of psychology, 15
    improving lives, guidelines for, 574
    menopause, 312
    middle-age concerns, 312
    in politics, 526, 573
    poverty, effects on, 505
    rape, 345–346
    sexual harassment, 346
    stress, response to, 504–505
    widowed, status of, 323
    in workplace, 593–594
    See also Feminist psychology; Gender
        differences
Women for Sobriety (WFS), 143
Working memory, 193–195
Working-memory model, 198–199
Wundt, Wilhelm, 7

X

Xanax, 144

Z

Zone of proximal development (ZPD), 290
Zygote, 278–279